Lecture Notes in Computer Science 14301

Founding Editors

Gerhard Goos
Juris Hartmanis

Editorial Board Members

The series Lecture Notes in Computer Science (LNCS), including its subseries Lecture Notes in Artificial Intelligence (LNAI) and Lecture Notes in Bioinformatics (LNBI), has established itself as a medium for the publication of new developments in computer science and information technology research, teaching, and education.

LNCS enjoys close cooperation with the computer science R & D community, the series counts many renowned academics among its volume editors and paper authors, and collaborates with prestigious societies. Its mission is to serve this international community by providing an invaluable service, mainly focused on the publication of conference and workshop proceedings and postproceedings. LNCS commenced publication in 1973.

Pradipta Maji · Tingwen Huang · Nikhil R. Pal ·
Santanu Chaudhury · Rajat K. De
Editors

Pattern Recognition and Machine Intelligence

10th International Conference, PReMI 2023
Kolkata, India, December 12–15, 2023
Proceedings

 Springer

Editors
Pradipta Maji (iD)
Indian Statistical Institute
Kolkata, West Bengal, India

Nikhil R. Pal (iD)
Indian Statistical Institute
Kolkata, West Bengal, India

Rajat K. De (iD)
Indian Statistical Institute
Kolkata, West Bengal, India

Tingwen Huang (iD)
Texas A&M University at Qatar
Doha, Qatar

Santanu Chaudhury (iD)
Indian Institute of Technology Jodhpur
Jodhpur, India

ISSN 0302-9743   ISSN 1611-3349 (electronic)
Lecture Notes in Computer Science
ISBN 978-3-031-45169-0   ISBN 978-3-031-45170-6 (eBook)
https://doi.org/10.1007/978-3-031-45170-6

This Springer imprint is published by the registered company Springer Nature Switzerland AG
The registered company address is: Gewerbestrasse 11, 6330 Cham, Switzerland

Paper in this product is recyclable.

Foreword

Writing the Foreword for the conference proceedings of the 10th Anniversary of Pattern Recognition and Machine Intelligence (PReMI) is an immense honour for me.

Over the years, from its inaugural conference in 2005 to its 10th anniversary edition in 2023, I got the chance to follow the evolution and impact of the PReMI conferences on diverse scientific groups. The scientific results reported during the PReMI conferences, the scope of the foundational research, and applications in so many different fields made the PReMI progression exceptional.

The main conference organizers, associated with the Machine Intelligence Unit at the Indian Statistical Institute, were extremely successful engaging their exceptional scientific and organizational talents to spreading cutting-edge scientific research not only in India but also in various other countries, including Poland.

The cooperation with Poland that was initiated years ago by Professors Sankar Kumar Pal and Mihir Kumar Chakraborty, especially with Professor Zdzisław Pawlak with whom I was so lucky to cooperate, have resulted in a number of excellent results, which include the foundations and applications of Pawlak's rough sets, especially methods based on combination of rough sets with other domains like fuzzy sets, granular computing, and neural networks to name a few.

I would like especially to convey my sincere gratitude to Professors Sankar Kumar Pal and Mihir Kumar Chakraborty as well as to many other researchers from the Machine Intelligence Unit and other research institutes from India for their collective effort in fostering this successful collaboration. That an excellent work has been done can be recognized as it also resulted in the development of friendships that endure.

I wish all Members of Committees of the PReMI 2023 Conference to successfully continue the collaboration that has produced such impressive outcomes. I would like to thank the Organizing Committee, Program Committee, Keynote and Invited Speakers, Authors of submitted and accepted papers, Reviewers as well as all Participants of the PReMI 2023 conference for their effort and excellent contribution to the success of the conference.

I wish all the Participants of PReMI 2023 to have a chance of witnessing a successful and academically rich conference from all respects that in particular will bring results making a significant step toward solving the main challenge of Artificial Intelligence that according to Professor Leslie Valiant, Turing Award winner, is related to the characterization of computational building blocks (which one can call complex granules) for cognition.

August 2023

Andrzej Skowron
Honorary Chair of PReMI 2023

Preface

It is our pleasure to welcome you all to the 10th International Conference on Pattern Recognition and Machine Intelligence (PReMI'23), held at the Indian Statistical Institute, Kolkata, India, during December 12–15, 2023. The primary goal of the conference is to provide a platform for presenting state-of-the-art scientific results, enabling academic and industrial interactions, and promoting collaborative research activities in Pattern Recognition, Machine Intelligence, and related fields, involving scientists, engineers, professionals, academicians, and students. This premier biennial event is an ideal forum for people to share their views and experiences in the said areas. This is the tenth conference in this series.

The conference has four keynote talks, four invited lectures, and two special talks, all by very eminent and distinguished researchers from around the world. It also has some special events such as Doctoral Colloquium, Student Research Workshop, and Industrial Session. The conference had a very good response in terms of paper submissions. It received 311 submissions from across the globe. Each paper went through a rigorous review (double-blind) process and was critically reviewed by at least three experts of the technical program/review committee. Based on the review reports, only 94 top-quality and highly relevant submissions are accepted. Among them, 91 submissions are included in the proceedings. The acceptance rate of PReMI'23 is 30%. Accepted papers are divided into fifteen groups, although there could be some overlaps. Abstracts of the keynote and invited speeches are also included in the proceedings.

We wish to express our appreciation to the Technical Program Committee members and reviewers who worked hard to ensure the quality of the contributions of this volume. We are thankful to Professor Trevor Hastie of Stanford University (USA), Professor Bernhard Schölkopf of Max Planck Institute for Intelligent Systems (Germany), Professor Dacheng Tao of University of Sydney (Australia), and Professor Alison Noble of University of Oxford (UK) for accepting our invitation to be the keynote speakers at this conference. We take this opportunity to express our gratitude to Professor Balaraman Ravindran of Indian Institute of Technology Madras, Professor SP Arun of Indian Institute of Science Bangalore, Professor Gajendra P. S. Raghava of Indraprastha Institute of Information Technology, New Delhi and Professor Richa Singh of Indian Institute of Technology Jodhpur for agreeing to be the invited speakers of the conference. We are also grateful to Professor Dipankar Banerjee of Aryabhatta Research Institute of Observational Sciences (India) and Dr. Balasubramanian Narasimhan of Stanford University (USA) for accepting our invitation to deliver the special lectures in this conference. We thank Dr. Soma Biswas of Indian Institute of Science Bangalore, Professor Animesh Mukherjee of Indian Institute of Technology Kharagpur, Dr. Sangheeta Roy of TCS Research Lab, and Dr. Anirban Santara of Google Research India for accepting our invitation to deliver pre-conference tutorial lectures. We gratefully acknowledge the staff of Springer for their co-operation in the publication of the PReMI'23 proceedings. Finally, we would like to thank all the contributors for their enthusiastic response.

We believe that you will find the proceedings to be a valuable source of reference for your ongoing and future research.

August 2023

Pradipta Maji
Tingwen Huang
Nikhil R. Pal
Santanu Chaudhury
Rajat K. De

Message from the Honorary Chair

The Machine Intelligence Unit (MIU) of Indian Statistical Institute (ISI) is going to organize the tenth edition of the biennial International Conference on Pattern Recognition and Machine Intelligence, PReMI-23 at ISI, Calcutta in the year when our Nation is in its "AmritKaal". I am delighted to see that the event PReMI, which was originated in 2005 at ISI, has now reached its tenth edition when the mother department MIU has completed its 30th year of glorious existence with numerous national and international achievements.

Since its inception in 2005, PReMI had always been drawing big responses globally in terms of paper submissions. This year, PReMI-23 received more than 300 submissions, and after a rigorous review process, only 91 papers are accepted. The conference has a nice blend of Plenary and Invited talks, and high-quality research papers, covering different aspects of pattern recognition and machine intelligence with real-life state-of-the-art applications. A balanced mixture of both classical and modern computing paradigms is there. Special emphasis has been given to different kinds of ML tasks ranging from shallow to deep learning, and forthcoming research areas such as cognitive computing and computational neurology, on the top of medical imaging, image and video processing, and information security. These are organized through regular as well as special sessions. Some pre-conference tutorials from academia and industry are also arranged for the beginners. All these make the PReMI 2023 an ideal state-of-the-art platform for researchers and practitioners to exchange ideas and enrich their knowledge for the benefit of science, society, and mankind.

I thank all the speakers, reviewers, different Chairs, and members of various committees for making this event a grand success. No conference is successful without the active involvement of the participants. I owe a special thanks to them. My thanks are also due to the sponsors for their support, and to Springer for publishing the PReMI proceedings under its prestigious LNCS series.

I believe the participants would have an academically fruitful and enjoyable stay in Calcutta, the city of everything.

August 2023   Sankar K. Pal

Organization

PReMI'23 Organizing Committee

Honorary Chairs

Sankar K. Pal	Indian Statistical Institute, Kolkata, India
Andrzej Skowron	University of Warsaw, Poland

Conference Chairs

Nikhil R. Pal	Indian Statistical Institute, Kolkata, India
Santanu Chaudhury	Indian Institute of Technology Jodhpur, India
Rajat K. De	Indian Statistical Institute, Kolkata, India

Program Chairs

Pradipta Maji	Indian Statistical Institute, Kolkata, India
Tingwen Huang	Texas A&M University at Qatar, Doha

Organizing Chairs

Deba Prasad Mandal	Indian Statistical Institute, Kolkata, India
B. Uma Shankar	Indian Statistical Institute, Kolkata, India

Special Session Chairs

Kuntal Ghosh	Indian Statistical Institute, Kolkata, India
Monidipa Das	Indian Institute of Technology-ISM Dhanbad, India

Tutorial Chairs

Pabitra Mitra	Indian Institute of Technology Kharagpur, India
Swapna Agarwal	Tata Consultancy Services, Kolkata, India

Special Issue Chairs

Hongmin Cai	South China University of Technology, China
Sanjoy K. Saha	Jadavpur University, Kolkata, India
Malay Bhattacharyya	Indian Statistical Institute, Kolkata, India

Doctoral Symposium Chairs

B. S. Daya Sagar	Indian Statistical Institute, Bangalore, India
Tanmay Basu	Indian Institute of Science Education and Research, Bhopal, India

Industry Liaisons

Narayan Bhamidipati	InMobi, USA
Utpal Garain	Indian Statistical Institute, Kolkata, India

International Liaisons

Dominik Ślęzak	University of Warsaw, Poland
Sergei Kuznetsov	Higher School of Economics, Moscow, Russia

Publicity Chairs

Francisco de A. T. de Carvalho	Universidade Federal de Pernambuco, Brazil
Abhirup Banerjee	University of Oxford, UK

Student Workshop Chairs

Guo Chen	University of New South Wales, Australia
Angshuman Paul	Indian Institute of Technology, Jodhpur, India

Web Chair

Ekta Shah	Max Planck Institute for Molecular Genetics, Germany

PReMI'23 Advisory Committee

Anil K. Jain	Michigan State University, USA
Bayya Yegnanarayana	International Institute of Information Technology, Hyderabad, India
Bhargab B. Bhattacharya	Indian Statistical Institute, Kolkata, India
Bidyut Baran Chaudhuri	Indian Statistical Institute, Kolkata, India
B. L. Deekshatulu	IDRBT, Hyderabad, India
David W. Aha	U.S. Naval Research Laboratory, USA
Edwin Hancock	University of York, UK
Farzin Deravi	University of Kent, UK
Jayaram K. Udupa	University of Pennsylvania, USA
Josef Kittler	University of Surrey, UK
Malay K. Kundu	Indian Statistical Institute, Kolkata, India
Nasser M. Nasrabadi	West Virginia University, USA
Ning Zhong	Maebashi Institute of Technology, Japan
Ramalingam Chellappa	Johns Hopkins University, USA
Witold Pedrycz	University of Alberta, Canada

Patron

Sanghamitra Bandyopadhyay	Indian Statistical Institute, India

PReMI'23 Program Committee

Animesh Mukherjee	Indian Institute of Technology, Kharagpur, India
Arun Ross	Michigan State University, USA
Ashish Ghosh	Indian Statistical Institute, Kolkata, India
Atiqur Rahman Ahad	University of East London, UK
Bart Lamiroy	Universitè de Reims Champagne-Ardenne, France
Bhabatosh Chanda	Indian Statistical Institute, Kolkata, India
Bhabesh Deka	Tezpur University, India
C. V. Jawahar	International Institute of Information Technology, Hyderabad, India
Dhruba K. Bhattacharyya	Tezpur University, India
Hemant Ishwaran	University of Miami, USA
Hisao Ishibuchi	Southern University of Science and Technology, China
Jayadeva	Indian Institute of Technology, Delhi, India
João Manuel R. S. Tavares	Universidade do Porto, Portugal

Kolin Paul	Indian Institute of Technology, Delhi, India
Lawrence O. Hall	University of South Florida, USA
Lipo Wang	Nanyang Technological University, Singapore
Patrick Siarry	University Paris Est Creteil, France
P. N. Suganthan	Qatar University, Qatar
Salvador García López	University of Granada, Spain
Sambhu N. Biswas	Indian Statistical Institute, Kolkata, India
Shalabh Bhatnagar	Indian Institute of Science, Bangalore, India
Shubhra Sankar Ray	Indian Statistical Institute, Kolkata, India
Sung-Bae Cho	Yonsei University, South Korea
Sushmita Mitra	Indian Statistical Institute, Kolkata, India
Valentina E. Balas	Aurel Vlaicu University of Arad, Romania

PReMI'23 Technical Review Committee

Abhijit Dasgupta	St. Jude Children's Research Hospital, USA
Ananda Chowdhury	Jadavpur University, Kolkata, India
Anindya Halder	North-Eastern Hill University, Shillong, India
Anish Turlapaty	IIIT Sri City, India
Anjeneya Swami Kare	University of Hyderabad, India
Ankita Mandal	Harvard Medical School, USA
Ankita Sharma	IIT Jodhpur, India
Anupam Ghosh	Netaji Subhash Engineering College, India
Ansuman Mahapatra	NIT Puducherry, India
Aparajita Khan	Stanford University, USA
Arpan Pal	TCS Research and Innovation, India
Ashish Phophalia	IIIT Vadodara, India
Chandra Das	Netaji Subhash Engineering College, Kolkata, India
Chandra Mohan Dasari	IIIT Sri City, India
Chen-Ching Lin	National Yang-Ming University, Taiwan
Debashis Sen	IIT Kharagpur, India
Debashree Devi	IIIT Guwahati, India
Debdoot Sheet	IIT Kharagpur, India
Deepak Ranjan Nayak	MNIT Jaipur, India
Dinabandhu Bhandari	Heritage Institute of Technology, Kolkata, India
Dinesh Singh	IIT Mandi, India
Francesco Masulli	University of Genoa, Italy
Gaurav Dixit	IIT Roorkee, India
Gugan Thoppe	IISc Bengaluru, India
Hemant Arjun Patil	DA-IICT Gandhinagar, India

Jagat Sesh Challa	BITS Pilani, India
Jaya Prakash	IISc Bengaluru, India
Jaya Sil	IIEST Shibpur, India
Jaya Sreevalsan-Nair	IIIT Bangalore, India
Jit Mukherjee	BIT Mesra, India
Mohammed Javed	IIIT Allahabad, India
Mohona Ghosh	IGDTUW Delhi, India
Mridula Verma	IDRBT Hyderabad, India
Mrinmoy Ghorai	IIIT Sri City, India
Mukesh Kumar	NIT Patna, India
Nabendu Chaki	University of Calcutta, India
Navjot Singh	IIIT Allahabad, India
Niyati Baliyan	NIT Kurukshetra, India
Pankaj Yadav	IIT Jodhpur, India
Panthadeep Bhattacharjee	IIIT Guwahati, India
Parashjyoti Borah	IIIT Guwahati, India
Partha Garai	Kalyani Government Engineering College, India
Piyush Kumar	NIT Patna, India
Poonam Goyal	BITS Pilani, India
Pravin Pawar	BITS Pilani, India
Rajdeep Chatterjee	KIIT Bhubneshwar, India
Rakesh Sanodiya	IIIT Sri City, India
Ramesh Kumar Bhukya	IIIT Allahabad, India
Romi Banerjee	IIT Jodhpur, India
Rosy Sarmah	Tezpur University, India
Rubell Marion Lincy G.	IIIT Kottayam, India
Ruchira Naskar	IIEST Shibpur, India
Rusha Patra	IIIT Guwahati, India
Sanjay Singh	CSIR - Central Electronics Engineering Research Institute, India
Sanjit Maitra	ISI Tezpur, India
Sanjoy Pratihar	IIIT Kalyani, India
Saroj K. Meher	ISI Bangalore, India
Satchidananda Dehuri	Fakir Mohan University, India
Saurabh Das	IIT Indore, India
Selvi Chandran	IIIT Kottayam, India
Shaswati Roy	RCC-IIT Kolkata, India
Shiv Ram Dubey	IIIT Allahabad, India
Snehasis Banerjee	IIIT Guwahati, India
Somnath Tagore	Columbia University, USA
Soumi Chattopadhyay	IIIT Guwahati, India
Soumyadev Maity	IIIT Allahabad, India

Suchithra M. S.	IIIT Kottayam, India
Sudarsana Kadiri	Aalto University, Finland
Sudipta Roy	Jio Institute, Mumbai, India
Sujit Das	NIT Warangal, India
Sukanta Das	IIEST Shibpur, India
Suman Mahapatra	ISI Kolkata, India
Sumeet Agarwal	IIT Delhi, India
Sumeet Saurav	CSIR-CEERI Pilani, India
Surajeet Ghosh	IIEST Shibpur, India
Surendiran B.	NIT Puducherry, India
Swarup Roy	Sikkim University, India
Tandra Pal	NIT Durgapur, India
Tharun Kumar Reddy Bollu	IIT Roorkee, India
Triloki Pant	IIIT Allahabad, India
Upasana Talukdar	IIIT Guwahati, India
Vandana Agarwal	BITS Pilani, India
V. Shanmugasundaram	IIIT Kottayam, India

Sponsoring Organizations from Academia

- International Association for Pattern Recognition (IAPR)
- Center for Soft Computing Research: A National Facility, ISI, Kolkata
- International Rough Set Society (IRSS)
- Web Intelligence Consortium (WIC)

Abstracts of Keynote, Invited and Special Talks

Statistical Learning with Sparsity

Trevor Hastie

Stanford University, USA
hastie@stanford.edu

Abstract. In a statistical world faced with an explosion of data, regularization has become an important ingredient. Often data are "wide" - we have many more variables than observations - and the lasso penalty and its hybrids have become increasingly useful. This talk presents a general framework for fitting large-scale regularization paths for a variety of problems. We describe the approach, and demonstrate it via examples using our R package GLMNET. We then outline a series of related problems using extensions of these ideas.

* Joint work with Jerome Friedman, Robert Tibshirani, and many students, past and present

Progress in Learning to Simplify Ultrasound

Alison Noble

University of Oxford, UK
alison.noble@eng.ox.ac.uk

Abstract. Automating the human skill of clinical ultrasound acquisition and interpretation is proving surprisingly difficult. Deep learning, which has been around for over a decade now, has provided a computational tool to advance understanding of both why scanning is hard, and to define assistive technologies to support humans to perform diagnostic ultrasound. I describe two quite different approaches we have been investigating on this topic. The first approach builds computational models of ultrasound tasks from simple-to-learn bespoke ultrasound scan sweep protocols making the models potentially suitable for triage in global health settings. The second is to take a multi-modal video analysis approach, whereby we use human gaze, probe movements and audio together with video to build learning-based models of ultrasound-based tasks. As I will show, deep learning underpins these solutions, but demonstrating success requires thinking beyond the algorithm.

More Is Different - Beyond Wittgenstein's Philosophy

Dacheng Tao

University of Sydney, Australia
dacheng.tao@sydney.edu.au

Abstract. Unleashing the hidden wisdom within broad data has become a captivating pursuit for the community. Among the myriad of possibilities, one solution stands out: foundation models. These behemoth architectures, powered by transformers, possess the ability to extract and harness the enigmatic dark knowledge that resides within broad data. Parameters, computations, and data combine in a symphony of potential, demonstrating that in the world of transformers, "more is different", and reigniting our dreams for Artificial General Intelligence.

In this presentation, we embark on a thrilling journey into the world of foundation models. We begin by introducing the ground-breaking LLMs ChatGPT and the wave of innovation they have set in motion. Along the way, we discuss concerns about the singularity of these techniques and offer our insights into this emerging trend. We then delve into theoretical foundations, example designs in NLP and CV, efficient decentralized optimization algorithms, and useful applications that flourish under the influence of foundation models. Yet, this adventure also highlights the challenges and opportunities that lie ahead in the era of these models. As we conclude, we do so with unwavering optimism: foundation models will play a pivotal role in shaping artificial intelligence. Join us on this remarkable expedition into the seamless integration of data, computational power, and algorithms, where the future unveils itself in unprecedented ways.

Reinforcement Learning with Structured Actions and Policies

Balaraman Ravindran

Indian Institute of Technology Madras
ravi@cse.iitm.ac.in

Abstract. Deep Reinforcement Learning has been very successful in solving a variety of hard problems. But many RL architectures treat the action as coming from an unordered set or from a bounded interval. It is often the case that the actions and policies have a non-trivial structure that can be exploited for more efficient learning. In this talk, I will present several scenarios in which taking advantage of the structure leads to more efficient learning. In particular, I will talk about some of our recent work on learning representations for actions that capture the underlying spatial structures and on learning ensemble policies.

Improving Machine Vision using Insights from Neuroscience

SP Arun

Indian Institute of Science Bangalore
sparun@iisc.ac.in

Abstract. Deep neural networks have revolutionized computer vision with their impressive performance on vision tasks. Recently their object representations have been found to match well to the visual areas of the brain. Yet their performance is still worse than humans, and it has been challenging to derive insight into why deep networks work or how they can be improved. In our lab we have been comparing object representations in brains and deep networks with the aim of understanding how we see and to make machine see better. We have shown that systematic biases in deep networks can be identified by comparing with brain representations, and that fixing these biases can improve performance. We have also been testing deep networks for the presence or absence of a variety of classic perceptual phenomena. Taken together these results suggest that accumulated wisdom from vision neuroscience can help us understand and improve deep neural networks. For more information, visit our research group, the Vision Lab at IISc at https://sites.google.com/site/visionlabiisc/

Computer-Aided Healthcare in Era of Artificial Intelligence

Gajendra P. S. Raghava

Indraprastha Institute of Information Technology, New Delhi
raghava@iiitd.ac.in

Abstract. The field of health informatics encompasses a wide range of disciplines aimed at acquiring, processing, and interpreting data to improve human health and healthcare services. Within the healthcare domain, informatics encompasses several specialized fields, including cheminformatics, pharmacoinformatic, health informatics, and medical/clinical informatics, which collectively generate an extensive amount of biological and clinical data. Bioinformatics, in particular, plays a pivotal role in compiling, storing, annotating, and analysing this data, making it accessible to both biologists and non-biologists alike. In light of the escalating global healthcare burden caused by emerging infectious diseases, the need for efficient drug discovery and development has become paramount. Informatics advancements, such as cheminformatics and pharmacoinformatic, have significantly reduced costs and time associated with drug discovery by enabling the identification of drug targets, selection of lead compounds, and prediction of crucial drug properties. Moreover, the field of immunoinformatic has emerged as a crucial player in vaccine development, employing computational tools to expedite the discovery of potential vaccine candidates. Medical/clinical informatics deals primarily with patient data, clinical knowledge, and information related to patient care, playing a pivotal role in disease diagnosis through the identification of biomarkers and assisting healthcare professionals in providing personalized treatments. The advent of the Internet of Things (IoT) has further revolutionized healthcare by facilitating the development of mobile apps, telemedicine platforms, and wearable sensor-based devices that enable remote monitoring and real-time health data collection. This talk aims to provide a comprehensive overview of freely available computational tools and databases in key areas of healthcare, such as drug discovery, toxicity and adverse effects assessment, vaccine development, disease diagnosis, and IoT applications. The featured resources encompass databases, web servers, standalone applications, and mobile apps, offering a diverse range of support to researchers across various healthcare disciplines. By highlighting these valuable resources, researchers can leverage their functionalities to expedite their work and contribute to the advancement of human health and healthcare services (https://webs.iiitd.edu.in/)

Adventures and Impact of AI in Face Recognition and Deepfakes

Richa Singh

Indian Institute of Technology, Jodhpur
richa@iitj.ac.in

Abstract: The increasing capabilities of machine learning algorithms is enabling the research community to address a number of long standing computer vision problems. However, as the saying goes that beauty lies in the eyes of the beholder, a technology can be utilized for both positive and negative tasks. For instance, while face recognition can provide solutions to problems like missing children and injured face identification, it can also be misused for similar tasks. We will discuss research initiatives in face recognition and deepfake that we have been pursuing along with the technological contributions and the social impact in the community.

India's First Solar Space observatory: Aditya L1 and scope of AI

Dipankar Banerjee

Aryabhatta Research Institute of Observational Sciences, India
dipu@aries.res.in

Abstract: Aditya L1 mission is the first observatory class solar mission from the Indian Space Research organization, launched in September 2023. With a combination of four remote sensing and 3 in situ instruments covering multi-wavelength it provides a unique opportunity to have joint observations with other co temporal missions. I will give a quick summary update of the status of the mission. In the context of AI and ML I will demonstrate how these techniques will enable us to analyze the data from these instruments and help us performing predictive science as well.

Convex Optimization: Tools and Applications in Statistics and Data Science

Balasubramanian Narasimhan

Stanford University, USA
naras@stanford.edu

Abstract: Optimization plays an important role in Statistics and Data Science and many algorithms rely on estimators that result from solving convex optimization problem. I will introduce "Disciplined Convex Optimization" (DCP), a constructive approach to formulating such problems. DCP provides mathematical building blocks with known properties along with a set of rules to combine them. Although these rules are sufficient (but not necessary) conditions for convexity, the approach captures a sizeable class of problems researchers encounter. Specifically, I will describe our work on CVXR, which implements DCP in the R programming language. To solve a convex problem, one specifies an objective and constraints by combining constants, variables, parameters, and a library of functions in a manner that closely mirrors the actual mathematical description. CVXR then applies DCP rules to verify the problem's convexity. Once verified, the problem is converted into standard conic form using graph implementations and passed to a numerical solver. If time permits, I will demonstrate with some examples.

Contents

Deep Learning

Statistical Learning

Cognitive Computing

Information Security

Biometrics

Bioinformatics

Pattern Recognition

An Efficient Approach for Findings Document Similarity Using Optimized Word Mover's Distance

Atanu Dey[1(✉)], Mamata Jenamani[1], and Arijit De[2]

[1] Indian Institute of Technology Kharagpur, Kharagpur, India
atanu.dey.cse@kgpian.iitkgp.ac.in, mj@iem.iitkgp.ac.in
[2] The University of Manchester, Manchester, UK
arijit.de@manchester.ac.uk

Abstract. We introduce Optimized Word Mover's Distance (OWMD), a similarity function that compares two sentences based on their word embeddings. The method determines the degree of semantic similarity between two sentences considering their interdependent representations. Within a sentence, all the words may not be relevant for determining contextual similarity at the aspect level with another sentence. To account for this fact, we designed OWMD in two ways: first, it decreases system's complexity by selecting words from the sentence pair according to a predefined set of dependency parsing criteria; Second, it applies the *word mover's distance (WMD)* method to previously chosen words. When comparing the dissimilarity of two text sentences, the WMD method is used because it represents the minimal "journey time" required for the embedded words of one sentence to reach the embedded words of another sentence. Finally, adding an exponent function to the inverse of the OWMD dissimilarity score yields the resulting similarity score, called Optimized Word Mover's Similarity (OWMS). Using STSb-Multi-MT dataset, the OWMS measure decreases MSE, RMSE, and MAD error rates by 66.66%, 40.70%, and 37.93% respectively than previous approaches. Again, OWMS reduces MSE, RMSE, and MAD error rates on Semantic Textual Similarity (STS) dataset by 85.71%, 62.32%, and 60.17% respectively. For STSb-Multi-MT and STS datasets, the suggested strategy reduces run-time complexity by 33.54% and 49.43%, respectively, compared to the best of existing approaches.

Keywords: Word embedding · Document distance · Contextual similarity · Document similarity · Word mover's distance · NLP Optimization

1 Introduction

The endeavor of determining how similar in meaning two brief texts are to one another is called "Contextual Similarity" (CS) [1]. Assigning a number between 0 and 1 (or 0 and 5) is a common method of tagging this similarity,

P. Maji et al. (Eds.): PReMI 2023, LNCS 14301, pp. 3–11, 2023.
https://doi.org/10.1007/978-3-031-45170-6_1

with higher scores indicating greater levels of resemblance between the two texts [2]. Numerous research papers have addressed the issue of contextual similarity. Although supervised models perform well in this regard, labeled training data may be costly and fine-tuning hyper-parameter (HP) may be error-prone [4–7]. These issues can be addressed via unsupervised approaches such as ROUGE and BLEU, employed word-matching [8]. These methods also have limitations in terms of computational efficiency, and often miss the information that have been reworded or rearranged from the source text. Unsupervised embedding-based methods have been proposed to tackle this challenge; however, ensemble methods may increase complexity and cost [2]. Instead, word mover's distance (WMD) may be used to evaluate text in a continuous space using pre-trained word embeddings [9–11]. Many applications of WMD have found success, including automatic evaluation of essays, and identification of emotions [1,3]. Such Bag-of-word approaches particularly for lengthy sentences, are computationally costly and may not necessary for aspect-level contextual similarity [1,3]. Figure 1 shows two sample sentence pairs for contextual similarity. The blue-boxed words are recognized utilizing WMD techniques, whereas the green-underlined words are adequate to determine the optimal distance between two contexts.

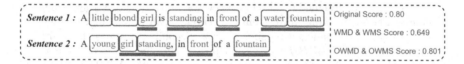

Fig. 1. An example of WMD and OWMD between two sentences

Considering above challenges towards findings aspect-level contextual similarity, the following contributions are as follows for this work: 1) We propose a dependency-parsing-based algorithm to select appropriate words for aspect-level contextual resemblance. It decreases the complexity and improves the accuracy of the system. 2) We have used embedding of aforesaid words as input to the WMD model [1], which is a hyper-parameter (HP) free unsupervised model and less complex than BOW model. 3) Apart from addressing the research challenges, we compare our work with three state-of-the-art methods ROUGE-L, WMS and Re-Eval-WMS on two benchmark datasets such as STSb-Multi-MT and STS.

Rest of the paper is organized as follows. The next section includes a literature review. Section 3 described the proposed method. Section 4 contains the outcomes of the experiment. Section 5 concludes the article and outlines its future applicability.

2   Literature Survey

Table 1 compares modern supervised and unsupervised document similarity methods. Labeled training data is expensive and time-consuming for supervised

Table 1. Comparison on supervised & unsupervised techniques for document similarity

Types	Methodology	Year	Features			Remarks
			HP Tuning	Ensemble	All Data	
Supervised	UWB [4]	2016	✓	✗	✓	Uses deep learning models and natural language processing (NLP) properties (called modified IDF weight).
	BIT [5]	2017	✓	✗	✓	Uses WordNet and British National Corpus to enrich the semantic space.
	ECNU [6]	2017	✓	✓	✓	Builds a global semantic similarity model using ensemble deep learning.
	Learn Short STS [7]	2019	✓	✗	✓	Uses word embeddings and semantic relatedness from other source.
Unsupervised	ROUGE-L [8]	2004	✗	✗	✓	One of the first efforts to employ an expensive Longest Common Word-Matching algorithm b/w two sentences.
	Meerkat Mafia [13]	2014	✓	✗	✓	Trains a Latent Semantic model using three billion English words.
	WMD [1]	2015	✗	✗	✓	Uses bag-of-word (BOW) embeddings to calculate word mover's distance (WMD).
	UESTS [2]	2019	✗	✓	✗	Introduces BabelNet-based synset-focused word aligner.
	WMD & WMS [3]	2019	✗	✗	✓	Uses WMD to compute Word mover's similarity (WMS) score b/w two texts.
	Re-eval WMD [12]	2022	✗	✗	✓	Uses WMD's values in high-dimension spaces, similar to L1-normalized BOW's.
	Proposed	2023	✗	✗	✗	Using dependency-parsing-based algo and WMD to compute Optimized Word mover's similarity (OWMS)

work [4–7]. Unsupervised approach is preferred when labeled training data is not available [1,3]. Several researchers have created unsupervised string-matching algorithms, but if the word sequence changes, they may lose accuracy [2,8]. To address this, a few authors have presented optimization-models for document similarity with accuracy, but they are time-consuming [1,3,12]. High computational cost is of no use for huge volume of datasets. This fact motivates us to simplify a document similarity optimization model without losing accuracy. Word embedding plays a vital role for such optimization models. The 100-dimensional pre-trained Glove vectors [9] beat Word2Vec [11], and BERT [10] on several document similarity datasets. Thus, we choose Glove for this piece of research.

3   Optimized Word Mover's Similarity

Dependency parsing selects words from two target sentences first in the proposed approach. Next, NLP steps remove stop words, symbols, numerical figures, and lemmatization from the selected words. Next, the WMD algorithm determines the optimal distance between the sentences. The detailed procedure is as follows:

3.1 Dependency Parsing Based Word Selection

Without regard to emotional tone, the similarity between two sentences may often be determined by their key contextual words. Therefore, we suggest a dependency parsing-based system for choosing appropriate words. In this regard, we tweak the method used by Qiu et al. (2011), which extracts the sentence's context by selecting just noun phrases [14]. Our deep research reveals that not just noun phrases ('NN', 'NNS') but also certain verb phrases ('VBD', 'VBG', 'VBZ', and 'VB') have contextual meaning at the aspect-level. As we have excluded emotional terms for the sake of similarity, hence no 'adverbs' or 'adjectives' are considered. For example, in Fig. 2, three nouns "girl", "front", "fountain" and one verb "standing" convey the whole meaning of the sentence regardless of other words.

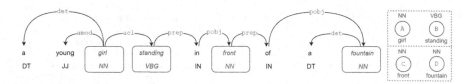

Fig. 2. Example of contextual word selection from a sentence

3.2 Word Mover's Distance (WMD)

WMD calculates text similarity using the discrete *Earth Mover's Distance (EMD)* based on transportation problem [1]. It uses text's bag-of-word (BOW) representations and word embedding similarities. For any two sentences $S1$ and $S2$, WMD is defined as the minimal cost required to transform one into the other. As shown in Eq. 1, the cost amount $F_{i,S1}$ of word i depends on it's relative frequency of the word in a sentence $S1$. Where, $|S1|$ is the total word count of the sentence S1. $F_{j,S2}$ is calculated similarly for sentence $S2$, where index j denotes each word.

$$F_{i,S1} = \frac{count(i)}{|S1|} \tag{1}$$

Now, let w_i represent the embedding of word i, where length of the embedding vector is denoted by d, i.e., $w_i \in \mathbb{R}^d$. The Euclidean distance between embeddings of words i and j is given by $\delta(i,j)$ as shown in Eq. 2.

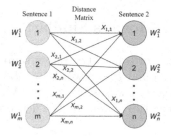

Fig. 3. Sentence to sentence distance measure using selected words and WMD

$$\delta(i,j) \;=\; ||w_i - w_j||^2 \tag{2}$$

Now, WMD can be realized as the solution of linear program as shown in Eq. 3, 4 and 5. Where, m is the number of words in sentence $S1$ and n is the number of words in sentence $S2$ after removing stop words. $\delta(i,j)$ is the Euclidean distance as described in Eq. 2. $X \in \mathbb{R}^{m \times n}$ is a non-negative matrix within which $X_{i,j}$ represents the cost of travelling from word i of sentence $S1$ (denoted by $W_i^1, i = 1..m$) to word j of sentence $S2$ (denoted by $W_j^2, j = 1..n$) as shown in Fig. 3. Specifically, WMD assures that the cost of total outgoing flow cost from each word (i) of $S1$ to all the words (j) in $S2$ is $F_{i,S1}$ in Eq. 4. In addition, Eq. 5 represents the cost of incoming flow to each word (j) of $S2$ from all the words (i) of $S1$ is $F_{j,S2}$.

$$WMD(S1, S2) \;=\; Minimize \sum_{i=1}^{m} \sum_{j=1}^{n} X_{i,j} \cdot \delta(i,j) \tag{3}$$

subject to:

$$\sum_{j=1}^{n} X_{i,j} = F_{i,S1}, \; \forall\, i \in S1 \tag{4}$$

$$\sum_{i=1}^{m} X_{i,j} = F_{j,S2}, \; \forall\, j \in S2 \tag{5}$$

As shown in Eq. 6, the exponent function transforms the dissimilarity measure (WMD) into a similarity score in the range of {0,1} (called "word mover's similarity" (WMS)), where higher values indicate greater similarity [3].

$$WMS(S1, S2) \;=\; exp\,(-WMD(S1, S2)) \tag{6}$$

We use the above describe process with selective words as explained in Sect. 3.1, which is supported by Hassan et al. [2]. Now, the proposed distance metric is called *optimized word mover's distance (OWMD)* and similarity metric as *optimized word mover's similarity (OWMS)*.

4 Result and Discussion

Following the discussion in Sect. 3, Table 2 shows WMD and OWMD approaches in action. WMD uses BOW technique to extract seven and five words from sentence 1 and 2 respectively, which are highlighted in orange. OWMD uses a dependency parsing (DP) strategy to select five and four words from both sentences, respectively, and underlined them in blue. As discussed in [1] and the pictorial representation of Fig. 3, each of these terms is treated as a node in the linear transportation problem. Multiplying the node counts of both sentences yields the number of decision variables, and adding the node counts yields the number of constraints.

We conduct experiments to compare three state-of-the-art methods with the proposed one using two real-world data sets. Due to a widespread use in various

Table 2. Example of WMD and OWMD methods using two sentences

Methods	Sentence 1	Sentence 2	Variables	Constraints
	a little blonde girl is standing in front of a water fountain	a young girl standing in front of a fountain		
WMD [1]	['little', 'blonde', 'girl', 'standing','front', 'water', 'fountain']	['young','girl', 'standing', 'front', 'fountain']	$7 \times 5 = 35$	$7 + 5 = 12$
OWMD	['girl','stand', 'front', 'water', 'fountain']	['girl','stand', 'front', 'fountain']	$5 \times 4 = 20$	$5 + 4 = 9$

research, the STSb-Multi-MT[1] (2021) and Semantic-Textual-Similarity (STS)[2] (2018) datasets are selected. Both the datasets comprise of 5750 and 13365 sentence pairings with contextual semantic similarity, respectively. Our annotator removes semantically comparable pairs but keeps contextually related ones. Thus, the STSb-Multi-MT and Semantic-Textual Similarity (STS) datasets have 1606 and 3510 sentences, respectively. For instance, "A woman is writing" and "A woman is swimming" should be around 50% similar based on the context of "woman", yet the original dataset solely analyzed semantic activities like "writing" and "swimming", giving just 10% similarity. Our annotators omit such combinations from the experiment because context affects the relevant score. Another pair of sentences, "a man is standing on a roof top playing a violin" and "a man is on a roof dancing", should be $30\% - 40\%$ similar, however the original dataset also gives 36%. Our annotators maintain those couples for the experiment with a context-relevant score. We compare proposed methods with three state-of-the-art methods in terms of three performance metrics: mean-square-error (MSE), root-means-square-error (RMSE), mean absolute deviation (MAD) and three processing times: 1) optimized processing time (OPT) which is responsible for linear programming solution; 2) dependency processing time (DPT) which is responsible for word selection using dependency parsing strategy; 3) total processing time (TPT) is the sum of aforementioned two processing times.

Table 3. Result comparison on STSB-Multi-MT dataset

Methods	Performance Metrics			Processing Time		
	MSE	RMSE	MAD	OPT	DPT	TPT
ROUGE-L (2004) [8]	0.210	0.459	0.363	-	-	-
WMS (2019) [3]	0.012	0.113	0.087	41.043	0.0	41.043
Re-Eval WMS (2022) [12]	0.149	0.387	0.323	41.793	0.0	41.793
OWMS (Ours)	0.004	0.067	0.054	18.423	8.850	27.274
Gain	0.008	0.046	0.033	22.62	-	13.769
Percentage decrease for proposed method	66.66%	40.70%	37.93%	51.11%	-	33.54%

---

[1] https://huggingface.co/datasets/stsb_multi_mt/viewer/en/train.

[2] https://github.com/anantm95/Semantic-Textual-Similarity/tree/master/data.

Table 4. Result comparison on Semantic Textual Similarity (STS) dataset

Methods	PerformanceMetrics			ProcessingTime		
	MSE	RMSE	MAD	OPT	DPT	TPT
ROUGE-L (2004) [8]	0.192	0.438	0.344	-	-	-
WMS (2019) [3]	0.021	0.146	0.113	106.317	0.0	106.317
Re-Eval WMS (2022) [12]	0.084	0.289	0.229	104.812	0.0	104.812
OWMS (Ours)	0.003	0.055	0.046	34.429	17.829	52.258
Gain	0.018	0.092	0.068	70.383	-	52.554
Percentage decrease for proposed method	85.71%	62.32%	60.17%	66.20%	-	49.43%

Tables 3 and 4 show that our contextual text similarity method outperforms "ROUGE-L", "WMS", and "Re-Eval WMS" on STSb-Multi-MT and Semantic-Textual Similarity (STS) datasets in terms of error evaluation metrics and time complexity. These tables highlight our findings in yellow in the fourth row, while orange represents the best performance among the other three techniques (best among first, second, and third rows). The fifth row shows the proposed technique's gain over the best method. The final row shows the proposed technique's % error and processing time reduction compared to the best-performing prior method. For instance, in Table 3, we minimize MSE, RMSE, and MAD errors by 66.66%, 40.70%, and 37.93%, respectively, compared to the previous approach WMS, which is superior among the three state-of-the-art methods. Our second main claim is that the proposed approach decreases system time complexity compared to prior optimization methods on both the datasets. ROUGE-L is not an optimization algorithm; hence we don't compare it's time complexity to other optimization algorithm. Moreover, in Table 3, we decreased total processing time (TPT) by 13.763 s over the best WMS methodology among two optimization techniques on the STSb-Multi-MT dataset. In Table 4, we reduced TPT by 52.554 s over the best Re-Eval-WMS strategy on the STS dataset. In other words, we reduce TPT by 33.54% and 49.43% on both the dataset respectively. We could have saved 8573.47 seconds (142.89 min or 2.38 h) and 14972.64 seconds (249.54 min or 4.16 h), respectively, if both the datasets contained 1 million identical records.

5   Conclusion

We present OWMD & OWMS, optimized word mover's distance and similarity method for identifying contextual similarity between two sentences at aspect-level irrespective to their semantic matching. This approach has two components: 1) it selects words from sentences using a dependency-parsing based strategy, and 2) it then uses WMD techniques on those words. We conducted experiments using two benchmark datasets namely STSb-Multi-MT and STS. We compare proposed methodology with three contemporary state-of-the-art approaches such as ROUGE-L, WMS and Re-Eval-WMS. OWMS decreases error rates on STSb-Multi-MT dataset by 66.66%, 40.70%, and 37.93% for MSE, RMSE, and MAD respectively, compared to previous approaches. On STS dataset, OWMS reduces error rates by 85.71%, 62.32%, and 60.17% for MSE, RMSE, and MAD respectively. The proposed solution decreases run-time complexity for STSb-Multi-MT and STS datasets by 33.54 and 49.44%, respectively, compared to previous ones. Thus, it may be used for large datasets containing millions of records and save hours of processing time. The proposed method is especially advantageous in the absence of training data since it is a hyper-parameter-less unsupervised method. In the future, we want to improve the suggested approach and conduct a rigorous mathematical analysis of its robustness.

References

1. Kusner, M., Sun, Y., Kolkin, N., Weinberger, K.: From word embeddings to document distances. In: International Conference on Machine Learning, pp. 957–966. PMLR (2015)
2. Hassan, B., Abdelrahman, S.E., Bahgat, R., Farag, I.: UESTS: an unsupervised ensemble semantic textual similarity method. IEEE Access **7**, 85462–85482 (2019)
3. Clark, E., Celikyilmaz, A., Smith, N.A.: Sentence mover' similarity: automatic evaluation for multi-sentence texts. In: Proceedings of the 57th Annual Meeting of the Association for Computational Linguistics, pp. 2748–2760 (2019)
4. Brychcín, T., Svoboda, L.: UWB at SemEval-2016 task 1: semantic textual similarity using lexical, syntactic, and semantic information. In: Proceedings of the 10th International Workshop on Semantic Evaluation (SemEval-2016), pp. 588–594 (2016)
5. Wu, H., Huang, H.Y., Jian, P., Guo, Y., Su, C.: BIT at SemEval-2017 task 1: using semantic information space to evaluate semantic textual similarity. In: Proceedings of the 11th International Workshop on Semantic Evaluation (SemEval-2017), pp. 77–84 (2017)
6. Tian, J., Zhou, Z., Lan, M., Wu, Y.: ECNU at SemEval-2017 task 1: leverage kernel-based traditional NLP features and neural networks to build a universal model for multilingual and cross-lingual semantic textual similarity. In: Proceedings of the 11th international workshop on semantic evaluation (SemEval-2017), pp. 191–197 (2017)
7. Nguyen, H.T., Duong, P.H., Cambria, E.: Learning short-text semantic similarity with word embeddings and external knowledge sources. Knowl.-Based Syst. **182**, 104842 (2019)
8. Lin, C.Y.: ROUGE: a package for automatic evaluation of summaries. In: Text Summarization Branches Out, pp. 74–81 (2004)
9. Pennington, J., Socher, R., Manning, C.D.: GloVe: global vectors for word representation. In: Proceedings of the 2014 Conference on Empirical Methods in Natural Language Processing (EMNLP), pp. 1532–1543 (2014)
10. Devlin, J., Chang, M.W., Lee, K., Toutanova, K.: BERT: pre-training of deep bidirectional transformers for language understanding. arXiv preprint arXiv:1810.04805 (2018)
11. Mikolov, T., Chen, K., Corrado, G., Dean, J.: Efficient estimation of word representations in vector space. arXiv preprint arXiv:1301.3781 (2013)

12. Sato, R., Yamada, M., Kashima, H.: Re-evaluating word mover' distance. In: International Conference on Machine Learning, pp. 19231–19249. PMLR (2022)
13. Kashyap, A.L., et al.: Meerkat mafia: multilingual and cross-level semantic textual similarity systems. In: Proceedings of the 8th International Workshop on Semantic Evaluation, pp. 416–423 (2014)
14. Qiu, G., Liu, B., Jiajun, B., Chen, C.: Opinion word expansion and target extraction through double propagation. Comput. Linguist. **37**(1), 9–27 (2011)

Aggregate Load Forecasting in Residential Smart Grids Using Deep Learning Model

Kakuli Mishra[1], Srinka Basu[2(✉)], and Ujjwal Maulik[1]

[1] Jadavpur University, Kolkata, India
[2] University of Kalyani, Kalyani, India
srinka.basu@gmail.com

Abstract. Since the integration of smart grids in power grid sector, large amounts of high frequency load consumption data gets accumulated at the microgrids which has been utilized for study and analysis. The rich data availability allows load forecasts from lower level, at buildings to aggregate levels. The aggregate level forecasts have recently gained importance because it acts as a dimensionality reduction approach, however as a result of the reduction, the information content is reduced too. The deep learning models have the capacity to extract the useful information from datasets, hence this paper aims to bring forward the performance of the deep models in case of multiple aggregation techniques. A comparative analysis is performed on the different aggregation techniques and the best is reported.

Keywords: Time series · Smart grids · Deep learning · Load forecasting · Aggregate Load · Clustering

1 Introduction

Load forecasting is a tool integration to the digitized smart grid system which estimates the future load of the grid with respect to the previous information collected from the grid. The forecasts at building level can yield substantial energy savings [8]. Two challenges involved in forecasting at building level are (i) handling the voluminous data. (ii) volatility of load at building level. The aggregate forecasting is a good solution to the above challenges because the granularity of the data is reduced. The dimensional reduction on the other hand, shown in SeriesNet [14] has also been successful in handling the voluminous data. The forecasts at individual building level help to capture the peak hours of usage [2] and accordingly plan for load shifting operations.

The literature shows several aggregation techniques, but limited works have discussed on the comparison between the different aggregation techniques using the state-of-the-art models. The authors in [13] have studied several aggregation levels for short term load forecasting using a deep learning model. Feng et al. in [3], discuss three different aggregation strategies- information aggregation (IA), model aggregation (MA) and hierarchical aggregation (HA). The IA is the

P. Maji et al. (Eds.): PReMI 2023, LNCS 14301, pp. 12–19, 2023.
https://doi.org/10.1007/978-3-031-45170-6_2

aggregation of external information [15], the MA is the aggregation at model building stage [9] and the HA is the load data aggregation at different levels [3].

A general categorization of aggregation techniques is- top-down and bottom-up aggregation [4]. In the former case, the data for individual buildings at the bottom level is aggregated to get a single timeseries and the forecasts are generated for the aggregated TS while in the latter case, the forecasts are obtained for all the buildings available and aggregated at the top. According to Peter et al. [12], there exist disadvantages of both the top-down and bottom-up approaches, the former causes information loss because of the single level aggregation and the latter has more noisy and dynamic TS which makes the forecasting difficult. Nystrup et al. in [12] combines the advantages of both top-down and bottom-up approaches.

The aim of this paper is to use deep learning model [11] for aggregate forecasts and study the comparative analysis of the different aggregation levels on the real life energy consumption data of residential homes and office buildings. Several works in literature [1] show that cluster based aggregation yield improved forecasting results as that of individual level forecasts. In this paper, the contribution is to experimentally prove that there exist other aggregate techniques that can yield good results other than the cluster based aggregation. The dilated convolution network [11], used in this paper, has wider filters that can capture the long-term dependencies from TS data. The aggregation techniques used are cluster-based aggregate, complete disaggregate and complete aggregate.

The rest of the paper is organized as- the proposed method in Sect. 2, experimental setup in Sect. 3, results and analysis in section and the conclusions and future work.

2   Proposed Method

In this section we discuss the proposed method to obtain the aggregate forecasts using multiple aggregation techniques and their complexity analysis.

2.1   Dilated Convolutional Dense Network

The components of dilated CNN is same as that of CNN with a change in the filter width. In case of dilated CNN, the filter size is increased by introducing gaps in between the filter values. The dilation factor controls the number of gaps to be introduced in the filter. In Fig. 1, we show the n layered *Dilated Convolutional Dense* Network (DaNSe) load forecasting model used in our study. The input to the model is a TS data obtained from the several aggregation techniques which is explained later in section. The residual connections in DaNSe help in learning the shallower counterpart of the model and makes the optimization easier. DaNSe uses two activation functions- Scaled Exponential Linear Unit (SeLu) and Rectified linear Unit (ReLu). The SeLu activation has a self-normalizing property that scales the model parameters within a range of 0 to 1 [7]. The SeLu activation enables a faster learning and a better convergence. The output from SeLu activation as shown in Fig. 1 is fed to 1×1 convolution so that the summation of the input with the output from SeLu is valid.

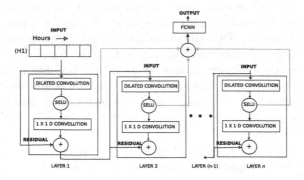

Fig. 1. Proposed DaNSe architecture in [11]

Fully Connected Neural Network (FCNN) is used at the output layer of DaNSe model. The output from the SeLu activation of each DaNSe layer is summed up and fed to the FCNN. The FCNN learns the features obtained from the DaNSe layers and gives the final output. The Relu activation [5] is used in the FCNN layers. For a negative input ReLu outputs zero and for a positive input, ReLu outputs the same value.

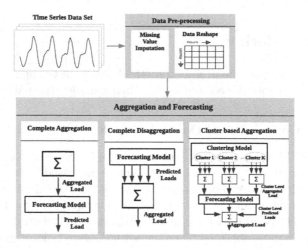

Fig. 2. Steps for the aggregation techniques. Three different aggregation techniques are shown, cluster based aggregation, complete disaggregate and complete aggregate. The $\sum$ represents the aggregation operation.

2.2   Aggregation Techniques

In this section, we discuss the aggregation techniques used. Let the TS dataset for n houses is given as $D = \{H_i\}_{i=1}^{n}$ where $H_i = \{h_i^x\}_{x=1}^{p}$, h_i^x represents the power consumed at time interval x and $|H_i| = p$. Figure 2 shows the steps of the aggregation techniques. The data preprocessing step, includes missing value identification. The missing values are replaced by moving averages.

Cluster Based Aggregation (CL-A): Hierarchical clustering (HC) with Dynamic Time Warping distance(DTW) is performed in the TS dataset D to group the houses with similar consumption. The number of clusters are decided based on cluster quality measures: Silhoutte score, Dunn index, Gamma score and Entropy. Let the clusters be represented as $C = \{c_k\}_{k=1}^{l}$ and $c_k = \{H_1, H_2, \ldots H_m\}$, $m << n$. Aggregate TS of the cluster is mean of power consumption of the houses in a cluster, given as: $\sum(c_k^{ag}) = \left\{ \frac{\sum_{i=1}^{m} h_i^1}{m}, \frac{\sum_{i=1}^{m} h_i^2}{m}, \ldots, \frac{\sum_{i=1}^{m} h_i^p}{m} \right\}$. The mean of (c_k^{ag}) is fed to the forecasting model and aggregate forecasts are obtained from respective clusters. The aggregate forecasts of the clusters are averaged to get the cluster based aggregated output.

Complete Disaggregation (CO-DA): In this case, the forecasting model is trained for each house H_i and the forecasts are obtained for each of them. The mean of the forecasted values of n houses is the CO-DA output. Let the forecast for house $H_i = \{\hat{h}_i^u\}_{u=1}^{v}$, where $\hat{h}_i^u$ is the forecasted value at u^{th} hour. The CO-DA output is: $\sum(D_{ag}) = \left\{ \frac{\sum_{i=1}^{n} \hat{h}_i^1}{n}, \frac{\sum_{i=1}^{n} \hat{h}_i^2}{n}, \ldots, \frac{\sum_{i=1}^{n} \hat{h}_i^v}{n} \right\}$.

Complete Aggregation (CO-A): In this case, the forecasting model is trained on the mean power consumption at each time interval over the entire dataset D. It is given as $\sum(D_{ag}) = \left\{ \frac{\sum_{i=1}^{n} h_i^1}{n}, \frac{\sum_{i=1}^{n} h_i^2}{n}, \ldots, \frac{\sum_{i=1}^{n} h_i^p}{n} \right\}$. The forecasting model is trained on D_{ag} to get the aggregated output.

2.3   Complexity Analysis

The CL-A includes DTW distance computation, HC, aggregation, future load forecasts and the outlier detection. The time complexity of DTW distance measure is $O(p \times q)$, where p and q is the length of TS H_i and H_j respectively. Total time complexity for distance matrix computation is $O(n^2)$. Time complexity of HC is $O(n^3)$. The time complexity of aggregate forecasting is a constant c. Hence the total time complexity for the CL-A technique is $O(n^3)$. In case of CO-DA and CO-A, technique, the time complexity for mean computation is $O(n)$.

3   Materials

Datasets: The model has been validated on three different datasets- Smart meter London dataset [10], residential and commercial buildings of IRISH dataset [6]. Some of the London households participated in the UK Power Networks based low carbon project between the year November 2011 and February 2014. The data consists of half hourly electricity consumption of the buildings. The IRISH dataset contains half hourly electricity consumption of the residential and commercial buildings of Ireland during the year 2009–10.

Other Models for Comparative Analysis: In addition to the SeriesNet architecture [14], the DaNSe architecture is compared with CNN and LSTM models.

The below performance measures are used to determine the number of clusters in case of CL-A technique and to compare the performance of the DaNSe model with the state-of-the-art.

Performance Measures: We choose the three different measures to decide the number of clusters - Silhoutte score, Dunn index and the Gamma score, and an entropy measure is used to check if the predicted number of clusters can carry sufficient information about the data or not.

The error metrics are used to compare the load forecasts obtained from the CL-A, CO-DA and CO-A techniques using the DaNSe architecture and the existing state-of-the-art models. Considering the dataset $D = \{H_i\}_{i=1}^{n}$, the error metrics are explained.

Symmetric Mean Absolute Percentage Error (SMAPE): SMAPE for TS H_i is represented as, $SMAPE(H_i) = \frac{1}{N} \sum_{x=1}^{N} \frac{|F_i^x - A_i^x|}{(|F_i^x| + |A_i^x|)/2}$

where, F_i^x and A_i^x represents the forecasted and the actual values for TS H_i, x is the number of predicted values in H_i. The overall $SMAPE$ of the dataset D is given as $S(D) = \frac{1}{n} \sum_{i=1}^{n} SMAPE(H_i)$.

Root Mean Square Error (RMSE): For a TS H_i, $RMSE(H_i) = \sqrt{\frac{\sum_{x=1}^{N}(F_i^x - A_i^x)^2}{N}}$. The overall $RMSE$ of the dataset D is given as $R(D) = \frac{1}{n} \sum_{i=1}^{n} RMSE(H_i)$

Mean Absolute Error (MAE): For a time series H_i, $MAE(H_i) = \frac{\sum_{x=1}^{N}|F_i^x - A_i^x|}{N}$. The overall MAE, of the dataset D is given as $M(D) = \frac{1}{n} \sum_{i=1}^{n} MAE(H_i)$.

3.1   Hyperparameters

The proposed DaNSe model has 7 layers and the dilation factor is increased exponentially with increase in number of layers, that is 1, 2, 4, 8, 16, 32 and 64. We choose 7 layers because a lesser number of layers gave poor results. The model gives the best result in case of truncated normal weight initialization technique . The Adaptive momentum (ADAM) learning algorithm is used with a learning rate of 0.0075, β_1 and β_2 is 0.9. To avoid the model overfitting, dropout and L2 regularization technique is used. The output layer has 3 fully connected layers and 32 hidden units with ReLu activation. The model is trained for 2500 epochs and mean absolute error is used to measure the performance. For comparative analysis, two layered CNN and LSTM models, with 32 hidden units are used. The increase in number of layers has shown negligible changes in accuracy of forecasts.

Table 1. Performance metrics of DaNSe and other models for different aggregation techniques.

Type	Model	London			Residential			SME		
		S(D)	R(D)	M(D)	S(D)	R(D)	M(D)	S(D)	R(D)	M(D)
CL-A	SeriesNet	0.18	**0.03**	0.03	**0.38**	1.27	0.71	**0.86**	3.59	3.32
	CNN	1.9	0.17	0.17	0.87	1.11	0.94	0.98	3.65	3.35
	LSTM	1.99	0.18	0.17	1.97	1.53	1.42	1.99	3.7	3.4
	DaNSE	**0.14**	**0.03**	**0.02**	0.5	1.55	**0.71**	0.93	3.6	**3.32**
CO-DA	SeriesNet	0.16	0.03	0.02	0.49	1.98	0.49	0.18	0.45	0.36
	CNN	1.81	0.17	0.17	1.2	1.25	1.12	1.42	1.72	1.68
	LSTM	1.99	0.18	0.17	1.98	1.53	1.42	1.99	2.04	2.01
	DaNSE	**0.09**	**0.02**	**0.01**	**0.24**	**0.4**	**0.3**	**0.17**	**0.41**	**0.34**
CO-A	SeriesNet	**0.22**	**0.06**	**0.04**	0.42	0.61	0.54	**0.2**	1.11	**0.7**
	CNN	1.76	0.17	0.16	1.69	1.69	1.32	1.54	1.8	1.75
	LSTM	1.99	0.18	0.17	1.99	1.55	1.44	1.99	2	2
	DaNSE	0.30	0.09	0.06	**0.4**	**0.6**	**0.51**	**0.2**	**1.04**	**0.7**

4   Results and Analysis

In this section, we discuss the results obtained from the three different aggregation techniques, the comparative study with the state-of-the-art models, and the comparative study amongst the aggregation techniques.

Following the elbow rule, the number of clusters for London and residential houses is, 6 and 26 for the SME buildings.

Table 1 shows a comparative analysis of the performance metrics obtained from DaNSe and the state-of-the-art models for the three aggregation techniques. For CL-A, the DaNSe model gives good results in the London dataset. In case of residential and SME houses, the SeriesNet wins over the other models. In case of CO-DA and CO-A forecasts, the DaNSe model wins over majority of the cases as compared to other models.

A comparison between the three aggregation techniques from Table 1 shows that in case of London and SME dataset, the three error metrics, $S(D), R(D)$ and $M(D)$ is minimum for the CO-DA case, obtained from the DaNSe model. For the residential dataset, minimum measures are obtained for the CO-A technique in case of DaNSe model. Hence the CO-DA technique gives best forecasts in two out of the three datasets.

In Fig. 3, we report the predicted versus actual plots for the three different aggregation techniques. For the London houses, the best predictions are obtained for CO-DA technique as shown in Fig. 3, second row, first column. The best predictions for residential houses is obtained in case of CO-A but the predicted pattern is shifted unlike the CO-DA predictions. For the SME houses, both the CO-DA and CO-A technique show good match with the actuals however, in the former case, predicted values are smaller than actuals in CO-DA and larger than actuals in CO-A technique.

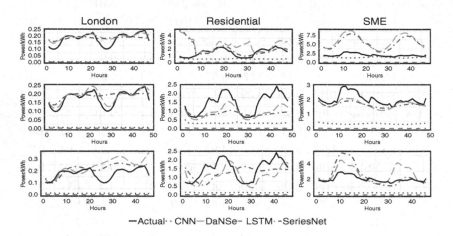

Fig. 3. Prediction versus actual plots. The first row represents the CL-A, second row represents the CO-DA and the third row represents the CO-A technique. Across the columns, the dataset names are shown.

5   Conclusions and Future Work

This paper uses different aggregation techniques to get the load forecasts using a dilated convolutional dense network. A comparative analysis with different deep learning models and the aggregated forecast techniques has been shown. The DaNSe architecture gives the best aggregated forecasts for complete disaggregate and complete aggregate techniques. Therefore, it is shown that there also exists the complete disaggregate and complete aggregate techniques that gives better prediction results that the cluster based aggregation – the commonly used aggregation technique.

As a future scope, we aim to apply the aggregation on streaming TS data. We also aim to automatically detect which type of aggregation will be suitable, based on the analysis of historic TS data.

Acknowledgments. The first author acknowledge the funding for this research from Department of Science and Technology, Women Scientist- B fellowship scheme (DST/WOS-B/ER-2/2021-G).

References

1. Bandara, K., Bergmeir, C., Smyl, S.: Forecasting across time series databases using recurrent neural networks on groups of similar series: a clustering approach. Expert Syst. Appl. **140**, 112896 (2020)
2. Chen, Z., Chen, Y., He, R., Liu, J., Gao, M., Zhang, L.: Multi-objective residential load scheduling approach for demand response in smart grid. Sustain. Cities Soc. **76**, 103530 (2022). https://doi.org/10.1016/j.scs.2021.103530
3. Feng, C., Zhang, J.: Assessment of aggregation strategies for machine-learning based short-term load forecasting. Electr. Power Syst. Res. **184**, 106304 (2020)
4. Gu, Y., Chen, Q., Liu, K., Xie, L., Kang, C.: GAN-based model for residential load generation considering typical consumption patterns. In: 2019 IEEE Power & Energy Society Innovative Smart Grid Technologies Conference (ISGT), pp. 1–5 (2019)
5. Hahnloser, R.H., Sarpeshkar, R., Mahowald, M.A., Douglas, R.J., Seung, H.S.: Digital selection and analogue amplification coexist in a cortex-inspired silicon circuit. Nature **405**(6789), 947–951 (2000)
6. ISSDA: CER smart metering project electricity customer behaviour trial accessed via the Irish social science data (2012). https://www.ucd.ie/issda
7. Klambauer, G., Unterthiner, T., Mayr, A., Hochreiter, S.: Self-normalizing neural networks. In: Advances in Neural Information Processing Systems, pp. 971–980 (2017)
8. Kolokotsa, D.: The role of smart grids in the building sector. Energy Build. **116**, 703–708 (2016)
9. Laurinec, P., Lóderer, M., Lucká, M., Rozinajová, V.: Density-based unsupervised ensemble learning methods for time series forecasting of aggregated or clustered electricity consumption. J. Intell. Inf. Syst. **53**(2), 219–239 (2019)
10. LondonDatastore: Smartmeter energy consumption data in London households (2015). https://data.london.gov.uk/dataset/smartmeter-energy-use-data-in-london-households
11. Mishra, K., Basu, S., Maulik, U.: DaNSe: a dilated causal convolutional network based model for load forecasting. In: Deka, B., Maji, P., Mitra, S., Bhattacharyya, D.K., Bora, P.K., Pal, S.K. (eds.) PReMI 2019. LNCS, vol. 11941, pp. 234–241. Springer, Cham (2019). https://doi.org/10.1007/978-3-030-34869-4_26
12. Nystrup, P., Lindström, E., Pinson, P., Madsen, H.: Temporal hierarchies with autocorrelation for load forecasting. Eur. J. Oper. Res. **280**(3), 876–888 (2020)
13. Shaqour, A., Ono, T., Hagishima, A., Farzaneh, H.: Electrical demand aggregation effects on the performance of deep learning-based short-term load forecasting of a residential building. Energy AI **8**, 100141 (2022)
14. Shen, Z., Zhang, Y., Lu, J., Xu, J., Xiao, G.: SeriesNet: a generative time series forecasting model. In: 2018 International Joint Conference on Neural Networks (IJCNN), pp. 1–8 (2018). https://doi.org/10.1109/IJCNN.2018.8489522
15. Xu, L., Wang, S., Tang, R.: Probabilistic load forecasting for buildings considering weather forecasting uncertainty and uncertain peak load. Appl. Energy **237**, 180–195 (2019)

Spot the Bot: Distinguishing Human-Written and Bot-Generated Texts Using Clustering and Information Theory Techniques

Vasilii Gromov and Quynh Nhu Dang(✉)

National Research University Higher School of Economics, Moscow, Russia
dqnhu00@gmail.com

Abstract. With the development of generative models like GPT-3, it is increasingly more challenging to differentiate generated texts from human-written ones. There is a large number of studies that have demonstrated good results in bot identification. However, the majority of such works depend on supervised learning methods that require labelled data and/or prior knowledge about the bot-model architecture. In this work, we propose a bot identification algorithm that is based on unsupervised learning techniques and does not depend on a large amount of labelled data. By combining findings in semantic analysis by clustering (crisp and fuzzy) and information techniques, we construct a robust model that detects a generated text for different types of bot. We find that the generated texts tend to be more chaotic while literary works are more complex. We also demonstrate that the clustering of human texts results in fuzzier clusters in comparison to the more compact and well-separated clusters of bot-generated texts.

Keywords: Semantic analysis · Clustering · Information theory

1 Introduction

With the development of NLP methods it has become increasingly more difficult to distinguish computer-generated texts from human literature. Many advances have been made in bot detection in various fields. However, state-of-the-art solutions are obtained using supervised methods and depend heavily on labelled data. Not as many works concentrate on self-supervised or unsupervised learning and those that do usually deal with particular bots. Our main objective is to conduct a careful study of semantic paths of both literature and bot-generated texts to find a black-box method for spotting bots. The goal is to find a procedure that distinguishes human-written texts from bot-generated texts without prior knowledge about the bot.

P. Maji et al. (Eds.): PReMI 2023, LNCS 14301, pp. 20–27, 2023.
https://doi.org/10.1007/978-3-031-45170-6_3

Our study provides a general view on how human-written texts and bot-generated texts differ on a semantic level and studies the compactness, separability and noisiness of clusters, as well as the types of text series (deterministic/chaotic/stochastic). Our hypothesis is that these characteristics should differ for human-written and bot-generated texts, and the findings can be used to create an algorithm for bot identification. The advantage of this algorithm lies in its universality and its ability to work with bots of different types - from simple Recurrent Neural Network models to more advanced GPT bots. Our study has shown that different methods highlight various properties of the semantic space. The analysis of the characteristics of semantic paths has shown that human-written texts are more complex, while the bot-generated texts tend to be simpler and more chaotic. The clustering of data has resulted in more compact and well-separated clusters for bot-generated texts and fuzzier clusters for human-written texts. The rest of this paper is organized as follows. In the next section we review recent advances in the bot detection field. Section 3 outlines the methods we have used for the analysis of semantic space. Section 4 provides the description of conducted experiments and presents the results. In Sect. 5 we give our conclusions.

2   Literature Review

Recent years have seen a surge of interest in the bot detection task. Most studies employ feature-based supervised learning algorithms and centre around constructing features which are then used to build a classification model. There are a variety of methods to build such features. [9] use simple lexical and syntactic features like letter frequency or average word length. [8] derive sentiment qualities of English and Dutch tweets by calculating their polarity. [3] model a Twitter user through a set of stylistic features and distinguish bots from human accounts by analysing the consistency of their post style. [4] combine text feature engineering and graph analytics. Similarly, [6] propose SentiBot, an architecture that combines graph-based and sentiment and semantic analysis techniques. In our study, we focus on unsupervised machine learning algorithms, rather than supervised learning methods, and engineer features by clustering texts, examining the resulting semantic space and extracting various characteristics.

Other approaches are based on information theory. [5] characterise the differences between bot and human activity on Twitter by calculating the entropy of account activity statistics. They have found that humans have higher entropy than bots, which highlights their more complex timing behaviour. In our work we apply similar ideas to semantic trajectories of text data instead of meta-data. In [7] the authors study a natural language as an integral whole and ascertain that it is a self-organised critical system, whereas a separate literature text is an avalanche' in a semantic space. The latter fact further reinforces the argument for considering a trajectory in a semantic space as a unified object.

3   Methodology

3.1   Data

For the human written corpus, the literary books were obtained via open sources. See Table 1 for corpora details and python libraries used for each language. To obtain bot-generated texts two models were utilised - a simple Long Short Term Memory recurrent neural network (LSTM), and a GPT-3. We use different models in order to design a working identification algorithm on both simple and complex bots. We train the LSTM model on subsets from the literary corpora and select pretrained GPT models from the huggingface database. To generate texts, for every 500th word from a literary piece we generate a text abstract of 500 words (the conventional size of a book page), therefore, the texts are generated of similar lengths as literary texts.

Table 1. Literature corpora details.

language	corpus size	unique bigrams	library
English	11008	8 m	spacy
Russian	12692	3 m	natasha
Vietnamese	1071	6 m	pyvi

3.2   Embeddings

Word embeddings are obtained using the SVD of a document-term matrix [1] and the word2vec models [12]. The decision to use these two techniques was based on their semantic properties - both SVD and word2vec embeddings capture the structural relationships between words. In order to study word order correlations, we split the texts into n-grams and obtain final embeddings by concatenating word embeddings for each word in an n-gram. The collection of n-gram embeddings for each text is further referred to as a semantic path.

3.3   Clustering

To analyse the semantic space, we use Wishart (density-based) [16] and K-Means [11] clustering techniques[1]. We additionally explore fuzzy implementations of these algorithms to allow for the noisiness and imprecise nature of real-life data. We consider two algorithms: fuzzy clustering C-Means, [2], which is similar to K-Means, and Wishart clustering on fuzzy numbers. To fuzzify the data, we use the notion of fuzzy numbers with trapezoidal membership functions [13]. For each j-th component of an m-dimensional object x we define the value for the fuzzy membership function as $\mu_j(x_j) = \frac{n_j}{\max\limits_{j} n_j}$, where n_j is the normalised frequency

---

[1] Each algorithm has its advantages—K-Means separates spherical clusters well, whereas Wishart algorithm does not make any assumptions about cluster shapes.

of j-th component in the text. With fixed parameter values of $l_j, r_j, \Delta c = m_{2j} - m_{1j}$ we construct the fuzzy number. The ordered set of fuzzy numbers for each component of x is the fuzzification of x.

To fuzzify n-grams, we join fuzzifications of the words from n-grams accordingly to the fuzzy logic, i.e. take the minimum of fuzzy number membership functions. Finally, to use Wishart clustering algorithm (which only requires pairwise distances) on fuzzy data, we calculate the fuzzy distance as defined in [13].

3.4 Entropy-Complexity Plane

The second method proposed in [14] distinguishes chaotic semantic paths from deterministic and stochastic ones. In order to test our hypothesis that the bot-generated texts are less complex and more chaotic, we calculate complexity and entropy measures of the word permutations. The position of the point in relation to the lower and upper theoretical boundaries points to the type of the series in question. Namely, simple deterministic processes occupy the bottom left corner of the plane, stochastic processes, the bottom right corner, whereas chaotic (complex deterministic) processes occupy areas adjacent to the vertex of the upper curve [14]. We also propose a modified variation for multidimensional use: for m-dimensional time series $(x^t)_{t=1}^L$, $x_t \in \mathbb{R}^m$ for each of m components of an n-gram we obtain permutation π_d as in one-dimensional case. For multidimensional case we define the final permutation as $\Pi = (\pi_1, \pi_2, \ldots, \pi_m)$.

4 Results

4.1 Clustering

Prior to text feature extraction using clustering results, we run experiments with the total collections of n-grams found in text corpora. For each type of corpora (human/bot, different languages) 3 million unique n-grams are selected. In order to differentiate bot-generated texts and human-written clusterisations, we study the compactness, separability and noisiness of their clusters. Both the Wishart and K-Means algorithms result in more compact and less separated clusters for bots measured by the RMSSTD and RS metrics [17]. The three languages share a resemblance—the clusters for literature corpora are less compact compared to those of bots. The nonparametric Wilcoxon test [15] shows statistically significant differences between RMSSTD distributions of literature and bots corpora: p-values are less than 0.05 (see Table 2).

Table 2. Wilcoxon test p-values for RMSSTD distribution.

	Russian		English		Vietnamese	
	LSTM	GPT	LSTM	GPT	LSTM	GPT
K-Means	5.63e−3	8.61e−88	7.47e−4	4.93e−2	2.12e−3	1.50e−2
Wishart	5.92e−3	8.15e−28	4.51e−3	2.29e−2	1.32e−5	9.33e−3

The Wishart clustering algorithm can also be used to find noisy data. We have found that out of all types of texts, those generated by LSTM model are the noisiest, while human written and GPT-generated texts are similar in the noise percentage (see Fig. 1). We propose a following interpretation for this observation—the LSTM texts are semantically simpler and the diversity of the texts are mainly achieved by the noise generation.

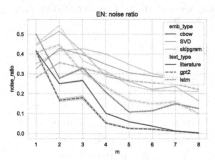

Fig. 1. Noise ratio in English data (found with Wishart algorithm on fuzzified data).

Table 3. Classification performance (accuracy) with intercluster distance measures.

Language	Literature vs.	LSTM+GPT		LSTM		GPT	
	Algorithm	Train	Test	Train	Test	Train	Test
English	K-Means	0.947	0.975	1.0	1.0	0.903	0.881
	Wishart	**0.953**	**0.975**	1.0	1.0	0.904	0.881
	C-Means	0.943	0.970	0.999	1.0	0.897	0.921
	Wishart+Fuzzy	0.945	0.947	1.0	1.0	**0.907**	**0.94**
Russian	K-Means	0.912	0.934	0.999	1.0	0.871	0.916
	Wishart	**0.937**	**0.954**	0.999	1.0	**0.913**	**0.944**
	C-Means	0.882	0.894	0.999	1.0	0.838	0.857
	Wishart+Fuzzy	0.882	0.913	0.991	1.0	0.904	0.911
Vietnamese	K-Means	0.862	0.903	1.0	1.0	0.887	0.881
	Wishart	0.902	0.896	1.0	1.0	0.893	0.900
	C-Means	0.887	0.893	1.0	1.0	0.871	0.871
	Wishart+Fuzzy	**0.929**	**0.942**	1.0	1.0	**0.893**	**0.926**

Based on these findings, we move on to clustering n-grams for each text in order to extract features. As previous experiments have shown that bots have more compact and less separated clusters, we use inter-cluster distances (average, maximum and minimum) as features. Simple SVC models (separate models for each set of parameters and text types) with L2 regularisation are trained and cross-validated on data subsets (1000 texts for each corpus). Table 3 shows the best results for each language. We found that the texts are better distinguished with features extracted from the Wishart algorithm. It is possible that K-Means, as well as its fuzzy variance C-Means, perform worse due to the abstract form of the noisy clusters. It is worth noting that fuzzification improves classification performance on English and Vietnamese texts.

4.2   Entropy-Complexity Plane

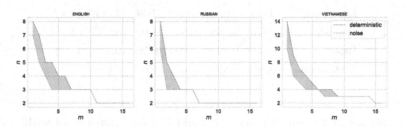

Fig. 2. Chaotic area parameter values for English, Russian and Vietnamese data with Skip-gram embeddings.

For certain parameter sets the entropy-complexity measures can fall into noise or deterministic areas, in which it is difficult to identify different types of texts. To account for this nuisance, we first analyse the values of m and n for which the literary texts fall into chaotic area on the entropy-complexity plane (i.e. close to the upper theoretical boundary). Such parameter sets are marked with the green area in Fig. 2. Sets below the area border result in texts appearing in noise area, above—deterministic area. Values differ significantly for each language: longer sequences fall into the chaotic area with values of n varying from 10 to 14 for $m = 1$ for Vietnamese, whereas for English and Russian the sequences are shorter—n varies from 7 to 8 and from 6 to 8 accordingly.

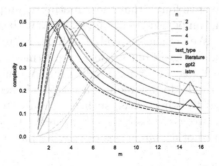

Fig. 3. Mean complexity measure on English data.

On average, the literary texts are more complex, although it is worth noting that for bigrams the more complex texts are LSTM-generated ones (Fig. 3). We believe this happens due to the vast variety of bigrams themselves: more logically coherent texts written by humans or generated by GPT models do not include as many bigrams as the simpler LSTM-generated texts.

Table 4. Classification performance (accuracy) based on entropy-complexity measures.

Literature vs.	LSTM+GPT		LSTM		GPT	
Language	Train	Test	Train	Test	Train	Test
English	0.937	0.965	0.999	1.0	0.997	1.0
Russian	0.879	0.890	0.991	0.992	0.889	0.893
Vietnamese	0.981	0.989	1.0	1.0	0.991	0.995

For the selected parameter sets we build classification model with entropy and complexity measures as features. Again, for the model we use a simple SVC with L2 regularisation. We originally tried classifying texts with the addition of m and n as numeric features, but such a model only achieved 0.57 accuracy on test set. The models for separate parameter sets perform much better, see Table 4 for the best models. LSTM texts are well separated on the entropy-complexity plane, a simple SVC achieves 100% accuracy. GPT texts are also distinguished well—for English and Vietnamese the accuracy is 99%, for Russian—90%. The binary classification model for both bots achieves highest accuracy on Skip-gram data, $m = 1, n = 3$ in English; for Russian—Skip-gram, $m = 1, n = 8$; for Vietnamese—SVD, $m = 3, n = 3$.

5   Conclusions and Further Directions

In order to differentiate generated texts from human literature, we have employed different techniques, such as crisp and fuzzy clustering and entropy-complexity plane construction. We have found that these methods, supplemented by a careful parameter selection, can be used to obtain features with significant differences for different text types. We are therefore able to build robust identification algorithms without prior knowledge of bot-model architecture. The final classification models achieve up to 99% accuracy for English and Vietnamese data and 94% for Russian. These methods do not require a lot of labelled data and thus can be easily downstreamed to other tasks, such as fraud detection. As a possible future direction for this work, we also propose an analysis of the methods of this research in application to other languages of varying language families.

Acknowledgements. This research was supported in part through computational resources of HPC facilities at HSE University [10]. The authors would also like to thank the HSE AI Center for the support throughout the research process.

References

1. Bellegarda, J.R.: Latent semantic mapping: principles & applications. Synthesis Lect. Speech Audio Process. **3**(1), 1–101 (2007)
2. Bezdek, J.C., Ehrlich, R., Full, W.: FCM: the fuzzy C-means clustering algorithm. Comput. Geosci. **10**(2–3), 191–203 (1984)
3. Cardaioli, M., Conti, M., Di Sorbo, A., Fabrizio, E., Laudanna, S., Visaggio, C.A.: It's a matter of style: detecting social bots through writing style consistency. In: 2021 International Conference on Computer Communications and Networks (ICCCN), pp. 1–9. IEEE (2021)
4. Chakraborty, M., Das, S., Mamidi, R.: Detection of fake users in twitter using network representation and NLP. In: 2022 14th International Conference on COMmunication Systems & NETworkS (COMSNETS), pp. 754–758. IEEE (2022)
5. Chu, Z., Gianvecchio, S., Wang, H., Jajodia, S.: Detecting automation of twitter accounts: are you a human, bot, or cyborg? IEEE Trans. Dependable Secure Comput. **9**(6), 811–824 (2012)
6. Dickerson, J.P., Kagan, V., Subrahmanian, V.: Using sentiment to detect bots on twitter: are humans more opinionated than bots? In: 2014 IEEE/ACM International Conference on Advances in Social Networks Analysis and Mining (ASONAM 2014), pp. 620–627. IEEE (2014)
7. Gromov, V.A., Migrina, A.M.: A language as a self-organized critical system. Complexity **2017** (2017)
8. Heidari, M., James Jr, H., Uzuner, O.: An empirical study of machine learning algorithms for social media bot detection. In: 2021 IEEE International IOT, Electronics and Mechatronics Conference (IEMTRONICS), pp. 1–5. IEEE (2021)
9. Kang, A.R., Kim, H.K., Woo, J.: Chatting pattern based game bot detection: do they talk like us? KSII Trans. Internet Inf. Syst. (TIIS) **6**(11), 2866–2879 (2012)
10. Kostenetskiy, P., Chulkevich, R., Kozyrev, V.: HPC resources of the higher school of economics. In: Journal of Physics: Conference Series, vol. 1740, p. 012050. IOP Publishing (2021)
11. MacQueen, J.: Classification and analysis of multivariate observations. In: 5th Berkeley Symposium on Mathematical Statistics and Probability, pp. 281–297 (1967)
12. Mikolov, T., Chen, K., Corrado, G., Dean, J.: Efficient estimation of word representations in vector space. arXiv preprint arXiv:1301.3781 (2013)
13. Novák, V., Perfilieva, I., Mockor, J.: Mathematical Principles of Fuzzy Logic, vol. 517. Springer, Heidelberg (2012)
14. Rosso, O.A., Larrondo, H., Martin, M.T., Plastino, A., Fuentes, M.A.: Distinguishing noise from chaos. Phys. Rev. Lett. **99**(15), 154102 (2007)
15. Wilcoxon, F.: Individual comparisons by ranking methods. In: Kotz, S., Johnson, N.L. (eds.) Breakthroughs in Statistics. Springer Series in Statistics, pp. 196–202. Springer, New York (1992). https://doi.org/10.1007/978-1-4612-4380-9_16
16. Wishart, D.: Numerical classification method for deriving natural classes. Nature **221**(5175), 97–98 (1969)
17. Xiong, H., Li, Z.: Clustering validation measures. In: Data Clustering, pp. 571–606. Chapman and Hall/CRC (2018)

Conditioning Covert Geo-Location (CGL) Detection on Semantic Class Information

Binoy Saha$^{(\boxtimes)}$ (iD) and Sukhendu Das (iD)

Visualization and Perception Lab, Department of CSE, IIT Madras, Chennai, India
binoysaha@cse.iitm.ac.in, sdas@iitm.ac.in

Abstract. To incorporate knowledge about non-object image regions (hideouts, turns, and other obscured regions) in machines, recently, a task for identification of potential hideouts termed Covert Geo-Location (CGL) detection was proposed by Saha et al. [14]. It involves identification of image regions which have the potential to either cause an imminent threat or appear as target zones to be accessed for further investigation to identify any occluded objects. Only certain occluding items belonging to certain semantic classes can give rise to CGLs. This fact was overlooked by Saha et al. and no attempts were made to utilize semantic class information, which is crucial for CGL detection. Thus in this paper, we propose a multitask-learning-based approach to achieve two goals - 1) extraction of features having semantic class information; 2) robust training of the common encoder, exploiting large standard annotated datasets as training set for the auxiliary task (semantic segmentation). To explicitly incorporate class information in the features extracted by the encoder, we have further employed attention mechanism in a novel manner. In this work, we have also proposed a better evaluation metric for CGL detection that gives more weightage to recognition rather than precise localization. Experimental evaluations performed on the CGL dataset, demonstrate a significant increase in performance of about 3% to 14% mIoU and 3% to 16% DaR on split 1 and ≈1% mIoU and 1% to 2% DaR on split 2 over SOTA, serving as a testimony to the superiority of our approach.

ACK: IMPRINT (MHRD/DRDO) GoI, for support

Keywords: CGL detection · hideouts · location detection · visual scene understanding · deep learning · Dimension-agnostic evaluation

1 Introduction

The majority of vision-related tasks [5, 6, 8–10] entail identifying only the objects present in an image. However, knowledge about the non-object image regions like hiding places, corners, bends, and other obscured areas of the scene can also provide helpful information for a variety of tasks like automated navigation, surveillance, etc. Detecting hidden spots or covert locations in a scene, for instance,

P. Maji et al. (Eds.): PReMI 2023, LNCS 14301, pp. 28–37, 2023.
https://doi.org/10.1007/978-3-031-45170-6_4

could provide a promising next step towards achieving a significant goal of better scene understanding. Thus, in this work, we attempt to tackle a recently proposed task [14] termed Covert Geo-Location (CGL) Detection, where, given an input image, the target is to identify and localize potential hideouts (Covert Geo-Locations) in the image.

In the absence of any prior work, Saha et al. [14] presented a novel dataset for CGL detection consisting of real-world images depicting diverse indoor environments, baseline models, and a detailed analysis of the challenges posed by CGL detection. Moreover, a novel segmentation-based Depth-aware Feature Learning Block (DFLB) was also proposed that facilitated the extraction of relevant depth features (with a single RGB image as input) required for the proposed task. However, in order to successfully detect or segment CGLs, the model needs to understand what kind of objects/occluding-items give rise to CGL and what items do not give rise to a CGL. This aspect was not considered by [14] while designing the model.

In this paper, we thus attempt to condition CGL detection on the semantic class of the occluding items. This information about the semantic class of occluding items can be implicitly extracted using a multitask learning setting. Thus, in this work, we exploit a multitask learning-based approach which also provides a way of leveraging large standard datasets for better training of the feature extractor. This work builds on top of [2], which first proposed multitask learning and provided evidence that learnings from one task indeed expedite learning for other tasks. We have further employed multi-head self/cross-attention-based decoders for explicit propagation of semantic class information to the CGL segmentation decoder. The proposed model manifests better semantic understanding and outperforms existing models.

The height and width of CGL cannot be defined precisely (in most cases) in the ground truth and thus the annotations inherently contain some uncertainty even though certain protocols were followed by Saha et al. [14] during annotation process. Thus, detection of all CGLs is more crucial than detecting CGLs of the same height and width (dimensions) as those in GT. So, ideally, we want an evaluation metric that can give more weightage to recognition than precise localization in the performance score. Mean IoU (which was also used by [14] for performance comparison of CGL detection models) is a standard evaluation metric for evaluating segmentation models, but it performs per-pixel evaluation by considering all corresponding image coordinate positions in GT and the output of the model, which is not desired for the evaluation of a CGL detection model. To tackle this problem, we have proposed a novel dimension (height and width) agnostic evaluation metric for CGL detection in this paper. More details about the proposed metric are included in Sect. 4.1.

2 Related Work

CGL detection requires context-aware detection and understanding of the complex 3D spatial relationships between edges of occluding items and their surroundings. Depth information is thus very crucial for the detection of CGLs. For

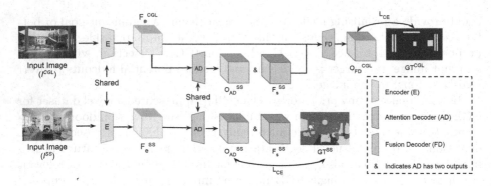

Fig. 1. Proposed architecture. Multi-task learning setting has been exploited with multi-head self-attention and cross-attention-based decoders.

this reason, authors of [14] developed an approach that can effectively extract RGB-based features as well as relevant depth features, using only a single RGB image as input. A novel DL-based technique was proposed which used an auxiliary decoder block, named Depth-aware Feature Learning Block (DFLB), to steer the common feature extractor towards extraction of necessary depth features (along with other RGB-based features). In this paper, we have used multitask learning and attention mechanism in a novel manner to design a model for CGL detection that considers the semantic class of the items present in the scene to perform the task at hand. In the subsequent subsections (2.1, 2.2, 2.3), we briefly present some technical details about these concepts.

2.1 Multi-Task Learning (MTL)

Multi-Task Learning (MTL) is a machine learning strategy that aims to learn many tasks concurrently while simultaneously minimizing multiple loss terms. In MTL, a single model is expected to learn to perform all of the tasks simultaneously rather than training separate models for each task. The model uses all of the available data from the various datasets (for various tasks) to learn generalized representations for the data. The simplest approach is to minimize a linear combination of the loss functions of the individual tasks [4,11–13,20,21].

2.2 Multi-head Attention

Spatial and feature-based attention (channel-wise attention) are two types of attention-based processes. In case of spatial attention [1,17,19], different weights are assigned to different spatial locations in spatial attention, but these weights are maintained throughout all feature channels at all spatial locations [18]. In comparison, channel-wise attention permits individual feature maps (channels) to be assigned their own weight/attention values [3]. Attention can be generalized and considered as the weighted sum of the values based on the query and the associated keys, given a set of key-value pairs (K, V) and a query (q). The query

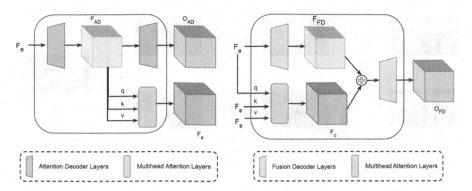

Fig. 2. Decoders. The attention decoder takes feature volume (F_e) extracted by the feature extractor as input and outputs a self-attended version of the feature volume (F_s) and per-pixel semantic classification (O_{AD}) as output. It employs multi-layered multi-head self-attention to obtain F_s from F_{AD}, which is the output of an intermediate layer in the attention decoder. q, k, and v represent the query, key, and value components respectively. The fusion decoder takes encoder feature map (F_e) and self-attended decoder feature volume (F_s) from attention decoder as input and outputs CGL segmentation mask (O_{FD}). It employs multi-layered multi-head cross-attention with F_e as query and F_s as key and value, and then fuses the cross-attended feature volume F_c with F_e.

"attends" to the values by choosing which keys to focus on. Multi-head attention uses an attention mechanism several times in parallel with different attention heads having a different set of learnable parameters. The attention outputs from all the attention heads are then concatenated and linearly transformed into the desired dimension. Intuitively, multiple attention heads allow for attending to feature vectors within a feature volume differently (calculating attention scores with different criteria). For example, in the case of image data, a few attention heads could model global spatial context and a few others could model local spatial context.

3   Proposed Approach

By concentrating on a single task, we can typically attain satisfactory results, but the model still misses out on information that could help it perform better on the metric we care about. Training the model simultaneously on multiple related tasks helps prevent this as the model gets to derive knowledge from multiple training signals coming from the various tasks being used for training. Also, we can improve the generalization of the model on our initial task by sharing representations between similar tasks. This method is known as Multi-Task Learning (MTL), and we have utilized it in this work.

Furthermore, in order to successfully detect or segment CGLs, the model needs to understand what kind of objects/occluding items give rise to CGL and what items cannot give rise to a CGL. This information about the semantic

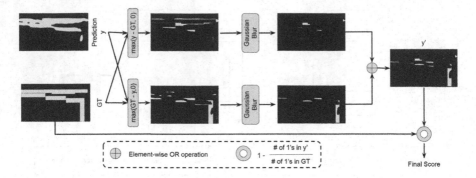

Fig. 3. The process used for computing the proposed Dimension-agnostic Recall (DaR) metric score. The whole process has been shown with the help of an example. The prediction (y) and the corresponding GT have been shown for a sample image from our CGL dataset. Yellow blobs indicate CGLs and purple regions indicate background/non-CGL regions. The white blobs in y' indicate regions of disagreement between prediction (y) and ground truth. (Color figure online)

class of occluding items can again be implicitly extracted using a multitask learning setting. The images from CGL dataset can also be then passed through a semantic segmentation decoder to get semantic class information. This semantic class information can be then used by the CGL segmentation branch yielding better performance.

Thus, to extract features having semantic class information and to exploit larger standard datasets for robust training of the common feature extractor, we have proposed a multitask learning-based architecture. Overall architecture is shown in Fig. 1. One of the decoder branches (Fusion Decoder) is trained to perform CGL segmentation (using CGL dataset for supervision) and the other decoder branch (Attention Decoder) is trained to perform semantic segmentation and is trained using the ADE20k dataset [22,23]. The attention decoder can also generalize and segment the input image from the CGL dataset and thus can provide additional semantic class information, which can further aid the fusion decoder in performing CGL segmentation.

The output of deeper layers of the decoder contains class-specific activation maps. These activation maps can be exploited for better propagation of semantic class information. We have employed multi-layered multi-head attention to achieve the same. Specifically, we propose to use multi-head self-attention layers to obtain better and more global features in the Attention Decoder (AD) and we propose to use multi-head cross-attention between encoder feature maps and the self-attended feature volume generated by AD in the Fusion Decoder (FD).

The architectures of attention decoder and fusion decoder are shown in Fig. 2(left) and Fig. 2(right) respectively.

3.1 Loss Functions

The proposed model is trained using the following loss function,

$$\mathcal{L} = \alpha * \mathcal{L}_{cgl} + \beta * \mathcal{L}_{ss} \tag{1}$$

where, α, β are hyperparameters. Hyperparameter tuning was performed using the K-fold cross-validation technique. Equations 2 and 3 represent $\mathcal{L}_{cgl}$ and $\mathcal{L}_{ss}$ loss terms respectively.

$$\mathcal{L}_{cgl} = \mathcal{L}_{ce}(O_{FD}^{CGL}, GT^{CGL}) \tag{2}$$

$$\mathcal{L}_{ss} = \mathcal{L}_{ce}(O_{AD}^{SS}, GT^{SS}) \tag{3}$$

where, $\mathcal{L}_{ce}$ is standard cross-entropy loss. GT^{SS} and GT^{CGL} represent the ground truth segmentation masks for the attention decoder and the fusion decoder respectively. O_{FD}^{CGL} represents the output of the fusion decoder for an image from the CGL dataset and O_{AD}^{SS} represents the output of the attention decoder from an image from ADE20k [22,23].

4 Results and Experiments

We have used the ADE20k dataset [22,23] along with the CGL detection dataset [14] for training our model. We evaluate our models for CGL segmentation using the proposed dataset. We use Adam optimizer and a similar training scheme to train all models. We report mean IoU, and CGL IoU (IoU for CGL class) for comparison of models. To provide a fair and informative study, we also report performance on the proposed **D**imension **a**gnostic **R**ecall (DaR) metric.

4.1 Proposed Evaluation Metric

Figure 3 shows the flowchart of the process used to obtain the score for the proposed metric named "Dimension-agnostic Recall" (DaR). At first, we obtain

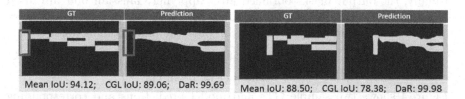

Mean IoU: 94.12;   CGL IoU: 89.06;   DaR: 99.69   Mean IoU: 88.50;   CGL IoU: 78.38;   DaR: 99.98

Fig. 4. Different rows show GT and prediction for two different samples and the corresponding Mean IoU, CGL IoU, and DaR scores are mentioned at the bottom of each row. Yellow blobs indicate CGL blobs and the background/non-CGL class has been indicated using purple color. Red bounding boxes enclose regions where there is a difference between the two masks. This figure provides evidence of the fact that DaR scores are more apt for the evaluation of CGL segmentation models. (Color figure online)

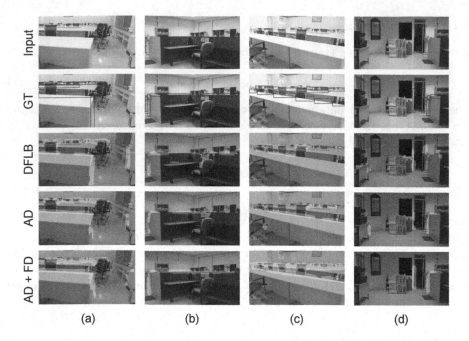

Input
GT
DFLB
AD
AD + FD

(a)   (b)   (c)   (d)

Fig. 5. Qualitative results on split 1 of CGL dataset. Image regions classified as CGL by the models have been indicated by overlaying translucent pink-colored blobs over the image. The last two rows show the output of the model proposed in this paper [with HRNetv2 as the encoder]. The third row shows the output of the model proposed in [14] with the same encoder. (Color figure online)

two relative complements, specifically, "$y - GT$" and "$GT - y$". Where "$y - GT$" represents false positives, "$GT - y$" represents false negatives, and "$-$" represents element-wise subtraction operation. Subsequently, to overlook minor mismatch in the dimensions of predicted CGLs, we make use of a symmetric Gaussian blur kernel with two parameters (σ, Th), where σ represents the standard deviation of the Gaussian kernel and Th is a threshold. We have empirically set σ to 3.0 and Th to 0.999.

Finally, the output masks obtained after applying Gaussian blur are fused using element-wise OR operation to obtain y'. Then the output of the OR operation (y') is used along with the GT to compute the final score as follows:

$$DaR = 1 - \frac{\text{Number of 1's in y'}}{\text{Number of 1's in GT}}$$

Figure 4 shows two sample GTs and model predictions and corresponding metric scores (Mean IoU, CGL IoU). We can see that even though the prediction is very close to GT, IoU scores are low (scores should have been very close to 1), as in IoU score computation, matching is done at each and every coordinate in the prediction with the corresponding coordinate in the GT. Pixel level matching is not appropriate for CGL detection as the height and width of CGLs may not always be precisely defined. The proposed evaluation metric (DaR) overcomes this challenge and it correctly ignores minor deviations in height and width of predicted CGLs as compared to GT CGLs. As a result, the DaR score for the two samples justifiably increases to more than 99%. Specifically, the DaR score for the sample shown in the first row is 99.38% and that for the sample in the second row is 99.69%.

Table 1. Performance comparison of existing models with our proposed models on CGL detection. All models have been trained and tested using split1/split2. The first row in each section of the table reports the performance of the baseline model (i.e. when the proposed modules and the semantic head are not used) and the rest of the rows report performance of models specifically designed to perform CGL detection with the encoder and decoder architectures having the same base architecture as the ones in the baseline model. [†] indicates model has been proposed in this paper.

Model	mIoU	CGL IoU	DaR
MobileNetv2 + C1 [15]	51.24/76.72	15.03/60.42	41.48/76.84
MobileNetv2 + C1 + DFLB [14]	54.19/78.46	20.62/63.40	44.78/80.32
MobileNetv2 + C1 + AD [†]	45.62/66.57	04.83/43.42	33.72/60.04
MobileNetv2 + C1 + AD + FD [†]	**57.38/78.47**	**26.21/63.42**	**47.17/80.51**
HRNetv2 + C1 [16]	55.31/81.95	23.36/69.75	44.16/85.35
HRNetv2 + C1 + DFLB [14]	57.76/83.55	27.64/72.38	51.73/87.64
HRNetv2 + C1 + AD [†]	66.27/83.76	42.25/73.53	59.61/87.95
HRNetv2 + C1 + AD + FD [†]	**67.55/84.08**	**44.74/74.12**	**61.23/89.01**
ResNet + PPMDeepsup [7]	55.23/80.60	22.50/67.30	48.05/83.27
ResNet + PPMDeepsup + DFLB [14]	56.21/83.21	23.55/71.98	52.30/87.27
ResNet + PPMDeepsup + AD [†]	56.86/83.62	24.02/72.45	53.25/87.77
ResNet+PPMDeepsup + AD+FD [†]	**70.46/83.98**	**49.58/73.19**	**68.26/88.84**

4.2 Qualitative Results

Figure 5 presents qualitative comparison between the proposed model and the DFLB-based model proposed in [14].

4.3 Quantitative Results

As evident from Table 1, the proposed CGL detection model outperforms the baseline and SOTA [14] model on CGL detection dataset [14]. Our proposed method effectively extracts and utilizes semantic class information to outperform other models on both train/test splits (irrespective of the encoder/decoder used). On split 1, we achieve a performance improvement of 3% to 14% mIoU and 3% to 16% DaR over SOTA and on split 2, performance improvement is ≈1% mIoU and 1% to 2% DaR. For details about baseline models refer [14]. Code is available here.

5   Conclusion

This paper introduces a novel approach that can facilitate effective extraction and utilization of semantic class information, through the use of multi-task learning combined with self/cross-attention mechanism. The proposed method additionally helps to overcome the problem of unavailability of a large dataset for the training of deep CNN models. Semantic segmentation (task of the attention decoder) is used as the auxiliary task (along with the target task of CGL segmentation). Attention mechanism is used to propagate semantic class information to the fusion decoder which is trained to perform CGL segmentation. Consequently, we discuss the shortcomings of the standard IoU score and propose a better evaluation metric, named Dimension-agnostic Recall (DaR) for CGL detection. DaR gives more weightage to recognition than precise localization by ignoring minor differences in the height and width of predicted CGLs with respect to the ground truth CGL instances.

References

1. Carion, N., Massa, F., Synnaeve, G., Usunier, N., Kirillov, A., Zagoruyko, S.: End-to-end object detection with transformers. In: Vedaldi, A., Bischof, H., Brox, T., Frahm, J.-M. (eds.) ECCV 2020. LNCS, vol. 12346, pp. 213–229. Springer, Cham (2020). https://doi.org/10.1007/978-3-030-58452-8_13
2. Caruana, R.: Multitask learning. Mach. Learn. **28**(1), 41–75 (1997)
3. Chen, L., et al.: SCA-CNN: spatial and channel-wise attention in convolutional networks for image captioning. In: Proceedings of the IEEE Conference on Computer Vision and Pattern Recognition, pp. 5659–5667 (2017)
4. Dai, J., He, K., Sun, J.: Instance-aware semantic segmentation via multi-task network cascades. In: Proceedings of the IEEE Conference on Computer Vision and Pattern Recognition, pp. 3150–3158 (2016)
5. Everingham, M., Eslami, S.M.A., Van Gool, L., Williams, C.K.I., Winn, J., Zisserman, A.: The pascal visual object classes challenge: a retrospective. Int. J. Comput. Vision **111**(1), 98–136 (2015)
6. Goyal, Y., Khot, T., Summers-Stay, D., Batra, D., Parikh, D.: Making the V in VQA matter: elevating the role of image understanding in visual question answering. In: Proceedings of the IEEE Conference on Computer Vision and Pattern Recognition (2017)
7. He, K., Zhang, X., Ren, S., Sun, J.: Deep residual learning for image recognition. In: Proceedings of the IEEE Conference on Computer Vision and Pattern Recognition, pp. 770–778 (2016)
8. Krishna, R., et al.: Visual genome: connecting language and vision using crowd-sourced dense image annotations (2016). https://arxiv.org/abs/1602.07332
9. Krizhevsky, A., Sutskever, I., Hinton, G.E.: ImageNet classification with deep convolutional neural networks. In: Advances in Neural Information Processing Systems, pp. 1097–1105 (2012)
10. Lin, T.-Y., et al.: Microsoft COCO: common objects in context. In: Fleet, D., Pajdla, T., Schiele, B., Tuytelaars, T. (eds.) ECCV 2014. LNCS, vol. 8693, pp. 740–755. Springer, Cham (2014). https://doi.org/10.1007/978-3-319-10602-1_48

11. Liu, S., Johns, E., Davison, A.J.: End-to-end multi-task learning with attention. In: Proceedings of the IEEE/CVF Conference on Computer Vision and Pattern Recognition, pp. 1871–1880 (2019)
12. Ma, J., Zhao, Z., Yi, X., Chen, J., Hong, L., Chi, E.H.: Modeling task relationships in multi-task learning with multi-gate mixture-of-experts. In: 24th ACM SIGKDD International Conference on Knowledge Discovery & Data Mining, pp. 1930–1939 (2018)
13. Misra, I., Shrivastava, A., Gupta, A., Hebert, M.: Cross-stitch networks for multi-task learning. In: Proceedings of the IEEE Conference on Computer Vision and Pattern Recognition (CVPR) (2016)
14. Saha, B., Das, S.: Catch me if you can: a novel task for detection of covert geo-locations (CGL). In: Proceedings of the Satellite Workshops of ICVGIP (2021). arXiv paper https://doi.org/10.48550/arXiv.2202.02567
15. Sandler, M., Howard, A., Zhu, M., Zhmoginov, A., Chen, L.C.: MobileNetV 2: inverted residuals and linear bottlenecks. In: Proceedings of the IEEE Conference on Computer Vision and Pattern Recognition, pp. 4510–4520 (2018)
16. Sun, K., et al.: High-resolution representations for labeling pixels and regions. arXiv preprint arXiv:1904.04514 (2019)
17. Wang, X., Girshick, R., Gupta, A., He, K.: Non-local neural networks. In: Proceedings of the IEEE Conference on Computer Vision and Pattern Recognition, pp. 7794–7803 (2018)
18. Xu, K., et al.: Show, attend and tell: neural image caption generation with visual attention. In: International Conference on Machine Learning, pp. 2048–2057. PMLR (2015)
19. Yuan, Y., Huang, L., Guo, J., Zhang, C., Chen, X., Wang, J.: OCNet: object context network for scene parsing. arXiv preprint arXiv:1809.00916 (2018)
20. Zhang, Z., Luo, P., Loy, C.C., Tang, X.: Facial landmark detection by deep multi-task learning. In: Fleet, D., Pajdla, T., Schiele, B., Tuytelaars, T. (eds.) ECCV 2014. LNCS, vol. 8694, pp. 94–108. Springer, Cham (2014). https://doi.org/10.1007/978-3-319-10599-4_7
21. Zhao, X., Li, H., Shen, X., Liang, X., Wu, Y.: A modulation module for multi-task learning with applications in image retrieval. In: Proceedings of the European Conference on Computer Vision (ECCV), pp. 401–416 (2018)
22. Zhou, B., Zhao, H., Puig, X., Fidler, S., Barriuso, A., Torralba, A.: Scene parsing through ADE20K dataset. In: Proceedings of the IEEE Conference on Computer Vision and Pattern Recognition, pp. 633–641 (2017)
23. Zhou, B., et al.: Semantic understanding of scenes through the ADE20K dataset. Int. J. Comput. Vision **127**(3), 302–321 (2019)

Search-Time Efficient Device Constraints-Aware Neural Architecture Search

Oshin Dutta$^{(\boxtimes)}$, Tanu Kanvar, and Sumeet Agarwal

Indian Institute of Technology, Delhi, India
{oshin.dutta,sumeet}@ee.iitd.ac.in

Abstract. Edge computing aims to enable edge devices, such as IoT devices, to process data locally instead of relying on the cloud. However, deep learning techniques like computer vision and natural language processing can be computationally expensive and memory-intensive. Creating manual architectures specialized for each device is infeasible due to their varying memory and computational constraints. To address these concerns, we automate the construction of task-specific deep learning architectures optimized for device constraints through Neural Architecture Search (NAS). We present DCA-NAS, a principled method of fast neural network architecture search that incorporates edge-device constraints such as model size and floating-point operations. It incorporates weight sharing and channel bottleneck techniques to speed up the search time. Based on our experiments, we see that DCA-NAS outperforms manual architectures for similar sized models and is comparable to popular mobile architectures on various image classification datasets like CIFAR-10, CIFAR-100, and Imagenet-1k. Experiments with search spaces—DARTS and NAS-Bench-201 show the generalization capabilities of DCA-NAS. On further evaluating our approach on Hardware-NAS-Bench, device-specific architectures with low inference latency and state-of-the-art performance were discovered.

Keywords: Neural Architecture Search · DARTS · Meta-Learning · Edge Inference · Constrained Optimization

1 Introduction

In recent years, there has been significant progress in developing Deep Neural Network (DNN) architectures for edge and mobile devices. However, designing DNN architectures for specific hardware constraints and tasks is a time-consuming and computationally expensive process [2]. To address this, Neural Architecture Search (NAS) [35] has become popular as it discovers optimal architectures given a task and network operations. Despite its success, traditional NAS techniques cannot guarantee optimal architecture for specific devices

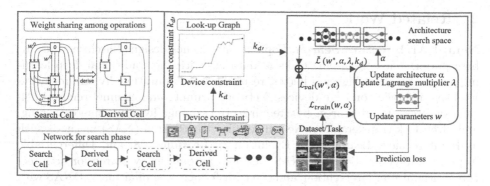

Fig. 1. DCA-NAS framework: Weight sharing in the search space and Derived cells lowers the search time from other DNAS. Target device constraint is used to query search constraint from look-up graph for constrained optimization.

with hardware constraints such as storage memory and maximum supported FLOPs. To address this concern, researchers have developed hardware-aware algorithms [3,25] that find optimal device architectures with low resource training overhead and search time. These methods often use inference latency [3], FLOPs [25] or a combination of hardware metrics [25] as constraints scaled by a tunable factor. However, the time to tune the scaling factor is often not considered within the NAS search time and can be ten times the reported search time. To address these issues, we propose the Device Constraints-Aware NAS (DCA-NAS), a principled differentiable NAS method that introduces total allowable model size or floating-point operations (FLOPs) as constraints within the optimization problem, with minimal hyper-parameter tuning. Unlike inference latency which is task dependent, FLOPs and memory are specified with a given hardware and thus appropriate for our generic method. The approach is adaptable to other hardware metrics such as energy consumption or inference latency using additional metric-measuring functions. The paper make the following significant contributions:

- It introduces a fast method that uses weight sharing among operations in the search space and channel bottleneck, along with a differentiable resource constraint, for continuous exploration of the search space.
- A training pipeline that allows a user to input device memory or FLOPs and search for optimal architecture with minimal hyper-parameter tuning.
- Our extensive experimentation on vision datasets- CIFAR-10, CIFAR-100, TinyImagenet, Imagenet-1k and inference-latency comparisons of trained models on Hardware-NAS-bench demonstrate the efficiency of our method. The generalization of our method to different search spaces is shown with experiments on DARTS and NAS-Bench.

2 Related Work

Neural Architecture Search. Popular approaches designed architectures for high performance on specific tasks or datasets with the traditional deep learning perspective that bigger is better, resulting in computationally and memory-intensive inference on edge devices. Network pruning and channel removal [24] can compress architectures, but require pre-training, hyperparameter tuning, and often lack transferability. Neural Architecture Search (NAS) methods such as Reinforcement Learning [3], Evolutionary Learning [28] and Differentiable Neural Architecture Search (DNAS) [18] can automatically search for architectures without user intervention, and can transfer across similar tasks. DNAS with surrogate metrics [30] have also been used to explore the architecture search space. However, architectures found by DNAS methods are not optimized for deployment on edge devices and smaller models obtained by reducing layers or channels are often sub-optimal.

Hardware-Aware Neural Architecture Search. Certain NAS methods optimize [2,3,13] for constraints such as latency, inference speed [29], FLOPS [26], memory usage [17]. Some use a separate DNN to predict constraint metrics and evolutionary search to obtain hardware-aware optimal models [2], while others consider real-time latencies of edge devices or provide specific architectures for specific devices [6,19]. However, these methods require significant search time and tuning of scaling factors controlling the trade-off between the performance and the constraint, and do not always account for optimal architectures. In contrast, we use a differentiable hardware-aware objective function with generic hardware metrics, and do not require a tunable scaling factor. Certain methods [2,7] train a supernet first and then search for a smaller architecture, but this is only efficient when there are more than fifteen different edge devices with different limitations or deployment scenarios [2] as training the supernet takes huge resources-32 V100s taking about 1,200 GPU hours. Search stage followed by evaluation, as done in our approach is more efficient when the different number of possible edge devices is less than fifteen.

3 DCA-NAS: Device Constraints Aware Fast Neural Architecture Search

We present the preliminary gradient-based NAS objective function in Sect. 3.1 and then formulate the problem of incorporating the hardware-awareness in NAS as a constrained optimization problem in Sect. 3.2 followed by techniques to reduce the search time in Sect. 3.3. The framework of our approach is illustrated in Fig. 1.

3.1 Gradient-Based NAS Objective Function

Popular DNAS techniques [18,34] have two stages, the search phase and the evaluation phase. During the search phase, given a task or a dataset the techniques search for a network of cells, which are directed acyclic graphs with N nodes. The edges of the graph are network layers, whose operations are to be selected from a pre-defined set $\mathcal{O}$ containing operations such as 3×3 separable convolution and identity operations with trainable weights w_o. The search is made differentiable by making the choice of a particular operation to be a softmax of architecture weights α of all operations. Thus, the intermediate output z_j at node j is given by,

$$z_j = \sum_{o \in \mathcal{O}} \frac{\exp\left\{\alpha_o^{i,j}\right\}}{\sum_{o' \in \mathcal{O}} \exp\left\{\alpha_{o'}^{i,j}\right\}} \cdot o\left(w_o^{i,j}, \mathbf{z}_i\right) \tag{1}$$

3.2 DCA-NAS Formulation

Previous DNAS approaches [18, 33, 34] did not prioritize searching architectures for resource-constrained inference. In contrast, we formulate the DNAS objective function as a constrained optimization problem by incorporating device resource constraints (memory or FLOPs) in the search objective function. The constrained bi-level optimization problem is written as,

$$\begin{aligned} &\min_\alpha \mathcal{L}_{\text{val}}\left(w^*(\alpha), \alpha\right) \\ &\text{s.t. } w^*(\alpha) = \text{argmin}_w \mathcal{L}_{\text{train}}\left(w, \alpha\right) \\ &\text{s.t. } k_s(\alpha) \leq K_d \end{aligned} \tag{2}$$

where training dataset is split into *train* and *val* sets to jointly optimize w and α in each iteration, while ensuring that the architecture's parameter or FLOPs count k_s remains within the device resource constraint K_d. The following equation calculates the architecture's number of parameters or FLOPs during search given the number of cells c_n. Our method can also be adapted to use other metrics such as latency and energy consumption with additional metric measuring functions.

$$k_s(\alpha) = c_n \sum_{(i,j) \in N} \sum_{o \in \mathcal{O}} \frac{\exp\{\alpha_o^{i,j}\} * b\,(o)}{\sum_{o' \in \mathcal{O}} \exp\{\alpha_{o'}^{i,j}\}} \tag{3}$$

Tackling the Difference in Search and Evaluation Networks. The size of the architecture in the search phase k_s is different from the architecture size in evaluation phase due to the softmax weighting factor in Eq. 3 (demonstration can be found in the supplementary material[1]). To address this, we introduce a tighter bound on the search constraint $K_{d'}$ than the device resource constraint K_d. A lookup graph (LUG) is made for each dataset by varying $K_{d'}$ within appropriate bounds and running the algorithm until convergence each time to obtain the corresponding device resource constraint K_d. The computation time of the LUG can be reduced by running the searches in parallel. Thus, on incorporating the tighter constraint by looking-up the graph for the given device

---

[1] https://github.com/oshindutta/DCA-NAS.

resource constraint K_d along with the trainable Lagrange multiplier λ in Eq. 2, the objective function is re-written as,

$$\widetilde{\mathcal{L}} = \mathcal{L}_{\text{val}} \left(w^*(\alpha), \alpha \right) + \lambda(k_s(\alpha) - LUG(K_d))$$
$$\text{s.t. } w^*(\alpha) = \text{argmin}_w \, \mathcal{L}_{\text{train}} \left(w, \alpha \right) \tag{4}$$

3.3 Techniques to Reduce Search Time

Channel Bottleneck. We use convolutional layers of 1×1 kernel to reduce the depth of output channels of operations in the search space to save computation time and memory overhead.

Derived Cell and Weight Sharing. During architecture search, a single cell with trainable architecture parameters α is used. The target network for inference is built by stacking cells with architectures derived from highly weighted operations. This derivation process, performed iteratively, reduces computation and memory overhead [34]. This derived cell saves computation and memory overhead. A weight sharing strategy among same operations with the same originating node i to all nodes $i < j < N$ has been applied within a cell. This is

Table 1. Performance comparison of architectures evaluated on visual datasets-CIFAR-10 and TinyImagenet. '(CIFAR-10)' indicates search with CIFAR-10. 'X M' in 'DCA-NAS-X M' denotes the input memory constraint. RCAS- Resource Constrained Architecture Search

Dataset	Search Strategy	Method	Accuracy (%)	Parameters (Million)	GPU Hours
CIFAR-10	manual	PyramidNet-110 (2017) [9]	95.74	3.8	–
	manual	VGG-16 pruned (2017) [11]	93.4	5.4	–
	evolution	Evolution + Cutout (2019) [28]	96.43	5.8	12
	random	NAO Random-WS (2019) [22]	96.08	3.9	7.2
	gradient	ENAS + micro + Cutout (2018) [21]	96.46	4.6	12
	gradient	DARTS + Cutout (2nd) (2018) [18]	97.24 ± 0.09	3.3	24
	gradient	SNAS + Cutout (2018) [31]	97.15	2.8	36
	gradient	PC-DARTS (2019) [33]	97.43 ± 0.07	3.6	2.4
	gradient	SGAS (2020) [16]	97.34	3.7	6
	gradient	DrNAS (2020) [5]	97.46 ± 0.03	4.0	9.6
	gradient	DARTS+PT (2021) [27]	97.39 ± 0.08	3.0	19.2
	gradient	Shapley-NAS (2022) [30]	97.53 ± 0.04	3.4	7.2
	RCAS	DCA-NAS- 3.5 M (CIFAR-10)	97.2 ± 0.09	**3.4**	**1.37**
Tiny ImageNet	manual	SqueezeNet (2016) [12]	54.40	–	–
	manual	PreActResNet18 (2020) [15]	63.48	–	–
	manual	DenseNet (2020) [1]	62.73	11.8	–
	gradient	DARTS+ Cutout (2018) [18]	62.15 ± 0.15	7.3	219
	RCAS	DCA-NAS- 3.5 M	61.34 ± 0.09	**3.5**	**12.5**
	RCAS	DCA-NAS- 3.5 M (CIFAR-10)	61.4 ± 0.15	3.4	1.37

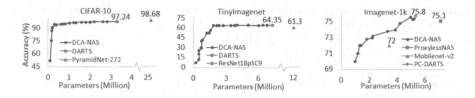

Fig. 2. Plots show that DCA-NAS method discovers models with fewer parameters than other NAS methods and manual architectures without sacrificing prediction performance to a large extent.

motivated by the observation that non-parametric operations operating on the representation of a node produce the same feature map irrespective of the output node and thereby extended to parametric operations. Thus, Eq. 1 may be re-written to the following,

$$z_j = \sum_{o \in \mathcal{O}} \frac{\exp\left\{\alpha_o^{i,j}\right\}}{\sum_{o' \in \mathcal{O}} \exp\left\{\alpha_{o'}^{i,j}\right\}} \cdot o\left(w_o^i, \mathbf{z}_i\right) \tag{5}$$

4   Experimental Results

Our approach is evaluated on two search spaces- DARTS and NAS-Bench with vision datasets- CIFAR10, TinyImagenet, Imagenet-16-20 and Imagenet-1k. The details of the search space and implementation is given in the supplementary material.

4.1   Results on DARTS Search Space

Transferability- Learning of Coarse Features During Search. We transfer the architecture searched on CIFAR-10 to train and evaluate the model weights on TinyImagenet in Table 1 and ImageNet-1k in Table 2. This transferred model yields higher performance than manually designed architectures [20,23] for the target dataset. It is observed that performance of the transferred model is comparable to the architecture searched on the target dataset itself which can be attributed to the architecture learning coarse features than objects during search.

Performance Versus Device-Constraints Trade-Off. DCA-NAS discovers 2 to 4% better-performing architectures than manual designs with a memory constraint of 3.5 million parameters on CIFAR-10 and similar performance on TinyImagenet as in Table 1. On Imagenet-1k, DCA-NAS yields models with similar performance to other NAS methods [5,30,33] with a constraint of 5.5 million parameters (taken to yield similar sized models as other NAS methods) as in Table 2. We vary the input device resource constraint and plot the performance

Table 2. Performance and comparison of architectures evaluated on Imagenet-1k. The label "(Imagenet)" indicates that the architecture has been searched and evaluated on Imagenet-1k.; else it is searched on CIFAR-10. 'X M' in 'DCA-NAS-X M' denotes the input memory constraint

Method	Test Error (%)		Parameters (Mil)	FLOPS (Mil)	Search Cost (GPU days)	Search Strategy
	top-1	top-5				
MobileNet_V2 (2018) [23]	72.0	91.0	3.4	300	–	manual
ShuffleNet 2× (v2) (2018) [20]	25.1	–	5	591	–	manual
MnasNet-92 (2020) [10]	25.2	8.0	4.4	388	–	RL
AmoebaNet-C (2019) [22]	24.3	7.6	6.4	570	3150	evolution
DARTS+Cutout (2018) [18]	26.7	8.7	4.7	574	1.0	gradient
SNAS (2018) [31]	27.3	9.2	4.3	522	1.5	gradient
GDAS (2019) [8]	26.0	8.5	5.3	545	0.3	gradient
BayesNAS (2019) [35]	26.5	8.9	3.9	–	0.2	gradient
P-DARTS (2018) [21]	24.4	7.4	4.9	557	0.3	gradient
SGAS (Cri 1. best) (2020) [16]	**24.2**	**7.2**	5.3	585	0.25	gradient
SDARTS-ADV (2020) [4]	25.2	7.8	6.1	–	0.4	gradient
Shapley-NAS (2022) [30]	24.3	–	5.1	566	0.3	gradient
RC-DARTS (2019) [14]	25.1	7.8	4.9	590	1	RCAS
DCA-NAS	25.1	8.1	**5.1**	578	**0.06**	RCAS
ProxylessNAS (GPU) (2019) [3](Imagenet)	24.9	7.5	7.1	465	8.3	gradient
PC-DARTS (2019) [33] (Imagenet)	24.2	7.3	5.3	597	3.8	gradient
DrNAS (2020) [5] (Imagenet)	24.2	7.3	5.2	644	3.9	gradient
DARTS+PT (2021) [27] (Imagenet)	25.5	–	4.7	538	3.4	gradient
Shapley-NAS (2022) [30] (Imagenet)	23.9	–	5.4	582	4.2	gradient
RCNet-B (2019) [32] (ImageNet)	25.3	8.0	4.7	471	9	RCAS
DCA-NAS- 5.5 M(Imagenet)	24.4	7.2	5.3	597	**1.9**	RCAS

of the searched models against the number of parameters in Fig. 2. As observed, DCA-NAS searched models can yield 15x lower sized models than manual architectures like PyramidNet-272 [9] with at most 1% reduction in accuracy on CIFAR-10. On TinyImagenet, DCA-NAS yields models similar in performance but 6x smaller in size than the manual Resnet variant. In comparison to ProxylessNAS [3] for Imagenet-1k, DCA-NAS yields 32% smaller model in terms of model parameters for similar accuracy. In comparison to DNAS methods [18,33] for each of the three datasets, we observe that the performance of the DCA-NAS searched models is retained to a certain extent as resources are further limited after which the model performance degrades. DCA-NAS model of similar size has the advantage of better performance (by 1%) and being automatically searched over MobileNet-v2 [23], a manually designed network on Imagenet-1k.

Search Time Comparison. For evaluation on TinyImagenet in Table 1, the architecture searched on CIFAR-10 with DCA-NAS demonstrates superior search-time efficiency, highlighting the transferability property. Our method requires about 4x lower search cost than SGAS [16] which performs the best among the other transferred architectures and 16x lower search time than the other resource-constrained approach [14] for similar performance as seen in Table 2. Moreover, ProxylessNAS [3] takes about 4x more search time than DCA-NAS whereas PC-DARTS takes about 2× more search time with no capability to constraint model size.

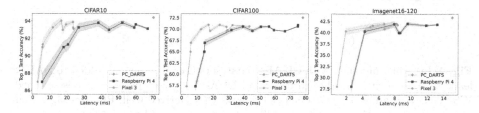

Fig. 3. Plots show DCA-NAS searched models with similar performance but lower inference latency (on two devices- Pixel 3 and Raspberry Pi 4) to previous SOTA NAS method- PC-DARTS when evaluated on NAS-Bench dataset.

4.2 Results on NAS-Bench-201 Search Space

Performance and Latency Comparisons on Different Devices. Our method reports the mean by averaging over five runs with different random seed. Figure 3 compares the performance of models searched with DCA-NAS and PC-DARTS by varying the latency constraints. It shows that unlike PC-DARTS, DCA-NAS can search for more efficient models which have lower inference latency for similar test accuracy. Moreover, we observe that models with similar performance have lower latency when tested on Pixel 3 than on Raspberry Pi 4 due to a faster RAM in Pixel 3. DCA-NAS takes the lowest search time among all the NAS methods due to the addition of search-time-efficient techniques while being at-par in terms of performance across all datasets.

5 Ablation Study

Effectiveness of Various Algorithmic Augmentations for Faster Search: We analyze the effectiveness of algorithmic augmentations mentioned preciously Sect. 3.3 to reduce search cost in our study. We sequentially add weight sharing, channel bottleneck, and derived cells to the baseline DARTS [18] method and measure search time and accuracy. Weight sharing, channel bottleneck, and derived cells was observed to significantly reduce search memory overhead, enabling us to use larger batch sizes and reducing overall search cost as seen in Fig. 4a. Adding the resource-constraint in the final DCA-NAS method negligibly increases search cost while maintaining performance.

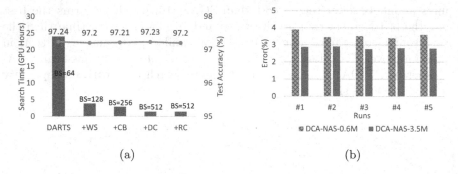

(a)   (b)

Fig. 4. (a) Ablation study with CIFAR-10 dataset- Each component added to DARTS leads to the reduction in the search cost of DCA-NAS while performance is retained. WS- Weight Sharing, CB- Channel Bottleneck, DC- Derived Cell, RC- Resource Constraint, BS- Batch Size (b) Shows stability of performance of DCA-NAS searched models for runs with varying seeds on CIFAR-10 dataset.

Stability of the Approach: We test stability by running the search algorithm independently five times with different initial seeds and the same constraints and hyperparameters. The architectures found during each run have similar performance when re-trained and evaluated as shown in Fig. 4b. Smaller models have lower performance due to restrictions in model complexity compared to larger models.

6   Conclusion

We present DCA-NAS, a device constraints-aware neural architecture search framework which discovers architectures optimized to the memory and computational constraints of an edge device in a time-efficient manner. It does so by incorporating a constraint in terms of the number of parameters or floating point operations (FLOPs) in the objective function with the help of a Lagrange multiplier. DCA-NAS in essence searches for a Pareto optimal solution given the edge device memory or FLOPs constraint. Moreover, it enables architecture search with search cost 4 to 17 times lower than the previous state-of-the-art Hardware-aware NAS approaches. DCA-NAS can discover models with size about 10 to 15 times lower than manually designed architectures for similar performance. In comparison to DARTS and its other NAS variants, DCA-NAS can discover models upto 3× smaller in size with similar performance. This hardware-aware approach can be generalized to any future updates to differential neural architecture search and possibly to training-free methods of NAS with some adaptation.

Acknowledgement. We thank the anonymous reviewers; Profs. Surendra Prasad and Brejesh Lall of IIT Delhi; and colleagues at Cadence India for their valuable feedback and inputs. This research is supported by funding from Cadence India; the first author is also supported by a fellowship from the Ministry of Education, India.

References

1. Abai, Z., Rajmalwar, N.: DenseNet models for tiny ImageNet classification (2020)
2. Cai, H., Gan, C., Wang, T., Zhang, Z., Han, S.: Once-for-all: train one network and specialize it for efficient deployment (2020). arXiv:1908.09791 [cs, stat]
3. Cai, H., Zhu, L., Han, S.: ProxylessNAS: direct neural architecture search on target task and hardware (2019)
4. Chen, X., Hsieh, C.J.: Stabilizing differentiable architecture search via perturbation-based regularization. In: International Conference on Machine Learning, pp. 1554–1565. PMLR (2020)
5. Chen, X., Wang, R., Cheng, M., Tang, X., Hsieh, C.J.: DRNAS: Dirichlet neural architecture search. arXiv preprint arXiv:2006.10355 (2020)
6. Chu, G., et al.: Discovering multi-hardware mobile models via architecture search. In: Proceedings of the IEEE/CVF Conference on Computer Vision and Pattern Recognition, pp. 3022–3031 (2021)
7. Ding, Y., et al.: NAP: neural architecture search with pruning. Neurocomputing **477**, 85–95 (2022)
8. Dong, X., Yang, Y.: Searching for a robust neural architecture in four GPU hours. In: Proceedings of the IEEE/CVF Conference on Computer Vision and Pattern Recognition, pp. 1761–1770 (2019)
9. Han, D., Kim, J., Kim, J.: Deep pyramidal residual networks. In: Proceedings of the IEEE Conference on Computer Vision and Pattern Recognition, pp. 5927–5935 (2017)
10. He, C., Ye, H., Shen, L., Zhang, T.: MileNAS: efficient neural architecture search via mixed-level reformulation. In: Proceedings of the IEEE/CVF Conference on Computer Vision and Pattern Recognition, pp. 11993–12002 (2020)
11. He, Y., Zhang, X., Sun, J.: Channel pruning for accelerating very deep neural networks. In: Proceedings of the IEEE International Conference on Computer Vision, pp. 1389–1397 (2017)
12. Iandola, F.N., Han, S., Moskewicz, M.W., Ashraf, K., Dally, W.J., Keutzer, K.: SqueezeNet: AlexNet-level accuracy with 50x fewer parameters and <0.5mb model size (2016)
13. Jiang, Q., Zhang, X., Chen, D., Do, M.N., Yeh, R.A.: EH-DNAS: end-to-end hardware-aware differentiable neural architecture search. arXiv:2111.12299 [cs] (2021)
14. Jin, X., et al.: RC-DARTS: resource constrained differentiable architecture search. arXiv preprint arXiv:1912.12814 (2019)
15. Kim, J.H., Choo, W., Song, H.O.: Puzzle mix: exploiting saliency and local statistics for optimal mixup (2020)
16. Li, G., Qian, G., Delgadillo, I.C., Müller, M., Thabet, A., Ghanem, B.: SGAS: sequential greedy architecture search (2020)

17. Lin, J., Chen, W.M., Lin, Y., Gan, C., Han, S., et al.: MCUNet: tiny deep learning on IoT devices. Adv. Neural. Inf. Process. Syst. **33**, 11711–11722 (2020)
18. Liu, H., Simonyan, K., Yang, Y.: DARTS: differentiable architecture search. arXiv preprint arXiv:1806.09055 (2018)
19. Lyu, B., Yuan, H., Lu, L., Zhang, Y.: Resource-constrained neural architecture search on edge devices. IEEE Trans. Netw. Sci. Eng. **9**(1), 134–142 (2022). https://doi.org/10.1109/TNSE.2021.3054583
20. Ma, N., Zhang, X., Zheng, H.T., Sun, J.: ShuffleNet V2: practical guidelines for efficient CNN architecture design. In: Proceedings of the European conference on computer vision (ECCV), pp. 116–131 (2018)
21. Pham, H., Guan, M.Y., Zoph, B., Le, Q.V., Dean, J.: Efficient neural architecture search via parameter sharing. In: ICML (2018)
22. Real, E., Aggarwal, A., Huang, Y., Le, Q.V.: Regularized evolution for image classifier architecture search (2019)
23. Sandler, M., Howard, A., Zhu, M., Zhmoginov, A., Chen, L.C.: MobileNetV 2: inverted residuals and linear bottlenecks. In: Proceedings of the IEEE Conference on Computer Vision and Pattern Recognition, pp. 4510–4520 (2018)
24. Srivastava, A., Dutta, O., Gupta, J., Agarwal, S., Prathosh, A.P.: A variational information bottleneck based method to compress sequential networks for human action recognition. In: Proceedings of the IEEE/CVF Winter Conference on Applications of Computer Vision, pp. 2745–2754 (2021)
25. Tan, M., et al.: platform-aware neural architecture search for mobile. In: 2019 IEEE CVF Conference on Computer Vision and Pattern Recognition (CVPR), pp. 2815–2823 (2019)
26. Tan, M., Le, Q.: EfficientNet: rethinking model scaling for convolutional neural networks. In: International Conference on Machine Learning, pp. 6105–6114. PMLR (2019)
27. Wang, R., Cheng, M., Chen, X., Tang, X., Hsieh, C.J.: Rethinking architecture selection in differentiable NAS. arXiv preprint arXiv:2108.04392 (2021)
28. Wistuba, M.: Deep learning architecture search by neuro-cell-based evolution with function-preserving mutations. In: Berlingerio, M., Bonchi, F., Gärtner, T., Hurley, N., Ifrim, G. (eds.) ECML PKDD 2018. LNCS (LNAI), vol. 11052, pp. 243–258. Springer, Cham (2019). https://doi.org/10.1007/978-3-030-10928-8_15
29. Wu, Y., et al.: Compiler-aware neural architecture search for on-mobile real-time super-resolution (2022). arXiv:2207.12577 [cs, eess]
30. Xiao, H., Wang, Z., Zhu, Z., Zhou, J., Lu, J.: Shapley-NAS: discovering operation contribution for neural architecture search (2022). arXiv:2206.09811 [cs]
31. Xie, S., Zheng, H., Liu, C., Lin, L.: SNAS: stochastic neural architecture search. In: International Conference on Learning Representations (2018)
32. Xiong, Y., Mehta, R., Singh, V.: Resource constrained neural network architecture search: will a submodularity assumption help? In: Proceedings of the IEEE/CVF International Conference on Computer Vision, pp. 1901–1910 (2019)
33. Xu, Y., et al.: PC-DARTS: partial channel connections for memory-efficient architecture search. arXiv preprint arXiv:1907.05737 (2019)
34. Yang, Y., You, S., Li, H., Wang, F., Qian, C., Lin, Z.: Towards improving the consistency, efficiency, and flexibility of differentiable neural architecture search. In: Proceedings of the IEEE/CVF Conference on Computer Vision and Pattern Recognition, pp. 6667–6676 (2021)
35. Zhou, H., Yang, M., Wang, J., Pan, W.: BayesNAS: a Bayesian approach for neural architecture search (2019)

Gödel Number Based Encoding Technique for Effective Clustering

Pankajbhai Narodia Parth and Kamalika Bhattacharjee[✉]

Department of Computer Science and Engineering, National Institute of Technology,
Tiruchirappalli 620015, Tamilnadu, India
kamalika.it@gmail.com

Abstract. In this paper, a Gödel number-based encoding technique is proposed to encode each object of a dataset before applying any clustering algorithm. This encoding technique converts the objects into a decimal string while maintaining the properties of the features. The results of all standard existing clustering algorithms after applying this encoding are evaluated based on benchmark metrics like, Silhouette Score, Davis Bouldin, Calinski Harabasz and Dunn Index. In comparison to the existing clustering algorithms if one uses Gödel number-based encoding over the dataset, it gives better performance.

Keywords: Gödel Number · Silhouette Score · Davis Bouldin · Calinski Harabasz · Dunn Index · Cellular Automata · K-Means

1 Introduction

Clustering is a grouping of objects based on similarity such that data points in one group are more similar to each other than the other group. It is a common unsupervised learning technique to analyze statistical data. Clustering can be perceived as a one-to-one function that evaluates the proximity between the items that require clustering. By definition, a one-to-one function splits the items in the domain into distinct, non-intersecting groups, with each group representing a single cluster. Clustering can be done using various algorithms such as K-Means [8], Hierarchical [11], DBSCAN [6] etc. which are based on some properties like centroid, connectivity, density, radius etc. Recently, reversible cellular automata (CAs) based clustering algorithms have been proposed that exploit the bijective global transition functions of the CAs to form the clusters [2]. In case of a reversible d-state cellular automaton (CA) of size n, the one-to-one global transition function distributes the configurations (all possible d-ary strings of length n) into some disjoint groups such that the configurations in each group are reachable from one another during the evolution of the CA. Each of these

This work is partially supported by Start-up Research Grant (File number: SRG/2022/002098), SERB, Govt. of India.

groups forms a cycle that uniquely characterizes a cluster. This metric of reachability is essential for forming clusters using reversible CAs [2].

However, in case of a CA-based clustering technique, the data objects need to be encoded into a string to be given as input to the CA. In Ref. [2], frequency-based encoding technique is used for this purpose. But, it has been observed that, the performance scores over the standard validation indices – Silhouette Score, Davis Bouldin, Calinski Harabasz and Dunn Index are not optimal. This may be due to loss of features' properties in the encoding process. In fact, none of the existing clustering algorithms actually give the optimal score in these standard validation indices, which indicates the clustering done by them are not perfect. This leads to the requirement of a new encoding technique that helps the clustering algorithms to achieve better performance score.

Furthermore, as the number of features increases, clustering becomes more challenging and computationally complex. Dimensionality reduction techniques are ineffective since they may lead to a loss of some features and suboptimal clustering results. Proper encoding technique may help in compressing the features to a great extent and reducing the length of the encoded string to a feasible level. To encode the features and reduce the encoded length, hashing techniques may be used (Sect. 3). But they do not preserve the property of the features leading to poor clustering. To address this, we propose Gödel number-based encoding function (Sect. 4). It encodes the features based on their values (weights) preserving the property of the features. Section 4.2 shows that this encoding technique effectively leads to better scores and meaningful clusters if applied over any existing algorithms.

2   Background

In this paper, we use data mining clustering algorithms K-Means [8], Hierarchical [11], DBSCAN [6], BIRCH [12] and Meanshift [4] as well as recent CA based clustering algorithm [2] as reference to compare the results with our technique. Our frame of reference, the clustering algorithm of Ref. [2] uses binary ($d = 2$) CA with 5-neighborhood dependency over null boundary condition and frequency based encoding is used for converting the data frames to CA configurations.

To evaluate the performance, Silhouette score [10], DB score [7], Calinski-Harabasz(CH) score [3] and Dunn index [5] are used. In the Silhouette score, its value ranges from -1 to 1. 1 means clusters are well distinguished and -1 means clusters are defined wrongly. Whereas, in case of Davis Bouldin (DB) score, a lower DB score indicates better clustering performance. A higher value of the Calinski Harabasz (CH) score indicates that the clusters are dense and well-separated. Same is for the Dunn index.

Datasets: The following datasets taken from Ref. [1] with only quantitative attributes have been used in the paper:

#Dataset	Dataset Name	No. of Instances	No. of Features
DS1	Seeds	199	8
DS2	User Knowledge Modelling	258	6
DS3	Heart Failure Clinical Record	299	13
DS4	BuddyMove	249	7

Data Preprocessing: Data may contain missing values or dirty values; in order to clean the data, preprocessing steps are applied over it. The following steps are conducted for this data preprocessing – data cleaning and data transformation. In data cleaning, to deal with missing data, imputation methods are used that estimate the missing values based on the observed data. We can use 'replace with previous values' (forward fill) or 'replace with next values' (backward fill). For example, in Python *data.fillna(method = 'ffill')* or *data.fillna(method = 'bfill')* package does this task. For categorical features, impute with the most frequent value can be used. Whereas, in data transformation, normalization of the data is performed so that data can fall under a given range. We can standardize the features by removing the mean and scaling it to unit variance. *Sklearn* library in Python is a preprocessing library for the preprocessing steps and *standard scalar* is used for this step. The standard scaler is calculated by $z = \frac{x-\mu}{\sigma}$ where μ is the mean of the data samples and σ is the standard deviation of the data samples. Scaling happens independently on each feature.

3 Hash-Based Encoding Function

We want to combine the dataset features into an encoded string so that the features are compressed for any high-dimensional datasets. If we directly combine the dataset features by just appending the feature values into a string, then the string length can be very large which is infeasible for effective computation. Thus we need an encoding function to encode the features. We can use an encoding technique that relies on the range of feature values to map data objects to encoded strings. While this technique is effective as the length of the string is reduced but it may cause a loss of data and may lead to poor clustering. If different unrelated data points are encoded to the same string, it can lead to poor clustering results as these points may belong to different clusters. To avoid this issue, it is important to use a unique encoding method so that two data points have the same encoding, if they are to be placed in the same cluster. In this section, we use hashing methods to compress the feature values and then encode them as a string.

3.1 Hash Based Encoding

There are many hashing functions available to compress the data, however all are not applicable to clustering. For example, if we use cryptographic hash function, a small change in the bit value can change the whole output. This implied that, two similar data objects may be hashed to two completely different strings. For example, if we round off the feature value then the hash function may produce different results as compared to the original feature value. So we need to use non-cryptographic hash functions that compress the feature values keeping the properties of the features intact. There are many hash functions available that generate up to 1024 bits of output. But as we want fewer bits we chose the following hashing algorithms that generate 4-byte compressed output – crc32, crc32c, MurmurHash3, xxHash, Adler32, fnv132 [9].

3.2 Implementation and Results

The hash functions are applied to the dataset row-wise, and for that, the value of the features are combined into string by appending each feature value one by one in a row-wise manner. This combined string is stored in a data structure. Hashing algorithms are applied on these combined strings producing 32-bit compressed strings as output. As the existing algorithms like K-Means, Hierarchical by default do not take encoded strings as input, we need to create a new data frame out of these hashed strings to be used as input. To create such a data frame, each of these compressed strings are divided into a number of parts, where each part is considered as a feature. In this paper, 32-bit compressed output string is generated, so we divide it into four parts making four 8-bit features. Now, clustering algorithms are applied to this newly created data frame. For example, *crc32* algorithm is applied through *zlib* library of Python which contains the hash function. In the same way, all other algorithms are used from various libraries i.e. *xxhash*, *mmh3*. Table 1 shows the comparison of hashing techniques based on evaluation metrics discussed in Sect. 2 for the *seeds* dataset.

Table 1. Comparison of hashing techniques over *Seeds* dataset

Hashing Function	Clustering Algorithm	Evaluation Metrics			
		Silhouette	Davis Bouldin	CH Score	Dunn Index
crc32	K-Means	0.272	1.501	77.298	0.0078
	Hierarchical	0.209	1.741	50.607	0.0072
crc32c	K-Means	0.229	1.650	65.813	0.0034
	Hierarchical	0.214	1.670	56.678	0.0022
xxhash	K-Means	0.241	1.597	68.101	0.0042
	Hierarchical	0.222	1.489	57.081	0.0035
mmh3	K-Means	0.269	1.442	77.923	0.0078
	Hierarchical	0.213	1.660	54.038	0.0063
adler32	K-Means	0.279	1.480	80.307	0.0073
	Hierarchical	0.222	1.692	56.468	0.0064
fnv132	K-Means	0.276	1.475	78.730	0.0032
	Hierarchical	0.186	1.853	46.046	0.0026

Table 2 shows the comparative results between the existing algorithms like K-Means, Hierarchical and CA-based along with the best result after applying the hashing technique over all existing algorithms. Both these tables indicate that, all hashing schemes have a lower benchmark score (see 5th column of Table 2 as example). This shows that the hash functions are not suitable for clustering because of their inability to preserve the property of the feature values which reflects in poor clustering score. In the next section, we introduce Gödel number-based encoding method which preserves the property of the features.

4   Gödel Number-Based Encoding Technique

The hash based encoding function compresses the data to 32-bits but this method fails to preserve the properties of the features, leading to poor clustering and accuracy scores. Our objective is to develop an encoding technique that can preserve the properties of the features and generate meaningful clusters. Here, we propose a new encoding technique based on Gödel numbers.

Table 2. Silhouette Score Comparison with Gödel number-based encoding

Dataset	K-Means	Hierarchical	Existing CA	Hash-based	Gödel number based
Seeds	0.531	0.495	0.502	0.279	0.988
User Knowledge Modelling	0.265	0.953	0.325	0.285	0.954
Clinical Heart Failure	0.583	0.679	0.612	0.266	0.761
BuddyMove	0.320	0.363	0.367	0.252	0.617

4.1   The Encoding Method

Gödel Number is a classical way of encoding symbols and numbers using a sequence of numbers. This sequence of numbers can again be represented as a single natural number. Given a sequence of numbers $(x_1, x_2, \cdots, x_n)$ of integers, the Gödel number of that will be the product of the first n primes raised to their corresponding values in the sequence. It works on the principle of the *fundamental theorem of arithmetic (or the unique-prime-factorization theorem)* that any number can be written as a unique product of the prime numbers. For example, any number c can be uniquely encoded as a product of the powers of the prime numbers as: $c = 2^{n_0} * 3^{n_1} * 5^{n_2} * \ldots * p_{k+1}^{n_k}$ where $2, 3, 5, \ldots, p_{k+1}$ are the sequence of the first k prime numbers and $n_0, n_1, n_2, \ldots, n_k$ are the natural numbers. For example, the number 600 can be encoded by Gödel numbering as $2^3 * 3^1 * 5^2$.

Gödel numbering is useful in many fields such as DNA coding, cryptography, and image analysis, etc. Here we use Gödel number for encoding each object of the dataset. Figure 1a shows 6 features of *buddymove* dataset having some numerical values. We can create Gödel number by taking each of the feature values and raising them to the power of the consecutive primes and multiply. For example, in the *buddymove* dataset, for the first two objects, the corresponding Gödel numbers are: $2^2 * 3^{77} * 5^{79} * 7^{69} * 11^{68} * 13^{95} = 5335406801306840660$ and $2^2 * 3^{62} * 5^{76} * 7^{76} * 11^{69} * 13^{68} = 6162014451816538124$.

To verify whether our Gödel number based encoding is preserving the properties of the features, we do the following:

1. Generate Gödel number for each row of the dataset.
2. Sort the Gödel numbers in ascending order based on their value. After sorting, automatically, the distribution of numbers will show some vacant positions where no numbers are there as per the dataset. Such vacant positions are called as *gaps*.
3. Find $k - 1$ largest gaps in the distribution of these numbers, where k is the desired number of clusters.
4. The rows corresponding to the Gödel numbers in each gap belong to the same cluster.

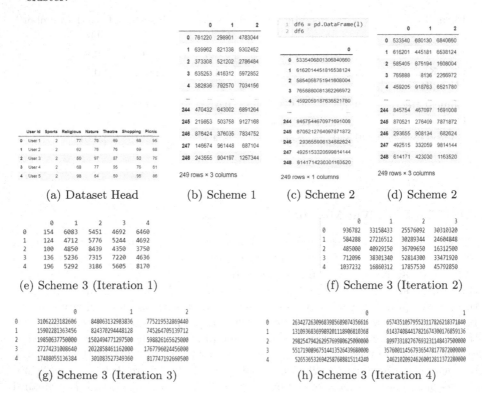

(a) Dataset Head   (b) Scheme 1   (c) Scheme 2   (d) Scheme 2

(e) Scheme 3 (Iteration 1)   (f) Scheme 3 (Iteration 2)

(g) Scheme 3 (Iteration 3)   (h) Scheme 3 (Iteration 4)

Fig. 1. Three Gödel number based encoding schemes over *BuddyMove* dataset

If we want k number of clusters then we find first $k - 1$ maximum distance between consecutive elements and split the data accordingly. We name this technique as *Sort Gödel* in this paper. Now, these clusters are tested by the standard validation indices. Table 3 shows a comparison result of this method with the K-Means algorithm. For example, if Gödel numbers are generated for the *seeds* dataset and the above method is applied, then silhouette score comes out to be 0.4934 which is very close to the score by K-Means (0.531). This means that Gödel number-based encoding function is able to preserve the property of the features.

Table 3. Comparison of hashing techniques based on evaluation metrics

Dataset	Clustering Technique	Evaluation Metrics			
		Silhouette	Davis Bouldin	CH Score	Dunn Index
Seeds	K-Means	0.531	0.659	345.488	0.0095
	Sort Gödel	0.493	0.824	318.944	0.0072
User Knowledge Modelling	K-Means	0.265	0.659	345.488	0.1279
	Sort Gödel	0.203	0.993	22910.758	0.0022
Clinical Heart Failure	K-Means	0.583	0.659	266.924	0.1285
	Sort Gödel	0.383	0.777	58.740	0.0035
BuddyMove	K-Means	0.320	1.336	119.97	0.045
	Sort Gödel	0.233	0.962	51.456	0.0080

Depending on the number of features, the corresponding Gödel number can be of a very large length. Likewise Sect. 3.2, we have to split the Gödel number into a number of parts. A completely new data frame is created from the original dataset and clustering is applied to that data frame. There are different ways to create a Gödel data frame, these are described in Table 4.

The Gödel numbers generated by each scheme are different for the same object and can be of different lengths. Figure 1 shows a sample way to apply these schemes over the *buddymove* dataset (Fig. 1a). Here, in the first scheme (Fig. 1b), three splits are considered, so the features are divided into three groups and for each group, the Gödel numbers are generated. Whereas, in the second scheme, the original number, generated by taking all the features together (Fig. 1c), is split into three parts to generate three features (Fig. 1d). Figures 1e to 1h shows four iterations of the third scheme where a window of two features is considered. Here, in the first iteration (Fig. 1e), Gödel numbers are generated considering each of the two consecutive features. In the next iteration, for that Gödel number and the next Gödel number, a Gödel number is generated and a overlapping window of length 2 is slided. Iteratively this is done until 2 attributes are left. The final Gödel numbers of these two attribute is considered as a new Data Frame (Fig. 1h).

Table 4. Different ways to create a data frame using Gödel numbering

Scheme 1	Split the features and generate Gödel number	Split the features and generate the Gödel number separately for each split and concatenate the generated number to get a data frame
Scheme 2	Generate Gödel Number and split	First generate the Gödel number for all the data objects, store it in a data frame and then split it into equal parts to create a new data frame where each part is considered as a feature
Scheme 3	Generate Gödel number by taking features in a window	Take a pre-defined window size, generating the Gödel number for the features coming under that window. Slide the window and Repeat the process till all features are covered in a window

Table 5. Comparison of all clustering techniques based on evaluation metrics

Clustering Technique	Scheme	Evaluation Metrics			
		Silhouette	Davis Bouldin	CH Score	Dunn Index
K-Means	Normal	0.531	0.659	345.488	0.0095
	Scheme 1	0.980	0.517	158.122	0.0083
	Scheme 2	0.952	1.615	150.607	0.0072
	Scheme 3	0.456	0.780	648.566	0.0070
Hierarchical	Normal	0.495	0.715	269.977	0.1050
	Scheme 1	0.988	0.005	12277.218	0.0080
	Scheme 2	0.948	0.137	710.927	0.0092
	Scheme 3	0.823	0.280	620.084	0.0045
BIRCH	Normal	0.346	0.913	129.199	0.0035
	Scheme 1	0.664	0.489	572.563	0.0068
	Scheme 2	0.978	0.152	3688.029	0.2143
	Scheme 3	0.925	0.366	700.067	0.2031
PAM	Normal	0.435	0.786	197.331	0.0053
	Scheme 1	0.553	0.584	497.994	0.0078
	Scheme 2	0.766	1.111	53.132	0.0093
	Scheme 3	0.777	0.663	361.559	0.0162
MeanShift	Normal	0.415	0.823	316.887	0.0012
	Scheme 1	0.629	0.523	778.277	0.0056
	Scheme 2	0.954	0.132	109806.136	0.2155
	Scheme 3	0.838	0.140	4026.506	0.1163
Existing CA	Normal	0.502	1.756	123.892	0.0010
	Scheme 1	0.456	0.956	236.842	0.0026
	Scheme 2	0.483	0.716	302.613	0.0036
	Scheme 3	0.301	0.530	224.650	0.0025

4.2 Results and Conclusion

To see the effectiveness of our Gödel number based encoding schemes, we apply this encoding over existing standard clustering techniques. Table 2 shows a comparison of the silhouette score of the Gödel number-based encoding result with the existing clustering algorithms. A detailed comparison over *seeds* dataset is shown in Table 5. It can be seen from these tables that Gödel number-based encoding drastically improves the scores in comparison to the existing clustering algorithms and hash-based encoding algorithm and helps to achieve the optimal performance. For example, if Gödel number based encoding is used over K-Means, it can achieve much better Silhouette score than the original. Other scores like DB score and CH score are also improved or is comparable to other algorithms. In fact, among the three schemes, the encoding of scheme 1 gives better results. As we are spiting the feature and generating Gödel number for them, the generated Gödel number is less when compared to other schemes. However, there is not much improvement over the score by CA-based clustering algorithm. This may be because, in the CA-based clustering technique of Ref. [2], binary CA has been used. So, again the Gödel numbers has to be converted into binary which looses the feature conservation property in that process. So, future work may be directed towards using decimal CA for clustering using this Gödel number based encoding technique.

Acknowledgment. The authors are grateful to Prof. Sukanta Das for his valuable comments.

References

1. UCI Machine Learning Repository, Center for Machine Learning and Intelligent Systems (2007). http://archive.ics.uci.edu/ml/index.php. Accessed January 2023
2. Abhishek, S., Dharwish, M., Das, A., Bhattacharjee, K.: A cellular automata based clustering technique for high-dimensional data. In: Das, S., Martinez, G.J. (eds.) ASCAT 2023. AISC, vol. 1443, pp. 37–51. Springer, Singapore (2023). https://doi.org/10.1007/978-981-99-0688-8_4
3. Caliński, T., Harabasz, J.A.: A dendrite method for cluster analysis. Commun. Stat. - Theory Methods **3**, 1–27 (1974)
4. Comaniciu, D., Meer, P.: Mean shift: a robust approach toward feature space analysis. IEEE Trans. Pattern Anal. Mach. Intell. **24**(5), 603–619 (2002)
5. Dunn, J.C.: Well separated clusters and fuzzy partitions. J. Cybern. **4**, 95–104 (1974)
6. Ester, M., Kriegel, H.-P., Sander, J., Xu, X.: A density-based algorithm for discovering clusters in large spatial databases with noise. In: Proceedings of the Second International Conference on Knowledge Discovery and Data Mining, KDD 1996, pp. 226–231. AAAI Press (1996)
7. Ester, M., Kriegel, H.-P., Sander, J., Xu, X.: A density-based algorithm for discovering clusters in large spatial databases with noise. In: Knowledge Discovery and Data Mining (1996)
8. Hartigan, J.A., Wong, M.A.: Algorithm AS 136: a K-Means clustering algorithm. Appl. Stat. **28**(1), 100–108 (1979)

9. Martín-Fernández, F., Caballero-Gil, P.: Analysis of the new standard hash function. In: Moreno-Díaz, R., Pichler, F., Quesada-Arencibia, A. (eds.) EUROCAST 2013. LNCS, vol. 8111, pp. 142–149. Springer, Heidelberg (2013). https://doi.org/10.1007/978-3-642-53856-8_18
10. Rousseeuw, P.: Silhouettes: a graphical aid to the interpretation and validation of cluster analysis. J. Comput. Appl. Math. **20**, 53–65 (1987)
11. Zepeda-Mendoza, M.L., Resendis-Antonio, O.: Hierarchical agglomerative clustering. In: Dubitzky, W., Wolkenhauer, O., Cho, K.H., Yokota, H. (eds.) Encyclopedia of Systems Biology, pp. 886–887. Springer, New York (2013). https://doi.org/10.1007/978-1-4419-9863-7_1371
12. Zhang, T., Ramakrishnan, R., Livny, M.: BIRCH: a new data clustering algorithm and its applications. Data Min. Knowl. Disc. **1**(2), 141–182 (1997)

Machine Learning

Unsupervised Discovery of Recurring Spoken Terms Using Diagonal Patterns

P. Sudhakar[1]([✉])[iD], K. Sreenivasa Rao[2][iD], and Pabitra Mitra[2][iD]

[1] Advanced Technology Development Centre, Indian Institute of Technology, Kharagpur, Kharagpur 721302, India
sudhakar.asp@iitkgp.ac.in
[2] Department of Computer Science and Engineering, Indian Institute of Technology, Kharagpur, Kharagpur 721302, India

Abstract. Spoken term discovery is a challenging task when a lot of spoken content is generated without annotation. The spoken term discovery task accomplished by pattern matching techniques resolves the challenge by directly capturing the resemblance of the spoken terms at the acoustic feature level. Despite feasibility, the pattern-matching approach generates more false alarms during the discovery task due to fluctuations that arise in natural speech; hence degradation in the performance was observed. In the proposed approach, the challenge that arises due to the variability is addressed in two stages. In the first stage, the RASTA-PLP spectrogram was used as an acoustic feature representation that reduces the variabilities among similar spoken contents. In the second stage, the novel Diagonal Pattern Search method unconstrainedly computes the pattern resemblance between the identical spoken terms at the segmental level. The proposed approach was evaluated using the IITKGP-SDUC speech corpus and inferred that a 10.11% improvement in the accuracy was achieved compared to other state-of-the-art systems in the spoken term discovery task.

Keywords: spoken term discovery · Diagonal Pattern Search · pattern matching · diagonal similarity

1 Introduction

In the recent communication era, a lot of spoken content generated without transcription challenges the Spoken Content Retrieval (SCR) task. In the conventional approach, the SCR task was achieved by converting the spoken query and spoken content into its equivalent text using Automatic Speech Recognition (ASR) system and text-based matching was applied to match similar spoken terms. The ASR-based system seeks a huge amount of annotated spoken content to achieve optimal performance [17]. Due to that, the spoken contents without annotation are unable to participate in the retrieval process. Pattern matching approach for spoken term detection is one of the alternate methods

P. Maji et al. (Eds.): PReMI 2023, LNCS 14301, pp. 61–69, 2023.
https://doi.org/10.1007/978-3-031-45170-6_7

that aim to capture the similarities in an unsupervised way by matching the pattern resemblances at the acoustic feature level itself. Such an approach does not seek annotations and is well-suitable for the SCR task without annotation.

Spoken Term Discovery (STD) without annotation is a subset of the SCR task that aim to discover similar spoken terms in the speech corpus in an unsupervised manner. In [1,9,10,12,14], an unsupervised STD task was attempted to resolve the resource constraints. However, a significant performance gap was observed in comparison to the ASR-based techniques. The existing approaches in the unsupervised STD tasks are broadly grouped into two categories: (i) Dynamic Time Warping (DTW) centric and (ii) template matching centric. In the DTW approach, temporal alignment between two acoustic feature representations is obtained, and similarities were computed [1,7,11,18]. The challenge in the DTW approach is global alignment. The segmental DTW approach [12] overcomes the challenge and achieves the task at the segmental level. Similarly, the statistical word discovery model in [4], the n-gram model [2] based on dynamic programming, Randomised Algorithm approach [9] and the audio motif discovery (MODIS) [6] utilised the segmental DTW-centric approach to accomplish the STD task in an unsupervised way. Despite its advantage, the segmental DTW approach completely relies on the segment size and deciding the segment size is another challenge due to the speech variabilities. The template matching approach discovers the pattern similarities from the acoustic feature representations. The syllable boundary-based n-gram approach [14] maps similar spoken terms at the syllable level and identifies the similarities. In [10], an embedded segmental K-means model was applied to capture similar spoken terms. Alternatively, an image processing-based approach [3] was studied to capture the pattern similarities at the image level. In [15], spoken content is segmented at the phoneme level in an unsupervised way, and the similarity match was detected based on the 3-NDFS traversal technique. Despite the feasibility, the aforementioned approaches introduce many false alarm matches during the discovery task and degrade the performance.

One of the major concern in the pattern discovery approach is eliminating the fluctuations that arise due to the speakers, language and environmental specific changes. As an effect, the pattern similarity between the same spoken term varies in three ways: (i) a total match in which two acoustic feature representations of the spoken terms match exactly in sequence for all frames (referred Type-I), (ii) a partial match happens at the prefix or the suffix portion of the spoken term in sequence (referred Type-II), and (iii) multiple non-contiguous partial matches in a spoken term region (referred Type-III). Therefore the pattern discovery approach should be robust enough to consider all possible matches and accomplish the STD task effectively. The proposed Diagonal Pattern Search (DPS) overcomes the drawbacks by capturing the similarities in all possible cases without constraint. Furthermore, the RASTA-PLP [8] spectrogram was employed as a feature representation that emphasises the significant matches of alike terms across the speakers and reduces the variabilities. As a result, a huge improvement in performance was achieved in the STD task in an unsupervised way.

2   Spoken Term Discovery

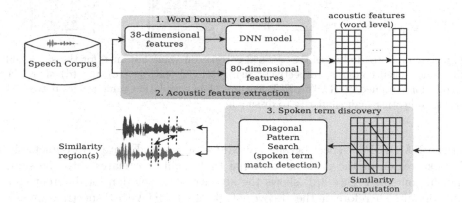

Fig. 1. The schematic view of the proposed spoken term discovery task.

The overall structure of the proposed work specified in Fig. 1 consists of two stages: (i) acoustic feature representation and (ii) pattern matching for spoken term discovery. In the first stage, the RASTA-PLP spectrogram was computed directly from the speech signal. In the second stage, the proposed DPS computes the spoken term similarity between two spoken documents.

2.1   Acoustic Feature Extraction

The spoken term discovery was achieved using RASTA-PLP spectrogram[1] as acoustic feature representation. In our approach, the RASTA-PLP spectrogram was obtained by processing the speech signal at multiple stages. At first, the speech signal is split into multiple frames of 20 ms duration without overlap. In the next stage, the hamming window was applied, and Discrete Fourier Transform (DFT)) was computed at each frame. Further, the DFT values were analysed using critical bands. In the later stage, the RASTA filter shown in Eq. 1 was applied over the log magnitude of the critical band values.

$$H(z) = 0.1z^4 * \frac{2 + z^{-1} - z^{-3} - 2z^{-4}}{1 - 0.98z^{-1}} \tag{1}$$

Furthermore, the filtered spectrum was multiplied with a factor to amplify the loudness and intensity. Finally, the all-pole model was applied over the spectrum, and cepstral coefficients were computed. The spectrum obtained from the cepstral coefficients is less sensitive to the low-frequency changes; hence higher similarity was observed even though two different speakers uttered the same spoken content. Figure 2 demonstrates the spectral correlation obtained based

---

[1] https://www.ee.columbia.edu/~dpwe/resources/matlab/rastamat/.

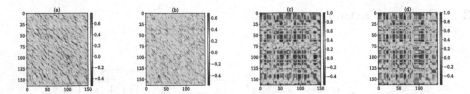

Fig. 2. (a) and (b) indicates the spectral correlation value obtained for the same and different spoken contents, respectively, using MFCC features. (c) and (d) show the correlation obtained by RASTA-PLP features. The correlation value ranges between 1 to −1, indicating high similarity to dissimilar.

on the RASTA-PLP spectrogram and MFCC features. Figure 2(c) depicts the line-like region at the principle diagonal that highly correlates with the same spoken content. Figure 2(d) shows the absence of correlation for different spoken content. Therefore, in the discovery task, the RASTA-PLP spectrogram was employed for the discovery task.

2.2   Spoken Term Discovery Using Diagonal Pattern Search

The objective of the proposed DPS is to consider all types (I, II and III) of matches between the spoken terms and capture the similarities. In the discovery task, the pattern similarity was obtained by processing the acoustic features at multiple stages. At first, the RASTA-PLP spectrogram representation $X = [x_1, x_2, ..., x_L], x \in \mathbb{R}^{80}$ for the document D^i was extracted. Similarly, for document D^j, the spectrogram representation $Y = [y_1, y_2, ..., y_M], y \in \mathbb{R}^{80}$ was obtained. In the next stage, the cosine similarity between D^i and D^j was computed frame-wise using Eq. 2 for all frames $l, m \in L, M$.

$$sim[l, m] = \frac{x_l . y_m}{\sqrt{x_l^2} . \sqrt{y_m^2}} \qquad (2)$$

The similarity matrix $sim[L, M]$ was binarised using Eq. 3 for all elements in u, v where $1 \leq u \leq L, 1 \leq v \leq M$.

$$sim_b[u, v] = \begin{cases} 1, & if\ sim[u, v] \geq \eta \\ 0, & otherwise. \end{cases} \qquad (3)$$

In sim_b, **1** indicates that the frames correspond to the two documents having higher similarity and **0** refers to dissimilarity (mismatch). Further, the sim_b was used to capture the pattern similarities that occur in the diagonal region of similar spoken terms. During the matching task, the proposed DPS approach captures the match(es) in three steps. At first, the sim_b was scanned diagonally to capture the segmental similarities by computing the depth of the similarity. Let $sim_b[u, v]$ represents a value of the similarity matrix at $u \times v$ position, then

$sim_d[u, v]$ was computed using Eq. 4.

$$sim_d[u, v] = \begin{cases} sim_b[u, v], & if\ u = 1\ or\ v = 1 \\ sim_b[u, v] + sim_b[u - 1, v - 1], & if\ u, v > 1 \end{cases} \qquad (4)$$

Similarly, for all matrix elements, the depth cost was computed, and the depth similarity matrix sim_d has arrived. The larger values in sim_d indicate the higher sequential similarity between the spoken terms. In the second stage, the diagonal cost was computed for all diagonal entries $(L + M - 1)$ in sim_d. The cost consideration in the diagonal path accounts for all types (I, II and III) of similarities and emphasises the similarity level. Based on the experiments conducted, it is observed that the affinity between two similar spoken content propagates diagonally in a contiguous or non-contiguous manner (see Fig. 2). This is due to the variability of natural speech. Hence, considering the diagonal matches of both contiguous and non-contiguous regions work for the variability issues. In the next step, the potential similarity region(s) were identified based on the diagonal cost obtained using Eq. 5.

$$dia\_sum[k] = \sum_{\forall k=1}^{L+M-1} diag(k) \qquad (5)$$

The $diag()$ function returns all cost values associated in the kth diagonal of the similarity matrix sim_d, and dia_sum list maintains the diagonal cost for each diagonal. Further, the best match can be easily retrieved by analysing the dia_sum cost alone. Finally, potential similarity region(s) in sim_d were identified by analysing the diagonal cost dia_sum with the threshold λ. The λ indicates the minimum depth of the similarity to be considered as a potential spoken term match. Figure 3 depicts the spoken term match detected between D^i and D^j containing the spoken content "spinar harabhajan sinh ne chaimpiyans trophee" and "chaimpiyans trophee ke lie"[2], respectively. From Fig. 3(b), it is observed that the diagonal cost for the spoken term similarity region is high (indicated by the line marked in blue colour) compared to other regions. By thresholding the diagonal cost with λ, the potential spoken term similarities were captured by the DPS approach. The DPS method differs from the DTW-centric techniques (subsequence DTW and segmental DTW) by identifying the spoken term matches without constraining the segment size. Figure 4 shows the comparison between the proposed approach and DTW-centric approaches for the spoken term detection task. The spoken term "chaimpiyans" in the x-axis was searched in the document containing "dakshin aphreeka ne bhee chaimpiyans trophee" in y-axis. Figure 4(a) and (b) indicates the cost matrix obtained from the proposed approach and its diagonal cost. Similarly, Fig. 4(c), (d), (e) and (f) indicate the subsequence DTW and its cost matrix, segmental DTW and its cost matrix, respectively. From the figure, it is clear that the proposed approach captures the similarity region and highlights the spoken term appropriately.

---

[2] transliterated from Hindi to English for readability.

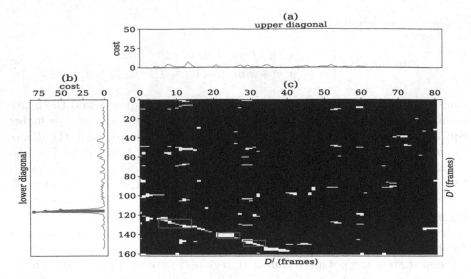

Fig. 3. Depicts the spoken term match detected by the proposed method. (a) and (b) indicate the upper and lower diagonal costs computed from the similarity matrix, respectively. (c) represents the document similarity (in white colour) computed between D^i and D^j. The rectangle region in red colour indicates the spoken term similarity detected by the proposed method.

3   Performance Evaluation

The proposed approach was evaluated based on the detection of spoken term matches in the corpus. The IITKGP-SDUC speech corpus[3] was used to measure the performance of the system. The standard performance metrics: precision, recall, F1 score and accuracy are used to measure the performance of both the proposed and other state-of-the-art systems [3,13,15,16].

The speech corpus designed for the unsupervised pattern discovery task consists of spoken contents from Hindi and Bengali. The speech signal was captured at IIT Kharagpur from two different native speakers in the age group of 20–30. The corpus consists of 2,072 spoken documents belonging to three different categories (politics, sports and weather). The total duration of the spoken content spans approximately three hours. All speech files are recorded in a noise-free condition and uniformly sampled at 16 kHz with 16 bits resolution. The key spoken terms (repeated more than once) in the corpus consist of 120,536 occurrences pairwise with a minimal phoneme sequence length of 5 in Hindi and 7 in Bengali. In the discovery task, there are 1,369,556 document pairs searched to capture the potential spoken term matches.

The performance measures hit (H), miss (M) and false alarms (FA) are computed for each pair of matches. The hit is counted if the discovered spoken term belongs to the ground truth document pair. Otherwise, it is a false alarm. The

---

[3] available at http://cse.iitkgp.ac.in/~ksrao/res.html.

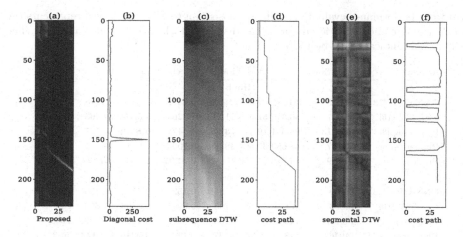

Fig. 4. (a) and (b) indicates the cost matrix and diagonal cost obtained from the proposed approach. (c) and (d) indicates the cost matrix and cost path for the subsequence DTW approach. Similarly, (e) and (f) represent the segmental DTW approach.

miss reveals the absence of the spoken term pair in the discovery task. Further, the standard performance measures: precision, recall, F1 score and accuracy [5] are calculated based on the hit, miss and false alarm scores.

In the proposed approach, the thresholding parameters η and λ were chosen empirically by maximising the hit and minimising the miss and false alarms. The optimal choices of $\eta \geq 0.95$ and $5 \leq \lambda \leq 15$ were obtained for 100 Hindi documents chosen randomly that maximise the hit and minimise the false alarms. From the results, it is inferred that the miss and false alarm ratio reaches a minimum when $\lambda = 9$ and $\eta = 0.97$; hence the same threshold values are retained for further experiments.

4   Results and Discussion

The outcome of the proposed approach in the STD task was specified in Table 1 in comparison with the other systems [3,13,15,16]. The IITKGP-SDUC speech corpus was used to measure the performance in terms of precision, recall, F1 score and accuracy.

In view of the hit ratio, the proposed approach achieves 96% in Bengali. Meanwhile, the Image-seg approach achieves 82% in Hindi. The least performance was observed in the CNN-QBE approach for both languages. A lot of false alarms generated during the discovery task degraded the performance, whereas the proposed approach reduced the false alarm significantly. In view of the false alarm ratio, the proposed approach attains a minimum of 17% in Hindi in comparison with all other methods. Meanwhile, in Bengali, the false alarm rises to 24%. In view of the other measures, the proposed approach improved by 10.2%, 9.5% and 10.11% in Hindi towards precision, F1 score and accuracy, respectively.

Table 1. Performance evaluation of the proposed approach. #Retrieved represents the number of documents retrieved during the discovery task. Acc indicates accuracy. The text in bold indicates the best score.

Approach	#Retrieved	Hit	Miss	FA	Precision	Recall	F1-score	Acc (%)
Hindi								
CNN-QBE [13]	294,388	46,285	62,001	248,103	0.1572	0.4274	0.2298	13.0
segDTW [16]	77,557	56,340	51,946	21,217	0.7264	0.5202	0.6063	43.5
Image-seg [3]	162,313	88,861	19,425	73,452	0.5474	**0.8206**	0.6567	48.9
Phoneme-seg [15]	97,347	68,689	39,597	28,658	0.7056	0.6343	0.6681	50.2
Proposed	89,859	74,518	33,768	15,341	**0.8292**	0.6881	**0.7521**	**60.2**
Bengali								
CNN-QBE [13]	17509	2673	9585	14836	0.1526	0.2180	0.1795	9.9
segDTW [16]	15693	10898	1352	4795	0.6944	0.8896	0.7800	63.9
Image-seg [3]	15929	11666	584	4263	0.7323	0.9523	0.8279	**70.6**
Phoneme-seg [15]	14946	11319	931	3627	**0.7573**	0.9240	**0.8324**	70.3
Proposed	16299	11830	420	4469	0.7258	**0.9659**	0.8287	**70.6**

In summary, the proposed DPS considers the significant spoken term similarities of all types (I, II and III) in the diagonal region and avoids the insignificant matches. As an effect, a reduction in false alarms and misses was observed. Based on the experimental results, it is inferred that the acoustic feature representation and the DPS method jointly contribute to the variability challenges. Thus the performance was improved in the unsupervised STD task in the absolute absence of annotations.

5 Summary and Conclusion

The objective of the proposed approach is to overcome the speech variability challenges in the STD task and improve the discovery performance. In the proposed method, the variability challenge is reduced by the RASTA-PLP spectrogram. Further, the proposed DPS method discovers the appropriate spoken term matches from the acoustic feature representation. Based on the experimental results, a 10.11% accuracy gain was achieved compared to the other state-of-the-art systems in the STD task by reducing false alarms. In future, we will explore the possible ways of DNN-based acoustic feature representation for the similarity detection task that reduces the false alarms further in the zero-resource constraint.

References

1. Park, A., Glass, J.R.: Towards unsupervised pattern discovery in speech. In: 2005 IEEE Workshop on Automatic Speech Recognition and Understanding, pp. 53–58 (2005)

2. Aimetti, G.: Modelling early language acquisition skills: towards a general statistical learning mechanism. In: Proceedings of the Student Research Workshop at EACL 2009, pp. 1–9 (2009)
3. Birla, L., et al.: A robust unsupervised pattern discovery and clustering of speech signals. Pattern Recogn. Lett. **116**, 254–261 (2018)
4. ten Bosch, L., Cranen, B.: A computational model for unsupervised word discovery. ISCA, Antwerp (2007)
5. Carterette, B., Voorhees, E.M.: Overview of information retrieval evaluation. In: Lupu, M., Mayer, K., Tait, J., Trippe, A. (eds.) Current Challenges in Patent Information Retrieval. The Information Retrieval Series, vol. 29, pp. 69–85. Springer, Heidelberg (2011). https://doi.org/10.1007/978-3-642-19231-9_3
6. Catanese, L., et al.: MODIS: an audio motif discovery software. In: Show & Tell-Interspeech 2013 (2013)
7. Gupta, V., Ajmera, J., Kumar, A., Verma, A.: A language independent approach to audio search. In: Twelfth Annual Conference of the International Speech Communication Association (2011)
8. Hermansky, H., Morgan, N.: Rasta processing of speech. IEEE Trans. Speech Audio Process. **2**(4), 578–589 (1994)
9. Jansen, A., Van Durme, B.: Efficient spoken term discovery using randomized algorithms. In: 2011 IEEE Workshop on Automatic Speech Recognition & Understanding, pp. 401–406. IEEE (2011)
10. Kamper, H., Livescu, K., Goldwater, S.: An embedded segmental k-means model for unsupervised segmentation and clustering of speech. In: 2017 IEEE Automatic Speech Recognition and Understanding Workshop (ASRU), pp. 719–726 (2017)
11. Karthik, P.D., Saranya, M., Murthy, H.A.: A fast query-by-example spoken term detection for zero resource languages. In: 2016 International Conference on Signal Processing and Communications (SPCOM), pp. 1–5. IEEE (2016)
12. Park, A.S., Glass, J.R.: Unsupervised pattern discovery in speech. IEEE Trans. Audio Speech Lang. Process. **16**(1), 186–197 (2008)
13. Ram, D., Miculicich, L., Bourlard, H.: CNN based query by example spoken term detection. In: Interspeech, pp. 92–96 (2018)
14. Räsänen, O., Doyle, G., Frank, M.C.: Unsupervised word discovery from speech using automatic segmentation into syllable-like units. In: Sixteenth Annual Conference of the International Speech Communication Association (2015)
15. Ravi, K.K., Krothapalli, S.R.: Phoneme segmentation-based unsupervised pattern discovery and clustering of speech signals. Circ. Syst. Signal Process. **41**(4), 2088–2117 (2022)
16. San, N., et al.: Leveraging pre-trained representations to improve access to untranscribed speech from endangered languages. In: 2021 IEEE Automatic Speech Recognition and Understanding Workshop (ASRU), pp. 1094–1101. IEEE (2021)
17. Weintraub, M.: Keyword-spotting using SRI's DECIPHER large-vocabulary speech-recognition system. In: 1993 IEEE International Conference on Acoustics, Speech, and Signal Processing, vol. 2, pp. 463–466. IEEE (1993)
18. Zhang, Y., Glass, J.R.: Towards multi-speaker unsupervised speech pattern discovery. In: 2010 IEEE International Conference on Acoustics, Speech and Signal Processing, pp. 4366–4369 (2010)

MuOE: A Multi-task Ordinality Aware Approach Towards Engagement Detection

Saumya Gandhi[✉], Aayush Fadia, Ritik Agrawal, Surbhi Agrawal,
and Praveen Kumar

Visvesvaraya National Institute of Technology, Nagpur, India
sgandhi@students.vnit.ac.in

Abstract. With the increasing adoption of online learning, decreasing student engagement is becoming rampant. Detecting this is the first step in making online education more viable and effective. We present MuOE, a Multi-task Ordinality-aware Engagement detection model to identify attention levels from students' webcam videos. MuOE uses a transformer with exceptional sequence-processing capability and a novel selector-based attention mechanism that picks important video frames. Facial cue detection is used as an auxillary task in our multi-task formulation of the problem, so the shared model base has more supervision. We leverage the ordinal nature of engagement levels by introducing a smooth loss function that penalizes predictions based on closeness to the true label. In this paper, we motivate each component of MuOE, and demonstrate its utility through a set of quantative experiments. We achieve a state-of-the-art accuracy of 57.65% (Top-2 accuracy 95.07%) on the DAiSEE dataset.

Keywords: Education · Engagement Detection · Deep Spatio-temporal Learning · Multitask Learning · Ordinal Regression · Transformers

1 Introduction

E-Learning has gained popularity recently owing to its affordable and high-quality nature. The COVID 19 pandemic accelerated this trend. This has led to reduced interaction, lack in engagement, lower retention, and higher dropout rates. According to [14], only 13% of students complete a Massively Open Online Course that they start. Technology-driven interventions can enhance learner engagement.

Computer Vision shows promise in detecting engagement. Classification of facial features from student videos outperforms behavior and sensor based methods. Deep learning models to extract facial features improve further upon methods based on hand-crafted features [12]. Even these methods struggle to achieve high accuracy on datasets like DAiSEE [9].

P. Maji et al. (Eds.): PReMI 2023, LNCS 14301, pp. 70–79, 2023.
https://doi.org/10.1007/978-3-031-45170-6_8

The challenge of such datasets is subjective and labourious annotation, leading to ambiguous and small datasets susceptible to overfitting. Existing methods for engagement detection, like DSFTN [12] and HybridTCN [1] use LSTMs and temporal convolutions. We build on these by using a transformer for sequential processing followed by a novel selector-based attention mechanism for identifying important frames. Moreover, we introduce an auxiliary task to predict Facial Action Unit intensities, a set of muscle movements related to emotion expression [7]. This auxiliary task is defined unambiguously, which reduces overfitting.

Existing methods treat engagement detection as a binary classification task, while engagement level is continuous [21]. Recent advances have shown the efficacy of finer-grained engagement detection [12]. These methods ignore the ordered nature of engagement levels by treating each level as orthogonal (Engagement Level Very Low is the same distance away from Low and High both, for example). We use a novel smooth-loss function to incorporate the order within engagement levels, and get predictions closer to the ground truth.

We propose a novel multi-task learning-based ordinality aware model (MuOE) for student engagement detection in an online learning scenario. Our major contributions are as follows:

- We are the first to introduce a multi-task learning paradigm for student engagement detection using a facial action unit-based auxiliary task.
- We utilize transformers for sequence modeling with a novel selector-based attention module to identify relevant frames.
- We propose a novel smooth-label-based ordinal loss, which incorporates the ordering between the engagement levels to tackle the classification problem.
- We demonstrate state-of-the-art performance across evaluation criteria on the DAiSEE dataset compared with several strong baselines.

2 Related Work

2.1 Student Engagement Systems

Traditionally, student engagement systems have been developed using self-reports, observational checklists and rating scales, evaluation indicators from e-learning systems and physiological indicators such as EEG signals [11]. These methods are intrusive and inconvinient.

In recent years, progress in computer vision has led to a rise in convinient, unintrusive video-based engagement detection [5]. Previously, handcrafted features, such as gaze keypoints, facial action units, and upper body pose were fed to classifiers for detecting engagement [5]. These methods lacked real-world robustness [12]. Recently, Deep learning has been utilized to solve shared tasks like the EmotiW challenge [5].

Apart from introducing the Dataset for Affective States in E-Environments (DAiSEE), [9] the authors provided several end-to-end baselines such as C3D [17], and Long-term Convolutional Neural Networks [6]. Similarly, the best performing model by Abedi et al. [1] formulates the problem as Spatio-temporal classification. They extract spatial features using a ResNet backbone [10] followed by dilated and causal 1D convolutions. However, these models overfit to possibly ambiguous annotations.

2.2 Ordinal Learning Objectives

Previous engagement detection approaches used binary classification [21]. Recently, fine grained assessment across several engagement levels has shown to be more accurate [1,9,12]. Existing loss functions such as Cross-entropy [9], Weighted Cross-entropy [21], focal loss, and center loss [12] are designed to work with orthogonal label classification, where all labels are different from each other, and no notion of closeness/order exists.

We use a loss function that exploits this order inherent in engagement levels, a method that has proved successful in tasks involving ordered labels like age classification and monocular depth estimation [8]. Several methods have been proposed for enforcing ordinality among classes such as K-rank, weight sharing [15] and kernel discrimination [16].

2.3 Multi-task Learning

The multitask learning (MTL) paradigm is used to jointly train multiple related tasks that may exhibit generalizable patterns. This improves the performance of each task and overall robustness of the model against adversarial attacks [13]. It has been effective across many Machine Learning applications such as Natural Language Processing, Speech Recognition, Computer Vision and Drug Discovery [4]. Facial action unit prediction have been used as an auxiliary task along with the main task of predicting engagement level. The MTL formulation is well suited to detecting academic engagement because features learned from predicting facial action units help predict engagement levels.

3 Methodology

3.1 Problem Formulation

Our goal is to assess the engagement level of a student given a video snippet $v_i \in V$, where $V = \{v_1, v_2, ..., v_n\}$. Each video $v_i = [f_1^i, f_2^i, ..., f_T^i]$ where f_t^i is the tth frame from the ith video and T is the total number of frames in each video. Following from [9,12], we formalize the assessment over four increasing levels of engagement: Very Low (VL) < Low (L) < High (H) < Very High (VH). Due to the inherent ordinal nature present between the engagement levels, we formulate engagement assessment as an ordinal classification problem. Formally, for each video v_i, we aim to classify v_i into an engagement level $y \in \{VL, L, H, VH\}$.

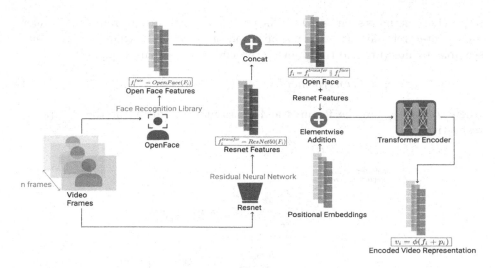

Fig. 1. Illustration of the first stage of our proposed model architecture.

3.2 Frame Level Feature Extraction

The face is the most expressive region to gauge emotional state, thus we require a robust representation of facial regions from each frame. We utilize a pre-trained ResNet50 [10] fine-tuned on the VGGFace2 dataset [3] as a backbone model for transfer-learning based feature extraction. Facial Landmarks, head pose estimation, and gaze direction are also essential for visual emotion recognition and non-verbal behavior systems [20]. We utilized the OpenFace 2.0 toolkit [2] to obtain many high-level facial analysis and behavior related features including head pose information, eye gaze direction and 3D facial landmarks.[1] As shown in Fig. 1, the 155-dimensional vector from these high-level features is concatenated with the lower-level pixel-based features learned via our fine-tuned ResNet50 model to create comprehensive representations of the facial region for each frame.

$$f_i^{face} = OpenFace(F_i), f_i^{transfer} = ResNet50(F_i) \qquad (1)$$

$$f_i = f_i^{transfer} \parallel f_i^{face} \qquad (2)$$

where $F_i \in R^{w \times h \times 3}$ is the ith frame of the video, and f_i are the features for the respective frame.

3.3 Sequential Modeling of Frames

We use the transformer architecture [18] which was proposed for Natural Language Processing tasks to replace recurrent models like LSTMs. In comparison

---

[1] We refrain from including Facial Action Units to avoid information leaking to the auxiliary task of predicting regressive action units.

to previous methods such as 3D CNNs for video classification, transformers offer higher interpretability (via the visualization of attention mechanism), an easily scalable architecture and the ability to process variable-length inputs.

$$v_i = TransformerEncoder(f_i + p_i) = \phi(f_i + p_i) \tag{3}$$

where f_i and p_i are the features and positional encodings for the ith frame, respectively.

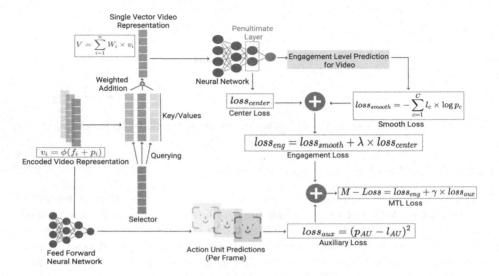

Fig. 2. Illustration of the second stage of our proposed MuOE model architecture.

3.4   Selector Based Attention Pooling

Every frame has a different importance with respect to judging engagement. For example, frames containing a yawn or prolonged eye closure are more important to engagement prediction and the model should pay more attention to those. We propose a novel selector-based attention mechanism that uses a trainable selector vector to produce a single-vector representation for the entire sequence with relevant information.

In the proposed mechanism, multiplicative attention is performed over the sequence of input vectors (keys/values) with the selector vector as the query. Weights are calculated for each vector in the input sequence as follows:

$$W_i = \frac{e^{s^T v_i}}{\sum_{j=1}^{n} e^{s^T v_j}} \tag{4}$$

where s is the trainable selector vector, v_i is vector representation of the ith video frame and W_i is the normalized weight for the corresponding video frame vector. Finally, as we see in Fig. 2, the video frames are aggregated into a single vector according to the weights that were calculated above:

$$V = \sum_{i=1}^{n} W_i \times v_i \qquad (5)$$

where V is the final vector representation of the entire video.

The selector vector acts as a template for what important frames might look like. It guides the mechanism to give higher weights to sequence vectors similar to itself and pass on that information into the single vector representation. Since the selector vector is trainable, it continually gets better at identifying important vectors from its input sequence during training.

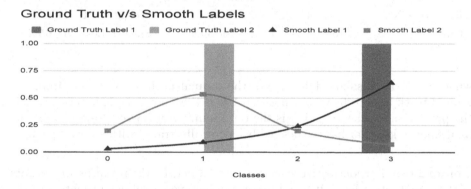

Fig. 3. Illustrative comparison of Smooth Labels and Ground Truth Labels. Ground truth labels are one-hot. They are 1 on the true class and zero everywhere else. Our smoothing operation distributes that one amongst the classes in proportion to how close each class is to the ground truth.

3.5   Smooth Contrastive Engagement Classifier

MuOE is optimized through a combination of center loss [19] and smooth loss.

Smooth Loss: While this is a classification problem with ordinal labels, not all incorrect pairs of (prediction, ground truth) should be penalized equally because the labels are ordered. For example, in a video where the ground truth engagement level was 3, predicting level 2 is more desirable than predicting 0 because class 2 is closer to 3 than 0. For this reason, we use the ordinal/smooth loss, which works by smoothing out the ground truth labels (illustrated in 3) and then applying cross-entropy loss.

$$d_c = |c - t| \; , \; l_c = \frac{e^{d_c}}{\sum_{j=1}^{C} e^{d_j}} \; , \; loss_{smooth} = -\sum_{c=1}^{C} l_c \times \log p_c \qquad (6)$$

Table 1. Performance comparison of examined models on the engagement level prediction task in terms of average accuracy over 5 runs. Author provided Source code and hyper-parameters used wherever available.

Model	Feature Extraction	Temporal Aggregation	Loss	Accuracy
InceptionNet Frame Level	CNN	None	CE	47.1%
InceptionNet Video Level	CNN	Aggregated Frame level outputs	CE	46.4%
C3D Training	3D CNN	3D CNN	CE	48.6%
LRCN	CNN	LSTM	CE	51.07%
Spatiotemporal Network Model	SE-ResNet-50	LSTM with global attention	Center Loss	54.2%
ResNet-TCN	ResNet	TCN	Weighted CE	55.47%
Ours	ResNet	Transformer	Smooth Loss	**57.65%**

where d_c is the absolute difference of the ordinal position of class c from the ground truth label ordinal class position t, l_c is the smooth label for class c, p_c is the prediction for class c and C is the total number of classes. $loss_{smooth}$ is the final smooth loss that has the desired behavior, illustrated with an example in 3.

Center Loss: is a contrastive loss function that acts on the penultimate outputs of the classification head. It maintains a running average of penultimate outputs ('centers') for every class. At every training iteration, the center loss places a penalty on how far away the penultimate outputs are from their corresponding classes' centers and updates the class centers. We calculate total engagement loss $loss_{eng}$ by adding $loss_{center}$ and $loss_{smooth}$, with a scaling parameter λ:

3.6 Multi-task Learning Problem Formulation

We frame engagement detection as a multi-task problem and predict a subset of Action Units from the Facial Actions Coding System. Specifically, we use Intensity Action units that can take continuous values from 0 to 5, representing how prominent that action is. This enables the two related tasks of engagement prediction and action unit prediction to be learned jointly and for information to be shared between the respective tasks. During training, the model predicts student engagement for the video and the intensity of Facial Action Units for each frame. The loss from this auxiliary task $loss_{aux}$ is simply the mean-squared error between the predicted and actual Action Unit intensities. Where p_{AU} and l_{AU} are the predicted and actual action unit intensities, respectively. Finally, the model is optimized using the total loss calculated as a sum of engagement loss and auxiliary loss, with a scaling parameter γ.

4   Experiments and Results

4.1   Ablation Study

We conduct our experiments on the DAiSEE dataset [9] which contains 10-second video snippets along with labels, and we report Accuracy and Top-2 accuracy averaged over 5 runs. In this subsection, we conduct ablation experiments to validate the performance of each of the proposed modules, i.e., Transformer module, MTL module, and Smooth loss, in MuOE.

Transformer: We attribute the increase in performance of the model after switching the LSTM block with a Transformer block to Transformers' superior sequence modeling capability.

Table 2. Ablation Study. Reported accuracies are averaged over 5 runs.

Model	MTL	C Loss	M-Loss	Accuracy	Top-2 Accuracy
LSTM	✗	✓	✗	43.2%	81%
LSTM	✗	✗	✓	47%	83.9%
LSTM	✓	✗	✓	52.4%	85.6%
Transformer	✓	✓	✗	49.8%	91.1%
Transformer	✗	✗	✓	54.2%	93.95%
Transformer	✓	✗	✓	57.65%	95.07%

Smooth Loss: The second part of the ablation study examines the effectiveness of smooth loss for tasks with ordinal classes. From Table 2 we can observe an increase in performance of both LSTM and Transformer based models after the introduction of smooth loss. Therefore the gain of smooth loss is not just limited to a particular model, and it has strong generalization capability.

MTL: Finally, we investigate the effectiveness of the MTL scheme. From 2 we observe a respectable increase in accuracy after the addition of the MTL component. This is due to better generalization caused by sharing of representations between related tasks, which in this case are classification of videos and prediction of action unit intensities. We can also observe that all the modules complement each other, resulting in an overall increase of an impressive 14.45% in accuracy from the baseline.

5 Conclusion

In this paper, we developed a novel approach for automated student engagement detection, which uses a transformer for superior sequence-processing, exploits the order amongst engagement levels with smooth loss, uses a related auxiliary task for robustness and a has a novel attention mechanism for selecting important parts of the video. Our experiments on the DAiSEE benchmark show a greater than 2% accuracy increase compared to existing state-of-the-art baselines. Our ablation studies confirm the effectiveness of each model component. We plan to extend our work to more datasets and understand the effects of hyperparameters better in the future.

References

1. Abedi, A., Khan, S.S.: Improving state-of-the-art in detecting student engagement with ResNet and TCN hybrid network. In: 2021 18th Conference on Robots and Vision (2021)
2. Baltrusaitis, T., Zadeh, A., Lim, Y.C., Morency, L.P.: Openface 2.0: facial behavior analysis toolkit. In: 2018 13th IEEE International Conference on Automatic Face & Gesture Recognition (FG 2018), pp. 59–66. IEEE (2018)
3. Cao, Q., Shen, L., Xie, W., Parkhi, O.M., Zisserman, A.: Vggface2: a dataset for recognising faces across pose and age. In: 2018 13th IEEE International Conference on Automatic Face & Gesture Recognition (FG 2018), pp. 67–74. IEEE (2018)
4. Collobert, R., Weston, J.: A unified architecture for natural language processing: deep neural networks with multitask learning. In: 25th ICML, pp. 160–167 (2008)
5. Dhall, A., Sharma, G., Goecke, R., Gedeon, T.: Emotiw 2020: driver gaze, group emotion, student engagement and physiological signal based challenges. In: Proceedings of the 2020 International Conference on Multimodal Interaction (2020)
6. Donahue, J., et al.: Long-term recurrent convolutional networks for visual recognition and description. In: IEEE CVPR (2015)
7. Ekman, P., Friesen, W.V.: Facial action coding system. Environ. Psychol. Nonverbal Behav. (1978)
8. Fu, H., Gong, M., Wang, C., Batmanghelich, K., Tao, D.: Deep ordinal regression network for monocular depth estimation. In: IEEE CVPR (2018)
9. Gupta, A., Jaiswal, R., Adhikari, S., Balasubramanian, V.: DAISEE: dataset for affective states in e-learning environments. CoRR abs/1609.01885 (2016)
10. He, K., Zhang, X., Ren, S., Sun, J.: Deep residual learning for image recognition. In: Proceedings of the IEEE Conference on Computer Vision and Pattern Recognition
11. Khedher, A.B., Jraidi, I., Frasson, C., et al.: Tracking students' mental engagement using EEG signals during an interaction with a virtual learning environment. J. Intell. Learn. Syst. Appl. 11(01), 1–14 (2019)
12. Liao, J., Liang, Y., Pan, J.: Deep facial spatiotemporal network for engagement prediction in online learning. Appl. Intell. 51(10), 6609–6621 (2021)
13. Mao, C., et al.: Multitask learning strengthens adversarial robustness. In: Vedaldi, A., Bischof, H., Brox, T., Frahm, J.-M. (eds.) ECCV 2020. LNCS, vol. 12347, pp. 158–174. Springer, Cham (2020). https://doi.org/10.1007/978-3-030-58536-5_10
14. Rothkrantz, L.: Dropout rates of regular courses and MOOCs. In: Costagliola, G., Uhomoibhi, J., Zvacek, S., McLaren, B.M. (eds.) CSEDU 2016. CCIS, vol. 739, pp. 25–46. Springer, Cham (2017). https://doi.org/10.1007/978-3-319-63184-4_3

15. Simonyan, K., Zisserman, A.: Very deep convolutional networks for large-scale image recognition. arXiv preprint arXiv:1409.1556 (2014)
16. Sun, B.Y., Li, J., Wu, D.D., Zhang, X.M., Li, W.B.: Kernel discriminant learning for ordinal regression. IEEE Trans. KDE **22**(6), 906–910 (2009)
17. Tran, D., Bourdev, L., Fergus, R., Torresani, L., Paluri, M.: Learning spatiotemporal features with 3d convolutional networks. In: IEEE ICCV (2015)
18. Vaswani, A., et al.: Attention is all you need. In: Advances in NIPS, vol. 30 (2017)
19. Wen, Y., Zhang, K., Li, Z., Qiao, Yu.: A discriminative feature learning approach for deep face recognition. In: Leibe, B., Matas, J., Sebe, N., Welling, M. (eds.) ECCV 2016. LNCS, vol. 9911, pp. 499–515. Springer, Cham (2016). https://doi.org/10.1007/978-3-319-46478-7_31
20. Whitehill, J., Serpell, Z., Lin, Y.C., Foster, A., Movellan, J.R.: The faces of engagement: automatic recognition of student engagement from facial expressions. IEEE Trans. Affect. Comput. **5**(1), 86–98 (2014)
21. Zhang, H., Xiao, X., Huang, T., Liu, S., Xia, Y., Li, J.: An novel end-to-end network for automatic student engagement recognition. In: 2019 IEEE 9th International Conference on Electronics Information and Emergency Communication (ICEIEC) (2019)

Handling Small Disjuncts and Class Skew Using Sequential Ellipsoidal Partitioning

Ranjani Niranjan$^{(\boxtimes)}$ and Sachit Rao

International Institute of Information Technology, Bangalore, Bengaluru, India
{ranjani.niranjan,sachit}@iiitb.ac.in

Abstract. Data irregularities, such as small disjuncts, class skew and imbalance, and outliers significantly affect the performance of classifiers. In this paper, we focus on identifying small disjuncts, which hitherto, has been addressed mainly by rule-based or inductive algorithms. Small disjuncts have been identified as distribution-based irregularities which provide significant learning, although they cover a subset of examples in the training set, which may be considered as being rare. Such samples are more error-prone than large disjuncts. Eliminating small disjuncts by removal or pruning is seen to affect the learning of the classifier adversely. Widely used non-rule-based learning algorithms like SVM, kNN, Logistic Regression, and Neural networks perform poorly in the presence of small disjuncts in the dataset. In this paper, a novel Sequential Ellipsoidal Partitioning method is proposed to identify small disjuncts in the dataset. This method is a supervised classifier that iteratively partitions the dataset into Minimum Volume Ellipsoids that contain points of the same label; this is performed based on the idea of Reduced Convex Hulls. By allowing an ellipsoid that contains points of one label to contain a few points of the other, such small disjuncts may be identified. As we discuss, the proposed technique is agnostic of underlying data distributions and is applicable as a supervised classifier when the datasets are highly skewed and imbalanced even. We demonstrate the performance of the approach using a few publicly available datasets.

Keywords: Small Disjuncts · Class Distribution Skew · Dataset Irregularities · Ellipsoidal Partitioning

1 Introduction

The performance of traditional supervised learning algorithms is dependent on the quality of the training dataset. Inherent irregularities such as class imbalance, skewness, small disjuncts, and outliers present in the training data influence the learning and reduce the accuracy of predictions. For example, class-distribution skew can increase the effect of class imbalance, especially around the overlapping region in the dataset. Preprocessing techniques such as Exploratory Data Analysis (EDA)(courtesy [13]) and Data Visualization are additionally used to identify such characteristics in the dataset. Although rule-based algorithms have been

© The Author(s), under exclusive license to Springer Nature Switzerland AG 2023
P. Maji et al. (Eds.): PReMI 2023, LNCS 14301, pp. 80–88, 2023.
https://doi.org/10.1007/978-3-031-45170-6_9

used to identify small disjuncts, non-concept-based or non-rule-based algorithms still face the challenge of giving correct predictions in presence of such small disjuncts. The proposed method, based on Sequential Ellipsoidal Partitioning, uses convex methods to identify one or more sub-concepts that are present in the training dataset. Once the small disjuncts are identified, new test samples that belong to the same feature space as these, can be classified with small error. As will be discussed, the proposed method is not dependent on the underlying data distribution and hence is immune to the presence of skewness in the training data.

In inductive systems, a rule consists of several disjuncts, where each disjunct is a conjunctive definition of a subconcept present in the dataset, [7]. While there is no formal definition which identifies a disjunct as being *small*, in the literature, samples of sizes 5, 10, or 15 are termed as *small disjuncts*. A review on data irregularities presented in [5] observes the assumptions that are made by traditional classification algorithms about the training dataset. Accordingly, each class in the dataset is assumed to comprise of one or more sub-concepts that are equally represented. This assumption is violated when a small number of rare cases are present in the dataset. These under-represented, rare samples give rise to the problem of *small-disjuncts* while learning. It is observed that non-rule based classification algorithms, for example, Support Vector Machines (SVM) and k-Nearest Neighbour (kNN) classifiers, fail to identify these small disjuncts. The errors in prediction due to small disjuncts become pronounced in presence of noisy data. The Decision-Tree classifier, which is rule-based, performs well on large disjuncts while Genetic Algorithm-based models score better in identifying the small disjuncts. The various research works discussed in [5] point out that pruning or reducing the importance of small disjuncts results in eliminating them, which is detrimental to the performance of the model when the rare cases represented by the small disjunct carry valuable learning for the classifier. Alternatively, assigning a new label to the small disjuncts, increases the number of classes in the dataset, converting the problem to multi-class classification. However, the literature does not indicate any practical application of this idea to solve the issues rising out of small disjuncts.

[14] explores the reasons for small disjuncts to be more error-prone and finds that the problem increases due to noise in attributes and class labels. Classifiers built using RIPPER and C4.5 algorithms have been analysed for the influence of disjunct size and training set size on errors in small disjuncts in [16]. This work on about 30 datasets, raises an objection to the definition given in [7] that a small disjunct is one that correctly classifies a few training examples. It emphasizes the need for a threshold for size that is also related to error rate, that can correctly define small disjuncts. Classifiers for balanced datasets are equally affected by their presence, [11]. Pruning is ineffective when skewness is observed in the dataset and oversampling to handle class imbalance can result in increase of small disjuncts. The problem of class imbalance, which is more common and well studied, has often been attributed to the failing performance of a classifier, but in [8], it is observed that cluster-based oversampling improves the accuracy

when the issues of class imbalance and small disjuncts are addressed together. Work on the effect of class imbalance, pruning, noise, and training set size in [15] highlights that identifying small disjuncts helps to improve the quality of classification to a large extent.

The proposed classifier, termed as the Sequential Ellipsoidal Partitioning Classifier (SEP-C), finds several hyperplanes, unlike a single separating hyperplane in traditional SVMs or its variants. Each hyperplane is found, similar to an SVM, so that points of different labels lie on either side of the hyperplane. SEP-C iteratively determines *non-overlapping* Minimum Volume Ellipsoids (MVEs), [3,9,12], using the Reduced Convex Hull (RCH) Algorithm, [1]. It should be remarked that each of these problems is a convex optimization problem, for which a global minimum exists and can be found if the problem is feasible. After each iteration, the covered samples from the dataset are removed and the process is repeated until all the data points in the training set are exhausted or the independence-dimension (I-D) inequality is violated, [4]. It is highlighted that in each iteration, the RCHs themselves are found iteratively and are not dependent on a single user-defined choice, as discussed in [1]. The removal of points in each iteration renders this approach as a sequential one. SEP-C emphasises the formation of non-overlapping MVEs, and if the dataset is heavily overlapped, then, the partitioning algorithm may terminate in the first iteration itself, thus making it similar to the conventional SVM. In such cases, SEP-C allows for a user-defined number of points of one label to be contained in the MVE of points of another label; this number, denoted by n_{Imp}, is the only hyper parameter used in SEP-C. With the introduction of such "impurities", the dataset can be partitioned finely.

In SEP-C, the presence of such impurities are interpreted as being small disjuncts, as these form a subset of points belonging to a label that have properties that are different than the majority of points of that label, hence, rare and under-represented. In clean datasets or even those with minimal overlap, that is, those can be defined by (nearly) disjoint ellipsoids, choosing a higher value of n_{Imp} does not affect the partitioning of the dataset. Thus, by choosing $n_{\text{Imp}} \geq 10$, it is possible to find small disjuncts of sizes $\leq n_{\text{Imp}}$; we show that such small disjuncts exist in some of the publicly available datasets. Unlike rule-based methods, where, a small training set is used to train the classifier to find small disjuncts in the much larger testing set, in SEP-C, the entire dataset is used to identify them. Once SEP-C terminates, the ellipsoidal partitions obtained represent the *landscape* of the training dataset, where some of the ellipsoids that may contain most of the points of one label also contain upto n_{Imp} points of the other label.

The main contributions of the paper are as follows:

1. Use of convex methods to partition a dataset into multiple ellipsoids that contain mostly points of the same label;
2. Identify under-represented points of one label that are "different" than most points of that same label - the small disjunct problem; and

3. Develop a method of classification that is immune to dataset irregularities such as skewness and imbalance.

The paper is organised as follows: In Sect. 2, SEP-C is introduced. In Sect. 3, the properties of SEP-C being independent of skew and its ability to identify small disjuncts is discussed. In Sect. 4, results of implementing SEP-C on a few datasets are presented, followed by Concluding Remarks in Sect. 5.

2   Sequential Ellipsoidal Partitioning Classifier

Consider the dataset in Fig. 1a, with points denoted by the sets $\mathcal{X} = \{x_i\}$, $x_i \in \Re^2$, $i = 1, \cdots, N$ and $\mathcal{Y} = \{y_j\}$, $y_j \in \Re^2$, $j = 1, \cdots, M$, where $N \geq M > 2$. The points in set $\mathcal{X}$ have label L_{+1} and those in $\mathcal{Y}$ have label L_{-1}. The MVEs, denoted by $\mathcal{E}_X$ and $\mathcal{E}_Y$, respectively, can be found such that each ellipsoid contains points of the respective set either in its interior or its boundary. By expressing an ellipsoid in the form $\mathcal{E} = \{z \mid \|\mathbf{A}z + \mathbf{b}\| \leq 1\}$, $z \in \Re^2$, for example, for set $\mathcal{X}$, $\mathcal{E}_X$ is found by solving the convex optimisation problem (CP)

$$
\begin{aligned}
&\min && \log \det \left(\mathbf{A}^{-1}\right) && (1)\\
&\text{subject to} && \|\mathbf{A}x_i + \mathbf{b}\| \leq 1, \ i = 1, \cdots, N,
\end{aligned}
$$

with the symmetric positive definite (SPD) matrix $\mathbf{A}$ and the vector $\mathbf{b}$ as the variables, [3]. It is highlighted that for the CP (1) to be feasible, the independence-dimension (I-D) inequality has to be satisfied, that is, $N > 2$, [4].

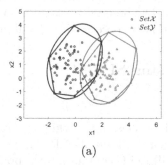 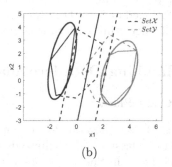

(a)   (b)

Fig. 1. 1a: Intersecting CHs, and MVEs, of the two sets; 1b: RCHs, and MVEs, that are non-intersecting (solid lines)

As can be seen in Fig. 1a, the ellipsoids $\mathcal{E}_X$ and $\mathcal{E}_Y$ intersect each other. SEP-C now partitions the dataset such that the MVEs for each dataset become non-intersecting by applying the RCH algorithm, [1]. First, the matrices $\mathbf{X} \in \Re^{N \times 2}$ and $\mathbf{Y} \in \Re^{M \times 2}$ that contain the datapoints x_i and y_j, respectively, are defined. Next, the RCHs of the sets $\mathcal{X}$ and $\mathcal{Y}$ are found. These are the set of all convex combinations $\mathbf{c} = \mathbf{X}^T \mathbf{u}$ and $\mathbf{d} = \mathbf{Y}^T \mathbf{v}$, respectively, where $\mathbf{u} = [u_i] \in \Re^2$, $\mathbf{v} =$

$[v_i] \in \Re^2$; $\sum u_i = 1$, $0 \leq u_i \leq D$, $\sum v_i = 1$, $0 \leq v_i \leq D$; and the scalar $D < 1$, which is a design parameter. The RCH algorithm finds the closest points in each RC-Hull by solving the CP

$$\min_{\mathbf{u},\mathbf{v}} \quad \frac{1}{2} \left\| \mathbf{X}^T\mathbf{u} - \mathbf{Y}^T\mathbf{v} \right\|^2 \tag{2}$$

$$\text{subject to} \quad \mathbf{e}^T\mathbf{u} = 1, \ \mathbf{e}^T\mathbf{v} = 1, \ 0 \leq \mathbf{u}, \mathbf{v} \leq D\mathbf{e}.$$

The vector $\mathbf{e}^T = [1 \ 1 \ \cdots]$. Now, if the solution to this CP exists for some $D < 1$, the RC-Hulls do not intersect and thus, the line normal to the line connecting the closest points is the separating hyperplane. Solving the CP (2) results in the non-intersecting RCHs for the two sets, as shown in Fig. 1b.

In SEP-C, the RCH algorithm is implemented differently. Beginning with $K = \min(N, M)$ and $D = (1/K)$, the CP (2) is solved iteratively, where K is reduced in each iteration until such time that the RCHs of both sets do not intersect or the RCH of points of one label contain at most n_{Imp} points of the other. To determine that the RCHs indeed do not intersect, the check on the intersection is performed on the MVEs that cover them. The RCHs intersect if their respective MVEs intersect. This approach is selected to minimize computational cost, especially for high-dimensional datasets. The MVEs shown in Fig. 1b are the first partitions of the dataset. Having found these partitions, the points contained in them are removed from the dataset and SEP-C continues to find similar partitions on the remainder of the training data. If the dataset is linearly separable, then SEP-C terminates in the first iteration itself. For datasets with significant overlap, additional iterations are performed. SEP-C is guaranteed to terminate in a finite number of iterations, as either there are no more points to be partitioned or the I-D inequality is violated. The pseudo-codes of SEP-C and the RCH algorithm with time complexity analysis are described in detail in [10].

3   Handling Data Irregularities Using SEP-C

3.1   Class Skew

We first discuss how SEP-C is not influenced by class skew while acting as a supervised classifier. The ellipsoids found in each iteration of SEP-C are a basis for classification. Since, by construction, the ellipsoids contain mostly points of the same label, if an unseen test point is now contained within one of them, it is assigned the label of the majority of the points in that ellipsoid; see [10] for issues on calculating the trust score for such classification rules. In any iteration of SEP-C, the CP (2) is solved to find the points $\mathbf{c}$ and $\mathbf{d}$. It can be observed that $\mathbf{c}$, or $\mathbf{d}$, is a convex combination of points in $\mathbf{X}$ *alone*, or $\mathbf{Y}$ *alone*, and not on any joint characteristics of the sets $\mathcal{X}$ and $\mathcal{Y}$. Further, if the solution to the CP (2) exists, then $\mathbf{c}, \mathbf{d}$, and the separating hyperplane, which is normal to the line joining these points, are also unique. The points $\mathbf{c}$ and $\mathbf{d}$ may lie in the region of intersection of the respective CHs, thus leading to points of both labels on either side of the obtained hyperplane. If the number of such points, which are in essence misclassifications, is less than the permitted number n_{Imp}, then SEP-C terminates in that iteration.

Since, for a "good" classifier, n_{Imp} should be low, SEP-C reduces the ellipsoids found in an iteration, using the RCH algorithm, but by iteratively changing the value of D. In this case, a reduced ellipsoid of one label is still independent of the ellipsoid found for the other label. This can be demonstrated by viewing the RCH algorithm akin to the classic Ellipsoid Algorithm discussed in [2], where a smaller ellipsoid in a later iteration is found after performing a cut on the ellipsoid found in the earlier iteration. In our case, the cut is exactly the hyperplane found in that iteration. According to the Ellipsoid Algorithm, the center, x_k, and the properties of an ellipsoid, given by an SPD matrix $\mathbf{B}_k$, found in iteration k, expressed as $\mathcal{E}_k = \{x \in \Re^n \mid (x - x_k)^T \mathbf{B}_k^{-1} (x - x_k) \leq 1\}$, which is then cut by a line $a^T x = b$, leads to a smaller ellipsoid in iteration $(k+1)$ that are functions of a^T and x_k and B_k *alone*. In our case, let in iteration k, the ellipsoid $\mathcal{E}_k^+$, that contains a majority of points with label L_{+1}, also contain $n_k > n_{\text{Imp}}$ number of points with label L_{-1}. Now, in the next iteration, the smaller ellipsoid, $\mathcal{E}_{k+1}^+$, is such that it contains $n_{k+1} \leq n_{\text{Imp}}$ points with label L_{-1}; indeed, $\mathcal{E}_{k+1}^+$ may also now have fewer points of label L_{+1}. The key observation is that finding $\mathcal{E}_{k+1}^+$ is not dependent on the properties of the corresponding ellipsoid, $\mathcal{E}_k^-$, found for the other label. The partitions found by SEP-C for a synthetic dataset with points obtained from skewed distributions are shown in Fig. 2 using $n_{\text{Imp}} = 2$. As can be seen, no ellipsoid contains more than 2 points of the other label and if a test point lies in one of these ellipsoids, it is assigned the label of majority of points in that label. The cases when the test point lies in the intersection of ellipsoids or outside all the ellipsoids are discussed in [10]. It is to be noted here that, if n_{Imp} is chosen to be too small, it may result in overfitting. By judiciously choosing this value, overfitting can be avoided.

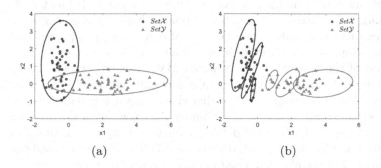

(a)   (b)

Fig. 2. Partitioning a Skewed 2-D Dataset

3.2   Identifying Small Disjuncts

The use of the SEP-C method to detect small disjuncts or rare cases is now discussed. As finding such rare cases is an exploratory exercise, the entire dataset is used for partitioning. Ideally, SEP-C should isolate these rare cases in their own ellipsoids. Consider the 2-D synthetic dataset shown in Fig. 3a, where a few points (ten) in set $\mathcal{Y}$ have characteristics that are different from the majority of points belonging to that set; it is evident that a single hyperplane will not be able to isolate this small cluster, thus leading to errors in classification. Indeed, kernels, such as radial basis functions may be used, but these require considerable tuning of the hyperparameters. As can be seen in Fig. 3b, SEP-C is able to isolate these points in their own ellipsoid. For this case, 2 iterations, with $n_{\text{Imp}} = 5$, are sufficient leading to 2 ellipsoids for each label.

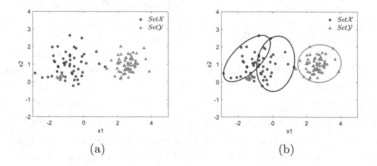

(a)   (b)

Fig. 3. Partitioning 2-D dataset with a small disjunct

It can happen that these rare cases are in proximity of points of another label or if the number of such rare cases is lesser than the dimension of the dataset; in the latter case, an MVE cannot be found exclusively as the I-D inequality fails. In both cases, choosing an appropriate value for n_{Imp} aids in identifying these rare, but non-trivial number of points. Suppose a small disjunct is defined as comprising of $5 < n_{\text{SD}} < 15$ number of points. Now, by choosing $n_{\text{Imp}} \geq n_{\text{SD}}$, SEP-C can find ellipsoids of one label to also contain n_{Imp} points, or fewer, of the other. Suppose an ellipsoid does contain $n_{\text{SD}} \geq n$ points, where n is the dimension of the feature space. Now, an MVE can be wrapped around these n_{SD} points and checked if it is contained completely in the larger ellipsoidal partition. If so, these points of the other class suggest a sub-concept, which can be a potential small disjunct. The number n_{SD} now gives the *coverage* of the disjunct. In higher dimensional datasets, where $n > n_{\text{SD}} > 15$, though an MVE cannot be found for the disjunct, density-based measures can be used to establish if the n_{SD} points qualify as a *small disjunct* or are just noise.

4   Results

SEP-C algorithm is implemented on the Vote, Pima Indian Diabetes (PID), and Chess Endgame datasets, [6]. The 3 partitions obtained for the Vote dataset, with $n_{\text{Imp}} = 17$, did *not* contain any small disjuncts in any of the partitions. On the other hand, SEP-C partitioned the PID dataset into 8 ellipsoids for both labels (no diabetes and diabetes), with $n_{\mathrm{Imp}}=10$, and 6 of these ellipsoids contained possible small disjuncts of sizes 9 and 8 respectively; the MVEs of these small disjuncts did not intersect with other ellipsoids of the same label, thus indicating that they are sub-concepts of points with that label. The ellipsoidal partitions obtained for $n_{\mathrm{Imp}} = 5, 10$ are listed in Table 1. The number in the brackets indicate the number of points of the other class in each ellipsoid. The Chess Endgame dataset, with 36 features and $n_{\mathrm{Imp}} = 37$, was partitioned into 5 ellipsoids each for both labels. 3 ellipsoids have potential small disjuncts of sizes 5, 11, and 5.

Table 1. Ellipsoidal Partitions of the PID dataset, and their coverage, for different values of n_{Imp}

	# of Ellipsoids	1	2	3	4	5	6	7	8	9	10	11	12	13
$n_{\mathrm{Imp}} = 5$	Class 0	58 (2)	73 (3)	64 (4)	27 (3)	44 (2)	25 (3)	15 (3)	23 (3)	35 (4)	24 (4)	21 (4)	27 (4)	22 (3)
	Class 1	58 (2)	73 (3)	64 (4)	27 (3)	44 (2)	25 (3)	15 (3)	23 (3)	35 (4)	24 (4)	21 (4)	27 (4)	22 (3)
$n_{\mathrm{Imp}} = 10$	Class 0	**64 (9)**	**150 (9)**	36 (5)	32 (6)	34 (6)	**26 (9)**	35 (7)	**52 (9)**					
	Class 1	57 (4)	37 (5)	35 (7)	14 (6)	18 (7)	**40 (8)**	22 (5)	**19 (8)**					

5 Conclusion

This paper presents the application of the novel SEP-C algorithm for identification of small disjuncts in a dataset, which, hitherto was achieved using rule-based or inductive approaches for the classifier. This approach does not require additional pre-processing techniques when underlying data distribution is unknown, skewed, shifted or imbalanced. In all the cases, the proposed method uses a single user-defined hyperparameter, which controls the number of misclassifications in the ellipsoidal partitions. SEP-C can fail to capture small disjuncts when the number of samples is less than the dimensionality of the dataset since ID-inequality constraint restricts the formation of an MVE. Applying density-based measures in such cases for determination of small disjuncts could be a direction in which future study can be conducted.

Acknowledgements. Ranjani Niranjan would like to thank Prateeksha Foundation for providing financial support for her doctoral program at IIIT-Bangalore.

References

1. Bennett, K.P., Bredensteiner, E.J.: Duality and geometry in SVM classifiers. In: Proceedings of the Seventeenth International Conference on Machine Learning, pp. 57–64. ICML 2000, Morgan Kaufmann Publishers Inc., San Francisco, CA, USA (2000)

2. Bland, R.G., Goldfarb, D., Todd, M.J.: The ellipsoid method: a survey. Oper. Res. **29**(6), 1039–1091 (1981). http://www.jstor.org/stable/170362
3. Boyd, S., Vandenberghe, L.: Convex optimization. Cambridge University Press, Cambridge (2004)
4. Boyd, S., Vandenberghe, L.: Introduction to Applied Linear Algebra: Vectors, Matrices, and Least Squares. Cambridge University Press, Cambridge (2018)
5. Das, S., Datta, S., Chaudhuri, B.B.: Handling data irregularities in classification: foundations, trends, and future challenges. Pattern Recogn. **81**, 674–693 (2018). https://doi.org/10.1016/j.patcog.2018.03.008
6. Dua, D., Graff, C.: UCI machine learning repository (2017). http://archive.ics.uci.edu/ml
7. Holte, R.C., Acker, L.E., Porter, B.W.: Concept learning and the problem of small disjuncts. In: Proceedings of the 11th International Joint Conference on Artificial Intelligence, vol. 1, pp. 813–818. IJCAI 1989, Morgan Kaufmann Publishers Inc., San Francisco, CA, USA (1989)
8. Jo, T., Japkowicz, N.: Class imbalances versus small disjuncts. ACM SIGKDD Explor. Newsletter **6**(1), 40–49 (2004). https://doi.org/10.1145/1007730.1007737
9. Kong, Q., Zhu, Q.: Incremental procedures for partitioning highly intermixed multi-class datasets into hyper-spherical and hyper-ellipsoidal clusters. Data Knowl. Eng. **63**(2), 457–477 (2007). https://doi.org/10.1016/j.datak.2007.03.006
10. Niranjan, R., Rao, S.: Classification with trust: a supervised approach based on sequential ellipsoidal partitioning (2023). http://arxiv.org/abs/2302.10487
11. Prati, R.C., Batista, G.E.A.P.A., Monard, M.C.: Learning with class skews and small disjuncts. In: Bazzan, A.L.C., Labidi, S. (eds.) SBIA 2004. LNCS (LNAI), vol. 3171, pp. 296–306. Springer, Heidelberg (2004). https://doi.org/10.1007/978-3-540-28645-5_30
12. Sun, P., Freund, R.M.: Computation of minimum-volume covering ellipsoids. Oper. Res. **52**(5), 690–706 (2004). https://doi.org/10.1287/opre.1040.0115
13. Tukey, J.W.: Exploratory Data Analysis. Addison-Wesley, Boston (1977)
14. Weiss, G.M.: Learning with rare cases and small disjuncts. In: Prieditis, A., Russell, S. (eds.) Machine Learning Proceedings 1995, pp. 558–565. Morgan Kaufmann, San Francisco (CA) (1995). https://doi.org/10.1016/B978-1-55860-377-6.50075-X
15. Weiss, G.M.: The impact of small disjuncts on classifier learning. In: Stahlbock, R., Crone, S., Lessmann, S. (eds.) Data Mining. Annals of Information Systems, vol. 8, pp. 193–226. Springer, Boston (2010). https://doi.org/10.1007/978-1-4419-1280-0_9
16. Weiss, G.M., Hirsh, H.: A quantitative study of small disjuncts. AAAI/IAAI **2000**(665–670), 15 (2000)

Error-Bounded Bimodal Isotropic Remeshing Using Curvature Map and Voronoi Tessellation

Preetam Chayan Chatterjee[ID] and Partha Bhowmick[✉][ID]

Department of Computer Science and Engineering, Indian Institute of Technology Kharagpur, Kharagpur, India
pb@cse.iitkgp.ac.in

Abstract. We introduce here a maiden problem of *bimodal isotropic remeshing* and present a GPU-based algorithm for the same. It takes as input a triangulated mesh (orientable 2-manifold closed surface) and produces an output mesh, subject to the following constraints: (i) the Hausdorff error between the input surface and the output surface is within a user-specified value; (ii) the constituent triangles of the output mesh are bimodal and isotropic, i.e., the triangles are almost equilateral in shape and have predominantly two well-separated sizes—the bigger triangles to fit low-curvature regions and the smaller ones to fit high-curvature regions. In order to parallelize the entire process, we use voxel processing. Our algorithm incorporates a novel concept of *bimodal curvature map* based on Poisson characteristics of discrete curvature. From this map, the sizes of the triangles are automatically determined and then a *curvature-adaptive centroidal Voronoi tessellation*, followed by Delaunay triangulation, is done to obtain the desired output. Experimental results on different models are found to be encouraging, and future extensions of the proposed concept are discussed at the end.

Keywords: Remeshing · Isotropic Mesh · Centroidal Voronoi tessellation · Discrete Curvature · GPU-based Algorithms · Surface Voxelization

1 Introduction

Today's high-performance graphical tools and devices are mostly designed with parallel computation in mind. The potential of parallel computation remains, however, underutilized if the mesh contains disproportionate or anisotropic triangles. Hence, a restructuring of the mesh—referred to as 'remeshing' in the literature—is often sought, so that the resulting mesh is almost isotropic; that is, it predominantly contains equilateral triangles with a limited variation in size. The main challenge with this kind of remeshing lies in satisfying the constraints like feature preservation in the new mesh and error minimization between the new mesh and the original.

© The Author(s), under exclusive license to Springer Nature Switzerland AG 2023
P. Maji et al. (Eds.): PReMI 2023, LNCS 14301, pp. 89–97, 2023.
https://doi.org/10.1007/978-3-031-45170-6_10

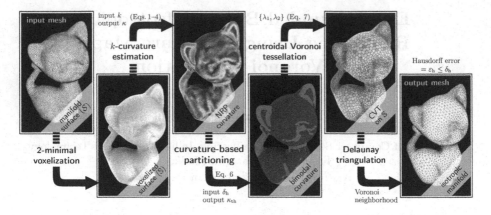

Fig. 1. The pipeline of our proposed algorithm (model: `Kitten`).

Many of the existing techniques for remeshing are based on Voronoi Tessellation (VT) and Centroidal Voronoi Tessellation (CVT). For isotropic remeshing, CVT is preferred. However, since CVT by itself is unable to satisfy all the necessary constraints, additional input are taken alongside, such as the number of seeds for tessellation [7], the density of seeds [2], and surface curvature [10]. Tuned to all these input parameters, a definite strategy is fixed for tessellation; some notable ones are based on L_p-metric [6], hyperbolic parameterization [9], and penalty functions [3,13]; some more can be seen in [5,8,11,12,14].

Our work encompasses a maiden concept of *bimodal isotropic triangulation*, where the triangles will be predominantly bimodal by size and equilateral by shape. This is aimed to restructure the high-curvature regions by small triangles and the low-curvature regions by large triangles, without violating the constraint of Hausdorff error supplied as input. Since the small triangles are almost equal in size, and so also the large ones, this will minimize the idling of cores while any such bimodal isotropic mesh is fed to a parallel-computing graphics system in a well-ordered manner. The entire concept is realized by incorporating several novel steps, which include estimation of bimodal curvature from the Poisson distribution of the surface curvature, fixing the sizes of small and large triangles based on the error bound, and judicious use of CVT to ensure mesh isotropy. The pipeline of the proposed algorithm is shown in Fig. 1. It may be noted that although there exist several techniques for isotropic remeshing, the concept of bimodal isotropy is not found in the literature.

2   Discrete Curvature Estimation

In order to make the pipeline work in a parallel computing platform, we first voxelize the input mesh S with a sufficiently high resolution. The resultant output is a set of voxels, $\mathbb{S}$, which is the union of the 2-minimal sets of voxels for all the triangles comprising S. As every 2-minimal voxelized triangle is topologically thinnest, the set $\mathbb{S}$ consists of a minimal set of voxels. In particular, if $\mathcal{S}$ is a closed orientable 2-manifold surface, then the interior and the exterior of $\mathbb{S}$ are 2-separable, i.e., any 2-path from any interior voxel to any exterior voxel of $\mathbb{S}$ must contain a voxel in $\mathbb{S}$. On the contrary, for any voxel $v \in \mathbb{S}$, the interior and the exterior of $\mathbb{S} \setminus \{v\}$ will not remain 2-separable. For further definitions and concepts related to connectedness, separability, minimality, and paths, we refer to [1].

For every voxel $v_i \in \mathbb{S}$, we consider a set $\mathcal{P}$ of nine real planes represented by the set of equations

$$\{ax + by + cz + d = 0 : a, b, c \in \{-1, 0, 1\}, |a| + |b| + |c| \in \{1, 2\}\},$$

with v_i at $(0, 0, 0)$ in the local coordinate system. For each $\Pi \in \mathcal{P}$, we consider a 0-path $\mathcal{C}_\Pi(v_i, k, \mathbb{S})$ in $\mathbb{S}$ consisting of $2k + 1$ voxels, such that their centers lie on Π and v_i is the middlemost voxel in this path. For brevity in notation, we denote the sequence of voxels in $\mathcal{C}_\Pi(v_i, k, \mathbb{S})$ as $\{v_j : j = i - k, i - k + 1, \ldots, i - 1, i, i + 1, \ldots, i + k - 1, i + k\}$. Notice that $\mathcal{C}_\Pi(v_i, k, \mathbb{S})$ is essentially a planar 0-minimal digital curve. Since curvature is the reciprocal of the radius of an osculating circle, we estimate the curvature at v_i using its chain-code sequence, as follows.

$$\kappa_\Pi(v_i, k, \mathbb{S}) = \frac{\theta_\Pi(v_i, k, \mathbb{S})}{s_\Pi(v_i, k, \mathbb{S})}, \tag{1}$$

where,

$$\theta_\Pi(v_i, k, \mathbb{S}) = \frac{1}{k-1} \sum_{j=1}^{k-1} \min \left\{ \min_{1 \leq \ell \leq 4} \left\{ m_{i,j}^{(\ell)}, 8 - m_{i,j}^{(\ell)} \right\} \right\} \tag{2}$$

$$\text{and } s_\Pi(v_i, k, \mathbb{S}) = \sum_{j=i-k}^{j=i+k-1} d_e(v_j, v_{j+1}). \tag{3}$$

Here, the chain code from v_{i-1} to v_i is denoted by m_i, the chain-code differences are denoted by $m_{i,j}^{(1)} = |m_{i+j} - m_{i-j+1}|$, $m_{i,j}^{(2)} = |m_{i+j+1} - m_{i-j+1}|$, $m_{i,j}^{(3)} = |m_{i+j} - m_{i-j}|$, $m_{i,j}^{(4)} = |m_{i+j+1} - m_{i-j}|$, and $d_e(v_j, v_{j+1})$ denotes the Eucledian distance between v_j and v_{j+1}. The rationale of Eq. 2 is that chain codes are integers in $[0, 7]$; hence, for a pair of voxels $(v', v'') \in \mathcal{C}_\Pi(v_i, k, \mathbb{S})$ lying on two opposite sides of v_i and with the same 0-path-distance from v_i, the difference (in modulo 8) between the chain codes of v' and v'' provides an estimate of the curvature at v_i. As the difference in the discrete space is likely to be erratic for a single pair, we consider k pairs. From the curvatures corresponding to nine real planes (NRP), we compute

$$\kappa_{\max}(v_i, k, \mathbb{S}) = \max_{\Pi \in \mathcal{P}} \{\kappa_\Pi(v_i, k, \mathbb{S})\}, \quad \kappa_{\min}(v_i, k, \mathbb{S}) = \min_{\Pi \in \mathcal{P}} \{\kappa_\Pi(v_i, k, \mathbb{S})\},$$

and estimate the final *NRP curvature* at v_i as

$$\kappa(v_i, k, \mathbb{S}) = \frac{1}{2} \big(\kappa_{\max}(v_i, k, \mathbb{S}) + \kappa_{\min}(v_i, k, \mathbb{S})\big). \tag{4}$$

(a) $k = 10$ (b) $k = 10$ (c) $k = 15$ (d) $k = 15$

Fig. 2. An illustration of curvature estimation and bimodal map on **Bunny** for different k values. Red to blue color in the spectrum denotes high- to low-curvature regions in (a) and (c). In (b) and (d), red and blue signify high and low curvatures respectively. (Color figure online)

Examples of estimated curvature are shown in Fig. 2(a, c). By simple calculations, we can see that $\theta_{II}(v_i, k, \mathbb{S}) \in [0, 4]$ and $s_{II}(v_i, k, \mathbb{S}) \in [2k, 2\sqrt{3}k]$, which implies

$$0 \leq \kappa(v_i, k, \mathbb{S}) \leq \tfrac{2}{k}. \tag{5}$$

3   Bimodal Curvature and Edge-Length Computation

To perform a curvature-guided CVT, we analyze the normalized curvature histogram and partition $\mathbb{S}$ into regions of high and low curvature, which we refer to as *bimodal curvature map* (Fig. 3). We adopt the technique proposed in [4]. Let K be the set of curvature values arranged in increasing order, and $\gamma(\kappa)$ be the normalized frequency for $\kappa \in K$. Let (K_1, K_2) be an *ordered partition* of K, i.e., $\kappa' < \kappa'' \ \forall \ (\kappa', \kappa'') \in K_1 \times K_2$. We fix the threshold curvature κ_{th} as the largest element in K_1^*, where

$$(K_1^*, K_2^*) = \underset{(K_1, K_2)}{\arg \min} \left\{ \sum_{j=1}^{2} \sum_{\kappa \in K_j} \kappa \cdot \gamma(\kappa) \left(1 - \ln \left(\frac{\sum\limits_{\kappa \in K_j} \kappa \cdot \gamma(\kappa)}{\sum\limits_{\kappa \in K_j} \gamma(\kappa)} \right) \right) \right\}. \tag{6}$$

A curvature is considered as 'high' if it is greater than κ_{th}, and 'low' otherwise (Fig. 2(b, d)).

Next, we find a feasible pair of edge-lengths, namely λ_1 and λ_2, that are used to compute the bimodal set of triangles comprising the output mesh. The triangles used to fit low-curvature regions will have edge-length λ_1, whereas those to fit high-curvature regions will have edge-length λ_2. Clearly, $\lambda_1 > \lambda_2$. We compute λ_1 and λ_2 as follows. Consider a real sphere S having a radius r_s, and a plane P passing through it. Let the circle formed from this intersection be C, with r_c as the radius. Let $\delta_{\text{h}} \leq r_s$ be the length of a/the smaller perpendicular

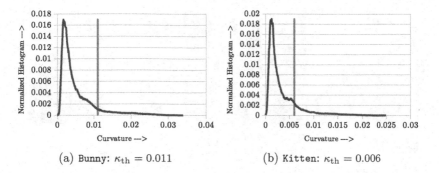

(a) Bunny: $\kappa_{\text{th}} = 0.011$ (b) Kitten: $\kappa_{\text{th}} = 0.006$

Fig. 3. The normalized curvature histograms for Bunny and Kitten, both voxelized to 1M voxels. The orange vertical line depicts the threshold κ_{th} of bimodal curvature.

drawn from the center of C to S. Then, the equilateral triangle inscribed in C has an edge length

$$\lambda = \sqrt{3} \cdot r_C = \sqrt{3} \cdot \sqrt{(r_S^2 - (r_S - \delta_{\text{h}})^2)} = \sqrt{3\delta_{\text{h}}(2r_S - \delta_{\text{h}})}. \tag{7}$$

In our case, the value of δ_{h} in Eq. 7 is the user-specified upper bound on the Hausdorff error, and S serves as an osculating sphere, i.e., $\kappa = \frac{1}{r_S}$. Thus, with $\kappa_1 = \kappa_{\text{th}}$ and $\kappa_2 = \max\{\kappa \in K\}$, we have

$$\lambda_j = \sqrt{3\delta_{\text{h}} \left(\frac{2}{\kappa_j} - \delta_{\text{h}} \right)} \text{ for } j = 1, 2. \tag{8}$$

4 Centroidal Voronoi Tessellation

Before discussing the steps of CVT, we introduce some terminologies related to our algorithm. For a set of seeds $\mathcal{X} \subset \mathbb{S}$, and for a seed $x \in \mathcal{X}$, the *Voronoi region* $\mathcal{R}_x$ is defined as $\mathcal{R}_x = \{v \in \mathbb{S} : \|v - x\| \leq \|v - y\|, \ \forall y \in \mathcal{X}\}$. For two seeds x and y, if $\mathcal{R}_x$ and $\mathcal{R}_y$ are adjacent, then x and y are called *Delaunay neighbors* of each other. We denote by $\mathcal{N}_x$ the set of Delaunay neighbors of x. The Voronoi tessellation of $\mathbb{S}$ is given by

$$\mathcal{T}(\mathbb{S}, \mathcal{X}) = \bigcup_{x \in \mathcal{X}} \mathcal{R}_x. \tag{9}$$

The *CVT energy* corresponding to $\mathcal{R}_x$ is given by

$$E_{\text{CVT}}(\mathcal{R}_x, x) = \sum_{v \in \mathcal{R}_x} \kappa_j \|v - x\|^2, \ j \in \{1, 2\}. \tag{10}$$

The total CVT energy is, therefore, given by

$$E_{\text{CVT}}(\mathbb{S}, \mathcal{X}) = \sum_{x \in \mathcal{X}} E_{\text{CVT}}(\mathcal{R}_x, x). \tag{11}$$

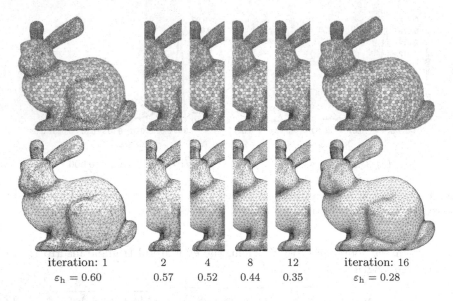

iteration: 1	2	4	8	12	iteration: 16
$\varepsilon_h = 0.60$	0.57	0.52	0.44	0.35	$\varepsilon_h = 0.28$

Fig. 4. Iterative progress of the proposed CVT technique on **Bunny**. $\lambda_1 = 13, \lambda_2 = 3$; top row: Voronoi tessellation; bottom row: Delaunay triangulation; ε_h: Hausdorff error.

Based on the values of λ_1 and λ_2 (Eq. 8), we construct an initial set of seeds, $\mathcal{X} \in \mathbb{S}$, and compute the VT on $\mathbb{S}$ using parallel BFS in GPU. After that, we update the Voronoi region of a voxel v from the current region $\mathcal{R}_x$ to a new region $\mathcal{R}_y$ if and only if $y \in \mathcal{N}_x \cup \{x\}$ and $\|v - y\| < \|v - y'\| \ \forall \ y' \in (\mathcal{N}_x \cup \{x\}) \smallsetminus \{y\}$. Next, we update the seed position by computing E_{CVT} for the 0-adjacent neighbors of all the seeds in the current iteration. We consider the voxels with the least energy as seeds in the next iteration. We then reconstruct VT on some updated seed x, which ensures that its distance from the weighted centroid of $\mathcal{R}_x$ reduces gradually, thus achieving isotropy. We terminate after a certain number of iterations or when the relative energy difference between two successive iterations is less than a predefined threshold. Finally, we perform Delaunay triangulation (DT) to get the resultant mesh. Some iterations of the proposed CVT technique are presented in Fig. 4.

5   Results and Discussions

The algorithm is completely implemented in C++, accessing the CUDA library (Ver. 11.4). We have used the NVIDIA GeForce GTX 1650 Ti GPU of the Acer Nitro 5 gaming laptop. The GPU has 1024 CUDA cores, 1290 clock rate, 4 GB GDDR5 GPU memory, and 1024 threads/block.

In Table 1, we have furnished a summary of statistics of our experimental results. The parameters n_v and n_f denote the respective numbers of vertices and faces in the input mesh; $|\mathbb{S}|$ denotes the number of voxels in $\mathbb{S}$; k is the input

Table 1. Statistics of characteristic parameters for four different models.

Model	n_v, n_f	$|\mathbb{S}|$	k	κ_1	κ_2	δ_h	$\{\lambda_1, \lambda_2\}$	ε_h	$\bar{\theta}_{min}$	GPU time (sec.)
Armadillo	7K, 14K	1M	15	0.009	0.122	0.3	$\{14, 3\}$	0.25	55.42	5.37
						0.5	$\{18, 4\}$	0.40	45.78	2.01
			30	0.004	0.066	0.3	$\{21, 5\}$	0.31	52.48	5.49
						0.5	$\{27, 6\}$	0.53	40.07	2.03
		2M	30	0.003	0.056	0.3	$\{24, 5\}$	0.28	56.33	12.72
						0.5	$\{31, 7\}$	0.45	49.28	5.99
Bunny	8K, 16K	1M	15	0.011	0.121	0.3	$\{13, 3\}$	0.28	51.01	4.26
Kitten	10K, 20K	1M	15	0.006	0.071	0.3	$\{18, 5\}$	0.30	47.98	3.76
Davidhead	25K, 50K	1M	15	0.004	0.111	0.3	$\{22, 4\}$	0.29	45.48	2.98

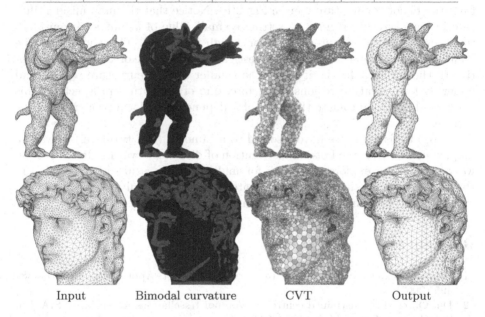

Input   Bimodal curvature   CVT   Output

Fig. 5. Results by our algorithm on `Armadillo` (top) and `Davidhead` (bottom).

parameter for curvature estimation; ε_h is the Hausdorff error of the output mesh w.r.t. the input mesh; $\bar{\theta}_{min}$ denotes the average of the minimum angles obtained, measuring the isotropy of the output mesh.

We have presented here some visual results on the models `Kitten` (Fig. 1), `Bunny` (Figs. 2 and 4), `Armadillo` (Fig. 5(top)), and `Davidhead` (Fig. 5(bottom)). On `Armadillo`, we have provided a little more detailed results to understand the effect of k on $\lambda_i (i = 1, 2)$ and ε_h. As noticed, for a higher value of k, the values of λ_i are larger, and hence ε_h is higher. This justifies our theoretical formulations: by Eq. 1, κ varies inversely with k, and by Eq. 8, it varies directly with λ_i. It can also be noticed that λ_i varies directly with $\bar{\theta}_{min}$. For example, on `Armadillo`, when $\{\lambda_1, \lambda_2\} = \{14, 3\}$, we get $\bar{\theta}_{min} = 55.42°$, which is close to the ideal value of 60∘. The value of ε_h is 0.25, which is also a good sign, indicating a feature-preserved remeshing. However, for the same model, when $\{\lambda_1, \lambda_2\} = \{27, 6\}$, the values of $\bar{\theta}_{min}$ and ε_h are not so good, clearly depicting the inherent inter-dependency among λ_is, ε_h, and $\bar{\theta}_{min}$. It is encouraging to note that the GPU time varies inversely with λ_i and ε_h. The rationale is that a higher value of δ_h allows larger values of λ_i and produces fewer Voronoi cells thereof, and being processed in GPU, reduces the execution time.

We also notice that, given a resolution of voxelization, an appropriate specification of k is needed so that ε_h does not exceed δ_h. In Table 1, for all models with 1M voxels and $k = 15$, we get $\varepsilon_h < \delta_h$. However, on Armadillo, for $|\mathbb{S}| = 1$M and $k = 30$, ε_h exceeds δ_h. The bound δ_h is not exceeded upon increasing the resolution of voxelization, as seen for $|\mathbb{S}| = 2$M. The reason for this is apparent from the bimodal curvature map in Fig. 2(b). Notice that the map misidentifies certain low-curvature regions on setting a small value of k, but again misidentifies certain high-curvature regions for a high value of k. This shows that the k-curvature technique needs deeper investigation. The value of k should be adaptive to the surface; that is, it should be smaller at high-curvature regions and larger at low-curvature regions. Therefore, one of the future prospects of this work would be to automate the value of k depending on local properties of the surface.

Also, in this work, we have resorted to a bimodal (i.e., two-level) curvature map, which rests on the Poisson distribution of discrete curvature. In the future, we would like to explore the scope for multi-level curvature map. Finally, in this paper, we have shown results for watertight surfaces only. We would like to extend it for open and non-orientable surfaces as well.

References

1. Brimkov, V., et al.: Digital planarity-a review. Discret. Appl. Math. **155**(4), 468–495 (2007)
2. Du, Q., et al.: Constrained centroidal Voronoi tessellations for surfaces. SIAM J. Sci. Comput. **24**(5), 1488–1506 (2003)
3. Du, X., et al.: Field-aligned isotropic surface remeshing. Comput. Graph. Forum **37**(6), 343–357 (2018)
4. Fan, J.: Notes on poisson distribution-based minimum error thresholding. Pattern Recogn. Lett. **19**(5), 425–431 (1998)
5. Leung, Y.S., et al.: A unified framework for isotropic meshing based on narrow-band Euclidean distance transformation. Comput. Visual Media **1**(3), 239–251 (2015)
6. Lévy, B., Liu, Y.: L_p Centroidal Voronoi tessellation and its applications. ACM ToG **29**(4), 119:1–11 (2010)
7. Liu, Y., et al.: On centroidal Voronoi tessellation–energy smoothness and fast computation. ACM ToG **28**(4), 101:1–17 (2009)
8. Liu, Y.J., et al.: Manifold differential evolution (MDE): a global optimization method for geodesic centroidal Voronoi tessellations on meshes. ACM ToG **35**(6), 243:1–10 (2016)
9. Shuai, L., et al.: GPU-based computation of discrete periodic centroidal Voronoi tessellation in hyperbolic space. Comput. Aided Des. **45**, 463–472 (2013)

10. Valette, S., et al.: Generic remeshing of 3D triangular meshes with metric-dependent discrete Voronoi diagrams. IEEE TVCG **14**(2), 369–381 (2008)
11. Wang, P., et al.: Robustly computing restricted Voronoi diagrams (RVD) on thin-plate models. Comput. Aided Geom. Des. **79**, 101–848 (2020)
12. Wang, X., et al.: Intrinsic computation of centroidal Voronoi tessellation (CVT) on meshes. Comput. Aided Des. **58**, 51–61 (2015)
13. Yan, D., Wonka, P.: Non-obtuse remeshing with centroidal Voronoi tessellation. IEEE TVCG **22**(9), 2136–2144 (2016)
14. Yan, D.M., et al.: Isotropic remeshing with fast and exact computation of restricted Voronoi diagram. Comput. Graph. Forum **28**(5), 1445–1454 (2009)

Multi-criteria Decision-Making Based Classifier Ensemble by Using Prioritized Aggregation Operator

Chandrima Debnath[1(✉)], Debashree Guha[1], Swati Rani Hait[2],
Soumita Guria[1], and Debjani Chakraborty[3]

[1] School of Medical Science and Technology, Indian Institute of Technology
Kharagpur, Kharagpur 721302, West Bengal, India
chandrima5debnath@gmail.com, debashree_smst@smst.iitkgp.ac.in ,
soumitaguriaphd22@kgpian.iitkgp.ac.in
[2] National Institute of Science Education and Research, Bhubaneswar 752050,
Odisha, India
[3] Department of Mathematics, Indian Institute of Technology Kharagpur, Kharagpur
721302, West Bengal, India
debjani@maths.iitkgp.ac.in

Abstract. This paper proposes a novel approach for classifier ensemble by employing the concepts of multi-criteria decision-making (MCDM) and aggregation operators. In this framework, a heterogeneous ensemble process has been incorporated where we consider varied set of classifiers to train the model. Each considered classifier is trained on the training data and a score correspondent to it is generated by utilizing the MCDM process. Subsequently, during the training phase, the priority is generated among the classifiers. For the testing phase, these prioritized classifiers are combined using prioritized aggregation operator. The priority order determined during the training phase is used to ensemble the classifiers during the testing phase. The proposed method is tested on UCI benchmark datasets and outperforms existing state-of-the-art methods.

Keywords: Ensemble learning · MCDM · Aggregation operator · Prioritized aggregation operator

1 Introduction

Ensemble classifiers represent a modern machine learning technique [3,12] that enhances classification accuracy by effectively amalgamating the class label predictions from multiple individual classifiers. These classifiers can be trained by using different learning procedures on the same training set [1,11], by training on a subset of the training set [7] or by using the same training set [11]. One of the most crucial aspects of ensemble learning is creating a diverse set of classifiers, which can be accomplished by using a single base learning classifier called the

P. Maji et al. (Eds.): PReMI 2023, LNCS 14301, pp. 98–105, 2023.
https://doi.org/10.1007/978-3-031-45170-6_11

homogeneous classifier with different parameters or by using a varied set of classifiers called the heterogeneous classifiers. In our approach, we develop a heterogeneous ensemble method where we will utilize different base learning classifiers which are to be ensembled together. To provide an unbiased evaluation, the classifiers are chosen randomly. First, we will provide priorities to these classifiers before accumulating the respective information. There are various methods to provide appropriate grading among classifiers during the classifier ensemble. In the current study, we utilize a multi-criteria decision-making (MCDM) process to prioritize those classifiers. When dealing with the MCDM process [10], we require a set of alternatives which are to be compared based on a set of criteria. Here, the alternatives are the classifiers, and the criteria are the performances of the classifiers, that is , accuracy, sensitivity, area under the receiver operating characteristic curve (AUC) and specificity, which make an evaluation matrix. The evaluation matrix is then converted into a vector representing the outcome for each alternative using an aggregating procedure. The prediction results from several classifiers can be thought of as the scores in the MCDM process, these scores can be utilized to provide priority among the classifiers.

The next step in any ensemble method is the accumulation process. Here we will utilize the concept of aggregation operators [5] to fuse the set of classifiers. Aggregation operators are mathematical functions that integrate the available information in the decision system. Various aggregation operators for assembling classifiers are discussed in [4]. In this study, we combine the classifier's output with the prioritized aggregation (PA) operator [14], an important family of averaging aggregation operators. Priority for different classifiers obtained from the MCDM procedure based on their respective score values can help identify which classifier results are more reliable and relevant to users. And then, the prioritized aggregation operator is utilized to generate respective weights of the classifiers. This enables more accurate and reliable classification results. This study's contribution can be summed up as follows:

1. At first, an MCDM-based approach for prioritizing the set of base learning classifiers has been presented.
2. The classifier accumulation technique has been proposed by utilizing priority based aggregation operator.
3. Experimental studies have been done over UCI dataset to check the efficacy of the proposed algorithm.

1.1   Basic Preliminaries

Definition 1 [5]. *An n-valued ($n > 1$) function A that maps to unit interval, i.e. $A : [0,1]^n \mapsto [0,1]$ is referred to as an aggregation operator if it possesses the following characteristics:*

1. *A is increasing in all of its arguments, i.e. if $y_1 \leq y_1'$, $y_2 \leq y_2'$, $\ldots$, $y_n \leq y_n'$ then we have $A(y_1, ..., y_n) \leq A(y_1', ..., y_n')$;*
2. *It satisfies the boundary condition i.e.; $A(0, ..., 0) = 0$, $A(1, .., 1) = 1$,*

Definition 2 [14]. *Let $\{g_1, g_2, \cdots, g_n\}$ be the set of criteria and let the criteria be strictly ranked in order of importance expressed by the strong priority rankings $g_1 > g_2 > \cdots > g_n$, where $g_i > g_{i+1}$ implies that the criterion g_i comes before g_{i+1} for every $i \in \{1, 2, \cdots, n-1\}$. Let $g_i(C)$ denote the performance of an alternative 'C' under the criteria g_i, where $g_i(C) \in [0, 1]$. The prioritized aggregation (PA) operator is given by*

$$PA(g_1(C), g_2(C), \cdots, g_n(C)) = \sum_{i=1}^{n} \xi_i g_i(C) \qquad (1)$$

where, normalized importance weights of criteria g_i is given by $\xi_i = \frac{T_i}{\sum_{i=1}^{n} T_i}$, for $i=1,...,n$; $T_1 = 1$, and $T_i = \prod_{l=1}^{i-1} g_l(C)$, for $i = 2, 3, \cdots, n$.

2 Methodology

MCDM is a problem-solving strategy that addresses the challenges of evaluation and selection among several alternatives based on multiple criteria or objectives. Here, we are taking the alternatives as classifiers $C_1, C_2, C_3, \ldots\ldots, C_N$ and respective criteria as accuracy, area under the receiver operating characteristic curve (AUC), sensitivity and specificity. In this study, at first, we generate scores for the individual classifiers in the training phase using TOPSIS (one of the well-known MCDM approach) [6], which are then used to provide priority among the classifiers based on their respective performances on the different criteria. Finally, a prioritized aggregation operator is used to ensemble the classifiers. The ensemble framework is described in Fig. 1.

2.1 MCDM Based Classifier Ranking

Assume that, the performances of the N classifiers with respect to M criteria is represented by the evaluation matrix $A = (a_{i,j})_{N \times M}$, with $i = 1, 2, ..., N$ and $j = 1, 2, ..., M$, contains N rows of classifiers and M columns of criteria. To assign relative importance to each criterion, we have used α_j with $j = 1, 2, ..., M$. For simplicity, we have taken the value of $\alpha_j = 1/M$, where M is the number of evaluation criteria. We will proceed as follows:

Step 1: Normalized the performance matrix A to bring all criteria on a common scale, given as

$$a_{\tilde{i},j} = \frac{a_{i,j}}{\sqrt{\sum_{i=1}^{N} a_{i,j}^2}} \qquad (2)$$

where, i=1,2,..,N, j=1,2,..,M.

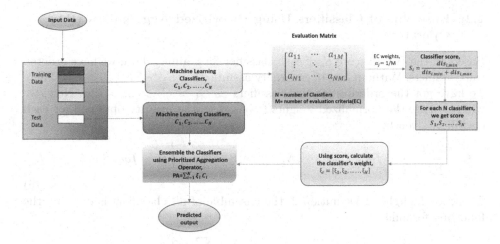

Fig. 1. Framework for classification ensemble in the proposed approach

Step 2: By including the relative importance of each criteria, calculate the weighted normalized matrix as follows:

$$\hat{a_{i,j}} = \tilde{a_{i,j}} \times \alpha_j, j = 1, 2, .., M \tag{3}$$

Step 3: In order to get the deviation of every classifier from the worst and best performances, calculate the euclidean distances $d_{i,min}$ and $d_{i,max}$ of the vector $\hat{a_i} = [\hat{a_{i,1}}, \hat{a_{i,2}}, \ldots, \hat{a_{i,j}}, \ldots, \hat{a_{i,M}}]$, from the maximum and minimum vectors $ec^{max} = [ec_1^{max}, \ldots, ec_j^{max}, \ldots, ec_M^{max}]$ and $ec^{min} = [ec_1^{min}, \ldots, ec_j^{min}, \ldots, ec_M^{min}]$ for every classifier i as

$$d_{i,min} = \sqrt{\sum_{j=1}^{M}(\hat{a_{i,j}} - ec_j^{min})^2}, i = 1, 2, ..., N$$

$$d_{i,max} = \sqrt{\sum_{j=1}^{M}(\hat{a_{i,j}} - ec_j^{max})^2}, i = 1, 2, ..., N$$

where,

$$ec_j^{max} = \{max(\hat{a_{i,j}})|i = 1, 2, ..., N\}, j = 1, 2, ..., M$$

$$ec_j^{min} = \{min(\hat{a_{i,j}})|i = 1, 2, ..., N\}, j = 1, 2, .., M$$

Step 4: Calculate the score or the relative performance for each classifier by

$$S_i = d_{i,min}/(d_{i,min} + d_{i,max}) \tag{4}$$

Step 5: Relative score of each classifier for trained data is obtained by

$$\hat{S_i} = \frac{S_i}{\sum_{k=1}^{N} S_k}, i = 1, 2, ..., N$$

2.2   Ensemble of Classifiers Using Prioritized Aggregation (PA) Operator

Based on the overall score $\hat{S}_i$ of each classifier for training data, we have ordered the classifiers. Without loss of generality assume that $\hat{S}_1 > \hat{S}_2 > ... > \hat{S}_N$. Then, we have got the ordering for the classifiers as $C_1 > C_2 > ... > C_N$. Now, we will calculate the normalized weights ξ_i based on the priority obtained for each classifier, given by:

$$\xi_i = \frac{T_i}{\sum_{i=1}^{N} T_i}, \quad for \quad i = 1, \cdots, N, \quad T_1 = 1, \quad T_i = \prod_{l=1}^{i-1} \hat{S}_l, \quad for \quad i = 2, \cdots, N.$$
(5)

Then, in the light of Definition 2, the ensemble of all classifiers is done by the following formula.

$$PA(C_1, C_2, ..., C_N) = \sum_{i=1}^{N} \xi_i C_i$$
(6)

The pictorial illustration of the proposed methodology is depicts in Fig. 1.

3   Experimental Analysis

We execute the tests on a few benchmark datasets from the UCI Machine Learning Repository [2] in order to compare the results of our proposed algorithm to those of other available techniques in the literature.

3.1   Datasets Description

The experimental data came from benchmark datasets in the UCI Machine Learning Repository. Table 1 contains information about these datasets. To compare our findings, we chose 8 UCI benchmark datasets. The feature space dimensions can be high with 166 or 60 features as in Musk and Sonar datasets or low with Liver or Diabetes with 6 and 8 features respectively, and the training set can be large (e.g., "Diabetes" and "German") or small (e.g., "Liver"). However, we have only two classes, i.e., we are considering a binary classification problem.

3.2   Performance Evaluation

Experimental results can be described by using several descriptors which can be used to estimate the performance of an algorithm. Various scales, including accuracy, precision, recall and F1-score, can be utilized to measure the algorithm's effectiveness [16].

Table 1. Dataset Description

Datasets	Number of Features	Number of Records
Breast Cancer	9	683
German	20	1000
Heart	13	270
Hepatitis	19	80
Diabetes	8	768
Sonar	60	208
Musk	166	476
Liver	6	200

3.3 Experimental Settings

In this study, we utilized Python 3.10 to implement the training and testing phase for our proposed approach. We split the available data into two sets, with 70% being used for training and 30% for testing, to ensure that the models could account for unpredictability. We employed a range of popular base learning classifiers, including support vector machine, decision tree, k-nearest neighbor, random forest, gradient boosting, adaBoost, bagging, xgboost, logistic regression, and naive bayes. This allowed us to explore each classifier's performance and compare their strengths and weaknesses. Also, during the training phase, priority is given to the classifiers using the scores obtained by utilizing the MCDM approach. Then, using prioritized aggregation operators these classifiers are ensembled. It is to be noted that we prioritize the classifiers in the training phase, and we calculate the weights, i.e., $\xi_1, \xi_2, ..., \xi_N$. Using these weights we ensemble the classifiers in the test phase.

3.4 Experimental Results and Comparative Analysis

In Table 2, performance evaluation of our proposed method has been shown. The proposed method is compared with the other five state-of-the-art approaches that are available in the literature [6,8,9,13,15]. The comparative analysis results are

Table 2. Performance Analysis of the Proposed Algorithm

Datasets	Accuracy	Precision	Recall	F1-Score
Breast Cancer	0.9619	0.9571	0.9306	0.9437
German	0.82	0.8513	0.9	0.875
Heart	0.844	0.8181	0.8577	0.8372
Hepatitis	0.875	1.00	0.25	0.4
Diabetes	0.745	0.7898	0.8267	0.8078
Sonar	0.833	0.8314	0.8214	0.8214
Musk	0.9021	0.8870	0.8870	0.8870
Liver	0.6923	0.6578	0.5682	0.6097

Table 3. Comparision of the Proposed approach with

Datasets	Proposed algorithm	MCF [6]	WMV [9]	CBEC [15]	result [8]	result [13]
Breast Cancer	0.9619	–	0.958	**0.9742**	**0.9742**	0.9624
German	**0.82**	–	–	–	–	0.7293
Heart	**0.844**	0.83	0.807	0.8396	0.839	0.8129
Hepatitis	**0.875**	–	0.8075	0.810	**0.875**	0.8307
Diabetes	0.745	–	0.757	–	0.753	**0.7595**
Sonar	0.833	**0.84**	0.759	0.801	0.801	0.8093
Musk	**0.9021**	0.90	–	–	–	–
Liver	0.6923	–	–	–	0.7185	**0.7642**

in Table 3. We have utilized accuracy measure for comparison of respective algorithms.

The performance of our model varied across several datasets and evaluation techniques, as shown in Table 3. In the Breast Cancer dataset, we found that our model performed better than techniques given in [6,8,9] and [13]. Our model performed exceptionally well for the German and Heart datasets. However, our model beat other techniques in the Musk dataset while gives a competitive result compared to the [8] method in the Hepatitis dataset and to the MCF method in the Sonar dataset.

4   Conclusions

We have developed a classifier ensemble technique that is based on the ideas of MCDM and aggregation operators. In order to prioritize the classifiers, scores are computed during the training phase using different base learning classifiers by utilizing an MCDM method. These prioritized classifiers are integrated using a prioritized aggregation operator during the testing phase. The normalized non-compensatory weights for these classifiers are obtained by utilizing those priority relation among the classifiers and then they are accumulated by utilizing an averaging operator. The proposed ensemble technique is significantly more trustworthy because it is based on the priority given to various classifiers obtained during the training phase, which helps prevent occurrences of mis-classification. Comparative research has demonstrated that the suggested approach out-performs the other algorithms in the majority of the datasets accessible from the UCI Machine Learning Repository. The strength of our study lies in prioritizing the classifiers based on multiple criteria during the ensemble process. The weakness of our study is that, we have assigned equal importance to all the criteria. In the future, we aim to expand our work by introducing a multi-modal hierarchical predictive scheme and conducting experiments on diverse datasets and domains for exploring the generalization capabilities of the proposed model.

Acknowledgements. The work of the second author is supported by the grant of ISIRD, IIT Kharagpur (Ref. No: IIT/SRIC/MM/DV H/2020-2021/143). The work of second and fifth author is supported by the grant of SERB, Government of India (Ref. No: SPG/2022/000045).

References

1. Bi, Y., Wu, S., Wang, H., Guo, G.: Combination of evidence-based classifiers for text categorization. In: 2011 IEEE 23rd International Conference on Tools with Artificial Intelligence, pp. 422–429. IEEE (2011)
2. Dua, D., Graff, C.: UCI machine learning repository (2017). http://archive.ics.uci.edu/ml/index.php
3. Gopika, D., Azhagusundari, B.: An analysis on ensemble methods in classification tasks. Int. J. Adv. Res. Comput. Commun. Eng. **3**(7) (2014)
4. Beliakov, G., Pradera, A., Calvo, T.: Aggregation Functions: A Guide for Practitioners, vol. 221. Springer, Heidelberg (2007). https://doi.org/10.1007/978-3-540-73721-6
5. Grabisch, M., Marichal, J.L., Mesiar, R., Pap, E.: Aggregation Functions, vol. 127. Cambridge University Press, Cambridge (2009)
6. He, Q., et al.: Feasibility study of a multi-criteria decision-making based hierarchical model for multi-modality feature and multi-classifier fusion: applications in medical prognosis prediction. Inf. Fusion **55**, 207–219 (2020)
7. Hothorn, T., Lausen, B.: Double-bagging: combining classifiers by bootstrap aggregation. Pattern Recognit. **36**(6), 1303–1309 (2003)
8. Jan, Z., Munos, J.C., Ali, A.: A novel method for creating an optimized ensemble classifier by introducing cluster size reduction and diversity. IEEE Trans. Knowl. Data Eng. **34**(7), 3072–3081 (2020)
9. Kuncheva, L.I., Rodríguez, J.J.: A weighted voting framework for classifiers ensembles. Knowl. Inf. Syst. **38**, 259–275 (2014)
10. Mufazzal, S., Muzakkir, S.M.: A new multi-criterion decision making (MCDM) method based on proximity indexed value for minimizing rank reversals. Comput. Ind. Eng. **119**, 427–438 (2018)
11. Rodriguez, J.J., Maudes, J.: Boosting recombined weak classifiers. Pattern Recognit. Lett. **29**(8), 1049–1059 (2008)
12. Rokach, L.: Ensemble-based classifiers. Artif. Intell. Rev. **33**, 1–39 (2010)
13. Wang, X., Wang, H.: Classification by evolutionary ensembles. Pattern Recognit. **39**(4), 595–607 (2006)
14. Yager, R.R.: Prioritized aggregation operators. Int. J. Approx. Reason. **48**(1), 263–274 (2008)
15. Jan, Z., Munos, J.C., Ali, A.: A novel method for creating an optimized ensemble classifier by introducing cluster size reduction and diversity. IEEE Trans. Knowl. Data Eng. **34**(7), 3072–3081 (2022)
16. Reddy, B.H., Karthikeyan, P.R.: Classification of fire and smoke images using decision tree algorithm in comparison with logistic regression to measure accuracy, precision, recall, F-score. In: 2022 14th International Conference on Mathematics, Actuarial Science, Computer Science and Statistics (MACS). IEEE (2022)

Federated Optimization with Linear-Time Approximated Hessian Diagonal

Mrinmay Sen[1,2(✉)], C. Krishna Mohan[1,2], and A. Kai Qin[1,2]

[1] IIT Hyderabad, Sangareddy, India
ai20resch11001@iith.ac.in
[2] SUT Melbourne, Melbourne, Australia

Abstract. Federated learning (FL) or federated optimization is a type of distributed optimization where multiple clients collaboratively train a global model without sharing local data. One of the key challenge in FL is the communication overhead due to slow convergence of the global model. In this paper, we propose a federated learning algorithm to handle this slow convergence by incorporating Hessian diagonal while training client's models. To reduce the computational and memory complexity in local clients, we introduce a linear time Hessian diagonal approximation technique by using only the first row of the Hessian. Our extensive experiments show that our proposed method outperforms state-of-the-art FL algorithms, FedAvg, FedProx, SCAFFOLD and DONE in terms of training loss, test loss and test accuracy.

Keywords: Federated learning · Slow convergence · Hessian diagonal approximation · Data heterogeneity

1 Introduction

Federated learning (FL) [11] is an emerging area of distributed learning where locally trained models from all the clients are sent to the central server and the server aggregates all these models to collaboratively train a global model. So, one communication round or global epoch of FL consists of two times of communication (sending global model to clients and sending clients model to server). This communications are the major issue with FL which needs to be minimized. The baseline FL algorithm FedAvg [11] suffers from slow convergence [9,16] when the data are heterogeneously distributed across all the clients which results in requirement of larger number of communication rounds while achieving a targeted accuracy from the global model. To reduce communication rounds in FL, several works have been done which are divided into two parts. One is first-order optimization based and another one is second-order optimization based. Existing first-order FL algorithms include FedProx [8], Fed-Nova [17], SCAFFOLD [5], MOON [6], FedDC [4]. The working principles of these algorithms are same as FedAvg. FedProx introduces a proximal term with the local loss function to control the direction of local gradient. FedNova uses

P. Maji et al. (Eds.): PReMI 2023, LNCS 14301, pp. 106–113, 2023.
https://doi.org/10.1007/978-3-031-45170-6_12

normalized averaging based local model aggregation. SCAFFOLD incorporates variance reduction while updating local models, MOON uses model level contrastive learning. FedDC uses an auxiliary local drift variable to control the local parameter's update. Even these first-order based algorithms work better than FedAvg, their convergence rate is still slow as these methods use only first-order gradient while optimizing model parameters which motivates us to use second-order optimization. Even the second-order optimization has quadratic convergence rate [1], it has major issue with calculation and storing of large Hessian matrix and its inverse ($O(d^2)$ space complexity and $O(d^3)$ time complexity). Existing second-order FL algorithms include DANE [14], GIANT [18], FedDANE [7], FedSSO [10], FedNL [13], Basis Matters [12], DONE [3] etc. which are either computationally expensive for local clients due to calculation of Hessian matrix or memory inefficient due to storing the Hessian matrix ($O(d^2)$ space complexity). FedSSO involves with storing of the full Hessian matrix in the server as it utilizes Quasi-Newton method while updating the global model in server. DANE, GIANT and FedDANE approximate local Hessian by using conjugate gradient method and DONE uses Richardson iteration to approximate the Hessian. DANE, GIANT, FedDANE and DONE use average gradient across all the clients while finding local Newton direction which leads to four times communications in each global round. Due to four times communication, requirement of per global iteration time is comparatively higher for these algorithms. FedNL and Basis Matters store previous step's Hessian matrix to approximate current step's Hessian in local clients. Storing, calculation and compression of local Hessian in FedNL and Basis Matters result in additional computational load to the local clients.

This paper focuses on improving the convergence of federated learning by taking into account of the problems of above mentioned existing methods. This paper incorporates linear time approximation of Hessian diagonal by using only the first row of the true Hessian and uses this Hessian diagonal along with gradient while optimizing the local models. Calculation and use of approximated Hessian diagonal while updating local models leads to better convergence of global model with linear-time space and time complexities. Our extensive experiments on image classification tasks of heterogeneously partitioned MNIST and FashionMNIST datasets show that our proposed method outperforms state-of-the-art FL algorithms, FedAvg, FedProx, SCAFFOLD and DONE in terms of global epoch wise training loss, test loss and test accuracy.

2 Problem Formulation

Suppose $\{C_i\}$ is the set of clients, where i = 1, 2, .., K. Client C_i contains its own local data D_i. The objective of federated optimization is to find the solution of function-1

$$\min_w F(w) = \frac{1}{K} \sum_{D_i} F_i(w; D_i) \tag{1}$$

where, $w \in R^d$ and $F_i(w) = \frac{1}{|D_i|} \sum_{\xi \in D_i} f_i(w; \xi)$ is the loss function of Client C_i

---

Algorithm 1. i^{th} Client's (C_i) model update

0: **Input:** T_l : Number of local iterations, w_0^i: Initial local model, which is initialized
   by global model w, η: Learning rate, ρ: Hessian regularization parameter

1: **for** $t = 0$ **to** $(T_l - 1)$ **do**
2:     $w_0^i \leftarrow w$
3:     Find gradient $g_t = \frac{\partial F_i(w_t^i, \beta_t)}{\partial w_t^i}$, where β_t is the mini batch at iteration t
4:     Find first row of the hessian $V = \frac{\partial g_t[0]}{\partial w_t^i}$, where $g_t[0]$ is the first element of g_t
5:     Approximate hessian diagonal $\Sigma_{approx} = \frac{V@V}{V[0]}$, where $V[0]$ is the first element of
       V and V@V is the dot product between V and V.
6:     Find inverse of $(\Sigma_{approx} + \rho I)$
7:     Update model parameters $w_{t+1}^i = w_t^i - \eta_t (\Sigma_{approx} + \rho I)^{-1} g_t$
8: **end for**

Algorithm 2. Proposed federated learning algorithm

0: **Input:** T : Number of global epochs, w^0: Initial global model

1: **for** $e = 0$ **to** $T - 1$ **do**
2:     Server sends global model w^e to all clients
3:     Each of all clients separately update this global model w^e by using Algorithm-1
       and finds w^i and sends this updated model to server
4:     Server receives all the locally updated models and aggregates (average) these
       and finds updated global model $w^{e+1} = \frac{1}{K} \sum_{i=1}^{K} w^i$
5: **end for**

---

3   Proposed Federated Learning Algorithm

Our proposed federated learning algorithm is presented in Algorithm-2. Our
proposed method follows the same strategy of FedAvg [11]. The only difference
is the calculation of local updates. In FedAvg, the local model is updated with
the help of gradient scaled by a learning rate (η) as shown in Eq.-2. But in our
proposed method, we scale the gradient with the help of inverse of the Hessian
diagonal along with learning rate. After finding local models, these models are
sent to server and the server performs aggregation on these models to find the
global model. Here, we propose a linear time Hessian diagonal approximation
technique by using only the first row of the true Hessian which helps us to reduce
the time complexity for Hessian diagonal calculation from $O(d^2)$ to $O(d)$. Further
scaling of the gradient with inverse of Hessian diagonal leads to faster local
convergence which results in faster global convergence. While approximating
Hessian diagonal, we assume two things. Hessian is symmetric positive semi-
definite matrix and the partial derivative of the loss function F with respect to
the first parameter (x_1) of the model (w) is a differentiable function which is
invertible. This is the only limitation of our proposed method. So, our algorithm
is applicable when the partial derivative of the loss function with respect to the
first parameter of the model is a differentiable function which is invertible. For

example, partial derivative of the log loss function (like cross entropy loss) with respect to the first parameter of the model is a differentiable and invertible. We show the validity of our claims with the practical implementations on MNIST and FashionMNIST datasets, where we use cross entropy loss function for image classification tasks.

$$w_t = w_{t-1} - \eta g_{t-1} \tag{2}$$

3.1 Linear Time Approximation of Hessian Diagonal with First Row the Hessian

Assumption-I. The loss function is twice differentiable with respect to the model parameters and the Hessian of the loss function is symmetric positive semi-definite matrix

Assumption-II. The partial derivative of the loss function F with respect to the first parameter (x_1) of the model (w) is a differentiable function which is invertible, i.e. $\frac{\partial F(w)}{\partial x_1}) = \frac{1}{\frac{\partial x_1}{\partial F(w)}}$, where $w = \{x_1, x_2, ..., x_d\}$

Statement-I. If assumption II holds, the diagonal of the Hessian (Σ_{approx}) can be approximated by Eq.-3.

$$\Sigma_{approx} = \frac{V@U}{\frac{\partial^2 F}{\partial x_1^2}} \tag{3}$$

where, V@U is the dot product between V and U vectors,
$V = \{\frac{\partial^2 F(w)}{\partial x_1^2}, \frac{\partial^2 F(w)}{\partial x_1 \partial x_2}, \frac{\partial^2 F(w)}{\partial x_1 \partial x_3}, ..., \frac{\partial^2 F(w)}{\partial x_1 \partial x_d}\}$ is the first row of the Hessian,
$U = \{\frac{\partial^2 F(w)}{\partial x_1^2}, \frac{\partial^2 F(w)}{\partial x_2 \partial x_1}, \frac{\partial^2 F(w)}{\partial x_3 \partial x_1}, ..., \frac{\partial 2^F(w)}{\partial x_d \partial x_1}\}$ is the first column of the Hessian

Proof of Statement-I. Let $\Sigma \in R^{d \times d}$ is a diagonal matrix which contains diagonal elements of true Hessian. Then $(i, i)^{th}$ the element of Σ is equal to $\Sigma^{(i,i)} = \frac{\partial^2 F}{\partial^2 x_i}$, where i $\in \{1, 2, 3, ..., d\}$

Now, according to Eq.-3, $(i, i)^{th}$ elements of Σ_{approx} is $\Sigma_{approx}^{(i,i)} = \frac{V^i \times U^i}{\frac{\partial^2 F}{\partial x_1^2}}$,

where $V^i = \frac{\partial^2 F}{\partial x_1 \partial x_i}$ and $U^i = \frac{\partial^2 F}{\partial x_i \partial x_1}$ are i^{th} elements of V and U respectively.

So, we can write

$$\Rightarrow \Sigma_{approx}^{(i,i)} = \frac{V^i \times U^i}{\frac{\partial^2 F}{\partial x_1^2}} = \frac{\frac{\partial^2 F}{\partial x_1 \partial x_i} \times \frac{\partial^2 F}{\partial x_i \partial x_1}}{\frac{\partial^2 F}{\partial x_1^2}} = \frac{\frac{\partial(\frac{\partial F}{\partial x_1})}{\partial x_i} \times \frac{\partial(\frac{\partial F}{\partial x_i})}{\partial x_1}}{\frac{\partial(\frac{\partial F}{\partial x_1})}{\partial x_1}}$$

If Assumption-II holds,

$$\Rightarrow \Sigma_{approx}^{(i,i)} = \frac{\partial(\frac{\partial F}{\partial x_1})}{\partial x_i} \times \frac{\partial(\frac{\partial F}{\partial x_i})}{\partial x_1} \times \frac{\partial x_1}{\partial(\frac{\partial F}{\partial x_1})} = \frac{\partial(\frac{\partial F}{\partial x_i})}{\partial x_i} = \frac{\partial^2 F}{\partial x_i \partial x_i} = \frac{\partial^2 F}{\partial^2 x_i}$$

$$\Rightarrow \Sigma_{approx}^{(i,i)} = \Sigma^{(i,i)}$$

Now, if assumption-I holds, we can say that the first column and the first row of the Hessian are identical. So we can say U=V. Putting U = V in Eq.-4 we get,

$$\Sigma_{approx} = \frac{V @ V}{\frac{\partial^2 F}{\partial x_1^2}} \tag{4}$$

So, under assumptions-I and II, Eq.-4 approximates the diagonal of Hessian with the help of only first row of the Hessian.

3.2   Updating Local Model with Approximated Diagonal Hessian

We use linear time approximated Hessian diagonal Σ_{approx} to scale the gradient vector g_t [15] while updating the local models which is presented in Algorithm-1. To overcome the problem of indefinite Hessian [2], we use the following regularized variant of newton method of optimization (Eq.-5). Here, instead of using full Hessian, we use only the diagonal elements of the Hessian.

$$w_{t+1} = w_t - \eta_t (\Sigma_{approx} + \rho I)^{-1} g_t \tag{5}$$

where, $\Sigma \in R^{dXd}$ is the matrix which contains only diagonal elements of the hessian, $\rho > 0$ is regularization parameter which helps us to make Σ invertible, I is identity matrix of size d and g_t is the gradient vector of the loss function $F_i(w_t)$ with respect to model parameters w_t.

3.3   Complexity Analysis

Local time complexity for calculating gradient is O(d) and the time complexity of calculating first row of the hessian is O(d). So the overall local time complexity of our algorithm is O(d) which is equal to the time complexity of FedAvg. The space complexity of our algorithm is O(2d) as our algorithm uses gradient and first row of Hessian.

4   Experimental Setup

We validate the applicability of our proposed method on heterogeneously partitioned MNIST and FashionMNIST datasets. Both MNIST and FashionMNIST datasets contains gray scale images of size 28 × 28. Each of these datasets has 10 number of classes. For both MNIST and FashionMNIST datasets, we use the same heterogeneous data partitioning strategy of the paper [11], where the data has been sorted with the class label and then divided. We create 150 number of shards of size 400 and then 3 shards has been assigned to each of the 50 clients. We use multinomial logistic regression (MLR) model with categorical cross entropy loss function for federated image classification tasks. We further consider that due to network connectivity issue, some of the clients may not be available in each iteration. We assume that 40% of total clients participate in each global epoch. We compare our proposed method with state-of-the-art

FL algorithms, FedAvg, FedProx, SCAFFOLD and DONE by using same initial states and same FL settings for all the methods. For FedAvg and FedProx, we use SGD with momentum (0.9) optimizer to update local models. To get the best performing models for both existing and proposed methods, we experiment with several sets of hyper-parameters and select the best model for each algorithm by considering minimum training loss, test toss and maximum test accuracy. We use learning rate $\eta \in \{0.5, 0.1, 0.01, 0.001, 0.0001\}$, FedProx proximal term $\in \{0.1, 0.01\}$, proposed method's regularization parameter $\rho \in \{0.1, 0.01\}$ and batch size $= 128$. In our proposed method, we use 1% learning rate decay per global iteration. For DONE, we use number of Richardson iterations $= 20$, $\alpha = 0.01$ and full batch data. We use full batch, as DONE performs better with full Batch than mini-batches. We use global epochs T = 30 and only one local epoch for all the methods. We implement all the methods using Tesla V100 GPU and PyTorch1.12.1+cu102. To make our experiments reproducible, we use seed $= 0$. For each dataset, we use same initialization and same settings for all the existing and proposed methods.

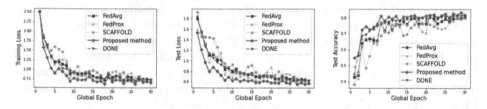

Fig. 1. Comparisons of training loss, test loss and test accuracy on MNIST

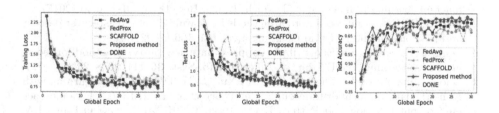

Fig. 2. Comparisons of training loss, test loss and test accuracy on FashionMNIST

4.1   Results

Our experimental results and comparisons have been depicted in Figs. 1 and 2. From these figures, it may be observed that in our proposed method, the global test and train losses decrease faster than existing state-of-the-art algorithms, FedAvg, Fedprox, SCAFFOLD and DONE which indicates that our algorithm needs comparatively less number of global epochs to reach a certain precision for convergence as we use the same initialization and same settings for all the methods. From Figs. 1 and 2, it also may be observed that the test accuracy achieved by our proposed method is better than others. To acheive 74% of test accuracy on FashionMNIST data, our proposed method takes 17 global epochs where DONE takes 29 global epochs. (FedAvg, Fedprox and SCAFFOLD can not able to achieve 74% within 30 global epochs). On MNIST dataset, to achieve 82% of test accuracy, our proposed method takes 22 global epochs where, DONE, SCAFFOLD, FedAvg and FedProx can not able to achieve 82% within 30 global epochs.

5   Conclusions

To overcome the problem of slow convergence in federated learning, we incorporate linear time approximated hessian diagonal along with gradient while updating local model parameters. We find the diagonal approximation by using only first row of the Hessian. Our method is easy to implement as it has same linear-time space and time complexities as first-order based algorithms. Our extensive experiments on heterogeneously partitioned datasets show that our proposed method outperforms state-of-the-art FL algorithms, FedAvg, FedProx, SCAFFOLD and DONE in terms of faster decreasing of train & test losses and faster incresing of test accuracy under the same settings for all the methods which indicates that our proposed optimization has better convergence than existing FL algorithms, FedAvg, FedProx, SCAFFOLD and DONE.

References

1. Agarwal, N., Bullins, B., Hazan, E.: Second-order stochastic optimization for machine learning in linear time. J. Mach. Learn. Res. **18**, 116:1–116:40 (2017)
2. Battiti, R.: First- and second-order methods for learning: between steepest descent and newton's method. Neural Comput. **4**(2), 141–166 (1992)
3. Dinh, C.T., et al.: DONE: distributed approximate newton-type method for federated edge learning. IEEE Trans. Parallel Distrib. Syst. **33**(11), 2648–2660 (2022)
4. Gao, L., Fu, H., Li, L., Chen, Y., Xu, M., Xu, C.: FedDC: federated learning with Non-IID data via local drift decoupling and correction. In: IEEE/CVF Conference on Computer Vision and Pattern Recognition, CVPR 2022, New Orleans, LA, USA, 18–24 June 2022, pp. 10102–10111. IEEE (2022)
5. Karimireddy, S.P., Kale, S., Mohri, M., Reddi, S.J., Stich, S.U., Suresh, A.T.: SCAFFOLD: stochastic controlled averaging for federated learning. In: Proceedings of the 37th International Conference on Machine Learning, ICML 2020, 13–18 July 2020, Virtual Event. Proceedings of Machine Learning Research, vol. 119, pp. 5132–5143. PMLR (2020)
6. Li, Q., He, B., Song, D.: Model-contrastive federated learning. In: IEEE Conference on Computer Vision and Pattern Recognition, CVPR 2021, virtual, 19–25 June 2021, pp. 10713–10722 (2021)
7. Li, T., Sahu, A.K., Zaheer, M., Sanjabi, M., Talwalkar, A., Smith, V.: FedDANE: a federated newton-type method. CoRR abs/2001.01920 (2020)

8. Li, T., Sahu, A.K., Zaheer, M., Sanjabi, M., Talwalkar, A., Smith, V.: Federated optimization in heterogeneous networks. In: Proceedings of Machine Learning and Systems 2020, MLSys 2020, Austin, TX, USA, 2–4 March 2020. mlsys.org (2020)
9. Li, X., Huang, K., Yang, W., Wang, S., Zhang, Z.: On the convergence of FedAvg on Non-IID data. In: 8th International Conference on Learning Representations, ICLR 2020, Addis Ababa, Ethiopia, 26–30 April 2020
10. Ma, X., et al.: Fedsso: a federated server-side second-order optimization algorithm. CoRR abs/2206.09576 (2022)
11. McMahan, B., Moore, E., Ramage, D., Hampson, S., y Arcas, B.A.: Communication-efficient learning of deep networks from decentralized data. In: Proceedings of the 20th International Conference on Artificial Intelligence and Statistics, AISTATS 2017, 20–22 April 2017, Fort Lauderdale, FL, USA, vol. 54, pp. 1273–1282. PMLR (2017)
12. Qian, X., Islamov, R., Safaryan, M., Richtárik, P.: Basis matters: better communication-efficient second order methods for federated learning. In: Camps-Valls, G., Ruiz, F.J.R., Valera, I. (eds.) International Conference on Artificial Intelligence and Statistics, AISTATS 2022, 28–30 March 2022, Virtual Event. Proceedings of Machine Learning Research, vol. 151, pp. 680–720. PMLR (2022)
13. Safaryan, M., Islamov, R., Qian, X., Richtárik, P.: FedNL: making newton-type methods applicable to federated learning. In: Chaudhuri, K., Jegelka, S., Song, L., Szepesvári, C., Niu, G., Sabato, S. (eds.) International Conference on Machine Learning, ICML 2022, 17–23 July 2022, Baltimore, Maryland, USA. Proceedings of Machine Learning Research, vol. 162, pp. 18959–19010. PMLR (2022)
14. Shamir, O., Srebro, N., Zhang, T.: Communication-efficient distributed optimization using an approximate newton-type method. In: Proceedings of the 31th International Conference on Machine Learning, ICML 2014, Beijing, China, 21–26 June 2014, vol. 32, pp. 1000–1008 (2014)
15. Sun, S., Spall, J.C.: SPSA method using diagonalized hessian estimate. In: 58th IEEE Conference on Decision and Control, CDC 2019, Nice, France, 11–13 December 2019, pp. 4922–4927. IEEE (2019)
16. Tan, A.Z., Yu, H., Cui, L., Yang, Q.: Towards personalized federated learning. CoRR abs/2103.00710 (2021)
17. Wang, J., Liu, Q., Liang, H., Joshi, G., Poor, H.V.: Tackling the objective inconsistency problem in heterogeneous federated optimization. In: Advances in Neural Information Processing Systems 33: Annual Conference on Neural Information Processing Systems 2020, NeurIPS 2020, 6–12 December 2020, virtual (2020)
18. Wang, S., Roosta-Khorasani, F., Xu, P., Mahoney, M.W.: GIANT: globally improved approximate newton method for distributed optimization. In: Advances in Neural Information Processing Systems 31: Annual Conference on Neural Information Processing Systems 2018, NeurIPS 2018, 3–8 December 2018, Montréal, Canada, pp. 2338–2348 (2018)

Deep Learning

Oscillatory Network and Deep Value Network Based Memory Replay Model of Hippocampus

Tamizharasan Kanagamani[1]($\boxtimes$), Madhuvanthi Muliya[1], V. Srinivasa Chakravarthy[1], Balaraman Ravindran[2], and Ramshekhar N. Menon[3]

[1] Laboratory for Computational Neuroscience, Department of Biotechnology, Bhupat and Jyoti Mehta School of Biosciences, Indian Institute of Technology Madras, Chennai, Tamil Nadu, India
tamizharasan.mit@gmail.com, schakra@ee.iitm.ac.in

[2] Department of Computer Science and Engineering, Robert Bosch Centre for Data Science and AI, Indian Institute of Technology Madras, Chennai, Tamil Nadu, India

[3] Cognition and Behavioural Neurology Section, Department of Neurology, Sree Chitra Tirunal Institute for Medical Sciences and Technology, Trivandrum, Kerala, India

Abstract. Memory replay is crucial for learning and consolidation. Hippocampal place cells demonstrate neuronal replay of behavioral sequences at a faster timescale in forward and reverse directions during resting states (awake and sleep). We propose a model of the hippocampus to demonstrate replay characteristics. The model comprises two parts - a Neural Oscillator Network to simulate replay and a Deep Value network to learn value function. The Neural Oscillator Network learns the input signal and allows modulation of the speed and direction of replay of the learned signal by modifying a single parameter. Combining reward information with the input signal and when trained with the Deep Value Network, reverse replay achieves faster learning of associations than forward replay in case of a rewarding sequence. The proposed model also explains the changes observed in the replay rate in an experimental study in which a rodent explores a linear track with changing reward conditions.

Keywords: Hippocampal Memory replay · Oscillatory Network · Value network

1 Introduction

Episodic memory represents the accumulation of past and present personal experiences. The key process in episodic memory is replaying these experiences, which is crucial for learning, consolidation, and planning [1–3]. The hippocampus plays a significant role in the replay process and this was first observed in rodent place cells [4]. Sequential place cell activity created as the animal explores the environment is recreated in the same or reverse order at a faster timescale during Sharp Wave Ripples (SWRs), which were observed to occur in the hippocampus in awake resting and sleep states [1, 5, 6]. It has been observed that the recurrent connections within the CA3 and the CA3 connections to CA1 in the hippocampus, generate the fast transient oscillations of the SWRs containing the forward and reverse replay events [1, 6–9].

P. Maji et al. (Eds.): PReMI 2023, LNCS 14301, pp. 117–127, 2023.
https://doi.org/10.1007/978-3-031-45170-6_13

Replay can occur at the start of an activity (preplay), after finishing an activity (awake-replay), and during slow-wave sleep (sleep-replay). The three types of replay are proposed to play specific roles viz., planning, learning, and consolidation, respectively [1]. Furthermore, the two key features of replay are its speed and direction (forward and reverse). Replay has been observed to occur at faster (compressed) timescales compared to the actual experience [1, 10]. Reverse replay has been observed primarily in the presence of a reward, while forward replay has been proposed to be involved in learning and planning [4, 11, 12].

In some animal studies, researchers found increased number of reverse replay events compared to forward replay events in the presence of reward [4, 11–13]. Similar results have been observed in human behavioral studies when the participants are presented with a sequence of images and asked to perform specific tasks [14–17]. The presentation of reward resulted in reverse replay at faster timescales in both awake and sleep replay [4, 10, 17–19].

Computational models of memory have resulted in a better understanding of replay. Levy (1996) modeled the hippocampal replay as a sequence prediction problem using a McCulloch-Pitts-neuron based recurrent excitatory neural network [7]. August et al. (1999) demonstrated temporal compression using integrate-and-fire neurons and Hebbian learning [20]. Shen et al. (1996) explained a replay of place cell activities using a single-layer recurrent network [21]. Milstein et al. (2022) demonstrated a recurrent network with spiking neurons for neuronal sequence generation [22]. Jahnke et al. (2015) proposed a leaky integrate-and-fire neuron model as a sequence prediction for demonstrating replay and SWR [23]. Biswas et al. (2021) proposed a complex-value-based oscillatory neural network for memorizing and reproducing complex signals [24]. Mattar et al. (2018) proposed a model that uses a priority-based replay mechanism using reward that helps learn the value representations [25].

Here we propose a model of hippocampal memory replay using a neural oscillator network. The model uses a Neural Oscillator Network to learn the multi-channel sequential input and replay the sequence in the forward and reverse order. The speed and direction of replay is controlled using a scalar multiplier that modulates the frequencies of all the oscillators. The model proposes a justification for replay, by formulating the sequence learning problem in Reinforcement Learning (RL) terms and applying it to a problem in spatial navigation. In spatial navigation problems, often, an RL agent learns to approach goal states where it receives a reward. At the point of reward delivery, as the agent trains its value function, it recalls its recent past states, a process resembling replay. In the present model, the past states are remembered using a network of neural oscillators.

To understand the effect of reward magnitude on the replay, we model the study of Ambrose et al. (2016) which observed that an increase (decrease) in reward leads to an increase (decrease) in the reverse replay rate [12]. In accordance with the study, the proposed model demonstrates the reward-based modulation of reverse replay by observing the number of epochs required to retrain the value network under altered reward conditions.

2 Methods and Results

The proposed model uses an Neural Oscillator Network that learns an n-channel input sequence. The learned sequences are replayed in the same order as observed. In the proposed model, the replay direction and speed are controlled by a single factor (β). When $\beta = 1$, the model replays the sequence in the same order and speed as the agent originally experienced it; when $\beta = -1$, replay occurs in the reverse order but at the original speed. When $|\beta| = 5$, replay occurs five times faster than the original speed in either direction depending on the sign.

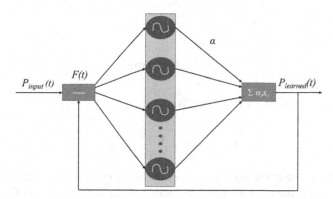

Fig. 1. Neural Oscillator Network for one channel

2.1 The Neural Oscillator Network

In this study, we use a Neural Oscillator Network which is a network of adaptive Hopf oscillators to learn sequences. Such networks have been proven to learn any periodic signal [24, 26, 27]. Each oscillator has an intrinsic frequency parameter ω, which can be adapted to the frequency components of the input signal; each oscillator has a weight parameter, α, that controls its amplitude. If the input signal has several frequency components, the network learns the signal by performing a Fourier-like decomposition of the signal.

The Neural Oscillator Network uses 50 neurons for each channel. Figure 1 displays the Neural Oscillator Network for a single channel. Training equations are given below (Eqns. 1–7).

$$x_i = r_i.\cos(\varphi_i) \tag{1}$$

$$\dot{r}_i = r_i(\mu - r_i^2) + k.F(t).\cos(\varphi_i) \tag{2}$$

$$\dot{\varphi}_i = \omega_i - k.F(t).\sin(\varphi_i)/r_i \tag{3}$$

$$\dot{\alpha}_i = \eta.x_i.F(t) \tag{4}$$

$$\dot{\omega}_i = -k.F(t).\sin(\varphi_i) \tag{5}$$

$$F(t) = P_{input}(t) - P_{learned}(t) \tag{6}$$

$$P_{learned}(t) = \sum_{i=0}^{N} \alpha_i x_i \tag{7}$$

where η, k, and μ are constants that control the learning rate. $P_{input}(t)$ is the teaching signal. $P_{learned}(t)$ is the learned signal, estimated as the weighted sum of the oscillator outputs. F(t) is the error predicted at a particular timestep, which is used for training the network. x_i represents the state, α_i represents the amplitude and ω_i represents the frequency of the ith oscillator. The iterative updating of these terms over time maximizes the correlation between F(t) and x_i. Here, α_i increases only if ω_i converges to any of the frequency components in F(t). φ_i represents the phase of the ith oscillator. The training model uses the constant values as follows: $\eta = 0.2$, $k = 5$, $\mu = 0.1$. The model is trained on a 5-channel input signal and uses 50 neurons for each channel.

During testing, since the prediction of the model is assumed to be correct, F(t) is set to 0. So only φ value gets updated as in Eq. 8. All the other three terms stay constant throughout. β is a scalar we use here to control the speed and direction.

$$\dot{\varphi}_i = \beta.\omega_i \tag{8}$$

2.2 Replay Using the Neural Oscillator Network

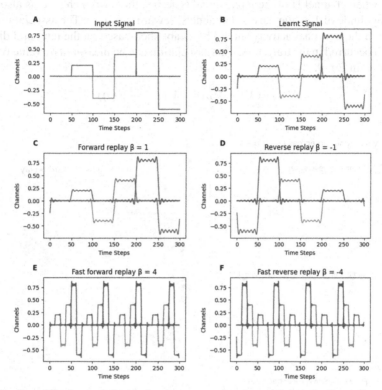

Fig. 2. Replay of the learned signals by the proposed replay model in the forward and reverse directions, and at different speeds.

The first part of this work demonstrates replay in the forward and reverse directions, and at different speeds (Fig. 2). The Neural Oscillator Network is used to learn and reproduce the input signals from multiple channels. The proposed model uses step signals from five channels as teaching input (Fig. 2A). Figure 2B shows the learned signal output. Since the Hopf oscillator learns the frequency, the direction and speed of the output signal can be controlled by multiplying a scalar β to ω, as shown in Eq. 8. Figure 2C and Fig. 2D display the output of the oscillator while using the β values as 1 and -1, respectively. $\beta = 1$ represents forward replay of the learned signal, and $\beta = -1$ shows reverse replay of the learned signal. The speed of replay is varied by using higher values of β. Figure 2E and Fig. 2F demonstrate forward and reverse replays at a faster timescale by using $\beta = 4$ and $\beta = -4$, respectively.

2.3 Reverse Replay with Reward

The second part of the work explains the need for reverse replay. This is done by value function estimation using a reward signal (Fig. 3). Here, eight input channels representing activity of a particular neuron, and an additional channel representing the reward signal are used. The sequential activity of these neurons represents place cell activity. For instance, when channel H of the input signal is active, the reward channel is also active with a magnitude of 1, while the other channels' rewards are zero. The association to the reward with the neuronal activity should be established based on the temporal distance at which it occurred in the trajectory. This association can be measured by value function estimated as in Eq. 9.

$$V(s) = V(s) + \rho(r + V\left(s'\right) - V(s)) \tag{9}$$

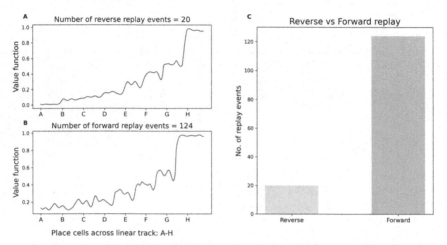

Value function across linear track

Fig. 3. Value learning comparison between forward and reverse replays

The learning of the value functions, V(s) depends on three terms: r - reward, V(s') - next state value function, and V(s) - the current state value function. In Eq. 9, ρ is the learning rate. Since the oscillatory model can replay the signal in either direction, the number of epochs required for learning the value function using both forward and reverse replay have been compared. The value function is estimated using a two-layered neural network (Deep Value Network) from the activity of the above 8 channels at a particular instant in time. The network receives an input of dimension 8 and has one hidden layer (6 neurons with leaky ReLU activity function) and an output layer with a single neuron (sigmoid activation function). The deep value network is trained using the loss function, the mean square of the temporal difference (TD) error calculated using the reward at the current state, and the current and next state value functions. Figure 3A and Fig. 3B show the value functions learned using reverse and forward replays. After learning, both replays generate similar value representations: the features close to the rewarding location estimate a higher value function compared to the features away from the rewarding location. Figure 3C shows the bar chart comparing the number of epochs required to learn the value functions using forward and reverse replay. Comparatively, reverse replay learns the value functions in significantly fewer epochs.

2.4 Reward Controlling the Number of Reverse Replay Events

The proposed replay-based value learning model is extended to demonstrate the results of an experimental study by Ambrose et al. (2016). The model simulates the increase or decrease in the number of reverse replay events per second (the replay rate) based on reward as observed in the experimental study (Fig. 4). In this study, the rat is allowed to run along a linear track with two reward wells at both ends. The replays were recorded during the idle states of the rat. The study conducted two experiments, each with three trials. The first experiment increased and then decreased the reward across trials, while the second experiment did the vice versa.

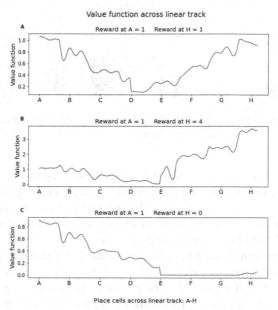

Fig. 4. Value representations across a linear track represented by 8 place cells, A–H, with increasing, decreasing, and constant rewards at the ends of the track.

Reward is varied only in one well (referred as the 'changing end') while the other well (called the 'unchanging end') has constant reward in all trials. In the first experiment, both wells are placed with a reward of 1× during the first trial. In the second trial, the reward was changed to 4× at the changing end. In the third trial, the reward was reset to 1× at the changing end. Among these three trials, the replay rate at both ends was observed to be similar in the first trial. In the second trial, the replay rate was higher at the 4× location than at the 1× rewarding location. Finally, the reverse replay rate at both ends was similar in the third trial.

In the second experiment, the reward was set to 0 at the changing end of the second trial. The rewards in the first and third trials were 1× at both ends. Like the first experiment, the replay rates are similar for both ends during the first trial. But during the second trial, the replay rate becomes very small at the decreased end (reward = 0). But the replay rate increases when the reward is reset to 1× at the changing end.

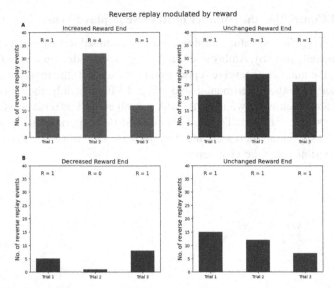

Fig. 5. Number of reverse replay events at the two rewarding ends of the linear track A-H across trials of increasing, decreasing, and constant rewards

The proposed model uses 9 channels: 8 channels (A–H) representing the activity of 8 place cells and 1 channel representing the reward. Here, activities of A and H are related to the rewarding locations (A – constant/unchanging reward, H - changing reward). This is input to the Neural Oscillator Network which is connected to the deep value network used in the second part of our work described earlier.

In the first experiment (increasing reward), for the first trial ($r_A = 1$, $r_H = 1$), values of the track A-H are learnt via reverse replay at H (H $\rightarrow$ A). The training is stopped when the TD error for all the states in the trajectory goes below the threshold of 0.1. Consequently, reverse replay at A (A $\rightarrow$ H) is used to train the value network. Similarly, the same value network is trained sequentially for the second ($r_A = 1$, $r_H = 4$) and the third ($r_A = 1$, $r_H = 1$) trials. The number of epochs required to train the value network at each case is observed. Similar training is carried out for the second experiment (0 reward at changing end; $r_H = 0$), and the number of epochs for each end is observed.

Figure 4 shows the value representations across the linear track for different reward conditions. Figure 5A shows the number of epochs, or the number of replay events, required to train the value network for each case at both ends (left- increased reward end, right- unchanged end) in the first experiment. Figure 5B compares the number of epochs required for each case (left- decreased reward end, right- unchanged end) of the second experiment. The results generated align with the experimental study's results [12].

3 Discussion

The proposed study focuses on modeling the characteristics of hippocampal memory replay. Existing models demonstrate replay as a sequence prediction method or a compression mechanism. As of now, there is no single model that controls the speed and direction of replay. Here we have proposed a model that uses a Neural Oscillator Network for simulating replay and a Deep value Network that controls the direction and speed. The model also explains how reward controls replay behavior. The first part of the study shows that the Neural Oscillator Network is a potential model for generating hippocampal replay and modulating the speed and direction by a single parameter. This effectively explains forward, reverse, fast forward, and fast reverse replays. This kind of model is biologically realizable since the learning parameters can be related to acetylcholine and TD error to dopamine [28, 29]. Although RNN-based models, such as bidirectional LSTM, can be trained to replay the sequential information in both directions, the advantage of the proposed model is that the replay direction and speed can be elegantly controlled by a single parameter which in turn is controlled by fluctuation in the value function, thereby enhancing the biological plausibility of the model.

The second part of the work explains the need for reverse replay using the Deep Value Network. Value learning depends on the reward, the current and succeeding state value functions. The value function learning was carried out separately using forward and reverse replays. Among these two approaches, reverse replay takes fewer number of epochs than forward replay to learn the value function. In another sense, the effect of reward is reflected in a single epoch throughout the trajectory when the reverse replay is carried out. In contrast, it takes more epochs for the forward replay to achieve the minimal effect of reward on all the states.

The third work demonstrates the modulation of the number of replays by the magnitude of reward based on reinforcement learning. In this task, the model takes a greater number of epochs when reward is increased to $4\times$ as compared to a reward of $1\times$, and similar number of epochs to learn the value representations if both ends have the same reward ($1\times$). On the other hand, when the reward at changing end is decreased from $1\times$ to $0\times$, the replay count decreases. When $0\times$ is changed to $1\times$, reverse replay events increase again. This trend in the number of reverse replay events mimics the observation of the replay rate as shown in the experimental study [12].

This proposed model gives insight into the different kinds of replay and why they might occur. Awake replay, which happens at the end of any activity, establishes the association of rewards to the positions on the trajectory using reverse replay. Reverse replay at the rewarding locations helps to learn the importance (value function) of the positions in the trajectory with immediate effect. Sleep replay comprises both forward and reverse replay. This could possibly establish the association between various overlapping trajectories. For example, a beneficial association between the start of one trajectory and the end of another trajectory is possible based on the value function if there is an overlap between trajectories. Preplay that happens at the start of an activity replays the trajectory of the best path from the learned trajectories in the forward direction is a component of planning. Though the model can control the speed and the direction of replay, it can learn only one sequence at a time. By building a model to learn more sequences and allowing it to replay based on context, we hope to explain and reconcile several existing theories of replay.

References

1. Carr, M.F., Jadhav, S.P., Frank, L.M.: Hippocampal replay in the awake state: a potential substrate for memory consolidation and retrieval. Nat. Neurosci. **14**, 147–153 (2011). https://doi.org/10.1038/NN.2732
2. Foster, D.J., Knierim, J.J.: Sequence learning and the role of the hippocampus in rodent navigation. Curr. Opin. Neurobiol. **22**, 294–300 (2012). https://doi.org/10.1016/J.CONB.2011.12.005
3. Pfeiffer, B.E., Foster, D.J.: Hippocampal place-cell sequences depict future paths to remembered goals. Nature **497**, 74–79 (2013). https://doi.org/10.1038/NATURE12112
4. Foster, D.J., Wilson, M.A.: Reverse replay of behavioural sequences in hippocampal place cells during the awake state. Nature **440**, 680–683 (2006). https://doi.org/10.1038/NATURE04587
5. Wilson, M.A., McNaughton, B.L.: Reactivation of hippocampal ensemble memories during sleep. Science **265**, 676–679 (1994). https://doi.org/10.1126/SCIENCE.8036517
6. Buzsáki, G.: Hippocampal sharp wave-ripple: a cognitive biomarker for episodic memory and planning. Hippocampus **25**, 1073–1188 (2015). https://doi.org/10.1002/HIPO.22488
7. Levy, W.B.: A sequence predicting CA3 is a flexible associator that learns and uses context to solve hippocampal-like tasks. Hippocampus **6**, 570–590 (1996)
8. Kali, S., Dayan, P.: The involvement of recurrent connections in area CA3 in establishing the properties of place fields: a model. J. Neurosci. **20**, 7463–7477 (2000). https://doi.org/10.1523/JNEUROSCI.20-19-07463.2000
9. Davoudi, H., Foster, D.J.: Acute silencing of hippocampal CA3 reveals a dominant role in place field responses. Nat. Neurosci. **22**, 337–342 (2019). https://doi.org/10.1038/S41593-018-0321-Z
10. Michelmann, S., Staresina, B.P., Bowman, H., Hanslmayr, S.: Speed of time-compressed forward replay flexibly changes in human episodic memory. Nat. Hum. Behav. **3**, 143–154 (2019). https://doi.org/10.1038/S41562-018-0491-4
11. Diba, K., Buzsáki, G.: Forward and reverse hippocampal place-cell sequences during ripples. Nat. Neurosci. **10**, 1241–1242 (2007). https://doi.org/10.1038/NN1961
12. Ambrose, R.E., Pfeiffer, B.E., Foster, D.J.: Reverse replay of hippocampal place cells is uniquely modulated by changing reward. Neuron **91**, 1124–1136 (2016). https://doi.org/10.1016/J.NEURON.2016.07.047
13. Singer, A.C., Frank, L.M.: Rewarded outcomes enhance reactivation of experience in the hippocampus. Neuron **64**, 910–921 (2009). https://doi.org/10.1016/J.NEURON.2009.11.016
14. Momennejad, I., Otto, A.R., Daw, N.D., Norman, K.A.: Offline replay supports planning in human reinforcement learning. Elife **7** (2018). https://doi.org/10.7554/ELIFE.32548
15. Schapiro, A.C., McDevitt, E.A., Rogers, T.T., Mednick, S.C., Norman, K.A.: Human hippocampal replay during rest prioritizes weakly learned information and predicts memory performance. Nat Commun. **9** (2018). https://doi.org/10.1038/S41467-018-06213-1
16. Liu, Y., Dolan, R.J., Kurth-Nelson, Z., Behrens, T.E.J.: Human replay spontaneously reorganizes experience. Cell **178**, 640-652.e14 (2019). https://doi.org/10.1016/J.CELL.2019.06.012
17. Schuck, N.W., Niv, Y.: Sequential replay of nonspatial task states in the human hippocampus. Science. **364** (2019). https://doi.org/10.1126/SCIENCE.AAW5181

18. Buhry, L., Azizi, A.H., Cheng, S.: Reactivation, replay, and preplay: how it might all fit together. Neural Plast. **2011** (2011). https://doi.org/10.1155/2011/203462
19. Findlay, G., Tononi, G., Cirelli, C.: The evolving view of replay and its functions in wake and sleep. Sleep Adv. **1** (2021). https://doi.org/10.1093/SLEEPADVANCES/ZPAB002
20. August, D.A., Levy, W.B.: Temporal sequence compression by an integrate-and-fire model of hippocampal area CA3. J. Comput. Neurosci. **6**, 71–90 (1999). https://doi.org/10.1023/A:1008861001091
21. Shen, B., McNaughton, B.L.: Modeling the spontaneous reactivation of experience-specific hippocampal cell assembles during sleep. Hippocampus **6**, 685–692 (1996)
22. Milstein, A.D., Tran, S., Ng, G., Soltesz, I.: Offline memory replay in recurrent neuronal networks emerges from constraints on online dynamics. J. Physiol. (2022). https://doi.org/10.1113/JP283216
23. Jahnke, S., Timme, M., Memmesheimer, R.M.: A unified dynamic model for learning, replay, and sharp-wave/ripples. J. Neurosci. **35**, 16236–16258 (2015). https://doi.org/10.1523/JNEUROSCI.3977-14.2015
24. Biswas, D., Pallikkulath, S., Chakravarthy, V.S.: A complex-valued oscillatory neural network for storage and retrieval of multidimensional aperiodic signals. Front. Comput. Neurosci. **15** (2021). https://doi.org/10.3389/FNCOM.2021.551111
25. Mattar, M.G., Daw, N.D.: Prioritized memory access explains planning and hippocampal replay. Nat. Neurosci. **21**, 1609–1617 (2018). https://doi.org/10.1038/S41593-018-0232-Z
26. Righetti, L., Buchli, J., Ijspeert, A.J.: From Dynamic hebbian learning for oscillators to adaptive central pattern generators. In: Proceedings of 3rd International Symposium on Adaptive Motion in Animals and Machines -- AMAM 2005, p. 45 (2005)
27. Righetti, L., Buchli, J., Ijspeert, A.J.: Adaptive frequency oscillators and applications. Open Cybern. Syst. J. **3**, 64–69 (2009). https://doi.org/10.2174/1874110X00903020064
28. Atherton, L.A., Dupret, D., Mellor, J.R.: Memory trace replay: the shaping of memory consolidation by neuromodulation. Trends Neurosci. **38**, 560 (2015). https://doi.org/10.1016/J.TINS.2015.07.004
29. Foster, D.J.: Replay comes of age. Annu. Rev. Neurosci. **40**, 581–602 (2017). https://doi.org/10.1146/ANNUREV-NEURO-072116-031538

Statistically Matched DWT Based Novel DNN Framework for Visual SLAM

Anvaya Rai[1,2]([✉]), Brejesh Lall[2], Astha Zalani[1], Raghwender Prakash[1], and Shikha Srivastava[1]

[1] Centre for Development of Telematics, New Delhi, India
anvayarai@gmail.com
[2] Indian Institute of Technology Delhi, New Delhi, India

Abstract. The foundation of any image processing tasks lies in an efficient representation of visual information and capturing significant information in an image concisely. The objective of this work is to present a novel classification framework that generates a concise representation of an indoor scene using a deep neural network (DNN) in conjunction with statistically matched directional wavelet filter banks. This representation is then used to accurately localize a subject in indoor environments by using the scene images captured from the subject's mobile phone camera. Suggested methodology can be used for various low compute robotic operations like indoor navigation, loop detection etc. We propose to construct multiresolution, lowpass and directional image expansions by using 2D non-separable filter banks. We apply this method in the domain of Visual SLAM and these representations of the indoor scene are then used to augment the featured extracted by deep neural networks during indoor positioning of a subject.

Keywords: Discrete Wavelet Transform (DWT) · Statistically Matched Wavelet · Nonseparable wavelet · Fractional Brownian Process · Directional Multirate Filter Bank · Indoor positioning

1 Introduction

Today, there are many real-world applications that depend on indoor positioning systems implemented using various techniques, such as positioning using Wi-Fi, Bluetooth, magnetic fields, image processing etc. The shortcomings of indoor positioning systems are usually related to the difficulty of having a general deployment strategy, either low accuracy or expensive hardware can be the obstacle. Examining the current positioning and navigation systems, vision-based methods can dominate various applications of indoor positioning systems. This work focuses on image processing based indoor localization method using an image captured by the mobile phone camera carried by the subject, that requires to be positioned or tracked while in motion. Specifically our contributions are towards the design of a novel framework that is robust to noisy indoor environments and capable of running on low compute edge devices.

© The Author(s), under exclusive license to Springer Nature Switzerland AG 2023
P. Maji et al. (Eds.): PReMI 2023, LNCS 14301, pp. 128–136, 2023.
https://doi.org/10.1007/978-3-031-45170-6_14

   The challenges of vision based indoor positioning systems further escalate with the presence of moving objects like humans, in the indoor scenario. To account for such challenges we augment the DNN with a directional multirate filter bank, constructed using filters that are statistically matched to the indoor scene. Thereby, precisely capturing only the relevant scene information in it's subbands and filtering out the noise due to moving objects. We pass the natural indoor scene image through this filter bank and generate a 2D signal representing the information captured by the HL-subband of the filter bank. We then use a pre-trained DNN to collectively extract features from the natural image and the generated 2D signal, and localise a user based upon these 2 sets of features.

   Abandoning the traditional approach of identifying image feature descriptors like ORB, SURF etc., and using deep neural networks to directly extract information from the image, results in effective computer vision based indoor positioning. The deep learning methods can simultaneously detect the feature points and also estimate their description from the image. Similar network was proposed by Yi et al. [4]. Xu et al. [2], introduced deep learning based representation of query image on object level and Taira et al. [3], represented it at feature level. Both the representations helped in improving the robustness of indoor image-based localization. Specifically, Taira et al. [3], achieved an accuracy of 40.7% at the localization of 0.5 meters. However, the accuracy suffered with the presence of moving people and objects in the scene. Also, the method compared every query image with all the images in the database, and thus with the increasing database, the retrieval performance decreases significantly. Also, it required huge compute and memory for near real time inference. Additionally, Detone et al. [5], demonstrated a new idea for generating feature point descriptors that combined the advantages of deep learning approach with traditional representations. They showed that CNN based models generate feature descriptors which provide a better image representation, but required huge compute for near real time performance. The varied scope of the receptive field of different layers, describes the varied characteristics captured between different layers. In the scene recognition task, stronger perception of objects is captured by the bottom receptive field, while the deeper layers focus on the information presented by the colour in the scene. Different set of feature descriptors are extracted by each layer, and the following layer generates information from the previous layer to improve the embedding. Therefore, the extracted descriptors using the deep neural networks, will be more suitable for visual positioning task.

   Motivated by the advancements achieved in the areas of image representation using deep neural networks, we suggest an indoor visual positioning pipeline that can be executed in real time on a subject's mobile phone and uses a pre-trained MobileNetv3-Small network [1] for feature point extraction and description. In this work, we use the concept of transfer learning and augment it with the traditional approach of PCA based feature space transformation and extract a manifold with lower dimension. Dimensionality reduction is important as it directly impacts the storage space and matching speed of the algorithm. The knowledge of MobileNetv3-Small network, pre-trained over ImageNet, is used to detect natural objects in the scene and construct features describing the natural scene. Additionally, MobileNetv3-Small network is optimised to run on low compute devices like mobile phone.

2 Methodology

In this section, we will discuss the proposed approach for augmenting a pre-trained MobileNetv3-Small network [1] with 2D filter bank, followed by a PCA based feature space transformation and generate the novel low-shot deep neural network based Visual SLAM technique for indoor environment. While the pre-trained DNN is used to generate feature point descriptors, PCA based feature transformation is used for optimising the dimension of these feature descriptors, there by leading to lesser storage space and faster matching speed. We also construct a multirate filter bank, using directional wavelets that are statistically matched to the indoor scenes and hence it generates an optimal representation of the indoor environment.

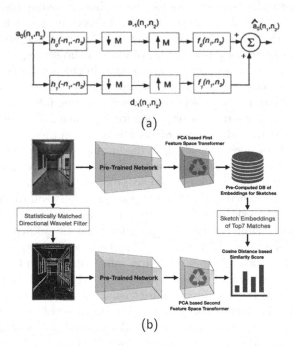

Fig. 1. (a) 2 Chanel 2D-multirate filter bank. (b) Suggested pipeline for inference and position the user based upon the scene image.

In the suggested framework, as shown in Fig. 1(b), we use a pre-trained DNN to create 2 channels for generating feature point descriptors. The input to first channel is the natural scene image while the input to the second channel is the

2D signal generated from the HL-subband of the filter bank. The output of the HL-subband of the filter bank, gives the information about the structure of the indoor scene, while suppressing the noise. This information is very helpful in precisely classifying the position of a user inside the building, especially when there is high amount of occlusion due to moving persons in the scene.

2.1   Estimation of Multidimensional Statistically Matched Wavelet Filter Bank

We estimate a 2-channel multidimensional nonseperable wavelet filters matched to the statistics of a multidimensional signal. The objective of the approach is to maximize the given signal energy onto successive scaling subspaces and minimizing it in the wavelet subspaces. In order to formulate the statistical nature of a multidimensional signal, we need to appropriately model it's attributes like roughness of the signal. As wavelet basis expansion behaves as Karhunen-Loeve type expansion for fractional Brownian processes [11,12] and the value of the Hurst exponent, characterizing a fBm process, is an estimate of the roughness of the signal, we assume this model for the given signal.

As shown in Fig. 1(a), when samples $a_0[n]$ of the multidimensional signal are given as input to the filter bank, the outputs of the analysis filter bank ($a_{-1}[n]$ and $d_{-1}[n]$) are defined as:

$$a_{-1}[n] = \sum_{k \in \mathbb{Z}^2} h_0[-k] a_0[\mathbb{M}n - k] \tag{1}$$

and

$$d_{-1}[n] = \sum_{k \in \mathbb{Z}^2} h_1[-k] a_0[\mathbb{M}n - k] \tag{2}$$

where $\mathbb{M}$ is the multidimensional decimation matrix, h_0 and h_1 are the scaling and wavelet filters respectively, $a_{-1}[n]$ corresponds to the energy in the lower scaling subspace and $d_{-1}[n]$ corresponds to the energy in the lower wavelet subspace [9–11]. As discussed by authors in [9], if we consider $\mathbb{M}$ to be a Quincunx decimation matrix, then the coefficients of h_1 are estimated, using the autocorrelation matrices, as:

$$\boldsymbol{H_1} = \boldsymbol{R}[n]^{-1} \boldsymbol{R_c}[n] \tag{3}$$

where,

$$\boldsymbol{R}[n] = \mathbb{E}\{\boldsymbol{A}[n]\boldsymbol{A}[n]^T\} \tag{4}$$

and

$$\boldsymbol{R_c}[n] = \mathbb{E}\{a_0[n_1 + n_2 + 1, n_1 - n_2 + 1]\boldsymbol{A}[n]^T\} \tag{5}$$

Generating Autocorrelation Matrix of a Multidimensional Signal. As we can recall that we had modeled the multidimensional signal as a fBm process, which is characterized through the value of its Hurst Exponent (H). The fBm process is called a 1st-order fbm process if $0 \leq H \leq 1$ and a 2nd-order fbm process if $1 \leq H \leq 2$. The correlation between any two position vectors $\boldsymbol{x}$ and $\boldsymbol{y}$ for a 2-dimensional 1st-order $(\boldsymbol{R^1}_{B_H})$ and 2nd-order $(\boldsymbol{R^2}_{B_H})$ fbm process is defined in Eq. (6) and (7) [6].

$$\boldsymbol{R^1}_{B_H}(\boldsymbol{x}, \boldsymbol{y}) = \frac{\sigma_H^2}{2}[\|\boldsymbol{y}\|^{2H} + \|\boldsymbol{x}\|^{2H} - \|\boldsymbol{y} - \boldsymbol{x}\|^{2H}] \tag{6}$$

$$\boldsymbol{R^2}_{B_H} = \frac{1}{2\pi}[\frac{\Gamma(-H)}{\Gamma(H+1)}(\|\boldsymbol{y}\|^{2H} + \|\boldsymbol{x}\|^{2H} - \|\boldsymbol{x} - \boldsymbol{x}\|^{2H}) - \frac{2\Gamma(-H+\frac{1}{2})}{\Gamma(H+\frac{1}{2})}(\|\boldsymbol{y}\|^{2H-1}\|\boldsymbol{x}\| + \|\boldsymbol{x}\|^{2H-1}\|\boldsymbol{y}\|)] \tag{7}$$

where $\sigma_H = \frac{2^{-1-2H}\Gamma(1-H)}{\Gamma(1+H)}$ and $\|\cdot\|$ denotes the norm. Thus, we can calculate $\boldsymbol{R}[\boldsymbol{n}]$ and $\boldsymbol{R}_c[\boldsymbol{n}]$ and there after $\boldsymbol{H}_1$, if we estimate the value of H.

Estimating Hurst Exponent of a Multidimensional Signal. Considering the inherent link between polyharmonic splines and fBms [8], we present an approach to estimate the Hurst Exponent (H) of a p-dimensional fBm process based on the values of the coefficients obtained from its polyharmonic spline wavelet analysis.

Theorem 1. *The polyharmonic spline wavelet transform of order $2\gamma \geq 2\gamma_0$, with $\gamma_0 \triangleq H/2 + p/4$, maps the nonstationary p-dimensional fBm process into a series of stationary (discrete) Gaussian processes [8].*

Theorem 2. *The variance of the polyharmonic wavelet coefficients depends exponentially on the Hurst exponent and the scale n [8]*

$$\mathbb{E}\{w_n^2[\boldsymbol{k}]\} = |D|^{\frac{(2H+p)n}{p}} \mathbb{E}\{w_0^2[\boldsymbol{k}]\} \tag{8}$$

$$\log_{\sqrt[p]{|D|}}(\mathbb{E}\{w_n^2[\boldsymbol{k}]\}) = (2H+p)n + \log_{\sqrt[p]{|D|}}(\mathbb{E}\{w_0^2[\boldsymbol{k}]\}) \tag{9}$$

Thus, slope of the linear Eq. (9), can be used to estimate the Hurst Exponent of an fBm process. In empirical form, the relationship is a regression problem defined as,

$$\left(n, \log_{\sqrt[p]{|D|}}(\mathbb{E}\{w_n^2[\boldsymbol{k}]\})\right) \tag{10}$$

where $\mathbb{E}\{w_n^2[\boldsymbol{k}]\}$ is the energy in HH, HL and LH subbands at scale n. $\boldsymbol{k}$ being the translation vector for mother wavelet.

Choice of Spline Wavelet for Estimating Hurst Exponent. We now present a family of orthogonal wavelets which uses Quincunx decimation [7] and the 2D analysis wavelet filter, as a function of their order (λ), is given by

$$H_\lambda(\boldsymbol{\omega}) = \frac{\sqrt{2(2 + \cos(\omega_1 + \omega_2))^\lambda}}{\sqrt{(2 + \cos(\omega_1 + \omega_2))^\lambda + (2 + \cos(\omega_1 - \omega_2))^\lambda}} \tag{11}$$

Since these have a frequency response similar to Daubechies filters, we can use them to play the role of Polyharmonic Spline Wavelet Filters and estimate the Hurst Exponent (H) for any input 2D signal. Hence we can estimate the analysis wavelet filters that is statistically matched to the input using the auto-correlation matrix, followed by the estimate of the scaling filter using the Perfect Reconstruction and Biorthogonality conditions of Multiresolution Analysis.

3   Results and Conclusion

The dataset curated to evaluate our approach, contained a total of 6880 scene image samples captured at 423 distinct locations inside the building. There were multiple images captured from multiple cell phone camera, from each of the locations and at various orientations. The dataset was split into a Novel Dataset with 4923 images and an Evaluation Dataset with 1957 image samples, referred as Original Evaluation Dataset henceforth. Various types of colour transformations like random Contrast, Brightness, Hue and Saturation were added to the raw images of the Original Evaluation Dataset, resulting in another Evaluation Dataset, called the BC-HSV. The objective of this dataset was to evaluate the performance of the proposed network under varying lighting conditions in indoor environment. The BC-HSV Evaluation Dataset was further augmented with random placement of 1, 2, 3 and 4 persons in the scene. This resulted in 4 more evaluation datasets called as BC-HSV-1P, BC-HSV-2P, BC-HSV-3P and BC-HSV-4P, respectively.

We have done our implementation by varying the captured variance of embedding generated from the DNN and identifying the corresponding number of eigen basis vectors required to efficiently and distinctly represent the indoor scenes. To evaluate the proposed approach, we have used Classification Accuracy and Latent Space Dimension as 2 metrics to compare the suggested pipeline. For each datset, initially the natural test image is passed through the feature space transformed DNN to identify the Top 7 matches and subsequently sketches of these 7 images along with the test sample, are passed through the 2nd feature space transformed DNN. The embedding generated for the natural and sketch images are independently fed into separate classifiers after dimensionality reduction and match probabilities ($P_{natural}$ and P_{sketch} respectively) are calculated independently. The final Top 3 predictions are generated from the weighted average of these 2 classification probabilities with an objective to maximise the score for the ground-truth class.

$$P = \alpha * P_{natural} + \beta * P_{sketch} \tag{12}$$

As shown in Table 1, the Classification Accuracy of the pre-trained DNN in the 576 dimensional Original Latent Feature Space (OLFS) is surpassed by 63 dimensional PCA transformed latent space with $\alpha = 1$ and $\beta = 0$ i.e. information in 2nd channel is not considered. This accuracy further increases with increase in the number of features captured. Further, in presence of moving objects like Persons, 2nd channel outperforms the 1st channel with equal number of features. This is depicted with $\alpha = 0$ and $\beta = 1$ i.e. information in 1st channel is not considered. Lastly, we get the best accuracy under all conditions, when the information in both the channels are used together i.e. $\alpha = 0.5$ and $\beta = 0.5$. The choice of Top 7 samples from 1st channel gives us a larger set of samples to extract refined Top 3 results (Fig. 2).

Table 1. Top 3 Match Accuracy vs Feature Space Dimension

Features#	(α,β)	Datasets					
		Orig	BC-HSV	BC-HSV-1P	BC-HSV-2P	BC-HSV-3P	BC-HSV-4P
576	OLFS	1352	1303	1069	807	610	469
27	(1, 0)	1176	1127	796	662	558	488
	(0, 1)	1124	1101	850	720	586	535
	(0.5, 0.5)	1153	1131	854	721	599	541
63	(1, 0)	1384	1319	1008	882	724	645
	(0, 1)	1310	1290	1063	906	802	730
	(0.5, 0.5)	1360	1328	1082	929	814	733
112	(1, 0)	1429	1386	1053	892	731	629
	(0, 1)	1375	1348	1120	947	828	719
	(0.5, 0.5)	1419	1395	1142	951	837	718
261	(1, 0)	1475	1436	1141	951	762	646
	(0, 1)	1421	1409	1167	1019	889	782
	(0.5, 0.5)	1466	1442	1198	1024	896	783
376	(1, 0)	1480	1445	1150	973	789	670
	(0, 1)	1433	1402	1183	1033	900	812
	(0.5, 0.5)	1487	1449	1211	1047	903	806

In our case, the calculated value of the hurst exponent was 0.49 and thus the estimated analysis scaling (h_0) and wavelet (h_1) filters are:

$$h_0 \triangleq \begin{pmatrix} -0.0201 & 0.0201 & -0.2299 \\ 0.2299 & -0.2299 & -1.0000 \\ -0.0201 & 0.0201 & -0.2299 \end{pmatrix} \quad h_1 \triangleq \begin{pmatrix} -0.0201 & -0.2299 & -0.0201 \\ -0.2299 & 1.0000 & -0.2299 \\ -0.0201 & -0.2299 & -0.0201 \end{pmatrix} \quad (13)$$

Since we are aiming to develop a nonseparable wavelet filter bank, the quincunx sampling using the corresponding decimation matrices becomes the first choice. The two generating matrices leading to quincunx sampling lattice (Q_0 & Q_1) [7] would be used alternately at each level of wavelet decomposition using

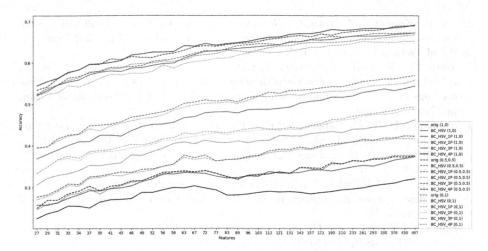

Fig. 2. Top 3 Accuracy for various (α, β) experimental setting over different dataset.

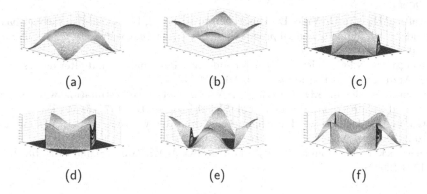

Fig. 3. Shapes of various Statistically Matched filters of the filter bank for (a)L (b)H (c)LL (d)LH (e)HL (f)HH subbands.

the statistically matched filters. and are defined as

$$Q_0 \triangleq \begin{bmatrix} 1 & -1 \\ 1 & 1 \end{bmatrix} Q_1 \triangleq \begin{bmatrix} 1 & 1 \\ -1 & 1 \end{bmatrix} \tag{14}$$

The shapes of the corresponding LL, HL, LH and HH subband wavelet filters are shown in Fig. 3.

References

1. Howard, A., et al.: Searching for mobilenetv3. In: Proceedings of the IEEE International Conference on Computer Vision, pp. 1314–1324 (2019)

2. Xu, H., Koppanyi, Z., Toth, C., Grejner-Brzezinska, D.: Indoor localization using region-based convolutional neural network. In: Proceedings of the 2017 International Technical Meeting of ION (2017)
3. Taira, H., Okutomi, M., Sattler, T., Cimpoi, M., Pollefeys, M., Sivic, J., et al.: InLoc: indoor visual localization with dense matching and view synthesis. In: Proceedings of the IEEE Conference on Computer Vision and Pattern Recognition, pp. 7199–7209 (2018)
4. Yi, K.M., Trulls, E., Lepetit, V., Fua, P.: LIFT: learned invariant feature transform. In: Leibe, B., Matas, J., Sebe, N., Welling, M. (eds.) ECCV 2016. LNCS, vol. 9910, pp. 467–483. Springer, Cham (2016). https://doi.org/10.1007/978-3-319-46466-4_28
5. DeTone, D., Malisiewicz, T., Rabinovich, A.: Superpoint: self-supervised interest point detection and description. In: CVPR Workshop on Deep Learning for Visual SLAM (2018)
6. Hager, P., Neuman, E.: The multiplicative chaos of $H = 0$ fractional Brownian fields. arXiv:2008.01385 (2020)
7. Feilner, M., Van De Ville, D., Unser, M.: An orthogonal family of quincunx wavelets with continuously-adjustable order. IEEE Trans. Image Process. **14**(4), 499–510 (2005)
8. Tafti, P.D., Van De Ville, D., Unser, M.: Invariances, Laplacian-like wavelet bases, and the whitening of fractal processes. IEEE Trans. Image Process. **18**(4), 689–702 (2009)
9. Kingsbury, N.: Complex wavelets for shift invariant analysis and filtering of signals. J. Appl. Comput. Harmonic Anal. **10**, 234–253 (2001)
10. Gupta, A., Joshi, S.D., Prasad, S.: A new method of estimating wavelet with desired features from a given signal. Signal Process. **85**, 147–161 (2005)
11. Gupta, A., Joshi, S.D.: Two-channel nonseparable wavelets statistically matched to 2-d images. Signal Process. **91**, 673–689 (2011)
12. Selesnick, I.: The double-density dual-tree dwt. IEEE Trans. Signal Proc. **53**, 1304–1314 (2004)

Compression of Large LSTM Networks for Inference on Space Constraint Systems

Suyash Saxena⬥, Varun Singh Negi(✉)⬥, and Kolin Paul

Indian Institute of Technology Delhi, Hauz Khas, New Delhi, India
suyash2896@gmail.com, varun.negi.varun@gmail.com

Abstract. In this paper, we propose a technique to compress the size of pre-trained LSTM and GRU models, which also improves their inference time. So that they can be deployed on space-constraint devices. We use KP-factorization (Kronecker Product factorization) to reduce the number of parameters that are used to compute the results, while improving inference time with little loss in accuracy. We take a pre-trained LSTM or GRU model and replace the weight matrix of each layer with its Nearest Kronecker Product Factors, which are smaller in size as compared to the original matrices. The difference between the original matrix multiplication and the Kronecker product is then adjusted using two sparse error matrices (we call them delta matrices) to reduce the loss in accuracy due to compression. These delta matrices are themselves reduced to NKP factors so as to save space. Once the compressed models are obtained then we retrain them on less than 40% of the original data and epochs to improve the accuracy of the compressed models. Compression up to a maximum of 185x and a speedup up to 5x was obtained. Experiments were performed on standard datasets like MNIST, PTB, WikiText, etc to demonstrate the effectiveness of our technique.

Keywords: LSTM · Space Compression · Runtime Efficient · Kronecker Product

1 Introduction

Long Short-Term Memory (LSTM) and Gated Recurrent Unit (GRU) are known to produce great results for problems that use time series or any sequential form of data. So they are a great fit for applications like Human Activity Recognition [1], Heart Sound Classification [2], etc. These state-of-the-art models are generally large in size and very compute-intensive. Presently, these models are deployed over the cloud due to constraints. Hosting a model over the cloud has its own challenges such as data security (as each time the data has to be delivered to the cloud so that the communication channel is secure), channel latency, hosting charges, etc. Deploying such large models in resource constraint devices is often an issue. This motivates the need for effective model compression. This

P. Maji et al. (Eds.): PReMI 2023, LNCS 14301, pp. 137–146, 2023.
https://doi.org/10.1007/978-3-031-45170-6_15

is also relevant as some of the challenges listed above are mitigated by deploying the model on edge devices.

As matrix multiplication is the key operation in LSTMs, we make use of Kronecker Products (KP) to compress the size of these models. Our approach is to compress pre-trained models so that they can produce effective results with meager retraining and a little drop in accuracy. The technique that we have used is capable of compressing models up to $185\times$ in size and up to $5\times$ in runtime. Our method is efficient as we use less than 40% of the data and epochs for retraining. The entire network then operates with the help of a custom LSTM layer that we have designed whose purpose is to convert the matrices that are being used in LSTM networks to their Nearest Kronecker Product (NKP), we reduce the conversion error with the help of delta matrices and use KP for forward propagation along with matrix multiplication on these smaller matrices. Once the models are compressed we convert them to Open Neural Network Exchange (ONNX) format, so that it can be readily used on edge devices.

1.1 Kronecker Product

The KP of $A \in R^{a_1 * b_1}$ and $B \in R^{a_2 * b_2}$ is represented as $C = A \otimes B$

$$
C = \begin{bmatrix}
a_{11} \circ B & a_{12} \circ B & \dots & a_1 b_1 \circ B \\
a_{21} \circ B & a_{22} \circ B & \dots & a_2 b_1 \circ B \\
. & . & . & . \\
. & . & . & . \\
a_{a_1 1} \circ B & a_{a_1 2} \circ B & \dots & a_{a_1 b_1} \circ B
\end{bmatrix}
$$

where A and B are said to be the Kronecker factors of $C \in R^{a \times b}$ where $a = a_1 \times a_2$ and $b = b_1 \times b_2$, $\circ$ is Hadamard Product. It can be observed that a large matrix C is represented using the Kronecker Product of two small matrices A and B.

1.2 Nearest Kronecker Product (NKP)

Given a large matrix C if we can factorize it into its Kronecker factors then it is possible to compress the neural network. The nearest Kronecker Product (NKP) gives us two matrices whose Kronecker Product is closest to the given matrix as it isn't always possible to obtain exact factorization.

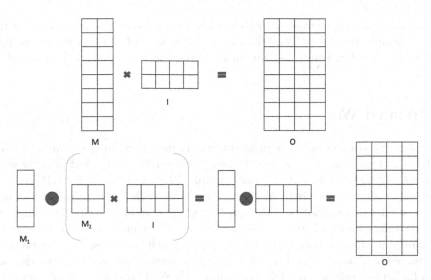

Fig. 1. Weight and Input matrix multiplication and Kronecker factors and input matrix multiplication

To compute the NKP factors of a matrix, we solve:

min $||M - M_1 \otimes M_2||_F$ where F is Frobenius Norm

Solution of this equation by Van Loan and Pitsianis (1993) [3] as:

$$arg \underset{M_1,M_2}{inf} \quad ||M - M_1 \otimes M_2||_F = arg \underset{M_1,M_2}{inf} \quad ||R(M) - vecM_1(vecM_2)^T||_F$$

where R(M) is a rearrangement of M in a block stack manner i.e., each block of matrix A is vertically stacked and so it is in the same manner as a vectorized product of M_1 and M_2. This is a 1-ranked approximation of the R(A) and we can get $M_1 and M_2$ by obtaining the leading singular vectors from the equation. It is to be noted that this is a lossy decomposition.

As an example take two matrices A and B each of size n × n

Now if A = $a_1 \otimes a_2$ and B = $b_1 \otimes b_2$ and a_1, a_2, b_1, b_2 each be of size $\sqrt{n} \times \sqrt{n}$ where a_1, a_2 are Kronecker factors of A and b_1, b_2 are Kronecker factors of B, then

$$A * B = (a_1 \otimes a_2) * (b_1 \otimes b_2)$$
$$= (a_1 * b_1) \otimes (a_2 * b_2) \qquad (Using \ Mixed \ sum \ property)(1)$$

The time complexity of $a_i * b_i = \mathcal{O}(n^{\frac{3}{2}})$ (matrix multiplication $\mathcal{O}(n^3)$ where n is replaced by $\sqrt{n}$)

The time complexity of $\otimes = \mathcal{O}(n^2)$

So total time complexity

$$= \mathcal{O}(n^{\frac{3}{2}} + n^{\frac{3}{2}} + n^2)$$
$$= \mathcal{O}(n^2)$$

We have used this property of Kronecker Products as it was observed in the above example that it reduces the size and number of operations to produce results of exact dimensions as standard matrix multiplication in the context of LSTM.

2   Related Work

The use of KPs differs from the most commonly used technique i.e., quantization [4]. KPs have been used in the deep learning community in the past [5]. Our work focuses on LSTM [6] and GRU [7] For example, Zhou and Wu [8] use KPs to compress fully connected layers in AlexNet. They start with a pre-trained model and use a low-rank decomposition technique to find the sum of KPs that best approximate the fully connected layer. KPs have been used for compressing sequence models before but such models were created from scratch as opposed to compressing pre-trained models [U. Thakker] [9]. We deviate from Zhou and Wu as we develop the solution for sequence models, not vanilla ANNs. Therefore generalizing it for all sequence models. Moreover, we are introducing delta matrices to stabilize the network error. So we are using two extra sparse matrices. The creation of delta matrices does not affect the training in any manner and does not require any user input as opposed to previous related work in LSTM compression. Although the delta matrices are trained at each training step it doesn't require modification of training method. The paper used Kronecker Product comparison with the help of delta matrices but the approach is quite different than used in [10]. They use it for CNN (Convolutional Neural Networks) and person re-identification. As the paper focuses on the inference part of the LSTM the approach is orthogonal to Mealy's paper [11] where they deal with quantization followed by binarization which is done specifically for FPGAs.

3   Custom LSTM Layer

A deep learning model has many layers and functions embedded into it. Now as we are compressing pre-trained LSTM models, so our first step is to extract all the parameters of all the LSTM layers of the model and then construct a new model with our Custom LSTM layers (layer capable of performing Kronecker Product) in place of the original layers. As the basis of all neural network calculations are matrices we replace these matrices to a non-conventional form. In order to replace matrices they are decomposed into NKP factors. NKP basically generates the factor matrices whose Kronecker Product is closest to the matrix that was decomposed. For e.g.: if $NKP(A) = B,C$ then $B \otimes C + X = A$, where X is a residual matrix.

Algorithm 1. Algorithm 1: Replacing original matrices with Kronecker matrices

---

Require: *Pre − trained LSTM model with concerned matrices of size $x1 \times x2$*
  $L \leftarrow All\ LSTM\ layers\ of\ the\ model$
  while *index $\leq$ length(L)* **do**
    $M_1, M_2 \leftarrow NKP(L_{ih}[index])$ ▷ NKP factorization of input-hidden
    $D_1 \leftarrow L_{ih}[index] - M_1 \otimes M_2$ ▷ delta matrix input-hidden
    $Q_1, Q_2 \leftarrow NKP(D_1)$ ▷ NKP factorization of delta input-hidden
    $D_2 \leftarrow L_{ih}[index] - (M_1 \otimes M_2 + Q_1 \otimes Q_2)$ ▷ second delta matrix of input-hidden
    $Q_3, Q_4 \leftarrow NKP(D_2)$ ▷ NKP factorization of second delta input-hidden
    $W_1, W_2 \leftarrow NKP(L_{hh}[index])$ ▷ NKP factorization of hidden-hidden
    $D_1 \leftarrow L_{hh}[index] - W_1 \otimes W_2$ ▷ delta matrix hidden-hidden
    $WQ_1, WQ_2 \leftarrow NKP(D_1)$ ▷ NKP factorization of delta hidden-hidden
    $D_2 \leftarrow L_{hh}[index] - (W_1 \otimes W_2 + WQ_1 \otimes WQ_2)$ ▷ second delta matrix of hidden-hidden
    $WQ_3, WQ_4 \leftarrow NKP(D_2)$ ▷ NKP factorization of second delta hidden-hidden
  end while

Algorithm 2. Algorithm 2: Forward Propagation

Require: *Model with matrices of LSTM layer replaced by Kronecker Product*
  $L \leftarrow All\ LSTM\ layers\ of\ the\ model$
  $I \leftarrow Input\ matrix$
  $H \leftarrow Last\ Hidden\ state$
  while *index $\leq$ length(L)* **do**
    $M_1 \otimes (M_2 \cdot I) + Q_1 \otimes (Q_2 \cdot I) + Q_3 \otimes (Q_4 \cdot I) + W_1 \otimes (W_2 \cdot H) + WQ_1 \otimes (WQ_2 \cdot H) +$
    $WQ_3 \otimes (WQ_4 \cdot H)$ ▷ Applying Mixed sum property as given in (1)
  end while

The algorithms are concentrated on the inference part of the network.

4 Methodology

To compress LSTM models we started with a simple Time series LSTM-based model trained on airline passengers dataset. We performed multiple experiments on this model such as using only NKP for decomposing weight matrices, the addition of delta matrices, and retraining of compressed model, etc. The problem of compressing an LSTM model hinges on representing weight matrices in the form of smaller decomposed matrices. As seen in Fig. 1, M is the original weight matrix and M1, M2 are decomposed matrices (using NKP) then M-(M1 $\otimes$ M2) should be as small as possible, where $\otimes$ is the Kronecker product operator.

After multiple tests it was observed that this method leads to the loss of vital information which we termed as "factorization loss" and due to this loss, the compressed model was not able to fit data correctly (as can be seen in the following plots) (Fig. 2).

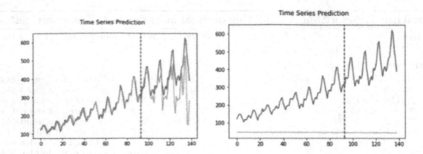

Fig. 2. Before and After NKP; Orange Line - Predicted Value; Blue Line - Actual Value (Color figure online)

4.1   NKP with Delta Matrices

"Factorization loss" happens as the decomposition of the weight matrix into Kronecker factors is lossy. To deal with it there are methods such as the "sum of Kronecker products" representation and we used a similar idea with some modifications. To deal with factorization loss, we decided to identify residual matrix (D) which was calculated as: $D = M - (M1 \otimes M2)$ And then we decomposed D into D1 and D2. We termed these matrices Delta matrices. We later found that with 2 sets of delta matrices, we were able to fit data better. $M' = (M1 \otimes M2) + (D11 \otimes D12) + (D21 \otimes D22)$

These delta matrices are used to produce output, by using the mixed product property of Kronecker Products and the distributive property of matrix multiplication, without having the need to generate M' before multiplying it with I. Also, the size of D11 and D21 is the same as M1, and the size of D12 and D22 is the same as M2.

After multiple tests, it was found that the model with delta matrices fit data better than the original NKP model but it still couldn't fit data as well as the original model (as can be seen in the following plot) (Fig. 3).

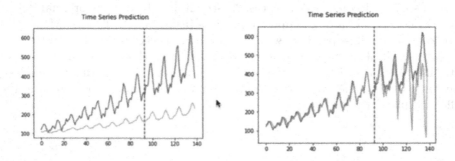

Fig. 3. Without and with retraining; Orange Line - Predicted Value; Blue Line - Actual Value (Color figure online)

4.2   Retraining NKP with Delta Matrices

The above images show that after introducing delta matrices, the compressed model couldn't fit data as well as the original model because decomposition is still lossy i.e.

$$\| \, M - (M1 \otimes M2) + (D11 \otimes D12) + (D21 \otimes D22) \, \| \geq 0$$

A few experiments showed that retraining the compressed model on some parts of the data and for fewer epochs resulted in the compressed model showing similar performance as the original model.

4.3   Factorisation Factor (FF)

The above methods were found to be effective for smaller models but as the number of trainable parameters increased performance loss started to increase with the high level of compression. To handle this, a factorization factor (FF) was introduced which enabled users to improve performance by adjusting compression. FF values range from 1 to layer size, with 1 indicating maximum compression.

Due to the FF parameter, a trade-off can be introduced between model compression and compressed model performance to work with larger models as well.

We tested on a Human Activity Recognition model, with FF as 8, and found that the compressed model's performance was marginally lower than the original model.

Model	Accuracy	Size
Original	84.23	194 KB
Compressed	84.09	32 KB

5   Results

To test the effectiveness of our methodology, we performed multiple experiments on models trained on real-world dataset.

5.1   Text Generation

A pre-trained text generation model with 16M trainable parameters in LSTM layers was compressed to 36K parameters in Custom LSTM layers (Fig. 4).

```
==================================================          ==================================================
Layer (type:depth-idx)              Param #                 Layer (type:depth-idx)              Param #
==================================================          ==================================================
LSTM2                                                       LSTM
├─Embedding: 1-1                    30,180,352              ├─Embedding: 1-1                    30,180,352
├─CustomLSTM: 1-2                   36,864                  ├─LSTM: 1-2                         16,793,600
├─Linear: 1-3                       30,209,825              ├─Linear: 1-3                       30,209,825
├─Dropout: 1-4                      --                      ├─Dropout: 1-4                      --
==================================================          ==================================================
Total params: 60,427,041                                    Total params: 77,183,777
Trainable params: 60,427,041                                Trainable params: 77,183,777
Non-trainable params: 0                                     Non-trainable params: 0
==================================================          ==================================================
```

Fig. 4. Before and After Compression

For retraining, multiple tests were run by selecting part of the dataset used for training and reducing the number of epochs. This experiment was started with 2 sets of delta matrices for input-hidden weights and hidden-hidden weights. Figure 5a shows the results with the setup mentioned above.

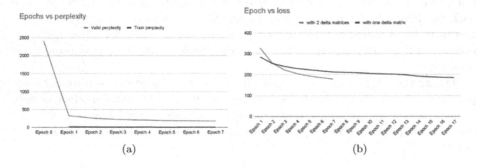

(a)   (b)

Fig. 5. a) Epochs and corresponding Loss after training b)Epochs and corresponding Loss comparison between 1 and 2 sets of delta matrices

Challenges with 2 sets of delta matrices setup include increased model size leading to a drop in compression rate, increased training time, and increased inference time which isn't ideal. To avoid this, we tried several FFs which improved run time and compression rate slightly but affected performance badly. Another experiment with just 1 set of delta matrices revealed that another set of delta matrices was redundant as with few more epochs runtime and compression rate improved without affecting the performance. A comparison can be seen in Fig. 5b.

It was also observed that a 5x speed up in run time was achieved.

A few more experiments, with only 1 set of delta matrices and only some part of the dataset available, and fewer epochs, were conducted and results were observed on the same lines and this can be seen in Table 1.

5.2   Pip Installable Library

We have packaged our approach and deployed it as a pip installable library that can compress PyTorch LSTM models. Conversion functions of the library can identify LSTM layers in a model and then convert them to Custom LSTM layers which perform compression operations on the model's LSTM layers and support forward propagation using Kronecker product operations (Table 2).

Table 1. More results

Model	Compression	Original Model Performance	Compressed Model Performance
Human Activity Recognition [1]	6×	84.23%	84.06%
MNIST classification [12]	20×	99.4%	98.29%
RUL (Remaining useful life) [13]	12×	25 RMSE	26 RMSE
Heart Sound classification [2]	3×	82%	81%
PTB language model [14]	38×	98 perplexity	125 perplexity
Text generation	182×	93 perplexity	147 perplexity

Table 2. Comparison of performance drop with respect to uncompressed model performance along with compression rate

Model	Our Approach	LMF	Magnitude Pruning	DKP	HKP
MNIST classification [12]	1.1% (20×)	2% (13×) [9]	2.9% (16.7×) [9]	–	1% (17×) [9]
PTB language model [14]	27.5% (46×)	31.7% (20×) [15]	28% (20×) [15]	1% (25×) [15]	21.7% (20×) [15]

6 Conclusion and Future Work

We have shown that LSTMs and GRUs can be compressed up to a great extent in size (tested until 185×) and over 5 times in speed. So that they can be deployed at space and energy-constraint edge devices. We have developed a library using PyTorch that is fully capable of compressing pre-trained sequence models. We have experimented with it on various language models, human-activity recognition, medical models, etc. All these models are relevant to edge devices. We have also benchmarked it against the standard MNIST dataset and received satisfactory results.

Our library is currently capable of compressing pre-trained LSTM and GRU models in PyTorch. We have also developed the codebase for converting these PyTorch models to ONNX (Open Neural Network Exchange). The advantage of converting these models to ONNX is, that after conversion to ONNX these models can be further converted to TFLite and TFLite is more easy to integrate on hardware platforms. Moreover, TFLite can also be run on STM32 microcontrollers. This strategy can be expanded to more complex deep learning architectures as well.

References

1. Chen, Y., Zhong, K., Zhang, J., Sun, Q., Zhao, X.: LSTM networks for mobile human activity recognition (2016)
2. Bentley, P., Nordehn, G., Coimbra, M., Mannor, S.: The PASCAL classifying heart sounds challenge 2011 (CHSC2011) results (2011). http://www.peterjbentley.com/heartchallenge/index.html
3. Van Loan, C.F., Pitsianis, N.: Approximation with Kronecker Products. In: Moonen, M.S., Golub, G.H., De Moor, B.L.R. (eds.) Linear Algebra for Large Scale and Real-Time Applications. NATO ASI Series, vol. 232, pp. 293–314. Springer, Dordrecht (1993). https://doi.org/10.1007/978-94-015-8196-7_17
4. Courbariaux, M., Hubara, I., Soudry, D., El-Yaniv, R., Bengio, Y.: Binarized neural networks: training deep neural networks with weights and activations constrained to +1 or −1 (2016)
5. Jose, C., Cisse, M., Fleuret, F.: Kronecker recurrent units (2017)
6. Hochreiter, S., Schmidhuber, J.: Long short-term memory. Neural Comput. 9(8), 1735–1780 (1997)
7. Cho, K., van Merrienboer, B., Gülçehre, Ç., Bougares, F., Schwenk, H., Bengio, Y.: Learning phrase representations using RNN encoder-decoder for statistical machine translation. CoRR, abs/1406.1078 (2014)
8. Zhou, S., Wu, J.-N.: Compression of fully-connected layer in neural network by kronecker product. CoRR, abs/1507.05775 (2015)
9. Thakker, U., et al.: Compressing RNNs to kilobyte budget for IoT devices using kronecker products. J. Emerg. Technol. Comput. Syst. 17(4), 1–18 (2021)
10. Shen, Y., Xiao, T., Li, H., Yi, S., Wang, X.: End-to-end deep kronecker-product matching for person re-identification (2018)
11. Mealey, T., Taha, T.M.: Accelerating inference in long short-term memory neural networks. In: NAECON 2018 - IEEE National Aerospace and Electronics Conference, pp. 382–390 (2018)
12. Deng, L.: The MNIST database of handwritten digit images for machine learning research. IEEE Signal Process. Mag. 29(6), 141–142 (2012)
13. Zheng, S., Ristovski, K., Farahat, A., Gupta, C.: Long short-term memory network for remaining useful life estimation. In: 2017 IEEE International Conference on Prognostics and Health Management (ICPHM), pp. 88–95 (2017)
14. Zaremba, W., Sutskever, I., Vinyals, O.: Recurrent neural network regularization (2015)
15. Thakker, U., Whatamough, P., Mattina, M., Beu, J.: Compressing language models using doped kronecker products (2020)

Deep Adaptive Pix-2-Pix Conditional Generative Adversarial Networks for Semantic Segmentation of Medium Resolution Google Earth Imagery

Bhuvanagiri V. Hari Priya$^{(\boxtimes)}$ and B. Sirisha

Maturi Venkata Subba Rao (MVSR) Engineering College, Hyderabad, India
bharipriya2498@gmail.com

Abstract. Land cover analysis using aerial images is vital for understanding how abiotic and biotic components are clustered on the earth's
surface. This research paper primarily focuses on the semantic segmentation of aerial remote sensing images using proposed adaptive Pix2Pix
conditional generative adversarial networks. The network model architecture contains a generator phase with a modified U-Net architecture. A
discriminator characterized by a convolutional PatchGAN as a classifier.
On the generator side, we replaced the backbone of the standard U-Net
feature extractor with two classical deep feature extractors, ResNet34
and InceptionNet-V3. The paper experimentally compares the effect of
modified Unets in Pix2Pix Conditional Generative Adversarial Nets for
semantic segmentation of aerial imagery for land cover application. A
comparison is made between the standard Pix2Pix GAN and the proposed adaptive Pix2Pix cGAN. Google Earth images are used to create
the dataset. The experimental results are evaluated and compared using
metrics like Root Mean Square Error (RMSE) and Structural Similarity Index (SSIM). The results signify that the proposed adaptive model
built using U-Net with Inception-Net: V3 backbone as Generator Pix2Pix
cGAN as Discriminator outperforms the standard approach, giving an
RMSE of 0.062 and an SSIM of 0.513. The subjective evaluation and
objective (visual) analysis both conclude that the proposed adaptive
pix2pix cGAN approach is accurate for the semantic segmentation of
aerial images.

Keywords: Semantic Segmentation · Generative Adversarial
Networks(GAN) · U-Net · Patch-GAN · Land Cover

1   Introduction

Aerial image classification is one of the most prominent applications of remote
sensing and photogrammetry. It is the prerequisite for several application
fields like land use and land cover analysis (LULC) [1,2], vegetation classification, determination of water bodies, disaster monitoring, change detection,

P. Maji et al. (Eds.): PReMI 2023, LNCS 14301, pp. 147–156, 2023.
https://doi.org/10.1007/978-3-031-45170-6_16

urban planning, etc. Most of the photogrammetry and remote sensing imagery employed for land cover classification is possessed by passive and active sensors. These sensors produce images of varied resolutions of hyper-spectral or multi-spectral bands [3].

Over a decade traditional Machine learning (ML) algorithm has played a key role in remote sensing image classification with high performance. ML algorithms like maximum likelihood estimator, decision tree, K-nearest neighbor, support vector machine and random forest, etc., can be employed for object-based and pixel-based classification of low resolution [4,5] and medium-resolution imagery [6,7]. Deep learning (DL) approaches have recently attracted a tonne of researchers for automatically classifying medium and high resolution remote sensing imagery. These algorithms are invariant to geometric deformations, and photometric variations and can manage the complexity of remote sensing imagery features and big data glitches. Deep Learning Algorithms in remote sensing have been successfully applied to image processing (Fusion, Registration, Segmentation [8,9]), change detection, accuracy assessment, and classification (Land cover/Land use classification), scene classification, and object recognition). In this research article, we explore the fitness of GANs to land cover classification (classes include: water, forest, bare soil, snow, deciduous grassland, etc.) This paper primarily focuses on the semantic segmentation of water bodies, bare soil, and deciduous forest from aerial imagery using proposed adaptive Pix2Pix conditional generative adversarial networks (Adaptive P2PcGAN). The network model architecture consists of modified U-Net architecture as a generator which is an auto-encoder with hop connections. This block of the network is capable of generating synthetic images alike to ground truth images. The discriminator is characterized by PatchGAN, which splits the input ground truth image and generated synthetic image into grids of patches and predicts the probability of each pixel class. The research contributions are twofold:

1. Adaptive Pix2Pix conditional generative adversarial networks are developed to automatically discriminate from numerous distinctive land cover classes.
2. A modified version of the UNet algorithm was built and employed as a generator in Adaptive Pix2Pix cGAN.

The experimental study establishes the competence of GANs for semantic segmentation of satellite imagery. The proposed approach is compared with the standard segmentation model. The rest of the paper is organized as follows. Section 2 focuses on related work, proposed method with step by step description of each module is given in Sect. 3. Section 4 discusses the dataset, evaluation metrics, and experimental results obtained. Lastly, Sect. 5 concludes the paper.

2   Related Work

In 2021 Zhifeng Zhang [10], employed the UC Merced land use dataset for classification using CaffeNet, VGG-S, and VGG-F CNN models. It is observed that multi-structured feature cascaded CNN models outperformed. Kotaridis (2021) explored metadata analysis of remote sensing imagery segmentation [11]. They analyzed statistical and quantitative pixel data from the segmentation algorithm and experimentally concluded that DL approaches work very well on complex imagery with a high spatial resolution (25 cm–10 m). High-resolution imagery is very expensive and will cover only a narrow area range. The authors recommended using medium-resolution (10–100 m) imagery for LC classification. Megharani. B (2021) compared five machine learning algorithms Random Forest, Minimum Distance, Gradient Tree Boost, Naïve Bayes, and CART for Land cover classification [12]. The landsat-8 dataset is used. Random Forest (72%) outperformed other classifiers. Le'an Qu(2021) employed random Forest and Recursive Feature Elimination (RFE) for performing pixel-based classification and K-means, G-means, and Simple Non-Iterative(SNIC) Clustering for Object-based classification. It is observed that object-based classification (96.01%) outperformed pixel-based (94.20%). Mengmeng Li (2020) explored graph-based convolutional networks and graph-based kernels to MAP Land Use from high-resolution aerial imagery. It is observed that graph convolutional networks outperformed the graph kernel-based approach [13]. In 2019 Poliyapram et al., segmented ice, water bodies, and land from a Landsat-8 Medium resolution imagery using a variant of U-Net Deep-CNN. The proposed model outpaced DeepWaterMap and the standard U-Net model [14]. In 2020 Victor [15] used Landsat 5/7 multispectral satellite imagery for LULC analysis. Resnet 101(88.25%) model outperformed FCN-Google LeNet (62.13%). Ali Jamali (2019) compared eight machine learning algorithms Random Forest, Decision Table, DTNB, J48, Lazy IBK, Multilayer Perceptron, Non-Nested Generalized Exemplars (NN ge), and Simple Logistic for LULC classification. Landsat 8 OLI/TIRS Level-2 image dataset is used. Non-Nested Generalized Exemplars outperformed other classifiers [16]. In our paper, we employed an adaptive Pix2Pix cGAN model with modified U-Net to perform semantic segmentation of remote sensing satellite imagery. The backbone-modified UNet is employed in the generator module and PatchGAN in the discriminator module.

3 Proposed Adaptive Pix2Pix cGAN Network Architecture

The proposed adaptive Pix2Pix cGAN network architecture intends to segment urban areas, water bodies, and forest features over medium spatial resolution aerial imagery from Google Earth. The proposed architecture inherits four stages to learn the extracted features and semantically segment the intricacy of land cover types. Stage-1: Dataset Preparation; Stage-2: Generator network module; Stage-3: Pix2Pix cGAN discriminator; Stage-4:Adversarial deep training.

3.1 Stage-1: Dataset Preparation

The dataset, comprises 1096 medium-resolution satellite imagery collected from Google Earth with a train-test split ratio of 0.8 (i.e., 876 images for training and

220 testing images). The geographical locations are specific regions of Gujarat, India. The images were obtained from Google Earth at a resolution of 1036 by 748, with a spatial resolution of about 50 m. Using Envi software, ground truth maps for the generated dataset were created. In ENVI, gold standard or ground truth data points are generated. The region of interest is converted to a polygon shapefile. In ArcMap the polygon file is converted to a point file and XY data points are added. This attribute table is exported and converted to kml file.

3.2   Stage-2: Generator Network Module

An image of 256*256 is fed into the generator G of the adaptive pix2pix CGAN architecture network, which produces a semantically segmented image. The Generator network uses the modified U-Net architecture, which uses residual networks as the backbones at both the encoder and decoder stages. In this research work, we experimentally determine an appropriate network model (U-Net or LinkNet) and its residual networks (backbones) to be used in the generator network. **U-Net:** Two components make up the fully convolutional neural network architecture known as U-Net. The feature extraction path makes up the first component, and the upsampling path makes up the second. The feature extraction path, sometimes referred to as the encoder, is made up of a number of layers that downsample the input image by extracting the features at each layer and producing a high-resolution feature map. While the decoder path, also known as the up-sampling path, uses skip connections to upsample the image of the feature map. These additional skip connections that are introduced from the encoder to the decoder, or across the feature map (bottleneck), can significantly increase the performance of the model. Firstly, we modified the U-Net architecture model with different backbones at the encoder and decoder paths. The backbones that we are introducing are Resnet34 and InceptionV3.

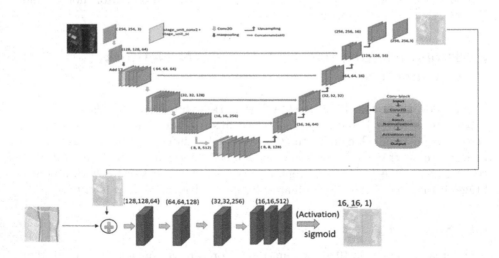

Fig. 1. Generator and Discriminator Network Architecture for Adaptive Pix2Pix cGAN

The Fig. 1 shows Generator Architecture for Adaptive Pix2Pix cGAN. The input data dimension of 256×256 pixels are fed to the first convolutional layer and convolutes with 64 filter banks. This layer learns and detects the prominent features using deep convolution. The output of this first layer is fed to the second convolution layer to increase the learning potential from varied feature dimensions with help of max-pooling algorithm. This algorithm will compress the feature map to $128 \times 128 \times 64$ dimension. This compression procedure further decreases the parameters of learning. Three more Convolution layers are applied to the extracted learning features. The number of filters employed are increased to enhance the learning potential of the features. The last convolutional layer feature map of dimension $8 \times 8 \times 512$ is maxpooled to compress the feature map to $8 \times 8 \times 128$ dimension. This output is applied to an upsampling algorithm for feature map enlargement in the decoder side to $16 \times 16 \times 64$ pixels. These generated feature maps will be fed to three convolution layers to the last decoder layer of this proposed modified U-Net architecture. The output synthetically generated image will be of dimension 256×256.

3.3   Stage-3: Pix2Pix cGAN Discriminator Network Module

To validate whether the generator has correctly segmented, satellite images are provided to the discriminator of Pix2Pix cGAN along with their segmented variants (ground truth). The Fig. 1 shows PatchGAN Discriminator. It seeks to determine if each NxN patch in the created image is real or fake by taking two images into consideration-one actual and the other generated by the generator. Convolutionally applying this discriminator to the image and averaging all replies yields the desired result. Updated the architecture to accept a pair of images-one ground truth and one produced by the U-Net generator-and to extract features from them using a PatchGAN discriminator in a CGAN with a modified U-Net generator. Employed convolution blocks, which incorporate a convolutional layer, batch normalisation, and an activation function, in our discriminator model D. Except for the second-to-last layer, which has a stride of 1, all convolutional layers are executed with a kernel size of 4 and a stride of 2. Leaky Relu is the activation function in use here. A dense layer with a sigmoid activation function is fed the output of the final convolutional layer after it has been flattened, and it produces a scalar value that represents the likelihood that the input image is real. Adam optimizer with a low learning rate 0.0002 and 0.5 beta is used to train the model with a batch size of one image.

3.4   Stage-4: Adversarial Deep Training

From the input image, the generator first creates an image. The Mean Absolute Error (L1 loss) between the input and target images is then calculated and multiplied by λ. We shall compute the cross entropy loss between the output of the discriminator and the matrix of 1. Because the purpose of the generator is to produce images that resemble real ones or to confuse the discriminator. A final loss function will be produced by adding the two losses. Gradients will be computed, and the generator's weights will be computed in accordance. The weights of the discriminator are updated in the following step. Because the discriminator is learning to distinguish between original real images and fake generated images, the original real image is compared to a matrix of all 1 s, and the fake generated image (the output of the generator) is compared to a matrix of all 0 s. The final loss function will be calculated by averaging the two. The same will be used to calculate gradients, and the updated weights of the discriminator will be based on that. The Eq.-1 can be used to model training mathematically.

$$L(\theta) = \frac{-1}{n} \Sigma_{j=1}^{n} [y^{(j)} log h(x^{(j)}, \theta) + (1 - y^{(j)}) log 1 - h(x^{(j)}, \theta)] \tag{1}$$

$$L(\theta) = -\iota_c GAN \tag{2}$$

$$Lc(\theta) = argmin_G max_D L(\theta) + \iota_{l1} GAN \tag{3}$$

The Binary Cross Entropy Loss (BCE loss), a fundamental learning equation for GAN, is shown in Eq. (1). Discriminator tries to minimize that equation whereas the generator tries to maximize it. The final equation, Eq. (3), is reached if we represent Eq. (1) as given in Eq. (2). Where $L(\theta)$ is the fundamental learning equation and $\iota_{l1} GAN$ is the L1 generator loss. The model is trained for varied learning rates (0.0002, 0.0003) and epochs. It is experimentally observed that the model performs better for 0.0002 learning rate for 10 epochs. ReLu activation function is employed at the hidden layers. The training hyperparameters utilized for the suggested architecture are detailed in Table 1.

Table 1. Training Hyperparameters

Hyperparameters	values
Batch size	1
Epochs	10
Generator	U-Net, Linknet
Generator Loss	Mae (mean absolute error)
G Activation function	Tanh
Discriminator	PatchGAN
Discriminator loss	Binary crossentropy
Discriminator Activation function	sigmoid
Learning rate	0.0002

4   Experimental Results and Discussion

This section presents the semantic segmentation outcomes generated by the proposed model. Mean square error (MSE) and structural similarity index measure (SSIM) were utilized to evaluate the proposed model and compare it to the standard approach. The activation and Loss functions used to train the proposed model are shown in Table 1. The model is trained for 10 epochs with batch size 1 and 0.0002 learning rate.

4.1   Results for Modified U-Net as Generator Pix2Pix cGAN as Discriminator:

Table 1 shows the mean square error(MSE) and SSIM recorded for standard Pix2Pix cGAN is 0.156 and 0.4839. Firstly experiments were conducted by replacing the feature extraction backbone of the U-Net is used in the Generator Network with Resnet34 and Inception-Net:v3 deep convolutional networks. It is observed that the average mean square error and SSIM recorded for modified U-Net with Inception-Net:V3 as backbone is 0.062 and 0.513 while for resnet34 as backbone is 0.118 and 0.426 (Tables 2 and 3)).

Table 2. Total number of instances generated for Angular rates parameters

Img.	Pix-2-Pix GAN		U-Net/Resnet-34		as U-Net/Inceptionv3	
	MSE	SSIM	MSE	SSIM	MSE	SSIM
Image 1	0.136	0.415	0.0023	0.391	0.305	0.388
Image 2	0.147	0.438	0.079	0.551	0.019	0.527
Image 3	0.154	0.51	0.1096	0.432	0.015	0.601
Image 4	0.2	0.283	0.2032	0.259	0.132	0.273
Image 5	0.125	0.641	0.022	0.49	0.018	0.64
Image 6	0.132	0.543	0.0373	0.501	0.025	0.57
Image 7	0.141	0.4707	0.209	0.432	0.013	0.55
Image 8	0.188	0.4601	0.07	0.343	0.004	0.516
Image 9	0.187	0.595	0.333	0.436	0.029	0.56
Average	0.156	0.4783	0.118	0.426	0.062	0.513

4.2   Results for Modified Link-Net as Generator Pix2Pix cGAN as Discriminator:

Experiments were conducted by replacing the U-Net with Link-Net with Resnet34 and Inception-Net:V3 as backbones. It is observed that the average mean square error and SSIM recorded for Link-Net as Generator with Inception-Net:V3 as the backbone is 0.085 and 0.481 while for resnet34 as the backbone

Table 3. Total number of instances generated for Angular rates parameters

Img.	Pix-2-Pix GAN		LINK-Net/Resnet-34		LINK-Net/Inceptionv3	
	MSE	SSIM	MSE	SSIM	MSE	SSIM
Image 1	0.136	0.415	0.0112	0.331	0.3177	0.34
Image 2	0.147	0.438	0.1299	0.477	0.0193	0.582
Image 3	0.154	0.51	0.1315	0.428	0.0583	0.546
Image 4	0.2	0.283	0.0804	0.176	0.2281	0.311
Image 5	0.125	0.641	0.2915	0.485	0.0256	0.625
Image 6	0.132	0.543	0.018	0.551	0.0499	0.56
Image 7	0.141	0.4707	0.0971	0.351	0.0406	0.37
Image 8	0.188	0.4601	0.0981	0.431	0.0066	0.476
Image 9	0.187	0.595	0.0968	0.417	0.0242	0.52
Average	0.156	0.4783	0.106	0.405	0.085	0.481

is 0.106 and 0.405. While comparing the three models we can conclude that modified U-Net with Inception-Net:V3 as backbone employed in Generator and Pix2Pix cGAN as Discriminator outperforms the other two models with minimum MSE (0.062) and maximum (0.513) SSIM.

Figure 2 shows the results of semantic segmentation using Pix2Pix model, Modified U-Net as Generator Pix2Pix cGAN as Discriminator and Link-Net as Generator Pix2Pix cGAN as Discriminator. It can be observed that the Pix2Pix-GAN model is unable to construct the segmented image, the result of Modified U-Net as Generator Pix2Pix cGAN as Discriminator is comparatively better than Link-Net as Generator Pix2Pix cGAN as Discriminator.

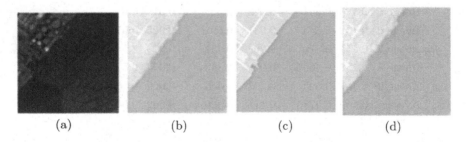

(a)   (b)   (c)   (d)

Fig. 2. a.Original Source Image b. Pix2Pix cGAN Segmented Image c. Segmented Image of Modified U-Net as Generator Pix2Pix cGAN as Discriminator d.Segmented Image of Link-Net as Generator Pix2Pix cGAN as Discriminator and Generated Data Signals of Parameters AR1 to AR5.

5   Conclusion

This study put forward deep learning based semantic segmentation algorithm to identify and extract land cover features using medium spatial resolution aerial Google earth imagery. The land cover dataset, which has three main classes (vegetation, urban, and water bodies) is envisioned for learning land cover feature patterns. The adaptive pix-2-pix cGAN architecture, which comprises U-Net with Inception-Net:V3 backbone as Generator Pix2Pix cGAN as Discriminator, is instigated for the supervised model. Multiple backbones (Resnet-34, InceptionNet-V3) are assessed for their performance to discriminate land cover. The results show that the performance of adaptive pix-2-pix cGAN outperforms standard pix-2-pix GAN deep learning algorithm. The proposed network architecture can identify, extract and classify land cover features accurately. It demonstrates improved performance compared to standard baseline network architectures in terms of error, similarity index assessments and segmentation results. The adaptive model can distinguish between vegetation, urban, and water bodies' features and can segment a narrow water bodies' precisely. For future works, time-series aerial data may possibly applied to improve the multiple viewpoint of land cover patterns.

References

1. Boonpook, W., et al.: Deep learning semantic segmentation for land use and land cover types using Landsat 8 imagery. ISPRS Int. J. GeoInf. **12**(1), 14 (2023). https://doi.org/10.3390/ijgi12010014
2. Singh, N.J., Nongmeikapam, K.: Semantic segmentation of satellite images using deep-UNet. Arab. J. Sci. Eng. **48**, 1193–1205 (2023). https://doi.org/10.1007/s13369-022-06734-4
3. Macarringue, L.S., Bolfe, É.L., Pereira, P.R.M.: Developments in land use and land cover classification techniques in remote sensing: a review. J. Geogr. Inf. Syst. **14**, 1–28 (2022). https://doi.org/10.4236/jgis.2022.141001
4. Anderson, J.R.: A Land Use and Land Cover Classification System for Use with Remote Sensor Data, USA (1976)
5. Senf, C., Hostert, P., van der Linden, S.: Using MODIS time series and random forests classification for mapping land use in South-East Asia (2012). https://doi.org/10.1109/IGARSS.2012.6352560
6. Amini, S., Saber, M., Rabiei-Dastjerdi, H., Homayouni, S.: Urban land use and land cover change analysis using random forest classification of landsat time series. Remote Sens. **14**(11), 2654 (2022). https://doi.org/10.3390/rs14112654
7. Qu, L.A., Chen, Z., Li, M., Zhi, J., Wang, H.: Accuracy improvements to pixel-based and object-based LULC classification with auxiliary datasets from google earth engine. Remote Sens. **13**(3), 453 (2021). https://doi.org/10.3390/rs13030453
8. Chaurasia, K., Nandy, R., Pawar, O., Singh, R.R., Ahire, M.: Semantic segmentation of high-resolution satellite images using deep learning. Earth Sci. Inf. **14**(4), 2161–2170 (2021). https://doi.org/10.1007/s12145-021-00674-7
9. Pranto, T.H., Noman, A.A., Noor, A., Deepty, U.H., Rahman, R.M.: Patch-wise semantic segmentation of sedimentation from high-resolution satellite images using

deep learning. In: Rojas, I., Joya, G., Catala, A. (eds.) IWANN 2021. LNCS, vol. 12861, pp. 498–509. Springer, Cham (2021). https://doi.org/10.1007/978-3-030-85030-2_41

10. Zhang, Z., Cui, X., Zheng, Q., Cao, J.: Land use classification of remote sensing images based on convolution neural network. Arab. J. Geosci. **14**(4), 1–6 (2021). https://doi.org/10.1007/s12517-021-06587-5

11. Kotaridis, I., Lazaridou, M.: Remote sensing image segmentation advances: a meta-analysis. ISPRS J. Photogrammetry Remote Sens. **173**, 309–322 (2021). https://doi.org/10.1016/j.isprsjprs.2021.01.020

12. Mayani, M.B., Itagi, R.: Machine learning techniques in land cover classification using remote sensing data. In: 2021 International Conference on Intelligent Technologies (CONIT) (2021). https://doi.org/10.1109/CONIT51480.2021.9498434

13. Li, M., Stein, A.: Mapping land use from high resolution satellite images by exploiting the spatia l arrangement of land cover objects. Remote sens. **12**(24), 4158 (2014). https://doi.org/10.3390/rs12244158

14. Poliyapram, V., Imamoglu, N., Nakamura, R.: Deep learning model for water/ice/land classification using large-scale medium resolution satellite images. In: IGARSS 2019–2019 IEEE International Geoscience and Remote Sensing Symposium, pp. 3884–3887 (2019). https://doi.org/10.1109/IGARSS.2019.8900323

15. Alhassan, V., Henry, C., Ramanna, S., Storie, C.: A deep learning framework for land-use/land-cover mapping and analysis using multispectral satellite imagery. Neural Comput. Appl. **32**(12), 8529–8544 (2019). https://doi.org/10.1007/s00521-019-04349-9

16. Jamali, A.: Evaluation and comparison of eight machine learning models in land use/land cover mapping using Landsat 8 OLI: a case study of the northern region of Iran. SN Appl. Sci. **1**(11), 1–11 (2019). https://doi.org/10.1007/s42452-019-1527-8

Fine-Grained Attribute-Object Feature Representation in Compositional Zero-Shot Learning

Nazir Shabbir[1], Ranjeet Kr. Rout[1(✉)], Saiyed Umer[2],
and Partha Pratim Mohanta[3]

[1] Department of CSE, National Institute of Technology, Srinagar, J&K, India
ranjeetkumarrout@nitsri.net
[2] Department of CSE, Aliah University, Kolkata, India
saiyed.umer@aliah.ac.in
[3] ECS Unit, Indian Statistical Institute, Kolkata, India
ppmohanta@isical.ac.in

Abstract. Compositional Zero-Shot Learning (CZSL) is designed to recognize unobserved (unseen) compositions of given objects (guava, orange, pear, etc.) and their states (sliced, peeled, ripe, etc.). The CZSL is challenging because it is sometimes difficult to separate the visual aspects of objects and states from their context in the images. In addition, the detailing feature of a state may vary considerably depending on its composition. For instance, the state *peeled* displays distinct visual characteristics in the *peeled apple* and *peeled guava* compositions. Existing research uses linguistic supervision and word embeddings to better segment and composes attribute-object relationships for recognition. We emphasize the visual embedding space and propose a Fine-grained Compositional Learning (FgCL) method capable of separating attributes from object features. We integrate visual fine-grained and Siamese-based features with word embedding into a shared embedding space that is representative of unseen compositions to learn our model more effectively. Extensive experiments are conducted and demonstrate a significant improvement over existing work (SymNet, TMN) on two benchmark datasets: MIT-States & UT-Zappos50K.

Keywords: Fine-grained · CZSL · Embedding space · Composition · Intra-class

1 Introduction

Humans can imagine and recognize Red Zebra creatures, even though they have never seen one in their lives. Compositionality is seen as an indicator of intelligence, beginning with Theaetetus [3] and extending to the early 19th century study of Frege [6]. The core assumption is that adding different simple concepts can create a more complex concept. Similarly, the concept of attributes

P. Maji et al. (Eds.): PReMI 2023, LNCS 14301, pp. 157–165, 2023.
https://doi.org/10.1007/978-3-031-45170-6_17

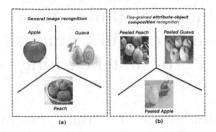

Fig. 1. Conventional Image recognition *versus* Fine-grained attribute-object composition recognition

and graphical methods representing Subject-verb-object (SVO) has been investigated in computer vision. The current state-of-the-art approach utilizes thousands of labeled samples to learn complex concepts instead of developing them from being composed. The collection of images in Fig. 1(a) contains images of apples, guava, and peach. An object recognition model would simply recognize a "apple" or "pear". However, it is challenging for a conventional image recognition model to distinguish between a peeled apple, peeled guava, and peeled peach, as shown in Fig. 1(b).

The concept of compositionality and contextuality are in conflict, and this can even be seen in philosophical debates. According to the contextuality principle, designing a simple concept without considering its context is impossible. It has frequently been cited as one of the primary arguments against adjectives (attributes), such as a peeled classifier in a peeled apple is notably distinct from a peeled classifier in a peeled pear or peeled guava, as shown in Fig. 1. A contradiction between compositionality and contextuality motivates a primary examination that will be conducted in this paper. It is to ask whether or not present vision models pose a compositional nature. Can we develop compositional spatial classifiers while still maintaining the notion of contextuality? One method for capturing context is using the text to determine the appropriate actions for modifiers. For instance, a modifier such as "peeled" should result in different visual alterations for correlated concepts such as "peeled apple" and "peeled guava". Text-based approaches [12] attempted to capture this concept and generate visual classifiers using text. However, it is necessary to use taxonomy and language-based knowledge [23] to acquire contextuality.

Compositional Zero-Shot Learning (CZSL) [7] consists of learning the compositionality of object-state pairs from training data to generalize to previously unseen combinations. In contrast to the conventional Zero-Shot Learning [13] approach, which uses intrinsic semantic representations to recognize unseen samples in test data, CZSL relies on transferable knowledge by using two compositional elements as image labels (objects and states). There are two common approaches: **(1)** In the first prevalent method [2], a single classifier is trained for recognition and transformation modules [16]. In [18], each state is represented as a linear transition of objects. In [25], a hierarchical representation of disentangled and compositional states-objects pair was proposed, and in [15], proposed a symmetrical model under attribute transitions. **(2)** In other approaches, [1] attempted to discover the joint representation of state-object pairs and intended to discover a modular network to rebuild new compositions based on the existing ones in [19] and [17] that establish the CZSL problems can be solved by employing causal graph methods. Moreover, both seen and unseen compositions consist of the same states and objects, and the domain gap between them could affect the model's efficiency.

Fine-grained-based feature recognition aims to extract the subtle and distinguish features among the classes. In [8], the pooling technique captures the interaction between discriminative feature maps. [22] proposed a superior method for learning global features that retain fine-grained details. An embedding function that integrates visual and semantic capabilities is proposed in [4] to handle unseen classes without training samples. Unseen classes are recognized depending on the distance between visual characteristics and unseen attribute representations. Zero-shot learning has been expanded in recent years by generative approaches [21] synthesizing features of unseen classes. Attention methods are introduced in [27] for zero-shot learning to extract finer descriptions. However, these works are intended for sequential input and inappropriate for image recognition. The organization of this paper is as follows: Sect. 2 describes our proposed methodology and the experimental setup with results and discussion have been demonstrated in Sect. 3. This work is concluded in Sect. 4.

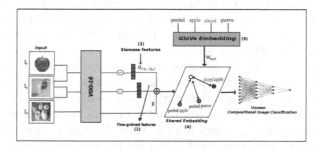

Fig. 2. Proposed FgCL architecture.

2   Proposed Method

In the proposed work, Compositional Zero-Shot Learning (CZSL) aims to identify unseen compositional samples wherein labels consist of a state such as "Red" and an object such as "Apple". In the CZSL framework, each image comprises two fundamental concepts, *i.e.* an object and a state. State-object pairs can be composed from $\mathcal{S}$ and $\mathcal{O}$, two sets of states and objects, $\mathcal{P} = \mathcal{S} \times \mathcal{O} = \{(s,o)|s \in \mathcal{S}, o \in \mathcal{O}\}$. In this research paper, we utilize the setup of ZSL [24] in which testing samples can be selected from seen or unseen compositions $(\mathcal{S}_s \cup \mathcal{S}_u)$, which is more difficult because of the larger prediction region and the bias towards seen compositions [19]. We assume that capturing the variation of visual features similarities and differences between image pairings of the full-view object (Apple) and attribute-modified object (Sliced-Apple) can lead to more effective use of attribute and object fine-grained visual features. Assembling these elements (fine-grained and siamese features) improves the recognition performance by helping to regularize the shared embedding space.

1. **Problem Formulation:-** Consider that I be an image with a class label l(attribute-object pair), $l=l_{a,o} \in L$, where l_a and l_o are the attribute and object label respectively. The data set is separated into seen pairs $l^s \in L^s$ and unseen pairs $l^u \in L^u$, where $L = L^s \cup L^u$ and $L^s \cap L^u = \emptyset$. However, $l^u = l_{a,o} \in L^u$ comprises of attribute l_a and object l_o that is never observed in training; they are only observed separately.

2. **Fine-grained Visual Features:-** To resolve the above problem formulation, a Fine-grained Compositional Learning (FgCL) architecture has been proposed (Fig. 2), where, from given an image I_a of a *peeled apple*, we additionally consider two more images: one I_f, a *full-view apple* with the same object as in I_a, and another one I_o, a *peeled guava* with the same attribute as in I_a. Here, **(1.)** the fine-grained feature extractor assembles the images (I_a, I_a) and extracts the f fine-grained feature vector using the $\odot$ (dot-product) layer, and **(2.)** the siamese-based feature extractor composes the images (I_a, I_f) and separates the $d_{(V_a - V_f)}$, 1-D feature vector using the $\ominus$ subtraction layer in the VGG-16 model. **(3.)** The GloVe word embeddings composes two word embeddings for attribute(peeled) and object(apple) and extract the compose word-feature vector $w_{(a,0)}$ for labels. **(4.)** Using the $\oplus$ operator, we integrate the $d_{(V_a - V_f)}$, f, g and $w_{(a,0)}$ and pass it to the 3-layer fully connected classification layers. To address the intra-class variation in the attribute modifier (Red in *Red-wine and Red-tomato*), the extraction of second-order texture information results in an improved **FgCL** proposed model with a better recognition rate. A dual VGG-16 model and a bilinear pooling layer are utilized to extract fine-grained features from I. After the final max-pooling layer, Z_1 and Z_2 can be represented by the feature maps of the two VGG-16 models. The bilinear pooling of Z_1 and Z_2 is formulated as $Q = Z_1 \cdot Z_2^\top$, and $\hat{Q} = \frac{sign(Q)\odot\sqrt{|Q|}}{||sign(Q)\odot\sqrt{|Q|}||_2}$, where Q is of dimension $c_1 \times c_2$. In general, bilinear representations are mapped from Riemannian manifolds into Euclidean spaces; the $\odot$ is an element-wise multiplication, square root transformation, and L2-normalization are used to minimize the effect of larger variance. Then $\hat{Q}$ is transformed into a feature vector and passed to fully connected layers for recognition.

3. **Siamese-based Visual Features:-** A proposed *FgCL* architecture to extract siamese-based visual features is composed of triple $R = (V_f, V_o, D)$, where V_f and V_o are feature-vector based on two symmetrical CNNs, D is a distance metric based on $\mathcal{D}_{V_f - V_o}$ function. A feature-vector function is a mapping function $V : \mathcal{P} \times \mathcal{I} \longrightarrow \mathbb{R}^{M \times N}$, that accepts an image-pair $(I_f, I_o) \in \mathcal{I}$ and a position $p \in \mathcal{P}$, and generates a feature of dimension $M \times N$ before

flattening into a *1-D vector*. A distance metric is employed to compute the transfer of variations from a full-view object(e.g., *Apple*) to an object-based image (e.g., *peeled Apple, sliced Apple*). The (variance-transfer) combination of V_f and V_o at any position is given in Eq. (1):

$$distance(p, I_f, I_o, V_f, V_o) = \mathcal{D}_{V_f - V_o} = V_f(p, I_f) \ominus V_o(p, I_o) \tag{1}$$

where $\ominus$ is the element-wise distance(subtraction) operator to calculate the transfer of variances from a full-view object image to an object-based image. V_f and V_o are generated with the following equation, as CNN_1 will generate the feature output as in Eq. (2)

$$V_f = \left\{ f(p_0^{I_f}, W_1), f(p_1^{I_f}, W_2), f(p_2^{I_f}, W_3) \cdots f(p_{l-1}^{I_f}, W_l) \right\} \tag{2}$$

Similarly, when an object-based image (I_o) passes through all layers, CNN_2 will generate the feature output as in Eq. (3)

$$V_o = \left\{ f(p_0^{I_o}; W_1), f(p_1^{I_o}; W_2), f(p_2^{I_o}; W_3) \cdots f(p_{l-1}^{I_o}; W_l) \right\} \tag{3}$$

where $p_0^{I_f}$ and $p_0^{I_o}$ represent the feature map generated at 0th layer from the image I_f and I_o, respectively.

4. **Word Embedding features:-** The word feature vector $w_o, w_a, w_{(o,a)}$ of object label o, attribute label a and attribute-object label *(o, a)* for the input image I are generated using [20]. It constructs word pair embedding by employing GloVe word embeddings as a feature extractor for *(o, a)* label.

5. **Unified Representation Learning:-** In this part, Unified Representation is constructed to produce discriminative features by modeling intra-class variation within the images. A flattened feature vector Q, $\mathcal{D}_{V_f - V_i}$, and $w_{(o,a)}$ are integrated with the concatenation operator and passed to the fully-connected layer block as input. Then a network will identify that specific indices (features) in the flattened vector correspond to the spatial map's specific locations of the object. The aggregate function $\mathcal{A}$ concatenates the Q, $w_{(o,a)}$, and features($\mathcal{D}_{V_f - V_i}$) generated by $\Psi(I_f, I_o, I_a) = \bigcup_{p \in \mathcal{P}} distance(p, I_f, I_o, V_f, V_o)$ $+\!\!+ Q(I_a, I_a) +\!\!+ w_{(o,a)}(W_o, W_a) = \bigcup_{p \in \mathcal{P}} (V_f(p, I_f) \ominus V_o(p, I_o)) +\!\!+ Q(I_a, I_a) +\!\!+ w_{(o,a)}(W_o, W_a)$, across all positions in the image to generate a global feature representation $\Psi(I_f, I_o, I_a)$, where $+\!\!+$ is a concatenation operator to aggregate variations within the images.

3 Experiments

Here, MIT-States [10] and UT-Zappos [26] benchmark datasets are employed to evaluate our methodology. MIT-States contains 53000 images containing 245 objects, 115 states, and 1252 are in compositions. The validation set consists of 300 compositions, while the test set contains 400 compositions. UT-Zappos is a fairly simple dataset with 16 states and 12 objects. The validation set consists of

15 unseen compositions, while the test set comprises 18 unseen compositions for 29000 images. These descriptions are demonstrated in Table 1. During implementation, the VGG-16 model is utilized to generate 512-dimensional feature vectors from the final max-pooling layer of each image. VGG-16 has been pre-trained on the ImageNet dataset. We train a three-layer fully-connected network with ReLU, LayerNorm, and Dropout while maintaining the feature extractor constant. While logistic regression is initially used to train the classifiers, stochastic gradient descent is used to fine-tune the entire network with parameters including a batch size of 16, momentum of 0.9, weight decay of 5×10^{-4}, and a learning rate of 10^{-3}. All experiments are conducted by using an NVIDIA Titan Xp GPU device with 64 GB RAM, NVIDIA- SMI 465.19.01 driver version, Python 3.7, Keras 2.4.3, CUDA-11.3, Tensorflow-2.4.1 in Linux-x86 64 and Intel Xeon(R) CPU E5-1650 v4 @ 3.60 GHz $\times$ 12 Processor. We adhere to the evaluation parameters proposed in [19]. Area Under Curve, Harmonic Mean, Seen Accuracy, and Unseen Accuracy are utilized to evaluate our methodology. The seen accuracy (SA) is computed on seen composition, while the unseen accuracy (UA) is computed on unseen compositions. Harmonic Mean (HM) is computed on $\frac{2 \ seen \ unseen}{seen+unseen}$ that calculates the average performance. Area Under Curve (AUC) is computed based on the variation within the seen and unseen composition.

Table 1. Datasets Description, Y_{seen} and Y_{unseen} are composition classes.

Datasets	Composition			Train		Validation			Test		
	A	O	$A \times O$	Y_{seen}	I	Y_{seen}	Y_{unseen}	I	Y_{seen}	Y_{unseen}	I
MIT-States	115	245	28175	1262	30338	300	300	10420	400	400	12995
UT-Zappos	16	12	192	83	22998	15	15	3214	18	18	2914

3.1 Results and Discussion

In Tables 2 and 3, we present the outcomes of our approach along with other competing methodologies applied to the MIT-States and UT-Zappos50K datasets. In Table 2, the AUC metric on the MIT-States dataset, our proposed method outperforms all other competing methods. However, compared to alternative methods on MIT-States, our proposed approach achieves results that are similar to or better than those of its competitive methods in terms of *seen composition* and *unseen composition* accuracy. Additionally, on metrics *Harmonic Mean(HM)*, our approach is also shown to outperform other competing methods. On the UT-Zappos50K dataset, Table 3 shows the AUC improvement is approximately 6.2% compared to SymNet [15], and it's anywhere from 0.8% to 4.4% range compared to other competitive methods. Compared to the two approaches TMN [18] and ymNet [15], our method achieves more or comparable results across the *seen and unseen composition* classes, while *Harmonic Mean(HM)* also improved by [0.4–3]% compared to other existing methods. Moreover, our method obtains better outcomes for all evaluation metrics on the UT-Zappos50K Dataset. As a

Table 2. Performance comparison on various metrics on MIT-States dataset.

Model	MIT-States			
	AUC	seen	unseen	HM
LabelEmbed+ [18]	2.0	15.0	20.1	10.7
AttrOpr [18]	1.6	14.3	17.4	9.9
TMN [19]	2.9	20.2	20.1	13.0
SymNet [15]	3.0	24.4	25.2	16.1
SCEN(with STM) [14]	3.9	22.5	21.9	13.3
Proposed Model	3.4	24.6	25.8	16.3

Table 3. Performance comparison on various metrics on UT-Zappos50K dataset.

Model	UT-Zappos50K			
	AUC	seen	unseen	HM
LabelEmbed+ [18]	25.7	53.0	61.9	40.6
AttrOpr [18]	25.9	59.8	54.2	40.8
TMN [19]	29.3	58.7	60.0	45.0
SymNet [15]	23.9	53.3	57.9	39.2
KG-SP(frozen backbone) [11]	22.9	58.0	47.2	39.1
SCEN(with CTS) [14]	26.4	60.0	61.2	44.2
Proposed Model	30.1	60.3	61.0	45.4

result, the proposed approach consistently attains well and, in many instances, outperforms the other baseline techniques on both datasets.

Here, we also experiment to validate the separate significance played by fine-grained and siamese feature representation in our proposed FgCL method, where the fine-grained visual-textual pattern produces discriminative *attribute* and *object* features to improve *unseen composition* classification. It creates sense in the context of the visual stream and then influences the entire approach. Tables 4 illustrate the effects of fine-grained visual embedding on visual-textual shared embedding space while a few examples of correct and incorrect classification results from the MIT States datasets are shown in Fig. 3.

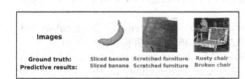

Images			
Ground truth:	Sliced banana	Scratched furniture	Rusty chair
Predictive results:	Sliced banana	Scratched furniture	Broken chair

Fig. 3. Results of correct classification (green) and incorrect classification (red) from MIT-States dataset. (Color figure online)

Table 4. Effects of fine grained and siamese features on Unseen composition.

Method (FgCL)	MIT- States	UT- Zappos 50K
Our approach	25.8	61
w/o fine-grained	22.3	57.2
w/o siamese	23.7	58.9
w/o fine-grained & siamese	20.4	56.6

4   Conclusions

Integrating fine-grained features and Siamese-based features and discovering an interaction between visual embedding and word embedding in a shared embedding space is the guiding principle of our methodology. In most instances, our approach outperforms the existing approaches on various parameters. In the future, we will attempt to modify our approach so that it can recognize multiple-states and single-object compositions, such as an apple that has been peeled and rotted.

References

1. Atzmon, Y., Kreuk, F., Shalit, U., Chechik, G.: A causal view of compositional zero-shot recognition. Adv. NIPS **33**, 1462–1473 (2020)
2. Biederman, I.: Recognition-by-components: a theory of human image understanding. Psychol. Rev. **94**(2), 115 (1987)
3. Bostock, D.: Plato's theaetetus (1991)
4. Changpinyo, S., Chao, W.L., Gong, B., Sha, F.: Synthesized classifiers for zero-shot learning. In: Proceedings of the IEEE Conference on CVPR, pp. 5327–5336 (2016)
5. Ding, Y., Zhou, Y., Zhu, Y., Ye, Q., Jiao, J.: Selective sparse sampling for fine-grained image recognition. In: Proceedings of the IEEE/CVF ICCV, pp. 6599–6608 (2019)
6. Frege, G.: Sense and reference. Psychol. Rev. **57**(3), 209–230 (1948)
7. Gu, Y., Deng, C., Wei, K.: Class-incremental instance segmentation via multi-teacher networks. In: Proceedings of AAAI Conference, vol. 35, pp. 1478–1486 (2021)
8. Hossain, S., Umer, S., Rout, R.K., Tanveer, M.: Fine-grained image analysis for facial expression recognition using deep convolutional neural networks with bilinear pooling. Appl. Soft Comput. **134**, 109997 (2023)
9. Huang, L., Wang, W., Chen, J., Wei, X.Y.: Attention on attention for image captioning. In: Proceedings of the IEEE/CVF ICCV, pp. 4634–4643 (2019)
10. Isola, P., Lim, J.J., Adelson, E.H.: Discovering states and transformations in image collections. In: Proceedings of the IEEE Conference on CVPR, pp. 1383–1391 (2015)
11. Karthik, S., Mancini, M., Akata, Z.: Kg-sp: knowledge guided simple primitives for open world compositional zero-shot learning. In: Proceedings of the IEEE/CVF CVPR, pp. 9336–9345 (2022)
12. Lei Ba, J., Swersky, K., Fidler, S., et al.: Predicting deep zero-shot convolutional neural networks using textual descriptions. In: Proceedings of the IEEE ICCV, pp. 4247–4255 (2015)
13. Li, X., Xu, Z., Wei, K., Deng, C.: Generalized zero-shot learning via disentangled representation. In: Proceedings of the AAAI, vol. 35, pp. 1966–1974 (2021)
14. Li, X., Yang, X., Wei, K., Deng, C., Yang, M.: Siamese contrastive embedding network for compositional zero-shot learning. In: Proceedings of the IEEE/CVF Conference on CVPR, pp. 9326–9335 (2022)
15. Li, Y.L., Xu, Y., Mao, X., Lu, C.: Symmetry and group in attribute-object compositions. In: Proceedings of the IEEE/CVF CVPR, pp. 11316–11325 (2020)
16. Misra, I., Gupta, A., Hebert, M.: From red wine to red tomato: composition with context. In: Proceedings of the IEEE CVPR, pp. 1792–1801 (2017)
17. Naeem, M.F., Xian, Y., Tombari, F., Akata, Z.: Learning graph embeddings for compositional zero-shot learning. In: Proceedings of the IEEE/CVF CVPR, pp. 953–962 (2021)
18. Nagarajan, T., Grauman, K.: Attributes as operators: factorizing unseen attribute-object compositions. In: Proceedings of ECCV, pp. 169–185 (2018)
19. Purushwalkam, S., Nickel, M., Gupta, A., Ranzato, M.: Task-driven modular networks for zero-shot compositional learning. In: Proceedings of the IEEE/CVF CVPR, pp. 3593–3602 (2019)
20. Saini, N., Pham, K., Shrivastava, A.: Disentangling visual embeddings for attributes and objects. In: Proceedings of the IEEE/CVF CVPR, pp. 13658–13667 (2022)

21. Schonfeld, E., Ebrahimi, S., Sinha, S., Darrell, T., Akata, Z.: Generalized zero- and few-shot learning via aligned variational autoencoders. In: Proceedings of the IEEE/CVF CVPR, pp. 8247–8255 (2019)
22. Shabbir, N., Rout, R.K.: Variation of deep features analysis for facial expression recognition system. MTAP **82**(8), 11507–11522 (2023)
23. Umer, S., Mondal, R., Pandey, H.M., Rout, R.K.: Deep features based convolutional neural network model for text and non-text region segmentation from document images. Appl. Soft Comput. **113**, 107917 (2021)
24. Xian, Y., Lampert, C.H., Schiele, B., Akata, Z.: Zero-shot learning's comprehensive evaluation of the good, the bad, and the ugly. IEEE Tran. PAMI **41**(9), 2251–2265 (2018)
25. Yang, M., Deng, C., Yan, J., Liu, X., Tao, D.: Learning unseen concepts via hierarchical decomposition and composition. In: Proceedings of the IEEE/CVF CVPR, pp. 10248–10256 (2020)
26. Yu, A., Grauman, K.: Fine-grained visual comparisons with local learning. In: Proceedings of the IEEE CVPR, pp. 192–199 (2014)
27. Zhu, Y., Xie, J., Tang, Z., Peng, X., Elgammal, A.: Semantic-guided multi-attention localization for zero-shot learning. In: Advances in NIPS, vol. 32 (2019)

Precise and Faster Image Description Generation with Limited Resources Using an Improved Hybrid Deep Model

Biswajit Patra(✉)⬤ and Dakshina Ranjan Kisku⬤

Department of Computer Science and Engineering, National Institute of Technology Durgapur, Durgapur 713209, India
bp.21cs1102@phd.nitdgp.ac.in, drkisku.cse@nitdgp.ac.in

Abstract. We propose a model that performs image captioning efficiently based on entity relations, followed by a deep learning-based encoder and decoder model. In order to make image captioning more precise, the proposed model uses Inception-Resnet(version-2) as an encoder and GRU as a decoder. To develop a less expensive and effective image captioning model in accordance with accelerating the training process by reducing the effect of vanishing gradient issues, residual connections are introduced in Inception architecture. Furthermore, the effectiveness of the proposed model has been significantly enhanced by associating the Bahadanu Attention model with GRU. To cut down the computation time and make it a less resource-consuming captioning model, a compact form of the vocabulary of informative words is taken into consideration. The proposed work makes use of the convolution base of the hybrid model to start learning alignment from scratch and learn the correlation among different images and descriptions. The proposed image text generation model is evaluated on Flickr 8k, Flickr 30k, and MSCOCO datasets, and thereby, it produces convincing results on assessments.

Keywords: Image captioning · hybrid pre-trained CNN model · Inception-Resnet-v2 · Attention · GRU · Compact Vocabulary · Evaluation metric

1 Introduction

Image description [14] is expressed as generating concise and natural descriptions concerning an image's visual content. It is very easy for a normal human being to describe an image precisely. However, it becomes complicated when we look for the visual recognition model developed on a machine. Precise and proper description generation of a picture is in great demand since it can be the eye for a blind or even partially blind person to sense the surroundings. It can be of great use in the area of the advertising industry, where automatic image caption generation is frequently used to get the attention of people towards their products, which are visualized in the sequence of videos or still images.

P. Maji et al. (Eds.): PReMI 2023, LNCS 14301, pp. 166–175, 2023.
https://doi.org/10.1007/978-3-031-45170-6_18

After significant success in machine translation [3], researchers often follow the encoder-decoder framework for generating textual descriptions of an image. In order to improve the quality of the generated captions, the proposed work has been developed based on the work discussed in [15]. However, capturing all primary and complex features to precisely describe an image as a whole is still a challenge. In the proposed work, memory-efficient precise descriptions are produced in less time by utilizing the capability of a wider and deeper hybrid CNN base [12], GRU [1] along with attention mechanism [3] and compact vocabulary model in the encoder-decoder framework [5,14,15]. The main contributions of the proposed work are summarized as follows.

- The proposed work uses the combination of an Inception-Resnet hybrid model, GRU, and attention mechanism to facilitate generating precise captions with more context information and faster the training process by improving the vanishing gradient issues.
- To generate more accurate descriptions, the attention mechanism exploits its inherent property of focusing useful context information in the image.
- The relationship among the features is modelled very efficiently once all the primary and complex features of the whole image are captured.
- Compact vocabulary, along with GRU, takes less memory and achieves computational efficiency to execute the algorithm fast.

The remaining part of the paper is organized as follows: Section 2 discusses some benchmark works about image description generation. Section 3 discusses the proposed image description model with baseline methods. The description of the datasets, implementation details, and experimental results have been presented in Sect. 4. The last section concludes the work with future directions.

2   Benchmark Works and Approaches

The image captioning tasks have attracted a good number of researchers in view of potential research outcomes and massive commercial applications. It can be performed using template-based [5], retrieval-based [5], and deep learning-based approaches [5,14,15]. In both template-based and retrieval-based approaches, diverse and precise description generation is not possible for complex images having challenging objects. Nowadays, deep learning-based encoder-decoder system is used in automatic image captioning tasks. Google NIC model presented in [14], further advanced in [15], which employed the Inception version-3 in the encoder and the LSTM in the decoder, and the combination of these two models produces good results. However, to the best of our knowledge, the attention-based approach was incorporated first into the image text generation in [11]. Some attention-based image text generation model [2,16] combines the top-down and bottom-up strategy and is able to focus selectively on words and extract the image's global features and concentrated local features of different areas.

3 Proposed Image Description Model

3.1 Motivation

Most of the existing image description models badly suffer from some inherent issues like the deviation from focusing key components and significant context of the image [14]. Sometimes, complex scenes that contain multiple objects find it difficult to establish spatial relationships between different objects [15] and seek object detection [1,9,17] to enhance the quality of the image captioning task. To overcome such inherent issues, complex scenes can be processed by a hybrid model of CNN that can learn alignments from scratch and obtain correlation among images [4]. The attention mechanism can be a solution to address the imprecise description issue often found in images. Moreover, in real-time scenarios obtaining a good description in a short time, GRU [1] can be used as a decoder which sometimes overcomes LSTM variant [15] for producing precise and appropriate image captions.

3.2 Baseline Models

Inception-Resnet V2: Inception-Resnet-v2 [12] is a variant of the CNN model that is trained on the Imagenet dataset [6] containing millions of images used for classification. It consists of 164 deep layers, which have the ability to detect rich and relevant features of the images. Further, these features can be used for different tasks ranging from image classification to image description generation. Its convolution base accepts an input of Volume $299 \times 299 \times 3$ and outputs a compact feature vector for 64 image regions, each having a 1536-dimensional representation.

Gated Recurrent Unit(GRU): GRU [1,7] a variant of recurrent networks which can identify long-term dependencies in sequences by eliminating the vanishing gradient, is used in the proposed model. In GRU, a couple of gating mechanisms are introduced, viz., update gate and reset gate. The update gate decides how much of the new input should be added to the hidden state, while the reset gate determines the portion of the prior hidden state information to remove.

Attention: Bahdanau attention described in [3] is a deterministic mechanism that can be used to simulate cognitive attention strategy. The concept is to apply greater computer resources to necessary image regions and discard the rest for each step while generating its description. The attention weight vector is formed by combining all encoded input vectors where the most relevant vector will obtain the highest weight and is further learned by gradient descent. Thus attention weight vector tells the relevance of each image region. The algorithm creates a focus on the image and predicts the most relevant word for that location which helps to fix the focus of attention for the next.

3.3 Proposed Methodology

To generate an image description, the proposed model framework shown in Fig. 1 consists of pre-processing, encoding, attention, and decoding processes as described as follows.

Text Processing: As part of pre-processing, text processing is carried out on a dataset consisting of images with a certain number of captions per image. These images get multiplied into several copies in accordance with the number of captions per image. Further, they are made to be available and sorted randomly during training. The random distribution of images with image captions thus, the model blocked from learning the same training sequence again and again in subsequent iterations. The results in the training process are found to be converged more quickly and free from bias. The dataset is partitioned into three disjoint sets, viz. training, validation, and test data. The text processing consists of the following steps.

- **Step 1:** In this step, after data cleaning, the tokenization of text to words and frequency count of the tokenized words are employed.
- **Step 2:** In this step, a dictionary is built with word frequencies, and further, the dictionary is sorted in terms of word frequencies in descending order.
- **Step 3:** In this step, the frequencies of words are replaced by the indices, starting from one.
- **Step 4:** In this step, vocabulary with a unique collection of words is built, and further, if the vocabulary is found to be too big, then infrequent words are removed and most frequent words are retained. In the proposed work 55% most frequently occured words are considered to generate compact vocabulary.
- **Step 5:** If the vocabulary is too big to handle, then we remove the infrequent words and keep the most frequent words in the vocabulary.
- **Step 6:** In this step, word embedding is employed in order to correspond to vocabulary having the most frequent words.

Encoding Process: The encoding process makes use of the convolution base of Inception ResNet-v2 [12] model to extract the visual elements from the image. The outcome of the last layer of the convolution base is a feature vector of dimension 1536 followed by an embedding process [1] that produces 256 key points. This embedded and reduced feature vector is then fetched to the attention module.

Attention: If s_{t-1} be the previous hidden state of the GRU and a_t be the attention weight vector at time step **t** the importance of each image region h_i for creating the subsequent word w_n can be depicted as [8]:

$$\text{score} = \tanh (q_h * h_i + k_s * s_{t-1} + b)$$
$$a_t = \text{softmax}(v * \text{score})$$

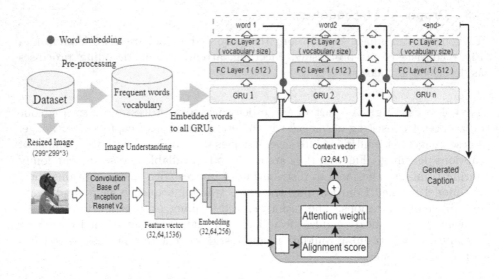

Fig. 1. Proposed Image Captioning architecture.

where $\mathbf{q}_h$, $\mathbf{k}_s$, and $\mathbf{v}$ are learnable parameters, and * denotes matrix multi-plication. The attention weight vector $\mathbf{a}_t$ is a probability distribution over the $\mathbf{i}$ image regions where, $\mathbf{i} = \mathbf{1,2,...,L}$ etc., and it is utilized further to generate the context vector i,e; the feature vector's h_i weighted sum:

$$c_t = \sum_i (a_t * h_i) \text{ , where i} = 1, 2, \ldots, \text{ L}$$

where, c_t is the context vector that holds the attended image features at the t, time step.

Decoding Process: Decoder [5,8] is responsible for word-by-word sentence generation as image caption. The decoder is a GRU [1] network for word-by-word caption sentence formation. The decoder computes the subsequent hidden state $\mathbf{s}_t$ and the subsequent word's probability distribution $\mathbf{w}_n$ for $\mathbf{t}$ time step by using the preceding word, $\mathbf{w}_{n-1}$ the preceding hidden state, $\mathbf{s}_{t-1}$ and the context vector $\mathbf{c}_t$. Thus next word probability distribution $\mathbf{p}_t$ can be derived as:

$$z_t = sigmoid(W_z * [w_{n-1}, c_t] + b_z)$$
$$r_t = sigmoid(W_r * [w_{n-1}, c_t] + b_r)$$
$$h_t = tanh(W_y * [r_t * w_{n-1}, c_t] + b_h)$$
$$s_t = (1 - z_t) * s_{t-1} + z_t * h_t$$
$$p_t = softmax(W_p * s_t + b_p)$$

Starting with the input image $\mathbf{I}$, the model is trained to maximize the log-likelihood [8] of the actual caption words, which are expressed as follows:

$$L = \sum_{n=1}^{N} log(p_t(w_n|w_1, ..., w_{n-1}, I))$$

where, $p_t(w_n|w_1, ..., w_{n-1}, I)$ is the likelihood of the next word being produced, w_n given the input image, I and the preceding words, $w_1, w_2..., w_{n-1}$.

During inference, the model creates the caption by keep appending generated words one after another in accordance with the word's probability distribution at every time step, and it stops on generating end token or reaches the length of the longest sentence. A softmax function can be further used to the decoder's output to get the final prediction and the distribution of probability over the vocabulary and can be depicted as:

$$p(w_n|w_1, ..., w_{t-1}, I) = softmax(W_p * w_t + b_p)$$

Here, W_p and b_p are learnable weight and bias.

4 Evaluation

4.1 Datasets and Evaluation Metrics

The proposed model is assessed on the benchmark datasets, such as Flickr 8k [15], Flickr 30k [15] and MS COCO [15] using the performance metrics, viz. Bilingual Evaluation Understudy Score (BLEU) [1], Metric for Evaluation of Translation with Explicit Ordering (METEOR) [1] and Consensus-based Image Description Evaluation (CIDEr) [1]. In Flickr 8k, Flickr 30k, and MSCOCO datasets, there exist 8091, 31783, and 123287 images, respectively. The datasets consist of images of salient activities, everyday objects, events, and humans. To utilize the complete dataset, images are split into three disjoint sets as 80:10:10 among the train, validation, and test sets. Since every image has five visible and impartial descriptions, for Flickr 8k, Flickr 30k, and MSCOCO datasets, a total of 40455, 158915, and 616435 instances are obtained, respectively.

4.2 Implementation Details

To begin with the image description generation process, the image features from the convolution base of the Inception-Resnet-v2 of shape $32 \times 8 \times 8 \times 1536$ (i,e; batch-size, patch-dimension, number-of-patches) are obtained for all three disjoint sets of a dataset. Image features generation is typically followed by an embedding layer to be fetched to the attention module. Later on, the context vector generated from the attention module is sent to the GRU blocks that predict the output words through two fully connected layers. The proposed framework employed Sparse Categorical Cross Entropy function [1] as a loss function that produces a category index of integers of the most likely matching caption. Further, the Adam optimizer is used to make the computation fast. To process the data, a batch size of 32 is chosen to accommodate limited GPU RAM. Thus, 253 batches of images for Flickr 8k, 994 batches of images for Flickr 30k, and 3853 batches of images for MSCOCO are processed.

4.3 Experimental Results

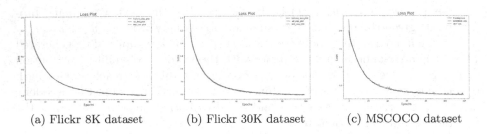

(a) Flickr 8K dataset   (b) Flickr 30K dataset   (c) MSCOCO dataset

Fig. 2. Train, validation, and Test loss plot.

As the image description model highly depends on the context information of the image as well as on the training captions, the combination of different deep models plays a vital role in generating precise descriptions. The proposed model assesses the performance using some performance metrics, such as BLEU-1, BLEU-2, BLEU-3, BLEU-4, Meteor, and CIDEr. The performance of the proposed image description is shown in Table 1, where the proposed system achieves

Table 1. Comparison with existing Image text generation models.

Model	BLEU-1	BLEU-2	BLEU-3	BLEU-4	METEOR	CIDEr
Evaluated on Flickr8k						
Show and Tell [14]	0.63	0.41	0.27	0.17	–	–
Show, Attend and Tell [15]	0.67	0.44	0.29	0.19	0.18	–
Neural Baby Talk [10]	0.68	0.48	0.36	0.26	0.20	0.55
Bottom-Up and Top-Down [2]	0.72	0.56	0.41	0.30	0.22	0.67
Proposed Model	**0.78**	**0.64**	**0.51**	**0.38**	**0.31**	**1.25**
Evaluated on Flickr 30k						
Show and Tell [14]	0.66	0.42	0.27	0.18	–	–
Show, Attend and Tell [15]	0.66	0.43	0.28	0.19	0.18	–
Neural Baby Talk [10]	0.69	0.50	0.38	0.27	0.21	0.57
Bottom-Up and Top-Down [2]	0.72	0.55	0.41	0.31	0.22	0.60
POS-SCAN [17]	0.73	0.56	0.42	0.30	0.22	0.69
OSCAR [9]	0.79	0.59	0.47	0.35	0.29	1.19
Proposed Model	**0.77**	**0.62**	**0.52**	**0.37**	**0.30**	**1.27**
Evaluated on MSCOCO						
Show and Tell [14]	0.66	0.46	0.32	0.24	–	–
Show, Attend and Tell [15]	0.70	0.49	0.34	0.24	0.23	–
Neural Baby Talk [10]	0.75	0.56	0.44	0.34	0.27	1.07
Bottom-Up and Top-Down [2]	0.77	0.60	0.46	0.36	0.27	1.13
POS-SCAN [17]	0.80	0.62	0.47	0.38	0.28	1.26
OSCAR [9]	0.77	0.60	0.46	0.37	0.30	1.27
Proposed Model	**0.77**	**0.63**	**0.51**	**0.39**	**0.32**	**1.29**

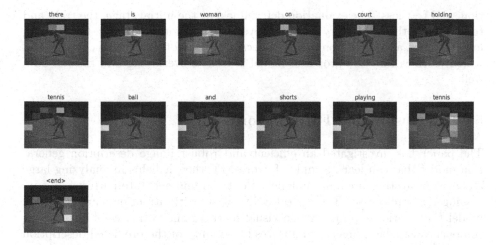

Fig. 3. Visualization of image description generation in sequence. **Real Caption:** there is woman on court holding tennis racket. **Prediction Caption:** there is woman on court holding tennis ball and shorts playing tennis.

superior performance over the existing state-of-the-art (SOTA) systems in terms of CIDEr score and other performance metrics also improve their scores. However, there is an incident where the BLEU-1 score of the proposed system is found to be less than that of POS-SCAN [17] while evaluating on MSCOCO dataset. Although this exception does not affect the overall efficiency of the proposed system, it emerges as a sustainable image captioning system. The similarity measures of a candidate sentence against a set of reference sentences give CIDEr [13] score. Moreover, it computes inverse document frequency to check whether a word element is common or rare using the provided reference sentences. The CIDEr score for a reference dataset with only one image will always be zero, and for some random image with a similar reference image in the validation set, the score may rise up to 5–10 as words of higher confidence are repeated over long sentences. So, for stable and reliable results, evaluation inverse document frequency is computed from the validation dataset by considering more model-generated captions and reference captions from the validation dataset, and the result is depicted in Table 1. Investigation shows that CIDEr scores rise as Inception-Resnet-v2 captures all necessary object features thoroughly, and the addition of an attention mechanism empowers the decoder. Further, it adaptably utilizes the most significant image feature by combining all encoded information into a weighted combination, with the most significant feature obtaining the highest weight, and this ensures the salient features of the image are described accurately by the generated captions. However, the most remarkable observation is that the predicted description of an image appears lively and is found to be more scene centric, as visualized in Fig. 3. The performance of the proposed model is also depicted in Figs. 2a, 2b and 2c while considering train, validation, and test loss. The evaluation determines, at the initial stage, the train and test losses both remain very high. However, as iteration progresses, the training loss, test loss, and validation loss keep decreasing smoothly towards convergence, which justifies that the proposed model is free of overfitting and fits the data well.

5   Conclusion and Future Works

The paper has investigated an efficient and robust image description generation model that can learn complex features. Further, it helps in analyzing large amounts of unstructured and unlabelled data to find accurate patterns by consuming fewer resources. The hybrid-CNN, along with attention, can effectively model the relationship among the visual features and, when combined with a compact vocabulary, precisely improves the quality of the predicted description of an image in less time. The performance of the proposed system outperforms the SOTA system while determining CIDEr, BLEU-1, 2, 3, 4 and Meteor scores.

However, the proposed work can have space for improvement. A better alignment of words with specific image regions in visual representation may provide a better understanding and improves the results. Adding self-attention and a prompt mechanism may be useful for better text guidance, and this is to be considered in future works too.

References

1. Al-Malla, M.A., Jafar, A., Ghneim, N.: Image captioning model using attention and object features to mimic human image understanding. J. Big Data **9**(1), 1–16 (2022)
2. Anderson, P., et al.: Bottom-up and top-down attention for image captioning and visual question answering. In: Proceedings of the IEEE Conference on Computer Vision and Pattern Recognition, pp. 6077–6086 (2018)
3. Bahdanau, D., Cho, K., Bengio, Y.: Neural machine translation by jointly learning to align and translate. arXiv preprint arXiv:1409.0473 (2014)
4. Bhatia, Y., Bajpayee, A., Raghuvanshi, D., Mittal, H.: Image captioning using Google's inception-resnet-v2 and recurrent neural network. In: 2019 Twelfth International Conference on Contemporary Computing (IC3), pp. 1–6. IEEE (2019)
5. Cho, K., Courville, A., Bengio, Y.: Describing multimedia content using attention-based encoder-decoder networks. IEEE Trans. Multimedia **17**(11), 1875–1886 (2015)
6. Deng, J., Dong, W., Socher, R., Li, L.J., Li, K., Fei-Fei, L.: ImageNet: a large-scale hierarchical image database. In: 2009 IEEE Conference on Computer Vision and Pattern Recognition, pp. 248–255. IEEE (2009)
7. Jyotsna, A., Mary Anita, E.: Enhancing IoT security through deep learning-based intrusion detection. In: Neri, F., Du, K.L., Varadarajan, V., San-Blas, A.A., Jiang, Z. (eds.) CCCE 2023, vol. 1823, pp. 95–105. Springer, Cham (2023). https://doi.org/10.1007/978-3-031-35299-7_8

8. Khan, R., Islam, M.S., Kanwal, K., Iqbal, M., Hossain, M.I., Ye, Z.: A deep neural framework for image caption generation using GRU-based attention mechanism. arXiv preprint arXiv:2203.01594 (2022)

9. Li, X., et al.: OSCAR: object-semantics aligned pre-training for vision-language tasks. In: Vedaldi, A., Bischof, H., Brox, T., Frahm, J.-M. (eds.) ECCV 2020. LNCS, vol. 12375, pp. 121–137. Springer, Cham (2020). https://doi.org/10.1007/978-3-030-58577-8_8

10. Lu, J., Yang, J., Batra, D., Parikh, D.: Neural baby talk. In: Proceedings of the IEEE Conference on Computer Vision and Pattern Recognition. pp. 7219–7228 (2018)

11. Song, X., Feng, F., Han, X., Yang, X., Liu, W., Nie, L.: Neural compatibility modeling with attentive knowledge distillation. In: The 41st International ACM SIGIR Conference on Research & Development in Information Retrieval, pp. 5–14 (2018)

12. Szegedy, C., Ioffe, S., Vanhoucke, V., Alemi, A.: Inception-v4, inception-resnet and the impact of residual connections on learning. In: Proceedings of the AAAI Conference on Artificial Intelligence, vol. 31 (2017)

13. Vedantam, R., Lawrence Zitnick, C., Parikh, D.: Cider: consensus-based image description evaluation. In: Proceedings of the IEEE Conference on Computer Vision and Pattern Recognition, pp. 4566–4575 (2015)

14. Vinyals, O., Toshev, A., Bengio, S., Erhan, D.: Show and tell: a neural image caption generator. In: Proceedings of the IEEE Conference on Computer Vision and Pattern Recognition, pp. 3156–3164 (2015)

15. Xu, K., et al.: Show, attend and tell: neural image caption generation with visual attention. In: International Conference on Machine Learning, pp. 2048–2057. PMLR (2015)

16. You, Q., Jin, H., Wang, Z., Fang, C., Luo, J.: Image captioning with semantic attention. In: Proceedings of the IEEE Conference on Computer Vision and Pattern Recognition, pp. 4651–4659 (2016)

17. Zhou, Y., Wang, M., Liu, D., Hu, Z., Zhang, H.: More grounded image captioning by distilling image-text matching model. In: Proceedings of the IEEE/CVF Conference on Computer Vision and Pattern Recognition, pp. 4777–4786 (2020)

Statistical Learning

Inverse Reinforcement Learning with Constraint Recovery

Nirjhar Das$^{(\boxtimes)}$ and Arpan Chattopadhyay

Indian Institute of Technology Delhi, New Delhi, India
{Nirjhar.Das.ee319,arpanc}@ee.iitd.ac.in

Abstract. In this work, we propose a novel inverse reinforcement learning (IRL) algorithm for constrained Markov decision process (CMDP) problems. In standard IRL problems, the inverse learner or agent seeks to recover the reward function of the MDP, given a set of trajectory demonstrations for the optimal policy. In this work, we seek to infer not only the reward functions of the CMDP, but also the constraints. Using the principle of maximum entropy, we show that the IRL with constraint recovery (IRL-CR) problem can be cast as a constrained non-convex optimization problem. We reduce it to an alternating constrained optimization problem whose sub-problems are convex. We use exponentiated gradient descent algorithm to solve it. Finally, we demonstrate the efficacy of our algorithm for the grid world environment.

1 Introduction

Reinforcement Learning (RL, [12, 21]) is a popular branch of artificial intelligence where an agent makes sequential decisions under uncertainty. Every time, the agent observes the *state* of the environment, chooses an *action* based on the current state, obtains a *reward* and transits to a random next state based on a probability distribution depending on the current state-action pair. The agent's goal is to choose the actions to maximize the expected sum of rewards over a time horizon; this gives rise to the problem of finding the optimal *policy* that, given the state at any time, prescribes an action to the agent. When the transition probability or reward function are unknown to the agent, RL is used to learn the optimal policy. RL has massive applications in various domains like autonomous driving, drug discovery, resource allocation in communication systems, robot learning, path planning, and large language models.

Inverse Reinforcement Learning (IRL) comes under the broad paradigm of learning from demonstrations [3, 19] where the goal is to learn behaviour from given expert demonstrations. Here, an inverse agent seeks to learn the reward function (and hence the objective) of an RL problem encountered by a forward agent. Typically, the inverse agent is provided with a set of trajectories of the RL problem of the forward agent. IRL is applied in several applications, such as autonomous driving and robotic manipulations. IRL is inherently ill-posed as several reward functions may conform with the same set of demonstrations.

P. Maji et al. (Eds.): PReMI 2023, LNCS 14301, pp. 179–188, 2023.
https://doi.org/10.1007/978-3-031-45170-6_19

However, there have been several works on IRL in the literature, such as [15] where IRL is posed as a linear program, [18] where IRL is posed as a structured maximum margin classification, and importantly [23] that proposes the new paradigm of maximum entropy IRL (MaxEnt IRL) that assumes that the demonstrated trajectories are sampled from a Boltzmann distribution with the negative sum reward of a sample trajectory as its potential function. In fact, several works [8,11,22] have used this maximum entropy principle to demonstrate strong performance on large-scale data sets.

In this work, we consider IRL where the forward agent encounters a constrained Markov decision process (CMDP [2]) problem, and the inverse agent seeks to recover both the reward and the constraint functions from a set of demonstrations. Many real-life tasks involve solving a CMDP. For example, while pouring water from a glass jar into a glass bottle, one must satisfy the constraint that neither glass vessel breaks. Similarly, path planning of an autonomous vehicle should ensure that the manoeuvring decision does not lead to an accident with neighbouring vehicles. Obviously, recovering the constraint function along with the reward function enables the IRL agent to obtain a realistic picture of the objectives of the forward agent.

Recent works on IRL for CMDP can be broadly categorized into two classes: (a) algorithms that recover rewards or policies given the knowledge of constraints and (b) algorithms that recover constraints given the reward function. The papers [6,7,13] belong to the first group, while [4,5,9,14,16,17,20] belong to the second group. In [6], the reward function is learnt when known multi-state combinatorial constraints restrict the distribution of trajectories. On the other hand, [7] considers learning the reward function when demonstrations are generated by the forward agent by using optimal control for the constrained problem. In [13], the authors propose an inverse Q-learning algorithm that updates the Q-estimates using the knowledge of the constraints. A notable work in the second class is [20], where the goal is to recover a maximum likelihood constraint set, which, when appended to the base MDP with known reward, conforms with the observed trajectories. In [14], the authors extend [20] to a parameterized policy setting with the objective to recover the forward agent's policy. In [9], the authors propose an algorithm to learn soft constraints that are bounded in expectation, from demonstrations in stochastic setting with continuous states and actions and known rewards. Moreover, [5,16,17] take Bayesian approaches to constraint learning when rewards are known.

In this paper, we consider the IRL problem where the inverse agent seeks to recover both the reward and constraint functions of the forward agent, given that the trajectory demonstrations have been obtained by executing an optimal policy for the forward agent's CMDP. We call this problem IRL with constraint recovery (IRL-CR). This problem is very important for scenarios that involve CMDPs, such as autonomous driving, healthcare and other safety-critical applications. To the best of our knowledge, this problem has not been solved before, and the authors of [9] claim that this problem is difficult to solve due to its ill-posed nature. However, we formulate a constrained optimization problem using the principle of maximum entropy and maximum likelihood estimation to tackle this challenge and provide a simple and efficient algorithm that achieves strong numerical performance. The main contributions of our work are:

1. We formulate a novel constrained optimization problem to recover the reward and the constraint simultaneously from demonstrations. Assuming a linear function approximation of the reward and constraint functions and by using the maximum entropy principle, we derive a Boltzmann distribution over trajectories parametrized by both the reward and constraint and use it to derive a non-convex constrained optimization problem.
2. We reduce the constrained, non-convex problem to an alternating constrained optimization problem whose sub-problems are convex. We use Exponentiated Gradient Descent to derive a simple and efficient algorithm for its solution.
3. We demonstrate strong empirical performance in a grid world environment.

2 Preliminaries

A CMDP is characterized by a septuple $(\mathcal{S}, \mathcal{A}, r, c, \alpha, p, \gamma)$, where $\mathcal{S}$ is the state space, $\mathcal{A}$ is the action space, r is the reward function, c is the constraint function, p is the state-transition probability set and $\gamma \in (0,1)$ is a discount factor. When an agent in state $s \in \mathcal{S}$ takes action $a \in \mathcal{A}$, then the agent receives a reward $r(s,a)$, incurs a penalty $c(s,a)$, and transits to the next state according to the probability distribution $p(\cdot|s,a)$. A *stationary, randomized policy* is a mapping $\pi : \mathcal{S} \to \triangle(\mathcal{A})$, where $\triangle(\mathcal{A})$ is the probability simplex over $\mathcal{A}$. Obviously, $\pi(a|s)$, denotes the probability of taking action a when the state is s. The *value functions* associated with the reward or the constraint is defined as:

$$V_x^\pi(s) = \mathbb{E}_\pi\left[\sum_{t=1}^{T} \gamma^{t-1} x(s_t, a_t)\Big| s_1 = s\right], \quad x \in \{r, c\} \tag{1}$$

where $\mathbb{E}_\pi$ denotes the expectation under policy π. The optimal policy π^* solves:

$$\max_\pi \ \sum_{s \in \mathcal{S}} p_0(s) V_r^\pi(s) \qquad \text{s.t.} \quad \sum_{s \in \mathcal{S}} p_0(s) V_c^\pi(s) \leq \alpha \tag{2}$$

where $p_0(\cdot)$ is the *known* initial state distribution. In this paper, we assume $\alpha > 0$ and $c(s,a) \geq 0 \ \forall \ s \in \mathcal{S}, \ a \in \mathcal{A}$. Also, we consider only one constraint, though an extension of our algorithm to more than one constraint is straightforward.

We denote by $\tau = \{s_1, a_1, s_2, a_2, \cdots, s_T, a_T\}$ a generic trajectory of the RL agent under policy π^*. The goal in the IRL-CR problem for an inverse agent is to learn both the reward $r(\cdot,\cdot)$ and the constraint $c(\cdot,\cdot)$ functions from a set of demonstrated trajectories $D = \{\tau_1, \ldots, \tau_m\}$ under π^*. However, we assume that the inverse agent knows the tuple $(\mathcal{S}, \mathcal{A}, p, \gamma)$.

3   Formulation

The maximum likelihood (ML) estimates of the unknown reward and cost functions are: $(r^*, c^*, \alpha^*) = \arg\max_{r,c,\alpha} \prod_{\tau \in D} p(\tau|r, c, \alpha)$, assuming that the demonstrated trajectories were generated by the RL agent under π^*.

First, we normalize the constraint function $c(\cdot, \cdot)$ to obtain a new constraint $c'(\cdot, \cdot) = c(\cdot, \cdot)/\alpha$, which eliminates the need to estimate α. In (2), we can see that the optimal policy is unchanged if this normalization is performed. Hence, our objective is to solve (subject to the constraint in (2)):

$$r^*, c^* = \arg\max_{r,c'} \prod_{\tau \in D} p(\tau|r, c', 1) \tag{3}$$

Now, we make some assumptions about the reward and constraint of the CMDP.

1. We assume that the reward and constraint are independent of the actions, that is: $r(s, a) = r(s)\forall\ s \in \mathcal{S},\ a \in \mathcal{A}$ and similarly for $c(\cdot, \cdot)$. This is a standard assumption in several prior works [1,22,23] in IRL, and it reduces computational complexity. However, the method developed here can be easily generalized to cases where this assumption does not hold since the actions will still be observable to the inverse agent in those cases.
2. We assume that the reward and cost functions are linear with respect to the features of the states denoted by $\Phi(\cdot)$; that is, $r(s) = \mathbf{w}_r^\mathsf{T}\Phi_r(s)$, $c(s) = \mathbf{w}_c^\mathsf{T}\Phi_c(s)$ for some unknown parameters $\mathbf{w}_r \in \mathbb{R}^{d_r}$ and $\mathbf{w}_c \in \mathbb{R}^{d_c}$, where $d_r < |\mathcal{S}|$. Henceforth, with a slight abuse of notation, we will represent $p(\tau|\mathbf{w}_r, \mathbf{w}_c)$ by $p(\tau)$, and hence, $p(\tau|r, c, 1) = p(\tau|\mathbf{w}_r, \mathbf{w}_c)$. This is a reasonable assumption since the inverse agent may be able to identify a set of meaningful feature vectors in realistic settings.

Now, for $x \in \{r, c\}$, we define the quantities *empirical feature expectation* (EFE) and *policy feature expectation* (PFE) as follows:

$$\text{EFE: } \tilde{\Phi}_x = \frac{1}{|D|}\sum_{\tau \in D}\Phi_x(\tau), \qquad \text{PFE: } \hat{\Phi}_x = \sum_{\text{all } \tau} p(\tau)\Phi_x(\tau) \tag{4}$$

where $\Phi_x(\tau) = \sum_{s_t \in \tau}\gamma^{t-1}\Phi_x(s_t)$. In order to compute the *PFE* for any policy π, we use the *state visitation frequency* defined as $\rho_\pi(s) = \sum_{t=1}^{\infty}\gamma^{t-1}\mathbb{P}_\pi(s_t = s)$. For a finite time horizon T, it can be approximated using the recursive equations:

$$d_1(s) = p_0(s) \quad \forall s \in \mathcal{S}$$

$$d_{t+1}(s') = \sum_{s \in \mathcal{S}}\sum_{a \in \mathcal{A}}\gamma \cdot d_t(s) \cdot \pi(a|s) \cdot p(s'|s, a) \quad \forall s' \in \mathcal{S},\ \forall t \geq 1 \tag{5}$$

With the help of the state visitation frequency, for $x \in \{r, c\}$, since $\rho_\pi(s) = \sum_{t=1}^{\infty}d_t(s)$., we can write (finite time approximation of) PFE as

$$\hat{\Phi}_x \approx \sum_{t=1}^{T}\sum_{s \in S}d_t(s)\Phi_x(s) \tag{6}$$

3.1   Obtaining the Boltzmann Distribution

In [1], the authors show that it is necessary and sufficient to match reward EFE and PFE to guarantee the same performance as the optimal policy under assumption (2), for the IRL problem without constraint recovery. We extend this to IRL-CR and ensure that the EFE and PFE for constraints also match. In formulating the optimization problem, we introduce a new constraint that $p(\tau|\mathbf{w}_r, \mathbf{w}_r)$ satisfies the constraint in (2). Next, we will use the principle of maximum entropy to determine the distribution $p(\tau|\mathbf{w}_r, \mathbf{w}_r)$ out of all possible distributions that satisfy these constraints. The problem can be formulated as:

$$\min_p \sum_{\text{all } \tau} p(\tau) \log(p(\tau)) \quad \text{s.t.} \quad \sum_{\text{all } \tau} p(\tau) \Phi_r(\tau) = \tilde{\Phi}_r, \quad \sum_{\text{all } \tau} p(\tau) \Phi_c(\tau) = \tilde{\Phi}_c$$
$$\sum_{\text{all } \tau} p(\tau) \mathbf{w}_c^\mathsf{T} \Phi_c(\tau) \le 1, \quad p(\tau) \in \triangle(\tau) \tag{7}$$

where $\triangle(\tau)$ is the probability simplex over all trajectories up to time T. This is a convex optimization problem in $p(\cdot)$. The Lagrangian $\mathcal{R}(p, \theta, \beta, \nu, \zeta, \delta)$ is:

$$\sum_{\text{all } \tau} p(\tau) \log(p(\tau)) + \theta^\mathsf{T} \Big(\sum_{\text{all } \tau} p(\tau) \Phi_r(\tau) - \tilde{\Phi}_r \Big) + \beta^\mathsf{T} \Big(\sum_{\text{all } \tau} p(\tau) \Phi_c(\tau) - \tilde{\Phi}_c \Big)$$
$$+ \nu \Big(\sum_{\text{all } \tau} p(\tau) \mathbf{w}_c^\mathsf{T} \Phi_c(\tau) - 1 \Big) + \zeta \Big(\sum_{\text{all } \tau} p(\tau) - 1 \Big) - \Big(\sum_{\text{all } \tau} \delta(\tau) p(\tau) \Big) \tag{8}$$

where $\theta, \beta, \nu, \zeta, \delta$ are Lagrange multipliers of appropriate dimensions. Also, note that $\nu \ge 0$ and $\delta(\tau) \ge 0 \; \forall \tau$. From the KKT condition, we have $\frac{\partial \mathcal{R}}{\partial p(\tau)} = 0 \forall \tau$ under the optimal $(p^*, \theta^*, \beta^*, \nu^*, \zeta^*, \delta^*)$. Hence, we obtain:

$$p^*(\tau) = \exp(-1 - \zeta^* + \delta^*(\tau)) \times \exp\Big(-\theta^{*\mathsf{T}} \Phi_r(\tau) - [\beta^* + \nu^* \mathbf{w}_c]^\mathsf{T} \cdot \Phi_c(\tau) \Big) \tag{9}$$

Now, we can interpret $-\theta^*$ as $\mathbf{w}_r$ since the higher the value of the term $-\theta^{*\mathsf{T}} \Phi_r(\tau)$, the higher will be the probability of that trajectory, thereby matching with the intuition that higher reward trajectories are more probable. Similarly, we can choose $\beta^* = \mathbf{w}_c$. We make a further simplifying assumption that $\delta^*(\tau) = 0 \; \forall \tau$ since it can be assumed that $p^*(\tau) > 0 \; \forall \tau$ and hence follows from complementary slackness condition. Thus, the expression (9) simplifies to $p^*(\tau|\mathbf{w}_r, \mathbf{w}_c) \propto \exp(\mathbf{w}_r^\mathsf{T} \Phi_r(\tau) - \lambda \mathbf{w}_c^\mathsf{T} \Phi_c(\tau))$ where $\lambda = 1 + \nu^* \ge 0$.

Thus, we observe the probability distribution over a trajectory is the Boltzmann distribution, according to the maximum entropy principle. This supports the intuition that the higher the reward and the lower the constraint value of a trajectory, the more likely it will be. Further, it is seen that $\lambda \ge 0$ acts as a Lagrange multiplier for (2). Now, we define a partition function $Z(\mathbf{w}_r, \mathbf{w}_c) = \sum_{\text{all } \tau} \exp(\mathbf{w}_r^\mathsf{T} \Phi_r(\tau) - \lambda \mathbf{w}_c^\mathsf{T} \Phi_c(\tau))$ as a proportionality constant and define:

$$p^*(\tau|\mathbf{w}_r, \mathbf{w}_c) = \frac{1}{Z(\mathbf{w}_r, \mathbf{w}_c)} \exp(\mathbf{w}_r^\mathsf{T} \Phi_r(\tau) - \lambda \mathbf{w}_c^\mathsf{T} \Phi_c(\tau)). \tag{10}$$

3.2   Solving the Optimization Problem

Clearly, (3) now becomes:

$$(\mathbf{w}_r^*, \mathbf{w}_c^*) = \arg \max_{\mathbf{w}_r, \mathbf{w}_c} \prod_{\tau \in D} p^*(\tau | \mathbf{w}_r, \mathbf{w}_c) \qquad \text{s.t.} \quad \mathbf{w}_c^\mathsf{T} \hat{\Phi}_c \leq 1 \tag{11}$$

Here, we once again enforce the constraint that the constraint value function should not exceed the budget so as to not allow arbitrary choices of $\mathbf{w}_r$ and $\mathbf{w}_c$ that would still produce the same $\mathbf{w}_r^\mathsf{T} \Phi_r(\tau) - \lambda \mathbf{w}_c^\mathsf{T} \Phi_c(\tau)$ as the original $\mathbf{w}_r$, $\mathbf{w}_c$. Simplifying (11) and taking the log-likelihood, the optimization becomes:

$$\min_{\mathbf{w}_r, \mathbf{w}_c} \underbrace{\left[\frac{1}{|D|} \sum_{\tau \in D} \left(-\mathbf{w}_r^\mathsf{T} \Phi_r(\tau) + \lambda \mathbf{w}_c^\mathsf{T} \Phi_c(\tau) \right) \right] + \log Z(\mathbf{w}_r, \mathbf{w}_c)}_{\doteq \mathcal{L}} \qquad \text{s.t.} \quad \mathbf{w}_c^\mathsf{T} \hat{\Phi}_c \leq 1$$

$$\tag{12}$$

The above form in (12) has a convex objective, but the constraint is non-linear and non-convex since $\hat{\Phi}_c$ involves an expectation over the distribution $p^*(\tau | \mathbf{w}_r, \mathbf{w}_c)$. Hence, we use an alternating optimization-based technique where this expectation is computed for a given $(\mathbf{w}_r, \mathbf{w}_c)$ pair, and then (12) is solved as a convex optimization in $(\mathbf{w}_r, \mathbf{w}_c)$. However, evaluating the partition function is computationally difficult as the number of trajectories grows at an exponential rate with T. Hence, we use gradient-based approaches. The gradient of the objective function $\mathcal{L}$ in (12) is:

$$\nabla_{\mathbf{w}_r} \mathcal{L} = -\frac{1}{|D|} \sum_{\tau \in D} \Phi_r(\tau) + \sum_{\text{all } \tau} \frac{\exp(\mathbf{w}_r^\mathsf{T} \Phi_r(\tau) - \lambda \mathbf{w}_c^\mathsf{T} \Phi_c(\tau))}{Z(\mathbf{w}_r, \mathbf{w}_c)} \cdot \Phi_r(\tau)$$

$$= -\tilde{\Phi}_r + \hat{\Phi}_r \tag{13}$$

Similarly, $\nabla_{\mathbf{w}_c} \mathcal{L} = \lambda(\tilde{\Phi}_c - \hat{\Phi}_c)$.

Note that, the inverse RL agent can compute $\tilde{\Phi}_r$ and $\tilde{\Phi}_c$ from the demonstrated trajectories, and can compute $\hat{\Phi}_r$ and $\hat{\Phi}_c$ for a given policy.

Now, we can formulate an algorithm to recover both $\mathbf{w}_r$ and $\mathbf{w}_c$. The essential idea is that starting from a random value of $\mathbf{w}_r$ and $\mathbf{w}_c$, we compute the optimal policy corresponding to it. Using the optimal policy, we calculate the state visitation frequency and hence, the PFE. After that, we apply a gradient step on $\mathbf{w}_r$ and $\mathbf{w}_c$. We alternate between the two steps till the change in $\mathbf{w}_r$ and $\mathbf{w}_c$ between two successive iterations are within a desired tolerance level. Algorithm 1 provides an outline of the proposed scheme. In steps 10 and 11 of the algorithm, we project $\mathbf{w}_r$ and $\mathbf{w}_c$ to a normalized set of 1-norm unity with non-negative coordinates using the usual Bregman divergence minimization [10] with negative entropy function $f(\mathbf{x}) = \sum_i \mathbf{x}_i \log(\mathbf{x}_i)$ for numerical stability. Also, note that the use of Exponentiated Gradient Descent as the intermediate gradient step in (12) requires such a projection for regularization (see sec. 5 of [10] for details). However, other forms of gradient updates can also be used with different regularizations. Once the algorithm computes optimal $\mathbf{w}_r$ and $\mathbf{w}_c$, the inverse RL agent can recover $r(s) = \mathbf{w}_r^\mathsf{T} \Phi_r(s)$, $c(s) = \mathbf{w}_c^\mathsf{T} \Phi_c(s)$.

4   Experiments

In this section, we use the gridworld environment to evaluate the proposed algorithm. We consider the grid of size 5×5. The agent always starts from the top left corner of the grid. At any time step, the agent has four actions available: up, down, left, and right. An action has 70% probability of success while with 30% probability, the agent moves into any of the neighbouring blocks. This adds stochasticity to the transition, which makes learning from data more difficult. The states feature vectors are: $\Phi_r((x,y)) = (2.5 \times 10^{-3}) [x, y]^\mathsf{T}$ and $\Phi_c((x,y)) = 0.1 \left[e^{-c_1(h_1-x)}, e^{-c_2(h_2-y)}, \min\{|4-x|, x\}, \min\{|4-y|, y\} \right]^\mathsf{T}$. The need for powerful representation for MaxEnt IRL [23] is well-known.

Algorithm 1. Iterative Algorithm for Reward and Constraint Recovery

---

Require: p_0, $p(s'|s,a)$, D, learning rate $= \kappa > 0$
1: Initialize $\mathbf{w}_r \in \mathbb{R}^{d_r}$ and $\mathbf{w}_c \in \mathbb{R}^{d_c}$ such that $|\mathbf{w}_r|_2 = |\mathbf{w}_c|_2 = 1$
2: Compute $\tilde{\Phi}_r$ and $\tilde{\Phi}_c$ using eq.(4)
3: **repeat**
4:     $\pi, \lambda \leftarrow$ Optimal Policy and Optimal Lagrange Multiplier for CMDP($\mathbf{w}_r, \mathbf{w}_c$)
5:     Calculate $d_t(s) \ \forall \ t = 1 \ldots, T, \ \forall \ s \in S$ under π using eq.(5)
6:     Compute $\hat{\Phi}_r$ and $\hat{\Phi}_c$ using eq.(6)
7:     Compute the gradients $\nabla_{\mathbf{w}_r}\mathcal{L}$ and $\nabla_{\mathbf{w}_c}\mathcal{L}$ using eq.(13)
8:     $\mathbf{w}_r \leftarrow \mathbf{w}_r \cdot \exp(-\kappa \nabla_{\mathbf{w}_r}\mathcal{L})$
9:     $\mathbf{w}_c \leftarrow \mathbf{w}_c \cdot \exp(-\kappa \nabla_{\mathbf{w}_c}\mathcal{L})$
10:    $\mathbf{w}_r \leftarrow \arg\min_{\mathbf{w}} \sum_i [\mathbf{w}]_i \log([\mathbf{w}]_i/[\mathbf{w}_r]_i)$ s.t $\sum_i[\mathbf{w}]_i = 1, \mathbf{w} \geq 0$
11:    $\mathbf{w}_c \leftarrow \arg\min_{\mathbf{w}} \sum_i [\mathbf{w}]_i \log([\mathbf{w}]_i/[\mathbf{w}_c]_i)$ s.t $\sum_i[\mathbf{w}]_i = 1, \ \mathbf{w} \geq 0, \ \mathbf{w}^\mathsf{T}\hat{\Phi}_c \leq 1$
12: **until** Convergence
13: **Return** $\mathbf{w}_r \ \mathbf{w}_c, \ \pi$

We choose $(c_1, c_2) \sim uniform[0,1]^2$ uniformly at random from the unit square, and (h_1, h_2) is chosen uniformly at random from the set of tuples $\{(i,j) : 1 \leq i, j \leq 3, \ i, j \in \mathbb{Z}\}$. The variable (h_1, h_2) corresponds to the location of a "hill" with "slopes" (c_1, c_2). In Fig. 1, we show results only for one realization of (c_1, c_2, h_1, h_2), though similar patterns were observed for numerical experiments using many other realizations. The true reward and the constraint parameters are chosen to be $\mathbf{w}_r = [q, 1-q]^\mathsf{T}$, $q \sim uniform[0,1]$ and $\mathbf{w}_c = [a, 1-a, b, 1-b]^\mathsf{T}$, $a, b \sim uniform[0,1]$. This has been done to keep the reward and constraint values normalized. We use 100 samples with $T = 2000$.

In Fig. 1, we can see that the reward and the constraints have been recovered well qualitatively, and the optimal policy for the recovered rewards and constraint is the same as the true policy. The simulation was run for 10 seeds, and the same trends were observed in each of them. This shows the effectiveness of our method, which is able to recover both the reward and the constraint from the given demonstrations. While experimenting, we observed that increasing T increased the accuracy of our method. This happens because the policy used to generate the trajectory corresponds to a stationary policy optimal for the

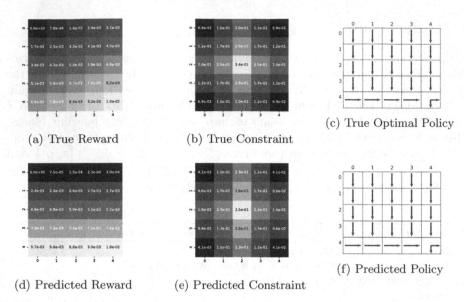

(a) True Reward   (b) True Constraint   (c) True Optimal Policy

(d) Predicted Reward   (e) Predicted Constraint   (f) Predicted Policy

Fig. 1. Pictorial demonstration of the performance of our algorithm in a grid-world setting. The numeric values of rewards and costs are written inside the boxes. The arrows denote the optimal action in a state.

infinite horizon discounted cost CMDP. Obviously, the longer the trajectory, the better it describes the policy. We also notice that the recovered reward follows the same pattern as the original reward (increasing from left to right and from top to bottom). However, the variation in numeric values in the recovered reward function is smaller, possibly because the principle of maximum entropy and normalization of $\mathbf{w}_r$ prevent any additional bias than what is strictly necessary to obtain the same data distribution as in the data set. Furthermore, we see that the peak of the penalty cost function (lightest colour) is well recovered through our method. Hence, we qualitatively demonstrate the effectiveness of our method. Since no previous work deals with the case of recovering both the reward and the constraint, we could not provide any comparison with other works.

5   Conclusion and Future Work

In this work, we focused on IRL-CR in the offline setting, in which the trajectory data is available in a batch. Though the problem is a difficult one and ill-posed, we have proposed a low-complexity algorithm to solve it. There has been no prior work on IRL-CR. Hence, there is a lack of a previous baseline to compare the performance of our work. However, we demonstrate strong results on a qualitative basis.

One immediate future step is to extend the framework to the settings where the data arrives in an online fashion. Also, though our work assumes known features for the states, this information may not be available in a real-world setting, and representation learning needs to be employed along with IRL-CR. Also, providing provable performance guarantees to the proposed algorithms will be very challenging, given that the problem is ill-posed. We will address these problems in our future research endeavours.

References

1. Abbeel, P., Ng, A.Y.: Apprenticeship learning via inverse reinforcement learning. In: Proceedings of the Twenty-First International Conference on Machine Learning, p. 1. ICML 2004, Association for Computing Machinery, New York, NY, USA (2004)
2. Altman, E.: Constrained Markov Decision Processes. Chapman and Hall, London (1999)
3. Argall, B.D., Chernova, S., Veloso, M., Browning, B.: A survey of robot learning from demonstration. Robot. Auton. Syst. **57**(5), 469–483 (2009)
4. Chou, G., Berenson, D., Ozay, N.: Learning constraints from demonstrations. In: Morales, M., Tapia, L., Sánchez-Ante, G., Hutchinson, S. (eds.) WAFR 2018. SPAR, vol. 14, pp. 228–245. Springer, Cham (2020). https://doi.org/10.1007/978-3-030-44051-0_14
5. Chou, G., Berenson, D., Ozay, N.: Uncertainty-aware constraint learning for adaptive safe motion planning from demonstrations. In: Conference on Robot Learning, pp. 1612–1639. PMLR (2021)
6. Ding, F., Xue, Y.: X-men: guaranteed xor-maximum entropy constrained inverse reinforcement learning. In: Cussens, J., Zhang, K. (eds.) Proceedings of the Thirty-Eighth Conference on Uncertainty in Artificial Intelligence. Proceedings of Machine Learning Research, vol. 180, pp. 589–598. PMLR (2022)
7. Englert, P., Vien, N.A., Toussaint, M.: Inverse KKT: learning cost functions of manipulation tasks from demonstrations. Int. J. Robot. Res. **36**(13–14), 1474–1488 (2017). https://doi.org/10.1177/0278364917745980
8. Finn, C., Levine, S., Abbeel, P.: Guided cost learning: Deep inverse optimal control via policy optimization. In: International Conference on Machine Learning, pp. 49–58. PMLR (2016)
9. Gaurav, A., Rezaee, K., Liu, G., Poupart, P.: Learning soft constraints from constrained expert demonstrations (2022)
10. Hazan, E., et al.: Introduction to online convex optimization. Found. Trends® Optim. **2**(3–4), 157–325 (2016)
11. Ho, J., Ermon, S.: Generative adversarial imitation learning. In: Advances in Neural Information Processing Systems, vol. 29 (2016)
12. Kaelbling, L.P., Littman, M.L., Moore, A.W.: Reinforcement learning: a survey. J. Artif. Intell. Res. **4**, 237–285 (1996)
13. Kalweit, G., Huegle, M., Werling, M., Boedecker, J.: Deep inverse q-learning with constraints. Adv. Neural. Inf. Process. Syst. **33**, 14291–14302 (2020)
14. Malik, S., Anwar, U., Aghasi, A., Ahmed, A.: Inverse constrained reinforcement learning. In: Meila, M., Zhang, T. (eds.) Proceedings of the 38th International Conference on Machine Learning. Proceedings of Machine Learning Research, vol. 139, pp. 7390–7399. PMLR (2021)

15. Ng, A.Y., Russell, S.J.: Algorithms for inverse reinforcement learning. In: Proceedings of the Seventeenth International Conference on Machine Learning, pp. 663–670. ICML 2000, Morgan Kaufmann Publishers Inc., San Francisco, CA, USA (2000)
16. Papadimitriou, D., Anwar, U., Brown, D.S.: Bayesian inverse constrained reinforcement learning. In: Workshop on Safe and Robust Control of Uncertain Systems (NeurIPS) (2021)
17. Park, D., Noseworthy, M., Paul, R., Roy, S., Roy, N.: Inferring task goals and constraints using Bayesian nonparametric inverse reinforcement learning. In: Kaelbling, L.P., Kragic, D., Sugiura, K. (eds.) Proceedings of the Conference on Robot Learning. Proceedings of Machine Learning Research, vol. 100, pp. 1005–1014. PMLR (2020)
18. Ratliff, N.D., Bagnell, J.A., Zinkevich, M.A.: Maximum margin planning. In: Proceedings of the 23rd International Conference on Machine Learning, pp. 729–736 (2006)
19. Schaal, S.: Learning from demonstration. In: Advances in Neural Information Processing Systems, vol. 9 (1996)
20. Scobee, D.R., Sastry, S.S.: Maximum likelihood constraint inference for inverse reinforcement learning. In: International Conference on Learning Representations (2020)
21. Sutton, R.S., Barto, A.G.: Reinforcement Learning: An Introduction. MIT press, Cambridge (2018)
22. Wulfmeier, M., Ondruska, P., Posner, I.: Deep inverse reinforcement learning. CoRR abs/1507.04888 (2015)
23. Ziebart, B.D., Maas, A.L., Bagnell, J.A., Dey, A.K., et al.: Maximum entropy inverse reinforcement learning. In: AAAI, vol. 8, pp. 1433–1438. Chicago, IL, USA (2008)

Transfer Learning: Kernel-Based Domain Adaptation with Distance-Based Penalization

Jainendra Prakash[✉][iD], Mrinmoy Ghorai[iD], and Rakesh Sanodiya[iD]

Indian Institute of Information Technology, Sri City, India
{jainendra.p19,mrinmoy.ghorai,rakesh.s}@iiits.in

Abstract. This paper introduces a novel approach to address the challenges of transfer learning, which aims to efficiently train a classifier for a new domain using supervised information from similar domains. Traditional transfer learning methods may fail to maintain the discriminative features of the target domain due to the scarcity of labelled data and the use of irrelevant source domain data distribution subspace, resulting in poor metrics. To overcome these challenges, the proposed approach, called KDADP, transforms the data distribution of both the source and target domains into a lower-dimensional subspace while preserving their discriminatory information. The KDADP model maximizes between-class variance and minimizes within-class variance with L1 penalization, enabling the recovery of the most useful characteristics and reducing the model's complexity. Experimental results on three real-world domain adaptation datasets demonstrate that the proposed KDADP model significantly improves classification performance and outperforms state-of-the-art primitive, shallow, and deeper domain adaptation methods.

Keywords: classification · domain adaptation · features space · transfer learning · supervised learning · semi-supervised learning

1 Introduction

Supervised learning relies on a substantial volume of labeled data. In contrast, transfer learning [2,12] is a more effective approach that allows knowledge to be acquired from readily available datasets and applied to scarce ones. This paper investigates the performance of Transfer Learning methods that consider both instance reweighing [1,4] and learning a new latent feature space [3,11]. The research paper focuses on unsupervised Transfer Learning, in this scenario, labeled data is available for the source domain while the target domain contains unlabeled data.

The existing domain adaptation methodologies lack critical objectives for optimum domain adaptation, such as preserving original data properties, addressing the disparity in marginal and conditional distributions between the source and target domains, and plotting the data into a new lower-dimensional

P. Maji et al. (Eds.): PReMI 2023, LNCS 14301, pp. 189–198, 2023.
https://doi.org/10.1007/978-3-031-45170-6_20

subspace. KDADP is an ideal domain adaptation model that learns a new lower-dimensional feature space while reducing the geometrical and distributional shift between source and target domain data points. By incorporating these objectives, KDADP can outperform existing Transfer Learning methods. The key contributions of our work include the following:

- In this study, we present an innovative approach to narrow the discrepancy between source and target domain data, simultaneously enhancing the separation between classes. Our framework involves training a novel projection matrix that maps the domains into a distinct subspace, effectively tackling the differences in marginal and conditional distributions between the two domains. To label the target domain data, we utilize pseudo-labelling, which enables us to generate appropriate labels for the data points.
- In order to showcase the efficiency of our model, we perform experiments on widely-used domain adaptation datasets, including SURF, DECAF, and PIE Face.

2   Previous Studies

Recent advancements in transfer learning and domain adaptation have focused on two approaches: instance re-weighting and learning new feature spaces. The former reduces the impact of irrelevant instances, narrowing domain distribution gaps, while the latter preserves class-wise features and minimizes geometric and distribution shifts. Several studies, such as TCA [7], JDA [5], JGSA [10], DICD [?], DIJDA [9], TJM [6], and Subspace-Based Transfer Joint Matching with Laplacian Regularization, have explored these techniques.

TJM combines instance re-weighting and feature learning, while the refined variant of TJM considers subspaces of both domains and integrates regularization conditions. These methods have shown varying levels of success in reducing the domain gap between source and target domain data points. However, finding an optimal method for reducing the domain gap remains a challenging task, and new methods such as KDADP, which preserves original data properties, addresses the disparity in marginal and conditional distributions between the source and target domains, and plots the data into a new lower-dimensional subspace, are still being developed.

3   Methodology

Within this segment, our main focus will be directed towards the problem statement and learning goal concerning domain adaptation. Subsequently, we will explore the approach we have implemented to address Domain Adaptation.

3.1   Problem Statement

[Definition 1] Target Domain(X_{td}) and Source Domain(X_{sd}): A Domain refers to a $d-$dimensional feature vector of Source and target domain X_{sd} and X_{td}. As we have data from two different domain D_{sd} and D_{td}, their distribution will have different feature space and marginal distribution i.e., $X_{sd} \neq X_{td}$ or $P_{sd}(X_{sd}) \neq P_{td}(X_{td})$

[Definition 2] Domain Adaptation: The objective of Domain Adaptation is to learn a new latent feature space using labelled samples from source domain and unlabelled samples from target domain such that $P_{sd} = P_{td}$ and $P_{sd}(y_{sd}/X_{sd}) = P_t(y_{td}/X_{td})$. where y_{td} is pseudo label of target domain samples.

3.2   Formulation

KDADP aims to minimize the disparity in marginal and conditional distributions between the source and target domains D_{sd} and D_{td}. It involves generating pseudo-labels for target domain samples using K-NN with source domain labelled data and transforming them into a lower-dimensional subspace. Optimization is carried out to obtain a new matrix ($\mathbf{A}$) that preserves the class-wise distribution and minimizes the domain gap.

3.3   Objective Function

We go into great depth in this part on each objective function's description that is employed to create our optimization task.

Preservation of Source Domain and Target Domain Discriminative Knowledge. LDA preserves both within-class and between-class characteristics based on label data. Challenges arise when using LDA for domain adaptation due to limited labelled data in the target domain. Pseudo-labels can be used in the target domain, predicted through source domain classifiers as discussed in JDA paper. An objective function for LDA can then be established for both domains.

$$opt = \underset{A}{\text{argmax}} \frac{A^T S_b A}{A^T S_w A} \tag{1}$$

where n_i is the number of data samples in the i-th class, m is the total mean vector of the source domain, m^i is the mean vector of the i-th class, and x_j^i is the j-th sample in the i-th class, S_b, S_w are between and within-class variance for given domain.

Target Domain Variance Optimization. If the pseudo-labels are inaccurate, the target domain's discriminative information may be lost, resulting in projection onto an irrelevant feature space. To address this, maximising variance in the target domain is essential.

$$\text{opt} = \arg \max_{A} A^T T_v A, \tag{2}$$

$$T_v = \mathbb{X}_t H_t \mathbb{X}_t^T, \tag{3}$$

where H_t is the centering matrix.

Maintaining the Original Resemblance of Every Set of Data Samples. The subspace data ($\mathbb{X} \in \mathbb{R}^{n \times d}$) can have structure or previous knowledge. We can maintain relationships between data samples using a p-nearest neighbour graph G as discussed in DIPDA paper, preserving a similarity link between x_i and x_j if they are close to each other. The similarity matrix S is defined as $S_{ij} = 1$ if x_i or x_j is among the p closest neighbours of each other, else $S_{ij} = 0$. To learn the projection vector matrix A, we calculate a regularizer,

$$J(A) = 2A^T \mathbb{X} L_f \mathbb{X}^T A, \tag{4}$$

where $L_f = \mathbb{X}L\mathbb{X}^T$ and $L = M - S$, with M being a diagonal matrix. This regularizer helps maintain similarity between data samples.

Aligning Source and Target Domain Distributions Using Maximum Mean Discrepancy (MMD). The maximum mean discrepancy (MMD) as per discussed in Rethink Maximum Mean Discrepancy for Domain Adaptation [8] can be used to align source and target domain distributions, without requiring density estimation. We can employ domain adaptation or transfer learning to learn a shared representation and minimize the gap between the distributions. This gap can be evaluated using the MMD matrix M_c, which can be computed using a given formula.

$$\left\| \frac{1}{n_s^k} \sum_{x_i \in \mathbb{X}_s^k} A^T x_i - \frac{1}{n_t^k} \sum_{x_j \in \mathbb{X}_t^k} A^T x_j \right\|^2 = \text{Tr}\left(A^T \mathbb{X} M_c \mathbb{X}^T A \right), \tag{5}$$

To align both marginal and conditional distributions, a variable approach called $D(A)$ is introduced, where we use a variable δ in both source and target distributions. The formula for $D(A)$ is the trace of the product of the transpose of A, the data matrix, and the distribution difference D_d. The MMD matrix M_c is defined based on the sample sets for each class in the source and target domains. We address the issue of relevance of the distributions by introducing δ in the evaluation of $D(A)$.

$$D(A) = (1 - \delta)\mathrm{Tr}\left(A^T \mathbb{X} M_d \mathbb{X}^T A\right) + \delta \mathrm{Tr}\left(A^T \mathbb{X} M_c \mathbb{X}^T A\right)$$
$$= \mathrm{Tr}\left(A^T \mathbb{X}((1 - \delta)M_d + \delta M_c)\mathbb{X}^T A\right)$$
$$= \mathrm{Tr}\left(A^T D_d A\right) \tag{6}$$

Minimizing Class-Wise Distribution-Gap of Source Domain and Target Domain. The L1 distance metric is a popular technique used in domain adaptation models to address the problem of distributional and marginal shift between source and target domains. This metric effectively reduces the shift by minimizing the intra-class distance between samples from the same source and target domains and maximizing the inter-class gap between samples from different domains. By penalizing the L1 distance metric, the model is encouraged to focus on the most relevant and informative features of the data while disregarding irrelevant or noisy features. This results in a more robust and accurate model that can better handle the challenges of domain adaptation, leading to significant improvements in performance and generalization.

$$S_t b = S_b - T_b \tag{7}$$
$$S_t w = S_w - T_w \tag{8}$$

S_b and T_b are between class scatter matrix, which is distance of mean of the source distribution and distance from mean of the class mean. S_w and T_w are within class scatter matrix, distance of class mean from it's data points. As referred in Eqs. 2 and 3.

KDADP Optimization Problem. To enhance KDADP's effectiveness, we combine multiple factors in the following equation:

$$\underset{A}{\mathrm{Max}} \, \mathrm{Tr}\left(\frac{A^T[\mu T_v + \alpha S_b + \beta T_b + \omega S_t b]A}{A^T D_d + [\gamma S_w + \eta T_w + \delta S_t w + \xi L_f]]A}\right) \tag{9}$$

Adjusting hyper-parameters such as $\mu, \alpha, \eta, \xi, \delta, \beta$, and γ, can optimize the equation, which considers Target Samples Variance, Source Domain inter-class variance, Target Domain inter-class variance, and other factors. The goal is to minimize intra-class differences while maximizing inter-class variation, while keeping the marginal and conditional distributions constant. Pseudo-labels for the target domain are updated through JDA and JGSA until convergence.

3.4   Optimization Function

To optimize Eqn. (9), the objective function may be recast in form of Langrange function:

$$f = \mathrm{Tr}\left(A^T[\mu T_v + \alpha S_b + \beta T_b + \omega S_t b]A\right) +$$

$$\mathrm{Tr}\left(\left(A^T[D_f + \gamma S_w + \eta T_w + \delta S_t w + \xi L_f]A - I\right)\Omega\right) \quad (10)$$

here I represent the identity matrix, and consider the equation $\frac{\partial f}{\partial A} = 0$ being set.

$$[\mu T_v + \alpha S_b + \beta T_b + \omega S_t b]A = [D_f + \gamma S_w + \eta T_w + \delta S_t w + \xi L_f]A\Omega$$

In this context, the matrix $\Omega = \mathrm{diag}(\omega_1, \ldots, \omega_k)$ represents the k-leading eigenvalues, and the matrix $A = [a_1, \ldots, a_k]$ contains the corresponding eigenvectors. The problem can be solved using a generalized eigenvalue decomposition approach. After obtaining matrix A, it becomes straightforward to compute the new latent feature space for both the source and target domains by projecting their respective data onto it.

4   Experiments

This section describes experiments comparing KDADP to state-of-the-art models on various domain adaptation benchmark datasets, and includes empirical studies on critical components of KDADP.

4.1   Dataset

The research paper made use of four sets of real-world domain adaptation data. Table 1 summarizes the statistics and provides a brief overview of each dataset. Performance evaluation was conducted on the Office-Caltech-256 dataset, which includes images from Caltech-256 and Office-31 datasets. The dataset is divided into ten groups, resulting in 12 cross-domain tasks. Feature extraction was performed using SURF and DeCAF6. Additionally, the PIE dataset with 68 individuals and 41,368 face images was utilized. Cross-domain experiments were conducted on five subsets of the PIE dataset, resulting in 20 tasks.

4.2   Results and Comparison

In this segment, a comparative analysis was conducted to evaluate traditional domain adaptation methods and KDADP using real-world visual domain adaptation datasets. KDADP emerged as the top-performing method in most tasks,

---

Algorithm 1: Kernel-Based Domain Adaptation with Distance-Based Penalization

---

Input : Input Data: X, Y_s; Hyperparameters: $\mu, \alpha, \eta, \xi, \delta, \beta, and \gamma$
         # iterations: total iterations ## pp -classifier: f_c

Output: Embeddings: $\mathbb{X}_s'$ and $\mathbb{X}_t'$; Transformation matrix: A.

1   Find initial low-dimensional subspace $\mathbb{X} \in \mathbb{R}^{(n_s+n_t) \times d}$, then obtain both domain subspaces $\mathbb{X}_s = \mathbb{X}[1 : n_s]$ and $\mathbb{X}_t = \mathbb{X}[n_s + 1 : n_s + n_t]$.

2   Initialize iter = 1 and pseudo labels Y_t' using f_c.

3   Construct matrices $S_b/T_b, S_w/T_w, T_v, S_{tw}/S_{tb}, L_f$, and D_f by using Eqs. (1), (1), (3), (7), (4), and (6), respectively.

4   **while** *iter* ≤ total *iterations* **do**

5   Solve the generalized eigen-decomposition problem as presented in Equation (9).

6   Select top k eigenvector and corresponding eigenvalues A.

7   Update the kernel space for source and target domain :$\mathbb{X}_s' = \mathbb{X}_s A$ and $\mathbb{X}_t' = \mathbb{X}_t A$

8   Update the KNN classifier model to generate updated pseudo labels for target domain samples f_c with $\mathbb{X}_s'$ and $\mathbb{Y}_s$ to update $Y_t' = f(\mathbb{X}_t')$

9   Iterate and update the matrix, using the optimization function and recalculating the matrices.

10   iter=iter+1;

11 **end**

Table 1. Summary of the key statistics for the four standard object/digit/face datasets.

Dataset	Type	Features	Classes	Samples	Subsets
Office-Caltech-10	Object	4096(DeCAF$_6$)	10	2533	A, W, D, C
Office-Caltech-10	Object	800(SURF)	10	2533	A, W, D, C
PIE	Face	1024	68	11,554	PIE1, . . . , PIE5

surpassing both subspace-centric and data-centric approaches. Specifically, it achieved the highest mean accuracy of 93.49% in the Office-Caltech-10 dataset and outperformed other techniques significantly in the PIE face dataset. Compared to TCA, JDA, and TJM, KDADP demonstrated considerable improvements of 90%, 42%, and 128%, respectively. Although LDADA and DICE methods preserved some target domain discriminative information, they fell short in comparison to KDADP due to overlooking other essential objectives (Tables 2, 3 and 4).

Table 2. Results for Surf Dataset

Data	TCA	NN	PCA	GFK	TJM	JDA	JGSA	LDAADA	DICD	DICE	DTLC	LDAPL	Proposed
C-A	45.6	23.7	39.5	46	46.8	43.1	51.5	54.8	47.3	50.2	50.3	57.2	**59.3**
C-W	39.3	25.8	34.6	37	39	39.3	45.4	60.2	46.4	48.1	54.4	53.22	53.56
C-D	45.9	25.5	44.6	40.8	44.6	49	45.9	41.5	49.7	51	52.4	52.87	**56.7**
A-C	42	26	39	40.7	39.5	40.9	41.5	38.4	42.4	42.7	46.6	43.54	**43.9**
A-W	40	29.8	35.9	37	42	38	45.8	49.3	45.1	52.2	48.1	53.22	**55.25**
A-D	35.7	25.5	33.8	40.1	45.2	42	47.1	39.1	38.9	49.7	45.4	55.41	**56.1**
W-C	31.5	19.9	28.2	24.8	30.2	33	33.2	31.7	33.6	37.8	33.8	34.73	**35.76**
W-A	30.5	23	29.1	27.6	30	29.8	39.9	35.1	34.1	37.5	33.5	42.48	**43.42**
W-D	91.1	59.2	89.2	85.4	89.2	92.4	90.5	74.6	89.8	87.3	87.3	95.54	94.64
D-C	33	26.3	29.7	29.3	31.4	31.2	29.9	29.9	34.6	33.7	32.1	34.6	**37.76**
D-A	32.8	28.5	33.2	28.7	32.8	33.4	38	40.6	34.5	41.1	36.2	41.75	**43.84**
D-W	87.5	63.4	86.1	80.3	85.4	89.2	91.9	74.7	91.2	84.1	92.9	94.58	**94.92**
Mean	46.24	31.38	43.57	43.14	46.34	46.77	50.05	47.49	48.97	51.28	51.08	54.93	**56.26**

Table 3. Results for Decaf Dataset

Data	TCA	NN	PCA	GFK	TJM	JDA	JGSA	LDAADA	DICD	DICE	DTLC	LDAPL	Proposed
C-A	89.8	87.3	88.1	88.2	88.8	89.6	91.4	92.5	90.1	92.3	92.8	93.74	93.43
C-W	78.3	72.5	83.4	77.6	81.4	85.1	86.8	86.4	92.2	93.6	98	96.27	95.1
C-D	85.4	79.6	84.1	86.6	84.7	89.8	93.6	88	93.6	93.6	93	95.54	**95.56**
A-C	82.6	71.4	79.3	79.2	84.3	83.6	84.9	88.6	86	85.9	88.2	88.78	93.21
A-W	74.2	68.1	70.9	70.9	71.9	78.3	81	90.5	81.4	86.4	93.6	90.85	**91.83**
A-D	81.5	74.5	82.2	82.2	76.4	80.3	88.5	85	83.4	89.8	87.3	90.45	91.72
W-C	80.4	55.3	70.3	69.8	83	84.8	85	87	84	85.3	88.1	88.25	89.12
W-A	84.1	62.6	73.5	76.8	87.6	90.3	90.7	92	89.7	90.7	92	93.01	**93.12**
W-D	100	98.1	99.4	100	100	100	100	96.8	100	100	100	100	100
D-C	82.3	42.1	71.7	71.4	83.8	83.8	86.2	86.6	86.1	87.4	89.31	89.31	89.5
D-A	89.1	50	79.2	76.3	90.3	90.3	90.9	92	92.1	92.5	92.9	93.95	**95.28**
D-W	99.7	91.5	98	99.3	99.3	99.3	95	99.7	99	99	100	100	100
Mean	85.62	71.08	81.67	81.52	85.96	87.93	89.50	90.42	89.80	91.38	92.93	93.35	**93.99**

5   Conclusion

The study presents KDADP, a novel framework that preserves discriminative data in both source and target domains, leading to better identification. Incorporating subspaces enhances classifier resilience to regional disruptions. The approach outperforms existing unsophisticated and complex domain adaptation methods across various datasets. Future work could explore multi-source unsupervised and semi-supervised DA, using particle swarm optimization for optimal parameter selection, and extending to a multi-metric unsupervised domain adaptation strategy for heterogeneous data distributions.

Table 4. PIE Dataset

Data	NN	PCA	TCA	GFK	JDA	TJM	JGSA	DICD	LDAADA	KUFDA	DICE	LDAPL	Proposed
5-7	26.09	24.8	40.76	26.15	58.81	29.52	68.07	73	34.5	67.67	84.1	86.43	**87.35**
5-9	26.59	25.18	41.79	27.27	54.23	33.76	67.52	72	44.9	70.34	77.9	75.98	**79.72**
5-27	30.67	29.26	59.63	31.15	84.5	59.2	82.87	92.2	61.5	86.06	95.9	96.22	95.98
5-29	16.67	16.3	29.35	17.59	49.75	26.96	46.5	66.9	35.4	49.02	66.5	66.54	**68.44**
7-5	24.49	24.22	41.81	25.24	57.62	39.4	25.21	69.9	31.4	72.62	81.2	87.18	**87.2**
7-9	46.63	45.53	51.47	47.37	62.93	37.74	54.77	65.9	34.9	74.34	74	87.19	86.5
7-27	54.07	53.35	64.73	54.25	75.82	48.8	58.96	85.3	53.5	87.86	88.6	90.96	90.5
7-29	26.53	25.43	33.7	27.08	39.89	17.09	35.41	48.7	26.4	61.7	68.8	70.47	**74.59**
9-5	21.37	20.95	34.69	21.82	50.96	37.39	22.81	69.4	38.2	73.91	78.8	80.79	79.36
9-7	41.01	40.45	47.7	43.16	57.95	35.29	44.19	65.4	30.5	72.56	76.7	82.75	**84.97**
9-27	46.53	46.14	56.23	46.41	68.45	44.03	56.86	83.4	60.6	86.96	85.2	95.01	94.82
9-29	26.23	25.31	33.15	26.78	39.95	17.03	41.36	61.4	40.7	69.85	70.8	71.88	**77.6**
27-5	32.95	31.96	55.64	34.24	80.58	59.51	72.14	93.1	61.3	90	93.3	96	**96.16**
27-7	62.68	60.96	67.83	65.92	82.63	60.5	88.27	90.1	56.7	88.4	95	96.56	**96.62**
27-9	73.22	72.18	75.86	73.35	87.25	64.88	86.09	89	67.8	84.62	92.3	94.42	93
27-29	37.19	35.11	40.26	37.38	54.66	25.06	74.32	75.6	50.4	75.24	81.1	84.44	**84.44**
29-5	18.49	18.85	26.98	20.35	46.46	32.86	17.52	62.9	31.3	54.05	73.8	76.53	**76.61**
29-7	24.19	23.39	29.9	24.62	42.05	22.89	41.06	57	24.1	67.46	71.2	78.6	**80.56**
29-9	28.31	27.21	29.9	28.42	53.31	22.24	49.1	65.9	35.4	70.77	74.1	81.56	**81.94**
29-27	31.24	30.34	33.6	31.33	57.01	30.72	34.75	74.8	48.2	76.78	81.8	90.3	89.76
Mean	34.76	33.85	44.75	35.49	60.24	37.24	53.39	73.09	43.38	74.01	80.55	84.49	**85.31**

References

1. Cai, H., Chen, H., Song, Y., Zhang, C., Zhao, X., Yin, D.: Data manipulation: towards effective instance learning for neural dialogue generation via learning to augment and reweight. arXiv preprint arXiv:2004.02594 (2020)
2. Li, M., Zhai, Y.M., Luo, Y.W., Ge, P.F., Ren, C.X.: Enhanced transport distance for unsupervised domain adaptation. In: Proceedings of the IEEE/CVF Conference on Computer Vision and Pattern Recognition, pp. 13936–13944 (2020)
3. Lin, T., Zha, H.: Riemannian manifold learning. IEEE Trans. Pattern Anal. Mach. Intell. **30**(5), 796–809 (2008)
4. Liu, F., et al.: Probabilistic margins for instance reweighting in adversarial training. In: Advances in Neural Information Processing Systems, vol. 34, pp. 23258–23269 (2021)
5. Long, M., Wang, J., Ding, G., Sun, J., Yu, P.S.: Transfer feature learning with joint distribution adaptation. In: Proceedings of the IEEE International Conference on Computer Vision, pp. 2200–2207 (2013)
6. Long, M., Wang, J., Ding, G., Sun, J., Yu, P.S.: Transfer joint matching for unsupervised domain adaptation. In: Proceedings of the IEEE Conference on Computer Vision and Pattern Recognition, pp. 1410–1417 (2014)
7. Pan, S.J., Tsang, I.W., Kwok, J.T., Yang, Q.: Domain adaptation via transfer component analysis. IEEE Trans. Neural Netw. **22**(2), 199–210 (2010)
8. Wang, W., Li, H., Ding, Z., Wang, Z.: Rethink maximum mean discrepancy for domain adaptation. arXiv preprint arXiv:2007.00689 (2020)

9. Yang, L., Zhong, P.: Discriminative and informative joint distribution adaptation for unsupervised domain adaptation. Knowl.-Based Syst. **207**, 106394 (2020)
10. Zhang, J., Li, W., Ogunbona, P.: Joint geometrical and statistical alignment for visual domain adaptation. In: Proceedings of the IEEE Conference on Computer Vision and Pattern Recognition, pp. 1859–1867 (2017)
11. Zhang, Z., Wang, J., Zha, H.: Adaptive manifold learning. IEEE Trans. Pattern Anal. Mach. Intell. **34**(2), 253–265 (2011)
12. Zhu, Y., et al.: Deep subdomain adaptation network for image classification. IEEE Trans. Neural Netw. Learn. Syst. **32**(4), 1713–1722 (2020)

A Contrastive Learning Approach for Infrared-Visible Image Fusion

Ashish Kumar Gupta[1]($\boxtimes$) (ID), Meghna Barnwal[2] (ID), and Deepak Mishra[3] (ID)

[1] Liquid Propulsion System Centre (ISRO), Thiruvananthapuram, India
ask812084@gmail.com
[2] Indian Institute of Technology, Guwahati, Guwahati, India
[3] Indian Institute of Space Science and Technology, Thiruvananthapuram, India
deepak.mishra@iist.ac.in

Abstract. Image processing and computer vision research have embraced deep learning. This paper offers a deep learning infrared-visible image fusion network using a contrastive learning framework and multi-scale structural similarity (MSSSIM). A novel contrastive learning loss combined with MSSSIM loss is introduced. The MSSSIM loss optimizes the mutual information between source and fused images from various viewpoints and resolutions, whereas contrastive loss reduces the artificially generated noise in the feature. The fusion network has an auto-encoder. The encoder extracts features from the infrared and visible images, and the decoder regenerates the fused image. Based on the similarity between the source and fused images, the loss function directs the network to extract silent targets and background textures from infrared and visible images, respectively. The proposed method outperforms the state-of-the-art in both qualitative and quantitative evaluations.

Keywords: Image Fusion · Infrared and Visible Image · Multi-Scale Structural Similarity (MSSSIM) · Contrastive Learning

1 Introduction

Infrared-Visible image fusion combines images from infrared and visual sensors or modalities of the same scene or objects into a single, high-resolution image. When these two modalities are integrated, they can reveal critical information about the scene, such as temperature, surface quality, and structural elements. High-quality fused images are commonly used in various applications, including but not limited to object identification, recognition, tracking, image enhancement, surveillance, remote sensing, and more [1]. Generally, a visible image is based on the visible light reflected by an object with a high spatial resolution and rich detail information. However, it is still impacted by low light levels, dark environments, bad weather, fog, smog, and other environmental interference. Omit, thermal radiation emitted by objects forms thermal images which provide silent target and global structural information in an interference environment with poor SNR and roughness.

P. Maji et al. (Eds.): PReMI 2023, LNCS 14301, pp. 199–208, 2023.
https://doi.org/10.1007/978-3-031-45170-6_21

Bavirisetti proposed the fusion technique for the infrared and visible images using two-scale decomposition and saliency. Mean, and median filters extract base and detail layers [2]. Li and Wang introduce deep decomposition using latent LRR, not SR, to extract features and nuclear norm and averaging strategy-based fusion to reconstruct the fused images in the low-rank category [3]. Deep neural networks' enormous feature extraction capabilities have advanced with the rise of deep learning in recent years. Yu Liu et al. create a decision map using CNN; they feed blurred versions of the input images into the CNN-Network during training. Fused images are combined with the decision map and the source image [4]. Li and Wu introduced DenseFuse, where the encoder is used for feature extraction and fused by addition and l1-norm fusion technique. After the fusion layer, the decoder network reconstructs the fused image. The previous techniques' loss functions include structure similarity and intensity gradient [5]. The loss function does not differentiate across sections of the source images, resulting in significant redundancy. DenseFuse proposes structural similarity (SSIM) loss with pixel loss, which computes the SSIM score adaptively by the comparison of pixel intensities of various source images in sliding windows [5]. The loss functions depend on the feature of the shallow image and only partially utilize in-depth features.

This paper proposes a novel fusion technique for the current self-supervised learning image fusion task motivated by contrastive learning methods and multi-scale structure similarity. It integrates variations in observing conditions with greater flexibility than single-scale techniques. We develop an adaptive framework for contrastive learning to reduce the noise in the image feature and preserve local features. A network can utilize a combination of contrastive loss and MSSSIM loss to facilitate feature extraction and reconstruction [6]. This technique identifies the salient targets and background textures from infrared and visible images.

This paper is divided into five sections, which are as follows: Sect. 2 briefly summarizes relevant efforts on image fusion methods. Section 3 describes the network architecture, fusion techniques as well as function. Section 4 describes the experimental results of the proposed technique. Section 5 concludes the paper.

2   Related Work

Deep learning has recently led to advancements in image fusion algorithms. Prabhakar introduced Deepfuse [7], a five-layer convolutional neural network autoencoder-based image fusion network. The encoder and decoder are used in feature extraction and image reconstruction, respectively. This model incorporates traditional visual information from each image to create a wholly artifact-free and visually stunning output. In contrast to Deepfuse's network architecture, The image fusion network DenseFuse [5] was developed by Li and Wu for the infrared and visible modality. They raised the number of network layers, implemented a dense block structure, and established an addiction and l_1-norm fusion technique. The feature map is integrated into a single feature map that contains salient infrared features and background visible image features. The decoder reconstructs the composite image. Hou et al. proposed VIF-Net [8], a simple end-to-end network. The encoder has five convolution layers for extracting the deep features of the infrared and visible images. To obtain fused features, the fusion layer directly concatenates deep features. A decoder from the fused feature reconstructs the fused image. Structural Similarity (SSIM) and the total variation (TV) loss function are used for guiding the network [9].

Contrastive learning is frequently employed in a wide range of image applications. Kang and Park introduced ContraGAN, which learns data-to-data and data-to-class relations via a conditional contrastive loss [10]. To improve the Mutual Information(MI) between crucial image regions in the fusion and source environments, Park et al. use contrastive learning [11]. Zhu and Yang proposed a CLF-Net [6], a fusion network that removes noise from feature maps using Noise Contrastive Estimation. Encoders and decoders are utilized for feature mapping and image reconstruction, while the Noice Contrastive estimation and SSIM function direct the network.

3   Method

This section discusses fusion network architecture, fusion algorithm, and loss function used in the process.

3.1   Network Architecture

The autoencoder is the fusion architecture's backbone. It comprises infrared and visible encoders and a decoder to reconstruct the image.

Color (RGB) images follow the same technique as grayscale images. The encoders extract the feature from the infrared and visible images, and the decoder regenerates the fused image. The framework uses two separate encoders

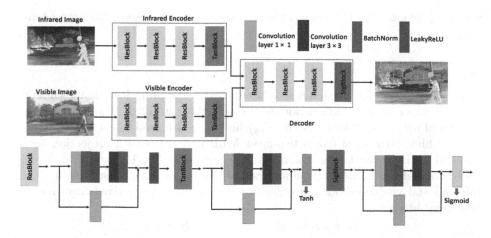

Fig. 1. Network Architecture: Encoders extract the features and decoder reconstructs the image

with the same architecture for feature extraction of infrared and visible images with independent parameters, respectively.

Encoder: As shown in Fig. 1, the encoder has three ResBlocks and one Tan-Block. Each ResBlock incorporates two convolution layers with kernel sizes of 1 × 1 and 3 × 3 and a LeakyRelu activation function. TanBlock incorporates two convolution layers with kernel 1 × 1 and 3 × 3 and a tanh activation function. Kernel 3 × 3 extracts the information, while kernel 1 × 1 transforms the input and output dimensions to maintain consistency.

Decoder: The decoder has three ResBlocks and one TanBlock, as shown in Fig. 1. SigBlock incorporates two convolution layers with kernel 3 × 3 and 1 × 1 and a sigmoid activation function. The sigmoid function ensures that the fused and the source image have the same dynamic range. The ResBlock, TanBlock, and SigBlock convolution layers are used throughout the feature extraction, fusion, and reconstruction operations. In particular, a stride of 1 and a padding of 0 are utilized for a 3 × 3 kernel, while a padding of 1 is added for a 1 × 1 kernel.

3.2 Contrastive Framework

The contrastive framework compares the distance between the network's outputs of positive and negative instances to the distance between positive and negative examples [12]. Positive samples are encoded to similar representations, while negative samples are encoded to dissimilar representations. Patch y and $\hat{y}$ from two images of the same spatial location. $\hat{y}$ is encoded into v, y is encoded into a positive k-dimensional vector $v^+ \in R^k$, and N other patches generate a negative vector $v^- \in R^{N \times k}$ [13]. The loss is minimal when v looks similar to positive vector v^+ but not negative vector v^-. The contrastive loss is given by:

$$l(v, v^+, v^-) = -\log \left[\frac{\exp\left(\frac{v.v^+}{\tau}\right)}{\exp\left(\frac{v.v^-}{\tau}\right) + \sum_{n=1}^{N} \exp\left(\frac{v.v_n^-}{\tau}\right)} \right]$$

where v_n denotes the nth negative vector and τ is a parameter to control temperature.

3.3 Loss

Noise Contrastive Estimation loss is a contrastive learning loss that estimates the parameters θ of a static model to identify the natural data and artificially generated noise [14]. Two encoders, E_{inf} and E_{vis}, are used to extract a feature stack, which is then fed into a two-layer MLP neural network projection head denoted as H in the image fusion network shown in Fig. 1. The infrared and visible modalities encoders produce the corresponding image features [6]. The infrared and visible encoders are generated from features derived from source and fused images.

$$z_{inf} = H(E_{inf}(I_{inf})) \quad z_{fuse\_inf} = H(E_{inf}(I_{fuse}))$$
$$z_{vis} = H(E_{vis}(I_{vis})) \quad z_{fuse\_vis} = H(E_{vis}(I_{fuse}))$$

patchNCE loss at a particular spatial site is given in (1)

$$l_{patchNCE}^{s}(Z^s) = \begin{cases} l(z_{fuse\_inf}^{s}, z_{inf}^{s}, z_{inf}^{\frac{S}{s}}) & \text{if } (z_{fuse\_inf}^{s} \cdot z_{inf}^{s}) \geq (z_{fuse\_vis}^{s} \cdot z_{vis}^{s}) \\ l(z_{fuse\_vis}^{s}, z_{vis}^{s}, z_{vis}^{\frac{S}{s}}) & \text{if } (z_{f\_inf}^{s} \cdot z_{inf}^{s}) < (z_{fuse\_vis}^{s} \cdot z_{vis}^{s}). \end{cases}$$
(1)

For a given location in the image, $zs \in R_C$ represents the patch's feature, while $z^{s/S} \in R^{(S-1) \times C}$ represents the features from other patches. The quantities S and C denote the total locations and channels, respectively. The contrastive loss for an image is calculated as shown in (2)

$$L_{patchNCE} = E_{x \sim X} \sum_{s=1}^{S} l_{patchNCE}^{s}(Z^s)$$
(2)

where $s \in \{1, \ldots, S\}$,

The loss function $L_{patchNCE}$ was used to improve the projection head and encoder to retain the equivalent feature of the infrared and visible images in the fused image [6].

The Structural Similarity (SSIM) [15] between image samples a and b can be calculated based on the comparison measurements: structure (s) (3), luminance (l) (4), and contrast (c) (5). The comparison functions are as follows:

$$s(a,b) = \frac{\sigma_{ab} + c_3}{\sigma_a \sigma_b + c_3}$$
(3)

$$l(a,b) = \frac{2\mu_a \mu_b + c_1}{\mu_a^2 + \mu_b^2 + c_1}$$
(4)

$$c(a,b) = \frac{2\sigma_a \sigma_b + c_2}{\sigma_a^2 + \sigma_b^2 + c_2}$$
(5)

where μ_a and μ_b represent the mean image a and b, respectively; σ_a^2 and σ_b^2 represent their variances, respectively; and σ_{ab} represents their covariance.

SSIM can be calculated as shown in (6):

$$SSIM(a,b) = [l(a,b)^{\alpha} \cdot c(a,b)^{\beta} \cdot s(a,b)^{\gamma}]$$
(6)

The single-scale approach SSIM was used to determine structural similarity. The single-scale technique may only be appropriate in certain situations. The multi-scale approach makes incorporating image information at various views and resolutions simple. Multi-scale structural similarity (MSSSIM) [16] can be expressed as shown in (7):

$$MSSSIM(a,b) = [l_m(a,b)]^{\alpha_M} \cdot \prod_{j=1}^{M} [C_j(a,b)]^{\beta_j} [s_j(a,b)]^{\gamma_j}$$
(7)

MSSSIM loss between the source and reconstructed image can be expressed as shown in (8)

$$L_{MSSSIM}(X, X_R) = \frac{1 - MSSSIM(X, X_R)}{2}$$
(8)

where X is the source, and X_R is the reconstructed images. The MSSSIM loss fusion network as shown in (9)

$$L_{MSSSIM} = L_{MSSSIM}(I_{inf}, I_{fuse}) + L_{MSSSIM}(I_{vis}, I_{fuse}) \qquad (9)$$

where I_{fuse}, I_{inf}, and I_{vis} are fused, infrared, and visible images, respectively. The total loss of fusion network is defined as shown in (10):

$$L_{fusion} = L_{patchNCE} + \lambda L_{MSSSIM} \qquad (10)$$

The hyperparameter λ controls the harmony between loss functions. Although the patchNCE loss is better at retaining deep features, the MSSSIM loss does a better job of preserving structural similarities from various viewpoints and resolutions across infrared, visible, and fused images. The network is guided towards optimal performance with the help of the loss functions.

4   Experiments

The experimental setup to evaluate the proposed technique and compare its performance with other existing techniques is described in this section.

4.1   Training and Testing Details

TNO and FLIR datasets were utilized throughout the whole training process. The TNO dataset [17] is the most popular for infrared-visible image fusion. It focuses mainly on describing scenarios involving the military. In addition, the FLIR dataset describes several road situations, such as roads, vehicles, and people, and it was built using FLIR movies.

The model has been trained on 18 TNO datasets and 20 FLIR datasets. It is necessary to have more than 38 data pairs to train the model. The training datasets size is increased after cropping. Each image is then divided into 128 × 128 smaller patches with a step size of 32. In the end, 8368 picture patch pairings were obtained. The model is trained using the Adam optimizer with an initial learning rate of 10^{-3} and a temperature constant $\tau = 0.07$ for 200 epochs with a batch size 16. Cropped and uncropped images of various sizes are input into the network during testing to reconstruct the fused image. All experiments for the proposed technique are conducted on the PyTorch framework on NVIDIA GeForce RTX A4000 GPU.

4.2   Evaluation Metrics

Qualitative evaluation relies on people's visual perception, whereas quantitative evaluation evaluates the integrity of the fused image. The image with prominent infrared targets and rich texture data has the greatest impact [6]. On the other hand, quantitative evaluation measures the performance of image fusion quantitatively using six objective evaluation metrics used in this research Entropy

(EN), Mutual Information (MI), Visual Information fidelity (VIF), Standard Deviation (SD), Average Gradient (AG) and Spatial Frequency (SF). These metrics serve as standard tools. Ma et al. use these metrics for quantitative analysis in image fusion [1].

4.3 Qualitative Evaluation

Due to space constraints, only discuss the performance of the image "courtyard", Fig. 2 depicts the infrared and visible images input into networks and the fused images obtained from existing fusion and proposed methods. Figure 2a and 2b show the visible and infrared images utilized as network input. Figure 2(c–m) shows fused images generated by distinct networks.

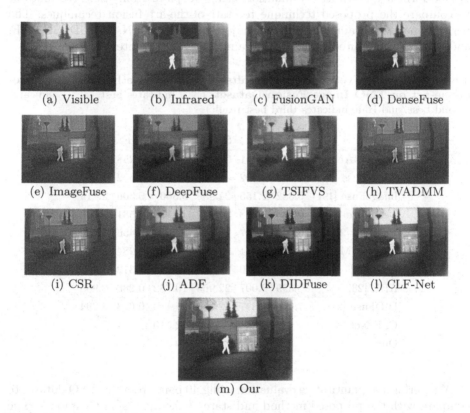

(m) Our

Fig. 2. Result of Qualitative Evaluation "courtyard" image: (a) Visible image, (b) Infrared Image, (c) FusionGAN, (d) DenseFuse, (e) ImageFuse, (f) DeepFuse, (g) TSIFVS, (h) TVADMM, (i) CSR, (j) ADF, (k) DIDFuse, (l) CLF-Net, and (m) output of our proposed method

As can be seen, the proposed technique preserves more detail and less noise. The image obtained through FusionGAN [18] contains more synthetic noise. ImageFuse [19], DeepFuse [7], TVADMM [20], and CSR [21] fused images contain synthetic structures around silent features. The fused image using DenseFuse [5], TSIFVS [2], and DIDFuse [22] has a fuzzy edge that hampers target recognition, and the sky is unclear. In contrast, the fused image derived via CLF-Net [6] and the proposed methods contain more silent features and maintain more detailed information with a clear sky, and details and background edges are preserved. The proposed method produces more natural-appearing fused images than other techniques. There is no distinction between CLF-Net and the proposed merger regarding human sensitivity. So, we will perform a quantitative evaluation in the next section.

4.4   Quantitative Evaluation

We perform a quantitative evaluation using 40 pairs from the TNO dataset to compare the proposed technique to state-of-the-art fusion techniques. The performance was evaluated using six objective metrics: EN, MI, SD, SF, VIF, and AG. The computed values for these metrics are presented in Table 1.

Table 1. Quantitative Evaluation results of proposed method and ten state-of-the-art on TNO Image Fusion Dataset: (Red indicates best, Green indicates second best, and Blue indicates third best result)

Metrics	EN	MI	SD	SF	VIF	AG
FusionGAN [18]	6.576	2.341	29.035	8.762	0.258	2.417
DenseFuse [5]	6.842	2.302	31.817	11.095	0.572	3.597
ImageFuse [19]	6.382	2.155	22.938	9.800	0.306	2.719
DeepFuse [7]	6.860	2.298	32.249	11.125	0.581	3.599
TSIFVS [2]	6.669	1.717	28.036	12.598	0.456	3.980
TVADMM [20]	6.402	2.041	23.007	9.034	0.284	2.518
CSR [21]	6.428	1.990	23.603	11.445	0.312	3.367
ADF [23]	6.399	2.007	22.963	10.782	0.286	2.988
DIDFuse [22]	7.006	2.347	42.657	13.126	0.623	4.294
CLF-Net [6]	7.147	4.261	46.992	12.610	0.782	4.880
Our	7.355	3.817	58.292	20.800	0.814	8.570

We perform a quantitative evaluation using 40 pairs from the TNO dataset to compare with the proposed method and state-of-the-art fusion techniques. The proposed methods attain the highest performance in EN, VIF, SD, AG, and SF and the second-highest performance in MI. CLF-Net performs the best in MI, second in EN, SD, VIF, and AG, and third in SF. While DIDFuse scored second in SF and third in EN, MI, VIF, SD, and AG, it was third in SF. According to the results, the VIF metric is highly correlated with human visual perception. The proposed technique attains the highest VIF value, indicating superior visual quality, consistent with the qualitative evaluation. Fused images with higher EN values contain more information. Since the proposed method yields a larger EN value, as shown in Table 1, the fused image has more information than others. Mutual Information (MI) metric quantifies information transmitted from input infrared and visible images to the fused image. Higher MI indicates that the fused image retains more information from infrared and visible images. The largest SD value implies that the fused image has the highest contrast, congruent with the qualitative evaluation. The highest SF value implies that the high-frequency components of the infrared image blend more naturally with the low-frequency components of the visible image. The fused image preserves sharp edges and precise detail. The highest AG value implies that the fused image contains more edges and sharp transitions, indicating preserved details and structures consistent with the quantitative evaluation. The proposed technique outperforms the other approach regarding the six quantitative metrics, indicating its effectiveness for fusing infrared and visible images. It consistently achieves the highest or second-highest results across all six metrics, demonstrating its superiority over state-of-the-art methods.

5   Conclusion

The paper proposed an infrared-visible image fusion network with the help of contrastive learning. The image fusion network introduces a contrastive learning framework with multiscale structural similarity. The contrastive loss emphasises feature similarity, while the multiscale structural similarity loss emphasises structural similarity from different viewpoints and resolutions. The loss function guides the network's extraction and fusion of features. The network retains the infrared image's silent feature and the visible image's rich background texture. The proposed technique is superior in qualitative and quantitative evaluation, outperforming state-of-the-art regarding visual perception and quantitative. In the future, we will develop various contrastive learning strategies, as well as structural similarity and multiscale structural similarity, to improve model accuracy. On the one hand, to increase model accuracy, we will create different contrastive learning strategies in the future, in addition to structural similarity and multiscale structural similarity. In contrast, we employ an image fusion technique for RGB-thermal object detection, recognition, and tracking.

References

1. Ma, J., Ma, Y., Li, C.: Infrared and visible image fusion methods and applications: a survey. Inf. Fusion **45**, 153–178 (2019)
2. Bavirisetti, D.P., Dhuli, R.: Two-scale image fusion of visible and infrared images using saliency detection. Infrared Phys. Technol. **76**, 52–64 (2016)
3. Wang, X., Yin, J., Zhang, K., Li, S., Yan, J.: Infrared weak-small targets fusion based on latent low-rank representation and DWT. IEEE Access **7**, 112 681–112 692 (2019)
4. Yang, Y., et al.: Infrared and visible image fusion based on infrared background suppression. Opt. Lasers Eng. **164**, 107528 (2023)

5. Li, H., Wu, X.-J.: DenseFuse: a fusion approach to infrared and visible images. IEEE Trans. Image Process. **28**(5), 2614–2623 (2018)
6. Zhu, Z., Yang, X., Lu, R., Shen, T., Xie, X., Zhang, T.: CLF-Net: contrastive learning for infrared and visible image fusion network. IEEE Trans. Instrum. Meas. **71**, 1–15 (2022)
7. Ram Prabhakar, K., Sai Srikar, V., Venkatesh Babu, R.: DeepFuse: a deep unsupervised approach for exposure fusion with extreme exposure image pairs. In: Proceedings of the IEEE International Conference on Computer Vision, pp. 4714–4722 (2017)
8. Hou, R., et al.: VIF-Net: an unsupervised framework for infrared and visible image fusion. IEEE Trans. Comput. Imaging **6**, 640–651 (2020)
9. Xu, H., Zhang, H., Ma, J.: Classification saliency-based rule for visible and infrared image fusion. IEEE Trans. Comput. Imaging **7**, 824–836 (2021)
10. Kang, M., Park, J.: ContraGAN: contrastive learning for conditional image generation. In: Advances in Neural Information Processing Systems, vol. 33, pp. 21 357–21 369 (2020)
11. Park, T., Efros, A.A., Zhang, R., Zhu, J.-Y.: Contrastive learning for unpaired image-to-image translation. In: Vedaldi, A., Bischof, H., Brox, T., Frahm, J.-M. (eds.) ECCV 2020, Part IX. LNCS, vol. 12354, pp. 319–345. Springer, Cham (2020). https://doi.org/10.1007/978-3-030-58545-7_19
12. Huang, D.-S., Jo, K.-H., Figueroa-García, J.C.: Intelligent Computing Theories and Application: 13th International Conference, ICIC 2017, Liverpool, UK, August 7–10, 2017, Proceedings, Part II, vol. 10362. Springer, Cham (2017). https://doi.org/10.1007/978-3-319-63309-1
13. Spiegl, B.: Contrastive unpaired translation using focal loss for patch classification. arXiv preprint arXiv:2109.12431 (2021)
14. Andonian, A., Park, T., Russell, B., Isola, P., Zhu, J.-Y., Zhang, R.: Contrastive feature loss for image prediction. In: Proceedings of the IEEE/CVF International Conference on Computer Vision, pp. 1934–1943 (2021)
15. Wang, Z., Bovik, A., Sheikh, H., Simoncelli, E.: Image quality assessment: from error visibility to structural similarity. IEEE Trans. Image Process. **13**(4), 600–612 (2004)
16. Zhao, H., Gallo, O., Frosio, I., Kautz, J.: Loss functions for image restoration with neural networks. IEEE Trans. Comput. Imaging **3**(1), 47–57 (2016)
17. Toet, A., et al.: TNO image fusion dataset. Figshare. Data (2014)
18. Ma, J., Yu, W., Liang, P., Li, C., Jiang, J.: FusionGAN: a generative adversarial network for infrared and visible image fusion. Inf. Fusion **48**, 11–26 (2019)
19. Li, H., Wu, X.-J., Kittler, J.: Infrared and visible image fusion using a deep learning framework. In: 2018 24th International Conference on Pattern Recognition (ICPR), pp. 2705–2710. IEEE (2018)
20. Guo, H., Ma, Y., Mei, X., Ma, J.: Infrared and visible image fusion based on total variation and augmented Lagrangian. JOSA A **34**(11), 1961–1968 (2017)
21. Liu, Y., Chen, X., Ward, R.K., Wang, Z.J.: Image fusion with convolutional sparse representation. IEEE Signal Process. Lett. **23**(12), 1882–1886 (2016)
22. Zhao, Z., Xu, S., Zhang, C., Liu, J., Li, P., Zhang, J.: DIDFuse: deep image decomposition for infrared and visible image fusion. arXiv preprint arXiv:2003.09210 (2020)
23. Bavirisetti, D.P., Dhuli, R.: Fusion of infrared and visible sensor images based on anisotropic diffusion and Karhunen-Loeve transform. IEEE Sens. J. **16**(1), 203–209 (2015)

A Supervised Approach for Efficient Video Anomaly Detection Using Transfer Learning

Rangachary Kommanduri$^{(\boxtimes)}$ ⓘ and Mrinmoy Ghorai ⓘ

Computer Vision Group, Indian Institute of Information Technology, Sri City, India
{rangachary.k,mrinmoy.ghorai}@iiits.in

Abstract. Video anomaly detection is a complex task that has numerous applications in video surveillance. It involves identifying unusual patterns or events in a video stream that deviate from the expected or typical behavior. This paper introduces a new framework for supervised video anomaly detection using transfer learning from a pre-trained model. The approach presented in this paper utilizes the MobileNetV2 architecture as a feature extractor, which is further fine-tuned using a small set of annotated data. The fine-tuned model is then utilized to classify video frames into normal or anomalous classes. The suggested methodology is evaluated on benchmark datasets and compared with state-of-the-art methods. The experimental results demonstrate the effectiveness and efficiency of the proposed method in detecting anomalies in videos with high accuracy and low computational cost.

Keywords: anomaly · classification · transfer learning · pre-trained model

1 Introduction

Anomaly refers to an observation or event that deviates significantly from the expected or normal pattern. Video anomaly detection (VAD) is a field within computer vision that focuses on automatically identifying and flagging abnormal events or behaviors in video data. While traditional approaches to VAD require a lot of manual effort and are often limited in their ability to accurately classify anomalies, recent advancements in deep learning have enabled the development of highly accurate and efficient models for anomaly detection. Despite the tremendous progress in deep learning, building a robust deep learning model from scratch remains a time-consuming process. Additionally, a substantial amount of training data is required to ensure that the model is capable of learning the underlying patterns and generalizing them effectively to new data. Moreover, while designing anomaly detection systems, it is not only important to consider the accuracy of detection but also to take into account the computational requirements in terms of time and memory to ensure that it can be practically deployed in real-world settings.

P. Maji et al. (Eds.): PReMI 2023, LNCS 14301, pp. 209–217, 2023.
https://doi.org/10.1007/978-3-031-45170-6_22

To address these challenges, transfer learning has emerged as a popular technique for building deep learning models with limited data. This approach entails initializing a model with pre-trained weights and subsequently fine-tuning it on a new task. By doing so, the model leverages the existing knowledge captured by the pre-trained weights, allowing it to effectively learn and adapt to the new task at hand. This article presents an approach based on transfer learning that utilizes MobileNetV2 as a pre-trained network for video frame classification. It achieves high accuracy across various image classification tasks while utilizing considerably fewer parameters and computational resources compared to other popular architectures such as ResNet and InceptionNet. The paper contributes the field of VAD are as follows;

- We introduce a novel framework for VAD that utilizes transfer learning with a fine-tuned MobileNetV2 pre-trained model.
- By evaluating our framework on four widely-used benchmark datasets, we demonstrate its exceptional performance, surpassing existing methods and achieving state-of-the-art results.
- We conduct ablation experiments on various pre-trained networks, highlighting the superior performance of MobileNetV2 compared to other networks.

2 Related Work

Video anomaly detection models can be classified into three main categories: prediction [3], classification [2], and reconstruction-based approaches [11]. Prediction-based techniques rely on predicting the future frames of a video sequence based on previous frames and identifying anomalies as deviations from the predicted frames. Reconstruction-based approaches aim to reconstruct the frames of the video sequence by modeling the normal behavior and identifying anomalies as deviations from the learned normal pattern. Classification-based techniques strive to classify video frames or sequences as normal or anomalous by leveraging learned features. However, this methodology necessitates annotated data for training, posing constraints in certain real-world scenarios. Temporally coherent Sparse Coding used by Luo *et al.* [9] to encode consecutive frames with similar content, which were then input to a stacked RNN for detecting anomalies in videos. An interesting method of training object-centric autoencoders with an SVM classifier used a two-stage training procedure [5]. In order to discriminate between abnormal and normal items, the SVM classifier was utilized once the autoencoders were trained to recognize objects. Bansod *et al.* [2] used a pre-trained VGG16 model for transfer learning to extract spatial features from anomalous and normal patterns. Meanwhile, Wan *et al.* [12] introduced the AR-Net, where they devised a weakly supervised dynamic multiple-instance learning loss and a center loss. The former aimed to enhance the dissimilarity between anomalous and normal instances, while the latter focused on reducing the intra-class distance of normal instances. Sulaiman *et al.* [1] utilized deep feature representations of a transfer learning model along with similarity measures to model normality in their proposed framework.

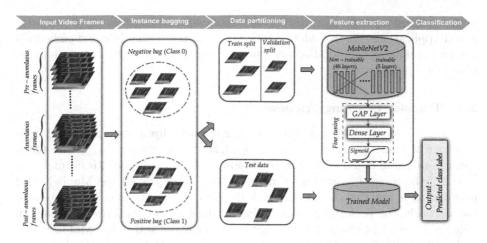

Fig. 1. The proposed network architecture is visually depicted in the form of a conceptual illustration, exhibiting five distinctive stages. The upper section of the figure highlights the individual functionalities attributed to each stage, symbolized by arrow marks.

In summary, transfer learning and fully supervised classification are two important approaches for effective video anomaly detection. While transfer learning can help leverage pre-trained models on extensive image datasets, while fully supervised classification requires a significant amount of labeled data but can deliver superior performance. A combination of these approaches has the potential to yield even more impressive results in video anomaly detection.

3   Our Approach

This section outlines the presented approach as illustrated in Fig. 1. Each of the framework's components is discussed in further detail in the following subsections.

3.1   Feature Extraction Network

For our anomaly detection task, we adopt MobileNetV2 as our pre-trained model. MobileNetV2 is a popular lightweight neural network architecture that was introduced by Sandler *et al.* in 2018. It contains 53 convolutional layers and one average pooling layer. The model has a computational cost significantly lower than other leading models such as ResNet or VGG. This makes MobileNetV2 an ideal choice for deployment on devices with limited resources, such as mobile phones, IoT devices, and embedded systems. We chose to use MobileNetV2 as our pre-trained model for several reasons. Firstly, it has undergone comprehensive pre-training on the ImageNet dataset, which comprises a vast collection of over 1.2 million images spanning 1,000 different classes. This pre-training allows the model to learn powerful features that are applicable to a diverse set of computer vision applications. Second, MobileNetV2 is optimized for mobile and embedded devices, making it computationally efficient and suitable for real-time anomaly detection applications.

3.2   Transfer Learning Framework

Consider a dataset X of n video clips, where each clip x_i is represented by a sequence of frames denoted as $x_i = I_1, I_2, ..., I_k$. Let $Y = y_1, y_2, ..., y_k$ be a set of corresponding labels for each video x_i, where $y_i = 0$ if the frame I_t is normal, and $y_i = 1$ if the frame I_t contains an anomaly. We can represent the MobileNetV2 network as a function $f_\theta(I_t)$, where θ denotes the pre-trained parameters of the network. For performing binary classification of video frames for anomaly detection, we adopt the transfer learning approach and utilize the MobileNetV2 architecture. We freeze the initial 48 layers of the model and add a Global Average Pooling (GAP) layer, dense layer parameters with w and b as trainable weights and bias, and a sigmoid activation layer on top of the pre-trained network, which is represented by a function $h_w b(z)$. The output of the fine-tuned MobileNetV2 network is fed as input to the GAP layer, which produces a feature vector z by computing the spatial average of each feature map in the pre-trained network's output. This can be formulated as:

$$z = GlobalAvgPool(f_\theta(I_t)) \qquad (1)$$

The feature vector z obtained is then passed to the dense layer, denoted as $h_w b(z)$. This layer can be mathematically represented as;

$$h_w b(z) = \sigma(w^T * z + b) \qquad (2)$$

where the sigmoid function σ, converts the dense layer's output to a probability between 0 and 1. To finetune the MobileNetV2 network for video anomaly classification, we need to optimize the parameters of the dense layer w and b to minimize the loss function $\mathcal{L}$ as:

$$\mathcal{L} = \frac{-1}{n} \sum_{i=1}^{n} [y_i * log(h_w b(GlobalAvgPool(f_\theta(I_t))))$$
$$+ (1 - y_i) * log(1 - h_w b(GlobalAvgPool(f_\theta(I_t))))] \qquad (3)$$

The parameters of the dense layer, represented by 'w' and 'b', can be optimized using an optimization algorithm such as stochastic gradient descent (SGD) with a specific learning rate (0.0001) and momentum (0.9). The objective is to minimize the loss function $\mathcal{L}$ through iterative updates of these parameters.

3.3   Video Anomaly Detection

To perform video frame classification, our model utilizes a final layer with a Sigmoid activation function. This activation function generates a scalar value

Table 1. Details of datasets utilized for video anomaly detection.

Dataset	# Videos	#Abnormal Events	Instance bagging		Data split	
			Class 0	Class 1	Training	Testing
Ped1	70	40	4156	4044	6560	1640
Ped2	28	12	1712	1648	2688	672
Avenue	37	47	4540	4454	7195	1799
UMN	3	11	1800	1620	2736	684

ranging from 0 to 1, representing the probability of the input frame containing an anomaly. In the train phase, the model is trained using labeled video frames, allowing it to learn the correlation between input frames and their corresponding labels. Through back-propagation, the model's weights are updated to minimize the binary cross-entropy loss, aligning the predicted labels with the true labels. During inference, the trained model is utilized to evaluate new video frames, with any frame having a probability value exceeding a threshold (usually 0.5) being classified as anomalous, and any frame below the threshold being classified as normal.

4   Experiments

4.1   Datasets and Evaluation Metric

The UCSD Ped1 and Ped2 datasets are captured by a stationary camera overlooking a pedestrian walkway, with a spatial resolutions of 158×238, 360×240 pixels, respectively. In these datasets, any objects other than pedestrians, including cyclists, skaters, wheelchairs, and carts are considered anomalies. The dataset from the University of Minnesota (UMN) comprises three distinct scenarios of crowd escape, namely lawn, indoor, and plaza, with a resolution of 320×240. Each scenario starts with a group of people walking around normally, and then all individuals start escaping suddenly, which is considered as an anomaly. Sample anomalous events in the CUHK Avenue dataset are throwing objects like paper and bag, loitering, and running across the camera. The dataset has a spatial resolution of 360×640. The frames in all these datasets are initially classified into two distinct classes, i.e., anomaly and non-anomaly. To facilitate model training and performance evaluation, the frames are further partitioned into two non-overlapping sets, namely train and test, in an 80:20 ratio. Further details about these datasets can be found in Table 1.

To evaluate the efficacy of the frame-level detection algorithm, the Receiver Operating Characteristic (ROC) curve serves as a valuable assessment tool. In addition to the ROC curve, two widely employed quantitative metrics, namely Area under the ROC Curve (AUC) and Equal Error Rate (EER), are utilized. Moreover, Accuracy, Precision, Recall, and F1 Score are commonly employed metrics to evaluate classification tasks.

Table 2. Performance comparison of various methods based on their AUC and EER metrics.

Method	AUC (%)				EER (%)			
	Ped1	Ped2	Ave.	UMN	Ped1	Ped2	Ave.	UMN
Ionescu *et al.* [5]	-	97.6	90.4	99.6	-	-	-	-
MGFC-AAE [7]	85	91.6	84.2	98.6	20	16	22.3	5
Anomaly-Net [13]	83.5	94.9	86.1	99.6	25.2	10.3	22	2.6
Tong *et al.* [8]	97.6	97.2	96.3	99.6	6.0	6.9	9.1	1.8
Guo *et al.* [4]	74.7	88.1	86.6	-	-	-	-	
Zhou *et al.* [14]	-	97.4	92.6	-	-	-	-	
FastAno [10]	-	96.3	85.3	-	-	-	-	
Ruchika *et al.* [6]	98.5	97.9	95.1	-	11	9	11.5	-
Ours	**98.6**	**99.4**	**95.5**	**99.7**	**4.2**	**2.6**	**8.9**	**1.2**

Table 3. Quantitative performance metrics for different datasets.

Dataset	Test Error	Test Accuracy	F1-Score	Precision	Recall
Ped1	0.155	0.947	0.948	0.943	0.954
Ped2	0.034	0.9941	0.994	1	0.988
CUHKAvenue	0.122	0.956	0.954	0.985	0.924
UMN	0.018	0.997	0.997	1	0.994

4.2 Results

We perform a series of experiments to assess and compare the effectiveness of the proposed framework against existing methods. The outcomes of these experiments are presented in Table 2. In order to maintain consistency and fairness across all datasets, we adopt identical network design and training parameters for each dataset. The AUC and EER values highlighted as bold in the table indicate the effectiveness of our framework in distinguishing anomalous and non-anomalous frames. Additionally, we provide comprehensive performance metrics such as accuracy, F1 score, precision, and recall, which are calculated and reported in Table 3. The computational complexity of our proposed model, when compared with other pre-trained models was evaluated based on the number of parameters and GFLOPs (Giga Floating Point Operations) and presented in Table 4. Upon analyzing the table, it becomes evident that our proposed method, considering MobileNetV2 as the baseline architecture achieves the highest AUC, outperforming other models, despite having the lowest number of parameters and operations.

Ablation Experiment. In order to assess the effectiveness of our proposed model, we conduct a comparative analysis with various pre-trained models,

Table 4. Comparative Analysis of parameters and GFLOPs for various architectures.

Baseline	Params	GFLOPs
ResNet50	23.59M	7.75
InceptionV3	21.8M	5.69
VGG16	14.7M	30.7
DenseNet201	18.32M	8.63
MobilenetV2	**2.26M**	**0.613**

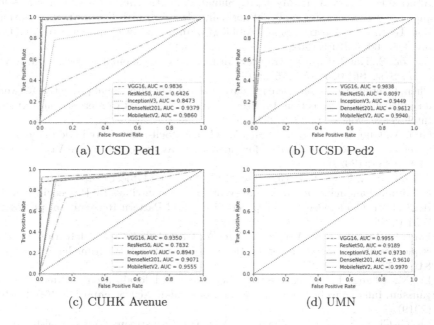

Fig. 2. Comparison of AUC scores for different pre-trained models on multiple datasets.

namely ResNet50, InceptionV3, VGG16, and DenseNet201. The results obtained from our study are visually presented in Fig. 2, which demonstrates the impact and improvement achieved by our model in detecting video anomalies.

5   Conclusion

This paper introduces a frame anomaly classification method using transfer learning with a fine-tuned Mobilenetv2 pre-trained model. The experimental findings indicate that the proposed framework substantially enhances the performance of anomaly detection, particularly on challenging datasets. The ablation experiments on multiple pre-trained networks highlighted the superiority of MobileNetV2 architecture over other networks. Despite the high effectiveness of the proposed approach, the study also identified a limitation when applied in real-time, where the number of anomalous events could be very small. This can make it challenging to balance anomalous and non-anomalous events to perform classification tasks effectively. Furthermore, the low requirements in terms of computing resources make the proposed framework suitable for real-time industrial applications.

References

1. Aburakhia, S., Tayeh, T., Myers, R., Shami, A.: A transfer learning framework for anomaly detection using model of normality. In: 2020 11th IEEE Annual Information Technology, Electronics and Mobile Communication Conference (IEMCON), pp. 0055–0061. IEEE (2020)
2. Bansod, S., Nandedkar, A.: Transfer learning for video anomaly detection. J. Intell. Fuzzy Syst. **36**(3), 1967–1975 (2019)
3. Chen, C.,et al.: Comprehensive regularization in a bi-directional predictive network for video anomaly detection. In: Proceedings of the AAAI Conference on Artificial Intelligence, vol. 36, pp. 230–238 (2022)
4. Guo, A., Guo, L., Zhang, R., Wang, Y., Gao, S.: Self-trained prediction model and novel anomaly score mechanism for video anomaly detection. Image Vis. Comput. **119**, 104391 (2022)
5. Ionescu, R.T., Khan, F.S., Georgescu, M.I., Shao, L.: Object-centric auto-encoders and dummy anomalies for abnormal event detection in video. In: Proceedings of the IEEE/CVF Conference on Computer Vision and Pattern Recognition, pp. 7842–7851 (2019)
6. Lalit, R., Purwar, R.K., Verma, S., Jain, A.: Crowd abnormality detection in video sequences using supervised convolutional neural network. Multimedia Tools Appl. **81**(4), 5259–5277 (2022)
7. Li, N., Chang, F.: Video anomaly detection and localization via multivariate gaussian fully convolution adversarial autoencoder. Neurocomputing **369**, 92–105 (2019)
8. Li, T., Chen, X., Zhu, F., Zhang, Z., Yan, H.: Two-stream deep spatial-temporal auto-encoder for surveillance video abnormal event detection. Neurocomputing **439**, 256–270 (2021)
9. Luo, W., Liu, W., Gao, S.: A revisit of sparse coding based anomaly detection in stacked RNN framework. In: Proceedings of the IEEE International Conference on Computer Vision, pp. 341–349 (2017)
10. Park, C., Cho, M., Lee, M., Lee, S.: FastANO: fast anomaly detection via spatio-temporal patch transformation. In: Proceedings of the IEEE/CVF Winter Conference on Applications of Computer Vision, pp. 2249–2259 (2022)
11. Sabokrou, M., Fayyaz, M., Fathy, M., Klette, R.: Deep-cascade: cascading 3D deep neural networks for fast anomaly detection and localization in crowded scenes. IEEE Trans. Image Process. **26**(4), 1992–2004 (2017)
12. Wan, B., Fang, Y., Xia, X., Mei, J.: Weakly supervised video anomaly detection via center-guided discriminative learning. In: 2020 IEEE International Conference on Multimedia and Expo (ICME), pp. 1–6. IEEE (2020)
13. Zhou, J.T., Du, J., Zhu, H., Peng, X., Liu, Y., Goh, R.S.M.: AnomalyNet: an anomaly detection network for video surveillance. IEEE Trans. Inf. Forensics Secur. **14**(10), 2537–2550 (2019)

14. Zhou, W., Li, Y., Zhao, C.: Object-guided and motion-refined attention network for video anomaly detection. In: 2022 IEEE International Conference on Multimedia and Expo (ICME), pp. 1–6. IEEE (2022)

Deep Sparse Representation Learning for Multi-class Image Classification

Amit Soni Arya(✉)(iD), Shreyanshu Thakur, and Sushanta Mukhopadhyay

Indian Institute of Technology (ISM), Dhanbad, Jharkhand, India
amitsoniuoh@gmail.com, msushanta2001@iitism.ac.in

Abstract. This paper presents a novel deep sparse representation learning for multi-class image classification (DSRLMCC). In our proposed DSRLMCC, we use dictionary learning for sparse representation to train the deep convolutional layers to work as coding layers. The dictionary-learning algorithm uses input training data to learn an exhaustive dictionary and sparse representation. The deep sparse coding layer enforces locality constraints for activated dictionary bases to achieve high convergence. With the second deep learning layer, fine-grained components are learned, which, in turn, are shared by all atoms in the input dictionary; thus, a low-level representation of the dictionary atoms can be learned that is more informative and discriminatory. Comparing the proposed model with several prominent dictionary learning strategies and deep learning models, we found that the proposed method outperforms them. We have executed the proposed method on three prominent datasets, and the results are satisfactory.

Keywords: Deep dictionary learning · Multiclass classification · Sparse representation · Deep sparse representation

1 Introduction

An important phase in image classification is obtaining feature representations containing label information. The most prevalent methods of representation learning in the past decade have been dictionary learning [5,16,22] and deep learning [11]. The dictionary method involves learning a set of atoms that could be combined into a sparse linear combination to approximate images, whereas the deep network method involves extracting deep representations for semantic features. The advancement of dictionary learning has been greatly aided by scholars from many research areas, including [21] and [5] from machine learning and statistics, and from signal processing [1], and from image processing and computer vision [16]. But what does a sparse representation really mean, and how is it useful? Our focus is on elucidating these two fundamental principles of sparse representation.

Dictionary learning [16] with deep learning has shown better outcomes in various image processing tasks, including denoising [30], deblurring [17], inpainting

© The Author(s), under exclusive license to Springer Nature Switzerland AG 2023
P. Maji et al. (Eds.): PReMI 2023, LNCS 14301, pp. 218–227, 2023.
https://doi.org/10.1007/978-3-031-45170-6_23

[3], and super-resolution [14]. One of the key techniques used in image processing is deep learning, which involves training a deep neural network (DNN) on a large dataset of images to identify patterns and features in the data [13]. However, its potential for image classification has not been fully explored since deep learning approaches often needed huge data and computational resources, making them challenging to use in many real-world applications. In addition, most dictionary learning investigations have employed a shallow network structure. Current resulting dictionary learning techniques, such as label consistent K-SVD (LC-KSVD) [9], discriminatory K-SVD (D-KSVD) [27], and K-SVD [1], seek to divide input data into complex sparse and basis coefficients. Nevertheless is challenging for shallow network structures to retrieve the inherent characteristics of the input image completely. In our initial examinations, we observed that both limitations result in a very poor performance in classification when data are scarce.

To address these challenges, we proposed a Deep Sparse Representation Learning for Multi-Class Image Classification (DSRLMCC) approach as shown in the Fig. 1. The proposed DSRLMCC model used dictionary-based deep learning methods, which rely on a sparse representation of the data in terms of a dictionary basis functions. In this approach, the input images are decomposed into sparse representations, which are then used to train a DNN. This allows for efficient use of data and computational resources while achieving high accuracy in image categorization tasks. The major key contributions of this research as fallows:

- We propose Deep Sparse Representation Learning for Multi-Class Image Classification (DSRLMCC) to combine the benefits of dictionary and deep learning.
- We present sparse coding and dictionary learning that can reduce the overhead of adding more convolutional layers in the deep learning framework, reducing the computational overhead.
- We generalise the proposed DSRLMCC model using a K-fold cross-validation strategy to evaluate the model efficacy.
- Comprehensive tests in a wider variety of data sets with limited training data indicate that the suggested approach outperforms cutting-edge dictionary learning and deep learning techniques and obtains competitive outcomes.

2   Related Work

This section contains a brief review dictionary learning including deep learning for image classification.

2.1   Dictionary Learning

Dictionary learning [5,16,22] employs sparse representation or sparse coding to represent signals as linear combinations of some items from a dictionary matrix comprising multiple sample signals. To linearly combine the original signal, employ the coefficient vector for choosing "useful" elements from the dictionary. Each entry is regarded as a weight that describes how much each selected atom comprises in the linear combination, and its value is considered a weight. Sparse representations [5] are very important because they allow complex signals to be represented concisely so that a simplified classifier (such as a linear classifier) can be utilized. Moreover, sparse-inducing regularization, as well as sparse representation [28], is extremely efficient at the representation of crucial signals. In sparse representation, audio, images, and video signals are mapped to condensed representations regularly or uniformly according to their original chaotic nature [7]. They are closely related to each other due to their over-inclusive dictionaries. In recent years, dictionary learning has gained significant attention in deep learning. It has been used to develop deep neural network architectures to learn more efficient and discriminative feature representations from raw data.

2.2   Deep Dictionary Learning

A recent study [4,8,20] showed how dictionary learning techniques can be used to develop deeper network architectures to address both limitations. Liu et al. [13] proposed have suggested using a dictionary learning layer in place of the conventional fully connected layer and rectified linear unit for scene recognition tasks. A locality constraint on image classification tasks was proposed by Song et al. [18]. According to Mahdizadehaghdam et al. [15], a new algorithm can be used to classify images by constructing a hierarchy of deep dictionaries. In contrast to conventional deep neural networks, deep dictionary learning derivations create patch-based representations of features before constructing global sparse feature representations based on those patches.

3   The Proposed Method

As shown in Fig. 1, the proposed method adopts some useful concepts from DNNs but differs from the dictionary learning method described previously. The dictionary is first explicitly learned from the input image and then serves to generate sparse representations for feature extraction. After that, the extracted features from sparse codes are fed into a DNN-based model for final image classification. In this proposed model, we combine deep learning (DNN-based model) and dictionary learning with improving the performance of tasks done by previous methods. A way to do this is through sparse coding, a technique used in dictionary learning to represent data using a small subset of the available atoms. This section presents every level of the proposed approach in order. Initially, we outline dictionary learning with a sparse coding approach. Later, we briefly discussed the feature extraction strategy. Finally, we present the DNN-based architecture for classification.

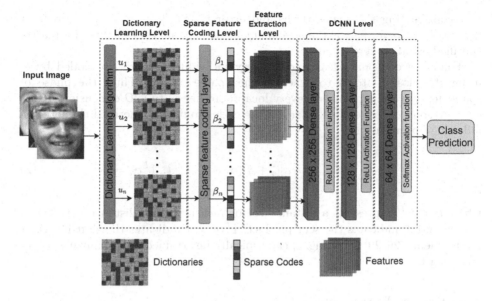

Fig. 1. Overview of the proposed deep sparse representation learning for multi-class image classification.

3.1 Dictionary Learning and Sparse Coding

Natural images are highly complex signals that are typically not sparse and comprise numerous structural and morphological elements. Multiple morphological components, such as shapes, edges, and wheel galleries, constitute an over-complete dictionary of base vectors in natural images (which is, the size of the basis in the dictionary is significantly smaller than the dimension of input images). The sparsely coded representation for an image in the dictionary is subsequently generated through sparse constraints subject to specific reconstructing errors.

Let x represent the overall images with different categories in the data set. The amount of dictionaries per category is represented by n. Next, we randomly choose k images from every class to train the respective category's dictionary. $D = x * n$ can therefore be used to determine the number of dictionaries. The following dictionary learning algorithm is then employed:

$$\min_{U_i,\beta_i} \left[\frac{1}{2} \|x_i - U_i\beta_i\|_2^2 \right] + \lambda \|\beta_i\|_0 , s.t. \|\beta_i\|_2 \leq 1 \tag{1}$$

Here, $U_i = [u_1, u_2, \cdot, u_n]$ is the ith class dictionary at the dictionary level of the proposed DSRLMCC model, which comprises of n atoms, i.e., u_i. After learning the dictionaries of every category separately, we group them to form a dictionary U. Thus, $U = [U_1, U_2, \cdots, U_x] = [u_1, u_2, \cdots, u_D] \in \mathbb{R}^{m \times D}$. β_i represents the sparse coefficient. The sparse coefficient $\beta_i = [\beta_1, \beta_2, \cdots, \beta_n]$ and the dictionary U could be jointly learned. Adjustments are made to the parameter to reconstructing the sparse terms and error terms. $\|.\|_2$ subscript by default denotes $l_2 - norm$. $\|.\|_0$ is the $l_0 - norm$, which is a non-zero value in a matrix specified as a non-zero number.

Following dictionary learning U, every individual feature is encoded by U using the closest atoms to generate the sparse coding. Thus, the phase of sparse feature coding converts every local identifier x_i to a D-dimensional code $\alpha_i = [\alpha_1, \alpha_2, \cdots, \alpha_l] \in \mathbb{R}^{D \times l}$. Each of the codes could be generated through the following optimization:

$$\min_{\alpha_i} [\sum_{i=1}^{m} \frac{1}{2} \|x_i - U\alpha_i\|_2^2 + \gamma \|\alpha_i \odot \zeta_i\|], s.t., 1^T \alpha_i = 1 \qquad (2)$$

where $\zeta_i \in \mathbb{R}^D$ represents a distance vector measuring the distance between u_i and x_i and $\odot$ indicates the scur product. $1^T \alpha_i = 1$ indicates the shift-invariant requirements [26, 29] of coding. ζ_i can typically be attained by minimizing reconstructing loss.

3.2   Feature Extraction

Following the sparse coding level, we use a feature extractor F to produce a set of features from sparse coding (S). To show the efficacy of the DSRLMCC approach, we perform our experiment using feature extractor, namely abstract feature extractor (AFE) to enhance performance of proposed model. The AFE has been extensively applied to DNN to reduce the overhead. Particularly, we obtain the AFE feature a_i from the sparse coding employing the feature extractor F, and this procedure can be expressed as $a_i = F(S), s[1, ..., l]$.

3.3   Deep Neural Network (DNN) Layers

We proposed a DNN framework to train the model using extracted features from sparse code as shown in Fig. 1. The DNN model comprises of three dense layers, each performing a different type of computation. Moreover, first two dense layers uses the rectified linear unit activation function (ReLU). Here, these two layers receives a AFE features as input and employs a linear transformation to produce a new set of values, which are then transmitted to the ReLU activation function. The resulting output is a vector with 256 elements from first dense layer and 128 elements from second dense layer. The last DNN layer is a dense 64-unit layer that employs a softmax activation function. In multi-class classification problems, the softmax function is frequently used to transform the final layer outcomes into a probability distribution across the predicted classes. In this model, the 64-dimensional outcome from the prior layer is utilised to generate the distribution of probabilities over possible classes. For a given input, the class with the largest probability is chosen as the final prediction class.

4   Experimental Results

4.1   Datasets Description

The proposed DSRLMCC model is evaluated on three standard dictionary learning data sets: MNIST [12], Fashion-MNIST [24], and Olivetti faces datasets [2]. For a fair comparison, each data set is evaluated according to the same criteria as prior research. The overview of three datasets are presented in Table 1.

Table 1. The detailed description of datasets used to evaluate the proposed model.

Dataset Name	Type	No. of samples	Image pixel size	No. of categories
Fashion-MNIST	Clothing and Accessories	70,000	28×28	10
MNIST	Hand written digits	70,000	28×28	10
Olivetti	Faces	400	64×64	40

4.2   System Implementation

The method described in the study is implemented using TensorFlow and the scikit-learn library under the Python framework on a Windows 10 platform. The system configurations are as follows: 64-bit operating system, 16 GB of RAM, and an Intel i7-10750H 2.60 GHz CPU. The parameters are used in the experiment as follows: The number of dictionary components (atoms) is set to 130 for dictionary learning. We have use the orthogonal matching pursuit optimization technique for sparse representation. The highest amount of iterations for dictionary learning is 600. The Adam optimisation algorithm and the sparse categorical cross-entropy loss function are employed to train the DNN. The accuracy of the DNN is used as a metric for evaluating its efficacy. The amount of epochs has been assigned to 60. We then evaluate the model's performance using K-fold cross validation to assess the performance of the model and ensure that it does not overfit the training data after training it in the dictionary learning phase. The maximum number of divisions (K-value) for K-fold cross-validation is set to 5.

4.3   Results and Analysis

We have compared the classification accuracy with the above mentioned datasets in the experiments. As shown in Table 2, we presented the comparative analysis for the three datasets (refer Table 1) for the state-of-the-art methods, including Deep Representation Learning [25], LC-KSVD [10], Convolution clustering [6], DDLCN-2 [19] and CNN-C1 [23].

It can be observed that the proposed DSRLMCC approach has better performance in accuracy when compared to other approaches for all three datasets

Table 2. Comparison proposed method with other methods in terms of classification accuracy

Methods	Datasets		
	MNIST	Fashion-MNIST	Olivetti faces
Deep Representation Learning [25]	85.47	83.66	90.03
LC-KSVD [10]	92.58	90.84	95.14
Convolution clustering [6]	98.60	94.27	99.58
DDLCN-2 [19]	96.56	93.46	98.79
CNN-C1 [23]	97.21	93.11	99.01
Proposed	**99.00**	**95.85**	**100**

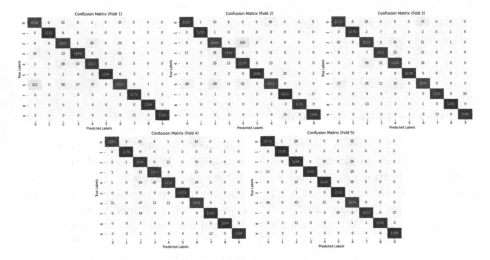

Fig. 2. Fold-wise confusion matrix for Fashion-MNIST dataset (*Please zoom the figure for better visualization*)

Table 3. 5-fold cross validation classification accuracy for proposed method

Datasets	Fold1	Fold2	Fold3	Fold4	Fold5	Average
MNIST	99.01	99.08	98.83	98.90	99.27	99.01
Fashion-MNIST	95.36	94.96	96.38	96.06	96.50	95.85
Olivetti faces	100	100	100	100	100	100

as shown in Table 2. Moreover, we provided the performance analysis for k-fold cross-validation for Fashion-MNIST dataset for reducing the overfitting problem in Table 3. Here we considered the K-value to 5. Moreover, we presented the confusion matrix in Fig. 2 for the Fashion-MNIST dataset for 5-folds. Where the diagonal part is represented as correctly classified and above and below the diagonal matrix represents miss-classified images. Furthermore, we showed the

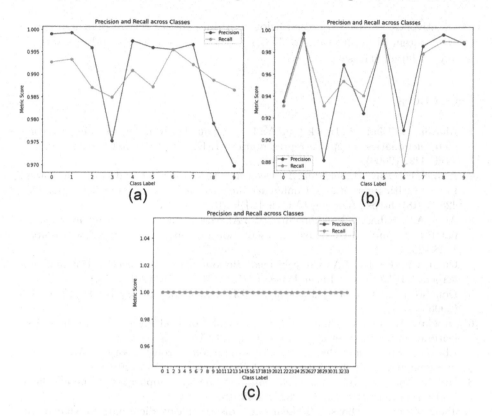

Fig. 3. The precision-recall curve (a) For the MNIST digit dataset (b) For Fashion MNIST dataset (c) For Olivetti faces dataset

precision and recall analysis in Fig. 3 for all classes in a specific dataset. It shows for each class label how the precision and recall is observed.

5 Conclusion

This article introduced DSRLMCC, an innovative approach for deep dictionary learning that combines deep learning and dictionary learning to improve the capability of deep sparse representational learning. Our method included a new dictionary learning and coding layer that replaces the traditional convolutional layers in CNNs, allowing us to learn from sparse representation to deep multi-layer architecture. We evaluated the performance of DSRLMCC on three public datasets with limited training data and compared it with premier dictionary learning methods and state-of-the-art CNN-based approaches.

Our experimental results have shown that DSRLMCC outperforms the leading dictionary learning methods and achieves comparable outcomes with cutting-edge CNN-based models. The results also suggested that DSRLMCC enhances the effectiveness of deep representation learning. In future, we plan to investigate the potential applications of DSRLMCC in various fields and evaluate its efficacy on larger datasets.

References

1. Aharon, M., Elad, M., Bruckstein, A.: K-SVD: an algorithm for designing overcomplete dictionaries for sparse representation. IEEE Trans. Signal Process. **54**(11), 4311–4322 (2006)
2. Altinel, F., Ozay, M., Okatani, T.: Deep structured energy-based image inpainting. In: 2018 24th International Conference on Pattern Recognition (ICPR), pp. 423–428 (2018). https://doi.org/10.1109/ICPR.2018.8546025
3. Arya, A.S., Saha, A., Mukhopadhyay, S.: ADMM optimizer for integrating wavelet-patch and group-based sparse representation for image inpainting. Vis. Comput. 1–28 (2023)
4. Chun, I.Y., Fessler, J.A.: Convolutional dictionary learning: acceleration and convergence. IEEE Trans. Image Process. **27**(4), 1697–1712 (2017)
5. Donoho, D.L.: Compressed sensing. IEEE Trans. Inf. Theory **52**(4), 1289–1306 (2006)
6. Dundar, A., Jin, J., Culurciello, E.: Convolutional clustering for unsupervised learning. arXiv preprint arXiv:1511.06241 (2015)
7. Elad, M.: Sparse and Redundant Representations: From Theory to Applications in Signal and Image Processing, vol. 2. Springer, New York (2010)
8. Hu, J., Tan, Y.P.: Nonlinear dictionary learning with application to image classification. Pattern Recogn. **75**, 282–291 (2018)
9. Jiang, Z., Lin, Z., Davis, L.S.: Learning a discriminative dictionary for sparse coding via label consistent K-SVD. In: CVPR 2011, pp. 1697–1704. IEEE (2011)
10. Jiang, Z., Lin, Z., Davis, L.S.: Label consistent K-SVD: learning a discriminative dictionary for recognition. IEEE Trans. Pattern Anal. Mach. Intell. **35**(11), 2651–2664 (2013)
11. LeCun, Y., Bengio, Y., Hinton, G.: Deep learning. Nature **521**(7553), 436–444 (2015)
12. LeCun, Y., Bottou, L., Bengio, Y., Haffner, P.: Gradient-based learning applied to document recognition. Proc. IEEE **86**(11), 2278–2324 (1998)
13. Liu, Y., Chen, Q., Chen, W., Wassell, I.: Dictionary learning inspired deep network for scene recognition. In: Proceedings of the AAAI Conference on Artificial Intelligence, vol. 32 (2018)
14. Maeda, S.: Image super-resolution with deep dictionary. In: Avidan, S., Brostow, G., Cissé, M., Farinella, G.M., Hassner, T. (eds.) ECCV 2022. LNCS, vol. 13679, pp. 464–480. Springer, Cham (2022). https://doi.org/10.1007/978-3-031-19800-7_27
15. Mahdizadehaghdam, S., Panahi, A., Krim, H., Dai, L.: Deep dictionary learning: a parametric network approach. IEEE Trans. Image Process. **28**(10), 4790–4802 (2019)
16. Mairal, J.: Sparse coding for machine learning, image processing and computer vision. Ph.D. thesis, Cachan, Ecole normale supérieure (2010)
17. Singhal, V., Majumdar, A.: Deep dictionary learning. Ph.D. thesis, IIIT-Delhi (2019)

18. Song, J., Xie, X., Shi, G., Dong, W.: Multi-layer discriminative dictionary learning with locality constraint for image classification. Pattern Recogn. **91**, 135–146 (2019)
19. Tang, H., Liu, H., Xiao, W., Sebe, N.: When dictionary learning meets deep learning: deep dictionary learning and coding network for image recognition with limited data. IEEE Trans. Neural Netw. Learn. Syst. **32**(5), 2129–2141 (2020)
20. Tariyal, S., Majumdar, A., Singh, R., Vatsa, M.: Greedy deep dictionary learning. arXiv preprint arXiv:1602.00203 (2016)
21. Tibshirani, R.: Regression shrinkage and selection via the lasso. J. Roy. Stat. Soc.: Ser. B (Methodol.) **58**(1), 267–288 (1996)
22. Wright, J., Yang, A.Y., Ganesh, A., Sastry, S.S., Ma, Y.: Robust face recognition via sparse representation. IEEE Trans. Pattern Anal. Mach. Intell. **31**(2), 210–227 (2008)
23. Xhaferra, E., Cina, E., Toti, L.: Classification of standard fashion MNIST dataset using deep learning based CNN algorithms. In: 2022 International Symposium on Multidisciplinary Studies and Innovative Technologies (ISMSIT), pp. 494–498. IEEE (2022)
24. Xiao, H., Rasul, K., Vollgraf, R.: Fashion-MNIST: a novel image dataset for benchmarking machine learning algorithms. arXiv preprint arXiv:1708.07747 (2017)
25. Yang, S., Luo, P., Loy, C.C., Shum, K.W., Tang, X.: Deep representation learning with target coding. In: Proceedings of the AAAI Conference on Artificial Intelligence, vol. 29 (2015)
26. Yu, K., Zhang, T., Gong, Y.: Nonlinear learning using local coordinate coding. In: Advances in Neural Information Processing Systems, vol. 22 (2009)
27. Zhang, Q., Li, B.: Discriminative K-SVD for dictionary learning in face recognition. In: 2010 IEEE Computer Society Conference on Computer Vision and Pattern Recognition, pp. 2691–2698. IEEE (2010)
28. Zhang, S., Wang, J., Tao, X., Gong, Y., Zheng, N.: Constructing deep sparse coding network for image classification. Pattern Recogn. **64**, 130–140 (2017)
29. Zheng, G., Yang, Y., Carbonell, J.: Efficient shift-invariant dictionary learning. In: Proceedings of the 22nd ACM SIGKDD International Conference on Knowledge Discovery and Data Mining, pp. 2095–2104 (2016)
30. Zheng, H., Yong, H., Zhang, L.: Deep convolutional dictionary learning for image denoising. In: Proceedings of the IEEE/CVF Conference on Computer Vision and Pattern Recognition, pp. 630–641 (2021)

A Novel Graph Representation Learning Approach for Visual Modeling Using Neural Combinatorial Optimization

Subhrasankar Chatterjee[(✉)], Subrata Pain, and Debasis Samanta

Indian Institute of Technology, Kharagpur 721302, India
subhrasanakrphd@iitkgp.ac.in
https://sites.google.com/view/subhrasankar-chatterjee/home

Abstract. The human visual system is a complex network of neurons that employs robust mechanisms to perceive and interpret the environment. Despite significant advancements in computer vision technologies in recent years, they still need to improve compared to human abilities, particularly in recognizing faces and interpreting scenes. As a result, there is a growing interest in understanding the underlying mechanisms of human vision. Artificial Intelligence (AI) systems, specifically computer vision models, represent the assigned task using a learned or systematically generated vector space known as the Latent Space. However, the field of brain representation space remains relatively less explored. Despite significant progress, a research gap exists in generating an optimal representation space for human visual processing. While graph-based representations have been proposed to better capture inter-region relationships in visual processing, learning an optimal graph representation from limited data remains a challenge, especially when there is no ground truth. Due to the lack of labeled data, supervised learning approaches are less preferred. The present study introduces a novel method for graph-based representation of the human visual processing system, utilizing Neural Combinatorial Optimization(NCO). We have obtained an accuracy of 60% from our proposed framework, which is comparable to other methods for eight class classification in Visual Modelling.

Keywords: Visual Modeling · Neural Combinatorial Optimization · AutoEncoder

1 Introduction

The human visual system is a remarkable network of neurons responsible for processing visual information from the surrounding environment. Despite advancements in computer vision technology, current systems still lag behind the capabilities of the human visual system, particularly in tasks like facial recognition and scene interpretation [11,20]. As a result, there is a growing interest in comprehending the mechanisms of the human visual system to enhance computer

P. Maji et al. (Eds.): PReMI 2023, LNCS 14301, pp. 228–237, 2023.
https://doi.org/10.1007/978-3-031-45170-6_24

vision capabilities. Neuroscientific visual models typically consist of encoding and decoding models [10,13,14,19]. These models utilize neural responses to predict either the stimulus or its properties or vice versa, employing an intermediate latent representation. Such models create a representation space that can replicate the behavior of neural responses, as illustrated in Fig. 1.

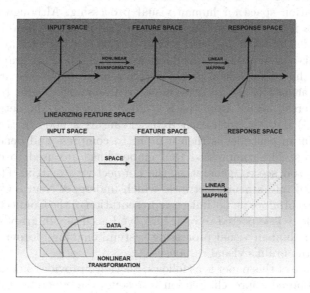

Fig. 1. Linearizing Feature Space.

Early attempts to model the visual system, such as the Gabor Wavelet Pyramid (GWP) [12], employed a pool of Gabor filters with varying orientation and spatial frequency to generate a feature space representing the stimulus-response relationship in early visual areas (V1). However, the GWP model fell short in capturing the patterns of late visual areas (V4 and IT). To address this limitation, the Semantic Labelling Modeling (SLM) approach was introduced, where objects in the stimulus were manually labeled, and a feature space was constructed based on these labels [19]. Nevertheless, SLM was susceptible to subject selection and judgment bias. Consequently, the field shifted towards adopting deep learning models.

Deep learning (DL) models, being trainable and capable of learning latent representations from training data, have shown promise in generating representation spaces for neural responses in late visual areas [1]. Subsequently, multiple DL models have been utilized for visual system analysis, demonstrating superior performance compared to earlier approaches [4,8,9,21,22]. Furthermore, graph representations have gained traction in decoding neural data, encompassing tasks such as stimulus categorization and image reconstruction [5–7,18]. Graph structures, such as functional connectivity and brain pathway analyses, have been successfully applied to fMRI data for analyzing neural responses [17]. Interpretable

Graph Neural Network (GNN) models, like BrainGNN, have been developed and proven effective in identifying neurological biomarkers for conditions like Autism Spectrum Disorder [15,16]. In 2023, Chatterjee et al. [3] proposed an adversarial game to develop an optimal graph representation for the human visual system using fMRI data.

Despite these advances, there remains a research gap in generating an optimal representation space for human visual processing. Although graph-based representations have shown promise in capturing neural response characteristics, these models are still data-driven and constrained by data availability. To address this, the present study introduces a novel method for graph-based representation of the human visual processing system, employing Neural Combinatorial Optimization (NCO) [2]. The proposed framework begins by identifying Regions of Interest (ROIs) from the Kay 2008 functional Magnetic Resonance Imaging (fMRI) dataset, with each ROI serving as a node in the graph representation. An autoencoder is then utilized to compress and denoise the ROI response vectors. The compressed ROI embeddings are used to calculate the inter-ROI Pearson scores, generating the connectivity matrix. This matrix is subsequently fed into a neural network, which undergoes Neural Combinatorial Optimization to produce an optimized representation of the Connectivity Graph. This methodology is expected to offer improved accuracy in graph-based representation of the human visual processing system, enabling deeper insights into the nature of the brain's visual responses.

The structure of this paper is as follows. Section 2 provides a detailed description of the proposed approach. Section 3 presents the experimental results and performance evaluation of the proposed method. Finally, Sect. 4 concludes the paper and discusses future research directions.

2 Methodology

2.1 Experimental Data

In this work, a publicly available dataset, introduced by Kay et al. (2008) and Naselaris et al. (2009), was employed to evaluate the proposed methods. The data collection process, as detailed in the studies mentioned earlier, involved the acquisition of BOLD fMRI responses from two male subjects (S1 and S2) while viewing natural images. The training image library consisted of 1,750 grayscale images, each presented twice, while the validation image library contained 120 different grayscale images, each presented 13 times. Each image was presented in successive 4-s trials, with each trial consisting of a 1-s presentation of the image, followed by 3 s of a gray background. The 1-s presentation of the image comprised five ON-OFF cycles, with each ON cycle corresponding to a 200 ms presentation of the image and each OFF cycle corresponding to a 200 ms presentation of the gray background. The BOLD signals were acquired using a 4-T Varian INOVA magnetic resonance scanner, and 18 coronal slices were obtained from the occipital cortex.

2.2 Proposed Framework

The proposed framework is comprised of two fundamental steps. Firstly, a graph generation stage where the raw ROI data is subjected to compression through an autoencoder. The compressed ROI data is utilized to generate an adjacency matrix, which represents the underlying graph. Secondly, the framework applies the Neural Combinatorial Optimization technique to the generated graph to optimize its edge connectivity.

2.3 Graph Generation

The Kay 2008 dataset is a collection of 1750 training images and their corresponding fMRI recordings, which have been preprocessed and analyzed to identify seven regions of interest (ROIs) within the human visual system. Specifically, the ROIs identified are V1, V2, V3, V3A, V3B, V4, and LatOcc. Each ROI is passed through an autoencoder to overcome this challenge, which compresses the information content and projects it onto a compressed latent space. This step allows for more efficient processing and analysis of the ROI data. The autoencoder used in this study is a neural network that aims to compress high-dimensional input data into a lower-dimensional representation while preserving essential input features.

Let x be the input data, and h be the hidden representation obtained by passing x through the encoder portion of the autoencoder. The encoder is typically a series of fully connected layers with nonlinear activations such as ReLU or sigmoid. The hidden representation h is then passed through the decoder portion of the autoencoder, which aims to reconstruct the original input x. The decoder is typically a mirror image of the encoder, with fully connected layers that progressively expand the hidden representation until the output has the same shape as the input.

The autoencoder is trained by minimizing a reconstruction loss that measures the difference between the input x and its reconstructed version obtained by passing h through the decoder. A common choice for the reconstruction loss is the mean squared error (MSE), defined as:

$$MSE(x, x') = \frac{1}{N} \sum_i (x_i - x'_i)^2 \tag{1}$$

where N is the number of elements in x and x', the sum is taken over all aspects i. The weights of the autoencoder are updated using backpropagation concerning the reconstruction loss.

Each ROI is passed through an autoencoder in the proposed framework to obtain a compressed representation that captures its essential features. The compressed ROI embeddings are then used to generate the connectivity matrix, representing the desired graph's edges. The autoencoder helps reduce the noise and variability in the fMRI data and reduce the dimensionality of each ROI to a manageable size.

Once the 7 ROIs have been identified and their respective embeddings have been compressed, the inter-region correlation is calculated for each pair of ROIs. The correlation matrix generated serves as the initial adjacency matrix for the desired graph, where each correlation value between connected regions is assigned as the weight of the corresponding edge.

To obtain the initial adjacency matrix, inter-region correlation is calculated for each ROI pair based on their respective ROI embeddings. Let $\mathbf{X}$ be the matrix that contains the ROI embeddings, where $\mathbf{x}_i$ denotes the embedding of the i-th ROI. The inter-region correlation matrix $\mathbf{C}$ is calculated as follows:

$$
\mathbf{C}_{i,j} = \begin{cases} corr(\mathbf{x_i}, \mathbf{x_j}), & \text{if } , i,j = 1, \ldots, 7, \& i \neq j \\ 0, & \text{otherwise} \end{cases} \tag{2}
$$

where $corr(\cdot, \cdot)$ is the Pearson correlation coefficient between two vectors. The initial adjacency matrix $\mathbf{A}$ is then obtained by setting the weight between each connected region to be equal to the corresponding element in $\mathbf{C}$:

$$
\mathbf{A_{i,j}} = \mathbf{C}_{i,j}, i,j = 1, \ldots, 7, \tag{3}
$$

The adjacency matrix is symmetric since $\mathbf{C}$ is symmetric.

2.4   Graph Optimization

Neural Combinatorial Optimization (NCO) is a method for optimizing combinatorial problems using neural networks. In this context, the combinatorial problem is to find an optimal edge connectivity pattern between nodes of a graph. We use the initial adjacency matrix $A_{i,j}$ generated from the inter-region correlations between the ROIs. The optimization criterion used is the modularity of the nodes. Modularity measures the strength of dividing a network into modules or communities. It is between -1 and 1, where values closer to 1 indicate a robust modular structure. The modularity Q of a network with n nodes and adjacency matrix A is given by:

$$
Q = \frac{1}{2m} \sum_{i,j} [A_{ij} - k_i k_j / 2m] \delta(c_i, c_j) \tag{4}
$$

where m is the total number of edges in the network, k_i is the degree of node i (i.e., the number of edges connected to node i), k_j is the degree of node j, c_i and c_j are the community assignments of nodes i and j, and $\delta(c_i, c_j)$ is the Kronecker delta function, which equals 1 when $c_i = c_j$ and 0 otherwise.

The optimization process involves finding the community assignments c_i that maximize the modularity Q. This is a combinatorial optimization problem that can be solved using NCO. In NCO, the adjacency matrix is fed into a neural network that generates a permutation of the nodes. The modularity Q is then calculated for the new permutation, and the network is trained to maximize Q using gradient descent.

Formally, let P be a permutation matrix that encodes the node ordering. Let F be a neural network that takes as input the adjacency matrix A and the permutation matrix P and outputs a score $S(P)$ for the given permutation. The optimization problem is to find the optimal permutation matrix P^* that maximizes $S(P)$:

$$P^* = \underset{P}{\mathrm{argmax}} S(P) \tag{5}$$

The score $S(P)$ is given by the modularity Q for the given permutation P:

$$S(P) = Q(P) \tag{6}$$

The optimization is performed using gradient descent:

$$P_{t+1} = P_t - \eta \frac{\delta S(P)}{\delta P} \tag{7}$$

where η is the learning rate, and $\frac{\delta S(P)}{\delta P}$ is the gradient of the score concerning the permutation matrix. The optimization continues until convergence or a maximum number of iterations is reached.

3 Experiment and Result

3.1 ROI Compression

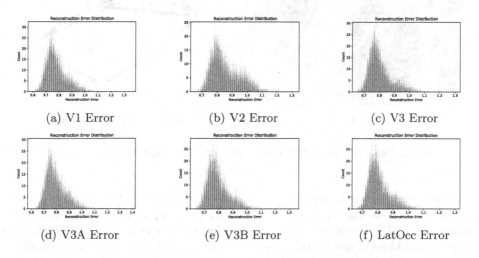

(a) V1 Error   (b) V2 Error   (c) V3 Error

(d) V3A Error   (e) V3B Error   (f) LatOcc Error

Fig. 2. Histograms of reconstruction error for the test data in the autoencoder model, showing the distribution of errors between the original and reconstructed input images.

In the study, ROI compression using an autoencoder resulted in an efficient representation of the raw fMRI data. The compressed representations of the

ROIs could capture a significant amount of the original data while reducing the dimensionality of the data. Each autoencoder had an input size similar to the original ROI vector. Two layers of 512 & 256 nodes each followed the input layer. The final latent layer had 128 nodes. The value of the nodes and no. of epochs to be trained was determined experimentally. The compressed ROIs were projected onto a 1 × 128-sized vector, which minimized the error for 180 epochs. This allowed for easier operation and inter-regional correlation calculations. The results showed that the compressed ROIs could generate an initial adjacency matrix, which represented inter-regional correlations well. These results demonstrate the effectiveness of the autoencoder approach for compressing ROI data in fMRI. The reconstruction error plots are given in Fig. 2.

3.2   Graph Generation

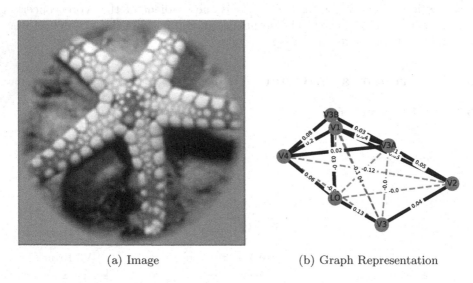

(a) Image   (b) Graph Representation

Fig. 3. Image on which fMRI was collected and Graph Representation.

The correlation matrix calculated between each pair of ROIs showed a high correlation within the same visual area and a low correlation between different visual areas. The adjacency matrix generated using the correlation matrix as weights exhibited a sparse structure with a few strong and many weak connections. The results showed that the proposed method successfully captured the underlying inter-regional connectivity of the visual system. This suggests that the graph-based approach can provide a powerful tool for investigating the functional connectivity of the brain and has potential applications in a wide range of neuroimaging studies. The adjacency matrix and graph structure are shown in Fig. 3

3.3   Classification Analysis

This study optimized the adjacency matrix using a Neural Combinatorial Optimization technique to obtain an optimized graph representation. The performance of the optimized graph was then evaluated by performing a classification task on the available dataset, which has 1750 instances and eight classes. The training was done by doing an 80:20 split and 10-fold cross-validation. Six standard classifiers were used to compare the optimized graph's performance, including AdaBoost, Decision Tree, Support Vector Machine, K-Nearest Neighbour, Naive Bayes, and Linear Discriminant Analysis. The obtained results revealed that the optimized graph outperformed both the compressed ROIs representation and initial adjacency matrix representation in expressing the functional and behavioral nature of the visual system. This suggests the proposed methodology could be a promising approach for representing complex neural systems using graph representations. The results are shown in Table 1. The obtained result clearly states that SVM achieved the highest accuracy for the Proposed Framework Representation.

Table 1. Classification performance of different components in comparison to the Optimized Graph Representation.

Classifier	AdaBoost	DT	SVM	KNN	NB	LDA
Compressed ROIs						
V1	42.2	31.2	45.0	38.8	22.4	17.6
V2	42.2	31.2	45.2	38.8	24	18
V4	48	37.6	48.8	40.4	39.2	20
LatOcc	48.8	36.0	47.6	38.8	41.6	46
Inital Corr Mat	49.2	38.8	54.8	44.8	38	45.6
Proposed Method	51.2	44.6	**60.2**	52.4	43.6	50.0

4   Conclusion

In conclusion, our research presents a novel methodology for generating a functional connectivity graph of the human visual system using fMRI data. Our proposed framework consists of two major steps: ROI compression using an autoencoder and graph optimization using Neural Combinatorial Optimization (NCO). The generated graph is optimized by maximizing the modularity of the nodes, which results in an optimal edge connectivity pattern among the ROIs. The performance of the final representation graph was evaluated using a classification task and compared to the compressed ROIs and the initial adjacency matrix.

Our experimental results demonstrate that the proposed methodology achieves a high accuracy of 60% on the classification task. This indicates that the generated graph adequately expresses the functional and behavioral nature of the visual system. Furthermore, the results indicate that the final representation graph outperforms the compressed ROIs and the initial adjacency matrix, indicating the effectiveness of the proposed methodology.

References

1. Agrawal, P., Stansbury, D., Malik, J., Gallant, J.: Pixels to voxels: Modeling visual representation in the human brain (07 2014)
2. Bello, I., Pham, H., Le, Q., Norouzi, M., Bengio, S.: Neural combinatorial optimization with reinforcement learning (2016)
3. Chatterjee, S., Pain, S., Samanta, D.: Adversarial policy gradient for learning graph-based representation in human visual processing (2023). https://openreview. net/forum?id=5-ROmmBJKV
4. Cui, Y., Qiao, K., Zhang, C., Wang, L., Yan, B., Tong, l.: GaborNet visual encoding: a lightweight region-based visual encoding model with good expressiveness and biological interpretability. Front. Neurosci. **15**, 614182 (2021). https://doi.org/10. 3389/fnins.2021.614182
5. Deshpande, G., Wang, Y.: Noninvasive characterization of functional pathways in layer-specific microcircuits of the human brain using 7T fMRI. Brain Sci. **12**, 1361 (2022). https://doi.org/10.3390/brainsci12101361
6. Dipasquale, O., et al.: Comparing resting state fMRI de-noising approaches using multi- and single-echo acquisitions. PLoS ONE **12**, e0173289 (2017)
7. Gilson, M., et al.: Network analysis of whole-brain fMRI dynamics: a new framework based on dynamic communicability. NeuroImage **201**, 116007 (2019). https:// doi.org/10.1016/j.neuroimage.2019.116007
8. Güçlü, U., van Gerven, M.A.J.: Deep neural networks reveal a gradient in the complexity of neural representations across the brain's ventral visual pathway (2014). https://doi.org/10.1523/JNEUROSCI.5023-14.2015. http://arxiv. org/abs/1411.6422https://doi.org/10.1523/JNEUROSCI.5023-14.2015
9. Han, K., et al.: Variational autoencoder: an unsupervised model for encoding and decoding fMRI activity in visual cortex. NeuroImage **198**, 125–136 (2019). https:// doi.org/10.1016/j.neuroimage.2019.05.039
10. Haxby, J.V.: Multivariate pattern analysis of fMRI: the early beginnings (2012). https://doi.org/10.1016/j.neuroimage.2012.03.016
11. Haynes, J.D., Rees, G.: Predicting the orientation of invisible stimuli from activity in human primary visual cortex. Nat. Neurosci. **8**, 686–91 (2005). https://doi.org/ 10.1038/nn1445
12. Kay, K., Naselaris, T., Prenger, R., Gallant, J.: Identifying natural images from human brain activity. Nature **452**, 352–5 (2008). https://doi.org/10.1038/ nature06713
13. Kay, K.N.: Principles for models of neural information processing (2018). https:// doi.org/10.1016/j.neuroimage.2017.08.016
14. Kriegeskorte, N.: Pattern-information analysis: from stimulus decoding to computational-model testing. NeuroImage **56**, 411–421 (2011). https://doi.org/ 10.1016/j.neuroimage.2011.01.061

15. Li, X., et al.: BrainGNN: interpretable brain graph neural network for fMRI analysis. Medical Image Analysis **74**, 102233 (2021). https://doi.org/10.1016/j.media.2021.102233
16. Li, Y., et al.: Brain connectivity based graph convolutional networks for infant age prediction. IEEE Trans. Med. Imaging, 1–1 (2022). https://doi.org/10.1109/TMI.2022.3171778
17. Meng, L., Ge, K.: Decoding visual fMRI stimuli from human brain based on graph convolutional neural network. Brain Sci. **12**, 1394 (2022). https://doi.org/10.3390/brainsci12101394
18. Mohanty, R., Sethares, W., Nair, V., Prabhakaran, V.: Rethinking measures of functional connectivity via feature extraction. Sci. Rep. **10**, 1298 (2020). https://doi.org/10.1038/s41598-020-57915-w
19. Naselaris, T., Kay, K.N., Nishimoto, S., Gallant, J.L.: Encoding and decoding in fMRI (2011). https://doi.org/10.1016/j.neuroimage.2010.07.073
20. Thirion, B., et al.: Inverse retinotopy: inferring the visual content of images from brain activation patterns. NeuroImage **33**, 1104–16 (2007). https://doi.org/10.1016/j.neuroimage.2006.06.062
21. Wen, H., Shi, J., Chen, W., Liu, Z.: Deep residual network predicts cortical representation and organization of visual features for rapid categorization. Sci. Rep. **8**, 3752 (2018). https://doi.org/10.1038/s41598-018-22160-9
22. Wen, H., Shi, J., Zhang, Y., Lu, K.H., Cao, J., Liu, Z.: Neural encoding and decoding with deep learning for dynamic natural vision. Cereb. Cortex **28**, 4136–4160 (2018). https://doi.org/10.1093/cercor/bhx268

Cognitive Computing

Explainable Decision Tree-Based Screening of Cognitive Impairment Leveraging Minimal Neuropsychological Tests

Km Poonam$^{(\boxtimes)}$, Aayush Prasad, Rajlakshmi Guha, Aritra Hazra,
and Partha P. Chakrabarti

Indian Institute of Technology Kharagpur, Kharagpur, West Bengal 721302, India
poonamk@iitkgp.ac.in, rajg@cet.iitkgp.ac.in,
{aritrah,ppchak}@cse.iitkgp.ac.in

Abstract. Cognitive impairment detection is challenging because it primarily depends on advanced neuroimaging tests, which are not readily available in small cities and villages in India and many developing countries. Artificial Intelligence (AI)-based systems can be used to assist clinical decision-making, but it requires advanced tests and a large amount of data to achieve reasonable accuracy. In this work, we have developed an explainable decision-tree-based detection model, which serves as a powerful first-level screening on a small basic set of cognitive tests. This minimum set of features is obtained through an ablation study. The Alzheimer's Disease Neuroimaging Initiative (ADNI) archive provided the data for this study. We obtained 93.10% accuracy for three classes: Cognitive Normal (CN), Mild Cognitive Impairment (MCI), Alzheimer's Disease (AD), and 78.74% accuracy for five classes: CN, Significant Memory Complaints (SMC), Early-MCI (EMCI), Late-MCI (LMCI), AD using Extreme Gradient Boosting (XGBoost) which is comparable to the accuracy of state-of-the-art methods which use a more sophisticated and expensive test like imaging. Current research pays little attention to explainability and is primarily concerned with enhancing the performance of deep learning and machine learning models. Consequently, clinicians find it challenging to interpret these intricate models. With the use of Tree Shapley Additive Explanations (TreeSHAP) values and Local Interpretable Model-agnostic Explanations (LIME), this work intends to give both global and local interpretability respectively. Moreover, we highlight the use of top-2 metrics (Accuracy, Precision, and Recall), which significantly improves corner cases and helps the clinician streamline diagnosis.

Keywords: Cognitive Impairment · Neuropsychological Tests · Machine Learning · Shapley Additive Explanations · Local Interpretable Model-agnostic Explanations

P. Maji et al. (Eds.): PReMI 2023, LNCS 14301, pp. 241–251, 2023.
https://doi.org/10.1007/978-3-031-45170-6_25

1   Introduction

The term cognitive impairment describes a variety of conditions ranging from subjective cognitive decline through mild cognitive impairment (MCI) and, finally, dementia [1]. MCI and dementia are diagnosed based on clinical decision-making, with neuropsychological tests, and Magnetic Resonance Imaging (MRI) scans assisting in determining the presence of cognitive impairment [2]. In India and other developing countries, only a small portion of the population has access to MRI machines. According to the article published in the magazine Swarajya[1], for every million persons, there is less than one MRI machine in developing countries like India and about fifteen MRI machines in nations that are a part of the Organization for Economic Cooperation and Development. This is even lower in small towns and villages. Since the MRI modality is challenging and expensive to obtain, using various cognitive tests to diagnose cognitive impairment in developing countries like India is imperative. A standardized neurocognitive test battery is a common starting point for a formal neuropsychological assessment of patients with cognitive problems [3]. In India, NIMHANS neuropsychological test battery or Addenbrooke's Cognitive Examination is used for MCI detection [4]. The emergence of machine learning algorithms capable of analyzing complex medical data may enhance the usage of Neuro-Psychological Tests (NPTs) more efficiently [5]. Several researchers have used machine learning for the differential diagnosis of dementia: Gurevich [6] investigated the potential of NPT to distinguish Alzheimer's Disease (AD) from other neurodegenerative diseases using ML methods. Most studies rely on a major modality to obtain reasonable accuracy, particularly neuroimaging. However, no prior study utilizing cognitive tests has attained classification performance equivalent to or better than studies employing neuroimaging modalities.

Previous research has focused exclusively on improving system performance while ignoring issues with explainability. Major advances in prediction were made by these investigations. These works are still not anticipated to be permitted in a clinical environment. The value of academic research findings and their relevance in clinical practice are very different. Because model performance and interpretability seem to be at odds, physicians typically don't rely on the newest technical approaches, such Machine Learning (ML) and Deep Learning (DL). A balanced performance-interpretability trade-off is necessary [7]. Most of these methods are unable to articulate how they arrived at a particular conclusion and their medical applicability [8]. To uncover patterns from databases, complex machine learning algorithms are applied. These patterns might not, however, necessarily indicate reliable outcomes. As a result, medical professionals are dubious of the conclusions drawn by black-box models because they demand more lucid and unambiguous justifications. Due to these limitations, clinical ML techniques focus on simpler, easier-to-comprehend models at the expense of accuracy rather than complicated models. By determining how precisely the

---

[1] https://swarajyamag.com/technology/innovative-india-made-mri-machine-can-make-medical-imaging-affordable-andaccessible.

model predicts, recent research has attempted to shed insight into the workings of complex models to explain their conclusions [9]. In this work, we have been able to find a balance between using simple cognitive tests and applying powerful ML methods to obtain accurate results that are explainable to a high degree.

In this research, first, a comprehensive ablation study was performed for optimal feature selection and establishment of robustness in terms of the number of features. We then used Extreme Gradient Boosting (XGBoost) model for classification. We obtained 93.10% accuracy for three classes: Cognitive Normal (CN), Mild Cognitive Impairment (MCI), Alzheimer's Disease (AD), and 78.74% accuracy for five classes: CN, Significant Memory Complaints (SMC), Early-MCI (EMCI), Late-MCI (LMCI), AD. Moreover, explanations of individual instances' predictions and contributions of features in diagnosis were studied using SHAP and LIME explainers on XGBoost classifier. Analysis of the top 2 metrics: accuracy, recall, and precision for the classification task provided us with discerning insights into types of misclassifications and emphasized the viability of our proposed model named XT-SCI-NT (eXplainable decision Tree-based Screening of Cognitive Impairment leveraging minimal Neuropsychological Tests) as a potential pre-screening tool for cognitive impairment detection. Our results match and improve upon known results on the same dataset, which uses more complex features.

2   Material and Methods

2.1   Dataset

The dataset used in this study is retrieved from the ADNI (Alzheimer's Disease Neuroimaging Initiative) database. The initial baseline dataset includes data from 1,737 patients on 1,907 features. The data was given five separate diagnostic labels by medical professionals: 417 CN, 310 EMCI, 562 LMCI, 106 SMC, and 342 AD. We converted the dataset to the three-class setting by merging SMC, EMCI and LMCI into the MCI class. We trained and validated the model on 80% of the data and tested on the remaining 20%. The order of techniques in Fig. 1 has been used for handling missing data, selecting the best features, and performing correlation analysis for efficient data preprocessing. The missing data were dealt with using the mode imputation method. Subsequently, a SHAP summary plot on the XGBoost model was drawn to order features based on their importance. Then, an ablation graph was drawn between the accuracy of the XGBoost model and the prefix array of ordered features. The peak of the ablation graph provides us with the possible optimal set of features. We removed the RAVLT_forgetting feature by analyzing the ablation graph. We used a heat map of features to perform correlation analysis. In order to do correlation analysis, we employed a heat map of features. Since ADAS13 had a greater feature importance than ADAS11 and the two were highly correlated (0.96), ADAS11 was left out. Finally, ten features were selected, consisting of eight neuropsychological test scores and two demographic attributes (age and education).

2.2 Machine Learning Models

The proposed framework's (XT-SCI-NT) development process includes several significant steps, as shown in Fig. 1. These steps were carried out in the specified order. First, neuropsychological tests and demographics (age and education) were chosen from the dataset. Second, mode imputation was applied to handle missing data. The third stage involves the assimilation of the feature selection step based on the heatmap correlogram, ablation graph, and SHAP summary plot. Fourth, to guarantee unbiased tuning of model hyperparameters, grid search was used to obtain the following optimal hyperparameters: learning rate = 0.1, number of estimators = 100, and maximum depth = 2. These optimal hyperparameters were used to train the XGBoost model and classify the patients as

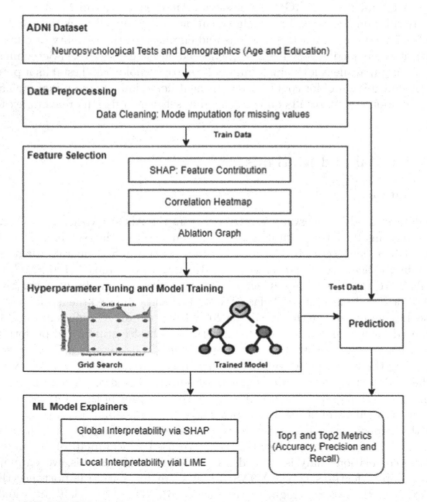

Fig. 1. XT-SCI-NT: Explainable Decision Tree-based Screening of Cognitive Impairment Leveraging Neuropsychological Tests Framework. LIME: Local interpretable model-agnostic explanations, SHAP: Shapley additive explanations

CN, SMC, EMCI, LMCI, and AD in five class settings and CN, MCI, and AD in three class settings.

3 Results and Discussion

Ablation Study: An ablation study for feature engineering was used through a sequence of trials in which a number of features are evaluated to determine their impact on the system's performance. We plotted an ablation graph between the ordered number of features and cross-validation accuracies for five class settings, as shown in Fig. 2. SHAP plots shown in Fig. 3 are used to get the ordered features according to their importance in the diagnosis. The ordered features are: CDRSB, MMSE, MOCA, ADAS13, FAQ, RAVLT percentage forgetting, RAVLT immediate, RAVLT learning, Age, Education ADAS11, and RAVLT_forgetting. An XGBoost model was used to obtain cross-validation scores for all prefix arrays of ordered features. The highest accuracy of 77.68% for five classes was obtained with the first eight features.

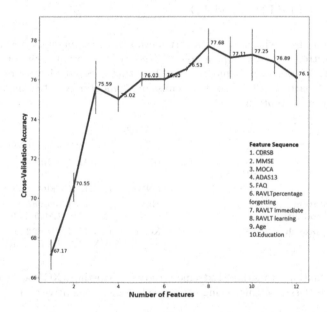

Fig. 2. Ablation Graph: Number of features vs. cross-validation accuracy for five classes setting, features importance order: Clinical dementia rating scale (CDR-SB), Mini-mental state exam (MMSE), Montreal cognitive assessment(MOCA), Alzheimer's disease assessment scale (ADAS13), Functional activities questionnaire (FAQ), Rey's auditory verbal learning test (RAVLT) percentage forgetting, RAVLT immediate, Education, RAVLT learning

Model Classification: Evaluation of the XT-SCI-NT method was carried out on the following metrics: accuracy, F1-score, precision, and recall for top-1 and top-2 labels reported class-wise (see Table.2.). We report test results to cor-roborate the models' performance. The XGBoost model achieves 78.74% and 93.10% accuracies for five classes and three classes, respectively. The obtained accuracy for three classes is comparable to the state-of-the-art accuracy, which uses various complex modalities [6] and is better than those obtained using MRI modality [5] as shown in Table.1. We can observe from the results in Table.2 that the precision for SMC is negligible for Top-1 precision. However, the top-2 precision for SMC is 100% for five classes. Thus, top-2 metrics act as an effi-cacious pre-screening measure when the uncommon cognitive impairment stage is incorrectly predicted. Top-2 accuracy, precision and recall all are 100% for three classes which represents there is no false positive and false negative top-2 prediction. Another observation is that CN's precision is 100% for three classes and for five classes' top-2, which implies that the model gives high-quality pos-itive predictions for the CN class. LMCI and EMCI classes have low precision which manifests that the classifier returns a lot of false positives, namely EMCI prediction for LMCI instance and vice versa. For an LMCI or AD instance, the actual class is always present in the top-2 prediction, which is indicated by the 100% top-2 recall for LMCI and AD.

Table 1. Comparison with state-of-the-art methods. MRI: magnetic resonance imag-ing, PET: positron emission tomography, CNN: convolutional neural network, RF: random forest, XGBoost: extreme gradient boosting, CS: cognitive score, NB: neu-ropsychological battery, PET: positron emission tomography, MH: medical history, MLP: multi-layer perceptron

Study	Modalities	Methods	Accuracy (%)
[11]	MRI	CNN	(NC/MCI/AD): 91.32
[12]	CS, NB, MRI, PET, MH, and genetic	RF	(CN/MCI/AD): 93.42
[13]	MRI+PET	CNN	(CN/EMCI/MCI/LMCI/AD): 86
Our implementation (MLP on CS Modality)	CS	MLP	(CN/MCI/AD): 87.06 (CN/SMC/EMCI/LMCI/AD): 72.7
XT-SCI-NT approach	CS	XGBoost	(CN/MCI/AD): **93.10** (CN/SMC/EMCI/LMCI/AD): **78.74**

Table 2. Evaluation of method Extreme Gradient Boosting (XGBoost) in the three classes and five classes settings using neuropsychological/cognitive tests.

Classes		Precision (%)	Recall (%)	F-1 Score (%)	Accuracy (%)	Top-2 Precision (%)	Top-2 Recall (%)	Top-2 Accuracy (%)
3	CN	100.00	91.00	93.08	93.10	100.00	100.00	100.00
	MCI	88.88	98.24			100.00	100.00	
	AD	95.59	84.42			100.00	100.00	
5	CN	85.15	91.49	76.60	78.74	100.00	93.62	96.84
	SMC	0.00	0.00			100.00	88.89	
	EMCI	67.27	57.81			88.40	95.31	
	LMCI	71.09	85.85			90.60	100.00	
	AD	95.23	90.90			95.65	100.00	

Model Explainability: Explainability is an important research agenda of the proposed contribution because it provides global and local interpretability of trained models, enabling a comprehensive understanding of the attributes' impact on class prediction. The model's interpretability can be divided into two categories: The first is global interpretability: The contribution of each predictor to the diagnostic label can be illustrated using SHAP methods, either positively or negatively. The second aspect is local interpretability. The LIME method has been used to generate local interpretable model-agnostic explanations. LIME creates an interpretable model by weighing predictions of perturbations of the input around its neighborhood.

Global Interpretability: For a global interpretation of the XGBoost models, we used TreeSHAP [9] graphs. Figure 3 illustrates how much every feature affects a certain group. When considering how each feature value in the data sample functions as a participant in a game where the prediction serves as the payoff, one can understand how the model makes predictions. The average marginal contribution of a feature value across all potential coalitions is what is known as the Shapley value, a strategy from coalitional game theory [10]. We obtained the ordered features according to their importance from the SHAP values plots. It can be observed that the CDRSB feature is most important in determining a subject's outcome. We looked at the summary plot for each diagnostic label (CN, SMC, EMCI, LMCI, and AD) presented in Fig. 3. to see if one attribute had a positive or negative influence on the result. The CN class summary plot shows that CDRSB values are very important in determining this class and are highly correlated with the low values. Furthermore, high FAQ and age values have a major positive impact. If we compare this analysis with the LMCI summary plot, it can be noticed color allocation is slightly different. For example, extremely high and low CDRSB values have a negative impact on the model's output. It is to be expected that high RAVLT-Immediate values have a negative impact here. The AD class's summary plot depicts drastically different trends from the CN diagnosis. High CDRSB values have a positive impact, while high MMSE results have a negative impact on this class's output. The critical aspect to notice in the SMC summary plot is how low age negatively influences the output to a large extent.

Local Interpretability: It is possible to isolate a single subject in order to graphically demonstrate how features affect a subject's labeling with a particular class. Any specific instance's prediction was explained using the LIME [9] approach. By producing locally valid interpretations, the LIME Python package aims to address the issue of model interpretability. We can enlarge a data point in a model to get a detailed look at the features that the model took into account to arrive at a certain result. The method makes an effort to understand the model by varying the input of data samples and examining how the predictions change. The plot in Fig. 4 corresponds to an EMCI diagnosis for a single subject. The majority of the traits have a significant positive effect, which explains why there is a high possibility that the person has EMCI. The patterns of people who were incorrectly predicted can be evaluated using this reasoning. We specifically

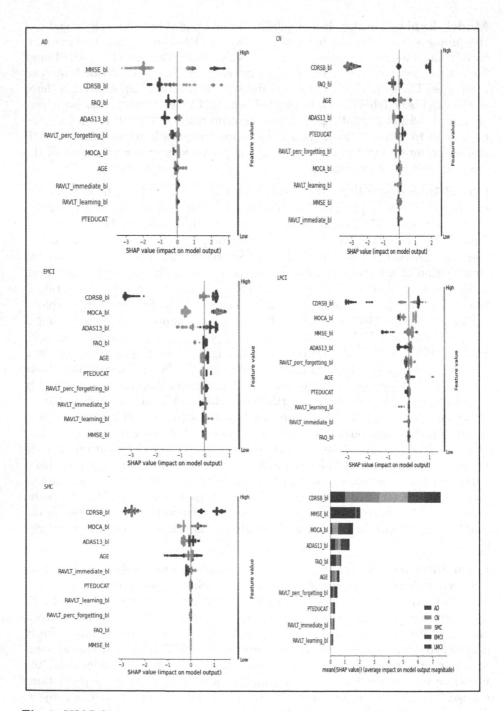

Fig. 3. SHAP feature importance measured as the mean absolute Shapley values using XGBoost Model and SHAP Summary Plot.

look at how features affect the expected and actual classes of randomly selected subjects.

Top-2 Metrics: We have taken three top-2 metrics: accuracy, precision and recall. Top 2 accuracy is the probability that a true class matches one of the model's two most likely classes.

This is an essential aspect for the clinician to know the probable diagnostic labels, especially in corner-case situations. Let's assume; c: class, x: actual label, [y1, y2]: predicted set. Either of y1 or y2 is x and x is equal to c for true positive t_p. For false positive f_p, x is neither y1 nor y2 and either of y1 or y2 is c. number of c class subjects where c is not in top2 prediction represents false negative f_n. So, we defined the precision and recall for Top-2 as follows:

$$Precision = \frac{t_p}{(t_p + f_p)} \quad \text{and} \quad Recall = \frac{t_p}{(t_p + f_n)}$$

In addition to performance evaluation, the system focuses on explainability. local explainability gives us the features that negatively and positively impact a subject's diagnostic decision. This extra information indicating which cognitive functions are majorly affected is valuable in dementia patient care as treatment plans may be structured accordingly. Global explainability provides a feature's average impact on predicting a particular diagnostic label. For example, MMSE has minimal impact on the prediction of CN and SMC.

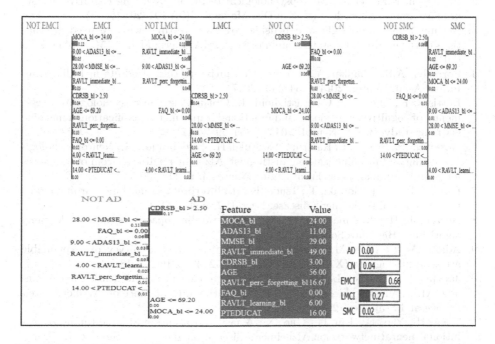

Fig. 4. Local Interpretability: LIME explains model predictions at the instance level.

4   Conclusion

We developed an explainable decision-tree-based detection model for cognitive impairment on a basic set of cognitive scores. First, we performed ablation to identify the possible optimal set of neuropsychological tests. Then, we trained our model using the classifier (XGBoost) to get the predictions. Moreover, The XGBoost method does not require high computing. Therefore, the complete XT-SCI-NT methodology can be implemented on-site using usual laptops and workstations even with augmented real data. The predictions were analyzed on various measures, and top-2 classification metrics, along with global and local explainability methodologies, were used to generate prediction explanations. Clinicians can use these explanations to provide important diagnostic decisions and assessment tool selection. The proposed XT-SCI-NT model can be a powerful pre-screening tool in low-resource settings of developing nations to obtain accurate outcomes comparable to the state-of-the-art results in high-resource settings.

References

1. Cheng, Y.W., Chen, T.F., Chiu, M.J.: From mild cognitive impairment to subjective cognitive decline: conceptual and methodological evolution. Neuropsychiatr. Dis. Treat. **13**, 491–498 (2017)
2. Baerresen, K.M., et al.: Neuropsychological tests for predicting cognitive decline in older adults. Neurodegenerative Dis. Manage. **5**(3), 191–201 (2015)
3. Newman, J.C.: Copyright and bedside cognitive testing: why we need alternatives to the mini-mental state examination. JAMA Intern. Med. **175**(9), 1459–1460 (2015)
4. Porrselvi, A.P., Shankar, V.: Status of cognitive testing of adults in India. Ann. Indian Acad. Neurol. **20**(4), 334–340 (2017)
5. Battista, P., Salvatore, C., Castiglioni, I.: Optimizing neuropsychological assessments for cognitive, behavioral, and functional impairment classification: a machine learning study. Behav. Neurol. **2017**, 1850909 (2017)
6. Gurevich, P., Stuke, H., Kastrup, A., Stuke, H., Hildebrandt, H.: Neuropsychological testing and machine learning distinguish Alzheimer's disease from other causes for cognitive impairment. Front. Aging Neurosci. **9**, 114 (2017)
7. Das, D., Ito, J., Kadowaki, T., Tsuda, K.: An interpretable machine learning model for diagnosis of Alzheimer's disease. Peer J. **7**, 6543 (2019)
8. Burrell, J.: How the machine "thinks": understanding opacity in machine learning algorithms. Big Data Soc. **3**(1) (2016)
9. Adadi, A., Berrada, M.: Peeking inside the black-box: a survey on explainable artificial intelligence (XAI). IEEE Access **6**, 52138–52160 (2018)
10. Janzing, D., Minorics, L., Blöbaum, P.: Feature relevance quantification in explainable AI: a causal problem. In: PMLR International Conference on Artificial Intelligence and Statistics (2020)
11. Tang, H., Yao, E., Tan, G., Guo, X.: A fast and accurate 3D fine-tuning convolutional neural network for Alzheimer's disease diagnosis. In: Zhou, Z.-H., Yang, Q., Gao, Y., Zheng, Yu. (eds.) ICAI 2018. CCIS, vol. 888, pp. 115–126. Springer, Singapore (2018). https://doi.org/10.1007/978-981-13-2122-1_9

12. El-Sappagh, S., Alonso, J.M., Islam, S.M.R., Sultan, A.M., Kwak, K.S.: A multilayer multimodal detection and prediction model based on explainable artificial intelligence for Alzheimer's disease. Sci. Rep. **11**(1), 2660 (2021)
13. Solano-Rojas, B., Villalón-Fonseca, R., Low-Cost, A.: Three-dimensional DenseNet neural network for Alzheimer's disease early discovery. Sensors **21**, 1302 (2021)

Semi-supervised Contrastive Regression for Estimation of Eye Gaze

Somsukla Maiti[✉] and Akshansh Gupta

CSIR- Central Electronics Engineering Research Institute, Pilani, India
somsuklamaiti@gmail.com, {somsukla,akshanshgupta}@ceeri.res.in

Abstract. With the escalated demand of human-machine interfaces for intelligent systems, development of gaze controlled system have become a necessity. Gaze, being the non-intrusive form of human interaction, is one of the best suited approach. Appearance based deep learning models are the most widely used for gaze estimation. But the performance of these models is entirely influenced by the size of labeled gaze dataset and in effect affects generalization in performance.

This paper aims to develop a semi-supervised contrastive learning framework for estimation of gaze direction. With a small labeled gaze dataset, the framework is able to find a generalized solution even for unseen face images. In this paper, we have proposed a new contrastive loss paradigm that maximizes the similarity agreement between similar images and at the same time reduces the redundancy in embedding representations. Our contrastive regression framework shows good performance in comparison to several state of the art contrastive learning techniques used for gaze estimation.

Keywords: Gaze Estimation · Contrastive Regression · Semi-supervised learning · Dilated Convolution

1 Introduction

Eye gaze is one of the most widely used human mode for developing human-machine interface system. Gaze controlled interface has become quite popular for virtual reality (VR) applications [1], navigation control of ground and aerial robots [2], control of robotic arms for surgery [3] and other commercial applications. With the advances in deep learning methods, gaze tracking has become an achievable task.

Appearance-based models are the most prominent approach that does not require an expensive and subject-dependent eye modeling. It mainly relies on annotated face images captured using camera/eye-tracker and learns a model to map gaze direction from the images. Most of the earliest methods relied on dedicated feature extraction [4,5] and feature selection steps, before performing the regression task [6]. This in effect makes the models more person-specific and generalization is not attained. At the same time, dedicated feature extraction also

© The Author(s), under exclusive license to Springer Nature Switzerland AG 2023
P. Maji et al. (Eds.): PReMI 2023, LNCS 14301, pp. 252–259, 2023.
https://doi.org/10.1007/978-3-031-45170-6_26

makes the computation time-taxing. With the advancements in deep learning [7], convolution neural networks(CNN) based frameworks [8,9] have become the most used architectures for gaze estimation. Mostly ResNet based CNN frameworks [10] have been developed that maps the gaze angles on the eye images. Dual branch CNN [11] has been another adopted approach for gaze estimation that reconstructs images with the gaze direction in supervision. Sequential models have also been used to learn the variation in gaze direction in subsequent frames, by leveraging LSTM models [12] on the residual features obtained using CNN. Capsule networks are another most promising approach for appearance-based models [13,14] as it emphasizes on learning equivariance instead of finding deeper features.

Generalization of appearance-based models is solely dependent on the volume of labeled data. Annotation of gaze direction in eye images is a difficult and time-consuming task. Even with the large gaze datasets available in the public domain, there are still issues in developing a domain-adaptive model due to varied background environment and illumination conditions. To deal with these problems, Semi-supervised learning(SSL) is one of the most promising solution.

SSL performs a pre-training [15] on the unlabeled data to learn an effective representation of the input. It further fine-tunes the solution using a small labeled dataset. Contrastive learning, a SSL technique, has been predominantly used in different computer vision applications in past few years. Contrastive learning based methods learn semantic embedding representation [16] of the input image by pulling the similar images together and pushing the disparate images away [17]. This facilitates the models to learn a suitable encoding of the images [18] using only the unlabeled data. Consequently, a limited gaze annotations are used to learn a model that can perform the final task of classification, segmentation or prediction. Wang [19] have first introduced the use of contrastive learning method for unsupervised regression learning of eye gaze direction.

In this paper, we present a semi-supervised regression technique to predict the eye gaze direction with two major contributions.

- We have developed a contrastive learning framework that learns an encoder architecture to compute embeddings and further uses the pre-trained embeddings to predict the gaze directions.
- We have proposed a new form of contrastive loss to maximize the agreement between similar images that can take care of both invariance and redundancy factors simultaneously.

2 Methodology

The designed framework is based on SimCLR framework [16] that performs the task in two stages. The first stage aims to learn an representation from the given images by maximizing the agreement between the vector representations learned from the images. The final stage uses the embeddings learnt in the pre-training stage and trains a model that performs the task of prediction by minimizing a loss function.

Mini-batches of batch size B are sampled from the dataset (X, G_{dir}), where X represents the images and G_{dir} represents the gaze direction labels for those images. Random data augmentation is performed to create two varied representations of the images in the mini-batches X_{a1} and X_{a2}. We have designed an encoder module $\mathcal{E}$ that learns latent space representations $f_1 = \mathcal{E}(X_{a1})$ and $f_2 = \mathcal{E}(X_{a2})$ from the augmented images. Latent space embeddings learns high-level features from the images. These embeddings are then passed to a projection head $\mathcal{P}$, which is designed as a multi-layer perceptron (MLP) to learn a non-linear projection vector for less complex processing. The learned embeddings are $p_1 = \mathcal{P}(f_1)$ and $p_2 = \mathcal{P}(f_2)$, which are then compared to minimize the contrastive loss for similar image pairs.

The designed encoder can learn local as well as global dependency in feature maps. The architecture of the encoder is shown in Fig. 1a. In order to learn global spatial dependency along with local spatial details, larger kernel size needs to be considered. But, larger kernel size increases the computation complexity of the model and can also lead to overfitting. Thus we have used dilated convolution with different dilation rates and local spatial dependency is learnt with each convolution. By using dilated convolution, we were able to attain larger receptive fields without increasing the computation complexity due to larger kernel size by using different dilation rates. Feature map of high spatial resolution is obtained by concatenating the coarse to fine feature maps learned. Convolution filters for different dilation rates have been shown in Fig. 1b, where each colour indicates kernel corresponding to each dilation rate in concatenated feature map.

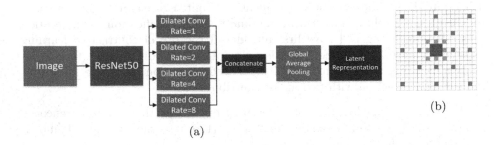

(a)

(b)

Fig. 1. .

An updated version of the Normalized temperature scaled cross-entropy (NT-Xent) loss [16] has been used to define our contrastive loss. The aim is to minimize the invariance in data as well as the redundancy in feature maps at the same time. The NT-Xent loss aims to maximize the similarity between two positive images and minimize the similarity between a positive and a negative image. We have used the concept of computing cross-correlation matrix as introduced in Barlow Twins [18] to analyze the correlation between the positive and negative images. The cross-correlation between the projections p_1 and p_2 is computed as C, where each element basically represents the similarity between each element of the projections. The contrastive loss defined in this paper is displayed in Equation [1], where the first term defines the **NT-Xent loss** that tries to **minimize the invariance**, whereas the second term **reduces the redundant** information in the output vector representation. The term γ represents loss coefficient factor to consider the redundancy term which has been set to $\gamma = 0.01$. The terms $sim(p_i, p_j)$ defines the cosine similarity between p_i and p_j and is defined by Equation [2].

$$\mathcal{L} = -\frac{1}{B} \sum_{i,j \in 1}^{B} log \frac{exp(sim(p_i, p_j)/\tau)}{\sum_{k=1}^{2B} \mathbb{1}_{k \neq i} \, exp(sim(p_i, p_k)/\tau)} + \gamma \sum_{i} \sum_{j \neq i} C_{ij}^2 \qquad (1)$$

$$sim(p_i, p_j) = \frac{p_i p_j}{\|p_i\| \, \|p_j\|} \qquad (2)$$

The framework pre-training stage and fine-tuning stage for regression is shown in Fig. 2a and Fig. 2b respectively. It uses the pre-trained encoder model and determines the values of latent space representations f_i. The latent vectors are used as an input to the regression network to predict the values of gaze directions G_{pred}. The regression fine-tuning network is optimized by minimizing the huber loss, which is a step-wise amalgamation of mean squared error and mean absolute error to tackle the outlier issue, as defined in Equation [3] where $d = G_{pred} - G_{dir}$. The loss parameter δ, that provides a measure of spread of the deviation error, ensures the loss function to generate large value of loss, by computing the squared value of deviation, for larger deviation values and smaller values of loss, by computing linear mean absolute error, for small deviation values.

$$L_\delta(d) = \begin{cases} \frac{d^2}{2}, & \text{if } |d| \leq \delta \\ \delta \left(|d| - \frac{\delta}{2} \right), & \text{otherwise} \end{cases} \qquad (3)$$

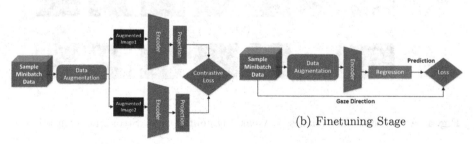

(a) Pre-training Stage

(b) Finetuning Stage

Fig. 2. Contrastive Regression Framework

3   Results and Discussion

3.1   Dataset

We have used the ETH-XGaze [20] dataset for evaluation of our model. ETH-XGaze is a large data set for gaze estimation that includes images with excellent resolution with consistent label quality, captured from 110 individuals representing a wide range of ages, genders, and ethnicities. The dataset contains around 1,083,492 images of 6000*4000 resolution with 18 cameras placed at different locations to get different views. The dataset covers a large scale of head-pose and gaze directions, which makes it a good choice for developing a generalized solution. Sample images with different gaze directions have been displayed in Fig. 3. Images from the train subset of the dataset has been first split into train and validation sets in 80:20 ratio. Train set images, without labels, are used to learn encoder in pre-training stage where validation set images with labels are used further in the fine-tuning stage. Augmented version of the face images are obtained by applying the following transfer functions such as, horizontal mirror imaging, rescaling, zooming and varying the brightness, contrast, hue and saturation. We have performed augmentation of mini-batches of images by randomly applying any three of the above mentioned operations. Figure 4 represents few samples of augmented images generated by weak and strong augmentation.

Fig. 3. Labeled Face images with Gaze direction

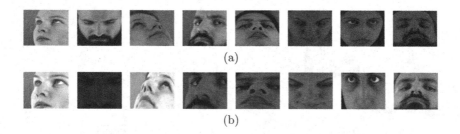

(a)

(b)

Fig. 4. Augmented Face images, a. Weak augmentation, b. Strong augmentation

3.2   Evaluation

The performance of developed architecture has been evaluated by computing the Mean Angular Error. The performance of our model has been compared with different state of the art architectures and the results have been enlisted in

Table [1]. Our model is able to generate significantly better result than SimCLR, which has been used for gaze estimation, and Barlow twins model. Our encoder computes features in an efficient manner by taking local dependencies in consideration. The encoder, when designed with a flatten layer at the output, provides slightly better result. We still prefer the model with global average pooling as displayed in Fig. 1a, as it reduces the number of parameters in the architecture. We can see that the model with flatten layer estimates with mean angular error of 2.152 degrees, whereas the model with reduced parameters generates mean angular error of 3.212 degrees.

Table 1. Mean Angular Error in degrees for gaze estimation

Method	Mean Angular Gaze Error
SimCLR	9.175°
Barlow Twins	9.390°
SimCLR with Deeplab Encoder	2.246°
Ours	**2.152°**
Ours (with reduced parameters)	3.212°

We have evaluated performance of models with other state of the art loss functions used in contrastive training for gaze estimation problem. The simultaneous optimization of invariance and redundancy provides us the upper hand in performance as shown in Table [2].

Table 2. Ablation study on using different Loss

Method	Mean Angular Gaze Error
NT-Xent loss	4.606°
Barlow Twins loss	4.3361°
Our Contrastive loss	3.212°

3.3 Ablation Study

In order to understand the role of second term in loss function defined in Eq. [1], which aims to minimize the redundancy, we have used a loss coefficient factor γ. By varying the value of γ, the performance of our model is evaluated. In Table [3], we can see that the performance improves as we increase the value of loss coefficient upto a certain value. The coefficient γ has been set as 0.1 for evaluation of our model.

Table 3. Ablation study on loss coefficient parameter

Method	Mean Angular Gaze Error
$\gamma = 0.005$	4.755°
$\gamma = 0.01$	4.549°
$\gamma = 0.1$	3.212°

4 Conclusion

This work has enlightened on semi-supervised learning for eye gaze prediction tasks by developing contrastive learning framework. The work has proposed a new form of contrastive loss to optimize the similarity agreement between augmented and captured face images considering two parameters, viz., invariant transformation and redundancy among images, to predict gaze direction. The proposed model has been tested on ETH-XGaze dataset. The evaluation of the proposed model has been done in terms of mean angular error. The model has outperformed different state of the art techniques such as SimCLR, Barlow twins as shown in the previous sections. In future we will experiment across different datasets and find a more generalized solution for cross-datasets scenarios.

Acknowledgements. Authors would like to acknowledge CSIR-Central Electronics Engineering Research Institute (CSIR-CEERI) for providing facilities and CSIR-AITS mission for providing fund to conduct this research work.

References

1. Konrad, R., Angelopoulos, A., Wetzstein, G.: Gaze-contingent ocular parallax rendering for virtual reality. ACM Trans. Graph. (TOG) **39**(2), 1–12 (2020)
2. Gerber, M.A., Schroeter, R., Xiaomeng, L., Elhenawy, M.: Self-interruptions of non-driving related tasks in automated vehicles: mobile vs head-up display. In: Proceedings of the 2020 CHI Conference on Human Factors in Computing Systems, pp. 1–9 (2020)
3. Ferrier-Barbut, E., Gauthier, P., Luengo, V., Canlorbe, G., Vitrani, M.A.: Measuring the quality of learning in a human-robot collaboration: a study of laparoscopic surgery. ACM Trans. Hum.-Robot Interact. (THRI) **11**(3), 1–20 (2022)
4. Rattarom, S., Uttama, S., Aunsri, N.: Model construction and validation in low-cost interpolation-based gaze tracking system. Eng. Lett. **27**(1), 87–96 (2019)
5. Yilmaz, C.M., Kose, C.: Local binary pattern histogram features for on-screen eye-gaze direction estimation and a comparison of appearance based methods. In: 2016 39th International Conference on Telecommunications and Signal Processing (TSP), pp. 693–696. IEEE (2016)
6. Aunsri, N., Rattarom, S.: Novel eye-based features for head pose-free gaze estimation with web camera: new model and low-cost device. Ain Shams Eng. J. **13**(5), 101731 (2022)
7. Pathirana, P., Senarath, S., Meedeniya, D., Jayarathna, S.: Eye gaze estimation: a survey on deep learning-based approaches. Expert Syst. Appl. **199**, 116894 (2022)

8. Cheng, Y., Wang, H., Bao, Y., Lu, F.: Appearance-based gaze estimation with deep learning: a review and benchmark. arXiv preprint arXiv:2104.12668 (2021)
9. Lemley, J., Kar, A., Drimbarean, A., Corcoran, P.: Convolutional neural network implementation for eye-gaze estimation on low-quality consumer imaging systems. IEEE Trans. Consum. Electron. **65**(2), 179–187 (2019)
10. Kanade, P., David, F., Kanade, S.: Convolutional neural networks (CNN) based eye-gaze tracking system using machine learning algorithm. Euro. J. Electr. Eng. Comput. Sci. **5**(2), 36–40 (2021)
11. Zhu, Z., Zhang, D., Chi, C., Li, M., Lee, D.J.: A complementary dual-branch network for appearance-based gaze estimation from low-resolution facial image. IEEE Trans. Cogn. Develop. Syst. **15**, 1323–1334 (2022)
12. Chong, E., Wang, Y., Ruiz, N., Rehg, J.M.: Detecting attended visual targets in video. In: Proceedings of the IEEE/CVF Conference on Computer Vision and Pattern Recognition, pp. 5396–5406 (2020)
13. Bernard, V., Wannous, H., Vandeborre, J.P.: Eye-gaze estimation using a deep capsule-based regression network. In: 2021 International Conference on Content-Based Multimedia Indexing (CBMI), pp. 1–6 IEEE (2021)
14. Mahanama, B., Jayawardana, Y., Jayarathna, S.: Gaze-net: appearance-based gaze estimation using capsule networks. In: Proceedings of the 11th Augmented Human International Conference, pp. 1–4 (2020)
15. Crawford, E., Pineau, J.: Spatially invariant unsupervised object detection with convolutional neural networks. Proc. AAAI Conf. Artif. Intell. **33**, 3412–3420 (2019)
16. Chen, T., Kornblith, S., Norouzi, M., Hinton, G.: A simple framework for contrastive learning of visual representations. In: International Conference on Machine Learning, pp. 1597–1607. PMLR (2020)
17. Grill, J.B., et al.: Bootstrap your own latent-a new approach to self-supervised learning. In: Advances in Neural Information Processing Systems, vol. 33, pp. 21271–21284 (2020)
18. Zbontar, J., Jing, L., Misra, I., LeCun, Y., Deny, S.: Barlow twins: self-supervised learning via redundancy reduction. In: International Conference on Machine Learning, pp. 12310–12320. PMLR (2021)
19. Wang, Y., et al.: Contrastive regression for domain adaptation on gaze estimation. In: Proceedings of the IEEE/CVF Conference on Computer Vision and Pattern Recognition, pp. 19376–19385 (2022)
20. Zhang, X., Park, S., Beeler, T., Bradley, D., Tang, S., Hilliges, O.: ETH-XGaze: a large scale dataset for gaze estimation under extreme head pose and gaze variation. In: Vedaldi, A., Bischof, H., Brox, T., Frahm, J.-M. (eds.) ECCV 2020. LNCS, vol. 12350, pp. 365–381. Springer, Cham (2020). https://doi.org/10.1007/978-3-030-58558-7_22

iBEHAVE: Behaviour Analysis Using Eye Gaze Metrices

S. Akshay[1]([✉])(iD), P. Kavya Bijith[1], S. Sanjana[1], and J. Amudha[2](iD)

[1] Department of Computer Science, School of Computing, Amrita Vishwa
Vidyapeetham, Mysuru, Karnataka, India
s_akshay@my.amrita.edu
[2] Department of Computer Science and Engineering, School of Computing, Amrita
Vishwa Vidyapeetham, Bengaluru, Karnataka, India
j_amudha@blr.amrita.edu

Abstract. Human behavior analysis is a fascinating and complex field
that has the potential to improve our understanding of social interactions and mental health. One approach to studying human behavior is
using eye gaze detection technology. Eye movements provide insights
into how people perceive and respond to their environment. Eye gaze
detection technology has many applications in human behavior analysis, such as understanding social interaction, detecting cognitive impairments, and improving mental health treatment. In this paper, we present
an overview of the field of human behavior analysis using eye gaze detection. We describe the technology behind eye gaze detection, the different
types of eye movements, and the methods used to analyze the data.
We then discuss how eye gaze can be used to predict social behavior,
detect cognitive impairments, and evaluate the effectiveness of mental
health treatments. The proposed system predicts human behavior such
as sadness and depression using a CNN model with an accuracy of 93%.
This shows that eye gaze detection has great potential for advancing
our understanding of social interactions and mental health as its use is
widespread in research and clinical settings.

Keywords: Behaviour analysis · Emotions · Eye gaze · Heatmap ·
Convolution Neural Network · Mental health

1 Introduction

Human behavior analysis is a field of study that seeks to understand how people
think, feel, and act in different situations. It includes a broad variety of academic
fields, such as anthropology, psychology, sociology, and neuroscience. The study
of human behavior is important because it can help us understand and predict
social interactions, improve mental health treatments, and promote overall wellbeing. One approach to studying human behavior is through the use of eye gaze
detection technology. Eye gaze detection is a non-invasive method for measuring

P. Maji et al. (Eds.): PReMI 2023, LNCS 14301, pp. 260–269, 2023.
https://doi.org/10.1007/978-3-031-45170-6_27

eye movements and has been used in various fields, including psychology, marketing, and human-computer interaction. It involves using a device to track the position and movement of the eyes, which can then be used to infer attention, focus, and emotional state. Eye gaze detection has many potential applications in human behavior analysis, including studying social interactions, identifying cognitive impairments, and evaluating the effectiveness of mental health treatments. For example, researchers have used eye gaze detection to study how people perceive and respond to different facial expressions, how individuals with autism spectrum disorder process social information, and how people with depression attend to emotional stimuli? This paper provides an overview of the field of human behavior analysis using eye gaze detection. We describe the technology behind eye gaze detection, the different types of eye movements, and the methods used to analyze the data. We then review how eye gaze can be used to predict social behavior. Finally, we discuss some of the challenges and future directions for the field. Previous research in behavior analysis has predominantly relied on facial expressions to interpret human emotions, intentions, and cognitive states. These methodologies have proved valuable in domains like affective computing, autism spectrum disorder diagnosis, and lie detection, but they have limitations in capturing the complexity of human behavior. Our research introduces a novel approach to behavior analysis by utilizing eye gaze metrics as an additional source of information. By tracking eye movements, fixations, saccades, and gaze patterns, we aim to gain insights into attentional focus, visual perception, decision-making processes, social interactions, and user experience. This innovative method enhances our understanding of human behavior and expands the scope of behavior analysis and provides a more comprehensive understanding of human behavior in various contexts.

2 Related Work

In order to explain how visual search and identification activities are carried out, eye tracking is increasingly often employed in medical imaging applications. This information can help people perform better. Work by [5] Examined the use of eye tracking to study attentional bias in anxiety disorders and concluded that attentional biases toward threat stimuli can be detected using eye-tracking technology. [14] use eye tracking to investigate the gaze behaviors of individuals with autism spectrum disorder in naturalistic social situations. [12] used eye tracking to assess social attention in children with autism spectrum disorder using a dual-target paradigm. A systematic review by [3] examined the use of eye-tracking measures of reading to detect cognitive impairment. The authors found that eye-tracking measures of reading can be a sensitive and specific tool for detecting cognitive impairment. The authors [17] found that eye-tracking metrics can distinguish between children with autism spectrum disorder and typically developing children as early as 6–12 months of age. The authors found that eye-tracking measures can predict behavior in social interactions with high accuracy [16]. The authors [7] describe various applications of gaze dynamics, such as object recognition and scene understanding. The use of eye tracking to investigate cognitive processes in bilingualism was proposed by [10] and found that it is a valuable tool for investigating cognitive processes in bilingualism. [11] examined the effect of emotion on eye movements. [6] The authors found that eye tracking can enhance the realism of virtual reality experiences and provide insights into user behavior. [8] Proposed a review that examined the use of eye-tracking metrics as biomarkers for psychiatric disorders. The authors found that eye tracking can provide insights into student engagement and learning outcomes [9]. [4] Examined the use of eye tracking in marketing research and found that eye tracking can provide valuable insights into consumer behavior and preferences. The authors found that gaze-based interaction can provide a more natural and intuitive way of interacting with virtual and augmented environments [8]. Insights into user behaviour and preferences may be gained by eye tracking, according to the authors, and this information can be utilised to enhance website design [15]. Work by [13]in schizophrenia, [1,2] in Parkinson's Disease emphasizes use of eye gaze. These works motivate us to use eye tracking for behavioral studies.

3   Proposed Methodology

3.1   Training Model

The training process for a CNN model in human behavior analysis using eye gaze metrics involves collecting and preparing a large dataset of labeled eye gaze data as depicted in Fig. 1. The input data may need to be pre-processed to remove noise or artifacts and to normalize the data for consistent analysis. Next, the pre-processed data is passed through a series of convolutional and pooling layers to extract meaningful features such as fixations, saccades, and pupil size. The resulting feature maps are flattened and passed through a series of fully connected layers to perform classification or regression tasks. The trained model is created by adjusting the weights and biases of the layers to minimize the error between the predicted output and the true labels. The CNN model is then designed and compiled using a suitable optimizer, loss function, and evaluation metrics. The validation set is used to assess the model's performance and prevent overfitting once the model has been trained on the training set.

Fig. 1. Training Model

3.2   Testing Model

The CNN model is used to classify the behavior being analyzed based on the eye gaze data as depicted in Fig. 2. The testing process for a CNN model in human behavior analysis using eye gaze metrics involves careful data collection, preprocessing, and analysis to generate accurate and reliable results. This process is crucial in evaluating the effectiveness of the CNN model and can inform future research in this field. The overall workflow of the system starts with camera optimization for capturing high-quality images of the eye. Frames are captured and synthesized using PCA eigen point detection, which helps to generate accurate representations of the eye's movements. Pupil identification is then performed to isolate the pupil from the surrounding area, and X and Y coordinates of the pupil's position are stored to generate the dataset. The generated dataset is then preprocessed to remove any outliers and normalized to ensure consistent results. The CNN model is then used to generate a heatmap, which highlights the areas of the image that are most relevant to the behavior being analyzed. The scan-path value, which is a measure of the complexity of eye movements, is calculated based on the heatmap. Finally, a CNN model is trained on the processed dataset to detect specific behaviors.

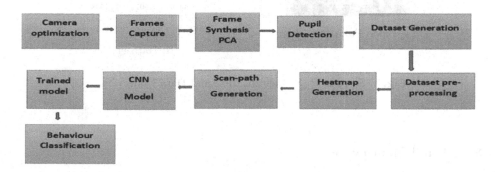

Fig. 2. Testing Model

3.3   Camera Optimization

Camera optimization is an essential step in eye tracking studies to ensure high-quality data collection. In this context, the camera should be optimized to capture clear and high-resolution images of the eye region. This can be achieved by adjusting camera settings such as focus, exposure, and aperture. The camera should also be positioned correctly to ensure that the eye is in the center of the image and that there is no distortion or occlusion. Moreover, ambient lighting conditions should be controlled to minimize any reflections or shadows that may interfere with eye tracking.

3.4   Frame Synthesis Using PCA Eigen Point Detection

Frame synthesis using PCA eigen point detection is a method of generating new frames based on the existing ones in the dataset. This technique involves identifying the key features of the eyes in each frame and using these features to generate new frames that are similar but not identical to the original ones as shown in Fig. 3a. In this context, PCA eigen point detection is used to identify the most important features of the eye region, such as the position of the iris, the shape of the eyelids, and the orientation of the eye. These features are then used to synthesize new frames that capture different viewing angles and eye movements. This process can help to increase the size of the dataset and improve the accuracy of subsequent analyses.

-0.10359	-1.03813	-0.3049
-0.34918	1.134523	-0.10673
1.645714	0.021385	1.337169
-0.52208	-0.92247	-1.54525
-0.74107	-0.70445	-0.06324
-1.16843	-0.79184	-0.51554
-1.10657	1.360777	2.033293
-1.1318	0.244911	-1.24419
-0.33872	1.889546	-0.3457
0.364486	-1.19072	-0.11033
-0.34279	-0.28076	-0.233
0.609446	1.00809	0.915554

(a) Eigen Point Detection

(b) Dataset

Fig. 3. Steps in Pupil Identification and Data Collection

3.5   Pupil Identification

Pupil identification is a crucial step in eye gaze analysis as it helps in accurately tracking the eye movements of the individual. In this context, pupil identification refers to the process of detecting and segmenting the pupil from the eye region in the captured frames. This process involves various image processing techniques such as thresholding, morphological operations, and edge detection to isolate the pupil from the rest of the eye area. After successful pupil identification, the center coordinates of the pupil are obtained, which are used in further processing and analysis. Accurate pupil identification is essential for generating reliable scan paths and heat maps, which can provide insights into an individual's visual attention and behavior.

3.6   Dataset Generation

A dataset as shown in Fig. 3b has been generated that includes the X and Y coordinates of the pupil viewed on the screen. The dataset can be used to train machine learning models to classify different eye behaviors based on gaze patterns. The dataset may also be analyzed to gain insights into patterns of eye movements during different tasks or in response to different stimuli. Proper labeling and cleaning of the dataset is crucial to ensure accurate training of the models. Techniques such as normalization, scaling, and data augmentation may also be applied to improve the robustness and generalization capability of the models.

3.7   Data Pre-processing

After generating the dataset consisting of X and Y coordinates of the pupil viewed in the screen, the next step is to process it. The dataset processing involves various operations like cleaning, normalization, and feature extraction. The cleaning process involves the removal of any redundant or noisy data points that may affect the accuracy of the results. After cleaning, the data is normalized to ensure consistency across different samples. Feature extraction involves the identification of important features that can be used to differentiate between different behaviors. This is done using techniques like Principal Component Analysis (PCA) and other statistical methods. Once the features are identified, they are used to generate heatmaps and scan path values for further analysis.

3.8   Heatmap Generation Based on View Index

After the dataset is processed, the next step is to generate a heatmap based on the view index. A view index represents the location of the point of gaze on the screen. Heatmaps provide a visual representation of the distribution of gaze points, indicating the regions of the screen that attract the most attention. To generate a heatmap, the view index data from the dataset is first binned into a grid of equal-sized cells. Each cell represents a region of the screen. The number of times a gaze point falls within a cell is then counted, and the count is normalized to the total number of gaze points in the dataset. The resulting normalized counts are then mapped onto a color scale, with high counts corresponding to a hot color (e.g., red) and low counts corresponding to a cool color (e.g., blue). The heatmap provides a visual representation of the gaze pattern, which can help identify regions of interest and attentional biases as depicted in Fig. 4.

(a) Stimuli 1

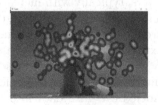

(b) Stimuli 2

Fig. 4. Generated Heatmaps

3.9   Scan Path Value Generation

In eye-tracking studies, scanpath analysis is an important tool used to understand how individuals view and process visual information. Scanpath refers to the sequence of fixations and saccades made by an individual while viewing an image or video. The scanpath can be used to extract important features such as the duration and frequency of fixations, saccade amplitudes and velocities, and the overall pattern of eye movements. In this context, scanpath values can be generated by analyzing the dataset of eye movements and identifying the sequence of fixations and saccades made by the participant while viewing the stimuli as in Fig. 5. These values can then be used to further analyze and interpret the eye tracking data, such as in comparison between different behaviors or in training a predictive model.

(a) Stimuli 1

(b) Stimuli 2

Fig. 5. Generated Scanpath Visualization

3.10   CNN Model Comparison

CNNs (Convolutional Neural Networks) are a type of deep learning algorithm that is particularly well-suited for image and video analysis. In the context of human behavior analysis using eye gaze metrics, CNNs can be used to analyze eye movement data and extract features such as fixations, saccades, and pupil size. A CNN consists of multiple layers that work together to extract meaningful features from the input data. A convolutional layer, which extracts features, a non-linear activation function, such as a ReLU (Rectified Linear Unit), a pooling layer. The resulting feature maps are passed through additional convolutional and pooling layers, typically with increasing numbers of filters and decreasing spatial dimensions. The final set of feature maps is then flattened into a vector and passed through a series of fully connected layers, which perform classification. In the context of human behavior analysis using eye gaze metrics, CNN is trained to classify eye movement data based on a variety of tasks or behaviors, such as detecting fixation points as depicted in Fig. 6. The training process involves feeding labeled eye gaze data into the network and adjusting the weights and biases of the layers to minimize the error between the predicted output and the true labels. We use a holdout validation approach, where a portion of the dataset is held out as a validation set for model evaluation.

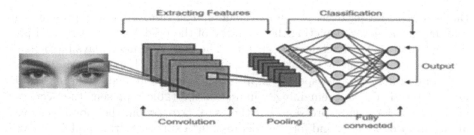

Fig. 6. The CNN Model Comparison

3.11   Prediction of Behavior

After the CNN models have been trained and compared using the generated dataset, the next step is to use the trained models to predict the behavior of individuals based on their eye movements. The prediction process involves inputting new eye-tracking data into the trained models and obtaining output predictions for the behavior being studied, such as attentional bias or social attention. The predictions can be used to gain insights into the underlying cognitive processes and inform interventions for individuals with behavioral disorders as in Fig. 7. It is important to evaluate the accuracy of the predictions using validation datasets and to continually refine the models to improve their performance.

(a) Sad   (b) Depression

Fig. 7. Prediction of Behavior

4   Results and Discussion

The overall work focused on utilizing eye-tracking technology and an Artificial Neural Network (ANN) algorithm to detect and predict specific behaviors, specifically focusing on behaviors related to sadness and depression. The generated dataset was specifically tailored to include information related to the X and Y axis of the pupil as viewed on the screen. By analyzing this dataset, heatmaps were generated based on the view index, providing visual representations of areas of focus during eye movements. Additionally, scan path values were generated to determine the path of eye movement during viewing, offering insights into the sequence and patterns of eye movements. The results Table 1 presents the findings of the study, depicting the accuracy of the model in detecting and predicting emotions for different participants. The first column displays participant numbers, with a total of 12 participants included for each expression. The second column indicates the specific expressions being examined, including "sad" and "depression". The remaining columns of the table represent the accuracy of the model for each expression. For the "sad" expression, the model achieved an accuracy of 93.35%. and for the "depression" expression, the model achieved an accuracy of 93.77%. This signifies a high level of accuracy in identifying depression-related eye behaviors in the participants. These results suggest that the proposed model demonstrated robust performance in accurately detecting and distinguishing between the expressions of sadness and depression based on the eye-tracking data.

Table 1. Performance of the proposed method

Total participants	Behaviour	Accuracy in %
12	Sad	93.35
12	Depression	93.76

5 Conclusion and Future Work

The proposed context for detecting eye behaviors using CNN model prediction has shown promising results in accurately predicting and classifying eye behaviors. The use of PCA eigen point detection and pupil identification techniques allowed for accurate and precise tracking of eye movements. The generated dataset and heatmap allowed for a comprehensive analysis of eye behavior. The model was tested on a set of unseen data, and the high accuracy and performance metrics demonstrated the effectiveness of the proposed approach. In the future, incorporating more diverse datasets, including those from individuals with different ages, backgrounds, and eye conditions, could help improve the generalizability of the model. The system could also be applied to other fields, such as psychology and marketing, to study human behavior and preferences. Furthermore, integrating real-time feedback mechanisms could enable the system to provide instant insights and recommendations for improving user engagement and interaction.

References

1. Akshay, S., Amudha, J., Kulkarni, N., Prashanth, L.K.: iSTIMULI: prescriptive stimulus design for eye movement analysis of patients with Parkinson's disease. In: Morusupalli, R., Dandibhotla, T.S., Atluri, V.V., Windridge, D., Lingras, P., Komati, V.R. (eds.) MIWAI 2023. LNCS, vol. 14078, pp. 589–600. Springer, Cham (2023). https://doi.org/10.1007/978-3-031-36402-0_55

2. Akshay, S., Amudha, J., Narmada, N., Bhattacharya, A., Kamble, N., Pal, P.K.: iAOI: an eye movement based deep learning model to identify areas of interest. In: Morusupalli, R., Dandibhotla, T.S., Atluri, V.V., Windridge, D., Lingras, P., Komati, V.R. (eds.) MIWAI 2023. LNCS, vol. 14078, pp. 659–670. Springer, Cham (2023). https://doi.org/10.1007/978-3-031-36402-0_61

3. Akshay, S., Megha, Y., Shetty, C.B.: Machine learning algorithm to identify eye movement metrics using raw eye tracking data. In: 2020 Third International Conference on Smart Systems and Inventive Technology (ICSSIT), pp. 949–955. IEEE (2020)

4. Andrzejewska, M., Stolińska, A.: Comparing the difficulty of tasks using eye tracking combined with subjective and behavioural criteria. J. Eye Mov. Res. **9**(3) (2016)

5. Bhattarai, R., Phothisonothai, M.: Eye-tracking based visualizations and metrics analysis for individual eye movement patterns. In: 2019 16th International Joint Conference on Computer Science and Software Engineering (JCSSE), pp. 381–384. IEEE (2019)

6. Boraston, Z., Blakemore, S.J.: The application of eye-tracking technology in the study of autism. J. Physiol. **581**(3), 893–898 (2007)

7. Castner, N., et al.: Deep semantic gaze embedding and scanpath comparison for expertise classification during opt viewing. In: ACM Symposium on Eye Tracking Research and Applications, pp. 1–10 (2020)

8. Gidlöf, K., Wallin, A., Dewhurst, R., Holmqvist, K.: Using eye tracking to trace a cognitive process: gaze behaviour during decision making in a natural environment. J. Eye Mov. Res. **6**(1) (2013)

9. Hasse, C., Bruder, C.: Eye-tracking measurements and their link to a normative model of monitoring behaviour. Ergonomics **58**(3), 355–367 (2015)

10. He, H., et al.: Real-time eye-gaze based interaction for human intention prediction and emotion analysis. In: Proceedings of Computer Graphics International 2018, pp. 185–194 (2018)

11. Hoppe, S., Loetscher, T., Morey, S.A., Bulling, A.: Eye movements during everyday behavior predict personality traits. Front. Hum. Neurosci. **12**, 105 (2018)

12. Jarang, S., Joshi, D., Deshpande, V.: Behaviour analysis using word embedding & machine learning on social media. In: 2019 5th International Conference On Computing, Communication, Control And Automation (ICCUBEA), pp. 1–6. IEEE (2019)

13. Kaushik, P.K., Pandey, S., Rauthan, S.S.: Facial emotion recognition and eye-tracking based expressive communication framework: Review and recommendations. International Journal of Computer Applications 975, 8887

14. Lévêque, L., Bosmans, H., Cockmartin, L., Liu, H.: State of the art: eye-tracking studies in medical imaging. IEEE Access **6**, 37023–37034 (2018)

15. Lewandowski, D., Kammerer, Y.: Factors influencing viewing behaviour on search engine results pages: a review of eye-tracking research. Behav. Inf. Technol. **40**(14), 1485–1515 (2021)

16. Panetta, K., et al.: ISeeColor: method for advanced visual analytics of eye tracking data. IEEE Access **8**, 52278–52287 (2020)

17. Podder, P.K., Paul, M., Debnath, T., Murshed, M.: An analysis of human engagement behaviour using descriptors from human feedback, eye tracking, and saliency modelling. In: 2015 International Conference on Digital Image Computing: Techniques and Applications (DICTA), pp. 1–8. IEEE (2015)

EngageDat-vL: A Multimodal Engagement Dataset Comprising of Emotional, Cognitive, and Behavioral Cues in Virtual Learning Environment

Sarthak Akre(✉)📷, Nilesh Palandurkar📷, Akshat Iyengar, Gourav Chayande, and Praveen Kumar📷

Visvesvaraya National Institute of Technology, South Ambazari Road, Nagpur 440010, Maharashtra, India
sarthak.akre@gmail.com

Abstract. To assess student engagement in an e-learning environment, this work proposes a novel learning analytics dataset collection that combines emotional, cognitive, and behavioral data. The dataset includes facial expressions recorded by a webcam during e-learning sessions and log data such as play, pause, seek, course views, course material views, lecture views, quiz responses, etc. The procedure for gathering the data and the difficulties encountered are covered in the study. Combining emotional, cognitive, and behavioral cues for engagement detection in e-learning settings is made possible by this dataset, which represents a significant advancement in the field of learning analytics.

Keywords: Learning analytics · Facial emotion recognition · Engagement detection

1 Introduction

A significant challenge in the realm of e-learning is the identification and enhancement of student engagement. Engagement encompasses emotional, cognitive, and behavioral aspects. Integrating emotional, cognitive, and behavioral aspects is crucial to assess student engagement effectively [2]. Log data analysis typically examines student engagement with the learning management system, specifically regarding course views and quiz responses. However, it lacks information regarding students' emotional and cognitive involvement. In contrast, self-report surveys depend on students' ability to assess their engagement levels accurately. Moreover, existing engagement detection systems often rely on a sole modality, such as facial expressions or log data, which might not accurately represent engagement. Facial expressions can provide insights into students' emotional engagement but do not offer information regarding their cognitive or behavioral involvement. Log data can provide insights into students' behavioral participation but offers no information regarding their emotional or cognitive engagement. This paper presents "EngageDat-vL", a novel learning analytics dataset collection that integrates emotional, cognitive, and behavioral data to detect engagement. This dataset offers a more comprehensive insight into student engagement in e-learning settings.

2 Background Work and Collecting the Data

We present our dataset, which includes videos of individuals in an e-learning environment that has been labeled with labels for attentive, frustration, confusion, and boredom along with log data for cognitive analysis. This dataset was collected during an active course with real-world reactions to content delivered to them via a Learning Management System and viewed on their personal laptops.

2.1 The Application

We developed a custom app with numerous functionalities to collect data from diverse users. This app had a variety of features and was designed primarily as a Learning Management System (LMS) with the added benefit of capturing various facial data through the webcam, and get it synchronized with the video lecture being played along with other logging data, such as the total number of problems attempted, the total number of videos watched, the number of days since the start of the course that a student accessed course content, the median number of days for access, and events like how many times a video was paused, rewound, fast-forwarded, etc. which can give us more insights into how students interact with the course [5].

2.2 Collecting Face Data

We begin by showing a video lesson to the students, and as soon as the videos start playing, the users' webcams activate and begin recording their faces. The data from the face cam is recorded at a rate of 10 frames per second and delivered via web sockets in the client's browser. In addition to gathering face data, we used BlazeFace [8], a neural network model for real-time face detection, to verify that the frames returned contain faces and that we can get more characteristics, and facial landmarks, such as eyes, nose, and mouth. BlazeFace is an anchor-free, single-stage model trained on a dataset of around 1 million faces. The video data captured is 720×480 pixels in dimension and captured on the client's machine. The video lectures can be viewed by the subjects at any time to ensure that emotions are as natural as possible.

2.3 Collecting the Log Data

In this dataset, we aimed to combine various aspects of student performance assessment, including emotional, behavioral, and cognitive factors. The study examines student behavior and their course interactions through log data. The

Table 1. Log Data

Action	Data stored in log
Login/Logout	Time when event triggered
Quiz /Test	Start time, end time, and marks
Video Lecture play/pause	Timestamp of the video when the event triggered, along with the cause of play/pause
Lecture Playback rate	Timestamp of the video when the event triggered, playback rate chosen
Notes about Lecture	Time when accessed, Time when closed
Popup Quiz in between lecture (when answered)	Start time, end time and marks
Lecture video rewind/seek to previous section	Timestamp of the video when the event triggered
Course Material	Time when accessed, Time when closed
Self Reporting (for affective states)	Timestamp of the video when the event triggered, the options are chosen by the user

cognitive study examines student performance in quizzes and tests throughout the course. The study examines students' emotional responses to various segments of video lessons by analyzing their facial data during lecture viewing. Regarding behavioral data, we record various video interactions, such as play and pause, the student's viewing speed during the Lecture, and additional data, all accompanied by a timestamp for mapping purposes. This data enables the identification of student engagement trends, including the frequency of LMS usage and the duration of specific activities. Data can track student progress over time, providing insight into their comprehension and engagement with the course material. This method facilitates the identification of course deficiencies and enables adjustments to the curriculum and teaching strategies to enhance student learning outcomes. [5] Table 1 provides a more comprehensive representation of the log data and the corresponding action-metadata pairs.

2.4 Background and Previous Work

We conducted an investigation into the domain of Facial Emotion Recognition (FER) [1,9] and E-Learning Based Learning Analytics (ELBLA) [3,4,7]. Our objective was to examine the integration of our dataset with these fields, to enhance educational resources, and explore potential real-world applications. The findings of the comparative analysis are presented in Table 2.

Table 2. Comparison of Research Papers

Title	Description	Emotions Captured	Data Collection Methods	Applications	Key Findings	Unique Feature
AffectNet dataset [6]	A large dataset of 450,000 images with labeled emotions, aiming to aid emotion recognition research	11	Web-crawling, manual filtering	Emotion recognition, facial expression analysis	Improved emotion recognition accuracy using AffectNet dataset	Large-scale dataset with diverse emotions
Belfast Natural Induced Emotion dataset [9]	A dataset of 1400 videos capturing natural, induced emotions in Belfast residents, focusing on cross-cultural emotion recognition	7	Inducing emotions through stimuli	Cross-cultural emotion recognition	Importance of cross-cultural validation in emotion recognition research	Capturing natural emotions in a cross-cultural context
DAISEE dataset [3]	A dataset of 9068 videos capturing emotions of students in a classroom setting, aiming to develop models for predicting and analyzing student engagement	4	Observational in a classroom setting	Predicting and analyzing student engagement	Models developed with DAISEE dataset show promising results in predicting student engagement	Focused on analyzing student engagement in a classroom setting
Prediction and Localization of Student Engagement in the Wild [4]	A study focusing on predicting and localizing student engagement in a large-scale, real-world classroom setting using 264 videos.	1	video conferencing and observation	Classroom engagement analysis, education research	Predicting and localizing student engagement can be achieved in a virtual classroom setting	Use of video conferencing for tracking student engagement
Towards Automated Understanding of Student-Tutor Interactions Using Visual Deictic Gestures [7]	A study using visual deictic gestures to analyze and understand student-tutor interactions using 20 videos	1	Video analysis	Student-tutor interaction analysis, education research	Visual deictic gestures can aid in analyzing and understanding student-tutor interactions	Use of visual deictic gestures for understanding student-tutor interactions

3   The Dataset

This section discusses our dataset, which includes video recordings of people in a virtual learning environment that have been tagged with labels for attentive, frustration, confusion, and boredom as seen in Fig. 1 along with log data of their actions on our learning management system and the results of any quizzes they have attempted throughout the duration of capturing. The dataset includes "in the wild" conditions that are commonly seen in the actual world. Our dataset is unique in that it integrates facial expression detection and log data-based learning analytics, whereas previous research has often employed only one or the other and thus is limited to some extent. We have built a more comprehensive understanding of student engagement during online lessons by merging these three elements: emotional states through facial emotion detection, behavior through log data analysis, and cognitive understanding through quizzes and evaluation results.

3.1 Dataset Details

To model real settings, we have used custom settings for capturing webcam data (720×480, 10 fps) to focus on the students watching the lectures. To emulate in-the-wild scenario, the students could watch lectures at any time at their own convenience. The lectures are of varying length but, on average, 46 min and emulate normal lectures as would be in an e-learning environment with quizzes in the middle to capture cognitive data of the students. There are 34 lectures totaling 500 h of recorded video. The distribution of the 4 states based on self-reported data is 59.2% Attentive, 21.9% Confused, 10.7% Bored, 8.2% Frustrated. The dataset contains 25 participants between the ages of 18 and 20, all of whom are currently enrolled students. The subjects are Asian, including 8 female and 17 male subjects. A sample of the dataset can be seen in Fig. 1.

Table 3. Self Reporting

Option	Label
Interesting and understandable	Attentive
Interesting but not understandable	Confused
Not interesting but understandable	Bored
Neither interesting nor understandable	Frustrated

3.2 Dataset Annotation

Our dataset includes labels for four affective states associated with user engagement: Attentive, frustrated, confused, and bored, similar to recent endeavors. Recent research has found that the seven fundamental emotions (anger, disgust, fear, joy, sadness, neutral, and surprise) lack reliability in long-term learning situations due to their propensity for rapid fluctuations. Two methods for annotating video datasets are manual annotation and automatic annotation. Due to constraints in time and resources, we opted for automatic annotations for our dataset. We initially employed Facial Action Units to train a model for detecting the four states of attentive, frustration, confusion, and boredom. Nevertheless, we encountered various obstacles with this methodology. There was insufficient FACS data available for the specific facial expressions of interest. Additionally, the process of FACS coding is both time-consuming and labor-intensive, necessitating specialized expertise and training that was not readily available to us. Limited research has been conducted on the relationship between FACS and the four states of interest that we aimed to detect. Therefore, we opted against pursuing this approach. We then investigated the potential of utilizing correlation analysis, as depicted in Fig. 3, to determine the correspondence between the four states and the combination of seven basic emotions. No previous research or empirical evidence was found to support the efficacy of this approach. Additionally, we had concerns regarding the generalizability of this approach to all frames in our dataset. Therefore, we opted against further pursuing this approach.

(a) Attentive   (b) Confused

(c) Bored   (d) Frustrated

Fig. 1. Various states in the dataset

Finally, we decided to use a machine learning model based on the MobileNet architecture, a lightweight and efficient neural network for mobile devices. We used the MobileNet model pre-trained on the AffectNet dataset [6], which contains over one million images labeled with one of the seven basic emotions. We then performed transfer learning on the DAISEE dataset [3], a publicly available dataset of facial expressions collected from students in real-world educational settings. We fine-tuned the MobileNet model on our dataset. We used self-reporting data as true labels for training the MobileNet model. Our dataset uses the labels obtained from the MobileNet model as pseudo-labels. For self-reporting, students are asked to answer a question based on their general mood for the past 10 min and 10 min prior to that. The question has 4 options, each corresponding to a particular label, as shown in Table 3. The resulting model achieved an accuracy of 71.46%, which was a significant improvement over our previous attempts. The graphs for accuracy and loss are given in Fig. 2, and Fig. 3 shows the confusion matrix of various emotions for the 4 states that they corresponded to.

3.3   Combining Log Data

We faced the challenge of integrating multiple modalities, namely log data and frames of faces, to obtain a more comprehensive understanding of student engagement. However, to accomplish this, we needed to find a way to synchronize the information obtained from both modalities. To address this issue, we devised a method of encoding log data into the video itself by using SRT (Sub-Rip Subtitle) files that contain the action performed synced with the time in the video. By doing so, we were able to fuse the data obtained from log events in a synchronized way with the video. However, to implement this approach, we had to first clean both the log files and the video frames. We kept the attempt where the student first viewed that part of the video and recorded the timestamp of their time. Then, we checked for log data in the same time interval and kept only the relevant logs for actions. The final step was to combine both the cleaned log files and frames of the video in a synchronized way by comparing the timestamps of the log files and the video frames, and generating an SRT file using FFmpeg accelerated over CUDA. The SRT file contains the actions performed synced with the time in the video, allowing us to fuse the data obtained from log events in a synchronized way with the video frames.

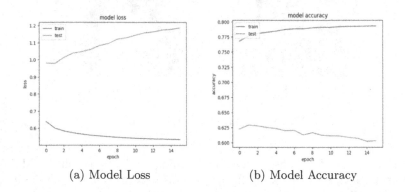

(a) Model Loss   (b) Model Accuracy

Fig. 2. Results Graphs

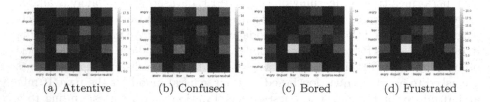

(a) Attentive   (b) Confused   (c) Bored   (d) Frustrated

Fig. 3. The confusion matrix for various states

3.4 Challenges for Dataset Collection

Although adequate care was taken when constructing the dataset, this does not mean that some improper samples did not appear; we encountered certain issues when gathering the dataset and compiled a list of all common issues for future reference.

- Low illumination: Reduced illumination can result in poor image quality and trouble identifying and tracking subjects in the video. This is problematic for post-processing.
- Occlusion: Face occlusion is another issue that arises when objects conceal parts of the face or if the individual does not face the camera, resulting in only a partial face profile being caught. This makes it challenging for algorithms to detect and recognize emotions in faces.
- Variation in emotions: A video dataset's wide range of emotional states might also be a challenge. Emotions are frequently subtle and difficult to detect and distinguish, especially in videos where individuals are moving, and the camera position isn't always perfect.

4 Privacy and User Agreements

All participants in the video clips have signed a consent form allowing the recordings to be captured and employed for future academic research. If consent is not granted, the acquired videos are erased. All subsequent uses will abide by the consent given by the participant and can only be used for academic and research purposes.

5 Future Work

Currently, we have used self-reported data as labels for training our model. In the future, we are looking into other alternatives to annotation, such as crowd annotation, which would provide a better, more consistent label for future models.

References

1. Benitez-Quiroz, C.F., Srinivasan, R., Martinez, A.M.: EmotioNet: an accurate, real-time algorithm for the automatic annotation of a million facial expressions in the wild. In: 2016 IEEE Conference on Computer Vision and Pattern Recognition (CVPR), pp. 5562–5570 (2016). https://doi.org/10.1109/CVPR.2016.600
2. Bosch, N.: Detecting student engagement: Human versus machine. In: Proceedings of the 2016 Conference on User Modeling Adaptation and Personalization, UMAP 2016, pp. 317–320. Association for Computing Machinery, New York (2016). https://doi.org/10.1145/2930238.2930371

3. Gupta, A., D'Cunha, A., Awasthi, K.N., Balasubramanian, V.N.: DAiSEE: towards user engagement recognition in the wild. arXiv Computer Vision and Pattern Recognition (2016). https://doi.org/10.48550/arXiv.1609.01885
4. Kaur, A., Mustafa, A., Mehta, L., Dhall, A.: Prediction and localization of student engagement in the wild. In: 2018 Digital Image Computing: Techniques and Applications (DICTA), pp. 1–8 (2018). https://doi.org/10.1109/DICTA.2018.8615851
5. Laveti, R.N., Kuppili, S., Ch, J., Pal, S.N., Babu, N.S.C.: Implementation of learning analytics framework for MOOCs using state-of-the-art in-memory computing. In: 2017 5th National Conference on E-Learning and E-Learning Technologies (ELELTECH), pp. 1–6 (2017). https://doi.org/10.1109/ELELTECH.2017.8074997
6. Mollahosseini, A., Hasani, B., Mahoor, M.: AffectNet: a database for facial expression, valence, and arousal computing in the wild. IEEE Trans. Affect. Comput. (2017). https://doi.org/10.1109/TAFFC.2017.2740923
7. Sathayanarayana, S., et al.: Towards automated understanding of student-tutor interactions using visual deictic gestures. In: 2014 IEEE Conference on Computer Vision and Pattern Recognition Workshops, pp. 480–487 (2014). https://doi.org/10.1109/CVPRW.2014.77
8. Shazeer, N., Kannan, A., Satheesh, S., Narayanan, S.K., Adam, H.: BlazeFace: submillisecond neural face detection. In: IEEE Conference on Computer Vision and Pattern Recognition (CVPR), pp. 9476–9484 (2019)
9. Sneddon, I., McRorie, M., McKeown, G., Hanratty, J.: The belfast induced natural emotion database. IEEE Trans. Affect. Comput. 3(1), 32–41 (2012). https://doi.org/10.1109/T-AFFC.2011.26

iGAME: Cognitive Game Analysis
Through Eye Movements of the Player

S. Akshay[1]([✉])(iD), B. Shreyas Bhargav[1], and J. Amudha[2](iD)

[1] Department of Computer Science, School of Computing, Amrita Vishwa
Vidyapeetham, Mysuru, Karnataka, India
s_akshay@my.amrita.edu

[2] Department of Computer Science and Engineering, School of Computing, Amrita
Vishwa Vidyapeetham, Bengaluru, Karnataka, India
j_amudha@blr.amrita.edu

Abstract. The main goal of this work is to use eye movement tracking
in classifying players based on their gameplay data and analyze their
experiences while playing Tic Tac Toe. We collected data by tracking
eye gaze and mouse movement of 20 participants while they played the
game. The collected data was pre-processed and cleaned to prepare it
for classification. We used six classification algorithms, including SVM,
Naive Bayes, KNN, Decision Tree Classifier, Random Forest, and XG
Boost, to classify players into beginner, intermediate, and expert levels. The accuracy of the classification algorithms ranged from 94.09% to
95.51%. We further evaluated the performance of each algorithm by generating classification reports. Our analysis of the collected data allowed
us to gain valuable insights into how different levels of players experience
Tic Tac Toe and which aspects of the game may be more challenging for
certain skill levels. This information can be used to inform game design
and optimize the gameplay experience for all players. The results of this
study have the potential to enhance player engagement.

Keywords: Eye Tracking · SVM · Naive Bayes · KNN · Decision Tree
Classifier · Random Forest · XG Boost · Gameplay Experience · Game
Design · Player Engagement

1 Introduction

Cognitive game analysis through eye tracking is an emerging area of research
that aims to understand the cognitive processes that occur during gameplay. In
particular, eye tracking technology is being used to gain insights into how players
perceive and interact with games. This information can be used to optimize game
design and enhance the overall gameplay experience for players. The goal of this
project is to collect eye gaze and mouse movement data from participants playing
the Tic Tac Toe game and use this data to classify players into different skill
levels and analyze their gameplay experiences. Tic Tac Toe is a simple game that

P. Maji et al. (Eds.): PReMI 2023, LNCS 14301, pp. 279–288, 2023.
https://doi.org/10.1007/978-3-031-45170-6_29

requires players to place X's and O's on a three-by-three grid, with the aim of getting three in a row. We recruited 20 participants from diverse backgrounds and tracked their eye gaze and mouse movement while playing the game. We also recorded their reaction times for each move. This data was pre-processed and cleaned to prepare it for classification. We used six different classification algorithms, including SVM, Naive Bayes, KNN, Decision tree classifier, Random Forest, and XG Boost, to classify players into beginner, intermediate, and expert levels based on their gameplay data. The accuracy of these algorithms ranged from 94.09% to 95.51%. Overall, this project aims to use eye gaze and mouse movement data to gain insights into how different levels of players experience the Tic Tac Toe game and identify areas of the game that may need improvement. The results of this project have the potential to inform game design and optimize the gameplay experience for all players.

2 Related Work

The study report suggests using gaze data stored as scanpath pictures to forecast players' decisions in economic games. The study by [3] found that traditional models in predicting players' choices and provide insights into the cognitive processes underlying decision-making. The platform by [4] included eye-tracking signals as Reliable biomarkers for assessing social and cognitive abilities might help in diagnostic and intervention techniques for kids with ASD. Authors [5] use feed-forward backpropagation neural networks to predict students' reading behavior and comprehension knowledge. Subjectivity and explicit ratings are predicted based on eye movement data. Work by [6] examined participants' eye movements (or "lookup patterns") as they played the games described in Di Guida and Devetag to see if the information search behaviors they exhibited were more consistent with the "best responding to beliefs" hypothesis or with "boundedly rational decision rules". System by [7] investigates the use of eye-tracking sensors to assess children's behaviour in attention-related cognitive treatments based on serious games, in order to identify the relevance of eye movements for attention enhancement therapies. Authors [8] stated that learning can be monitored constantly and inconspicuously from children if eye-tracking data can properly infer the learning increase from standardised pre-tests and post-tests. EEG and eye-tracking were discovered to be widely utilised methods for testing cognitive abilities during online learning after conducting a thorough literature review by [9]. Neurofeedback can be a useful tool, and synchronous video conferencing can improve student performance. Work by [10] presented a test to know the viability of eye tracking while playing a puzzle game and provide supplemental indicators for cognitive function using eye-tracking measurements. In the work done by [12] participants with glasses had calibration issues. Even after satisfactory calibration, there was still a constraint. Using the proposed work by [13] we discover that learners' in-game performance changes depending on their amount of prior knowledge. The suggested technique demonstrates that tonic pupil size was the most reliable ocular predictor of increasing effort in this scenario. The study by [14] examines expected differences in puzzle-solving abilities between healthy subjects and those with dementia. The proposed method by [15] to examine the use of visual observation in relevance to the keyboard and mouse input control and shows the difference. The methodology of the study [17] is to observe the players' interaction with the games before and after using eye tracking as an input method for the game. Work by [18] proposed a method to understand the player's interaction and emotional experience of video games. In order to supplement the information obtained from these more conventional methods of evaluating emotional reactions, non-invasive eye-tracking equipment is utilized. However, self-regulated videos can be effective in promoting learning outcomes. Other shreds of evidence for the use of eye gaze in cognition include [1], [2]. Applications in reading research include [11,16]. Overall eye movements analysis proves to be a definite choice for the detection of cognitive load.

3   Proposed Method

(See Fig. 1).

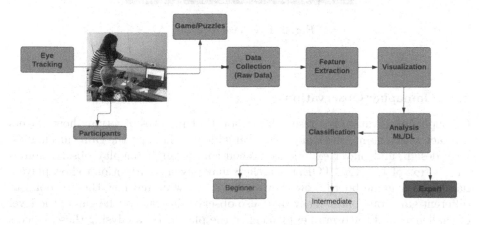

Fig. 1. iGAME

3.1   Eye Gaze Tracking

Eye gaze tracking involves web camera that track the movement of a player's eyes as they play the game using an openCV platform. Figure 2 represent detection of left and right eye with respect to mouse position. This can provide valuable information about what aspects of the game the player is looking at, how long they are spending on each element, and whether they are experiencing any difficulties or challenges. Mouse position tracking involves recording the movement of the player's mouse using pymouse input mapping as they play the game, while gaze position tracking records where the player is looking on the screen. By comparing these two data streams we gain insights into how players are using their mouse to interact with the game, and whether there are any discrepancies between where they are looking and where they are clicking. This information can be particularly valuable when analysing the gameplay of different levels of players, as it can provide insights into which aspects of the game are more challenging for different skill levels. For example, eye gaze tracking may reveal that beginner players are spending more time looking at the rules of the game or the placement of X's and O's, while expert players are spending more time anticipating their opponent's moves or developing advanced strategies.

Fig. 2. Eye Gaze Tracking

3.2 Gameplay Observation

Gameplay observation is a research method that involves observing how players interact with a game, and can provide valuable insights into the game mechanics, level design, and player experience. When conducting gameplay observation in the context of TIC TAC TOE, researchers may pay close attention to how players navigate the game board, how they strategize to win, and how they respond to different game outcomes. They may also observe the pace of the game, the level of challenge, and the overall enjoyment of the player. By analysing these aspects of the game, researchers can gain insights into what makes TIC TAC TOE engaging and enjoyable for players, as well as what aspects of the game may need improvement. For example, if players are consistently losing the game, this could indicate that the game is too challenging, and adjustments may need to be made to the difficulty level. In addition, researchers may classify players into different levels based on their gameplay performance, such as beginner, intermediate, and expert players. This can help to identify which aspects of the game are more challenging for different levels of players, and where adjustments may need to be made to optimize the gameplay experience for all levels of players. By combining gameplay observation with other methods of data collection, such as eye gaze tracking or surveys, researchers can gain a more complete understanding of how players are experiencing the game, and use this information to make data-driven design decisions that can improve the overall quality of the game (Fig. 3).

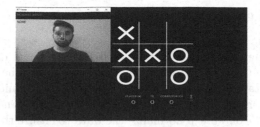

Fig. 3. Gameplay

3.3   Dataset Collection

We have successfully collected data from a group of 20 participants ranging from 16 years to 35 years, who played the TIC TAC TOE game while their eye gaze and mouse movement were tracked using a web camera. We made sure to select participants from a diverse range of ages and skill levels to capture a wide range of gameplay experiences. During the data collection process, each participant played the game while their web camera recorded their eye movements and mouse position. The web camera recorded the X and Y co-ordinates of where the participant was looking on the screen, while the mouse position tracking recorded the X and Y co-ordinates of where the participant clicked on the screen. In addition to tracking eye gaze and mouse movement, we also collected reaction time data for each participant (Fig. 4).

X	Y	duration	target
813	245	0.599142	1
773	434	0.506652	1
1046	262	0.252509	1
750	721	0.239104	0
762	325	0.053396	1
776	341	0.009374	1
884	409	0.232862	0
794	634	0.138534	0
974	455	0.476941	1

Fig. 4. Calculation of mouse movement and reaction time

This involved recording the amount of time it took for each player to place an X or O on the game board after their turn began. We then analyzed the X and Y co-ordinates of each participant's gaze and mouse movement, as well as their reaction time data. This analysis involved examining patterns and trends in the data, such as which areas of the game board the participants looked at most frequently, or how quickly they were able to place their X's and O's. By analysing the collected data, we gained insights into how different levels of players experienced the game, which aspects of the game were more challenging for different skill levels, and where adjustments may need to be made to optimize the gameplay experience for all players.

3.4 Data Pre-processing

After collecting the dataset, the next step is to pre-process the data to prepare it for analysis. The pre-processing steps will involve cleaning and formatting the data to ensure that it is consistent and free of errors. The first step in pre-processing the data will be to remove any missing or invalid data. This will involve checking for any incomplete or inaccurate records and removing them from the dataset. Next, we will normalize the data to ensure that all data points are on the same scale. This will involve scaling the X and Y co-ordinates of the gaze and mouse position data. We will also need to filter the data to remove any noise or outliers. This will involve removing any data points that fall outside a certain range or do not fit the expected patterns of gameplay. Additionally, we will need to synchronize the gaze and mouse position data to ensure that they are accurately aligned. Finally, we will aggregate the data to create summary statistics and visualizations that provide insights into the patterns and trends in the data. This will involve calculating metrics such as mean and standard deviation for various aspects of the gameplay, and creating visualizations such as heat maps to show the areas of the game board that are most frequently looked at by different player skill levels.

3.5 Classification of Players

Once the data has been pre-processed, we can use various classification algorithms to classify the players based on their gameplay data. Support Vector Machines (SVM), Naive Bayes, K-Nearest Neighbours (KNN), Decision Tree, Random Forest, and XG Boost are a few of the frequently used classification methods. Support Vector Machines (SVM) is a popular classification algorithm used to classify data points based on their properties. In both binary and multi-class classification issues may be solved with it. Another popular classification technique that relies on the Bayes theorem is naive Bayes. It calculates the probability of each class based on the input features. K-Nearest Neighbours (KNN) is a simple yet effective classification algorithm that assigns the class based on the majority of its K-nearest neighbor. Decision Tree is a tree-like model where each node represents a feature, and the edges represent the decision rule. Until a stopping condition is satisfied, it iteratively splits the data into smaller groups depending on the most important attribute. Random forest modeling blends many decision trees to increase the model's precision and decrease its variance. XG Boost is a powerful algorithm that uses gradient boosting to create a predictive model. It is known for its high performance and accuracy in both regression and classification tasks. By using these classification algorithms on the pre-processed dataset, we can classify the players based on their gameplay data, and gain insights into how different skill levels perform in the TIC TAC TOE game. This information can be used to make necessary adjustments to optimize the gameplay experience for all players (Fig. 5).

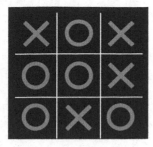

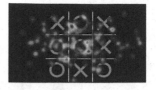

(b) Heat Map generation.

(a) Tic Tac Toe Game.

Fig. 5. Visualization of player's gaze

3.6 Heat Map Generation

A heat map is a graphical representation of data that uses color-coded cells to visualize the relationship between two variables. In the context of eye gaze tracking data, a heat map can be used to visualize where a user is looking on a screen. To generate a heat map from the generated CSV file, the X and Y coordinates for each gaze point can be plotted on a 2D plane. The frequency of gaze points in each area of the screen can then be calculated and represented as a colour gradient on the heat map. Areas with a higher frequency of gaze points will appear as a warmer colour, while areas with a lower frequency of gaze points will appear cooler. The resulting heat map can provide insights into the user's gaze patterns and areas of interest on the screen. It can also be used to evaluate the effectiveness of visual design elements, such as the placement of buttons or the layout of information.

4   Results

The graph in Fig. 6 displays the accuracy scores of six different machine learning algorithms used for player classification in the Tic Tac Toe game. Each algorithm was trained on the pre-processed dataset and tested to determine its accuracy in classifying players as beginners, intermediate, or experts. The results show that Decision Tree Classifier had the highest accuracy score of 95.51%. The results suggest that all of the algorithms performed well in classifying players, with most of them achieving accuracy scores above 94%. Naive Bayes, Decision Tree Classifier, and KNN are the top-performing algorithms, indicating that they may be the best choices for accurately classifying players in the Tic Tac Toe game.

The classification report in Fig. 7 provides a comprehensive evaluation of the performance of each machine learning model. Figure 8 illustrates the precision, recall, and F1 score of the machine learning algorithms used to classify players in our study. The KNN Classifier had the highest recall and f1 score of all models at 96%, with high precision and recall for all classes. Overall, all six models performed well in classifying the players based on their gameplay skill

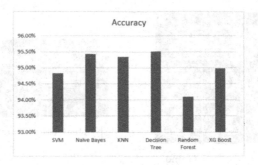

Fig. 6. Accuracy of Different Models

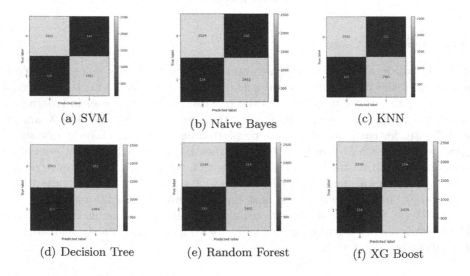

(a) SVM

(b) Naive Bayes

(c) KNN

(d) Decision Tree

(e) Random Forest

(f) XG Boost

Fig. 7. Classification Report

level. The classification report provides valuable insights into the strengths and weaknesses of each model, allowing for further optimization and improvement in future analysis. These scores indicate that all of the algorithms performed well in accurately classifying players, with some algorithms having higher precision, recall, or F1 scores than others. Overall, the results suggest that machine learning algorithms can effectively analyze player behavior and skill level through eye-tracking data, and can be used to classify players into meaningful categories.

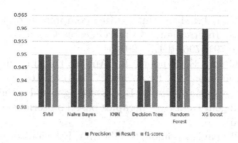

Fig. 8. Precision, Recall and F1-score

5 Conclusion and Future Scope

This study demonstrated the potential of using eye-tracking technology and machine learning algorithms to analyze and classify the gameplay behavior of players based on their skill levels. The study's findings showed that linear SVM achieved an accuracy of 95.25% in classifying players as beginner, intermediate, or expert. This high level of accuracy provides game designers with valuable insights into the gameplay behavior of different skill levels and can be used to develop games that cater to a wider audience. This study provides a framework for future research in this field. The use of eye-tracking technology and machine learning algorithms could potentially revolutionize the way games are designed, developed, and played in the future. In future research, it would be interesting to investigate the use of different machine learning algorithms and feature selection methods to improve classification accuracy. Additionally, applying this technique to other types of games or activities could provide insights into the cognitive processes underlying different types of gameplays.

References

1. Akshay, S., Amudha, J., Kulkarni, N., Prashanth, L.K.: iSTIMULI: Prescriptive stimulus design for eye movement analysis of patients with Parkinson's disease. In: Morusupalli, R., Dandibhotla, T.S., Atluri, V.V., Windridge, D., Lingras, P., Komati, V.R. (eds.) MIWAI 2023. LNCS, vol. 14078, pp. 589–600. Springer, Cham (2023). https://doi.org/10.1007/978-3-031-36402-0_55
2. Akshay, S., Amudha, J., Narmada, N., Bhattacharya, A., Kamble, N., Pal, P.K.: iAOI: an eye movement based deep learning model to identify areas of interest. In: Morusupalli, R., Dandibhotla, T.S., Atluri, V.V., Windridge, D., Lingras, P., Komati, V.R. (eds.) MIWAI 2023. LNCS, vol. 14078, pp. 659–670. Springer, Cham (2023). https://doi.org/10.1007/978-3-031-36402-0_61
3. Byrne, S.A., Reynolds, A.P.F., Biliotti, C., Bargagli-Stoffi, F.J., Polonio, L., Riccaboni, M.: Predicting choice behaviour in economic games using gaze data encoded as scanpath images. Sci. Rep. **13**(1), 4722 (2023)
4. Chien, Y.L., et al.: Game-based social interaction platform for cognitive assessment of autism using eye tracking. IEEE Trans. Neural Syst. Rehabil. Eng. (2022)

5. Copeland, L., Gedeon, T.: Measuring reading comprehension using eye movements. In: 2013 IEEE 4th International Conference on Cognitive Infocommunications (CogInfoCom), pp. 791–796. IEEE (2013)
6. Devetag, G., Di Guida, S., Polonio, L.: An eye-tracking study of feature-based choice in one-shot games. Exp. Econ. **19**, 177–201 (2016)
7. Frutos-Pascual, M., Garcia-Zapirain, B.: Assessing visual attention using eye tracking sensors in intelligent cognitive therapies based on serious games. Sensors **15**(5), 11092–11117 (2015)
8. Giannakos, M.N., Papavlasopoulou, S., Sharma, K.: Monitoring children's learning through wearable eye-tracking: the case of a making-based coding activity. IEEE Pervasive Comput. **19**(1), 10–21 (2020)
9. Jamil, N., Belkacem, A.N., Lakas, A.: On enhancing students' cognitive abilities in online learning using brain activity and eye movements. Educ. Inf. Technol. **28**, 1–35 (2022)
10. Krebs, C., et al.: Application of eye tracking in puzzle games for adjunct cognitive markers: pilot observational study in older adults. JMIR Serious Games **9**(1), e24151 (2021)
11. Kumar, U., Amudha, J., Chandrika, K.: Automatic feedback captions for eye-tracker based online assessment. In: 2023 International Conference on Advances in Intelligent Computing and Applications (AICAPS), pp. 1–6. IEEE (2023)
12. Lee, J.Y., Donkers, J., Jarodzka, H., Van Merriënboer, J.J.: How prior knowledge affects problem-solving performance in a medical simulation game: using game-logs and eye-tracking. Comput. Hum. Behav. **99**, 268–277 (2019)
13. Mallick, R., Slayback, D., Touryan, J., Ries, A.J., Lance, B.J.: The use of eye metrics to index cognitive workload in video games. In: 2016 IEEE Second Workshop on Eye Tracking and Visualization (ETVIS), pp. 60–64. IEEE (2016)
14. Morimoto, R., Kawanaka, H., Hicks, Y., Setchi, R.: Development of recreation game for measurement of eye movement using tangram. Procedia Comput. Sci. **192**, 4924–4932 (2021)
15. Muhammad, T.Q.K., Sharifi, H.O., Ghareb, M.I.: Eye tracking technique for controlling computer game objects. UHD J. Sci. Technol. **6**(1), 43–51 (2022)
16. Nagarajan, H., Inakollu, V.S., Vancha, P., Amudha, J.: Detection of reading impairment from eye-gaze behaviour using reinforcement learning. Procedia Comput. Sci. **218**, 2734–2743 (2023)
17. Polonio, L., Di Guida, S., Coricelli, G.: Strategic sophistication and attention in games: an eye-tracking study. Games Econom. Behav. **94**, 80–96 (2015)
18. Renshaw, T., Stevens, R., Denton, P.D.: Towards understanding engagement in games: an eye-tracking study. Horizon **17**, 408–420 (2009)

Cortical Circuits of Context Adaptability: Understanding the Neurobehavioral Mechanisms Underlying Flexible Behavior

Sweta Kaman[1]($\boxtimes$) , Ankita Sharma[2] , and Romi Banerjee[3]

[1] School of Artificial Intelligence and Data Science, IIT Jodhpur, Karwar, India
kaman.1@iitj.ac.in
[2] School of Liberal Arts, IIT Jodhpur, Karwar, India
ankitasharma@iitj.ac.in
[3] Department of Computer Science and Engineering, IIT Jodhpur, Karwar, India
romibanerjee@iitj.ac.in

Abstract. The present pilot study aims to investigate the cortical circuits involved in context adaptability and gain initial insights into the neurobehavioral mechanisms underlying flexible behavior. To accomplish this, we designed a novel first-person perspective picture-based decision-making task, using stick figures and objects, where eight participants were engaged in imagining themselves as stick figures for each depicted scenario. These scenarios were portrayed through objects and emotional contexts of positivity, negativity, and neutrality. Our results showed a significant link (p = 0.020) between the absolute power values of the alpha frequency band (8–12 Hz) and ratings for positive context stimuli in one group. This suggests that alpha power may affect how people rate positive situations. We also found a significant association between the absolute power values of theta (4–7 Hz) and alpha frequency bands for neutral context stimuli in both group 1 (p = 0.023 and p = 0.022) and group 2 (p = 0.047 and p = 0.020). However, we found no significant associations between absolute power values of frequency bands (theta, alpha, beta1, beta2, beta3 and gamma) and ratings for negative stimuli in both the groups (p = 0.099, p = 0.105). Nonetheless, the linear regression models demonstrated strong fits, capturing variance in the data. Findings provide initial insights into emotional processing and decision-making, warranting further research with larger samples.

Keywords: Event-related potentials (ERPs) · context adaptability · decision making · flexible behavior · emotional stimuli · alpha frequency band · theta frequency band · emotional processing

1 Introduction

Context adaptability is the ability to adapt to different settings. Ecker [1] showed that situations alter primary visual cortex cell activity and cognitive flexibility. Contextual knowledge helps the brain filter out irrelevant information and

P. Maji et al. (Eds.): PReMI 2023, LNCS 14301, pp. 289–298, 2023.
https://doi.org/10.1007/978-3-031-45170-6_30

focus on crucial information. The **cocktail party effect** allows people to ignore background noise and focus on their conversation in a noisy space [2]. We learn new information in the context of other knowledge. This makes fresh knowledge memorable. Decision-making requires context [3]. Context adaptability in decision making can reveal the brain underpinnings of cognitive flexibility, the ability to adapt to environmental changes [4]. Understanding the neural processes of cognitive flexibility can help create strategies to increase this ability in people with cognitive impairments, such as traumatic brain injuries or neurodegenerative disorders [5]. A novel first-person perspective picture-based decision-making task will investigate the neurobehavioral processes of flexible behaviour and context adaption. In today's fast-paced environment, adaptability is key to social success and decision-making. These adaptive behaviours' brain pathways are poorly understood. To fill this gap, we conducted a pilot study with eight individuals who imagined positive, negative, or neutral emotional experiences. Participants made hypothetical decisions and judged their knowledge in this activity. Event-Related Potentials (ERPs) confirmed the visuals' emotional nature. This study establishes the intricate relationship between emotions, brain activity, and decision-making, influencing future research on emotional processing and individual variability in adaptive behaviours.

2   Methodology

2.1   Participants

This pilot study recruited eight graduate students from our institute (4 male and 4 female, ages 20–30 with a mean of 27.1). Participants gave written informed consent and reported normal or corrected-to-normal vision and no neurological issues. The research involved two four-person groups. Groups 1 and 2 were randomly assigned similar demographics (age, gender, etc.). Group 1 received positive, negative, and neutral stimuli in that order. Group 2 received a neutral, negative stimulus, and a positive one.

2.2   Experimental Task

2.2.1   Design and Structure of the Performance-Based Task This is a performance based think aloud task where we have six picture vignettes. Participants of both the groups were presented with the same set of six picture vignettes. Each one showed a different situation with stick figures and objects. The scenarios were carefully thought out to cover a wide range of moral dilemmas and emotional situations that people face every day. Importantly, linguistic elements of the visual cues were left out on purpose so that the task would be easy for people of different ages and languages to understand. The purpose of this experiment is to find out how people react to emotional situations and if the order in which they are exposed to these situations affects how they make decisions. We wanted to test possible order effects and find how people change their decision-making strategies in response to positive, negative, and neutral stimuli by showing them different emotional contexts in different orders. In real life, people have to deal with emotional situations in different orders. By simulating these dynamic emotional changes in the study, we wanted to see how the changing emotional landscape affects the participants' ability to make decisions, which is similar to how hard it is to make decisions in the real world. The six picture vignettes were divided into three emotional contexts: two scenarios that evoked positive emotions (like feelings of joy when helping someone), two scenarios that evoked negative emotions (like fear or sadness), and two scenarios where the emotional valence was minimized to act as a control condition. The goal of the task was to see how people make decisions when they are feeling different kinds of emotions. Fig. 1. shows a vignette for each emotional setting. In each scenario, the participants were asked to imagine themselves as the stick figures shown, and then they were asked to make hypothetical decisions based on what they saw. In particular, they were asked, **What would you do if you were in that situation?** This approach from the first-person point of view got people to think about decisions that made sense in the context and matched their own possible experiences. After each scenario, people in both groups were asked to put their hypothetical decisions on a scale from 1 to 10 based on how wise they thought they were. This rating scale let people judge for themselves how wise and flexible their decisions were in each emotional situation.

2.3 EEG Data Acquisition and Analysis

A 32-channel Brain Vision Amplifier [3] acquired EEG (sampling rate = 512 Hz; high pass filter = 0.1 Hz; low pass filter = 70 Hz; impedances below 11 kOhm). Participants sat in a comfortable chair during the recordings. EEG data were processed and analyzed using EEGLAB [4]. After downsampling to 250 Hz, we re-filtered the data with 1 Hz low-frequency and 45 Hz high-frequency filters. Average referencing reduced noise and increased signal-to-noise ratio. EEG data were epoched −500 to 4000 ms around stimulus onset. Baseline corrected EEG data removed the average of activity between −500 and stimulus onset. Then, Darbeliai (EEGLAB plugin) Fast Fourier Transform was used to calculate electrode absolute frequency powers. The following frequency bands of the mean absolute power spectra were considered: theta (4–7 Hz), alpha (8–12 Hz), beta 1 (13–18 Hz), beta 2 (19–21 Hz), beta 3 (22–30 Hz), and gamma (31–45 Hz). The anatomical regions studied are C3, C4, CP1, CP2, CP5, CP6, Cz, F3, F4, F7, F8, FC1, FC2, FC5, FC6, FT10, FT9, Fp1, Fp2, O1, O2, Oz, P3, P4, P7, P8, Pz, T7, T8, TP10, and TP9.

3 Experimental Results

3.1 Early ERP Components

Please see Table 1 for a full comparison of ERP components (P1, P2, N1, N2, and P3) between two groups (Group 1 and Group 2) and across stimuli conditions (positive, negative, and neutral). In the table, **A** stands for the affect

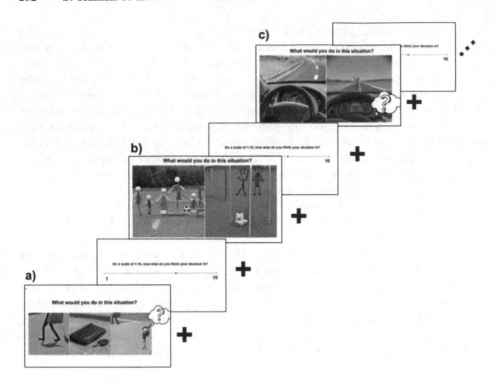

Fig. 1. Illustrative Vignettes Depicting Emotional Contexts (a) Positive Context Stimuli; (b) Negative Context Stimuli; (c) Neutral Context Stimuli. Each vignette is followed by a visual analog scale, allowing participants to rate the perceived wisdom of their hypothetical decisions on a scale ranging from 1 to 10, following a brief fixation period of 500 ms.

of the stimulus, and **(L, A)** stands for the latency (ms) and amplitude (μV), respectively. **R** shows the area where the effect is strongest. The table gives a lot of information about the differences in ERP sizes and their effects on different parts of the brain for each group and emotion. This analysis sheds light on how neural processing and emotional responses might be different between participant groups and stimulus conditions. This helps us learn more about the neurobehavioral mechanisms that allow people to adapt to their surroundings and behave in different ways.

3.2   Later Components

Late Positive Potential(LPP): Cuthbert [5] found that high-arousing stimuli make the LPP components more positive over a wide range of latency intervals. Hajcak [6] found that the LPP (600–1000, 1200–1800 ms) for arousing pictures was bigger at centro-parietal sites when the person was just looking at them. In our study we found that for group 1, LPP related to positive stimuli and negative stimuli was significantly greater than LPP related to neutral stimuli

Table 1. Comparison of ERP components (P1, P2, N1, N2, and P3) between two groups (Group 1 and Group 2) and across stimuli conditions (positive, negative, and neutral).

Comparative ERP Analysis			
ERP Components	Our Findings for Group 1	Our Findings for Group 2	Literature Reference
P1 (112–124 ms)	A: $Neu > pos, Pos > neg$, $Neu > neg$ (L,A): (120, 2.956), (112, 1.216), (120, 2.956) R: Occipital (permutation test, FDR corrected $P < 0.05$)	A: $pos > neu, pos > neg$, $neu > neg$ (L,A): (124, 0.5713), (124, 0.5713), (0.2141) R: Occipital (permutation test, FDR corrected $P < 0.05$)	117 ms [P1] by Smith [7], 150–165 ms [late P1] by Delplanque [8]
N1 (148–172 ms)	A: $Pos > neg, Pos > neg$, $Pos > neu$ (L,A): (148, −3.254), (148, −200) R: Occipito-temporal, Parietal (permutation test, FDR corrected $P < 0.01$)	A: $neg > neu, neg > pos$, $pos > neu, neg > neu$ (L,A): (148, −3.339), (152, −2.577), (172, −2.424), (152, −2.577) R: Occipito-temporal (permutation test, FDR corrected $P < 0.05$)	160–224 ms [N1] by Schupp [9]
P2 (200–220 ms)	A: $Pos > neu, neg > pos$ (L,A): (212, 1.397), (220, 2.236) R: Fronto-central, Occipito-temporal (permutation test, FDR corrected $P < 0.05$)	A: $Neg > pos, Neg > pos$, $Neg > Neu$ (L,A): (212, 0.6612), (200, 0.6048), (200, 0.257) R: Fronto-central, Occipito-temporal, Posterior (permutation test, FDR corrected $P < 0.05$)	180–213 ms [P2] by Delplanque [8], 150–250 [P2] by Spreckelmeyer [10]
N2 (228–264 ms)	A: $pos > neg, neu > neg$, $neu > pos$ (L,A): (264, −2.805), (236, −3.933), (236, −3933) R: Fronto-central (permutation test, FDR corrected $P < 0.05$)	A: $Neg > pos, neg > neu$, $neu = pos$ (L,A): (228, −1.652), (228, −1.652), (228, −0.6629) R: Fronto-central (permutation test, FDR corrected $P < 0.05$)	240 ms [N2] by Carretié [11]
P3b (540–564 ms)	A: $Neg > neu, Pos > neg$ (L,A): (560, 1.49), (540, 1.265) R: Posterior, Fronto-central (permutation test, FDR corrected $P < 0.05$)	A: $Neg > neu, Pos > neg$ (L,A): (564, 2.823), (548, 2.823) R: Posterior, Fronto-central (permutation test, FDR corrected $P < 0.05$)	406–603 ms [P3b] by Delplanque [8], 439–630 ms [P3b] by Delplanque [8]

at an interval of 800–1100 ms (permutation test, FDR corrected $P < 0.05$) in centro-parietal region. In group 2, we found significantly greater LPP for negative stimuli than neutral stimuli (permutation test, FDR corrected $P < 0.05$), but we did not find any significance for LPP in positive vs neutral(see Fig. 2 and 3).

3.3 Statistical Results

The regression analysis explored the relationship between the average absolute power values of six frequency bands (theta, alpha, beta1, beta2, beta3, and gamma) as independent variables and participants' ratings for positive, negative, and neutral stimuli for both groups as the dependent variable.

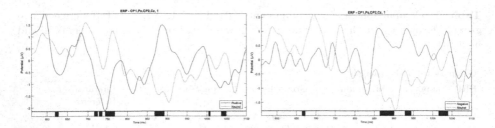

Fig. 2. Late Positive Potential [800–1100 ms] related to positive stimuli is greater than neutral stimuli for group 1 (permutation test, FDR corrected $P < 0.05$)(left). Late Positive Potential [800–1100 ms] related to negative stimuli is greater than neutral stimuli for group 1 (permutation test, FDR corrected $P < 0.05$)(right).

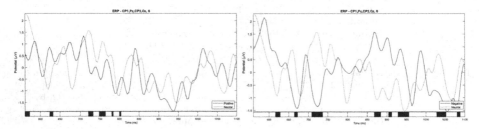

Fig. 3. Late Positive Potential [800–1100 ms] related to positive stimuli and neutral stimuli for group 2 (no significance)(left).Late Positive Potential [800–1100 ms] related to negative stimuli is greater than neutral stimuli for group 2 (permutation test, FDR corrected $P < 0.05$)(right).

Group 1 (Positive Stimuli): The alpha frequency band's absolute power value correlated with positive stimulus ratings ($p = 0.020$). Other five frequency bands i.e. theta, beta1, beta2, beta3 and gamma showed no significant relationships having p values 0.479, 0.553, 0.448, 0.418, 0.789 respectively. The analysis showed a strong linear relationship with an R^2 value of 0.975, indicating that the variance in the alpha frequency band's absolute power value explained 97.5% of group 1's ratings for positive stimuli (see Fig. 4). These findings suggest that alpha oscillations modulate positive emotional stimuli in this group.

Group 1 (Negative Stimuli): P value 0.099 was not statistically significant at 0.05. However, the analysis showed a strong linear relationship with an R^2 value of 0.862, indicating that 86.2% of the variance in participants' ratings for negative stimuli could be explained by the variance in the frequency bands' average absolute power values (see Fig. 4).

Group 1 (Neutral Stimuli): The average absolute power values of the theta and alpha frequency bands were significantly associated with neutral stimuli ratings ($p = 0.023$ and 0.022, respectively). Other four frequency bands showed no significant relationships. The analysis showed a robust linear relationship, with an R^2 value of 0.976, indicating that the variance in theta and alpha frequency bands' absolute power values could explain 97.6% of group 1's neutral stim-

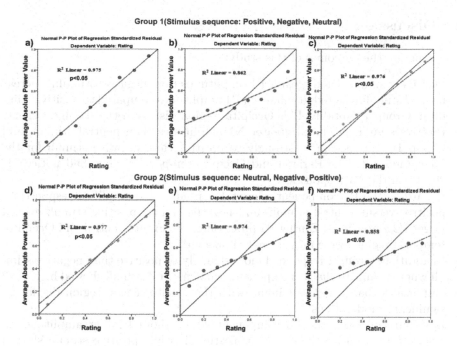

Fig. 4. Linear regression between average absolute power values for frequency bands and ratings associated with each condition.

uli ratings (see Fig. 4). These findings suggest that theta and alpha oscillations modulate neutral emotional stimuli in this group.

Group 2 (Neutral Stimuli): Theta ($p = 0.047$) and alpha ($p = 0.020$) frequency bands were significantly associated with neutral stimuli ratings (see Fig. 4). Other four frequency bands showed no significant relationships. The analysis showed a robust linear relationship, with an R^2 value of 0.977, indicating that the variance in theta and alpha frequency bands' absolute power values explained 97.7% of group 2 participants' neutral stimuli ratings.

Group 2 (Negative Stimuli): The frequency bands did not correlate with negative stimulus ratings ($p = 0.105$). An R^2 value of 0.974 (Fig. 4) showed a strong linear relationship. Despite the lack of statistical significance, the high R^2 value suggests that the variance in frequency band absolute power values could explain 97.4% of group 2 participants' ratings for negative stimuli.

Group 2 (Positive Stimuli): The frequency bands did not correlate with positive stimulus ratings ($p = 0.54$). An R^2 value of 0.858 (Fig. 4) showed a strong linear relationship. Multicollinearity from significant correlations between frequency band absolute power values may have affected the significance result.

4   Discussion

Following are the outcomes of this study:

- Positive stimuli elicited greater P1 amplitudes than negative stimuli, whereas neutral stimuli resulted in enhanced P1 amplitudes compared to positive stimuli in Group 1. Notably, P1's Occipital region displayed the strongest effect.
- Positive stimuli produced greater N1 amplitudes than neutral stimuli, and Group 1 responded more strongly to positive than negative stimuli for the N1 component. The Parietal and Occipito-temporal regions had noticeable effects on the N1 responses.
- Regarding the P2 component, Group 1 demonstrated amplified responses to positive versus neutral stimuli, and negative versus positive stimuli evoked larger P2 amplitudes. During P2 processing, the Fronto-central and Occipito-temporal regions were most heavily impacted.
- In addition, Group 1 responded more strongly to positive than negative stimuli when it came to the N2 component, while neutral stimuli showed higher N2 amplitudes than negative stimuli, with the Fronto-central region displaying significant modulations.
- Last but not least, the P3 component (P3b) showed larger amplitudes in response to negative than to neutral stimuli, while positive stimuli showed larger P3b amplitudes than negative stimuli.
- In our study, we have also used linear regression analyses to examine the relationship between average absolute power values related to six EEG frequency bands (theta, alpha, beta1, beta2, beta3 and gamma) and participants' ratings of stimuli that were positive, negative, and neutral in two separate groups (Group 1 and Group 2) which is explained in Sect. 3.3.
- The results of our study's LPP analysis shed important light on how the brain processes emotional stimuli and how this processing relates to flexible behaviour and context adaptability.
- According to Cuthbert [5], the LPP component, which reflects elevated positivity to highly arousing stimuli, is linked to emotional engagement and attentional processing.
- When compared to neutral stimuli, both positive and negative LPP amplitudes in Group 1 were significantly higher, indicating increased emotional responsiveness to emotionally upsetting situations. This increased emotional responsiveness may indicate that members of Group 1 are more emotionally engaged and sensitive to both positive and negative situations.
- This increased responsiveness may have an impact on their ability to adapt and respond flexibly to various emotional contexts.
- In contrast, Group 2 showed no significant difference between positive and neutral stimuli but significantly higher LPP amplitudes in response to negative stimuli compared to neutral stimuli.
- This pattern suggests that members of Group 2 may be selective in their emotional responsiveness, focusing more of their attention and involvement on distressing emotional situations. The lack of significant differences for positive

stimuli could be a sign that people's adaptive reactions to happy emotional contexts are limited.

- In general, these LPP findings provide insight into the neurobiological underpinnings of adaptable behaviour and context adaptability.
- Regardless of valence, people who exhibit stronger LPP responses to emotionally upsetting stimuli may be better able to handle a variety of emotional situations.
- On the other hand, people who have particular LPP enhancements in response to adverse stimuli may show a more targeted and focused adaptive response to difficult or dangerous situations.

5 Limitation and Conclusion

A drawback with this study is that the sample size was small, with only two groups of people taking part. This small sample may restrict the generalizability of our findings to a broader population. In summary, our study gives us important information about how the brain processes emotional stimuli and what that means for understanding flexible behaviour and adaptability to different situations. The significant associations between LPP amplitudes and positive or negative stimuli in both groups show how important emotional responsiveness is decision-making. Individuals with heightened emotional engagement to emotionally arousing stimuli may display more adaptable behavior across various emotional contexts. Moreover, individuals with selective LPP enhancements to negative stimuli might demonstrate a focused adaptive response to challenging situations. While the study's findings are valuable, future research with larger and more diverse samples and exploration of other emotional contexts is needed.

References

1. Ecker, A.S., et al.: Decorrelated neuronal firing in cortical microcircuits. Science 327(5965), 584–587 (2010)
2. Pollack, I., Pickett, J.M.: Cocktail party effect. J. Acoust. Soc. Am. 29(11), 1262–1262 (1957)
3. Analyzer, B.V.: User manual. Brain Products GmbH (2006)
4. Delorme, A., Makeig, S.: EEGLAB: an open source toolbox for analysis of single-trial EEG dynamics including independent component analysis. J. Neurosci. Methods 134(1), 9–21 (2004)
5. Cuthbert, B.N., Schupp, H.T., Bradley, M.M., Birbaumer, N., Lang, P.J.: Brain potentials in affective picture processing: covariation with autonomic arousal and affective report. Biol. Psychol. 52(2), 95–111 (2000)
6. Hajcak, G., Nieuwenhuis, S.: Reappraisal modulates the electrocortical response to unpleasant pictures. Cogn. Affect. Behav. Neurosci. 6, 291–297 (2006)
7. Smith, N.K., Cacioppo, J.T., Larsen, J.T., Chartrand, T.L.: May I have your attention, please: electrocortical responses to positive and negative stimuli. Neuropsychologia 41, 171–183 (2003)

8. Delplanque, S., Lavoie, M.E., Hot, P., Silvert, L., Sequeira, H.: Modulation of cognitive processing by emotional valence studied through event-related potentials in humans. Neurosci. Lett. **356**, 1–4 (2004)
9. Schupp, H.T., Junghöfer, M., Weike, A.I., Hamm, A.O.: Attention and emotion: an ERP analysis of facilitated emotional stimulus processing. NeuroReport **14**, 1107–1110 (2003)
10. Spreckelmeyer, K.N., Kutas, M., Urbach, T.P., Altenmuller, E., Münte, T.F.: Combined perception of emotion in pictures and musical sounds. Brain Res. **1070**, 160–710 (2006)
11. Carretie, L., Hinojosa, J.A., Martin-Loeches, M., Mercado, F., Tapia, M.: Automatic attention to emotional stimuli: neural correlates. Hum. Brain Mapp. **22**, 290–299 (2004)

Computational Intelligence

Generation of Multi-Layered QR Codes with Efficient Compression

Pratheesh Suresh[1], Debanjan Sadhya[1(✉)], and Amitesh Singh Rajput[2]

[1] ABV-Indian Institute of Information Technology and Management Gwalior,
Gwalior, India
{mtis_202008,debanjan}@iiitm.ac.in
[2] Birla Institute of Technology and Science, Pilani, India
amitesh.singh@pilani.bits-pilani.ac.in

Abstract. In this modern data-centric era, securing information that is transferred over the internet is a serious concern. Various cryptographic and stenographic methods play a vital role in this purpose. In this work, we develop a multi-layered steganographic system capable of hiding payloads in different hidden layers inside QR codes. Furthermore, each layer is compressed and encrypted separately to secure the payload data. Hence, we use the QR (Quick Response) Code as the cover medium to achieve and implement the above principles. In the proposed multi-layered QR Code approach, the top layer works as a standard QR Code while the layers beneath it act as private data. The secret is efficiently compressed to accommodate more information within the same space provided, thereby increasing the holding capacity of the QR code. The data in each layer are retrieved using different methods according to the type of compression used during the encoding process of the specified layer. The proposed model can store up to nine hidden layers of data. Various robustness tests are carried out to validate the efficiency of the hidden layers in the QR code and to check whether the hidden layers can withstand alterations without any data loss. Importantly, the resulting QR code works identically to a normal version upon scanning with any typical QR code scanner.

Keywords: QR Code · Compression · Payload · Steganography

1 Introduction

Quick Response codes are basically a form of 2D bar code that can be scanned quickly by a digital device. These codes store information as a series of black and white pixels in a square-shaped grid format. The initial QR code was developed in 1994 by a Japanese company named Denso Wave, currently a Toyota subsidiary[1]. QR codes are convenient, simple, and faster to use when it comes to sharing information/data. In comparison to standard barcodes, QR codes have become

---

[1] http://www.densowave.com/qrcode/aboutqr-e.html.

© The Author(s), under exclusive license to Springer Nature Switzerland AG 2023
P. Maji et al. (Eds.): PReMI 2023, LNCS 14301, pp. 301–311, 2023.
https://doi.org/10.1007/978-3-031-45170-6_31

more popular due to their immense data-holding capacity and fast readability. Consequently, QR codes are now found in everyday products, ranging from small food packets to large shipments and advertisements. The current standard of QR codes is ISO/IEC 18004:2015; the subsequent standard ISO/IEC CD 18004 is under development.

Several stenography techniques can be realized by using QR Codes as containers. These codes provide an easy-to-use alternative for embedding and sharing data across multiple users. However, there are several challenges in the existing techniques for using QR Codes as containers. Firstly, no mechanism exists (according to the best of the authors' knowledge) for embedding hidden layers of sensitive information in the QR Codes without affecting the baseline message or the image quality. Furthermore, existing techniques can be augmented with dynamic compression while considering the nature of the data to be shared. The resulting codes would maximize the efficiency of the sharing model. The existing QR Code models use an identical algorithm to process diverse data. This process reduces the data storage capacity, and they are more prone to attacks if an attacker can decode one layer of information. Hence, there is always a need for an efficient way of securing valuable hidden data in each layer against attacks.

In this work, we design an effective multi-layer steganographic framework capable of hiding payloads in different hidden layers inside QR codes. The modified QR code comprises of a dynamic compression technique that analyzes the nature of the given data and accommodates more data in the same space. The compressed payload in each layer is separately fed into an encryption algorithm to make it resistant to cryptographic attacks before packing into the QR code. To the adversary, the resultant QR Code works identically to a normal QR upon scanning with typical QR code scanners. Thus, we develop an efficient and secure data-hiding mechanism with higher resistance to damage or adversarial attacks.

2   Related Work

Several approaches exist which efficiently use QR Codes, not just as containers. Alajmi et al. [1] implemented a model with a hidden layer to carry secret information along with a standard message displayed by the QR Code. The model mainly contains two sections. The first part deals with payload embedding, and the latter part is about payload extraction. However, the model was prone to attacks like regular-singular steganalysis and fall of boundary problems. Rani and Euphrasia [8] introduced a mechanism that uses QR codes combined with images. Herein, the message was encrypted and stored inside the QR Code, which was subsequently masked inside a cover image to increase the system's security. However, the QR code was embedded inside the cover image rather than the QR code itself. Dey et al. [4] presented a method that takes a randomized intermediate QR Host embedded with the payload that must be securely transmitted. The model uses embedding techniques and double encryption to make the system more efficient and robust to various attacks. However, the authors used an image as the cover (instead of the QR code itself).

Now we discuss some security applications of QR codes apart from embedding. Sahu and Swain [9] proposed a data hiding technique that is created with pixel value difference as well as the modulus function. The authors present two variants of their approach, both of which use the difference between a pair of consecutive pixels to embed the secret data based on an adaptive range table. The modulo operation was specifically used to reduce the distortion in the stego-image. Barrera et al. [2] introduced a mechanism that utilizes QR codes in optical encryption and also as a container. The withstand power against alterations was the primary reason for choosing the QR Code as a container. However, the system was eventually more prone to noise. Chow et al. [3] developed an approach for secret sharing using QR codes. The proposed model uses the error correction mechanism inherent in the QR code for distributing and encoding information about a secret message within various *shares*. A secret QR-sharing approach for safeguarding sensitive QR data in a distributed manner was proposed in [5]. Importantly, the model can resist the print-and-scan operation.

3 Methodology

Most of the current data-hiding techniques use images as containers. In comparison to images, QR Codes need lesser space and computational time. However, the currently available models are not fully used in terms of the usability of QR codes. This study aims to design an effective multi-layer steganographic system capable of hiding payloads in different hidden layers inside QR codes. The modified QR code will have a dynamic compression technique that analyzes the nature of the given data and is subsequently efficiently compressed to accommodate more data in the same space. The compressed payload in each layer is separately fed into an encryption algorithm. This process makes the payload more resistant to adversarial attacks before packing it into the QR code. The resultant QR Code gives the adversary a piece of dummy information upon scanning with typical QR code scanners. The dummy message can be scanned from the resulting QR code using any QR code reader. The proposed system implementation can be broadly divided into four phases - 1) Data Collection, 2) Data Preparation, 3) Layering and Packing, and 4) Pixel Embedding. The final output from these phases is a normal scannable QR code embedded with all the hidden layers. The secret layer information can only be read using a custom-created algorithm that accepts the password allocated for each layer. The hidden layers are encrypted, compressed, and stored separately inside the QR code, thus ensuring security between the layers.

3.1 Data Collection Phase

The initial requirements are collected from the user in this phase. The public/dummy message that needs to be outputted while regular QR code scanning is initially fetched from the user. We represent this data by D_p. The hidden layer messages D_{s1}-D_{s9} are subsequently captured in the plain-text format, which is compressed and encrypted in the next phase. The icon or logo that needs to be embedded (visible) in the middle of the QR code is also captured. This optional step is done in organizations to distinguish their QR codes from normal ones.

3.2 Data Preparation Phase

In the second phase, the collected data is processed to match the constraints of making an embedded QR code. The input to this module is the assembled plain-text hidden data blocks. This hidden information is then fed into the dynamic compression algorithm, where the suitable method is selected according to the type of data supplied. The map-key of the used compression algorithm is prepended to the data for marking which algorithm is set by the dynamic compression module at the time of compression. Noticeably, the map-key is a unique identifier for each algorithm in the compression module that identifies the specific algorithm used during compression. This key plays a significant role in determining the compression algorithm used during the decompression stage at the receiver side when the legitimate user of that hidden layer is trying to extract the data in the specified layer.

The input to the compression module is the text file containing the plain text of the confidential data. We initially find the efficient compression method for the given input file, and subsequently prepend the map key corresponding to the selected algorithm. The algorithm selection entirely depends on the nature of the contents inside the plain text data. The use of dynamic algorithm selection reduces the possibility of a weak performance by choosing the optimum algorithm for the input data [13]. After the compression module task, the output is fed into the encryption module. Herein, the compressed data gets encrypted to increase its security. In the encryption module, the current industry-standard AES algorithm [11] is implemented. Each layer is encrypted separately with different keys, which the generator and the legitimate user of the hidden layer only know. The output of this phase is the series of efficiently compressed encrypted forms of hidden layer data. Thus, we obtain a series of efficiently compressed encrypted forms of hidden layer data. This received data is ready for layering and packing in the dummy message QR code.

3.3 Layering and Packing Phase

The compressed and encrypted hidden layer data are embedded into the dummy QR code. Every QR code reader/decoder works on the key pixel module recognition principle, which means for every module (black/white), the center portion of the module is only considered for decoding [6]. Thus, if the decoder reads a dark pixel in the center of a block, the entire block is regarded as dark irrespective of the surrounding pixels. The same working principle applies to the white area as well. Hence as shown in Fig. 1, we can use the surrounding pixels in a module to hide the data blocks. The entire module is divided accordingly so that we can serially accommodate the hidden blocks.

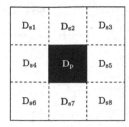

Fig. 1. The composition of the recognition module.

To use the remaining spaces, we first convert every hidden layer message into the QR code form. The version of the QR code is determined by considering the most lengthy message among all the hidden layers and the dummy message. This process ensures that no data loss occurs on any of the layers (hidden and dummy). After creating the hidden layer data and dummy layer messages QR codes, the layering process begins. Ds_1 till Ds_8 represents the area of the corresponding module from hidden layer 1 data to hidden layer 8 data, respectively. Thus, we obtain the QR code embedded with the eight layers of hidden data.

3.4 Pixel Embedding Phase

An additional layer of the hidden layer is introduced in the pixel embedding phase. This extra layer is added on top of the aforementioned layers, but it works using the concept of least significant bit data (LSB) embedding [7]. Consequently, this layer can only be used in electronically transmitted QR codes. The core idea behind this technique is that the resultant image visually looks the same for every QR code taken if we modify the final bit value for each pixel inside the code. This pattern occurs since changing the last bit never fully alters the color profile of that pixel. Theoretically, a slightly lighter/darker shade will happen, but the image visually remains the same. This data layer also goes through the compression and encryption phases prior to embedding, thus ensuring that the data is compact and secure enough like other hidden layers.

Figure 2 represents the entire workflow of the proposed model. D_1-D_9 are the plain text hidden data that are fed into the dynamic lossless compression module. This compressed data is subsequently fed into the encryption module, which further encrypts the compressed data. After this process, the D_1-D_8 processed data goes through the layering module while D_9, the hidden layer goes through the LSB embedding technique. After packing D_9 along with the dummy message, the final QR code with all the active hidden layers is ready for transmission.

4   Experiments and Results

We have considered some sample data which we embed inside each layer. The details of the data are presented in Table 1. As observable, we have considered the

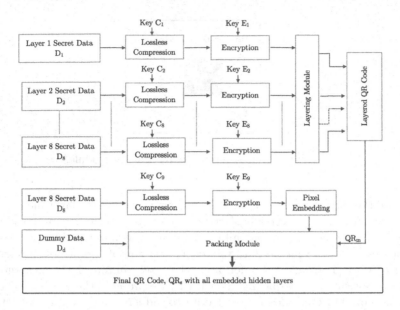

Fig. 2. Process flow diagram of the holistic proposed model.

structure of the input message in the format '**The meeting is at X pm. Password: enter@meetX.**', where '**X**' is the layer ID. Alternatively, the dummy data is considered as '**The meeting is at 11 am.**'. In total, nine different messages are taken as input for embedding in the nine layers.

4.1   Robustness Analysis

We test the robustness of the generated QR codes against benchmark tests. The robustness of the code is validated if the embedded data inside the QR code can be successfully retrieved (without data loss) from the tampered code.

Gaussian Blur Addition: Gaussian blur (Gaussian Smoothing) [10] is an image processing technique in which we blur the actual image by using the Gaussian function. It is often used in graphics editors to decrease an image's detail or noise. The output image will be similar to the actual image looked through a translucent screen. In two dimensions, the Gaussian function can be represented as $G(x,y) = \frac{1}{\sqrt{2\pi\sigma^2}} e^{-\frac{x^2+y^2}{2\sigma^2}}$. In Fig. 3, the first QR code is the output after applying the Gaussian blur function with intensity 1.0. It is followed by the QR codes applied with intensities of 2.5, 5.0, and 7.5, respectively. The greater the intensity value, the more blurred the final image is. The robustness of the produced QR codes against Gaussian blur is tested by retrieving all the dummy and hidden layer data. Hence, the ability to retrieve the data embedded inside the QR code is evaluated for each level of applied intensity.

Distortion: Distortion is defined as the modifications in the original image which alter the image's fundamental physical properties. Consequently, the out-

Table 1. Tabular representation of the input data taken from the user and their compressed-encrypted form.

Layer	Data	Compressed-Encrypted Form
D_d	The meeting is at 11 am.	n/a
D_1	The meeting is at 1 pm. Password: enter@meet1.	WMh/i7s7ZvX+JsUgU9ZlAvCepGvJTifQquDJkzr2ySnMp0l+V MB0gBa6X/8XbWa8OB3ah78Sax9eubAIXBXepWiApPGKyc PHMgEzrkcylAM=
D_2	The meeting is at 2 pm. Password: enter@meet2.	uGJvuSpfVsxfB1bFPAZog2Hi6fYqCIPI0ghPuIAR2GIFFxxas 4dTxVaQRt1abQNXz39VAv34kLaRDLhdw7uAP2c/yHKnq1 GsiyCV2faC5Yg=
D_3	The meeting is at 3 pm. Password: enter@meet3.	vytOLZkV1zcUbAIoHBMDJB6OKm4NKJDWIJz8Hn5X+ WCRNn2Frh W0wxSV5YqEoThxSP7URvY2D4JWwGKmEl2CB1iCEu3m+ sGwmqGodl1/Chs=
D_4	The meeting is at 4 pm. Password: enter@meet4.	Mh28nay1XAIFuCL9DcwwEHS77xf1DPW3dmGDfYEzMn 74yvQ d/gSAxC5lEoBGUlQ5+GOWOLOpvnwk/dE7Mfk2c255 iKi6NBCPsTiggbxwoV0=
D_5	The meeting is at 5 pm. Password: enter@meet5.	qPauc6m6p8h+ujtVxiFfGnO/LKV2mVLCsMm2e1F/lqPukjFwzp 52/CWcduePIbhsThSPjVh2gLS/BHb5q9hAH4ujNf3YFc3HNIx8r9z42Zg=
D_6	The meeting is at 6 pm. Password: enter@meet6.	X/SX9LWv24fdAt/VA3YHjL4jm9TDRSFrnvOL60+doTqjXBsgu 6aFJoxarNa47F3hymyQr99zprfoSVLe2Zsi/alypLHv+u41qLiEyCmYC84=
D_7	The meeting is at 7 pm. Password: enter@meet7.	zgoDkegUqz3AhWexizUbPpFNp4auypc5V1fvkCjrngy0noJDdq7+q AbuTrR96vRHgsrQuV2DulV3CIiY/ZWfm5mmgdYEgrBZi+50gE/ZgCU=
D_8	The meeting is at 8 pm. Password: enter@meet8.	i8HemXIIyD7kG/7IXi4FMx9CPjF7/9/eHeuL8vvfSnRDycUNZ9xM AgqsPEqJuQeD0Jw0uEjylkYRXSvIOr4u6dsOvZ03vg92lF5iKvrIsCg=
D_9	The meeting is at 9 pm. Password: enter@meet9.	Gnk/tHPQiNl+5VHTIYvmp78n+DxQluWN6N9MjLtz0HFAU/MbCv vNSzeHhVxwC3OH63cO6xcMt5xkZqdL/b20PzJsP3Ruq1eGCdh2antJ1pQ=

Fig. 3. Effects of Gaussian blur on the produced QR code. The intensity values of 1.0, 2.5, 5.0, and 7.5 are used respectively.

put image losses its original shape or structure. The most common distortions are shear, squeeze, stretch, and skew. In Fig. 4, the first QR code is the output after applying the corner squeeze. It is followed by the QR codes applied with shear, compress and stretch, respectively. Robustness against distortions in the final QR code is tested by treating it with four different types of distortion.

Gaussian Noise Addition: Gaussian noise in images is the noise signal added to the original image with a probability density function similar to the Gaussian distribution. For a Gaussian random variable z, the probability density function p is expressed as $p(z) = \frac{1}{\sigma\sqrt{2\pi}}e^{-\frac{(z-\mu)^2}{2\sigma^2}}$. Here, the Gaussian random variable z indicates the grey level. The mean grey value is represented as μ and σ is the

Fig. 4. Effects of distortion on the produced QR code. The employed distortion operations are shear, squeeze, stretch, and skew respectively.

standard deviation. In Fig. 5, the first QR code corresponds to the output after applying the compression with $\mu = 20$, which is followed by the QR codes applied with μ values of 50, 70, 80 respectively. The greater the μ value, the more noisy the final image will be.

Fig. 5. Effects of Gaussian noise addition on the produced QR code. Different values of $\mu = \{20, 50, 70, 80\}$ are used respectively.

Rotation: Rotation is the process of tilting the original image with respect to the center or axis. In Fig. 6, the first QR code corresponds to the rotation at an angle of 45°. It is followed by the QR codes applied with rotation 90°, 135°, and 270° respectively.

Fig. 6. Effects of rotation on the produced QR code. The base code was rotated at angles of 45°, 90°, 135°, and 270°.

In all the above tests and their various intensities and variations, the data inside hidden layers (viz. D_1 to D_8) was retrieved without any data loss. These were subsequently decompressed to get back the original text. The proposed method is resistant to all the above robustness tests at given intensities and variations since the hidden data is retrieved successfully in all scenarios. However, the data embedded using Least Significant Bit (viz. D_9) does not pass the above tests. This happens because all the simulated tests alter the entire pixels of the QR code, which consequently alters the LSBs. Hence, this layer of data can be retrieved successfully if no tampering has happened to the final code.

4.2 Data Holding Capacity

Data holding capacity refers to the amount of data that can be embedded inside the QR code. Theoretically speaking, a QR code has a maximum symbol size of 177×177 modules. Consequently, it can contain 31,329 squares which can encode 3 KB of data. A QR code also has four levels of error correction for accurately handling data. The Reed-Solomon error correction scheme is generally used in QR codes to achieve the validation of the data inside it. There are four types of error correction schemes used - Level L [Low], Level M [Medium], Level Q [Quartile], and Level H [High] [12]. In Level L, only 7% bytes of data can be corrected. The ability to recover can be increased by using a higher Error Correction Level (ECL) like M, Q or H. These can recover 15%, 25%, and 30% bytes of data, respectively. When comparing the data holding capacity of the proposed method with existing methods, the proposed scheme outperforms others in terms of the data (in bits) corresponding to all four error correction schemes. As presented in Fig. 7, our scheme comprehensively outperforms all other works. Our model achieves such high data-holding capacity since it is possible to embed data from up to nine different sources in a single QR code.

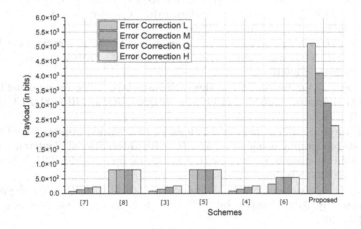

Fig. 7. Comparative analysis of payload capacity of QR codes.

5 Conclusion

Our work presents a multi-layered information-hiding architecture capable of embedding payloads in different hidden layers inside QR codes. Each layer in the model is encrypted separately to secure the payload data. The proposed model can take up nine layers of hidden layer data, while the current implementations are only up to three layers of hidden layer data. The model also implements a dynamic compression module that can compress the data efficiently. Importantly, each layer has been encrypted and compressed separately to provide maximum safety and ownership. We believe that our model would be especially useful when a single cover medium (QR code in our case) is used to convey distinct messages to multiple parties. Our future attempts would be to modify the existing framework for catering to dynamic QR codes, wherein the information or data is available on a website that can be changed dynamically.

References

1. Alajmi, M., Elashry, I., El-Sayed, H.S., Allah, O.S.F.: Steganography of encrypted messages inside valid QR codes. IEEE Access **8**, 27861–27873 (2020). https://doi.org/10.1109/access.2020.2971984
2. Barrera, J.F., Mira, A., Torroba, R.: Optical encryption and QR codes: secure and noise-free information retrieval. Opt. Express **21**(5), 5373–5378 (2013). https://doi.org/10.1364/oe.21.005373
3. Chow, Y.-W., Susilo, W., Yang, G., Phillips, J.G., Pranata, I., Barmawi, A.M.: Exploiting the error correction mechanism in QR codes for secret sharing. In: Liu, J.K., Steinfeld, R. (eds.) ACISP 2016. LNCS, vol. 9722, pp. 409–425. Springer, Cham (2016). https://doi.org/10.1007/978-3-319-40253-6_25
4. Dey, S., Mondal, K., Nath, J., Nath, A.: Advanced steganography algorithm using randomized intermediate QR host embedded with any encrypted secret message: ASA_QR algorithm. Int. J. Modern Educ. Comput. Sci. **4**(6), 59–67 (2012). https://doi.org/10.5815/ijmecs.2012.06.08
5. Lin, P.Y.: Distributed secret sharing approach with cheater prevention based on QR code. IEEE Trans. Industr. Inf. **12**(1), 384–392 (2016). https://doi.org/10.1109/TII.2015.2514097
6. Liu, S., Fu, Z., Yu, B.: Rich QR codes with three-layer information using hamming code. IEEE Access **7**, 78640–78651 (2019). https://doi.org/10.1109/ACCESS.2019.2922259
7. Masud Karim, S.M., Rahman, M.S., Hossain, M.I.: A new approach for LSB based image steganography using secret key. In: 14th International Conference on Computer and Information Technology (ICCIT 2011), pp. 286–291 (2011). https://doi.org/10.1109/ICCITechn.2011.6164800
8. Rani, M.M.S., Euphrasia, K.R.: Data security through QR code encryption and steganography. Adv. Comput. Int. J. **7**(1/2), 1–7 (2016). https://doi.org/10.5121/acij.2016.7201
9. Sahu, A.K., Swain, G.: An optimal information hiding approach based on pixel value differencing and modulus function. Wirel. Pers. Commun. **108**(1), 159–174 (2019). https://doi.org/10.1007/s11277-019-06393-z
10. Singhal, P., Verma, A., Garg, A.: A study in finding effectiveness of gaussian blur filter over bilateral filter in natural scenes for graph based image segmentation. In: 2017 4th International Conference on Advanced Computing and Communication Systems (ICACCS), pp. 1–6 (2017). https://doi.org/10.1109/ICACCS.2017.8014612

11. Information Technology Laboratory, National Institute of Standards and Technology: Announcing the Advanced Encryption Standard (AES) [electronic resource]. Computer Security Division, Information Technology Laboratory, National Institute of Standards and Technology Gaithersburg, MD (2001)
12. Wu, W.C.: Quantization-based image authentication scheme using QR error correction. EURASIP J. Image Video Process. **2017**(1), 13 (2017)
13. Senturk, A., Kara, R.: Comparison of image compression algorithms used in wireless multimedia sensor networks. In: 2016 24th Signal Processing and Communication Application Conference (SIU), pp. 269–272 (2016). https://doi.org/10.1109/SIU.2016.7495729

Analysis of Segmented Spectrograms for Human Activity Recognition via Neural Network

Avinash Dixit[1]([⊠]) [iD], Vinay Kulkarni[1,2], and V. V. Reddy[1]

[1] International Institute of Information Technology, Bengaluru, India
{avinash.dixit,vinay.kulkarni,vinod.reddy}@iiitb.ac.in
[2] Ignitarium Technology Solutions Pvt Ltd., Bengaluru, India

Abstract. Identification of human activities without intruding into their privacy appeals to the use of radar. The micro-movements of the body parts of any activity induce unique micro-Doppler signatures in the spectrogram. We design two neural network architectures that can effectively identify activities. The networks are designed to have a reduced number of model parameters for their adoption in embedded hardware. To observe the sensitivity of these networks, we verify their performance with varying duration of spectrograms.

Keywords: Human Activity Classification · LSTM · Convmixer

1 Introduction

Human Activity classification is a problem of significant interest in applications such as the identification of infiltrator activities along the border [18], suspicious activities in public places, and specific gait positions of elderly at home [4], to mention a few. Although camera [7] provides a wider scope for precise activity identification, radar-based activity classification is preferred to operate under different lighting conditions [9] and maintain the privacy of the subjects.

The additional movements of human parts along with the entire body introduce micro-Doppler [15] signature in the received radar signal. Since each human activity involves the unique movement of body parts against time, the received signal is hypothesized to preserve unique characteristics that help in the identification of the activities performed by the subject under consideration. In other applications, micro-Doppler signature has been used for the detection [11] and classification of unmanned aerial vehicles [10] and estimation of breath-rate and heart-rate of human subjects [12], to mention a few.

The frequency of the micro-Doppler signature varies with time by the rate of change of micro-motions within the body. Joint time-frequency transforms are commonly employed to study these micro-Doppler signatures [3]. In most practical applications, short-time Fourier transform (STFT) generates a spectrogram that reveals the instantaneous variations in the spectral content over time.

P. Maji et al. (Eds.): PReMI 2023, LNCS 14301, pp. 312–320, 2023.
https://doi.org/10.1007/978-3-031-45170-6_32

Deep neural networks (DNN) are known to be effective for nonlinear processing and decision-making. Of the numerous networks available, Convolutional neural networks (CNN) [8] have been widely employed in the context of radar for multi-target detection [5], object detection, and human activity classification [20]. This prowess of DNN can be attributed to its ability to successfully extract hidden patterns embedded within the data.

Noting the success of DNN/CNN for image classification, the problem of human activity classification fits into this framework using spectrogram images that preserve unique time-varying spectral information for each activity. CNN extracts local and global features to give representations in the latent space that captures the spatial dependencies in the spectrogram. Autoencoder, realized using CNN, is shown in [14] to achieve a fall detection accuracy of 87%. An encoder-decoder network is trained using transfer learning and unsupervised learning in [13] to classify 12 indoor activities. To exploit the temporal information in the spectrograms, 3D-CNN with temporal attention module (TAM) has been used to classify six activities in [2]. Classification of six different suspicious activities has been demonstrated in [1] using CNN. In another work [19], 17-layered CNN is used for classifying human activities using W-band radar. Another promising work [17] is where a tinyML-based single-chip radar solution has been proposed for implementing Convolutional Neural Network (CNN) for human activity classification. But here the number of activities is restricted to four and as the number of classes increases their distribution overlaps, thus making it difficult for the proposed network to accurately predict, thereby requiring a more complex network for the same. Although classification on real data has shown promising results in [1,2,13,14,17,19], there exists scope for improving the accuracy of activity classification.

In this work, we intend to not only improve the classification accuracy for human activity recognition but also analyze the performance of accuracies across different time segments of spectrogram with the help of diverse kinds of neural networks. This study enables us to not only observe the subject behavior transitions between activities but also helps to determine the type of neural network that performs better in real-time scenarios with predominant activity transitions. We adopt two custom neural network architectures built with an emphasis on accuracy and model size. The architectures include (i) Long short-term memory (LSTM)-based Neural Network and (ii) patch-based CNN architecture (ConvMixer). The networks are trained and evaluated on openly available CI4R activity recognition dataset [6].

The paper is organized as follows: we formulate the problem in Section II. Proposed networks are discussed in Section III, Section IV presents the results and discussions before concluding Section V.

2   Problem Formulation

In the presence of a single human target in the scene, the radar response can be decomposed into components scattered by the body mainframe and various parts of the body. Ignoring the negligible second-order term in the phase, the down-converted signal can be written as

$$z(t,l) \approx \alpha^{(b)} e^{j\left[2\pi f_{R_0} t + 2\pi f_0 t_{0,l}^{(b)}\right]} + \sum_{b=1}^{K_B} \alpha_b^{(p)} e^{j\left[2\pi (f_{R_0} + \delta f_R^{(p)}) t + 2\pi f_0 t_{b,l}^{(p)}\right]} + \eta(t,l), \qquad (1)$$

where $f_{R_0} = \frac{2\mu R_0}{c}$ is range frequency, K_B is the number of moving parts of the human body, $\alpha^{(b)}$ and $\alpha_b^{(p)}$ are the response magnitude from the body mainframe and the moving parts of the body, respectively. Since the body parts are in the vicinity of the body, we approximate the range frequency to $f_{R_0} + \delta f_R^{(p)} \approx f_{R_0}$.

Denoting the slow-time variable as $\tilde{t}_l \approx (l-1)T_{\text{cri}}$, the propagation delay for the body and b^{th} part can be written as

$$t_{0,l}^{(b)} = \frac{2}{c}\left[R_0 + v_0 \tilde{t}_l\right] \text{ and } t_{b,l}^{(p)} = \frac{2}{c}\left[R_0 + v_0 \tilde{t}_l + m_b(\tilde{t}_l)\right], \qquad (2)$$

where $m_b(\tilde{t}_l)$ denotes the time-varying delay due to the movement of the bth body part. The slow-time signal at R_0 from the radar can be obtained as

$$\overline{z}(l) = \alpha^{(b)} e^{j[2\pi f_D \tilde{t}_l + \phi]} + \sum_{b=1}^{K_B} \alpha_b^{(p)} e^{j[2\pi f_D \tilde{t}_l + m_b(\tilde{t}_l) + \phi]} + \overline{\eta}(l), \qquad (3)$$

where $\phi = e^{j[2\pi f_0 2R_0/c]}$ is a constant phase and $f_D = (2v_0/c)f_0$ is the Doppler frequency. We note that the signal constitutes the Doppler sinusoidal component and K_B modulating signals, each of which varies with the movement of the corresponding body part. Background clutter is suppressed from (3) by a moving target indicator (MTI) filter. The spectrogram is then obtained by the STFT of the filtered signal to yield

$$\overline{Z}(m,f) = \sum_{l=0}^{\infty} \overline{z}(l) w(l-m) e^{-j2\pi f l T_{\text{cri}}}, \qquad (4)$$

where $w(.)$ is the sliding window function and m is the time-frame index. For each human activity, the moving body parts introduce unique patterns as a function of time in the spectrogram. Based on this hypothesis, a spectrogram is used to identify various human activities in this work.

It is also important to understand the minimum necessary duration used to generate the spectrogram for accurate identification of human activities. In Section V, we present the sensitivity of the proposed solution to the spectrogram duration.

3   Proposed Approach

The signal nonstationarity due to the unique patterns of individual activities manifests nonlinearly in the spectrogram. Neural networks are therefore employed in the literature for effective classification of these activities, albeit with limited success [13]. We present two custom-made different architectures to enhance classification accuracy for this problem. These networks have been designed to enhance accuracy while maintaining a small model size to suit real-time deployment.

3.1 LSTM-Based Architecture

Since the micro-motions for each activity evolve with time, we consider an LSTM-based network to identify the activity. With its capability to remember the temporal sequence, the LSTM network will be able to characterize the evolution of micro-Doppler variations over time embedded within the spectrogram (4). The LSTM network designed for human activity classification is shown in Fig. 1.

The spectrogram is fed as the input x to the network with the temporal variations (m) of the spectrogram associated with time-space $(< t >)$, and frequency variations of micro-Doppler (f) associated with feature space of the LSTM layers. The two LSTM layers of 32 units and 16 units are designed, with each LSTM layer followed by a layer normalization (LN) to normalize the features. A dense layer of 11 neurons with softmax activation classifies human activities.

As an example for associativity, an activity acquired over a duration of 20 s yields a spectrogram of size 804×1475 (frequency bins × time frames). The 1475 time frames are associated with the time axis of the input LSTM layer and 804 frequency bins at each time frame index constitute the feature vector for the network.

Fig. 1. Proposed LSTM network architecture.

The network is trained using an ADAM optimizer having a learning rate of 0.001 and decay 1e−6 for 50 epochs. This compact network constitutes only 80 k parameters, thus making it suitable for easy deployment on embedded hardware.

3.2 Patch-Based CNN Architecture

Each spectrogram has a frequency spread due to the micro-motions of the body that does not rapidly change across the time axis. This stationary property within a short duration of the spectrogram has to be effectively extracted for the local features. The patch-based CNN [16] architecture uses depthwise or pointwise convolutions by dividing them into small patches, for local features. This concept is used in our design of the architecture shown in Fig. 2.

The spectrogram is divided into patches of size 2×2 by feeding it to a convolutional layer having 256 filters, with kernel size and stride equal to the patch size. The layer employs GELU as the activation function. These patches are fed to a block of depth 4. Each block contains a depthwise convolution having a kernel size of 5×5 and stride of 1×1. The output from the convolutional layer is batch normalized and added to the input. This output is then passed through a point-wise convolutional layer having 256 filters and a kernel size of 1 as shown in Fig. 2(b). This output from the first block is fed to three such blocks sequentially before a global-average pool layer followed by a dense layer having 11 neurons and softmax as an activation function for classification as shown in Fig. 2 (a).

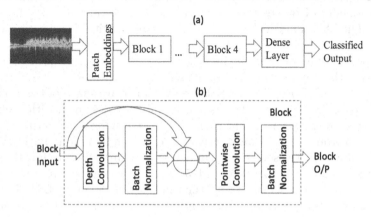

Fig. 2. (a) ConvMixer network architecture, (b) Block of depth and point convolutions.

The entire network is trained using sparse categorical cross-entropy loss for 50 epochs with ADAM optimizer having a learning rate of 0.001 and weight decay of $1e-6$. It is evident from Fig. 2 that the proposed network, with as low as 300k model parameters, is simple and lightweight compared to the benchmark networks such as Resnet-50, InceptionNET, and others.

As can be noticed, the proposed networks adopt different architectures that are customized to handle spectrograms. The intent here has been to understand the network that is most suited for the context of activity recognition. Besides, the networks are designed to be computationally light in order to operate in real-time within an embedded system. The comparative performance of these networks alongside the discussion of computational complexity is presented in the next section. We also study their performance against the signal duration employed for the construction of the spectrogram image.

4   Numerical Results and Discussion

4.1   Dataset

In order to evaluate the performance of the proposed networks, we employ the open-source dataset shared by the Laboratory of Computational Intelligence for RADAR (CI4R), University of Alabama [6]. The data consists of 56 − 62 spectrograms per class. With 11 different activities, the dataset provides a total of 648 samples. The down-converted raw signal from 77 GHz FMCW radar is subjected to 4096-point STFT with a hop length of 59 samples and window size of 256 samples to generate the spectrogram. The RGB image thus obtained for a raw signal duration of 20 s is of size $804 \times 1475 \times 3$.

The eleven human activities to be classified are walking towards radar (59 samples), walking away from the radar (58), picking up an object (56), bending (59), sitting (57), kneeling (62), crawling (61), walking on toes (58), limping (59), short steps (60) and scissors gait (59). We augment the data using additive Gaussian noise, impulse noise, Gaussian blur and sharpening. Since the spectrograms shared by [6] are constructed over 20 s duration, decisions are provided at the same interval. For the sensitivity analysis of the proposed networks against varying spectrogram duration, we construct 6 s, 8 s, 10 s, 12 s, and 16 s spectrograms from the available ones as shown in Table 1.

4.2   Results

The proposed networks are realized using Keras tensorflow and trained on Nvidia K80 GPU. LSTM and ConvMixer networks employ sparse categorical cross-entropy loss. Both networks were trained with Adam Optimizer.

The efficacy of the networks for test samples is presented using t-SNE. Fig. 3 (a) shows the t-SNE plot for the input spectrogram image. The 11 classes are color coded for better visualization. Fig. 3 (b-c) shows the t-SNE representation obtained at the output of network over 6 s duration.

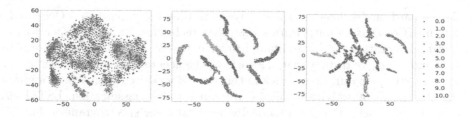

Fig. 3. t-SNE plots for (a) Input spectrogram images (b) Convmixer (c) LSTM architectures.

We next study the classification accuracy of the two networks for various durations of the spectrogram along with their complexity measured in FLOPS. This study enables one to decide on the minimum duration of the spectrogram required for human activity classification with the desired accuracy and complexity. Each row of Table 1 provides the accuracy of the two networks for specific spectrogram duration.

The real-time computational load, determined by the model parameter size, is tabulated in the last row of Table 1. The consolidated observation of two networks with their importance in the duration of activity along with suitable edge

Table 1. Performance and complexity comparison of the models.

Spectrogram Time Segments (sec)	LSTM (%)	ConvMixer (%)
0–6, 4–10, 8–14, 12–18, 14–20	81	92
0–8, 4–12, 8–16, 12–20	92	98
0–10, 4–14, 8–18, 10–20	95	99
0–12, 4–16, 8–20	98	98
0–16, 4–20	98	99
0–20	99	99
Model parameter size	69.6k	300k

Table 2. Observations.

Model	Memory Imprint	FLops	Duration Suitability	Comments
Convmixer	3.2 MB	0.776G	>8 s	Patch-based CNN architecture (ConvMixer) outperforms the LSTM network for all spectrogram durations and this can be attributed to its patch-based representation and mixing of distant spatial locations. Due to its size, it is not suitable for edge devices with limited memory.
LSTM	898 KB	0.000106 G	>12 s	It is a lightweight network that uses a minimal number of Flops, thus making it suitable for edge-based devices but they require a longer duration of temporal sequences in order to derive the important frequency components which contribute more to the classification

device hardware is listed in Table 2. We note that the patch-based CNN architecture (ConvMixer) outperforms the other technique for all the spectrogram durations and this can be attributed to their power of patch-based representation and mixing of distant spatial locations The accuracy of convMixer is $\geq 98\%$ for a spectrogram duration of 8 s and hence is better suited than other for studying transitions of activities and also Human activity classification. LSTM also provides accuracies that are practically acceptable for spectrogram of duration ≥ 10 s i.e. they require a longer duration of temporal sequences in order to derive the important frequency components which contribute more to the classification. This observation is in line with the inherent capability of LSTM to exploit temporal sequences.

From this study, it is evident that human activity can be effectively classified with spectrogram duration ≥ 6 s with the proposed patch-based ConvMixer network. The other proposed network strikes a good trade-off between the computational load, spectrogram duration, and accuracy. The system designer can appropriately decide on one among the proposed network for effective human activity classification.

5   Conclusions

Classification of 11 human activities from the openly available spectrograms was performed. Two custom neural network architectures were devised to enhance classification accuracy based on the human activity duration. Both networks exhibit effective classification accuracy. Besides the classification performance, the networks are lightweight and therefore suitable for realization on embedded hardware. These networks are shown to effectively classify activities from spectrogram with duration ≥ 8 s.

References

1. Chakraborty, M., et al.: DIAT-μ radhar (micro-doppler signature dataset) & μ Radnet (a lightweight DCNN)-for human suspicious activity recognition. IEEE Sens. J. **22**(7), 6851–6858 (2022)
2. Chen, H., et al.: Human activity recognition using temporal 3DCNN based on FMCW radar. In: IEEE MTT-S International Microwave Biomedical Conference (IMBioC), pp. 245–247. IEEE (2022)
3. Chen, V.C.: Analysis of radar micro-Doppler with time-frequency transform. In: Proceedings of the10th IEEE Workshop on Statistical Signal and Array Processing, pp. 463–466 (2000)
4. Cippitelli, E., et al.: Radar and RGB-depth sensors for fall detection: a review. IEEE Sens. J. **17**(12), 3585–3604 (2017)
5. Furukawa, H.: Deep learning for end-to-end automatic target recognition from synthetic aperture radar imagery. arXiv preprint arXiv:1801.08558 (2018)
6. Gurbuz, S.Z., Rahman, M.M., Kurtoglu, E., Macks, T., Fioranelli, F.: Cross-frequency training with adversarial learning for radar micro-Doppler signature classification (rising researcher). In: Radar Sensor Technology XXIV, vol. 11408, pp. 58–68 (2020)
7. Hossain, M.S.: Patient status monitoring for smart home healthcare. In: IEEE International Conference on Multimedia & Expo Workshops (ICMEW), pp. 1–6 (2016)
8. Krizhevsky, A., Sutskever, I., Hinton, G.E.: ImageNet classification with deep convolutional neural networks. Commun. ACM **60**(6), 84–90 (2017)
9. Li, H., et al.: Bi-LSTM network for multimodal continuous human activity recognition and fall detection. IEEE Sens. J. **20**(3), 1191–1201 (2019)
10. Molchanov, P.T.: Classification of small UAVs and birds by micro-Doppler signatures. Intl. J. Microwave Wirel. Technol. **6**(3), 435–444 (2014)
11. Reddy, V.V., Peter, S.: UAV micro-doppler signature analysis using FMCW radar. In: IEEE Radar Conference, pp. 1–6 (2021)
12. Salmi, J., Luukkonen, O., Koivunen, V.: Continuous wave radar based vital sign estimation: modeling and experiments. In: IEEE Radar Conference, pp. 564–569 (2012)
13. Seyfioğlu, M.S., Gürbüz, S.Z.: Deep neural network initialization methods for micro-Doppler classification with low training sample support. IEEE Geosci. Remote Sens. Lett. **14**(12), 2462–2466 (2017)
14. Seyfioğlu, M.S., Gürbüz, S.Z., Özbayoğlu, A.M., Yüksel, M.: Deep learning of micro-Doppler features for aided and unaided gait recognition. In: IEEE Radar Conference, pp. 1125–1130. IEEE (2017)

15. Tahmoush, D.: Review of micro-doppler signatures. IET Radar Sonar Navig. **9**(9), 1140–1146 (2015)
16. Trockman, A., Kolter, J.Z.: Patches are all you need? arXiv preprint arXiv:2201.09792 (2022)
17. Yadav, S.S., Agarwal, R., Bharath, K., Rao, S., Thakur, C.S.: TinyRadar: MmWave radar based human activity classification for edge computing. In: IEEE International Symposium on Circuits and Systems (ISCAS), pp. 2414–2417. IEEE (2022)
18. Yessad, D., Amrouche, A., Debyeche, M., Djeddou, M.: Micro-Doppler classification for ground surveillance radar using speech recognition tools. In: San Martin, C., Kim, S.-W. (eds.) CIARP 2011. LNCS, vol. 7042, pp. 280–287. Springer, Heidelberg (2011). https://doi.org/10.1007/978-3-642-25085-9_33
19. Zhang, R., Cao, S.: Real-time human motion behavior detection via CNN using MmWave radar. IEEE Sens. Lett. **3**(2), 1–4 (2018)
20. Zhu, J., Lou, X., Ye, W.: Lightweight deep learning model in mobile-edge computing for radar-based human activity recognition. IEEE Internet Things J. **8**(15), 12350–12359 (2021)

Modified Group Delay Features for Emotion Recognition

S. Uthiraa$^{(\boxtimes)}$, Aditya Pusuluri, and Hemant A. Patil

Speech Research Lab, DA-IICT, Gandhinagar, Gujarat, India
{uthiraa_s,aditya_pss,hemant_patil}@daiict.ac.in

Abstract. As technological advancements progress, dependence on machines is inevitable. Therefore, to facilitate effective interaction between humans and machines, it has become crucial to develop proficient techniques for Speech Emotion Recognition (SER). This paper uses phase-based features, namely Modified Group Delay Cepstral Coefficients for SER. To the best of our knowledge, this paper is the first attempt to use the MGDCC feature on emotions. Experiments were performed using the EmoDB database on emotions, anger, happy, neutral, and sad. The proposed feature outperformed the baseline Mel Frequency Cepstral Coefficients (MFCC) and Linear Frequency Cepstral Coefficients (LFCC) by **7.7 %** and **5.14 %**, respectively. The noise robustness characteristics of MGDCC were tested on stationary and non-stationary noise and the results were promising. The latency period was also analysed and MGDCC proved to be the most practically suitable feature.

Keywords: Speech Emotion Recognition · Narrowband Spectrogram · Group Delay Function · Modified Group Delay · EmoDB · Vocal Tract Features

1 Introduction

The easiest and most effective way of communication is through speech and the emotional aspect of speech is what leads to effective interpersonal communication. One can infer someone's emotions using facial expressions [1], speech [2], body language [3], etc. To that effect, this work focuses on emotion detection using *only* speech signals. As important as it is, it comes with its own challenges as well [4]. After examining emotions, their causes, and their effects, researchers have categorised them using a 4-D model, where each dimension-duration, quality, intensity, and pleasure-is distinct from the others [5].

The increasing technological advancements have led to a commensurate growth in human reliance on machines. Notably, the distinction between human-human interaction and human-machine interaction lies in the absence of emotional elements in the latter. This aspect has prompted the emergence of a novel research domain, namely, Speech Emotion Recognition (SER). Its applications include monitoring patients, call centre services [6], analysing driver's behaviour, etc.

© The Author(s), under exclusive license to Springer Nature Switzerland AG 2023
P. Maji et al. (Eds.): PReMI 2023, LNCS 14301, pp. 321–330, 2023.
https://doi.org/10.1007/978-3-031-45170-6_33

Characteristics related to prosody, such as pitch, fundamental frequency (F_0), pitch frequency, duration, energy, and others, are widely employed for SER in the literature [7]. Nonetheless, these features are limited to characterizing only the vocal folds state. Therefore, incorporating a feature that characterizes both the vocal tract and vocal fold state would enhance the emotion classification performance.

This paper explores the applicability of phase spectrum in SER due to its demonstrated effectiveness in speech recognition [8] and source/system information extraction [9]. To extract intricate details from the spectral envelope, the study employs group delay and modified group delay functions, which have been found to capture system information more effectively than the magnitude or Linear Prediction (LP) spectrum. The robustness of these proposed features is also tested with state-of-the-art features used for SER.

2   Phase Based Features

Extracting phase-based features is a challenging task since the phase spectrum is discontinuous in the frequency domain. For the phase to be used, it has to be unwrapped to make it a continuous function, however, the phase unwrapping technique is computationally complex due to the non-uniqueness associated with it. On the other hand, the group delay and modified group delay techniques have similar properties to the unwrapped phase and are known to be extracted directly from the signal [10].

2.1   Group Delay and Modified Group Delay Functions

The group delay function is characterized as the negative derivative of the unwrapped Fourier transform phase. It is also possible to compute the group delay of the signal p(n) from the signal itself using the following method-

$$T_m(\omega) = -Im\frac{d(P(\omega))}{d\omega}, \tag{1}$$

upon solving the Eq. (1) as stated in [10], we arrive at:

$$T_m(\omega) = \frac{P_R(\omega)Q_R(\omega) + P_I(\omega)Q_I(\omega)}{|P(\omega)|^2}. \tag{2}$$

where $P(\omega)$ and $Q(\omega)$ are Fourier transforms of $p(n)$ and $np(n)$, respectively. The $P_R(\omega)$ and $P_I(\omega)$ indicates the real and imaginary parts of $p(\omega)$, respectively. The representation of the group delay function using cepstral coefficients is given by [11]:

$$T_m(\omega) = \sum_{n=1}^{+\infty} nc(n)cos(n\omega), \tag{3}$$

where $c(n)$ indicates the n-dimensional cepstral coefficients. This operation is replicated by applying Discrete Cosine Transform (DCT). The two most important properties of group delay feature that gives them an edge compared to magnitude-based features are **additivity** and **high resolution**. Nevertheless, despite the numerous advantages it offers, the group delay function can be effectively applied in speech processing tasks only when the signal satisfies the *minimum phase* condition. If the signal is a non-minimum phase, the presence of the roots of the Z-transformed signal outside (or) close to the unit circle gives rise to the spikes in the group delay spectrum causing distortion of the fine structure of the envelope contributed by the vocal tract system and masking the formant location [11]. These spikes are due to a smaller denominator term in Eq. (2) indicating that the distance between the corresponding zero location and the frequency bin on the unit circle is small.

Any meaningful use of the phase-based features comes with the reduction of inadvertent spikes due to the smaller denominator value in Eq. (2). One such representation is the **modified group delay function (MODGF)** introduced to maintain the dynamic range of the group delay spectrum. The MODGF is given by [11]:

$$T_m(\omega) = \frac{T(\omega)}{|T(\omega)|}|T(\omega)|^\alpha, \tag{4}$$

where

$$T(\omega) = \frac{P_R(\omega)Q_R(\omega) + P_I(\omega)Q_I(\omega)}{|S(\omega)|^{2\gamma}}, \tag{5}$$

where $S(\omega)$ represents the cepstrally-smoothed version of $|P(\omega)|$. It was seen that introducing $|S(\omega)|$, very low values can be avoided. The parameters α and γ are introduced to reduce the spikes and restore the dynamic of the speech spectrum, respectively. Both parameters α and γ vary from 0 to 1. In order to obtain the cepstral coefficients, DCT is applied to convert the spectrum to cepstral features. The first coefficient of the cepstral coefficients is ignored as this value corresponds to the average value in the GDF. Including the effect of linear phase due to window and location of pitch peaks w.r.t window, the importance of the value is yet to be explored [11].

2.2   Robustness of Modified Group Delay Function

In this section, we demonstrate the resilience of the modified group delay function to additive noise through analytical means. Let $u(n)$ represent a clean speech signal, which has been degraded by the addition of uncorrelated, additive noise $v(n)$ with zero mean and variance σ^2. The resulting noisy speech $c(n)$ can be represented as follows:

$$c(n) = u(n) + v(n). \tag{6}$$

Taking the Fourier Transform and obtaining the power spectrum, we have,

$$P_c(\omega) = P_u(\omega) + P_v(\omega). \tag{7}$$

Considering low SNR situation, we have:

$$P_c(\omega) = \sigma^2(\omega)(1 + \frac{P_u(\omega)}{\sigma^2(\omega)}). \tag{8}$$

Taking the logarithm on both sides and using the Taylor series expansion results in:

$$ln(P_c(\omega)) \approx ln(\sigma^2(\omega)) + \frac{P_u(\omega)}{\sigma^2(\omega)}. \tag{9}$$

Since $P_u(\omega)$ is a continuous, periodic function of ω, it can be expanded using the Fourier series, we get:

$$ln(P_c(\omega)) \approx ln(\sigma^2(\omega)) + \frac{1}{\sigma^2(\omega)}\left[\frac{d_0}{2} + \sum_{k=1}^{+\infty} d_k cos(\frac{2\pi}{\omega_0}\omega k)\right]. \tag{10}$$

where d_k's are the Fourier series coefficients. Since $P_u(\omega)$ is an even function of ω, the coefficients of sine terms are zero. Assuming the additive noise as a minimum phase signal [11], we can obtain the cepstral coefficients as [12]:

$$T_c(\omega) \approx \frac{1}{\sigma^2(\omega)}\sum_{k=1}^{+\infty} k d_k cos(\omega k). \tag{11}$$

Eq. (11) reveals that the group delay function exhibits an inverse relationship with the noise power in regions where the noise power surpasses the signal power. For the high SNR case, upon repeating the Eq. (7)-Eq.(11), we arrive at the conclusion indicating that the group delay function is directly proportional to the signal power [12]. This conveys that the group delay spectrum follows the envelope of the signal rather than that of noise. Hence, it preserves the formant peaks well in presence of additive noise [12].

3   Experimental Setup

3.1   Dataset Details

The present study employed the widely-used EmoDB dataset, developed in 2005, to assess the performance of phase based features on SER. EmoDB is a German speech corpus comprising ten actors (5 Male and 5 Female), who uttered ten German phrases under favorable recording conditions, expressing seven emotions, namely anger, joy, neutral, sadness, disgust, boredom, and fear [13]. The current investigation focused on four emotions, namely anger, happiness, neutrality, and sadness, with one male speaker reserved for test.

3.2   Classifier Used

The utilization of deep learning models, specifically Convolutional Neural Networks (CNN), has become prominent in SER, leading us to apply the same for MGDCC. Our model comprises of 2 convolution layers with filter sizes of *8* and

16, respectively. To mitigate the issue of vanishing gradients and reduce computational complexity, we employ the Rectified Linear Unit (ReLU) activation function. The kernel size considered is (3×3). A dropout layer of *0.2*, strides of *2*, and learning rate at *0.001* is employed. *5* fold cross-validation split of *80%* and *20%* for train and test, *adam* optimizer and *categorical cross entropy* as loss function and *accuracy* as evaluation metrics is used.

3.3 Baseline Considered

The state-of-the-art features, Mel Frequency Cepstral Coefficients (MFCC) and Linear Frequency Cepstral Coefficients (LFCC) are used for comparison. To maintain uniformity among features, *20*-D feature vectors with a window length of *25* ms and a hop length of *10* ms is used for all.

4   Experimental Results

To restore the dynamic range of phase based features, MGDCC has two additional constraint parameters, alpha (α), and gamma (γ). The CNN classifier is used to fine-tune these parameters by varying them from 0 to 1 with a step size of *0.1*. The optimal parameters thus found by classification accuracy is $\alpha = \mathbf{0.1}$, $\gamma = \mathbf{0.1}$.

4.1   Spectrographic Analysis

Panel-A, Panel-B, and Panel-C of Fig. 1 represent the Spectrogram, Mel Spectrogram, and MGDCC-gram analysis of various emotions, respectively. Figure 1(a), Fig. 1(b), Fig. 1(c), and Fig. 1(d) show the analysis for anger, happy, sad, and neutral, respectively. Mel spectrograms give broaden and dull representation of utterance and thus have obstructed the ability to identify the fine formant structures and energy distribution. It can be observed from the plots that the fine structure of the formants that can be observed in the magnitude spectrum (Panel-A) can also be seen in the spectrogram obtained by the modified group delay spectrum. Hence, there is no information loss while using phase-based cepstral coefficients. Additionally, the resolution between the formants is high in the phase-based, i.e., modified group delay spectrum resulting in a better distinction among the formants. This is due to the fact that the denominator term at the formant frequencies becomes 0 (as the pole radius approaches to unit circle) resulting in peaks that give a higher resolution formants. Additionally, phase features are able to capture irregularities in the speech signal. The presence of turbulence in a speech signal changes with emotion and these irregularities are captured better through phase signal rather than the magnitude spectrum (Fig. 2).

326   S. Uthiraa et al.

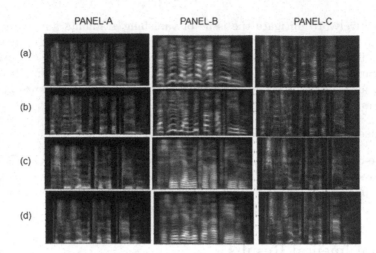

Fig. 1. Panel-A, Panel-B, and Panel-C represent the Spectrograms *vs.* Mel Spectrograms *vs.* MGD spectrogram of a male speaker uttering the same sentence in emotions-(a) anger, (b) happy, (c) sad, and (d) neutral, respectively

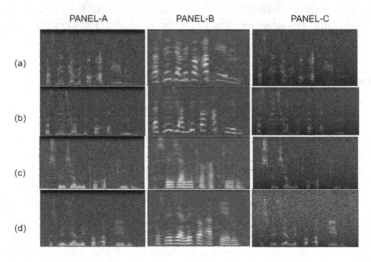

Fig. 2. Panel-A, Panel-B, and Panel-C represent the Spectrograms *vs.* Mel Spectrograms *vs.* MGD spectrogram of white noise added speech of a male speaker uttering the same sentence in emotions- (a) anger, (b) happy, (c) sad, and (d) neutal, respectively

4.2   Comparision with Baseline Features

From Table 1, it can be observed that LFCC is the best-performing baseline feature. The MGDCC feature outperforms the magnitude-based features i.e., MFCC and LFCC by a margin of **7.7**% and **5.14** %, respectively. This might be because of the high-resolution property of the modified group delay function which can be noticed in Fig 1. They capture the fine structures of spectral envelope and thus formant structures are emphasized well. However, GDCC fails to achieve similar performance. This is because of the noisy structure resulting from the GDCC occurring from the presence of zeros close to or outside the unit circle. These spikes cause formant masking, making it difficult to obtain valuable features for the classification task. It is also observed LFCC captures emotion information well in higher frequency regions as compared to MFCCs as in MFCC, the width of the triangular filters increases with frequency and thus, ignoring fine details (Sect. 4.1). The emotions, in particular, anger and happy operate in higher frequency regions, which is captured better by LFCC due to constant difference between the width of filterbanks throughout.

Table 1. Classification Accuracy on CNN

Feature Set	MFCC	LFCC	GDCC	MGDCC
Test Acccuracy	71.79	74.35	56.41	**79.49**

4.3 Robustness Under Signal Degradation

The robustness of the proposed features is tested using various noise types, such as white, pink, babble, and street noise with SNR levels of -10 dB, -5 dB, 0 dB, 5 dB, 10 dB, and 15 dB. When we consider additive white noise for evaluation, due to the nature of AWGN, the noise is distributed across all the bands of frequency. From Table 2, at the low SNR values, MGDCC clearly outperforms both magnitude-based features, MFCC and LFCC by a significant margin of **3.41 %**, **10.25 %**, respectively. Similarly, at higher SNR values, MGDCC outperforms baseline features MFCC and LFCC by **17.95 %**, **7.79 %**, respectively. Considering that the signal is degraded by the pink noise, which has higher noise power in lower frequencies rather than the higher frequencies, the MGDCC feature set outperforms both MFCC and LFCC features. Additionally, when considered non-stationary noises (noises which vary w.r.t time) such as street noise or traffic noise and babble noise are considered. The MGDCC noise robustness is evident in any kind of noise. Based on these findings, it can be inferred that the performance of the baseline features is degraded in the presence of stationary and non-stationary noise, whereas the performance of MGDCC remains intact across various noise types. These results prove the additive noise robustness property, and also that the emphasis of the group delay spectrum on the signal spectrum, rather than the noise spectrum, is a well-known characteristic. This can also be attributed to the nature of the MGDCC feature set pushes the zeros into the unit circle in an attempt of making the signal a minimum phase, which may also help in the suppression of noise. Additionally, it can be noted that LFCC and MFCC are not equally robust in white noise as the energy in higher frequency speech regions is weak making it more susceptible to noise corruption. The LFCC contains more subband filters at higher frequencies than MFCC, making it less robust to white noise. As the noise power decreases, the LFCC feature set still outperforms MFCC due to its linearly-spaced subband filters instead of the Mel filterbank. This reasoning also explains the comparable performance of MFCC to LFCC, when the signal is corrupted with pink noise.

Table 2. Classification Accuracy on CNN with different noise types on EmoDB

NOISE	FEATURE	−10 dB	−5 dB	0 dB	5 dB	10 dB	15dB
Babble	MGDCC	79.48	81.29	82.05	81.66	81.66	82.66
	MFCC	74.35	76	79.48	79.48	79.48	79.48
	LFCC	61.53	66.66	79.48	76.92	79.48	79.48
Street	MGDCC	75.35	80	81.66	81.66	71.79	86.66
	MFCC	74.35	76	76.92	79.48	88.48	82.05
	LFCC	74.35	70.23	79.48	71.79	76.92	79.48
White	MGDCC	76.92	79.48	74.35	71.79	76.92	74.35
	MFCC	69.23	76.92	74.35	43.58	82.05	43.58
	LFCC	71.79	64.10	64.10	58.97	71.79	69.23
Pink	MGDCC	74.35	69.23	71.79	71.79	71.79	74.35
	MFCC	41.79	38.46	41.02	43.58	70.35	71.79
	LFCC	71.79	66.66	66.66	61.53	71.79	71.79

4.4 Analysis of Latency Period

In this study, we explored the latency period of MGDCC feature set in comparison to the baseline features, i.e., MFCC and LFCC. To evaluate the performance of CNN based on different feature sets, we measured the accuracy % with respect to latency period, as depicted in Fig. 3. The latency period denotes the time elapsed between the utterance of speech and the system's response, expressed as a percentage fold accuracy that represents the number of frames utilized for utterance classification. Therefore, if the system demonstrates superior performance at lower latency periods, it implies that it can classify the speech utterance effectively without requiring a prolonged duration of speech. The duration of utterance is upto *3* s and is plotted at an interval of *0.5* s. It is observed that MGDCC features give significant classification performance throughout, the highest accuracy being *79.48* % at 1.5 s (Fig. 3). On the contrary, the baseline features constantly down-perform and take longer duration to achieve comparable performance. This encourages the practical suitability of proposed MGDCC feature set.

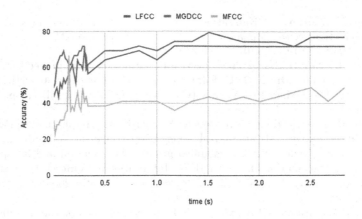

Fig. 3. Latency Period of MFCC, LFCC, and MGDCC.

5   Summary and Conclusions

In this study, phase-based vocal tract features were proposed for emotion recognition. Other spectral features MFCC and LFCC were used for comparison. The objective was to capture the irregularities in speech signal and the formant structure better for efficient SER. MGDCC also proved to perform well for stationary and non-stationary noise-added dataset due to its additive noise robustness property. The significance of linear filterbanks over Mel filterbanks was observed for emotion classification. The practical suitability of MGDCC was also calculated and promising results were seen. Further, this work can be extended by testing the robustness of convolution-type noise and its performance in SER for the mentally challenged.

References

1. Tarnowski, P., Kołodziej, M., Majkowski, A., Rak, R.J.: Emotion recognition using facial expressions. Procedia Comput. Sci. **108**, 1175–1184 (2017)
2. Basu, S., Chakraborty, J., Bag, A., Aftabuddin, M.: A review on emotion recognition using speech. In: 2017 International Conference on Inventive Communication and Computational Technologies (ICICCT), pp. 109–114. IEEE (2017)
3. Abramson, L., Petranker, R., Marom, I., Aviezer, H.: Social interaction context shapes emotion recognition through body language, not facial expressions. Emotion **21**(3), 557 (2021)
4. Khalil, R.A., Jones, E., Babar, M.I., Jan, T., Zafar, M.H., Alhussain, T.: Speech emotion recognition using deep learning techniques: a review. IEEE Access **7**, 117327–117345 (2019)
5. Cabanac, M.: What is emotion? Behav. Proc. **60**(2), 69–83 (2002)
6. Sethu, V., Ambikairajah, E., Epps, J.: Group delay features for emotion detection. In: Eighth Annual Conference of the International Speech Communication Association (2007)

7. Swain, M., Routray, A., Kabisatpathy, P.: Databases, features and classifiers for speech emotion recognition: a review. Int. J. Speech Technol. **21**(1), 93–120 (2018). https://doi.org/10.1007/s10772-018-9491-z
8. Schluter, R., Ney, H.: Using phase spectrum information for improved speech recognition performance. In: 2001 IEEE International Conference on Acoustics, Speech, and Signal Processing. Proceedings (Cat. No. 01CH37221), vol. 1, pp. 133–136. IEEE (2001)
9. Murthy, H.A.: Algorithms for processing Fourier transform phase of signals, Ph.D. dissertation, Indian Institute of Technology, Department of Computer ... (1992)
10. Murthy, H.A., Gadde, V.: The modified group delay function and its application to phoneme recognition. In: 2003 IEEE International Conference on Acoustics, Speech, and Signal Processing, 2003. Proceedings. (ICASSP 2003), vol. 1, pp. I-68. IEEE (2003)
11. Hegde, R.M., Murthy, H.A., Gadde, V.R.R.: Significance of the modified group delay feature in speech recognition. IEEE Trans. Audio Speech Lang. Process. **15**(1), 190–202 (2006)
12. Parthasarathi, S.H.K., Rajan, P., Murthy, H.A.: Robustness of group delay representations for noisy speech signals. Technical report, Idiap (2011)
13. Burkhardt, F., Paeschke, A., Rolfes, M., Sendlmeier, W.F., Weiss, B.: A database of German emotional speech. In: Interspeech, vol. 5, pp. 1517–1520 (2005)

Formal Concept Analysis for Evaluating Intrinsic Dimension of a Natural Language

Sergei O. Kuznetsov⊙, Vasilii A. Gromov⊙, Nikita S. Borodin$^{(\boxtimes)}$⊙,
and Andrei M. Divavin

HSE University, Moscow 109028, Russia
borodinik.s@gmail.com

Abstract. Some results of a computational experiment for determining the intrinsic dimension of linguistic varieties for the Bengali and Russian languages are presented. At the same time, both sets of words and sets of bigrams in these languages were considered separately. The method used to solve this problem was based on formal concept analysis algorithms. It was found that the intrinsic dimensions of these languages are significantly less than the dimensions used in popular neural network models in natural language processing.

Keywords: Intrinsic dimension · Formal concept analysis · Language manifold

1 Introduction

The emergence of methods for representing words and n-grams of a natural language as real-valued vectors (embeddings) allows one to ask about the definition of *intrinsic dimensions* of sets of words and bigrams observed in a given natural language. As a manifestation of the concept of intrinsic dimensions, let us consider a sphere, which is a two-dimensional object, where every point is given by two coordinates - latitude and longitude. Being embedded in three-, five- and ten-dimensional space, it will be given by a set of vectors, respectively, with three, five and ten coordinates, however, but it will remain a two-dimensional object, and its intrinsic dimension will be equal to two. The problem of intrinsic dimension is important from the practical point of view: its solution will allow one to judge the appropriateness of using very large vectors of embeddings (first of all, neural network models like BERT, etc.) in NLP domain.

2 Related Work

Turning to methods for estimating the intrinsic dimension, we note, first of all, the work of V. Pestov on intrinsic dimension of a dataset [17], where the

P. Maji et al. (Eds.): PReMI 2023, LNCS 14301, pp. 331–339, 2023.
https://doi.org/10.1007/978-3-031-45170-6_34

requirements for the definition of intrinsic dimension and methods for obtaining it were formulated. The introduced axiomatics is based on the results of M. Gromov [9].

It seems to us that the approaches known from the literature can be divided into three large classes: methods using a method for estimating the dimension of the strange attractor [12]; graph-based methods [4,5,14]; methods based to one or another variant of persistent homology analysis [20]. Let us take a look at the three above approaches.

First of all, among the works related to the establishment of the dimensions of the strange attractor we note a classical monograph by Kantz and Schreider [12]. It considers a set of classical approaches to the definition of the concept dimension of a strange attractor (topological, Hausdorff, spectrum, generalized entropy dimensions, etc.) and methods for their evaluation. Unfortunately, the classical approaches to determining the dimension of the strange attractors suffer from two disadvantages: firstly, they usually require very significant computing power and, secondly, are often non-robust with respect to sample changes. These circumstances necessitated creation of a new generation of methods for estimating the intrinsic dimension.

Kozma et al. [14] proposed a method of estimating the upper box dimension using a minimum spanning tree and statistics based on it. J.A. Costa et al. [4] and A. Farahmand et al. [5] in numerous papers have developed the idea of estimating intrinsic dimension by examining nearest neighbor graphs. In 2013 M.R. Brito et al. [3] proposed an approach based on nearest neighbor graph (KNN), minimum weight spanning tree (MST) and sphere of influence (SOI) analysis to determine the Euclidean dimension of i.i.d. geometric dataset.

Adams et al. [1] suggested a way to computing intrinsic dimension using persistent homology (Persistent homology dimension). The idea is to investigate the properties of random variables of the following form:

$$E_\alpha^i(x_1, \ldots, x_n) = \sum_{I \in PH_i(x_1, \ldots, x_n)} |I|^\alpha, \tag{1}$$

where $\{x_j\}_{j \in \mathbb{N}}$ are i.i.d. samples from a probability measure on a metric space, $PH_i(x_1, \ldots, x_n)$ denotes the i-dimensional reduced persistent homology of the Čech or Vietoris-Rips complex of $\{x_1, \ldots, x_n\}$, and $|I|$ is the length of a persistent homology interval. Schweinhart [20] carried out a rigorous formal analysis of this estimates, its connection is established with the upper box dimension. Jaquette and Schweinhart extended the methodology to the case of fractal systems, characterized by non-integer dimensions.

We also note a stand-alone work [11], based on the concept of distance between metric spaces, introduced by M.Gromov [9] and formal concept analysis [6,15].

3 Main Definitions and Problem Statement

3.1 Formal Concept Analysis and Pattern Structures

Here we give basic definitions and facts related to Formal Concept Analysis [15] and Pattern structures from [6].

In basic FCA binary data are given by a *formal context* $K = (G, M, I)$, where G is the set of objects, M is the set of (binary) attributes, and I is a incidence relation between objects and attributes: $I \subseteq G \times M$.

Derivation (prime) operators $(\cdot)'$ are defined as follows: A' gives the subset of all attributes shared by all objects from $A \subseteq G$. Similarly, B' gives the subset of all objects having all attributes from $B \subseteq M$.

$$A' = \{m \in M \mid \forall g \in A : gIm\}, \qquad (2)$$
$$B' = \{g \in G \mid \forall m \in B : gIm\}, \qquad (3)$$

A *formal concept* is a pair (A, B) of subsets of objects A and attributes B, such that $A = B'$, and $B = A'$.

The generality order $\leq$ on concepts is defined as follows:

$$(A_1, B_1) \leq (A_2, B_2) \text{if} A_1 \subseteq A_2 (\Leftrightarrow B_2 \subseteq B_1).$$

The set of all concepts makes an algebraic lattice, called *concept lattice*, w.r.t. the partial order $\leq$, so that every two concepts have supremum and infimum w.r.t. $\leq$.

Pattern structures [6,15] propose a generalization of FCA so that objects, instead of sets of binary attributes, can be described by complex descriptions, the set of which is ordered w.r.t. subsumption (containment) relation.

Let G be a set of objects, let $(D, \sqcap)$ be a meet-semilattice of *descriptions*, and let $\delta : G \to D$ be a mapping that assigns a description to each object from G. Then $(G, \underline{D}, \delta)$, where $\underline{D} = (D, \sqcap)$; is called a *pattern structure* w.r.t. "similarity operation" $\sqcap$, provided that the set $\delta(G) := \{\delta(g) \mid g \in G\}$ generates a complete subsemilattice $(D_\delta, \sqcap)$ of $(D, \sqcap)$, i.e., every subset X of $\delta(G)$ has an infimum $\sqcap X$ in $(D, \sqcap)$ and D_δ is the set of these infima.

If $(G, \underline{D}, \delta)$ is a pattern structure, the *derivation (prime) operators* are defined as

$$A^\diamond := \underset{g \in A}{\sqcap} \delta(g) \text{ for all } A \subseteq G$$

$$d^\diamond := \{g \in G \mid d \sqsubseteq \delta(g)\} \text{ for all } d \in D$$

The set D is partially ordered w.r.t. the following *subsumption* relation:

$$c \sqsubseteq d: \iff c \sqcap d = c$$

A *pattern concept* of $(G, \underline{D}, \delta)$ is a pair (A, d) satisfying

$$A \subseteq G, d \in D, A^\diamond = d \text{ and } A = d^\diamond$$

The set of all pattern concepts forms the *pattern concept lattice*.

In this paper we will use interval pattern structure [13,15], an important case of pattern structures where descriptions from D are tuples of closed numerical intervals of the form $[s,t]$, $s,t \in \mathbb{N}$ and the similarity operation on two interval tuples is given component-wise as their convex hull:

$$[s,t] \sqcap [q,r] = [\min\{s,q\}, \max\{t,r\}].$$

The intuition of this definition is explained by interpreting numerical intervals as uncertainty intervals, so that their similarity is a minimal convex cover of both uncertainties.

3.2 Intrinsic Data Dimension and Problem Statement

In Hanika et al. [11], the authors suggest using approaches based on Gromov's metric [9] and Pestov's axiomatic approach [18] to estimate the intrinsic dimension of data. So, given tabular data in the form of a formal context $\mathbb{K} = (G, M, I)$ and measures ν_G, ν_M on sets G and M of objects and attributes, respectively, the complexity of the dataset (called *observed diameter*) is defined as

$$Diam(\mathbb{K}, \alpha) = \max\{\nu_G(A) \mid (A, B) \in \mathfrak{B}(\mathbb{K}), \alpha < \nu_M(B) < 1 - \alpha\}, \quad (4)$$

where α is a parameter. If datatable is not binary, but e.g., given by an interval pattern structure $\mathbb{PS}$, then this definition can be extended as follows:

$$Diam(\mathbb{PS}, \alpha) = \max\{\nu_G(A) \mid (A, d) \in \mathfrak{B}(\mathbb{PS}), \alpha < \nu_M(d) < 1 - \alpha\}, \quad (5)$$

where α is a parameter. A natural specification of the general form of ν_M in this definition would be

$$\sum_{i \in M} \nu_i \cdot \mathbb{K}_{(y_i - x_i) \leq \theta},$$

where $[x_i, y_i]$ is the ith interval component of tuple d, ν_i is the measure (weight) associated to attribute $i \in M$, and θ is a parameter.

The intrinsic dimension of the context (dataset) is then defined as follows:

$$Dim(\mathbb{K}) = \left(\int_0^1 Diam(\mathbb{K}, \alpha)\, \delta\alpha \right)^{-2}, \quad (6)$$

Now the problem we solve in this paper can formally be stated as follows.

Given a set of natural language texts $C = \{T_1, \ldots, T_N\}$; $d \in \mathbb{N}$, the dimension of the embedding space; $n \in \mathbb{N}$, the number of words in n-grams (it is assumed that the set of texts C is a representative sample of texts of the corresponding natural language)

1. compute the sets $E_n(d), n \in \mathbb{N}$ of embeddings of texts from C, construct the set F of respective threshold binary attributes F, where $f(e) \in F$ means $e > 0$ for $e \in E_n(d)$,
2. compose the context $\mathbb{K} = (C, F, I)$, with the relation

$$I = \{(T, f(e)) \mid e(T) > 0 \text{ for embedding } e \text{ of text } T\},$$

3. calculate the approximate value of (6) by using the trapezoid method for integration:

$$Dim(\mathbb{K}; \ell) = \left(\frac{1}{2\ell} \sum_{i=1}^{\ell} \left[Diam\left(\mathbb{K}, \frac{i-1}{\ell}\right) + Diam\left(\mathbb{K}, \frac{i}{\ell}\right) \right] \right)^{-2}, \quad (7)$$

here ℓ is the number of intervals used for approximation.

4 Realization of the Model

4.1 Computing Data Dimension

To compute data dimension according to (7) one does not need to compute the set of all concepts, which can be exponentially large w.r.t. initial data. One can use the properties of monotonicity of measures ν_G and ν_M and antimonotonicity of prime operators $(\cdot)'$. The general idea of computing the observed diameter is as follows: start with largest possible concept extents (corresponding to one-element sets of attributes), which have largest ν_G measure, and decrease them until the measure ν_M of respective concept intents falls in the interval $[\alpha; 1 - \alpha]$.
More formally:

1. For every attribute $m \in M$ compute m' and m'', generating concepts (A, B), where $A = m'$, and $B = m''$.
2. If some of the generated concepts satisfy (4), take concept (A, B) with the largest $\nu_G(A)$ as the solution to the problem.
3. If there are no (A, B) satisfying (4), for every (A, B) generated so far compute $((B \cup \{n\})', (B \cup \{n\})''$, where $n \notin B$.
4. Iterate steps 1, 2 and 3 until solution is obtained for all given $\alpha_i \in \{\alpha\}_\ell \subseteq [0; 1]$.
5. Compute $Dim(\mathbb{K}; \ell)$.

Since the cardinality of intents are growing with every iteration of Steps 2 and 3, finally the process will attain intents satisfying $\alpha < \nu_M(B) < 1 - \alpha$. It is no need to go further by increasing intents, because with increasing intents, extents will decrease with no more chance to obtain a concept extent with the largest measure ν_G satisfying (4).
What is the computational complexity of first four steps for a single value of α? If $\alpha = 0$, then, by monotonicity of measure ν_G, the algorithm terminates at the first iteration of step 2 by outputting $\max \nu_G(m')$ for $m \in M$, which takes

$O(|M|)$ applications of prime operation $(\cdot)'$. If $\alpha \neq 0$, then one needs to generate intents with $\nu_M \leq \alpha$ until the subsequent generation in step 3 would produce intents with $\nu_M > \alpha$, so that the observed diameter would be the maximal ν_G of respective extents. For $\alpha > 0$ let $k(\alpha)$ denote the number of concepts (A, B) with $\alpha < \nu_M(B) < 1 - \alpha$. Then, applying the argument of "canonicity check" [16], one can show that the algorithm terminates upon $O(|M| \cdot k(\alpha))$ applications of $(\cdot)'$.

4.2 Preprocessing Text Corpora

To compute language dimensions we take standard open source Internet language corpora that represent national prose and poetry for Bengali, English and Russian languages. The preprocessing of corpora consists of several steps.

1) Removal of stop words: some words are found in large numbers in texts that affect a variety of subject areas and, often, are not in any way informative or contextual, like articles, conjunctions, interjections, introductory words;
2) Tokenization: other words can provide useful information only by their presence as a representative of a certain class, without specificity; good examples for tokenization are proper names, sentence separators, numerals;
3) Lemmatization: it is useful to reduce the variability of language units by reducing words to the initial form

Then we apply standard techniques based on tf-idf measure to select keyterms from obtained n-grams of the texts, so that every text in the corpus is converted to a set of keyterms and the text-keyterm matrix is generated. Upon this we apply SVD-decomposition of this matrix and select first high-weight components of the decomposition to obtain semantic vector-space of important features of the language and allow for computing respective embeddings of the texts from the corpus. This results in obtaining text-features matrix, which is originally numerical. Then the numerical matrix can be either converted to binary one by selecting value thresholds or treated directly by means of interval pattern structures described above.

5   Computer Experiments

We used the approach described above to estimate the intrinsic dimension of Russian, Bengali, and English languages. To do this, we form groups of sample sets of n-grams for different parameters n and d. Then, for each $n \in 1, 2$ (103952 and 14775439 Russian words and bigrams; 209108 and 13080621 for Bengali words and bigrams; 94087 and 9490603 English words and bigrams), we average the obtained intrinsic dimensions over d and round it to the nearest integer. We took the most obvious realization of the measures as $\nu_M(X) = |X|$ and $\nu_G(Y) = |Y|$. The results are presented in the Tables (1, 2) for 1,2-grams, respectively.

Table 1. Intrinsic dimension estimation for natural languages, n = 1.

Language	d	Intrinsic dimension
Bengali	5	6.2509
	8	5.2254
	14	4.7445
	20	4.5318
Russian	5	6.2505
	8	5.2308
	14	4.6470
	20	4.4438
English	5	6.2509
	8	5.2302
	14	4.6437
	20	4.4369

Table 2. Intrinsic dimension estimation for natural languages, n = 2.

Language	d	Intrinsic dimension
Bengali	5	5.6792
	8	5.6346
Russian	5	5.8327
	8	5.6610
English	5	5.4013
	8	5.6058

6   Conclusion and Future Directions

We have applied the combination of Formal Concept Analysis [15] with an approach based on M. Gromov metrics [9,11] to estimating intrinsic dimensions of linguistic structures with complex statistical characteristics. It is striking that for natural languages we observe very small values of intrinsic dimensions.

Namely, the indicated dimension was found to be ≈ 5 for all given languages. This fact allows us to conclude that the orders of intrinsic dimension are equal for the above languages.

Obvious directions for future research can be analysis of other definitions of language dimension; extending the list of languages for similar analysis, including languages from various language families.

Acknowledgement. The work of Sergei O. Kuznetsov was supported by the Russian Science Foundation under grant 22-11-00323 and performed at HSE University, Moscow, Russia.

References

1. Adams, H., et al.: A fractal dimension for measures via persistent homology. In: Baas, N.A., Carlsson, G.E., Quick, G., Szymik, M., Thaule, M. (eds.) Topological Data Analysis. AS, vol. 15, pp. 1–31. Springer, Cham (2020). https://doi.org/10. 1007/978-3-030-43408-3_1
2. Bellegarda, J.: Latent Semantic Mapping: Principles & Applications. Morgan & Claypool, New York (2007)
3. Brito, M., Quiroz, J., Yukich, E.: Intrinsic dimension identification via graph-theoretic methods. J. Multivar. Anal. **116**, 263–277 (2013)
4. Costa, J., Girotra, A., Hero, A.: Estimating local intrinsic dimension with k-nearest neighbor graphs. In: IEEE/SP 13th Workshop on Statistical Signal Processing, IEEE Conference Publication, pp. 417–422 (2005)
5. Farahmand, A., Szepesvári, C., Audibert, J.-Y.: Manifold-adaptive dimension estimation. In: Z. Ghahramani (Ed.), Proceedings of the 24th International Conference on Machine Learning, ACM, New York, pp. 265–272 (2007)
6. Ganter, B., Kuznetsov, S.O.: Pattern structures and their projections. In: Delugach, H.S., Stumme, G. (eds.) ICCS-ConceptStruct 2001. LNCS (LNAI), vol. 2120, pp. 129–142. Springer, Heidelberg (2001). https://doi.org/10.1007/3-540-44583-8_10
7. Ganter, B., Wille, R.: Formal Concept Analysis: Mathematical Foundations. Springer, Cham (1999). https://doi.org/10.1007/978-3-642-59830-2
8. Golub, G., Kahan, W.: Calculating the singular values and pseudo-inverse of a matrix. J. Soc. Ind. Appl. Math. Ser. B: Numer. Anal. **2**(2), 205–224 (1965)
9. Gromov, M.: Metric structures for Riemannian and non-Riemannian spaces. Transl. from the French by Sean Michael Bates. With appendices by M. Katz, P. Pansu, and S. Semmes. Edited by J. LaFontaine and P. Pansu. English, Boston, MA: Birkhäuser, pp. xix + 585 (1999)
10. Gromov, V., Migrina, A.: A language as a self-organized critical system. Complexity 9212538 (2017)
11. Hanika, T., Schneider, F., Stumme G.: Intrinsic dimension of geometric data sets. In: Tohoku Mathematical Journal (2018)
12. Kantz, H., Schreiber, T.: Nonlinear Time Series Analysis. Cambridge University Press, Cambridge (2004)
13. Kaytoue, M., Kuznetsov, S., Napoli, A., Duplessis, S.: Mining gene expression data with pattern structures in formal concept analysis. Inf. Sci. **181**(10), 1989–2001 (2011)
14. Kozma, G., Lotker, Z., Stupp, G.: The minimal spanning tree and the upper box dimension. Proc. Am. Math. Soc. **134**(4), 1183–1187 (2006)
15. Kuznetsov, S.O.: Pattern structures for analyzing complex data. In: Sakai, H., Chakraborty, M.K., Hassanien, A.E., Slezak, D., Zhu, W. (eds.) RSFDGrC 2009. LNCS (LNAI), vol. 5908, pp. 33–44. Springer, Heidelberg (2009). https://doi.org/ 10.1007/978-3-642-10646-0_4
16. Kuznetsov, S.: A fast algorithm for computing all intersections of objects from an arbitrary semilattice. Nauchno-Tekhnicheskaya Informatisya Ser. **2**, 17–20 (1993)
17. Pestov, V.: Intrinsic dimension of a dataset: what properties does one expect?. In: IJCNN, pp. 2959–2964 (2007)
18. Pestov, V.: An axiomatic approach to intrinsic dimension of a dataset. Neural Netw. **21**(2–3), 204–213 (2008)

19. Piantadosi, S.: Zipf's word frequency law in natural language: a critical review and future directions. Psychon. Bull. Rev. **21**(5), 1112-1130 (2014). https://www.ncbi. nlm.nih.gov/pubmed/?term=Piantadosi%20ST%5BAuthor%5D&cauthor=true& cauthor_uid=24664880Piantadosi.   https://www.ncbi.nlm.nih.gov/entrez/eutils/ elink.fcgi?dbfrom=pubmed&retmode=ref&cmd=prlinks&id=24664880
20. Schweinhart, B.: Fractal dimension and the persistent homology of random geometric complexes. Adv. Math. **372**, 107291 (2020). https://doi.org/10.1016/j.aim. 2020.107291
21. Shopen, T.: Language Typology and Syntactic Description: Volume 3 Grammatical Categories and the Lexicon, vol. 3. Cambridge University Press, Cambridge (2007)
22. Tanaka-Ishii, K.: Data. In: Statistical Universals of Language. MM, pp. 217–222. Springer, Cham (2021). https://doi.org/10.1007/978-3-030-59377-3_22

User Interest Drift Identification Using Contextual Factors in Implicit Feedback-Based Recommender Systems

Vinnakota Saran Chaitanya$^{(\boxtimes)}$, Sayali Deo, and P Santhi Thilagam

National Institute of Technology Karnataka, Surathkal, Mangalore, India
vsaranchaitanya@gmail.com, santhi@nitk.edu.in

Abstract. The modeling of appropriate recommendations using the session interactions in the implicit feedback-based recommender systems necessitates the identification of user interest drift. But this identification is challenging due to the presence of unintentional interactions (noise) made by the user. Most of the existing literature focused on understanding the correlation between ongoing session interactions but did not explore the contextual factors, such as the time of occurrence of the session and the item's popularity, that led the user to perform that specific interaction. This has resulted in the wrongful categorization of interactions between user interest drift and noise. To overcome these limitations, this work proposes a deep learning-based approach that uses both ongoing session information and contextual information. Depending on availability, this work also considers the user's previous interactions to generate personalized recommendations. In comparison with the existing works, this work effectively identifies the user interest drift and generates the appropriate recommendations for the users. The proposed approach demonstrates superior performance over state-of-the-art baselines in terms of Recall and MRR, as evidenced by experimental results on benchmark datasets.

Keywords: Recommender system · Session-based recommender system · Session-aware recommender system · User interest drift · noise

1 Introduction

Recommender Systems (RS) are software tools that recommend items of interest to users based on their preferences [1]. These preferences are obtained either implicitly or explicitly. Due to the massive availability of items online, implicit feedback-based systems have gained significance. The implicit feedback is obtained through user-item interactions made by the user in a session, where the session is a logical time period that makes up the session data. In essence, the session data consists of data such as the time stamp of the interaction and item details (item-id) that give the short-term (ongoing) preferences of the user [3].

© The Author(s), under exclusive license to Springer Nature Switzerland AG 2023
P. Maji et al. (Eds.): PReMI 2023, LNCS 14301, pp. 340–347, 2023.
https://doi.org/10.1007/978-3-031-45170-6_35

The dwell time, which is calculated by subtracting two consecutive start timestamps, is the length of time a user spends viewing an item. Session-Based Recommender Systems (SBRS) consider the intra-session data such as the session interactions and dwell time to generate recommendations for the users. The accurate identification of user preferences is essential to generate appropriate recommendations which is difficult due to less number of interactions or due to the presence of noisy (unintentional) interactions in the user clicks. Moreover, the preferences of the user might continuously change known as User Interest Drift (UID) [3].

Assume the following interactions on an e-commerce site by a user: pink color collarless t-shirt, yellow color collarless t-shirt, blue color collarless t-shirt, a TV set and a green color collarless t-shirt. Through sequential analysis of the user's clicks, it is understood that the user has interest toward t-shirts. But the fourth interaction is with the TV set. It can be interpreted as a noisy interaction made by the user due to its least correlation with the other interactions (t-shirt). But it also might be due to the UID by the user that cannot be accurately determined. Thus, it is essential and challenging to identify the UID and generate recommendations according to the ongoing user preferences of the user.

Dwell time can be used as an indicator to analyze the user's interest in an item and it exhibits direct proportionality to the user's interest, which helps to segregate an interaction as UID or noise [6]. But it is not necessary for a user to spend a long time viewing an item. Even in the case of the first scenario, it might be possible that the user might be interested in viewing a TV set if the user gets a better recommendation than what the user might have thought of previously.

Apart from the consideration of intra-session information, the inter-session data such as the user's long-term preferences (if the user logs in to the application) plays a significant role in UID identification. Session-Aware Recommender Systems (SARS) generate recommendations to the users by consideration of the ongoing preferences along with the previous session interactions of the user. Along with it, the consideration of contextual information obtained from inter-session data such as the time of the session's occurrence might also help to understand user preferences by rightly identifying UID. The time of session occurrence tells the user's preference towards that item irrespective of the correlation between the items.

Also, the user might exhibit their interest drift towards a popular (trending) item anytime during a session. The popularity here refers to an item that has a larger number of interactions at that point in time. But an item's popularity might be interesting to users at a specific point in time. However, it is not necessary that every user exhibit interest in the popular items.

Existing works in the literature have tried identifying the UID in different ways. The MBPI model proposed by Zhang et al. [4] has compared the ongoing session information with the ongoing parallel session to identify user preferences. The work by Bogina et al. [6] has used dwell time to identify users interests. The model identifies an interaction with a low dwell time as a noisy interaction. The

CASER model proposed by Tang et al. [5] uses sequential mining to understand user preference in the current session.

To overcome the above limitations, this work proposes a methodology known as the Contextual Factors-based RECommendation model (*CFREC*) that identifies UID based on both intra- and inter-session information. The intra-session information is passed to the GRU layer, The user's history are given as input to the GRU layer on availability. The inter-session information is passed to the convolutional layer to extract the significance of the current session using contextual factors. The two intermediate outputs are passed to the softmax function to give the final probabilities of items and generate recommendations. The use of the above said different parameters helps the *CFREC* model effectively capture the UID. The objectives of the work are to:

- Use contextual factors along with the session interactions to understand user preferences by distinguishing between UID and noise.
- Generate appropriate recommendations to users.

The paper's organization is as follows: Sect. 2 covers the related work, Sect. 3 presents the proposed methodology, and Sect. 4 discusses the results. The paper concludes in Sect. 5 by outlining future work.

2   Related Work

This section discusses the existing literature related to the detection of UID and generating recommendations.

Hidasi et al. [8] was the first one to introduce neural networks for the task of SBRS. This work proposed the use of Recurrent Neural Networks (RNN) for the task of recommendation generation in SBRS. The performance of RNN models depends on receiving a few interactions. The use of dwell time in generating recommendations was first explored by Bogina et al. [6] and later it was further explored by Dallman et al. as a measure of user interest. The CASER model by Tang has used past interactions along with the session data to generate recommendations. Chen et al. [7] have used the cross-session information along with the user's past interactions to model the recommendations. Zhang et al. [4] have considered ongoing neighborhood sessions to model the recommendations. Thus, it is evident that the existing literature was unable to segregate an interaction as UID or noise accurately. Thus, the proposed *CFREC* methodology overcomes the above limitation by considering the various inter and intra-session parameters.

3   Contextual Factors-Based Recommendation Model

The proposed Contextual Factors-based RECommendation model (*CFREC*) consists of four steps that are explained in the below sub-sections. The neural architecture of the proposed *CFREC* model is depicted in Fig. 1.

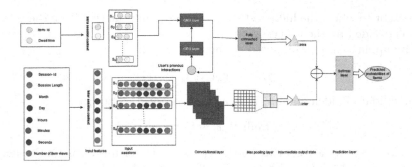

Fig. 1. Architecture of the proposed *CFREC* model

3.1   Input Construction

The input to the *CFREC* model consists of the raw session data that consists of user-item interactions of a session S_n in the form of $\{i_1, i_2, ..., i_n\}$. The sessions of length one are removed from the dataset as the model does not learn anything from the sessions of length one and sessions up to length 10 are considered. The input to the intra-session context module is the dwell time denoted as dt, and item-id (iid). Upon user login to the application, the previous user interactions are inputted.

The input to the inter-session context module is the session-id, session length, time of occurrence of the session, and the number of item interactions across all the sessions that gives the popularity of the item. The session length is calculated by adding up the individual dwell times of the items within a particular session and is measured in seconds. On the other hand, the inter-session context features make up a two-dimensional structure analogous to a 2D image with the intention of being passed into the convolutional layer. The date of session occurrence is further expanded into day, month, and year, while the time is split into hours, minutes, and seconds.

3.2   Intra-session Context Module

A gated Recurrent Unit (GRU) known for modeling sequential data is used to model the intra-session context embeddings. The *CFREC* model passes the intra-session context embeddings, and previous interactions (on availability) to the GRU_{intra} layer. The model consists of three hidden layers. The learning rate, batch size, and dropout are 0.01, 500, and 0.2 respectively.
Consider the sth session interactions made by user u_k. The event context embeddings are passed into the GRU layer one after another. The hidden state h_i of the GRU at the ith interaction x_i is obtained by linearly interpolating between the previous hidden state h_{i-1} and the candidate hidden state h'_i, as specified in Eq. 1.

$$h_i = z_i h_{i-1} + (1 - z_i)h'_i \tag{1}$$

The extent to which the hidden states updates its information from the previous state is decided by the update gate z_i.

The update gate is computed as shown in Eq. 2:

$$z_i = \sigma(w_z x_i + U_z h_{i-1}) \tag{2}$$

The candidate hidden state h_i' is computed as given in Eq. 3:

$$h_i' = \tanh(W x_i + U(r_i \oplus h_{i-1})) \tag{3}$$

Here r_i represents the reset gate and $\oplus$ represents the element-wise multiplication operator. x_i is the event-context embedding denoted as C_{eve}.

The reset gate r_i is computed in a similar manner to the update gate, as described in Eq. 4.

$$r_i = \sigma(W_r x_i + U_r h_{i-1}) \tag{4}$$

where W_z, U_z, W_r, and U_r are update matrices for the ith interaction x_i and the previous hidden state h_{i-1}. W and U are weight matrices. σ is the sigmoid function. Ultimately, the final hidden state h_n is used for updating the user context (C_{usr}) that updates the long-term preferences of the current user. At the start of the session, the user embeddings (usd_i) of the current user of the ith session is passed along with item embeddings in another GRU layer, say GRU_{usr}. This GRU_{usr} consists of weights that train upon the individual user's context and thus save the long-term preferences of the user within. This ensures that the user's preferences are updated after every session. The output of this is concatenated with the final hidden state h_n and fed into a fully connected layer for flattening into a high-level non-linear combination. This combination is represented by Δ_{intra} and is given in Eq. 5:

$$\Delta_{intra} = \sigma(W_{mn} * x_{ij} + b_i) \tag{5}$$

where W_{mn} are the weights of the fully connected layer and σ is the non-linearity introduced in this component. Δ_{intra} is then passed into the softmax layer for further consideration.

3.3 Inter-session Context Module

The convolution filters of Convolutional Neural Networks (CNN) are used to extract the spatial characteristics from the session features. In this approach, each I*d matrix formed from the session context is used as an image vector, where I is the number of I previous items and d is the number of dimensions in the C_{inter}. The C_{inter} consists of eight-dimensional session embeddings i.e. $< sid, sl, mm, dd, hr, min, ss, nov >$ which make up the columns of the image. In this case, the image comprises a single channel. The pre-nonlinearity input to the unit x_{ij}^l in the lth layer can be computed by taking the weighted sum of the contributions from the previous layer cells, as described in Eq. 6:

$$x_{ij}^l = \sum_{a=0}^{m-1} \sum_{b=0}^{m-1} w_{ab} y_{(i+a)(j+b)}^{l-1} \tag{6}$$

The next layer used is the max pooling layer. Following the application of the convolutional filter, max pooling is employed to extract significant features. Δ_{inter} represents the output of the max pooling layer as given in Eq. 7.

$$\Delta_{inter} = \sum_{k=1}^{n} p_k^{max}(x_{ij}^l) \tag{7}$$

3.4 Combination and Recommendation Generation

Δ_{intra} and Δ_{inter} are then aggregated together and passed into the softmax layer. Here, the softmax outputs a probabilistic distribution for each item in the form of Δ_{prob} where the size of Δ_{prob} is the aggregate quantity of items. Equation 8 presents the recommended set of items, determined based on their highest probabilities, which are then displayed to the users.

$$\Delta_{prob} = softmax(\Delta_{intra} + \Delta_{inter})$$

$$\Delta_{prob}[i] = \frac{e^{z_i}}{\sum_{j=1}^{k} e^{z_j}} \tag{8}$$

where $\Delta_{prob}[i]$ is the probability of item i and k is the total number of items.

4   Results and Discussion

The primary objective of the RS is to generate a list of items that the user would prefer to interact with. Mean Reciprocal Rank (MRR) and recall are the most frequently used evaluation metrics in the RS domain. The recommendation of the top K items from the list of items, where the value of K is taken as 20, is the standard accepted by most of the recent works. The *CFREC*'s model performance is evaluated using two benchmark datasets Xing and Retailrocket. The sessions of length above ten are removed as they form a negligible fraction of the dataset. The details of the datasets after preprocessing are presented in Table 1. The train and test split are in the ratio of 80 and 20.

Table 1. Dataset Description

Description	XING	Retailrocket
Number of items	20,775	70,849
Number of users	65,346	68,605
Total Sessions	5,38,601	4,89,971
Number of sessions having length>1 and length<10	5,03,592	4,48,323

The performance evaluation of the *CFREC* model is conducted by comparing it against several baselines. Among the non-neural network baselines, the Popularity Predictor (POP) and Factorizing Personalized Markov Chains (FPMC) are chosen. Additionally, neural network baselines such as the Mixed Behaviors and Preference Interaction (MBPI) model [4] and the Convolutional Sequence Embedding Recommendation Model (CASER) [5] are also selected. Furthermore, the performance of *CFREC* is individually assessed by considering its constituent components: the intra-session context (referred to as $CFREC_{intra}$) and the inter-session context (referred to as $CFREC_{inter}$) with the MBPI model, while the $CFREC_{inter}$ is compared with the CASER model, as these models share similar parameters. Table 2 shows this comparison.

Table 2. Comparison of *CFREC* model with the baselines

Baseline	XING		Retailrocket	
	RECALL	MRR	RECALL	MRR
POP	7.31 (**+65.53**)	0.84 (**+30.57**)	6.14 (**+68.62**)	0.69 (**+32.59**)
FPMC	35.9 (**+36.94**)	11.73 (**+19.68**)	40.44 (**+34.32**)	18.94 (**+14.34**)
MBPI (Zhang et al. [4])	52.01	24.87	51.73	21.74
$CFREC_{Intra}$	56.83 (**+4.82**)	25.12 (**+0.25**)	55.9 (**+4.17**)	24.32 (**+2.58**)
CASER (Tang et al. [5])	41.89	21.65	42.34	20.57
$CFREC_{Inter}$	61.12 (**+19.23**)	27.28 (**+5.63**)	63.17 (**+20.83**)	29.10(**+8.53**)
CFREC	**72.84**	**31.41**	**74.76**	**33.28**

The following observations are made from the results:

- The *CFREC* model clearly outperforms POP by a very large margin over the XING dataset. POP uses a very naive and traditional approach in which it recommends only the top-N most frequent items throughout the dataset. A similar trend is observed in the Retailrocket dataset, although the ratio of users to items is not very low.
- The *CFREC* model shows a clear improvement on both datasets compared to FPMC, though FPMC is known for the usage of Markov chains and matrix factorization that aim at capturing the adjacent sequential transitions between items. It is because the FPMC model lacks temporal dynamics, which cannot detect the change in user preferences appropriately.
- The intra-session context module of *CFREC* ($CFREC_{intra}$) provides better results than the MBPI model for both datasets on both metrics of MRR and Recall. This is because the passing of the user id as a separate input to the GRU layer enables the model to learn user preferences appropriately. The wrongful categorization of a user's preference change as noise in comparison with ongoing neighbor sessions can be observed in the MBPI model. This approach severely affects the quality of recommendations for users with unique tastes.
- $CFREC_{inter}$ module provides notable improvements over the CASER model on both datasets and on both metrics. This is because the CASER model

uses the item sequences and item ids alone to model the recommendations, while the $CFREC_{inter}$ model uses multiple session features along with item sequences that have proven beneficial for mapping onto convolutional filters.
– The overall model of $CFREC$ provides improvements over the existing as well as the proposed sub-modules ($CFREC_{inter}$ and $CFREC_{intra}$) over both the datasets. It's due to the usage of different parameters that enabled the $CFREC$ model to correctly identify the user preferences.

5   Conclusion

UID identification is essential in the generation of effective recommendations for users. This work proposed a model that uses contextual information along with both inter and intra-session information in understanding user preferences. The proposed model had been evaluated on benchmark datasets and had given better results. As part of future work, this work shall be extended to consider the ongoing neighbor sessions.

References

1. Ricci, F., Rokach, L., Shapira, B.: Introduction to recommender systems handbook. In: Ricci, F., Rokach, L., Shapira, B., Kantor, P.B. (eds.) Recommender Systems Handbook, pp. 1–35. Springer, Boston, MA (2011). https://doi.org/10.1007/978-0-387-85820-3_1
2. Lu, J., Dianshuang, W., Mao, M., Wang, W., Zhang, G.: Recommender system application developments: a survey. Decis. Support Syst. **74**, 12–32 (2015)
3. Wang, S., Cao, L., Wang, Y., Sheng, Q.Z., Orgun, M.A., Lian, D.: A survey on session-based recommender systems. ACM Comput. Surv. (CSUR) **54**(7), 1–38 (2021)
4. Zhang, J., Ma, C., Zhong, C., Mu, X., Wang, L.: MBPI: mixed behaviors and preference interaction for session-based recommendation. Appl. Intell. **51**(10), 7440–7452 (2021). https://doi.org/10.1007/s10489-021-02284-8
5. Tang, J., Wang, K.: Personalized top-n sequential recommendation via convolutional sequence embedding. In: Proceedings of the Eleventh ACM International Conference on Web Search and Data Mining, pp. 565–573 (2018)
6. Bogina, V., Kuflik, T.: Incorporating dwell time in session-based recommendations with recurrent neural networks. In: RecTemp@ RecSys, pp. 57–59 (2017)
7. Chen, T., Wong, R.C.W.: An efficient and effective framework for session-based social recommendation. In: Proceedings of the 14th ACM International Conference on Web Search and Data Mining (2021)
8. Hidasi, B., Karatzoglou, A., Baltrunas, L., Tikk, D.: Session-based recommendations with recurrent neural networks. arXiv preprint arXiv:1511.06939 (2015)

Spot the Bot: Coarse-Grained Partition of Semantic Paths for Bots and Humans

Vasilii A. Gromov[ID] and Alexandra S. Kogan[✉][ID]

National Research University Higher School of Economics,
Moscow, Russian Federation
stroller@rambler.ru, kogana00@gmail.com

Abstract. Nowadays, technology is rapidly advancing: bots are writing comments, articles, and reviews. Due to this fact, it is crucial to know if the text was written by a human or by a bot. This paper focuses on comparing structures of the coarse-grained partitions of semantic paths for human-written and bot-generated texts. We compare the clusterizations of datasets of n-grams from literary texts and texts generated by several bots. The hypothesis is that the structures and clusterizations are different. Our research supports the hypothesis. As the semantic structure may be different for different languages, we investigate Russian, English, German, and Vietnamese languages.

Keywords: Natural language processing · Clustering · bots

1 Introduction

The Internet is a rich source of information. However, not all the information is trustworthy. There are special programs (bots) whose main aim is to write spam, malicious content, fake news, or reviews. Consequently, it is crucial to know whether a particular text was written by a human or a bot.

The majority of modern research deals with a particular bot, but, as far as we know, there is no in-depth research on the semantic paths of natural language texts. Coarse-grained partition of semantic paths may help find the structure of «human» language, and detect text generated by various bots.

A semantic path is defined as a sequence of embeddings of the words of the text. To gain a coarse-grained partition we split the semantic path into n-grams, concatenate the corresponding vectors and apply a clustering algorithm.

The main idea is that humans and bots write using different n-grams ($n > 1$ because bots can use the same set of words as humans). Humans can produce more complex and «flowery» phrases while bots use more standard phrases and may be repetitive. Therefore the clusterizations will differ.

2 Related Works

There are a lot of papers devoted to bot detection. Many of them use metadata or/and interaction of accounts (authors of the texts) [4–6,14].

P. Maji et al. (Eds.): PReMI 2023, LNCS 14301, pp. 348–355, 2023.
https://doi.org/10.1007/978-3-031-45170-6_36

However, the problem statement when bot detection is based purely on texts seems to be more practicable. Various neural networks, such as BiLSTM [19], GPT [9], BERT [7], DDN [21], etc. Graph Convolutional Networks are widely used for detecting bots in social media [8,11]. Linguistic alignment can help detect bots in human-bot interactions [3].

In [10] language was investigated as a whole and it was shown that the number of words in the texts obeys power-law distribution, so it is possible to analyze «human» language not only on the level of particular texts.

In contrast to other research, our work is not focused on detecting a particular bot. We are trying to explore the structure of a natural language and use this structure to distinguish human-written and bot-generated texts.

3   Methodology

3.1   Corpora

We employ corpora of literary texts, because, from our point of view, literature is the clear reflection of the national language.

The methods for finding the structure of the language may differ for different languages or different families/branches, therefore we investigate several languages.

The majority of available datasets contain Wikipedia or news articles, blog posts, or only fragments of texts (the SVD embedding method requires full texts). Due to this fact, we collect corpora ourselves from open sources, such as Project Gutenberg[1].

The preprocessing includes lemmatization and tokenization. Also, pronouns, proper nouns, numbers, and determiners (in German) are replaced with special tokens. For preprocessing we use pretrained models[2].

The overview of corpora can be found in Table 1

Table 1. Overview of the corpora

Language	Family	Branch	number of texts	avg. size of text, words
Russian	Indo-European	Balto-Slavic	12692	1000
English	Indo-European	Germanic	11008	21000
German	Indo-European	Germanic	2300	25000
Vietnamese	Austroasiatic	Vietic	1071	55000

---

[1] https://www.gutenberg.org/.

[2] Russian https://github.com/natasha/natasha, English https://spacy.io/models/en (en_core_web_lg), German https://spacy.io/models/de (de_core_news_lg), Vietnamese https://github.com/trungtv/pyvi.

3.2 Bots

We employ 2 bots for every language: LSTM (trained on our corpora) and GPT-2/3 (pretrained).[3]

To generate texts similar to texts in the corpus, every 100th word in the literary text is used as a prompt for the model and about 100 words are generated.

3.3 Embeddings

We employ SVD [2] and Word2Vec[4] [17] embeddings. We train embeddings on our literary corpora.

The SVD embeddings rely on co-occurrences of the words in the texts, while Word2Vec ones (Skip-Gram, CBOW) take into account the local context.

3.4 Dataset Creation

To create a dataset we need:

- n - size of n-gram;
- R - size of the embedding;
- A corpus of preprocessed texts;
- A dictionary (a word and corresponding vector)

For every text in the corpus, all n-grams are investigated. For every word in the n-gram, the corresponding vector of size R is taken from the dictionary. The vector for n-gram is the concatenation of vectors of its words. The resulting dataset contains vectors for n-grams, which have size $R \times n$.

In this research $n = 2$, $R = 8$.

3.5 Clustering

The Wishart clustering technique[5] [20] was chosen during preliminary explorations (we compared several clustering techniques on synthetic datasets and dataset of literary texts).

Calinski-Harabasz index[6] (CH) [1] was chosen as a clustering metric in preliminary experiments.

However, the clusterization chosen via CH may not always be useful because of the enormous number of noise points. To decrease it we adjust the metric: $CH_{adj} = CH \times (ratio\_not\_noise)^T$, where T is a hyperparameter, and $ratio\_not\_noise$ is number of point not marked as noise divided by total number of points.

---

[3] GPT-2 for Russian https://huggingface.co/sberbank-ai/rugpt3large_based_on_gpt2, English https://huggingface.co/gpt2, German https://huggingface.co/dbmdz/german-gpt2 and GPT-3 for Vietnamese https://huggingface.co/NlpHUST/gpt-neo-vi-small.

[4] https://radimrehurek.com/gensim/models/word2vec.html.

[5] https://github.com/Radi4/BotDetection/blob/master/Wishart.py.

[6] https://scikit-learn.org/stable/modules/generated/sklearn.metrics.calinski_harabasz_score.html.

3.6 Comparing Clusterizations

To compare clusterizations of datasets corresponding to humans and bots, for every cluster metrics are computed. As a result, there are 2 arrays for every metric. The hypothesis that the arrays belong to the same distribution is tested.

We compute 8 metrics, their formulas and descriptions can be found in Table 2.

Notation

NC - number of clusters

C_i - cluster i

n_i - number of unique points in cluster i

$\overline{n}_i$ - total number of points (with duplicates) in cluster i

c_i - centroid of cluster i

Table 2. Metrics for clusters

№	description	formula
1	Number of unique vectors in the cluster Normalized by the size of the biggest cluster	$\xi_i = \frac{n_i}{max_{j=1}^{NC} n_j}$
2	Number of unique vectors in the cluster Normalized by the total number of unique vectors in the dataset	$\xi_i = \frac{n_i}{\sum_{j=1}^{NC} n_j}$
3	Number of vectors with duplicates in the cluster Normalized by the size (number of vectors with duplicates) of the biggest cluster	$\xi_i = \frac{\overline{n}_i}{max_{j=1}^{NC} \overline{n}_j}$
4	Number of vectors with duplicates in the cluster Normalized by the total number of vectors with duplicates in the dataset	$\xi_i = \frac{\overline{n}_i}{\sum_{j=1}^{NC} \overline{n}_j}$
5	Maximum distance to the centroid	$\xi_i = \max_{x \in C_i} d(x, c_i)$
6	Average distance to the centroid	$\xi_i = \frac{\sum_{x \in C_i} d(x, c_i)}{n_i}$
7	Maximum distance between points in the cluster	$\xi_i = \max_{x,y \in C_i, x \neq y} d(x, y)$
8	Average distance between points in the cluster	$\xi_i = \frac{\sum_{x,y \in C_i, x \neq y} d(x,y)}{n_i(n_i - 1)}$

To test the hypotheses the Mann-Whitney-Wilcoxon test[7] is used [16]. However, as the 8 hypotheses are tested, the multiple comparisons problem arises. To tackle it we employ the Holm-Bonferroni method[8] [12].

---

[7] https://docs.scipy.org/doc/scipy/reference/generated/scipy.stats.mannwhitneyu.html.

[8] https://www.statsmodels.org/dev/generated/statsmodels.stats.multitest.multipletests.html.

3.7 Taking the Subset

Clustering the big dataset (> 3 million points) is time- and memory-consuming. Hyperparameter optimization will be impossible. To handle this problem we conduct preliminary experiments on literary data using nested datasets ($D_1 \subset D_2 \subset ... \subset D_l$) to find the significantly lesser dataset which will be representative.

4 Results

For every language, we conduct separate experiments on all embeddings on our dataset (literary texts) to find the best number of unique points and the best T. See Table 3 for the final choices. .The numbers of unique points in datasets corresponding to bots are significantly lesser than in ones corresponding to humans, so the whole datasets are taken.

Let us stress that all the methods (Wishart technique, CH metric), and hyperparameters (R, n, T, size of the literary subsets) were chosen based on only literary data. The comparison with bot generated texts is the final step of the research.

Table 3. The number of points in literary texts and T for different languages

Language	Number of unique points	T
Russian	$\approx 650K$	2
English	$\approx 175K$	4
German	$\approx 400K$	2
Vietnamese	$\approx 700K$	2

The results of the comparison can be found in Table 4. For particular language, embedding and bot there are 2 numbers in the cell: the number of metrics (out of 8) with significant differences before and after correction for multiple testing.

The Skip-Gram embedding seems to be insufficient for the task as it fails to distinguish the clusterization of humans and bots for the majority of languages. The SVD works fine in Russian, and German, but is useless in the Vietnamese and English languages. The CBOW embedding shows the best results because it can spot the difference for all languages and all bots.

Table 4. Results of comparison. For all languages, embeddings, and bots.

Embedding \ Language	Russian		English		German		Vietnamese	
	LSTM	GPT2	LSTM	GPT2	LSTM	GPT2	LSTM	GPT3
SVD	5-3	5-4	2-0	3-0	4-4	4-4	2-0	0-0
CBOW	**3-1**	**6-4**	**8-8**	**6-6**	**4-2**	**7-7**	**6-4**	**4-4**
Skip-Gram	0-0	0-0	6-0	7-0	6-6	8-8	0-0	0-0

The t-SNE[9] visualization [15] for the Russian language the SVD and CBOW embeddings can be seen in Fig. 1 and Fig. 2 correspondingly. The pink (light gray in grayscale), and green (dark gray) colors correspond to LSTM and GPT-2 bots and black is the color for humans (literature). It can be seen, that for the SVD method, there is a giant cluster for both bots and humans, and for the CBOW embedding there are a lot of little clusters. We also can notice that there are «human» clusters that are remote from bot clusters and vice versa, but t-SNE visualization cannot provide enough evidence and additional experiments are required.

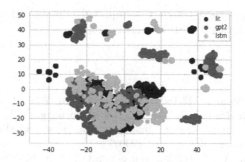

Fig. 1. t-SNE visualization of clusters. Language: Russian. Embedding: SVD

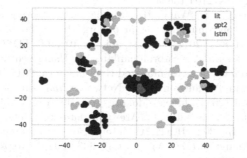

Fig. 2. t-SNE visualization of clusters. Language: Russian. Embedding: CBOW

5 Further Research

At this point, we have found differences between semantic paths for bots and humans while using a significant number of texts. We have not proposed a classifier for particular text yet. We plan to create a classifier with respect to results of this research.

---

[9] https://scikit-learn.org/stable/modules/generated/sklearn.manifold.TSNE.html.

We plan to investigate more advanced multilingual bots, such as mGPT [18] and more modern embeddings.

6 Conclusion

We can conclude that there are significant differences in coarse-grained partitions of semantic paths for bots and humans. We found them for all investigated languages and bots. The best results can be obtained using the CBOW embeddings.

Acknowledgments. This research was supported in part through computational resources of HPC facilities at HSE University [13].

References

1. Aggarwal, C.C., Reddy, C.K. (eds.): Data Clustering: Algorithms and Applications. CRC Press, Boca Raton (2014). http://www.charuaggarwal.net/clusterbook.pdf
2. Bellegarda, J.R.: Latent semantic mapping: principles & applications. Synth. Lect. Speech Audio Process. **3**(1), 1–101 (2007)
3. Bhatt, P., Rios, A.: Detecting bot-generated text by characterizing linguistic accommodation in human-bot interactions (2021). https://doi.org/10.48550/ARXIV.2106.01170, https://arxiv.org/abs/2106.01170
4. Chakraborty, M., Das, S., Mamidi, R.: Detection of fake users in SMPs using NLP and graph embeddings (2021). https://doi.org/10.48550/ARXIV.2104.13094, https://arxiv.org/abs/2104.13094
5. Chu, Z., Gianvecchio, S., Wang, H., Jajodia, S.: Detecting automation of twitter accounts: are you a human, bot, or cyborg? IEEE Trans. Dependable Secure Comput. **9**(6), 811–824 (2012). https://doi.org/10.1109/TDSC.2012.75
6. Dickerson, J.P., Kagan, V., Subrahmanian, V.: Using sentiment to detect bots on twitter: are humans more opinionated than bots? In: 2014 IEEE/ACM International Conference on Advances in Social Networks Analysis and Mining (ASONAM 2014), pp. 620–627 (2014). https://doi.org/10.1109/ASONAM.2014.6921650
7. Dukić, D., Keča, D., Stipić, D.: Are you human? Detecting bots on twitter using BERT. In: 2020 IEEE 7th International Conference on Data Science and Advanced Analytics (DSAA), pp. 631–636 (2020). https://doi.org/10.1109/DSAA49011.2020.00089
8. Feng, S., Wan, H., Wang, N., Luo, M.: BotRGCN. In: Proceedings of the 2021 IEEE/ACM International Conference on Advances in Social Networks Analysis and Mining. ACM (2021). https://doi.org/10.1145/3487351.3488336
9. Garcia-Silva, A., Berrio, C., Gomez-Perez, J.M.: Understanding transformers for bot detection in twitter (2021). https://doi.org/10.48550/ARXIV.2104.06182, https://arxiv.org/abs/2104.06182
10. Gromov, V.A., Migrina, A.M.: A Language as a self-organized critical system. Complexity **2017**, 1–7 (2017). https://doi.org/10.1155/2017/9212538, https://ideas.repec.org/a/hin/complx/9212538.html
11. Guo, Q., Xie, H., Li, Y., Ma, W., Zhang, C.: Social bots detection via fusing BERT and graph convolutional networks. Symmetry **14**(1), 30 (2022). https://doi.org/10.3390/sym14010030, https://www.mdpi.com/2073-8994/14/1/30

12. Holm, S.: A simple sequentially rejective multiple test procedure. Scand. J. Stat. **6**(2), 65–70 (1979). http://www.jstor.org/stable/4615733
13. Kostenetskiy, P.S., Chulkevich, R.A., Kozyrev, V.I.: HPC resources of the higher school of economics. In: Journal of Physics: Conference Series, vol. 1740(1), p. 012050 (2021). https://doi.org/10.1088/1742-6596/1740/1/012050
14. Kudugunta, S., Ferrara, E.: Deep neural networks for bot detection. Inf. Sci. **467**, 312–322 (2018). https://doi.org/10.1016/j.ins.2018.08.019
15. van der Maaten, L., Hinton, G.: Visualizing data using t-SNE. J. Mach. Learn. Res. **9**(86), 2579–2605 (2008). http://jmlr.org/papers/v9/vandermaaten08a.html
16. Mann, H.B., Whitney, D.R.: On a test of whether one of two random variables is stochastically larger than the other. Ann. Math. Stat. **18**(1), 50–60 (1947). https://doi.org/10.1214/aoms/1177730491
17. Mikolov, T., Chen, K., Corrado, G., Dean, J.: Efficient estimation of word representations in vector space (2013). https://doi.org/10.48550/ARXIV.1301.3781, https://arxiv.org/abs/1301.3781
18. Shliazhko, O., Fenogenova, A., Tikhonova, M., Mikhailov, V., Kozlova, A., Shavrina, T.: mGPT: few-shot learners go multilingual (2022). https://doi.org/10.48550/ARXIV.2204.07580, https://arxiv.org/abs/2204.07580
19. Wei, F., Nguyen, U.T.: Twitter bot detection using bidirectional long short-term memory neural networks and word embeddings (2020). https://doi.org/10.48550/ARXIV.2002.01336, https://arxiv.org/abs/2002.01336
20. Wishart, D.: Numerical classification method for deriving natural classes. Nature **221**(5175), 97–98 (1969). https://doi.org/10.1038/221097a0
21. Zhang, J., Dong, B., Yu, P.S.: FakeDetector: effective fake news detection with deep diffusive neural network (2018). https://doi.org/10.48550/ARXIV.1805.08751, https://arxiv.org/abs/1805.08751

Medical Imaging

Self-supervised Diffusion Model
for Anomaly Segmentation in Medical
Imaging

Komal Kumar, Snehashis Chakraborty[ID], and Sudipta Roy[(✉)][ID]

Artificial Intelligence and Data Science, Jio Institute, Navi Mumbai 410206, India
{komal2.kumar,snehashis1.C,sudipta1.roy}@jioinstitute.edu.in

Abstract. A powerful mechanism for detecting anomalies in a self-supervised manner was demonstrated by model training on normal data, which can then be used as a baseline for scoring anomalies. Recent studies on diffusion models (DMs) have shown superiority over generative adversarial networks (GANs) and have achieved better-quality sampling over variational autoencoders (VAEs). Owing to the inherent complexity of the systems being modeled and the increased sampling times in the long sequence, DMs do not scale well to high-resolution imagery or a large amount of training data. Furthermore, in anomaly detection, DMs based on the Gaussian process do not control the target anomaly size and fail to repair the anomaly image, which led us to the development of a simplex diffusion and selective denoising ($(SD)^2$) model. $(SD)^2$ does not require a full sequence of Markov chains in image reconstruction for anomaly detection, which reduces the time complexity, samples from the simplex noise diffusion process that have control over the anomaly size and are trained to reconstruct the selective features that help to repair the anomaly. $(SD)^2$ significantly outperformed the publicly available Brats2021 and Phenomena detection from X-ray image datasets compared to the self-supervised model. The source code is made publicly available at https://github.com/MAXNORM8650/SDSquare.

Keywords: Anomaly detection · Self-supervise learning · MRI · X-rays · Diffusion models · Simplex noise

1 Introduction

Anomaly detection in medical image analysis is an important application of deep-learning models in healthcare. This involves identifying abnormal or unexpected features in images that may indicate the presence of an abnormal disease. Obtaining pixel-wise annotated ground truths can be a challenging and time-consuming task in medical image analysis (MIA). This is because medical images, such as CT scans, MRIs, and X-rays, often contain complex and

© The Author(s), under exclusive license to Springer Nature Switzerland AG 2023
P. Maji et al. (Eds.): PReMI 2023, LNCS 14301, pp. 359–368, 2023.
https://doi.org/10.1007/978-3-031-45170-6_37

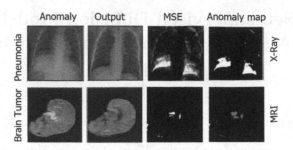

Fig. 1. Self-supervised learning for anomaly detection

subtle abnormalities that require expert knowledge for identification and annotation. Moreover, obtaining ground-truth data requires extensive manual annotation [1,2] by trained medical professionals, which can be a time-consuming and costly process. In addition, there may be inter-observer variability among experts, which can lead to inconsistencies in annotations [3]. To overcome these challenges, several techniques have been developed to reduce the number of manual annotations required for training machine-learning models. These include weakly supervised, transfer, active, and self-supervision. A powerful mechanism for detecting anomalies in a self-supervised manner was demonstrated by model training on normal reference data, which can then be used as a baseline for scoring anomalies, as shown in Fig. 1. Generative modeling has been shown to provide powerful models for anomaly detection in MIA and improve the efficiency of disease screening and diagnosis. In Anomaly detection, autoencoder-based models [4] spatially VAEs [5] are used to train on image-to-image labels of healthy references, and then reflected in high-anomaly score anomaly images. This technique is applied to a wide range of anomaly detection methods in a self-supervised manner, where anomalies are detected using the difference between the anomaly image and its healthy reconstruction. Other approaches [6] use Generative Adversarial Networks (GAN) [7] for anomaly detection. However, training GANs is challenging and requires considerable hyperparameter tuning. In a recent study, transformer networks [8] were used to detect and segment brain anomalies [9] from MRI images. Semi-supervised thresholding-based methods [10] have also achieved better performance in medical anomaly segmentation. Recent studies on DMs such as Denoising Diffusion Probabilistic Models (DDPMs) [11] and denoising diffusion implicit models (DDIM) [12] have beaten GANs for quality image synthesis [13]. In a recent study [14], the authors proposed a weakly supervised anomaly detection method for medical images based on guided diffusion models. However, these DMs do not scale well to high-resolution imagery and a large amount of training data because of the inherent complexity of the systems and the increased sampling times in long sequences. AnoDDPM [15] proposed the idea of Simplex Noise for the diffusion forward process to corrupt the anomaly in the image, which results in a healthy prediction. The scalability and sampling times of AnoDDPM are improved by not requiring full-length

Markov chain diffusion, but more research is needed to assess its robustness. In this work, $(SD)^2$ samples from a simplex noise diffusion process that has control over the anomaly size and is trained to reconstruct the selective features that help repair the anomaly. $(SD)^2$ can be used as partial diffusion, which does not require a full Markov chain for diffusion as in AnoDDPM.

The main contributions of this study are as follows.

- We develop a diffusion anomaly detection model based on a partially observed Markov chain.
- A multi-scale simplex noise diffusion process that gives control over the target anomaly size and repairs the anomaly better than the Gaussian process.
- Selective convolutional denoising block to increase the robustness of the model to repair the anomaly.

2 Methodology

2.1 Overview of DDPM

DDPMs [11] is based on a diffusion process that can be viewed as a series of steps in a Markov chain, where each step involves sampling from a Gaussian distribution with a mean that depends on the current state of the chain. As the number of steps increased, the distribution over the chain converged to a Gaussian distribution. For data $x_0 \sim q(x_0)$ and Markov chain process q from x_1 to x_χ which adds the noise at each step to produce a noisy sample based on Gaussian noise with a variance schedule β_t:

$$q\left(x_t \mid x_{t-1}\right) = N\left(x_t; \sqrt{1 - \beta_t} x_{t-1},\ \beta I\right) \tag{1}$$

In DDPM, q is not applied repeatedly to sample $x_t \sim q(x_t|x_0)$ instead, it expresses $q(x_t|x_0)$ in a Gaussian distribution for $\eta \sim N(0, I)$:

$$q\left(x_t \mid x_0\right) = N\left(x_t; \sqrt{\bar{\alpha}_t}\, x_0,\ (1 - \bar{\alpha}_t)\, I\right) \tag{2}$$

$$= \sqrt{\bar{\alpha}_t}\, x_0 + \eta \sqrt{1 - \bar{\alpha}_t} \tag{3}$$

For $1 - \alpha_t = \beta_t$, $\bar{\alpha}_t = \prod_{s=0:\chi} \alpha_s$, and $1 - \bar{\alpha}_t$ can be used as a noise scheduler instead of β_t. Given that the posterior is also Gaussian based on Bayes' theorem, we can sample $q(x_0)$ by sampling from each reverse step of the distribution $q(x_{t-1}|x_t)$ for t from χ to 1 to reach $q(x_0)$. We can estimate the parameters (mean vector and covariance matrix) of $q(x_{t-1}|x_t)$ using the neural network to approximate $q(x_{t-1}|x_t)$. The objective of such neural networks is to minimize the dissimilarity between two probability distributions from t^{th} step to $(t-1)^{th}$ step by the Kullback-Leibler divergence (D_{KL}). In the first step, we can minimize entropy. A neural network can be viewed as a mapping from a simpler Gaussian distribution to a more complex distribution of images. This mapping can be considered as a non-parametric method for defining the mean function of a Gaussian process. A network $\eta_\theta(x_t, t)$ with θ parameters for predicting η can be trained to simplify the objective and result in better sampling. For a given $x_0 \sim q(x_0)$, $\eta \sim N(0, I)$ in each step $t \sim [0, \chi]$ is defined as follows:

$$L_{Final} = \frac{1}{\chi} \sum_{t=0:\chi} ||\eta - \eta_\theta(x_t, t)||^2 \tag{4}$$

2.2   Simplex Diffusion and Selective Denoising $(SD)^2$

$(SD)^2$ is based on the DDPM, which consists of χ forward and backward process steps, as shown in Fig. 2. For image X_0 and after $\lambda - 1$ step of the nosing process, the corrupted image $X_{\lambda-1}$ is used to sample X_λ from $q_\phi(X_\lambda|X_{\lambda-1})$ where ϕ is the set of parameters in simplex noise such that frequency, octave value, and persistence. X'_λ was approximated using an encoder (En.) Decoder (de.) and a selective denoising (SD) feature-map module. These two forward and backward process is described as follows:

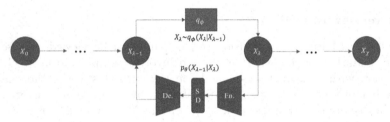

Fig. 2. Proposed model for anomaly detection for image-to-image translation. X_0 is an input image, and X_χ is a noisy image of the input using q_ϕ for parameter ϕ. The backward process represents the denoising process using the encoder (En.) to the decoder (De.) through selective denoising (SD) block. (Color figure online)

Simplex Noise Forward Process: In a power law distribution, the frequency of an event (in this case, the occurrence of a certain pixel intensity) is proportional to the power of the event size (in this case, the intensity value). In images, this means that there are many low-intensity pixels and few high-intensity pixels and that the distribution of pixel intensities follows a power law. In the white noise process, the noise values at each point in time are independent and identically distributed (i.i.d.) random variables that follow a Gaussian distribution with zero mean and constant variance, and the noise is spread equally across all frequencies, which is not good for low-intensity pixels. In images, anomalies or outliers can appear as high-frequency components that are distinct from the rest of the image. By adding noise that strongly affects low-frequency components, we can smooth out these anomalies while preserving the overall structure of the image. A power law distribution for the applied noise can be particularly effective in this case because it tends to affect low-frequency components more strongly than high-frequency components. Perlin noise is a type of gradient noise generated by combining multiple octaves of noise, where each octave is a higher-frequency version of the noise in the previous octave. Each octave is weighted by decreasing amplitude and increasing frequency, which creates a more complex and detailed noise pattern. The result is a noisy texture that varies smoothly and gradually across space. Simplex noise [16] was introduced by the author of Perlin noise as an improvement over the earlier Perlin noise algorithm. Simplex noise is also a type of gradient noise but is more computationally efficient, produces better results in higher dimensions, and uses a more efficient method for determining the closest grid points and calculating the gradient vectors. The steps for the simplex noise are shown in Algorithm 1.

Algorithm 1. Simplex Noise

- Define a regular grid of points by dividing the space into a grid of cells.
- Determine the position of the input point within the grid by finding the closest grid points to the input point.
- Calculate the pseudo-random gradient vector for each point of the grid.
- Calculate the dot products between the gradient vectors and the vectors from the closest grid points to the input point.
- Interpolate the dot products using a smooth function.
- Repeat the process for multiple octaves of different frequencies and amplitudes.

Selective Denoising Backward Process: We used a U-net-based model to model the backward diffusion process. In DDPM, the U-net architecture consists of an encoder and decoder network, where the encoder network extracts features from X_λ at λ^h step, and the decoder network generates $X'_{\lambda-1}$ with the training of $(X_\lambda, X_{\lambda-1})$ labels. Although the Simplex noise forward process helps to produce smoother noise with fewer visible artifacts, to increase the robustness of U-Net in the denoising step, inspired by SSPCAB [17] we selectively mask the feature map from the encoder, which helps to repair the anomaly and quality image reconstruction. The selective denoising backward process consists of three steps: first, encoder-based feature extraction, selectively masking the feature by masked convolutional layers (MCL) followed by a squeeze-and-excitation block [18] for selective denoising (SD), as shown in Fig. 2 with a detailed diagram in Fig. 3, and a decoder to generate the output. For $X \in \mathbb{R}^{C \times H \times W}$ input for the MCL is the output of the encoder block of U-Net, where C is the number of features with spatial dimension $H \times W$. For MCL, $\Psi_{k', D}$ is performed to obtain the K_i regions, where $i \in 1, 2, 3, 4$ for a two-dimensional input, k' is the spatial dimension of the sub-kernel that needs to be tuned, and D is the distance from the masked region shown in Fig. 2 (blue).

$$\widetilde{X} = \Psi_{k', D}(X) \tag{5}$$

where $\widetilde{X} \in \mathbb{R}^{N \times C \times k' \times k'} = K_i \in \mathbb{R}^{C \times k' \times k'} : i \in \{1, 2, 3, 4\}, k' \in \mathbb{N}^+$ shown in the Fig. 3. Values other than $\widetilde{X}$ are ignored. Then, we apply the convolution operation in this region, with the filter size F calculated as follows:

$$F = 2k' + 2D + 1 \tag{6}$$

The output from all convolution layers is combined and shared with the SE block. Thereafter, it is passed through fully connected layers activated by ReLU, which reduces the number of feature maps C by $\frac{C}{r}$ where r is the reduction ratio followed by the fully connected layers to compute C important features corresponding to the image label. The step is as follows:

$$Y = \sigma\left(ReLU\left(W_1 \bullet s\right) \bullet W_2\right) \tag{7}$$

where $W_1 \in \mathbb{R}^{\frac{C}{r} \times C}$ are the weights of the first fully connected layer (FC) activated by ReLU, followed by the second fully connected layer in which $W_2 \in \mathbb{R}^{C \times \frac{C}{r}}$ are the weights. The first FC layer consists of $\frac{C}{r}$ nodes, where the information is squeezed by a reduction ratio of r. Finally, a tensor Z with the same spatial dimension as F is generated as follows:

$$Z = Y \bullet F(X) \tag{8}$$

where $\bullet$ is element-wise multiplication, and $Z \in \mathbb{R}^{C \times H \times W}$ is the final tensor containing the recalibrated attention map.

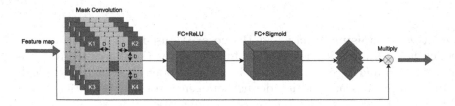

Fig. 3. Figure represents the selective denoising block for feature map reconstruction.

The objective is modified by adding the self-supervised reconstruction $L_{SD}(Z, X)$ loss to the original loss L_{Final} for $\alpha \in \mathbb{R}^{+}$ as follows:

$$L_{Total} = L_{Final} + \alpha\left(Z - X\right)^2 \tag{9}$$

3   Experiments

3.1   Experimental Setting

$(SD)^2$ uses the updated U-Net architecture from guided diffusion [13] by adding a self-supervised block, as discussed in the selective denoising process, and the block shown in Fig. 2 for the prediction of η_θ. This architecture uses a transformer [19] sinusoidal positional embedding for time-step encoding based on a Wide ResNet. $(SD)^2$ hyperparameters included 1000 simplex diffusion steps with a cosine noise schedule, 128 base channels, 2 heads, $\{32, 16, 8\}$ attention resolution and 0.9999 exponential moving average (EMA). We optimized the objective function with the AdamW optimizer ($\beta_1 = 0.9$, $\beta_2 = 0.999$), initial learning rate

1×10^{-4} and a batch size of 1 on an RTX A4000 GPU. $(SD)^2$ uses Pytorch as the codebase. We trained the $(SD)^2$ parameters for 3000 iterations. BRATS2021 and Pneumonia X-Ray were used for the experiments with $(SD)^2$ model.

BRATS2021: From the BRATS 2021(Brain Tumor Segmentation) [20] dataset, we first preprocess BRATS2021 in healthy and anomaly datasets with the help of segmentation mask for training and testing the model respectively. We used the top 1306 (40%) $2D$ $4 \times 240 \times 155$ slices with all four modalities, as anomalies are easier to spot from this view. For preprocessing of the input volumes, the first random rotation of either positive or negative 3 degrees is applied, a random translation of 0.02 times the width and 0.09 times the height is applied, and a center crop of size 235 is taken from the preprocessed, a center crop of size 235 is taken from the preprocessed, and finally, it is resized to 256×256. For the testing, we used the top 1935 (60%) $2D$ $4 \times 240 \times 155$ slices with a segmentation mask.

Pneumonia X-Ray: The Chest X-Ray Images for pneumonia detection [21] is a publicly available dataset having two categories: normal and pneumonia. We train on normal inference, which consists of 1341 (25%) images, and test on the pneumonia dataset, which consists of 3875 (75%) images.

3.2   Performance of the Model

To evaluate $(SD)^2$, we segmented 1935 images of brats2021 and reported the segmentation results in Table 1 for comparison with different self-supervised methods for anomaly detection. $(SD)^2$ performed better for our brats2021 test dataset. $(SD)^2$- based anomaly repairing for healthy image reconstruction and anomaly segmentation, Fig. 4 represents the anomaly image, its reconstruction, anomaly map from $(SD)^2$, and mask as ground truth. Typically, pneumonia appears as a cloudy or hazy area on an X-ray, which may be white, gray, or yellow. We prepared the ground truth for pneumonia with the help of a doctor, as shown in Fig. 4, in the yellow bounded box. In Fig. 4, we show some examples that illustrate our methods for creating a realistic-looking image while preserving all the details that lead to a quality anomaly map.

Table 1. Segmentation evaluation for Brats2021 dataset with sample distance of $\lambda = 800$ with simplex noise of octave = 6 and frequency = $2^{-6}(64)$.

Models	Dice ($\uparrow$)	IoU($\uparrow$)	Precision ($\uparrow$)	Recall ($\uparrow$)
VAE [5]	0.191 ± 0.002	0.014 ± 0.001	0.016 ± 0.001	0.018 ± 0.024
Con. En. [22]	0.309 ± 0.200	0.248 ± 0.058	0.351 ± 0.092	0.368 ± 0.113
AnoGAN [23]	0.228 ± 0.008	0.018 ± 0.009	0.422 ± 0.007	0.007 ± 0.005
DDPM [11]	0.201 ± 0.111	0.016 ± 0.005	0.018 ± 0.003	0.022 ± 0.019
$(SD)^2$ (Proposed)	$\mathbf{0.511 \pm 0.103}$	$\mathbf{0.349 \pm 0.078}$	$\mathbf{0.477 \pm 0.108}$	$\mathbf{0.580 \pm 0.120}$

3.3 Ablation on $(SD)^2$

To verify the effect of simplex diffusion and selective denoising as an ablation study, we report the results in Fig. 5 for segmentation evaluation on 64 slices of the test brats2021 dataset. We compared Gaussian diffusion (GD), simplex diffusion (SD), and simplex diffusion with selective denoising $(SD)^2$. This was performed with a sample size of 800. In Fig. 5, $(SD)^2$ shows the improvement in the other two strategies.

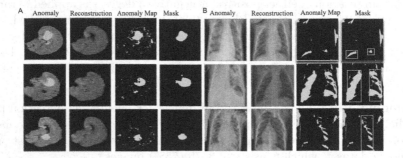

Fig. 4. Visualization of the results from $(SD)^2$. (A) Brats 2021 dataset. (B) Pneumonia dataset.

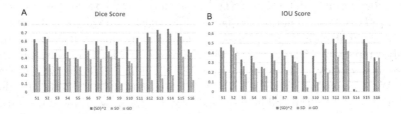

Fig. 5. Effect of $(SD)^2$ over simplex diffusion and Gaussian diffusion on segmentation evaluation for the 16 slices with sample distance 800. (A) Dice Coefficient, (B) IoU.

4 Conclusion

Using a self-supervised anomaly detection model based on a partially observed Markov chain, we develop denoising a diffusion anomaly detection model. In addition to a simplex noise diffusion process that controls the size of the target anomaly, we used selective convolutional denoising blocks to increase the robustness of the model, thereby repairing the image. We applied our method to two different medical image datasets and achieved quality results in self-supervised learning, which does not require annotated data for training to achieve a quality anomaly map. In the future, we aim to extend the model performance to various medical anomaly detection problems. In addition, we will consider three-dimensional data in domains other than anomaly detection.

References

1. Roy, S., Bhattacharyya, D., Bandyopadhyay, S.K., Kim, T.H.: Heterogeneity of human brain tumor with lesion identification, localization, and analysis from MRI. Inform. Med. Unlocked **13**, 139–150 (2018)
2. Roy, S., Shoghi, K.I.: Computer-aided tumor segmentation from T2-weighted MR images of patient-derived tumor xenografts. In: Karray, F., Campilho, A., Yu, A. (eds.) ICIAR 2019. LNCS, vol. 11663, pp. 159–171. Springer, Cham (2019). https://doi.org/10.1007/978-3-030-27272-2_14
3. Kabiraj, A., Meena, T., Reddy, P.B., Roy, S.: Detection and classification of lung disease using deep learning architecture from x-ray images. In: Bebis, G., et al. (eds.) ISVC 2022. LNCS, vol. 13598, pp. 444–455. Springer, Cham (2022). https://doi.org/10.1007/978-3-031-20713-6_34
4. Kumar, K., Kumar, H., Wadhwa, P.: Encoder-decoder (LSTM-LSTM) network-based prediction model for trend forecasting in currency market. In: Thakur, M., Agnihotri, S., Rajpurohit, B.S., Pant, M., Deep, K., Nagar, A.K. (eds.) Soft Computing for Problem Solving. Lecture Notes in Networks and Systems, vol. 547, pp. 211–223. Springer, Singapore (2023). https://doi.org/10.1007/978-981-19-6525-8_17
5. Kingma, D.P., Welling, M.: An introduction to variational autoencoders. Found. Trends Mach. Learn. **12**(4), 307 (2019)
6. Baumgartner, C.F., Koch, L.M., Tezcan, K.C., Ang, J.X., Konukoglu, E.: Visual feature attribution using Wasserstein GANs. In: Proceedings of the IEEE Conference on Computer Vision and Pattern Recognition, pp. 8309–8319 (2018)
7. Goodfellow, I.J., et al.: Generative adversarial networks. arXiv preprint arXiv:1406.2661 (2014)
8. Pirnay, J., Chai, K.: Inpainting transformer for anomaly detection. In: Sclaroff, S., Distante, C., Leo, M., Farinella, G.M., Tombari, F. (eds.) ICIAP 2022. LNCS, vol. 13232, pp. 394–406. Springer, Cham (2022). https://doi.org/10.1007/978-3-031-06430-2_33
9. Pinaya, W.H.L., et al.: Unsupervised brain anomaly detection and segmentation with transformers. arXiv preprint arXiv:2102.11650(2021)
10. Meissen, F., Kaissis, G., Rueckert, D.: Challenging current semi-supervised anomaly segmentation methods for brain MRI. In: Crimi, A., Bakas, S. (eds.) Brainlesion: Glioma, Multiple Sclerosis, Stroke and Traumatic Brain Injuries, BrainLes 2021. Lecture Notes in Computer Science, vol. 12962, pp. 63–74. Springer, Cham (2021). https://doi.org/10.1007/978-3-031-08999-2_5
11. Ho, J., Jain, A., Abbeel, P.: Denoising diffusion probabilistic models. In: Advances in Neural Information Processing Systems, vol. 33, pp. 6840–6851 (2020)
12. Song, J., Meng, C., Ermon, S.: Denoising diffusion implicit models. arXiv preprint arXiv:2010.02502 (2020)
13. Dhariwal, P., Nichol, A.: Diffusion models beat GANs on image synthesis. In: Advances in Neural Information Processing Systems, vol. 34, pp. 8780–8794 (2021)

14. Wolleb, J., Bieder, F., Sandkühler, R., Cattin, P.C.: Diffusion models for medical anomaly detection. In: Wang, L., Dou, Q., Fletcher, P.T., Speidel, S., Li, S. (eds.) MICCAI 2022. Lecture Notes in Computer Science, vol. 13438, pp. 35–45. Springer, Cham (2022). https://doi.org/10.1007/978-3-031-16452-1_4
15. Wyatt, J., Leach, A., Schmon, S.M., Willcocks, C. G.: AnoDDPM: anomaly detection with denoising diffusion probabilistic models using simplex noise. In: Proceedings of the IEEE/CVF Conference on Computer Vision and Pattern Recognition, pp. 650–656 (2022)
16. Perlin, K.: Association for computing machinery. In: SIGGRAPH (vol. 2, p. 681) (2002)
17. Ristea, N.C., et al.: Self-supervised predictive convolutional attentive block for anomaly detection. In: Proceedings of the IEEE/CVF Conference on Computer Vision and Pattern Recognition, pp. 13576–13586 (2022)
18. Hu, J., Shen, L., Sun, G.: Squeeze-and-excitation networks. In: Proceedings of the IEEE Conference on Computer Vision and Pattern Recognition, pp. 7132–7141 (2018)
19. Vaswani, A., et al.: Attention is all you need. In: Advances in Neural Information Processing Systems, vol. 30 (2017)
20. Baid, U., et al.: The RSNA-ASNR-MICCAI BraTS 2021 benchmark on brain tumor segmentation and radiogenomic classification. arXiv preprint arXiv:2107.02314 (2021)
21. Kermany, D., Zhang, K., Goldbaum, M.: Labeled optical coherence tomography (OCT) and chest X-ray images for classification. Mendeley Data 2(2), 651 (2018)
22. Pathak, D., Krahenbuhl, P., Donahue, J., Darrell, T., Efros, A.A.: Context encoders: feature learning by inpainting. In: Proceedings of the IEEE Conference on Computer Vision and Pattern Recognition, pp. 2536–2544 (2016)
23. Schlegl, T., Seeböck, P., Waldstein, S.M., Schmidt-Erfurth, U., Langs, G.: Unsupervised anomaly detection with generative adversarial networks to guide marker discovery. In: Niethammer, M., et al. (eds.) IPMI 2017. LNCS, vol. 10265, pp. 146–157. Springer, Cham (2017). https://doi.org/10.1007/978-3-319-59050-9_12

Ensemble Methods with [18F]FDG-PET/CT Radiomics in Breast Cancer Response Prediction

Moumita Dholey[1]($\boxtimes$), Ritesh J. M. Santosham[2], Soumendranath Ray[2], Jayanta Das[2], Sanjoy Chatterjee[2], Rosina Ahmed[2], and Jayanta Mukherjee[1]

[1] Indian Institute of Technology Kharagpur, Kharagpur, West Bengal, India
dholey.moumita5@iitkgp.ac.in
[2] Tata Medical Center, Kolkata, West Bengal, India

Abstract. Pathological complete response (pCR) after neoadjuvant che-motherapy (NAC) in patients with breast cancer was found to improve survival, and it has a great prognostic value in the aggressive tumor subtype. This study aims to predict pCR before NAC treatment with a radiomic feature-based ensemble learning model using both positron emission tomography/computed tomography (PET/CT) images taken from the online QIN-Breast dataset. It studies the problem of constructing an end-to-end classification pipeline that includes a large-scale radiomic feature extraction, a hybrid iterative feature selection and a heterogeneous weighted ensemble classification. The proposed hybrid feature selection procedure can identify significant radiomic predictors out of 2153 features extracted from delineated tumour regions. The proposed weighted ensemble approach aggregates the outcomes of four weak classifiers (Decision tree, Naive Bayes, K-nearest neighbour, and Logistics regression) based on their importance. The empirical study demonstrates that the proposed feature selection-cum-ensemble classification method has achieved 92% and 88.4% balanced accuracy in PET and CT, respectively. The PET/CT aggregated model performed better and achieved 98% balanced accuracy and 94.74% F1-score. Furthermore, this study is the first classification work on the online QIN-Breast dataset.

Keywords: Breast cancer · Ensemble learning · Radiomics · PET/CT · Pathologic complete response

1 Introduction

Breast cancer is a major source of cancer-related death in women around the world. There were 2,261,419 new female breast cancer cases and 684,996 deaths reported in 2020, worldwide [14]. Locally advanced and operable breast cancers are usually treated with neoadjuvant chemotherapy (NAC) [17]. In the NAC trials, the pathological complete response (pCR) was the primary endpoint for

P. Maji et al. (Eds.): PReMI 2023, LNCS 14301, pp. 369–379, 2023.
https://doi.org/10.1007/978-3-031-45170-6_38

overall disease-free survival [10]. Radiomics has been used for breast tumor detection, diagnosis, and response monitoring for prognosis and treatment [2]. Li et al. [8] have developed a pCR prediction method using ^{18}F-FDG PET/CT radiomic features for NAC treatment. They have extracted 2210 radiomic features from PET/CT images, and used supervised and unsupervised learning models for the identification of prognostic predictors. In another study, Ou et al. [12] worked with 44 patients for breast lymphoma and carcinoma differentiation using ^{18}F-FDG PET/CT radiomic features. Boughdad et al. [1] studied pCR, morphological response and metabolic response of breast cancer in neoadjuvant endocrine therapy treatment.

The ensemble learning algorithm has recently become popular in the machine learning domain because it can provide better prediction performance than single classifiers and reduce overfitting issues. This study tried to explore the efficacy of ensemble models in breast cancer early response prediction. Dogan and Birant [4] worked on a weighted majority voting-based heterogenous ensemble approach to evaluate the performance of each classifier independently and adjust the weights for the final decision. Tanveer et al. [15] used twin k-class SVM, least squares twin SVM, twin bounded SVM, robust energy-based least square twin SVM and least square twin SVM classifiers for their ensemble study.

This work contributes to the development of a pCR prediction algorithm using ^{18}F-FDG PET/CT scans taken pre NAC. The main contributions of this paper are enlisted below:

1. We generate tumour-delineated ground-truth images and develop a large-scale radiomic features dataset extracted from both PET/CT samples.
2. We propose a novel hybrid ensemble feature selection technique that combines filtering, wrapper and embedded feature selection method for selecting consistent and significant radiomic features.
3. We introduce a heterogenous weighted ensemble algorithm where the weight and bias of base learners are assigned based on model performance and error, respectively.
4. We perform experiments on multiple online datasets to demonstrate the advantage of the proposed method compared to state-of-the-art (SOTA) models.

The Sect. 2 demonstrates the proposed algorithm for breast cancer prediction. Section 3 addresses the data analysis results of the proposed method. Finally, the concluding remarks are presented in Sect. 4.

2   Materials and Methods

The abstract workflow diagram of the proposed work is shown in Fig. 1. Initially, the target tumor or volume of interest (VOI) is segmented. Next, various radiomic features are extracted from the VOI of PET and CT images. Later, a hybrid ensemble feature selection technique is introduced. Finally, a weighted ensemble classifier is proposed to predict pCR accurately.

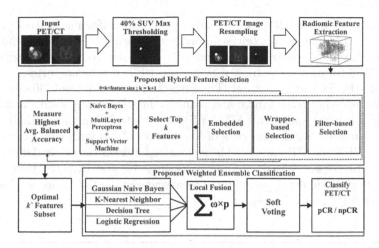

Fig. 1. Abstract workflow of the proposed methodology.

2.1   Sample Collection

The sample PET/CT images from an online dataset named *QIN-BREAST* (under The Cancer Imaging Archive, Award: U01 CA142565, PI: Thomas E. Yankeelov) are used in this study [9]. 43 patient data with Longitudinal PET/CT modalities are available for the assessment of breast cancer in NAC. FDG administration is performed intravenously via a vein (antecubital) contralateral to the affected breast. A response sheet of QIN-Breast treatment i.e., pCR and npCR for 36 data samples are present. Based on this information, the sample PET and CT images are categorized into two classes (pCR:10, npCR:26).

2.2   Target Tumor Region Delineation

The target VOI is delineated from the PET image series only. It is an automated process where 40% max SUV thresholding is used for a rough segmentation. Later, the 3D Snake algorithm is used for fine-tuned VOI generation. The proposed VOI delineation process is conducted under the supervision of radiologists, and later the output is cross-verified by multiple experts.

2.3   Radiomic Feature Extraction

The CT images are downsampled and transformed into similar PET dimensions (128 × 128 × 83). Features are extracted from VOI regions of both PET and resampled CT samples. It is executed in two stages i.e. filtered image set generation and feature extraction [16]. A combination of nine linear and non-linear filtering methods is considered in filtered image generation i.e., laplacian of gaussian, square, wavelet, square root, exponential, logarithm, gradient, and local binary pattern (2D and 3D). Finally, for feature mining, multiple radiomic feature extraction algorithms are considered, namely shape-based (3D), first-order statistics, shape-based (2D), neighbouring gray tone difference matrix (ngtdm), gray level run length matrix (glrlm), gray level dependence matrix (gldm), gray level co-occurrence matrix (glcm), and gray level size zone matrix (glszm). A total of 2153 features are extracted from each PET/CT image series.

QIN-BREAST feature dataset: The extracted feature dataset $[36 \times 2154]$ contains imbalanced class instances and requires data balancing with the adaptive synthetic sampling approach (ADASYN). The data balancing method creates two new synthetic feature datasets of size $[3000 \times 2154]$ with equal class distribution for PET and CT samples. The similarity between the original dataset and the synthetic dataset based on Chi-square statistic and Inverted Kolmogorov-Smirnov D statistic is calculated [3]. The average evaluation score is 77.4% and 71.25% for PET and CT, respectively.

Algorithm 1: Proposed hybrid feature selection

Result: Best significant feature subset F'
$F \leftarrow full\ feature\ dataset$;
Declare accuracy[len(F)];
Declare featurenames[len(F)];
for $k \leftarrow 1\ to\ len(F)$ **do**
$\quad [S^1]_{1 \times k} \leftarrow$ applyFilteringMethod(F, k);
$\quad [S^2]_{1 \times k} \leftarrow$ applyWrapperMethod(F, k);
$\quad [S^3]_{1 \times k} \leftarrow$ applyEmbeddedMethod(F, k);
$\quad [S']_{1 \times k} \leftarrow$ rank($[S^1, S^2, S^3]$, k);
$\quad accuracy[k] \leftarrow$ computeWeightedClassificationAccuracy($F[:, S']$);
$\quad featurenames[k] \leftarrow S'$;
end
$topaccuracyidx \leftarrow index(max(sort(\ accuracy\ )))$;
$sigfeaturesidx \leftarrow minimum([topaccuracyidx])$;
$F' \leftarrow F[:, featurenames[sigfeaturesidx]]$;

Online benchmark dataset: A total of eight online benchmark datasets from the University of California, Irvine (UCI) machine learning repository [5] are considered for validation. The considered datasets are Dermatology, Wisconsin, Chronic kidney disease, Breast cancer, Cardiotocography, Image segmentation, Letter recognition, and Diabetic retinopathy dataset.

2.4   Hybrid Ensemble Feature Selection

The pseudocode of the proposed hybrid ensemble feature selection algorithm is illustrated in Algorithm 1. Here, three different feature selection techniques viz., filter (Pearson correlation coefficient and chi-squared test), wrapper (Recursive feature elimination) and embedded method (Random forest) are used. An iterative process (forward selection) is adopted where all three said methods have picked a feature subset (S^1, S^2, S^3) of size k independently. It is observed that

---

Algorithm 2: Proposed weighted ensemble classifier

Result: Predicted class values $\hat{C}$ of test samples

$D_{train} \leftarrow training\ feature\ dataset;$

$D_{test} \leftarrow testing\ feature\ dataset;$

$M \leftarrow base\ classifiers\ list;$

Declare $model\_weight[len(M)];$

Declare $model\_loss[len(M)];$

for $j \leftarrow 1...m$, **do**

    1. Train model M_j with datset D_{train}

    2. Compute model performance using 10-fold cross validation

    3. Calculate weight factor $model\_weight_j =$

        $(balanced\ accuracy + precision + recall + F - measure + mcc + kappa)/6$

    4. Measure model error using hamming loss

        $model\_loss_j = hamming\_loss(M_j, D_{train})$

end

for $i \leftarrow 1...t$, **do**

    for $j \leftarrow 1...m$, **do**

        1. Predict class prediction probalities $p_{i,j} = Classify(D_{test,i}, M_j)$

        2. Compute class-wise weighted probabilits

        $[P_k]_{i,j} = ([p_k]_{i,j} - model\_loss_j) \times model\_weight_j$

        ; for all class values k=1...c

    end

    $\hat{C}_i = arg\ \underset{i}{max} \left[\frac{\sum_{j=1}^{m}[P_k]_{i,j}}{\sum_{j=1}^{m} model\_weight_j} \right]_{k=1}^{c}$

end

---

the features present in each three selected subsets were not the same. However, the size of the resultant feature subset (S') will be k after the aggregation of three feature subsets. Hence, a rank dictionary is formed where features are ordered based on their presence in all three selected feature subsets. The features which are present in all the subsets get high priority. Whereas, unique features that are only present in one subset get low priority. Next, the resultant feature subset (S') is generated using the ranking method by choosing the top features from the dictionary. Later, the selected feature dataset ($F[:, S']$) is trained and tested with multiple classifiers (train:70%, test:30%). The weighted classification accuracy (AC) (($accuracy[k]$)) and the feature subset (S') are recorded in a list at each step. The above iteration process is repeated for N times, where N is equals to feature size. Next, the best feature subset is selected with the highest weighted accuracy. The ($topaccuracyidx$) returns a single index value of the highest weighted accuracy ($accuracy$) and in the case of a tie of accuracies, it returns all the indexes. The selection is made based on the minimum size of the corresponding feature subset ($minimum(topaccuracyidx)$). The ($sigfeaturesidx$)

denotes the index of the selected highest accuracy value. Finally, the optimum feature dataset (F') is segmented from the original feature dataset (F).

2.5 Weighted Ensemble Classifier

The proposed ensemble model combines multiple heterogeneous predictive models and combines their weighted outcomes for final classification. The proposed global averaging strategy follows four fundamental steps:

- Select different types of base learners, which are the most appropriate models for the given problem. We have selected a total of four different SOTA classifiers viz., Decision tree (DT), Gaussian Naïve Bayes (GNB), Logistics regression (LR), and K-nearest neighbour (KNN).
- Assign weights to each predictive model. The models are individually trained on the training dataset, and their performance metrics are recorded on the testing dataset. The weight of each model is proportional to its weighted performance.
- Quantify model diversity to learn the model's bias. The bias is proportional to estimating the average error during model testing.
- Aggregate model outcomes to classify data instances. The soft voting mechanism is adopted to select class labels with maximum weighted probability.

The pseudocode of the proposed ensemble method is presented in Algorithm 2. Initially, individual base learners (M) are trained and tested with the training dataset (D_{train}) under 10-fold cross-validation. Here, the number of base learners is $m = 5$. The base classifier's performance is used to compute its weight and bias factors. The weight of each base learner $(model\_weight_j)$ is the mean value after adding six performance metrics, i.e., balanced accuracy, precision, recall, F-measure (F1), Mathews' correlation coefficient (MCC), and kappa score. Similarly, the bias of each base learner $(model\_loss_j)$ is the hamming loss generated by the classifier. Next, the class probabilities of each test instance (D_{test}) are computed for each base learner $(p_{i,j})$. The modified probability for each class (c) is calculated based on the formula as stated $[P_k]_{i,j} = ([p_k]_{i,j} - model\_loss_j) \times model\_weight_j$. Finally, the soft voting technique is considered to get the final class of each test instance $(\hat{C}_i)$. The class value with the highest probability value is selected as the outcome.

3 Results and Discussion

We have adopted a SOTA pipeline that includes feature extraction, feature selection, and supervised classification. The performance of proposed feature selection and ensemble model are evaluated. Here, the online benchmark datasets are divided into two sets where 60% of the dataset is used in model training, and 40% is utilized in testing. Whereas, the local QIN-Breast synthetic feature dataset is used for model training, and the original imbalanced dataset is applied to model testing. The proposed feature selection method hybridized two concepts i.e., independent assessment of feature importance and selecting the best feature space. At each iteration, top k ($features\ size \geq k \geq 1$) significant features are selected, and the weighted accuracy of the three classifiers is recorded. The accuracy results for PET and CT samples are plotted in Fig. 2. In this experiment, it is observed that the weighted accuracy decreases gradually when the value of k is above 100 in both cases. The classification accuracy is maximum when the feature subset size is 8 and 76 for PET and CT, respectively.

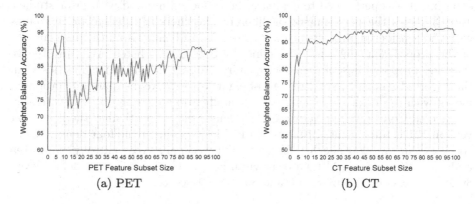

(a) PET   (b) CT

Fig. 2. Classification accuracy with incremental features.

The proposed ensemble model is evaluated on the online datasets. The performances based on the balanced accuracy is presented in the Table 1. The results present the performance of the individual classifiers and a general voting classifier that aggregates all four base classifiers. In most cases, our proposed ensemble model performs better than other models. The working principle of both voting and the proposed is similar. The voting classifier model aggregates the base learners' outcomes based on majority voting. In comparison, the proposed model calculates each base classifier's importance (weight and bias) and then performs a probabilistic majority voting. The weight factor indicates the strength of a base classifier, and the bias value signifies the diversity. The class-wise prediction probabilities are subtracted by the model bias and then multiplied by the weight factor. The modified prediction probability tries to improve the probability generated by the better-performing classifiers and penalize the poor-performing classifiers' results. In the end, class-wise probabilities by all four base classifiers are aggregated, and the class value with maximum probability is selected as the outcome. We have implemented the critical difference diagram (CDD) [3] to check the statistical significance. This significance is based on post-hoc Wilcoxon signed rank tests [3] for each pair of classifiers. The computed CDD diagram for this study is shown in Fig. 3. The lowest rank corresponds to the highest accuracy. The proposed ensemble model is the best choice for the overall classification task. After evaluating classifiers on online datasets, the performance of the proposed ensemble model is compared with and without applying the feature selection method on local dataset. The assessment result is presented in Table 2. The proposed model achieved higher accuracy when tested on the significant feature dataset. The proposed model achieved 92% and 88.4% balanced accuracy on PET and CT datasets with feature selection, respectively. As we have already worked on model ensemble, a similar approach also experimented on PET/CT fusion where the prediction probabilities of PET and CT-based models were jointly considered. The ensemble classification approach achieved 98% balanced accuracy, 90 % precision, 100% recall, and 94.74% F1-score. Next, the important experiment was performed to compare the proposed method with prior studies. Table 3 shows the performance of different classifiers adopted in prior studies with the considered online benchmark datasets. In comparison, the performance of the proposed model on these online datasets is also listed. We can observe that the proposed ensemble model acquired higher classification metrics than the reported studies in six cases out of eight. Finally, we compare our proposed model with recent deep learning based classification algorithm i.e., 3D Densely Connected Convolutional Networks (3D-DenseNet). In particular, the DenseNet version 121 is implemented that has [6,12,24,16] layers in the four dense blocks. After executing 3000 epochs, the loss values (Binary cross entropy) and area under the ROC curve (AUC) are shown in Fig. 4. The DenseNet model achieved 89.58% precision, 87.50% recall, and 86.82% F1-score.

Table 1. Classification balanced accuracy of models

Dataset	GNB	DT	KNN	LR	Voting	Proposed
Dermatology	0.874	0.92	0.973	0.961	0.98	0.992
Wisconsin	0.962	0.943	0.961	0.959	0.959	0.972
Kidney	0.971	0.951	0.97	0.986	0.981	0.998
Breast Cancer	0.958	0.955	0.975	0.979	0.97	0.988
Cardiotocography	0.939	0.976	0.976	0.977	0.969	0.98
Image Segmentation	0.789	0.943	0.932	0.927	0.95	0.956
Letter Recognition	0.651	0.858	0.914	0.776	0.909	0.931
Diabetic Retinopathy	0.61	0.605	0.593	0.668	0.675	0.716

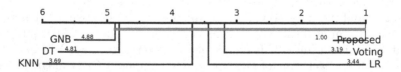

Fig. 3. Critical difference diagram.

Table 2. Importance of feature selection on proposed model

Dataset	With feature selection				Without feature selection			
	B Accuracy	F1	Precision	Recall	B Accuracy	F1	Precision	Recall
PET	0.92	0.818	0.75	1	0.844	0.727	0.615	0.888
CT	0.884	0.8	0.73	0.89	0.824	0.695	0.571	0.889

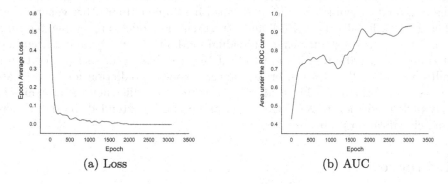

(a) Loss   (b) AUC

Fig. 4. DenseNet model performance.

Table 3. Model performance comparison with prior arts

Dataset	Prior study			Proposed
	Author	Method	Performance	
Dermatology	Kaya and Kuncan [6]	Extreme learning machine (ELM)	AC: 0.963	**AC: 0.966**
Dermatology	Kaya and Kuncan [6]	Factor analysis + ELM	AC: 0.969	
Wisconsin	Kaya and Kuncan [6]	Extreme learning machine (ELM)	AC: 0.971	AC. 0.971
Wisconsin	Kaya and Kuncan [6]	Factor analysis + ELM	AC: 0.972	
Kidney	Pal [13]	Bagging	AC:0.972	**AC: 0.994**
Cardiotocography	Kim and Lee [7]	Log-likelihood Naive Bayes	AC:0.943	**AC:0.986**
Image Segmentation	Kim and Lee [7]	Log-likelihood Naive Bayes	AC:0.987	**AC:0.99**
Letter Recognition	Kim and Lee [7]	Log-likelihood Naive Bayes	AC:0.991	AC:0.93
Diabetic Retinopathy	Memis et al. [11]	Fuzzy soft classifier	AC: 0.659	**AC: 0.702**
Breast cancer	Memis et al. [11]	Fuzzy soft classifier	AC: 0.95	**AC:0.991**

4   Conclusion

This study introduced two novel algorithms for feature selection and classification. A ^{18}F-FDG PET/CT radiomic feature extraction process was discussed that developed nearly 2153 features. The proposed hybrid feature selection method combined filter, wrapper, and ensemble methods. We have introduced a new weighted ensemble classification algorithm. The predicted class probabilities were adjusted by two factors i.e., the base classifier's weight and bias. The proposed ensemble classifier performed best among four other generic classifier models. Finally, both PET and CT ensemble models are aggregated, and it achieved higher accuracy than individual modalities (98% balanced accuracy, 90 % precision, 100% recall, and 94.74% F1-score). The results suggested to use multi-modality (PET/CT) in breast cancer response prediction for better classification performance. This study demonstrated the efficiency of radiomics in early pCR prediction to NAC treatment and could be extended to other supervised classification problems.

References

1. Boughdad, S., et al.: Early metabolic response of breast cancer to neoadjuvant endocrine therapy: comparison to morphological and pathological response. Cancer Imaging **20**(1), 11 (2020)
2. Conti, A., Duggento, A., Indovina, I., Guerrisi, M., Toschi, N.: Radiomics in breast cancer classification and prediction. In: Seminars in Cancer Biology. Elsevier (2020)
3. Demšar, J.: Statistical comparisons of classifiers over multiple data sets. J. Mach. Learn. Res. **7**, 1–30 (2006)
4. Dogan, A., Birant, D.: A weighted majority voting ensemble approach for classification. In: 2019 4th International Conference on Computer Science and Engineering (UBMK), pp. 1–6. IEEE (2019)
5. Dua, D., Graff, C.: UCI machine learning repository (2017)
6. Kaya, Y., Kuncan, F.: A hybrid model for classification of medical data set based on factor analysis and extreme learning machine: FA+ ELM. Biomed. Sign. Process. Control **78**, 104023 (2022)
7. Kim, T., Lee, J.S.: Exponential loss minimization for learning weighted Naive Bayes classifiers. IEEE Access **10**, 22724–22736 (2022)
8. Li, P., et al.: ^{18}F-FDG PET/CT radiomic predictors of pathologic complete response (pCR) to neoadjuvant chemotherapy in breast cancer patients. Eur. J. Nuclear Med. Mol. Imaging **47**(5), 1116–1126 (2020). https://doi.org/10.1007/s00259-020-04684-3
9. Li, X., Abramson, R.G., Arlinghaus, L.R.: Data from QIN-breast. The Cancer Imaging Archive (2016)
10. Matsuda, N., et al.: Change in sonographic brightness can predict pathological response of triple-negative breast cancer to neoadjuvant chemotherapy. Breast Cancer **25**(1), 43–49 (2018)
11. Memiş, S., Enginoğlu, S., Erkan, U.: A classification method in machine learning based on soft decision-making via fuzzy parameterized fuzzy soft matrices. Soft. Comput. **26**(3), 1165–1180 (2022)

12. Ou, X., et al.: Radiomics based on 18F-FDG PET/CT could differentiate breast carcinoma from breast lymphoma using machine-learning approach: a preliminary study. Cancer Med. **9**(2), 496–506 (2020)

13. Pal, S.: Chronic kidney disease prediction using machine learning techniques. Biomed. Mater. Dev. 1–7 (2022)

14. Sung, H., et al.: Global cancer statistics 2020: GLOBOCAN estimates of incidence and mortality worldwide for 36 cancers in 185 countries. CA Cancer J. Clin. **71**(3), 209–249 (2021)

15. Tanveer, M., Ganaie, M.A., Suganthan, P.N.: Ensemble of classification models with weighted functional link network. Appl. Soft Comput. **107**, 107322 (2021)

16. Van Griethuysen, J.J.M., et al.: Computational radiomics system to decode the radiographic phenotype. Can. Res. **77**(21), e104–e107 (2017)

17. Yang, L., et al.: Prediction model of the response to neoadjuvant chemotherapy in breast cancers by a Naive Bayes algorithm. Comp Meth. Programs Biomed. **192**, 105458 (2020)

3-D Attention-SEV-Net for Segmentation of Post-operative Glioblastoma with Interactive Correction of Over-Segmentation

Swagata Kundu[1]([✉])([ID]), Subhashis Banerjee[3], Dimitrios Toumpanakis[2],
Johan Wikstrom[2], Robin Strand[3], and Ashis Kumar Dhara[1]

[1] Electrical Engineering Department, National Institute of Technology Durgapur,
Mahatma Gandhi Avenue, 713209 Durgapur, West Bengal, India
`swagatakundu2103@gmail.com`
[2] Department of Surgical Sciences, Neuroradiology, Uppsala University,
751 05 Uppsala, Sweden
[3] Department of Information Technology, Centre for Image Analysis, Uppsala
University, 751 85 Uppsala, Sweden

Abstract. Accurate localization and volumetric quantification of post-operative glioblastoma are of profound importance for clinical applications like post-surgery treatment planning, monitoring of tumor regrowth, and radiotherapy map planning. Manual delineation consumes more time and error prone thus automated 3-D quantification of brain tumors using deep learning algorithms from MRI scans has been used in recent years. The shortcoming with automated segmentation is that it often over-segments or under-segments the tumor regions. An interactive deep-learning tool will enable radiologists to correct the over-segmented and under-segmented voxels. In this paper, we proposed a network named Attention-SEV-Net which outperforms state-of-the-art network architectures. We also developed an interactive graphical user interface, where the initial 3-D segmentation of contrast-enhanced tumor can be interactively corrected to remove falsely detected isolated tumor regions. Attention-SEV-Net is trained with BraTS-2021 training data set and tested on Uppsala University post-operative glioblastoma dataset. The methodology outperformed state-of-the-art networks like U-Net, V-Net, Attention U-Net and Residual U-Net. The mean dice score achieved is 0.6682 and the mean Hausdorff distance-95 got is 8.96 mm for the Uppsala University dataset.

Keywords: Attention-SEV-Net · Post-operative Glioblastoma ·
Interactive Correction

1 Introduction

Glioblastoma is an aggressive tumor that occurs in the central nervous system of humans which has heterogenous properties when it comes to shape and

P. Maji et al. (Eds.): PReMI 2023, LNCS 14301, pp. 380–387, 2023.
https://doi.org/10.1007/978-3-031-45170-6_39

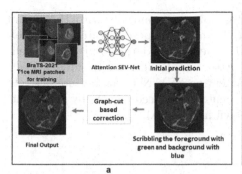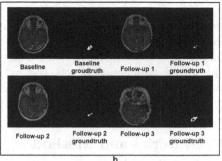

a   b

Fig. 1. (a)Block diagram of the proposed strategy. It shows the steps undertaken for the proposed method, that is initial segmentation with Attention SEV-Net and final interactive correction to remove false positive voxels with graph cut. (b) The post-operative baseline and three follow-ups of a subject

appearance. There is a very less prognosis for patients with glioblastoma. The common treatment is neuro-surgery followed by radiotherapy and chemotherapy. Accurate localization and delineation of brain tumors from MRI is important for clinical diagnosis and treatment planning. Accurate delineation helps in surgical planning so that glioblastoma is resected safely by preserving neurological functions. For post-operative cases, volumetric quantification becomes an important factor for precise radiotherapy treatments. The amount of residual tumor often influences the prognosis after the resection of glioblastomas. The knowledge of this residual tumor size is crucial for response evaluation and survival prediction after chemotherapy and radiotherapy. Manual volumetric quantification of brain tumors is high time taking, tedious, prone to inter-observer errors, and requires expert knowledge. Thus automatic tool for precise 3-D brain segmentation of tumors is necessary, which is robust and reproducible for different scanners. The state-of-the-art algorithms for brain tumor segmentation can be categorized into three broad categories: supervised, unsupervised, and hybrid. Unsupervised learning mainly deals with the intrinsic characteristics of unlabeled data for segmentation. Unsupervised learning uses methods like clustering, gaussian modeling, and other techniques [1,3]. Deep learning networks for supervised learning have become very popular in recent years. Some of the promising deep-learning architectures which are being extremely used for the segmentation of medical images include U-Net [8], V-Net [5], Attention U-Net [6], Residual U-Net [9], UNet++ [10], and U^2Net [7]. There are a number of reasons which makes the segmentation of post-operative brain tumor and their follow-ups challenging. Some of the challenges are, inter scanner data variability for a particular patient's follow-ups, class imbalance, radiotherapy effects, and post-surgical cavities.

Several authors have proposed many variants of U-Net architectures for precise segmentation of pre-operative brain tumors. In most of the previous works segmentation of pre-operative glioblastoma has been the focus but there is very little work on the automatic delineation of post-operative glioblastoma. Dhara *et al.* [2] performed 2D segmentation of glioblastoma initially with U-Net and reduced the false-positive by smart paint [4]. In our proposed strategy, we developed a novel network named Attention-SEV-Net, which outperformed other well-known architectures like U-Net, V-net, Attention U-Net and Residual U-Net. The initial segmentation achieved by Attention-SEV-Net can be interactively corrected to remove the isolated over-segmented enhanced tumors by graph-cut. The overall framework of the work is shown in Fig. 1(a).

2   Material and Method

2.1   Dataset

The proposed network is trained on the BraTS-2021 training dataset. The BraTS-2021 dataset comprises 1251 MRI scans along with its annotations for training. The MRI scans are skull stripped with an isotropic resolution of $1mm^3$ with dimensions of (240,240,155) voxels. Each subject has four modalities that is T1, post-contrast T1-weighted (T1ce), T2, and T2-FLAIR. Annotations consist of four classes edema, enhanced tumor, necrosis and background. Out of four modalities, only T1ce is considered for training in our work to segment the enhanced tumors. For testing Uppsala University post-operative glioblastoma dataset is used. The Uppsala University dataset has a total of 85 3D MRI volumes of 15 subjects. The MRI sequence is only post-contrast T1-weighted with annotations of enhanced residual tumors. Each subject has undergone surgery and has a post-surgery baseline and follow-up MRI scans. The number of follow-ups ranges from 1 to 9. The baseline and follow-ups of one subject and the annotations are shown in Fig. 1(b). It is observed from the follow-ups of this patient that with time the tumor volume has reduced but has recurred again in the last follow-up scan. Each MRI is of dimensions (256,256,208). The MRI scans were skull stripped and extrapolated to $1mm^3$ of voxel resolution. The ground truths for the dataset were done by two expert radiologists having 25 years of clinical experience. The radiologists manually segmented the enhanced tumor regions on the axial slices using the freely available tool called 3D-Slicer.

2.2   Method

The proposed strategy has two steps. Initially, each post-contrasted T1 MRI of the Uppsala University dataset was tested using Attention SEV-Net. The segmented results had shown some isolated false positive voxels. These false positives could be removed interactively by graph cut correction. For the correction step, The region of interest (foreground) is marked with a color and the isolated false positive voxels (background) with another color.

2.3   Network Architecture

The proposed Attention-SEV-Net shown in Fig. 2 has the baseline structure that of Residual U-Net. The contraction path has 4 contraction blocks with filter sizes

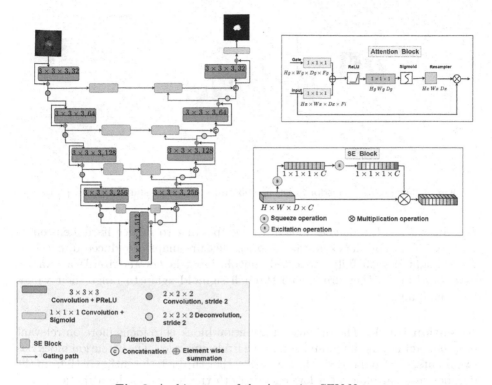

Fig. 2. Architecture of the Attention-SEV-Net.

of 32, 64, 128, and 256. At each block, there are two 3D convolutional layers of kernel size of $3 \times 3 \times 3$. The PReLU activation function and batch normalization follow each convolution layer. A dropout of 0.4 is used after each residual block. A convolution layer with a kernel size of $2 \times 2 \times 2$ and stride 2 was implemented for the task of downsampling at each stage of the encoder structure. The bottleneck region has a residual block with two convolutional layers and the filter size is 512. The expansion path follows the same filter sizes as that of the encoder. The size of the matrix is upsampled in the decoder structure, and for upsampling operation, a deconvolution layer with a kernel size of $2 \times 2 \times 2$ and stride 2 was used. At each stage of the encoder-decoder structure, there is a bridging with two blocks, squeeze and excitation (SE) block, and attention block. These blocks are attached in series with each other along the skip-connected path at each stage of the encoder and decoder.

SE Block. The main aim of using the SE block is to emphasize more on the channel information and reduce the dependency on the spatial information. It basically squeezes the information along the spatial domain and re-weights along the channel domain. To achieve its operation, the input feature map size of

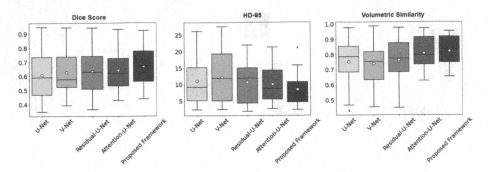

Fig. 3. Dice score, Hausdorff distance-95 and volumetric similarity box plots.

$H \times W \times D \times C$ undergoes global average pooling to reduce its dimension to $1 \times 1 \times 1 \times C$. For the excitation step, the feature maps of reduced dimensions were weighted with fully-connected convolutional layers and ReLU activation function. Finally, they are passed through sigmoid again to range their values between 0 and 1.

Attention Block. The purpose of attention block is to focus more on relevant or important feature maps and ignore the irrelevant ones. The attention block has two inputs, one from the SE block and the other through the gating path from the decoder residual block at a lower level. Both the inputs to the attention block are first brought to the exact dimensions and then passed through the ReLU activation function, followed by another convolution layer, and finally through the sigmoid. The attention coefficients are in the range between 0 and 1.

2.4   Implementation Details

To train the proposed network named Attention SEV-Net, overlapped patches of dimensions $128 \times 128 \times 64$ were extracted from BraTS-2021 training T1ce MRI scans. It was ensured that patches were extracted in a biased manner such that some amount of tumor regions were present in each training patch. The training patches were augmented so that the number of training samples increased to 13,000. All 85 MRI scans of the Uppsala University dataset were skull-stripped and isotropic resolutions were extrapolated to $1mm^3$. Attention-SEV-Net and all the other competing networks were trained using DICE loss and ADAM optimizer having a learning rate of 0.0001. The number of epochs was 50 for all the experiments with a batch size of 5. The experiments were conducted in Keras with TensorFlow 2.10.0 using python 3.9. The workstation used is equipped with NVIDIA-Quadra RTX 6000 which has 24 GB VRAM.

3   Segmentation Results

The performance metrics that were used for evaluating the performance of the proposed methodology and that of the other competing networks are dice score,

Table 1. Evaluation results of Uppsala University dataset. The table shows comparative results of the proposed methodology with that of the state-of-the-art networks like U-Net, V-Net, Residual U-Net, and Attention U-Net

Network Architecture	Dice Score	VS	Precision	HD-95
3D U-Net	0.6070	0.75305	0.5837	11.11
	±0.166	±0.155	±0.214	±7.06
3D V-Net	0.625	0.7387	**0.7390**	12.16
	±0.0152	±0.145	**±0.146**	±7.98
3D Residual U-Net	0.6315	0.7654	0.577	10.65
	±0.155	±0.161	±0.189	±6.31
3D Attention U-Net	0.6399	0.8104	0.6720	10.00
	±0.142	±0.1051	±0.190	±6.06
Proposed Method	**0.6682**	**0.8229**	0.7210	**8.96**
	±0.139	**±0.100**	±0.177	**±5.268**

volumetric similarity (VS), precision, and Hausdorff Distance-95 (HD-95). As mentioned before, the Attention-SEV-Net was trained with the BraTS-2021 dataset (1251 T1ce MRI scans), and its performance was evaluated on the 85 T1ce MRI volumes of the Uppsala University post-operative glioblastoma dataset. Figure 4 shows the segmentation results for four subjects of the Uppsala University post-operative glioblastoma dataset. Figure 4(a) provides a comparative segmentation output for attention SEV-Net with that of the other well-known architectures, U-Net, V-Net, Residual U-Net, and Attention U-Net. It can be clearly observed from the output segmentation results that Attention SEV-Net performed better compared to the rest of the architectures. Here true positive pixels(TP) are in red, false positive pixels(FP) are in green and false negative pixels(FN) are in blue. It is seen that the false positive candidates are quite low for the segmentation results of Attention SEV-Net compared to the outputs of the other networks. Figure 4(b) depicts the segmentation results of Attention SEV-Net and the corresponding outputs after undergoing graph cut interactive correction. On analyzing Fig. 4(b) it is clearly seen that the graph cut correction can remove the isolated false positives (shown in green). This removal of false positives improved the segmentation results significantly and thus improvement in mean dice score and mean volumetric similarity and mean HD-95 are quite prominent. Table. 1 and Fig. 3 provide the performance analysis of the proposed method with that of the competing state-of-the-art networks. The mean dice score achieved with Attention SEV-Net and graph cut correction is 0.6682, which is 2.83% more than its nearest competitor, Attention U-Net. The mean Hausdorff distance-95 with the proposed methodology is 8.96mm, which is again less than the Attention U-Net by 1.04mm. The mean volumetric similarly and mean precision with the proposed method are 0.8229 and 0.7210, respectively.

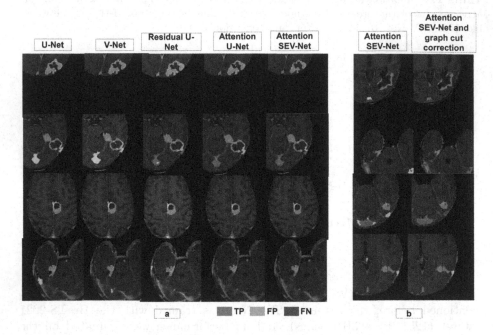

Fig. 4. (a) The comparative segmentation results of Attention SEV-Net with that of the state-of-the-art networks that are U-Net, V-Net, Residual U-Net, and Attention U-Net are shown. (b) The improvement in the segmentation results on using the interactive graph cut correction method after initial segmentation by Attention-SEV-Net.

4   Conclusion

When deep learning networks are tested with the datasets available in clinics, there are always chances of over-segmentation and under-segmentation. An interactive method would help the radiologists to get the nearly correct delineation with minimum human effort. In this paper, we proposed an interactive correction method whereby the falsely detected isolated voxels can be removed efficiently. A novel network called Attention-SEV-Net has also been put forward. This network performed better in terms of dice score, volumetric similarity, and Hausdorff distance-95 than its nearest competitors, and the interactive post-processing boosted the performance further. Though the post-processing technique is quite fast, it is also necessary to compare its interaction time with other competing algorithms in future.

Acknowledgment. The authors are thankful to the Department of Biotechnology (DBT), Government of India (No.BT/PR41121/swdn/1357/020) and Vinnova, The Agency for Innovation Systems (No.2020-03616), Government of Sweden for supporting this work.

References

1. Chander, A., Chatterjee, A., Siarry, P.: A new social and momentum component adaptive PSO algorithm for image segmentation. Expert Syst. Appl. **38**(5), 4998–5004 (2011)
2. Dhara, A.K., et al.: Segmentation of post-operative glioblastoma in MRI by U-Net with patient-specific interactive refinement. In: Crimi, A., Bakas, S., Kuijf, H., Keyvan, F., Reyes, M., van Walsum, T. (eds.) BrainLes 2018. LNCS, vol. 11383, pp. 115–122. Springer, Cham (2019). https://doi.org/10.1007/978-3-030-11723-8_11
3. Ji, S., Wei, B., Yu, Z., Yang, G., Yin, Y.: A new multistage medical segmentation method based on superpixel and fuzzy clustering. Comput. Math. Meth. Med. **2014** (2014)
4. Malmberg, F., Strand, R., Kullberg, J., Nordenskjöld, R., Bengtsson, E.: Smart paint: a new interactive segmentation method applied to MR prostate segmentation. In: MICCAI 2012 (2012)
5. Milletari, F., Navab, N., Ahmadi, S.A.: V-Net: fully convolutional neural networks for volumetric medical image segmentation. In: 2016 Fourth International Conference on 3D Vision (3DV), pp. 565–571. IEEE (2016)
6. Oktay, O., et al.: Attention U-Net: learning where to look for the pancreas (2018)
7. Qin, X., Zhang, Z., Huang, C., Dehghan, M., Zaiane, O.R., Jagersand, M.: U2-Net: going deeper with nested U-structure for salient object detection. Pattern Recogn. **106**, 107404 (2020)
8. Ronneberger, O., Fischer, P., Brox, T.: U-Net: convolutional networks for biomedical image segmentation. In: Navab, N., Hornegger, J., Wells, W.M., Frangi, A.F. (eds.) MICCAI 2015. LNCS, vol. 9351, pp. 234–241. Springer, Cham (2015). https://doi.org/10.1007/978-3-319-24574-4_28
9. Zhang, Z., Liu, Q., Wang, Y.: Road extraction by deep residual U-Net. IEEE Geosci. Remote Sens. Lett. **15**, 749–753 (2017)
10. Zhou, Z., Siddiquee, M.M.R., Tajbakhsh, N., Liang, J.U.: A nested U-Net architecture for medical image segmentation (2018). arXiv preprint arXiv:1807.10165

Local Binary Pattern Induced Optimized CNN for Brain Tumor Diagnosis from MRI Data

Pranay Nath[1](✉), Surajit Mondal[1], and Lidia Ghosh[2]🆔

[1] Maulana Abul Kalam Azad University of Technology, Kolkata, West Bengal, India
pranay15nath@gmail.com
[2] Institute of Engineering and Management, Kolkata, University of Engineering and Management, Kolkata, West Bengal, India

Abstract. Advancements in medical science have led to new approaches for preventing, diagnosing, and treating brain tumors, studied by researchers across different fields. The accurate identification of tumors in MRI scans can assist in disease identification, treatment evaluation, and radiation-based therapies. Currently, humans manually perform this task, but research has explored the integration of computer processing in MRI analysis. While MRIs provide a comprehensive view of the brain to identify tumors, they lack accuracy in pinpointing their location and size. To address this, an improved version of Local Binary Pattern (LBP) encoded optimized Convolutional neural network is proposed to improve diagnostic accuracy. LBP captures texture information in a local neighborhood of each pixel, providing additional features to learn from and enhancing the accuracy of texture-based image classification. The model is evaluated on the Figshare dataset through multiple experiments.

Keywords: Optimized Convolutional Neural Network · Local Binary Pattern · Brain tumor · Figshare dataset · MRI analysis

1 Introduction

The body's cells are in a constant state of growth and proliferation, with new cells replacing old and damaged ones [16]. A tumor is a harmful mass of cells that grow uncontrollably. Tumors can be benign or malignant with varying degrees of severity [7]. Brain tumors are abnormal masses that grow in the brain and are considered as one of the most serious life-threatening conditions [15]. Brain tumors have numerous kinds based on its location, intensity, texture, and shape [5] such as lymphoma, acoustic neuroma, glioma, pituitary and meningioma [12]. Glioma, the most deadly primary tumor, occurs due to abnormal increament in the Glial cells which make up 80% of the human brain [9]. Meningioma is another form of primary tumor that evolves in the protective membrane of the brain and meninges spinal cord [5]. Early detection and prompt treatment of tumors can significantly improve patients' life expectancy.

P. Maji et al. (Eds.): PReMI 2023, LNCS 14301, pp. 388–396, 2023.
https://doi.org/10.1007/978-3-031-45170-6_40

Magnetic resonance imaging (MRI) [16] techniques are widely used for brain tumor recognition because they provide high-quality images of internal structures. Automated methods for examining MRI images may prove useful in improving the accuracy and efficiency of brain tumor diagnosis [7]. Brain tumor diversity can make it difficult to draw accurate inferences from MRI images alone [12]. Underdiagnosis can lead to reduced treatment response and lower survival rates. The use of artificial intelligence (AI) as well as computer-aided diagnosis (CAD) systems [5,12] has become essential in improving diagnosis accuracy.

2 Literature Survey

The CAD system is composed of multiple stages, including noise removal [15], *segmentation* of the lesion area from the rest of the images [16], *feature extraction* [15], and *classification* [2]. There exist plenty of research works that implement various machine learning algorithms [1,2,5–8,10–13,15,16] and deep learning algorithms [2,5,16] to address the problem. Among these, Support Vector Machine (SVM) and k-Nearest Neighbor (KNN) are the most commonly used for MRI image classification [5,7].

Various algorithms and models have been utilized to detect brain tumors. These include fuzzy brainstorm optimization [14], Cat Swarm Optimization (CSO), Decision-based Couple Window Median Filter (DBCWMF), scale-invariant feature transform (SIFT), Statistical Region Merging (SRM) as well as CSO-SIFT extraction and Backpropagation Neural Network (BPNN) [4]. Pretrained deep convolutional neural networks (DCNNs), such as ResNet50, ResNet101, VGG16, InceptionV3, AlexNet, GoogLeNet, and InceptionResNetV2, have also been employed, mostly on the Figshare repository [12,13]. A model called Regions with CNN (R-CNN) has been developed for brain tumor detection and classification, using the Region Proposal Network and VGG-16 as the primary seed [11]. Recurrent Neural Networks (RNNs) have also been cascaded with CNN for multi-tier feature processing, but it suffers from the vanishing gradient problem when the input feature vector dimension is high [13]. Finally, a DenseNet-41-based Mask-RCNN architecture has been deployed to execute the accurate segmentation, localization, and classification of brain tumors [6].

Despite the introduction of various automatic procedures for brain tumor diagnosis, each has its pros and cons. Thus, the present study aims to design an improved version of Local Binary Pattern (LBP) [4] encoded optimized CNN that enhances brain tumor diagnosis efficiency from images. Here, the main objective is to develop a deep learning-based architecture for early detection of brain tumor with the highest accuracy and lowest computational time.

The paper is arranged as follows. Section 2 provides the proposed methodology. Section 3 is dedicated to Simulation and results including the details of the dataset. The proposed work is concluded in Sect. 4.

3   Proposed Methodology

3.1   Pre-processing

The raw images from Figshare brain MRI dataset have been resized to 224×224 pixels to accelerate the process of training and reduce the space requirement. For the sake of better visualization, some pre-processing measures including skull-stripping [9], contrast enhancement [15], and grayscale [1] transformation extraction have been performed. Fig. 1 shows an example of pre-processed image from a brain tumor raw image.

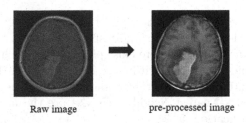

Raw image   pre-processed image

Fig. 1. Image Pre-processing

3.2   Traditional Convolutional Neural Network

Convolutional Neural Networks (CNNs) incorporate hyperparameters in various layers, such as kernel number, activation function, kernel size, and stride in convolutional layers, learning rate and kernel size in pooling layers, and size of layer and number of layers in dense layers. These hyperparameters play a crucial role in CNN's performance. An image can be represented mathematically as a tensor with certain dimensions:

$$d_{image} = (s_H, s_W, s_C) \tag{1}$$

where: s_H and s_W are respectively the size of the height and width of the image, and s_C is the number of image channels.

Dimension of kernel K can be given as follows

$$d_{kernel} = (f, f, s_C) \tag{2}$$

for an odd dimension f. Therefore, for an image I and kernel K, the convolution function and its dimension can be defined as:

$$conv(I, K)_{x,y} = \sum_{m=1}^{s_H} \sum_{n=1}^{s_W} \sum_{p=1}^{s_C} K_{i,j,k} I_{x+m-1,y+n-1,p} \tag{3}$$

$$dim(conv(I, K)) = (\lfloor \frac{s_H + 2r - f}{s} + 1 \rfloor, \lfloor \frac{s_W + 2r - f}{s} + 1 \rfloor); s > 0$$

$$= (s_H + 2r - f, s_W + 2r - f); s = 0 \tag{4}$$

where s is the number of strides and r is the padding size.

3.3   The Optimized CNN Architecture

The Optimized CNN [1] is essentially a Multilayer Perceptron (MLP) that includes an activation function linking weighted inputs to outputs in each neuron. Finding their optimal configuration is a challenging task. The present study proposes an effective optimization solution for improving CNN performance as represented in Table 1. This architecture enables it to be both translation and rotation invariant i.e., the proposed architecture shows efficacy in identifying and classifying actual classes accurately regardless of their position or orientation in the input image.

Table 1. Pre and post-optimization performance of the proposed CNN

Performance Metric	Pre-Optimization	Post-Optimization
Classifier Accuracy	91.78%	96.91%

In the present context, the base CNN architecture is considered as the foundation for the subsequent hyperparameter optimization. The proposed optimized architecture is composed of an input layer, five convolutional layers, five max-pooling layers as well as a classification block comprising two fully connected layers and one dropout layer as described in Fig. 2. Through experimentation, this topology is found to be the most suitable for the specific classification task. Table 2 depicts the summary of the hyper-parameter settings for the optimized CNN architecture implemented here.

Table 2. Summary of the hyperparameter settings for the Optimized CNN

Layers	Type	Output shape	Parameters
1	Input	$224 \times 224 \times 3$	0
2	Convolution	$224 \times 224 \times 6$	456
3	Maxpooling	$112 \times 112 \times 6$	0
4	Convolution	$112 \times 112 \times 16$	2416
5	Activation	$112 \times 112 \times 16$	0
6	Maxpooling	$56 \times 56 \times 16$	0
7	Convolution	$54 \times 54 \times 64$	9280
8	Maxpooling	$27 \times 27 \times 64$	0
9	Flatten	46656	0
10	Dense	128	5972096
11	Dropout	128	0
12	Dense	2	258

3.4 Proposed Local Binary Pattern Encoded Optimized CNN

Although the optimized CNNs are powerful models for image classification, still it can sometimes struggle to capture the local texture information of an MRI image. MRI brain tumor data contains complex textures and structures that can be difficult to capture using optimized CNN. In this scenario, Local Binary Pattern (LBP), a robust texture descriptor, can be a useful tool where the local texture information is important for accurate classification, especially while dealing with texture-rich MRI images. Additionally, the robustness of the LBP operator to grayscale variations and rotation makes it useful in tasks where changes in illumination and orientation are likely to occur.

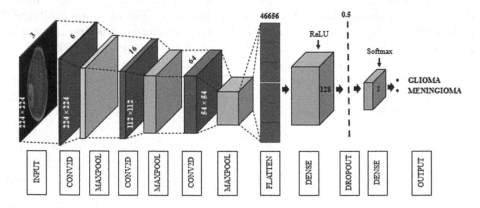

Fig. 2. Detailed architecture of the Optimized CNN used for brain tumor classification

The LBP operator works by defining a matrix of size 3×3 around a central pixel, which is utilized as a threshold. The adjacent eight pixels are then compared to the central pixel, and if the value of the neighboring pixel is greater than the central pixel, it is set to 1, otherwise, it is set to 0. This generates an 8-bit binary number which is then converted to a decimal number, replacing the value of the central pixel. This LBP code expresses the textural feature of the image [4]. LBP can be represented by the following formula:

$$LBP_{P,R} = \sum_{i=0}^{n-1} S(g_i - g_c) \times 2^i \tag{5}$$

$$S(x) = \begin{cases} 1 & \text{if } x > 0 \\ 0 & \text{if } x \leq 0 \end{cases} \tag{6}$$

where P is the number of sample points, R is the radius, g_c denotes the value of the central pixel and g_i is the value of the surrounding pixel. Thus, the LBP operator generates an LBP code for every pixel present in an image. By using this encoding method, it becomes possible to create a locally coded image of binary patterns based on the original image.

To mitigate the impact of illumination and occlusion on brain MRI images, this study utilizes the LBP descriptor to extract LBP codes from the images. These LBP-coded images are then used as inputs for the optimized CNN architecture as depicted in Fig. 3.

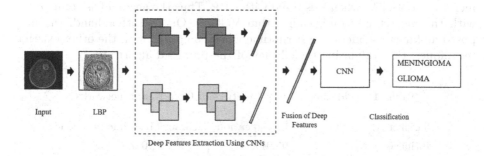

Fig. 3. Classification of brain tumor by LBP infused deep learning architectures

4   Simulation and Results

4.1   Dataset Description

The proposed architecture is trained and validated on the Figshare dataset, which consists of 3064 functional MR images, all in the .mat file format, collected from 233 patients with 3 types of brain tumors: glioma, meningioma and pituitary. We consider only 2 classes: meningioma and glioma. The details of training and testing data dimensions for both classes are depicted in Table 3. All the contrast-enhanced images have been converted into Grayscale for better visualization [3].

Table 3. Cardinality of images used in Simulation.

Tumor type	No. of images	Dimension	Training samples	Testing samples
Glioma	1426	512×512	1026	400
Meningioma	708	512×512	530	178

4.2 Performance Analysis of the Proposed Architecture

The experimental simulation demonstrating the effectiveness of the aforesaid method has been depicted in this section. In this experiment, six pre-trained CNN models, like VGG 16, VGG 19, NasNet Mobile, GoogLeNet, ResNet152V2, DenseNet-201, as mentioned in Table 4, have been trained on the Figshare dataset using the transfer learning approach. All the six classifier algorithms along with the proposed one are trained in two ways: without LBP and with LBP. For the later case, after processing the brain tumor image dataset through LBP texture descriptor, the LBP transformed images have been passed through each of the aforesaid same set of architectures. It is observed that LBP-infused deep Learning models offer better performance as compared to its counter part. For the space economy, we here depicted the performance of the classfier algorithms fused with LBP.

It is evident from Table 4 that the proposed optimized CNN architecture achieves accuracy of classification 96.91% without LBP, but the accuracy increases to 98.57% when it is fused with LBP. Thus the accuracy is comparable with the highest performing algorithm VGG19. On the other hand, the proposed architecture offers lowest runtime when compared with the other existing techniques, thus validating the efficacy of the proposed algorithm.

Table 4. Validation Accuracy metrics of Deep Neural networks

Classifier Algorithm	Classification Accuracy	Runtime in second
Optimized CNN	96.91%	10.09
LBP+Optimized CNN	**98.57%**	**9.76**
LBP+VGG 16	98.98%	15.67
LBP+VGG 19	99.00%	13.83
LBP+ResNet 152 V2	97.39%	12.89
LBP+GoogleNet	93.38%	11.87
LBP+NasNet Mobile	97.14%	10.77
LBP+DenseNet 201	97.60%	11.12

4.3   Training and Validation Profile of the Proposed Method

The training and validation profile of both the optimized CNN and LBP induced optimized CNN are portrayed in Fig. 4. It is evident from the figure that both the training and validation accuracy remain consistently high for the later one.

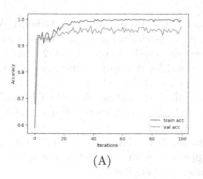
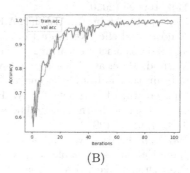

(A)   (B)

Fig. 4. Training and validation profile of (A) Optimized CNN (B) LBP+Optimized CNN.

5   Conclusion

The identification and segmentation of tumors or irregular areas in MRI can be beneficial for cancer research and clinical treatment. However, accurately identifying tumors through manual review by radiologists is a time-intensive process. To overcome this challenge, a new approach to categorize brain tumors into two classes, Glioma and Meningioma, using an automated method is presented in this study. The proposed model is evaluated on the Figshare brain tumor dataset and its performance is compared to existing methods to confirm its validity.

The proposed algorithm utilizes an optimized CNN to diagnose brain tumors in medical images. The raw MRI images of brain tumor are preprocessed through skull stripping and contrast enhancement, before being fed into an optimized CNN for classification. The performance of the optimized CNN is compared with the existing dense CNN models where the DenseNet 201 model performs best with 99.80% accuracy. However, when LBP is introduced to the same set of models, their performance was inverted, with less dense architectures such as optimized CNN, VGG16, and VGG19 exhibiting higher performance. It is validated through the experimentation that the inclusion of LBP increases the efficiency of the architecture with less number of layers that evidently reduces the time complexity and space complexity of the procedure.

References

1. Ait Amou, M., Xia, K., Kamhi, S., Mouhafid, M.: A novel MRI diagnosis method for brain tumor classification based on CNN and Bayesian optimization. In: Healthcare, vol. 10, p. 494. MDPI (2022)

2. Amin, J., Sharif, M., Haldorai, A., Yasmin, M., Nayak, R.S.: Brain tumor detection and classification using machine learning: a comprehensive survey. Complex Intell. Syst. 1–23 (2021)
3. Cheng, J.: Brain tumor dataset (2017)
4. Kaplan, K., Kaya, Y., Kuncan, M., Ertunç, H.M.: Brain tumor classification using modified local binary patterns (LBP) feature extraction methods. Med. Hypotheses **139**, 109696 (2020)
5. Kibriya, H., Amin, R., Alshehri, A.H., Masood, M., Alshamrani, S.S., Alshehri, A.: A novel and effective brain tumor classification model using deep feature fusion and famous machine learning classifiers. Comput. Intell. Neurosci. **2022** (2022)
6. Masood, M., et al.: A novel deep learning method for recognition and classification of brain tumors from MRI images. Diagnostics **11**(5), 744 (2021)
7. Mohsen, H., El-Dahshan, E.S.A., El-Horbaty, E.S.M., Salem, A.B.M.: Classification using deep learning neural networks for brain tumors. Future Comput. Inform. J. **3**(1), 68–71 (2018)
8. Nayak, D.R., Padhy, N., Mallick, P.K., Bagal, D.K., Kumar, S.: Brain tumour classification using noble deep learning approach with parametric optimization through metaheuristics approaches. Computers **11**(1), 10 (2022)
9. Pereira, S., Pinto, A., Alves, V., Silva, C.A.: Brain tumor segmentation using convolutional neural networks in MRI images. IEEE Trans. Med. Imaging **35**(5), 1240–1251 (2016). https://doi.org/10.1109/TMI.2016.2538465
10. Rasool, M., et al.: A hybrid deep learning model for brain tumour classification. Entropy **24**(6), 799 (2022)
11. Salçin, K., et al.: Detection and classification of brain tumours from MRI images using faster R-CNN. Tehn. Glas. **13**(4), 337–342 (2019)
12. Senan, E.M., Jadhav, M.E., Rassem, T.H., Aljaloud, A.S., Mohammed, B.A., Al-Mekhlafi, Z.G.: Early diagnosis of brain tumour MRI images using hybrid techniques between deep and machine learning. Comput. Math. Methods Med. **2022** (2022)
13. Shahzadi, I., Tang, T.B., Meriadeau, F., Quyyum, A.: CNN-LSTM: cascaded framework for brain tumour classification. In: 2018 IEEE-EMBS Conference on Biomedical Engineering and Sciences (IECBES), pp. 633–637. IEEE (2018)
14. Sharif, M.I., Li, J.P., Khan, M.A., Saleem, M.A.: Active deep neural network features selection for segmentation and recognition of brain tumors using MRI images. Pattern Recogn. Lett. **129**, 181–189 (2020)
15. Siar, M., Teshnehlab, M.: A combination of feature extraction methods and deep learning for brain tumour classification. IET Image Process. **16**(2), 416–441 (2022)
16. Vidyarthi, A., Agarwal, R., Gupta, D., Sharma, R., Draheim, D., Tiwari, P.: Machine learning assisted methodology for multiclass classification of malignant brain tumors. IEEE Access **10**, 50624–50640 (2022)

iPyrDAE: Image Pyramid-Based Denoising Autoencoder for Infrared Breast Images

Kaushik Raghavan[1]([✉]) [iD], B. Sivaselavan[1], and V. Kamakoti[2]

[1] Indian Institute of Information Technology, Design and Manufacturing,
Kancheepuram, Chennai, India
`kaushik.gr@gmail.com, sivaselvanb@iiitdm.ac.in`
[2] Indian Institute of Technology Madras, Chennai, India
`kama@cse.iitm.ac.in`

Abstract. An early and accurate breast cancer diagnosis will reduce the death rate and improve survival chances. Thermography is a promising non-invasive early detection modality for breast cancer. Artificial intelligence-based classification systems are being used to classify thermographic infrared images. The success of these classification systems also depends on the quality of infrared images. However, the thermographic images acquired using digital infrared cameras are inevitably degraded by noise. In this paper, we propose novel denoising auto-encoders using image pyramids. The denoising auto-encoders are forced to learn the non-local noises by corrupting the input images in the image pyramid domain. We also propose a method to estimate the noise probability distribution in infrared images using statistical methods. The proposed denoising auto-encoder framework will learn better data representations from the corrupted images generated using image pyramids and estimated noise probability distribution. The Experimentation with four different infrared breast image data sets demonstrates robust representation learning by the agent showing promising improvements in the peak signal-to-noise ratio.

Keywords: Denoising auto-encoder · Infrared Imaging Denoising · Infrared Breast Imaging

1 Introduction and Literature Background

1.1 Infrared Breast Imaging

Breast cancer (BC) is one of the most common malignancies among women worldwide. In India, the incidence of breast cancer has rapidly increased by almost 50% from 1965 to 1983 [1]. Imaging techniques and Artificial Intelligence (AI) framework make early BC detection more reliable. Mammography is one of the most commonly used and accepted examinations. But the low doses of X-rays used in mammography can harm patients. Other imaging techniques, such

P. Maji et al. (Eds.): PReMI 2023, LNCS 14301, pp. 397–406, 2023.
https://doi.org/10.1007/978-3-031-45170-6_41

as MRI and Ultrasound, are being used to support the early diagnosis. Infrared (IR) thermography is a potential imaging technique that has proven effective in the early detection of BC in recent times. Thermography is a skin-surface temperature screening method. It is a non-invasive technique, and there is no contact involved. Thermography is considered very safe and involves no radiation like a mammogram [2]. ANNs and deep learning techniques are widely used for classifying IR breast images (as cancerous or non-cancerous). The success of the classification algorithm mainly depends on the quality of the Acquired Infrared breast images. The quality of the IR images is mainly affected by the presence of noise in the IR images. IR images have a low Signal-to-noise ratio, and their contrast is low, making further processing a problematic task. This makes IR image denoising a critical image pre-processing step before attempting segmentation and classification.

The main reason for the noise in IR images is the sensor and the interference from the signal processing circuit. The variation in the pixel values can measure the noise [3] as shown by Budzan and Wyżgolik. From the literature, it can be observed that infrared thermographic breast images contain different kinds of noise like 1) Gaussian Noise, 2) Speckle Noise, 3) Salt and Pepper Noise, 4) External Noise, and 5) Poisson Noise.

1.2 Literature Review

Although a significant amount of literature exists in the area of image denoising, in this section, we will focus on the research on the image-denoising techniques used for IR images, especially on medical and breast IR images. Block matching and 3D (BM3D) filtering techniques enhanced the image quality. Applying collaborative filtering and grouping at each step of the BM3D [4] process improved the signal-to-noise ratio of denoised thermal image increased by 32%. Wavelet-based denoising techniques were evaluated to denoise the IR-based medical images. Raheleh and Rabbani [5] modeled the local noise variance and substituted the wavelet-based maximum a posterior (MAP) estimator for noise removal. In a 2015 paper [6], the authors evaluated several wavelet types with different vanishing moments, like Biorthogonal, Haar, and Meyer. The best results were obtained using the Biorthogonal wavelets with a vanishing moment of coiflets = 5. Non-linear filters can also be used to denoise the IR thermal images. The model is validated with SNR and shows an average increase of 30 dB. Soft wavelet thresholding can also be applied to IR beast images [7]. Initially, a soft threshold is applied in wavelet transform separately on each red, green, and blue channel. Then an inverse transform is performed to obtain the smoothed image. The co-occurrence filtering (CoF) technique is also used to denoise the IR images [8]. The co-occurrence matrix-based filtering was used to improve the Signal-to-Noise ratio. The paper shows that the accuracy of the KNN algorithm increased from 75% to 83.33% when the images were denoised using a Co-occurrence filter [9]. The literature shows that deep learning techniques have been used to denoise infrared images. Techniques like convolution neural networks (CNN) have been used [10]. Deep reinforcement techniques were also used to denoise the infrared medical images [11]. As a part of the research, we present a variation of auto-encoder where the noisy image is created using image pyramid operation.

Although the literature discusses several denoising techniques, the authors have not attempted to estimate the noise in the infrared images. Most of the papers assume that infrared images have noise and go on to apply various denoising techniques. This paper proposes a technique to estimate the noise distribution of infrared breast images captured from multiple sources. Then we use the estimated noise distribution to corrupt the images at multiple scales and train a Denoising Auto-encoder to enhance the infrared breast images without blurring the edges. The following are the main contribution of the paper.

1. We propose a methodology to estimate the noise probability distribution in infrared medial images.
2. We implement a novel Denoising auto-encoder using image pyramids that we will learn both local and non-local noises.
3. We have trained and validated the model with multiple data-sets.

2   Infrared Image Denoising - Proposed Methodology

The proposed methodology consists of two major steps. The first step is to estimate the noise distribution of each image in the data set. Based on the type of noises discussed in Sect. 1.1, we will segregate the images based on the noise distribution as Gaussian, Gamma, and Poisson. The second step is to train an image-denoising auto-encoder using image pyramids. The details of the implementation are discussed in the following steps.

2.1   Data-Sets Used for Experimentation

For experimentation purposes, we use four different infrared breast data sets. We chose multiple thermal image data sets to make the results reproducible across multiple data sets. The first two data sets mentioned above had enough samples. We could only get sample images from the rest of the data sets. So, we augmented the images to get more examples. We used TorchIO [12] to perform the augmentation process. We sampled 2000 random images from all data-sets and divided the data into test and train. The following is the list of data sets used for IR image denoising.

1. DMR [13] - Database For Mastology Research
2. MammoTherm - Thermographic mammary [13] images database
3. Sample images from The DBT-TU-JU Breast Thermogram data-set [14]
4. Case study images from ABT (Amrita Breast Thermography) [10]

2.2 Estimating the Noise Distribution of IR Breast Images

We begin by assuming a null hypothesis that noise belongs to a known probability density function (PDF). Using the distribution, we need to extract the noisy features of the image. The homogeneous regions in the image are identified using the technique present in the paper [15]. We do this by selecting suitable texture-less areas. We use Haraliks co-occurrence matrices to capture the homogeneity metric using the geometric content of the data. High values are associated with high textural variations and vice versa. The co-occurrence matrix of an arbitrary point is represented using $P(i,j)$. The normalized version of the same is represented using $p(i,j) = P(i,j)/N$, where N is constant. The second-order measure, the homogeneity metric, is represented using Eq. 1 (see Equation. 1).

$$Hm = \sum_i \sum_j \frac{1}{1+(i-j)^2} p(i,j) \tag{1}$$

The above value is computed for each of the coordinates. Initially, we start with a small matrix, say 5X5, and then combine the adjacent regions not differing much from the homogeneity measure as one region. Once the homogeneous regions are identified, the null hypothesis is tested by estimating the noise parameters' maximum likelihood estimate of the assumed PDF. To test the null hypothesis, we must estimate the noise parameters using the Maximum Likelihood estimate (MLE) for the assumed PDF. The mean and variance are the parameters for the Normal/Gaussian distribution with PDF (as shown in Eq. 2) are $\widehat{u}^n$ and σ^2 as shown in Eq. 3 and Eq. 4

$$p(x \mid \mu, \sigma) = \frac{1}{\sqrt{2\pi\sigma_0^2}} \exp\left(-\frac{1}{2}\frac{(x-\mu_0)^2}{\sigma_0^2}\right) \tag{2}$$

$$\widehat{u}^n = \frac{1}{n}\sum_{j=1}^n x_j \tag{3}$$

$$\sigma^2 = \frac{1}{n}\sum_{j=1}^n (x_j - \hat{\mu})^2 \tag{4}$$

For the gamma distribution with PDF as shown in Eq. 5, the Noise parameters k and scale σ are arrived using the MLE as shown in Eq. 6 and Eq. 7

$$p(x \mid k, \sigma) = \frac{x}{\sigma^k \Gamma(k)} \exp\left(-\frac{x}{\sigma}\right) \tag{5}$$

$$\hat{k} = \frac{n\sum X_i}{n\sum X_i \ln X_i - \sum \ln X_i \sum X_i} \tag{6}$$

$$\hat{\alpha} = \frac{1}{n^2}\left(n\sum X_i \ln X_i - \sum \ln X_i \sum X_i\right) \tag{7}$$

In the same way for Poisson distribution with the PDF as shown in Eq. 8 the noise parameter λ is given by the MLE in Eq. 9.

$$p(x \mid \lambda) = \exp\left(-\lambda_0\right)\frac{1}{x!}\lambda^x \tag{8}$$

$$\hat{\lambda} = \frac{1}{n}\sum x_j \tag{9}$$

Once the PDF curves are fit, the next step is numerically analyzing the distributional characteristics of the PDFs using Kullback-Leibler(KL)/ Jensen-Shannon (JS) divergences. Assuming P and Q are the estimates and fitted distributions, the value of KLD is given by $KLD(P,Q) = -\sum_i P(i)\log\frac{Q(i)}{P(i)}$ and the value of JS is given by $JSD(P,Q) = 1/2(KLD(P,M) + KLD(Q,M))$. A higher value indicates more deviation from the fitted distribution.

The next important test is to conduct hypothesis testing for the assumed PDF. To begin with, we make an assumption on the PDF of the input noise feature. We then conduct a t test using KLD and JSD that we obtained using the homogeneous regions calculation. The t statistic is calculated using $t = \frac{\hat{x}-\mu}{s/\sqrt{n}}$. based on the t-value (or the p-value obtained from t-distribution), the hypothesis is either accepted or rejected. We will repeat the steps until we find the right PDF for the noise features. Based on the PDFs, the images will be separated for further processing. The following Table 1 shows the KLD and JSD values of various homogeneous regions from four different data sets. The noise distributions of various images are shown in Fig. 1 (see Fig. 1)

Table 1. Table showing the KLD and JSD values for various images.

Images	Regions			
	Red	Blue	Green	Yellow
DMR	[0.0194, 0.0462]	[0.0086, 0.0049]	[0.0116, 0.0118]	[0.0143, 0.0330]
ABT	[0.0198, 0.0396]	[0.0196, 0.0387]	[0.0176, 0.0337]	[0.0178, 0.0356]
MammoTherm	[0.0228, 0.0451]	[0.0253, 0.0504]	[0.0296, 0.0603]	[0.0291, 0.0594]
DBT-TU-JU	[0.0456, 0.1653]	[0.0426, 0.1613]	[0.0770, 0.2851]	[0.0665, 0.2509]

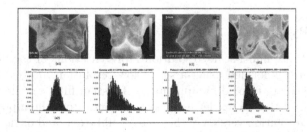

Fig. 1. a2, d2 shows that a1, d1 has noise Gaussian noise PDF, b2 shows that image b1 has Gamma noise PDF and c2 shows shows that c1 has Poisson Noise distribution

2.3 iPyrDAE: Denoising IR Breast Images

In this paper, we propose a Denoising Auto Encoder (DAE) using image pyramids to denoise the infrared images, which is a low-level pixel predicting task. We present a DAE that uses representations from other gradient domains, such as Laplace and Gaussian. A conventional DAE uses a clean image to generate a noisy image by adding noise using the encoder-decoder network [16]. In this work, we generate the noisy image by corrupting the clean image at a larger scale in other domains, which are more complex to remove. The idea is to train a network to learn complex and robust representations at varied scales. This will enforce the DAE to exploit the data structures in different domains making the learning process resilient to different kinds of noise that are part of the infrared images. DAEs accomplish this task by using a loss function that compares the output images with the original input, not the corrupted input. By this, the network will learn to denoise the image from the corrupted images. Let us consider the input image to be x and the corrupted version to be $\bar{x}$, which will be mapped to the hidden representation using the following Eq. 10 in the auto-encoder. In the context of denoising autoencoders, we trained separate models for different noise distributions. When training a denoising autoencoder, the process typically involves introducing a form of noise to the input data and then training the autoencoder to reconstruct the clean version of the data. The choice of noise distribution is arrived at using the noise estimation technique discussed in Sect. 2.1.

$$y = f_\theta(\bar{x}) = s(W\bar{x} + b) \tag{10}$$

The reconstruction using the hidden representation (y) is given as the following Eq. 11

$$z = g_{\theta'}(y) \tag{11}$$

The θ and θ are the network hyper-parameters learned by minimizing the reconstruction error, which can be a mean squared error, as shown in the below Eq. 12. Such DAEs are known to learn better as compared to traditional auto-encoders.

$$L_2(x, z) = \|z - x\|^2 \tag{12}$$

2.4 Image Pyramids

Image pyramids are multi-scale/resolution representations of the images. Gaussian pyramid [18] is formed using a set of low-resolution images. These lower-resolution images are formed by applying a Gaussian filter on the input image. For the purpose of this paper, let us denote the data from the input image as x, then the lower resolution version of the image will be denoted using x_l^G. Here the level of the pyramid will be denoted by l. In the image pyramid, the bottom level will be the original image itself which is $x_0^G = x$ and $x_{(l+1)}^G = downsample(x_l^G)$. Laplace pyramids [18] are constructed using the Gaussian pyramid. At each level of the Laplace pyramid, the image will contain the pixels that are present in the Gaussian pyramid and not pixels in the lower level of the Gaussian pyramid. By subtracting the neighboring levels in the Gaussian pyramid, we get the Laplace pyramid x_i^L. We can represent this using $x_i^L = x_l^G - upsample(x_{(l+1)}^G)$. If N denotes the top level of the pyramid, then $x_N^L = x_N^G$, meaning the top level of the Gaussian pyramid is the same as that of the Laplacian pyramid and are the residuals of the pyramid operations. These corrupt images will be part of the DAE. Once the Image pyramids are formed, we also add noise to the images based on the noise distribution PDF estimated in the Sect. 2.6. The image corruption process is showing in Fig. 2 (see Fig. 2).

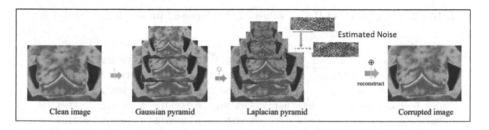

Fig. 2. Figure show the image corrution process. The noise showing in the image is generated using the noise estimation technique

2.5   iPyrDAE Architecture

We propose to retrieve important representations from the data input data set by training a convolutional neural network (CNN) to reconstruct the data $x \in X$ from the noisy data $\tilde{x} \in \widetilde{X}$. We use the image pyramids to generate the corrupted data $\bar{x}$ from x. Initially, we construct image pyramids from the clean data x and then corrupt a random level of the pyramid to generate a corrupted image $\tilde{x}$. By corrupting the input data $\tilde{x}$ across a variety of scales, we attempt to capture the non-local information along with the local information. This makes the representation learning (RL) phase learn a diverse variety of corruptions. We also add noise to the images in the pyramid based on the noise distribution PDF estimated in Sect. 5.6. This makes the DAE network "learn harder". The following Fig. 3 (see Fig. 3) shows the implementation of the iPyrDAE.

Let us denote the corrupted image as $\tilde{x} = iPyr(x : \tilde{x})$. For consistency purposes, we will be denoting the pyramid data using $\widetilde{x_l}$ in place of $\widetilde{x_l^L}$ (for Laplace Image) and $\widetilde{x_l^G}$ (for Gaussian Image). The corrupted input space will be represented as Eq. 13

$$I = \{iPyr(x : \tilde{x})_c, C \in C\} \tag{13}$$

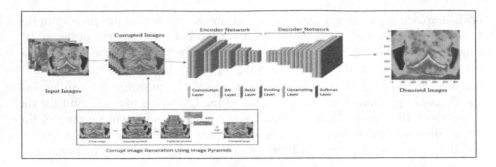

Fig. 3. The iPyrDAE showing the Denoising Architecture using auto-encoders

Table 2. Comparison of PNSR values of the denoised images from the test set

Algorithm	SNR	MSE	RMSE	PSNR
FastNlMeansDenoising	8.7424012	0.3047012	0.5520012	36.7379
Wavelet Denoising (skImage)	11.0797112	0.1252012	0.3538389	36.7402
Total-variation denoising	16.6118012	0.0447012	0.2116012	36.745
Denoise image using a bilateral filter	25.0637012	0.0183012	0.1352012	36.7594
Robust wavelet-based estimator	35.0815012	0.0050012	0.0709012	36.7703
Standard DAE	37.5651012	0.0007634	0.0276297	39.651641
DAE with Gaussian Pyramid	38.3837012	0.0002057	0.0143422	42.49923
DAE with Laplace Pyramid	38.8451012	0.0001531	0.0123734	43.140526
iPyrDAE + ReLU	35.7454012	0.0000119	0.0034496	48.687667
iPyrDAE + ReLU + Estimated Noise	40.3837012	0.0000062	0.00249	50.103443

Here C is the corrupted image set from the pyramid. The encoder with hyper-parameter θ will map the corrupted image space to the hidden representation in the encoder network. The representation space is denoted using $Y = F_\theta(I)$. The network is trained in mini-batches where the corrupted image is picked from one of the pyramids (Gaussian/Laplace) with a random level of the pyramid. The mini-batch optimizes based on the following objective function as defined below Eq. 14.

$$I_{rec} = \sum_{c \in C} \mathbf{E}_x \left\| x - z_c \right\|^2 \tag{14}$$

2.6   Implementation and Results

We implemented the iPyrDAE using python. TensorFlow and OpenCV were the main packages used for training and testing purposes. The models were statistically using used Signal-to-Noise ratio (SNR) and Peak-Signal-to-noise ratio. SNR is defined as the ratio of power and signal in the image. It is measured in dB. In the following equation, P stands for power. PSNR is the ratio between the maximum possible power to the actual power of the noise.

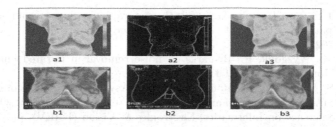

Fig. 4. a1, b1 shows the Original images; a2, b2 shows the identified noise and a3, b3 shows the denoised images.

$$SNR_{db} = 10 \left(\log_{10} \left(\frac{P_{signal}}{P_{Noise}} \right) \right) \tag{15}$$

$$PSNR = 10 \left(\log_{10} \left(\frac{255}{\sqrt{MSE}} \right) \right) \tag{16}$$

These metrics are calculated using the Eq. 15 and Eq. 16. The following Table 2 shows the improvement wit average PSNR values of the denoised test images. We evaluated several other denoising techniques and tabulated the results in the Table 2. The above table and Fig. 4 (see Fig. 4) show that the iPyrDAE performs well when compared to traditional Denoising methods. From the Above results, it can be observed that the proposed iPyrDAE method with image pyramids shows considerable improvement in the PNSR values when compared to the other techniques.

3   Conculsion

In this paper, we have introduced a new unsupervised representation learning-based denoising auto-encoder. This work shows that by corrupting the data using the image pyramids and passing these corrupted images as input, the denoising auto-encoder eliminates the noise more efficiently. We showed that by corrupting the data of a randomly chosen image pyramid and a level applied, the corruptions at multiple scales. This kind of random corruption forces the model to learn global noises in the underlying data structures from multiple scales. Compared to the conventional DAE, the proposed iPyrDAE agent is forced to learn better representations of the underlying data. The model's effectiveness is demonstrated with the aid of extensive experimentation results.

References

1. Mehrotra, R., Yadav, K.: Breast cancer in India: present scenario and the challenges ahead. World J. Clin. Oncol. **13**(3), 209–218 (2022)

2. Sarigoz, T., Ertan, T.: Role of dynamic thermography in diagnosis of nodal involvement in patients with breast cancer: a pilot study. Infrared Phys. Technol. **108**, 103336 (2020)
3. Budzan, S., Wyżgolik, R.: Remarks on noise removal in infrared images. Meas. Autom. Monit. **61**(6), 187–190 (2015)
4. Prabha, S., Sujatha, C. M., Ramakrishnan, S.: Asymmetry analysis of breast thermograms using BM3D technique and statistical texture features. In: 2014 International Conference on Informatics, Electronics & Vision (ICIEV), pp. 1–4 (2014). https://doi.org/10.1109/ICIEV.2014.6850730
5. Kafieh, R., Rabbani, H.: Wavelet-based medical infrared image noise reduction using local model for signal and noise. In: 2011 IEEE Statistical Signal Processing Workshop (SSP), pp. 549–552 (2011)
6. Moraes, M.S., Borchartt, T.B., Conci, A., MacHenry, T.: Using wavelets on denoising infrared medical images. In: 2015 IEEE International Conference on Industrial Technology (ICIT), pp. 1791–1798 (2015)
7. Wippig, D., Klauer, B., Zeidler, H.C.: Denoising of infrared images by wavelet thresholding. In: Elleithy, K., Sobh, T., Mahmood, A., Iskander, M., Karim, M. (eds.) Advances in Computer, Information, and Systems Sciences, and Engineering, pp. 103–108. Springer, Dordrecht (2007). https://doi.org/10.1007/1-4020-5261-8_18
8. Indumathi, T.V., Sannihith, K., Krishna, S., Remya Ajai, A.S.: Effect of co-occurrence filtering for recognizing abnormality from breast thermograms. In: 2021 Second International Conference on Electronics and Sustainable Communication Systems (ICESC), pp. 1170–1175 (2021)
9. Li, Q., Li, W., Zhang, J., Xu, Z.: An improved k-nearest neighbour method to diagnose breast cancer. Analyst. **143**(12), 2807–2811 (2018)
10. Lai, F., Kandukuri, J., Yuan, B., Zhang, Z., Jin, M.: Thermal image enhancement through the deconvolution methods for low-cost infrared cameras. Quant. Infrared Thermogr. J. **15**(2), 223–239 (2018)
11. Zhang, Z., Zheng, W., Ma, Z., Yin, L., Xie, M., Wu, Y.: Infrared star image denoising using regions with deep reinforcement learning. Infrared Phys. Technol. **117**, 103819 (2021)
12. Pérez-García, F., Sparks, R., Ourselin, S.: TorchIO: a Python library for efficient loading, preprocessing, augmentation and patch-based sampling of medical images in deep learning. Comput. Methods Programs Biomed. **208**, 106236 (2021)
13. Silva, L.F., Saade, D.C.M., Sequeiros, G.O., Silva, A.C., Paiva, A.C., Bravo, R.S., et al.: A new database for breast research with infrared image. J. Med. Imaging Health Inform. **4**(1), 92–100 (2014)
14. Bhowmik, M.K., Gogoi, U.R., Majumdar, G., Bhattacharjee, D., Datta, D., Ghosh, A.K.: Designing of ground-truth-annotated DBT-TU-JU breast thermogram database toward early abnormality prediction. IEEE J. Biomed. Health Inform. **22**(4), 1238–1249 (2017)
15. Gomez, L., Ospina, R., Frery, A.C.: Unassisted quantitative evaluation of despeckling filters. Remote Sens. **9**(4), 389 (2017)
16. Sun, Q., Liu, X., Bourennane, S., Liu, B.: Multiscale denoising autoencoder for improvement of target detection. Int. J. Remote Sens. **42**(8), 3002–3016 (2021)
17. Yan, L., et al.: Infrared and visible image fusion via octave Gaussian pyramid framework. Sci. Rep. **11**(1), 1–12 (2021)
18. Wang, Z., Cui, Z., Zhu, Y.: Multi-modal medical image fusion by Laplacian pyramid and adaptive sparse representation. Comput. Biol. Med. **123**, 103823 (2020)

Domain Adapted Few-Shot Learning for Breast Histopathological Image Classification

Anindita Mohanta[1][✉], Sourav Dey Roy[1], Niharika Nath[2],
and Mrinal Kanti Bhowmik[1]

[1] Computer Science and Engineering Department, Tripura University (A Central University),
Agartala, Tripura 799022, India
aninditamohanta01@gmail.com, souravdeyroy49@gmail.com,
mrinalkantibhowmik@tripurauniv.ac.in
[2] Biological and Chemical Sciences Department, New York Institute of Technology, New York,
NY 10023, USA
nnath@nyit.edu

Abstract. The inaccessibility of high numbers of annotated data and imbalance dataset's classes is a common phenomenon in medical microscopic image datasets. Also, collecting data from the same domain is a challenging task in microscopic imaging (e.g. same magnification factor, staining method, cancer type, imaging modality). A Conventional Deep Learning model with lack of labeled training data and domain shift could result in a misdiagnosis for such datasets. To overcome this problem, we formulated a domain adaptive few-shot learning (DA-FSL) problem and measured the perception capability of DA-FSL benchmark for medical histopathological image classification (especially for breast histopathological imaging). DA-FSL model overcomes a few-shot learning problem with domain shift by training the network on available source domain data but being able to test on target domain data with less number of available samples. DA-FSL models are validated on two publicly available breast cancer histopathological image datasets i.e., BreakHis and BreastCancer_IDC_Grade (BCIG). The presented DA-FSL framework has shown promising outcomes on both datasets. For performance evaluation we compared DA-FSL framework with other transfer learning and few-shot learning methods with different settings.

Keywords: Breast Cancer · Histopathological Images · Few-Shot Learning · Domain Adaptation · Classification

1 Introduction

An automatic and robust image classification system can assist pathologists and doctors for early and accurate disease diagnosis with confidence in some complex disease patterns such as breast cancer [1–3]. Histopathological analysis of breast tissue samples plays a crucial role in breast cancer diagnosis [4]. In the medical field histopathological image classification for breast abnormality detection is a challenging task due to

P. Maji et al. (Eds.): PReMI 2023, LNCS 14301, pp. 407–417, 2023.
https://doi.org/10.1007/978-3-031-45170-6_42

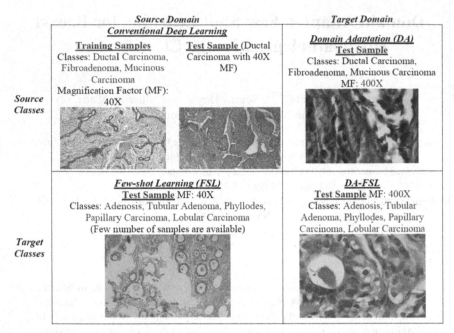

Fig. 1. Exemplar illustration of four types of classification problems in breast histopathological imaging. In DA-FSL problem, we have few samples of target classes with domain shift. Domain shifting is measured by: a) Magnification factor; b) Cancer type; c) Staining color etc.

the high complexity of the images. However, obtaining a sufficient amount of annotated histopathological images at the same imaging domain is often expensive and time-consuming task. Therefore, collecting histopathological image data from the same domain (e.g., same magnification factor, staining color, cancer types, and imaging modality) is not always possible. The diagnosis of breast abnormality using traditional deep learning (DL) models to obtain accurate classification results from such datasets is a difficult task. In the medical field, researchers are motivated to design DL based automatic decision making systems with faster learning capability with less number of samples. Nowadays, the concept of few-shot learning (FSL) which is inspired by human intelligence is quite popular among the deep learning researchers to overcome the challenges of data shortage in the medical field. In medical imaging, FSL mainly focuses on classifying rare diseases with less availability of data. In Fig. 1 shows the FSL and domain adaptation (DA) problems together in histopathological imaging.

In this paper, we investigated a domain adaptive few-shot learning (DA-FSL) problem and formulated DA-FSL framework for breast histopathological image classification. Presented DA-FSL framework can overcome insufficient and unbalanced dataset problems by leveraging model's learning from a source domain (e.g. lung and colon cancer data) to classify images in a target domain (i.e., breast cancer data with different magnification factor) with few samples. To meet up the specific necessities of the DA-FSL problem, we have integrated benchmark FSL models with Meta fine-tuning (Meta FT) for domain adaptation. The DA-FSL framework can be roughly show in three stages: i) Meta-leaning the model on the source domain; ii) Meta fine-tuning the pre-trained model such that it can able to adapt new domain fast; and iii) Evaluating the model on a test set from the target domain.

2 Related Work

Few-shot learning (FSL) has recently gained significant attention in computer vision due to its ability to learn new concepts with few number of samples. FSL can be a great supporting tool for analysis and validation of microscopic images. For accurate histopathology image classification and grading, which requires a significant amount of expert annotated data. To overcome this problem, Xue et al. (2021) [5] proposed a conditional GAN (Generative Adversarial Network) model for generating synthesize histopathology image patches condition on class labels for FSL classification. To address the same issue, Singh et al. (2021) [3] proposed a FSL meta-learning based model to overcome the problem of unavailability of annotated data. Yang et al. (2022) [6] proposed a contrastive learning approach with latent augmentation to build a FSL model for histopathological image classification. Also, [7–10] proposed FSL based methods for histopathological images classification to reduce the need of balanced and labelled data on medical datasets. Furthermore, more extensive research on FSL for histopathology imaging is required. Although, there is no research work conducted so far which focus on domain adaptation (DA) problems in microscopic imaging. To the best of our knowledge, there is no literature still date which addresses both FSL problem and DA problem jointly for histopathological image classification.

3 Methodology

3.1 Problem Definition

We define a domain as a joint distribution D over input space I and label space L. We use the pair (i, l) to denote an image i and the corresponding label l. In the domain shift problem, we have a source domain (I_{SD}, L_{SD}) with joint distribution D_S and a target domain (I_{TD}, L_{TD}) with joint distribution D_T where $D_S \neq D_T$. In FSL problem, we have a set of source classes (C_S) denoted as (I_{CS}, L_{CS}) with large sample set and a few-shot sample of target classes (C_T) denoted as (I_{CT}, L_{CT}), where $C_S \cap C_T = \emptyset$ and $I_{CT} \in \{1, 2, 3, ..., 20\}$. A FSL model is presented with a set of source classes C_S and a set of few-shot target classes $C_T = \{I_j, L_j\}_{j=1}^{N \times K}$, where N is the number of classes and K is the number of samples per class. This configuration is called as "N-way K-shot" FSL, as target set consisting of N classes with K samples from each class. In DA-FSL problem setting, we consider domain adaptation (DA) and few-shot learning (FSL) problems both in the same subject. In DA-FSL setting, we have $D_S \neq D_T$; $C_S \cap C_T = \emptyset$; $D_S \cap C_T = \emptyset$; $C_S \cap D_T = \emptyset$; and $I_{CT} \in \{1, 2, 3, ..., 20\}$. Our goal is to train a model using source classes C_S with source domain D_S such that it can adopt and classify target classes C_T with target domain D_T easily with very few number of samples i.e. $I_{CT} \in \{1, 2, 3, ..., 20\}$.

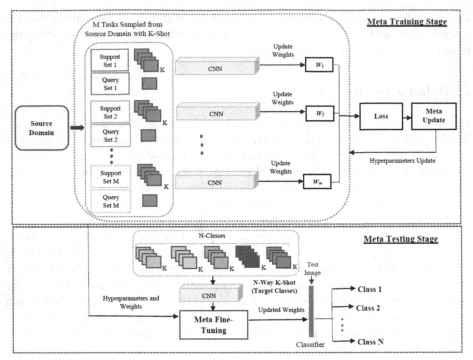

Fig. 2. Overview of DA-FSL Meta learning framework for Histopathological Image Classification.

3.2 Few-Shot Learning for Histopathological Image Classification

Few-shot learning (FSL) [11] promises to solve unavailability of large dataset problems by acquiring features with few samples. FSL methods can be categorized into three groups i.e. data generation based, transfer learning based, and meta-learning based methods. In microscopic imaging data generative based methods like GANs [12] which generate synthetic images are not effective enough because of image's complexity and information sensitivity. The basic idea of the transfer learning [13] based approaches is to reuse the features learned from the source classes for the target classes. For domain adaptation (DA) related problems, transductive fine-tuning (FT) [14, 15] is quite popular. But transfer learning based methods require a large dataset of source classes which is very challenging for medical images. The meta-learning (ML) based methods which aim to learn learners that can be able to quickly learned using a few samples [16]. Considering the facts of complexity and information sensitivity of histopathological images, we considered ML based approach for FSL classification. Each task T_i is assumed to be presented from a fixed distribution. In ML, each task T_i is a small set $C_i = \{I_i, L_i\}_{i=1}^{N \times K}$. C_S (T) and C_T (T) are used to denote source and target classes task distribution respectively. During meta training and testing stages, the model is trained on T tasks $\{T_i\}_{i=1}^{T} \in C_S$ (T) and expected to be fast learned to a new task $T_j \sim C_T$ (T), respectively.

Table 1. The experimental results of transfer learning and meta-learning models in the same domain setting (only for FSL problem).

Methods	5-Way Classification Accuracy (%)		
	5-Shot	10-Shot	20-Shot
Transductive FT [15]	43.24 ± 0.58	58.10 ± 0.43	72.75 ± 0.65
ProtoNet [18]	**66.85 ± 0.54**	**77.40 ± 0.86**	**89.83 ± 0.78**
ProtoNet + Meta FT	45.51 ± 0.58	58.30 ± 0.77	70.12 ± 0.22
RelationNet [19]	51.04 ± 0.87	66.29 ± 0.86	74.02 ± 0.37
RelationNet + Meta FT	36.38 ± 0.76	47.02 ± 0.97	58.39 ± 0.60
GnnNet + Meta FT [20]	54.08 ± 0.65	67.56 ± 0.89	74.47 ± 0.56
GnnNet-MAML + Meta FT	54.51 ± 0.65	68.42 ± 0.65	76.20 ± 0.88
Transductive FT + Aug	65.49 ± 0.54	73.60 ± 0.78	84.53 ± 0.73
ProtoNet + Aug	**84.70 ± 0.33**	**93.39 ± 0.75**	**98.58 ± 0.40**
ProtoNet + Meta FT + Aug	67.62 ± 0.65	74.34 ± 0.31	85.10 ± 0.44
RelationNet + Aug	69.57 ± 0.12	80.53 ± 0.52	92.24 ± 0.52
RelationNet + Meta FT + Aug	54.88 ± 0.78	62.56 ± 0.48	74.82 ± 0.71
GnnNet + Meta FT + Aug	74.50 ± 0.65	83.57 ± 0.98	90.85 ± 0.28
GnnNet-MAML + Meta FT + Aug	76.56 ± 0.67	88.43 ± 0.10	96.22 ± 0.69

* Aug- Data augmentation during fine-tuning.

3.3 Domain Adaptive Few-Shot Learning (DA-FSL) Method for Histopathological Image Classification

Meta-learning (ML) methods learn the initial model m_θ on the source class data [15]. In Graph Neural Network (GnnNet) [17] use graph-based convolutions that can produce data representations that are more adaptable beyond a simple Euclidean space for FSL. The Model-Agnostic Meta-Learning (MAML) [16] learns the initial parameter θ of the learning model that can quickly learn new tasks with few samples. This is accomplished by using a two-stage optimization process to optimize the model parameter. In this paper, we integrate GnnNet with MAML (GnnNet-MAML) for performance enhancement of the GnnNet. ProtoNet [18] represents the mean vector of embedded support samples for each class k as $C_k = 1/N \sum_{j=1}^{N} m\theta(xj)$. The distance between the query image and the prototype representations of each class is then calculated to perform a few-shot classification. In RelationNet [19] the nearest neighbour classifier metric is meta-learned using a Siamese network for the best comparison between query and support sets. All of the ML models implicitly consider that $D_S = D_T$. Therefore the knowledge gained during the meta-training phase can be used to learn the target classes quickly. However, in DA-FSL problem $D_S \neq D_T$ which carry a number of additional challenges for current FSL techniques. For domain shifting problems, we integrate Meta fine-tuning (Meta FT) [20] into the episodic training process for learning a set of initial parameters that can be easily fine-tuned on the test domain. In this paper, we integrate Meta FT into the meta-learning model (e.g. ProtoNet, RelationNet) that exploits domain related features of the source and target. Overview of the DA-FSL meta-learning framework is shown in Fig. 2.

4 Experiments

4.1 Used Datasets

For experimental study we used three publicly available histopathological image datasets: Lung_Colon Dataset [21], BreastCancer_IDC_Grades (BCIG) Dataset [22], BreakHis Dataset [23]. Lung_Colon dataset contains 25,000 images of lung and colon cancer in 5 classes. Each class has 5,000 images of the entities: benign lung tissue, lung squamous cell carcinoma, lung adenocarcinoma, colon adenocarcinoma, and benign colonic tissue. BCIG dataset contains 922 images of breast invasive ductal carcinomas (IDC) of 124 patients with IDC in 3 classes with 4x, 10x, 20x and 40x magnification factors (MFs). The images were stained with H&E and labelled based on their grade (IDC Grade I, Grade II, and Grade III). On the other hand, BreakHis dataset contains 7,909 breast cancer images of 82 patients in 8 classes with 40x, 100x, 200x, and 400x MFs entities as: Adenosis (444 images), Fibroadenoma (1,014 images), Phyllodes Tumor (453 images), Tubular Adenoma (569 images), Ductal Carcinoma (3,451 images). Lobular Carcinoma (626 images), Mucinous Carcinoma (792 images), Papillary Carcinoma (560 images), which were processed using H&E staining method.

4.2 Parameter Configuration

First, we test DA-FSL models only on FSL problems using the same domain setting. For that, we train on breast cancer classes entities as: IDC Grade I, IDC Grade II, Ductal Carcinoma, Fibroadenoma, Mucinous Carcinoma in 40x magnification factor (MF) and test on breast cancer classes entities as: Adenosis, Phyllodes Tumor, Papillary Carcinoma, Tubular Adenoma, Lobular Carcinoma in 40x MF with few samples. Secondly, we test DA-FSL models on DA-FSL problem settings using different domains or domain shifts. For that, we train on lung and colon cancer images from Lung_Colon dataset [21] which contains 5 classes with unknown image MF and staining information. And tests on breast cancer images from BreakHis dataset [23] in 40x MF and 400x MF and BCIG dataset [22] in 4x MF and 40x MF. During the training stage of FSL models (e.g. ProtoNet, RelationNet), models are trained for 600 epochs. In the training stage of FSL with Meta FT models (e.g. ProtoNet + Meta FT), models are trained for 400 epochs, followed by 200 epochs of Meta FT. Transductive FT [15], ProtoNet [18] and RelationNet [19] models are adopting the recommended hyper-parameters from their own papers for fair comparison. During testing, meta-learning based models that require adaptation on the target set of the test episodes used Adam optimizer. The learning rate is set to 0.01. For data augmentation during the meta-testing stage (if applicable), we sample 15 additional images from the target set by applying jitter, random flips, and random crops on a randomized basis.

4.3 Results and Discussions

Table 1 shows the experimental results of DA-FSL models in the same domain setting on BreakHis dataset. All the models showed increasing classification accuracy with

Table 2. The experimental results of transfer learning and meta-learning models in the different domain setting for DA-FSL problem on BreakHis dataset.

Methods	MF	5-Way Classification Accuracy (%)		
		5-Shot	10-Shot	20-Shot
Transductive FT [15]	40X	43.19 ± 0.53	50.17 ± 0.68	62.86 ± 0.31
	400X	34.28 ± 0.23	42.82 ± 0.52	53.25 ± 0.62
ProtoNet [18]	40X	49.77 ± 0.69	60.67 ± 0.26	73.53 ± 0.34
	400X	36.35 ± 0.32	48.96 ± 0.62	57.82 ± 0.62
ProtoNet + Meta FT	40X	51.08 ± 0.64	64.68 ± 0.36	78.24 ± 0.38
	400X	38.25 ± 0.46	47.31 ± 0.73	59.61 ± 0.93
RelationNet [19]	40X	34.84 ± 0.77	47.36 ± 0.78	56.96 ± 0.76
	400X	27.33 ± 0.16	38.49 ± 0.27	49.95 ± 0.68
RelationNet + Meta FT	40X	40.54 ± 0.38	54.99 ± 0.47	62.28 ± 0.72
	400X	33.73 ± 0.70	45.21 ± 0.69	54.76 ± 0.35
GnnNet + Meta FT [20]	40X	45.86 ± 0.58	52.73 ± 0.54	64.85 ± 0.64
	400X	36.97 ± 0.55	46.73 ± 0.23	55.36 ± 0.46
GnnNet-MAML + Meta FT	40X	**57.90 ± 0.68**	**66.47 ± 0.43**	**80.36 ± 0.23**
	400X	**46.15 ± 0.48**	**58.53 ± 0.24**	**69.86 ± 0.64**
Transductive FT + Aug	40X	52.12 ± 0.53	63.58 ± 0.47	71.16 ± 0.46
	400X	43.65 ± 0.35	51.36 ± 0.86	62.48 ± 0.40
ProtoNet + Aug	40X	60.68 ± 0.71	71.83 ± 0.38	83.57 ± 0.37
	400X	48.81 ± 0.43	57.75 ± 0.48	70.93 ± 0.43
ProtoNet + Meta FT + Aug	40X	63.42 ± 0.64	75.82 ± 0.32	86.99 ± 0.53
	400X	54.79 ± 0.39	65.23 ± 0.67	77.86 ± 0.65
RelationNet + Aug	40X	46.89 ± 0.89	57.38 ± 0.20	68.23 ± 0.86
	400X	37.06 ± 0.61	46.97 ± 0.31	57.86 ± 0.27
RelationNet + Meta FT + Aug	40X	58.83 ± 0.73	69.81 ± 0.37	78.39 ± 0.78
	400X	49.38 ± 0.87	57.37 ± 0.78	68.72 ± 0.22
GnnNet + Meta FT + Aug	40X	63.40 ± 0.66	75.33 ± 0.58	84.14 ± 0.43
	400X	54.14 ± 0.63	63.87 ± 0.75	77.48 ± 0.62
GnnNet-MAML + Meta FT + Aug	40X	**70.65 ± 0.61**	**80.77 ± 0.52**	**90.79 ± 0.40**
	400X	**56.24 ± 0.62**	**68.95 ± 0.76**	**79.57 ± 0.80**

* MF- Magnification Factor; Aug- Data augmentation during fine-tuning.

Table 3. The experimental results of transfer learning and meta-learning models in the different domain setting for DA-FSL problem on BreastCancer_IDC_Grades (BCIG) Dataset.

Methods	MF	3-Way Classification Accuracy (%)		
		5-Shot	10-Shot	20-Shot
Transductive FT [15]	4X	52.17 ± 0.56	56.09 ± 0.74	60.15 ± 0.42
	40X	52.90 ± 0.45	56.89 ± 0.68	60.57 ± 0.76
ProtoNet [18]	4X	53.64 ± 0.53	57.12 ± 0.14	61.02 ± 0.23
	40X	54.74 ± 0.50	57.87 ± 0.37	61.88 ± 0.62
ProtoNet + Meta FT	4X	56.11 ± 0.76	59.04 ± 0.65	61.87 ± 0.16
	40X	56.54 ± 0.45	59.79 ± 0.42	62.72 ± 0.56
RelationNet [19]	4X	43.28 ± 0.79	46.82 ± 0.76	49.23 ± 0.10
	40X	43.89 ± 0.87	47.11 ± 0.67	49.87 ± 0.68
RelationNet + Meta FT	4X	45.23 ± 0.62	48.04 ± 0.23	42.70 ± 0.82
	40X	45.80 ± 0.79	48.98 ± 0.51	42.98 ± 0.55
GnnNet + Meta FT [20]	4X	58.23 ± 0.65	61.78 ± 0.68	68.25 ± 0.56
	40X	58.94 ± 0.58	62.27 ± 0.65	68.68 ± 0.46
GnnNet-MAML + Meta FT	4X	**59.28 ± 0.87**	**63.05 ± 0.44**	**69.53 ± 0.57**
	40X	**59.98 ± 0.25**	**63.92 ± 0.67**	**69.89 ± 0.71**
Transductive FT + Aug	4X	54.94 ± 0.37	59.37 ± 0.35	66.18 ± 0.77
	40X	55.16 ± 0.45	60.38 ± 0.78	66.70 ± 0.51
ProtoNet + Aug	4X	55.78 ± 0.38	60.31 ± 0.72	64.11 ± 0.33
	40X	56.20 ± 0.67	60.68 ± 0.58	64.46 ± 0.42
ProtoNet + Meta FT + Aug	4X	58.73 ± 0.50	61.34 ± 0.43	65.16 ± 0.42
	40X	59.11 ± 0.94	62.10 ± 0.87	65.96 ± 0.33
RelationNet + Aug	4X	46.89 ± 0.18	49.37 ± 0.67	53.27 ± 0.85
	40X	47.82 ± 0.53	49.66 ± 0.44	53.98 ± 0.71
RelationNet + Meta FT + Aug	4X	49.02 ± 0.32	52.18 ± 0.70	56.89 ± 0.79
	40X	49.76 ± 0.75	52.87 ± 0.32	57.14 ± 0.47
GnnNet + Meta FT + Aug	4X	61.67 ± 0.59	65.79 ± 0.84	70.42 ± 0.55
	40X	62.18 ± 0.60	66.28 ± 0.53	72.89 ± 0.23
GnnNet-MAML + Meta FT + Aug	4X	**63.08 ± 0.61**	**67.37 ± 0.32**	**73.11 ± 0.65**
	40X	**63.71 ± 0.48**	**67.89 ± 0.67**	**73.65 ± 0.82**

* MF- Magnification Factor; Aug- Data augmentation during fine-tuning.

data augmentation (Aug) techniques. For the same domain setting, we performed 5-way classification using 5-shot, 10-shot and 20-shot. Among all the shot levels, the average accuracies are 74.54% (±0.68) for Transductive FT (Aug), 92.22% (±0.49)

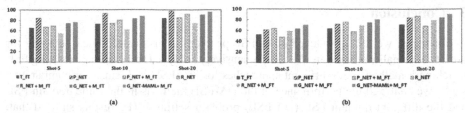

Fig. 3. Comparisons of DA-FSL models in the (a) same domain; and (b) different domain settings. **T_FT:** Transductive FT; **P_NET:** ProtoNet; **P_NET + M_FT:** ProtoNet + Meta FT; **R_NET:** RelationNet; **R_NET + M_FT:** RelationNet + Meta FT; **G_NET + M_FT:** GnnNet + Meta FT; **G_NET-MAML + M_FT:** GnnNet-MAML + Meta FT.

for ProtoNet (Aug), 75.68% (±0.46) for ProtoNet + Meta FT (Aug), 80.78% (±0.38) for RelationNet (Aug), 64.08% (±0.65) for RelationNet + Meta FT (Aug), 82.97% (±0.63) for GnnNet + Meta FT (Aug), 87.07% (±0.48) for GnnNet-MAML + Meta FT (Aug). In the same domain FSL problem setting ProtoNet gives the best classification accuracy 92.22% (±0.49). Table 2 and Table 3 show the experimental results of DA-FSL models in the different domain settings. In Table 2, we performed 5-way classification using 5-shot, 10-shot and 20-shot on BreakHis dataset in DA-FSL problem setting. Among all the shot levels, the average accuracies are 57.38% (±0.51) for Transductive FT (Aug), 65.59% (±0.46) for ProtoNet (Aug), 70.68% (±0.53) for ProtoNet + Meta FT (Aug), 52.39% (±0.52) for RelationNet (Aug), 63.75% (±0.62) for RelationNet + Meta FT (Aug), 69.72% (±0.61) for GnnNet + Meta FT (Aug), 74.49% (±0.61) for GnnNet-MAML + Meta FT (Aug). In Table 3, we performed 3-way classification (for shortage of classes) using 5-shot, 10-shot and 20-shot on BCIG dataset in DA-FSL problem setting. Among all the shot levels, the average accuracies are 60.45% (±0.53) for Transductive FT (Aug), 60.25% (±0.51) for ProtoNet (Aug), 62.06% (±0.58) for ProtoNet + Meta FT (Aug), 50.16% (±0.56) for RelationNet (Aug), 52.97% (±0.55) for RelationNet + Meta FT (Aug), 66.53% (±0.55) for GnnNet + Meta FT (Aug), 68.13% (±0.59) for GnnNet-MAML + Meta FT (Aug). In DA-FSL problem setting, GnnNet-MAML + MetaFT model gives the highest accuracies 74.49% (±0.61) and 68.13% (±0.59) on BreakHis and BCIG datasets, respectively. The performance of ProtoNet was decreased on domain shifting (in DA-FSL problem). The ProtoNet + MetaFT model underperformed and outperformed ProtoNet in the same domain (only FSL problem) and the different domain (DA-FSL problem) settings, respectively. In DA-FSL settings, performance of ProtoNet was increased by 1 to 5% by the use of Meta FT (ProtoNet + MetaFT). Moreover, in the DA-FSL problem, all the FSL models with the combination of Meta FT for domain adaptation give the improved accuracies. However, GnnNet-MAML + MetaFT model gives consistently good results in all of the settings for histopathological image classification. By the use of MAML, GnnNet + MetaFT performance was increased dramatically. Finally we conclude that, GnnNet with the combination of MAML and Meta FT (GnnNet-MAML + MetaFT) outperformed all the other transfer learning and FSL models for both FSL and DA-FSL problem settings for histopathological image classification. Graphical representation of the experimental results are shown in Fig. 3.

5 Conclusion

In this paper, we first introduced a DA-FSL problem in histopathological imaging for breast abnormality prediction. We comprehensively analyzed and evaluated existing FSL benchmark methods with different approaches for DA-FSL problems. For comparative study, we analyzed the performance of the DA-FSL methods in the same domain FSL and the different domain FSL (DA-FSL) problem settings. The results showed that, GnnNet-MAML + MetaFT gives best accuracy in all shot levels as compare to other DA-FSL methods for histopathological image classification with 74.49% ($\pm$0.61) and 68.13% ($\pm$0.59) average accuracies on BreakHis and BCIG datasets, respectively. In conclusion, we believe this study will help the research community to understand what techniques are most effective for DA-FSL scenarios in microscopic imaging and drive further advances in deep learning approaches to benefit real-world medical applications.

Acknowledgment. The work presented here is being conducted in the Bio-Medical Infrared Image Processing Laboratory of the Computer Science and Engineering Department, Tripura University, India. This work is supported by the Department of Biotechnology (DBT), Government of India under Grant No. BT/PR33087/BID/7/889/2019, Dated: 23rd March 2022. The first author is also grateful to All India Council for Technical Education (AICTE), Government of India for providing her AICTE Doctoral Fellowship (Application No. 1638385211866).

References

1. Dai, Z., et al.: PFEMed: few-shot medical image classification using prior guided feature enhancement. Pattern Recogn. **134**, 109108 (2023)
2. Hipp, L.E., Hulswit, B.B., Milliron, K.J.: Clinical tools and counseling considerations for breast cancer risk assessment and evaluation for hereditary cancer risk. Best Pract. Res. Clin. Obstet. Gynaecol. **82**, 12–29 (2022)
3. Singh, R., Bharti, V., Purohit, V., Kumar, A., Singh, A.K., Singh, S.K.: MetaMed: few-shot medical image classification using gradient-based meta-learning. Pattern Recogn. **120**, 108111 (2021)
4. Xu, Y., et al.: Large scale tissue histopathology image classification, segmentation, and visualization via deep convolutional activation features. BMC Bioinf. **18**(1), 1–17 (2017)
5. Xue, Y., et al.: Selective synthetic augmentation with HistoGAN for improved histopathology image classification. Med. Image Anal. **67**, 101816 (2021)
6. Yang, J., Chen, H., Yan, J., Chen, X., Yao, J.: Towards better understanding and better generalization of few-shot classification in histology images with contrastive learning. arXiv preprint arXiv:2202.09059 (2022)
7. Medela, A., et al.: few shot learning in histopathological images: reducing the need of labeled data on biological datasets. In: 2019 IEEE 16th International Symposium on Biomedical Imaging (ISBI 2019), pp. 1860–1864. IEEE (2019)
8. Chen, J., Jiao, J., He, S., Han, G., Qin, J.: Few-shot breast cancer metastases classification via unsupervised cell ranking. IEEE/ACM Trans. Comput. Biol. Bioinf. **18**, 1914–1923 (2019)
9. Deuschel, J., et al.: Multi-prototype few-shot learning in histopathology. In: Proceedings of the IEEE/CVF International Conference on Computer Vision 2021, pp. 620–628 (2021)
10. Chao, S., Belanger, D.: Generalizing few-shot classification of whole-genome doubling across cancer types. In: Proceedings of the IEEE/CVF International Conference on Computer Vision 2021, pp. 3382–3392 (2021)

11. Lake, B.M., Salakhutdinov, R., Tenenbaum, J.B.: Human-level concept learning through probabilistic program induction. Science **350**(6266), 1332–1338 (2015)
12. Mao, X., Li, Q.: Generative Adversarial Networks for Image Generation. Springer, Cham (2021). https://doi.org/10.1007/978-981-33-6048-8
13. Pan, S.J., Yang, Q.: A survey on transfer learning. IEEE Trans. Knowl. Data Eng. **22**(10), 1345–1359 (2010)
14. Dhillon, G.S., Chaudhari, P., Ravichandran, A., Soatto, S.: A baseline for few-shot image classification. arXiv preprint arXiv:1909.02729 (2019)
15. Guo, Y., et al.: A broader study of cross-domain few-shot learning. In: Vedaldi, A., Bischof, H., Brox, T., Frahm, J.M. (eds.) Computer Vision – ECCV 2020, ECCV 2020, vol. 12372, pp. 124–141. Springer, Cham (2020). https://doi.org/10.1007/978-3-030-58583-9_8
16. Finn, C., Abbeel, P., Levine, S.: Model-agnostic meta-learning for fast adaptation of deep networks. In: International Conference on Machine Learning, pp. 1126–1135. PMLR (2017)
17. Garcia, V., Bruna, J.: Few-shot learning with graph neural networks. arXiv preprint arXiv: 1711.04043 (2017)
18. Snell, J., Swersky, K., Zemel, R.: Prototypical networks for few-shot learning. In: Advances in Neural Information Processing Systems (2017)
19. Sung, F., Yang, Y., Zhang, L., Xiang, T., Torr, P.H., Hospedales, T.M.: Learning to compare: relation network for few-shot learning. In: Proceedings of the IEEE Conference on Computer Vision and Pattern Recognition, pp. 1199–1208 (2018)
20. Cai, J., Shen, S.M.: Cross-domain few-shot learning with meta fine-tuning. arXiv preprint arXiv:2005.10544 (2020)
21. Borkowski, A.A., Bui, M.M., Thomas, L.B., Wilson, C.P., DeLand, L.A., Mastorides, S.M.: Lung and colon cancer histopathological image dataset (lc25000). arXiv preprint arXiv:1912. 12142 (2019)
22. Bolhasani, H., Amjadi, E., Tabatabaeian, M., Jassbi, S.J.: A histopathological image dataset for grading breast invasive ductal carcinomas. Inf. Med. Unlocked **19**, 100341 (2020)
23. Spanhol, F.A., Oliveira, L.S., Petitjean, C., Heutte, L.: A dataset for breast cancer histopathological image classification. IEEE Trans. Biomed. Eng. **63**(7), 1455–1462 (2015)

Attention-CNN Model for COVID-19 Diagnosis Using Chest CT Images

S. Suba$^{(\boxtimes)}$ and Nita Parekh

International Institute of Information Technology, Hyderabad, Hyderabad, India
suba.s@research.iiit.ac.in, nita@iiit.ac.in

Abstract. Deep learning assisted disease diagnosis using chest radiology images to assess severity of various respiratory conditions has garnered a lot of attention after the recent COVID-19 pandemic. Understanding characteristic features associated with the disease in radiology images, along with variations observed from patient-to-patient and with the progression of disease, is important while building such models. In this work, we carried out comparative analysis of various deep architectures with the proposed attention-based Convolutional Neural Network (CNN) model with customized bottleneck residual module (Attn-CNN) in classifying chest CT images into three categories, COVID-19, Normal, and Pneumonia. We show that the attention model with fewer parameters achieved better classification performance compared to state-of-the-art deep architectures such as EfficientNet-B7, Inceptionv3, ResNet-50 and VGG-16, and customized models proposed in similar studies such as COVIDNet-CT, CTnet-10, COVID-19Net, etc.

Keywords: Attention model · Computed Tomography · Convolutional Neural Network · COVID-19

1 Introduction

Epidemics and pandemics are not rare now and healthcare facilities can benefit from deep learning-based image analysis due to their non-invasiveness, fast and accurate predictions. Though real-time reverse transcription polymerase chain reaction (RT-PCR) tests have been popular in detecting COVID-19 infection, some practical issues associated with it are delayed results, high false negative rates during early phase of infection (<8 days), and shortage of kits worldwide. Low sensitivity and non-uniformity of results across laboratories led to the use of Chest X-rays (CXRs) and Computed Tomography (CT) scans for rapid triaging of patients in hospitals during the pandemic situation. CTs give an elaborate view of the lungs and associated parts such as air passages, soft tissue, blood vessels, etc., thus being sensitive in assessing the progression and severity of disease. For disease diagnosis, chest CT manifestations, both typical manifestations (ground glass opacities (GGOs), consolidations, etc.) and atypical manifestations (airway changes, pleural changes, fibrosis, nodules, etc.), can supplement limitations of RT-PCR assays [1]. Earlier works have cited advantages of the usage of

P. Maji et al. (Eds.): PReMI 2023, LNCS 14301, pp. 418–427, 2023.
https://doi.org/10.1007/978-3-031-45170-6_43

these in addition to RT-PCR to confirm the diagnosis and restrict the spread of infection [2,3], particularly in the screening of asymptomatic patients and those for whom RT-PCR tests remained negative despite persistent clinical suspicion. The most common feature of COVID-19, GGOs, are predominantly observed in the peripheral regions and mostly localized in the posterior lobes, resulting in sparse distribution of these patterns in the CT images. Though difficult to detect visually in the early phase of the disease, convolution neural networks (CNNs) are powerful in picking up such fine motifs in images and even in monitoring the changes with the progression of disease. Several DL based studies have reported high performance in detection of COVID-19, but many of them are clinically unsuitable due to various reasons such as methodological flaws and/or underlying biases [4]. For example, initial studies had been trained on very few COVID images, while later models are trained on predominantly COVID images (>5–10× than normal and other pneumonia images). Apart from class imbalance, several demographic factors such as race, ethnicity, and age of the cohort on which the models have been trained can affect their overall accuracy and performance in a different clinical setting. The characteristic features, such as GGOs, consolidations, etc., that are relevant for differentiating COVID-19 pneumonia from other pneumonia being sparsely distributed, using the entire image can introduce noise in the analysis and affect the model's performance. Attention mechanism models are best suited for such image analysis tasks by appropriately weighting relevant areas in the image. Here we propose an attention-based CNN model with a customized bottleneck residual module (Attn-CNN) for multi-class classification of chest CT scan images by appropriately assigning weights to the pixels that are relevant in discriminating the COVID class from others. Further, mapping the weighted pixel regions onto the image would provide visual clues to radiologists on how the model arrived at the decision.

2   Data

For the training and validation of models, version-3 of the benchmark dataset of COVID-19 CT images, COVIDx CT-3A, was downloaded from Kaggle Datasets [5]. It consists of chest CTs belonging to normal/pneumonia/COVID-19 categories, collated from various repositories worldwide and spanning 16 countries. Despite the large quantity and diversity, the dataset is geographically biased with 85% of the patients from China, France, Russia, and Iran. Out of the 425,024 images (5312 patients) 310,593 images belong to 3731 COVID-19 patients. Covid images with supporting RT-PCR or radiology reports were only included. It may be noted from Table 1 that the dataset is highly imbalanced with the Covid class comprising 74% of the total images, while pneumonia and normal classes cover only 15% and 11%, respectively. 84:8:8 was the split ratio for training/validation/testing and only images labelled by radiologists were included in validation and test sets.

Table 1. Number of images (patients) from COVIDx CT-3A dataset used in the 3-class classification is summarized. It is divided into training, validation and test sets as given.

Type	Normal	Pneumonia	Covid	Total
Train	35996 (321)	26970 (592)	294552 (3336)	357518 (4249)
Validation	17570 (164)	8008 (202)	8147 (194)	33725 (560)
Test	17922 (164)	7965 (138)	7894 (201)	33781 (503)
Total	–	–	–	425024 (5312)

3   Related Works

Due to scarcity of RT-PCR kits and delayed results, faced worldwide, there has been increased use of chest X-rays and CT scan images in hospitals for faster triaging of patients. This has led to a surge in publications with wide variety of deep learning models being proposed for automated analysis of chest radiographs to address COVID-19 detection. These studies may be broadly classified into binary classification (COVID-19 *vs* Normal/Bacterial/ Viral Pneumonia) and multi-class classification (COVID-19, Normal and Other Pneumonia, or, COVID-19, Normal, Bacterial Pneumonia and Other Viral Pneumonia) tasks. The studies cover different types of convolution-based deep learning architectures *viz.* VGG, ResNet, InceptionNet, DenseNet, MobileNet, EfficientNet, etc., or a customized version of one or more of these networks pre-trained on ImageNet Database. Various additional features such as transfer learning [6], residual networks [7], LSTMs [8], attention models, etc. have been proposed along with lung segmentation, marking regions of interest (ROI), background removal, etc. Major issues with most of these studies include - diversity in the data, data imbalance across different classes, etc. [4]. Very few studies have discussed about the generalizability of their models in an unseen setup [9]. Most of the early studies are trained and tested on small datasets with very few COVID images [8].

One of the pioneering works in this field has been the COVIDNet-CT [10] and its update, COVID-NET CT-2 [11], based on tailored deep convolution neural network for separating CT scan images into classes *viz.* Normal, non-Covid Pneumonia and COVID-19, proposed a large, curated benchmark dataset, COVIDx CT. For performance evaluation we have considered the latest version of this dataset, COVIDx CT- 3. Using a machine-driven design exploration strategy they designed their model based on ResNet framework. After pre-training on ImageNet, it resulted in an accuracy of 99% on COVIDx CT-2. Another early study that used transfer learning classified COVID-19 from other viral pneumonia that exhibits similar radiologic features as COVID-19 using a GoogleNet Inception v3 network [6]. Regions of interest (ROI) marked images were used for classification in this case. The model achieved an accuracy of 79.3%, true negative rate of 0.83, and true positive rate of 0.67 on an external test set. Several earlier works have proposed extracting lung parenchyma and abnormalities from the CTs for better performance [12, 13]. They claim that these models were more generalizable than models trained on non-segmented scans. Methods that combined CT data with patient's age, gender, travel history, other clinical indications, and COVID19 test results were proposed in [14]. In this study, only the CT slices identified to have lung infection were used for training the model to differentiate COVID-19 & non-COVID-19 classes.

Recently there has been interest in using attention models for COVID detection from CTs. Such models focus on ROIs ignoring irrelevant areas and doing away with annotations or lung segmentations for removing background noise. It is observed that most CT slices of COVID patients contain abnormalities in very few regions of the image. This can be leveraged using pixel based attention mechanisms. Few recent studies have used either channel attention or spatial attention methods, or both [15–17]. A 'parallel attention module' that includes both spatial and channel attention methods was proposed in [18], while in [15] Convolutional Block Attention Module (CBAM) is used to fuse across channel and spatial attentions and Long Short Term Memory (LSTM) to acquire axial dependency of the slices. Another spatial attention based CNN model uses a customized architecture with 1×1 convolution followed by 'relu' and a second 1×1 convolution followed by 'sigmoid' activation to classify four types of pneumonia, *viz.*, COVID-19 pneumonia, non-COVID-19 pneumonia, bacterial pneumonia, mycoplasma pneumonia and normal CT images [16]. A multi-scale attention network proposed concatenation of spatial features extracted by the attention blocks from three different layers of the CNN for binary classification of CT images [17].

4 Methods

The architecture of the proposed attention-based CNN model with a customized bottleneck residual module (Attn-CNN) is described in Sect. 4.2. Two important features of the proposed Attention-based CNN model are: (1) Lower number of training parameters, and (2) Generalizable model for classification of chest CT scan images.

4.1 Data Pre-processing

The chest CT images used for training and evaluating the models were subjected to following pre-processing methods.

Image Resizing: The input images being sourced from various hospitals across the world, are of different sizes because of different capturing modalities and different equipment standards. Hence all the images were processed to have the same uniform dimensions of 224×224 pixels.

Normalization: Each image in the dataset is normalized in the range (0, 1) by multiplying each pixel by a factor of $1/255$. This is done to make the dataset consistent in terms of pixel intensity.

Augmentation: COVIDx CT-3A dataset considered in this study suffer from class imbalance problem: the number of images in COVID-19 category is ~10× more in comparison with that in pneumonia and normal categories. DL models, when trained on such datasets are likely to be biased towards the majority class, leading to biased models and unreliable performances. Augmentation techniques such as rotation, horizontal flip and width shift, height shift and zoom were carried out to address the data imbalance problem.

4.2 Network Design

The framework of the proposed network, Attn-CNN given in Fig. 1 consists of couple of standard Conv blocks (brown) and 'depthwise' Conv block (orange), a residual block (dark blue) and an Attention Map Generator (AMG) block (purple). The model takes CT image of size $224 \times 224 \times 3$ as input and outputs an attention map of the image from the AMG block. This is followed by the classification module consisting of a 'Dropout' layer and a 'Dense' layer that takes the attention map as input and outputs a label (Normal/COVID-19/Pneumonia) for the image. The detailed architecture of each block is also given in Fig. 1. Number of kernels in each block decreases hierarchically as 256, 128, 64, 32 and 16. After each Conv block, 'maxpool' and 'batchnormalization' layers, colour-coded as green and yellow, respectively, are added. Conv blocks 1 and 2 consists of normal convolutional kernels while blocks 3 and 4 consist of 'depthwise' and pointwise convolutional kernels. The kernel sizes are 3×3 except for pointwise kernel which is of size 1×1. The Residual block consists of a residual connection with a 'pointwise' Conv and a direct connection with 2 'depthwise' Conv and one 'pointwise' Conv. After this a 'Leaky Relu' layer and 'maxpool' and 'batchnormalization' layers are added. The AMG block is inserted after this series of Conv blocks to turn all the relevant pixels 'on' and others 'off' before the succeeding 'globalaveragepooling' layer. This is done by connecting two Conv2D layers through a 'locallyconnectd2D' layer having separate kernels for all the pixels and turning the pixels 'on' through a 'sigmoid' activation function based on its relevance. These selected pixel positions act as a mask for the features from the Conv2D layer before the attention module. The selected positions are element wise multiplied with the features extracted from the previous Conv layer. The features extracted from the attention module are sent to a 'globalaveragepooling' layer along with the masks to do a rescaling of the features. The rescaled features are sent to the classification module with a dense layer for classification. The number of parameters in this model is very low, ~$1M$. Optimizer was Adam and learning rate was $5e-5$.

Attention Map Generator. The Attention Map Generator (AMG) extracts subtle features that may help in improving the discriminating power of the classifier. The residual connection ·is introduced to address the vanishing gradient problem and also to take care of any loss in accuracy due to reduction in number of parameters with 'depthwise' convolutions. The 'depthwise' convolutions and

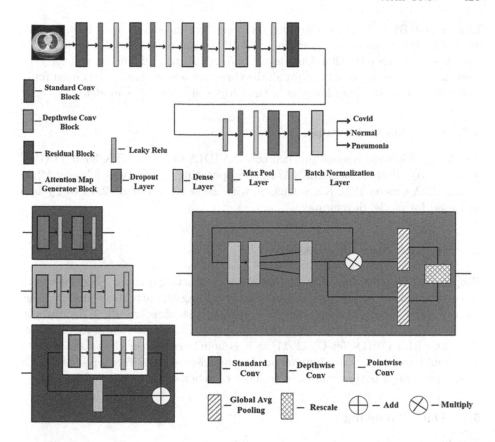

Fig. 1. The proposed Attn-CNN's framework is given. The colour codes given identifies CONV blocks, Residual block, Attention Map Generator (AMG) block, pooling, normalization and dropout layers. Detailed architecture of each of the colour coded Standard Conv (brown), Depthwise Conv (orange), Residual (dark blue) and AMG blocks (purple) are expanded in the lower half of the figure. The Conv layers and other layers in each block such as Global Average Pooling (GAP) and Rescale are also colour coded as shown. The Residual block includes an 'addition' operation and the Attention block includes a 'multiplication' operation. (Color figure online)

pointwise convolutions in the 3rd and 4th Conv blocks reduce the computational complexity. The features generated after the Global Average Pooling (GAP) layer can be defined as:

$$F_{GAP}^T = GAP[\sigma(f^{1\times1}(F_{max}^\tau))] \tag{1}$$

where $(F_{max}^\tau) \in \Re^{1 \times H \times W}$ represents the 2D tensors obtained from Maxpooling operation on the output tensor from the 4th Conv block, and H, W denote height, width of the tensor.

For performance evaluation of the Attn-CNN model, four SOTA deep learning models, VGG-16 ($\sim$138M), ResNet-50 ($\sim$23M), Inception-v3 ($\sim$25M) and

EfficientNet-B7 ($\sim$60M), pre-trained on ImageNet database, have been considered. The fully connected layers in VGG-16, Inception-v3 and EfficientNet-B7 models were replaced with 4 dense layers of 512, 128, 64 and 3 nodes respectively. Learning rate was set to 0.0001 for all the three models. Softmax activation function was used in the final layer as in the proposed Attn-CNN model.

4.3   Experimental Setup

All the models were trained on dual core NVIDIA GeForce RTX 3080 Ti GPU with 32 GB DDR4 3200 MHz RAM. The operating system was Ubuntu 22.04 with CUDA version 12.0. Keras package with Tensorflow version 2.4.1 in Python was used for model development.

5   Results and Discussion

Proposed Attn-CNN model is evaluated by conducting various experiments to assess the impact of data imbalance and of adding the attention module. The metrics used for evaluation include accuracy, precision, recall, F1-score and Receiver Operating Characteristic (ROC) curves. Comparative analysis was carried out with COVID-Net CT-2 [11] as it is benchmarked on COVIDx CT data and would provide a fair comparison. On multi-class classification, Attn-CNN model performed better compared to most of other studies reviewed here.

5.1   Data Balancing

To address the data imbalance problem, following augmentation operations were applied on training set: rotation, width shift, height shift, zoom, and horizontal flip. The test accuracies of Attn-CNN, VGG-16, ResNet-50, Inception-v3 and EfficientNetB7 after training for 10 epochs are 94%, 87%, 71%, 79% and 82% respectively. Precision, recall and F1-scores (Table 2) shows that the Attn-CNN model performs remarkably better compared to the four deep convolution networks. Though the training accuracy for all the models (except ResNet-50) was better than Attn-CNN model, however, the validation and test accuracies are significantly higher for the Attn-CNN model. Except for recall for covid class (0.93 for EfficientNet *vs* 0.88 for Attn-CNN) and precision for pneumonia class (0.94 for VGG *vs* 0.92 for Attn-CNN), all the metrics are higher for the proposed model. This indicates attention module's capability to extract the discriminating features and hence outperform the DL models. The ROC curves were obtained for the three classes and area under the curve (AUC) value calculated for covid, normal and pneumonia class is 0.98, 0.99 and 0.99 respectively, for the Attn-CNN model. However, from Table 2, it can be noted that the model performed better on normal and pneumonia classes compared to covid class. This is the case for all models (see F1-scores). A similar trend was also reported in [11] for the earlier version of the data. The reason might be that normal and pneumonia images are from legacy databases which are well curated compared to the covid images collected during pandemic. As a result of data augmentation, bias in performance due to class imbalance is not observed.

COVID-Net CT-2's accuracy [11] on COVIDx CT-2 (earlier version of data) was 98% and achieved a sensitivity of 0.99 for Covid class. The proposed Attn-CNN model also achieved 98% accuracy on COVIDx CT-2 dataset with a sensitivity of 0.98 and precision of 0.97. COVIDx CT-3 is the latest and largest set of Covid images in the Open Source Initiative and as expected there is a drop in performance of all the models, due to the large data imbalance, including for the proposed model, though its performance is better compared to other DL models. For comparison with other attention based models, [15] reported an accuracy of 78%, [16] had 97%, [17] and [18] had 98% accuracies in binary classification of CT slices except for [16] which had 5 class classification but the slice selection was done by radiologist for training and testing.

Table 2. Attn-CNN's performance along with VGG-16, ResNet50, Inception-v3 and EfficientNet-B7 models for classifying CT images using balanced datasets after data augmentation is given.

Attn-CNN	Precision	Recall	F1-score
COVID-19	0.89	0.88	0.89
Normal	0.97	0.98	0.97
Pneumonia	0.92	0.91	0.92

VGG-16	Precision	Recall	F1-score
COVID-19	0.69	0.90	0.78
Normal	0.96	0.85	0.90
Pneumonia	0.94	0.88	0.91

ResNet-50	Precision	Recall	F1-score
COVID-19	0.47	0.76	0.58
Normal	0.91	0.70	0.79
Pneumonia	0.79	0.70	0.74

Inception-v3	Precision	Recall	F1-score
COVID-19	0.54	0.93	0.69
Normal	0.97	0.72	0.83
Pneumonia	0.93	0.81	0.86

EfficientNet-B7	Precision	Recall	F1-score
COVID-19	0.59	0.93	0.72
Normal	0.96	0.76	0.85
Pneumonia	0.95	0.86	0.90

5.2   Without Data Balancing

An ablation study was conducted to assess if data balancing techniques did indeed improve the model's performance. The accuracy of Attn-CNN model is observed to drop significantly by ~10%, while a marginal drop of 1% and 2% is observed for VGG-16 and EfficientNet-B7, respectively without data augmentation. For the other two DL models, *viz.*, ResNet-50 and Inception-v3, an improved performance was observed without data augmentation (11% and 5% respectively). These results show mixed response of the models towards data augmentation and clearly highlights the need of ablation studies.

6 Conclusion

In this study a novel attention based CNN model architecture with customized residual bottleneck module has been proposed for classifying chest CT images into three classes, *viz.*, covid, normal and pneumonia. The model is easily extendable to include other classes of pneumonia for classification. The proposed model with only 1M trainable parameters performed relatively better compared to other popular CNN-based SOTA models that require tens and hundreds of times more parameters for training. Also, the proposed model is as good as the customized model COVID-Net CT-2 which has a machine-generated architecture. High sensitivity and lightweight makes Attn-CNN model easily deployable in clinical settings. Its architecture can be easily extended to any similar chest CT classification tasks for diagnosis of other diseases/conditions using radiology images, such as cancer, tuberculosis, pulmonary embolism, etc. In future work we hope to modify the proposed framework to accept whole CT volume files as input to the model. This would facilitate in accepting CT volume data directly from the machine, thereby generating the diagnostics along with the CT scan images in hospital settings.

References

1. Ye, Z., Zhang, Y., Wang, Y., Huang, Z., Song, B.: Chest CT manifestations of new coronavirus disease 2019 (COVID-19): a pictorial review. Eur. Radiol. **30**, 4381–4389 (2020)
2. Xie, X., Zhong, Z., Zhao, W., Zheng, C., Wang, F., Liu, J.: Chest CT for typical coronavirus disease 2019 (COVID-19) pneumonia: relationship to negative RT-PCR testing. Radiology **296**(2), E41–E45 (2020)
3. Cleverley, J., Piper, J., Jones, M.M.: The role of chest radiography in confirming COVID-19 pneumonia. BMJ **370** (2020)
4. Roberts, M., et al.: Common pitfalls and recommendations for using machine learning to detect and prognosticate for COVID-19 using chest radiographs and CT scans. Nat. Mach. Intell. **3**(3), 199–217 (2021)
5. Gunraj, H.: COVIDx CT. Kaggle. https://www.kaggle.com/datasets/hgunraj/covidxct
6. Wang, S., et al.: A deep learning algorithm using CT images to screen for corona virus disease (COVID-19). Eur. Radiol. **31**, 6096–6104 (2021)
7. Wang, J., et al.: Prior-attention residual learning for more discriminative COVID-19 screening in CT images. IEEE Trans. Med. Imaging **39**(8), 2572–2583 (2020)
8. Sedik, A., et al.: Deploying machine and deep learning models for efficient data-augmented detection of COVID-19 infections. Viruses **12**(7), 769 (2020)
9. Wang, S., et al.: A fully automatic deep learning system for COVID-19 diagnostic and prognostic analysis. Eur. Respiratory J. **56**(2) (2020)
10. Gunraj, H., Wang, L., Wong, A.: COVIDNet-CT: A tailored deep convolutional neural network design for detection of COVID-19 cases from chest CT images. Front. Med. **7**, 608525 (2020)
11. Gunraj, H., Sabri, A., Koff, D., Wong, A.: COVID-Net CT-2: enhanced deep neural networks for detection of COVID-19 from chest CT images through bigger, more diverse learning. Front. Med. **8**, 3126 (2022)

12. Rezaeijo, S.M., Ghorvei, M., Alaei, M.: A machine learning method based on lesion segmentation for quantitative analysis of CT radiomics to detect COVID-19. In: 2020 6th Iranian Conference on Signal Processing and Intelligent Systems (ICSPIS), pp. 1–5. IEEE (2020)
13. Zhang, K., et al.: Clinically applicable AI system for accurate diagnosis, quantitative measurements, and prognosis of COVID-19 pneumonia using computed tomography. Cell **181**(6), 1423–1433 (2020)
14. Mei, X., et al.: Artificial intelligence-enabled rapid diagnosis of patients with COVID-19. Nat. Med. **26**(8), 1224–1228 (2020)
15. Mohammed, A., et al.: Weakly-supervised network for detection of COVID-19 in chest CT scans. IEEE Access **8**, 155987–156000 (2020)
16. Wong, P.K., et al.: Automatic detection of multiple types of pneumonia: open dataset and a multi-scale attention network. Biomed. Signal Process. Control **73**, 103415 (2022)
17. Hong, G., Chen, X., Chen, J., Zhang, M., Ren, Y., Zhang, X.: A multi-scale gated multi-head attention depthwise separable CNN model for recognizing COVID-19. Sci. Rep. **11**(1), 1–13 (2021)
18. Xiao, B., et al.: PAM-DenseNet: a deep convolutional neural network for computer-aided COVID-19 diagnosis. IEEE Trans. Cybern. **52**(11), 12163–12174 (2021)

Image and Video Processing

Multi-focus Image Fusion Using Reorganized DTT Moments and Sparse Representation

Manali Roy$^{(\boxtimes)}$ and Susanta Mukhopadhyay

Indian Institute of Technology (Indian School of Mines), Dhanbad 826004,
Jharkhand, India
manalir66@gmail.com

Abstract. Multi-focus image fusion is a widely accepted solution to
solve the problem of narrow depth-of-field suffered by optical lenses in
an imaging system that fails to capture an all-in-one focused image.
This article puts forward a focus fusion framework in the transform
domain using moments derived from orthogonal Tchebichef polynomials. The input images are represented as 8×8 coefficient images using
discrete Tchebichef basis functions. The coefficients across all the sub-
images are reordered to resemble a decimated multiscale decomposition
with directional subbands at three scales and an approximation band.
Inter-scale spectral significance is used to fuse the mid-level detail coefficients whereas the finest details having the highest resolution employ
the sparse-coding technique. The approximation subband also utilizes
the same sparse dictionary to select the relevant features. After reposi-
tioning the fused coefficients back to their initial locations, inverse DTT
is applied to generate the final fused image. Empirical results support
the efficacy of the approach in multi-focus fusion in terms of perceptual
clarity and quantitative metrics.

Keywords: Multi-focus · Tchebichef transform · Sparse
representation · Image fusion · Multi-resolution analysis

1 Introduction

The shallow depth-of-field exhibited by optical lenses mounted in imaging equipment relies on multiple factors: the size of the lens aperture, the focal length,
and the distance between the lens and the subject. Due to the refraction of light
through the lenses, an image is in partial focus when there is an increase in
the aperture or a decrease in the separation between the lens and the subject.
Consequently, it fails to capture a single image focused on its entirety, posing a severe problem in real-time applications like macro-photography or optical
microscopy. Multi-focus fusion resolves the issue by fusing multiple semi-focussed
images taken at varying focal lengths to generate an explicitly focused image for
a high-level interpretation [4].

© The Author(s), under exclusive license to Springer Nature Switzerland AG 2023
P. Maji et al. (Eds.): PReMI 2023, LNCS 14301, pp. 431–440, 2023.
https://doi.org/10.1007/978-3-031-45170-6_44

Transform domain constitutes a powerful framework in image fusion literature as it can; a) encode non-redundant spatial information into a set of decorrelated coefficients, b) pack most of the energy (information) in fewer coefficients,
and c) offer multi-resolution analysis to describe the scale and orientation-specific
features [8]. Tchebichef moments, using discrete orthogonal polynomials, overcome the limitations of continuous moments (like Zernike or Legendre) by avoiding discrete approximation, eliminating coordinate space normalizations, reducing reconstruction errors from truncation, and being more robust in the presence
of noise. In this work, we employ discrete Tchebichef polynomial transform to
represent the input images into multiple blocks of orthogonal moments [13]. Individual coefficient within a block captures unique spatial frequencies concerning
the input image. Hence, the moments from multiple blocks are restructured to
mimic a wavelet-like multi-resolution decomposition consisting of low and high-
frequency information [7]. A sparse dictionary is adopted to fuse the moments
in two ways, the high-frequency moments at the finest level and approximation
moments at the coarsest level. The frequencies lying at the middle scales are
fused exploiting the inherent inter-scale dependencies among the DTT coefficients. The fused coefficients are shifted back to their original position within
the blocks before the inverse transform. The algorithm was executed over multi-
focus datasets and thorough evaluations report its qualitative and quantitative
efficiency. The primary highlights of the article are:

- Wavelet-like multiresolution analysis rendered from local orthogonal
  tchebichef moments to capture spatial frequencies within multiple subbands.
- Sparse representation is adopted to fuse the approximation band and details
  with the highest resolution.
- Interband coefficient dependencies are exploited to fuse the mid-band frequencies components.

The rest of the article is as follows: Sect. 2 briefly introduces the pre-requisite concepts needed for the work. The proposed method is presented in Sect. 3 followed
by experimental discussions in Sect. 4. The conclusion is presented in Sect. 5.

2   Preliminaries

2.1   Local Discrete Tchebichef's Moments

The tchebichef's moments [17] are coefficients of a 2D image computed using
convolution masks obtained from two separable 1D ($f(x)$) tchebichef polynomials (Fig. 1)(c) of degree p, denoted by $t_p(x)$, satisfying the following recurrence
relation,

$$t_p(x) = (\beta_1 x + \beta_2)t_{p-1} + \beta_3 t_{p-2}(x) \qquad (1)$$

where $x = 0, 1, \ldots N - 1$, $p = 2, \ldots N - 1$ and $\beta_1 = \frac{2}{p}\sqrt{\frac{4p^2-1}{N^2-p^2}}$,
$\beta_2 = \frac{1-N}{p}\sqrt{\frac{4p^2-1}{N^2-p^2}}$, and $\beta_3 = \frac{1-p}{p}\sqrt{\frac{2p+1}{2p-3}}\sqrt{\frac{N^2-(p-1)^2}{N^2-p^2}}$

The starting values for the above recurrence are given by,

$$t_0(x) = \frac{1}{\sqrt{N}}, \quad t_1(x) = (2x + 1 - N)\sqrt{\frac{3}{N(N^2-1)}}$$

The discrete local tchebichef's moments of an image block $(f(x, y))$ of size $M \times N$ (say 8×8) require polynomials up to degree 0 to 7.

$$T_{pq} = \sum_{x=0}^{M=7} \sum_{y=0}^{N=7} t_p(x)t_q(y)f(x, y) \quad p, q = 0, 1, \ldots 7 \qquad (2)$$

where, $t_p(x)$ and $t_q(x)$ are Tchebichef polynomial of order p in x and q in y respectively [5]. Inversely,

$$f(x, y) = \sum_{p=0}^{M=7} \sum_{q=0}^{N=7} T_{pq} \underbrace{t_p(x)t_q(y)}_{\text{convolution mask}} \qquad (3)$$

where $C_{pq} = t_p(x)t_q(y)$ is a set of 64 basis images [Fig. 1(a)] which can be used to identify directional patterns in an image. For blocks of 8×8, it is defined as,

$$C_{pq} = \begin{bmatrix} t_p(0)t_q(0) \ldots t_p(0)t_q(7) \\ \ldots \\ t_p(7)t_q(0) \ldots t_p(7)t_q(7) \end{bmatrix} \qquad (4)$$

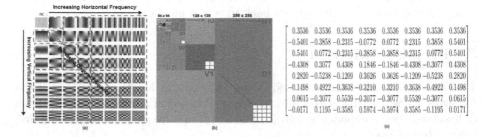

Fig. 1. (a) 8×8 DTT basis images; (b) Multi-resolution decomposition and inter-band dependency; (c) Tchebichef's polynomials for N = 8

2.2 Sparse Representation

Sparse representation (SR) exploits the sparse nature of signals and simulates the characteristics of human visual system [15]. In SR, a signal, $y \in \mathbb{R}^p$ is approximated by a linear combination of sparse (fewer number) basis elements or atoms of an over-complete (redundant) dictionary, $\mathbf{D} \in \mathbb{R}^{p \times Q}(p < Q)$ where Q is the number of atoms in it. Mathematically, $y \approx \mathbf{D}\alpha$, where α is the sparse coefficient vector. SR aims to calculate the sparsest α with the least non-zero entries amongst all the possible solutions for an under-constrained system by optimizing the following inequality,

$$\min_{\alpha} \|\alpha\|_0 \text{ subject to} \|\mathbf{D}\alpha - y\| < \epsilon, \ \epsilon > 0 \ \epsilon : \text{tolerance factor} \qquad (5)$$

The construction of the dictionary largely impacts the ability of sparse coding. Here, patch wise SR is adopted with greedy-based OMP (Orthogonal Matching Pursuit) [11] algorithm to select the dictionary atoms. The source images are divided into J multiple patches of size $n \times n$ which are lexicographically ordered as column vectors $v_{j=1...J}$. For every column vector v_j, a sparse vector is obtained w.r.t to a dictionary atom such that, $v_{j=1...J} = \sum_{q=1}^{Q} \alpha^{j=1...J}(q) d_q$. Collectively, all such vectors constitute a matrix, V can be expressed as,

$$V = [d_1 \, d_2 \ldots d_Q]_{1 \times Q} \begin{bmatrix} \alpha^1(1) & \alpha^2(1) \ldots \alpha^J(1) \\ \alpha^1(2) & \alpha^2(2) \ldots \alpha^J(2) \\ \ldots & \ldots \\ \alpha^1(Q) & \alpha^2(Q) \ldots \alpha^J(Q) \end{bmatrix}_{Q \times J} \quad (6)$$

where $\mathbf{D} = [d_1 \, d_2 \ldots d_Q]$ is the dictionary of atoms and $\alpha = [\alpha^1, \alpha^2, \ldots \alpha^J]$ are sparse vectors obtained using Eq. 5. Fusion of K registered images ($I_{k=1...K}$), will require $V_{k=1...K}$ such matrices. The activity level of individual sparse vectors of kth source image, I_k is measured as,

$$A_{k_{j=1...J}} = \|\alpha_{k_{j=1...J}}\|_1 \quad (7)$$

The corresponding columns of all sparse matrices, $\alpha_1, \alpha_2, \ldots \alpha_K$ are fused using their activity levels (choose-max) to generate α_F such that $\alpha_{F_j} = \alpha_{F_j^*}$, where $F_j^* = arg\max_{k_j}(A_{k_j})$. The fused vectors, $V_F = \mathbf{D}\alpha_F$ reconstructs the fused image, I_F by reshaping the vectors back to $n \times n$ patches.

3   Proposed Method

This section discusses the proposed fusion approach at length, consisting of the following steps, a) MST decomposition using Tchebichef's coefficients, b) Fusion of low-frequency components, and (c) Fusion of high-frequency components and inverse transform.

3.1   MST Decomposition Using reorganized DTT Coefficients

The forward transformation formula to obtain local Tchebichef's moments (8×8) using Eq. 4 can be expressed as the product of following matrices,

$$F(x, y) = C \times f(x, y) \times C^{-1} \quad (8)$$

where f and C are image block and DTT transform matrix of size 8×8 respectively. Equation 8 contains 63 DTT AC components along with one DC component thus capturing unique spatial frequencies. Hence, moments corresponding to a specific location for all the image blocks can be reorganized into a new matrix to resemble a 3-scale wavelet structure with an approximation and nine detail subbands. It isolates the frequency contents based on their strength and gives a more accurate representation. Due to the property of energy compaction, there is a gradual decrease in the magnitude of, a) horizontal frequencies along the row, b) vertical frequencies along the column, and c) diagonal frequencies along the diagonal, with $F(0,1)$, $F(1,0)$ and $F(1,1)$ having the highest magnitude along horizontal, vertical and diagonal directions respectively [Fig. 1(a)].

- The DC coefficient, $F(0,0)$ from all the blocks are merged to generate the approximation or low pass band, A_3 with the least resolution (64×64).
- The AC coefficients from location $F(0,1)$, $F(1,0)$, $F(1,1)$ from all the blocks are combined to generate the horizontal (H_3), vertical (V_3) and diagonal (D_3) subbands respectively at coarsest level (Level 3) with a resolution of 64×64.
- At next higher resolution (Level 2) with dimension 128×128, 4×4 coefficient matrices with indices $\underset{i=0,1\ j=2,3}{F(i,j)}$, $\underset{i=2,3\ j=0,1}{F(i,j)}$ and $\underset{i=2,3\ j=2,3}{F(i,j)}$ gives the horizontal, vertical and diagonal bands respectively.
- For the highest resolution (Level 3) with dimension 256×256, the subsequent 8×8 coefficient matrices with indices $\underset{i=0,1,2,3\ j=4,5,6,7}{F(i,j)}$, $\underset{i=4,5,6,7\ j=0,1,2,3}{F(i,j)}$ and $\underset{i=4,5,6,7\ j=4,5,6,7}{F(i,j)}$ gives the horizontal, vertical and diagonal bands respectively.

3.2   Fusion of Low Frequency Components

To fuse low pass bands, sparse representation approach is adopted as follows:

- The input images (say, L_a, L_b) are raster scanned and divided into $n \times n$ overlapping patches.
- Individual patches from source images are converted into column vectors (v_{L_a}, v_{L_b}) and normalized with respect to mean (v'_{L_a}, v'_{L_b}).
- For each normalized column vector, the sparse coefficient vectors (α_{L_a}, α_{L_b}) are calculated by OMP using a dictionary $\mathbf{D}$, learned from K-SVD method [1].
- The activity level of the sparse vectors corresponding to the input images are compared using Eq. 7 (max-L_1 rule). The vectors with the highest activity levels get absorbed as fused sparse vectors (α_{L_f}).
- The fused vectors (v_{L_f}) are generated from the sparse vectors using the same dictionary $\mathbf{D}$, as follows, $v_{L_f} = \mathbf{D}\alpha_{L_f}$. The fused vectors are reshaped back into their original patches to reconstruct the final fused low pass image (L_f).

3.3   Fusion of High Frequency Components

From Sect. 3.1, 3 levels of directional details ($V_3, H_3, D_3, V_2, H_2, D_2, V_1, H_1, D_1$) are obtained with nine subbands. Instead of conventional level-specific fusion of bands, inter-level dependency among the coefficients for each direction is exploited. To evaluate the weight of coefficients at a specific level, the absolute magnitude of coefficients from the current level upto the finest level of decomposition are taken into account, i.e., $w_{l_3} \rightarrow l_3, l_2, l_1$, $w_{l_2} \rightarrow l_2, l_1$. A strong feature of an image can withstand repeated decompositions, whereas a weak one gradually diminishes, therefore higher-valued coefficients at a location in an intermediate level carry a certain weightage to its next coarser level at corresponding locations. The weight (w) of a coefficient at level 3 (w_{cl_3}) and level 2 (w_{cl_2}) are computed as:

$$w_{cl_3}(i,j) = |c_{l_3}| + \sum_{r_1=0}^{1}\sum_{s_1=0}^{1}|c_{l_2}(2i-r_1,2j-s_1)| + \sum_{r_2=0}^{3}\sum_{s_2=0}^{3}|c_{l_1}(4i-r_2,4j-s_2)| \quad (9)$$

$$w_{cl_2}(i,j) = |c_{l_2}| + \sum_{r_1=0}^{1}\sum_{s_1=0}^{1}|c_{l_1}(2i-r_1,2j-s_1)| \quad (10)$$

Since the resolution of each level increases at a power of 2, the general expression for coefficient weight at level 'k' for 'm' decomposition levels is given by,

$$w_{cl_k}(i,j) = |c_{l_k}| + \sum_{r_1=0}^{1}\sum_{s_1=0}^{1}|c_{l_{k-1}}(2^1i-r_1,2^1j-s_1)|$$

$$+ \sum_{r_2=0}^{3}\sum_{s_2=0}^{3}|c_{l_{k-2}}(2^2i-r_2,2^2j-s_2)| + \cdots + \sum_{r_m=0}^{2^m-1}\sum_{s_m=0}^{2^m-1}|c_{l_{k-m}}(2^mi-r_m,2^mj-s_m)|$$

$$(11)$$

All the intermediate high-pass bands till the penultimate level are fused by weighted averaging, $c_f(i,j) = \frac{c_a(i,j)w_a(i,j)+c_b(i,j)w_b(i,j)}{w_a(i,j)+w_b(i,j)}$ where the weights with respect to a coefficient are evaluated using Eq. 11. The coefficients at the last level (with no subsequent levels further) are fused using the similar sparse coding approach as discussed in Sect. 3.2. The fused coefficients are repositioned back to their original blocks (F_f) and inverse DTT transform is applied using Eq. 12 to get the final fused image.

$$I_{f(x,y)} = C^{-1} \times F_f(x,y) \times C \quad (12)$$

4   Experimental Results and Discussion

This section discusses the experimental settings adopted for testing the proposed algorithm along with subjective and objective evaluation. Experiments are conducted on two different registered datasets; Lytro(20 pairs) [14] and MFI-WHU(120 pairs) [19] along with some unregistered pairs from MFIFB (40 pairs) [20]. The algorithm is executed on Matlab R2017b installed on 64-bit windows 11 operating system, Intel 2.60 Hz Core i7 CPU, and 16 GB RAM. The perceptual quality of the algorithm is assessed against four competing fusion algorithms, SR [2], MGFF [3], SESF [9] and Swinfusion [10] using five quality measures, Q_o and Q_w [16], FMI [6], Q_{AB}^F [18] and $NIQE$ [12]. For all the metrics, a higher value indicates better perceptual results except $NIQE$. The patch size for sparse coding is 8×8 with a stride of 6 pixels and an error tolerance of 0.1. The average value of quality metrics corresponding to the datasets and the visual results are presented in Table 1 and Fig. 2 respectively.

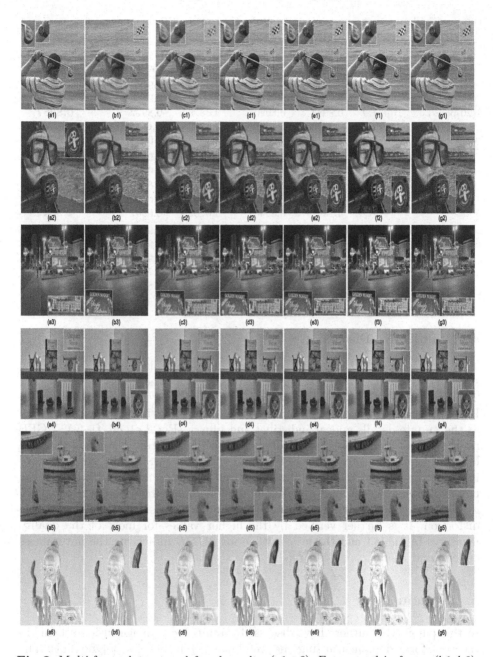

Fig. 2. Multi-focus dataset and fused results: (a1–a6): Foreground in focus; (b1–b6): Background in focus; (c1–c6): SR results; (d1–d6): MGFF results; (e1–e6): SESF results; (f1–f6): Swinfusion results; (g1–g6): Proposed results

Table 1. Average objective evaluation on multifocus image sets

Images	Metrics	Methods				
		SR [2]	MGFF [3]	SESF [9]	Swinfusion [10]	Proposed
Lytro [14]	Q_o	0.9224	0.9327	0.9339	0.9150	**0.9419**
(512 × 512)	Q_w	0.8746	0.9227	0.9252	0.9304	**0.9392**
(20 pairs)	FMI	0.8984	0.8920	0.8879	0.8972	**0.8987**
	Q_{AB}^F	0.5658	0.6681	0.6703	**0.6794**	0.6792
	$NIQE$	3.6945	3.2858	3.1051	3.0655	**2.9907**
MFI-WHU [19]	Q_o	0.9147	0.9140	0.9328	0.9253	**0.9432**
(512 × 512)	Q_w	0.8953	**0.9340**	0.9333	0.9252	0.9311
(40 pairs)	FMI	0.8870	0.8770	0.8848	0.8789	**0.8896**
	Q_{AB}^F	0.5980	0.6679	0.6197	0.6617	**0.6917**
	$NIQE$	4.1652	3.8303	3.0152	3.0957	**2.9644**
MFIFB [20]	Q_o	0.9030	0.9286	0.9133	0.9052	**0.9396**
(512 × 512)	Q_w	0.8629	0.9403	0.9306	0.9127	**0.9452**
(40 pairs)	FMI	0.9152	0.9138	**0.9180**	0.9114	0.9101
	Q_{AB}^F	0.6591	0.7681	0.8030	0.7352	**0.8101**
	$NIQE$	3.8672	4.1592	3.9903	3.8501	**3.4513**

4.1 Subjective Discussion

This section presents the subjective judgement of the said approach with a few state-of-art fusion algorithms. Visual results from all the datasets, Lytro (1st, 2nd row), MFI-WHU (3rd, 4th row) and MFIFB (5th, 6th row) are presented in Fig. 2. Evidently, results from SR and Swinfusion suffer from low visual clarity as the minute details appear indistinct and blurry (Fig. 2 c1–c6, f1–f6). MGFF results appear to have enhanced colors along with a feature distortion near the boundary for unregistered datasets (Fig. 2, d5, d6). SESF-based method have introduced severe blotches in its results (Fig. 2 e6) possibly resulting from the non-explainable nature of deep learning models in feature selection. Exemplary results are exhibited by the proposed method which is free from any visible distortion. It is further verified by the higher values for most of the quality measures in Table 1 and the lowest value for $NIQE$ indicating the naturalness of the fused results.

5 Conclusion

In this paper, the authors have discussed a multi-focus image fusion scheme in the transform domain utilizing the well-known Tchebichef's polynomials. The input images are expressed in terms of local Tchebichef's basis and the coefficients are rearranged to mimic a wavelet-like multiscale decomposition with approximation and detail subbands. The mid-frequency coefficients are fused using weighted averaging where the weight is calculated from the coefficients at the current level and all its subsequent finer levels of resolution. The sparse-coding approach is used to fuse the finest details at the highest resolution.

In addition, the same sparse dictionary is used to fuse features from the approximation subband. The fused coefficients are relocated back to their initial blocks, followed by the application of inverse DTT to generate the final fused image in the spatial domain. The subjective judgement and fusion metrics on the results display the superiority of the proposed approach.

References

1. Aharon, M., Elad, M., Bruckstein, A.: K-SVD: an algorithm for designing overcomplete dictionaries for sparse representation. IEEE Trans. Signal Process. **54**(11), 4311–4322 (2006)
2. Aymaz, S., Köse, C.: A novel image decomposition-based hybrid technique with super-resolution method for multi-focus image fusion. Inf. Fusion **45**, 113–127 (2019)
3. Bavirisetti, D.P., Xiao, G., Zhao, J., Dhuli, R., Liu, G.: Multi-scale guided image and video fusion: a fast and efficient approach. Circ. Syst. Signal Process. **38**, 5576–5605 (2019)
4. Bhat, S., Koundal, D.: Multi-focus image fusion techniques: a survey. Artif. Intell. Rev. **54**, 5735–5787 (2021)
5. Deng, C., Gao, X., Li, X., Tao, D.: A local Tchebichef moments-based robust image watermarking. Signal Process. **89**(8), 1531–1539 (2009)
6. Haghighat, M.B.A., Aghagolzadeh, A., Seyedarabi, H.: A non-reference image fusion metric based on mutual information of image features. Comput. Electr. Eng. **37**(5), 744–756 (2011)
7. Kumar, B.S., Swamy, M., Ahmad, M.O.: Multiresolution DCT decomposition for multifocus image fusion. In: 2013 26th IEEE Canadian Conference on Electrical and Computer Engineering (CCECE), pp. 1–4. IEEE (2013)
8. Liu, Y., Wang, L., Cheng, J., Li, C., Chen, X.: Multi-focus image fusion: a survey of the state of the art. Inf. Fusion **64**, 71–91 (2020)
9. Ma, B., Zhu, Y., Yin, X., Ban, X., Huang, H., Mukeshimana, M.: SESF-Fuse: an unsupervised deep model for multi-focus image fusion. Neural Comput. Appl. **33**, 5793–5804 (2021)
10. Ma, J., Tang, L., Fan, F., Huang, J., Mei, X., Ma, Y.: SwinFusion: cross-domain long-range learning for general image fusion via swin transformer. IEEE/CAA J. Autom. Sinica **9**(7), 1200–1217 (2022)
11. Mallat, S.G., Zhang, Z.: Matching pursuits with time-frequency dictionaries. IEEE Trans. Signal Process. **41**(12), 3397–3415 (1993)
12. Mittal, A., Soundararajan, R., Bovik, A.C.: Making a "completely blind" image quality analyzer. IEEE Signal Process. Lett. **20**(3), 209–212 (2012)
13. Mukundan, R., Ong, S., Lee, P.A.: Image analysis by Tchebichef moments. IEEE Trans. Image Process. **10**(9), 1357–1364 (2001)
14. Nejati, M., Samavi, S., Shirani, S.: Multi-focus image fusion using dictionary-based sparse representation. Inf. Fusion **25**, 72–84 (2015)
15. Olshausen, B.A., Field, D.J.: Emergence of simple-cell receptive field properties by learning a sparse code for natural images. Nature **381**(6583), 607–609 (1996)
16. Piella, G., Heijmans, H.: A new quality metric for image fusion. In: Proceedings 2003 International Conference on Image Processing (Cat. No. 03CH37429), vol. 3, pp. III-173. IEEE (2003)

17. Wang, G., Wang, S.: Recursive computation of Tchebichef moment and its inverse transform. Pattern Recogn. **39**(1), 47–56 (2006)
18. Xydeas, C., Petrovic, V.: Objective image fusion performance measure. Electron. Lett. **36**(4), 308–309 (2000)
19. Zhang, H., Le, Z., Shao, Z., Xu, H., Ma, J.: MFF-GAN: an unsupervised generative adversarial network with adaptive and gradient joint constraints for multi-focus image fusion. Inf. Fusion **66**, 40–53 (2021)
20. Zhang, X.: Multi-focus image fusion: a benchmark. arXiv preprint arXiv:2005.01116 (2020)

Universal Detection and Source Attribution of Diffusion Model Generated Images with High Generalization and Robustness

Sanandita Das[ID], Dibyarup Dutta[ID], Tanusree Ghosh[✉][ID],
and Ruchira Naskar[ID]

Department of Information Technology, Indian Institute of Engineering,
Science and Technology, Shibpur, Howrah 711103, India
{510819041.sanandita,510819047.dibyarup,
2021itP001.tanusree}@students.iiests.ac.in, ruchira@it.iiests.ac.in

Abstract. The proliferation of synthetic media over the internet is posing a significant social threat. Recent advancements in Diffusion Models (DM) have made it easier to create astonishingly photo-realistic synthetic media with high stability and control. Moreover, applications like DALLE-2, powered by DM and Large Language Models (LLM), permit visual content generation from natural language description, enabling opportunities for everyone to generate visual media. Hence, there is an immediate need to identify synthetic images and attribute them to their source architectures. In this work, we propose a synthetic image detector as universal detector and a source model attributor based on a popular transfer-learning model ResNet-50 and compare the results with other popular models, including Visual Geometry Group (VGG) 16, Xception-Net and InceptionNet. The proposed universal detector attains over 96% accuracy, with a source attribution, accuracy over 93% for detection of Diffusion Model generated images. The model also succeeds in achieving significant generalization and robustness capabilities under different training-testing configurations, as proven by our experiments.

Keywords: Diffusion Model · Generative Adversarial Network · Source Attribution · Synthetic Media · Transfer Learning · Universal Detection

1 Introduction

The field of synthetic image generation has seen tremendous growth after Goodfellow et al. [1] proposed the idea of Generative Adversarial Networks (GANs) in 2014. After that, generative models kept improving with more complex architectures resulting in extreme photo-realistic picture quality. Interestingly, Lago et al. in [2] showed that humans consider StyleGAN2 [3] synthesized faces as more 'real' than real faces. While such synthetic images have their use cases in

P. Maji et al. (Eds.): PReMI 2023, LNCS 14301, pp. 441–448, 2023.
https://doi.org/10.1007/978-3-031-45170-6_45

(a)   (b)   (c)   (d)   (e)

Fig. 1. Synthetic images generated by DALL-E [6] and Stable Diffusion [7] using text prompts: (a) An Indian girl with a red earring & (b) A dog in a suit and tie & (c) Bengali foods served on a banana leaf & (d) A bird sitting on a tree with red flower & (e) A realistic portrait of an Indian woman wearing white 'kalamkari' printed saree

the entertainment industry for low-cost, royalty-free image generation, malicious users often misuse this capability of generative models for artificial synthesis of non-consensual obscene contents. An article[1] published by CNN in 2020 reported the perilous role of AI-generated pictures used in fake social media profiles in cyberbullying and harassment cases.

In addition to causing detrimental social impacts and deluding courtroom proceedings, AI synthesized fake media may also lead to troubled psychological and memory experiences for the victims [4].

While GANs learn to generate images from latent code employing two generator-discriminator networks in an adversarial setting, Diffusion Models (DMs) [5], constituting another set of data-driven generative model, learn to synthesize images by adding noise gradually to a source image and then performing a reverse de-noising step. Diffusion Models, in combination with large language models have given rise to Large Text-to-Image (LTIM) models such as DALL-E 2 [6], Stable Diffusion [7], etc., which have the capability to generate astonishingly high-quality realistic images from a text prompt. This gives users a better control over the synthesized image content. Such models have been used to synthesize images of any style: artistic or realistic. While this has provided an outstanding opportunity for creative thinkers to materialize any idea with a proper text description, such models are highly vulnerable to misuse with malicious intent.[2] A painting titled "Portrait of Edmond Belamy", claimed to have been created by an AI network, was sold for $432,500 at an auction by Christie's[3] (Fig. 1).

The detection of GAN-synthesized images is a well-explored field. Deep learning-based detectors have proved to be efficient in this task [8]. However, the primary drawback with the majority of such detectors is that they fail to identify images from networks other than those present in the training set and perform unsatisfactorily when test images get compressed, which is a very common operation for images circulated over social networks. Both these generalization and robustness problems should be considered for designing synthetic image detectors, as suggested in [9].

---

[1] https://edition.cnn.com/2020/02/20/tech/fake-faces-deepfake/.

[2] https://www.theregreview.org/2023/01/24/penava-ai-art-is-in-legal-greyscale/.

[3] https://www.christies.com/features/A-collaboration-between-two-artists-one-human-one-a-machine-9332-1.aspx.

DM-generated image detection is comparatively an unexplored domain. Corvi et al. [10] explored the generalization capabilities of existing GAN-specific models on DM-synthesized image detection task and concluded that they work poorly in this task with the average accuracy of detection ranging from 51.9% to 75.9%. They also showed that DM models like DALLE2 and ADM lack patterns in the frequency domain, unlike GAN models resulting in poor detection performance. Sha et al. [11] included text modality with images to design a DM-synthesized image detector. Even though their detection performance was well, their scope of work was limited to LTIMs so their generalization and robustness capability cannot be commented on.

In this paper, we propose a synthetic image detector and source attributor based on ResNet-50 [12] transfer learning model, with enhanced generalization and robustness capabilities. We trained our model on images generated by five diffusion models, viz., Latent Diffusion [13], Stable Diffusion [7], GLIDE [14], DALL-E mini [15] and DALL-E 2 [6] vs. real images collected from Flickr8k dataset [16]. We have compared the model's performance to other transfer learning based models like VGG-16 [17], XCeptionNet [18], and InceptionNet [19], and have conducted generalization and robustness study of our model to ensure the model's usability in practical scenarios.

Rest of the paper is structured as follows. In Sect. 2, we present the proposed model for synthetic image detection as well as source attribution of synthetic images. Section 3 presents experimental results pertaining to performance of the model, along with generalization and robustness investigations. Finally, in Sect. 4 we discuss future research directions and conclude our paper.

2   Proposed Universal Synthetic Image Detector with Source Attribution

The proposed model is based on Resnet 50 [12], a Convolutional Neural Network(CNN) which utilizes residual connections to mitigate the vanishing gradient problem and has a hierarchical structure of five stages, each containing multiple residual blocks. In order to address the challenges of limited dataset size and to enhance generalization capabilities of the model, we leverage pre-training on the *ImageNet* dataset [20] to extract critical features (Fig. 2).

Our proposed approach involves freezing the first four convolution stages of ResNet-50 trained on ImageNet to utilize their capability of extracting features such as textures, styles and noise artifacts, etc. We re-initialise the weights of the final convolution stage of the ResNet-50 architecture, and trained the model on our dataset, using the features extracted by the frozen layers. It was observed that this resulted in the best accuracy and helped us to mitigate over-fitting, given that our training dataset is relatively small.

Next, we added a classification head. We used fully connected layers instead of traditional machine learning models (such as Gradient Boosting, SVM, Logistic Regression, etc.) on top of the features extracted by pretrained ResNet-50,

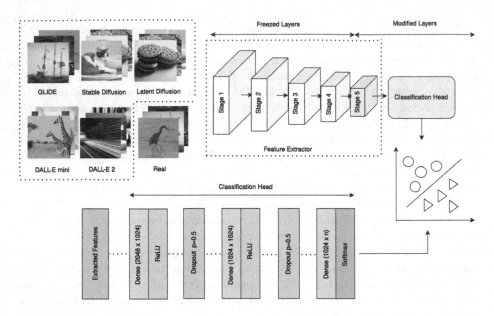

Fig. 2. Proposed model for universal detection and source attribution with $n = 2$ and $n = 5$ neurons in the last dense layer for Universal detector and source attributor, respectively.

to obtain a classifier since they can learn complex, non-linear relationships between features and labels better. The classification head is constructed as follows:

- Two fully connected layers using the ReLU activation function to introduce non-linearity.
- Two dropout layers with a dropout parameter of 0.5.
- A softmax layer to calculate probability distribution of the classes.

Activation function is used to introduce non-linearity into the model. We use the ReLU activation function ($f(x) = max(0, x)$) due to its sparsity in the activation of neurons with simple and efficient computation.

Dropout is turned off during inference when the model is used for predictions. Softmax is a mathematical function used to provide a probability distribution over the predicted classes. Mathematically, softmax function can be represented as $\sigma(\mathbf{z})_j = \frac{\exp(z_j)}{\sum_j \exp(z_j)}$ where $\sigma(\mathbf{z})_j$ is the j-th output of the softmax function, z_j is the j-th input to the function, and K is the number of classes.

Our training procedure was done using ADAM optimizer, due to its fast convergence and ability to adaptively adjust the learning rate for each parameter in the network with an initial learning rate of 0.0001. We kept the loss function uniform for the task of universal detection and source attribution by using *categorical cross entropy loss*.

Table 1. Performance Evaluation and Comparison of the Proposed Universal Detector and Source DM Attribution Models in terms of testing accuracy (%) and F1 score

Transfer Learning Models	Universal Detection		Source Attribution	
	Accuracy (%)	F1 Score	Accuracy (%)	F1 Score
Inception V3	91.19	0.9756	86.39	0.8701
Xception	90.42	0.9733	92.89	0.9237
VGG-16	88.65	0.9686	87.67	0.8788
Proposed Model	96.55	0.9762	93.11	0.9330

3   Experimentation, Results and Discussion

We have used a subset of the Corvi et al.'s dataset [10] for training in both universal detection and source attribution cases. The subset contains 3000 GLIDE [14], 1000 DALL-E 2 [6], 1000 DALL-E mini [15], 1000 Stable Diffusion [7] and 3000 Latent Diffusion [21] generated images. To balance the dataset classwise, we perform data augmentation using *random flip*, *random rotation* and *random brightness*. We have also tested the generalization capability of the proposed model on a second dataset, which is a subset of the Corvi et al.'s dataset [10], consisting of 1000 BigGAN [22], 1000 ProGAN [23] and around 2000 StyleGAN [3] images.

We have evaluated the performance efficiency of the proposed model in terms of classification accuracy, in case of both fake vs. real classification as well as source attribution. The results are also compared with other state-of-the-art CNNs, viz. Inception V3 [19], Xception [18], and VGG-16 [17]. The performance evaluation and comparison results have been presented in Table 1, where we have shown both training and testing accuracy.

In generalizability test, as reported in the literature by Corvi et al. [10], the highest accuracy achieved with Grag et al.'s [24] classifier trained only on Latent Diffusion [13] images was 73.9% when tested on GLIDE, DALL-E 2 and DALL-E mini generated images and accuracy of only 59.3% when tested on GAN generated images. The classifier showed high accuracy for GAN generated images when trained using ProGAN generated images, however the accuracies for DM generated images were extremely low. Our model achieved an accuracy of above 92% (highest reported accuracy 100% and lowest 92.43%) while being tested on GAN-generated images, as evident from Table 2. This proves that Real-Fake image detectors trained on a small set of DM generated images have significantly higher generalization power as compared to models trained on single GAN or single DM. Additionally, we also tested the proposed model's performance on a dataset of synthetic artistic images [25], and in this case, we observed an accuracy of 84.30%.

We evaluated the robustness of multiple models trained with different training settings against three types of post-processing operations. Specifically, we have used *JPEG compression*, *Additive White Gaussian Noise* (AWGN) induction, and *Gaussian Blur* operation. Figure 3 shows the performance of models trained with

Table 2. Comparison of Generalization Capability of Universal Detector (Accuracy %)

Model	Training Dataset	GLIDE	Stable Diffusion	Latent Diffusion	DALL-Emini	DALL-E 2	Pro-GAN	Style-GAN	Big-GAN
Grag et al. [24]	Latent Diffusion	62.5	99.7	97.1	73.9	50.4	52.0	58.0	52.9
Sinitsa and Fried [26]	LTIM and GAN	90.3	99.3	–	99.0	79.5	57.7	91.5	96.9
Wang et al. [27]	ProGAN	74.5	61.7	–	78.3	74.7	100	72.2	96.9
Proposed	Our dataset[†]	96.53	100	97.37	95.05	94.22	92.71	95.27	92.43

[†]Subset of Corvi et al.'s [10] dataset

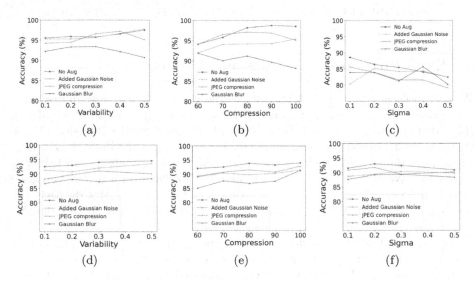

(a) (b) (c)

(d) (e) (f)

Fig. 3. Robustness of Proposed Model: Accuracy (%) obtained with varied degrees of augmentation. (a)-(c) Robustness of Universal Detector. (d)-(f) Robustness of Source Attributor. (a) and (d) are trained on varied levels of AWGN induction,(b) and (e) are trained on varied levels of JPEG compression, and (c) and (f) are trained on varied levels of Gaussian Blur

each type of augmentation. Our training data underwent different levels of JPEG compression ranging between 60 to 100. AWGN levels were between 0.1 to 0.5 variability (equivalent to 1/SNR), and Gaussian Blur was in the range $\sigma \in [0, 0.5]$. The test samples were made to undergo random post-processing operations in order to simulate a real world scenario, where the impairments of the test images are unknown. This study helped us understand the effect of different pre-processing operation and select a combination of pre-processing settings to make our model more robust. The robustness test results with the best model are presented in Table 3 for fake vs. real detector, and in Table 4 for source attribution, respectively.

Table 3. Robustness Results of Proposed Universal Detector (in Accuracy %)

Augmentation on Test Set	AWGN					JPEG Compression					Gaussian Blur				
Parameter	Variability					Quality					σ				
Value	0.1	0.2	0.3	0.4	0.5	100	90	80	70	60	0.1	0.2	0.3	0.4	0.5
Proposed Model	94.27	93.56	92.78	90.05	88.81	96.73	96.41	93.59	92.93	91.07	86.79	84.23	83.52	83.17	80.29
Proposed Robust Model	96.75	96.35	95.38	95.23	93.47	97.31	95.93	95.28	94.68	94.47	91.20	89.96	89.13	87.48	85.67

Table 4. Robustness Results of Proposed Source Attributor (Accuracy %)

Augmentation on Test Set	AWGN					JPEG Compression					Gaussian Blur				
Parameter	Variability					Quality					σ				
Value	0.1	0.2	0.3	0.4	0.5	100	90	80	70	60	0.1	0.2	0.3	0.4	0.5
Proposed Model	88.86	87.06	86.43	84.65	83.07	88.67	87.91	85.69	83.54	78.83	84.18	83.23	82.49	78.87	73.50
Proposed Robust Model	92.35	91.75	90.87	90.39	89.61	91.50	89.77	89.39	87.50	87.23	88.11	87.96	86.13	85.67	84.67

4 Conclusion

We present a transfer learning model for effective classification of diffusion model generated fake vs. real images, as well as source attribution of diffusion models. Our model achieves exceptional generalization and robustness capacities, highlighting its potential for practical application in image forensics. Future research will involve investigation of frequency domain traits of diffusion model synthesized images and development of a significantly large dataset of such images to be used in related researches.

References

1. Goodfellow, I., et al.: Generative adversarial networks. Commun. ACM **63**(11), 139–144 (2020)
2. Lago, F., Pasquini, C., Böhme, R., Dumont, H., Goffaux, V., Boato, G.: More real than real: a study on human visual perception of synthetic faces [applications corner]. IEEE Signal Process. Mag. **39**(1), 109–116 (2021)
3. Karras, T., Laine, S., Aittala, M., Hellsten, J., Lehtinen, J., Aila, T.: Analyzing and improving the image quality of styleGAN. In: Proceedings of the IEEE/CVF Conference on Computer Vision and Pattern Recognition, pp. 8110–8119 (2020)
4. Hancock, J.T., Bailenson, J.N.: The social impact of DeepFakes. Cyberpsychol. Behav. Soc. Netw. **24**(3), 149–152 (2021). PMID: 33760669
5. Dhariwal, P., Nichol, A.: Diffusion models beat GANs on image synthesis. In: Advances in Neural Information Processing, vol. 34, pp. 8780–8794 (2021)
6. Nichol, A., Ramesh, A., Dhariwal, P.: Hierarchical text-conditional image generation with clip Latents (2022)
7. Lorenz, D., Rombach, R., Blattmann, A.: High-resolution image synthesis with latent diffusion models (2022)

8. Passos, L. A., Jodas, D., da Costa, K. A., Júnior, L. A. S., Colombo, D., Papa, J. P.: A review of deep learning-based approaches for DeepFake content detection. arXiv preprint arXiv:2202.06095 (2022)

9. Cozzolino, D., Gragnaniello, D., Poggi, G., Verdoliva, L.: Towards universal GAN image detection. In: 2021 International Conference on Visual Communications and Image Processing (VCIP), pp. 1–5. IEEE (2021)

10. Zingarini, G., Corvi, R., Cozzolino, D.: On the detection of synthetic images generated by diffusion models (2022)

11. Yu, N., Sha, Z., Li, Z.: De-fake: detection and attribution of fake images generated by text-to-image generation models (2023)

12. He, K., Zhang, X., Ren, S., Sun, J.: Deep residual learning for image recognition. In: Proceedings of the IEEE Conference on Computer Vision and Pattern Recognition, pp. 770–778 (2016)

13. Rombach, R., Blattmann, A., Lorenz, D., Esser, P., Ommer, B.: High-resolution image synthesis with latent diffusion models. In: Proceedings of the IEEE/CVF Conference on Computer Vision and Pattern Recognition, pp. 10684–10695 (2022)

14. Ramesh, A., Nichol, A., Dhariwal, P.: GLIDE: towards photorealistic image generation and editing with text-guided diffusion models (2022)

15. Dayma, B.: Dall·e mini, vol. 7 (2021)

16. Hodosh, M., Young, P., Hockenmaier, J.: Framing image description as a ranking task: data, models and evaluation metrics. J. Artif. Intell. Res. **47**, 853–899 (2013)

17. Simonyan, K., Zisserman, A.: Very deep convolutional networks for large-scale image recognition. arXiv preprint arXiv:1409.1556 (2014)

18. Chollet, F.: Xception: deep learning with depthwise separable convolutions. In: Proceedings of the IEEE Conference on Computer Vision and Pattern Recognition, pp. 1251–1258 (2017)

19. Szegedy, C., Vanhoucke, V., Ioffe, S., Shlens, J., Wojna, Z.: Rethinking the inception architecture for computer vision. In: Proceedings of the IEEE Conference on Computer Vision and Pattern Recognition, pp. 2818–2826 (2016)

20. Deng, J., Dong, W., Socher, R., Li, L.-J., Li, K., Fei-Fei, L.: ImageNet: a large-scale hierarchical image database. In: 2009 IEEE Conference on Computer Vision and Pattern Recognition, pp. 248–255. IEEE (2009)

21. Towsley, D., Atwood, J.: Diffusion-convolutional neural networks (2016)

22. Simonyan, K., Brock, A., Donahue, J.: Large scale GAN training for high fidelity natural image synthesis (2018)

23. Laine, S., Lehtinen, J., Karras, T., Aila, T.: Progressive growing of GANs for improved quality, stability, and variation (2018)

24. Marra, F., Gragnaniello, D., Cozzolino, D.: Are GAN generated images easy to detect? A critical analysis of the state-of-the-art (2021)

25. Wang, Z.J., Montoya, E., Munechika, D., Yang, H., Hoover, B., Chau, D.H.: DiffusionDB: a large-scale prompt gallery dataset for text-to-image generative models. arXiv:2210.14896 [cs] (2022)

26. Fried, O., Sinitsa, S.: Deep image fingerprint: accurate and low budget synthetic image detector (2023)

27. Zhang, R., Wang, S.-Y., Wang, O.: CNN-generated images are surprisingly easy to spot... for now (2020)

Semi-supervised Video Object Segmentation Using Parallel Coattention Network

Sangramjit Chakraborty(✉)[iD], Monalisha Mahapatra[iD], and Anup Nandy[iD]

Machine Intelligence and Bio-Motion Lab, Department of Computer Science
and Engineering, National Institute of Technology, Rourkela, Rourkela, Odisha, India
chsangram99@gmail.com

Abstract. In this work, a novel method is proposed for video object segmentation. The temporal correlation is measured between subsequent frames in a video sequence to propagate a reference segmentation mask through the video sequence. The aim is to develop a novel deep learning based holistic method for video object segmentation. For this purpose, a parallel coattention module is used to capture the rich temporal information between two subsequent frames and mask. An autoencoder architecture with a siamese encoder module is applied with three inputs, and skipped connections are utilized between the encoder and decoder networks. No auxiliary information such as optical flows are used in this network. The method is validated on DAVIS16 and FBMS datasets with mean region similarity ($\mathcal{J}_{mean}$) of 91.2 and 83.2 respectively.

Keywords: Coattention · Deep learning · Autoencoder · Video Object Segmentation

1 Introduction

Video Object Segmentation(VOS) plays a pivotal role in numerous applications. It is involved in intelligent behaviour of vision based agents which depends on holistic understanding of scenes. Humans inherently have the ability to understand complex scenes. The same level of coherent understanding of scenes is important to build systems that can mimic human abilities [2]. Accurate detection of objects in scenes can have revolutionary effects on diverse applications.

An object can be defined as a foreground object in a video sequence if it satisfies two important properties: (i) the object must be prominent and distinguishable in a single frame (local saliency), (ii) the object must appear consistently and frequently throughout the video sequence (temporal consistency) [8]. However, there are major challenges currently encountered in VOS such as occlusion, deformation, and clutter [19].

The contribution of this research is to develop a VOS method that can provide pixel level segmentation with higher accuracy in comparison to other state-of-the-art methods. Therefore, a novel methodology using coattention mechanism is

P. Maji et al. (Eds.): PReMI 2023, LNCS 14301, pp. 449–456, 2023.
https://doi.org/10.1007/978-3-031-45170-6_46

proposed to achieve this task. It captures rich spatial and temporal relationships for performing segmentation without calculating any auxiliary information like optical flow.

The paper is arranged as follows: Sect. 2 discusses some of the previous works done in VOS. Section 3 offers an overview of the experimental methodology. Section 4 discusses the proposed method. The results are highlighted in Sect. 5. Finally, Sect. 6 presents the conclusion and future works.

2   Previous Work

Shelhamer et al. [12] first introduced the fully convolutional neural network architecture, which had the ability to take input images in arbitrary sizes and directly produce pixel level segmentation maps. Subsequently, deep learning was used for video object segmentation in multiple new techniques [1,7,13,15].

Previous deep learning based methods have utilized differences in motion to perform the detection of foreground objects. Calculating optical flows was a popular method [4,14,15,19] of capturing the motion information in consecutive frames. Recurrent Neural Network based methods [13] were also utilized.

Lu et al. [8] proposed COSNet, or Coattention Siamese Network. This is an unsupervised method that incorporates a gated coattention mechanism to learn foreground object segmentation. Huang et al. [3] proposed CoMatchNet. It contains a coattention module which calculates the correlation between the query frame and its previous frame along with the first frame of the sequence.

However, no methods are used to propagate the segmentation mask by capturing the correlation between two consecutive frames.

3   Materials and Methods

First, the proposed model is pre-trained on MSRA10K [2] saliency dataset to bring the foreground object representations closer in the embedding space. The images along with their corresponding masks are transformed in various ways. They are used as the query while the actual image and mask are utilized as the reference. Then, the network is fine-tuned using the DAVIS16 [10] and FBMS [9] dataset with two successive frames from the same sequence as input.

3.1   Dataset

The pre-training dataset MSRA10K [2] is a saliency detection dataset which has 10 thousand images with pixel level masks for salient objects. The model is also fine-tuned and tested on two VOS dataset such as DAVIS16 [10] and FBMS [9]. DAVIS16 is a dataset containing 50 video sequences (30 training, 20 testing), with pixel level object masks for all frames of the videos. FBMS dataset contains 59 video sequences (29 training, 30 testing). It is sparsely annotated with pixel level masks for 720 frames.

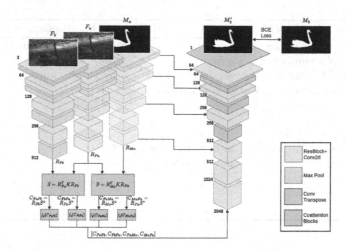

Fig. 1. Network architecture for the proposed method

Standard evaluation methods [10] are adopted for testing the performance on DAVIS16. Mean, recall, and decay metrics for $\mathcal{J}$ (region similarity), $\mathcal{F}$ (boundary accuracy), and mean for $\mathcal{T}$ (temporal stability) are calculated for the DAVIS16 dataset. For testing with FBMS dataset, mean $\mathcal{J}$ (region similarity) is calculated for the testing subset containing 30 videos following standard procedure [4,13, 18,19].

4   Proposed Methodology

This section discusses the proposed technique for VOS using coattention mechanism.

4.1   Coattention Mechanism

Vanilla Coattention: Let F_a and F_b be two video frames, and let their feature representations be R_{F_a}, R_{F_b} in $\mathbb{R}^{W \times H \times C}$ where the width is W, the height is H, and the number of channels is C, the coattention [6,8] between F_a and F_b is as follows

The affinity matrix S is first computed as

$$S = R_{F_b}^T K R_{F_a} \in \mathbb{R}^{(WH) \times (WH)} \tag{1}$$

where K is a weight matrix of size $C \times C$, and the representations are flattened to $R_{F_a}, R_{F_b} \in \mathbb{R}^{C \times (WH)}$. The similarity between each row of $R_{F_b}^T$ and R_{F_a} is represented by each element of S.

Then, it is normalized by taking its row-wise and column-wise softmax

$$S^c = softmax(S), S^r = softmax(S^T) \tag{2}$$

Algorithm 1: Algorithm for inference pipeline of the proposed method

---

Input : V - sequence of video frames, M_0 - Segmentation mask for V_0,
       N - number of video frames
Output: M' - predicted segmentation masks for the video sequence
1 Initialize predicted segmentation mask array M' with size N.
2 Set $M'_0 = M_0$.
3 Initialize $i = 1$.
4 **while** $i \leq N - 1$ **do**
5   Give V_{i-1}, V_i and M_{i-1} as inputs to the model.
6   Get O_i as the output from the model.
7   Set $M'_i = O_i$.
8   Set $i = i + 1$.
9 **end**

Next, the attention summaries are calculated as follows

$$C_a = R_{F_b}S^c = [C_a^{(1)}C_a^{(2)}...C_a^{(i)}...C_a^{(WH)}] \in \mathbb{R}^C \times (WH) \tag{3}$$

$$C_a^{(p)} = R_{F_b} \otimes S^{c(p)} = \sum_{q=1}^{WH} R_{F_b}^{(q)} . s_{pq}^c \in \mathbb{R}^C \tag{4}$$

where $C_a^{(p)}$ denotes the p-th column of C_a, $\otimes$ is a matrix times vector operation, $S^{c(p)}$ is the p-th column of S^c, $R_{F_b}^{(q)}$ indicates the q-th column of R_{F_b} and s_{pq}^c is the q-th element in $S^{c(p)}$. The features for F_b is computed as $C_b = R_{F_a}S^r$.

Symmetric Coattention: When the weight matrix is limited to being symmetric, the projection matrix K transforms into an orthogonal matrix [8,11]. The equation for symmetric coattention is described as follows

$$S = R_{F_b}^T P^T D P R_{F_a} = (P R_{F_b})^T D P R_{F_a} \tag{5}$$

Gated Coattention: The information in the input image may not be homogenous. Therefore weighting the pixels can be advantageous. A self-gate mechanism [8] can be implemented for this purpose. The attention summaries are calculated as follows

$$C_a = C_a * \sigma(wC_a + b) \in [0,1]^{WH}, C_b = C_b * \sigma(wC_b + b) \in [0,1]^{WH} \tag{6}$$

where b and w denote the bias and the convolution kernel respectively, and σ symbolises the sigmoid function.

4.2   Network Architecture

The proposed network consists of three modules, the encoder, the parallel coattention module, and the decoder. The encoder module consists of resblock and

Table 1. Proposed VOS method compared to other methods for DAVIS16 dataset using $\mathcal{J}$ (), $\mathcal{F}$ (region similarity), and $\mathcal{T}$ (temporal stability).

	Method	PDB [13]	LSMO [15]	COSNet [8]	AGNN [16]	MATNet [19]	EGMN [7]	F2Net [5]	MiVOS [1]	Proposed
$\mathcal{J}$	Mean	77.2	78.2	80.5	81.3	82.4	82.5	83.1	89.7	**91.2**
	Recall	93.1	91.1	93.1	93.1	94.5	94.3	95.7	97.5	**97.9**
	Decay	0.9	4.1	4.4	0	5.5	4.2	0	6.6	0
$\mathcal{F}$	Mean	74.5	75.9	79.4	79.7	80.7	81.2	84.4	92.4	**94.9**
	Recall	84.4	84.7	89.5	88.5	90.2	90.3	92.3	96.4	**97.4**
	Decay	−0.2	3.5	5	5.1	4.5	5.6	0.8	5.1	0
$\mathcal{T}$	Mean	29.1	21.2	18.4	33.7	21.6	19.8	20.9	**16.9**	23.6

2D convolutional modules (conv2D) with (2×2) max pooling layers in between. Each combination of resblock and max pooling layers reduces the image size by half. The encoder is modeled as a siamese network where three input streams are computed using the same network. Two frames and a supporting mask are provided as inputs to the encoder network. This makes the proposed technique a semi-supervised VOS method, as compared to COSNet [8] which is an unsupervised method. A supporting mask for the previous frame is provided as a third input to the network. This enables the network to learn the initial configuration of the foreground objects. The addition of skipped connections also significantly boosts the spatial stability of the results.

The decoder module consists of resblock and conv2D with transposed convolutions to upscale the inputs. Each resblock and transposed convolution pair upscales the image by a factor of 2. Feature channels from the mask encoder are concatenated to the corresponding decoder channels via skipped connections.

Let F_a, F_b be two successive frames of a video, and M_a, M_b be the corresponding segmentation masks. The frame F_a is designated as the reference frame, the mask M_a as the reference mask, and the frame F_b as the query frame. The frames F_a, F_b and the reference mask M_a is first encoded through the encoder network to obtain the feature representations $R_{F_a}, R_{F_b}, R_{M_a}$. Then, R_{F_a} and R_{F_b} are passed through a coattention module to obtain the representations $C_{F_aF_b}$ and $C_{F_bF_a}$. R_{F_a} and R_{M_a} are passed through a coattention module to obtain the representations $C_{F_aM_a}$ and $C_{M_aF_a}$. Finally, the output segmentation mask M_b' is produced by the decoder module from $[C_{F_aF_b}, C_{F_bF_a}, C_{F_aM_a}, C_{M_aF_a}]$. The complete network architecture is shown in Fig. 1.

5   Result Analysis and Discussion

All training and testing tasks are performed with a single Nvidia RTX^{TM} A4000 GPU, 64 GB of memory, Intel® Xeon processor, and Windows 10(64-bit) Operating System.

The training is performed with a batch size of 4 and optimized using Adam optimizer with initial learning rate of 10^{-5}. Efficiency techniques such as autocasting and gradient scaling are used. The model is pre-trained for 100 epochs and fine-tuned for 60 epochs on each dataset with Binary Cross-Entropy Loss.

Table 2. Proposed VOS method compared to other methods for FBMS dataset using $\mathcal{J}$ (jaccard index).

	Method	PDB [13]	UMOD [18]	MGA [4]	COSNet [8]	DyStaB [17]	MATNet [19]	Proposed
$\mathcal{J}$	Mean	74	63.6	82.8	75.6	75.8	76.1	**83.2**

Fig. 2. Qualitative results on DAVIS16 and FBMS dataset. On top: *dance-twirl* from DAVIS16 dataset, on bottom: *giraffes01* from FBMS dataset

During the testing phase, the reference mask for the first frame is taken from the ground truth annotations. The user is expected to provide the manually segmented mask for the first frame. The rest of the masks for subsequent frames are generated pairwise by the trained model. This is shown in Algorithm 1.

Different results are obtained on various dataset used in this research experiment. The experimental results in Table 1 demonstrate the evaluation of the proposed model on DAVIS16 dataset. The comparisons are shown with several other methods. The results obtained from experiments performed on the FBMS dataset are mentioned in Table 2. It is evident from the comparisons that the model exhibits better performance than state-of-the-art methods.

Qualitative Results: Figure 2 shows the qualitative results on the segmentation task. A subset of the video sequences "dance-twirl" and "giraffes0" is presented from the DAVIS16 and FBMS dataset respectively. It can be seen that multiple foreground objects are tracked accurately in spite of motion and deformation.

5.1   Ablation Study

The impact of vanilla coattention (Eq. 3) and symmetric coattention (Eq. 5) is investigated, in addition to a version with no coattention. The results are demonstrated in Table 3. Vanilla coattention and symmetric coattention perform significantly better as compared to no coattention. Symmetric coattention yields marginally better results.

The effects of varying the inputs to the model are also shown in Table 3. The model performs significantly better when provided with the Reference Frame and Query Frame together. On adding the Reference Mask, the model experiences a further improvement in performance. Thus it is clear that all three input branches contribute significantly to the model performance.

Table 3. Ablation Study of proposed technique on DAVIS16 and FBMS dataset

Variant	$\mathcal{J}Mean$		Variant	$\mathcal{J}Mean$	
	DAVIS	FBMS		DAVIS	FBMS
Coattention Variant			Input Branches		
No coattention	80.8	77.1	QF Only	77.6	64.4
Vanilla coattention (Eq. 3)	90.6	81.7	QF + RF	79.9	71.3
Symmetric coattention (Eq. 5)	91.2	83.2	QF + RF + RM	91.2	83.2

Variant	$\mathcal{J}Mean$	
	DAVIS	FBMS
Network Architecture		
Skipped Connections	91.2	83.2
No Skipped Connections	79.5	74.2

A significant drop in performance is noticed if the skipped connections are removed from the network. This is also demonstrated in Table 3 which shows the skipped connections are integral to the optimal performance of the model.

6   Conclusion and Future Work

In this study a novel technique for video object segmentation is proposed. The task is modeled as a temporal coherence capturing problem. This is achieved by relating semantic segmentation to propagation of segmentation masks across frames. The correlation between two consecutive frames and the semantic mask is modeled using parallel coattention. The method is proven to be superior in performance as compared to several other state-of-the-art methods ($\mathcal{J}_{mean}$: 91.2 on DAVIS16, $\mathcal{J}_{mean}$: 83.2 on FBMS). The proposed method efficiently propagates the given segmentation mask even when the objects are occluded or deformed, and with varied amounts of background clutter. This method can also be generalised to other video related temporal propagation task like optical flow estimation. However, it is observed that this method has slow computational efficiency for estimating the segmentation masks. Consequently, further research can be carried out to perform video object segmentation efficiently by modifying the model architecture.

References

1. Cheng, H.K., Tai, Y.W., Tang, C.K.: Modular interactive video object segmentation: interaction-to-mask, propagation and difference-aware fusion. In: Proceedings of the IEEE/CVF Conference on Computer Vision and Pattern Recognition (CVPR), pp. 5559–5568 (2021)
2. Cheng, M.M., Mitra, N.J., Huang, X., Torr, P.H.S., Hu, S.M.: Global contrast based salient region detection. IEEE TPAMI **37**(3), 569–582 (2015)

3. Huang, L., Sun, F., Yuan, X.: COMatchNet: co-attention matching network for video object segmentation. In: Pattern Recognition, pp. 271–284 (2022)
4. Li, H., Chen, G., Li, G., Yu, Y.: Motion guided attention for video salient object detection. In: Proceedings of the IEEE/CVF International Conference on Computer Vision, pp. 7274–7283 (2019)
5. Liu, D., Yu, D., Wang, C., Zhou, P.: F2Net: learning to focus on the foreground for unsupervised video object segmentation. In: Proceedings of the AAAI Conference on Artificial Intelligence, vol. 35, no. 3, pp. 2109–2117 (2021)
6. Lu, J., Yang, J., Batra, D., Parikh, D.: Hierarchical question-image co-attention for visual question answering. In: Proceedings of the 30th International Conference on Neural Information Processing Systems, pp. 289–297 (2016)
7. Lu, X., Wang, W., Danelljan, M., Zhou, T., Shen, J., Van Gool, L.: Video object segmentation with episodic graph memory networks. In: Vedaldi, A., Bischof, H., Brox, T., Frahm, J.-M. (eds.) ECCV 2020. LNCS, vol. 12348, pp. 661–679. Springer, Cham (2020). https://doi.org/10.1007/978-3-030-58580-8_39
8. Lu, X., Wang, W., Ma, C., Shen, J., Shao, L., Porikli, F.: See more, know more: unsupervised video object segmentation with co-attention Siamese networks. In: Proceedings of the IEEE/CVF Conference on Computer Vision and Pattern Recognition, pp. 3623–3632 (2019)
9. Ochs, P., Malik, J., Brox, T.: Segmentation of moving objects by long term video analysis. IEEE Trans. Pattern Anal. Mach. Intell. $36(6)$, 1187–1200 (2014)
10. Perazzi, F., Pont-Tuset, J., McWilliams, B., Van Gool, L., Gross, M., Sorkine-Hornung, A.: A benchmark dataset and evaluation methodology for video object segmentation. In: Proceedings of the IEEE Conference on Computer Vision and Pattern Recognition, pp. 724–732 (2016)
11. Rodríguez, P., Gonzàlez, J., Cucurull, G., Gonfaus, J.M., Roca, F.X.: Regularizing CNNs with locally constrained decorrelations. CoRR abs/1611.01967 (2016)
12. Shelhamer, E., Long, J., Darrell, T.: Fully convolutional networks for semantic segmentation. IEEE Trans. Pattern Anal. Mach. Intell. $39(4)$, 640–651 (2017)
13. Song, H., Wang, W., Zhao, S., Shen, J., Lam, K.M.: Pyramid dilated deeper ConvLSTM for video salient object detection. In: Proceedings of the European Conference on Computer Vision (ECCV), pp. 715–731 (2018)
14. Tokmakov, P., Alahari, K., Schmid, C.: Learning video object segmentation with visual memory. In: 2017 IEEE International Conference on Computer Vision (ICCV), pp. 4491–4500 (2017)
15. Tokmakov, P., Schmid, C., Alahari, K.: Learning to segment moving objects. Int. J. Comput. Vision $127(3)$, 282–301 (2019)
16. Wang, W., Lu, X., Shen, J., Crandall, D.J., Shao, L.: Zero-shot video object segmentation via attentive graph neural networks. In: Proceedings of the IEEE/CVF International Conference on Computer Vision, pp. 9236–9245 (2019)
17. Yang, Y., Lai, B., Soatto, S.: DyStaB: unsupervised object segmentation via dynamic-static bootstrapping. In: Proceedings of the IEEE/CVF Conference on Computer Vision and Pattern Recognition (CVPR), pp. 2826–2836 (2021)
18. Yang, Y., Loquercio, A., Scaramuzza, D., Soatto, S.: Unsupervised moving object detection via contextual information separation. In: Proceedings of the IEEE/CVF Conference on Computer Vision and Pattern Recognition, pp. 879–888 (2019)
19. Zhou, T., Wang, S., Zhou, Y., Yao, Y., Li, J., Shao, L.: Motion-attentive transition for zero-shot video object segmentation. In: Proceedings of the AAAI Conference on Artificial Intelligence, pp. 13066–13073 (2020)

SoccerKDNet: A Knowledge Distillation Framework for Action Recognition in Soccer Videos

Sarosij Bose[1]([✉])[iD], Saikat Sarkar[2][iD], and Amlan Chakrabarti[3][iD]

[1] Department of Computer Science and Engineering, University of Calcutta,
Kolkata, India
sarosijbose2000@gmail.com
[2] Department of Computer Science, Bangabasi College, University of Calcutta,
Kolkata, India
[3] A.K. Choudhury School of Information Technology, University of Calcutta,
Kolkata, India
acakcs@caluniv.ac.in

Abstract. Classifying player actions from soccer videos is a challenging problem, which has become increasingly important in sports analytics over the years. Most state-of-the-art methods employ highly complex offline networks, which makes it difficult to deploy such models in resource constrained scenarios. Here, in this paper we propose a novel end-to-end knowledge distillation based transfer learning network pre-trained on the Kinetics400 dataset and then perform extensive analysis on the learned framework by introducing a unique loss parameterization. We also introduce a new dataset named "SoccerDB1" containing 448 videos and consisting of 4 diverse classes each of players playing soccer. Furthermore, we introduce an unique loss parameter that help us linearly weigh the extent to which the predictions of each network are utilized. Finally, we also perform a thorough performance study using various changed hyperparameters. We also benchmark the first classification results on the new SoccerDB1 dataset obtaining 67.20% validation accuracy. The dataset has been made publicly available at: https://bit.ly/soccerdb1.

Keywords: Soccer Analytics · Knowledge Distillation · Action Recognition

1 Introduction

Recognition of player actions in soccer video is a challenging computer vision task. Existing vision-based soccer analytics models either rely heavily on manpower which is responsible for tracking every aspect of the game or other offline network based analytics products that are used for analyzing the game closely once it's over [11,12]. It has been established that deep learning based methods exceed their traditional counterparts in performance. Recently, deep reinforcement learning based models [13,14] have been used for the estimation of ball

© The Author(s), under exclusive license to Springer Nature Switzerland AG 2023
P. Maji et al. (Eds.): PReMI 2023, LNCS 14301, pp. 457–464, 2023.
https://doi.org/10.1007/978-3-031-45170-6_47

possession statistics in broadcast soccer videos. But, there is an issue regarding employing such deep networks, which are often trained on large image based datasets such as ImageNet. These offline models may deliver superior accuracy but suffers due to a significant domain gap. As a result, there is a need for domain specific data or, at the very least, fine tuning on sports specific datasets.

Soccer Action Recognition: We also look into the existing literature in the action recognition domain for soccer videos. However, work has been very limited regarding this aspect. One of the very few public soccer video datasets is the Soccernet v2 benchmark [4] released very recently. Other attempts to classify actions from soccer videos such as in [3] have focused on specific localization tasks instead of classification. Therefore, we believe that our newly contributed soccer dataset (SoccerDB1) and knowledge distillation based action recognition framework (SoccerKDNet) would help progress the research on vision-based action recognition in soccer videos.

In summary, we present SoccerDB1, a datset for action recognition in soccer video. We also present SoccerKDNet, a knowledge distillation based action recognition framework. We have achieved 67.20% accuracy on action recognition task. Next, we describe our SoccerDB1 dataset in detail.

2   SoccerDB1 Dataset

We introduce a new soccer dataset named SoccerDB1 consisting of 448 soccer video clips. The dataset contains videos of 4 action classes namely: Dribble, Kick, Run, and Walk. There are over 70 video clips per class. Sample frames of different action classes are shown in Fig. 1. The video clips are created manually from openly available broadcast soccer match videos available on YouTube. The frames were sampled uniformly and each video clip contains 25–26 frames. The proposed action recognition framework is discussed next.

Actual: Dribble | Actual: Kick | Actual: Run | Actual: Walk
Predicted: Run | Predicted: Kick | Predicted: Run | Predicted: Walk
(i) | (ii) | (iii) | (iv)

Fig. 1. Sample frames from SoccerDB1 dataset, their actual and predicted labels.

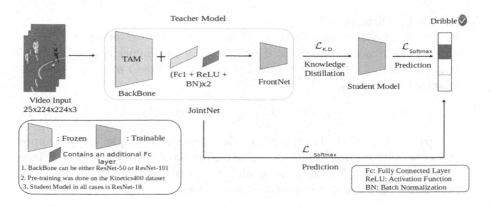

Fig. 2. SoccerKDNet: Schematic Architecture of Proposed End-to-End network.

3   Methodology

3.1   Knowledge Distillation Based Transfer Learning

We propose the SoccerKDNet network to classify actions from soccer video clips as shown in Fig. 2. Here, we use the Temporal Adaptive Module (TAM) [9] with backbones as both ResNet-50 and ResNet-101 [7]. We then add a few fully connected layers with BatchNorm in front of the backbone network in order to enable it to have some learnable parameters. The features from this setup are then passed on to the frontnet which is shown in Fig. 3. This entire setup is referred to as the 'jointnet' throughout the rest of the paper.

We use ResNet-18 as the student network in all our experiments. The 'jointnet' serves as the Teacher Network and is initially trained on the Soccer Dataset. We use both ResNet-50 and ResNet-101 as backbones alongwith the Temporal Adaptive Module (TAM). We perform uniform sampling with all the video frames in all our experiments since it is known to yield better results than dense sampling [2].

In our network as shown in Fig. 2, the various losses employed are described below:-

- Cross Entropy Loss:-
  The Cross Entropy Loss is given by the following formula:-

$$\mathcal{L}_{\text{softmax}} = -\sum_{c=1}^{M} y_{o,c} \log(p_{o,c}) \tag{1}$$

- KullBack-Liebler Divergence Loss:-
  The KullBack Liebler Divergence Loss can be given by the following formula:-

$$\mathcal{L}_{\text{KL}} = \sum_{c=1}^{M} \hat{y}_c \log \frac{\hat{y}_c}{y_c} \tag{2}$$

We have also applied a Temperature (τ) hyperparameter to this equation.

– Knowledge Distillation Loss:-
  If there is a given Teacher Network D and a Student Network S and the loss
  of the student network is denoted by $\mathcal{L}_{\text{softmax}}$ and a hyperparameter α such
  that $(0 \leq \alpha \leq 1)$, then the knowledge distillation Loss can be given by the
  following formula:-

$$\mathcal{L}_{\text{k.d.}} = \alpha * \mathcal{L}_{\text{softmax}} + (1 - \alpha) * \mathcal{L}_{\text{KL}} \tag{3}$$

The $y_{o,c}$ represents the truth label for that particular sample, and $p_{o,c}$ represents the softmax probabilities obtained after the final fully connected layer
(Fc4) $L \in R^{128 \times 4}$. Further, the $\hat{y}_c$ and y_c are the predicted and the actual
probability distributions respectively for a given soccer frame sample.

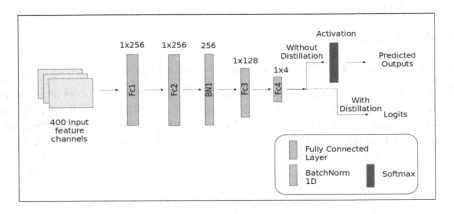

Fig. 3. Architecture of the FrontNet Module. The Backbone network in Fig. 2 has an
output of 400 classes so the obtained feature output serves as it's input in this case.

3.2 Experiments

Datasets Used. Here, we use two datasets for our work. The first dataset is
the Kinetics 400 dataset which consists of 400 diverse action classes of everyday
activities with over 300, 000 videos. We used this dataset for pre-training our
backbone model as it can learn more generalized features.

For benchmarking our results, we used SoccerDB1. Further details regarding
our dataset have already been discussed in detail in Sect. 2.

Implementation Details. We first train the jointnet on the Soccer Dataset for
100 epochs. The batch size was kept to 64 and the Cross Entropy Loss function
was used. The Adam optimizer was chosen with a learning rate of 0.0001 and
CosineAnnealing rate decay scheduler.

Next, we train the student model which is a ResNet-18. We take a batch
size of 128 and train the student model for 200 epochs. The KullBack-Liebler
divergence loss function was used here alongwith the distillation loss as described
in Eq. 3. Table 1 illustrates the considerable change in accuracy with the changing

Table 1. Alpha vs Model accuracy comparison

Alpha (α)	Model Accuracy
0.95	66.31%
0.90	**67.20%**
0.97	62.8%

value of α, and we found the optimal value to be 0.90. The value of Temperature (τ) was taken to be 6, SGD Optimizer was used here with a constant learning rate of 0.0001, momentum of 0.9 and a constant weight decay of 5e−4. Then the obtained student model was simply plugged into the evaluation framework to obtain the corresponding accuracy. As evident from Fig. 4 in Sect. 4, experiments were run for 200 epochs till the validation accuracy started saturating.

All the input video frames were resized to 224 × 224 RGB images using the spatial cropping strategy as outlined in [2]. All the accuracies reported were sampled over 5 runs to ensure the reproducibility of results. All models were trained on a 32 GB NVIDIA V100 GPU.

4   Experimental Results

Accuracy Metrics. All accuracies reported here are Top-1 accuracies. All figures were sampled over 5 runs. The student model is ResNet-18 in all cases. In our setting, we have used the Top-1/Top-5 accuracy metric for evaluation in all our experiments as used in several previous works [6]. Top-1 accuracy refers to when the 1st predicted model label matches with the ground truth label for the particular frame. Using this metric, a particular soccer video is considered to be classified correctly only when atleast half or more of it's total frames match with the corresponding ground truth label. Thus, we report the accuracies obtained using various backbones in Table 2.

Table 2. Top-1 validation accuracies obtained on the soccer dataset using various network backbones.

BackBone	Teacher Acc	Student Acc
ResNet-50	60.00%	65.26%
ResNet-101	62.10%	**67.20%**

We note that directly using the pre-trained backbone model yields a very poor accuracy of 7.7% highlighting the need for a generalized network. We also see that the student model, with proper training and sufficient number of epochs exceeds the teacher model in accuracy.

When the fine-tuning dataset is small, it is very difficult to ensure the model does not overfit to the dataset. Here, pre-training is carried out on the Kinetics 400 dataset, which is significantly larger in comparison to our Soccer Dataset. To prevent overfitting, we rigorously apply regularizers such as Batch Normalization on both the TAM and FrontNet module and dropout on the Student Model. However, such concerns may still remain to some extent as highlighted in [1].

Table 3. Comparison of accuracy of SoccerKDNet with similar methods.

Model	Dataset	Accuracy*
Russo et al. [10]	300	32.00%
Kukleva et al.[†] [8]	4152	94.50%
SoccerKDNet (R50)	448	65.26%
SoccerKDNet (R101)	448	**67.20%**

As it can be seen from Table 3, our model outperforms all other existing models. The SoccerData dataset by Kukleva et al. [8] is an image dataset not video dataset. On that particular dataset, the model requires digit level bounding boxes and human keypoint annotations which our dataset does not have and there are no trained models provided by the authors to be used publicly for testing. Further, our models are trained on video data which cannot be ideally tested on image datasets without compromising on crucial information such as the temporal sequence present in a video.

Several earlier works such as Two Stream Networks [5] have millions of parameters and hence are unsuitable for edge deployment. Using knowledge distillation here, we show that even simple 2D networks such as ResNet-18 can be used for action classification. Table 1 highlights this aspect by listing the networks used in our work - all of them have fewer than 50 mil. parameters and the backbone network is frozen. For context, 3D networks such as C3D [15] has 73 million parameters.

From Fig. 4, it can be seen that the student Model is able to achieve a Train accuracy as high as 77.9% and validation accuracies above 60% underscoring the generalizability and effectiveness of our proposed network. On the right, the corresponding validation loss curve obtained using a ResNet-18 student and a ResNet-50 teacher model is shown.

4.1   Ablation Study

We also perform a mini ablation study on a variety of factors: the backbone network, stage in which distillation is applied, layers in frontnet module and various hyperparameters.

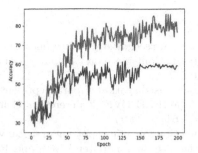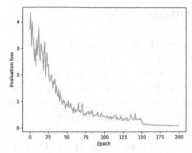

Fig. 4. On the left: red and blue curves denote the train and validation accuracies respectively. On the right, the validation loss is shown. (Color figure online)

- *Backbone Network:* As it can be seen from Table 2, we experimented with 2 backbone networks. The TAM-ResNet101 backbone model performs the best for both the teacher and student models. Further, employing parameter heavy models such as ResNet-152 as the backbone would not only defeat the purpose of moving towards a more online solution but the relatively small size of the target dataset for fine-tuning means there will be considerable concerns in performance due to model over-fitting.
- *Distillation Stage:* There are two possibilities: directly distill the frozen TAM backbone module and then use the distilled model as a plug-in within the network. We call this as the early distillation where the distillation is done early on in the network. However, performance using this approach is not satisfactory: taking the TAM-ResNet50 as the backbone Teacher model, we get only 8.3% accuracy on the Kinetics400 dataset using the ResNet-18 as the student model. We suspect this is due to the inability of the student model to directly learn features from the heavy teacher model. Therefore, we chose to go with the late stage distillation process.
- *FrontNet Module and Hyperparameters:* We found adding dropout layers decreased the accuracy by 1.2%, adding more fully connected layers in the latter half of the FrontNet module decreased accuracy as much as 4.9% of the teacher module to 57.2%. We did not find much difference in accuracy on using NLL loss instead of CrossEntropy so we chose to keep it. We found a learning rate of 0.0001 and batch size of 64 and 128 to be optimal for all our experiments as bigger batches lead to better performance.

5   Conclusion

In this paper, we introduce a new Soccer Dataset consisting of 4 diverse classes and over 70 video clips per class. The network not only provides the flexibility of using any of the original (teacher) model as the classifier but also has the option of using a smaller network (ResNet-18 in our case) as the student network. In future, we plan to add more action classes in our dataset. Also we plan to utilize SoccerKDNet for soccer event detection based on the actions of the players.

References

1. Carreira, J., Zisserman, A.: Quo vadis, action recognition? A new model and the kinetics dataset. In: proceedings of the IEEE Conference on Computer Vision and Pattern Recognition, pp. 6299–6308 (2017)
2. Chen, C.F.R., et al.: Deep analysis of CNN-based spatio-temporal representations for action recognition. In: Proceedings of the IEEE/CVF Conference on Computer Vision and Pattern Recognition, pp. 6165–6175 (2021)
3. Cioppa, A., et al.: A context-aware loss function for action spotting in soccer videos. In: Proceedings of the IEEE/CVF Conference on Computer Vision and Pattern Recognition, pp. 13126–13136 (2020)
4. Deliege, A., et al.: SoccerNet-v2: a dataset and benchmarks for holistic understanding of broadcast soccer videos. In: Proceedings of the IEEE/CVF Conference on Computer Vision and Pattern Recognition, pp. 4508–4519 (2021)
5. Feichtenhofer, C., Pinz, A., Zisserman, A.: Convolutional two-stream network fusion for video action recognition. In: Proceedings of the IEEE Conference on Computer Vision and Pattern Recognition, pp. 1933–1941 (2016)
6. Girdhar, R., Tran, D., Torresani, L., Ramanan, D.: DistInit: learning video representations without a single labeled video. In: Proceedings of the IEEE/CVF International Conference on Computer Vision, pp. 852–861 (2019)
7. He, K., Zhang, X., Ren, S., Sun, J.: Deep residual learning for image recognition. In: Proceedings of the IEEE Conference on Computer Vision and Pattern Recognition, pp. 770–778 (2016)
8. Kukleva, A., Khan, M.A., Farazi, H., Behnke, S.: Utilizing temporal information in deep convolutional network for efficient soccer ball detection and tracking. In: Chalup, S., Niemueller, T., Suthakorn, J., Williams, M.-A. (eds.) RoboCup 2019. LNCS (LNAI), vol. 11531, pp. 112–125. Springer, Cham (2019). https://doi.org/10.1007/978-3-030-35699-6_9
9. Liu, Z., Wang, L., Wu, W., Qian, C., Lu, T.: TAM: temporal adaptive module for video recognition. In: Proceedings of the IEEE/CVF International Conference on Computer Vision, pp. 13708–13718 (2021)
10. Russo, M.A., Filonenko, A., Jo, K.H.: Sports classification in sequential frames using CNN and RNN. In: 2018 International Conference on Information and Communication Technology Robotics (ICT-ROBOT), pp. 1–3. IEEE (2018)
11. Sarkar, S., Chakrabarti, A., Mukherjee, D.P.: Estimation of ball possession statistics in soccer video. In: Proceedings of the 11th Indian Conference on Computer Vision, Graphics and Image Processing, pp. 1–8 (2018)
12. Sarkar, S., Mukherjee, D.P., Chakrabarti, A.: From soccer video to ball possession statistics. Pattern Recogn. **122**, 108338 (2022)
13. Sarkar, S., Mukherjee, D.P., Chakrabarti, A.: Watch and act: dual interacting agents for automatic generation of possession statistics in soccer. In: Proceedings of the IEEE/CVF Conference on Computer Vision and Pattern Recognition, pp. 3560–3568 (2022)
14. Sarkar, S., Mukherjee, D.P., Chakrabarti, A.: Reinforcement learning for pass detection and generation of possession statistics in soccer. IEEE Trans. Cogn. Dev. Syst. **15**(2), 914–924 (2023)
15. Tran, D., Bourdev, L., Fergus, R., Torresani, L., Paluri, M.: Learning spatiotemporal features with 3D convolutional networks. In: Proceedings of the IEEE International Conference on Computer Vision, pp. 4489–4497 (2015)

DeFlare-Net: Flare Detection and Removal Network

Allabakash Ghodesawar, Vinod Patil, Ankit Raichur,
Swaroop Adrashyappanamath, Sampada Malagi, Nikhil Akalwadi$^{(\boxtimes)}$,
Chaitra Desai, Ramesh Ashok Tabib, Ujwala Patil, and Uma Mudenagudi

Center of Excellence in Visual Intelligence (CEVI), KLE Technological University,
Hubballi, Karnataka, India
{nikhil.akalwadi,chaitra.desai,ramesh_t,ujwalapatil,uma}@kletech.ac.in

Abstract. In this paper, we propose DeFlare-Net to detect, and remove flares. Typically, flares in hand-held devices are inherent due to internal reflection of light and forward scattering of lens material. The distortions due to flares limit the applications in the field of computer vision. Research challenges towards detection and removal of flare persist due to multiple occurrences of flare with varying intensities. The performance of existing flare removal methods are sensitive to the assumption of underlying physics and geometry, leading to artefacts in the deflared image. The current approaches for deflaring involve elimination of light-source implicitly, whilst removal of flare from the image leading to loss of information. Towards this, we propose DeFlare-Net for detection, and removal of flares, while retaining light-source. In this framework, we include Light Source Detection (LSD) module for detection of light-source, and Flare Removal Network (FRN) to remove the flares. Unlike state-of-the-art methods, we propose a novel loss function and call it as DeFlare loss $L_{DeFlare}$. The loss $L_{DeFlare}$ includes flare loss L_{flare}, light-source loss L_{ls}, and reconstruction loss L_{recon} towards removal of flare. We demonstrate the results of proposed methodology on benchmark datasets in comparison with SOTA techniques using appropriate quantitative metrics.

Keywords: Flare Detection · Flare Removal · Lightsource

1 Introduction

In this paper, we propose DeFlare-Net to detect, and remove flares. During image acquisition, inclusion of light-source in Field of View (FoV), and due to the physical construction of the camera, the reflection and scattering of light internally produces flares in the image. Flares in images causes artefacts and results in performance degradation of downstream tasks like, object detection, image restoration, semantic segmentation, depth estimation, and scene understanding.

Factors affecting the formation of flares, include the lens properties, scene conditions such as the camera angle, position of the light-source, resulting in flares of varied intensities, sizes and shapes. Flares appear as circles, and streaks

P. Maji et al. (Eds.): PReMI 2023, LNCS 14301, pp. 465–472, 2023.
https://doi.org/10.1007/978-3-031-45170-6_48

leading to occlusion of scene under the flare region. Typically, removal of flare in an image demands use of specialized lenses, lens coating, adjusting camera parameters and use of additional filters. It is inevitable to completely remove flare, despite use of professional accessories and equipments.

Traditional methods like Bayesian estimation [14], Markov Random Fields [4] and point spread functions (PSF) identify and remove the flares based on exemplars. These methods fail to generalize well over vast amount of images and demand for a robust algorithm to detect and remove flares. Recently, learning-based techniques have taken a leap due to vast availability of data and computational resources. Learning-based methods in literature employ convolutional neural networks and generative models to detect and eliminate flares. However, these methods eliminate light-source implicitly whilst removal of flare from the image, leading to loss of information.

CNN-based methods like [8] use deconvolution for removal of flares. Authors in [1,2] adopt a multi-stage approach for detecting flares of different shapes, location and intensities. Authors in [3], employ in-painting approach to iteratively refine the flare region. The method proposed in [3], implicitly considers light-source along with flare region for generating flare free observations. [11,13], use direct-indirect separation and light-field based approaches for identifying the light-source and consistent removal of flares without creating additional artefacts. Methods discussed in [10,12] adopt GAN-based and U-Net like architectures to deflare images. However, the methods discussed in literature fail to detect the origin of light-source, resulting in implicit removal of light-source along with flare. Towards this, the contributions of this work include:

- We propose a DeFlare-Net, a network for light-source detection (LSD), and removal of flares (FRN).
  - A Flare Removal Network (FRN) to detect and remove flare inclusive of light-source (Sect. 2).
  - We propose to include a Light Source Detection (LSD) module to detect and localise the light-source (Sect. 2).
- We propose a novel DeFlare loss $L_{DeFlare}$ which includes lightsource loss L_{ls}, flare loss L_{flare}, and reconstruction loss L_{recon} towards removal of flare (Sect. 2.1).
- We demonstrate the results of proposed methodology on benchmark datasets in comparison with SOTA techniques using appropriate quantitative metrics.

2 DeFlare-Net: Flare Detection and Removal Network

The proposed DeFlare-Net comprises of two main modules: a) Flare Removal Network (FRN), and b) Light Source Detection (LSD) module [6] as shown in Fig. 1. Given a flared image I_{flare} as input, the aim of the proposed DeFlare-Net is to generate flare-mask, light-source mask and reconstruct a flare-removed image. Flare removal module M_{FRN} detects and removes flare by masking the region as given as,

$$X_{flare} = M_{FRN}(I_{flare}) \tag{1}$$

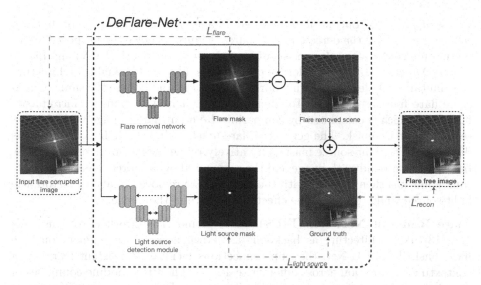

Fig. 1. The proposed framework of DeFlare-Net. DeFlare-Net includes two modules; Flare Removal Network (shown in blue color) for removal of flares inclusive of light-source; Light Source Detection (LSD) (shown in green color) for detection and generation of light-source mask. (Color figure online)

where, M_{FRN} learns the mapping from I_{flare} to X_{flare}, and X_{flare} is the segmented flare-mask. M_{FRN} implicitly segments light-source along with flare. The removal of light-source from the scene creates additional artefacts resulting in unpleasant observations. Towards this we introduce a light-source detection module LSD, to retain the light-source in accordance with groundtruth I_{GT}.

M_{LSD} module segments the light-source from the scene and generates a mask consisting of light-source in accordance with the true scene. The process of segmenting the light-source mask is given by,

$$X_{ls} = M_{LSD}(I_{GT}) \tag{2}$$

where, X_{ls} is the segmented light-source mask, M_{LSD} is a function to learn the light-source, and I_{GT} is the groundtruth image. The flare-mask X_{flare} is subtracted from I_{flare} to obtain the flare-removed scene, and is given by,

$$I_{fr} = I_{flare} - X_{flare} \tag{3}$$

where, I_{fr} is the flare-removed scene. The flare removed scene I_{fr}, implicitly removes the light-source along with the flares resulting in loss of information. Towards this, we consider to add the flare-removed scene I_{fr}, and light-source mask X_{ls},to obtain the blended output I_{res}. The blended deflared observation includes the light-source of the scene under consideration. The process of blending the flare-removed scene I_{fr}, and light-source mask X_{ls} is given by,

$$I_{res} = I_{fr} + X_{ls} \tag{4}$$

where, I_{res} is the output flare-removed image. I_{res} comprises of both flare-removed scene and the detected light-source. Figure 1, shows the proposed architecture for DeFlare-Net. It consists of Flare-Removal Network (FRN) and Light-source Detection (LSD) module. We propose an end to end trainable architecture to simultaneously learn the light-source in the scene and deflare the same to generate flare free observations. To efficiently learn flare detection, we introduce a flare loss, which is calculated by comparing the input flared image with the corresponding flare-mask. The generated flare-mask includes a light-source, and is discarded. The light-source mask is iteratively refined while considering the loss between the groundtruth image and the segmented light-source mask. The light-source mask is then blended with the output flare-removed image to restore the light-source while removing the effect of the flare in the image.

Flare Removal Network (FRN). Flare Removal Network (FRN) uses U-Net [13] like architecture as backbone as shown in Fig. 1 to segment out the flare-mask. Unlike U-Net, the skip connections facilitate consistent learning of contextual information across different scales [7]. The FRN module comprises of encoder and decoder for segmenting the flare-mask. Encoder consist of a series of convolutional layers for progressive downsampling of the input flared image I_{flare} to generate feature maps comprising of local contextual information. The decoder progressively upsamples the intermediate feature representations to obtain the flare-mask X_{flare}. Given an input flared image I_{flare}, FRN iteratively learns to detect and localise the region of interest i.e., flare region. FRN implicitly learns to detect light-source along with the flare region, as the distribution of pixels under RoI are similar. The detected RoI is given as,

$$X_R = f(X_{flare}, X_{ls}) \tag{5}$$

where, X_R is the region of interest, and is function of flare X_{flare}, and light-source X_{ls}. The RoI X_R is purged from the flare image I_{flare}. FRN purges X_{ls} along with flare X_{flare}, from the scene. The removal of light-source from the scene creates additional artefacts resulting in unpleasant observations. Towards this we introduce a light-source detection module LSD, to retain the light-source in accordance with groundtruth I_{GT}.

Light-Source Detection Module (LSD). Light Source Detection Network (LSD) uses U-Net [13] style architecture as shown in Fig. 1. Given an input flared image I_{flare}, LSD iteratively learns to detect and localise the region of interest i.e., light-source region in the scene X_{ls}. LSD learns to detect and segment light-source as given in Eq. 2.

Fusion of X_{ls} with I_{fr}. The segmented light-source mask X_{ls} is fused with I_{fr} as shown in Eq. 4 to obtain the flare-removed image I_{res}.

2.1   Loss Functions

Flare Loss: For flare detection, we incorporate flare loss [12]. Flare loss L_{flare} is computed between input flared image I_F and flare-mask X_{flare}. As shown in

Fig. 1, the input flared image I_{flare} is fed to the FRN, for detecting and masking the flare region. The flare loss quantifies the pixel-wise discrepancy between the predicted flare-mask obtained from the input image and the updated flare-mask provided by the model as given by,

$$\mathbb{L}_{flare} = \sum \left\| X_{flare} - \hat{X}_{flare} \right\|_1 \tag{6}$$

where, X_{flare} is the groundtruth flare-mask in corresponding to the input image, $\hat{X}_{flare}$ is the the generated mask. The flare-mask is subtracted from the input image I_{flare} for rendering the flare-removed image $I_{flarefree}$, however the generated sample still lacks the light-source in the image. To overcome this, we propose to use a light-source detection module to mask out the light-source region so as to blend with the flare-removed scene/image.

Light-Source Loss: To generate the light-source mask, the light-source module is optimized using light-source loss which measures the pixel-wise difference between generated light-source masks. light-source loss is given by,

$$\mathbb{L}_{ls} = \sum \left\| X_{ls} - \hat{X}_{ls} \right\|_1 \tag{7}$$

where, X_{ls} represents the light-source mask derived from the input flared image I_{flare}, while $\hat{X}ls$ corresponds to the light-source mask from the generated flare-removed image $Iflarefree$. The light-source mask is then combined with the flare-removed image $I_{flarefree}$ using pixel-wise multiplication, resulting in the ultimate refined flare-removed output.

Reconstruction Loss: For reconstructing the deflared image, we incorporate reconstruction loss between the flare-removed I_{res} image and the groundtruth I_{GT}. L_{recon} measures the pixel-wise difference between the I_{res}, and I_{GT} and is given by,

$$\mathbb{L}_{recon} = \sum \| I_{GT} - I_{res} \|_1 \tag{8}$$

Proposed Weighted Combinational Loss. We propose $L_{DeFlare}$ as a weighted combination of L_{flare}, L_{ls}, and L_{recon}, and is given as,

$$\mathbb{L}_{DeFlare} = \alpha * \mathbb{L}_{flare} + \beta * \mathbb{L}_{ls} + \gamma * \mathbb{L}_{recon} \tag{9}$$

where α, β, and γ are weights and we heuristically set $\alpha = \beta = \gamma = 0.33$.

3   Results and Discussions

In this section, we discuss on the datasets used for training the proposed DeFlare-Net. We demonstrate the results of DeFlare-Net on benchmark datasets in comparison with SOTA methods using appropriate quantitative metrics.

Fig. 2. Qualitative comparison of proposed DeFlare-Net. 1st column shows input flared images, 2nd column corresponds to light-source masks segmented using LSD, 3rd column corresponds to the segmented flares from the flare scene using FRN, and 4th column corresponds to results of proposed DeFlare-Net. We infer, the light-source masks, and the flare-masks, are segmented without any artefacts in the deflared image.

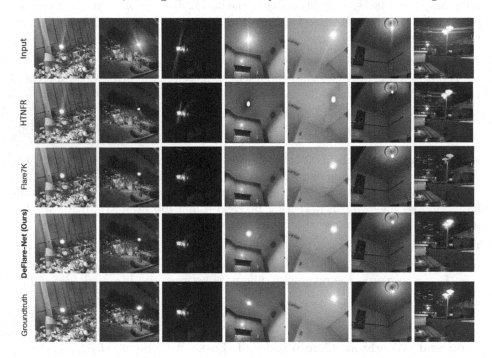

Fig. 3. Qualitative comparison of the proposed DeFlare-Net with SOTA methods. The 1st row shows input flared images, 2nd row shows the results from authors in [10], 3rd row shows results of authors in [5], the 4th row corresponds to results of proposed DeFlare-Net, and the 5th row shows groundtruth images. We observe the proposed DeFlare-Net preserves contextual information well, and removes flares thereby outperforming SOTA methods.

3.1   Experimental Setup

The proposed DeFlare-Net is implemented using the PyTorch framework, coupled with Python (v3.8), and trained on NVIDIA RTX 3090 with 24 GB VRAM. To ensure the robustness and generalizability of our model, we preprocess the input images by resizing them to a resolution of 512 × 512 pixels and apply random flip augmentations. We use Adam optimizer, with $\beta_1 = 0.9$ and $\beta_2 = 0.9999$, and ϵ set to $8e^{-2}$. We train the model for 100 epochs with learning rate set to $lr = 0.0001$. We heuristically set the loss weights $\alpha = \beta = \gamma = 0.3$.

3.2 Results

Results on Flickr24K Dataset, and Flare7K Dataset [5]. We compare the performance of proposed DeFlare-Net on benchmark dataset using appropriate quantitative metrics. In Fig. 3, we show the deflaring performance comparison with SOTA methods on Flickr24K Dataset, and Flare7K Datasets [15]. Figure 2 shows qualitative results of proposed DeFlare-Net in comparison with SOTA methods on Flickr24K dataset [15]. From Fig. 2 we infer proposed DeFlare-Net outperforms SOTA methods in every scenario and eliminates flare artefacts. For instance, in Fig. 3 results from authors in [10] in 2nd row consist of flare artefacts around the light-source in comparison to the results of proposed DeFlare-Net in the 3rd row. From Fig. 3, it is evident, the proposed DeFlare-Net consistently removes flares in low-light conditions (Table 1).

Table 1. Performance comparison of DeFlare-Net with SOTA methods on Flare24K Dataset [15]. First highest value is highlighted in ▪, and second highest value is highlighted in ▪.

Methods	PSNR (in dB)	SSIM
Dehaze [9] (2010)	17.47	0.745
Flare spot removal [2] (2015)	18.53	0.782
[10] + U-Net [13] (2015)	25.55	0.850
Flare spot removal [1] (2019)	18.57	0.787
Dereflection [15] (2018)	22.28	0.822
Flare spot removal [1] (2019)	18.57	0.787
[10] + Network [15] (2019)	24.21	0.834
Ours(DeFlare-Net)	25.76	0.953

4   Conclusions

In this paper, we have proposed DeFlare-Net, a Flare Detection and Removal Network. Unlike existing methods, we have proposed two modules to learn flare-mask and light-source mask towards removal of flares. We have proposed DeFlare loss $L_{DeFlare}$ for flare detection, removal, and reconstruction of flare free image. We have demonstrated the performance of the proposed DeFlare-Net on benchmark datasets, employing appropriate quantitative metrics.

Acknowledgement. This project is partly carried out under Department of Science and Technology (DST) through ICPS programme- Indian Heritage in Digital Space for the project "Digital Poompuhar" (DST/ ICPS/ Digital Poompuhar/2017 (General)).

References

1. Asha, C., Bhat, S., Nayak, D., Bhat, C.: Auto removal of bright spot from images captured against flashing light source. In: 2019 IEEE International Conference on Distributed Computing, VLSI, Electrical Circuits and Robotics, DISCOVER 2019 - Proceedings. Institute of Electrical and Electronics Engineers Inc., USA (2019). https://doi.org/10.1109/DISCOVER47552.2019.9007933
2. Chabert, F.: Automated lens flare removal. Technical report, ArXiv e-prints (2015). arXiv:1503.04212
3. Chen, L.C., Zhu, Y., Papandreou, G., Schroff, F., Adam, H.: Encoder-decoder with atrous separable convolution for semantic image segmentation. In: Proceedings of the European Conference on Computer Vision (ECCV), p. 10 (2018)
4. Clifford, P.: Markov random fields in statistics. Disorder in physical systems: a volume in honour of John M. Hammersley, pp. 19–32 (1990)
5. Dai, Y., Li, C., Zhou, S., Feng, R., Loy, C.C.: Flare7K: a phenomenological night-time flare removal dataset. In: Thirty-Sixth Conference on Neural Information Processing Systems Datasets and Benchmarks Track (2022)
6. Dai, Y., et al.: MIPI 2023 challenge on nighttime flare removal: methods and results. In: Proceedings of the IEEE/CVF Conference on Computer Vision and Pattern Recognition (CVPR) Workshops, pp. 2852–2862 (June 2023)
7. Desai, C., Benur, S., Tabib, R.A., Patil, U., Mudenagudi, U.: DepthCue: restoration of underwater images using monocular depth as a clue. In: Proceedings of the IEEE/CVF Winter Conference on Applications of Computer Vision (WACV) Workshops, pp. 196–205 (2023)
8. Faulkner, K., Kotre, C., Louka, M.: Veiling glare deconvolution of images produced by X-ray image intensifiers. In: International Conference on Image Processing and its Applications, p. 2 (1989)
9. He, K., Sun, J., Tang, X.: Single image haze removal using dark channel prior. IEEE TPAMI 6, 7 (2010)
10. Ignatov, A., Timofte, R.: AI benchmark: running deep neural networks on android smartphones. In: Proceedings of the IEEE Conference on Computer Vision and Pattern Recognition Workshops, pp. 27–35 (2018). https://doi.org/10.1109/CVPRW.2018.00009
11. Li, C., Yang, Y., He, K., Lin, S., Hopcroft, J.E.: Single image reflection removal through cascaded refinement, p. 2 (2020)
12. Qiao, X., Hancke, G.P., Lau, R.W.: Light source guided single-image flare removal from unpaired data. In: Proceedings of the IEEE/CVF International Conference on Computer Vision, pp. 4177–4185 (2021)
13. Ronneberger, O., Fischer, P., Brox, T.: U-net: convolutional networks for biomedical image segmentation. In: Navab, N., Hornegger, J., Wells, W.M., Frangi, A.F. (eds.) MICCAI 2015. LNCS, vol. 9351, pp. 234–241. Springer, Cham (2015). https://doi.org/10.1007/978-3-319-24574-4_28
14. Wu, T.P., Tang, C.K.: A Bayesian approach for shadow extraction from a single image. In: Proceedings of the Tenth IEEE International Conference on Computer Vision (ICCV), pp. 1–7 (2005)
15. Zhang, X., Ng, R., Chen, Q.: Single image reflection separation with perceptual losses. In: Proceedings of the IEEE Conference on Computer Vision and Pattern Recognition, pp. 4786–4794 (2018)

A Novel Network Architecture for Microplankton Classification in Digital Holographic Images

A. Shrihari[1]([✉])([iD]), Prithwijit Guha[1,2]([iD]), and Rishikesh Dilip Kulkarni[1,2]([iD])

[1] Centre for Intelligent Cyber Physical Systems, Indian Institute of Technology Guwahati, North Guwahati 781039, Assam, India
a.shrihari@iitg.ac.in
[2] Department of EEE, Indian Institute of Technology Guwahati, North Guwahati 781039, Assam, India

Abstract. Planktons are the building blocks of marine food webs and key indicators of ocean health. Monitoring of plankton populations help study the biological diversity of microbial eukaryotes. Recent years have witnessed the wide usage of digital holographic microscopes (DHM) for in situ detection of underwater microplanktons. Holography has an edge over other imaging techniques due to its unique ability to provide a 3D hologram of the microplankton without disturbing its orientations. In this paper, a novel network architecture with 5.29 GFLOPs is developed for the classification of microplanktons in digital holographic images. The proposed method achieved a class-wise F1-scores above 80% at a lower computational cost. The proposal provided competitive performance with respect to six baseline network architectures. This technique has the potential to be appealing for future applications of in situ classification of microplanktons.

Keywords: Convolutional Neural Network · Digital Holographic Images · Classification · Microplanktons

1 Introduction

Planktons make up a large part of aquatic particle fields and impact several areas of research, including ocean optics, aquatic ecology, and climate change [3,7]. Therefore, knowing the temporal and geographical distribution of planktons in different aquatic environments is very important and is the subject of much limnological and oceanographic research [3,11].

To characterize the distribution of microplankton (MP) in water, many measurement methods have been explored. The acoustic backscatter tool was one such method developed to assess the plankton size distribution [10]. Several other methods obtained size information by optical scattering and by absorption measurements [19]. However, these methods had limited size ranges and required manual intervention for collecting the sample volumes.

P. Maji et al. (Eds.): PReMI 2023, LNCS 14301, pp. 473–482, 2023.
https://doi.org/10.1007/978-3-031-45170-6_49

In the recent decade, digital holographic microscope (DHM) has emerged as a promising technology for fully characterizing plankton distributions over a 3D volume [1,14]. The amplitude and phase information of objects can be obtained by digital holography from holograms recorded by the digital sensor in the form of interference patterns [6]. It has been employed for particle classification and in situ mapping of plankton distribution [7]. Dyomin et al. [5] proposed a rapid marine particle identification method using underwater digital holograms to identify morphological features. Wang *et al.* [20] presented a deep learning architecture to optimize the reconstruction of an image from a digital hologram by reconstructing its phase and magnitude information at the same time. Liam *et al.* [13] performed the classification of MPs, detected with a portable digital in-line holographic microscope (The HoloSea), using four different pre-trained deep neural networks and transfer learning. The major setback in the field of automatic MP detection using digital holographic microscope is the dataset availability for training the deep neural networks. Aditya Nayak *et al.* [1,14] conducted *in situ* field experiments in 3 different deployments during 2014 to 2017, and created a database of different types of MPs. Buyu *et al.* [7] used this dataset to classify 10 different types of planktons with ShuffleNetV2 architecture.

A technique for classification of holographic images of MPs is proposed in the present work using a novel deep neural network. With parallel convolutions, depthwise seperable convolutions and group convolutions, the proposed model termed as Shuffled-Inception (ShincNet), achieved a good accuracy with ∽6 million parameters and 5.29 GFLOPs. The performance is evaluated quantitatively using F1-scores and compared against six other state-of-art network architectures.

2   Microplankton Dataset

The dataset reported in [7] has been used in the present work. The holograms were captured by a submersible digital holographic imaging system (HOLO-CAM) with a 660 nm pulsed Nd-YAG laser as its illumination source and a 2048×2048 pixel CCD camera to record holograms with a frame rate of 15 FPS [14]. The dataset consists of 50 classes of microplanktons. Background-subtracted holograms and in-focus MP images are provided for each class. Background-subtracted holograms are formed by subtracting time-averaged background from raw holograms. This was done to remove noise and unusual patterns in the hologram prior reconstruction. Later, these holograms were numerically reconstructed using Fresnel diffraction formulation [9] and a grayscale equalization process applied to yield in-focus images. Detailed descriptions of these strategies can be found in [14]. Ten prominent classes which have been mentioned in [7] are used for the classification (see Fig. 1). Since the training data is imbalanced (Fig. 3), data augmentation techniques [15] such as random horizontal flip followed by vertical flip, random shift followed by random rotation (10°) and random rotation (10°) with vertical flip, as shown in Fig. 2, were used. Out of

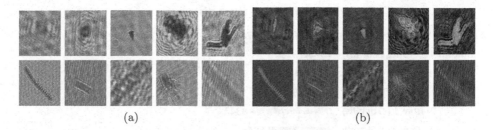

Fig. 1. Amplitude images of the 10 classes obtained from [7]. From top left to bottom right: *Ceratium furca (singular), Ceratium muelleri (singular), Ciliate, Copepod Nauplii, Copepod, Diatom 1 (c. debilis), Diatom 2, Diatom 3 (ditylum sp.), Diatom 4 (c. concavicornus), Thalassiosira sp.* (a) Background-subtracted holograms. (b) Conventionally reconstructed in-focus images.

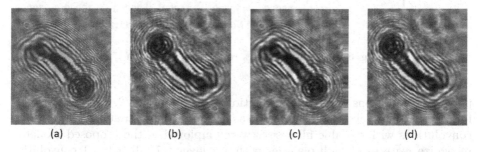

Fig. 2. Data augmentation techniques used: (a) Original image (b) Random horizontal flip followed by vertical flip (c) Random shift followed by random rotation (10°) (d) Random rotation (10°) with vertical flip.

250 holograms per class, 100 and 150 holograms were used for testing and training the network, respectively. Using the data augmentation methods, additional 450 holograms, for training, were generated. Thus, the training set consisted of 600 holograms per class.

3 Proposed Network Architecture: ShincNet

The combination of parallel convolutions, rectified linear units (ReLU) and weighted pooling layers is the basic building block in our network, repeated multiple times before leading to the final feature extraction module. These steps are grouped as the backbone feature extraction module. The main purpose of this module is to identify the underlying characterization of the hologram data. Finally, the extracted feature representation is fed into the fully connected layer.

The proposed network architecture, termed as Shuffled-Inception Network (ShincNet), is inspired by InceptionV3 [18] and ShuffleNetV2 [12] architectures. The main intuition behind the proposed architecture is to incorporate the

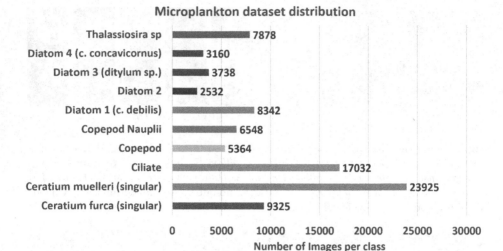

Fig. 3. Number of images recorded per class in [7].

parallel convolutions with 1×1 convolution as in InceptionV3, and group convolutions with channel shuffling operation as in ShuffleNetV2 architectures. Parallel convolutions with variable filter sizes were employed in the proposed model to recognize features of multiple sizes within a layer [17]. The 1 × 1 convolution blocks were added to reduce the number of channels and compress information for model complexity reduction [2]. Spatial and depth-wise separable convolutions were used to reduce the memory complexity and number of FLOPs in the model. Point-wise group convolutions along with a channel shuffle operation perform better in smaller models, than the normal convolution, by enabling the communication between different groups of channels and improving the accuracy [22]. As shown in Fig. 4(a), the architecture consists of four processing stages, each composed of processing blocks (PB553). The PB553 (Fig. 4)(b) is made up of two parallel layers of convolution blocks with ReLU activation. The top layer consists of 1 × 1 point-wise convolution followed by 3 × 3 depth-wise separable convolution. The bottom layer consists of 4-group grouped convolution followed by channel shuffling operation. Later, a spatially separable convolution of 5 × 5 and 3 × 3 are used in different stages. Output of this parallel layers are then concatenated and fed to 1 × 1 convolution block to further improve the generalizabilty between channels. A residual connection from the previous unit is then added to the processed output. Weighted pooling is used to obtain the feature maps of small regions as weighted average of the feature embeddings of the region. This process significantly reduces the size of the representation and hence, the computations. The output of this feature extraction module is fed to the Global Average Pooling (GAP) stage to provide one-dimensional embedding. A fully connected layer transforms this embedding to the output layer. The output layer with 10 nodes hosts *SoftMax* activation functions and produces a

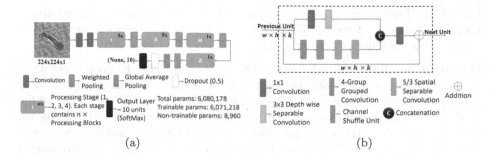

Fig. 4. (a) Overview of the proposed Shuffled-Inception architecture. (b) Detailed view of PB553.

class probability distribution specific to the ten MP categories [8]. The network is trained by minimizing the cross-entropy loss.

4 Experiments and Results

This section describes the baseline methods, implementation details, quantitative performance analysis of ShincNet and associated ablation studies. The results of the ShincNet are compared with the ShuffleNetV2 architecture used in [7], along with other baseline models.

Baseline Methods – The planktons in our dataset were classified with six different CNNs along with our proposed network: VGG16, InceptionV3, ResNet50V2, ResNet152V2, ShuffleNetV2 and Xception. VGG16 is the shallowest in terms of model depth with 3×3 convolution and max pooling layers. ResNets and InceptionV3 are of near equal depth [13] with identity connections between the blocks and parallel convolution filters, respectively. Xception is the deepest with depthwise seperable convolutions. ShuffleNetV2 is a lightweight architecture [12] with group convolutions and channel shuffling operations. Since the plankton dataset was small, a transfer learning strategy was employed in which each model was pretrained on 1.4 M images binned into over 1000 classes from the ImageNet dataset [4]. This provided powerful baseline networks for feature extraction [13]. The last-4 layers of each of the six models were finetuned for the plankton dataset, while freezing the feature extraction layers of the state-of-the-art models [13].

Implementation Details – The ShincNet was trained by minimizing the cross-entropy loss with the Adam optimizer. The learning rate was set to 0.001 with a batch size of 16. Dropout is used at a probability of 0.4 to prevent overfitting [16]. The training dataset was further split into train and validation sets during model training. The model was trained using stratified 2-folds [13,21] with 50 epochs for each fold. The average of the performance scores is reported as the final prediction score. The networks were implemented on the NVIDIA CUDA Toolkit using NVIDIA Tesla V100 GPU with 32 GB RAM. Keras, a deep learning toolbox for Tensorflow, was used to train and execute the model. The accuracy, GFLOPs, number of model parameters and class-wise F1-scores are used to evaluate the classifier performance [13].

Quantitative Results – Figure 5 shows the class-wise F1-scores obtained through the proposed network. For the hologram images as training input dataset (blue), minimum and maximum F1-scores of 70.1% and 94.4% were achieved for *Thalassiosira sp* and *diatom 4 (c. concaviconous)*, respectively. For the reconstructed in-focus as training input dataset (red), minimum and maximum F1-scores of 76.0% and 92.9% were achieved for *diatom 3 (ditylum sp.)* and *diatom 4 (c. concaviconous)*, respectively. The F1-scores were found to be consistent among classes. Figure 6 show the plots of average F1-score achieved by each network against their total number of model parameters (in millions) and Floating point operations (in Giga-FLOPS or GFLOPs). The proposed network achieved an average F1-score of 80.21%, for hologram images, with 6 million parameters and 5.29 GFLOPs.

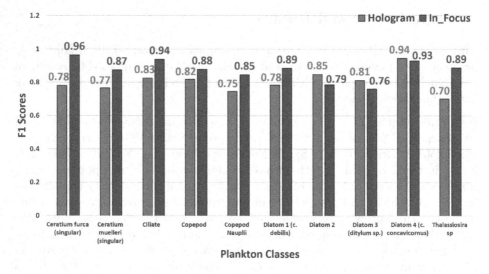

Fig. 5. Class-wise F1-scores for Shuffled-Inception Network. F1-scores of hologram images are shown as blue bars and F1-scores of in-focus images are shown as red bars. Best viewed in color.

Table 1 shows the overall classifier performance comparison as a function of accuracy, precision, recall, and F1 scores for the hologram images and reconstructed in-focus images, as training input dataset. The proposed model performance was found to be comparable to that of Xception with the accuracy of 80.4% and 84.8%, respectively.

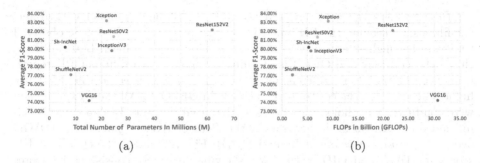

(a)   (b)

Fig. 6. (a) Average F1-score vs. Total Model Parameters plot. (b) Average F1-score vs. GFLOPs plot.

Table 1. Overall metrics comparison of the proposed network with state-of-the-art networks for hologram images (H) and reconstructed in-focus images (IF).

Metrics	VGG16		ShuffleNetV2		Xception		ResNet50V2		ResNet152V2		InceptionV3		ShincNet	
	H	IF	H	IF	H	IF	H	IF	H	IF	H	IF	H	IF
Accuracy	0.739	0.783	0.77	0.814	0.828	0.872	0.811	0.855	0.818	0.862	0.795	0.839	**0.804**	**0.848**
Recall	0.723	0.768	0.759	0.804	0.821	0.865	0.802	0.847	0.808	0.853	0.783	0.828	**0.791**	**0.836**
Precision	0.764	0.828	0.793	0.857	0.844	0.908	0.826	0.891	0.836	0.901	0.814	0.878	**0.822**	**0.887**
F1-score	0.742	0.791	0.771	0.821	0.831	0.881	0.813	0.863	0.821	0.871	0.798	0.847	**0.802**	**0.851**
GFLOPs	30.7		2.09		9.14		6.99		21.9		5.7		**5.29**	
Total Parameters (Million)	15.28		8.25		21.93		24.63		61.81		23.94		**6.08**	

Ablation Analysis – The processing stages in the ShincNet contain certain number of repetitions of the processing block (PB) along with different filter sizes for the spatial separable convolution layer. First stage has 5 PBs with filter size of 5, second stage has 5 PBs with filter size of 5, third stage has 1 PB with filter size of 3 and fourth stage has 1 PB with no spatial separable layer. This is represented in the following notation: b551_f553 where, b is for PB repetitions and f for filter sizes, each number is associated with a stage. Final stage is always kept constant while experimented with first 3 stages along with filter sizes.

Table 2. Overall accuracy and GFLOPs of ShincNet model with different filter sizes at b551.

Spatial Filter Sizes	Accuracy	GFLOPs
f553	80.45%	5.29
f353	78.40%	5.02
f533	77.90%	5.04
f531	74.76%	4.89
f511	72.43%	4.95
f331	69.01%	4.21

Table 3. Overall accuracy and GFLOPs of ShincNet model with different PB repetitions at f553.

PB Repetition	Accuracy	GFLOPs
b551	80.45%	5.29
b544	79.56%	5.31
b433	76.99%	5.21
b542	75.99%	5.02
b322	67.25%	4.19
b421	67.15%	4.27

Table 2 shows the accuracy and GFLOPs of ShincNet model with different filter sizes keeping the PB repetitions constant at b551. It can be observed that f553 has highest accuracy at the cost of little increase in GFLOPs. Table 3 shows the accuracy and GFLOPs of ShincNet model with different PB repetitions keeping the filter size constant at f553. It can be observed that b551 has highest accuracy at the cost of little increase in GFLOPs. All these experiments were conducted with hologram images as the input dataset. Table 4 shows a significant improvement in the accuracy of the *Dataset With Augmentation* (DWA) over the *Original Imbalanced Dataset* (OID). Figure 7 shows the class-wise F1-scores for DWA and OID, with DWA showing relatively consistent F1-scores among all classes whereas OID having variations of scores due to the imbalanced nature of the dataset. Here, the proposed ShincNet architecture was used for the comparison in order to justify the need of data augmentation techniques.

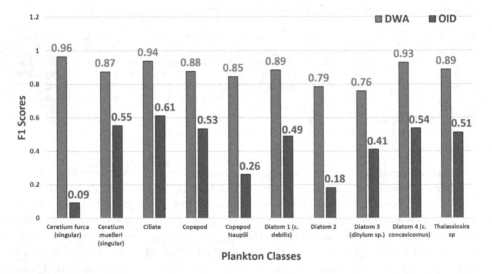

Fig. 7. Class-wise F1-scores for the in-focus images using ShincNet. F1-scores of the Dataset With Augmentation (DWA) are shown as blue bars and F1-scores of the Original Imbalanced Dataset (OID) are shown as red bars. Best viewed in color.

Table 4. Performance metrics comparison for DWA and OID. The analysis was performed with ShincNet b551_f553 architecture using hologram images (H) and reconstructed in-focus images (IF).

Metrics	DWA		OID	
	H	IF	H	IF
Accuracy	0.804	0.848	0.383	0.429
Recall	0.791	0.836	0.269	0.303
Precision	0.822	0.887	0.455	0.502
F1-score	0.802	0.851	0.301	0.368

5   Conclusion

A method for automatic classification of microplanktons in digital holography was designed, mainly focusing on small and imbalanced dataset of underwater holograms. Classification of MPs was performed using holograms and corresponding reconstructed in-focus images. The performance of the proposed Shinc-Net was compared against six state-of-art baseline network architectures. With the model parameters of 6.08M and 5.29 GFLOPS, the proposed model obtained an accuracy of 80.4% for hologram images and 84.8% for reconstructed in-focus images, outperforming InceptionV3, VGG16 and ShuffleNetV2. It demonstrated comparable performance with respect to the heavier networks such as ResNet50V2, ResNet152V2 and Xception. The proposed method is a robust, computationally minimal and effective tool for automatic microplankton classification.

Performance metrics for reconstructed in-focus images have an upper hand to that of holograms due to the better resolution of the objects after reconstruction. However, the major drawback of conventional reconstruction is high computation time and cost, which sets a trade-off for the accuracy. Further research on classifying the microplanktons through hologram images with a better accuracy is underway. The holographic properties of plankton lack the means of creating clear images at multiple scales. Further research on scale-invariant feature detection could overcome this limitation and help identify the diversity of plankton features that are more or less resolvable at different scales. Further research may focus on the detection of underwater microorganisms. In addition, an underwater holographic imaging experiment is a potential research direction to better determine the true distribution of microplanktons in the rivers.

References

1. Arnone, R.A., Hou, W.W., Sullivan, J.M., Twardowski, M.S., McFarland, M.N., Nayak, A.R.: On plankton distributions and biophysical interactions in diverse coastal and limnological environments (2018). Ocean Sensing and Monitoring X
2. Chen, L., Li, S., Bai, Q., Yang, J., Jiang, S., Miao, Y.: Review of image classification algorithms based on convolutional neural networks. Remote Sens. **13**(22), 4712 (2021)
3. Chivers, W.J., Walne, A.W., Hays, G.C.: Mismatch between marine plankton range movements and the velocity of climate change. Nat. Commun. **8**(1), 14434 (2017)
4. Deng, J., Dong, W., Socher, R., Li, L.J., Li, K., Fei-Fei, L.: ImageNet: a large-scale hierarchical image database. In: 2009 IEEE Conference on Computer Vision and Pattern Recognition, pp. 248–255. IEEE (2009)
5. Dyomin, V.V., Polovtsev, I.G., Davydova, A.Y.: Fast recognition of marine particles in underwater digital holography. In: 23rd International Symposium on Atmospheric and Ocean Optics: Atmospheric Physics, vol. 10466, pp. 467–471. SPIE (2017)
6. Goodman, J.W.: Introduction to Fourier Optics. Roberts and Company Publishers (2005)

7. Guo, B., et al.: Automated plankton classification from holographic imagery with deep convolutional neural networks. Limnol. Oceanogr. Methods **19**(1), 21–36 (2021)
8. Janocha, K., Czarnecki, W.M.: On loss functions for deep neural networks in classification. arXiv preprint arXiv:1702.05659 (2017)
9. Katz, J., Sheng, J.: Applications of holography in fluid mechanics and particle dynamics. Annu. Rev. Fluid Mech. **42**(1), 531–555 (2010)
10. Kim, H., Kang, D., Jung, S.W.: Development and application of an acoustic system for harmful algal blooms (HABs, red tide) detection using an ultrasonic digital sensor. Ocean Sci. J. **53**, 91–99 (2018)
11. Kirby, R.R., Beaugrand, G.: Trophic amplification of climate warming. Proc. Roy. Soc. B: Biol. Sci. **276**(1676), 4095–4103 (2009)
12. Ma, N., Zhang, X., Zheng, H.T., Sun, J.: ShuffleNet v2: practical guidelines for efficient CNN architecture design. In: Proceedings of the European Conference on Computer Vision (ECCV), pp. 116–131 (2018)
13. MacNeil, L., Missan, S., Luo, J., Trappenberg, T., LaRoche, J.: Plankton classification with high-throughput submersible holographic microscopy and transfer learning. BMC Ecol. Evol. **21**(1), 1–11 (2021)
14. Nayak, A.R., McFarland, M.N., Sullivan, J.M., Twardowski, M.S.: Evidence for ubiquitous preferential particle orientation in representative oceanic shear flows. Limnol. Oceanogr. **63**(1), 122–143 (2018)
15. Shorten, C., Khoshgoftaar, T.M.: A survey on image data augmentation for deep learning. J. Big Data **6**(1), 1–48 (2019)
16. Srivastava, N., Hinton, G., Krizhevsky, A., Sutskever, I., Salakhutdinov, R.: Dropout: a simple way to prevent neural networks from overfitting. J. Mach. Learn. Res. **15**(1), 1929–1958; 1532–4435 (2014)
17. Szegedy, C., et al.: Going deeper with convolutions. In: Proceedings of the IEEE Conference on CVPR, pp. 1–9 (2015)
18. Szegedy, C., Vanhoucke, V., Ioffe, S., Shlens, J., Wojna, Z.: Rethinking the inception architecture for computer vision. In: Proceedings of the IEEE Conference on Computer Vision and Pattern Recognition, pp. 2818–2826 (2016)
19. Twardowski, M.S., Jamet, C., Loisel, H.: Analytical model to derive suspended particulate matter concentration in natural waters by inversion of optical attenuation and backscattering. In: Ocean Sensing and Monitoring X, vol. 10631, pp. 152–166. SPIE (2018)
20. Wang, K., Dou, J., Kemao, Q., Di, J., Zhao, J.: Y-net: a one-to-two deep learning framework for digital holographic reconstruction. Opt. Lett. **44**(19), 4765–4768 (2019)
21. Yadav, S., Shukla, S.: Analysis of k-fold cross-validation over hold-out validation on colossal datasets for quality classification. In: 2016 IEEE 6th International Conference on Advanced Computing (IACC), pp. 78–83 (2016)
22. Zhang, X., Zhou, X., Lin, M., Sun, J.: ShuffleNet: an extremely efficient convolutional neural network for mobile devices. In: Proceedings of the IEEE Conference on Computer Vision and Pattern Recognition, pp. 6848–6856 (2018)

Generation of Data for Training Retinal Image Segmentation Models

Srinjoy Bhuiya[1]([✉])(iD), Suchandra Chakraborty[1](iD), Subhopriyo Sadhukhan[1](iD),
Deba Prasad Mandal[2](iD), and Dinabandhu Bhandari[1](iD)

[1] Heritage Institute of Technology, Kolkata 700107, West Bengal, India
{srinjoy.bhuiya.cse23,suchandra.chakraborty.cse23,
subhopriyo.sadhukhan.cse23}@heritageit.edu.in,
dinabandhu.bhandari@heritageit.edu
[2] Indian Statistical Institute, Kolkata, Kolkata 700108, West Bengal, India
dpmandal@isical.ac.in

Abstract. Biomedical image segmentation requires pixel-wise labelling which is extremely time-consuming and the availability of additional training data is highly beneficial for training Deep Learning models. In addition to using Classical Image augmentation, generative adversarial networks have been used to augment the training data. This work is an investigation of the usefulness of generated medical images for Deep Learning segmentation models. An attempt has been made to create a computer-generated retinal image segmentation dataset using various state-of-the-art image generative deep learning models and use that dataset to train a supervised image segmentation model. Our experiments demonstrate that the generated data can be used successfully for medical segmentation tasks and improves the model's performance over using classical augmentations.

Keywords: Retinal Image Segmentation · Image Generation · Image Augmentation · Image Translation

1 Introduction

Biomedical imaging is essential for practitioners in the field of medical study. However, clinically verified labelling of biomedical image data is extremely time-consuming with many legal barriers for their use. The scarcity of high-quality data causes overfitting and poor generalizability in many learning models. Data augmentation has been used to generate additional data points that can alleviate these problems to a certain degree. Classically, only simple affine and non-affine image transformations have been used in this data augmentation process. Recently, Generative Adversarial Networks (GANs) have emerged as a promising solution for generating additional medical images, where data scarcity and imbalanced data categories are common challenges. Wasserstein GANs (WGAN) [1] are proposed to produce synthetic multi-sequence brain magnetic resonance

P. Maji et al. (Eds.): PReMI 2023, LNCS 14301, pp. 483–491, 2023.
https://doi.org/10.1007/978-3-031-45170-6_50

images (MRI) to improve the accuracy and consistency of medical diagnoses. For high-resolution images, progressively grown GANs [2,3] are utilized to generate synthetic medical image data for retinal fundus photographs and multimodal MRI of glioma. Conditional GANs [4] are exploited for denoising, superresolution, modality conversion, and reconstruction in MRI and for computing tomography images. CycleGan and Pix2pix [5] are utilized in detecting ischemic strokes. In MRI imaging, Swin-transformer-based GANs [6] for multi-modal medical image translation are used to perform the missing and corrupted modalities from the available existing ones using image-to-image translation architectures.

The objective of this investigation is to demonstrate the effectiveness of the generated retinal fundus images in training a segmentation model. Initially, we have incorporated the Perceptual path length (PPL) regularization [22] to get smooth and continuous changes in the latent space while generating images. Subsequently, an image-to-image GAN [7,8] is applied to generate the corresponding vessel masks. A fully convolutional neural network based image segmentation model is developed to examine the usefulness of our generated data. In this model, a custom loss function [9,10] is considered instead of the popularly used binary cross entropy. The proposed image generation framework diverges from traditional image augmentation methods and focuses on the benefits of using images generated using generative adversarial networks for deep learningbased model training. Through experiments, the results show that training with generated data leads to notable improvements compared to conventional augmentation methods.

Section 2 describes our proposed image generation model and the corresponding image segmentation model. The experimental results with the generated retina image dataset are presented in Sect. 3. Section 4 finds the conclusions and future scope of this investigation.

2   Proposed GAN Based Image Generation Model

In this work, we are concerned with generating retinal image data and verifying its effectiveness. Here, three different tasks are performed: firstly, the retinal images are generated using a GAN; then the respective masks (pixel-wise labels) are generated corresponding to each generated fundus image using a conditional GAN; and finally, the utility of using generated datasets in retinal vasculature segmentation is verified using a CNN model. Moreover, some additional experiments are performed using a mixture of real, generated and classicallyaugmented datasets to verify the usefulness of using additional generative data in such tasks. The generated dataset aims to capture and mimic the distribution of disease markers present in the input dataset used for training. The focus is on replicating the overall distribution of the entire dataset, rather than generating images based on specific visual characteristics or disease markers. This approach ensures that the generated data aligns with the distribution of disease markers in the original dataset.

2.1 Retinal Image Generation

The image generation model described in [11] is utilized here for retinal image generation. The weight modulation and demodulation in the generator structure helped eliminate any artefacts by normalizing them with estimated statistics. A hierarchical generator with skip connections, similar to MSG-GANs, has been exploited to reduce the phase artefacts. Additionally, Adaptive Discriminator Augmentation (ADA) regularization has been used to improve the training stability and sample quality by dynamically adjusting the complexity of the discriminator during training. Path length regularization [11] was employed in the generator loss to encourage smooth and continuous changes in the latent space, increasing the training stability of the generator. The real and generated images are processed using a residual connection network as a discriminator. An R1 regularization penalty was used in the nonsaturating discriminator loss to stabilize the training of the discriminator, thereby improving the quality of the generated images.

2.2 Vasculature Retinal Masks Generation

The GAN framework introduced in [7] by Phillip Isola et al. is exploited for an image-to-mask translation system. This model includes a Conditional GAN [8] that creates images based on an input retinal image, in this instance the retinal image, and the output is a vascular structure segmentation mask. The generating network is a U-style autoencoder connected by skip connections, similar to the architecture provided in [7]. The encoder extracts the features of the input retinal image into a latent feature vector and the decoder uses the latent feature vector to generate the translated image. Finally, the output from the decoder network is passed through a $Tanh$ activation function. A PatchGAN discriminator [7] is being used to downsample the input using convolutions and strided-convolutions to produce a single-channel prediction map. 70×70 image patches are used as the discriminator input. The model uses the Leaky ReLU as the activation function, batch normalization for regularization and the Wasserstien loss function to maintain the Lipchitz continuity of the critic function.

2.3 Image Segmentation Model

To compare the performance of the generated retinal image segmentation dataset with that of a real retinal dataset. Here a lightweight self-attention-based medical image segmentation model showing state-of-the-art performance retinal vasculature segmentation available in [23] is chosen. As shown in Fig. 1, the model uses a simple U-style autoencoder CNN and incorporates the concept of a convolutional self-attention mechanism [24] as the bottleneck. In the proposed model, a down-sampling block to the decoder part of the autoencoder is added resulting a feature vector width of 256 channels. The final segmentation model used in this work is fully convolutional and has approximately 7 million learnable parameters. The model is then trained on two different datasets. The first was

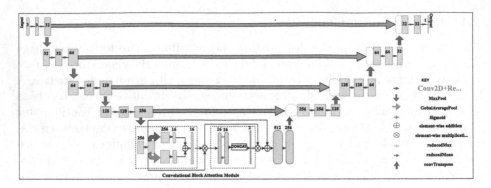

Fig. 1. Architecture of the segmentation model used

the clinician-labelled data of 4000 training image-mask pairs, the other was a generated dataset of the same size. Additional image-mask pairs are generated for use as the validation dataset. The performance of both models is tested using real data. To deal with the high levels of the background to vessel pixels imbalance, a custom loss function [9,10] based on a combination of dice and focal loss is incorporated. The aim of the proposed work is to evaluate the effectiveness of generated retinal image rather than proposing a novel architecture or method for retinal image generation. The methodology involves leveraging pre-existing image generation models and adapting them through parameter adjustments and modifications to suit retinal image generation. The fine-tuned models are subsequently trained on a carefully curated dataset.

3   Results

To generate data in training the segmentation model, two datasets were created to train two separate deep-learning models viz., the retinal image generation and the retinal mask generation models. The first dataset for retinal image generation was compiled from six publicly available benchmark datasets - DRIVE [12], CHASE_DB1 [13], RIDB [14], DIARETDB1 V2.1 [15], HRF [16], and IDRiD [17], totalling 5000 retinal images. The second dataset for retinal vessel mask generation was created by collecting image and mask pairs from DRIVE, CHASE_DB1, ARIA [18], FIVES [19] and STARE [20], totalling 1500 image pairs. The images were resized to a resolution of 512 × 512 while maintaining their aspect ratio. Centre cropping was also performed on all images.

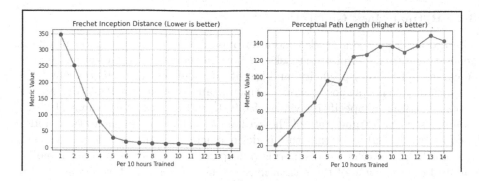

Fig. 2. FID and PPL Metric

3.1 Retinal Image Generation

The proposed image generation system has achieved satisfactory results in generating high-quality retinal fundus images with a fully generated vasculature structure. The Frechet Inception Distance (FID) [21] and Perceptual Path Length Metric [22] are used to evaluate the image generation model. After 50 epochs the model resulted in an FID score of 9.55 and a Perceptual Path Length value of 143.54. As illustrated by Fig. 2, the performance of the model has increased steadily with the increase in the number of epochs trained. Figure 3 presents some examples of the retinal images generated from the model, centred on the macula with proper focus. A good visualization of the parafoveal vessels was achieved over the two disk diameters around the fovea. To further demonstrate the model's superiority, it is compared to another image generation model discussed in [22] that was unable to generate connected vasculature and contained noisy artefacts; its FID score was only 25.46, indicating significantly inferior performance than the proposed approach. The average computation time required to generate the retinal images was 0.2446 s per image an Nvidia P100 Graphics Processor.

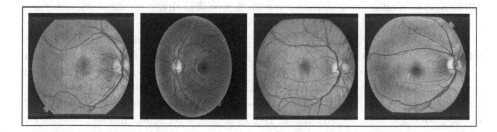

Fig. 3. Samples of the Retinal Fundus images Generated

3.2   Retinal Mask Generation

The proposed image-to-Mask generation model has also shown good results in generating retinal vasculature masks for both generative and real retinal images. Accuracy, F1-Score, Specificity, and Sensitivity metrics are used to evaluate its performance. The proposed model achieves an Accuracy of 94.456%, an F1-Score of 0.8232, a Specificity value of 0.954, and a Sensitivity value of 0.875. Comparisons with some state-of-the-art supervised binary segmentation models such as [23,25] indicates that the model has achieved comparable performance to even the above-referenced supervised deep convolutional segmentation model. Figure 4 depicts some of the retinal masks generated, most of which show all of the major retinal vessels with only some of the finest vessels being either missing or deviating from the ground truth. The average computation time required to generate the vessel masks was 0.455 s per image on an Nvidia P100 Graphics Processor.

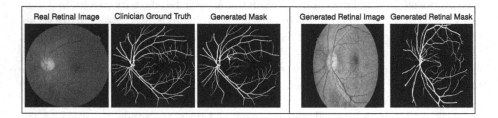

Fig. 4. A sample of the masks generated from the model

3.3   Real-Data Versus Generated-Data

To demonstrate the benefits of generated (fake) data, the segmentation model is trained on four different datasets. The first contains real images and clinically verified vessel segmentation masks, the next has generated images and vessel masks, and the third has only the real images but was augmented with some affine and non-affine transformation techniques. Finally, a segmentation dataset containing both real images and generated images together is chosen; this dataset is used to compare the utility of using classical image augmentation techniques with the GANs-based image generation process mentioned in earlier an section.

Table 1 shows the performance of all the different models on a fixed testing dataset comprising real test images and clinically verified segmentation masks. Figure 5 depicts samples of generated masks in comparison to the ground truth masks. Metrics such as Accuracy, DICE Score, Precision, Recall, Specificity, and Sensitivity are used for assessing the performance between real data and generated data for training image segmentation models. It has been found that the generated data leads to better results than merely using the real data- this is primarily due to a low number of real training image-mask pairs. The model trained with generated data yield a high IoU score of 0.871, a Precision value

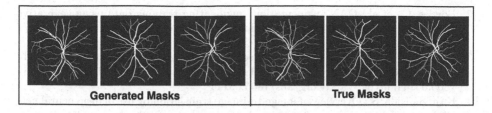

Fig. 5. Generated and True Masks

Table 1. Performance metrics of segmentation model based on different data-sets

Dataset	Accuracy	IOU	DICE	F1	Precision	Recall	Specificity	MCC
Real Data	0.978	0.728	0.842	0.842	0.864	0.822	0.990	0.832
Generated Data	0.981	0.762	0.864	0.864	0.895	0.836	0.992	0.855
Real + Gen	**0.992**	0.871	**0.931**	**0.932**	**0.925**	**0.937**	0.993	**0.905**
Real + Augmented	0.983	**0.892**	0.887	0.888	0.905	0.894	**0.994**	0.903

of 0.925, and a recall value of 0.937. These metrics indicate that generated data can be used to train medical image segmentation models for real-life applications without any serious complications. The use of combined datasets of the real and generated datasets together is found to perform better than when either real and augmented data together or only generated data is used. This may suggest that using medical images created through GANs leads to better training outcomes than only applying affine and non-affine transformations on real datasets.

4   Conclusions

This paper presents a high-resolution retinal fundus image generation pipeline that generates retinal images and vasculature masks. The pipeline was rigorously tested on the medical image generation task and was able to reproduce high-quality medical images that can enhance the training of deep-learning models in medical imaging. The use of additional generated training samples was able to significantly improve the performance of the segmentation model. It is also shown that augmenting medical datasets with generative data results in better performance than using simple transformations for data augmentation. In future work, the generative model architecture used to create a medical-specific image generator will be modified, compare and contrast the use of various types of regularization techniques in the loss function and explore the use of diffusion models for medical image generation.

References

1. Han, C., et al.: GAN-based synthetic brain MR image generation. In: 2018 IEEE 15th International Symposium on Biomedical Imaging (ISBI 2018) (2018). https://doi.org/10.1109/ISBI.2018.8363678

2. Bowles, C., et al.: GAN augmentation: augmenting training data using generative adversarial networks (2018). https://doi.org/10.48550/arXiv.1810.10863, https://arxiv.org/abs/1810.10863

3. Beers, A., et al.: High-resolution medical image synthesis using progressively grown generative adversarial networks (2018). https://doi.org/10.48550/arXiv.1805.03144, https://arxiv.org/abs/1805.03144

4. Kaji, S., Kida, S.: Overview of image-to-image translation by use of deep neural networks: denoising, super-resolution, modality conversion, and reconstruction in medical imaging - radiological physics and technology (2019). https://doi.org/10.1007/s12194-019-00520-y, https://link.springer.com/article/10.1007/s12194-019-00520-y

5. Platscher, M., Zopes, J., Federau, C.: Image translation for medical image generation: ischemic stroke lesion segmentation. Biomed. Signal Process. Control **72**, 103283 (2022). https://doi.org/10.1016/j.bspc.2021.103283

6. Yan, S., Wang, C., Chen, W., Lyu, J.: Swin transformer-based GAN for multimodal medical image translation. Front. Oncol. **12**, 942511 (2022). https://doi.org/10.3389/fonc.2022.942511

7. Isola, P., Zhu, J.-Y., Zhou, T., Efros, A.A.: Image-to-image translation with conditional adversarial networks (2018). https://doi.org/10.48550/arXiv.1611.07004, https://arxiv.org/abs/1611.07004

8. Mirza, M., Osindero, S.: Conditional generative adversarial nets (2014). https://doi.org/10.48550/arXiv.1411.1784, https://arxiv.org/abs/1411.1784

9. Lin, T.-Y., Goyal, P., Girshick, R., He, K., Dollar, P.: Focal loss for dense object detection. IEEE Trans. Pattern Anal. Mach. Intell. **42**, 318–327 (2020). https://doi.org/10.1109/TPAMI.2018.2858826

10. Sudre, C.H., Li, W., Vercauteren, T., Ourselin, S., Jorge Cardoso, M.: Generalised dice overlap as a deep learning loss function for highly unbalanced segmentations. In: Cardoso, M.J., et al. (eds.) DLMIA/ML-CDS -2017. LNCS, vol. 10553, pp. 240–248. Springer, Cham (2017). https://doi.org/10.1007/978-3-319-67558-9_28

11. Karras, T., Aittala, M., Hellsten, J., Laine, S., Lehtinen, J., Aila, T.: Training generative adversarial networks with limited data (2020). https://doi.org/10.48550/arXiv.2006.06676, https://arxiv.org/abs/2006.06676

12. Staal, J., Abramoff, M.D., Niemeijer, M., Viergever, M.A., van Ginneken, B.: Ridge-based vessel segmentation in color images of the retina. IEEE Trans. Med. Imaging **23**, 501–509 (2004). https://doi.org/10.1109/tmi.2004.825627

13. Fraz, M.M., et al.: An ensemble classification-based approach applied to retinal blood vessel segmentation. IEEE Trans. Biomed. Eng. **59**, 2538–2548 (2012). https://doi.org/10.1109/tbme.2012.2205687

14. Akram, M.U., Abdul Salam, A., Khawaja, S.G., Naqvi, S.G., Khan, S.A.: RIDB: a dataset of fundus images for retina based person identification. Data Brief **33**, 106433 (2020). https://doi.org/10.1016/j.dib.2020.106433

15. Kauppi, T., et al.: The DIARETDB1 diabetic retinopathy database and evaluation protocol. In: Proceedings of the British Machine Vision Conference 2007 (2007). https://doi.org/10.5244/c.21.15

16. Budai, A., Bock, R., Maier, A., Hornegger, J., Michelson, G.: Robust vessel segmentation in fundus images. Int. J. Biomed. Imaging **2013**, 1–11 (2013). https://doi.org/10.1155/2013/154860

17. Porwal, P., et al.: Indian diabetic retinopathy image dataset (IDRiD): a database for diabetic retinopathy screening research. Data **3**, 25 (2018). https://doi.org/10.3390/data3030025

18. Farnell, D.J.J., et al.: Enhancement of blood vessels in digital fundus photographs via the application of multiscale line operators (2008). https://research.manchester.ac.uk/en/publications/enhancement-of-blood-vessels-in-digital-fundus-photographs-via-th

19. Jin, K., et al.: FIVES: a fundus image dataset for artificial intelligence based vessel segmentation. Sci. Data **9**, 475 (2022). https://doi.org/10.1038/s41597-022-01564-3

20. Hoover, A.D., Kouznetsova, V., Goldbaum, M.: Locating blood vessels in retinal images by piecewise threshold probing of a matched filter response. IEEE Trans. Med. Imaging **19**, 203–210 (2000). https://doi.org/10.1109/42.845178

21. Heusel, M., et al.: GANs trained by a two time-scale update rule converge to a local nash equilibrium (2019). https://arxiv.org/abs/1706.08500, https://doi.org/10.48550/arXiv.1706.08500. Accessed 12 Jan 2018

22. Karras, T., Laine, S., Aila, T.: A style-based generator architecture for generative adversarial networks. In: IEEE/CVF Conference on Computer Vision and Pattern Recognition (CVPR) (2019)

23. Bhuiya, S., Choudhury, S.R., Aich, G., Maurya, M., Sen, A.: Retinal blood vessel segmentation and analysis using lightweight spatial attention based CNN and data augmentation. In: 2022 IEEE Calcutta Conference (CALCON) (2022). https://doi.org/10.1109/CALCON56258.2022.10060189

24. Woo, S., Park, J., Lee, J.-Y., Kweon, I.S.: CBAM: convolutional block attention module. In: Computer Vision - ECCV 2018, pp. 3–19 (2018). https://doi.org/10.1007/978-3-030-01234-2_1

25. Alom, M.Z., Hasan, M., Yakopcic, C., Taha, T.M., Asari, V.K.: Recurrent residual convolutional neural network based on U-net (R2U-net) for medical image segmentation (2018). https://doi.org/10.48550/arXiv.1802.06955

Computer Vision

Object Detection with YOLO Model on NAO Humanoid Robot

Sougatamoy Biswas$^{(\boxtimes)}$, Anup Nandy , and Asim Kumar Naskar

National Institute of Technology Rourkela, Odisha, India
521CS6015@nirkl.ac.in, {nandya,naskara}@nitrkl.ac.in

Abstract. Object detection is an important part in the field of robotics as it enables robots to understand their surroundings. The NAO humanoid robot is extensively used in human-robot interaction research. In this study a novel approach combining the VGG16 network and You Only Look Once (YOLO) algorithm is used for object detection using the NAO robot. YOLOv7 is selected for its best balanced information retention, quick inference, accurate localization, and identification of objects as compared to several bounding box algorithms. VGG16 network is adopted as a feature extractor to optimize the performance of object detection for NAO low-resolution camera images. Once feature extraction is completed then it's output layer is combined with our fine tuned YOLOv7 model for object detection. The fine-tuned YOLOv7 model is proposed with some pre-processing techniques such as image augmentation, angle movement, and scale resizing for the performance improvement. The efficiency of the proposed model is compared with the performance of other state-of-the-art models.

Keywords: Object detection · Computer Vision · Humanoid robots · Object recognition

1 Introduction

Object detection is a foundational robotics task that enables intelligent interaction between robots and their environment. Enabling robots to detect and recognize objects is necessary for effective manipulation and real-time decision-making. NAO robots have been utilized by researchers for applications such as interaction therapy, assisted living, and non-verbal sign analysis. The primary objective of this research is to empower the NAO robot with real-time object detection, classification, and localization abilities within its field of view, facilitating the execution of actions based on the identified objects. The low computing power [1] and memory of NAO robots make object detection tasks difficult.

Researchers have presented different techniques of object detection based on the NAO robots. The earliest object-finding algorithm was Viola-Jones object detection method [2] that is useful for real time object identification. The Region-based convolutional network (R-CNN), introduced by Girshick et al. [3], achieved

P. Maji et al. (Eds.): PReMI 2023, LNCS 14301, pp. 495–502, 2023.
https://doi.org/10.1007/978-3-031-45170-6_51

substantial performance improvement of 50% over previous approaches on the VOC 2012 dataset, reaching a mean average precision (mAP) of 62.4%. The introduction of Region Proposal Networks (RPN) in 2016 further enhanced the speed and accuracy of Faster R-CNN [4] by replacing the traditional region proposal generation process. However, the YOLO network and its derivatives demonstrated superior test speeds ranging from 45 to 150 frames per second and surpassed the performance of the Region-based models.

Real-time inference will be performed using the camera on the NAO robot, and the effectiveness of the model will be evaluated in terms of latency and accuracy. Through performance tests, it has been observed that YOLOv7 outperforms other algorithms when handling low-resolution images. The pre-trained VGG16 network is applied for feature extraction for NAO captured images to solve the problem of object detection with low resolution images captured by NAO. The feature extraction layer output is combined with the fine-tuned YOLOv7 for object detection. The proposed method works efficiently with the low resolution images of NAO humanoid robot and shows better result compared to other methods. This paper's remaining sections are structured as follows. Section 2 outlined the motive of this work. Section 3 discusses proposed methods. Section 4 describes the evaluation metrics. Section 5 describes the experimental datasets. Section 6 describes the experimental results and compares the performance of numerous YOLO algorithms. The final section concludes the work.

2   Problem Definition

The goal is to recognize and localize items in the image acquired by the NAO robot's low-resolution camera. An agent, such as a robot, needs these data to act in response to an object's name and location. To illustrate the model's predictions and enhance visual understanding, it is necessary to draw bounding boxes around the identified items. The identified object's class name and its coordinates inside the image's reference frame are the two pieces of information that will be produced by the neural network.

3   Proposed Methodology

The NAOv6 robot with VGG16 as feature extractor and the YOLO algorithm are used to make the proposed method for detecting objects. The captured image from the NAO robot is pre-processed using data augmentation, horizontal flip, and changes of data rotation between $-30°$ and $+30°$.

Due to the lower image resolution of NAO camera the model performance can be impacted. To solve this problem and optimize the performance, pre-trained VGG16 convolution network is used as feature extractor for the input images. Once the features are extracted from the images then the output layer of VGG16 is combined with our fine-tuned version of YOLOv7 [5]. The proposed YOLOv7 version is modified with optimal hyperparameters. The ADAM optimizer with confidence threshold of 0.25 is used which defines the lowest possible prediction

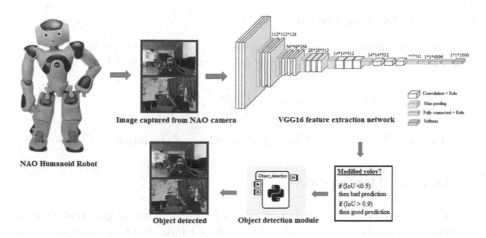

Fig. 1. Methodology of the object detection process [8]

score before it accepts as valid (otherwise it will entirely ignore this prediction). The hyper-parameters and configurations as in YOLOv7 (as in hyp.scratch.yaml) is modified to optimize the performance of our model. Intersection Over Union (IoU) threshold for the prediction is set to 0.45. The overlapping degree between the predicted and ground truth box must be greater than the IoU threshold to return the best bounding box for an object. The model batch size is set to 16 with a learning rate of 0.001. Also, the image is scaled to 640 × 640. First, the NAO camera is used to take pictures of various objects and store them in a predetermined place. Once the YOLOv7 model [6] is trained using the extracted features from the VGG16 network, the whole model is included in the NAO "Choregraphe" software tool. Then, the images are utilized which are acquired by the NAO camera and feed them into the object detection model [7]. The entire methodology is shown in Fig. 1.

4   Performance Evaluation Metrics

Performance evaluation metrics are used to measure the accuracy of object detection models. The metrics used in this work to measure the performance of object detection model include:

4.1   Intersection over Union (IoU)

IoU is used to measure the overlapping area by two boxes [9]. The cost of IoU is defined by Eq. (1).

$$IoU = \frac{A}{B} \tag{1}$$

where A represents the intersection between the predicted and ground truth boxes, while B denotes the result obtained from merging the two.

4.2   Mean Average Precision (mAP)

First, average precision of each class is calculated for obtaining the average of number of classes which calculates the mAP value [10]. It is defined in Eq. (2).

$$mAP = \frac{1}{N} \sum_{i=1}^{N} AP_i \qquad (2)$$

The **Average Precision (AP)** of class i is AP_i and the number of classes is N.

5   Dataset Description

The dataset consists of 1900 images which includes training and test images. The images are labeled and annotated in YOLO format [11,12] with an open-source software program LabelImg. The dataset is mainly categorized into 5 categories like Person, Ball, Bottle, cell phone, and chair. In each category, there exists a total of 380 images. To train and test the model, the dataset is divided into separate sets, with 80% of the total data allocated for training and 20% for testing purposes. The experiment makes use of Pytorch 1.13.1 and Python 3.10.9 and the whole module is incorporated in the NAO Choregraphe 2.8.6.23 software.

Fig. 2. Image acquisition from the camera of the NAO robot.

6   Result Analysis and Discussion

The experimental setup for collecting images from the NAO robot camera is shown in Fig. 2. The proposed neural network model is able to identify the objects [13,14] in the image with an accurate bounding box [15,16] as shown in Fig. 3. The usual detection accuracy threshold is 0.5 IoU. The detection is accurate if the predicted and ground truth bounding boxes overlap at least 50%. The mAP@0.5 assesses model accuracy at a single IoU threshold of 0.5, whereas mAP@0.5:0.95 measures model accuracy over a range of IoU thresholds from 0.5 to 0.95. The performance of the model improves gradually after 90 epochs and at the 100 epoch it shows the mean Average Precision mAP@0.5 is 93.7% and mAP@0.5:0.95 is 76.5% (Fig. 4).

Fig. 3. Object detection results with corresponding output frames, bounding boxes and object labels.

The model performs well at several IoU levels and proves that it is more robust and trustworthy. The Box loss, Class loss, and Object loss vs. epochs graph are shown in Fig. 5. It illustrates the model's capacity to recognize and categorize objects in pictures. Box loss is anticipated in bounding boxes which firmly contain image objects. Class loss is the mistake in expected class labels, which identify the bounding box's objects. Object loss is defined by predicting the bounding box which contains an item. As epochs rise, the model improves bounding box, class label, and item presence predictions by decreasing the loss. The Learning rate vs the number of epochs graph shown in Fig. 6 illustrates how the learning rate changes throughout training. It controls how fast the model modifies parameters to minimize the loss function. Higher learning rates speed up convergence but potentially overshoot the ideal solution and produce unstable training. Lower learning rates may impede convergence, but they are more stable and provide better solutions. The x/lr0, x/lr1, and x/lr2 graphs represent the number of iterations or epochs. These values are usually calculated by multiplying the initial learning rate (lr0) by a schedule of scaling factors (lr1 and lr2), which are typically set to decrease the learning rate over time.

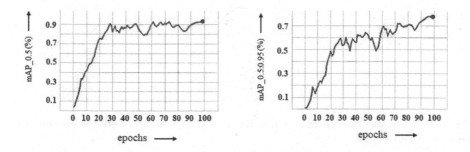

Fig. 4. Comparison between mAP values and the number of epochs for the proposed YOLOv7 model.

Table 1. Result analysis and performance comparison of different models.

Model Name	mAP@0.5	mAP@0.5:0.95	Completion time (hours.)
YOLOv5	83.5%	63.2%	0.205
YOLOv7	91%	69%	0.262
YOLOv7-tiny	83.9%	65.2%	0.105
YOLOv8	86.7%	67.1%	0.354
Modified YOLOv7	93.7%	76.5%	0.186

Fig. 5. Comparison between Box loss, Class loss, and Object loss Vs the epochs for the proposed YOLOv7 model.

The mean Average Precision (mAP) scores for different versions of YOLO, including YOLOv5, YOLOv7, YOLOv7-tiny, and YOLOv8, were determined on our dataset. The respective mAP values for these versions are 83.5%, 91%, 83.9% and 86.7%. The comparative analysis of different models is presented in Table 1. We have achieved an adequate mAP@0.5 value of 93.7% and mAP@0.5:0.95 as 76.5% with a quicker inference rate (0.186 h). It justifies that our proposed model outperforms other state-of-the-art models.

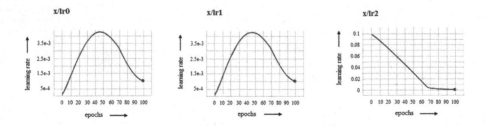

Fig. 6. Comparison between variation of learning with number of epochs for the proposed YOLOv7 model.

7   Conclusion and Future Work

This research aims to investigate the challenges associated with instructing a humanoid robot, such as NAO, in the domain of computer vision, specifically in the tasks of object identification, recognition, and localization. The study focuses on utilizing a customized YOLOv7 network model for this purpose. In the future, this object detection module can be incorporated for real-time object detection with high FPS. Moreover, this technique can be used for the treatment of autistic children [17] and to identify different objects using the NAO robot. We plan to utilize NAO's robot in-built "Say" module to produce speech to the textual information about the identified item For interacting with the autism children.

Acknowledgements. We would like to extend our sincerest appreciation to everyone who helps to make this study a success. We are thankful to the Science and Engineering Research Board (SERB), Government of India for funding this research work with FILE NO: CRG/2021/004701.

References

1. Vahrenkamp, N., Asfour, T., Dillmann, R.: Simultaneous grasp and motion planning: humanoid robot ARMAR-III. IEEE Robot. Autom. Mag. **19**, 43–57 (2012)
2. Viola, P., Jones, M.: Rapid object detection using a boosted cascade of simple features. In: Conference on Computer Vision and Pattern Recognition (2001)
3. Girshick, R., Donahue, J., Darrell, T., et al.: Region-based convolutional networks for accurate object detection and segmentation. IEEE Trans. Pattern Anal. Mach. Intell. **38**(1), 142–158 (2016)
4. Ren, S., He, K., Girshick, R., et al.: Faster R-CNN: towards real-time object detection with region proposal networks. In: International Conference on Neural Information Processing Systems, pp. 91–99. MIT Press (2015)
5. Wang, C., Bochkovskiy, A., Liao, H.: YOLOv7: trainable bag-of-freebies sets new state-of-the-art for real-time object detectors. arXiv/abs/2207.02696 (2022). Accessed 30 Apr 2023
6. Duan, X., Chen, H., Lou, H., Bi, L., Zhang, Y., Liu, H.: A more accurate mask detection algorithm based on Nao robot platform and YOLOv7. In: 2023 IEEE 3rd International Conference on Power, Electronics and Computer Applications (ICPECA) (2023)
7. Jayawardana, J.T.H., et al.: Train a robot to climb staircase using vision-base system. In: 2022 IEEE 10th Region 10 Humanitarian Technology Conference (R10-HTC) (2022)
8. Understanding VGG16: Concepts, Architecture, and Performance. https://datagen.tech/guides/computer-vision/vgg16/
9. Steffi, D., Mehta, S., Venkatesh, V.: Object detection on robosoccer environment using convolution neural network. Indonesian J. Electr. Eng. Comput. Sci. **29**, 286 (2022)
10. Diana Steffi, D.D., Mehta, S., Venkatesh, K.A., Dasari, S.K.: HOG-based object detection toward soccer playing robots. In: Bansal, J.C., Engelbrecht, A., Shukla, P.K. (eds.) Computer Vision and Robotics. AIS, pp. 155–163. Springer, Singapore (2022). https://doi.org/10.1007/978-981-16-8225-4_12

11. Hui, J.: Real-time Object Detection with YOLO, YOLOv2 and now YOLOv3. https://jonathan-hui.medium.com/real-time-object-detection-with-yolo-yolov2-28b1b93e2088
12. Zhou, J., Feng, L., Chellali, R., Zhu, H.: Detecting and tracking objects in HRI: YOLO networks for the NAO "I See You" function. In: 2018 27th IEEE International Symposium on Robot and Human Interactive Communication (RO-MAN) (2018)
13. Redmon, J., Farhadi, A.: YOLO9000: better, faster, stronger. In: IEEE Conference on Computer Vision and Pattern Recognition, pp. 6517–6525. IEEE Computer Society (2017)
14. Wang, Z.: Deep learning-based approach for object detection in robot football competition. In: 2022 International Conference on Frontiers of Artificial Intelligence and Machine Learning (FAIML) (2022)
15. Liu, J., Zhu, X., Zhou, X., Qian, S., Yu, J.: Defect detection for metal base of TO-Can packaged laser diode based on improved YOLO algorithm. Electronics **11**, 1561 (2022)
16. Chatterjee, S., Zunjani, F.H., Nandi, G.C.: Real-time object detection and recognition on low-compute humanoid robots using deep learning. In: 2020 6th International Conference on Control, Automation and Robotics (ICCAR) (2020)
17. Yun, S.-S., Kim, H., Choi, J., Park, S.-K.: A robot-assisted behavioral intervention system for children with autism spectrum disorders. Robot. Auton. Syst. **76**, 58–67 (2016)

Scene Estimation for Making Active Decisions

Sambhunath Biswas[1,2]([✉]) and Sabyasachi Moitra[1]

[1] Techno India University, Kolkata, West Bengal, India
sambhunathbiswas17@gmail.com
[2] Ex-Machine Intelligence Unit, ISI, Kolkata, India

Abstract. Scene estimation problem has been examined along with the structural description of differents objects in the scene. The data structure of scenes is established through a tree structure. This uses depths of different objects in the scene. Depth map is computed using Horn's reflectance map and Shah's linearization technique of the reflectance map. The center of mass is considered for the localized rectangle of each object to define the hierarchy of objects present in the scene. The localization of objects is based on least square estimation technique on YOLO output images. The localization method is fully free from any kind of thresholds and is a new concept. Comparison with other methods shows our method is more effective. Finding the structural description is also a new scheme. The nearness of objects at different levels of the hierarchical tree for the scene is based on some weights that help for making active decisions on the positions of objects relative to the camera observer. Finally, some applications shows the merits of the proposed scheme in some details.

Keywords: Localization · Least square · Adaptive · Structural descriptions · Active decisions

1 Introduction

Scene estimation is an important problem for its wide spread applications in many different fields, *e.g.*, in self-driving cars, video surveillance, crowd counting, etc. By scene estimation, we mean not only finding different objects present in the scene but also the localization of each object and its positional relationship between all other objects. Basically, a scene is an image with many objects in it, in general. However, a scene, in a special case, may contain a single object. As yet, we do not have the best possible localization of objects in the scene and a suitable mathematical description for an arbitrary scene. Since, each object can have a relation with all other objects; we formulate a scene as a tree with all of its objects having the best possible localizations.

In our approach, we view the localization as an estimation problem. Thus, neither confidence threshold nor IoU threshold (NMS-based method) is required for localization of objects, as described in [1–3]. In other words, the proposed approach is free from NMS. We estimate the bounding box in the least square

P. Maji et al. (Eds.): PReMI 2023, LNCS 14301, pp. 503–513, 2023.
https://doi.org/10.1007/978-3-031-45170-6_52

sense from the vertices of the multiple detection bounding boxes. It thus requires only the YOLO output images for the proposed method. Comparison of our results with those of NMS shows that our results are superior. Hence, the major aspect in scene estimation is two folds. One is finding the best possible localization of objects in the scene without using any kind of thresholds and second, the formulation of the structural description of the scene for an effective scene description. Such a description of scenes can be used in a number of applications. The applications, described in the present paper, show the merit of the paper in the practical domain. The proposed approach is altogether a new concept.

2   Scene Estimation

To estimate an arbitrary scene, we first find out the number of objects in the scene, and then we localize each object. Such number of objects, collectively provide important information about the scene, which can successfully be used in different applications. The information carried out by a scene can also be used for active decision making.

2.1   Detection of the Number of Objects in the Scene

For this, we choose the center of each bounding box of the YOLO output image corresponding to a particular object. This forms a cluster and so, for different objects in the scene we get different clusters. The number of such clusters can be easily determined by K-means clustering technique. The value of K is obtained following the method given in [4]. The clusters are separated and labeled properly. This provides the number of objects in the scene. Figure 1 explains the method for an input YOLO output image.

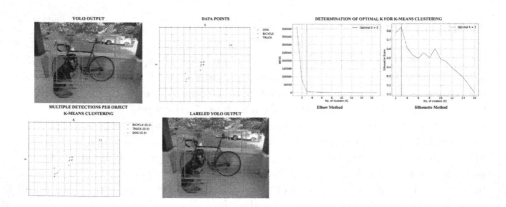

Fig. 1. Detection of the number of objects in an arbitrary scene.

2.2   Least Square Estimate for the Localization Rectangle

Next we localize each object in the scene. We collect all the vertices of rectangles for an object in the YOLO output image. Hence, for an object we get four different sets of vertices-data. Taking each pair of them, we fit a straight line in the least square sense. This helps to obtain four different lines; the lines in order are orthogonal to each other. Their intersection provides the required vertices of the localized rectangle. Thus, one obtains all the objects in the scene, localized in the image plane. Figure 2 explains the method for the best possible localized objects for an YOLO output image. We discuss in the Sect. 4 our results on a set of different YOLO output images.

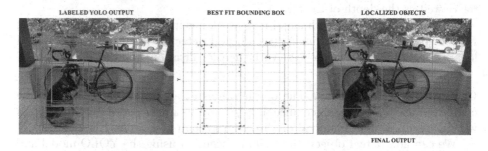

Fig. 2. Estimation of best possible localized rectangles for objects in an arbitrary scene.

3   Structural Description and Relationship Between Objects in a Scene

We have already seen that a scene may contain, in general, many objects in it. But, unfortunately no one has described so far any relation between them, though the area has some potential applications. The relationship between objects define a structure in the scene which is equally important from the data structure point of view. This section describes the nearness of objects or how far away the objects are from the viewer. The near-by as well as far away objects help to provide a structural description of a scene. In other words, one can estimate a data structure of different objects present in a scene. The comparison between such data structure of two scenes can easily tell how one scene is different from the other. This phenomenon can have immense use in many areas, e.g., in the medical domain if we compare the growth pattern of tumours, we can say whether they are slowly varying or rapidly growing tumours. This can be helpful in cancer treatment. On the other hand, the structure can also predict the positional configuration of subjects in a sprint. In fact, there are many more applications in many areas.

To compute the structural description, we have computed the depth information for all the localized objects in the scene using the linearized Horn's reflectance map [5,6]. The distances between such computed depth values of different objects were also computed. So, depending on depth values, it is not difficult to find out all the nearer objects to the observer in succession. The nearer objects were thought to have higher weights while the far away objects have lesser weights. This information may effectively provide a tree structure with the objects as nodes and edges as the distance between them.

3.1 Computation of Camera-Object Distance

Camera-object distance is the distance of all points on the object from the camera. This distance is basically the depth of each point on the object from the camera. The center of mass of all such points may be taken as their representative point. Hence, the object's distance from the camera may be taken as the distance of the center of mass of the object from the camera. This distance may be viewed as the depth of the object.

The computation of depth map in our work has its framework in [6]. For this, we consider the same RGB image (scene) and detect different objects in it and localize them suitably. The objects with their localization are as shown in Sect. 2.

Computation of Depths. The depth values at all the object points can be computed using Horns's reflectance map [5] and its linearization by Shah [6], in which the albedo and illumination direction is computed using Elhabian [7].

We can now detect objects in the input scene, S using the YOLO model and localize them using the proposed least square method as described in Sect. 2. Let the ith object o_i in the scene be described as the vector $S([x_1^i, y_1^i, x_2^i, y_2^i, cls^i]^T)$. With all such objects, the scene can be viewed as,

$$S_{OBJ} = S([x_1^i, y_1^i, x_2^i, y_2^i, cls^i]_{i=1 \text{ to } N}^T), \tag{1}$$

where the arguments in $[x_1^i, y_1^i, x_2^i, y_2^i, cls^i]^T$ indicate the ith bounding box coordinates with (x_1^i, y_1^i) and (x_2^i, y_2^i) as the top-left and bottom-right corners and cls^i as the class of the ith object in the scene respectively.

We can construct the depth map Z from the localized image for each object, say, $Z_{OBJ} = \{Z_1, Z_2, \ldots, Z_i, \ldots, Z_N\}$ from it, where $Z_i = Z((x_1^i, x_2^i), (y_1^i, y_2^i))$. Figure 3 shows the depth map for different objects for an arbitrary scene.

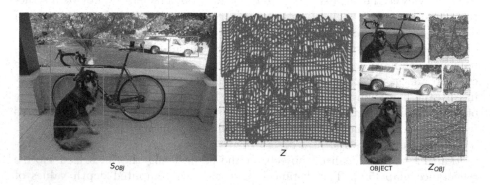

Fig. 3. Depth map for different objects for an arbitrary scene.

With the depth values computed at every point on the objects in the scene, we compute the center of mass (x_c^i, y_c^i, z_c^i) of the ith object using

$$x_c^i = \frac{\sum_{j=1}^k m_j^i x_j^i}{\sum_{j=1}^k m_j^i}, y_c^i = \frac{\sum_{j=1}^k m_j^i y_j^i}{\sum_{j=1}^k m_j^i}, z_c^i = \frac{\sum_{j=1}^k m_j^i z_j^i}{\sum_{j=1}^k m_j^i}, \tag{2}$$

where m_j^i is the weight of the ith object for which we consider its intensity value and z_j^i is its depth value. The value of m can be calculated in the following way:

$$m = Ae^{-\alpha z}. \tag{3}$$

At $z \to z_\infty$, $m \to 0$.
Let $m = m_{max} = 1$ when $z = z_{min}$
And $m = m_{min}$ when $z = z_{max}$.
Furthermore, assuming $m_{min} = 0.05 m_{max} = 0.05$, one can show,

$$\alpha = -\frac{\log(0.05)}{(z_{max} - z_{min})} \tag{4}$$

and

$$A = e^{\alpha z_{min}}. \tag{5}$$

We compute the distance d_i of the ith object from the camera as the distance of the center of mass of the ith object from the camera as,

$$d_i = \sqrt{x_c^2 + y_c^2 + z_c^2}. \tag{6}$$

If the scene consists of N number of objects, we normalize their distance as,

$$D = \left\{ d : d = \frac{d_i}{\sum_i d_i}, 1 \le i \le N \right\}. \tag{7}$$

The distances of different objects in the scene in Fig. 3 are shown in the Table 1 for clarification.

Table 1. Distance of different objects

No. of Objects	Distance	Sorted Distance
3	0.292603 (BICYCLE)	0.256259 (DOG)
	0.451138 (TRUCK)	0.292603 (BICYCLE)
	0.256259 (DOG)	0.451138 (TRUCK)

3.2 Scene Data Structure

We formulate the scene data structure using the hierarchy of detected objects in a scene. Objects' relative position computed in Sect. 3.1 with respect to an observer provides the camera-object distance D. Thus, $D = \{d_i\}$ with $i = 1, 2, ..., N$ for N different objects in the scene. However, this distance is not ordered. One can sort it in the decreasing order to get an ordered scene where the ordered scene means a scene with its objects successively positioned, or the nearest object has the first position and the farthest object is at the last. Such a scene can be considered as $S(= S_{OBJ}^{NEW})$ with objects $(o_1, o_2, ..., o_N)$. The scene itself is the root and the objects are its different nodes.

The root node resides at the top of the hierarchy for which the level is L_0, whereas the non-root nodes are at different lower levels $(L_1, L_2, ..., L_M)$ based on the camera-object distance information. Objects within a distance d'_{L_1} from the root level L_0 are in level L_1, while objects within a distance d'_{L_2} but greater than d'_{L_1} are in level L_2. Thus, all the objects with an arbitrary distance d satisfying $d'_{L_{l-1}} < d \le d'_{L_l}$ are in level L_l, $l = 1, 2, ..., M$. Objects in a particular level are positioned from left to right in increasing order of camera-object distance, provided they satisfy the threshold condition. Object(s) o_i at level L_l is considered a child(ren) of a node of its previous level L_{l-1}. The scene thus can be viewed to have a tree data structure. Such a data structure is significant and very effective in diverse applications. The hierarchy of different objects in Fig. 3 is shown in Fig. 4.

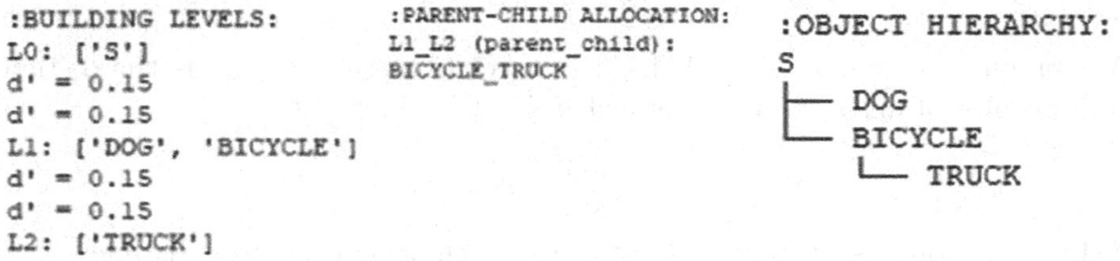

```
:BUILDING LEVELS:          :PARENT-CHILD ALLOCATION:    :OBJECT HIERARCHY:
L0: ['S']                  L1_L2 (parent_child):
d' = 0.15                  BICYCLE_TRUCK                S
d' = 0.15                                               ├── DOG
L1: ['DOG', 'BICYCLE']                                  └── BICYCLE
d' = 0.15                                                   └── TRUCK
d' = 0.15
L2: ['TRUCK']
```

Fig. 4. Hierarchy of different objects.

Note that different objects within certain minor distances may belong to a single level, which can well define the structure of the scene but it is rather difficult to examine or predict the decision for objects at the same level to occupy its positional configuration according to some merit sequence. This problem is significant in many applications, such as in the area of athletics and medical surgery etc. To resolve this problem, we assign weights to different objects using a weight assignment principle as given below.

3.3   Weight Assignment Principle for Objects

The weight assignment principle explicitly computes weights of each object in the hierarchy. The assignment is such that, as the camera-object distance increases, object weight decreases. This means weights of the nearby objects are larger than those of the far away objects. The algorithm for computing the weights for different objects at different levels in the scene is described below.

Let us suppose we have M number of levels $L_1, L_2, ..., L_M$ in the hierarchy. We also assume that L_1 has t_1 objects $o_1, o_2, ..., o_{t_1}$ objects, L_2 has t_2 objects, and so on. The weights of different objects at the ith level, L_i are given by,

$$L_i : w_j = \frac{t_i - (j-1)}{t_1 t_2 ... t_i} \cdot \frac{M - (i-1)}{M+1} \tag{8}$$
$$i = 1, 2, \ldots, M, j = 1, 2, \ldots, t_i.$$

If the camera-object distance of two consecutive objects is same, their weights are also same. Figure 5 shows the weights of different objects in the scene shown in Fig. 3.

```
:OBJECT WEIGHTS:
OBJECT              W
   DOG   0.666667
BICYCLE   0.333333
 TRUCK   0.166667
```

Fig. 5. Weights of different objects.

4   Results and Discussion

Our method for localization of objects in a scene does not need any thresholds. The results of our method along with comparison with other methods are shown below. Experiments involve data generation from the bounding boxes to obtain the number of objects in the scene. The centres of bounding boxes are considered as the data point and so, they form different clusters for different objects, which are subsequently labeled for nonambiguous understanding of objects. Thus, we get labeled bounding boxes for each object in the scene. Also, data is extracted from the vertices of these bounding boxes. These data sets are used for the least square estimate for the localization of objects. Figure 6 shows results of our method on the detection of the number of objects in the scene and the best possible localization for the YOLO output images, where bestness is in the least square sense. We have already provided a comparison between an analytic, heuristic and existing NMS-based methods [3], where we have seen the heuristic-based method is the best. In the present section, we therefore provide the comparison between the least square (LS) and the heuristic-based methods. Table 2 and Fig. 7 provide this comparison (we have considered R^2 Score and Mean Absolute Error (MAE) for quantitative comparison). The comparison shows the LS-based method is somewhat superior to all cases.

For the structural description of a scene, we have already seen that the weight-computing algorithm plays a crucial role in defining the tree objects in the scene and this tree can solve many practical problems in real-life. Such tree structures of the scenes are described in Fig. 8 for a complete understanding.

Precisely speaking, we have carried out the experiments with the same data as in [3]. But unfortunately, for page limitation, the results are provided for a few.

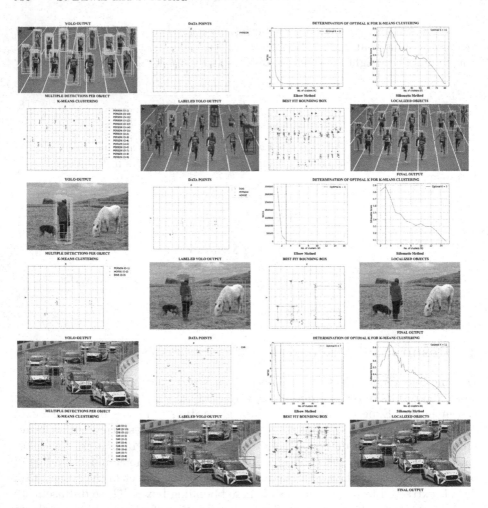

Fig. 6. Detection of the number of objects in the scene and the best possible localization for the YOLO output images.

Table 2. Performance comparison between the two methods

LS-Based Method	Heuristic Method
Absolutely free from thresholds for object detection in a scene.	Thresholds are detected adaptively using regression model for object detection.
Objects are well localized.	Sometimes, the localization is not as superior as to the LS-based method.
No chance of information loss for an object or multiple rectangles.	Chance of information loss for an object or multiple rectangles.

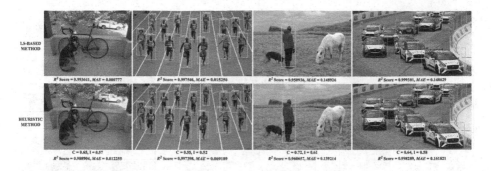

Fig. 7. Localization of objects in arbitrary scenes using the two methods.

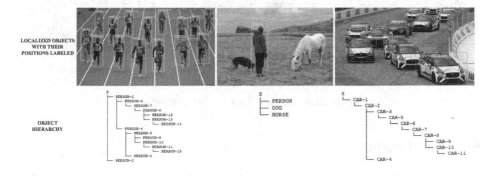

Fig. 8. Tree structure for different scenes.

5   Application of Scene Data Structure

The scene data structure is highly effective in different fields of applications, such as, to make running commentary, make decisions or priority for medical surgery or in civil/defence aircrafts tracking etc. The first application that we have considered is the final scene or the finishing scene for a sprint as shown in Fig. 9a, where our objective is to infer different positions, mainly first, second and third position. The next scene comprises a car/motor racing, Fig. 9b wherein we infer their positions in the final finishing end. The last one indicates the positions of different airplanes, shown in Fig. 9c. It is noted that the scene data structure and the corresponding weights are the key parameters for inference.

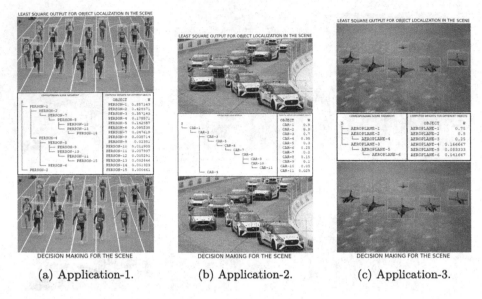

| (a) Application-1. | (b) Application-2. | (c) Application-3. |

Fig. 9. Applications of scene data structure.

6   Conclusion

Localization of objects in YOLO output images, in general, requires thresholds which are arbitrary in nature. This is one of the great drawbacks. Our objective is to develop a threshold free algorithm. Since the localization in our method uses the least square technique, it is threshold independent and so does not need any human interaction. For the structural description of a scene, we find objects' successive positions in the scene by measuring the distance between an object and an observer (the camera). The camera-object distance is computed using the depth map of objects. The data structure might be helpful in faster processing of scenes. Computation of objects' weights from the hierarchy defines the objects' positional configuration which provides merit for making active decisions, such as, positions in the merit list of athletics. Decisions can also be made in the field of medical science and various defence applications. The robustness of the structural description of scenes under various noises will be reported elsewhere.

Acknowledgements. The authors would like to acknowledge Techno India University, West Bengal for its support to this work.

References

1. Moitra, S., Biswas, S.: Object detection in images: a survey. Int. J. Sci. Res. (IJSR) **12**(4), 10–29 (2023)
2. Hosang, J., Benenson, R., Schiele, B.: Learning non-maximum suppression (2017)

3. Moitra, S., Biswas, S.: Human interaction-free object localization in a scene. In: 2023 International Conference on Computer, Electrical & Communication Engineering (ICCECE), pp. 1–5 (2023)
4. Mahendru, K.: How to determine the optimal k for k-means? (2019)
5. Horn, B., Brooks, M.: Shape from Shading, vol. 2 (1989)
6. Ping-Sing, T., Shah, M.: Shape from shading using linear approximation. Image Vis. Comput. **12**(8), 487–498 (1994)
7. Elhabian, S.Y.: Hands on shape from shading (2008)

Quantized Disentangled Representations for Object-Centric Visual Tasks

Daniil Kirilenko[1], Alexandr Korchemnyi[2], Konstantin Smirnov[3],
Alexey K. Kovalev[1,4(✉)], and Aleksandr I. Panov[1,4]

[1] Federal Research Center "Computer Science and Control"
of the Russian Academy of Sciences, Moscow, Russia
{kovalev,panov}@airi.net
[2] Moscow Institute of Physics and Technology, Dolgoprudny, Russia
[3] Innopolis University, Innopolis, Russia
[4] AIRI, Moscow, Russia

Abstract. Recently, the pre-quantization of image features into discrete latent variables has helped to achieve remarkable results in image modeling. In this paper, we propose a method to learn discrete latent variables applied to object-centric tasks. We assign objects to slots which are represented as vectors generated by sampling from non-overlapping sets of low-dimensional discrete variables. We empirically demonstrate that embeddings from the learned discrete latent spaces have the disentanglement property. We use set prediction and object discovery as downstream tasks. The model achieves state-of-the-art results on the CLEVR dataset among a class of object-centric methods for the set prediction task. We also demonstrate manipulation of individual objects in a scene with controllable image generation in the object discovery setting.

Keywords: Disentangled representations · Object-centric methods · Slot quantization

1 Introduction

The well-known problem of neural networks is that they cannot generalize at the human level [6]. The reason for this is thought to be the binding problem, i.e., the inability of modern neural networks to dynamically and flexibly bind the information distributed in them. This problem affects the ability of neural networks to 1) construct meaningful representations of entities from unstructured sensory inputs; 2) maintain the obtained separation of information at a representation level; 3) to reuse these representations of entities for new inferences and predictions. One way to solve this problem is to constrain the neural network to learn disentangled object-centric representations of a scene [1,5].

The disentangled object-centric representation can potentially improve generalization and explainability in many machine learning domains such as structured scene representation and scene generation [20], reinforcement learning [24,25], reasoning [26], and object-centric visual tasks [7,23]. However, with few

P. Maji et al. (Eds.): PReMI 2023, LNCS 14301, pp. 514–522, 2023.
https://doi.org/10.1007/978-3-031-45170-6_53

exceptions [1,5,18], recent research has focused on either object-centric or disentangled representations and has not paid enough attention to combining them.

We propose a model that obtains the disentangled representation of objects by quantizing the corresponding slot representation. We call it Vector Quantized Slot Attention (VQ-SA). The quantization of slots obtained in an unsupervised manner [19] involves two steps. First, we initialize discrete latent spaces each corresponding to the one of generative factors in the data. Second, we initialize each latent space with embeddings by the number of corresponding generative factor values. This two-step quantization allows the model to assign a particular generative factor value to a particular embedding. The proposed object-centric disentangled representation improves the results of the conventional model [19] on object-centric visual tasks, such as set prediction, compared to specialized models [27]. We demonstrate this through extensive experiments on CLEVR [10].

Commonly used disentanglement metrics [8,11] are based on the assumption that disentanglement is achieved at the vector coordinate level, i.e., each coordinate corresponds to the generative factor. In our approach, generative factors are expressed by vectors, and separate coordinates are not interpretable. Thus, such metrics are not suitable, and the problem of quantitative evaluation of disentanglement remains an open question. Nevertheless, we propose DQCF-micro and DQCF-macro methods that qualitatively evaluate the disentanglement in the object discovery task. The original Slot Attention model [19] achieves remarkable results in the object discovery task, but our model allows not only to separate distributed features into object representations, but also to separate these features into representations of their properties.

Our main contributions are: 1) We propose a discrete representation of object-centric embeddings that maps them to latent spaces; 2) Quantization produces a disentangled representation where disentanglement is achieved at the level of latent embeddings; 3) The learned discrete representations allow us to manipulate individual objects in a scene by manipulating embeddings in the latent space; 4) The VQ-SA model achieves state-of-the-art results on the set prediction task on the CLEVR dataset among a class of object-centric methods; 5) We propose DQCF-micro and DQCF-macro methods that qualitatively evaluate the disentanglement of the learned discrete variables represented by vectors.

2   Related Work

Disentanglement. Most approaches to obtaining disentangled representations are based on the Variational Autoencoder (VAE). VAE tends to match the distribution of the latent representation of the input data and the standard Gaussian distribution. Thus, each representation is generated from a continuous distribution and may not reflect the discrete nature of some generative factors. Beta-VAE [8] and Factor-VAE [11] use additional constraints during training to enforce better disentanglement. As an architecturally different approach, Info-GAN [2] maximizes the mutual information between a subset of latent variables and the generated samples to aid disentanglement. There is also work that uses Hyperdimensional Computing [14] to achieve disentanglement [15].

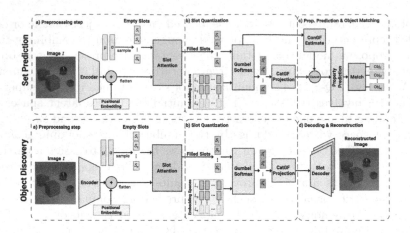

Fig. 1. Overall architecture of the proposed VQ-SA model.

Set Prediction. Although the set structure is natural for many types of data, traditional deep learning models are not inherently suitable for representing sets. There are some approaches that are built to reflect the unordered nature of sets: the Deep Set Prediction Network (DSPN) [27] reflects permutation symmetry by running an inner gradient descent loop that changes a set to encode more similar to the input; iDSPN [28] is an improved version of DSPN with approximate implicit differentiation that provides better optimizations with faster convergence and state-of-the-art performance on CLEVR. Slot Attention [19] and TSPN [16] use set-equivariant self-attention layers to represent the structure of sets.

3   Method

Overview. We obtain quantized disentangled object representations by first discovering objects in an unsupervised manner with Slot Attention [19] and then transforming their representations into desired ones. The idea of slot representation is to map an input (image) to a set of latent variables (slots) instead of a single latent vector [12,22] such that each slot describes a part of an input [3,4,19]. We assign each object to a slot of a dimension d_s and transform each slot into a desired latent representation. We take inspiration from the discrete latent representation proposed in [21]. Instead of using a single discrete latent space to map slots, we use multiple latent spaces with a small embedding dimension d_l ($d_l < d_s$) and the small number of embeddings in each latent space.

The main assumption behind this design choice is that each object is generated by a fixed number of generative factors. Thus, it is possible to represent each object as a combination of embeddings corresponding to values of the generative factors. For the data used, most of the generative factors are discrete, and an appropriate choice of the generative distribution would be the categorical one. We choose the number of categorical distributions equal to that of the generative factors, with the number of possible categories equal to the number of values. The overall architecture of the proposed model VQ-SA is shown in Fig. 1.

The VQ-SA pipeline for the set prediction task consists of three stages. In the preprocessing stage (Fig. 1a), the image I is flattened by Encoder, combined with positional embeddings, and objects are assigned to slots by a slot attention mechanism. In the second stage (Fig. 1b), we perform separate processing of categorical generative factors (CatGF) and continuous generative factors (ConGF). We use slot quantization by multiple discrete latent spaces to represent categorical generative factors and estimate values of continuous generative factors. In the third step (Fig. 1c), we combine both types of generative factors and predict object properties. We match the predicted objects with the ground truth using the Hungarian algorithm [17]. For the object discovery task, we process continuous generative factors similarly to generative factors (Fig. 1b) and use the same decoding strategy as in Slot Attention (Fig. 1d).

Slot Representation. We follow the procedure proposed in [19] to represent an image I as a set of slots $S_i, i = 1 \ldots N$, where the slots are vectors of dimension d_s. Each slot S_i is randomly initialized $S_i = \mu + \sigma \cdot N(0, 1)$ and is used to iteratively assign an object $O_m, m = 1 \ldots M$ or a background from an image in I. The main feature of a slot attention mechanism is that slots compete with each other for the assignment of an object, i.e. the attention coefficients are normalized over the slots.

Slot Quantization. After assigning the objects to the slots, each slot S_i is represented in discrete latent spaces $L_k, k = 1 \ldots K$, K is the number of latent spaces corresponding to the number of categorical generative factors ($K = 4$ for the CLEVR dataset). Each latent space L_k is initialized with embeddings $e_j^k, j = 1 \ldots n_k$ with dimension d_l ($d_l < d_s$). n_k is the number of embeddings in the latent space L_k, i.e. the number of categories of a generative factor. We linearly project a slot S_i to a lower dimension d_l: $S_i' = M S_i$ ($S_i' \in \mathbb{R}^{d_l \times 1}$, $M \in \mathbb{R}^{d_l \times d_s}$, $S_i \in \mathbb{R}^{d_s \times 1}$). Then, we construct a new representation of a slot S' in each discrete latent space L_i by the Gumbel-Softmax trick [9]. First, we compute the similarity between the slot S_i' and each embedding e_j^k in the latent space L_k to get posterior distributions $q(e_j^k | S_i')$ by normalizing with a Softmax function:

$$sim^k = (S_i')^T L_k = (S_i')^T [e_1^k, e_2^k, \ldots, e_{n_k}^k], \quad q(e_j^k | S_i') = \frac{\exp(sim_j^k)}{\sum_j \exp(sim_j^k)}. \quad (1)$$

To get the continuous approximation y^k of the one-hot-encoded representation of the discrete variable e^k we use the Gumbel-Softmax trick with a constant temperature parameter $t = 2$.

$$y_j^k = \frac{\exp\left(\frac{(g_j + \log(q(e_j^k | S_i')))}{t}\right)}{\sum_j \exp\left(\frac{(g_j + \log(q(e_j^k | S_i')))}{t}\right)}, \quad (2)$$

where g denotes random samples from a Gumbel distribution.

The resulting representation $\hat{e}_i^k$ of the slot S_i' in the discrete latent space L_k is a weighted sum of all embeddings $e_j^k \in L_k$ from L_k with weights $y^k = [y_1^k, y_2^k, \ldots, y_{n_k}^k]$: $\hat{e}_i^k = (y^k)^T L_k = [y_1^k, y_2^k, \ldots, y_{n_k}^k]^T [e_1^k, e_2^k, \ldots, e_{n_k}^k]$.

Then, the representations of S_i' from all discrete latent spaces $L_k, k = 1 \ldots K$ are concatenated: $S_i^D = [\hat{e}_i^1, \ldots, \hat{e}_i^K]$. S_i^D is further used as a quantized representation of the slot S_i'. The concatenation can be seen as the construction of a new vector representation S_i^D from separate generative factors $\hat{e}_i^1, \ldots, \hat{e}_i^K$.

Coordinates Representation. Encoding continuous generative factors, such as coordinates, by discrete latent spaces can lead to significant quantization errors. Also, there is no unique way to represent a continuous value by a discrete segment, as the length of a segment could be considered as a hyperparameter.

In the set prediction task, we explicitly split generative factors into categorical (shape, color, etc.) and continuous (x, y, z coordinates). We use slot quantization to represent categorical generative factors and obtain a quantized slot representation S_i^D. We use a two-layer multilayer perceptron (MLP) to predict object coordinates. In the object discovery task, we also process coordinates separately, but in a manner similar to categorical generative factors. The only difference is that we use a single latent space instead of multiple latent spaces.

Encouraging Disentanglement. To facilitate disentanglement between discrete latent spaces, we add the following well-known term to the loss function: $-\sum_k \mathrm{KL}(q(L_k|S')\|p(L_k))$, where $p(L_k)$ is a true prior uniform categorical distribution over a discrete latent space L_k, $q(L_k|S')$ is a posterior categorical distribution over a discrete latent space predicted by a neural network. Using this loss term, we force the posterior distributions over each latent space $q(L_k|S')$ to be independent and closer to the prior distributions, resulting in better disentangling between spaces.

4   Experiments

For all tasks, we first trained the original Slot Attention for 600K iterations and used its encoder and slot attention weights to initialize the corresponding modules of VQ-SA. We also experimented with end-to-end learning, but the model converges more slowly, making it difficult to set up multiple experiments.

Set Prediction. In the set prediction task, the model receives an image as an input and predicts target features as an unordered set of object vectors. The vectors of predicted and target features are matched using the Hungarian algorithm [17]. To quantify the quality of the model, the Average Precision (AP_{thr}) metric with a threshold is used. A detected object is considered a true positive if: 1) the set of its predicted features exactly matches the ground truth, and 2) the position is predicted within a threshold thr relative to the ground truth. The threshold ∞ means that we do not use the distance threshold. As shown in Table 1, VQ-SA significantly improves the results for small thresholds, more than two times for the 0.25 threshold and more than 2.5 times for the 0.125

threshold. Compared to a highly specialized model for the set prediction task, iDSPN [28], VQ-SA shows comparable results for the thresholds greater than one and moderate results for smaller thresholds. The reason for this is that the architecture of our model was not specifically tuned for the set prediction task and could be used for other tasks such as object discovery.

Setup. To ensure correct comparisons with the Slot Attention model, we use the same hyperparameters during training: batch size of 512, three iterations of Slot Attention, and 150,000 training iterations. The model is trained using the Adam [13] optimizer with a learning rate of 0.0004. We also use a learning rate warm-up with an exponential decay schedule after that. The number of slots is 10 as we use CLEVR [10] images with 10 or less objects.

Table 1. Performance on the CLEVR object set prediction task.

Model	AP_∞ (%)	AP_1 (%)	$AP_{0.5}$ (%)	$AP_{0.25}$ (%)	$AP_{0.125}$ (%)
Slot MLP	19.8 ± 1.6	1.4 ± 0.3	0.3 ± 0.2	0.0 ± 0.0	0.0 ± 0.0
DSPN T=30	85.2 ± 4.8	81.1 ± 5.2	47.4 ± 17.6	10.8 ± 9.0	0.6 ± 0.7
DSPN T=10	72.8 ± 2.3	59.2 ± 2.8	39.0 ± 4.4	12.4 ± 2.5	1.3 ± 0.4
Slot Attention	94.3 ± 1.1	86.7 ± 1.4	56.0 ± 3.6	10.8 ± 1.7	0.9 ± 0.2
VQ-SA (ours)	$\mathbf{96.1 \pm 0.4}$	$\mathbf{91.2 \pm 0.5}$	$\mathbf{71.8 \pm 2.3}$	$\mathbf{22.2 \pm 2.1}$	$\mathbf{2.4 \pm 0.2}$
iDSPN	98.8 ± 0.5	98.5 ± 0.6	98.2 ± 0.6	95.8 ± 0.7	76.9 ± 2.5

Object Discovery. In the object discovery task, the model receives a raw image, separates distributed scene features into individual object features, and uses them to reconstruct objects, combining them into the original scene image. The original Slot Attention achieves remarkable results in the object discovery task, while our extension allows the model not only to separate distributed features into object representations, but also to separate distributed features of the objects into representations of their properties. Figure 2 illustrates the ability to manipulate individual objects in a scene with our model: the columns correspond to the changing discrete component of the object representation to the discrete latent variable from the same space.

Setup. We use the same training setup as in the original Slot Attention: the main term in the loss is the mean squared image reconstruction error, the batch size is 64, and the optimizer and learning rate setup are the same as in set prediction. We also use an additional loss term, which aids disentanglement.

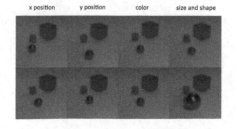

Fig. 2. Manipulation of individual objects in the scene.

Ablation Studies. In the ablation studies (Table 2), we examined the effect of increasing the number of embeddings in each space (to eight and 16) and using only a single common space (cspace) in the supervised set prediction task. These modifications did not affect the performance.

Table 2. Ablation studies results. In parentheses is the total number of embeddings.

Model	AP_∞ (%)	AP_1 (%)	$AP_{0.5}$ (%)	$AP_{0.25}$ (%)	$AP_{0.125}$ (%)
Slot Attention	94.3 ± 1.1	86.7 ± 1.4	56.0 ± 3.6	10.8 ± 1.7	0.9 ± 0.2
VQ-SA (ours)	$\mathbf{96.1 \pm 0.4}$	91.2 ± 0.5	$\mathbf{71.8 \pm 2.3}$	$\mathbf{22.2 \pm 2.1}$	$\mathbf{2.4 \pm 0.2}$
VQ-SA(8, cspace)	41.8 ± 27.5	38.2 ± 26.5	27.6 ± 18.3	7.0 ± 4.4	0.7 ± 0.4
VQ-SA(16, cspace)	83.3 ± 7.7	79.3 ± 7.2	58.8 ± 4.5	15.3 ± 1.2	1.5 ± 0.1
VQ-SA(32, cspace)	92.3 ± 1.4	88.1 ± 1.4	66.0 ± 2.4	17.7 ± 1.6	1.8 ± 0.2
VQ-SA(64, cspace)	94.2 ± 0.6	90.3 ± 0.5	69.2 ± 2.6	19.1 ± 2.2	1.9 ± 0.3
VQ-SA(32)	95.9 ± 0.2	$\mathbf{92.1 \pm 0.4}$	70.4 ± 1.6	18.9 ± 1.4	1.9 ± 0.2
VQ-SA(64)	96.1 ± 0.1	92.1 ± 0.3	69.6 ± 1.1	18.5 ± 1.0	1.8 ± 0.1

5   Disentangled Representations

To qualitatively evaluate the disentanglement of the trained discrete variables, we propose the methods DQCF-micro and DQCF-macro (DQCF stands for Disentanglement Quality of Categorical generative Factors). DQCF-micro evaluates the disentanglement with respect to all other vectors from all discrete spaces, while DQCF-macro evaluates it on the level of discrete spaces. For DQCF-micro, for each set of objects from the validation data, we calculate the frequency of sampling each latent vector as the most similar vector. This statistic with Hungarian matching gives us frequency probabilities of each property with values conditioned on the sampled latent vectors. The results for the first latent space are shown in Fig. 3 (left). A strong proximity of the property values distribution to a uniform distribution means that this vector is not specific to objects with a particular property value and does not contain information that is unique to that property.

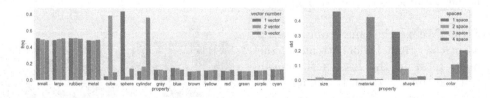

Fig. 3. Left: results of DQCF-micro. Right: results of DQCF-macro.

For DQCF-macro, we calculate the standard deviation over all values of the corresponding properties and obtain the mean over all vectors from the same space. The results are shown in Fig. 3 (right). These values show how much the change in the object properties affects the change in the distribution over a given space. High values indicate that the latent variables from that space contain information specific to that property. It can be seen that the information specific to the property "color" is contained in the vectors of both the third and the fourth space, i.e. they are entangled, while the information about other properties is distributed over vectors of single spaces.

6   Conclusion and Discussion

In this paper, we propose the VQ-SA model, which obtains the disentangled representation of objects by quantizing the corresponding slot representation. This makes it possible to achieve state-of-the-art results among the class of object-centric methods on a set prediction task. We also show that by manipulating the learned discrete representations, we can generate scene objects with the given property. To qualitatively evaluate the disentanglement in the object discovery task, we propose DQCF-micro and DQCF-macro methods.

The important feature of our model is that we use the number of latent discrete spaces equal to the number of generative factors in the data. Therefore, our model cannot be directly applied to data with a different number of generative factors. As with most object-oriented models, we show results on relatively simple data. Modifying our model for more complex scenes, real or simulated, is a promising and challenging task and will be considered in future work.

Acknowledgements. This work was supported by the Russian Science Foundation (Project No. 20-71-10116).

References

1. Burgess, C., et al.: Monet: unsupervised scene decomposition and representation. arXiv (2019)
2. Chen, X., et al.: InfoGAN: interpretable representation learning by information maximizing generative adversarial nets. In: NeurIPS (2016)
3. Engelcke, M., et al.: Genesis: generative scene inference and sampling with object-centric latent representations. arXiv (2020)
4. Engelcke, M., et al.: Genesis-v2: inferring unordered object representations without iterative refinement. In: NeurIPS (2021)
5. Greff, K., et al.: Multi-object representation learning with iterative variational inference. In: ICML (2019)
6. Greff, K., et al.: On the binding problem in artificial neural networks. arXiv (2020)
7. Groth, O., et al.: Shapestacks: learning vision-based physical intuition for generalised object stacking. arXiv (2018)
8. Higgins, I., et al.: Beta-VAE: learning basic visual concepts with a constrained variational framework. In: ICLR (2017)
9. Jang, E., et al.: Categorical reparameterization with Gumbel-softmax. arXiv (2016)
10. Johnson, J., et al.: CLEVR: a diagnostic dataset for compositional language and elementary visual reasoning. In: CVPR (2017)

11. Kim, H., Mnih, A.: Disentangling by factorising. In: ICML (2018)
12. Kingma, D.P., Welling, M.: Auto-encoding variational bayes. arXiv (2013)
13. Kingma, D.P., et al.: Adam: a method for stochastic optimization. In: ICLR (2015)
14. Kleyko, D., et al.: A survey on hyperdimensional computing aka vector symbolic architectures, Part I: Models and data transformations. arXiv (2021)
15. Korchemnyi, A., et al.: Symbolic disentangled representations in hyperdimensional latent space. In: ICLR 2023 NeSy-GeMs Workshop (2023)
16. Kosiorek, A.R., et al.: Conditional set generation with transformers. arXiv (2020)
17. Kuhn, H.W.: The Hungarian method for the assignment problem. Nav. Res. Logist. Q. **2**(1–2), 83–97 (1955)
18. Li, N., et al.: Learning object-centric representations of multi-object scenes from multiple views. In: NeurIPS (2020)
19. Locatello, F., et al.: Object-centric learning with slot attention. arXiv (2020)
20. Matsumori, S., et al.: Unified questioner transformer for descriptive question generation in goal-oriented visual dialogue. In: ICCV (2021)
21. van den Oord, A., et al.: Neural discrete representation learning. In: NeurIPS (2017)
22. Rezende, D.J., et al.: Stochastic back-propagation and variational inference in deep latent Gaussian models. arXiv (2014)
23. Singh, G., et al.: Illiterate Dall-e learns to compose. arXiv (2021)
24. Sun, C., et al.: Stochastic prediction of multi-agent interactions from partial observations. arXiv (2019)
25. Watters, N., et al.: Cobra: data-efficient model-based RL through unsupervised object discovery and curiosity-driven exploration. arXiv (2019)
26. Yang, J., et al.: Object-centric diagnosis of visual reasoning. arXiv (2020)
27. Zhang, Y., et al.: Deep set prediction networks. In: NeurIPS (2019)
28. Zhang, Y., et al.: Multiset-equivariant set prediction with approximate implicit differentiation. In: ICLR (2022)

RGB-D Fusion Based on Fuzzy Optimization for Salient Object Detection

Sudipta Bhuyan$^{(\boxtimes)}$, Debashis Sen , and Sankha Deb

Indian Institute of Technology, Kharagpur, Kharagpur 721302, West Bengal, India
sudiptabhuyan1@gmail.com, dsen@ece.iitkgp.ac.in,
sankha.deb@mech.iitkgp.ac.in

Abstract. The objective of RGB-D salient object detection is to identify visually distinct objects from both depth and RGB images. The fusion of depth information with RGB has gained significant research attention in this field since salient objects can appear in one or more modalities. This paper proposes a fusion scheme for detecting multiple salient objects from RGB-D data by integrating multiple prior maps using a fuzzy optimization framework. First, We generate several prior maps, which are considered to be fuzzy. A fuzzy divergence measure is then utilized to minimize the discrepancies between the different prior maps during the fusion process, ultimately maximizing the number of detected salient objects in the final fused map. Our proposed framework estimates the optimal fuzzy membership parameters to address the boundary ambiguity between salient regions and non-salient backgrounds. Experimental results on different databases demonstrate the efficiency of the proposed method compared to existing RGB-D salient object detection methods.

Keywords: RGB-D fusion · Salient object detection · Fuzzy optimization

1 Introduction

Salient object detection (SOD) is a crucial process that automatically identifies the most visually appealing object in an image. Its utility extends to numerous intelligent tasks, including robotic applications, object pose estimation, and robot task planning. Numerous studies have been conducted on salient object detection, however, most of them focus on color images. The algorithms based on color images show encouraging results. However, their performance tends to decline in the presence of complex background and when an object bears a resemblance to the background. In these scenarios, depth information can be useful to distinguish the object from the background as depth data provides shape, and edge information and is more robust to light variation.

The existing state-of-the-art (SOTA) models on RGB-D SOD can be categorized as 1) Input or early fusion 2) Mid-level fusion 3) Late fusion. Early fusion techniques [1–3] incorporate depth data as an additional channel, which is combined with RGB channels to extract and process RGB and depth features together throughout the model. In middle fusion techniques [4,5], first, features are extracted separately from RGB and depth streams and then fused using a dedicated fusion module at each stage to obtain

© The Author(s), under exclusive license to Springer Nature Switzerland AG 2023
P. Maji et al. (Eds.): PReMI 2023, LNCS 14301, pp. 523–531, 2023.
https://doi.org/10.1007/978-3-031-45170-6_54

a final salient object map. Late fusion techniques [6–8] involve processing RGB and depth data separately to produce a prediction map for each modality, which are then fused to obtain a final SOD map. The fusion of inputs, features and prediction maps in early and late fusion techniques are performed by directly concatenating them or taking addition or multiplication (element-wise) of generated predictions by two modalities, thus inadequate for complementary information fusion [4]. In addition, all these data-hungry CNN based techniques require a huge number of data pairs for training in order to achieve satisfactory performance. These deep learning-based RGB-D fusion models are typically trained on RGB-D benchmark datasets, and while they perform very well on similar sets of images, they often fail to achieve satisfactory performance on arbitrary images. In real world scenarios, like industrial environments, it is not always possible to obtain sufficient image pairs for training. Additionally, these models are susceptible to over-fitting on the trained datasets, which can be problematic.

In this paper, we propose a fuzzy optimization based decision level fusion technique for the detection of multiple salient objects using RGB-D data. A set of prior maps generated from the RGB and depth data are fused through the proposed framework as shown in Fig. 1. Our technique has an upper hand as compared to deep networks when data is scarce, as these networks require a high volume of data for training. Our fusion method will adapt to concurrence between the individual prior maps, in contrast to the over-fitting that can occur in the fusion modules of deep RGB-D methods. The prior maps obtained from individual processing of RGB and depth data usually contain imprecise boundaries, that is, they lack a clear distinction between the object region and its background. Fuzzy set theory is commonly utilized to represent and model the uncertainty that arises from indistinct region boundaries [9]. This approach allows for more flexible and accurate handling of imprecise information. Inspired by this, to address the ambiguity that arises at region boundaries, we treat each prior map as a fuzzy map and represent it using multiple Gaussian membership functions with varying parameters. A swarm evolutionary based optimization technique estimates the optimum parameters for these membership functions using fuzzy divergence [9] as an optimization function. The fuzzy divergence is well known to model the discrepancy between fuzzy sets. Hence, we adopt the fuzzy divergence as an optimization function in our approach to reduce the disagreement in selecting the salient regions between the different input prior maps and the output fused map. This enables us to effectively fuse the input maps while preserving the salient regions and minimizing any discrepancies between them. The estimated parameters along with the input prior maps are fed into a fuzzy inference system to obtain the fused salient object map. The proposed fusion method's efficacy and efficiency in detecting multiple salient regions are demonstrated through both qualitative and quantitative evaluations on publicly available databases. Our model is the first of its kind that handles boundary ambiguities while fusing the prior maps for the SOD task.

2   The Proposed RGB-D Fusion Method for Salient Object Detection

The block diagram of our proposed RGB-D fusion for salient object detection is depicted in Fig. 1. After acquiring RGB and depth data from the RGB-D sensor, prediction maps from RGB (RGB prediction map) and depth data (depth prediction map) are generated. To handle true negative and false positive regions in the predicted maps, we generate additional three maps like RGB distance map, depth distance map and depth ratio map. We consider the obtained maps as fuzzy sets and integrate them based on some predefined fuzzy rules. For fuzzification of the prior maps, we use the Gaussian membership function whose parameters are optimized using the fuzzy divergence as an optimization function. Then, the fuzzified maps are combined using predefined fuzzy if-then rules and defuzzified to get the final fused salient map.

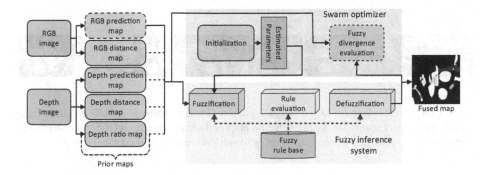

Fig. 1. Block diagram of the proposed fusion technique

2.1 Generation of Prior Maps

In this section, we describe the prediction map generation from the RGB and depth data along the lines of [10] to obtain multiple salient regions. In addition, we generate another three prior maps taking into account the area ratio, spatial extend, and depth ratio to reduce the detected false negative regions.

Generation of Prediction Maps. First, we conduct proto-object partitioning taking into account uniformity of color (for RGB image) and depth data (for depth image) between different image locations to make the generated map local structure-aware. Each proto-partition represents a candidate object region in the image, where objects are composed of one or more proto-partitions. To proto-partition an input image appropriately into uniform regions, we employ the gPb-owt-ucm [11] procedure. The gPb-owt-ucm method uses a combination of the globalized boundary probability-based contour detector and the oriented watershed transform to produce an ultrametric contour map (UCM) in the form of real values for an image.

The UCM is first thresholded to produce a boundary map containing a set of closed boundaries. From this boundary map, regions that are too small are removed, and the resulting map is converted into a set of proto-partition, $P_i(i = 1, \ldots, n)$. Adopting this same procedure, we generate proto-partitions for both RGB and depth images. The next step involves creating operation masks [10] using the image proto-partition that was obtained earlier. The operation masks are designed to be adaptable to the local region around each pixel in the image. To obtain prediction maps, center-surround operations are applied at multiple scales around each pixel of the input image using the generated masks. Then, prediction maps obtained considering all the scales are normalized and added to generate a prediction map for an image. The same procedure is adopted for both RGB and depth images. Prediction maps with multiple salient regions are obtained as shown in Fig. 2(c) and (d) from RGB and depth images, respectively. It can be observed in Fig. 2(c) and (d) that few regions are detected in the RGB prediction map but not in the depth prediction map and vice versa. However, in the fused map, all the regions are detected properly.

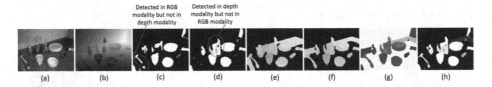

Fig. 2. (a) Original image (b) Depth image (c) detected salient regions in RGB prediction map (d) detected salient regions in depth prediction map(e) distance map from RGB proto-partitions (f) distance map from depth proto-partitions (g) depth ratio map (h) Fused salient map

Generation of Distance Map in RGB and Distance Map in Depth. To eliminate true negative and false positive regions from the predicted map, a weight measure is assigned to each proto-partition (of RGB and depth) based on its location or distance from the boundary of the image as well as based on its extend or area. Usually, typical characteristics of the background include a high area ratio and a widespread presence close to the border of the image [12]. In contrast, salient regions are characterized by a small area ratio, a small extent, high variance and a high probability of being located in the center of the image. Considering all these factors, we adopt a measure similar to [12] to assess the location of a proto-partition within an image. Furthermore, we suggest incorporating the spatial coverage of each proto-partition in computing its weight. This is due to the fact that the distance between the center pixel and the image content is a crucial determinant in determining the informative value of a pixel [13]. For a proto-partition P_i, the position is defined as:

$$R(P_i) = 1 - (min_j \|\bar{p}_i, c_j\| / d_c) \tag{1}$$

where p_i is the center position of proto-partition P_i, c_j corner positions of the image and d_c represents the distance from the image center to its corners. The value of R will be high for objects located near the corners of the image and low for objects positioned closer to the center of the image. Similarly, for a proto-partition P_i, the spatial extend measure is defined as [10]: Let the leftmost and rightmost values for a proto-partition P_i be $x_l^{P_i}, x_r^{P_i}, y_l^{P_i}, y_r^{P_i}$. Let the measure of the extent of a proto-partition P_i with reference to its center pixel (x_c, y_c) be denoted as:

$$D_i = \max[\left|x_c - x_l^{P_i}\right|, \left|x_c - x_r^{P_i}\right|] + \max[\left|y_c - y_l^{P_i}\right|, \left|y_c - y_r^{P_i}\right|] / (M + N) \tag{2}$$

By normalizing D_i using M+N, which represents the maximum extent of the image, we can ensure that D_i lies within the range [0, 1]. D_i will have larger values for smaller image partitions and smaller values for larger image partitions. Now, the distance measure for a proto-partition D_{Pi} is defined as:

$$D_{Pi} = 1 - exp(-(R + D_i)^2) \tag{3}$$

This distance measure effectively assigns weight to a proto-partition P_i based on its distance from the image boundary and its spatial extent. It effectively assigns a smaller weight to background regions and a comparatively larger weight to object regions.

It is very unlikely that a proto-partition attached to the corner of an image belongs to the salient region. Similarly, if a proto-partition is heavily connected to the image boundary, its probability of being background is higher. Considering these notions, if a proto-partition contains an image corner, a zero weight is assigned to it. The boundary ratio measure is used to evaluate the extent to which a proto-partition is connected to the image border. This ratio is calculated by dividing the perimeter of the region that is in contact with the image boundary by the total perimeter of the region [14]. Zero weight is assigned to a proto-partition if its boundary ratio is greater than 0.3. The distance maps obtained from RGB and depth are shown in Fig. 2(e) and (f).

Generation of Depth Ratio Map. Usually salient regions are considered to have a small area with high variance where as background regions are interpreted to have high area and high depth value. Considering this notion we propose a measure called the depth ratio of a proto-partition P_i which is defined as:

$$D_{ratio}(P_i) = (d_{max} - d_{min})/(D_{max} - D_{min}) \tag{4}$$

where d_{max} and d_{min} indicate maximum and minimum depth values of a proto-partition P_i. D_{max} and D_{min} are maximum and minimum depth values in the whole image, respectively. Here, the high value of $(d_{max} - d_{min})$ indicates more probability of a proto-partition to be the background. The generated depth ratio map is shown in Fig. 2(g).

2.2 Fused Salient Map Generation via Fusion of Prior Maps in a Fuzzy Framework

Through the above-mentioned process, we obtain a set of prior maps corresponding to each input RGB-D data. We treated each prior map as a fuzzy set and utilized fuzzy divergence to handle the boundary ambiguities while fusing them to generate a fused salient map. The Mamdani fuzzy inference system [15], in conjunction with the Cuckoo search optimization method [16], is employed to generate the fused salient map.

To integrate different maps, first, a set of fuzzy if-then rules (refer Table 1) are defined to classify the obtained regions in different maps either as a salient object or non-salient object region. For the fuzzification of prior maps, instead of using a membership function with fixed parameters, we optimize the parameters for each prior map to produce a fused map with minimum discrepancy with the prior maps. Here, we select a Gaussian function as a membership function whose mean and standard deviation are optimized. Fuzzification of a prior map I is given as:

$$\mu_{I_k}(x,y) = exp\left(-(I(x,y) - m_{I_k})^2/2\sigma_{I_k}^2\right) \tag{5}$$

where, $k \in \{Lower, Intmed, Higher\}$, denotes three different regions (background, intermediate and object region) based on the saliency value. The value of $m_{I_{Lower}}$ and $m_{I_{Higher}}$ is considered as 0 and 1, respectively. Therefore, corresponding to a prior map I, four parameters $\{m_{I_{Intmed}}, \sigma_{I_{Lower}}, \sigma_{I_{Intmed}}, \sigma_{I_{Higher}}\}$ and considering all the five prior maps and one fused map, 24 parameters are to be optimized. After generating a set of 24 parameters from the optimization framework, the obtained prior maps are fused using a predefined fuzzy if-then rule to obtain a rule strength. A consequence of each rule is obtained by combining rule strength with the output membership function $\mu_{O_k}(x,y)$ which takes the same form as Eq. 5. The consequences of each rule are combined to generate an output distribution which is considered as intermediate map. The intermediate map F_i corresponds to the i_{th} set of 24 parameters. The i_{th} intermediate map for which the optimization function value (fuzzy divergence) is minimum, that means, the disagreement between each prior map and the intermediate map F_i is minimum, that is considered as optimum one and the fused salient map O. The objective function for n number of prior maps with MN elements is defined as:

$$f_{obj}(I,F) = \sum_n d[I_n, F_i] = d[I_1, F_i] + d[I_2, F_i] + d[I_3, F_i] + d[I_4, F_i] + d[I_5, F_i] \tag{6}$$

where, the fuzzy divergence $d(I_n, F_i)$ between two fuzzy sets I_n and F_i is given by:

$$d(I_n, F_i) = \sum_{j=1}^{MN} \left[\mu_{I_n}(x_j)ln\{\mu_{I_n}(x_j)/\mu_{F_i}(x_j)\} + (1 - \mu_{I_n}(x_j))ln\{(1 - \mu_{I_n}(x_j))/(1 - \mu_{F_i}(x_j))\}\right]$$

Table 1. Fuzzy if-then rules for fusion

M1	M2	M3	M4	M5	Out
Higher	Higher	Higher	Higher	Lower	Higher
Lower	Higher	Lower	Lower	Higher	Lower
Higher	Lower	Lower	Lower	Higher	Lower
Lower	Higher	Higher	Higher	Lower	Higher
Higher	Lower	Higher	Higher	Lower	Higher
Intmed	Intmed	Higher	Higher	Lower	Higher
Higher	Higher	–	–	–	Higher
Lower	Lower	–	–	–	Lower

M1: RGB prediction map
M2: depth prediction map
M3: RGB distance map
M4: depth distance map
M5: depth ratio map
Out: Output fused map
- : Maps are not considered
Higher indicates salient pixel,
lower indicates non salient pixel.

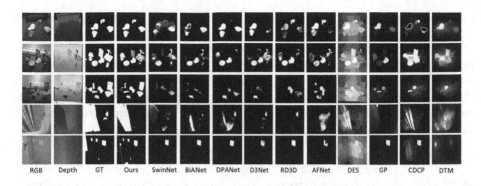

| RGB | Depth | GT | Ours | SwinNet | BiANet | DPANet | D3Net | RD3D | AFNet | DES | GP | CDCP | DTM |

Fig. 3. Qualitative comparison of proposed method with different state-of-the-art algorithms.

Table 2. Comparison of our proposed method with SOTA methods on multiple object databases (GIT and RGB-D scene). Best three results are indicated in red, green and blue, resp.

Classification method→		Deep learning							Classical methods			
Database	Measures	Proposed fusion	AFNet 2019	DPANet 2020	D3Net 2020	ASIF 2020	RD3D 2021	BiANet 2021	SwinNet 2022	DES 2014	GP 2015	CDCP 2017	DTM 2019
GIT	$AUC\uparrow$	0.7642	0.7082	0.7204	0.7169	0.6396	0.7414	0.6897	0.7302	0.7000	0.6361	0.7408	0.7055
	$S_\alpha\uparrow$	0.5698	0.4850	0.5456	0.5290	0.4988	0.5445	0.5296	0.5106	0.4767	0.4796	0.5425	0.5010
	$F\uparrow$	0.5219	0.3951	0.4878	0.4550	0.3746	0.4931	0.4509	0.4192	0.2245	0.4037	0.4433	0.3997
	$F_w^\beta\uparrow$	0.4225	0.2553	0.3532	0.3279	0.2812	0.3540	0.3368	0.3337	0.2652	0.2428	0.3318	0.2507
	$E_\phi\uparrow$	0.6829	0.6381	0.6382	0.6674	0.6222	0.6440	0.6322	0.6159	0.4803	0.6074	0.6671	0.6568
RGB-D scene	$AUC\uparrow$	0.8965	0.8793	0.8557	0.8532	0.7671	0.8565	0.7941	0.8230	0.8357	0.7353	0.8425	0.8417
	$S_\alpha\uparrow$	0.7395	0.6990	0.7004	0.6673	0.6277	0.6704	0.6335	0.5785	0.5242	0.3942	0.5312	0.6049
	$F\uparrow$	0.6713	0.6047	0.7085	0.7330	0.6625	0.6817	0.6868	0.5162	0.4245	0.5575	0.5729	0.5175
	$F_w^\beta\uparrow$	0.5645	0.6047	0.6130	0.5560	0.5293	0.5545	0.5140	0.3865	0.2752	0.3555	0.4989	0.3200
	$E_\phi\uparrow$	0.7987	0.8138	0.7870	0.7889	0.7179	0.7768	0.7345	0.6415	0.6328	0.7265	0.8016	0.7239

3 Evaluation of Proposed RGB-D Fusion Method for Multiple SOD

For the evaluation of our proposed RGB-D fusion method for multiple salient object detection, we choose images with multiple objects. We selected GIT [17] and RGB-D scenes database [18] as these contain indoor images with multiple salient objects. The effectiveness of the proposed method is evaluated using widely used measures, the Area under Receiver Operating Characteristic (AUC), S-measure (S_α) [19], F-measure (F), weighted F-measure (F_w^β) and E-measure (E_ϕ) [20]. For comparison, eleven (seven deep learning and four classical) recent state-of-the-art methods like DTM [21], DES [22], CDCP [23], GP [24], AFNet [6], DPANet [25], ASIFNet [26], D3Net [1], RD3D [27], BiANet [28] and SwinNet [29] with publicly available implementation codes are chosen. For deep learning based models, results are generated using the pre-trained model provided by the authors for RGB-D SOD task.

The quantitative comparison results on multiple object databases based on the five evaluation measures are presented in Table 2. As depicted in Table 2, our proposed method ranks as best compared to the state-of-the-art methods in terms of all the evaluation measures for the GIT database and ranks among the top three in RGB-D scenes database, except for the *F* measure.

Figure 3 shows the visual comparison between our proposed method and state-of-the-art RGB-D SOD methods. The qualitative result indicates the outperformance of our method in detecting all the salient objects present in an image. In addition, our method results in a complete structure and preserves object boundaries. All the quantitative and qualitative results validate the efficiency and effectiveness of the proposed method.

4 Conclusion

This paper proposes a novel RGB-D fusion method for SOD tasks based on a fuzzy optimization concept. The experimental results show the efficiency of our method in detecting multiple salient objects as compared to SOTA methods.

References

1. Fan, D.-P., Lin, Z., Zhang, Z., Zhu, M., Cheng, M.-M.: Rethinking RGB-D salient object detection: models, data sets, and large-scale benchmarks. IEEE TNNLS **32**(5), 2075–2089 (2020)
2. Fu, K., Fan, D.-P., Ji, G.-P., Zhao, Q.: JL-DCF: joint learning and densely-cooperative fusion framework for RGB-D salient object detection. In: CVPR, pp. 3052–3062. IEEE (2020)
3. Zhao, X., Zhang, L., Pang, Y., Lu, H., Zhang, L.: A single stream network for robust and real-time RGB-D salient object detection. In: Vedaldi, A., Bischof, H., Brox, T., Frahm, J.-M. (eds.) ECCV 2020. LNCS, vol. 12367, pp. 646–662. Springer, Cham (2020). https://doi.org/10.1007/978-3-030-58542-6_39
4. Chen, H., Li, Y.-F., Su, D.: Attention-aware cross-modal cross-level fusion network for RGB-D salient object detection. In: IROS, pp. 6821–6826. IEEE (2018)
5. Zhao, J.-X., Cao, Y., Fan, D.-P., Cheng, M.-M., Li, X.-Y., Zhang, L.: Contrast prior and fluid pyramid integration for RGBD salient object detection. In: CVPR, pp. 3927–3936. IEEE (2019)
6. Wang, N., Gong, X.: Adaptive fusion for RGB-D salient object detection. IEEE Access **7**, 55 277–55 284 (2019)
7. Peng, H., Li, B., Xiong, W., Hu, W., Ji, R.: RGBD salient object detection: a benchmark and algorithms. In: Fleet, D., Pajdla, T., Schiele, B., Tuytelaars, T. (eds.) ECCV 2014. LNCS, vol. 8691, pp. 92–109. Springer, Cham (2014). https://doi.org/10.1007/978-3-319-10578-9_7
8. Ding, Y., Liu, Z., Huang, M., Shi, R., Wang, X.: Depth-aware saliency detection using convolutional neural networks. J. Vis. Commun. Image Represent. **61**, 1–9 (2019)
9. Bhandari, D., Pal, N.R.: Some new information measures for fuzzy sets. Inf. Sci. **67**(3), 209–228 (1993)
10. Bhuyan, S., Sen, D., Deb, S.: Structure-aware multiple salient region detection and localization for autonomous robotic manipulation. IET Image Process. **16**, 1135–1161 (2022)
11. Arbelaez, P., Maire, M., Fowlkes, C., Malik, J.: Contour detection and hierarchical image segmentation. IEEE Trans. PAMI **33**(5), 898–916 (2010)
12. Jiang, L., Koch, A., Zell, A.: Salient regions detection for indoor robots using RGB-D data. In: ICRA, pp. 1323–1328. IEEE (2015)
13. Yan, Q., Xu, L., Shi, J., Jia, J.: Hierarchical saliency detection. In: CVPR, pp. 1155–1162. IEEE (2013)

14. Zhou, Y., Mao, A., Huo, S., Lei, J., Kung, S.-Y.: Salient object detection via fuzzy theory and object-level enhancement. IEEE Trans. Multimed. **21**(1), 74–85 (2018)
15. Mamdani, E.H., Assilian, S.: An experiment in linguistic synthesis with a fuzzy logic controller. Int. J. Man-Mach. Stud. **7**(1), 1–13 (1975)
16. Yang, X.-S., Deb, S.: Engineering optimisation by cuckoo search. Int. J. Math. Modell. Numer. Optim. **1**(4), 330–343 (2010)
17. Ciptadi, A., Hermans, T., Rehg, J.M.: An in depth view of saliency. Georgia Institute of Technology (2013)
18. Lai, K., Bo, L., Ren, X., Fox, D.: A large-scale hierarchical multi-view RGB-D object dataset. In: ICRA, pp. 1817–1824. IEEE (2011)
19. Fan, D.-P., Cheng, M.-M., Liu, Y., Li, T., Borji, A.: Structure-measure: a new way to evaluate foreground maps. In: ICCV, pp. 4548–4557. IEEE (2017)
20. Fan, D.-P., Gong, C., Cao, Y., Ren, B., Cheng, M.-M., Borji, A.: Enhanced-alignment measure for binary foreground map evaluation. In: IJCAI, pp. 698–704 (2018)
21. Cong, R., Lei, J., Fu, H., Hou, J., Huang, Q., Kwong, S.: Going from RGB to RGBD saliency: a depth-guided transformation model. IEEE Trans. Cybern. **50**, 3627–3639 (2019)
22. Cheng, Y., Fu, H., Wei, X., Xiao, J., Cao, X.: Depth enhanced saliency detection method. In: ICIMCS, pp. 23–27 (2014)
23. Zhu, C., Li, G., Wang, W., Wang, R.: An innovative salient object detection using center-dark channel prior. In: ICCV Workshops, pp. 1509–1515. IEEE (2017)
24. Ren, J., Gong, X., Yu, L., Zhou, W., Ying Yang, M.: Exploiting global priors for RGB-D saliency detection. In: CVPR, pp. 25–32. IEEE (2015)
25. Chen, Z., Cong, R., Xu, Q., Huang, Q.: DPANet: depth potentiality-aware gated attention network for RGB-D salient object detection. IEEE TIP **30**, 7012–7024 (2020)
26. Li, C., et al.: ASIF-Net: attention steered interweave fusion network for RGB-D salient object detection. IEEE Trans. Cybern. **51**(1), 88–100 (2020)
27. Chen, Q., Liu, Z., Zhang, Y., Fu, K., Zhao, Q., Du, H.: RGB-D salient object detection via 3D convolutional neural networks. AAAI AI **35**(2), 1063–1071 (2021)
28. Zhang, Z., Lin, Z., Xu, J., Jin, W.-D., Lu, S.-P., Fan, D.-P.: Bilateral attention network for RGB-D salient object detection. IEEE TIP **30**, 1949–1961 (2021)
29. Liu, Z., Tan, Y., He, Q., Xiao, Y.: SwinNet: swin transformer drives edge-aware RGB-D and RGB-T salient object detection. IEEE TCSVT **32**(7), 4486–4497 (2021)

AfforDrive: Detection of Drivable Area for Autonomous Vehicles

Mahek Jain, Guruprasad Kamat, Rochan Bachari, Vinayak A. Belludi, Dikshit Hegde[✉], and Ujwala Patil

KLE Technological University, Vidyanagar, Hubballi 580031, Karnataka, India
dikshithegde@gmail.com, ujwalapatil@kletech.ac.in

Abstract. In this paper, we propose "AfforDrive": a novel approach for detecting drivable surfaces using affordance segmentation for autonomous vehicles. Affordance segmentation is the detection of potential regions for different sets of actions in the surrounding area. The research advancement in sensor technology has paved the way for a new paradigm in achieving higher levels of autonomy in intelligent mobility. However, sensor-based solutions demand in-situ measurements and skilled personnel for data capture and analysis. To address this, we propose a vision-based pipeline, AfforDrive, a model to generate affordance toward achieving a higher level of autonomy. We combine depth information and surface normals as midlevel cues along with RGB images to generate an affordance map. We infer the highest probable area for driving from the affordance map and facilitate the ADAS to achieve safe and intelligent mobility. We also extend our framework to perform vehicle dodging to maneuver around the static/dynamic objects in the space of affordance. This framework finds potential applications in intelligent mobility and drone-based applications. We demonstrate the results of the proposed methodology using Cityscapes dataset, and KITTI-Dataset. Additionally, we also perform an ablation study to generate affordance segmentation using different state of art techniques.

Keywords: Affordance segmentation · Depth image · Surface normals

1 Introduction

Intelligent mobility has become the need of the hour in modern lifestyle. Advanced Driver Assistance Systems (ADAS) are one of the potential research and development areas in the automobile industry. The ongoing trend in the automobile industry revolves around safe and comfortable transportation. As a result, finding drivable surfaces has become vital in the fields of autonomous driving in both urban and rural settings. Inclement weather, such as rain, fog, varying topography, and low light conditions, makes it harder to locate the drivable area. Typically multi-sensor data is used to perceive and infer the surrounding area more correctly and accurately. Typically LIDAR, RADAR, and camera are deployed to perceive the information about the scene at different levels. However,

© The Author(s), under exclusive license to Springer Nature Switzerland AG 2023
P. Maji et al. (Eds.): PReMI 2023, LNCS 14301, pp. 532–539, 2023.
https://doi.org/10.1007/978-3-031-45170-6_55

multi-sensor data capture is less feasible as it demands in situ measurements and trained personnel. With the availability of processing infrastructure, computer vision-based deep learning frameworks are promising alternatives for scene perception in the autonomous transportation domain [6]. From the literature [12] we observe the generation of an affordance map aids in robotic functionality by detecting suitable areas to sit, walk, sleep, climb, etc. We provide a deep-learning system in this paper to discover drivable locations to facilitate autonomous driving as we strive towards a higher level of autonomy.

Generation of affordance provides a solution for several applications such as robot navigation, path planning [4], and autonomous driving [5] and it demands that the spatial (and temporal) relationships between the scene's objects be preserved. Mid-level visual cues are commonly used in current research [12] to help subjects remember the spatial (and temporal) relationships between objects in a scene. The authors of [7] address the role of mid-level cues in comprehending the geometry of the scene, including depth maps, semantic cues, and occlusion maps. The authors in [8] use a neural network-based road-detecting approach. Authors in [9] proposed the detection of roads, drivable area, and highway lane under unfavorable conditions based on the paradigm of image enhancement.

However, these methods underperform when provided with an unstructured road with no lane markings as they fail to detect the lanes and thus the drivable surface. These methods also fail to detect the drivable surface if there are water spots or shadow spots on the road. To do this [13], the authors created a road map detection method based on semantic segmentation to locate open driving spaces for autonomous vehicles. A transfer learning-based Hybrid-SRD technique for road detection are discussed in [2]. However, the frameworks mentioned lack a robust dataset with other vehicles or objects in the way, and fail to foresee a drivable surface.

To address this, we propose a pipeline to detect drivable surfaces for autonomous vehicles using computer vision based deep learning technique. We generate depth images and surface normals as mid-level cues from the RGB images and use an auto-encoder model to generate an affordance map to detect the drivable surface. Towards this, our contributions are:

- We propose a pipeline to generate affordance for the drivable surface,
    - Generate an affordance map to detect the highest probale area for safe drive.
    - Generate surface normals and depth map to provide additional clue along with RGB information to generate affordance map.
- To help drivers anticipate the road ahead and the obstacle in front of their ego car, we provide a unique architecture for obstacle dodging.
- We illustrate and evaluate the performance of the suggested pipeline in comparison to cutting-edge affordance segmentation techniques.
    - We train and demonstrate the results of proposed pipeline on the Cityscapes dataset
    - We demonstrate the generalisability of our model over the KITTI dataset.

2   AfforDrive

In this section, we discuss the proposed pipeline, AfforDrive, for detecting the drivable area in the dynamic and static road scenario. In this pipeline we concatenate mid-level cues like depth images, surface normals of a given RGB image to retain spatial and temporal relation among the objects and the scene. We foresee to infer shape, texture, orientation, and distance of various objects in the scene towards the complete understanding of the scene. This enables us to generate a drivable affordance map. Along with this, we present object dodging to assist the driver with a vague sense of direction of the road, by considering the borderline of drivable surface and detecting the midpoint of it throughout the drivable surface. In what follows we discuss the modules of the proposed pipeline in detail (Fig. 1).

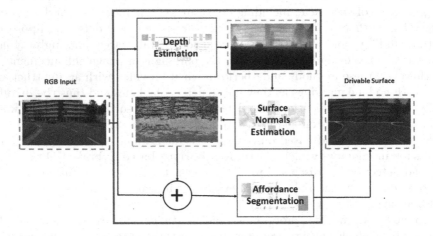

Fig. 1. Proposed model of drivable surface estimation. The RGB image along with, depth and surface normals facilitate to detect drivable area in the road scene.

Depth Estimation: We use depth information of the scene as one of the cue and have used the state of art LeRes architecture [15] to estimate the depth. LeRes is a pre-trained model. Unlike in typical residual architecture, LeRes uses residual blocks to allow the network to learn residual functions and facilitate the network to learn deeper features and overcomes the problem of vanishing gradient.

The LeRes monocular depth estimation model uses a mathematical loss function to measure the error between the predicted depth map and the ground truth depth map. Typically, it uses the mean absolute error (MAE) between the predicted depth map D and the ground truth depth map G:

$$Loss(D, G) = \frac{1}{N} \sum_{i=1}^{N} |D_i - G_i| \qquad (1)$$

where N is the maximum number of pixels in the depth map
  where i is the number of pixels in the depth map.
   The MAE loss is a commonly used loss function in computer vision tasks like depth estimation because it is less sensitive to outliers.

Surface Normals Estimation: Surface normals estimated from depth images play a significant role in providing the normals information about the image to enhance the judgement of the surface that can be driven on.
   In Algorithm 1:

- The top vector (t) is defined as $[i, j-1, \dim[j-1, i, 0]]$.
- The bottom vector (f) is defined as $[i-1, j, \dim[j, i-1, 0]]$.
- The center vector (c) is defined as $[i, j, \dim[j, i, 0]]$.

The cross product of the vectors (f-c) and (t-c) is calculated to obtain the surface normal at each pixel location (i, j). The resulting normal vector is then normalized to obtain a unit normal vector, which is stored in the output array. The algorithm from [3] involved in obtaining surface normals from depth image is as follows:

Algorithm 1 An Algorithm to obtain Surface normals using Depth image

---

Require: *Depthimage* ← *depth*
Ensure: *Surfacenormals* ← *Normals*
   Get the height *(h)*, width *(w)* and depth *(d)* of the depth image: h, w, d ← dim.shape
   for i=1 to $w-1$ **do**
      for j=1 to $h-1$ **do**
         Define the top and bottom vectors:
         t ← np.array([i, j-1, dim[j-1, i, 0]]
         f ← np.array([i-1, j, dim[j, i-1, 0]]
         Define the center vector:
         c ← np.array([i, j, dim[j, i, 0]])
         Compute the surface normals:
         d ← np.cross(f-c, t-c)
         n ← d/np.sqrt(np.sum(d**2))
         Store the surface normals in the output array:
         Normals[j,i,:] ← n
      end for
   end for

Affordance Segmentation: We use depth information and surface normals to achieve Affordance Segmentation. We perform ablation using DeepLabv3-Plus [10] and U-Net [14] to achieve the affordance segmentation. From the experimentation we observe DeepLabv3-Plus outperforms the U-Net. In what follows we brief about the DeepLabv3-Plus.

– **DeepLabv3-Plus** is a state-of-the-art semantic segmentation algorithm that was developed by Google Research. It is an extension of the DeepLabv3 architecture that improves its performance by adding an encoder-decoder structure with an atrous spatial pyramid pooling module. The structure includes an encoder network that downsamples the input image and a decoder network that upsamples the output to the original image size.

The total loss function used in DeepLab-v3 Plus is a weighted sum of the cross-entropy loss and the Lovasz-Softmax loss:

$$\mathcal{L}_{total}(y, \hat{y}) = \mathcal{L}_{CE}(y, \hat{y}) + \lambda \mathcal{L}_{LS}(y, \hat{y}) \tag{2}$$

where, λ is a hyperparameter that controls the weight of the Lovasz-Softmax loss relative to the cross-entropy loss and $\mathcal{L}_{CE}(y, \hat{y})$ is cross-entropy loss and $\mathcal{L}_{LS}(y, \hat{y})$ is Lovasz-Softmax loss.

3 Obstacle Dodging

In this section, we discuss about obstacle dodging with the help of center line marking. Generation of only the drivable surface is not enough to provide proper insight of the road. Thus, we also attempt to generate the center line marking on the road for obstacle dodging. We consider the entire drivable surface from the bottom, compute the width of the drivable surface and draw in line at the middle of the drivable surface. This line acts as the Center-Line for the segmented drivable surface thus helping in obstacle dodging.

4 Results and Discussions

In this section, we discuss dataset and the results of proposed pipeline.

4.1 Dataset

A Cityscapes [1] focuses on the semantic interpretation of urban street scenes. It offers 30 classes, divided into 8 groups, semantic, instance-wise, and dense pixel annotations with 5000 finely annotated photos and 20,000 coarsely annotated images. We use around 2975 images to train and 500 images to test along with the ground truth labels (Fig. 2).

Fig. 2. The sample images of Cityscapes dataset.

4.2   Training

We conducted exhaustive ablation study to check the effect of mid-level cues both individually and in combination. The above experiments were conducted for 100 epochs each, with a batch size of 16 on 2975 training images of Cityscapes [1] and tested on 500 test images. We use binary cross-entropy loss as loss function:

$$L(y, \hat{y}) = -[y \log(\hat{y}) + (1 - y) \log(1 - \hat{y})] \tag{3}$$

where, y is the true label (0 or 1), $\hat{y}$ is the predicted probability of the positive class (0 to 1) and log is the natural logarithm. The results are shown in Table 1.

4.3   Experimental Results

In this subsection, we discuss about the experiments conducted to demonstrate the performance of our pipeline. We use MIOU as a qualitative metric to demonstrate the performance of different affordance segmentation architectures, that are U-Net and DeepLabv3-Plus. We also experimented by providing depth and surface normals individually as a cue and also together. The same is demonstrated in Table 1. We also check the generalizabilty of our pipeline using KITTI dataset and same is demonstrated on Fig. 4, the proposed pipeline "AfforDrive" performs well for detection of drivable area and obstacle dodging (Fig. 3).

We infer from Table 1 that depth-surface normal as the cue and for DeepLabv3-Plus performance is better. We also compare our results with the state of art method for detection of drivable area as shown in Table 2.

Table 1. Comparison of quality metric MIOU across ablation. We observe with Depth-Surface Normal as the cue and for DeepLabv3-Plus performance is better.

Input	Mid-level Cues	U-Net	DeepLabv3-Plus
RGB	None	0.8180	0.8306
RGB	depth	0.8089	0.7859
RGB	depth-surface normals	0.9984	**0.99989**
RGB	depth and depth-surface normals	0.9961	0.9872

Table 2. Comparison with state of art technique Pixel Segmentation for detection of drivable area [11], and observe ours is better

	AfforDrive	Pixel Segmentation [11]
MIOU	0.99989	0.9833

Fig. 3. Detection of drivable area on Cityscapes dataset. First row indicates the input RGB Images. Second and third rows indicate detection of drivable area corresponding to the affordance segmentation generated using DeepLabv3-Plus and U-Net architectures respectively, fourth row indicates obstacle dodging.

Fig. 4. Detection of drivable area on KITTI dataset. First row indicates the input RGB images. Second row indicate detection of drivable area and third row indicates obstacle dodging.

5   Conclusions

In this paper, we have proposed "AfforDrive": a novel approach for detecting drivable surfaces through affordance segmentation for autonomous vehicles. We used depth information and surface normals as midlevel cues along with RGB images to generate an affordance map. We extended our pipeline to perform vehicle dodging to bypass the front vehicle, moving in the space of affordance.

References

1. Andersson, E.: Urban landscapes and sustainable cities. Ecol. Soc. **11**(1) (2006)
2. Bayoudh, K., Hamdaoui, F., Mtibaa, A.: Transfer learning based hybrid 2D–3D CNN for traffic sign recognition and semantic road detection applied in advanced driver assistance systems. Appl. Intell. **51**, 124–142 (2021)
3. Bradski, G., Kaehler, A., et al.: OpenCV. Dr. Dobb's J. Softw. Tools **3**(2) (2000)
4. Dhanakshirur, R.R., Pillai, P., Tabib, R.A., Patil, U., Mudenagudi, U.: A framework for lane prediction on unstructured roads. In: Thampi, S.M., Marques, O., Krishnan, S., Li, K.-C., Ciuonzo, D., Kolekar, M.H. (eds.) SIRS 2018. CCIS, vol. 968, pp. 178–189. Springer, Singapore (2019). https://doi.org/10.1007/978-981-13-5758-9_16
5. Gupta, A., Kembhavi, A., Davis, L.S.: Observing human-object interactions: using spatial and functional compatibility for recognition. IEEE Trans. Pattern Anal. Mach. Intell. **31**(10), 1775–1789 (2009)
6. Hegde, D., Hegde, D., Tabib, R.A., Mudenagudi, U.: Relocalization of camera in a 3D map on memory restricted devices. In: Babu, R.V., Prasanna, M., Namboodiri, V.P. (eds.) NCVPRIPG 2019. CCIS, vol. 1249, pp. 548–557. Springer, Singapore (2020). https://doi.org/10.1007/978-981-15-8697-2_51
7. Hoiem, D., Efros, A.A., Hebert, M.: Recovering surface layout from an image. Int. J. Comput. Vis. **75**, 151–172 (2007)
8. Li, K., Xiong, H., Yu, D., Liu, J., Wang, J., et al.: An end-to-end multi-task learning model for drivable road detection via edge refinement and geometric deformation. IEEE Trans. Intell. Transp. Syst. **23**(7), 8641–8651 (2021)
9. Li, Q., Chen, L., Li, M., Shaw, S.L., Nüchter, A.: A sensor-fusion drivable-region and lane-detection system for autonomous vehicle navigation in challenging road scenarios. IEEE Trans. Veh. Technol. **63**(2), 540–555 (2013)
10. Liu, M., et al.: Comparison of multi-source satellite images for classifying marsh vegetation using DeepLabV3 plus deep learning algorithm. Ecol. Ind. **125**, 107562 (2021)
11. Rasib, M., Butt, M.A., Riaz, F., Sulaiman, A., Akram, M.: Pixel level segmentation based drivable road region detection and steering angle estimation method for autonomous driving on unstructured roads. IEEE Access **9**, 167855–167867 (2021)
12. Roy, A., Todorovic, S.: A multi-scale CNN for affordance segmentation in RGB images. In: Leibe, B., Matas, J., Sebe, N., Welling, M. (eds.) ECCV 2016. LNCS, vol. 9908, pp. 186–201. Springer, Cham (2016). https://doi.org/10.1007/978-3-319-46493-0_12
13. Shao, M.E., Haq, M.A., Gao, D.Q., Chondro, P., Ruan, S.J.: Semantic segmentation for free space and lane based on grid-based interest point detection. IEEE Trans. Intell. Transp. Syst. **23**(7), 8498–8512 (2021)
14. Siddique, N., Paheding, S., Elkin, C.P., Devabhaktuni, V.: U-Net and its variants for medical image segmentation: a review of theory and applications. IEEE Access **9**, 82031–82057 (2021)
15. Sun, L., Bian, J.W., Zhan, H., Yin, W., Reid, I., Shen, C.: SC-DepthV3: robust self-supervised monocular depth estimation for dynamic scenes. arXiv preprint arXiv:2211.03660 (2022)

Revealing the Unseen: A Single-Stage Attention Based Occluded Object Detection Model in Remote Sensing Imagery

Nandini Saini[1($\boxtimes$)], Chiranjoy Chattopadhyay[2], and Debasis Das[1]

[1] Computer Science and Engineering, IIT Jodhpur, Jodhpur 342037, India
{saini.9,debasis}@iitj.ac.in
[2] School of Computing and Data Sciences, FLAME University, Pune 412115, India
chiranjoy.chattopadhyay@flame.edu.in

Abstract. Object detection based on deep learning has achieved promising results on traditional datasets, but detecting objects in remote sensing imagery with diverse occlusions remains challenging. This is due to the fact that natural occlusions are common in real-world images, and there is a lack of adequate datasets and neglect of latent information that can be useful for identification. Our research endeavors to tackle this challenge by presenting an innovative single-stage image-adaptive YOLO-transformer framework that leverages attention-based mechanisms to enable the model to concentrate on important regions and extract more distinctive features. To optimize the model's accuracy while maintaining its lightweight and suitability for real-time applications, we employed a depthwise convolution and SiLU activation function in lieu of the standard convolution. These modifications allow our framework to attain high levels of precision. Our approach is evaluated on synthetically generated occluded datasets from publicly available NWPU-VHR10 and demonstrated adaptive processing of images in both normal and three types of environmental occlusions (foggy, rainy, and cloudy). The experimental results are highly promising, as our approach achieved an inference speed of 6 ms with 11.9 GFLOPs on the NVIDIA Tesla T4 while maintaining effectiveness in all three occlusion types.

Keywords: Object Detection · Environmental Occlusion · Remote Sensing Images · CNN-Transformer · Attention Mechanism

1 Introduction

In recent years, there has been a growing focus on remote sensing imagery due to its potential for numerous applications in both the military and civil domains [9], including traffic supervision [13] and environmental monitoring [10]. Despite the great strides made by object detection algorithms in natural images over the past

© The Author(s), under exclusive license to Springer Nature Switzerland AG 2023
P. Maji et al. (Eds.): PReMI 2023, LNCS 14301, pp. 540–547, 2023.
https://doi.org/10.1007/978-3-031-45170-6_56

decade, there are still significant challenges to overcome when it comes to applying these algorithms to remote sensing images. These challenges include non-uniform object distribution, multi-scale objects, illumination variations, occlusions, and other factors that are unique to remote sensing data.

Several recent studies focus on different aspects of object detection, such as detecting small-scale objects [16], oriented and clustered objects [17,18]. These studies are trained on ideal remote sensing data, but in real-world scenarios, objects in images can be affected by multiple factors i.e. occlusion, illumination, uneven distributions. Among these factors, occlusion is particularly challenging, as it is a common occurrence in remote sensing images due to environmental and man-made objects, vegetation, and atmospheric conditions. In the paper [19], authors have mentioned that an image affected by occlusion can be divided into two components: a clean image and occlusion-specific information. The degradation in image quality is primarily attributed to the interaction between the occlusion and objects, resulting in subpar object detection performance.

Other pre-processing techniques, such as occlusion-based filtering [8] and image enhancement [4], have been proposed to improve detection performance, but these methods add complexity to the detection network and require separate training under pixel-level supervision. In order to overcome the challenge of environmental occlusion in remote sensing object detection, we propose the lightweight image adaptive single stage attention based YOLO-Transformer framework to obtain feature information effectively. To evaluate the effectiveness of our proposed framework, we used a synthetically generated occluded dataset with three different environmental occlusions (cloudy, foggy, and rainy), which we created from the publicly available NWPU-VHR10 dataset.

The following is a summary of the contributions made by our work:

- A novel image adaptive single stage YOLO-Transformer detection framework is proposed that using an attention-based mechanism to allow the model to focus on the most significant regions in the image and extract more discriminative features.
- A lightweight feature extraction network is designed where depthwise convolution with SiLU activation function is leveraged in place of simple convolution to reduce the complexity, parameters and improve the inference speed, making it suitable for real-time applications.
- An algorithm to augment publicly available NWPU-VHR10 [12] dataset with three types of environmental occlusion, namely cloudy, foggy, rainy
- Experimental results are performed on the publicly available and the occluded (augmented) dataset, which lead to notable gains in mean average precision (mAP), inference speed.

2   Related Work

The literature is divided into two sections based on their types of work.

2.1   Aerial Image Based Object Detection

Recent advancements in deep learning have led to the classification of object detection methods into two main categories: multi-stage object detection and single-stage object detection. Multi-stage approaches i.e., R-CNN [3] and Cascade R-CNN [2], detect objects in two stages. First, they create the region of interests (ROIs) from an image, and then they predict the object class for each region using a Convolutional Neural Network (CNN). In [11], authors have used semantic segmentation along with bounding-box regression to improve detection precision, but these methods are computationally expensive and have slower inference speed. Single-stage object detectors i.e., YOLO series [1] and Efficient-Det [14], predict distinct bounding boxes and classes simultaneously using a single CNN. These methods were designed to improve object detection speed and support real-time detection. Yet, due to the intricate nature of aerial images, including object scale fluctuations, occlusion, and dynamic object distribution, these methods are limited in their ability to detect objects with high accuracy.

2.2   Object Detection Under Occlusion in Aerial Images

In comparison to general object detection, few research efforts have been conducted on occluded object detection in an aerial image. Real-time occlusion can happen as a result of the overlap of physical objects, a transition in the natural atmosphere, or the dense scattering of a group of objects. Recent works have attempted to address these challenges with image enhancement techniques [4] and kernel-based approaches [7]. It is probable that the detection performance may not consistently improve with solely enhanced image quality. In the presence of weather-specific occlusions, certain prior-based methods utilize a combination of image enhancement and domain adaptation techniques [5,6]. Various techniques have enhanced the learning of non-occluded semantic parts through the incorporation of deformable part-based models. These models explicitly represent objects as compositions of parts and subsequently merge them using a voting mechanism [15].

3   Methodology

This section briefly describes the model's architecture and training.

3.1   Attention Based Feature Enhancement

The proposed single-stage image adaptive architecture consists of three main modules, as shown in Fig. 1: first backbone as feature extraction, the second neck as feature fusion, and the head as prediction result. The backbone network represents focus structure, depthwise separable convolution, batch normalisation, and the SiLU layer. The focus structure is the slicing operation, which first divides an input image into slices of the feature map after concatenation

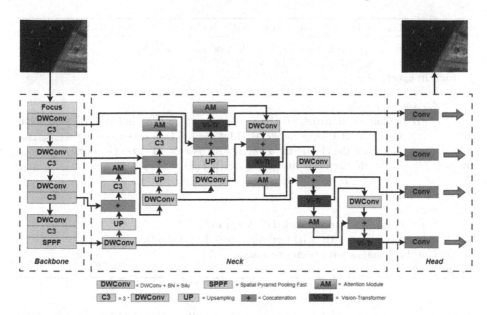

Fig. 1. The proposed single-stage image adaptive architecture which uses a lightweight feature extraction network with attention module to focus on occluded objects.

operations apply. Depthwise convolution (DW) along with the SiLU activation function can reduce the parameters and speed up the detection process, which can be defined by the Eq. 1.

$$DW_{i,j,m} = \sum_{p=1}^{k}\sum_{q=1}^{k} X_{i+p-1,j+q-1,m} K_{p,q,m} \tag{1}$$

where i and j are the spatial indices of the output tensor, and m is the channel index. The summation is performed over the kernel size k, and the values of the kernel K are shared across all channels of the input tensor X. The SiLU activation function is defined in Eq. 2 which is a non-monotonic, differentiable activation function that leads to faster convergence during training of the model.

$$SiLU(x) = \frac{x}{1+e^{-x}} \tag{2}$$

To enhance feature learning for occluded objects, we have added an attention-based module in the neck of the model. The attention module (AM) can be summarised by the Eq. 3 which helps the model focus on important regions of an image while suppressing irrelevant regions.

$$AM(Q,K,V) = softmax(QK^{T}/\sqrt{d_{k}}) * V \tag{3}$$

where Q, K, and V represent Query, Key, and Value, respectively, and d_{k} is the dimensionality of the Key vector K for calculating attention module (AM).

Algorithm 1. The training procedure with occluded data generation

---

1: Initialize the proposed network D^W with random weight W
2: Set epochs = 100, batch_size = 16, N=10
3: **for** i in epochs **do**
4:     Take a batch images N from original data;
5:     **for** j in batch_size **do**
6:         **if** random.randint(0,4)>0 **then**   ▷ occluded data generation
7:             Generate the foggy image M(j) by $f(x) = (1 - \alpha) * x + \alpha * x_{fog\_overlay}$
8:             Generate the cloudy image M(j) with $f(x) = (1 - \beta) * x + \beta * x_{cloud\_overlay}$
9:             Generate the rainy image M(j) with $f(x) = (1 - \gamma) * x + \gamma * x_{rain\_overlay}$
10:            where $(\alpha, \beta, \gamma) \in (0, 1)$
11:        **end if**
12:    **end for**
13:    Send image batch to network D^W for training
14:    Update gradient with SGD optimizer based on detection loss
15:    Untill all images have been processed
16: **end for**

Finally, to improve the fusion of features for small occluded objects, we utilized four prediction heads in the head network. The loss function is composed of three components: confidence, location, and classification. We aim to output a single bounding box for each object detected in the image. Thus, out of the n predicted bounding boxes, we select the one with the highest Intersection over Union (IoU) score.

3.2 Hybrid Data Training

In order to achieve superior detection performance in both normal and environmental occlusion scenarios, our proposed method employs a hybrid data training approach which is summarized in the Algorithm 1. During the training process, we randomly select 40% of images in each batch and apply occlusion transformations to them to generate synthetic occluded images for cloudy, foggy, and rainy conditions. The resultant dataset is then used to train the entire pipeline with YOLOv5 detection loss, using the SGD optimizer. By adopting this hybrid approach, our model is effectively trained to handle both normal and occluded conditions. This allows the model to dynamically process images based on their content, leading to superior detection performance.

4   Experiments

Our method is evaluated in three distinct occlusion scenarios caused by the weather: cloudy, foggy, and rainy situations and normal conditions.

4.1 Dataset and Experimental Setup

We used publicly available aerial image benchmark dataset NWPU-VHR10 [12] as source dataset. The dataset has 800 images divided into 10 categories (aeroplane (AE), ship (SP), storage tank (ST), baseball diamond (BD), tennis court (TC), basketball court (BC), ground track field (GTF), harbour (HR), bridge (BE), and vehicle (VE)), which are collected from satellite images and Google Earth. Our target dataset consisted of occluded aerial images, which we generated synthetically by augmenting the source dataset with three occlusion types (fog, rain, and clouds) while maintaining the same annotation information. We have conducted training and testing using PyTorch on a workstation with a 32 GB NVIDIA Tesla T4 GPU. We preprocessed the image by resizing the image to $(640 \times 640 \times 3)$ before training. Initially, the learning rate is set to 10, and then it is reduced by a factor of 10 every 20 epochs for total 100 epochs.

4.2 Experimental Results

To showcase the effectiveness of our proposed approach, we conducted a comparative study with YOLOv5 baseline on four datasets, namely three synthetically generated occluded datasets (cloudy, foggy, rainy) and a normal dataset. Table 1 summarizes the precision values for each class under three different settings corresponding to cloudy (A), foggy (B), and rainy (C) occlusion. Our proposed model exhibits improvements over the baseline (YOLOv5) for all three types of occlusion, which indicates the strength of the adaptive process to handle occluded images. The overall performance of our method in terms of mean average precision (mAP) compared to the baseline is illustrated in Fig. 3. Our proposed model achieves 73% mAP on the normal dataset and 67.4%, 61.9%, and 68.4% on the cloudy, foggy, and rainy occluded datasets, respectively. The object detection visualization results for all three occlusions as well as the normal dataset are presented in Fig. 2. It can be observed that our model effectively detects objects in the normal and cloudy settings. However, for other types of occlusion, some objects are missed to detect due to presence of highly occluded regions.

Table 1. Performance evaluation of detection task with three occlusion setting

Setting	Method	AE	SP	ST	BD	TC	BC	GTF	HR	BE	VE
A	YOLOv5(baseline)	0.90	0.79	0.96	0.86	0.42	0.15	0.71	0.79	0.35	0.34
	YOLO-Transformer	0.92	**0.87**	0.97	0.92	**0.49**	**0.09**	0.68	**0.95**	0.29	0.39
	Ours	**0.93**	0.74	**0.98**	**0.94**	0.45	0.08	**0.88**	0.93	**0.44**	**0.41**
B	YOLOv5(baseline)	0.82	0.36	0.70	0.78	0.15	0.03	0.45	0.81	0.10	0.18
	YOLO-Transformer	0.93	0.57	**0.83**	0.91	0.25	0.06	0.60	0.83	0.17	0.33
	Ours	**0.95**	**0.75**	0.72	**0.96**	**0.34**	**0.07**	**0.88**	**0.87**	**0.29**	**0.37**
C	YOLOv5(baseline)	0.95	0.71	0.95	0.95	0.31	0.10	0.65	0.47	0.18	0.49
	YOLO-Transformer	0.96	0.60	**0.98**	0.96	0.52	0.06	0.76	0.95	**0.34**	**0.60**
	Ours	**0.98**	**0.76**	0.95	**0.97**	**0.61**	**0.12**	**0.88**	0.82	0.32	0.46

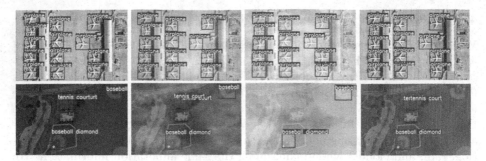

Fig. 2. Object detection results on normal test images (column 1) and synthetic occluded images under cloudy, foggy and rainy occlusion (column 2, 3, 4)

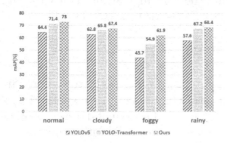

Fig. 3. Overall performance comparison of each occlusion with baseline

Table 2. Analysis of speed and complexity of the proposed model

Method	FR	IT(ms)	GFLOPs
YOLOv5(baseline)	13.69	7.3	15.9
YOLO-Transformer	13.33	7.5	15.7
Ours	16.67	6.0	11.9

Table 2 presents an analysis of our proposed model's performance in terms of two metrics: frame rate (FR) in frames per second (FPS) and inference time (IT), which measures the rate at which the object detection model processes input and makes predictions. The FPS metric is calculated as $FPS = 1/IT$. We also measured the model's computational complexity in terms of GFLOPS (Giga Floating Point Operations per Second), which is a parameter used to estimate the amount of computational complexity to execute the model. The results show that our proposed model outperforms the YOLOv5 baseline in terms of mAP, speed, and model's complexity, demonstrating its effectiveness for object detection in environmental occlusion conditions.

5   Conclusion

Our work proposes a novel approach for enhancing the recognition of occluded objects in remote sensing imagery by employing a single-stage adaptive attention-based strategy. Specifically, we developed a lightweight feature extraction network augmented with an attention module based on YOLOv5. We improved the model's accuracy and reduced its complexity by integrating depth-wise separable convolution with the SiLU activation function. To facilitate hybrid data training, we generated three synthetic occluded datasets with varying weather conditions, including cloudy, foggy, and rainy scenarios. In real-time applications, we evaluated the proposed method's accuracy and inference speed, as well as its model complexity. For future investigations, we plan to leverage numerous aerial image datasets to explore the detection of occluded man-made objects.

References

1. Bochkovskiy, A., Wang, C.Y., Liao, H.Y.M.: Yolov4: optimal speed and accuracy of object detection. arXiv preprint arXiv:2004.10934 (2020)
2. Cai, Z., Vasconcelos, N.: Cascade r-cnn: delving into high quality object detection. In: CVPR, pp. 6154–6162 (2018)
3. Girshick, R., Donahue, J., Darrell, T., Malik, J.: Rich feature hierarchies for accurate object detection and semantic segmentation. In: CVPR, pp. 580–587 (2014)
4. Guo, C., et al.: Zero-reference deep curve estimation for low-light image enhancement. In: CVPR, pp. 1780–1789 (2020)
5. Hnewa, M., Radha, H.: Multiscale domain adaptive yolo for cross-domain object detection. In: ICIP, pp. 3323–3327. IEEE (2021)
6. Huang, S.C., Le, T.H., Jaw, D.W.: DSNET: joint semantic learning for object detection in inclement weather conditions. IEEE T-PAMI **43**(8), 2623–2633 (2020)
7. Kim, B., Lee, J., Lee, S., Kim, D., Kim, J.: Tricubenet: 2d kernel-based object representation for weakly-occluded oriented object detection. In: CVPR, pp. 167–176 (2022)
8. Liu, X., Ma, Y., Shi, Z., Chen, J.: Griddehazenet: attention-based multi-scale network for image dehazing. In: ICCV, pp. 7314–7323 (2019)
9. Maiti, S., Gidde, P., Saurav, S., Singh, S., Chaudhury, S.: Real-time vehicle detection in aerial images using skip-connected convolution network with region proposal networks. In: PReMI, pp. 200–208. Springer, Heidelberg (2019). https://doi.org/10.1007/978-3-030-34869-4_22
10. Saini, N., Chattopadhyay, C., Das, D.: E2alertnet: an explainable, efficient, and lightweight model for emergency alert from aerial imagery. Remote Sens. Appl. Soc. Environ. **29**, 100896 (2023)
11. Schweitzer, D., Agrawal, R.: Multi-class object detection from aerial images using mask r-cnn. In: IEEE BigData, pp. 3470–3477. IEEE (2018)
12. Su, H., Wei, S., Yan, M., Wang, C., Shi, J., Zhang, X.: Object detection and instance segmentation in remote sensing imagery based on precise mask r-cnn. In: IGARSS, pp. 1454–1457. IEEE (2019)
13. Sun, W., Dai, L., Zhang, X., Chang, P., He, X.: RSOD: real-time small object detection algorithm in UAV-based traffic monitoring. AI, 1–16 (2021)
14. Tan, M., Pang, R., Le, Q.V.: Efficientdet: scalable and efficient object detection. In: CVPR, pp. 10781–10790 (2020)
15. Wang, A., Sun, Y., Kortylewski, A., Yuille, A.L.: Robust object detection under occlusion with context-aware compositionalnets (2020)
16. Wang, J., Yang, W., Guo, H., Zhang, R., Xia, G.S.: Tiny object detection in aerial images. In: ICPR, pp. 3791–3798. IEEE (2021)
17. Yang, F., Fan, H., Chu, P., Blasch, E., Ling, H.: Clustered object detection in aerial images. In: ICCV, pp. 8311–8320 (2019)
18. Yi, J., Wu, P., Liu, B., Huang, Q., Qu, H., Metaxas, D.: Oriented object detection in aerial images with box boundary-aware vectors. In: WACV, pp. 2150–2159 (2021)
19. You, S., Tan, R.T., Kawakami, R., Mukaigawa, Y., Ikeuchi, K.: Adherent raindrop modeling, detection and removal in video. IEEE T-PAMI **38**(9), 1721–1733 (2015)

A Study of Quantifying the Deviation of Remotely Sensed Objects from Multi-spectral Images

Prateek Tewary[✉] and Jit Mukherjee[ID]

Birla Institute of Technology Mesra, Mesra, Jharkhand, India
prats2241@gmail.com, jit.mukherjee@bitmesra.ac.in

Abstract. Land use and land change ($LULC$) has several widely discussed research challenges. However, there is a significant research gap in detecting the direction of change of any remotely sensed object. Detection of such deviation has several environmental and social consequences. Further, it has direct correspondence for disaster management, early indication of natural phenomenon, and planning. In the past, different machine and deep learning techniques have been employed for $LULC$ detection using different remote sensing paradigms such as aerial, multi-spetral, and hyper-spectral images. However, few works have studied the shape features of these land class changes to comprehend the deviation. Majority of them use complex shape features and employ multi-modal analysis. Therefore, the primary objective of this work is to quantify the direction of such change using multi-spectral images explicitly. Characteristics of intersecting lines are studied here to achieve this. Thus, the proposed technique can detect the deviation of any concave and convex remote sensing objects without holes using linear equations.

Keywords: Remotely Sensed Objects · Deviation of Shapes · Shape Features · Multi-spectral Images

1 Introduction

One of the crucial areas of remote sensing based monitoring is to detect the direction of change in different land classes. This is predominantly related to describing the detected land classes and their features which has close correspondence to low-level image processing. The detection of different land classes from remotely sensed images has been studied thoroughly in the literature. Different combinations of reflectance values of particular bands, such as normalized difference water index ($NDWI$), bare soil index (BI), coal mine index (CMI), etc. enhance spatial features of specific land classes. Such band combinations are utilised to detect land classes without any labeled dataset. Aerial crop datasets are studied to detect different crop types from heterogeneous sparse labels using meta-learning [12]. Different ground truth datasets are also proposed to detect

P. Maji et al. (Eds.): PReMI 2023, LNCS 14301, pp. 548–556, 2023.
https://doi.org/10.1007/978-3-031-45170-6_57

diverse land classes [1]. Majority of the techniques in literature does not compute the direction of change and seldom mid-resolution multi-spectral images are considered. Mid-resolution satellite images enhance the spectral features of natural objects over a larger region. Therefore, they help to understand the dynamics and changes of such natural objects in several applications such as disaster management, urban planning, resource planning, and others [11]. Formerly, field studies were the common practise to determine such changes [13]. Presently, remote sensing and machine learning based change detection techniques are utilised frequently. An ensemble approach using Pixel-Based Image Analysis (PBIA), Geographic Object-Based Image Analysis (GEOBIA), and a Deep Neural Network (DNN) is applied for $LULC$ [3]. Transfer learning [11] and recurrent neural networks [2] are used for $LULC$. Change detection using multi-modal approaches through synthetic aperture radar, hyperspectral, and multi-spectral images are also discussed [14]. Although these techniques can detect the $LULC$ with high accuracy, they do not provide the direction of the change of these objects. Very few works have been conducted to understand the dynamics of such changes [4]. In [4], the direction of change of retrogressive thaw slumps in the Tibetan Plateau is quantified using DeepLabv3+ and a series of medial circles of the changed sections from *CubeSat* and digital elevation model (*DEM*) images. Though $LULC$ has been a widely researched domain, there are very few works that detect the direction of changes of a natural object from mid-resolution satellite images. Various properties of an image such as, centroid, polygon evolution, convex hull, Fourier descriptor, and others can be treated as a shape feature [5]. Identifying the deviation of natural objects using multi-spectral images explicitly, needs further experimentation. This is treated as the primary objective of this paper. To the best of the author's knowledge, shape features primarily based on linear equations are rarely used for quantification of such deviation. Shape features using linear equations are easily interpretable, and more robust [8]. Hence, they are prioritised here. In this work, primarily, water bodies are considered and a highly dynamic complex object i.e. coal seam fire, is also briefly studied. The proposed technique does not require labeled dataset in any stage.

2   Methodology, Data, and Study Area

Two images with different timestamps are considered in this work. First, the contours of the objects are detected. An approximation of the polygon is computed to reduce the number of vertices. Further, intersecting lines from the centroid of the changed polygon to the sides of the initial polygons are studied. The approximation, over image with earlier and later timestamp are referred to as the initial and new polygon, respectively. Let n, and m be the number of points in initial and new polygon, respectively. Vertices of initial and new polygon are in the form of points P_i $(1 \leq i \leq n)$, and p_j $(1 \leq j \leq m)$, respectively. Let the centre of the new polygon be G. Each pair of points p_j and p_{j+1} correspond to the side s_j. The set of points of initial polygon is joined with centroid G.

The line segment through P_i and G denoted by $\overline{P_iG}$ detects inward deviation whereas $\vec{PG}$ detects outward deviation. The lines are studied through equations in 2-D Cartesian plane. These notations are used throughout.

Given the set of vertices of a figure, polygon approximation reduces the number of edges by forming approximate digital straight line segments ($ADSS$), which are almost collinear based on the approximation parameter τ. Among various techniques for such approximation, in this work, a technique close to [7] has been used. The proposed algorithm's complexity depends on the number of sides of the polygon, which further depends on approximation parameter τ. High τ implies a lesser number of sides, which decreases the time complexity. The proposed technique focuses on non-complex features. Hence, the perpendicular distance of a point from a line, i.e. $\delta = \frac{Ax_1+By_1+C}{\sqrt{A^2+B^2}}$, is considered here. (x_1, y_1) and $\{Ax + By + C = 0\}$ are denoted as a vertex of the polygon, and the equation of a side, respectively. If δ is less than τ, the point is considered almost on the line and it is removed. Otherwise, it is retained and the next set of points is analysed. It provides the approximated polygon (V), given the original polygon (P), number of vertices (ϖ) and approximation parameter (τ).

The centroid G of the new polygon is computed as $G = (\frac{\sum_{i=1}^{m} x_i}{m}, \frac{\sum_{i=1}^{m} y_i}{m})$. The aim is to find a point as close as the visual center of the polygon. There are two cases, either the centroid can lie within new polygon or outside. As the centroid of a triangle always lies inside it, in the second case, triangulation on the new polygon is performed. Triangulation divides a polygon P, into a set of non-overlapping triangles such that union of all the triangles form the polygon. Here, the polygon is decomposed into trapezoids and these trapezoids are decomposed into monotone polygons, which can be computed in linear time [10]. Each triangle provides a centroid. Deviations from all initial points are computed from each of the centroids. Two cases can arise. First, the initial polygon has shrunk over a period of time, then deviation is towards centre and it is detected using $\overline{PG}$. Second, the initial polygon has expanded and the deviation is in opposite direction to the center, detected using $\vec{PG}$. Intersecting lines with G and vertices P_i is computed ($\overline{P_iG}$) and side s_j is formed by joining adjacent points of the new polygon. Here, a restriction on abscissa and ordinate is used. For a side, along with the coefficients of the line, its limits are also studied for validation. Let $p_1 = (x_1, y_1)$ and $p_2 = (x_2, y_2)$ be the vertices of the side s. The limits are defined as $x_{max} = \max(x_1, x_2)$, $x_{min} = \min(x_1, x_2)$, $y_{max} = \max(y_1, y_2)$, and $y_{min} = \min(y_1, y_2)$. The direction of change is determined by comparing the slope and coordinates of the intersecting lines. For each point of the initial polygon, the intersecting lines are computed to detect both inwards and outward deviation.

Let the point of intersection between line $\overline{P_iG}$ with side s_j be (x_{ij}, y_{ij}). For each line $\overline{P_iG}$ ($1 \leq i \leq n$), for all the sides s_j the point of intersections are computed. The equation for $\overline{P_iG}$ along with $x_{max}, x_{min}, y_{max}$ and y_{min} validate the intersection point. If the conditions $x_{min} \leq x_{ij} \leq x_{max}$ and $y_{min} \leq y_{ij} \leq y_{max}$ are satisfied, a valid change is obtained for P_i with slope of line being direction of change. Similar process is followed for $\vec{PG}$. Let

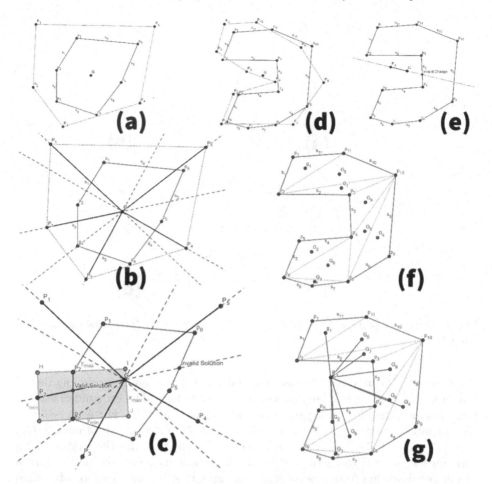

Fig. 1. (a) Initial Polygon (*blue*) and New Polygon, (b) Formation of Initial Points joining the Centroid, (c) Finding Valid and Invalid Change (*red*), (d) Centroid lying outside Concave Polygon, (e) No Deviation can be Measured, (f) Triangulation to obtain Central Points within Polygon, (g) Finding Deviation (Color figure online)

$n = 5, P = \{P_1, P_2, P_3, P_4, P_5\}$ and $m = 6, p = \{p_1, p_2, p_3, p_4, p_5, p_6\}$ as shown in Fig. 1(a). The sides of the new polygon from the given vertices p are formed as $s = \{s_1 = \overline{p_1 p_2}, s_2 = \overline{p_2 p_3}, s_3 = \overline{p_3 p_4}, s_4 = \overline{p_4 p_5}, s_5 = \overline{p_5 p_6}, s_6 = \overline{p_6 p_1}\}$. Next, centroid G of the new polygon is computed. The intersecting lines joining P with centroid G i.e., $\overline{P_i G}$ are generated (Fig. 1(b)). For each $\overline{P_i G}$ and s_j, $x_{max}, x_{min}, y_{max}$ and y_{min} are determined. From the intersection point of $\overline{P_i G}$ with s_j, the validity is checked (Fig. 1(c)). The valid point of intersection provides the deviation from point P_i. As all the computations are on the 2-D coordinate, it is necessary to check that the intersection lies on the line segments $\overline{P_i G}$ and s_j rather than their extended parts. A polygon may be concave and thus the centroid of the polygon may lie outside the polygon. In such a case,

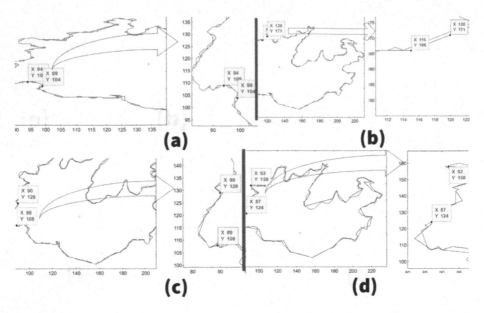

Fig. 2. Portion of polygon for validation (a)–(b) with $\tau = 0.0$, (c)–(d) as compared in Table 1.

the segment $\overline{P_i G}$ may not intersect any side and it will not provide any deviation (Fig. 1(d) and (e)). Triangulation is performed here. The centroid of each of these triangles is taken as separate central points (Fig. 1(f)). For each centroid G_k, an intersecting line is formed with each of P_i. Intersection of each $\overline{P_i G_k}$, $(1 \le i \le n$ and $1 \le k \le m - 2)$ with s_j $(1 \le j \le m)$ provides the change along each initial point (Fig. 1(g)). A suitable statistical measure like mean can be chosen for deviation from a point when triangulation is performed for obtaining centroid. Similarly, outward deviation can be obtained using $\vec{PG}$.

Landsat 8 $L1$ multi-spectral data from February and December 2017 is used here. It has a spatial and temporal resolution of 30 meters, in most of the bands, and 16 days, respectively. It provides top of atmosphere reflectance. Patratu lake (23°37′58.4″ N and 85°18′11.88″ E, Jharkhand, India) is chosen here as the primary study area. Waters from river Nalkari and waterfalls from surrounding hills contribute to Patratu lake. Jharia coal field, a coal mining region in Jharkhand, India, (23°38′ N, to 23°50′ N and 86°07′E, to 86°30′E) is chosen for coal seam fires.

3   Results and Discussion

Satellite images of Patratu lake of Jharkhand, India on February, and December 2017, respectively are chosen as the primary study area (Fig. 3(a) and (b)). These images are detected using $NDWI$ and manual threshold values. As a polygon with a hole has a different topology, it is treated as a future direction.

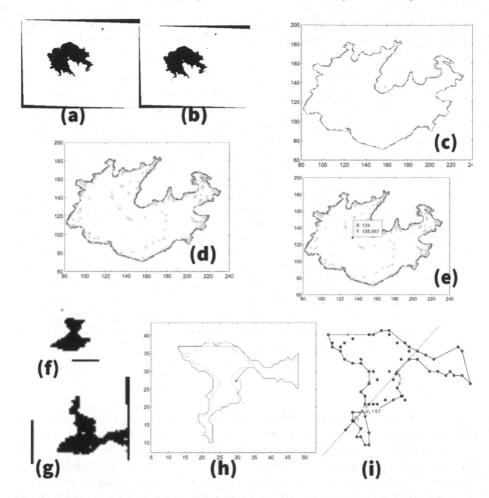

Fig. 3. (a) Water body at (a) T_1, (b) T_2, (c) Polygon without approximation and center is outside, (d) Triangulation and their centroid, (e) One centroid chosen for validation, (f)-(g) Coal seam fire detected, (h) Initial and New polygon with centroid, (i)Sample deviation in one direction.

Therefore, the hole detected inside the water body (Fig. 3(a) and (b)) is not considered here. Let, the detected regions in Fig. 3(a) and (b) be the initial polygon at timestamp T_1, and new polygon at timestamp T_2, respectively. It is observed that the centre of the initial polygon lies outside the polygon (Fig. 3(c)). Here, the initial polygon, new polygon and centroid are shown in the blue contour, red contour, and green point, respectively (Fig. 3(c)). Triangulation is performed as the centroid lies outside the polygon (3(c)) to obtain set of centre points (3(d)). The minimum deviation to all center points is obtained. The left images of Fig. 2(b) and (a) show the polygon without approximation. The right images of Fig. 2(b) and (a) are chosen for validation of the outcome of the proposed

Table 1. Comparison: Ground Truth and Outcome for $\tau = 0.5$ (Fig. 2(c)) from Sl.no 1–7 and $\tau = 0.85$ (Fig. 2(d)) from Sl.no 8–16

	Result by plotting						Result by algorithm			
Sl. no	Initial Polygon point	Vertex to Centroid line	Equation of side	Intersection point	Angle of Deviation	Deviation	Type	Intersection point	Angle of Deviation	Deviation	Type
1	(86, 122)	y = −0.093x + 130.046	y = x + 37	(85.085, 122.085)	174.654	0.918443	Outward	(85.085, 122.086)	174.655	0.918	Outward
2	(82, 115)	y = 0.027x + 112.759	y = 4x − 218	(83.258, 115.034)	1.565	1.259	Inward	(83.009, 115.028)	1.565	1.009	Inward
3	(82, 113)	y = 0.060x + 108.070	y = 3x − 134	(82.340, 113.020)	3.440	0.340	Inward	(82.3401, 113.02)	3.440	0.340	Inward
4	(85, 109)	y = 0.132x + 97.763	y = −2x + 279	(85, 109)	7.530	0	Inward	(85,109)	7.530	1.42e−14	Inward
5	(86, 107)	y = 0.169x + 92.414	y = −2x + 279	(86, 107)	9.625	0	Inward	(86,107)	9.625	0	Inward
6	(88, 108)	y = 0.157x + 94.132	y = −2x + 279	(85.682, 107.634)	8.955	2.346	Outward	(85.682, 107.635)	8.955	2.346	Outward
7	(89, 109)	y = 0.141x + 96.363	y = −2x + 279	(85.265, 108.469)	8.080	3.772	Outward	(85.265, 108.47)	8.081	3.772	Outward

	Result by plotting						Result by algorithm			
Sl. no	Initial Polygon point	Vertex to Centroid line	Equation of side	Intersection point	Angle of Deviation	Deviation	Type	Intersection point	Angle of Deviation	Deviation	Type
8	(93, 153)	y = −1.026x + 248.430	y = 0.571x + 91.857	(98.007, 147.861)	134.260	7.174	Inward	(98.007, 147.861)	134.26	7.174	Inward
9	(95, 153)	y = −1.068x + 254.461	y = 0.571x + 91.857	(99.182, 148.532)	133.116	6.119	Inward	(99.182, 148.533)	133.115	6.119	Inward
10	(99, 148)	y = −1.051x + 252.132	y = 0.571x + 91.857	(98.735, 148.277)	133.552	0.383	Outward	(98.736, 148.278)	133.551	0.383	Outward
11	(99, 148)	y = −1.051x + 252.132	y = −0.25x + 174	(97.441, 149.639)	133.552	2.262	Outward	(97.441, 149.64)	133.551	2.262	Outward
12	(96, 147)	y = −0.965x + 239.666	y = 0.571x + 91.857	(96.185, 146.820)	136.012	0.258	Inward	(96.185, 146.821)	136.011	0.258	Inward
13	(96, 137)	y = −0.756x + 209.666	x = 94	(94, 138.513)	142.876	2.508	Outward	(94, 138.514)	142.875	2.508	Outward
14	(91, 133)	y = −0.610x + 188.515	y = 0.666x + 72.333	(91, 133)	148.614	0	Inward	(91, 133)	148.614	0	Inward
15	(88, 131)	y = −0.541x + 178.666	y = −1.5x + 263	(88, 131)	151.557	0	Outward	(88, 131)	151.556	0	Outward
16	(87, 123)	y = −0.391x + 157.087	y = x + 37	(86.281, 123.281)	158.604	0.771	Outward	(86.281, 123.282)	158.604	0.771	Outward

technique. Similarly, experimentation of the proposed technique over different τ values is also conducted as shown in Fig. 2(c) ($\tau = 0.5$) and Fig. 2(d) ($\tau = 0.85$).

For validation a center point is randomly chosen (Fig. 3 (e), black point). The outcome is compared with actual deviation obtained by graphically plotting points. Validation is performed for polygon with approximation of $\tau = 0.5$ and 0.85. Triangulation on a closed polygon with k vertices produces $k - 2$ triangles [10]. New polygon with 644 points, produces 622 ($\neq k - 2$) triangles with $\tau = 0.0$. This is due to limited precision and many points being very close to each other. First, two portions of the polygon with $\tau = 0.0$ (Fig. 2(a) and (b)) are chosen. Their corresponding ground truth obtained by manual plotting and outcome of algorithm is compared. The proposed algorithm correctly computes angle of deviation, deviation and type of deviation. Polygon approximation with $\tau = 0.5$ gives initial and new polygon having 230 and 251 points respectively. Further experimentation with higher polygon approximation ($\tau = 0.85$) gives initial and new polygon with 113, and 120 points, respectively. Portions of the polygon with $\tau = 0.5$ (Fig. 2(c)) and $\tau = 0.85$ (Fig. 2(d)) have been studied. Their corresponding ground truth obtained by manual plotting and outcome of algorithm are also compared. The proposed algorithm can correctly compute the angle of deviation, deviation and type of deviation (Table 1). However, approximation with high τ may affect the shape of the polygon (Fig. 2(d)). This may provide wrong outcome in certain scenarios. Hence, it is observed that $\tau = 0.5$ provides optimal results in terms of accuracy and performance. Further, the technique is applied with coal seam fires (*CSF*). In this work, surface and sub-surface *CSF* are detected as studied in [6] from February, and December of 2017 (Fig. 3(f), and (g)). It can be inferred that the algorithm correctly detects deviation from the sample deviation in one direction (Fig. 3(i)). The proposed technique can be applied to any remotely sensed object. However the proposed algorithm may fail, when two objects merge into one or split into several parts. This is treated as a future direction of our work. In [9], edges of two polygons are mapped by segment to segment matching to detect change in shape. However, this technique may be found inefficient for complex polygons. Changes in retrogressive thaw slumps in Tibetan Plateau are quantified using complex features such as medial circle with CubeSat and *DEM* images [4]. The proposed technique uses multi-spectral images explicitly through linear equations to detect the change of any concave and convex shaped object.

4   Conclusion

In this paper, a novel technique has been proposed to detect the deviation of land classes through linear equations and multi-spectral images explicitly. Although *LULC* is an active research area, experimentation on the detection of deviation needs further attention. Such deviations can be found beneficial in disaster management, and the planning of resources. In the past, a few works have employed multi-modal analysis over complex shape features to detect such change. In this work, properties of intersecting lines are studied to identify the deviation. It is observed that the proposed technique can detect such deviation for any concave and convex shape. Here, no labeled dataset for training is required. The proposed technique may not perform correctly for polygon with holes and when there is many to many multi-temporal mapping of objects. These are treated as the future directions of the proposed work.

References

1. Boguszewski, A., Batorski, D., Ziemba-Jankowska, N., Dziedzic, T., Zambrzycka, A.: LandCover. AI: Dataset for automatic mapping of buildings, woodlands, water and roads from aerial imagery. In: IEEE/CVF Conference CVPR, pp. 1102–1110 (2021)
2. Campos-Taberner, M., et al.: Understanding deep learning in land use classification based on sentinel-2 time series. Sci. Rep. **10**(1), 17188 (2020)
3. Castelo-Cabay, M., Piedra-Fernandez, J.A., Ayala, R.: Deep learning for land use and land cover classification from the Ecuadorian paramo. Int. J. Digit. Earth **15**(1), 1001–1017 (2022)
4. Huang, L., Liu, L., Luo, J., Lin, Z., Niu, F.: Automatically quantifying evolution of retrogressive thaw slumps in Beiluhe (tibetan Plateau) from multi-temporal CubeSat images. Int. J. Appl. Earth Obs. Geoinf. **102**, 102399 (2021)
5. Mingqiang, Y., Kidiyo, K., Joseph, R., et al.: A survey of shape feature extraction techniques. Pattern Recogn. **15**(7), 43–90 (2008)

6. Mukherjee, J.: A study on automated detection of surface and sub-surface coal seam fires using isolation forest from Landsat 8 OLI/TIRS images. In: IEEE IGARSS, pp. 5512–5515 (2022)
7. Pratihar, S., Bhowmick, P.: On the Farey sequence and its augmentation for applications to image analysis. Int. J. Appl. Math. Comput. Sci. **27**(3), 637–658 (2017)
8. Quackenbush, L.J.: A review of techniques for extracting linear features from imagery. Photogram. Eng. Remote Sens. **70**(12), 1383–1392 (2004)
9. Rowe, N.C., Grewe, L.L.: Change detection for linear features in aerial photographs using edge-finding. IEEE TGRS **39**(7), 1608–1612 (2001)
10. Seidel, R.: A simple and fast incremental randomized algorithm for computing trapezoidal decompositions and for triangulating polygons. Comput. Geom. **1**(1), 51–64 (1991)
11. Storie, C.D., Henry, C.J.: Deep learning neural networks for land use land cover mapping. In: IEEE IGARSS, pp. 3445–3448. IEEE (2018)
12. Tseng, G., Kerner, H., Nakalembe, C., Becker-Reshef, I.: Learning to predict crop type from heterogeneous sparse labels using meta-learning. In: IEEE/CVF Conference CVPR, pp. 1111–1120 (2021)
13. Wang, M., Wander, M., Mueller, S., Martin, N., Dunn, J.B.: Evaluation of survey and remote sensing data products used to estimate land use change in the united states: evolving issues and emerging opportunities. Environ. Sci. Policy **129**, 68–78 (2022)
14. You, Y., Cao, J., Zhou, W.: A survey of change detection methods based on remote sensing images for multi-source and multi-objective scenarios. Remote Sens. **12**(15), 2460 (2020)

Soft Computing

Multi-objective Non-overlapping Front Generation: A Pivot-Based Deterministic Non-dominated Sorting Approach

Sourab Mandal$^{(\boxtimes)}$ and Paramartha Dutta

Department of Computer & System Sciences, Visva-Bharati University, Santiniketan, Bolpur, West Bengal, India
smvb.rs@gmail.com

Abstract. Multiobjective/Many-objective Optimization Genetic Algorithm (MOGA) is a method that utilizes a stochastic search inspired by nature to find solutions in a multiobjective optimization framework. Examples of MOGA include NSGA-II and NSGA-III, both of which rely on fast non-dominated sorting during execution. Non-dominated sorting is a difficult task in this field. This paper presents an alternative deterministic approach to fast non-dominated sorting that is both correct and complete. The approach focuses on pivots, which enables it to handle data with multiple or many objectives. The proposed method has been applied to relevant benchmark data sets and has been proven effective.

Keywords: NSGA-II · NSGA-III · Pivot · Non-dominated Sorting · Decision Space · Objective Space · Multiobjective Optimization

1 Introduction

MOGA is extensively employed in diverse fields such as engineering, science, medicine, management, finance, etc. A couple of examples [1, 2] showcase its effectiveness in addressing crucial multi-objective optimization problems in recent times. The widespread adoption of MOGA in industrial applications has significantly elevated its significance, making it a highly valued domain.

1.1 Prerequisites

This portion presents an exploration of the essential terminologies and pertinent concepts related to multi-objective optimization problems.

Definition 1 (Multi-objective Optimization Problem(MOP)). *Multiobjective optimization is a method utilized to improve multiple objectives concurrently, considering their mutual influence and any existing constraints. It aims to find optimal solutions that enhance two or more objectives simultaneously. The formal definition of the MOP is as follows:*

P. Maji et al. (Eds.): PReMI 2023, LNCS 14301, pp. 559–567, 2023.
https://doi.org/10.1007/978-3-031-45170-6_58

$$Min/Max \quad z_m(x), \quad m = 1, 2, \ldots, M;$$
$$s.t., \quad w_j(x) \geq 0, \quad j = 1, 2, \ldots, J; \quad y_k(x) = 0, \quad k = 1, 2, \ldots, K;$$
$$x_i^{(L)} \leq x_i \leq x_i^{(U)} \quad i = 1, 2, \ldots, n;$$

A solution[1], denoted as $x \in \mathbb{R}^n$, is a vector consisting of n decision variables: $x = (x_1, x_2, \ldots, x_n)^T$. In this context, M, J, and K represent the number of objectives that require optimization, denoted by z_m, the number of inequality constraints denoted by w_j, and the number of equality constraints denoted by y_k, respectively. The lower and upper bounds of x_i are denoted as $x_i^{(L)}$ and $x_i^{(U)}$, respectively, where $i = 1, 2, \ldots, n$ [3]. The mapping of decision space points to objective space points is illustrated in Fig. 1.

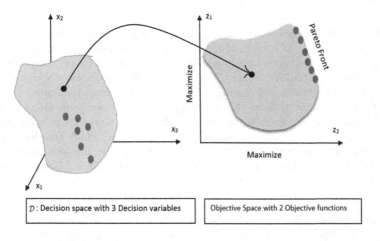

Fig. 1. Decision Space to Objective Space Mapping. The red points found in the objective space represent the members of the Pareto front. (Color figure online)

Definition 2 (Domination Relation). *A solution $\alpha \in \mathcal{D}$ (Decision Space) is said to dominate another solution $\beta \in \mathcal{D}$ if both the following conditions hold together:*

1. *In terms of all the objective functions, the solution α can not be worse than the solution β.*
2. *There exists at least one objective function for which α is strictly better than β [3].*

Definition 3 (Pareto Optimal Set). *A solution is deemed Pareto optimal when there is no other solution that can improve one objective without worsening another. The set of all Pareto optimal solutions is the "Pareto optimal set", and their corresponding objective points form the "Pareto front" [3].*

---

[1] Here "solution" refers to the elements of the decision space and "point" refers to the elements of the objective space respectively.

For example, in Fig. 1, the red solutions in the decision space form the Pareto optimal set, while the red points in the objective space depict the Pareto front.

1.2   Literature Survey

There have been several mechanisms to solve the MOPs, including SPEA2 [4], MOGA [5], NSGA-II [6], IBEA [7], NSGA-III [8], and more. Among these, NSGA-II stands out as one of the most popular approaches. NSGA-II comprises two main constituents: Fast Non-dominated Sorting (FNDS) and Crowding Distance. FNDS having the computational complexity of $O(MN^2)$, generates non-dominated fronts, with M and N being the number of objective functions and population size respectively. Although other non-dominated sorting approaches exist, for example, a recursive mechanism having a computational complexity of $O(Nlog^{M-1}N)$ by Jensen et al. [9], they become ineffective when two different solutions are with the same objective function value. Tang et al. introduced a fast approach for generating the non-dominated set using the arena's principle [10]. Zhang et al. introduced an important method called Efficient Non-dominated Sorting (ENS), which encompasses two variations: one employing sequential search (ENS-SS) and the other utilizing binary search (ENS-BS) [11]. However, no existing algorithm in the literature achieves better time complexity in the worst-case scenario than $O(MN^2)$ for non-dominated sorting while remaining complete.

1.3   Gap Identification and Motivation

To address the issues discussed in Sect. 1.2, we have offered a pivot-based non-dominated sorting that intends to provide a complete, correct, and time-efficient algorithm that generates non-dominated fronts.

1.4   Structure of the Paper

This paper is structured into the following four sections. First, "Introduction" in Sect. 1, covers the background information, literature review, and gap analysis. Followed by "Methodology" in Sect. 2, which explains the proposed technique and provides information about the relevant dataset. Section 3 is dedicated to "Result and Analysis", where the completeness and accuracy of the proposed method are demonstrated and discussed. Finally, the "Conclusion" is presented in Sect. 4.

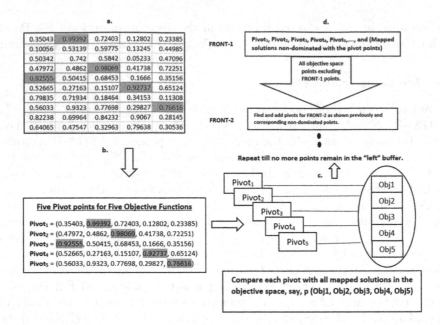

Fig. 2. Flow Diagram of the Pivot-based Deterministic Non-dominated Sorting Approach. **a.** Snippet of a demo data set in an objective space with each column representing five different objective functions. **b.** Five Pivot points for five objective functions. **c.** Comparing all points in the objective space with the pivot point(s) to check whether they are worse or in a non-dominated relation with the pivot point(s). **d.** The recursive process of generating fronts until the "left" buffer, used to hold all other elements excluding the current front's pivot points and its non-dominated points, is empty.

2   Methodology

For a clear understanding of the methodology, we introduce the concept of *Pivot*.

Definition 4 (Pivot). *Pivot points refer to the mapped solutions from a decision space to an objective space where there is at least one objective function that achieves the optimal value. This optimal value can be either the maximum value if the objective function aims to maximize or the minimum value if the objective function aims to minimize. In a typical multi-objective optimization, there can be a combination of possibilities for both maximization and minimization. Figure 2 depicts the flow diagram of the mechanism, with an explanation of pivot points.*

2.1   Benchmark Data-Set Specification

Zitzler-Deb-Thiele-1 (ZDT-1) Test Suite. The construction of the ZDT problem suite is rooted in a 30-variable problem ($n = 30$) that exhibits a convex Pareto-optimal set [14].

$$\min z_1(x); \min z_2(x) = g(x)h(z_1(x), g(x));$$

where two objectives need minimization, the function g(x) is typically used to represent convergence, and it is common for $g(x) = 1$ for Pareto-optimal solutions. The definition of the ZDT-1 test suite is as follows:

$$z_1(x) = x_1; \quad g(x) = 1 + \frac{9}{n-1}\sum_{i=2}^{n}x_i; \quad h(z_1, g) = 1 - \sqrt{\frac{z_1}{g}}; \quad 0 \le x_i \le 1$$

where, $i = 1, \ldots, n$.

The Vehicle Crashworthiness Problem. This real-life application-based benchmark involves optimizing the level of safety in the event of a crash and is characterized as a problem with three objectives and no constraints [13]. This problem involves five decision variables, x_1, x_2, x_3, x_4, and x_5. Three objective functions: z_1, z_2, and z_3 are depicted as follows:

$$z_1(x) = 1640.2823 + 2.3573285x_1 + 2.3220035x_2$$
$$+ 4.5688768x_3 + 7.7213633x_4 + 4.4559504x_5$$

$$z_2(x) = 6.5856 + 1.15x_1 - 1.0427x_2 + 0.9738x_3 + 0.8364x_4 - 0.3695x_1x_4$$
$$+ 0.0861x_1x_5 + 0.3628x_2x_4 - 0.1106x_1x_1 - 0.3437x_3x_3 + 0.1764x_4x_4$$

$$z_3(x) = -0.0551 + 0.0181x_1 + 0.1024x_2 + 0.0421x_3 - 0.0073x_1x_2 + 0.024x_2x_3$$
$$- 0.0118x_2x_4 - 0.0204x_3x_4 - 0.008x_3x_5 - 0.0241x_2x_2 + 0.0109x_4x_4$$

Deb-Thiele-Laumanns-Zitzler-1 (DTLZ-1). This involves n decision variables and is defined as follows [15]:
Minimize:
$$f_1(\vec{x}) = \frac{1}{2}x_1x_2\cdots x_{M-1}(1 + g(\vec{x}))$$
$$f_i(\vec{x}) = \frac{1}{2}x_1x_2\cdots(1 - x_{i-1})\cdots(1 - x_{M-1})(1 + g(\vec{x})), \quad i = 2, \ldots, M-1$$
$$f_M(\vec{x}) = \frac{1}{2}(1 - x_1)(1 + g(\vec{x}))$$

where $\vec{x} = (x_1, x_2, \ldots, x_K)$ depicts the decision variables, and $g(\vec{x})$ is a nonlinear function given by:

$$g(\vec{x}) = \sum_{i=K-M+1}^{K}(x_i - 0.5)^2 - \cos(20\pi(x_i - 0.5))$$

The decision variables are subject to the following constraints:

$$0 \le x_i \le 1, \quad i = 1, \ldots, K$$

OneMinMax and Leading Ones and Trailing Zeros (LOTZ). The One-MinMax benchmark was originally suggested by Giel and Lehre (2010) as a two-objective version of the well-known ONEMAX benchmark. Laumanns, Thiele, and Zitzler (2004) introduced a benchmark called LOTZ. The benchmarks mentioned here contain objective functions that are of maximization type [12].
$z : \{0,1\}^n \rightarrow \mathbb{N} \times \mathbb{N}$
OneMinMax Function is defined by:

$$z(x) = (z_1(x), z_2(x)) = (n - \sum_{i=1}^{n} x_i, \sum_{i=1}^{n} x_i); \forall x = (x_1, x_2, \ldots, x_n) \in \{0,1\}^n$$

The LOTZ function is defined as follows:

$$z(x) = (z_1(x), z_2(x)) = (\sum_{i=1}^{n} \prod_{j=1}^{i} x_j, \sum_{i=1}^{n} \prod_{j=1}^{n} (1 - x_j)); \forall x \in \{0,1\}^n$$

2.2   Pivot-Based Deterministic Non-dominated Sorting

The algorithm takes input as the mapped solutions from the decision space and outputs non-overlapping decomposed Front(s), where the first Front represents the Pareto Front. Algorithm 1 shows the Pivot-based Deterministic Non-dominated Sorting.

3   Result and Analysis

The result yielded for different benchmark functions are shown in Fig. 3. The result of the suggested Pivot-based algorithm is evaluated using the ZDT-1 bi-objective benchmark function to compare the fast non-dominated sorting and the proposed approach. In the sample of 500 elements in the objective space, both methods successfully position all elements on the Pareto Front. This indicates the presence of a single front, where all 500 elements in the sample are mutually non-dominated. This information is visualized as a diamond shape in Fig. 3. The analysis extends to the "Vehicle Crashworthiness" benchmark, which involves three objective functions and is examined using both fast non-dominated sorting and the proposed approach. In this case, the entire objective space is divided into eight fronts, with each front containing an equal number of elements for both methods. These fronts are represented by a brown-coloured asterisk sign. The consistency of this outcome is observed across all other benchmark functions showcased in Fig. 3 where yellow square, green triangle, and brown cross are used respectively for DTLZ - 1, LOTZ, and OneMinMax front representation, thereby affirming the validity of the proposed algorithm.

3.1   Completeness and Correctness of the Algorithm

Formation of pivots followed by placement of an objective space element in a suitable front in respect of the pivot undergo exhaustive exploration in a deterministic sense. Hence, assigning a newly explored element in an appropriate Front can not but be procedurally complete.

Algorithm 1 Pivot-based Deterministic Non-dominated Sorting Algorithm

---

1: Find the pivot points (min/max depending on the objective function(s)) and assign them to the head of the current level
2: Save the remaining tuples (or points) in a buffer named left
3: **for** each Tmp_{tpl} from **left** fetch one by one and **do**
4:     $swap_{flg} \leftarrow 0; move_{flg} \leftarrow 0$
5:     **for** each ith element of both Tmp_{tpl} and $Head_{tpl}$ **do**
6:         $lower_{flg} \leftarrow 0; greater_{flg} \leftarrow 0; equi_{flg} \leftarrow 0$
7:         **if** $Tmp_{tpl} == Head_{tpl}$ **then**
8:             Insert the Tmp_{tpl} into current Head and go to **step-3**.
9:         **end if**
10:         **for** $i \leftarrow 0$ to M **do**   ▷ M: Number of objective functions
11:             **if** $(Tmp_{tpl})_i > Head_{tpl}$ **then**
12:                 $greater_{flg} + = 1$
13:             **end if**
14:             **if** $(Tmp_{tpl})_i < Head_{tpl}$ **then**
15:                 $lower_{flg} + = 1$
16:             **end if**
17:             **if** $(Tmp_{tpl})_i == Head_{tpl}$ **then**
18:                 $equi_{flg} + = 1$
19:             **end if**
20:         **end for**
21:         **if** $(greater_{flg} + equi_{flg}) == M$ **then**
22:             move $Head_{tpl}$ from head list to left
23:             $swap_{flg} + = 1$
24:         **end if**
25:         **if** $(greater_{flg} == 0$ and $lower_{flg} \neq 0)$ **then**
26:             move $Temp_{tpl}$ to left
27:             $swap_{flg} \leftarrow 0, move_{flg} \leftarrow 0$
28:             goto **step-3**
29:         **end if**
30:         **if** $(greater_{flg} \neq 0$ and $lower_{flg} == 0)$ **then**
31:             $move_{flg} + = 1$
32:         **end if**
33:         **if** $(swap_{flg} > 0$ or $move_{flg} > 0)$ **then**
34:             move/add Tmp_{tpl} in the $Head$(current Head)
35:             goto **step-3**
36:         **end if**
37:     **end for**
38: **end for**
39: **if** left is not empty **then**
40:     Create next level and goto **step-1**
41: **end if**

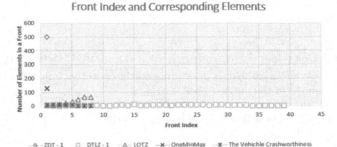

Fig. 3. Number of Fronts and corresponding elements generated using the proposed method and the Fast Non-dominated Sorting.

3.2 Complexity of the Proposed Algorithm

The Algorithm proposed in Algorithm 1 consists of two nested for loops in steps 3 and 5, which iterate N times, where N represents the number of mapped solutions in the objective space. In the worst-case scenario, this algorithm requires $O(N^2)$ time to finish. Additionally, step 10 includes another loop that iterates M times, where M is the number of objective functions. Step 1, on the other hand, takes $O(MN)$ time to complete. Consequently, the algorithm's best-case, average-case, and worst-case time complexity is respectively, $\Omega(MN^2)$, $\Theta(MN^2)$, $O(MN^2)$, which is similar to respective cases of the Fast Non-dominated Sorting phase in NSGA-II and NSGA-III. Furthermore, no worse than any existing non-dominated sorting algorithm, which is complete, in the worst-case scenario.

4   Conclusion

The pivot-based framework has a number of benefits. First off, the idea is simple and straightforward to put into practice. Second, it covers all the solutions in the decision space by effectively dividing them into non-overlapping fronts using the mapped objective space values, needless to mention which ensures the categorization of the quality of the solutions. Last but not least, it accomplishes these advantages in a time-efficient way that isn't worse than current state-of-the-art methods. The effectiveness of the suggested approach is validated by comparisons with multiple benchmark multi-objective optimization functions that exist in the literature. Despite being a novel, complete, and correct approach, the algorithm cannot handle streamed or online data. Our efforts in the future will be directed towards addressing this particular issue in the algorithm.

References

1. Mei, Y., Wu, K.: Application of multi-objective optimization in the study of anti-breast cancer candidate drugs. Sci. Rep. **12**, 19347 (2022). https://doi.org/10.1038/s41598-022-23851-0

2. Winiczenko, R., Kaleta, A., Górnicki, K.: Application of a MOGA algorithm and ANN in the optimization of apple drying and rehydration processes. Processes **9**(8), 1415 (2021). https://doi.org/10.3390/pr9081415
3. Deb, K.: Multiobjective Optimization Using Evolutionary Algorithms. Wiley, New York (2001)
4. Zitzler, E., Laumanns, M., Thiele, L.: SPEA2: improving the strength pareto evolutionary algorithm. In: Evolutionary Methods for Design, Optimization and Control With Applications to Industrial Problems. Proceedings of the EUROGEN 2001, Athens, Greece, 19–21 September 2001 (2001)
5. Fonseca, C.M., Fleming, P.J.: Genetic algorithms for multiobjective optimization: Formulation, discussion and generalization. In: Forrest, S. (Ed.), Proceedings of the Fifth International Conference on Genetic Algorithms, pp. 416–423. Morgan Kauffman Publishers (1993)
6. Deb, K., Pratap, A., Agarwal, S., Meyarivan, T.: A fast and elitist multiobjective genetic algorithm: NSGA-II. IEEE Trans. Evol. Comput. **6**(2), 182–197 (2002). https://doi.org/10.1109/4235.996017
7. Zitzler, E., Künzli, S.: Indicator-based selection in multiobjective search. In: Yao, X., et al. (eds.) PPSN 2004. LNCS, vol. 3242, pp. 832–842. Springer, Heidelberg (2004). https://doi.org/10.1007/978-3-540-30217-9_84
8. Deb, K., Jain, H.: An evolutionary many-objective optimization algorithm using reference-point-based nondominated sorting approach, Part I: solving problems with box constraints. IEEE Trans. Evol. Comput. **18**(4), 577–601 (2014)
9. Jensen, M.T.: Reducing the run-time complexity of multiobjective EAs: the NSGA-II and other algorithms. IEEE Trans. Evol. Comput. **7**(5), 503–515 (2003)
10. Tang, S., Cai, Z., Zheng, J.: A fast method of constructing the non-dominated set: Arena's principle. In: 2008 Fourth International Conference on Natural Computation, pp. 391–395. IEEE Computer Society Press (2008)
11. Zhang, X., Tian, Y., Cheng, R., Jin, Y.: An efficient approach to nondominated sorting for evolutionary multiobjective optimization. IEEE Trans. Evol. Comput. **19**(2), 201–213 (2015)
12. Zheng, W., Liu, Y., Doerr, B.: A first mathematical runtime analysis of the non-dominated sorting genetic algorithm II (NSGA-II). In: Proceedings of the AAAI Conference on Artificial Intelligence, vol. 36, no. 9, pp. 10408–10416 (2022). https://doi.org/10.1609/aaai.v36i9.21283
13. Liao, X., Li, Q., Yang, X., Zhang, W., Li, W.: Multiobjective optimization for crash safety design of vehicles using stepwise regression model. Struct. Multidiscip. Optim. **35**(6), 561–569 (2008)
14. Zitzler, E., Deb, K., Thiele, L.: Comparison of multiobjective evolutionary algorithms: empirical results. Evol. Comput. **8**(2), 173–195 (2000). https://doi.org/10.1162/106365600568202
15. Deb, K., Thiele, L., Laumanns, M., Zitzler, E.: Scalable multi-objective optimization test problems. In: Proceedings of the 2002 Congress on Evolutionary Computation. CEC 2002 (Cat. No.02TH8600), vol. 1, pp. 825–830. IEEE, Honolulu, HI, USA (2002). https://doi.org/10.1109/CEC.2002.1007032

Elephant Swarm Water Search Algorithm (LESWSA) for Solving Constrained Optimization Problems: A List Based Randomized Approach

Joy Adhikary and Sriyankar Acharyya[✉]

Department of Computer Science and Engineering, Maulana Abul Kalam Azad University of
Technology, Kolkata, West Bengal, India
srikalpa8@gmail.com

Abstract. Elephant Swarm Water Search Algorithm (ESWSA) is a Swarm
Intelligence-based metaheuristic algorithm that follows the water search strategy
of groups of elephants. This paper has introduced LESWSA (List based Elephant
Swarm Water Search Algorithm), newly version of ESWSA. It uses two lists (P_{list}
and G_{list}) which enables the search process to explore search space in a more efficient way and make a balance between exploration and exploitation. These two
lists store different local and global best solutions having equal cost. Moreover,
a randomized move with the student's t-distributed random numbers is used to
enhance the exploration. The proposed variant has outperformed ESWSA on 23
benchmark functions out of 30 (CEC 2014). Results have been verified by comparing with the results obtained by existing meta-heuristic techniques like GSA,
Firefly, CL-PSO, DE, ESWSA, and CM-ESWSA on CEC 2014 benchmark functions. It has also been used to find solutions to constrained optimization problems
existing in real-world domains, and its performance is superior to that of other
promising metaheuristics in most of the cases.

Keywords: Metaheuristics · Elephant Swarm · Optimization · Constrained
problem

1 Introduction

Metaheuristic algorithms [1, 2] are normally used to solve various hard real-life problems
within a reasonable time. These algorithms are normally nature-inspired, simple, and
problem-domain independent [1, 2, 10]. The basic structure of these algorithms remains
the same while solving problems in different domains. Exploration and exploitation
[2] are the main characteristics of the meta-heuristic search process. It balances the
effectiveness between exploration and exploitation to make the search more efficient [1,
2, 10].

In [10], researchers divided metaheuristic algorithms into two categories: trajectory-
based and population-based. A trajectory-based algorithm [1, 10] (Simulated Annealing

© The Author(s), under exclusive license to Springer Nature Switzerland AG 2023
P. Maji et al. (Eds.): PReMI 2023, LNCS 14301, pp. 568–576, 2023.
https://doi.org/10.1007/978-3-031-45170-6_59

(SA) [9], Iterated Local Search (ILS) [1], and others) starts its execution with a single solution. The population-based (Genetic Algorithm (GA) [4], Particle Swarm Optimization (PSO) [5], Grey Wolf Optimizer (GWO) [2, 8], and others) algorithms start with a randomly generated population of solutions. Then, the initial population of solutions will be progressively updated through iterations.

Swarm Intelligence (SI) [2, 3] based algorithms are the most simple and popular population-based metaheuristic algorithms which use a swarm of intelligently behaving search agents. Throughout the course of iterations, they keep track of movements and exchange information about the search space, and they store the most promising solutions explored so far. [2]. These techniques are mainly motivated by the collective behavior of various animals/creatures in the natural environment. Elephant Swarm Water Search Algorithm (ESWSA) [3, 11] is of this type where a group of elephants explores together to find a water body by controlling local and global search processes using the context switching probability (p_{cs}). In [11], a different version of ESWSA, namely, CM-ESWSA (Chaotic Move Elephant Swarm Water Search Algorithm) is proposed and implemented. Researchers made use of the chaotic movements in the search process to improve the explorative behaviour so that it can avoid the problem of early convergence.

In this paper, ESWSA has been modified to a new variant LESWSA (List based Elephant Swarm Water Search Algorithm) to enhance exploration characteristics in the search process by incorporating two lists P_{list} (local or personal best solutions) and G_{list} (global or swarm best solutions). Solutions stored in P_{list} have cost very close to each other and so also for the solutions stored in G_{list}. In any step, the personal or global best solutions are selected in a random manner from the corresponding lists. So, the variant LESWSA enhances the exploration capability of the searching procedure, which helps avoid local optimum in the search space and resists premature convergence. Apart from this, LESWSA has used a randomized approach based on student's t-distributed [2] random numbers in the local water search strategy instead of LDIW [3, 11].

Following is the arrangement of the remaining sections: A cocise explanation of ESWSA and its proposed variation (LESWSA) are provided in Sects. 2 and 3. Experimental observations are discussed in Sect. 4. Section 5 concludes the work and raises some future issues.

2 Elephant Swarm Water Search Algorithm (ESWSA)

The Elephant Swarm Water Search algorithm (ESWSA) [3, 11] was designed based on the tactics used by elephants to find water resources. Elephants move in multiple groups (elephant swarms) in search of water when there is a drought. The leader of each group decides the next movement of the group to reach the best water source. The group leader will inform other groups when a group locates a water source [3, 11]. The algorithm considers that each elephant group is considered a solution identified by its own position. Two types of search strategies are undertaken, namely, local and global water search and they are controlled by context switch probability (p_{cs}) [3]. In the local strategy of water search, the best (nearest) position of the source of water discovered by a swarm of elephants in their journey is taken as the local best solution. In the global strategy of water search, the closest position of the water source discovered by all groups or swarms is considered as the global best solution. The global and local water searches are expressed by Eqs. (1) and (2), respectively.

$$V_i = V_i * w + rand(1, d) \odot (Gbest - X_i) \tag{1}$$

$$V_i = V_i * w + rand(1, d) \odot (Pbest_i - X_i) \tag{2}$$

In Eqs. (1) and (2), $rand(1, d)$ refers to an array of random values within the range [0, 1] with dimension d. Linear Decreasing Inertia Weight (LDIW) [3] is expressed by w (Eq. 3). V_i denotes the velocity of propagation of the elephants in the i-th group and X_i is the existing location of the group. $Pbest_i$ denotes the local best solution obtained by the i-th group and $Gbest$ denotes the global best solution. The best solution in the set of all local best solutions is taken as the global best solution. In Eq. (3), t and t_{max} indicates the iteration number and the maximum limit on iterations taken into account respectively. Here, w_{max} and w_{min} are control parameters. The position of a group of elephants is modified by Eq. (4).

$$w = w_{max} - \left\{ \frac{w_{max} - w_{min}}{t_{max}} \right\} * t \tag{3}$$

$$X_i = V_i + X_i \tag{4}$$

3   List Based Elephant Swarm Water Search Algorithm (LESWSA)

The proposed variant List based Elephant Swarm Water Search Algorithm (LESWSA) enhances the rate of exploration in searching water resources by maintaining two lists: P_{list} and G_{list}. P_{list} And G_{list} store solutions (local best and global best) with costs very close to each other. The personal and global best solutions are choosen at random from their corresponding lists (P_{list} and G_{list}) after each iteration. In the next iteration, any best solution from each list will be selected randomly to update solutions. This random selection of $Pbest$ and $Gbest$ enhances the explorative behavior without sacrificing the quality (exploitation). Thus, a balance is established between exploration and exploitation. The details about P_{list} and G_{list} have been given in Sects. 3.1 and 3.2 respectively. Apart from this, LESWSA has used another randomized move strategy using student's t distributed random numbers [2] (Eq. 5) in case of local search only whereas the earlier version ESWSA used Linear Decreasing Inertia Weight (LDIW) [3] in case of both search (local and global). Student's t-distributed random number generator provides an uncertain jump in generating random numbers which is absent in LDIW. In exploring the search space, this abruptness is used [2]. $trnd(v, 1, d)$ Generates random numbers ($1 \times d$ student's t distributed) [2] where v = degrees of freedom and d = dimension [2].

$$wt = u * trnd(v, 1, d) + u * trnd(v, 1, d) \tag{5}$$

3.1 Implementation of P_{list}

For each group of elephants, Eq. 4 updates the position. Then the cost of the updated position of i-th group $(cost(X_i))$ is matched with its personal best cost $(cost(Pbest_i))$. If the $cost(X_i)$ is less than $cost(Pbest_i)$, then perform the following steps.

i. Reset the P_{list} (as the previous best solutions are worse than the current best solutions the lists are made empty to hold new best solutions)
ii. Store X_i into P_{list} and it has been considered as $Pbest_i$ (Fig. 1).

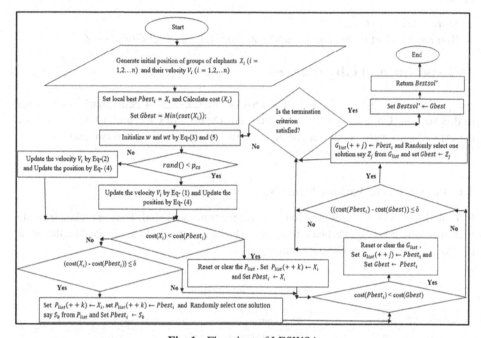

Fig. 1. Flowchart of LESWSA

Here in this proposed method P_{list} stores all solutions having equal cost or with a small difference within a limit. If cost (X_i) is not less than cost $(Pbest_i)$, then the difference of the cost is checked. If the cost difference between X_i and $Pbest_i$ (cost (X_i) - cost $(Pbest_i)$) is within the specified threshold (δ) value, then perform the following steps.

i. Store X_i and $Pbest_i$ into P_{list}.
ii. Randomly select one solution such as S_k from P_{list} and set $Pbest_i \leftarrow S_k$

3.2 Implementation of G_{list}

G_{list} Will be used while comparing the cost of the personal best solution with that of the globally best solution. The cost of the solution (local or personal best) achieved by the i-th group of elephants (cost $(Pbest_i)$) is matched with that of the global best solution (cost (*Gbest*)). If the cost (*Pbest$_i$*) is less than the cost (*Gbest*), then perform the following steps.

i. G_{list} has been cleared or reset.
ii. Store *Pbest$_i$* into G_{list} and consider it as *Gbest*.

The similar concept has been incorporated in the case of G_{list}. If the cost (*Pbest$_i$*)) of elephants (i-th group) is not better than that of the global best solution (cost (*Gbest*)), then the difference of their cost is checked. If the cost difference of *Pbest$_i$* and *Gbest* (cost (*Pbest$_i$*) - cost (*Gbest*)) is within the threshold (δ) value, then perform the following steps.

i. Store *Gbest* into G_{list}.
ii. Randomly select one solution such as Z_j from G_{list} and set *Gbest* $\leftarrow Z_j$.

4   Experimental Observations

The performance of ESWSA and LESWSA on the CEC 2014 benchmark is examined in this section. On a computer with a Pentium Dual-Core CPU and 4 GB of memory, the experiments were conducted. Matlab R2012b is used as the platform, and Microsoft Windows 7 is the software environment.

4.1   Parameters of Various Algorithms

In Table 1, parameter values used in various algorithms are listed. They are taken from the literature where tuning has been done on the basis of sensitivity analysis. The threshold parameter δ is tuned here experimentally.

Table 1. Parameter values

Algorithm	Parameters	Algorithm	Parameters
Firefly[7]	$\beta_0 = 0.5, \alpha = 0.2,$ $\lambda = 1.5, \Upsilon = 0.01$ and $m = 1$	ESWSA [3, 11], CM-ESWSA [11], LESWSA	$w_{max} = 0.9, w_{min} = 0.4,$ $\delta = 0.3, p_{cs} = 0.6, u = 0.5$ and $t_{max} = 10{,}000$
DE [12]	$F = 0.5$ and $C_p = 0.9$	GSA[6]	$G_0 = 100$ and $\alpha = 20$

4.2   Analysis of Benchmark Function Results and Comparative Analysis

According to CEC 2014 criteria [2, 8], each function of the benchmark set is optimized over 51 runs. The CEC 2014 provides 30 different types of functions. It calculates the error ($|Cost - Cost^*|$), where $Cost$ = computed cost and $Cost^*$ = cost reported in CEC 2014 [2, 8]. From the errors obtained the mean, standard deviation, and median are measured. The performance of LESWSA is measured based on all three metrics: mean, standard deviation, and median. Results of ESWSA and LESWSA on dimension 10 are shown in Table 2. In unimodal functions (1 to 3), LESWSA is best for all functions.

LESWSA performed well in 8 multimodal functions out of 13 (4 to 16). The performance of LESWSA is extremely good in all hybrid functions (17 to 22) except function 19. In composite functions (23 to 30), LESWSA performed well in 7 functions out of 8. It clearly shows that LESWSA is better than ESWSA in 23 benchmark functions out of 30.

This section analyses the cost convergence of LESWSA along with other meta-heuristic algorithms like Gravitational Search Algorithms (GSA) [6], Firefly [7], Comprehensive Learning PSO (CL-PSO) [5], Differential Evolution (DE) [12], Elephant Swarm Water Search Algorithm (ESWSA) [3] and Chaotic Move Elephant Swarm Water Search Algorithm (CM-ESWSA) [11]. Figure 2 shows that LESWSA does not fall prey to early convergence and has reached the best value compared to others.

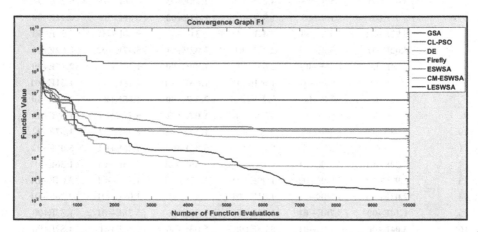

Fig. 2. Convergence analysis of LESWSA and other metaheuristics

4.3 Performance on Real-World Problems

The effectiveness of LESWSA with ESWSA is compared on constrained real-life optimization problems [2]. Here, tension/compression string design [2, 8] and pressure vessel design [2, 8] problems have been considered. The cost functions of these problems are represented in Eq. (6) and (7). In Eq. (6), d_1, d_2 and d_3 are decision variables, where d_1 = diameter of wire, d_2 = mean of coil diameter and d_3 = count of coils active [2, 8]. In Eq. (7), d_1, d_2, d_3 and d_4 are decision variables, where d_1 = the thickness of the shell, d_2 = The dish's thickness end, d_3 = radius of the shell and d_4 = length of the shell [2, 8]. The penalty function [2] considered here is used to control the effect of constraints. Whenever some constraint is violated a penalty value is generated which is used to increase the cost function [2].

$$C_1(d) = (d_3 + 2)d_2 d_1^2 \qquad (6)$$

$$C_2(d) = 0.6224 d_1 d_3 d_4 + 1.7781 d_2 d_3^2 + 3.1661 d_1^2 d_4 + 19.84 d_1^2 d_3 \qquad (7)$$

The efficacy of other metaheuristic algorithms is matched with that of LESWSA and the results on these problems are given in Tables 3 and 4. Results produced by all other algorithms are collected from [8]. In both cases, LESWSA has achieved the lower cost value.

Table 2. Mean, Standard Deviation, and Median error value on CEC14 benchmark instances [For a function, better results are bolded].

ESWSA				LESWSA		
Function	Mean	Std dev	Median	Mean	Std dev	Median
1	4.83E+04	1.50E+05	8.33E+03	**1.01E+04**	**1.35E+04**	**4.28E+03**
2	3.67E+03	7.57E+03	4.24E+02	**2.48E+03**	**3.36E+03**	9.73E+02
3	2.99E+02	1.16E+03	1.97E+01	**1.47E+02**	**3.80E+02**	**6.12E+00**
4	**5.97E−01**	**1.09E+00**	**2.42E−01**	4.31E+00	9.30E+00	3.22E+00
5	**2.02E+01**	8.30E−02	**2.02E+01**	2.02E+01	**5.47E−02**	2.02E+01
6	2.64E+00	**1.36E+00**	2.60E+00	**1.80E+00**	1.47E+00	2.15E+00
7	1.92E−01	1.01E−01	1.69E−01	**1.65E−01**	**7.18E−02**	**1.51E−01**
8	9.40E+00	5.74E+00	7.95E+00	**2.25E+00**	**1.85E+00**	**1.99E+00**
9	1.72E+01	6.85E+00	1.79E+01	**1.62E+01**	**6.71E+00**	**1.59E+01**
10	2.08E+02	1.35E+02	2.12E+02	**1.34E+02**	**1.08E+02**	**1.37E+02**
11	6.28E+02	2.37E+02	6.11E+02	**5.02E+02**	**2.26E+02**	**5.07E+02**
12	5.29E−01	**3.35E−01**	4.19E−01	**4.80E−01**	4.93E−01	**1.36E−01**
13	**1.97E−01**	**7.80E−02**	**1.90E−01**	3.12E−01	1.19E−01	3.04E−01
14	**2.03E−01**	**9.00E−02**	**1.81E−01**	2.41E−01	1.09E−01	2.28E−01
15	**1.14E+00**	**3.76E−01**	**1.14E−01**	1.38E+00	5.38E−01	1.33E+00
16	**3.04E+00**	**4.13E−01**	**3.03E+00**	5.03E+00	1.12E+01	4.87E+00
17	1.97E+04	6.52E+04	3.67E+03	**7.40E+03**	**8.60E+03**	**3.57E+03**
18	7.97E+03	8.19E+03	5.53E+03	**7.57E+03**	8.40E+03	**5.25E+03**
19	**1.36E+00**	**4.19E−01**	**1.52E+00**	1.55E+00	5.23E−01	1.60E+00
20	1.58E+03	4.63E+03	2.91E+02	**8.48E+02**	**2.27E+03**	**6.79E+01**
21	2.59E+02	3.24E+02	1.39E+02	**1.87E+02**	**1.81E+02**	**1.25E+02**
22	2.83E+01	2.84E+01	2.15E+01	**2.73E+01**	**8.38E+00**	2.17E+01
23	3.30E+02	**1.00E+01**	**3.29E+02**	3.22E+02	3.09E+01	**3.29E+02**
24	**1.29E+02**	**1.36E+01**	**1.27E+02**	1.33E+02	1.97E+01	1.28E+02
25	2.02E+02	**4.58E+00**	2.00E+02	**1.87E+02**	2.50E+01	**2.00E+02**
26	**1.00E+02**	1.59E−01	**1.00E+02**	**1.00E+02**	**1.35E−01**	**1.00E+02**
27	8.94E+02	2.00E+02	9.56E+02	**3.84E+02**	**5.92E+01**	**4.00E+02**
28	4.61E+02	7.03E+01	4.30E+02	**3.17E+02**	**3.19E+01**	**3.06E+02**
29	2.27E+02	3.24E+01	2.13E+02	**2.05E+02**	**2.92E+01**	**2.05E+02**
30	9.03E+02	3.04E+02	8.65E+02	**2.85E+02**	**5.88E+01**	**2.62E+02**

Table 3. Results on compression string design

Algorithm	Optimal decision vector			Optimum value
	d_1	d_2	d_3	
LESWSA	0.05	0.348	10.648	**0.011**
ESWSA	0.05	0.348	10.562	**0.011**
RW-GWO [8]	0.051	0.356	11.330	0.0126
GWO [8]	0.051	0.353	11.504	0.127
GA(Coello) [8]	0.051	0.351	11.632	0.0127
GSA [8]	0.050	0.323	13.525	0.0127

Table 4. Results on pressure vessel design

Algorithm	Optimal decision vector				Optimum value
	d_1	d_2	d_3	d_4	
LESWSA	**0.7791**	**0.3980**	**40.3493**	**200.0000**	**5935.31**
ESWSA	0.7868	0.3899	40.7686	193.8424	5903.154
GWO [8]	0.87500	0.43750	44.98072	144.10807	6136.660
GSA [8]	1.12500	0.62500	55.98866	84.45420	8538.836
PSO [8]	0.81250	0.43750	42.09127	176.74650	6061.078
GA [8]	0.81250	0.43450	40.32390	20.00000	6288.745

5 Conclusions

The proposed variant LESWSA significantly improves the overall search performance compared to ESWSA. LESWSA has introduced two lists, which store all the locally and globally best solutions with the same cost/fitness in iteration. From the list, the local and global best solutions are randomly selected for the next operation. It helps the search process reach the important area of the search space by balancing the contributions obtained from exploration and exploitation. The algorithm's performance has been tested against ESWSA on CEC 14 benchmark functions and LESWSA has achieved better results in most of the benchmark functions. Moreover, LESWSA has also performed better on most of the constrained optimization problems in the real world.

References

1. Abdel-Basset, M., Abdel-Fatah, L., Sangaiah, A.K.: Metaheuristic algorithms: a comprehensive review. In: Computational Intelligence for Multimedia Big data on the Cloud with Engineering Applications, pp. 185–231 (2018)
2. Adhikary, J., Acharyya, S.: Randomized balanced grey wolf optimizer (RBGWO) for solving real life optimization problems. Appl. Soft Comput. **117**, 108429 (2022)
3. Mandal, S., Saha, G., Paul, R.K.: Recurrent neural network-based modeling of gene regulatory network using elephant swarm water search algorithm. J. Bioinform. Comput. Biol. **15**(04), 1750016 (2017)

4. Bhowmik, S., Acharyya, S.: Image cryptography: the genetic algorithm approach. In: IEEE International Conference on Computer Science and Automation Engineering, vol. 2, pp. 223–227 (2011)
5. Liang, J.J., Qin, A.K., Suganhan, P.N., Baskar, S.: Comprehensive learning particle swarm optimizer for global optimization of multimodal functions. IEEE Trans. Evol. Comput. **10**(3), 281–295 (2006)
6. Rashedi, E., Nezamabadi-Pour, H., Saryazdi, S.: GSA: a gravitational search algorithm. Inf. Sci. **179**(13), 2232–2248 (2009)
7. Yang, X.S.: Firefly algorithm, Levy flights and global optimization. In: Bramer, M., Ellis, R., Petridis, M. (eds.) Research and development in intelligent systems XXVI, pp. 209–218. Springer, London (2010). https://doi.org/10.1007/978-1-84882-983-1_15
8. Gupta, S., Deep, K.: A novel random walk grey wolf optimizer. Swarm Evol. Comput. **44**, 101–112 (2019)
9. Biswas, S., Acharyya, S.: A bi-objective RNN model to reconstruct gene regulatory network: a modified multi-objective simulated annealing approach. IEEE Trans. Evol. Comput. Biol. Bioinform. **15**(6), 2053–2059 (2018)
10. Gendreau, M., Potvin, J.Y.: Metaheuristics in combinatorial optimization. Ann. Oper. Res. **140**(1), 189–213 (2005)
11. Adhikary, J., Acharyya, S.: Identification of biologically relevant biclusters from gene expression dataset of duchenne muscular dystrophy (DMD) disease using elephant swarm water search algorithm. In: Hassanien, A.E., Bhattacharyya, S., Chakrabati, S., Bhattacharya, A., Dutta, S. (eds.) Emerging Technologies in Data Mining and Information Security. AISC, vol. 1286, pp. 147–157. Springer, Singapore (2021). https://doi.org/10.1007/978-981-15-9927-9_15
12. Guo, S.M., Yang, C.C., Hsu, P.H., Tsai, J.S.H.: Improving differential evolution with a successful-parent-selecting framework. IEEE Trans. Evol. Comput. **19**(5), 717–730 (2015)

Fuzzy Rule-Based Approach Towards Cognitive Load Measurement During Mental Task Using fNIRS

Subashis Karmakar[1(✉)], Chiranjib Koley[2], Aniruddha Sinha[3],
Sanjoy Kumar Saha[4], and Tandra Pal[1]

[1] Department of Computer Science and Engineering, National Institute of
Technology Durgapur, Durgapur, West Bengal, India
`sk.21cs1108@phd.nitdgp.ac.in`
[2] Department of Electrical Engineering, National Institute of Technology Durgapur,
Durgapur, West Bengal, India
[3] Tata Consultancy Services Ltd., TCS Research, Kolkata, West Bengal, India
[4] Department of Computer Science and Engineering, Jadavpur University, Kolkata,
West Bengal, India

Abstract. Every individual utilizes a different level of cognitive load for the same mental task. Measuring cognitive levels helps to design personalized instructional materials to enhance teaching-learning process and diagnose possible learning disabilities or neurodegenerative disorders. To acquire brain signals and measure the cognitive load, functional near infrared spectroscopy (fNIRS) is one of the popular non-invasive techniques. It is challenging to draw clear distinctions between the various cognitive states of the brain because of the complexity of the brain. A fuzzy system is designed where fuzzy inferencing rules and fuzzy membership functions are generated based on fuzzy c-means clustering. Three levels of cognitive load of the subjects as *low*, *medium* or *high* are considered based on the domain of the crisp output. The proposed fuzzy logic based model distinguishes the subjects based on their cognitive levels during mental tasks. We have worked on two available open-access fNIRS datasets. The outcomes shows the effectiveness of the proposed model.

Keywords: Brain-computer interface (BCI) · fNIRS · Cognitive Load · Mental Task · Fuzzy c-means Cluster · Fuzzy Logic

1 Introduction

Recently, there have been significant developments in the field of brain-computer interface (BCI). The primary objectives of BCI are finding a suitable communication medium to interact with the brain and analyze neurological changes based

This work is supported by Ministry of Electronics & Information Technology, Government of India (Sanctioned number: 4(16)/2019-ITEA).

P. Maji et al. (Eds.): PReMI 2023, LNCS 14301, pp. 577–586, 2023.
https://doi.org/10.1007/978-3-031-45170-6_60

on different mental and physical activities. In BCI, brain signals are recorded in the form of electrical potential or concentration changes in blood oxygenation level by using external stimulus on the subjects (or participants). Due to the high cost and risk of an invasive method, researchers prefer a non-invasive system like functional magnetic resonance imaging (fMRI), electroencephalogram (EEG) and functional near infrared spectroscopy (fNIRS). fNIRS is a well-established non-invasive neuroimaging technique that can measure hemoglobin concentration changes by passing infrared light inside the brain. By applying modified Beer-Lambert Law (MBLL) [2], optical density (let's say, A) is computed in order to determine the variation in oxyhemoglobin (HbO) and deoxyhemoglobin (HbR), as shown in (1).

$$A = log_{10}(\frac{I_{inc}}{I_{det}}) = (\epsilon \times C \times DPF) + G \tag{1}$$

Here, I_{inc} denotes incident light intensity, I_{det} denotes intensity of the detected light, ϵ denotes the molar absorption coefficient, C represents the concentration of substance in the media, DPF denotes the differential path length factor and G is the factor that account for measurement geometry (intensity lost due to scattering). Compared to other systems, fNIRS is portable, less sensitive to movement [8] and easy to setup.

Shin et al. [13] have performed experimentations on three different types of tasks: (i) left-hand motor imagery (LMI) and right-hand motor imagery (RMI) tasks, (ii) mental arithmetic (MA) and baseline (BL) tasks and (iii) motion artifacts. They have demonstrated that shrinkage linear discriminant analysis (sLDA) offers promising outcomes for the first and second experiments, respectively, with an accuracy of 66.5% and 80.7%. In [14], the authors have worked on three distinct types of cognitive tasks: (i) 0, 2 and 3 back tasks; (ii) discrimination/selection response tasks and (iii) word generation tasks. In order to categorize cognitive tasks and the rest, they also used sLDA, which has a classification accuracy of 74.3%.

To asses the mental workload, prefrontal cortex (PFC) plays a significant role. The study in [16] shows significant changes in the working memory performance in prefrontal activation based on the age of the subjects. Hemodynamic changes can also measure mental workload and expertise level of the subject. In [4], it is observed that task performance, mental effort and level of competence are all associated with the dorsolateral prefrontal cortex (DLPFC). It shows that experimentation with two types of subjects, expert (with high practice) and novice, have relatively lower oxygenation at low to moderate levels of the workload associated with more expertise and oxygenation level is higher at moderate level of workload for novice. For a given task assigned to the subjects over multiple sessions, there are wide variations in hemodynamic responses in different brain regions. Due to variations in responses, some features of different classes are overlapped, which is a challenging task to distinctly classify by traditional classifiers whether a brain state is active or not.

A fuzzy rule-based classifier plays a significant role in classifying different classes with overlapped feature space. Several studies [6,15]show that the fuzzy rule base approach provides promising results in real-life applications. Clustering

techniques help to analyze the feature distribution or data pattern. Soft clustering like fuzzy c-means (FCM) provides fuzzy belongingness on overlap features.
The design of the fuzzy rules and membership functions determines the performance of a fuzzy expert system. The subtractive clustering algorithm is employed
to automatically generate the tuned membership functions in accordance with
the domain knowledge. A. Priyono et al., [11] implement a traffic control system where they generate Takagi-Sugeno-Kang (TSK) fuzzy rule by subtractive
clustering technique. The self-organized genetic algorithm-based rule generation
(SOGARG) [10] method shows promising outcomes without any human expert.
After dimensionality reduction, Dey et al. [5] show satisfactory results using fuzzy
classifier to differentiate three classes of cognitive load as low, moderate and high.

The current work deals with the measurement of the cognitive load of subjects
as *low, medium* or *high* while performing mental task. This study will help to
identify any learning disabilities and develop personalized learning materials to
enhance teaching-learning process. For this purpose we have used fNIRS brain
signal while subjects are performing mental tasks. Based on the mean of HbO
concentration, FCM cluster is formed. Fuzzy rules are generated based on FCM
cluster. Fuzzy inference system has been designed to evaluate three different
levels of cognitive load of a subject which are labeled as *low, medium* or *high*.
The effectiveness of the proposed model is evaluated on two open-access datasets
that are available in [13] and [14]. The ground truth of the subjects are not
mentioned in these datasets.

The remaining sections of the paper are organized as follows. The detailed
descriptions of the available open-access datasets, including experimental
paradigms and recording methods, are discus in Sect. 2. Section 3 provides the
detail description of the proposed methodology. Results and discussion are
reported in Sect. 4. Thereafter, the paper is concluded in Sect. 5.

2   Dataset Description

In order to measure the effectiveness of the proposed model, we have used two
open-access datasets which are available in [13] and [14] generated by BCI experimentation using EEG and fNIRS. In this experiments, we have considered only
fNIRS data which are named as Dataset I [13] and Dataset II [14].

Dataset I [13]: fNIRS system of 36 channels and 12.5 Hz sampling frequency
with fourteen sources and sixteen detectors is used as shown in Fig. 1. A total
of 29 healthy subjects consisting of 15 females and 14 males with an average
age of 28.5 ± 3.7 (mean ± standard deviation) is considered for assessment of
cognitive load. In Dataset I, following three different datasets are available.

- **Dataset A (MI):** Three sessions of right-hand motor imagery (RMI) vs
  left-hand motor imagery (LMI).
- **Dataset B (MA):** Three sessions of MA vs BL. BL stands for baseline
  indicating resting state.
- **Dataset C (Artifacts):** Motion Artifacts including eye movement, eye
  blinking, head movement, mouth opening, etc.

Since we are interested to assess the cognitive load while performing a mental task, we only consider MA, i.e., Dataset B, to analyze the effectiveness of the proposed model. The time sequence diagram of the experimental setup is shown in Fig. 2a. In total there are three sessions on MA related tasks, each comprising 2 s of instruction, 10 s of mental arithmetic task and 15 or 17 s of rest period. Each session is repeated 20 times, excluding 1 min of the pre and post-experiment resting periods.

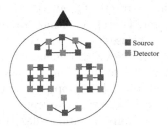

Fig. 1. Placement of sources (denoted by red squares) and detectors (denoted by green squares) of fNIRS where black lines represent channels. (Color figure online)

Dataset II [14]: A total of 26 healthy participants, consisting of 17 females and 9 males with an average age of 26.1 ± 3.5 years (mean $\pm$ standard deviation), are participated in 3 different experimentations: Dataset A (n-back tasks), Dataset B (discrimination/selection response (DSR) tasks) and Dataset C (word generation (WG) tasks). For acquisition of data, 36 channels fNIRS system of 10.4 Hz sampling rate, consisting of sixteen sources and sixteen detectors, is used. Figure 2b shows the time sequence diagram of the experimental setup. The following three datasets are available in Dataset II where each dataset contains 3 sessions.

- **Dataset A:** In each session, three sets of tasks (0, 2 and 3 back) were presented in counterbalanced order. For each of the individual, nine sets of n-back tasks were carried out.
- **Dataset B:** In a counterbalanced order, three sets of discrimination/selection response tasks (DSR) were presented during each session. For each individual, nine sets of DSR tasks were performed.
- **Dataset C:** Each of the session consists of ten numbers of trials on word generation (WG) and BL. In each session a total of twenty trials consist of ten number of WG and ten number of BL were randomly repeated.

Here, we have considered WG and excluded BL for Dataset C to measure the effectiveness of the proposed model. During WG, the subjects were instructed to keep thinking of words as fast as possible, beginning with the letter that was previously given. A single trial contained an instruction of 2 s showing a single initial letter indicates WG or the fixation cross that denots BL, a task for 10 s and a rest period of 13–15 s by representing a fixation cross in the center of the monitor.

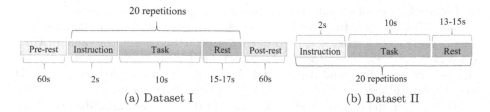

(a) Dataset I   (b) Dataset II

Fig. 2. Time sequence diagram of the experimental setup

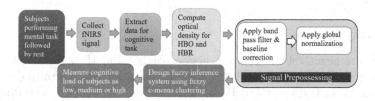

Fig. 3. Block diagram of the proposed methodology

3   Proposed Methodology

In this section, we elaborate the proposed methodology. Here, we consider only the mental state and use the data generated by mental tasks excluding the data of resting state, as we work on measuring cognitive load during mental tasks. The of changes concentration of HbO and HbR are first computed from the acquired fNIRS data. To eliminate the noise and unwanted contamination from the signal data, a bandpass filter and baseline correction are performed after global normalisation. After that, among thirty-six, nine frontal channels are selected that are primarily responsible for the mental task. Based on FCM clustering, fuzzy rules are generated. From the output domain of the fuzzy system, cognitive loads of the subjects are measured as *low, medium* or *high*. Figure 3 represents the block diagram of the proposed methodology and the details are discussed below in different subsections.

3.1   Preprocessing and Noise Removal

For Dataset I and Dataset II, we have considered 10 s from MT (i.e., MA or WG), and 2 s from BL (i.e., the rest) to include the transition from MT to BL. As the sampling rate is 12.5 Hz, for a total of 12 s data, a total of 1500 samples (150 × 10 repetitions) are generated for each of 29 subjects for Dataset I. In case of Dataset II, the sampling rate is 10.4 Hz and for 12 s data, a total 3600 samples (120 × 10 repetitions × 3 sessions) are generated for 26 subjects.

Optical density is computed for both HbO and HbR using MBLL. It is observed [7] that the frontal and pre-frontal cortex play a significant contribution in processing of MT. Different channel positions (frontal: 9 channels, central: 24 channels and occipital: 3 channels) of the fNIRS device are shown in Fig. 1. So, we select only the available 9 frontal channels among 36 channels of fNIRS device. In order to reduce the temporal drifts that changes over time, baseline correction is carried out by subtracting the mean value of HbO concentration between −5 to −2 s. Bandpass filter (Butterworth filter [12] with sixth-order zero-phase and a passband of 0.01–0.1 Hz) is applied on both HbO and HbR to filter out additional noise [9] related frequencies, like cardiac (1–1.5 Hz), respiration (0.2–0.5 Hz), Mayer wave ($\leq$0.1 Hz), motion artifacts and eye movement. Furthermore, global normalization is performed for uniform scaling of data.

3.2   Fuzzy System

As there are negatively correlation between HbO and HbR, and HbO is more sensitive towards cognitive load [17], we only consider HbO data to develop the fuzzy system. In Dataset I and Dataset II, MT are not labeled according to the complexity of the task. Fuzzy c-means (FCM) clustering [3], a well used unsupervised method, is used to form the clusters. Three clusters of HbO data for MT are formed to represent three levels of cognitive loads (i.e., *low, medium* and *high*) for both the Datasets. From 3 clusters, three Gaussian membership functions are generated as fuzzy sets for each of the input variables, where the channels correspond to input variables. We have considered three Gaussian membership functions also for the output variable representing three different levels of cognitive load also as *low, medium* and *high.*

Fuzzy rules are generated from the clusters based on the Mamdani-Assilian fuzzy inference system. For defuzzification purpose 'centroid' method is performed to transform the fuzzy output into crisp value. From the mean of the crisp output, the threshold values are computed by using (2) and (3) as given below.

$$max_{crisp\_mean} = max \left(\left[\frac{\sum_{j=1}^{S} crisp\_output_j}{S} \right]_{i=1}^{N} \right) \tag{2}$$

$$min_{crisp\_mean} = min \left(\left[\frac{\sum_{j=1}^{s} crisp\_output_j}{S} \right]_{i=1}^{N} \right) \tag{3}$$

Here, S = total no. of samples and N = total no. of subjects. Based on the range between min_{crisp_mean} and max_{crisp_mean}, three intervals of equal length are computed, where i_1 and i_2 denote the upper bound of first and second intervals, respectively, as shown in (4).

$$min_{crisp\_mean} \leq low < i_1;$$
$$i_1 \leq medium < i_2; \tag{4}$$
$$i_2 \leq high < max_{crisp\_mean}$$

The intervals determine the belongingness of subjects among three cognitive levels as *low, medium* and *high.*

4   Results and Discussion

The results and the effectiveness of the proposed model on two datasets are discuss in this section. The experiment is carried out in the Matlab environment (Matlab 2021a) on an Intel Core i5 computer at 3.10 GHz with 8 GB of RAM. For designing and testing purpose, Matlab based Fuzzy Logic Toolbox is used.

Table 1. Ranges of different levels of cognitive load

Cognitive Load	Ranges	
	Dataset I	Dataset II
Low	1.637–1.844	1.774–1.901
Medium	1.844–2.051	1.901–2.027
High	2.051–2.258	2.027–2.153

For the purpose of visualization of the clusters, generated by fuzzy c-means clustering, we have used 3D scatter plot by using three channels as it is not possible to show the clusters considering all the channels. Figure 4 shows three clusters of HbO data for MT, representing three levels of cognitive loads as *low, medium* and *high* for both the Datasets. However, we have experimented with all of 9 channels and observed the same type of clusters.

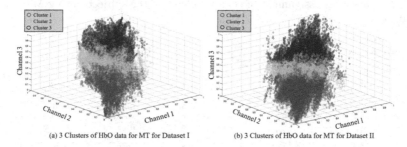

(a) 3 Clusters of HbO data for MT for Dataset I   (b) 3 Clusters of HbO data for MT for Dataset II

Fig. 4. Cluster formation of HbO data for MT for both the Datasets

The set of three fuzzy rules that are generated based on FCM clustering is given below.

Rule 1: *If (ch1 is in cluster1) and (ch2 is in cluster1) and (ch3 is in cluster1) and (ch4 is in cluster1) and (ch5 is in cluster1) and (ch6 is in cluster1) and (ch7 is in cluster1) and (ch8 is in cluster1) and (ch9 is in cluster1) then (output is in cluster1)*

Rule 2: *If (ch1 is in cluster2) and (ch2 is in cluster2) and (ch3 is in cluster2) and (ch4 is in cluster2) and (ch5 is in cluster2) and (ch6 is in cluster2) and (ch7 is in cluster2) and (ch8 is in cluster2) and (ch9 is in cluster2) then (output is in cluster2)*

Rule 3: *If (ch1 is in cluster3) and (ch2 is in cluster3) and (ch3 is in cluster3) and (ch4 is in cluster3) and (ch5 is in cluster3) and (ch6 is in cluster3) and (ch7*

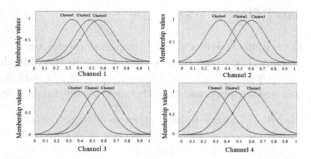

Fig. 5. Fuzzy membership functions of four input variables (or channels) for Dataset I

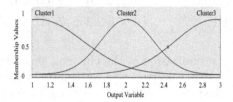

Fig. 6. Fuzzy membership functions for output variable for Dataset I

Table 2. Class label assignment of cognitive load of the subject during MT for both the datasets

(a) Results for Dataset I

Subjects #	Cognitive Load of Subject	Value of Cognitive Load
1	Medium	2.041
2	High	2.258
3	High	2.102
4	Low	1.698
5	High	2.096
6	Medium	1.920
7	Medium	2.022
8	Low	1.822
9	High	2.072
10	High	2.056
11	Medium	1.999
12	High	2.229
13	Low	1.739
14	Medium	2.010
15	Medium	1.927
16	High	2.051
17	Medium	1.970
18	Medium	2.025
19	High	2.110
20	High	2.151
21	High	2.204
22	High	2.094
23	Low	1.715
24	Low	1.638
25	Low	1.721
26	High	2.065
27	High	2.139
28	High	2.149
29	High	2.102

(b) Results for Dataset II

Subject #	Cognitive Load of Subject	Value of Cognitive Load
1	Low	1.892
2	Medium	1.907
3	High	2.111
4	Medium	1.960
5	High	2.153
6	Medium	1.935
7	Medium	1.923
8	High	2.132
9	High	2.049
10	Low	1.872
11	Low	1.884
12	Low	1.774
13	Low	1.879
14	Low	1.828
15	Medium	1.941
16	High	2.104
17	Low	1.839
18	High	2.067
19	High	2.142
20	High	2.036
21	High	2.033
22	Medium	2.008
23	Low	1.795
24	Low	1.808
25	Low	1.895
26	Low	1.886

is in cluster3) and (ch8 is in cluster3) and (ch9 is in cluster3) then (output is in cluster3)

There are a total of nine input variables corresponding to 9 channels in the fuzzy inference system. However, due to some space complexity, among nine, the membership functions of 4 input variables (channels 1, 2, 3 and 4) and the output variable are respectively shown in Figs. 5 and 6 for Dataset I. Similar membership functions are also generated for Dataset II. By using (2), (3) and (4), the interval values for each of the three cognitive levels are computed for both the datasets, which are shown in Table 1. The minimum and the maximum values of cognitive load for Dataset I are respectively 1.637 and 2.258, whereas, for Dataset II, they are, respectively, 1.774 and 2.153. The range of cognitive load of different levels may vary based on the type of experimentation and the age of the subjects. A label is assigned to each subject based on the three interval values as shown in Table 1. For Dataset I and Dataset II, the assignment of class levels of cognitive load to the subjects during MT are shown, respectively, in Table 2a and Table 2b.

5 Conclusion

It is important to measure the cognitive load of a subject to design and develop effective instructional materials to detect possible learning disability or neurodegenerative disorder. The study focuses on a fuzzy logic approach to measure the cognitive load of a subjects as *low, medium,* or *high* while performing the mental task. The interval value for each level of cognitive load is computed based on the domain of crisp output. We have used two open-access datasets to evaluate the cognitive load of the subjects by using our proposed model while performing mental task. As the ground truth of the subjects is not mentioned in the datasets, so in this study, the performance of the proposed model cannot be evaluated. From the cluster, it is observed that some outliers are there in the datasets. The anomaly detection technique is an unsupervised method that can be used to address this problem and to improve the results. In this study, we have used frontal channels which are primarily responsible for MT. Alternatively, different feature selection techniques [1] can be incorporated to find out the significant as well as optimal number of features or channels which are more sensitive for MT.

References

1. Aydin, E.A.: Subject-specific feature selection for near infrared spectroscopy based brain-computer interfaces. Comput. Methods Prog. Biomed. **195**, 105535 (2020)
2. Baker, W.B., Parthasarathy, A.B., Busch, D.R., Mesquita, R.C., Greenberg, J.H., Yodh, A.G.: Modified beer-lambert law for blood flow. Biomed. Opt. Express **5**(11), 4053–4075 (2014)
3. Bezdek, J.C., Ehrlich, R., Full, W.: FCM: the fuzzy c-means clustering algorithm. Comput. Geosci. **10**(2–3), 191–203 (1984)
4. Bunce, S.C., Izzetoglu, K., Ayaz, H., Shewokis, P., Izzetoglu, M., Pourrezaei, K., Onaral, B.: Implementation of fNIRS for monitoring levels of expertise and mental

workload. In: Schmorrow, D.D., Fidopiastis, C.M. (eds.) FAC 2011. LNCS (LNAI), vol. 6780, pp. 13–22. Springer, Heidelberg (2011). https://doi.org/10.1007/978-3-642-21852-1_2

5. De, A., Bhattacharjee, T., Konar, A., Ralescu, A.L., Nagar, A.K.: A type-2 fuzzy set induced classification of cognitive load in inter-individual working memory performance based on hemodynamic response. In: 2017 IEEE Symposium Series on Computational Intelligence (SSCI), pp. 1–7. IEEE (2017)

6. Hadrani, A., Guennoun, K., Saadane, R., Wahbi, M.: Fuzzy rough sets: survey and proposal of an enhanced knowledge representation model based on automatic noisy sample detection. Cogn. Syst. Res. **64**, 37–56 (2020). https://doi.org/10.1016/j.cogsys.2020.05.001

7. Herff, C., Heger, D., Fortmann, O., Hennrich, J., Putze, F., Schultz, T.: Mental workload during n-back task-quantified in the prefrontal cortex using fnirs. Front. Hum. Neurosci. **7**, 935 (2014)

8. Lloyd-Fox, S., Blasi, A., Elwell, C.: Illuminating the developing brain: the past, present and future of functional near infrared spectroscopy. Neurosci. Biobehav. Rev. **34**(3), 269–284 (2010)

9. Nguyen, H.D., Yoo, S.H., Bhutta, M.R., Hong, K.S.: Adaptive filtering of physiological noises in fNIRS data. Biomed. Eng. Online **17**(1), 1–23 (2018)

10. Pal, T., Pal, N.R.: Sogarg: a self-organized genetic algorithm-based rule generation scheme for fuzzy controllers. IEEE Trans. Evol. Comput. **7**(4), 397–415 (2003)

11. Priyono, A., Ridwan, M., Alias, A.J., Rahmat, R.A.O., Hassan, A., Ali, M.A.M.: Generation of fuzzy rules with subtractive clustering. Jurnal Teknologi, 143–153 (2005)

12. Selesnick, I.W., Burrus, C.S.: Generalized digital butterworth filter design. IEEE Trans. Signal Process. **46**(6), 1688–1694 (1998)

13. Shin, J., et al.: Open access dataset for EEG+NIRS single-trial classification. IEEE Trans. Neural Syst. Rehabil. Eng. **25**(10), 1735–1745 (2017). https://doi.org/10.1109/TNSRE.2016.2628057

14. Shin, J., Von Lühmann, A., Kim, D.W., Mehnert, J., Hwang, H.J., Müller, K.R.: Simultaneous acquisition of EEG and NIRS during cognitive tasks for an open access dataset. Sci. Data **5**(1), 1–16 (2018)

15. Vasconez, J.P., Viscaino, M., Guevara, L., Cheein, F.A.: A fuzzy-based driver assistance system using human cognitive parameters and driving style information. Cogn. Syst. Res. **64**, 174–190 (2020). https://doi.org/10.1016/j.cogsys.2020.08.007

16. Vermeij, A., Van Beek, A.H., Olde Rikkert, M.G., Claassen, J.A., Kessels, R.P.: Effects of aging on cerebral oxygenation during working-memory performance: a functional near-infrared spectroscopy study. Plos One (2012)

17. Zhu, Q., Shi, Y., Du, J.: Wayfinding information cognitive load classification based on functional near-infrared spectroscopy. J. Comput. Civ. Eng. **35**(5), 04021016 (2021)

A Grammatical Evolution Based Automated Configuration of an Ensemble Differential Evolution Algorithm

M. T. Indu and C. Shunmuga Velayutham[✉][iD]

Department of Computer Science and Engineering, Amrita School of Computing,
Amrita Vishwa Vidyapeetham, Coimbatore, India
cs_velayutham@cb.amrita.edu

Abstract. Designing/configuring ensemble Differential Evolution (DE) algorithms with complementary search characteristics is a complex problem requiring both in-depth understanding of the constituent algorithm's dynamics and tacit knowledge. This paper proposes a Grammatical Evolution (GE) based automated configuration of a recent ensemble DE algorithm - Improved Multi-population Ensemble Differential Evolution (IMPEDE). A Backus Naur Form grammar, with nine ensemble and DE parameters, has been designed to represent all possible IMPEDE configurations. The proposed approach has been employed to evolve IMPEDE configurations that solve CEC'17 benchmark optimization problems. The evolved configurations have been validated on CEC'14 suite and a real-world optimization problem - economic load dispatch (ELD) problem - from CEC'11 suite. The simulation experiments demonstrate that the proposed approach is capable of evolving IMPEDE configurations that exhibit statistically superior or comparable performance against the manual configuration of IMPEDE as well as against other prominent ensemble DE algorithms.

Keywords: automated algorithm configuration · parameter tuning · grammatical evolution · ensemble differential evolution · meta-evolutionary approach

1 Introduction

Differential Evolution (DE) [20] is both a simple and efficient Evolutionary Algorithm (EA) employed in a number of optimization scenarios [2,18,19]. Numerous guidelines for setting the DE algorithm parameters as well as several parameter tuning and adaptation schemes have been proposed in the literature [4,6]. Consequently, given an optimization problem, a practitioner of DE is confronted with dizzying design choices of heuristics to set parameter values, parameter tuning and control methods. The recent research in DE literature attempts to combat the above said problem through *ensemble DE algorithms* [23]. These algorithms often employ a number of constituent DE algorithms (with different strategies)

P. Maji et al. (Eds.): PReMI 2023, LNCS 14301, pp. 587–596, 2023.
https://doi.org/10.1007/978-3-031-45170-6_61

which cooperatively/competitively solve a given optimization problem. However the effectiveness of ensemble DE rests on the complementary search characteristics of its constituent DE algorithms/algorithmic strategies [23]. In addition, the ensemble DE paradigm brings with itself more design parameters. Consequently, to use ensemble DE, the algorithm should be *configured* by choosing optimal set of above mentioned typical DE parameters and parameters related to multi-population ensemble models. The huge design space and the lack of clarity in understanding the effect of design parameters on the performance of the algorithm makes the configuration process of ensemble DE difficult even for experienced DE researchers with tacit knowledge [14]. This state of affairs demands automating the ensemble DE configuration task. This paper proposes to employ the meta-evolutionary approach to automatically configure the parameters of ensemble DE algorithms.

In this paper, a Grammatical Evolution (GE) [17] based parameter configuration of a low-level multi-population ensemble differential evolution has been presented. The capability of this method has been illustrated on a recently proposed ensemble algorithm namely *IMPEDE* (*Improved Multi-population Ensemble Differential Evolution*) [22] algorithm. The approach has been studied by evolving IMPEDE algorithm configuration to solve the functions in CEC'17 [1] benchmark suite. CEC'14 [11] benchmark suite and a real-world optimization problem - static economic load dispatch (ELD) problem from CEC'11 suite [5] have been used to validate the proposed approach. From the simulation experiments, it has been found that GE based automated method can successfully evolve statistically comparable and often better parameter configurations for IMPEDE, against its manual configuration [22] and other prominent ensemble DE algorithms like MPEDE [24], eMPEDE [9], MPMSDE [10] and EDEV [25]. The approach has also been demonstrated to be competitive against the prominent algorithm configurator – *irace* [12]. The observed results suggest the meta-evolutionary paradigm as a potential automated approach for practitioners of DE to configure effective ensemble of DE algorithms even without having the theoretical foundations about DE algorithm itself.

In the remaining part of this paper, Sect. 2 briefs the background study, Sect. 3 outlines the meta-evolutionary approach for configuring ensemble DE algorithm using GE, Sect. 4 explains the empirical study and results and Sect. 5 summarizes the work.

2   Background Study

The *IMPEDE* [22] algorithm, chosen for the automated configuration in this paper, has been proposed as an enhancement of *MPEDE* algorithm [24]. In IMPEDE, the population of size ($NP = 250$) is split into three *indicator* sub-populations of equal sizes ($0.2 \times NP$) employing separate variation strategies (*current-to-pbest/1/bin,current-to-rand/1, pbad-to-pbest/1/bin*) and a *reward* population of greater size. The reward population initially randomly uses the strategy of any one indicator sub-population. The evolution continues for a pre-specified number of generations ($ng = 20$), after which, the most promising variation technique is employed in the reward population. Information sharing among sub-populations is facilitated by combining and re-allocating the individuals in sub-populations. Weighted Lehmer mean strategy is used in IMPEDE to improve the parameter adaptation approach of MPEDE. Though Tong et al. [22] reports NP as the only sensitive parameter, the candidate choice of parameters subjected for sensitivity analysis were the typical DE parameters while some of the important parameters like the number of indicator sub-populations, the choice of constituent mutations, crossovers, etc. have not been considered. Consequently, in this proposed work, it has been decided to include an exhaustive list of IMPEDE parameters to be evolved by GE.

The capability of GE to evolve the parameters of a classical DE algorithm was studied in [8]. In addition, GE has been used in several scenarios to evolve parameters and local search strategies [3,13,15,16,21]. However automatic configuration of an ensemble EA has not been taken up well in ensemble literature.

3 Grammatical Evolution Based Automated Configuration of IMPEDE

The GE based automated parameter configuration approach outlined in this section essentially involves identifying the design parameters of *IMPEDE* and the possible values those parameters can have. The list of IMPEDE parameters decided to be evolved by GE follows: population size (NP), number of indicator sub-populations (ns), their sizes as a proportion (r), period of generations (ng), p in *current-to-pbest/1* mutation, p' of *pbad-to-pbest/1* mutation, c of JADE adaptation, mutations to be performed on the indicator sub-populations (*mutations*), crossovers to be performed on the indicator sub-populations (*crossovers*).

The ingredients for a GE based automated configuration approach include not only the parameters but also the possible options (values) for each of the parameter. Together, they create the configuration space in which GE searches to find effective configurations for the IMPEDE algorithm for a given optimization problem. In this paper, CEC'17 suite with dimension $D = 30$ have been employed. NP has been decided to take values from the range $(150, 300)$ [20] in intervals of 10. The parameter ns is allowed to take values 2, 3, 4 or 5. The size of indicator sub-population (r) is a proportion of population size (taking values from $\{0.1,0.15,0.2,0.25,0.3\}$ according to the number of sub-populations) such that $NP_i = r \times NP$, for $i = 1$ to ns. The remaining population is kept as reward sub-population. The possible values for number of generations (ng) have been decided to be in the range $(10, 100)$ in the intervals of 10. The parameters p and c take values from the range $(5\%,20\%)$ [26] and the parameter p' takes values from the range $(0,1)$ [22]. The set of standard mutation strategies comprising *rand/**, *best/**, *current-to-best/**, *current-to-rand/** and *rand-to-best/** with one as well as two difference vectors, together with the two new mutations *current-to-pbest/1* and *pbad-to-pbest/1* form the mutation choices for each sub-population. Each mutation strategy has been given a choice in grammar

Table 1. BNF grammar for translating GE chromosome to IMPEDE parameters

$\langle PARAMS \rangle$ ::= $\langle NP \rangle$ $\langle NSM \rangle$ $\langle NG \rangle$ $\langle P \rangle$ $\langle P' \rangle$ $\langle C \rangle$

$\langle NP \rangle$ ::= 150 | 160 | 170 | 180 | 190 | 200 | 210 | 220 | 230 | 240 | 250 | 260 | 270 | 280 | 290 | 300

$\langle NSM \rangle$ ::= $\langle LS \rangle \langle MUT \rangle \langle MUT \rangle \langle CROSS \rangle \langle CROSS \rangle | \langle MS \rangle \langle MUT \rangle \langle MUT \rangle \langle MUT \rangle$ $\langle CROSS \rangle \langle CROSS \rangle \langle CROSS \rangle | \langle SS \rangle \langle MUT \rangle \langle MUT \rangle \langle MUT \rangle \langle MUT \rangle \langle CROSS \rangle \langle CROSS \rangle$ $\langle CROSS \rangle \langle CROSS \rangle | \langle SS \rangle \langle MUT \rangle \langle MUT \rangle \langle MUT \rangle \langle MUT \rangle \langle MUT \rangle \langle CROSS \rangle \langle CROSS \rangle$ $\langle CROSS \rangle \langle CROSS \rangle \langle CROSS \rangle$

$\langle LS \rangle$ ::= 0.1 | 0.15 | 0.2 | 0.25 | 0.3

$\langle MS \rangle$ ::= 0.1 | 0.15 | 0.2

$\langle SS \rangle$ ::= 0.1 | 0.15

$\langle NG \rangle$ ::= 10 | 20 | 30 | 40 | 50 | 60 | 70 | 80 | 90 | 100

$\langle MUT \rangle$ ::= rand/1 | rand/2 | best/1 | best/2 | current-to-best/1 | current-to-best/2 | current-to-rand/1 | current-to-rand/2 | rand-to-best/1 | rand-to-best/2 | current-to-pbest/1 | pbad-to-pbest/1

$\langle CROSS \rangle$ ::= binomial | exponential | nil

$\langle P \rangle$ ::= 0.05 | 0.06 | 0.07 | 0.08 | 0.09 | 0.10 | 0.11 | 0.12 | 0.13 | 0.14 | 0.15 | 0.16 | 0.17 | 0.18 | 0.19 | 0.2

$\langle P' \rangle$ ::= 0.1 | 0.2 | 0.3 | 0.4 | 0.5 | 0.6 | 0.7 | 0.8 | 0.9

$\langle C \rangle$ ::= 0.05 | 0.06 | 0.07 | 0.08 | 0.09 | 0.10 | 0.11 | 0.12 | 0.13 | 0.14 | 0.15 | 0.16 | 0.17 | 0.18 | 0.19 | 0.2

design to operate either without crossover (*nil*) or along with *binomial* (*bin*) or *exponential* (*exp*) crossover to exploit the advantages of all combinations.

The BNF grammar designed for representing IMPEDE candidate configurations, using the above mentioned parameter list and their possible values, is given in Table 1. The start symbol is $\langle PARAMS \rangle$. The non-terminals $\langle NP \rangle$, $\langle NG \rangle$, $\langle NSM \rangle$, $\langle P \rangle$, $\langle P' \rangle$ and $\langle C \rangle$ respectively denote the parameters NP and ng, configuration of constituent sub-populations, parameter p of *current-to-pbest/1* mutation, p' of *pbad-to-pbest/1* mutation and c of JADE adaptation. The number of indicator sub-populations ns is represented by the number of $\langle MUT \rangle$ and $\langle CROSS \rangle$ non-terminals which respectively represent *mutations* and *crossovers*. The proportion r is represented by the non-terminals $\langle LS \rangle$, $\langle MS \rangle$ and $\langle SS \rangle$ to ensure that the reward sub-population will always be larger than indicator sub-populations.

The GE based meta-evolutionary automated paradigm for evolving effective IMPEDE configurations for a given problem is presented in Algorithm 1. The outer meta-evolutionary algorithm, GE, begins with a random population of 20 candidate solutions which, after fitness evaluation, are subjected to variation (fixed one point crossover at a probability of 0.85 and int flip per codon mutation at a probability of 0.1), evaluation and selection cycle. Each candidate solution in GE is a linear genome which gets mapped to the BNF grammar to result in a specific IMPEDE configuration. There has been no deliberate attempt to fine-tune the GE parameters as it is intended to show both the ease of employing the automated paradigm as well as its effectiveness. The evaluation of each GE

Algorithm 1 Algorithm for GE based automated configuration of IMPEDE

1: **function** GrammaticalEvolution()
2: Initialize chromosomes $C_1, C_2, ..C_N$
3: **for** $i = 1$ to N **do**
4:     Evaluate(C_i)
5: **end for**
6: **for** $gen = 1$ to $Maxgen$ **do**
7:     Select parents and do crossover
8:     Perform mutation
9:     **for** $i = 1$ to $offspring\_count$ **do**
10:         Evaluate(O_i)
11:     **end for**
12:     Replace the current population with the next population
13: **end for**

14: Return the best chromosome C^* which encodes the best IMPEDE configuration to solve the optimization functions
    end function
15: **function** Evaluate(C_i)
16: Translate chromosome C_i to IMPEDE parameters
17: Apply IMPEDE algorithm with these parameters to minimize the optimization functions for multiple runs
18: Return the overall fitness of X_i
    end function

---

candidate (IMPEDE configuration) amounts to solving all the functions in the CEC'17 suite. 5 runs per function have been executed to take into account the stochastic nature of ensemble DE algorithm. Each candidate IMPEDE configuration has been given a maximum of $10000 \times D$ fitness evaluations to solve each of the function. The fitness then is considered to be the root mean square error of all best fitness values. The mutation, crossover, fitness evaluation and selection operators work on the population marking one generation for GE run. After a specified number of generations ($Maxgen\_GE = 15$) the best individual returned by GE represents the best IMPEDE configuration to solve all functions in the given benchmark suite.

4   Experiments and Results

The implementation of grammatical evolution, employed in this paper, has been adopted from Fenton et al. [7]. The experiments to evolve IMPEDE configurations using GE have been executed in a High Performance Computing cluster. The client node configuration comprises DELL PowerEdge R740 with Dual Intel Xeon Gold 5120 @ 2.2 GHz with 14 core processors and 256 GB RAM. To study whether the randomness in GE execution affects the performance of the proposed approach, five runs of GE have been conducted to evolve configurations for IMPEDE algorithm to optimize the CEC'17 benchmark suite at 30 dimensions. Table 2 lists the evolved IMPEDE configurations (R_1 - R_5). It is important to note that all these configurations are different from the manual design in [22].

The performance validation of IMPEDE with GE evolved configurations (referred to as GE-IMPEDE hereafter) R_1 - R_5 has been carried out on CEC'14 benchmark suite at 50 dimensions. 51 simulation runs of GE-IMPEDE with the evolved configurations and the compared ensemble DE algorithms have been

Table 2. GE-evolved IMPEDE configurations R_1- R_5

Conf	NP	ns	λ	*mutations* and *crossovers*	ng	p	p'	c
R_1	200	5	0.15	{current-to-pbest/1}, {current-to-pbest/1/bin}, {current-to-rand/2/exp}, {current-to-rand/1/exp}, {rand-to-best/1/exp}	40	0.12	–	0.15
R_2	170	5	0.15	{rand/2/exp}, {rand/1/exp}, {current-to-pbest/1}, {current-to-best/2/bin}, {current-to-rand/1/bin}	30	0.1	–	0.17
R_3	200	5	0.15	{pbad-to-pbest/1}, {pbad-to-pbest/1/exp}, {current-to-best/2}, {current-to-rand/1/bin}, {current-to-best/1/exp}	20	–	0.6	0.2
R_4	190	4	0.15	{rand/1/exp}, {current-to-best/2/bin}, {pbad-to-pbest/1}, {current-to-best/2/exp}	40	–	0.6	0.08
R_5	170	4	0.15	{current-to-best/2/bin}, {current-to-best/1/exp}, {pbad-to-pbest/1/bin}, {pbad-to-pbest/1}	30	–	0.4	0.06

performed and the outputs of Wilcoxon rank sum test (at 5% significance level) has been summarized in Table 3 to evaluate and benchmark the former against the rest of the algorithms. The columnwise entries in the format $+/\approx/-$ in the table represent the number of functions out of the 30 CEC'14 functions for which GE-IMPEDE-R_i statistically outperformed, displayed comparable performance or was outperformed by the algorithm in the row. The total number of better and comparable performances by R_1 against the compared algorithms were on as high as 23–28 functions and by R_2-R_5 were on 22–28, 23–28, 21–27 and 22–28 functions respectively. The competitive performance across multiple GE runs observed in this table demonstrates the reliability of the GE based meta-evolutionary approach in evolving robust GE-IMPEDE configurations. The convergence plots of IMPEDE with manual and GE evolved configuration R_1 are presented in Fig. 1 on three representative 50 dimensional CEC'14 functions (F_3, F_8 and F_{11}). The plots show that GE-IMPEDE with configuration R_1 exhibited better convergence than that of the manually configured IMPEDE on the unimodal function F_3 and multimodal functions F_8 and F_{11}. These plots thus reiterate the better performance of GE-IMPEDE as compared to the manual configuration of IMPEDE.

Table 3. Comparison of GE-IMPEDE (with configurations R_1 to R_5) with prominent ensemble DE methods on 50 dimensional CEC'14 suite

Algorithms	R_1	R_2	R_3	R_4	R_5
MPEDE	16/7/7	13/10/7	17/6/7	16/5/9	18/4/8
eMPEDE	15/9/6	14/8/8	19/6/5	17/4/9	18/6/6
MPMSDE	21/7/2	21/7/2	23/5/2	22/5/3	24/4/2
EDEV	17/8/5	16/7/7	19/5/6	21/5/4	24/2/4
IMPEDE	17/10/3	16/8/6	20/6/4	19/6/5	20/4/6

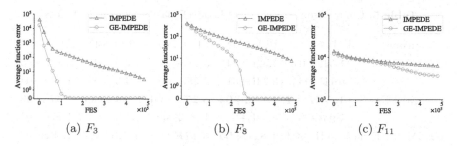

| (a) F_3 | (b) F_8 | (c) F_{11} |

Fig. 1. Convergence plots of IMPEDE with manual configuration and GE-IMPEDE configuration R_1 on three representative CEC'14 functions

The significance of the validation results is further statistically verified with Friedman test. The results of Friedman test are presented in Table 4. It is worth noting that GE-IMPEDE is ranked as the best performing algorithm in all the 5 runs. These results show that the proposed meta-evolutionary approach evolves several effective configurations, different from the manual one [22], and offers robust performance, despite the randomness in GE algorithm execution.

Table 4. Average ranks obtained in Friedman test

Algorithm	Average Rank				
	Run_1	Run_2	Run_3	Run_4	Run_5
GE-IMPEDE-R_i	2.35	2.27	2.07	2.27	2.10
eMPEDE	3.20	3.13	3.27	3.17	3.27
MPEDE	3.23	3.23	3.30	3.27	3.27
EDEV	3.73	3.73	3.67	3.80	3.77
IMPEDE	4.08	4.08	4.12	3.98	4.12
MPMSDE	4.40	4.55	4.58	4.52	4.48

The performance of the GE-IMPEDE configurations has been benchmarked against a popular algorithm configurator – *irace* [12]. Since the GE population with 20 individuals underwent evaluation once for the initial population and later for 15 generations, each for 29 functions, a total of 9280 experiments was decided to be the tuning budget for *irace*. The IMPEDE configuration returned by *irace* execution (C_{irace}) was {NP: 190, ns: 5, r: 0.15, *mutations* and *crossovers*: rand/2/bin, pbad-to-pbest/1, current-to-best/1/bin, current-to-pbest/1, current-to-pbest/1/exp, ng: 80, p: 0.19, $p^{'}$: 0.3, c: 0.19}. The performance of IMPEDE algorithm with the configuration C_{irace} has been compared against GE-IMPEDE-R_1 to GE-IMPEDE-R_5 on 50 dimensional CEC'14 functions. The results of Wilcoxon rank sum test reported that the evolved configurations R_1-R_5 performed statistically better or comparable to C_{irace} on 21,

Table 5. Comparison on Economic Load Dispatch problem instances

Algorithms	ELD 6D	ELD 13D	ELD 15D	ELD 40D	ELD 140D
IMPEDE	1.54E+04	1.82E+04	3.28E+04	1.26E+05	1.88E+06
	6.11E-06	8.74E+01	2.28E+01	9.42E+02	1.20E+04
GE-IMPEDE-R_1	**1.54E+04**	**1.81E+04**	**3.27E+04**	**1.26E+05**	1.89E+06
	1.93E-06	6.43E+01	1.96E+00	8.16E+02	1.07E+04
GE-IMPEDE-R_2	**1.54E+04**	**1.81E+04**	**3.27E+04**	**1.26E+05**	1.89E+06
	2.52E-06	3.40E+01	1.28E+00	7.90E+02	1.33E+04
GE-IMPEDE-R_3	**1.54E+04**	**1.82E+04**	**3.28E+04**	**1.25E+05**	**1.87E+06**
	9.76E-06	6.65E+01	2.35E+01	8.31E+02	1.26E+04
GE-IMPEDE-R_4	**1.54E+04**	1.85E+04	**3.28E+04**	1.27E+05	1.91E+06
	1.50E-05	7.33E+01	1.67E+01	6.56E+02	1.67E+04
GE-IMPEDE-R_5	**1.54E+04**	1.84E+04	**3.28E+04**	1.27E+05	1.90E+06
	4.57E-02	6.54E+01	1.76E+01	4.36E+02	1.25E+04

19, 20, 20 and 19 functions respectively out of the 30 CEC'14 functions at 50 dimensions.

The potential of the GE based meta-evolutionary approach for automated configuration was further studied by analyzing the performance of the evolved IMPEDE configurations on a real world application problem namely the Static Economic Load Dispatch (ELD) problem from CEC'11 suite [5]. GE-IMPEDE with the configurations R_1-R_5 and IMPEDE algorithm with configuration in Tong et al. [22] were applied to solve ELD instances on 6, 13, 15, 40 and 140 dimensions, as per the CEC'11 evaluation criteria, 25 times. The average and standard deviation of fitness obtained by the algorithms are listed in Table 5. The GE-IMPEDE configurations which gave a better or same mean value as that of IMPEDE algorithm are highlighted with bold face. It is noted that the on ELD instance with 6 and 15 dimensions, all the five evolved configurations gave better or same mean value as that of IMPEDE, on 13 and 40 dimensions, three configurations gave better or same mean value and on 140 dimensions, one configuration could give a better mean value. This experiment of validating the configurations on problems which are completely unknown at the time of meta-evolution clearly demonstrates the potential of the proposed approach in evolving robust parameters for the considered ensemble algorithm.

5   Conclusion

The parameter configuration problem in ensemble DE has been solved by a meta-evolutionary technique using GE in this paper. The potential of this approach has been illustrated on a recently proposed ensemble DE - IMPEDE. The GE searches for effective IMPEDE configurations through evolving a population of candidate IMPEDE configurations. From the simulation experiments, it has been noted that GE based automated method can successfully evolve several IMPEDE configurations different from the manual configuration [22], and all the evolved configurations exhibited statistically comparable and often superior performance against the manually configured IMPEDE, other prominent ensembles and the configuration produced by the algorithm configurator *irace*. The results suggest the meta-evolutionary paradigm as a potential automated approach for practitioners of EA in general to evolve effective configuration for any EA as a matter of fact.

References

1. Awad, N.H., Ali, M.Z., Liang, J.J., Qu, B.Y., Suganthan, P.N.: Problem definitions and evaluation criteria for the CEC 2017 special session and competition on single objective real-parameter numerical optimization. Technical report, Nanyang Technological University (2016)
2. Bilal, P.M., Zaheer, H., Garcia-Hernandez, L., Abraham, A., et al.: Differential evolution: a review of more than two decades of research. Eng. Appl. Artif. Intell. **90**, 103479 (2020)
3. Burke, E.K., Hyde, M.R., Kendall, G.: Grammatical evolution of local search heuristics. IEEE Trans. Evol. Comput. **16**(3), 406–417 (2011)
4. Das, S., Mullick, S.S., Suganthan, P.N.: Recent advances in differential evolution-an updated survey. Swarm Evol. Comput. **27**, 1–30 (2016)
5. Das, S., Suganthan, P.N.: Problem definitions and evaluation criteria for CEC 2011 competition on testing evolutionary algorithms on real world optimization problems. Technical report, Nanyang Technological University (2010)
6. Dhanalakshmy, D.M., Akhila, M., Vidhya, C., Jeyakumar, G.: Improving the search efficiency of differential evolution algorithm by population diversity analysis and adaptation of mutation step sizes. Int. J. Adv. Intell. Paradigms **15**(2), 119–145 (2020)
7. Fenton, M., McDermott, J., Fagan, D., Forstenlechner, S., Hemberg, E., O'Neill, M.: PonyGE2: grammatical evolution in python. In: Proceedings of the Genetic and Evolutionary Computation Conference Companion, pp. 1194–1201. ACM (2017)
8. Indu, M.T., Shunmuga Velayutham, C.: Towards grammatical evolution-based automated design of differential evolution algorithm. In: Sharma, H., Saraswat, M., Yadav, A., Kim, J.H., Bansal, J.C. (eds.) CIS 2020. AISC, vol. 1335, pp. 329–340. Springer, Singapore (2021). https://doi.org/10.1007/978-981-33-6984-9_27
9. Li, X., Dai, G.: An enhanced multi-population ensemble differential evolution. In: Proceedings of the 3rd International Conference on Computer Science and Application Engineering, pp. 1–5. ACM (2019). https://doi.org/10.1145/3331453.3362054
10. Li, X., Wang, L., Jiang, Q., Li, N.: Differential evolution algorithm with multi-population cooperation and multi-strategy integration. Neurocomputing **421**, 285–302 (2021)
11. Liang, J., Qu, B., Suganthan, P.: Problem definitions and evaluation criteria for the CEC 2014 special session and competition on single objective real-parameter numerical optimization. Technical report, Nanyang Technological University (2013)
12. López-Ibáñez, M., Dubois-Lacoste, J., Cáceres, L.P., Birattari, M., Stützle, T.: The irace package: iterated racing for automatic algorithm configuration. Oper. Res. Perspect. **3**, 43–58 (2016). https://doi.org/10.1016/j.orp.2016.09.002

13. Lourenço, N., Pereira, F.B., Costa, E.: The importance of the learning conditions in hyper-heuristics. In: Proceedings of the 15th Annual Conference on Genetic and Evolutionary Computation, pp. 1525–1532 (2013)
14. Ma, H., Shen, S., Yu, M., Yang, Z., Fei, M., Zhou, H.: Multi-population techniques in nature inspired optimization algorithms: a comprehensive survey. Swarm Evol. Comput. **44**, 365–387 (2019)
15. Mweshi, G., Pillay, N.: An improved grammatical evolution approach for generating perturbative heuristics to solve combinatorial optimization problems. Expert Syst. Appl. **165**, 113853 (2021)
16. Nyathi, T., Pillay, N.: Comparison of a genetic algorithm to grammatical evolution for automated design of genetic programming classification algorithms. Expert Syst. Appl. **104**, 213–234 (2018)
17. O'Neill, M., Ryan, C.: Grammatical evolution. IEEE Trans. Evol. Comput. **5**(4), 349–358 (2001). https://doi.org/10.1109/4235.942529
18. RV, S.D., Kalyan, R., Kurup, D.G., et al.: Optimization of digital predistortion models for RF power amplifiers using a modified differential evolution algorithm. AEU-Int. J. Electron. Commun. **124**, 153323 (2020)
19. Sree, K.V., Jeyakumar, G.: An evolutionary computing approach to solve object identification problem for fall detection in computer vision-based video surveillance applications. In: Hemanth, D.J., Kumar, B.V., Manavalan, G.R.K. (eds.) Recent Advances on Memetic Algorithms and its Applications in Image Processing. SCI, vol. 873, pp. 1–18. Springer, Singapore (2020). https://doi.org/10.1007/978-981-15-1362-6_1
20. Storn, R., Price, K.: Differential evolution-a simple and efficient heuristic for global optimization over continuous spaces. J. Global Optim. **11**(4), 341–359 (1997). https://doi.org/10.1023/A:1008202821328
21. Tavares, J., Pereira, F.B.: Automatic design of ant algorithms with grammatical evolution. In: Moraglio, A., Silva, S., Krawiec, K., Machado, P., Cotta, C. (eds.) EuroGP 2012. LNCS, vol. 7244, pp. 206–217. Springer, Heidelberg (2012). https://doi.org/10.1007/978-3-642-29139-5_18
22. Tong, L., Dong, M., Jing, C.: An improved multi-population ensemble differential evolution. Neurocomputing **290**, 130–147 (2018)
23. Wu, G., Mallipeddi, R., Suganthan, P.N.: Swarm Evol. Comput. **44**, 695–711 (2019). https://doi.org/10.1016/j.swevo.2018.08.015
24. Wu, G., Mallipeddi, R., Suganthan, P.N., Wang, R., Chen, H.: Differential evolution with multi-population based ensemble of mutation strategies. Inf. Sci. **329**, 329–345 (2016). https://doi.org/10.1016/j.ins.2015.09.009
25. Wu, G., Shen, X., Li, H., Chen, H., Lin, A., Suganthan, P.N.: Ensemble of differential evolution variants. Inf. Sci. **423**, 172–186 (2018)
26. Zhang, J., Sanderson, A.C.: JADE: adaptive differential evolution with optional external archive. IEEE Trans. Evol. Comput. **13**(5), 945–958 (2009)

Scalable Centroid Based Fuzzy Min-Max Neural Network Ensemble Classifier Using MapReduce

Vadlamudi Aadarsh$^{(\boxtimes)}$ [ID] and P. S. V. S. Sai Prasad [ID]

School of Computer and Information Sciences, University of Hyderabad, Hyderabad 500046, Telangana, India
{19mcpc09,saics}@uohyd.ac.in

Abstract. Fuzzy Min-Max Neural Network (FMNN) Classifier has acquired significance owing to its unique properties of single-pass training, non-linear classification, and adaptability for incremental learning. Since its inception in 1992, FMNN has witnessed several extensions, modifications, and utilization in various applications. But very few works are done in the literature for enhancing the scalability of FMNN. In recent years, MapReduce framework is used extensively for scaling machine learning algorithms. The existing MapReduce approach for FMNN (MRFMNN) is found to be having limitations in load balancing and in achieving good generalizability. This work proposes MRCFMNN Algorithm for overcoming these limitations. MRCFMNN induces an ensemble of centroid-based FMNN Classifiers for achieving higher generalizability with load balancing. Four ensemble strategies are proposed for combining the individual classifier results. The comparative experimental results using benchmark large decision systems were conducted on Apache Spark MapReduce cluster. The results empirically establish the relevance of the proposed MRCFMNN by achieving significantly better classification accuracy in most of the datasets over MRFMNN.

Keywords: Fuzzy Min-Max Neural Network · Ensemble classification · Hyperbox · MapReduce · Apache spark · Distributed Machine Learning

1 Introduction

Patrick K. Simpson proposed Fuzzy Min-Max Neural Network (FMNN) [8] classifier. FMNN is the association of Fuzzy sets with Neural networks. FMNN is a supervised algorithm that works as a pattern classifier. It is an online adaptive algorithm and Single-pass learning classifier. FMNN classifier uses hyperboxes to classify input patterns. A Min Point (V) and Max Point (W) define a Hyperbox [8]. The significant steps in FMNN's training process are Membership value calculation, Expansion, Overlap test, and Contraction.

P. Maji et al. (Eds.): PReMI 2023, LNCS 14301, pp. 597–607, 2023.
https://doi.org/10.1007/978-3-031-45170-6_62

Several attempts were made by researchers in enhancing the membership function, Contraction process. There were a few improvements made to the membership function of traditional FMNN. Data-Core Based FMNN for Pattern Classification [10], An Enhanced FMNN for Pattern Classification [5], A modified FMNN for clustering and inspecting internal data [4], A FMNN Classifier With Architecture of Compensatory Neuron [6], A modified FMNN with rule extraction and classification [7] are few of those which suggested improvements to traditional FMNN to improve the performance.

Traditional FMNN works well for small decision systems and there was need of a parallel/distributed paradigm for scaling to large-scale decision systems. The MapReduce [1] programming model is a parallel/distributed programming paradigm that helped in improving the scalability of systems. There are many MapReduce frameworks such as Apache Hadoop, Apache Spark, Twister, etc. Apache spark [9] has been chosen to implement the proposed approach because of its in-memory feature.

In the literature, we observed one work on improving the scalability of FMNN through MapReduce. Algorithm MRFMNN [2] was proposed by Shashikanth Ilager et al. using Twister's iterative MapReduce. MRFMNN uses a novel space partitioning strategy and builds FMNN through map-level parallelism. Our theoretical and practical analysis of the MRFMNN algorithm has lead to the identification of the following limitations. (1) Load balancing in MRFMNN is very poor as the partitioning of the dataset is of varying sizes. This is resulting in more computational time for the map phase. (2) MRFMNN is an implementation of classical FMNN which is proved [3] to have generalization issues resulting from information loss due to the contraction step.

Intending to overcome the limitations of MRFMNN, this work proposes a MapReduce-based centroid FMNN (MRCFMNN) Algorithm. The important contributions of the work are: (1) retaining load balancing through Random Partitioning (2) Map-level construction of Centroid-based FMNN classifiers (3) Ensemble classifiers through the formation of four ensemble strategies.

MRCFMNN Algorithm is implemented in Apache Spark iterative MapReduce framework. And a comparative experimental study is done with MRFMNN for assessing its merits and demerits.

The remaining paper is organized as follows: Sect. 2 gives an overview of Fuzzy Min-Max Neural Network and the existing approach. Section 3 describes the proposed approach that is Scalable Centroid based Fuzzy Min-Max Neural Network Ensemble classifier using MapReduce. Section 4 is the discussion of results and Sect. 5 is the conclusion.

2   Preliminaries

2.1   Fuzzy Min-Max Neural Network

FMNN is applied on numeric decision systems $Dt = (U, C \cup \{d\})$. Here U represents a set of the universe of objects which are defined over a set of numeric conditional attributes 'C' and a categorical decision attribute 'd'. FMNN requires the normalization of conditional attributes to the range of [0,1]. In the remaining discussion, 'n' represents $|C|$ and I^n represents the n-dimensional unit queue which is the pattern space formed by n-normalized conditional attributes. The objective of FMNN training is to form Hyperboxes in I^n where each Hyperbox contains objects of a particular decision class. A jth hyperbox(B_j) is represented by two corner points,i.e, a minimum point $V_j = (v_{j1}, v_{j2}, .., v_{jn})$, maximum point $W_j = (w_{j1}, w_{j2}, .., w_{jn})$. A Hyperbox is treated as a fuzzy set over U and for any object $A_h = (a_{h1}, a_{h2}, ..., a_{hn})$, the membership into b_j is defined by the membership function given in Eq. 1.

$$b_j(A_h) = \frac{1}{2n} \sum_{i=1}^{n} [max(0, 1 - max(0, \gamma min(1, a_{hi} - w_{ji}))) + max(0, 1 - max(0, \gamma min(1, v_{ji} - a_{hi})))]$$

$$(1)$$

Here γ is a sensitivity parameter and as recommended in [8] $\gamma = 4$ is used in our implementation.

FMNN Training Algorithm. FMNN training is a single-pass algorithm. Starting with an empty set of hyperboxes, each training object is used only once. The training process for the input pattern A_h involves an expansion step followed by overlap and contraction.

Since there will be no hyperboxes initially, the first input pattern is created as a point Hyperbox. That means that the input pattern is treated as Min Point(V) and Max Point(W) of the point hyperbox and is represented as $V_j = W_j = A_h$. If there are hyperboxes of the same decision class of the input pattern, then the fuzzy membership value is calculated for all those hyperboxes of the same decision class. If that input pattern is fully member of any hyperbox (membership value $= 1$), then that training object is included into that hyperbox. If the membership value is less than 1, then the highest membership value is considered and expansion criteria is checked for that identified hyperbox. The selected hyperbox is enlarged to accommodate the input pattern based on the below criteria.

$$\sum_{i=1}^{n} (max(w_{ji}, a_{hi}) - min(v_{ji}, a_{hi})) \leq n\theta \qquad (2)$$

where θ is a user-defined parameter with a range of 0 to 1 that controls the size of a hyperbox. We used $\theta = 0.3$ as recommended in [3]. If expansion criteria is satisfied, hyperbox is expanded by adjusting either V or W in any dimension to make that training object a member of that Hyperbox according to the expansion process as follows.

$$v_{ji}^{new} = min(v_{ji}^{old}, a_{hi}) \forall i = 1, 2, ..n \qquad (3)$$

$$w_{ji}^{new} = max(w_{ji}^{old}, a_{hi}) \forall i = 1, 2, ..n \qquad (4)$$

If expansion criteria is not satisfied, then a point hyperbox is created for that training object. After each expansion, an overlap test is conducted to identify overlap between hyperboxes of different classes. If any overlap exists, contraction is applied to remove the overlap among hyperboxes. More about membership function, expansion, overlap test, and contraction process is mentioned in detail in [8].

FMNN Testing Algorithm. The membership value of the test pattern is computed with respect to all hyperboxes using the membership function referred to in Eq. 1. The decision class of the hyperbox to which the highest membership value is obtained is returned.

2.2   MRFMNN Algorithm

Currently, the only approach available for scalable FMNN Algorithm using MapReduce is the MRFMNN algorithm proposed by Shashikant Ilager et al. [2]. In this approach, a novel space partitioning technique is used and the given data is partitioned in the object space such that a hyperbox created in one partition has no overlapping with hyperboxes of the other partitions. Using a map-only job, the traditional FMNN algorithm is applied in parallel on individual partitions to obtain hyperboxes for the respective space regions. Hence the aggregation of hyperboxes obtained over all partitions becomes equivalent to a stand-alone FMNN classifier. Here testing process involves a mapping job for identifying the local best membership hyperbox and through reduce process the global best decision has arrived.

3   Proposed Work

MRFMNN algorithm has provided a scalable approach for the FMNN algorithm. The theoretical and experimental study of this approach has led to the identification of the following limitations.

1. The space partitioning strategy which helps in obtaining non-overlapping partitions has also resulted in load balancing problem. It is observed for almost all the datasets in our analysis, there is a significant variance among the sizes of the partitions. This has become one important factor in resulting in higher training times of MRFMNN algorithms.
2. MRFMNN results in a single FMNN classifier whose set of hyperboxes are distributed among the partitions. As it follows the traditional FMNN algorithm the problems arising from the contraction process affect MRFMNN too. This has resulted in the misclassification resulting from the contraction process limiting the generalizability of the MRFMNN classifier.

To overcome the limitations of MRFMNN, the following solution design choices are considered in our proposed approach.

1. In the proposed solution, we have adopted randomized partitioning of the dataset into equal-sized partitions. The number of partitions is set to the number of cores available in the spark cluster. This overcomes the problem of load balancing in MRFMNN. But any partition here covers the entire pattern space. Hence, unlike MRFMNN we construct a separate FMNN classifier trained on each partition data which are random sample subsets of original training data. Hence in our approach, we construct an ensemble of FMNN classifiers and propose several strategies to ensemble the local classifier results.
2. Construction of an ensemble of classifiers itself helps in achieving better-generalized classification. To enhance it further and to overcome the problems associated with the contraction step, we construct centroid-based FMNN classifiers. The centroid-based FMNN approach involves the only expansion step and uses the centroid of the hyperbox for decision-making for the test pattern in case of ambiguity. We have formulated the centriod based FMNN approach such that the incremental learning property of FMNN is retained. We hope the utilization of centroid-based FMNN as a partition-level classifier and the strategies of ensembling will achieve better generalizability in the proposed approach.

The algorithms for the training phase of the proposed MRCFMNN are provided in algorithms 1,2. The testing of MRCFMNN for an input test pattern is depicted in algorithms 3,4.

3.1 MRCFMNN Training

Input dataset $Dt = (U, C \cup \{d\})$ is pre-processed before the training process. Random partitioning is applied to the Input dataset using the count of Mappers 'N'. The input dataset is partitioned into N partitions horizontally. With a horizontal partitioning strategy, the dataset is distributed over object space, and the data partitions are dispersed among several cluster nodes. This implies that each node in a cluster that has the dataset horizontally partitioned has access to data on all attributes for a subset of objects.

On the partitioned datasets $Dt^i = (U^i, C \cup \{d\})$; where $U^i \subseteq U$, $i \in \{1, 2, ...N\}$ mapPartitions method (Algorithm 2) is invoked in parallel.

Algorithm 1: Driver - MRCFMNN - Training

Input: Dataset $Dt = (U, C \cup \{d\})$; N: Number of Mappers
Output: HBRDD $< V, W, dec, Cent, Sum, Count >$
1 Split the dataset Dt horizontally using N randomly so that each data partition becomes $Dt^i = (U^i, C \cup \{d\})$, $\forall i \in 1, 2, ...p$ where p is the number of data partitions in the cluster. And dataset is DTRDD after partitioning
    `// DTRDD=sc.textFile(DT)`
2 HBRDD<
    $V, W, dec, Cent, Sum, Count >$=DTRDD.mapPartitions(MRCFMNN_Training)
3 Return HBRDD $< V, W, dec, Cent, Sum, Count >$

The proposed centroid-based FMNN is inspired from [10]. A Hyperbox is represented by $< V, W, dec, Cent, Sum, Count >$. Here $Cent$ represents centroid and is equal to *Sum* divided by *Count* where *Sum* represents the summation of training patterns of decision class *dec* belonging to H and *Count* is the cardinality of such objects, V is Min Point, W is Max Point of Hyperbox, dec is decision class. We maintain *Sum, Count* for easy updation of centroid when a new training becomes a member of H. As described in Algorithm 2 in CFMNN only the expansion step is involved and appropriate updation of centroid parameters is done. As the contraction step is avoided, after the training, there will be overlapping among hyperboxes of different classes.

Algorithm 2: *Training – MRCFMNN*

Input: *Dataparition*; $Dt^i = (U^i, C \cup \{d\})$
Output: HBList $< V, W, dec, Cent, Sum, Count >$

1 HBList$= \phi$
2 **for** $a \in U^i$ **do**
3   a. Find the maximum membership of 'a' to all $H \in HBList$ where $H_{dec} = dec(a)$. Let H_{max} denote the hyperbox giving maximum membership.
4   b.**if** $H_{max} = \phi$ **then**
5   Create point Hyperbox $H^{new} < C(a), C(a), dec(a), -, C(a), 1 >$
6   Add H^{new} to HBList
7   **end**
8   **else**
9   **if** $b_{H_{max}}(a) == 1$ **then**
10   continue
11   **end**
12   **else**
13   Test for expansion criteria using $\theta = 0.3$
14   **if** *Expansion criteria is satisfied* **then**
15   Update $V(H_{max}), W(H_{max})$ using expansion criteria
                     $Sum(H_{max}) = Sum(H_{max}) + c(a)$
                     $Count(H_{max}) = Count(H_{max}) + 1$
16   **end**
17   **else**
18   Create point Hyperbox $H^{new} < C(a), C(a), dec(a), -, C(a), 1 >$
19   Add H^{new} to HBList
20   **end**
21   **end**
22   **end**
23 **end**
24 **for** $HB \in HBList$ **do**
25      $count(HB) = Sum(HB)/Count(HB)$
26 **end**
27 Return HBList

3.2 MRCFMNN Testing

In the driver for testing (Given in Algorithm 3), the test pattern 'x' is broadcasted to HBRDD and Algorithm 4 is invoked on each partition in parallel through mapPartitions method of RDD. At each partition, a collection $WinList$ of Hyperboxes having maximum membership for 'x' is constructed. As hyperboxes can overlap $|WinList|$ can be more than 1 in which case the nearest Hyperbox H^* of $WinList$ is selected based on Cartesian distance of x to the centroid of Hyperboxes in $WinList$. If $|WinList|$ is 1, then that single hyperbox becomes H^* without ambiguity. For assisting in the ensemble process algorithm4 returns $(b_{H^*}, dec(H^*), dist(x, Cent(H^*)))$. In the driver, the local best results from the partitions are collected into LB_Results variable. A given ensemble method $Ensemble\_Function$ is applied on LB_results for computing the predicted decision class d(x).

Algorithm 3: Driver - MRCFMNN- Testing

Input: HBRDD $< V, W, dec, Cent, Sum, Count >$; Test Pattern: x; Ensemble function
Output: d(x): Predicted decision class of test pattern 'x'
1   Broadcast test pattern 'x'
2   perform local partition-based testing using HBRDD for test pattern 'x'
3   TRRDD$< LB_{mem}, LB_d, LB_{dist} >=$
    HBRDD$< V, W, dec, Cent, Sum, Count >$.mapPartitions(MRCFMNN-Testing)
4   LB_Results=TRRDD.collect()
5   EnsembleResults $< d(x) >= Ensemble_Function(LB\_Results)$
    // Return predicted decision class after applying ensemble function
    for test pattern 'x'

Algorithm 4: MRCFMNN-Testing: A MapReduce Approach

Input: Test pattern $'x'$, HBList
Output: local best result($b_{H^*}, dec(H^*), dist(x, Cent(H^*))$)   of each partition for test pattern $'x'$
1   for $Hyperbox H \in HBList$ do
2 | Calculate membership of x; $b_H(x)$
3   end
4   Let WinList denote the set of Hyperboxes obtaining the highest membership.
5   if $|WinList| == 1$ then
6 | Let H^* denote the single Hyperbox in WinList.
7   end
8   if $|WinList| > 1$ then
9 | 1. Calculate Euclidean distance(dist) from test pattern 'x' to $Cent(H)$
    | $\forall H \in WinList$
10 | 2. Let H^* denote the hyperbox in WinList whose centroid is nearest to $'x'$.
11 end
12 return $(b_{H^*}, dec(H^*), dist(x, Cent(H^*)))$

Ensemble Approaches. The following ensemble functions are used in Algorithm 3.

1. **Max_occurrences**: Max_occurrences technique considers the decision class which occurs a maximum number of times in local results as global best.
2. **Min_Distance class**: Min_Distance class returns the decision class of least distance Hyperbox among local results.
3. **KNN_DClass**: KNN_Dclass considers k nearest neighbors of test pattern based on distances and chooses the decision class of hyperbox having maximum membership.
4. **Highest_Membership_MinDist**: Highest_Membership_MinDist Consider the decision class of the local best hyperbox having the highest membership. If a tie occurs, it breaks the tie by considering the distance values among tied and returning the decision class of the nearest hyperbox.

4 Experimental Observations & Analysis of Results

A Comparative experimental study is conducted between the proposed MRCFMNN algorithm with MRFMNN algorithm. Both algorithms are implemented in Apache Spark's iterative MapReduce framework. The purpose of the study is to assess the benefits and drawbacks of MRCFMNN over MRFMNN in the aspects of classification accuracy, Training time (Seconds), and cardinality of Hyperboxes.

4.1 Experimental Setup

The tests are run using Apache Spark on a cluster of six nodes, with one fixed as the master and the rest serving as slaves. The Intel (R) Xeon (R) Silver 4110 CPU @2.10 GHz processor, with 32 cores and 64 GB of main memory, powers the master node. Each worker node has an Intel (R) Core (TM) i7-8700 CPU running at 3.20 GHz, with 12 cores, and 32 GB of main memory. All nodes utilize the Ubuntu 18.04 LTS operating system and have 1000 Mbps Ethernet connections. Java 1.8.0 171, Apache Spark 2.3.1, and Scala 2.11.4 are all installed on every node. In the experiment, a few benchmark numerical decisions from the UCI machine learning repository [1] are employed [11].

Table 1. Benchmark Datasets

Data Set	No.of Attributes	Objects	Decision classes
CoverType	54	581012	7
Crop mapping using fused optical-radar	175	325834	7
Skin Segmentation	4	245057	2
Sepsis Survival	4	110341	2
Statlog (Shuttle)	9	58000	7
Thyroid	21	7200	3

4.2 Comparative Experiment Results

Each dataset is randomly divided into 80% as training data and 20% as test data. Distributed FMNN models are constructed on training data using MRCFMNN and MRFMNN algorithms. The model accuracy is evaluated over the test data. The obtained results are summarized in Table 2. MRFMNN algorithm is applied repeatedly conducted 5 times as the space partitioning strategy depends on randomly selected features [2]. Hence we have reported minimum and maximum values obtained for Hyperbox count(HBcount), Classification accuracy as accuracy, and Training_time(seconds). The classification accuracy of MRCFMNN is reported for each ensemble strategy used, in the order of 1. Max_occurrences 2. Min_Distance class 3. KNN_Dclass 4. Highest_Membership_MinDist. For the KNN_DClass approach k=3 is considered for experimentation.

Table 2. Comparative results

SNo	DATASET NAME	Approach	HB Count*	Accuracy * (%)	Training time* (Sec)
1	CoverType	MRFMNN	69 (m), 75 (M)	43.75 (m), 50.63 (M)	84.33 (m), 87.11 (M)
		MRCFMNN	707	60.34, 51.00, 49.29, 50.97	41.42
2	Crop mapping using fused optical-radar	MRFMNN	931 (m), 960 (M)	95.17 (m), 97.41 (M)	30.70 (m), 33.62 (M)
		MRCFMNN	1272	98.54, 98.19, 97.93, 98.34	16.78
3	Skin Segmentation	MRFMNN	65 (m), 73 (M)	73.00 (m), 89.00 (M)	14.39 (m), 16.10 (M)
		MRCFMNN	178	97.63, 90.17, 88.31, 90.17	6.42
4	Sepsis Survival Primary Cohort	MRFMNN	27 (m), 34 (M)	31.09 (m), 54.29 (M)	10.28 (m), 11.11 (M)
		MRCFMNN	86	68.76, 61.59, 65.53, 61.83	4.61
5	Shuttle	MRFMNN	21 (m), 24 (M)	88.74 (m), 89.91 (M)	6.02 (m), 6.39 (M)
		MRCFMNN	73	94.04, 94.62, 94.78, 94.67	2.53
6	Thyroid	MRFMNN	43 (m), 51 (M)	87.09 (m), 95.82 (M)	2.14 (m), 2.52 (M)
		MRCFMNN	170	96.90, 96.47, 94.52, 97.26	1.14

*Note: In Table 2, m denotes minimum and M indicates Maximum out of 5 repeated experiments in MRFMNN. Results of MRCFMNN are mentioned only once because no randomization was involved in partitioning

4.3 Analysis of Results

From the results reported in Table 2 following observations are made in classification accuracy results. The proposed MRCFMNN achieved better generalizability than MRFMNN in all the datasets. MRCFMNN could achieve significantly better results in CoverType, Skin Segmentation, and Sepsis Survival datasets even when the comparison is done with Maximum accuracy obtained by MRFMNN. Among the ensemble strategies used in MRCFMNN, Strategy1, i.e., Max_Occurrences performed consistently better than other strategies. And Hence the same is recommended. These significant results of MRCFMNN are majorly due to utilizing centroid-based FMNN as the base classifier and the ensemble strategy used.

But MRFMNN resulted in significantly fewer Hyperboxes than MRCFMNN in all the datasets. This is because the space partitioning in MRFMNN results in the formation of Hyperboxes in different portions of pattern space across partitions. Hence Hyperboxes are formed only once in a region of pattern Space (I_n). Due to Random Partitioning involved in MRCFMNN, Hyperboxes are constructed in the entire pattern space in every partition. On the positive side, this factor alone helped in the construction of a meaningful Ensemble classifier and in achieving better classification results.

The training time of MRCFMNN is significantly less than that of MRFMNN in all the datasets. The reason for the faster training time of MRCFMNN is majorly due to load balancing through Random partitioning, restricting FMNN training to only the expansion step and construction of centroid being done with less number of computations. Overall the results established the relevance of MRCFMNN and the approach is horizontally scalable as most computations are done through narrow transformations of mapPartitions.

5   Conclusion

The Algorithm MRCFMNN is proposed as a hybridization of FMNN with the centroid of Hyperbox using better ensemble techniques to overcome the limitations of MRFMNN. The experimental results have established that MRCFMNN achieved better classification accuracy than existing approaches. In the future, attempts will be done for proposing a better system that reduces the count of Hyperboxes and improves accuracy.

References

1. Dean, J., Ghemawat, S.: MapReduce: simplified data processing on large clusters. Commun. ACM **51**(1), 107–113 (2008)
2. Ilager, S., Prasad, P.S.: Scalable mapreduce-based fuzzy min-max neural network for pattern classification. In: Proceedings of the 18th International Conference on Distributed Computing and Networking, pp. 1–7 (2017)
3. Kumar, A., Prasad, P.S.V.S.S.: Scalable fuzzy rough set reduct computation using fuzzy min-max neural network preprocessing. IEEE Trans. Fuzzy Syst. **28**(5), 953–964 (2020). https://doi.org/10.1109/TFUZZ.2020.2965899
4. Liu, J., Ma, Y., Zhang, H., Su, H., Xiao, G.: A modified fuzzy min-max neural network for data clustering and its application on pipeline internal inspection data. Neurocomputing **238**, 56–66 (2017)
5. Mohammed, M.F., Lim, C.P.: An enhanced fuzzy min-max neural network for pattern classification. IEEE Trans. Neural Netw. Learn. Syst. **26**(3), 417–429 (2014)
6. Nandedkar, A.V., Biswas, P.K.: A fuzzy min-max neural network classifier with compensatory neuron architecture. IEEE Trans. Neural Netw. **18**(1), 42–54 (2007)
7. Quteishat, A., Lim, C.P.: A modified fuzzy min-max neural network with rule extraction and its application to fault detection and classification. Appl. Soft Comput. **8**(2), 985–995 (2008)
8. Simpson, P.K.: Fuzzy min–max neural networks–part 1: classification. IEEE Trans. Neural Netw. **3**(5), 776–786 (1992)
9. Spark, A.: Apache spark: lightning-fast cluster computing, pp. 2168–7161 (2016). http://spark.apache.org

10. Zhang, H., Liu, J., Ma, D., Wang, Z.: Data-core-based fuzzy min-max neural network for pattern classification. IEEE Trans. Neural Netw. **22**(12), 2339–2352 (2011)
11. Dua, D., Graff, C.: UCI Machine Learning Repository (Technical report, University of California, Irvine, School of Information and Computer Sciences) (2017)

Membership Adjusted Superpixel Based Fuzzy C-Means for White Blood Cell Segmentation

Arunita Das[1]([✉])[ID], Amrita Namtirtha[2][ID], and Animesh Dutta[1][ID]

[1] Department of Computer Science and Engineering, National Institute of Technology Durgapur, Durgapur 713209, West Bengal, India
`arunita17@gmail.com, animesh@cse.nitdgp.ac.in`
[2] Department of Computer Science and Engineering, JIS College of Engineering, Kalyani, Nadia 741235, India

Abstract. Fuzzy C-means (FCM) is a well-known clustering technique that is efficiently used for image segmentation. However, the performance of the FCM degrades for noisy images and slow convergence due to the repeated calculation of the distance among pixels and cluster centers. Therefore, this study develops a Membership Adjusted superpixel-based Fuzzy C-Means (MASFCM) to overcome both issues. The proposed MASFCM utilizes superpixel image as input to make the clustering method fast and noise robust. Membership scaling based on triangle inequality has been employed to speed up performance by avoiding unnecessary distance calculations. Lastly, the final membership matrix has been filtered using morphological reconstruction to enhance the robustness of the MASFRFCM. Furthermore, the proposed MASFCM has been efficiently applied to segment the White Blood Cell (WBC) from pathology images. The visual and numerical results clearly demonstrate that the proposed MASFCM produces promising outcomes compared to other tested state-of-the-art clustering techniques over clean as well as noisy pathology images.

Keywords: Image Segmentation · Noise · Superpixel · Membership Scaling · Membership Filtering

1 Introduction

Image segmentation is a key step in computer vision for classification and object identification. However, image segmentation is a very challenging task, especially for pathology images, due to noise, illumination effects, complex backgrounds, etc. [1]. WBC segmentation from hematopathology images plays a crucial role in the computer-assisted automatic diagnosis of several critical diseases, like cancer. Several segmentation techniques have been developed in the literature for the fast and accurate segmentation of WBC. Clustering is a simple and efficient technique for image segmentation and has proven its efficacy in the WBC segmentation domain. FCM and K-Means (KM) are the most popular image clustering strategies [2]. The main issues with FCM and KM are local trapping due to random initialization, large computation times due to repetitive distance computation and image size dependency, and noise sensitivity [2,3]. Therefore, researchers developed improved variants of KM and FCM for the proper segmentation of WBC. For example, a robust WBC segmentation technique had been developed based on the adaptive KM technique by Makem et al. [4], where arithmetic operation, texture enhancement, and mean-shift operation were utilized as preprocessing techniques. The proposed method achieved nearly 90% accuracy over different public datasets. Umamaheswari and Geetha [5] applied FCM for WBC segmentation, and then watershed transform and morphological reconstruction were used as preprocessing techniques to improve segmentation quality. However, computational time, local trapping, and noise robustness were the main concerns of the two above-mentioned techniques. Nature-inspired optimizers (NIOs) were efficiently incorporated into KM and FCM to overcome the local trapping problem [6,7]. However, NIOs needed large computation times for clustering, which hampered real-time construction [6,7]. For example, Vishnoi et al. [6] developed roulette wheel whale optimizer based fuzzy clustering (RWWOFC) for nucleus segmentation to overcome the local trapping problem and found it to be a capable clustering technique compared to KM and FCM. A Stochastic Fractal Optimizer-based KM (SFO-KM) had been developed and applied for WBC segmentation and provided promising results by outperforming KM and FCM [7]. The limitations of both the proposed methods, i.e., RWWOFC and SFO-KM, were noise sensitivity and higher execution times. Dwivedi et al. [8] designed an improved FCM variant called MLWIFCM based on the incorporation of weighted local information and the Golden Eagle Optimizer (GEO). Incorporation of weighted local information made the method noise-robust, whereas GEO reduced the local trapping problem. But the main limitation was the higher computational effort. To reduce the computation time, image histogram-based clustering approaches have been developed [9]. For example, histogram-based fast fuzzy clustering depending on the Archimedes Optimizer (AO) [9] and Firefly Algorithm [10] had been designed. Both the proposed methods outperformed FCM [10], FCM with mean filter-based spatial constraints (FCM_S1), FCM with median filter-based spatial constraints (FCM_S2), histogram-based Enhanced FCM (EnFCM), Fast Generalized FCM (FGFCM), Fuzzy Local Information C-Means Clustering (FLICM), and fast and robust FCM (FRFCM) [3]. However, AO and FA increased the computational time, and histogram-based clustering failed in the color image segmentation as finding the histogram of a color image was hard. Then a superpixel-based preprocessed image was used to surmount the problems of noise sensitivity and large computation times. Mendi and Budak [11] employed Simple Linear Iterative Clustering (SLIC), Quick Shift, Watershed, Felzenszwalb, and graph based superpixel generation techniques as preprocessing techniques for KM and FCM-based WBC segmentation. The authors claimed that KM and FCM gave the best results with SLIC and Quick Shift. Ray et al. [12] developed SLIC with a Particle Swarm Optimizer (PSO)-based clustering strategy for nucleus segmentation and found promising results by outperforming KM. Mittal and Saraswat [13] developed SLIC with an Improved Gravitational Search Optimizer (SLIC-IGSO)-based clustering strategy for nucleus segmentation and achieved good accuracy. But noise sensitivity and large computational times were the main problems in Ref. [12, 13]. Therefore, it can be noticed from the above literature that the development of noise robust and low computational time-based clustering techniques is the main challenge in the WBC segmentation domain, and this is the main motivation of the work. The proposed work selects FCM over KM because FCM is a soft clustering technique that is flexible and robust for ambiguity in overlapped pixels in pathology images. This study develops an improved version of FCM called Membership Adjusted Superpixel-based Fuzzy C-Means (MASFCM) for WBC segmentation, and this is the main contribution of the study. The excellent feature of MASFCM is that it is an exceptionally fast and noise-robust color image clustering technique due to the Multiscale Morpho-logical Gradient Reconstruction with Watershed Transform (MMGRWT) based super-pixel, membership scaling, and Morphological Reconstruction (MR)-based final membership matrix filtering.

In the rest of the paper, Sect. 2 describes the methodology. Section 3 presents the experimental results. Section 4 discussed the conclusion and future works.

2   Methodology

FCM is considered the most popular soft clustering method which is developed by Bezdek's fuzzy extension of the least-square error approach [10]. FCM based image procedure is presented as follows. Consider an image (I) that consists of N number pixels with L number of gray levels. Now, let we want to cluster I into K clusters. So, I is regarded as the set of pixels. Let, z_p is the d components of pixel p. Here, d is dimension. Here, in FCM the main aim is to minimize the objective function stated following:

$$J_e = \arg\min_k \sum_{i=1}^{N} \sum_{j=1}^{K} u_{ij}^e \|z_p^i - m_j\|^2 \tag{1}$$

Here, $\|.\|$ is an inner product-induced norm in d dimensions. Basically, it computes the distance between i^{th} pixel (denoted by z_p^i) and j^{th} cluster center (denoted by m_j). Next, the membership or partition matrix is estimated as $U = [u_{ij}]^{N \times K}$. Here, $\sum_{(j=1)}^{K} u_{ij} = 1$ and $e\,(1 \le e \le \infty)$ is the fuzzy exponent parameter. In FCM, the cluster centers are randomly initialized. Then, the fuzzy membership of each pixel element is calculated at each iteration based on the following expression:

$$u_{ij} = \frac{\left(\frac{1}{\|z_p^i - m_j\|^2}\right)^{\frac{1}{e-1}}}{\sum_{k=1}^{K} \left(\frac{1}{\|z_{pi} - m_k\|}\right)^{\frac{1}{e-1}}}, \; for\, 1 \le j \le K; 1 \le i \le N; \tag{2}$$

Next, the cluster centers are computed by applying the expression stated following:

$$m_j = \frac{(\sum_{(i=1)}^{N} u_{ij} z_p^i)}{(\sum_{(i=1)}^{N} u_{ij})}, 1 \leq j \leq K \tag{3}$$

2.1 Membership Scaling

Membership scaling [14] accelerates the clustering convergence and maintains high clustering quality of FCM by using a triangle inequality. The brief mathematical discussion of membership scaling is as follows. Suppose, the distance between z_p^i and m are $d_{ij} = \|z_p^i - m_j\|, for 1 \leq j \leq K; 1 i \leq N$ and they are rearranged in ascending order as $D_i^1 \leq D_i^2 \leq .... \leq D_i^K$. Displacement of centre $\delta_j^t = d(m_j^{t+1} - m_j^t)$. According to the triangle inequality [14] the following lemma can be written.

Lemma 1. *A pixel z_p^i cannot change its nearest cluster after one update, if*

$$D_i^2 - \max_{1 \leq j \leq K} \delta_j \geq D_i^1 + \delta_{\zeta_i^*}, where\, \zeta_i^* = arg \min_{1 \leq j \leq K} d_{ij} \tag{4}$$

The pixels whose closeness relationship do not change after one update are filtered out by using triangle inequality as per Eq. (4) and Q is taken as the index set of the filtered pixels. The membership grades of the filtered pixels are scaled to accelerate the convergence of FCM. Therefore, the new update scheme for U^{t+1} is as follows:

$$u_{ij}^{(t+1)} = \begin{cases} M_i^t, & i \in Q^t, j = \zeta_i^{*t}, \\ \beta_i^t u_{ij}^t, & i \in Q^t, j \neq \zeta_i^{*t}, \\ u_{ij}^t, & i \notin Q^t, 1 \leq j \leq K \end{cases} \tag{5}$$

where $M_i^t = [1 + (k-1)(D_i^1/D_i^K)^{\frac{2}{e-1}}]^{-1}, \beta_i^t = \frac{1-M_i^t}{1-u_{\zeta_i^t,i}^t}$. Then the update of m is also Eq. (3). This membership scaling helps FCM to filter out the pixels in the update of their non-affinity centers and increases the participation of the filtered pixels in the update of the remaining centers by scaling the membership. Therefore, membership scaling helps to reduce the number of iteration, lower time consumption, and higher cluster quality [14]. In this study, superpixel image has been taken as input for clustering and therefore, the pixel must be replaced by superpixel in Eq. (4) for MASFCM.

2.2 Membership Filtering

Membership matrix filtering (MMF) is a nice way to make FCM better in a noisy environment. The proposed MASFCM modifies the final membership matrix using morphological reconstruction (MR) [3]. Only the final MMF is performed to reduce the execution time significantly. In fact, MMF is equivalent to the inclusion of local spatial information.

To verify the effectiveness of MMF, a test is conducted by selecting a synthetic image which is presented as Fig. 1(a) having 256×256 size and three different gray values (0, 85, 170). Salt & Pepper noise (20%) is added to Fig. 1(a) and clustering (with 3 cluster numbers) has been done by FCM, FCM with median filter based MMF, FCM with MR based MMF. The filtering window of the median filter and square structure element for MR are set o 3×3. The results in Fig. 1 clearly confirmed the supremacy of MR based MMF.

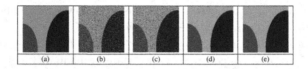

Fig. 1. Results with MMF. (a) Original image; (b) Noisy image; (c) FCM; (d) FCM with Median filter; (e) FCM with MR.

2.3 Superpixel Strategy

Recently, image clustering techniques utilized superpixel images as input to make the method fast and noise-robust, especially for color images. Although histogram-based clustering methods are fast and image size independent, they failed for color images. Consideration of superpixel image for clustering is equivalent to the inclusion of local spatial information [2]. SLIC [2], Mean-Shift (MS) [2] and MMGRWT [15] are the most commonly used superpixel techniques, and MMGR-WT proves its supremacy over SLIC and MS [2]. MMGRWT performs better in noisy environments and has a strong capacity to cut down on computation time for color image segmentation. As a result, this study has chosen to use this superpixel generating technique.

The MMGR technique is used to produce superpixel images with accurate limits while using adaptive neighbouring information and minimizing the variety of pixels in a color image. Since WT just uses the region minima of gradient images to generate pre-segmentation, its complexity is incredibly low. For pre-segmentation, the MMGRWT [2,15] can give better results than SLIC and Mean Shift while taking less time to run.

Therefore, the MASFCM technique has been designated as Algorithm 1 based on the membership scaling, filtering, and superpixel strategy. According to the theoretical analysis discussed above, the proposed MASFCM offers two key benefits that make it a real-time segmentation technique, namely speed and noise resistance.

Algorithm 1. Procedure of MASFCM

Input: Image (I), clusters number (c), and fuzzification parameter (e).
Output: Membership Matrix (U), and cluster center vector m.
1: Compute the superpixel image using MMGRWT technique.
2: Compute the cluster center $m^{(}(1))$ by the initial membership matrix U^0
3: **while** $\max(U^t - U^{t+1}) \geq 10^{-5}$ **do**
4:    Compute the distance between superpixels and cluster centers.
5:    Compute the membership matrix and cluster centers.
6:    Filtering out the subset using triangular inequality as per Eq. (4)
7:    Perform membership scaling using Eq. (5)
8:    Compute cluster centers based on updated membership matrix.
9: **end while**
10: Perform MR based membership filtering to derive final membership matrix

---

3   Experimental Results

This section presents the results over WBC segmentation using proposed cluster-ing technique called MASFCM and other tested clustering algorithms, namely SLIC-IGSO [13], SFO-KM [7], RWWOFC [6], MLWIFCM-GEO [8], SLIC-KM [11], SLIC-FCM [11], KM [2], and FCM [2]. For all SLIC-based clustering, num-ber of superpixels is taken as 400 from exhaustive experiments. c is set to 3 optimally through a trial-and-error strategy. e is set to 2 for fuzzy clustering. Population size (n) and maximum iteration (MI) are set to 50 and 150, respec-tively, for a fair comparison among NIOs-based clustering strategies. For MAS-FCM, r_1, η , size of structuring element of MR are set to 3, $10^{(} - 4)$, and 3×3 respectively; $\rho = 0.7$ for GSO; MDN is et to 1 for SFO; for RWWOFC, a is et to 2; and lastly, $[p_a^0 - p_a^T$], $[p_c^0 - p_c^T$] in MLWIFCM-GEO set to [0.5–2], [1–0.5] respectively from experience and the source papers of the methods.

The experiment has been carried out using MatlabR2018b and Windows-8 OS on an x64-based PC with an IntelI Intel Core-i7 CPU running at 2.20 GHz and 8 GB of RAM. Experiments have been tested using 200 images from the Raabin-white blood cells (WBC) dataset [16]. Each image (575×575) in the Raabin-WBC dataset is accompanied by a set of ground truth images. In this study, four quality evaluation parameters [2] - Accuracy (ACC), Matthews Cor-relation Coefficient (MCC), Dice (DI), and Jaccard (JC) are computed to eval-uate the clustering algorithms. The higher values of the mentioned parameters indicate better results.

The original WBC and the associated ground truth images are shown in Fig. 2. The segmented result, which is assessed by the eight comparing algorithms and the proposed algorithm, is shown in Fig. 3. The visual inspection of Fig. 3 makes it very evident that the MASFCM produces the best WBC segmentation results. In addition to visual examination, average values of quality parameters and execution time in Table 1 clearly revealed that MASFCM based clustering technique produces faster and more accurate segmentation results compared to other SLIC-based clustering methods, NIOs based clustering methods, and clas-

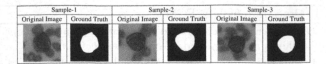

Fig. 2. Original WBC images with corresponding ground truth

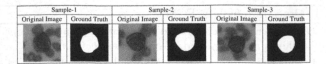

Fig. 3. Segmented results by the tested clustering algorithms over original WBC images

sical methods. So, MMGRWT based superpixels are best fit for WBC segmentation. MASFCM achieves 94% accuracy, which proves the significant efficacy of MASFCM over other algorithms. The proposed MASFCM takes the least execution time due to the MMGRWT based superpixel image and membership scaling. On the other hand, NIOs based clustering strategies are associated with execution time. Classical FCM and KM consider all pixels for clustering, which is why they take more time compared to SLIC-KM and SLIC-FCM. MLWIFCM-GEO is the worst clustering algorithm when considering execution time only. The bold font in tables indicates the best numerical values.

A comparison analysis of the clustering methods in the noisy image segmentation domain has been conducted in order to demonstrate that the proposed MASFCM is resilient against noise. Two different types of noise, Gaussian and Salt & Pepper, are externally applied to pathology images in this investigation. Figure 4 shows the original, ground truth, and noisy WBC images following the addition of Gaussian noise (mean 0 and variance 0.3) and Salt & Pepper noise (density 30%) to the original WBC images. The segmentation outcome using the suggested method and other methods is shown in Fig. 5. The visual inspection of Fig. 5 makes it very evident that the MASFCM produces the best WBC segmentation results. The MASFCM is resistant to Salt & Pepper noise as well as Gaussian noise since it employs MMGRWT and MR-based membership filtering. The performance of various approaches for segmenting noisy images was assessed using quality parameters. The average values for the segmentation quality parameters over Salt & Pepper and Gaussian noisy WBC images, are provided in Table 2. The quality parameter values demonstrate that in noisy conditions, MASFCM outperforms other comparable algorithms in terms of results. Additionally, high quality segmented WBC could not be produced using SLIC

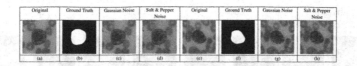

Fig. 4. Original and noisy WBC images

super-pixel-based approaches. The worst visual results are produced by other pixel-based NIOs-clustering approaches, traditional FCM, and KM. This leads to the conclusion that the suggested MASFCM is also a powerful clustering method for noisy WBC images.

Table 1. Numerical results and execution time over original images

Method	ACC	MCC	DI	JC	Time (Sec.)
MASFCM	**0.9459**	**0.8619**	**0.8697**	**0.8069**	**1.10**
SLIC-IGSO	0.9102	0.6998	0.7624	0.6238	13.47
SLIC-KM	0.8888	0.6872	0.7378	0.6113	1.25
SLIC-FCM	0.8776	0.6565	0.7084	0.6001	2.05
SFO-KM	0.8661	0.6319	0.6928	0.5982	15.21
RWWOFC	0.8589	0.6237	0.6822	0.5823	18.29
MLWIFCM-GEO	0.8591	0.6241	0.6827	0.5819	21.99

Table 2. Numerical results over noisy images

Method	Gaussian Noisy Images				Salt & Pepper Noisy Images			
	ACC	MCC	DI	JC	ACC	MCC	DI	JC
MASFCM	**0.9211**	**0.8010**	**0.8187**	**0.7684**	**0.9065**	**0.7555**	**0.7898**	**0.6847**
SLIC-IGSO	0.852	0.6317	0.6731	0.5658	0.8811	0.6822	0.7244	0.5998
SLIC-KM	0.8312	0.6118	0.6618	0.5599	0.8654	0.6687	0.7101	0.5989
SLIC-FCM	0.8233	0.6091	0.6372	0.3893	0.8469	0.6566	0.7032	0.5781
RWWOFC	0.8011	0.5234	0.6075	0.5013	0.8015	0.5117	0.6011	0.4668
MLWIFCM-GEO	0.8015	0.5238	0.6079	0.5016	0.8018	0.5121	0.6015	0.4676
SFO-KM	0.8171	0.4413	0.5448	0.3771	0.7899	0.4178	0.5261	0.3612
KM	0.8169	0.4406	0.5442	0.3767	0.7896	0.4174	0.5258	0.3593
FCM	0.7662	0.4363	0.5351	0.3675	0.7835	0.4091	0.5172	0.3508

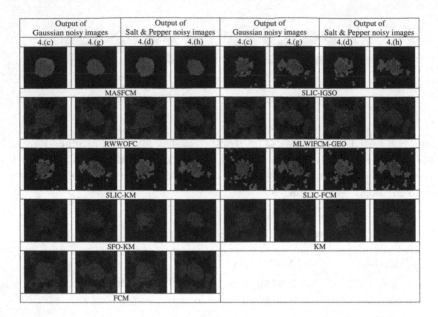

Fig. 5. Segmentation results of the tested clustering algorithm over noisy images

4 Conclusion

This work introduces a new fuzzy clustering technique called Membership Adjusted superpixel-based Fuzzy C-Means (MASFCM). The suggested MAS-FCM has two primary characteristics: (i) remarkably fast due to the use of MMGRWT-based superpixel and membership scaling; (ii) noise-resistant due to superpixel and MR-based final membership matrix filtering. As a result, MAS-FCM solves the noise sensitivity and long computing time concerns of traditional FCM. The MASFCM has been effectively used to segment WBC from clean and noisy pathology pictures. Experiment findings reveal that the suggested MAS-FCM is particularly effective at accurately segmenting the WBC in noisy environments when compared to the other eight tested clustering approaches. The MASFCM's execution time is likewise relatively short, making it suitable for real-time applications. The proposed technique's key shortcoming is that the cluster number is user defined. Another problem of the proposed MASFCM is local optimum trapping. Additionally, the suggested MASFCM should be employed in other image segmentation domain.

References

1. Dhal, K.G., Ray, S., Das, S., Biswas, A., Ghosh, S.: Hue-preserving and gamut problem-free histopathology image enhancement. Iran. J. Sci. Technol. Trans. Electr. Eng. **43**, 645–672 (2019)

2. Sasmal, B., Dhal, K.G.: A survey on the utilization of Superpixel image for clustering based image segmentation. Multimedia Tools Appl. **82**, 35493–35555 (2023). https://doi.org/10.1007/s11042-023-14861-9

3. Lei, T., Jia, X., Zhang, Y., He, L., Meng, H., Nandi, A.K.: Significantly fast and robust fuzzy C-means clustering algorithm based on morphological reconstruction and membership filtering. IEEE Trans. Fuzzy Syst. **26**(5), 3027–3041 (2018)

4. Makem, M., Tiedeu, A., Kom, G., Nkandeu, Y.P.K.: A robust algorithm for white blood cell nuclei segmentation. Multimedia Tools Appl. **81**(13), 17849–17874 (2022). https://doi.org/10.1007/s11042-022-12285-5

5. Umamaheswari, D., Geetha, S.: Fuzzy-C means segmentation of lymphocytes for the identification of the differential counting of WBC. Int. J. Cloud Comput. **10**(1–2), 26–42 (2021)

6. Vishnoi, S., Jain, A.K., Sharma, P.K.: An efficient nuclei segmentation method based on roulette wheel whale optimization and fuzzy clustering. Evol. Intell. **14**, 1367–1378 (2021). https://doi.org/10.1007/s12065-019-00288-5

7. Dhal, K.G., Gálvez, J., Ray, S., Das, A., Das, S.: Acute lymphoblastic leukemia image segmentation driven by stochastic fractal search. Multimedia Tools Appl. **79**, 12227–12255 (2020). https://doi.org/10.1007/s11042-019-08417-z

8. Dwivedi, A., Rai, V., Joshi, S., Kumar, R., Pippal, S.K.: Peripheral blood cell classification using modified local-information weighted fuzzy C-means clustering-based golden eagle optimization model. Soft. Comput. **26**(24), 13829–13841 (2022). https://doi.org/10.1007/s00500-022-07392-2

9. Dhal, K.G., Ray, S., Rai, R., Das, A.: Archimedes optimizer: theory, analysis, improvements, and applications. Arch. Comput. Methods Eng. **30**, 2543–2578 (2023). https://doi.org/10.1007/s11831-022-09876-8

10. Bezdek, J.C., Ehrlich, R., Full, W.: FCM: the fuzzy C-means clustering algorithm. Comput. Geosci. **10**(2–3), 191–203 (1984)

11. Mendi, G., Budak, C.: Automatic cell nucleus segmentation using superpixels and clustering methods in histopathological images. Balkan J. Electr. Comput. Eng. **9**(3), 304–309 (2021)

12. Ray, S., Dhal, K.G., Naskar, P.K.: Superpixel image clustering using particle swarm optimizer for nucleus segmentation. In: Thakur, M., Agnihotri, S., Rajpurohit, B.S., Pant, M., Deep, K., Nagar, A.K. (eds.) SocProS 2022. LNNS, vol. 547, pp. 445–457. Springer, Singapore (2023). https://doi.org/10.1007/978-981-19-6525-8_34

13. Mittal, H., Saraswat, M.: An automatic nuclei segmentation method using intelligent gravitational search algorithm based superpixel clustering. Swarm Evol. Comput. **45**, 15–32 (2019)

14. Zhou, S., Li, D., Zhang, Z., Ping, R.: A new membership scaling fuzzy C-means clustering algorithm. IEEE Trans. Fuzzy Syst. **29**(9), 2810–2818 (2020)

15. Lei, T., Jia, X., Zhang, Y., Liu, S., Meng, H., Nandi, A.K.: Superpixel-based fast fuzzy C-means clustering for color image segmentation. IEEE Trans. Fuzzy Syst. **27**(9), 1753–1766 (2018)

16. Kouzehkanan, Z.M., et al.: Raabin-WBC: a large free access dataset of white blood cells from normal peripheral blood. bioRxiv (2021)

Information Security

MSPIS: Multimodal Suspicious Profile Identification System in Online Social Network

Monika Choudhary[1]([✉]), Satyendra Singh Chouhan[1],
Emmanuel Shubhankar Pilli[1], and Nehul Singh[2]

[1] Malaviya National Institute of Technology, Jaipur, Rajasthan 302017, India
{2019rcp9186,sschouhan.cse,espilli.cse}@mnit.ac.in
[2] Indian Institute of Information Technology SriCity, Sri City,
Andhra Pradesh 517646, India
nehul.s20@iiits.in

Abstract. Easy access to social media platforms and effortless profile creation have enabled users to create online profiles in large numbers. Apart from general interaction, user profiles can be created to spread fake news and target individuals, organizations, and communities by bullying, trolling, and spreading hate content. Identifying these suspicious profiles is one of the crucial research issues in online social media. Most research works in this domain focus on a single attribute, like either profile features or post content, thereby proposing unimodal models capable of processing numeric data or text. This paper presents a multimodal approach to identifying suspicious user profiles. The multimodal features in our experiments are extracted from profiles, posts, and their engagement. The baseline experiments and comparison with unimodal approaches show the effectiveness of the proposed multimodal model. The proposed *MSPIS* framework gives high accuracy of 93.6% in detecting suspicious users by using rich multimodal features to assess user credibility.

Keywords: Suspicious profiles · Multimodal analysis · Social media

1 Introduction

With the increasing use of social media, suspicious user activities have received wide attention. The simplified process of creating profiles and making new connections with little or no direct ownership of the content posted has led to an increase in suspicious activities. Suspicious accounts that indulge in such activities tend to spread spam content and fake news, troll and bully celebrities and rivals, and favor or oppose individuals, organizations, and products. With little or no background verification of new users, Online Social Networks (OSNs) are used by unethical users to create suspicious profiles for personal or organizational benefit. Facebook took down approximately 1.9 billion spam posts in the

P. Maji et al. (Eds.): PReMI 2023, LNCS 14301, pp. 621–628, 2023.
https://doi.org/10.1007/978-3-031-45170-6_64

first quarter of 2020 [1]. Over 500 fake accounts, 131 Instagram accounts, 78 network groups, and 146 pages worldwide were removed for indulging in inauthentic behavior during this period [1].

Several researchers have worked to identify fake accounts, bots, and bullying profiles. In general, genuine user accounts are not used directly to spread suspicious content on online social media. People create separate automated or manual accounts to perform malicious and suspicious activities. Researchers have worked on identifying individual and groups of fake accounts [11], compromised accounts [8,15], bullying accounts [14,17], spam accounts [5,10], and bots [7] performing suspicious activities. The approaches for identifying suspicious profiles have mainly relied on features data [2], pattern matching [12], graph theory [13], and behavioral analysis [15]. The proposed models have used different clustering and classification algorithms for assessing profile credibility. In this paper, our work identifies profiles that spread 'hate content' and are involved in bullying. Together, they are referenced as 'suspicious profiles' throughout this paper.

Researchers have used static and dynamic user profile and post-text-based features to identify suspicious profiles. Researchers in [3] created a supervised model that examined Facebook users' emotions to detect fake accounts. Their research revealed that fake profiles frequently used negative terms such as "hate", "kill", and "ugly". Akyon et al. [4] suggest Support Vector Machine (SVM) and Neural Network (NN) based methods for fake account detection. The existing approaches focus only on user characteristics and do not consider using the content users post. Most of the research in this field relies on user profile characteristics, while a few studies have centered on analyzing the sentiment in user posts. Many of these investigations concentrate on a sole attribute, either profile traits or post content, and propose unimodal models that can handle textual or numerical data. But, user profile information and the content they post encompass multiple modalities.

This paper presents the Multimodal Suspicious Profile Identification System (*MSPIS*) to identify suspicious profiles on social platforms. It considers user and post metadata along with the post content (text and image) to identify the user profiles' credibility. To the best of our knowledge, we are the first to present a multimodal system considering various 'modes' (such as numeric, text, and visual features) to classify a user as 'suspicious' or 'non-suspicious'. The multimodal features in our experiments comprise profile features, text and images of users' posts, and post-engagement features. The presented system works in three stages. In the first stage, there are three parallel encoders to obtain numeric features (from the user profile and post engagement), text, and image features. In the second stage, these features from multiple encoders are fused to obtain a combined feature vector. In the last stage, the dense layer performs the final classification on the combined feature vector to classify the input user profile as 'suspicious' or 'not-suspicious'. The key findings of this paper can be summarized as follows

– It presents a multimodal system, *MSPIS*, based on numeric, textual, and visual features to identify suspicious profiles.

– Different DL-based text and image feature extraction module combinations are studied and analyzed.
– Ablation study of unimodal and multimodal models is performed.
– Performance comparison of *MSPIS* with other state-of-the-art models is made to assess the viability of the presented framework.

The rest of the paper is organized as follows. Section 2 presents the methodology, including the proposed *MSPIS* framework. Section 3 discusses the experiments conducted and the analysis of the results. It first describes the experimental setup and the dataset characteristics, followed by experimental outcomes. Section 4 concludes the paper.

2   Methodology

In this section, we formulate the formal problem definition and discuss the *MSPIS* framework in detail.

2.1   Problem Statement

Given a dataset $\mathcal{D}$ of labeled user profiles consisting of user metadata, text, and images. These user profiles have labels L as either suspicious (1) or not suspicious (0). A user profile $P \in \mathcal{D}$ consists of user metadata (U), text (T), and image (I). Let P be a user profile composed of user metadata (U), $U = [u_1, u_2, \ldots, u_n]$ contain n user features, text (T), and I is an attached image of the text T. Here, user metadata also includes engagement features associated with the user post.

The objective of this research is to design a multimodal model M, such that, given a user profile P with user metadata U, text T, and image I, the model M classifies P into label $L \in \{Suspicious(1), NotSuspicious(0)\}$ by learning a profile assessment function $F : F(U, T, I) \rightarrow (L)$.

2.2   *MSPIS* Framework

In this section, we propose a multimodal framework to identify suspicious profiles. The proposed framework works in three stages, as shown in Fig. 1. In the first stage, three parallel encoders generate user, text, and image features. In the second stage, features extracted by parallel encoders are fused to generate a combined feature vector. In the last stage, the dense layer performs the final classification on the combined feature vector to classify the input user profile as 'suspicious' or 'not-suspicious'.

The formal details are as follows. Let $D = \{d_j\}_{j=1}^{m}$ represent the dataset with m instances, $d_j = (u_j, t_j, i_j, l_j)$ where u_j represent user metadata, t_j is text related to jth post, i_j is image related to j-th post and $l_j \in \{0(not - suspicious), 1(suspicious)\}$ is label assigned to d_j. Let e_u, e_t, e_i denote parameters of the user metadata encoder, text encoder and image encoder, respectively. The output of encoders can be expressed as

$$E_j^U = f_U(u_j; e_u) \qquad (1)$$

$$E_j^T = f_T(t_j; e_t) \tag{2}$$

$$E_j^I = f_I(i_j; e_i) \tag{3}$$

where $E^U, E^T, E^I \in \mathbb{R}^{p \times m}$.

The resultant feature vector is passed through fully connected and dense layers with sigmoid activation for generating the final classification.

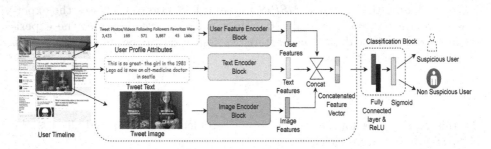

Fig. 1. *MSPIS* framework

The Dense Neural Network (DNN) is used for user feature concatenation and encoding in the user feature encoder. The text encoder tokenizes the input text, and embeddings are generated. BERT, Roberta, and Universal Sentence Encoders (USE) have been used at the text encoder level, and their performance is analyzed. Resnet, InceptionNet, and EfficientNet models have been used in the image encoder. The embeddings generated from the user feature, text, and image encoders are passed through dense and dropout layers and normalized before concatenation and single feature vector generation.

User features considered for experiments include numeric data such as the count of friends, followers, tweets, retweets, likes, user sentiment, and verified flags. They also include post-engagement features such as likes and post sentiment. Text and image features are derived from the text and corresponding images. User metadata, text, and image features have been considered in the *MSPIS* framework.

3   Experiments and Results

The performance of the *MSPIS* framework for identifying suspicious profiles is evaluated through multiple experiments. We introduce the following research questions and aim to find their answers through detailed experiments.

RQ1: How do the proposed multimodal framework *MSPIS* perform in identifying suspicious profiles?

RQ2: Whether *MSPIS* is statistically significant over unimodal models in identifying suspicious profiles?

RQ3: Does the *MSPIS* framework outperform the existing state-of-the-art systems?

We perform several experiments to find answers to the above research questions and analyze the results, as discussed in the next section.

3.1 Experimental Setup

The implementation is done in python language using various DL libraries such as Keras, Scikit learn, and Pandas. The model is trained using a batch size of 32, a dropout rate of 0.1, and projection dimensions of 256. The Adam optimizer is employed along with the categorical cross-entropy loss function.

We use the multimodal suspicious profile dataset curated from Twitter. This dataset includes temporal and post-engagement attributes, including user profile and post features, textual and image content of user posts, profile, and banner pictures. The dataset has 810 unique suspicious users with 5,50,042 distinct tweets with text and 493 non-suspicious users with 5,03,157 distinct tweets. The dataset is available at GitHub repository[1].

3.2 RQ1: Performance of MSPIS Framework

Several experiments are performed using different DL-based models in the *MSPIS* framework. The results are shown in Table 1.

Table 1. Performance of DL Algorithms using different feature set combinations

Features	Model	P	R	A	F1
User Only	DNN	11.39	33.76	33.76	17.04
Text Only	BERT	84.41	84.67	84.46	83.95
	USE	88.39	88.52	88.69	88.4
	RoBERTa	88.17	87.13	87.13	85.67
Image Only	ResNet	82.51	82.25	82.24	79.52
	InceptionNet	80.95	80.24	80.62	76.85
	EfficientNet	81.55	82.44	82.44	81.18
User+Text	DNN + BERT	90.87	90.89	90.97	90.91
	DNN + USE	91.17	91.84	91.84	91.74
	DNN + RoBERTa	89.21	89.32	89.27	89.54
User+Image	DNN + ResNet	89.48	89.47	89.47	89.09
	DNN + InceptionNet	89.23	88.78	88.85	88.06
	DNN + EfficientNet	86.92	86.28	86.04	86.26
User+Text+Image	DNN + BERT + ResNet	92.55	92.3	92.24	91.84
	DNN + BERT + InceptionNet	92.28	92.04	92.04	91.64
	DNN + BERT + EfficientNet	**93.55**	**93.60**	**93.60**	**93.53**
	DNN + USE + ResNet	93.16	92.49	92.87	92.52
	DNN + USE + InceptionNet	93.01	92.89	92.93	92.66
	DNN + USE + EfficientNet	92.75	92.41	92.24	92.01
	DNN + RoBERTa + ResNet	92.67	92.34	92.46	92.23
	DNN + RoBERTa + InceptionNet	91.79	91.43	91.47	91.03
	DNN + RoBERTa + EfficientNet	92.37	92.04	92.04	92.36

Note: P: Precision, A: Accuracy, R: Recall, F: F1 Score

[1] https://github.com/20199186/MmDs.

It is observed that multimodal models performed significantly better than unimodal models (either user metadata, text, or image model). The performance of unimodal models had accuracy in the range of 33.76% to 88.69% and an F1 score in the range of 17.04% to 88.4%. Deep learning-based multimodal models combining all user, text, and image features had accuracy in the range of 91.47% to 93.60% and F1 scores from 91.03% to 93.53%. Thus, concatenating user, text, and image features improved performance over unimodal models.

3.3 RQ2: Statistical Significance of *MSPIS* over other models

The Mann-Whitney U test is conducted to analyze the significance of multimodal models over other models. The results are shown in Table 2.

Table 2. Mann Whitney U test results

Min performing multimodal model	Models	p-value	Z-score	Significance
DNN+RoBERTa+ EfficientNet Vs.	DNN	0.01208	2.50672	Yes
	BERT	0.01208	2.50672	Yes
	USE	0.01208	2.50672	Yes
	RoBERTa	0.01208	2.50672	Yes
	ResNet	0.01208	2.50672	Yes
	InceptionNet	0.01208	2.50672	Yes
	EfficientNet	0.01208	2.50672	Yes
	DNN + BERT	0.01208	2.50672	Yes
	DNN + USE	0.29834	−1.04447	No
	DNN + RoBERTa	0.01208	2.50672	Yes
	DNN + ResNet	0.01208	2.50672	Yes
	DNN + InceptionNet	0.01208	2.50672	Yes
	DNN + EfficientNet	0.01208	2.50672	Yes

It can be observed from the results that the minimum-performing multimodal model (with user, text, and image features) is significant over almost all unimodal or bi-modal models. The results indicate the importance of rich features to identify suspicious profiles correctly.

3.4 RQ3: Comparison with State-of-the-art Models

The multimodal *MSPIS* framework presented in this paper is also compared with other state-of-the-art models. Table 3 summarises the comparative analysis. Authors in [9] used machine learning algorithms on profile and content-based numerical features. The authors got the best result with Decision Tree with an F1 Score of 81%. Other researchers have also worked on the Twitter platform

Table 3. Comparison with state-of-the-art models

Related Work	Learning Model	Features	Results reported	Platform
Azab et al. [9]	ML Techniques (Decision Tree)	Profile & content-based (numeric)	F1-Score 81.00%	Twitter
BalaAnand et al. [6]	EGSLA (Graph based)	Content-based (numeric)	Accuracy 90.3%	Twitter
Adhikari et al. [2]	Data Mining Techniques (PCA & SVM)	Profile-based (static)	Accuracy 87.00%	LinkedIn
Walt et al. [16]	ML Techniques (Random Forest)	Profile-based (numeric)	Accuracy 87.11%	Twitter
Presented Work	*MSPIS* (multimodal DL based)	Content(image, text) & profile-based	Accuracy 93.60%	Twitter

using data mining [2] and graph-based approaches [6]. These approaches typically use numeric data that may not give complete information about user behavior by ignoring the content users post. The presented multimodal *MSPIS* framework considers numeric, text and visual features and is better capable of identifying suspicious users giving an accuracy of 93.6%.

4   Conclusion and Future Scope

With the increasing use of social media, suspicious user activities have received wide attention. Several researchers have proposed unimodal approaches largely based on user profile features to identify suspicious users. However, with the advanced media sharing capabilities on social platforms, multimodal models considering rich features are required to enhance the classification capabilities of models. In this paper, we have proposed a multimodal framework *MSPIS* for identifying suspicious profiles by considering user features and text and visual features of user posts. An accuracy of 93.6% and an F1 score of 93.53% has been obtained with *MSPIS* framework. We also present a comparative analysis of unimodal models and multimodal models. In the future, additional capabilities like processing short videos and identifying malicious URLs embedded in user posts can be considered to improve model performance. Further, the model can be made more powerful by including cross-modal ambiguity learning skills.

References

1. August 2020 coordinated inauthentic behavior report (2020). https://about.fb.com/news/2020/09/august-2020-cib-report/. Accessed 12 Nov 2022
2. Adikari, S., Dutta, K.: Identifying fake profiles in Linkedin. arXiv preprint arXiv:2006.01381 (2020)

3. Agarwal, N., Jabin, S., Hussain, S.Z.: Analyzing real and fake users in Facebook network based on emotions. In: 11th International Conference on Communication Systems and Networks (COMSNETS), pp. 110–117 (2019)
4. Akyon, F.C., Kalfaoglu, M.E.: Instagram fake and automated account detection. In: Innovations in Intelligent Systems and Applications Conference (ASYU), pp. 1–7 (2019)
5. Alom, Z., Carminati, B., Ferrari, E.: Detecting spam accounts on twitter. In: International Conference on Advances in Social Networks Analysis and Mining (ASONAM), pp. 1191–1198 (2018)
6. Balaanand, M., Karthikeyan, N., Karthik, S., Varatharajan, R., Manogaran, G., Sivaparthipan, C.: An enhanced graph-based semi-supervised learning algorithm to detect fake users on twitter. J. Supercomput. **75**, 6085–6105 (2019)
7. Cresci, S., Di Pietro, R., Petrocchi, M., Spognardi, A., Tesconi, M.: DNA-inspired online behavioral modeling and its application to spambot detection. IEEE Intell. Syst. **31**(5), 58–64 (2016)
8. Egele, M., Stringhini, G., Kruegel, C., Vigna, G.: Compa: Detecting compromised accounts on social networks. In: Network and Distributed System Symposium (2013)
9. El Azab, A., Idrees, A.M., Mahmoud, M.A., Hefny, H.: Fake account detection in twitter based on minimum weighted feature set. Int. J. Comput. Inf. Eng. **10**(1), 13–18 (2015)
10. Fu, H., Xie, X., Rui, Y.: Leveraging careful microblog users for spammer detection. In: 24th International Conference on World Wide Web, pp. 419–429 (2015)
11. Gupta, A., Kaushal, R.: Towards detecting fake user accounts in Facebook. In: ISEA Asia Security and Privacy (ISEASP), pp. 1–6 (2017)
12. Gurajala, S., White, J.S., Hudson, B., Matthews, J.N.: Fake twitter accounts: profile characteristics obtained using an activity-based pattern detection approach. In: International Conference on Social Media & Society, pp. 1–7 (2015)
13. Mohaisen, A., Hollenbeck, S.: Improving social network-based sybil defenses by rewiring and augmenting social graphs. In: International Workshop on Information Security Applications, pp. 65–80 (2013)
14. Nakano, T., Suda, T., Okaie, Y., Moore, M.J.: Analysis of cyber aggression and cyber-bullying in social networking. In: 10th International Conference on Semantic Computing (ICSC), pp. 337–341 (2016)
15. Ruan, X., Wu, Z., Wang, H., Jajodia, S.: Profiling online social behaviors for compromised account detection. IEEE Trans. Inf. Forensics Secur. **11**(1), 176–187 (2015)
16. Van Der Walt, E., Eloff, J.: Using machine learning to detect fake identities: bots vs humans. IEEE Access **6**, 6540–6549 (2018)
17. Zhao, R., Zhou, A., Mao, K.: Automatic detection of cyberbullying on social networks based on bullying features. In: 17th International Conference on Distributed Computing and Networking (ICDCN), pp. 1–6 (2016)

Ignore-and-Recalculate Strategy for a Lossless and Low-Cost Secret Image Sharing Scheme

Krishnendu Maity$^{(\boxtimes)}$ (ID), Satyam Kumar, and Susanta Mukhopadhyay

Department of Computer Science and Engineering, Indian Institute
of Technology (ISM), Dhanbad 826004, Jharkhand, India
krishnendu.18dr0066@cse.iitism.ac.in

Abstract. The field of secret image sharing is of utmost importance in safeguarding the confidentiality of images while sharing them among numerous participants. This article proposes a simple, low-cost and lossless secret image-sharing method based on *'ignore-and-recalculate'* strategy. Even if any of the shares falls outside the intensity range of an image, the proposed scheme prevents pixel tampering while allowing the process of sharing to be repeated. Thus proposed method reduces the overhead of sharing process compared to the existing schemes. This method is capable of preventing information leakage, either individually or collectively, up to $(n-1)$ shares without any *encryption* techniques before sharing. The efficacy of the proposed scheme has been successfully demonstrated through qualitative, quantitative, and experimental security analyses.

Keywords: Polynomial SIS · lossless SIS · low-cost SIS

1 Introduction

In contemporary society, images are extensively used entities for sharing information over the public domain; at the same time, securing them is also crucial. Since only a single copy of a hidden image is transmitted, methods like encryption and steganography have limits. In contrast, secret image sharing (SIS) enables sharing an image among n participants with a (k,n) threshold scheme, where any k shares can reconstruct the secret image. Thus, SIS is fault-tolerant and ensures security as any number of shares fewer than k cannot reveal the secret image.

The concept of a (k,n) threshold secret sharing (SS) was first proposed by Shamir [1] using a k degree polynomial in a Galois Field (GF) framework. Moreover, an *interpolation* technique is needed for secret reconstruction. Thein and Lin [2] (TL-SIS) first applied the SS concept for sharing an image among n participants in $GF(251)$. A $(k-1)$ degree polynomial has been chosen for sharing so that interpolating any k shadow/share images can reconstruct the secret image. However, it has a lossy reconstruction due to the use of $GF(251)$ for input pixels $\in [0, 255]$. Yang *et al.* [4] demonstrated that image encryption is necessary to

P. Maji et al. (Eds.): PReMI 2023, LNCS 14301, pp. 629–637, 2023.
https://doi.org/10.1007/978-3-031-45170-6_65

prevent information leakage from individual shares in a polynomial secret image sharing (PSIS) scheme that follows the TL-SIS scheme. However, the TL-SIS scheme has led to various research works aimed at improving the quality and reducing the cost of the reconstruction.

Wu et al. [6] proposed an SIS scheme to reduce the sharing cost using simple modular arithmetic. It incorporates P_G (largest prime $< 2^N$) for modulo operation with varying window size ranging $8 \leq N \leq 17$, where N is the number of bits considered to represent a secret value. The LSB modification and optimal pixels adjustment process (OPAP) have been applied when the pixel value is $> P_G$. This scheme is analysed for different N values to suggest an optimal value of N, but the reconstructed image has some distortions. Then, Yang et al. [5] proposed a hybrid scheme for enhancing recovered image quality by the modify-and-recalculate strategy that uses mod P_S (smallest prime $\geq 2^N$) and shared pixels were modified when exceeding $(2^N - 1)$. The minimum number of bit-flipping operations was followed to reduce image distortion. However, the recovered image had distortion, which depends on the N value. Another scheme proposed by Lou et al. [7] achieves lossless recovery with high efficiency, which needs a post-processing calculation on distorted pixels to achieve the original pixels of the reconstructed image. Apart from that, there are some existing SIS schemes that concentrate on exciting features rather than the performance of a scheme, like two-in-one recovery, meaningful shares, and progressive SIS [8–10].

1.1 Motivation and Contribution

As of now, a majority of PSIS schemes have been designed with a modulo operation by a prime number q that follows *simple modular arithmetic* and is computationally more efficient than $GF(2^8)$ [6]. In summary, $GF(P_G)$ [6] leads *secret pixel modification* when pixel value is larger than P_G. Similarly, for $GF(P_S)$ [5], *'modify-and-recalculate'* strategy has been followed if any of the share pixels does not $\in [0, 2^N - 1]$, as shown in Fig. 1. Of late, Lou et al. [7] proposed a lossless scheme with mod P_S (where $N = 16$), i.e. 65, 537. In this scheme, the pixel value of any share is considered as *invalid* share when $2^N \leq$shared pixel value$\leq (P_S - 1)$ and that is modified to '0'. Although this scheme has designed a lossless SIS, it incorporates Neighbourhood Consistency Calculation (NCC) for handling the distorted pixels due to this modification. Therefore, we propose another novel *lossless* and *low-cost* SIS scheme to overcome this extra calculation overhead of NCC. The key contributions of the proposed scheme are given as follows:

1. We have followed the *'ignore-and-recalculate'* strategy to a secret pixel when any of the produced shares does not $\in [0, 2^N - 1]$. For a (k, n) threshold-sharing scheme with random coefficients except c_0, which consists of secret image pixels, a polynomial of degree $(k - 1)$ is needed. Due to the $(k - 1)$ random coefficients, the mentioned strategy provides another set of shares for that particular secret value while repeating the sharing process.
2. To prevent the leakage of secret image information from individual shares, the PSIS demands encryption of the secret image prior to sharing. On the

other hand, the proposed method eliminates the requirement of encryption by incorporating randomness while sharing each secret value, which reduces the overall cost of sharing. Moreover, the incorporated randomness increases the security of the scheme against differential attacks.

3. We have applied a *Pixel Linking* operation to two consecutive (horizontal) secret pixels to make a 16-bit secret pixel to reduce the size of the shared image. As a result, the size of the shared image is decreased to $N \times N/2$ for a secret image of $N \times N$, which reduces the overall cost of storage and transmission.

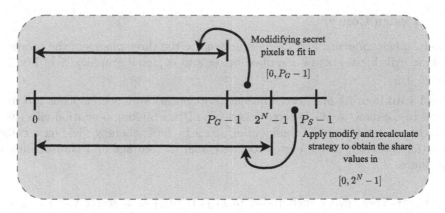

Fig. 1. Distribution of P_G, 2^N and P_S

The rest of this article is organised as follows. Section 2 presents the background of the proposed scheme. Details about the scheme are mentioned in Sect. 3, and the results are provided in Sect. 4. Finally, Sect. 6 represents the conclusion and future scope of our scheme.

2 Background

2.1 Polynomial Secret Sharing

Secrets are shared using a polynomial function, and all calculations are accomplished under modular arithmetic and GF framework. A polynomial of degree $(k-1)$ is needed for an (k,n) PSS scheme, as shown in Eq. (1).

$$p(x) = \left(c_0 + c_1 x + c_2 x^2 + \ldots + c_{k-1} x^{k-1}\right) \mod q \tag{1}$$

$$p(x) = \sum_{j=1}^{k} \left(p(x_j) \prod_{l=1, l \neq j}^{k} \frac{x - x_l}{x_j - x_l}\right) (mod\ q) \tag{2}$$

In order to simplify the modular operation, it is preferable that q be a prime integer. TL-SIS utilises consecutive k number of unprocessed pixels as the coefficients of a polynomial of degree $(k-1)$ for reducing the share image sizes by $1/k$ times. Sharing involves simply calculating the terms $\{y_i = p(i)\}_{i=1}^{n}$ according to Eq. 1, where q is 251 and they are distributed as n individual shares among the participants. Moreover, we can determine the secret value by evaluating the polynomial $p(x)$ derived by Lagrange's interpolation method with the help of any k data pairs (x_1, y_1), (x_2, y_2), (x_3, y_3), ... (x_k, y_k), as shown in Eq. 2.

3   Proposed Method

3.1   Design Concept

Pixel Linking, *Sharing*, and *Reconstruction* are the three phases of the proposed scheme. All the stages are described below and depicted graphically in Fig. 2.

Pixel Linking: At first, two adjacent (horizontal) 8-bit secret pixels are combined to construct a 16-bit secret pixel. The Pixel Linking operation effectively reduces the total count of confidential pixels by 50%, thereby yielding a consequential reduction in the cost associated with the storage and transmission of the shares.

Sharing: Then, every such 16-bit pixel is treated as a secret value and, one by one, is shared among the n participants with the help of the *'ignore-and-recalculate'* strategy. We have selected a $(k-1)$ degree polynomial similar to the polynomial presented in Eq. 1. However, the polynomial includes $(k-1)$ arbitrary coefficients c_1, c_2, c_3 and c_{k-1} in addition to the coefficient c_0, which carries a 16-bit secret value. Here, the smallest prime number $\geq 2^{16}$, i.e. $q = 65,537$, has been chosen for the modulo operation. Therefore, only $65,536$ ($\notin 0$ to $2^{16}-1$) is the invalid pixel value for a 16-bit image. The proposed strategy implies ignorance of the sharing operation when a secret pixel provides at least one invalid share and follows the repetition of the share-making procedure until all shares are valid for that secret pixel. The combination of the Pixel Linking and Sharing stages of the proposed scheme is defined in Algorithm 1.

Reconstruction: The reconstruction process we have followed in this scheme is similar to the other existing PSIS scheme. As usual, Lagrange's interpolation technique has been applied to the shares to find out the secret value, as shown in Eq. 2. After reconstructing the 16-bit secret pixel, two 8-bit pixels are extracted and re-positioned in the corresponding positions.

3.2   Salient Features

Here, we have analysed the proposed sharing technique and listed out the salient features.

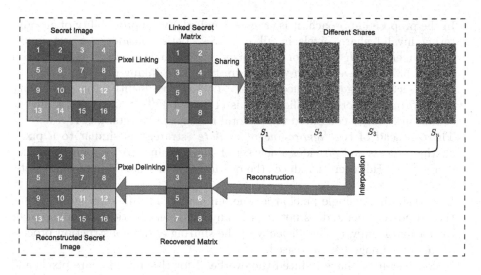

Fig. 2. Schematic diagram

Algorithm 1. Ignore-and-recalculate($\mathcal{S}[N,N]$)

Input: Secret image of size $R \times C$, and threshold parameters (k,n) where $2 \leq k \leq n$.

Step 1: Generate, *Secret Matrix* $\mathcal{S}'$ of size $R \times C/2$ using pixel-linking operation on secret image $\mathcal{S}$.

Step 2: Select the next unprocessed 16-bit secret from $\mathcal{S}'$ and consider as c_0 coefficient (all the remaining $k-1$ coefficients are random) of a $(k-1)$ degree polynomial selected for sharing, as follows:

$$p(x) = \left(c_0 + c_1 x + c_2 x^2 + \ldots + c_{k-1} x^{k-1}\right) \mod 65{,}537 \qquad (3)$$

Then, calculate the n number of shares according to the SS technique.

Step 3: Check if any of the shares is $65{,}636$, then repeat the **Step 2** until all shares are valid.

Step 4: Then, n shares are stored in $\mathcal{SS}_i$ corresponding to the position of the secret value.

Step 5: *Goto* the **Step 2** until all the secrets of $\mathcal{S}'$ are not processed.

Output: The n number of shares $\mathcal{SS}_1, \mathcal{SS}_2 \cdots \mathcal{SS}_n$ each of size $R \times C/2$.

- We have selected a prime number $65{,}537$ for modulo operation, which reduces the cost of calculation under the GF framework. Moreover, the chosen prime can accommodate the whole range (0 to $65{,}535$) of the pixel's value for a 16-bit image.
- Pixel linking operation reduces the size of the secret and shared images by 50%, i.e. secret values that need to be shared are half of the original image pixels.

- In the proposed approach, it is crucial to calculate the probability of encountering invalid share pixels in all n shares. Let's consider a secret image with dimensions $R \times C$. For each pixel, the probability of it being invalid is $1/65,537$. However, when we perform the pixel linking operation, the size of the secret image is reduced to $R \times C/2$. Consequently, the probability of the total number of invalid pixels is $(1/65,537)^{nRC/2}$. This probability is significantly lower compared to the total number of secrets, i.e., $R \times C$.
- The overhead of the *'ignore-and-recalculate'* strategy is similar to a pixel-sharing process and provides a new set of shared values corresponding to that secret pixel. However, it reduces the overhead of the *'modify-and-recalculate'* strategy.
- Due to sharing a single pixel at a time, unlike the TL-SIS sharing technique, the proposed scheme does not require any image encryption technique prior to sharing. However, the efficiency of the sharing and reconstruction process for a secret image has decreased.
- In conclusion, we have reduced the overhead for the invalid share pixels and successfully designed a simple, effective and low-cost PSIS technique.

4   Experimental Results

All the experimental works have been conducted in MatLab(2020b) platform in a system with Ryzen 9 4900H 3.30 GHz, RAM 16 GB and Windows 10.

In this section, we have presented the results of the proposed scheme qualitatively and quantitatively. In qualitative results, we have plotted the secret, all the shares, and the reconstructed image as shown in Fig. 3. Table 1 presents the results of quality measured parameters such as Mean Square Error (MSE), Peak Signal to Noise Ratio (PSNR), Structural Similarity Index Measure (SSIM), and Correlation-Coefficient (CC) for *quantitative analysis*. All the images selected for the analysis have achieved the desired outcome, with an MSE value of '0' and a $PSNR$ value of 'infinity'. The $SSIM$ and CC are also optimal for all the images. Hence, the proposed scheme achieves lossless SIS since the reconstructed images are exact replicas of the original secret images.

In addition, we conducted a comparison of the reconstruction cost (measured in seconds) between the proposed scheme and several state-of-the-art methods. The reconstruction costs of various SIS [2,3,13,14] and Visual Secret Sharing (VSS) [15] schemes are presented in Table 2. It is important to note that the scheme [3] has a higher cost than other schemes due to the use of $GF(2^8)$ to increase the image reconstruction quality. Furthermore, the existing schemes incorporating P_G (65521) and P_S (65537) also demonstrate favourable results regarding reconstruction cost. However, in our proposed scheme, we integrate a pixel-linking operation to reduce the number of secret pixels and employ GF(65537) to achieve the most optimal reconstruction cost.

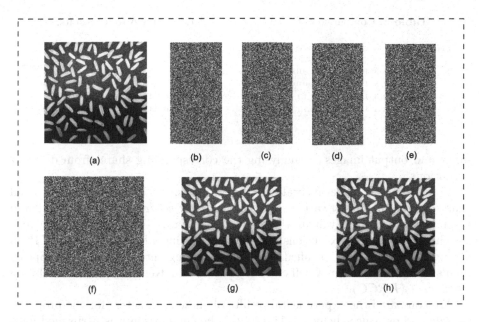

Fig. 3. Qualitative measurements of $(3,4)$ threshold scheme: (a) Secret image, (b) S_1, (c) S_2, (d) S_3, (e) S_4, (f) Reconstruction with S_1 and S_2, (g) Reconstruction with S_1, S_2, and S_3, (h) Reconstruction with S_1, S_2, S_3, and S_4.

Table 1. Results of the parameters for quantitative measurements.

Image name	CAMERAMAN	LENA	MALE	RICE	BABOON	COUPLE	BOAT	TESTPAT1	CLOCK	PENTAGON
MSE	0	0	0	0	0	0	0	0	0	0
PSNR	Inf	Inf	Inf	Inf	Inf	Inf	Inf	Inf	Inf	Inf
SSIM	1	1	1	1	1	1	1	1	1	1
CC	1	1	1	1	1	1	1	1	1	1

Table 2. Comparison of reconstruction time (in seconds)

Scheme	GF(251) [2]	GF(2^8) [3]	GF(65537) [13]	GF(65521) [13]	Soreng et al. [14]	VSS [15]	**Proposed scheme**
$(2,2)$	1.3169	95.4635	0.9994	1.0273	2.3068	1.2284	**0.5575**
$(3,3)$	1.6127	114.1649	1.2402	1.2076	2.6647	1.8379	**0.6193**
$(4,4)$	1.8332	132.9753	1.4596	1.3659	3.0256	2.3916	**0.6531**
$(5,5)$	2.0508	149.3193	1.5406	1.4854	3.3980	2.8790	**0.7039**
$(10,10)$	4.4384	249.9161	2.1215	2.1033	6.4326	5.6328	**0.9098**

5   Experimental Security Analysis

The security of PSIS scheme is well-established and does not require additional proof. However, it is important to assess the resilience of the proposed scheme against differential attacks. These attacks aim to establish a relationship between

Table 3. Comparison of $NPCR$, $UACI$, $SRCC$ and $KRCC$ results.

Parameters	Images	Yang et al. [12]	Soreng et al. [14]	Luo et al. [7]	Bao et al. [11]	Proposed Scheme
NPCR	Share 1, 2, 3, 4	0,0,0,0	0,0,0,0	0,0,0,0	98.87,98.91,98.90,98.92	100,99.99,100,99.99
UACI	Share 1, 2, 3, 4	0,0,0,0	0,0,0,0	0,0,0,0	33.18,33.09,33.20,33.00	13.06.13.10,13.05,13.07
SRCC	Share 1, 2, 3, 4	1,1,1,1	1,1,1,1	1,1,1,1	0.0215,0.0158,0.0145,0.0201	0.0060,0.0034,0.0042,0.0021
KRCC	Share 1, 2, 3, 4	1,1,1,1	1,1,1,1	1,1,1,1	0.0144,0.0158,0.0145,0.0201	0.0040,0.0022,0.0028,0.0014

input and output images by analysing the corresponding shares from different executions.

To conduct an experimental security analysis, we collected the set of all shares corresponding to various executions of our scheme. We then calculated several parameters to evaluate the degree of similarity or dissimilarity between the shares of different executions. The parameters included the Number of Pixel Change Rate ($NPCR$), Unified Average Changing Intensity ($UACI$), Spearman's Rank Correlation Coefficient ($SRCC$), and Kendall Rank Correlation Coefficient ($KRCC$).

We compared the experimental results of these parameters for the proposed scheme and existing schemes [7,11,12,14]. The comparison was performed for a $(4,4)$ scheme using the CAMERAMAN image with dimensions (256×256). The results are presented in Table 3.

A value of '0' against $UACI$ and $NPCR$ indicates that the existing schemes [7,12,14] provide identical shares in different executions. Similarly, a value of '1' for $SRCC$ and $KRCC$ suggests a high correlation between the corresponding shares from different executions. Specifically, the parameter values of the existing methods [7,12,14] imply that their shares are identical in every execution, making them vulnerable to differential attacks. On the other hand, one of the state-of-the-art schemes [11] demonstrates excellent results for these parameters.

Based on the tabulated data, we can conclude that the proposed scheme effectively mitigates differential attacks and outperforms existing schemes in terms of security.

6   Conclusion and Future Scope

In this article, we have successfully designed a lossless and low-cost sharing technique that transparently overcomes the need for encryption before sharing and avoids the need to modify shared pixels under $GF(65,537)$. We handle all the *invalid* shared pixels without any heavy processing cost, using the *ignore-and-recalculate* strategy. The quantitative analysis proves the lossless reconstruction of the proposed scheme. According to the experimental security analysis, the proposed approach can severely restrict differential attacks. While prioritising the *efficiency* of the sharing process, such as processing a larger number of pixels at once, is a crucial consideration, it is worth noting that our current scheme involves certain compromises. However, we recognise that the development of a scheme with *enhanced efficiency* remains a potential future objective for our research.

References

1. Shamir, A.: How to share a secret. Commun. ACM **22**(11), 612–613 (1979)
2. Thien, C.C., Lin, J.C.: Secret image sharing. Comput. Graph. **26**(5), 765–770 (2002)
3. Yang, C.N., Chen, T.S., Yu, K.H., Wang, C.C.: Improvements of image sharing with steganography and authentication. J. Syst. Softw. **80**(7), 1070–1076 (2007)
4. Yang, C.N., Chang, W.J., Cai, S.R., Lin, C.Y.: Secret image sharing without keeping permutation key (2014)
5. Wu, X., Yang, C.N., Yang, Y.Y.: A hybrid scheme for enhancing recovered image quality in polynomial based secret image sharing by modify-and-recalculate strategy. J. Inf. Secur. Appl. **51**, 102452 (2020)
6. Wu, X., Yang, C.N., Zhuang, Y.T., Hsu, S.C.: Improving recovered image quality in secret image sharing by simple modular arithmetic. Sig. Process. Image Commun. **66**, 42–49 (2018)
7. Luo, S., Liu, Y., Yan, X., Yu, Y.: Secret image sharing scheme with lossless recovery and high efficiency. Sig. Process. **206**, 108931 (2023)
8. Lin, P.Y., Chan, C.S.: Invertible secret image sharing with steganography. Pattern Recogn. Lett. **31**(13), 1887–1893 (2010)
9. Yang, C.N., Ciou, C.B.: Image secret sharing method with two-decoding-options: lossless recovery and previewing capability. Image Vis. Comput. **28**(12), 1600–1610 (2010)
10. Yan, X., Lu, Y., Liu, L.: A general progressive secret image sharing construction method. Sig. Process. Image Commun. **71**, 66–75 (2019)
11. Bao, L., Yi, S., Zhou, Y.: Combination of sharing matrix and image encryption for lossless (k, n)-secret image sharing. IEEE Trans. Image Process. **26**(12), 5618–5631 (2017)
12. Yang, C.N., Zheng, C.E., Lu, M.C., Wu, X.: Secret image sharing by using multi-prime modular arithmetic. Sig. Process. **205**, 108882 (2023)
13. Yang, C.N., Wu, X., Chung, M.J., Zhang, X.: AMBTC-based secret image sharing by simple modular arithmetic. J. Vis. Commun. Image Represent. **84**, 103482 (2022)
14. Soreng, A.V., Kandar, S.: Verifiable varying sized (m, n, n) multi-image secret sharing with combiner verification and cheater identification. J. Vis. Commun. Image Represent. **84**, 103466 (2022)
15. Kannojia, S.P., Kumar, J.: XOR-based visual secret sharing scheme using pixel vectorization. Multimedia Tools Appl. **80**(10), 14609–14635 (2021). https://doi.org/10.1007/s11042-020-10352-3

Cyberbully: Aggressive Tweets, Bully and Bully Target Profiling from Multilingual Indian Tweets

Suman Karan and Suman Kundu[✉][iD]

Department of Computer Science and Engineering, IIT Jodhpur, Jodhpur, India
{karan.1,suman}@iitj.ac.in

Abstract. The present work proposes an end-to-end solution to identify a potential bully and bully-targets from multilingual aggressive tweets in Indian Twitter-o-sphere. The proposed work uses two LSTM based classifiers in pipeline to detect the tweet's language and aggressiveness. The model was trained with over 150,000 tweets of Hindi, English, Bengali, and Hinglish languages. F1 scores achieved for English, Hindi, Bengali, and Hinglish are 0.73, 0.83, 0.69, and 0.91, respectively. The paper further reported the patterns identified for several different attributes such as followers count, friends count, frequencies of tweets, and percentage of aggressive tweets of such potential bully and target users.

1 Introduction

People's ability to speak their minds freely on social media also leads to an increase in the use of profanity. For instance, tweets such as 'This incident happened in ****** r**di. Majority of muzlim nowadays. What can we expect' or 'I literally want to punch this b**ch' certainly hurt the target person emotionally or psychologically. Instead of having a firm mechanism to deal with such cases immediately, platforms like Twitter only support reporting/flagging. This kind of action takes time and hence becomes ineffective. Thus, automatic detection of aggression will aid in developing a self-quarantine system. Finding a potential bully or their victims can also help build community resilience.

Bullying is a common issue with young children, and research has been conducted on it for a long time [1, 2]. The earliest work on understanding the risk of violence in the digital world was studied by [3]. About a decade after, intensified research has been started on cyberbully [4–7]. The majority of the work is based on text analysis [5, 8–10]. Major studies on aggression detection are for the English language [4,5,8–10] while Work for multilingual texts is limited [11,12]. Existing bi/multilingual algorithms either translate texts to English or manually segregate the documents and use separate language-based classifiers. India is a country of many languages, and its social media produces material in diverse languages. There is significantly less work on Indian languages.

This study proposed an end-to-end solution for identifying potential bullies and vulnerable targets from multilingual Indian Tweets. Experiments include

P. Maji et al. (Eds.): PReMI 2023, LNCS 14301, pp. 638–645, 2023.
https://doi.org/10.1007/978-3-031-45170-6_66

Tweets in English, Hindi, Hinglish (Hindi written in Roman Script), and Bengali. The procedure detects the language and selects the appropriate aggression detection classifier. Further, we use Twitter's public data to identify the behavior patterns of potential bullies and their victims.

The rest of the paper is organized as follows. The proposed multilingual aggression detection methodologies are presented in Sect. 2. Section 3 describes the bully and bully target identification and analysis along with experiments and results. Finally, Sect. 4 concludes the findings of the research.

2   Multilingual Aggressive Tweet Detection

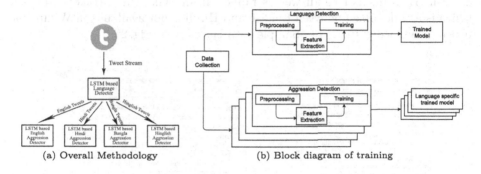

(a) Overall Methodology   (b) Block diagram of training

Fig. 1. Working model of the propose method

The proposed end-to-end solution takes a tweet and predicts its language on-the-go. According to the language, the text is passed to the respective language-specific aggression predictor. One trained language detector and four different aggression detector LSTM classifiers are trained (Fig. 1a) for Hindi, Hinglish, English, and Bengali texts. Unlike existing research, no translation is performed. The memory cell of LSTM helps to retain the essential parts of the sentence and reject the insignificant parts. Each LSTM unit has three gates to control what information to keep, and what to get rid of. These are the sigmoid function ($\sigma(.)$) where output 0 means block all information and 1 means keep all information. In order to remember long-term dependencies we have cell state (c_t). The following update equations are used in the experiments:

$$f_t = \sigma(W_f[x_t, h_{t-1}] + b_f)$$
$$i_t = \sigma(W_i[x_t, h_{t-1}] + b_i)$$
$$o_t = \sigma(W_o[x_t, h_{t-1}] + b_o)$$

$$c_t = f_t * c_{t-1} + i_t * \tilde{c}_t$$
$$\tilde{c}_t = tanh(W_c[x_t, h_{t-1}] + b_c)$$

where f_t, i_t, o_t are function of the forget, input, and output gates respectively, h_{t-1}, x_t is the output of previous and input of the current LSTM unit, and W_x, b_x are the weight and bias of the respective neuron. $\tilde{c}_t$ is the candidate cell-state and c_t is the cell-state at timestamp t. The final output pass to the next cell is calculated by $h_t = tanh(c_t) \times o_t$. The model designed here is scalable in terms of languages, allowing us to add a new language by updating and retraining the language detector model, and prepare a new aggression detector for the concerning language without tinkering with other models. The block diagram of the training is shown in Fig. 1b.

2.1 Data Collection

Different layers of LSTM are trained on different data collected from different sources such as Twitter and Wikipedia. The data and codes are available at https://figshare.com/s/ce91ed033c29f7379cdb.

Data for Language Detection Model: Data for three regular languages, English, Bengali, and Hindi were scrapped from Wikipedia articles. Hinglish which is a code mixed between English and Hindi is not available on Wikipedia, hence, downloaded from [13]. Sample data is shown in Fig. 2a.

মাতৃভাষীর সংখ্যায় বাংলা ইন্দোইউরোপীয় ভাষা পরিবা-রের চতুর্থ ও বিশ্বের ষষ্ঠ বৃহত্তম ভাষা	Bangla
অনেক বাঙালি এমনকি ইংরেজি কিংবা সংস্কৃত থেকে ধারকৃত শব্দ উচ্চারণের ক্ষেত্রেও এই ধারাটি বজায় রাখে যেমন গ্রাম উচ্চারণ করেন গেরাম, স্কুল উচ্চারণ করেন ইস্কুল হিসেবে'	Bangla
They seem to be a mainstay of condominium resorts like The Margate at Winnepesaukee a Premier Lakes Region Resort which suggests ownership Winterberry a Resort Village and Moon Ridge a Point of View which contains a nice whimsy	English
The White House Inn for example has become The White House a Country Inn	English
अगर आप गेट की परीक्षा पास करके एम टेक करेंगे तो आपको एक अच्छी स्कालरशिप भी मिलेगी	Hindi
इन कॉलेजो में प्रवेश गेट स्कोर साक्षात्कार लिखित परीक्षा तथा अनुभव के आधार पर मिलता है	Hindi
doktar grant mujhe yada kada varneriyan sosayati kee sabhaon men bhi le jate the	Hinglish
san kee garmiyon men mainne apane do-dos-ton ko sath liya apaneapane pitthoo thaile lade aur north vels kee sair ko paidal hi nikal gae	Hinglish

(a) For language detection model

ভাগ্য ভাল ভিডিওটা করার সময় বুঝতে পারেনি ওরা না হলে তোমাকে ও চু* দিতো	AG
৮০% পতিতা নিজের ইচ্ছায় এই কাজ করের না মা durga 'র murti এই পতিতাসের বাড়ির মাটি দিয়ে তৈরী হয় মেয়েদের somman করতে শেখ	NAG
Confused! Guys new video is up, do check it out, thank you. https://goo.gl/XuclJV	NAG
What has so far Mr.Yechuri done for this Country. Ask him to shut down his bloody p**hole for good or I if given the chance will crap on his mouth hole.	AG
भारतीय मीडिया को मिला दलाली का प्रमाणविश्वसनीयता पर 180 देशों में 136 वां स्थान !	AG
जेडीयू ने मांग की कि लोकसभा में विपक्ष का नेता कांग्रेस से होना चाहिए	NAG
Pad nahi Mila to bhavuk hona to lazimi he. Amanatullah ne konsa jhooth bola tha	NAG
Chl be fake account jyada na bol Himmat hi ni h.Ja na apne page me Baar 2 pta ehi hu pakistan k page jaNi h na to bna leTra desh kya ho rha h bhut acche se pta nikl lo and wlt and watch india ku6 t9 krega zarur fir puchenge	AG

(b) For aggression detection model

Fig. 2. Sample Data

Data for Aggression Detection Model: We used TRAC data sets [14,15] with label OAG (Openly Aggressive), CAG (Covertly Aggressive), and NAG (Non-Aggressive) and converted them into binary by considering OAG and CAG as Aggressive (AG). A combined TRAC 1 and 2 data sets are used for training the model to increase accuracy. We collected 4952, 1583, 12210, and 17169 rows of data for Hindi, Bengali, Hinglish, and English respectively. Figure 2b shows a sample data set used in the model.

Language Specific Slang Words: Slang words or curse words are often used by users to vent their aggression. We did not find any organized collection of slang words. We created lists of slang words from various websites and personal experiences. The lists consists of 67 English ([16–18]), 40 Bengali [19,20], 71 Hindi [21–23] slang words. We converted Hindi slang words into code mixed Hinglish which resulted in 125 slang words for Hinglish language.

2.2 Data Preprocessing

We removed punctuation, numbers, and URLs from language and aggression detection data as these do not have any significance. All letters in English and Hinglish texts are converted to lowercase. No stop words were removed from the sentences while used for the language detection model. Stop words play a significant role in language detection, as their frequent presence helps the model better learn what language it is. Apart from the this, we removed language-specific stop words, white spaces, and new line characters from aggression detection data. As it is common to have user mentions in tweets, these names are used latter to identify vulnerable users but removed as part of preprocessing.

2.3 Language Detector Model

Feature Extraction: We first vectorized the texts by text tokenizer function (Python Tensorflow Keras library) with the most frequently used 500K words. A fixed length of 250 words is used for representing any text. We truncated the input sequence when it is more than 250, and padded with 0 if it is less than 250. As Twitter only allows 280 characters, 250 words are sufficient.

   The Model: LSTM is used for classification. The embedding layer encodes the input sequence into a sequence of dense vectors of size 100. Dropout and recurrent dropout are set to 0.2, and SoftMax is used as an activation function. We used adam optimizer. Categorical cross entropy $\rho = -\sum_{c=1}^{C} y_{o,c} \log(p_{o,c})$ is used as a loss function where C is the set of classes (e.g., 4 languages here), $y_{o,c}$ is a binary value (0 or 1) if class c is the correct classification for the observation o, and $p_{o,c}$ is the predicted probability for the observation o is of class c

2.4 Aggression Detection

Feature Extraction: We vectorized the text using the tokenizer (Python Tensorflow Keras library), limiting the corpus size to 50K most frequent words for each language. The maximum number of words in a text is kept to 250. Density of slang words, i.e., the number of slang words in a sentence and emojis are considered as features. Density of capital letters is used as another feature as it is generally used for screaming. Similarly, we observed frequent use of question marks and exclamation marks leads to aggressive text. We counted the occurrence of those as a feature. Note that this feature is extracted from the original text rather than the preprocessed text. Polarity in sentiment analysis is identifying sentiment orientation, while subjective expressions are opinions that describe people's feelings towards a specific subject or topic. We used polarity and subjectivity scores of each sentence as features.

The Model: An LSTM classifier is used with embedding dimension, output vector size, dropout, and recurrent dropout set to 100, 128, 0.2, and 0.2. SoftMax is used as the activation function, and cross-entropy is used as a loss function.

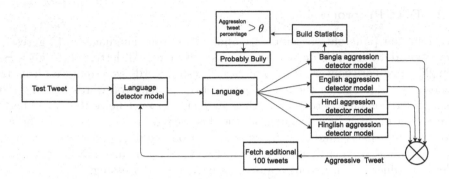

Fig. 3. Block diagram of bully detection

3   Bully and Bully Target Identification and Analysis

Figure 3 depicts the method by which we detect bullies using the trained model described previously. Once a tweet is determined to be aggressive, the system retrieves 100 of the author's most recent tweets. The model then evaluates and categorizes all of these tweets as aggressive or not. If θ (user-defined) percent, of these tweets, are aggressive, the user is flagged. In addition, we extracted every user mentioned in the aggressive tweet and designated them as potential targets. Our experiment evaluates the user profiles, number of friends, and followers of bully and bully targets by identifying hidden patterns in it.

Table 1. Precision, Recall and F1 score for aggression detection.

Language	Precision	Recall	F1 Score
English	0.7255	0.7382	0.7318
Hindi	0.8427	0.8255	0.8341
Bengali	0.8125	0.6046	0.6933
Hinglish	0.8735	0.9512	0.9107

3.1   Experiments and Results

All the experiments are conducted on Windows 10 PC with Intel Core i5, 2.2 GHz processor, and 16 GB ram. Python 3.6 with TensorFlow is used. The batch size of 64, and 15 epoch is used for both the language and aggression detection. The epoch size is kept low as the loss is found to be converged before 15 and no further significant reduction in loss value is observed. The data set for language detection contains 176681 samples, 57991 English, 54920 Hindi, 50954 Bengali, and 12816 Hinglish data. The overall accuracy achieved is 99.97% on the test data set. On the other hand, the data set for aggression detection has 35,914 data samples with 4952 Hindi, 1583 Bengali, 12210 Hinglish, and 17169 English data. For both cases, we used 80% for training, 10% for validation, and the rest 10% for testing. Table 1 shows the comparison matrices for all four languages.

3.2   Analysis of Bully and Vulnerable Targets

We ran our algorithm on approximately 50000 tweets and discovered 1515 users to be aggressive. These users are suspected of being the bully. However, it may be a one-time outburst instead of a personality trait, so additional 100 recent tweets are retrieved. In addition, we extracted all mentioned users from aggressive tweets. These are potential targets. 100 tweets from target accounts were also extracted. In case users have less than 100 tweets we retrieved them all. Further, we collected public information about users, including follower and following counts. We calculated tweet frequency per day using tweets that we retrieved.

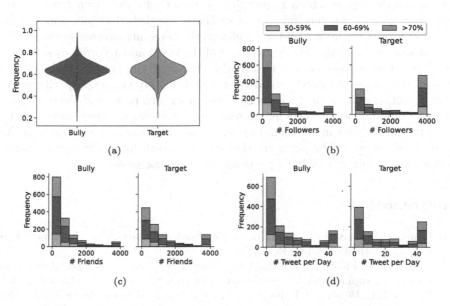

Fig. 4. Different statistics for predicted bully and target users.

Patterns in Bully: Experimental results show that many users post high (60% or more) aggressive tweets (Fig. 4a). We further study these suspected bully users. Most suspected bullies have followers (Fig. 4b) below 500. There are, however, a significant number of users with followers of more than 4000. Similarly, most bullies follow (Fig. 4c) less than 1000 people, specifically, with less than 500 following. It is also found that most of the suspected bully tweets between 0 to 10 tweet (Fig. 4d) per day. However, there are a significant number of users who have tweets between 60 to 80 per day.

Patterns in Predicted Targets: Our experiment found about 1100 mentions (target) in the aggressive tweets. Interestingly, many of these targets themselves post aggressive tweets (Fig. 4a). Hence, we also analyzed target users in the same glass as of the bully. Similar to the prospective bully, where the majority have 50% or more aggressive tweets, most of their targets have aggressive tweets between more than 50% (Fig. 4a). Users having a follower count greater than 4000 is more for target users (Fig. 4b). It indicates that these targets, with more than 4000 followers, are celebrity users and are subject to aggressive targets. As we can see, the targets of aggressive tweets may also have bully characteristics, so a deeper understanding of the profile is required apart from just classifying a post as aggressive or bully-post. It may not be that a target user is always a victim.

4   Conclusion

In this paper, we presented a multilingual cyberbully detection from Twitter. The work is done on the Indian text of Hindi, English, Bengali, and Hinglish languages. The model is found to be effectively detecting aggressive tweets. The model automatically detects the language of the tweet and accordingly selects the corresponding aggression detection model. Although the present work only consider 4 languages, it can be extended by attaching any language specific aggression detection module in the pipeline. The paper also presented the patterns in the users' public profiles who like to post aggressive tweets. One interesting fact reported here is that mentions in the bully posts are also very aggressive in their own tweets. It would be an interesting research work for the future to analyze further the reciprocity of bully posts and its contagiousness.

References

1. Chang, F., Burns, B.M.: Attention in preschoolers: associations with effortful control and motivation. Child Dev. **76**, 247–263 (2005)
2. Rodkin, P.C., Farmer, T.W., Pearl, R., Acker, R.V.: They're cool: social status and peer group supports for aggressive boys and girls. Soc. Dev. **15**, 175–204 (2006)
3. Berson, I.R., Berson, M.J., Ferron, J.M.: Emerging risks of violence in the digital age: lessons for educators from an online study of adolescent girls in the United States. J. Sch. Violence **1**, 51–71 (2002)
4. Yin, D., et al.: Detection of Harassment on Web 2.0. In: Content Analysis in the WEB 2.0 (CAW2.0) Workshop at WWW2009, (Madrid) 2009
5. Dinakar, K., Reichart, R., Lieberman, H.: Modeling the detection of textual cyberbullying. In: Proceedings of the International AAAI Conference on Web and Social Media, vol. 5, no. 3, pp. 11–17 (2021)
6. Hinduja, S., Patchin, J.W.: Social influences on cyberbullying behaviors among middle and high school students. J. Youth Adolesc. **42**(5), 711–722 (2013)

7. Kontostathis, A., Reynolds, K., Garron, A., Edwards, L.: Detecting cyberbullying: query terms and techniques. In: Proceedings of the 5th Annual ACM Web Science Conference, pp. 195–204 (2013)
8. Van Hee, C., et al.: Detection and fine-grained classification of cyberbullying events. In: International Conference Recent Advances in Natural Language Processing (RANLP), pp. 672–680 (2015)
9. Nandhini, B.S., Sheeba, J.I.: Cyberbullying detection and classification using information retrieval algorithm. In: Proceedings of the International Conference on Advanced Research in Computer Science Engineering & Technology, pp. 1–5 (2015)
10. Zhong, H., Miller, D.J., Squicciarini, A.: Flexible inference for cyberbully incident detection. In: Brefeld, U., et al. (eds.) ECML PKDD 2018. LNCS (LNAI), vol. 11053, pp. 356–371. Springer, Cham (2019). https://doi.org/10.1007/978-3-030-10997-4_22
11. Malte, A., Ratadiya, P.: Multilingual cyber abuse detection using advanced transformer architecture. In: TENCON IEEE Region 10 Conference, pp. 784–789 (2019)
12. Si, S., Datta, A., Banerjee, S., Naskar, S.K.: Aggression detection on multilingual social media text. In: Proceedings of the International Conference on Computing, Communication and Networking Technologies, pp. 1–5. IEEE (2019)
13. KaggleDataset, Code Mixed (Hindi-English) Dataset (2018)
14. Kumar, R., Reganti, A.N., Bhatia, A., Maheshwari, T.: Aggression-annotated corpus of hindi-english code-mixed data. In: Proceedings of the Eleventh International Conference on Language Resources and Evaluation (LREC 2018), (Miyazaki, Japan), European Language Resources Association (ELRA) (2018)
15. Bhattacharya, S., et al.: Developing a multilingual annotated corpus of misogyny and aggression. In: Proceedings of the 2nd Workshop on Trolling, Aggression and Cyberbullying, (Marseille), pp. 158–168. European Language Resources Association (ELRA) (2020)
16. 26 English swear words that you should use very very carefully. https://www.rypeapp.com/blog/english-swear-words. Accessed 02 Feb 2021
17. Category:english swear words. https://en.wiktionary.org/wiki/Category:English_swear_words. Accessed 02 Feb 2021
18. A definitive ranking of every swear word from worst to best. https://tinyurl.com/ranking-swear. Accessed 02 Feb 2021
19. Urban thesaurus. https://tinyurl.com/bnslang. Accessed 02 Feb 2021
20. Bengali slang words with meaning (Bengali slang dictionary). https://tinyurl.com/bengali-slang. Accessed 02 Feb 2021
21. 40+ Hindi Gaaliyan in English that you have to know being Indian!. https://tinyurl.com/Hindi-Gaaliyan. Accessed 02 Feb 2021
22. Hindi language blog. https://tinyurl.com/slang-in-hindi-i. Accessed 02 Feb 2021
23. Slay the chats with the most popular Hindi texting slang!. https://tinyurl.com/hindi-text-slang. Accessed 02 Feb 2021

Financial Misinformation Detection via RoBERTa and Multi-channel Networks

Ashraf Kamal, Padmapriya Mohankumar, and Vishal Kumar Singh[✉]

PayPal, Chennai, India
{askamal,pamohankumar,vishalksingh}@paypal.com

Abstract. Financial misinformation has been a potential threat to online social communities in the current era of macroeconomic conditions. However, there is less attention in this direction of research. This paper presents a new study for financial misinformation detection. A new model called `Fin-MisID` is introduced, consisting of input, `RoBERTa` in the embedding layer and multi-channel networks (CNNs, BiGRU, and attention layers). The performance of the proposed `Fin-MisID` model is investigated on a new financial misinformation-based dataset. It shows comparatively better results than two existing studies and several baseline methods.

Keywords: Online social media · Misinformation detection · Financial misinformation detection · Information retrieval · Multi-channel Networks

1 Introduction

In the last two decades, the rapid growth of user-generated information (UGI) has remarkably increased [1]. It has become the giant source for online social interaction and propagate non-literal information, like humor, sarcasm, fake news, etc. [2,3]. However, such UGI is also used to mislead people globally. Such dubious information has immense potential to create false suspicion and uncertainty. It is available in varied forms, including satire, parody, fake content, hoax, spam, rumor, etc. Furthermore, a huge amount of such misleading content originated and propagated using UGI, which has reflected a possible threat to online communities. It gives a negative impact on numerous online activities, like e-commerce shopping, stock price movement, and financial purchases [4].

The financial market surveillance provides the efficient flow of the finance-based business and solutions [5]. The available online data has been perceived as a valuable source to spread unverified financial information massively, like the spread of false rumors, financial fake news, etc. [6]. Also, the manual verification of online financial misinformation is tedious and time-consuming tasks. Therefore, identification of financial misinformation is the need of the hour for proper functioning of the financial activities which is less explored by researchers.

P. Maji et al. (Eds.): PReMI 2023, LNCS 14301, pp. 646–653, 2023.
https://doi.org/10.1007/978-3-031-45170-6_67

1.1 Our Contributions

The extraction of semantic and syntactic information in line with context is crucial for any particular domain, like finance [6]. Considering this, we investigate a new study for financial misinformation detection. To the best of our knowledge, this is a first study towards the financial misinformation detection, wherein a new relevant dataset is created and a novel deep learning-based model called Fin-MisID is introduced to perform classification task. Fin-MisID constitutes an input layer, RoBERTa in embedding layer followed by multi-channel networks. Each channel consists of convolutional neural network (CNN) to extract semantic and syntactic information with respect to the different window sizes, kernel values, etc., bidirectional gated recurrent unit (BiGRU) to obtain latent contextual sequences, and attention layer which is used to emphasise important and relevant financial and misinformation tokens in the input data. The combined output generated from the summation of each channel is passed to the dense and output layers, wherein classification is done via *sigmoid*. The key contributions are given below:

- Proposed a new financial misinformation detection problem.
- Created a new dataset based on the financial misleading texts.
- Development of a new Fin-MisID model to detect financial misinformation.
- Performed an empirical evaluation of the proposed model and compared the results with existing studies and baselines methods.

The remaining portion of this study is presented as follows: Section 2 presents the existing studies. Section 3 presents the problem description and dataset preparation. Section 4 presents the proposed model. Section 5 presents the experimental setup and evaluation results. Lastly, Sect. 6 presents the conclusion of this study and future works.

2 Related Work

This section presents the existing studies for misinformation detection (MID) problem on online content. In [7], authors extracted word-based features for MID and obtained less recall due to unwanted tags in fake contents. In [8], authors extracted 23 features and used graph kernel-based hybrid machine learning-based classifier to detect rumor. In [9], authors applied recurrent neural network (RNN) to capture the contextual information of rumors posts on two real-world datasets.

In [10], authors proposed hierarchical recurrent convolutional neural network to learn contextual information. In [11], authors proposed deceptive review identification using recurrent CNN to identify the deceptive text. In [12], authors presented a system for hoax detection in mail system by taking benefit of intelligent automation. In [13], authors proposed hoax detection framework for prior diagnosis of available hoaxes in digital social media. In [15], authors proposed fake news detection and applied CNN and LSTM models in financial domain. In [14], authors authors proposed satire detection and they extracted lexical and feature groups.

3 Problem Description and Dataset Preparation

This section presents the problem description and preparation of a newly created dataset.

3.1 Problem Description

The online Cambridge dictionary defines misinformation as "wrong information, or the fact that people are misinformed"[1]. This study presents the financial misinformation detection as a two-class problem. Hence, a portion of textual data is classified either as financial misinformation (FMI) or true financial information (TFI).

3.2 Dataset Preparation

This section presents the dataset collection and data pre-processing steps.

Dataset Collection. In this study, data is collected from `Politifact`[2], a popular fact-check website using `BeautifulSoup4`[3] wrapper/html parsing tool. We consider key financial topics from [5] work which is given in Table 1 to collect financial misinformation only. Also, each data is labelled as either *half true, true, mostly true, pants on fire, false, mostly false.*

Table 1. A list of finance-based topics

A list of finance-based topics
'income', 'debt', 'loan', 'mortgage', 'economy', 'job', 'poverty', 'salary', 'money', 'bank', 'savings', 'fund', 'payroll' 'earning', 'wage', 'revenue', 'payoff', 'wealth'

Data Pre-processing. After data collection, we have done several cleaning steps to receive pre-processed textual data which can be used further for classification tasks. To this end, we have removed numbers, comma, exclamations, quotation, full-stop, punctuation marks, etc. Lastly, convert the raw data into its lower-case form.

4 Proposed Model

This section presents the layer-wise complete description of the proposed `Fin-MisID` model, as given in Fig. 1.

---

[1] https://dictionary.cambridge.org/dictionary/english/misinformation.
[2] https://www.politifact.com/.
[3] https://beautiful-soup-4.readthedocs.io/en/latest/.

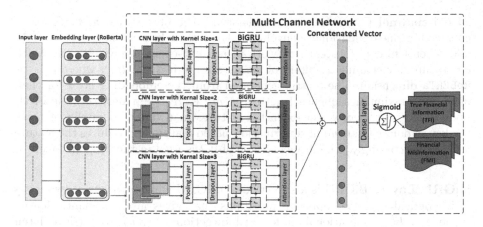

Fig. 1. Work-flow of the proposed `Fin-MisID` model

4.1   Input Layer

The input layer receives pre-processed text as an input text and that tokenizes each word from it, accordingly. Each token is assigned a number as an index. It results in a dictionary and finally converted into a numeric vector n as per the index value of the dictionary. Each numeric vector is of different size due to the varying length. Hence, a fixed-length f of 100 is taken as a padding value for each input vector and it is considered as a padded vector p such that $|p| = f \geq |n|$. The fixed-length of the resulting vector as $p \in R^{1 \times f}$ is passed to the succeeding layer.

4.2   Embedding Layer

In the study, `RoBERTa`[4] is used in embedding layer. The resultant input vector is received by the embedding layer to retrieve relevant contextual financial misinformation in both directions. In this line, we have taken 768-dimensional word vector representation to cover contextual information in bidirectional mode using `Transformer`. The encoded representation from `RoBERTa` gives a relevant and enrich contextual representation. Finally, the vector generated from this layer is forwarded to the next layer (i.e., multi-channel network).

4.3   Multi-channel Networks

This section briefly describe the multi-channel networks. Each channel is consisted of a CNN with varying kernel sizes, pooling and dropout, followed by BiGRU, and attention layers. A detailed description of each layer is given below:

---

[4] https://huggingface.co/docs/transformers/model_doc/roberta.

Multi-channel CNN Layer. In this study, the proposed `Fin-MisID` model considers a one-dimensional convolution layer with kernel sizes of 1, 2, and 3 and several filters, f to each network in a multi-channel environment. Mathematically, for channel x, filters of kernel size, k is $f^x \in R^{kd}$, where d is the `RoBERTa` dimension. The matrix generated from the embedding layer for channel c via maximum sequence length p is $m^c \in R^{pd}$. Further, the role of the pooling layer is to receive the extracted features-map. The max pooling extracts the key semantic financial misinformation-based feature and reduces the feature-map size accordingly. The dropout value of 0.2 is used in the dropout layer.

BiGRU Layer. BiGRU is a special kind of GRU which consists of two gates. It is applicable in two opposite directions that gives latent semantic feature sequences. It is operational in forward direction as $\overrightarrow{gru_f}$ to retrieve latent semantic representation of misinformation-based on financial tokens as forward sequences (f_t to f_{32}). On the other hand, GRU operational in backward direction as $\overleftarrow{gru_b}$ to retrieve latent semantic representation of misinformation-based on financial tokens as backward sequences (f_{32} to f_t). The final hidden representation of GRU is obtained by combining the outcome of both forward and backward directions of GRU, as given in Eq. 1, and it is passed further to the next layer.

$$gru_i = [\overleftarrow{gru_b}, \overrightarrow{gru_f}] \tag{1}$$

Attention Layer. In this study, the attention layer is employed to apply varying weights for tokens in the input text to highlight the important financial misinformation-related keyword-based features. It also minimizes the effect of normal keywords in parallel. The latent representation, u_t, received using $tanh(.)$, is given in Eq. 2. The normalized similarity α_t is given in Eq. 3 for u_t via `softmax`. Lastly, Eq. 4 measures the resultant vector s_i.

$$u_t = \tanh(W_w f_c + gru_i) \tag{2}$$

$$\alpha_t = \frac{\exp(u_t)}{\sum_t (\exp(u_t))} \tag{3}$$

$$s_i = \sum_{i=1}^{t} \alpha_t f_c \tag{4}$$

4.4   Concatenated Layer

This layer refers to the concatenated vector which is obtained by combining all vectors received across multi-channel networks. The resultant concatenated vector is forwarded to the dense and output layers for final classification steps.

4.5   Dense and Output Layers

The fully connected dense layer gives financial misinformation-related features set from the resultant concatenated vector from the previous layer and divisible into two classes as FMI and TFI. *Sigmoid* and *binary cross-entropy* are applied to perform the final classification of input data labeled as FMI or TFI.

5   Experimental Setup and Results

In this section, we discuss the experimental setup and evaluation results. We have taken `Intel Haswell` machine, Ubuntu-20.04 operative system, 32 GB RAM, and `NVIDIA Tesla A100` GPU as hardware components. The proposed `Fin-MisID` model is implemented in `Keras` with `Python` 3.7. The neural network-based parameter settings used in this study include 100 batch-size, 30 padding, 0.4 spatial dropout at BiGRU, 25 epoch with early stopping, $1e - 5$ learning rate, and `Adam` as optimizer.

5.1   Dataset

As discussed in Subsect. 3.2, we have prepared a financial misinformation dataset, wherein only *true* and *false* labels are taken and replace them as *TFI* and *FMI*, respectively. We have called this newly created dataset as `FMID` dataset, as shown in Table 2.

Table 2. Final statistics of the newly created `FMID` dataset

Actual labels	Final labels	Total
True	TFI	1791
False	FMI	3179

5.2   Evaluation Results and Comparative Analysis

The performance evaluation results of the proposed `Fin-MisID` model are given in Table 3. It shows that the proposed `Fin-MisID` model receives impressive results as *f-score* of 0.85, *training accuracy* of 0.88, and *test accuracy* of 0.83, respectively. It also compares the evaluation results of the `Fin-MisID` with recent studies. It shows that the `Fin-MisID` outperforms as compared to the existing studies. `Fin-MisID` performs 13.33%, 10.00%, and 10.66% better than [15] work in terms of *f-score*, *training accuracy*, and *testing accuracy*, respectively. It also compares the results with several baseline methods based on neural networks and `Fin-MisID` shows better results. It can be seen that the performance of BiGRU is better across several baseline methods. `Fin-MisID` performs 21.42% better than

Table 3. Performance evaluation results on newly created FMID dataset

Methods ↓	Precision	Recall	F-score	Train Acc.	Test Acc.
Fin-MisID	**0.82**	**0.88**	**0.85**	**0.88**	**0.83**
Zhi et al. [15]	0.73	0.77	0.75	0.80	0.75
Raza and Ding [16]	0.71	0.75	0.72	0.71	0.70
CNN	0.65	0.69	0.67	0.72	0.68
GRU	0.64	0.65	0.65	0.74	0.70
LSTM	0.65	0.63	0.64	0.68	0.64
BiGRU	0.68	0.72	0.70	0.69	0.74
BiLSTM	0.67	0.60	0.63	0.61	0.70
CNN+BiGRU	0.61	0.67	0.64	0.65	0.68
CNN+BiLSTM	0.66	0.63	0.64	0.61	0.67
BERT	0.78	0.74	0.76	0.78	0.74

BiGRU in terms of *f-score*. Likewise, Fin-MisID performs 18.91% better than GRU in terms of *training accuracy* and 12.16% better than BiGRU in terms of *testing accuracy*. The proposed model also performs better than BERT.

These results indicate that the proposed Fin-MisID model shows impressive results with fine-grained new labeled dataset. It shows that contextual information and extraction of semantic features using several multi-channel layers also play a significant role in classification performance.

6   Conclusion and Future Works

This study has presented a new problem for financial misinformation detection. A new labeled dataset based on financial information/misinformation has created for experimental evaluation. We have proposed a new model called Fin-MisID for financial misinformation detection mainly based on a contextualize embedding followed by multi-channel networks. The proposed model shows impressive results and outperforms in comparison to the existing studies and baseline methods. The inclusion of multi-modal settings and multi-lingual data could be an interesting research direction for this work.

References

1. Kamal, A., Abulaish, M.: An LSTM-based deep learning approach for detecting self-deprecating sarcasm in textual data. In: Proceedings of the 16th International Conference on Natural Language Processing (ICON), pp. 201–210. ACL, IIIT Hyderabad, India (2019)
2. Kamal, A., Abulaish, M.: Self-deprecating humor detection: a machine learning approach. In: Nguyen, L.-M., Phan, X.-H., Hasida, K., Tojo, S. (eds.) PACLING 2019. CCIS, vol. 1215, pp. 483–494. Springer, Singapore (2020). https://doi.org/10.1007/978-981-15-6168-9_39

3. Abulaish, M., Kamal, A., Zaki, M.J.: A survey of figurative language and its computational detection in online social networks. ACM Trans. Web **14**(1), 1–52 (2020)
4. Kamal, A., Anwar, T., Sejwal, V.K., Fazil, M.: BiCapsHate: attention to the linguistic context of hate via bidirectional capsules and hatebase. IEEE Trans. Comput. Soc. Syst. 134–141 (2023)
5. Kamal, A., Mohankumar, P., Singh, V. K.: IMFinE: an integrated BERT-CNN-BiGRU model for mental health detection in financial context on textual data. In: Proceedings of the 19th International Conference on Natural Language Processing (ICON), pp. 139–148. IIIT Delhi, India (2022)
6. Mohankumar, P., Kamal, A., Singh, V.K., Satish, A.: Financial fake news detection via context-aware embedding and sequential representation using cross-joint networks. In: Proceedings of the 15th International Conference on COMmunication Systems & NETworkS (COMSNETS), pp. 780–784. IEEE, Bengaluru, India (2023)
7. Benamira, A., Devillers, B., Lesot, E., Ray, A.K., Saadi, M., Malliaros, F.D.: Semi-supervised learning and graph neural networks for fake news detection. In: Proceedings of the ASONAM, pp. 568–569. Vancouver, Canada (2019)
8. Wu, K., Yang, S., Zhu, K.Q.: False rumors detection on sina weibo by propagation structures. In: Proceedings of the ICDE, pp. 651–66. Seoul, South Korea (2015)
9. Ma, J., et al.: Detecting rumors from microblogs with recurrent neural networks. In: Proceedings of the IJCAI, pp. 3818–3824, New York City, USA (2016)
10. Lin, X., Liao, X., Xu, T., Pian, W., Wong, K.F.: Rumor detection with hierarchical recurrent convolutional neural network. In: Proceedings of the NLPCC, pp. 338–348, Dunhuang, China (2019)
11. Zhang, W., Du, Y., Yoshida, T., Wang, Q.: DRI-RCNN: an approach to deceptive review identification using recurrent convolutional neural network. Inf. Process. Manage. **54**(4), 576–592 (2018)
12. Vuković, M., Pripužić, K., Belani, H.: An intelligent automatic hoax detection system. In: Velásquez, J.D., Ríos, S.A., Howlett, R.J., Jain, L.C. (eds.) KES 2009. LNCS (LNAI), vol. 5711, pp. 318–325. Springer, Heidelberg (2009). https://doi.org/10.1007/978-3-642-04595-0_39
13. Santoso, I., Yohansen, I., Warnars, H.L.H.S., Hashimoto, K.: Early investigation of proposed hoax detection for decreasing hoax in social media. In: Proceedings of the IEEE CyberneticsCom, pp. 175–179. Phuket Thailand (2017)
14. Burfoot, C. and Baldwin, T.: August. Automatic satire detection: Are you having a laugh?. In: Proceedings of the ACL-IJCNLP, pp. 161–164, Suntec, Singapore (2009)
15. Zhi, X., Xue, L., Zhi, W., Li, Z., Zhao, B., Wang, Y., Shen, Z.: Financial fake news detection with multi fact CNN-LSTM model. In: proceedings of the International Conference on Electronics Technology (ICET), pp. 1338–1341, Chengdu, China (2021)
16. Raza, S., Ding, C.: Fake news detection based on news content and social contexts: a transformer-based approach. Int. J. Data Sci. Anal. **13**(4), 335–362 (2022)

Quantum Image Teleportation Based on Probabilistic Bit-Encoding Strategy

Arnab Chatterjee[iD], Subrata Sarkar, Ishan Dutta,
and Suvamoy Changder[✉][iD]

Department of Computer Science and Engineering, National Institute of Technology
Durgapur, Durgapur 7000139, India
ac.21cs1101@phd.nitdgp.ac.in, suvamoy@cse.nitdgp.ac.in

Abstract. Quantum teleportation of images has been a long-awaited and necessary operation in the domain of Quantum Information Processing. Various Quantum Image Representations have been proposed to suit the different requirements of Quantum Image processing, such as edge detection, inversion, color operation, geometric transformation, etc. To meet the Quantum Teleportation of an Image, the existing algorithm is not capable of teleporting the Quantum Image. Instead, the algorithm can only transport classical bits via quantum channels, making it a superdense coding algorithm rather than actual quantum teleportation. In this paper, we demonstrate a simulation of quantum image teleportation to overcome the challenge mentioned above. To do this, we have presented a new Quantum Image Representation technique so that Quantum Teleportation can be simulated using Quantum Simulator. This technique converts the classical image into a superposition state of α and β components, generated using a probabilistic bit encoding strategy. The measurement was performed 50000 times on the superposition state to retrieve the classical image. To verify the correctness of this method, the proposed algorithm was tested using different parametric tests between the classical image and the images after measurement. The results indicate the correctness of the proposed method, paving the path for applications of Quantum Image Teleportation.

Keywords: Quantum Image Representation (QIR) · Classical to Quantum Converter (C2Q) · Quantum to Classical Converter (Q2C)

1 Introduction

Quantum Information Theory and Quantum Computation are rapidly emerging as promising research fields due to the parallelism properties of Quantum Mechanics. Quantum teleportation, which enables the transfer of quantum information from one location to another using an already created entanglement pair, is one of the most exciting applications of this theory. While the paper [7] claims to have achieved the practical implementation of an image teleportation protocol for the first time, some essential points need to be addressed.

P. Maji et al. (Eds.): PReMI 2023, LNCS 14301, pp. 654–662, 2023.
https://doi.org/10.1007/978-3-031-45170-6_68

According to the study [7], the objective is to transmit a classical (digital) image using a quantum configuration. A complex mathematical model is used to map classical bits into equivalent computational basis states (CBS), where 0 is represented by $|0\rangle$ and 1 is represented by $|1\rangle$ [6]. However, it should be noted that these states ($|0\rangle$ and $|1\rangle$) are not in a superposition state, but rather are utilized to represent the two distinct logical states of the qubits [8]. These logical states are said to be teleported from sender to receiver. Hence, the proposed C2Q encoding [6,7] technique does not create superposition states but provides an encoding scheme from classical bits to computational basis states (CBS). As a result, the protocol can be considered a variation of superdense coding rather than actual teleportation.

In order to carry out actual quantum image teleportation in quantum simulator, a quantum image is necessary. Over the last a couple of years, researchers have proposed multiple Quantum Image Representation (QIR) techniques that aim to use quantum mechanical principles to represent classical images in a quantum computer [10]. However, using the classical encoding of bits for quantum image representation has raised questions about whether these images can be truly considered as quantum images [6]. To address these challenges, the QuBoIP Algorithm [5] has been proposed as a potential solution, although several difficulties have been identified [4]. The practical implementation of QIR techniques requires a classical-to-quantum interface to enable classical bits to be used for QIR [5]. Developing a Classical-to-Quantum (C2Q) data encoding strategy and its reverse process is necessary [2] to enable the utilization of classical images for processing on a quantum computer.

In this paper, classical images are converted to quantum images (C2Q) using a Probabilistic Encoding Strategy to implement quantum image teleportation. To achieve this, a prototype based on Amplitude Encoding [9] and Bit-Pixel to Quantum Pixel conversion [3] has been used for classical to quantum pixel encoding. Unlike positive or negative superposition [3], our proposed quantum pixels are expressed as a superposition of states, which are described as a linear combination of quantum states. To regenerate the classical image (Q2C), a quantum measurement operation is to be performed.

The primary contribution of our work are: Firstly, A quantum image has been created successfully, with each pixel being represented as a superposition state of a qubit. Secondly, we have successfully implemented the simulation of image teleportation in quantum simulator, which involves transmitting the quantum information across a distance through entanglement pair and the original image is recovered with high accuracy after teleportation, at the receiving end after multiple measurements.

2   Mathematical Model

This section presents a practical approach for classical to quantum pixel transform utilizing Bit-Pixel to Quantum-Pixel conversion [3]. The classical pixel $I[i][j]$ is transformed into superposition states $|\psi_{ij}\rangle = [|\alpha_{ij}\rangle, |\beta_{ij}\rangle]$ after applying unitary operator on the empty image matrix. Here, α and β are tow probability components and depends on the value of each classical pixel.

2.1   Mathematical Model for C2Q Data Encoding

This subsection presents the mathematical model for the proposed C2Q Data Encoding. A pixel in a Grey-scale image is represented in an eight-bit binary stream. The Polynomial expression of a greyscale pixel $I[i][j]$ is expressed as:

$$I[i][j] = \sum_{i=0}^{q-1}[f(Y,X)] = a_{q-1}2^{q-1} + a_{q-2}2^{q-2} + ... + a_0 2^0 = \sum_{i=0}^{q-1} a_i 2^i \quad (1)$$

where q is the number of bits to represent the image. For binary bit stream, each bit is either 0 or 1. This means: $a_i = 0$ or 1 and $q = 2$. The values that correspond to 0 and the values that correspond to 1 are categorized separately. These two groups are added independently as two different probability states. This process is shown as follows:

$$P(I[i][j]) = \sum_{i=0}^{m-1} \frac{a_i}{2^q - 1}|0\rangle + \sum_{j=m}^{q-1} \frac{b_j}{2^q - 1}|1\rangle = \frac{1}{2^q - 1}\left[\sum_{i=0}^{m-1} a_i|0\rangle + \sum_{j=m}^{q-1} b_j|1\rangle\right]$$
$$(2)$$

where a_i correspond to the 0's and b_i correspond to the 1's in the bit stream. Let

$$\sum_{i=0}^{m-1} \frac{a_i}{2^q - 1} = \alpha^2 \quad and \quad \sum_{j=m}^{q-1} \frac{b_j}{2^q - 1} = \beta^2 \quad (3)$$

From Eq. (3), we get:

$$\alpha = \sqrt{\frac{\sum_{i=0}^{m-1} a_i}{2^q - 1}} \quad and \quad \beta = \sqrt{\frac{\sum_{j=m}^{q-1} b_j}{2^q - 1}} \quad (4)$$

Using α and β, the superposition state $|\psi\rangle$ is represented as:

$$|\psi\rangle = \alpha|0\rangle + \beta|1\rangle = \alpha \begin{bmatrix} 1 \\ 0 \end{bmatrix} + \beta \begin{bmatrix} 0 \\ 1 \end{bmatrix} = \begin{bmatrix} \alpha \\ \beta \end{bmatrix} \quad (5)$$

In general, the corresponding superposition state $|\psi_{ij}\rangle$ for a classical pixel $(I[i][j])$ can be expressed as:

$$|\psi_{ij}\rangle = k.[\alpha_{ij}, \beta_{ij}] \quad (6)$$

where k= Normalized integer constant in the range of [0–255] for scaling the superposition state to classically visualise during simulation.

2.2 Quantum to Classical (Q2C) Conversion Using Quantum Measurement

Measurement operation is performed to get the classical state from the superposition state [8]. The classical state is obtained after collapse of the wave-function to either of the basis states. Mathematically after measurement, the Born Probability of getting $|0\rangle$ is $|\alpha^2|$ and probability of getting $|1\rangle$ is $|\beta^2|$.

From Eq. (6), the mathematical representation after the measurement is performed, is expressed as:

$$\mathcal{M}_i = (2^q - 1).random(|0\rangle, |1\rangle) \tag{7}$$

where $k = (2^q - 1)$ is the same normalization constant utilized in classically visualizing the superposition state after simulation as shown in Eq. (6).

Quantum Measurement Problem: During measurement, the superposition state collapses randomly to either of the CBS with probabilities $|\alpha^2|$ and $|\beta^2|$. This can lead to erroneous output, so multiple measurements are necessary to reduce measurement errors. The classical simulation of this process is demonstrated in the Results and Analysis section using standard images.

2.3 Application of Data Encoding in Image Representation

We use the above C2Q technique to represent images in the following ways. The size of the classical image we consider is $2^{n_1} \times 2^{n_2}$. Hence the superposition state of the image will be of size $2^{2n_1} \times 2^{n_2}$. After measurements, the regenerated classical image is of $2^{n_1} \times 2^{n_2}$ dimension. Instead of using classical encoding of bits, $|\psi_{ij}\rangle$ is used as pixels to produce an actual quantum image in which all the pixels are superposition states. The mathematical representation of quantum greyscale image is as follows:

$$|\psi_{grey}\rangle = \frac{1}{2^{\frac{n_1+n_2}{2}}} \sum_{j=0}^{2^{n_2}-1} \sum_{i=0}^{2^{n_1}-1} |\psi_{ij}\rangle |ji\rangle \tag{8}$$

Using Eq. (6), the above expression is re-written as:

$$|\psi_{grey}\rangle = \frac{K}{2^{\frac{2n_1+n_2}{2}}} \sum_{j=0}^{2^{n_2}-1} \sum_{i=0}^{2^{2n_1}-1} [\alpha_{ij}, \beta_{ij}] |ji\rangle \tag{9}$$

where $K = k.n_1.n_2$, K is a normalisation operator used for visualisation.

3 Proposed Algorithm

This section outlines the algorithm for converting classical images to quantum images and vice versa. This process is shown in Fig. 1.

Figure 1 represents the flowchart of the bit encoding and ecoding strategy , which converts a classical pixel to it's corresponding superposition state and vice versa.

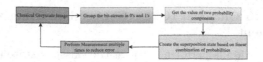

Fig. 1. Flow Diagram of C2Q and Q2C procedure

3.1   Grey Scale Image Transformation

Algorithm 1 converts Classical greyscale images to Quantum greyscale images. Algorithm 2 reverses the process to create classical images from quantum greyscale images after the collapse of the superposition state.

Algorithm 1. Algorithm for Classical to Quantum Greyscale Image Conversion

---

Input: A Classical Greyscale Image
Output: Equivalent Quantum Superposition Greyscale Image

Initialization of variables: Create empty image matrix using Unitary Operator **H** and **I**
while each pixel in classical image matrix **do**
    Read the greyscale image $P_{classical} = [f(Y, X)]_{2^{n_1} \times 2^{n_2}}$
    The 8-bit Greyscale image is encoded using probabilistic encoding technique
    while end of CBS matrix **do**
        The superposition states of the corresponding pixels are represented as: $|\psi_{ij}\rangle = k \cdot [\alpha_{ij}, \beta_{ij}]$
        Substitute this quantum pixel $|\psi_{ij}\rangle$ in the empty image matrix.
    end while
    Repeat this step for all pixels in the Greyscale image
end while

---

4   Results and Analysis

We have implemented the proposed QIR based on Classical to Quantum data Encoding technique using Python 3.0. Due to the unavailability of an advanced quantum computer, our algorithm was simulated on a classical simulator for complex 256 × 256 images. The Quantum Image Teleportation was simulated in Python and IBM Qiskit 0.42 for a 64 × 64 image. Classical simulations were conducted on an Intel(R) Core(TM) i3-3470 CPU @ 3.20 GHz with 4.00 GB RAM and a 64-bit operating system.

4.1   Classical Gray Scale Image Simulation

A sample data set of classical grey scale 256 × 256 image is used to simulate the pixel transform algorithm. Figure 2 shows the classical simulation of the

---

Algorithm 2. Algorithm for Quantum Greyscale Image to Classical Image Conversion (Measurement Operation)

Input: Quantum Superposition State of Greyscale Image
Output: Equivalent Classical Greyscale Image after Measurement

  Initialization of variables: Pixel Superposition states from the Quantum Image
  while each superposition state from image matrix **do**
    The probability α^2 or β^2 is obtained from the superposition state $|\psi\rangle$
    while random probability from state$|\psi\rangle$ **do**
      Measuring randomly, $|0\rangle$ is obtained with α^2 probability
      Else $|1\rangle$ is obtained with β^2 probability
      The equivalent classical image is generated based on every random outcome.
    end while
    Repeat this step for all superposition pixels in the image
    Perform this measurement multiple times to get accurate result.
  end while

---

proposed Algorithm. Fig. 1(a) is the classical greyscale image. After applying C2Q Algorithm to Fig. 2(a) and as shown in Eq. (9), the superposition image Fig. 2(b) is obtained. Quantum measurement operation is applied to the superposition state to regain the classical image (Q2C). The classical image after a single measurement is shown in Fig. 2(c). Measurements are made 100 and 1000 times accordingly to obtain more exact and accurate results. These results are shown in Fig. 2(d) and Fig. 2(e), respectively. Different parametric tests have been conducted between two additional images, Baboon and Pepper, and we got a similar result from all these. The results are shown in Table 1 below.

(a) Classical Lake   (b) Superposition state   (c) 1 Shot Measurement   (d) 100 Shot Measurement   (e) 1000 Shot Measurement

Fig. 2. Sample 256×256 Greyscale Images Simulation for C2Q and Q2C Conversion

Comparison of Classical Image and Classical-to-Quantum-to-Classical (C2Q2C) Restored Image. Different Parametric tests, such as MSE, RMSE, PSNR, RASE, SSIM, UQI, etc., are conducted between pixels and is shown in Table 1. Here the classical image is pixel-wise compared with 1st shot, 100-shot, and 1000-shot measurement. The results shown in Fig. 2 and Table 1 prove that the image is nearer to the classical image if the number of iterations increases during the measurement operation. It has been proved that just a few hundred repetitions of the algorithm are sufficient to decrease the probability of error to less than 10^{-20} [8]. Our proposed method provides a unique advantage in comparison to other existing QIR approaches. Unlike previous methods that primarily rely on mathematical calculations to determine the number of shots, our approach goes beyond theoretical modeling and includes actual result simulations. This additional step enhances the accuracy and reliability of our proposed method, enabling a more comprehensive and practical comparison with other QIR techniques.

Table 1. Information Loss Table for Measurement [accurate upto two decimal points and time in seconds](1, 100, 1000 shots for Greyscale Image)

Title	Lake	Lake	Lake	Baboon	Baboon	Baboon	Pepper	Pepper	Pepper
Shots	1	100	1000	1	100	1000	1	100	1000
Time	2.24	51.11	997.39	1.89	49.52	835.21	3.71	54.83	1079.61
MSE	11188.47	198.57	97.87	14508.65	369.22	239.54	12757.53	433.23	323.54
RMSE	105.77	14.09	9.89	120.45	19.21	15.47	112.94	20.81	17.98
PSNR	7.64	25.15	28.22	6.51	22.45	24.33	7.07	21.76	23.03
SSIM	0.14	0.80	0.95	0.08	0.82	0.94	0.11	0.74	0.92
UQI	0.65	0.97	0.98	0.63	0.97	0.98	0.57	0.92	0.93
MSSSIM	0.54	0.95	0.98	0.41	0.90	0.93	0.49	0.94	0.98
ERGAS	31513.34	4252.33	3059.15	29013.90	4335.93	3089.67	39511.44	8065.66	7063.83
SCC	0.10	0.57	0.81	0.12	0.71	0.91	0.05	0.40	0.72
SAM	0.64	0.10	0.07	0.76	0.15	0.12	0.77	0.14	0.11

4.2   Teleportation of Quantum Image Using Qiskit

Quantum Teleportation has already been implemented as simulation in classical computer using IBM Qiskit. Feynman accurately stated [1] that simulating quantum mechanics requires a quantum computer, as classical computers are incapable of achieving certain unique quantum operations, such as entanglement. While classical computers can simulate the logical aspects of quantum mechanics through mathematical modeling, but they cannot replicate the true essence of quantum phenomena. Since actual quantum computers are not yet available, the image teleportation algorithm is simulated using IBM QSAM simulators.

In this case, a single logical quantum state $|\psi\rangle$ is teleported from Alice to Bob using an already created entanglement pair. The teleportation of the quantum superposition state of an image is not performed earlier. In this example, let us assume there are two persons: Alice and Bob. Alice wants to send an image to Bob, as shown in Fig. 3(a). Now Alice will use the C2Q interface to convert the image to a superposition state as shown in 3(b). Alice teleports state 3(b) to Bob, one state at a time. When Bob gets the state 3(b), he performs measurement, in the same order. After a single measurement, Fig. 3(c) is obtained. When Bob increases the number of measurements, Figs. 3(d), 3(e), and 3(f) are obtained for 100 shots, 1000 shots, and 2000 shots, respectively. As the number of measurements increases, the loss of information decreases, and it becomes difficult to discern the differences visually. In Table 2, the information loss between the classical and regenerated images after teleportation up to 50000 shots of measurement are shown. This result proves that if the number of measurement increases, we get a result similar to the classical image. A comparison with respect to the execution time and number of shots is also shown. The simulation demonstrates a direct correlation between the number of shots and the execution time. Though the precision of outcome is increased after multiple measurements, but as claimed in literature [7], it will never reach 100%. This is due to the Measurement Problem and Uncertainty Principle of Quantum Mechanics.

(a) Classical Image (b) Superposition State (c) 1 Shot measurement (d) 100 Shot measurement (e) 1000 Shot measurement (f) 2000 Shot measurement

Fig. 3. Illustration of Quantum Image Teleportation of 64 × 64 image

Table 2. Information Loss Table for Quantum Image Teleportation using Qiskit

Shots	1	100	1000	2000	3000	4000	5000	50000
Time(sec)	0.12	4.84	41.24	75.37	102.15	135.11	151.87	1620.55
MSE	12028.997	154.258	46.486	40.759	38.728	38.081	37.625	35.154
RMSE	109.677	12.42	6.818	6.384	6.223	6.171	6.134	5.929
PSNR	7.329	26.248	31.458	32.029	32.251	32.324	32.376	32.671
SSIM	0.246	0.934	0.981	0.984	0.984	0.985	0.985	0.987
UQI	0.697	0.994	0.998	0.998	0.998	0.998	0.998	0.999
MSSSIM	0.691	0.988	0.997	0.997	0.997	0.998	0.998	0.998
ERGAS	26424.094	2860.218	1343.696	1182.86	1116.904	1098.147	1090.882	993.78
SCC	0.222	0.838	0.926	0.939	0.936	0.946	0.943	0.95
SAM	0.665	0.088	0.048	0.045	0.044	0.044	0.043	0.042

5   Conclusion

The implementation of Quantum Image Teleportation using the Probabilistic Bit Encoding Strategy has been successfully demonstrated in this paper. The approach involves converting a classical image into a superposition state and then teleporting it from sender to receiver using quantum simulator. At receiver's end, the classical image is generated after multiple measurements on the quantum image. The conversion between classical and quantum pixels approach effectively answers the queries raised by different researchers. The paper confirms the correctness of the proposed method by demonstrating the similarity between the classical image and the measured image in two different experiments. By conducting 50,000 measurements using the teleportation protocol, results were obtained that closely resemble classical images, indicating a high level of similarity. In classical simulation, it is not possible to create an entanglement pair between sender and receiver. Therefore, Alice needs to send the superposition to Bob, which might appear as information transfer. However, in real quantum computing, the transmission of superposition state is not required due to their entanglement. In teleportation, the measurement basis is sent from Alice to Bob through a classical channel instead of the actual superposition state. To create a quantum RGB image, the three greyscale planes (red, green, and blue) are converted into quantum greyscale images and then merged. In future, complex RGB images to be simulated along with complete mathematical description. Additionally different experiments related to quantum mechanics will be performed to validate our claim. Furthermore, the quantum image teleportation can provide the way for developing new communication algorithms, cryptography, and steganography techniques. The potential applications of this approach are vast and can contribute to the advancement of various fields in Quantum Information Processing.

References

1. Feynman, R.P.: Simulating physics with computers. Int. J. Theor. Phys. **21**(6), (1982)
2. Ghosh, K.: Encoding classical data into a quantum computer (2021)
3. Laurel, C.O., Dong, S.H., Cruz-Irisson, M.: Equivalence of a bit pixel image to a quantum pixel image. Commun. Theor. Phys. **64**(5), 501 (2015)
4. Li, H.S., Fan, P., Xia, H.Y., Zhou, R.G.: A comment on "quantum image processing?". Quantum Inf. Process. **19**(5), 1–10 (2020)
5. Mastriani, M.: Quantum Boolean image denoising. Quantum Inf. Process. **14**(5), 1647–1673 (2014)
6. Mastriani, M.: Quantum image processing? Quantum Inf. Process. 16(1) (2016)
7. Mastriani, M.: Teleporting digital images. Optical and Quantum Electr. **55**(1572–817X) (2023)
8. Nielsen, M.A., Chuang, I.L.: Quantum Computation and Quantum Information: 10th Anniversary Edition. Cambridge University Press, Cambridge (2010)
9. Schuld, M., Bocharov, A., Svore, K.M., Wiebe, N.: Circuit-centric quantum classifiers. Phys. Rev. A **101**, 032308 (2020)
10. Su, J., Guo, X., Liu, C., Li, L.: A new trend of quantum image representations. IEEE Access **8**, 214520–214537 (2020)

Annihilation of Image Stegogram Through Deep Texture Extraction Based Sterilization

Sreeparna Ganguly$^{(\boxtimes)}$ ⓘ, Ankit Mishra ⓘ, and Imon Mukherjee ⓘ

Indian Institute of Information Technology Kalyani, Kalyani, India
{sreeparna_phd21,ankit20538,imon}@iiitkalyani.ac.in

Abstract. This work presents a deep feature-based image sterilization algorithm that effectively mutilates stego-secrets concealed within lossless cover images using any steganography scheme without oppressing the perceptual quality of the cover. The proposed method learns the possible steganalytic features such as edges, corners, textures, blobs etc., through a convolution based deep feature extractor network and produces an edge map locating probable stego-secret rich regions of a suspected stego-image. Sterilization by pixel modification is performed by constructing a hexagonal skeleton of the given image using the edge map. The use of deep features and the hexagonal neighbourhood reduces the degradation of visual quality caused by spatial modifications of image pixels. The efficacy of the method is assessed on an experimental image set of size 45,135 containing 5,015 images from USC-SIPI and Boss-Base 1.01 dataset and their secret-embedded versions generated by eight benchmark steganography schemes. The proposed method is observed to produce optimal outcomes in terms of sterilization percentage, sterilization time and visual quality among the relevant state-of-the-art works.

Keywords: Image Sterilization · Steganalysis · Steganography Removal · Convolutional Neural Network

1 Introduction

The malicious use of image steganography for transmitting harmful content hiding in benign-looking image files poses a great threat to societal wellbeing [1]. Traditional steganalysis attempts to resolve the issue by applying various statistical and analytical methods to identify the presence of secret data within a cover image [2]. The highly undetectable nature of modern steganographic algorithms [3–5] makes it difficult to provide accurate steganalysis with a low false-alarm rate. Instead of providing such binary answers, active steganalysis or image sterilizaton [9–12,14] manipulates a suspected cover in such a way that the stego secret becomes mutilated beyond reconstruction. Image sterilization for steganography removal is reported for the first time in the work of Paul and

P. Maji et al. (Eds.): PReMI 2023, LNCS 14301, pp. 663–671, 2023.
https://doi.org/10.1007/978-3-031-45170-6_69

Mukherjee [3] which uses a flip function to sterilize one bit of LSB of suspicious image pixels. The extension to this model is demonstrated in [4] where the authors improve the sterilization strategy to incorporate other steganography methods such as PVD. To increase the robustness of modification sterilization, the method discussed in [15] employs alpha-blending in the coefficients of Integer Wavelet Transform. Since the changes made to the transform domain coefficients reflect in the spatial domain intensities of an image, method [15] is robust against LSB PVD, EMD, DE and other adaptive techniques such as UNIWARD and HUGO. Methods [5] and [13] employ various filters for removing parts of the image where steganographic secrets are likely to be present. Ameen [5] uses wiener and gaussian filters and denoising algorithms Visushrink, Bayeshrink and Sureshrink to remove the secret data from a suspected cover image. Amritha et al. [13] propose a filter shower method that simultaneously applies 27 filters in combination for mutilating stego messages generated from various algorithms. [14] applies autoencoder based sterilization.

This work proposes a Deep Feature Map based active image sterilization algorithm that provides steganography removal by modifying spatial intensities of a suspected cover image. Feature Extractor CNN (FECNN) has been proposed to find image segments preferred by various stego-embedding methods. For preventing the degradation in visual quality, a hexagonal skeleton matrix is constructed to limit the cover modification within the desired range.

2   Proposed Method

The overall architecture of the proposed sterilization system is presented in Fig. 1. Deep Feature Extraction Network (FECNN) identifies the portions of image where the chance of steganographic embedding is higher. Suspected stego images are passed through FECNN to produce a deep feature map. The image sterilization algorithm traces the image according to the deep feature map and performs steganography removal by constructing hexagonal skeleton markings as discussed in the subsections below.

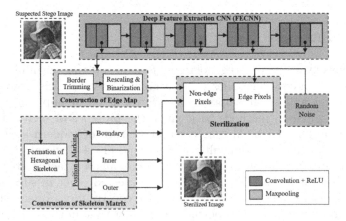

Fig. 1. System Architecture of the Proposed Model

2.1 Deep Feature Extraction

The proposed algorithm adaptively sterilizes a suspected cover image by tracing the edges of a deep feature map. The deep feature map is produced by superimposing the intermediary feature maps generated from Deep Feature Extraction CNN (FECNN). **Deep Feature Extraction CNN (FECNN)** is a five-block convolutional neural network without any fully connected layer. The first two blocks of FECNN consist of two convolutional layers followed by a max pooling layer. Each of the third, fourth and fifth blocks has three convolution layers in place of two and a max pooling layer at the end like the previous blocks. All the convolution layers use kernels of dimension 3×3 with padding as same. ReLU has been used as the activation function in every convolution layer. The input dimension of FeCNN is $1 \times 256 \times 256$. The max pooling operation with 2×2 stride 2 is applied. The input dimensions and the number of kernels for each convolution layer are provided in Table 1. The FECNN architecture does not include any fully connected layer. The dense layers result in a substantial increase in computational complexity which directly affects the training time of any neural network. Since the network is not intended to provide any classification results, the proposed model has eliminated the use of dense layers. It is important to note that the FECNN contains max pooling layers at every block. Max pooling operation not only decreases the input dimension of the deep layers but also helps to locate the highest intensity pixels where stego-secrets may be hidden.

Table 1. Blockwise Detail of FECNN

Layer	Input Dimension	Number of Kernel	Output Dimension (after maxpooling)
1	$1 \times 256 \times 256$	64	$64 \times 128 \times 128$
2	$64 \times 128 \times 128$	128	$128 \times 64 \times 64$
3	$128 \times 64 \times 64$	256	$256 \times 32 \times 32$
4	$256 \times 32 \times 32$	512	$512 \times 16 \times 16$
5	$512 \times 16 \times 16$	512	$512 \times 8 \times 8$

Construction of the Deep Feature Map. The deep feature map is constructed by performing pixel-wise disjunction of feature maps taken from the last convolution layers of each block. Due to padding at the convolution layers, the combined feature map contains visible artefacts at the upper rows and the leftmost columns. These are trimmed out by crop operation. The cropped feature map is then binarized to produce the Deep feature Map containing *Non-Edge Pixels* and *Edge Pixels* to be used for image sterilization.

2.2 Sterilization in the Edge Pixels and the Non-Edge Pixels

The **Non-Edge Pixels** are located in the smoother regions of the image where the pixel intensity does not vary much. To sterilize a non-edge pixel, initially, its position in the skeleton matrix is traced. If it is an Inner pixel, a neighbour pixel is selected from its container hexagon. The sterilized value of the selected pixel is obtained by bitwise XORing of 2LSBs of the non-edge pixel and the selected neighbour pixel. If the pixel is Outer, a similar operation is performed by selecting the neighbour from a 3×3 block surrounding it. If the pixel is in the Boundary, it is likely to be a part of two or more hexagons. In this case, one neighbour is selected from each hexagon to perform the 2-bit XOR operation. The formation of neighbourhoods and the process of sterilization are illustrated in Fig. 2. As the **Edge Pixels** have good noise resilience, adaptive steganography algorithms tend to have a high embedding rate in the edge region. For sterilizing an edge pixel I^{Edge}, XOR operation is performed on the three least significant bits of I^{Edge} i.e., $\{i_2 i_1 i_0\}$ using three randomly selected binary bits $\{r_2 r_1 r_0\}$.

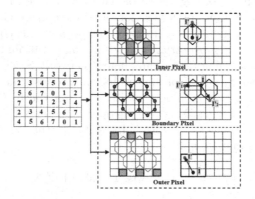

Fig. 2. Sterilization of Non-Edge Pixels

3   Experimental Results

The experimental dataset for training the FECNN is prepared by taking 5,000 and 15 grayscale images of size 256×256 taken from BossBase 1.01 [17] and USC-SIPI [16] datasets respectively. To evaluate the universality of the sterilizer, test dataset is prepared from steganographic images generated by eight benchmark steganography algorithms including spatial domain based LSB, PVD [6], EMD [7], DE [8] and adaptive methods such as UNIWARD [9], HUGO [10], MiPOD [12], and WOW [11]. The FECNN model is trained, validated and tested in the ratio of $6:1:3$ using 10,000 images from BossBase 1.01.

3.1   Analysis of Perceptibility

To investigate the visual quality of the proposed sterilization scheme observation test and histogram analysis are performed. **Observation test** attempts to find dissimilarity or artefact induced due to sterilization by observing a random stego image and its corresponding sterilized image. The proposed algorithm withstands the observation test as the stego and sterilized images presented in

Fig. 3 looks identical on observation. **Histogram Comparison** seeks for global visual dissimilarity between stego and sterilized images. For assessing local dissimilarity after sterilization, Pixel Difference Histogram (PDH) has been used. Figure 4 presents the histograms of stego images produced by applying various embedding schemes on image Elaine and their respective sterilized versions generated by the proposed algorithm. In Fig. 5 the PDHs of the same stego and sterilized images generated from Elaine are depicted. Both types of histograms show no significant altercations between stego and sterilized images in any of the embedding methods.

3.2   Analysis of Quality Metrics

The visual quality of the current work is evaluated on metrics PSNR, RMSE, SSIM, MAE, UIQI and NCC [2]. For better visual quality, the desirable value of PSNR is greater than 30 dB. The values of RMSE and MAE should be as low as possible. SSIM, UIQI and NCC are measured as probabilities so their permissible range is $(0, 1)$ where 1 signifies the best image quality. From Table 2 it is seen that the results obtained on benchmark images Elaine, Mandrill and Peppers from USC-SIPI database provide good visual quality for all the embedding schemes.

Table 2. Analysis of Quality Metrics.

Technique	Image	PSNR	RMSE	SSIM	MAE	UIQI	NCC
LSB	Elaine	44.1779	2.4848	0.9857	0.6822	0.9968	0.9994
	Peppers	44.0616	2.5522	0.9858	0.8102	0.9970	0.9995
	Mandrill	44.1903	2.4777	0.9920	0.6813	0.9978	0.9992
PVD [6]	Elaine	44.0945	2.5330	0.9855	0.7025	0.9967	0.9994
	Peppers	44.0977	2.5311	0.9837	0.6918	0.9967	0.9996
	Mandrill	44.0860	2.5379	0.9921	0.6983	0.9978	0.9992
EMD [7]	Elaine	44.1083	2.5250	0.9850	0.6932	0.9966	0.9994
	Peppers	44.0829	2.5397	0.9839	0.7360	0.9967	0.9996
	Mandrill	44.1019	2.5287	0.9919	0.6980	0.9978	0.9992
DE [8]	Elaine	44.0842	2.5390	0.9899	0.7012	0.9974	0.9994
	Peppers	44.1235	2.5161	0.9887	0.7110	0.9975	0.9996
	Mandrill	44.0938	2.5334	0.9935	0.6975	0.9982	0.9993
UNIWARD [9]	Elaine	44.1159	2.5205	0.9850	0.6895	0.9966	0.9994
	Peppers	44.0464	2.5612	0.9856	0.8082	0.9969	0.9996
	Mandrill	44.0985	2.5306	0.9918	0.6960	0.9978	0.9992
HUGO [10]	Elaine	44.1197	2.5183	0.9851	0.6905	0.9966	0.9994
	Peppers	44.0783	2.5425	0.9859	0.8109	0.9970	0.9996
	Mandrill	44.0945	2.5330	0.9918	0.6969	0.9978	0.9992
WOW [11]	Elaine	44.1117	2.5229	0.9851	0.6921	0.9966	0.9994
	Peppers	44.0678	2.5486	0.9855	0.8077	0.9969	0.9996
	Mandrill	44.1017	2.5288	0.9919	0.6975	0.9978	0.9992
MiPOD [12]	Elaine	44.1086	2.5247	0.9850	0.6908	0.9966	0.9994
	Peppers	44.0657	2.5498	0.9857	0.8100	0.9969	0.9995
	Mandrill	44.1058	2.5264	0.9919	0.6959	0.9978	0.9992

3.3   Analysis of Data Recovery

For this experiment, we apply the extraction algorithm on embedded sample images before and after sterilization. The secret is in the form of string and the payload is 100% in each case. The amount of embedded data being corrupted by the proposed sterilization scheme is computed as the ratio of the number of mismatched characters to the total number of embedded characters in the secret (Table 3).

Stego Image   Sterilized Image

Fig. 3. Observation test on Sample Image Elaine

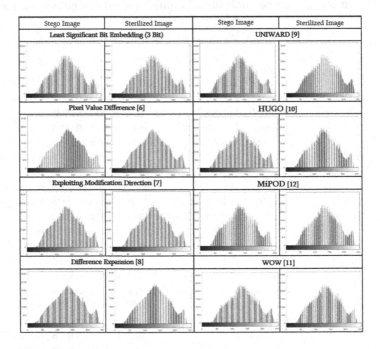

Fig. 4. Histogram Comparison between Stego image and Sterilized image

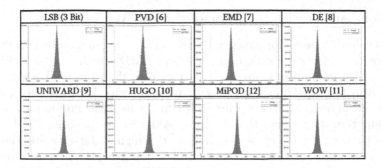

Fig. 5. Comparison of Pixel Difference Histogram

Table 3. Technique-wise Data Loss Ratio.

Image/ Technique	Elaine	Lena	Mandrill	Boat	Lake	Indian	Goldhill	Peppers
LSB	0.9430	0.9407	0.9427	0.9427	0.9407	0.9639	0.9392	0.9604
PVD [6]	0.9956	0.9954	0.9953	0.9961	0.9958	0.9957	0.9957	0.9954
EMD [7]	0.9987	0.9991	0.9984	0.9985	0.9987	0.9988	0.9987	0.9983
DE [8]	0.9938	0.9961	0.9942	0.9943	0.9935	0.9949	0.9957	0.9933

Table 4. Comparison on PSNR/Steganography Removal/Elapsed Time between Stego and Sterilized Images.

Method	Ameen [5]	Amrita [13]	Mukherjee [4]	Proposed
Lena(PVD)	29.93/0.4947/0.53	34.24/0.4891/0.61	47.57/0.4892/24.11	43.59/0.4933/1.67
Lena(EMD)	30.18/0.5094/0.54	34.89/0.4919/0.63	46.28/0.4368/27.90	43.90/0.5122/1.66
Mandrill(PVD)	27.62/0.4938/0.53	28.73/0.4924/0.61	46.57/0.4895/27.39	44.08/0.4940/1.58
Mandrill(EMD)	27.81/0.5093/0.51	29.04/0.4949/0.63	46.36/0.4312/27.86	44.10/0.5027/1.62
Peppers(PVD)	29.47/0.4925/0.54	33.09/0.4926/0.59	46.57/0.4897/28.90	44.09/0.4952/1.84
Peppers(EMD)	29.79/0.5094/0.55	33.73/0.4950/0.59	46.05/0.4456/27.64	44.08/0.5011/1.91

Table 5. Quality metrics for LSB payload on BossBase 1.01.

Technique	RMSE	PSNR	SSIM	UIQI
Bicubic Inter	6763.73	9.83	0.22	0.51
Wavelet Filter	6935.08	9.72	0.19	0.50
Autoencoder [14]	5.63	40.62	0.98	0.99
DDSP [14]	5.09	41.05	0.98	0.99
Proposed	2.53	44.12	0.99	0.99

3.4   Comparison with the State-of-the-Art Works

Table 4 evaluates the performance of PSNR, bitwise steganography removal score and time taken for sterilization on PVD and EMD scheme on USC-SIPI [16]. The proposed method has superior visual quality than the methods of Ameen [5] and Amrita [13]. Though the scheme of Mukherjee [4] overcomes the quality issue of [5] and [13], the sterilization time is for real-time implementation. The tabulation data shows that the proposed method provides the best sterilization time vs. PSNR while maintaining the highest bit-wise steganography removal rate among all the algorithms. Table 5 compares the proposed algorithm on BossBase 1.01 [17] considering RMSE, PSNR, SSIM and UIQI. The Bicubic interpolation and Wavelet filtering cause loss in image content so the sterilized image looks visibly distorted. The Autoencoder-based model and DDSP model overcome the visible distortion issue by training with steo-sterilized pair of images having adaptive embeddings such as UNIWARD and HUGO. The proposed model performs best among all the above-mentioned techniques as the deep feature extractor provides active identification of the possible stego-data rich locations for quality-preserving adaptive sterilization.

4   Conclusion

This paper proposes an adaptive sterilization algorithm for removing malicious contents from stego images without compromising visual perceptibility. The method extracts the steganalytic features of the image by the proposed Feature Extraction CNN (FECNN) architecture and constructs a hexagonal neighbourhood structure to sterilize the smoother regions identified by FECNN. The proposed algorithm is universal as it effectively sterilizes both spatial and transform domain based benchmark steganography algorithms including UNIWARD and LSB. Our method withstands the test of perceptibility, the analysis of image quality and provides a superior stego-destruction rate than state-of-the-art image sterilizers.

Acknowledgement. We would like to thank UGC for providing the NET Fellowship. We thank Vinay Singh and Rahul Kumar for their assistance.

References

1. Ker, A.D., Pevný, T.: The steganographer is the outlier: realistic large-scale steganalysis. IEEE Trans. Inf. Forensics Secur. **9**(9), 1424–1435 (2014)
2. Mandal, P.C., Mukherjee, I., Paul, G., Chatterji, B.N.: Digital image steganography: a literature survey. Inf. Sci. **609**, 1451–1488 (2022)
3. Paul, G., Mukherjee, I.: Image sterilization to prevent LSB-based steganographic transmission. arXiv preprint arXiv:1012.5573 (2010)
4. Mukherjee, I., Paul, G.: Double bit sterilization of stego images. In: Proc. of the International Conference on Security and Management (SAM), p. 1. The World Cong. in Comp. Sc., Comp. Engg. and Appl. Comp. (WorldComp) (2011)

5. Ameen, S. Y., Al-Badrany, M. R.: Optimal image steganography content destruction techniques. In: International Conference on Systems, Control, Signal Processing and Informatics, pp. 453–457 (2013)

6. Wu, D.C., Tsai, W.H.: A steganographic method for images by pixel-value differencing. Pat. Rec. Lett. **24**(9–10), 1613–1626 (2003)

7. Zhang, X., Wang, S.: Efficient steganographic embedding by exploiting modification direction. IEEE Comm. Lett. **10**(11), 781–783 (2006)

8. Tian, J.: Reversible data embedding using a difference expansion. IEEE Trans. Circ. Syst. Video Technol. **13**(8), 890–896 (2003)

9. Holub, V., Fridrich, J., Denemark, T.: Universal distortion function for steganography in an arbitrary domain. EURASIP J. Inf. Secur. **2014**(1), 1–13 (2014). https://doi.org/10.1186/1687-417X-2014-1

10. Filler, T., Fridrich, J.: Gibbs construction in steganography. IEEE Trans. Inf. Forensics Secur. **5**(4), 705–720 (2010)

11. Holub, V., Fridrich, J.: Designing Steganographic Distortion Using Directional Filters. In: In 2012 IEEE International Workshop on Information Forensics and Security. Canary Islands (2012)

12. Sedighi, V., Cogranne, R., Fridrich, J.: Content-adaptive steganography by minimizing statistical detectability. IEEE Trans. Inf. Forensics Secur. **11**(2), 221–234 (2015)

13. Amritha, P., Sethumadhavan, M., Krishnan, R., Pal, S. K.: Anti-forensic approach to remove stego content from images and videos. J. Cyber Secur. Mobility, pp. 295–320 (2019)

14. Corley, I., Lwowski, J., Hoffman, J.: Destruction of image steganography using generative adversarial networks. arXiv:1912.10070 (2019)

15. Ganguly, S., Mukherjee, I.: Image Sterilization through Adaptive Noise Blending in Integer Wavelet Transformation. In: Image Sterilization through Adaptive Noise Blending in Integer Wavelet Transformation, pp. 1–6 (2022)

16. USC-SIPI. http://sipi.usc.edu/services/database/Database.html

17. Bas, P., Filler, T., Pevný, T.: "Break our steganographic system": the Ins and outs of organizing BOSS. In: Filler, T., Pevný, T., Craver, S., Ker, A. (eds.) IH 2011. LNCS, vol. 6958, pp. 59–70. Springer, Heidelberg (2011). https://doi.org/10.1007/978-3-642-24178-9_5

Signal Processing

Heterogeneous Stacked Ensemble Framework for Surface Electromyography Signal Classification

Suman Samui[1] , Soumen Garai[1(✉)] , Anindya Ghosh[2],
and Anand Kumar Mukhopadhyay[3]

[1] National Institute of Technology Durgapur, Durgapur, India
soumengoroi@gmail.com
[2] Indian Institute of Engineering Science and Technology Shibpur, Howrah, India
[3] MathWorks India Private Limited, Bengaluru, India

Abstract. Surface electromyography (sEMG) signal is essential for accurately controlling prosthetic devices with numerous degrees of freedom in human-machine interfaces for robotics and assistive technologies. The controlling method of the upper-limb prosthesis device depends on electromyogram (EMG) pattern recognition, which requires the efficient blending of conventional signal processing and machine learning. This paper focuses on stacked ensemble models, one of the popular methods for reducing generalization error. The proposed work uses a dataset of sEMG signals from different upper-limb positions in subjects. The raw signals are transformed into correlated time-domain descriptors (cTDD) for feature extraction, which are then used to train the stacked ensemble framework. The framework includes four base classifiers (support vector machine (SVM), K-nearest neighbours (KNN), logistic regression (LR), and decision tree (DT)) and two meta-classifiers (random forest (RF) and multi-layer perceptrons (MLP). The performance of the meta-classifiers is evaluated on two test sets, showing superior classification accuracy compared to the basic classifiers. The proposed approach demonstrates the capability to accurately classify limb position invariant EMG signal classification for prosthetic device control.

Keywords: sEMG signal classification · Stacking ensemble learning · Myoelectric control · Human-computer interaction · Supervised learning

1 Introduction

In numerous applications, the electromyogram (EMG) signal is crucial. EMG has been successfully used for task discrimination in the myoelectric control of powered prosthetics for amputees because it is beneficial in identifying repeatable patterns of muscle movements [1]. Modern biomedical signal processing and machine learning developments have transformed the design of diverse human-computer interfaces for prosthetic devices [5,6,9]. Other than prosthesis devices,

P. Maji et al. (Eds.): PReMI 2023, LNCS 14301, pp. 675–682, 2023.
https://doi.org/10.1007/978-3-031-45170-6_70

gaming control, and nowadays, various technical features (e.g., volume or brightness control) are being introduced to intelligent devices using EMG-based gesture recognition. In recent years, three primary factors have been considered to advance supervised learning-based systems: data collection methods, preprocessing feature extraction techniques, and appropriate classifier design [7]. EMG signals are produced when the neurological system activates muscles, which create electric potential. Traditionally, invasive EMG involves inserting needle electrodes directly into the muscle tissue to capture the signals. However, noninvasive methods have been developed to collect EMG signals without needle electrodes. The surface EMG (sEMG) signals are recorded via surface electrodes from the individual's upper limbs using multiple electrode channels at various limb postures. Surface electrodes are adhesive electrodes placed on the skin's surface above the muscle of interest. These electrodes detect the electrical activity the muscle fibres generate beneath the skin. Surface EMG is the most widely used non-invasive method and is relatively simple and cost-effective.

Myoelectric signals collected from the upper limbs have been classified using a variety of pattern recognition algorithms over the past ten years. These strategies can be broadly divided into several essential types, such as statistical models, discriminative models, and evolutionary algorithm-based methods. The most successful methods for real-time EMG-based control have been built on discriminative models, including multi-layer perceptrons (MLP), linear discriminant analysis (LDA), support vector machine classifiers, and most recently DNN-based architectures [3,7,8]. We have recently observed that deep learning has achieved incredible success in machine perception, extracting helpful information from unstructured data and big datasets. However, the ensemble architecture with decision tree methods continues to be considered the best when using medium to small datasets [2]. This study looked at stacking ensemble models with heterogeneous base classifiers for diverse hand gestures utilizing EMG signals. It may be used to create control systems with multiple degrees of freedom in prosthetic devices for amputees. The following are the article's main contributions:

- This study investigated a multi-class categorization of upper arm-hand activities utilizing the sEMG signals using the stacking ensemble model with heterogeneous base classifiers. Using five different limb locations with multi-electrode channels, we studied the dataset comprising the myoelectric signal recorded from the upper limb of various patients [5]. The classifier mentioned above was trained using a collection of characteristics known as correlated Time-Domain Descriptors (cTDD) [4], which have been utilized for training the classifier as mentioned above and be highly effective in maintaining the limb position invariance effect [5,6].

- The sEMG data, collected from various limb positions [7], has been used to train the stacking ensemble framework. Here, we considered two sets of data: Test Set 1(utterly disjoint from the train set, which will aid in verifying the proposed system's ability to generalize while carrying out the same movements with varied limb positions) and Test Set 2 (contained all the limb position for capture for a real-time testing session).

- For heterogeneous stacking ensemble, grid Search model-based optimization has been used to adjust each hyperparameter individually, which provides acceptable accuracy for both meta-classifiers while reducing the generalization error.

The remaining portion of the work is organized as follows. The dataset used in these studies has been described in Sect. 2. The process of feature extraction is presented in Sect. 3. The stacking ensemble classifier and how it was used in this current work are discussed in Sect. 4. Sections 5 and 6 present an experimental setup and result discussion. Finally, the work is concluded in Sect. 7.

2 Description of sEMG Dataset

This research use of a dataset made up of myoelectric signals that were non-invasively acquired from the surface of eleven participants' upper limbs using seven electrode channels at five different limb locations [5][1]. Wrist flexion (C0), wrist extension (C1), wrist pronation (C2), wrist supination (C3), open hand (C4), power grip (C5), pinch grip (C6), and rest (C7) are the eight classifications of hand movements that are taken into consideration, which is shown in Fig. 1(a). Furthermore, Fig. 1(b) shows five different hand movements recorded. This dataset's advantage is that it can create EMG-based control schemes for trans-radial amputees' prosthetic hand controllers and various EMG-based innovative control applications, like gaming muscle-computer interfaces.

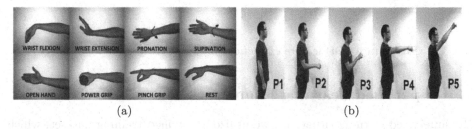

(a)   (b)

Fig. 1. (a) shows the five different limb orientations used to collect the eight various hand movements taken into consideration in this work [5,7]. and (b) various limb positions considered in this research [5].

3 Data Analysis and Feature Extraction

Each time-domain sEMG signal waveform has a set of power spectrum parameters extracted from it. Since the energy of an EMG signal is not evenly distributed, a sliding window approach has been used since the energy's fluctuation

---

[1] https://www.rami-khushaba.com/biosignals-repository.

over time provides crucial characteristics for muscle action. A data sample is qualified using a 100 ms window size, which will be advanced by 25 ms every time to assess the system throughput [7]. In this analysis, six time-domain power spectral density features (shown in Fig. 2(a)) were used in this investigation and are taken into consideration: m0 (root squared zero-order moment), m2 (root squared fourth-order moment), m4 (root square eighth-order moment), IF (irregularity factor), sparseness, and WL ratio [5]. The terms m0, m2, and m4 are used to determine the features (f2-f5). The EMG signal's first and second derivatives (d1 and d2) are used to create the feature f6. The collection of features is hence also known as associated time-domain descriptors. By joining the elements that were taken out of each EMG signal channel, a 42-Dimensional cTDD feature set was created (Each 6-dimensional channel's cTDD features * 7 Channels) [4].

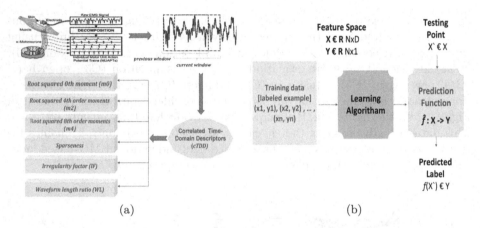

(a)   (b)

Fig. 2. (a) cTDD feature extraction. (b) Supervised Learning Task.

4   Supervised Learning Framework

In supervised learning situations, we utilize a specified training dataset, which is a set of labelled examples $\{(x_i, y_i)\}_{i=1}^{N}$. A design matrix with the notation $X \in \mathbb{R}^{N \times D}$, where D stands for the dimension of the feature vector, can provide the composite representation of feature space. In a multiclass situation, the label y_i could be classified under one of a finite number of classes that are $\{1, 2, ..., C\}$, where C is the total number of classes in the dataset. Using the design matrix and related labels, a supervised learning algorithm's goal is to create a hypothesis or function $h : X \Rightarrow Y$ in order to make $h(x)$ a reliable predictor of the corresponding value of y. If the i.i.d. assumptions, which claim that the train set and the test set are independent of one another and have an identical distribution, are valid, then a well-trained model can produce relatively low generalization error on a test set. Figure 2(b) represents the actual definition of supervised learning.

5 Stacking Ensemble Method

The stacking ensemble, a separate classifier known as a *meta*-classifier or *Blender*, is trained to aggregate the outputs of different base classifiers. The training dataset is divided into subsets to train the base classifiers and predict their outcomes. The predicted probabilities of the base classifiers are used to create a new dataset for training the meta-classifier. The stacking process can be extended to multiple levels by adding additional subsets for predicting higher-level classifiers [2]. The choice of heterogeneous base classifiers is essential for maximizing the benefits of the stacking method. Stacking helps to estimate and correct for biases in the classifiers using multiple partitions of the training set [10]. In this work, as shown in Fig. 3, SVM, DT, KNN, and LR are used as base classifiers, while RF and MLP are used as meta-classifiers in a two-step stacking model. The stacking ensemble method is chosen for its ability to account for correcting the classifiers' biases and improve the system's overall performance.

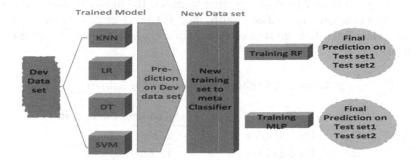

Fig. 3. Training method of stacking using the new dataset.

6 Experimental Results

This work was conducted using Python 3.8. The mlxtend[2] package and grid search were used to implement the stacking ensemble model and fine-tune hyperparameters, respectively. The relevant parameters of each classifier are listed in Table 1. The study focuses on a multiclass classification problem with eight classes. Subject-specific [9] analysis was performed, considering 11 healthy subjects (nine male, two female) separately, and the average accuracy across subjects was calculated. The study also addresses limb position invariance and evaluates whether the model trained on data from fewer limb positions can still achieve good accuracy on unseen positions. The data distribution is illustrated in Table 1. The training set, consisting of data from positions Pos1, Pos3, and Pos5, effectively trained the classifiers. Two test sets were used for evaluation. Test set

---

[2] https://rasbt.github.io/mlxtend/.

1 (TS1) contains data from positions Pos2 and Pos4, while test set 2 (TS2) represents a real-time testing scenario with data from all positions. The open-source implementation of the proposed method is available online[3]. Two training steps have been conducted for stacking, requiring two training datasets. The dev dataset, a subset of the training data, was used to obtain training data from the prediction probabilities of the base classifiers. Meta-classifiers, namely RF and MLP, were chosen for designing the meta-classifier. Hyperparameters such as $n\_estimator$ and maximum depth were tuned for RF, while hidden layer size, alpha, and learning rate were tuned for MLP. The average accuracy across the 11 subjects is shown in Table 2. It is observed that the meta-classifiers (MLP and RF) outperformed the base classifiers for TS2. The TS2 achieved higher accuracy than TS1 since it included data from all possible positions. For TS1, LR and SVM also performed well, but the RF meta-classifier performed comparably to MLP. It is approx 0.357% more accurate than the MLP meta-classifier. We can observe from the confusion matrix that both the meta-classifiers can provide the best possible accuracy for class 2 (wrist pronation) and class 5 (power grip) on both test datasets. IIt is evident that from all the confusion matrices, class 4 (open hand) and class 7 (rest) are getting confused the most. In most cases, class 4 (open hand) is getting confused with class 6 (pinch grip) and class 7 (rest); similarly, class 7 (rest) is getting confused with class 4 (open hand) and class 6 (pinch grip) (Fig. 4, 5).

Table 1. Distribution of data for any subject

Subject	Positions	Amount of data point
Train	Pos1, Pos3, and Pos5	28368
TS1	Pos2 and Pos4	12168
TS2	All position (Pos1- Pos5)	7040

Table 2. List of parameters and Overall Accuracy and F1 score of all classifiers taking an average of 11 subjects.

Classifier	Parameters	Accuracy for Test set 1	Accuracy for Test set 2	F1 score for Test set 1	F1 score for Test set 2
LR	Learning rate (Alpha)	0.844383	0.925775	0.838142	0.925700
KNN	K	0.777270	0.911777	0.771791	0.911722
SVM	C, Gamma	0.810374	0.924574	0.802445	0.92435
DT	Max depth, Criterion, min samples leaf.	0.750732	0.901485	0.744961	0.929968
Stack model-1 (RF)	$n\_estimators$, max depth.	0.821596	**0.930178**	0.814467	**0.929968**
Stack model-2 (MLP)	Hidden layer, size, Learning rate(Alpha)	0.817046	0.928706	0.810643	0.928637

---

[3] https://github.com/sumansamui/EMG_Signal_Classification.git.

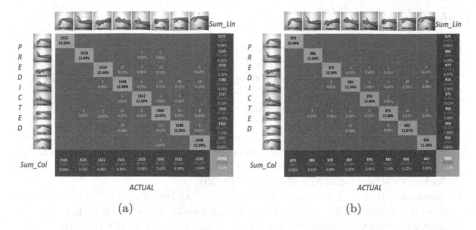

(a)   (b)

Fig. 4. Confusion matrix of (a) Test Set1 with RF. and (b) Test Set 2 with RF.

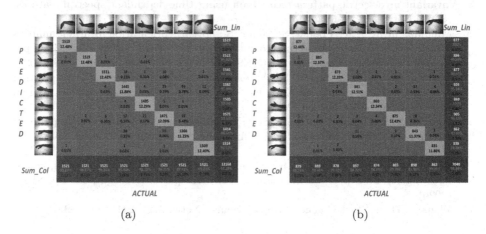

(a)   (b)

Fig. 5. Confusion matrix of (a) Test Set 1 with MLP. and (b) Test Set2 with MLP.

7   Conclusions

This paper suggests a stacking ensemble framework with heterogeneous classifiers for classifying hand movements from sEMG data. Reducing the generalization error of base classifiers is the primary objective of stacking ensemble learning. We observed that the meta-classifiers (RF and MLP) could provide, on an average 5.65% improved accuracy than the base classifiers when evaluated on the two subsets of unseen test data. In the future, popular deep learning techniques like convolutional neural networks or LSTM can be used for the same work. Moreover, the complexity can be reduced if we use raw EMG data and employ windowing techniques to implement EMG signal classification.

References

1. Farina, D., Jiang, N., Rehbaum, H., Holobar, A., Graimann, B., Dietl, H., Aszmann, O.C.: The extraction of neural information from the surface EMG for the control of upper-limb prostheses: emerging avenues and challenges. IEEE Trans. Neural Syst. Rehabil. Eng. **22**(4), 797–809 (2014)
2. Géron, A.: Hands-on machine learning with Scikit-Learn, Keras, and TensorFlow. " O'Reilly Media, Inc." (2022)
3. Jabbari, M., Khushaba, R.N., Nazarpour, K.: EMG-based hand gesture classification with long short-term memory deep recurrent neural networks. In: 2020 42nd Annual International Conference of the IEEE Engineering in Medicine & Biology Society (EMBC), pp. 3302–3305. IEEE (2020)
4. Khushaba, R.N., Al-Ani, A., Al-Timemy, A., Al-Jumaily, A.: A fusion of time-domain descriptors for improved myoelectric hand control. In: 2016 IEEE Symposium Series on Computational Intelligence (SSCI), pp. 1–6. IEEE (2016)
5. Khushaba, R.N., Takruri, M., Miro, J.V., Kodagoda, S.: Towards limb position invariant myoelectric pattern recognition using time-dependent spectral features. Neural Netw. **55**, 42–58 (2014)
6. Mukhopadhyay, A.K., Poddar, S., Samui, S.: Forearm orientation invariant analysis for surface myoelectric pattern recognition. In: 2020 IEEE International Symposium on Smart Electronic Systems (iSES)(Formerly iNiS), pp. 86–90. IEEE (2020)
7. Mukhopadhyay, A.K., Samui, S.: An experimental study on upper limb position invariant EMG signal classification based on deep neural network. Biomed. Signal Process. Control **55**, 101669 (2020)
8. Samui, S., Chakrabarti, I., Ghosh, S.K.: Time-frequency masking based supervised speech enhancement framework using fuzzy deep belief network. Appl. Soft Comput. **74**, 583–602 (2019)
9. Samui, S., Mukhopadhyay, A.K., Ghadge, P.K., Kumar, G.: Extreme gradient boosting for limb position invariant myoelectric pattern recognition, pp. 81–85 (2020)
10. Wolpert, D.H.: Stacked generalization. Neural Netw. **5**(2), 241–259 (1992)

Audio Fingerprinting System to Detect and Match Audio Recordings

Kaushal Kishor, Spoorthy Venkatesh$^{(\boxtimes)}$, and Shashidhar G. Koolagudi

Department of Computer Science and Engineering,
National Institute of Technology, Karnataka, India
vspoorthy036@gmail.com, koolagudi@nitk.edu.in

Abstract. The emergence of a sizable volume of audio data has increased the requirement for audio retrieval, which can identify the required information rapidly and reliably. Audio fingerprint retrieval is a preferable substitute due to its improved performance. The task of song identification from an audio recording has been an ongoing research problem in the field of music information retrieval. This work presents a robust and efficient audio fingerprinting method for song detection. This approach for the proposed system utilizes a combination of spectral and temporal features extracted from the audio signal to generate a compact and unique fingerprint for each song. A matching algorithm is then used to compare the fingerprint of the query recording to those in a reference database and identify the closest match. The system is evaluated on a diverse dataset of commercial songs and a standardized dataset. The results demonstrate the superior identification accuracy of the proposed method compared to existing approaches on a standardized dataset. Additionally, the method shows comparable identification performance for recordings, particularly for shorter segments of 1 s, with an improvement in accuracy by 14%. Moreover, the proposed method achieves a reduction in storage space by 10% in terms of the number of fingerprints required.

Keywords: Audio Fingerprinting · Mel Spectrogram · Hashing

1 Introduction

Significant improvements in multimedia have resulted in a considerable rise in information communication in audio and visual formats. The widespread usage of the Internet has further hastened this expansion. Many unclassified audio data and misspelled file names have been produced due to the growth of multimedia platforms like YouTube, Spotify, and BitTorrent. Audio fingerprinting is a method that identifies audio recordings from the audio signal alone without the requirement for filenames, metadata, or tags.

Audio fingerprinting is a powerful technique for detecting and identifying audio recordings in large databases. The process involves analyzing audio signals and creating a compact and unique signature, or "fingerprint," for each

P. Maji et al. (Eds.): PReMI 2023, LNCS 14301, pp. 683–690, 2023.
https://doi.org/10.1007/978-3-031-45170-6_71

recording. These fingerprints can then be used to quickly and accurately detect matching recordings in a database, even if the audio has been altered, compressed, or partially degraded. In recent years, the development of audio fingerprinting algorithms has enabled the creation of robust and efficient systems for audio song recording detection, with applications in areas such as music industry monitoring [10], copyright enforcement [7], and content distribution.

Despite the effectiveness of existing audio fingerprinting algorithms, there is room for improvement, especially in robustness and computational cost. To address these challenges, this work presents a novel approach to audio fingerprinting that significantly improves existing algorithms. This approach is based on the Shazam fingerprinting algorithm [11], which uses the local critical points of an audio stream, which are spectrogram peaks. Then Shazam uses specific pairs of these critical points to produce a local descriptor. The local descriptor is based on the frequency and temporal differential between two nearby peaks. The collected fingerprints are extremely resistant to noise, foreground voices, and audio compression. The working of the system can be categorized into three parts. The first part uses time and frequency analysis with the help of feature extraction of audio. In the second part, this system stores the generated patterns in the first step using a hashing function. At last, to detect the song, this system applies the matching algorithm. The basic block diagram of the working system is shown in Fig. 1. The key aim of this work is to build a system that can retrieve the correct audio with a shorter segment (example: 1 s) of an audio song with noise efficiently and using fewer resources.

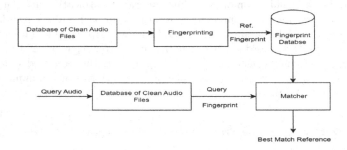

Fig. 1. Basic Block Diagram of Working System

The rest of the paper is structured as follows: Section 2 thoroughly examines the numerous studies in this area and the current systems. Section 3 describes the proposed system's design and experimental setup. The experimental results attained after implementing the suggested system are further described in Sect. 4. At last, Sect. 5 provides final conclusions of the proposed work.

2   Related Work

The researchers' community has made numerous contributions to address the issue of audio fingerprinting, with each approach motivated by its unique set of problems. As Philips audio fingerprinting algorithm is one among the most well-known algorithms [4] is. By comparing the energy in nearby bands, it generates fingerprints. The technique can sustain retrieval performance even when the audio signal is interfered with, and it is very robust to many signal degradations. It also has a short granularity of approximately 3 s. In [11], the proposed method provides basics of the famous algorithm employed by Shazam limited.

In recent studies, a new hashing method is presented in [9] for audio fingerprinting using the geometrical properties to calculate the similarities among the audio contents. To make the space efficient and more scalable system for audio fingerprinting, a method was proposed in [13] in which they sub-sample one-fourth of the original fingerprints so that less space is required and search speed is increased while maintaining a recall rate of approximately 98%. A comprehensive survey was done on already-developed algorithms for audio fingerprinting and considered four major of them to analyze and identify the potential hurdles that can affect their results [8].

In [6], a local linear embedding (LLE)-based low-dimensional audio fingerprint extraction approach and an effective hierarchical retrieval method was proposed. To create an audio fingerprint, also known as a database of audio tracks, to look for the source audio, a methodology was proposed to employ a two-stage feature-extraction-based approach [3]. Here, Mel-Spectrograms and Mel Frequency Cepstral Coefficients (MFCC) are two prominent aspects. The fundamental audio features are coefficients taken from a simple spectrogram, which are then treated independently by an advanced feature extraction technique to create the final composite fingerprint. In order to determine the coefficient of the optimum wavelet packet, an algorithm was developed in [5] that is based on the lifting wavelet packet and the improved optimal-basis selection.

3 Proposed System

This section explains the methodology used for the proposed system, which is based on [11], and as it is already mentioned above, this system contains three parts. The first two parts include fingerprint extraction, and the last matches the query song. Section 3.1 explains all the steps in extracting the fingerprints, and Sect. 3.2 contains information about the matching algorithm.

3.1 Extraction of Fingerprints

The step-by-step procedure to extract fingerprints is explained in brief as follows:

- **Sampling:** Analog signals are converted into digital format through sampling, where the continuous signal is divided into discrete portions. The choice of sampling interval, such as one millisecond, is crucial. It must accurately capture the analog signal while minimizing storage space. The Nyquist sampling theorem guides the selection of intervals, ensuring accurate data collection and avoiding anomalies during the conversion process using analog-to-digital converters or video cameras [12]. Sampling intervals are vital in audio fingerprinting, preserving the fidelity of the digital representation of the analog signal.

– **Mel-Spectrogram:** Having digitalized data from audio signals requires converting it into frequencies. For that, the proposed system uses the mel-spectrogram. Mel-spectrogram is used because the Mel-scale defines a linear relation in frequency, which is traditionally logarithmic. As a result, even though the numerical difference between two frequencies is the same, people tend to perceive the difference between two different low frequencies much better than two different high frequencies. Figure 2 shows the Mel-spectrogram of an audio song in which the x-axis shows the time-domain and the y-axis for frequency in Hertz, and the color represents the amplitude in decibels.

– **Finding the Peaks:** After obtaining the Mel-spectrogram, the proposed system now determines the amplitude peaks. A peak is a pair of frequencies and times corresponding to an amplitude value that is the highest in its immediate vicinity. Since they are nearby and have smaller amplitudes, it is less likely to survive noise than other (time, frequency) pairs. It uses the SciPy image processing toolbox and methods to locate peaks while treating the Mel-Spectrogram as an image. Combining a highpass filter (accentuating high amplitudes) and SciPy local maxima structs do the trick.

– **Hashing the Fingerprints:** When given an integer as input, a hash function will produce another integer as the output. The beauty is that a decent hash function will rarely produce the same result from two separate inputs, in addition to returning the same output number whenever the input is the same. The proposed system groups the peaks into specific numbers concerning each peak. The hash function created using these peaks discovered in the previous phase creates an index for the actual audio segments stored in the database, speeding up the search process. A small number of anchor points are selected for an audio segment linked to a target location in order for the hash function to function. The hash index is created by combining each anchor point with a point in the matching target zone to produce two frequency components and the time difference between each component. The same procedure is used to generate a hash table, a straightforward data structure that stores the song ID and an audio segment in tandem.

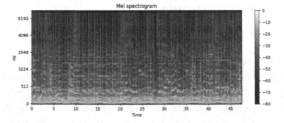

Fig. 2. An example for Mel-spectrogram for a song (Sean.mp3)

3.2   Matching Process

The query song is taken as input and processed in the same way as above for fingerprint extraction, and to find out the metadata of the query song, all the fingerprints, i.e., hash values generated in the previous step, are compared with all hash values stored in the database and the resultant matching songs are grouped for further action. Getting the matching songs to match the start time is crucial because the recording's start time differs from the source files. However, because the relative offsets will be spaced at the same distance apart, the difference between the database offset from original songs and the sample offset from recordings will be the same for all accurate matches. After calculating the differences for each matching song, the resultant song will have the most number of matches having the same difference. Algorithm 1 contains the pseudo-code for this algorithm.

Algorithm 1 Pseudo Code for Matching Algorithm

---

audioChannels=loadAudio()
matchedFingerprints=[]
for audioChannelSamples in audioChannels **do**
   hashes=processingAudio(audioChannelSamples)
   matchedFingerprints+=databaseMatches(hashes)
end for
songPredicted=startTimeMatching(matchedFingerprints)

3.3   Implementation Details and Dataset Collection

The presented research work uses two datasets. One of them is a standardized dataset called Free Music Archive (FMA Small) [1] dataset, which has 8000 audio tracks of 30 s, each divided into eight genres, and the format of every song is ".wav." The other is a collection of 42 Bollywood songs collected from the Internet and stored into two classes; one contains original songs, and the other has recordings recorded with a mobile recorder while playing on a laptop. All 42 songs are in ".mp3" format, and recordings also have noise, so the system can be tested for noisy recordings. For calculation, the Mel spectrogram settings are listed in Table 1. In Table 1, STFT is an acronym for "Short Time Fourier Transform." "Hann" is a window function that performs Hann smoothing to get better frequency resolution and leakage security. "T" represents the number of time frames or samples used to describe the signal in the STFT spectrogram and "Dynamic range" refers to the ratio between the highest and lowest values of the Mel spectrogram. Besides these, the parameters used while computing the peaks are set by brute force to balance the accuracy and the number of fingerprints. The presented work uses the "XXHash128" hash function for the hashing purpose. XXHash128 is a non-cryptographic hash function well-suited for applications requiring high throughput, as it can quickly hash. All the work is executed on a desktop computer having 8 GB RAM and a 3.40 GHz CPU.

Table 1. Configuration for Mel Spectrogram

Parameters	Value
Sampling rate	44.1 kHz
STFT window function	Hann
STFT window size	4096
STFT Hop Length	2048
Overlap ratio	0.5
STFT spectrogram size	2049× T
log-power Mel spectrogram size	128× T
Dynamic range	80 dB

4 Result Analysis and Discussion

For testing purposes, the system is tested in two ways. Firstly, retrieving original songs from disk without noise and second and recovering original songs from recordings with noise. For testing, pieces are taken in 1–6 seconds segments.

1. **Testing Songs without Noise:** For this, both datasets are employed. While examining the Bollywood dataset without noise system provides 100% recall for all 1–6 seconds segments. And also, for the FMA dataset, this system offers 100% matching accuracy for all 2–6 seconds segments except for a 1-second segment, which is better than that of the proposed approach in [3]. The reason for comparing it with [3] is that [3] is the most recent research proposing an audio fingerprinting system using Mel spectrogram, MFCCs, and based on a similar algorithm. The results are shown in Table 2.

2. **Recovering Songs with Noise:** Here, the Bollywood dataset is tested as it contains recordings with noise. For comparison purposes, the system is compared with Dejavu [2], an open-source system that uses spectral and temporal features to build the system for audio fingerprinting is taken as it is. The Bollywood dataset is tested on both systems and collected the results. The results are listed below in Table 3 (Fig. 3).

Table 2. Results for FMA Dataset

Num. of Seconds	System in [3]		Proposed System	
	Num. Of Correct	Accuracy(%)	Num. of Correct	Accuracy(%)
1	24/45	53	48/54	90.7
2	40/45	88	54/54	100
3	42/45	93	54/54	100
4	44/45	97	54/54	100
5	45/45	100	54/54	100
6	45/45	100	54/54	100

Table 3. Results for Bollywood Dataset

Num. of Seconds	Dejavu		Proposed System	
	Num. Of Correct	Accuracy(%)	Num. of Correct	Accuracy(%)
1	25/42	59.5	31/42	73.8
2	39/42	92.9	38/42	90.2
3	41/42	97.6	40/42	95.2
4	40/42	95.2	41/42	97.6
5	41/42	97.6	41/42	97.6
6	41/42	97.6	41/42	97.6

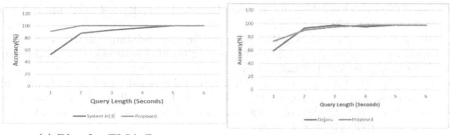

(a) **Plot for FMA Dataset**   (b) **Plot for Bollywood Dataset**

Fig. 3. Plots of Query Length and Accuracy

Besides, this proposed system takes *10% less space in terms of the number of fingerprints* for the Bollywood dataset than that of the Dejavu system. While doing hashing, the system is tested with SHA and XXHash128, and XXHash128 is immensely improving concerning *hashing time as the number of seconds takes 15% less time*. Here the plots for both tests have been included in Fig 4.

5   Conclusion

In conclusion, the system proposed in this work has successfully tackled the retrieval of audio recordings of shorter segments. The results show improved performance compared to existing methods while utilizing less storage space. To further advance the field of audio fingerprinting, potential research directions include:

1. Enhanced Retrieval of Short Segments
2. Speed-Invariant Song Retrieval
3. Performance Evaluation Metrics
4. User Feedback and Usability Studies
5. Hybrid Approaches

Exploring these research directions can lead to further improvements in the system's accuracy, robustness, and user experience.

References

1. Defferrard, M., Benzi, K., Vandergheynst, P., Bresson, X.: FMA: a dataset for music analysis. In: 18th International Society for Music Information Retrieval Conference (ISMIR), pp. 1–8. Paris, France (2017)
2. Drevo, W.: Dejavu: Open-source audiofingerprinting project (2014). https://github.com/worldveil/dejavu. Accessed 10 Aug 2023
3. Gupta, A., Rahman, A., Yasmin, G.: Audio fingerprinting using high-level feature extraction. In: Das, A.K., Nayak, J., Naik, B., Dutta, S., Pelusi, D. (eds.) Computational Intelligence in Pattern Recognition. AISC, vol. 1349, pp. 281–291. Springer, Singapore (2022). https://doi.org/10.1007/978-981-16-2543-5_24
4. Haitsma, J., Kalker, T.: A highly robust audio fingerprinting system. In: International Conference on Music Information Retrieval (ISMIR), vol. 2002, pp. 107–115. Paris, France (2002)
5. Jiang, Y., Wu, C., Deng, K., Wu, Y.: An audio fingerprinting extraction algorithm based on lifting wavelet packet and improved optimal-basis selection. Multimedia Tools Appl. **78**, 30011–30025 (2019)
6. Li, T., Jia, M., Cao, X.: A hierarchical retrieval method based on hash table for audio fingerprinting. In: Huang, D.-S., Jo, K.-H., Li, J., Gribova, V., Bevilacqua, V. (eds.) ICIC 2021. LNCS, vol. 12836, pp. 160–174. Springer, Cham (2021). https://doi.org/10.1007/978-3-030-84522-3_13
7. Malekesmaeili, M., Ward, R.K.: A local fingerprinting approach for audio copy detection. Signal Process. **98**, 308–321 (2014)
8. Mehmood, Z., Ashfaq Qazi, K., Tahir, M., Muhammad Yousaf, R., Sardaraz, M.: Potential barriers to music fingerprinting algorithms in the presence of background noise. In: 6th Conference on Data Science and Machine Learning Applications (CDMA), pp. 25–30. Riyadh, Saudi Arabia (2020)
9. Son, H.S., Byun, S.W., Lee, S.P.: A robust audio fingerprinting using a new hashing method. IEEE Access **8**, 172343–172351 (2020)
10. Sonnleitner, R., Arzt, A., Widmer, G.: Landmark-based audio fingerprinting for DJ mix monitoring. In: International Society for Music Information Retrieval Conference (ISMIR), pp. 185–191. New York City, USA (2016)
11. Wang, A.: An industrial strength audio search algorithm. In: 4th International Conference on Music Information Retrieval (ISMIR), pp. 1–7 Barcelona, Spain (2003)
12. Weik, M.H.: Nyquist Theorem, pp. 1127–1127. Springer, Boston (2001)
13. Yang, G., Chen, X., Yang, D.: Efficient music identification by utilizing space-saving audio fingerprinting system. In: IEEE International Conference on Multimedia and Expo (ICME), pp. 1–6. Chengdu, China (2014)

Analysis of Speaker Recognition in Blended Emotional Environment Using Deep Learning Approaches

Shalini Tomar$^{(\boxtimes)}$ and Shashidhar G. Koolagudi

Department of Computer Science and Engineering, National Institute of Technology, Surathkal, Mangalore, Karnataka, India
{jrf.shalinitomar,koolagudi}@nitk.edu.in

Abstract. Generally, human conversation has some emotion, and natural emotions are often blended. Today's Speaker Recognition systems lack the component of emotion. This work proposes a Speaker Recognition approaches in Blended Emotion Environment (SRBEE) system to enhance Speaker Recognition (SR) in an emotional context. Speaker Recognition algorithms nearly always achieve perfect performance in the case of neutral speech, but it is not true from an emotional perspective. This work attempts the recognition of speakers in blended emotion with the Mel-Frequency Cepstral Coefficients (MFCC) feature extraction using the Conv2D classifier. In the blended emotional environment, calculating the accuracy of the Speaker Recognition task is complex. The blend of four basic natural emotions (happy, sad, angry, and fearful) utterances tested in the proposed system to reduce SR's complexity in a blended emotional environment. The proposed system achieves an average accuracy of 99.3% for blended emotion with neutral speech and 92.8% for four basic blended natural emotions (happy, sad, angry, and fearful). The dataset was prepared by blending two emotions in one utterance.

Keywords: Blended emotion · Mel Frequency Cepstral Coefficients · Convolutional Neural Network · Speaker Recognition · Speaker Recognition in Blended Emotion Environment · Valence

1 Introduction

Speaker Recognition aims to extract, characterize and recognize the information of speech signals that convey Speaker Identification. Speaker Recognition contains two processes Speaker Identification which identifies a speaker from a set of known speakers, and Speaker verification, which determines whether the speaker is the claimed one [14]. Speaker Recognition is divided into two sets: an Open and a Close-set. These are reference models for unknown speakers that may not exist or should exist accordingly. Various studies focused on SR in neutral emotion, [17] using spectral and suprasegmental features. The proposed work focused on the emotions neutral, happy, sad, angry, and fearful and the blending of happy, sad, angry, and fearful emotions.

P. Maji et al. (Eds.): PReMI 2023, LNCS 14301, pp. 691–698, 2023.
https://doi.org/10.1007/978-3-031-45170-6_72

1.1 Speaker Recognition Using Various Emotions

Speaker Recognition models trained on neutral speech could not perform better in emotional states. A rising number of applications, including security protocols, biometric verification, criminal investigation, medical conditions, and customer service, have increased the demand for emotional SR. Several studies looked into the various SR approaches for emotional expression itself. Many studies focused on Emotional Environment Speaker Recognition (EESR), using various speech features and classifiers. The Hidden Markov Model (HMM) [15] generate a set of subsequences of feature vectors, Mel-Frequency Cepstral Coefficient (MFCC) and Support Vector Machine (SVM) [1] was used as feature extraction and a classifier for SR process for various emotions. Gaussian Mixture Models (GMM) [5], Second Order Hidden Markov Model (CHMM2s), and Suprasegmental Hidden Markov Model [16] were used for EESR. Speaker Recognition with emotional speech using transformation of speech features with Auto Associative Neural Network (AANN) [3] were proposed as SR models for the emotional environment. Analysis of emotions in terms of valence was required to understand the validity of speaker recognition for emotional content [11]. Neural network methodologies were also used to analyze the SR in an emotional environment, like capsule network [10], but still, there is a lack of improvement in the performance of SR in emotional content. Blended emotion is a form of real-time speech because people mainly talk with various emotions in a conversation. The proposed method aims to recognize the speaker in blended emotions so that a speaker can be recognized in a real-time environment conversation.

1.2 Speaker Recognition in Blended Emotional Environment

Valence is the term used to describe the pleasantness or unpleasantness of an emotional event. A moderately positive valence is assigned to happiness, a very positive valence to enthusiasm, a moderately negative valence to sadness, and a highly negative valence to anger. It is difficult to identify the speaker when expressing two oppositely valenced emotions (fear and happiness), for example, simultaneously [7]. There have been efforts in psychology to comprehend how to assess blended emotions [6]. The main work for the SR system is done in a neutral state, but there is a lack of emotional content in SR system. It is challenging to achieve ideal results when including timbre, pitch, rhythm, loudness [13] and spectral features for SR due to the complexity of the emotional context. After being trained with each emotion separately, the model was first evaluated with blended emotions for SR. The SRBEE aims to make the SR system less complex in an emotional setting. The suggested approach Conv2D using MFCC feature extraction addresses evaluating the model's performance with blended emotions. A novel introduction by modeling various emotions in a blended context is a Speaker Recognition task for Blended Emotions. The framework tried to discover how the combination of emotions affected the selection process of the right speaker for various emotional states. Blending fundamental emotions such as Happy, Angry, Fear, Sad, and neutral might create new emotion types. The proposed model for Speaker Recognition in a blended emotional environment is shown in Fig. 1.

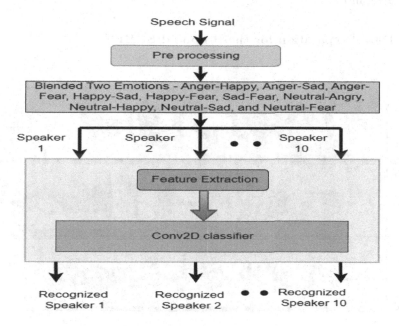

Fig. 1. Block diagram for Speaker Recognition in Blended Emotional Environment.

The rest of the paper is structured as follows: Sect. 2 briefly explains the proposed method of Speaker Recognition in a Blended Emotional Environment. Results analysis are discussed in Sect. 3. The conclusions and acknowledgment are given in Sects. 4 and 5.

2 A Proposed Methodology: Speaker Recognition in a Blended Emotional Environment

The suggested approach used a blend of different emotions to observe the performance of the proposed model. This methodology is also helpful in creating complex emotions like embarrassment, awe, envy, disgust, gratitude, and guilt by blending different emotions for the SR system. Honest conversations have blended emotions, and the proposed method tried to find an SR system for short blended emotional utterances. Further, it may be implemented for long utterances or conversations with different emotions to recognize the speaker. The core steps of the proposed method are pre-processing feature extraction and classification. The proposed work started with the creation of a blended dataset. Many emotional datasets are available in different languages like EmoDB, RAVDESS dataset, Telugu dataset, Hindi dataset, and Kannada dataset. Still, the blended emotions dataset was not available, so the blended dataset was created for the short utterances.

2.1 Data Preparation for the Proposed SRBEE

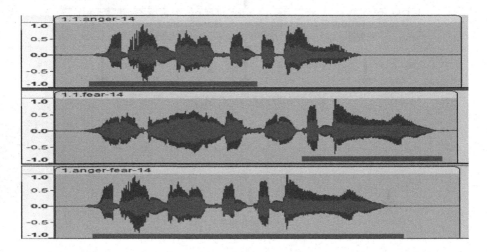

Fig. 2. Blended waveform of Anger-Fear emotion using Audacity

In the proposed system, the Hindi dataset [4] was used to create the blended dataset. There were 15 utterances for each emotion; 10 speakers dataset was considered for the proposed dataset. Audacity [2] software was used to combine emotions. The speech signal blended for Anger-Fear from Anger and Fear utterance as represented in Fig. 2 using Audacity. Here the first half of the Anger speech combined with the second half of the Fear speech signal and created a blended Anger-Fear speech signal. There were two experiments to analyze the performance of the proposed methodology. For the first experiment, there were a total of 1200 utterances (12 Neutral utterances, 10 Speakers, and 10 sessions) as the training dataset and 1020 (102 Blended utterances, 10 Speakers) utterances as the test data. Five emotions (Angry, Happy, Fear, Sad, and Neutral) were used to prepare the test dataset. 10 combinations of emotions (Angry-Happy, Angry-Sad, Angry-Fear, Happy-sad, Happy-fear, Sad-Fear, Neutral-Angry, Neutral-Happy, Neutral-Sad, and Neutral-Fear) were used for the test data. For the second experiment, there were 1500 (15 Neutral utterances, 10 Speakers, and 10 sessions) utterances as the training dataset and 900 (90 Blended utterances, 10 speakers) utterances as the test data. Six combinations of emotions (Angry-Happy, Angry-Sad, Angry-Fear, Happy-sad, Happy-fear, Sad-Fear) were used for the test data.

2.2 Feature Extraction Technique Used for Blended Emotional Speech

MFCC is widely used for extracting features from a speech signal to identify speakers. [9]. The steps that make up the feature extraction process by MFCC are as follows:

1. Framing and Windowing, 2. Discrete Fourier Transform (DFT), 3. Mel-Filter Bank, 4. Discrete Cosine Transform (DCT) 5. Delta Energy and Spectrum.

To identify voice-based phones, the MFCC approach analyzes the audio signal for feature extraction that can be used, and the DFT transform's employed signal's domain with time and frequency. Mel-Filter Bank asserts that there are distinctions between the sound perception of human ears and machines. The core idea of DCT is to appropriately describe the local spectral characteristics by correlating the values of the mel spectrum. The features' first- and second-order derivatives were considered by the MFCC.

2.3 Convolutional Neural Network 2D Model (Conv2D)

The proposed model built by a convolutional 2D neural network contained three layers merged to produce the architecture shown in Fig. 3. Convolutional and pooling layers and the filter dimension determined the dropout probability, the learning rate, batch size, and the number of epochs [12]. This study's suggested technique created a sequential convolutional neural network model using 2D convolutional layers (Conv2D), a batch normalization, two dense layers, and the output layer as the final layer. ReLU was chosen as the activation function for this layer. The second layer input shape was $20 \times 5 \times 64$, and it had 128 filters. Additionally, it includes a 30% dropout rate to reduce overfitting. A MaxPooling2D layer follows each of the two Conv2D levels [8].

Batch normalization reduces learning rates, causes parameter initialization to over-saturate the model with nonlinearities, and causes the prior layers' parameters to vary during training. The model was processed using one output layer and two dense layers. Each of the two dense layers contained 512 and 256 nodes, and the output layer contained ten nodes. Because ReLU reduces gradient descent time by turning all negative activation to zero, it was chosen as the nonlinear function for the two dense layers. The model was trained and classified the speakers according to input MFCC features in a blended and neutral emotional speech. The correctness of the model was then evaluated by comparing the labels of each speaker.

3 Result Analysis and Discussion

The proposed method used a Hindi-blended dataset. The SR task was performed with a Conv2D classifier using MFCC feature extraction. In the SRBEE system, combinations of emotions used for testing and neutral emotions were used for training in two experiments. Experiment 1 included the neutral test dataset,

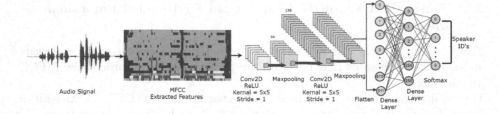

Fig. 3. Proposed Conv2D Model for SRBEE.

and Experiment 2 did not include the neutral test dataset. The model's performance was better observed if a neutral test set with other emotions was also taken with blended emotions. The proposed model provided better results for blended emotions than single emotions. The blended emotional dataset contained a combination of two emotions. It was observed in Fig. 4 that neutral emotion accuracy was highest at 98.84%, blended with happy emotion, and increased the performance of anger, sadness, and fear emotion accuracy. Positive valence feelings like happiness and joy impacted the model's performance. The model's performance was also considered in the case of a single emotion concerning all emotions, as shown in Table 1. The model's performance was better than other emotions regarding neutral and happy emotions.

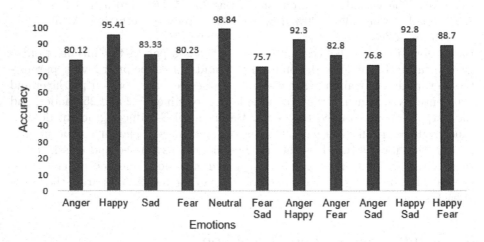

Fig. 4. Average accuracy of different emotions trained with neutral emotion for ten speakers.

The model's accuracy increased with positive valence emotion blended rather than single emotion negative valence. The model's performance was degraded

Table 1. Single Emotion accuracy with other Emotions

HINDI DATASET	ANGER	HAPPY	NEUTRAL	SAD	FEAR
ANGER	88.7	38.8	72.1	23.3	43.1
HAPPY	38.7	94.8	84.5	30.5	17.9
NEUTRAL	75.4	69.7	99.6	73.4	86.2
SAD	22.7	33.8	66.7	90.2	15.2
FEAR	43.5	38.1	70.9	16.5	86.3

because of two negative valences, blended emotions like Anger, Sad, and Fear. For some cases, like instant or sudden emotion, the SRBEE system can be used. In some medical, panic, or critical emergencies, the SRBEE system can recognize the person and provide help according to a particular combination of emotions in less time. The blended emotions can improve the accuracy of recognizing speakers in an unorganized emotional dataset.

4 Conclusion

The proposed architecture performs better when paired with the different emotional statements suggested in work due to the impact of positive emotional valence. A blended dataset that contained the voices of 10 speakers were employed for the performance assessment. Using the obtained dataset, 92.8 % accuracy for multi-emotions and 99.3% accuracy for neutral were considered. Comparing performance for this task is difficult because there are various dataset conditions, like the number of speakers and the utterance of each emotion. The classification method Conv2D with Mel-Frequency Cepstral Coefficients and voice feature extraction skills precisely combined the various emotions. The recommended method can combine various deep-learning strategies with additional feature extraction methods.

Acknowledgement. This work was supported by the Cognitive Science Research Initiative (CSRI), Department of Science & Technology, Government of India, under project DST/CSRI/2018/400(G)".

References

1. Ghiurcau, M.V., Rusu, C., Astola, J.: Speaker recognition in an emotional environment. Proc. Signal Process. Appl. Math. Electron. Commun. (2011)
2. GNU General Public License, A.i.a.r.t.: Audacity® software is copyright 1999–2021 audacity team (1999–2021)
3. Koolagudi, S.G., Fatima, S.E., Rao, K.S.: Speaker recognition in the case of emotional environment using transformation of speech features. In: Proceedings of the CUBE International Information Technology Conference, pp. 118–123 (2012)

4. Koolagudi, S.G., Reddy, R., Yadav, J., Rao, K.S.: IITKGP-SEHSC : Hindi speech corpus for emotion analysis. In: 2011 International Conference on Devices and Communications (ICDeCom), pp. 1–5 (2011). https://doi.org/10.1109/ICDECOM.2011.5738540

5. Koolagudi, S.G., Sharma, K., Sreenivasa Rao, K.: Speaker recognition in emotional environment. In: Mathew, J., Patra, P., Pradhan, D.K., Kuttyamma, A.J. (eds.) ICECCS 2012. CCIS, vol. 305, pp. 117–124. Springer, Heidelberg (2012). https://doi.org/10.1007/978-3-642-32112-2_15

6. Kreibig, S.D., Gross, J.J.: Understanding mixed emotions: paradigms and measures. Curr. Opin. Behav. Sci. 15, 62–71 (2017)

7. Larsen, J.T., McGraw, A.P.: The case for mixed emotions. Soc. Pers. Psychol. Compass 8(6), 263–274 (2014)

8. Mishra, A.P., Harper, N.S., Schnupp, J.W.H.: Exploring the distribution of statistical feature parameters for natural sound textures. PLoS ONE 16, e0238960 (2020)

9. Nakagawa, S., Asakawa, K., Wang, L.: Speaker recognition by combining MFCC and phase information. In: Eighth Annual Conference of the International Speech Communication Association. Citeseer (2007)

10. Nassif, A.B., Shahin, I., Elnagar, A., Velayudhan, D., Alhudhaif, A., Polat, K.: Emotional speaker identification using a novel capsule nets model. Expert Syst. Appl. 193, 116469 (2022)

11. Parthasarathy, S., Busso, C.: Predicting speaker recognition reliability by considering emotional content. In: Seventh International Conference on Affective Computing and Intelligent Interaction (ACII), pp. 434–439. IEEE (2017)

12. Piczak, K.J.: Environmental sound classification with convolutional neural networks. 2015 IEEE 25th International Workshop on Machine Learning for Signal Processing (MLSP), pp. 1–6 (2015)

13. Plutchik, R.: The Emotions. University Press of America (1991)

14. Quatieri, T.F.: Discrete-Time Speech Signal Processing: Principles and Practice (2001)

15. Shahin, I.: Speaker recognition systems in the emotional environment. In: 2008 3rd International Conference on Information and Communication Technologies: From Theory to Applications, pp. 1–5. IEEE (2008)

16. Shahin, I.: Speaker identification in emotional environments (2009)

17. Yegnanarayana, B., Prasanna, S.R.M., Zachariah, J.M., Gupta, C.S.: Combining evidence from source, suprasegmental and spectral features for a fixed-text speaker verification system. IEEE Trans. Speech Audio Process. 13, 575–582 (2005)

Spatiotemporal Co-occurrence Index Using Spatiotemporal Variability Signals

Rahul Dasharath Gavas[1,2]($\boxtimes$), Debatri Chatterjee[3], Soumya Kanti Ghosh[1],
and Arpan Pal[3]

[1] Department of Computer Science and Engineering, Indian Institute of Technology
Kharagpur, Kharagpur, India
rahulgavas@kgpian.iitkgp.ac.in
[2] TCS Research, Bangalore, India
rahul.gavas@tcs.com
[3] TCS Research, Kolkata, India
{debatri.chatterjee,arpan.pal}@tcs.com

Abstract. Spatiotemporal climatic variables like temperature, precipitation, humidity vary in a co-occurring fashion across different geographical zones. It is intuitive to believe that the co-occurrence is higher for signals sampled from nearby locations whereas, the extent decreases for signals which are spatially far apart. However, nearby zones, sometimes have lower climatic co-occurrence if any of those zones have variations in terms of urbanization, population, and other unforeseen variables. This study makes an attempt to study the nature of spatiotemporal co-occurrence of climatic variables like temperature, by considering their spatial variation. We thus define this variation signal as spatiotemporal variability signal (SVS) and use it get insights of the co-occurring nature of climatic variables. Frequency domain analysis of this SVS reveals interesting patterns which is quantified in the form of an index of spatiotemporal co-occurrence and is used to test an assortment of real world signals sampled from near and far-off locations, across the globe.

Keywords: Spatiotemporal Variability Signal · Co-Occurrence ·
Climatic variables

1 Introduction

Spatiotemporal co-occurrence analysis is gaining wide applications in the domain of epidemiology, ecology and climatic studies [1]. The degree of co-occurrence in both space and time pertaining to objects or events is an important measure for studying the trends and patterns in spatiotemporal data. This can help in coming up with better economical models and also help in climatological predictions and anomaly detection. Co-occurrences primarily refer to features for which there is frequent occurrence of events and is broadly classified into 3 categories based on the type of target dataset used [2], viz., (i) rules of association derived from transaction datasets, (ii) Co-occurrences in spatial patterns

P. Maji et al. (Eds.): PReMI 2023, LNCS 14301, pp. 699–707, 2023.
https://doi.org/10.1007/978-3-031-45170-6_73

from spatial datasets and (iii) spatiotemporal co-occurrence patterns derived from spatio-temporal datasets [3]. In case of spatiotemporal co-occurrence pattern mining, the literature largely models geographic phenomena like diseases, accidents, crimes at given location and time points as boolean features and instances [3]. The authors in [4] harnessed the spatiotemporal transitions in electroencephalogram time series to extract discriminating features for mental stress classification. The study focussed on finding the maximal changes (co-occurrences) in a given feature across time steps and spatial brain lobes, however, the relationships are used in a classification problem and not primarily on the quantification of the co-occurrences. This study primarily focusses on quantifying spatiotemporal relationships or co-occurrences pertaining to climatic time series data. In case of climatic studies, the modelling of spatiotemporal relationships is largely seen as a problem restricted to specific narrowed domains. This has resulted in deriving relations like the Nino index, southern oscillation index, and so on [5]. These indexes are beneficial for pin-pointed analysis of the target phenomenon/regions under consideration. The detailed review of these considerations for each of the indexes can be found in [5]. However, there is a need to first establish a holistic relationship between the spatiotemporal signals before targeting a particular event in it. This study majorly focusses on studying the spatiotemporal relationships in terms of co-occurrence of Earth surface temperature signals, as it is one of the prominent climatic variables. Surface temperature is of paramount importance in case of climate and weather, owing to its relevance in agriculture, human health, ecosystem services, economic activity and national development. Several unforeseen variables like loss of vegetation cover, urbanization, drought, solar radiations, local, global and regional climate changes contribute to the variations in land surface temperature [6,7]. Also, other factors like latitude, longitude, isotherms and so on, play a direct role in deciding the spatiotemporal co-occurrence in climatic variables like temperature. The authors in [8] provide an assortment of standardized and non-standardized pluviometric indices for temperature, precipitation and agricultural drought. These indices like the several others reported in existing works [5] focus primarily on the time domain features of the spatiotemporal signals. It is seen from literature that spatiotemporal co-occurrence indexes designed so far lack the following properties, viz., (i) handling spatiotemporal climatic time series signals across two or more geographic zones for deriving a standardized score, (ii) modelling the periodic frequency components in the climatic signals (iii) a simple standardized score for co-occurrence in non-categorical and non-boolean type spatiotemporal events (iv) variation in data from one zone should decrease the overall co-occurrence. To meet this goal, the current study first defines a new signal, termed as spatiotemporal variation signal and followed by the designing of an index of spatiotemporal co-occurrence from the frequency domain aspects. Our core contributions are, (i) Defining a spatiotemporal variation signal for the data obtained from a group of geographic locations. (ii) Studying the nature of SVS signal by its pulse harmonics with respect to their physical significance. (iii)

Analysing the SVS signals for near and far-off locations for deriving an index of spatiotemporal co-occurrence.

2 Spatiotemporal Co-occurrence Index

Spatiotemporal Variation Signal: Let $X_Z(t)$ be the spatiotemporal signal under consideration. This can be any signal like Earth surface temperature, precipitation, humidity and so on collected from Z number of zones over the time period t. In this study, we limit this to Earth surface temperature signals only. Consider Fig. 1 which shows the generation of SVS signals. The dotted ovals shows the signal values at a given time instant t across Z zones (here $Z = 4$). The diameter of the green circles indicate signal's amplitude. The red circle signifies the standard deviation σ_t across Z at t. Several such values of σ contribute towards the SVS signal shown in red. The magnitude of σ is shown using the red circle's diameter and its elevation along the Y-axis for illustration purposes. It is to be noted that when all the amplitude values across the zones are same, the value of $\sigma \to 0$. If any one zone contributes towards different amplitudes then it results in increase of σ. Thus, SVS signals posses the information regarding non-association and co-occurrence of signals across zones. Figure 2 (a) shows the raw time domain view of Earth skin temperature signals sampled from 4 nearby zones/locations (Karwar, Ankola, Gokarna and Kumta) from the coastal regions of Uttara Kannada district of Karnataka state, India, from the year 1981 to 2021. These cities have similar climatic conditions owing to their spatial closeness (as per Tobler's first law of geography). Figure 2 (b) shows the frequency spectrum of 'Zone 1' signal and similar frequencies where seen in the rest of the zones and are skipped for the sake of brevity. The SVS signal corresponding to these 4 zones is shown in the bottom most row of Fig. 2 (a) and its frequency spectrum is shown in Fig. 2 (c). On closer observation we see an additional dominant frequency in SVS spectrum which is missing in the zonal raw signal (Fig. 2 (b)). The first frequency f_1 translates to annual seasonality component while the second one (f_2) corresponds to the ~6-month, semi-annual seasonality component in Fig. 2

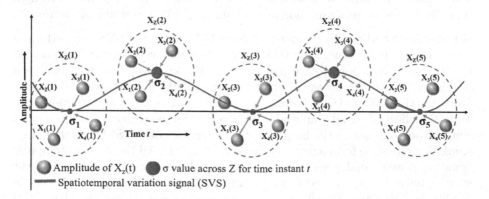

Fig. 1. Illustration of spatiotemporal variation signal (SVS) generation

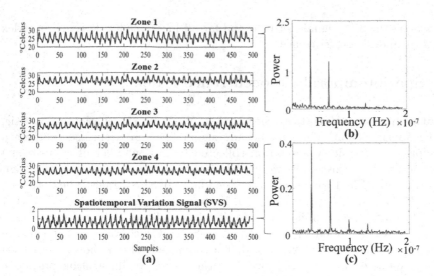

Fig. 2. (a) Temperature signals from 4 nearby zones. (b) Frequency spectrum of zone 1 signal. (c) Frequency spectrum of SVS

(b). The existence of f_3 in the SVS spectrum is indicative of the quarter-annual patterns, however, its presence in the raw signal's frequency spectrum, is very minimal. The latter points to the fact that the f_3 patterns are less frequent over the temporal spread of the Zone 1's data; nevertheless, its dominance in SVS explains that it may have been prevalent in one of the zones among the cluster of zones considered from the nearby regions. These pulse harmonics in temperature signals are results of seasonal cycles of solar radiations culminating in cyclical cooling and heating of the land surface. According to Tobler's law, the nearby zones should posses high similarity but the SVS spectrum points to the existence of anomalies in one of the regions. Among the 4 zones, Karwar is more urbanized than the rest 3, and hence, even if they are spatially very close to each other; the frequency spectrum view of SVS reveals the variability. From Fig. 2 it is evident that temperature variation seasonality as seen in the SVS, is not only transpired annually, but is an amalgamation of semi-annual and quarter-annual patterns.

Simulation Studies: To further understand the nature of SVS, we perform a simulation study by generating signals with 4 dominant frequency components f_1 through f_4 analogous to the real world Earth skin temperature signals seen in Fig. 2. We set the power, ω corresponding to the frequencies, f_1 through f_4 in $X_Z(t)$ to follow the relation - $\omega_1 > \omega_2 > \omega_3 > \omega_4$. The intention is to study the effect of signal amplitude and phase difference among spatiotemporal signals from Z zones on the frequency characteristics of the SVS signal. Thus 4 simulation cases are formulated as follows. (i) `Case 1`: All the Z spatiotemporal signals are same, analogous to data from very close regions having exactly the same climatic conditions. (ii) `Case 2`: All the Z spatiotemporal signals vary in amplitude. (iii) `Case 3`: All the Z spatiotemporal signals vary in phase. (iv) `Case 4`: All the Z spatiotemporal signals vary in amplitude and in phase.

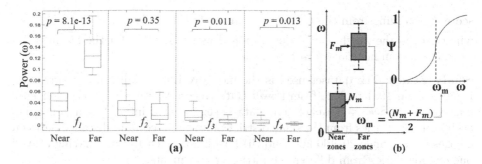

Fig. 3. (a) SVS pulse harmonics for near and far regions (b) Scoring mechanism used

Quantification of Spatiotemporal Co-occurrence: We first analyse the features that are significant markers of spatiotemporal co-occurrence using the spread of ω values for close and far-off places as shown in Fig. 3 (a). It is seen that other than ω_2, the rest shows significant differences with $p < 0.05$ for close and far-off places. However, the F-value of ANOVA is 110.73 for ω_1 whereas, it is 7.13 and 6.65 for ω_3 and ω_4, respectively. Hence, ω_1 is used for the estimation of spatiotemporal co-occurrence index. In order to have an interpretable score for assessing spatiotemporal co-occurrence, the significant feature/s needs to be normalized in a range and hence, a mapping function is required. We use such a mapping function ($\Psi_Z : \mathbb{R}^+ \rightarrow [0, 1]$) analogous to the one proposed in [9]. The spatiotemporal co-occurrence index, Ψ_Z across Z zones is given by,

$$\Psi_Z = 1 - \frac{1}{1 + e^{-\delta \times (\omega - \omega_m)}} \tag{1}$$

δ is scaling parameter for a given value of ω_m which must satisfy the condition,

$$\max_{\delta} \left\{ 1 - \frac{1}{1 + e^{-\delta \times (\omega - \omega_m)}} \right\} \quad \text{s.t.} \quad \sum_{i=0}^{N} \sigma_i = 0 \implies \omega = 0 \tag{2}$$

where N is the number of samples in X_Z. ω_m is the center point taken as the average of the two median values coming from the boxplots of near and far-off regions (illustrated in Fig. 3 (b)). Ψ_Z takes the values in the range [0,1], with higher values depicting larger degree of spatiotemporal co-occurrence. It is to be noted that higher values of δ yields larger separation in the scores for the near and far-off regions, however; the dynamic range is reduced. To handle this, the following approach is used. Figure 4 (a) shows the distance between Ψ_Z corresponding to near and far-off locations for different values of δ along with its 1st and 2nd order derivatives. The distance function is a 2nd order norm computed between the mean of the Ψ_Z scores among the near and far-off zones. The change in inflexion point is at around $\delta = 18$ (shown using dotted line in Fig. 4 (a)) and hence, we consider this value in our study for the computation of the spatiotemporal co-occurrence index. In case of more than 1 feature being considered for the computation of the spatiotemporal co-occurrence index, the score Ψ_{Z_k} coming from the kth feature can be fused as, $\Psi_{fused} = \frac{\sum_{k=1}^{K} W_k \times \Psi_{Z_k}}{\sum_{k=1}^{K} W_k}$, where, W_k is the weighted F-value obtained using ANOVA for the features (ω) considered from near and far-off regions.

Study Zones: The dataset used is the monthly Earth skin temperature data from the year 1981 to 2021 from Power Data Access Viewer (https://power.larc.nasa.gov/data-access-viewer/). The data is seggregated into (i) near zones, i.e. each group has cities from the same district or state (maximum distance between 2 cities in the range 20–400 km) and (ii) far-off zones, each group having atleast one or more cities from different countries or continents.

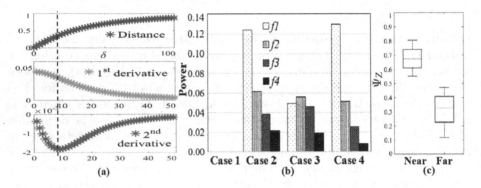

Fig. 4. (a) Analysis of Ψ_Z for different values of δ. The distance between Ψ_Z for near and far regions in row 1; followed by its 1st and 2nd derivatives in rows 2 and 3, respectively. (b) Simulation results. (c) Ψ_Z scores for $\delta = 18$ for real world signals

3 Results and Discussions

Simulation Results: Figure 4 (b) shows the normalized power values of the 4 dominant frequencies, f_1, f_2, f_3 and f_4 for the 4 simulation cases for $Z = 4$ zones. The power values of the 4 frequencies are zero for Case 1 as the SVS signal is just a DC like signal. In Case 2, where all the Z signals have different amplitudes, the powers of f_1 through f_4 in the resulting SVS, still follows the relation $\omega_1 > \omega_2 > \omega_3 > \omega_4$ as seen in the parent spatiotemporal signals. Case 3 deals with change in phase, and hence, ω_1 is largely impacted, whereas the trend of $\omega_2, \omega_3, \omega_4$ still follow the same pattern as that of Case 2. In Case 4, where both the amplitude and phase change occurs among the Z spatiotemporal signals, we notice the relation, $\omega_1 > \omega_2 > \omega_3 > \omega_4$ still persists in the SVS signals. Here the effect of amplitude dominates the phase change and hence, the trend is similar to Case 2, except that the value of ω_1 is slightly higher than that of Case 2. This simple simulation points to the fact that the variations in amplitude and phase has a direct impact on the magnitude of power values corresponding to the 4 important frequencies under consideration.

Analysis of Ψ on Real World Signals: It is straightforward to think that Ψ_Z is a function of spatial distances between the study zones selected. However, we found that the pearson correlation coefficient is least for the index Ψ_Z vs the maximum distance between the group of zones. The correlation coefficient values are -0.19 and -0.08 for near and far-off zones, respectively. Thus we can conclude that there is more to co-occurrence rather than just a function of spatial distances in between, although distance plays a major role. Figure 4 (c) shows the boxplot of Ψ_Z and a good separation in Ψ_Z is seen for the near and far groups. Table 1 shows the p and F values obtained from ANOVA analysis of the feature ω_1 and the proposed score Ψ_Z. It can be seen that the values improved further which is indicates that the mapping function is capable of effectively discriminating between the spatiotemporal co-occurrence between the near and far-off regions. Table 2 shows the extreme scenarios of Ψ_Z values obtained, i.e. highest and lowest values of Ψ_Z over near and far-off regions considered in this study. The highest value of Ψ_Z obtained among the 20 near zone group is for the Scenario 1 (with a value of 0.8055) in Table 2 considering the following places: Dandeli, Haliyal, Sirsi and Yellapur from Uttara Kannada district of Karnataka, India. These 4 cities are very close to each other and have similar climatic conditions as they are located amidst the thick forests of Western ghat regions of India. Hence, there is not much change in the climatic conditions between these 4 places and hence, a high spatiotemporal co-occurrence is expected and is seen in case of the proposed index. Considering the Scenario 2 in Table 2 where although the study zones are near to each other, the value of Ψ_Z is comparatively higher. The zones in Scenario 2 are taken from the Indian state of Punjab having large variations in temperature [10]. Moga and Jagraon fall in western region where the weather is mostly arid to dry. Faridkot and Firozpur fall in western plain region where the climate is much more humid. Moreover, according to a report, Faridkot is facing erratic climate change from the last decade [10]. Thus, even though these cities are close to each other, the value of Ψ_Z is comparatively higher when considering other near zones used in the study. The least value of Ψ_Z is in case of the following far-off cities (Scenario 3 in Table 2): Helsinki, Kolhapur, Montreal and Seoul with a value of 0.1174. This is intuitive as these 4 cities are from 4 different countries. Although they 4 hail from northern hemisphere of Earth, it is to be noted that they belong to different isotherm belts. Also, Kolhapur is below the Tropic of Cancer when compared to the rest. As a result, these 4 regions have completely different climatic and weather conditions and a least value of Ψ_Z is found. Considering Scenario 4 in Table 2, Dakhla and Solapur fall under same isothermic belt whereas, Helsinki and Longyearbyen belong to the top same isothermic regions. The former two cities are closer to equator whereas the latter two are closer to Arctic region. Thus 50% of the zones are hot and humid and the rest 50% are colder. Therefore, although they are far-off, the score is slightly above the average value. Thus the index Ψ_Z is capable of establishing the spatiotemporal co-occurrence in climatic data.

Table 1. Analysis of p and F values of ANOVA for the proposed score

Feature/score	p values	F values	Significant	Remarks
ω_1	8.10E−13	110.73	Yes	Good separation as evident from p and F values
Ψ_Z	2.43E−14	140.64	Yes	The score further improved both p and F values

Table 2. Analysis of Ψ_Z for selected extreme cases

Scenario	Type	Ψ_Z	Cities	Max distance (km)
1	Near	0.8055	Dandeli, Haliyal, Sirsi, Yellapur	79.13
2	Near	0.5515	Faridkot, Firozpur, Jagraon, Moga	82.95
3	Far	0.1174	Helsinki, Kolhapur, Montreal, Seoul	12371.87
4	Far	0.4712	Dakhla, Helsinki, Longyearbyen, Solapur	9402.85

4 Conclusions

Spatiotemporal co-occurrence among different geographic regions is a vital parameter that helps in understanding the inter-relationships in the target climatic variable. This study aims at quantifying this association with an index termed as the spatiotemporal co-occurrence index. This aids in analysing how related the study regions are with respect to each other without having to deal into the underlying complex natural phenomenon. The study a new signal named SVS in which the power corresponding to the fundamental frequency is a good indicator of spatiotemporal co-occurrence. The impact of pulse harmonics is also studied and its seen that the bi-yearly seasonal component (2nd harmonic) is the least contributor whereas, the third and the fourth harmonic contributes towards the determination of spatiotemporal co-occurrence. In future, we would like to test other climatic variables like precipitation, humidity, rainfall, and so on for determining the spatiotemporal co-occurrence. A fusion of these variables can be studied to get more insights into the climatic conditions to detect anomalies, predict climate change and so on.

References

1. Shekhar, S., et al.: Spatiotemporal data mining: a computational perspective. ISPRS **4**(4), 2306–2338 (2015)
2. Chen, Y., Cai, J., Deng, M.: Discovering spatio-temporal co-occurrence patterns of crimes with uncertain occurrence time. ISPRS **11**(8), 454 (2022)
3. Cai, J., et al.: A statistical method for detecting spatiotemporal co-occurrence patterns. Int. J. Geograph. Inf. Sci. **33**(5), 967–990 (2019)
4. Chatterjee, D., Gavas, R., Saha, S.K.: Detection of mental stress using novel spatio-temporal distribution of brain activations. Biomed. Signal Process. Control **82**, 104526 (2023)
5. Araghinejad, S., Meidani, E.: A review of climate signals as predictors of long-term hydro-climatic variability. Climate variability-regional and thematic patterns (2013)

6. NourEldeen, N., et al.: Analysis of the spatiotemporal change in land surface temperature for a long-term sequence in Africa. Remote Sens. **12**(3), 488 (2020)
7. Jan, M.: Land surface temperature differences within local climate zones, based on two central European cities. Remote Sens. **8**(10), 788 (2016)
8. Vergni, L., Todisco, F.: Spatiotemporal variability of precipitation, temperature & agricultural drought indices in central Italy. Agric. Forest Meteorol. **151**, 301–313 (2011)
9. Sinha, A., Chaki, R., De, B.K., Guha, R., Saha, S.K., Basu, A.: Multiscale analysis of textual content using eyegaze. In: Gavrilova, M.L., Tan, C.J.K., Saeed, K., Chaki, N. (eds.) Transactions on Computational Science XXXV. LNCS, vol. 11960, pp. 12–35. Springer, Heidelberg (2020). https://doi.org/10.1007/978-3-662-61092-3_2
10. Prabhjyot, K., et al.: Climate change in Punjab - some facts. In: National Innovations on Climate Resilient Agriculture, Department of Climate Change and Agricultural Meteorology, Punjab Agricultural University, Ludhiana, India, p. 16 (2020)

Noise Robust Whisper Features for Dysarthric Severity-Level Classification

Siddharth Rathod(✉)⬧, Monil Charola⬧, and Hemant A. Patil⬧

Dhirubhai Ambani Institute of Information and Communication Technology,
Ganghinagar, India
{siddharth_rathod,monil_charola,hemant_patil}@daiict.ac.in

Abstract. Dysarthria is a speech disorder caused by improper coordination between the brain and the muscles that produce intelligible speech. Accurately diagnosing the severity of dysarthria is critical for determining the appropriate treatment and directing speech to a suitable Automatic Speech Recognition systems. Recently, various methods have been employed to investigate the classification of dysarthria severity-levels using spectral features, including Short-Time Fourier Transform (STFT) and Mel Frequency Cepstral Coefficients (MFCC). This study proposes utilizing Web-scale Supervised Pretraining for Speech Recognition (WSPSR), also known as Whisper, pre-trained encoder module for dysarthric severity-level classification. Whisper model is an advanced machine learning model used for speech recognition, which is trained on a large scale of 680,000 h of labeled audio data. The proposed approach also demonstrates that the whisper features are significantly more noise robust compared to the MFCC. A high accuracy rate of 97.49% is obtained using whisper features, surpassing the accuracies achieved by MFCC (96.48%). In addition, experimental results obtained indicate that the performance of whisper features relatively more robust compared to the MFCC.

Keywords: Dysarthria · Encoder-Decoder Transformer · Whisper · Babble Noise · AWGN

1 Introduction

Dysarthria is a speech disorder that can impede the dynamic movements of the articulators and the upper respiratory system responsible for producing intelligible speech. This condition may arise from a range of neurological disorders, such as cerebral palsy, muscular dystrophy, stroke, brain infection, brain injury, facial paralysis, tongue or throat muscular weakness, and nervous system disorders. These neurological conditions disrupt the coordination between the brain and the muscles involved in speech production, leading to various speech disorders, including dysarthria, stuttering, apraxia, and dysprosody [7].

© The Author(s), under exclusive license to Springer Nature Switzerland AG 2023
P. Maji et al. (Eds.): PReMI 2023, LNCS 14301, pp. 708–715, 2023.
https://doi.org/10.1007/978-3-031-45170-6_74

The precise classification of dysarthric severity-level is of critical importance for clinical practice, as it can facilitate the development of personalized treatment plans by healthcare professionals, leading to improved outcomes for individuals with dysarthria. Furthermore, such classification systems have the potential to detect dysarthria at an early stage, which could be especially beneficial in areas where healthcare services are not readily available. Additionally, severity-level classification can be applied to Automatic Speech Recognition (ASR) systems, diverting speech signals to an appropriate ASR system based on the severity-level of dysarthria [6].

In recent years, the Short-Time Fourier Transform (STFT) [3], and other acoustical parameters have been widely used to classify dysarthria severity-levels [1]. To capture the global spectral envelope information of speech signals, state-of-the-art feature sets, such as STFT-based spectrogram, and Mel Frequency Cepstral Coefficients (MFCC) have been commonly employed [5]. These feature sets are preferred as they are known to capture perceptual information and effectively characterize dysarthric speech. Recently, transfer learning techniques have been explored for the classification of dysarthric speech. Specifically, Bidirectional Long-Short Term Memory (BLSTM) networks have been used to classify dysarthric speech into intelligible (I) and non-intelligible (NI) [2]. In [8], the ResNet-50 model pre-trained on the ImageNet dataset was employed for a transfer learning approach on a Convolutional Neural Network (CNN) classifier to classify speech into two classes, as done in [2]. However, the pre-trained ResNet-50 model does not account for sequential information as it treats the audio signal as an image. Furthermore, the model was trained on ImageNet, which is a visual dataset, and may not be optimized for speech signals. This study proposes making use of the pre-trained **W**eb-scale **S**upervised **P**retraining for **S**peech **R**ecognition [9], also referred to as **Whisper**, encoder model for dysarthric severity-level classification. The Whisper model was initially trained for speech recognition tasks.

The Whisper model is trained using weakly supervised audio matched with corresponding transcripts collected from various sources on the Internet. This approach results in a highly diverse dataset that includes a wide range of sounds from different acoustical environments, recording setups, speakers, and languages, making it well-suited for transfer learning in various speech applications. In this study, the transformer encoder of the Whisper model, which has been pre-trained on a large speech dataset, is proposed for classifying dysarthric speech from the TORGO corpus into four severity classes. In addition, due to the Whisper model's training on a broad and extensive dataset, we hypothesize that it would exhibit better performance in noisy conditions. To validate this hypothesis, we conducted experiments on signals that were augmented with noise. The contributions of this paper are summarized as follows:

- Proposes end-to-end pre-trained Whisper transformer encoder, using a transfer learning approach to classify dysarthria into four classes of severity.
- Accurate diagnosis of the severity-level is crucial in determining the course of treatment for dysarthria, and it is necessary to be able to achieve this even

for shorter durations of speech. Therefore, our study includes an analysis of latency periods, and its comparison with state-of-the-art feature sets.

- Since research on dysarthria requires high performance, it is crucial to evaluate the precision of model re-training. This study reports the experiments for this purpose.
- Given that microphone conditions are not always optimal in practical applications, it is crucial for the system to be robust to noise. Therefore, this study also includes an analysis of the system's performance under noisy signal degradation conditions.

2 Proposed Work

2.1 Introduction to Whisper Model

Whisper is pre-trained on a massive amount of labelled audio transcription data, in contrast to many of its predecessors, such as *wav2vec 2.0* [4], which is pretrained on unlabelled audio data. Whisper is an open source pre-trained automated speech recognition (ASR) model released in September 2022, at https://github.com/openai/whisper. Whisper is derived from the acronym **WSPSR**, which stands for **W**eb-scale **S**upervised **P**retraining for **S**peech **R**ecognition [9]. Whisper essentially highlights the fact that training on a substantial and varied supervised dataset and focusing zero-shot transfer significantly improves the endurance and performance of the system.

The Whisper model is an encoder-decoder transformer architecture similar to that described in [11]. It has been trained to perform various tasks, such as transcription, voice activity detection, alignment, translation, and language identification on audio samples. The input audio is broken into 30 s segments, and if necessary, padded before being resampled at a frequency of 16 kHz. A Log-Mel Spectrogram with 80 channels is then computed using a window length of 25 ms and a stride of 10 ms, as outlined in [9].

2.2 Dataset Used to Train Whisper

The dataset created to train the whisper model consists of 680,000 h of audio from which 117,000 h covers other languages, and 125,000 h of the dataset is translation from other languages to English [9]. This results in a diversified dataset, encompassing a wide range of sounds from several different environments, recording setups, speakers, and languages. The huge volume and enormous variety in audio quality certainly helps in the training the model with high performance and robustness.

This study proposes using pre-trained Whisper-Encoder model for the classification of dysarthric severity-levels. Specifically, we hypothesize that the Transformer Encoder module of the pre-trained Whisper model captures all relevant information for this task. To test this hypothesis, we utilized the pre-trained Whisper encoder combined with a CNN acting as a classifier, utilizing the learned representations from the Whisper encoder's last layer, called as Whisper encoder features.

Using a pre-trained model has proven effective in various natural language processing and speech recognition tasks. Leveraging the pre-trained Whisper encoder enables us to benefit from its ability to extract high-level features from audio data. We chose this specific approach as the variability of the dataset used for training makes the model more robust and suitable for our problem. The proposed transfer learning approach allows us to leverage the model's ability to generalize unseen data, which is essential for our task of dysarthric severity-level classification.

2.3 Training Pipeline

The training pipeline of our work is shown in Fig. 1. The speech signal is preprocessed and made ready to be given as input to the Whisper encoder block. Upon this, the input is processed by two convolution layers of kernel size 3×3 [9]. In order to help the Whisper encoder learn the relative positions within the input speech signal, sinusoidal embeddings are applied to it [11]. The processed signal is then directed to the Whisper encoder block, which depending upon the size of Whisper model, gives a vector output of fixed dimensions in its last hidden state. This output, Whisper features, is then taken as input by a CNN, which classifies the speech signal into four classes of dysarthric severity.

For the training process, the weights of the Whisper encoder are kept *frozen*, and only the weights of CNN classifier are updated during backpropagation.

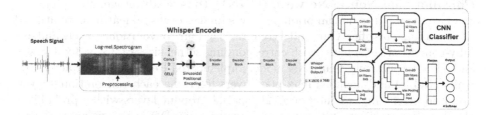

Fig. 1. Functional Block Diagram of Proposed Whisper Encoder Transfer Learning Pipeline in Tandem with CNN Classifier.

3   Experimental Setup

3.1   Datasets Used

This study employs the TORGO dataset, as referenced in [10], to analyze a sample of $1,982$ utterances that fall into three distinct severity-level classes. Of these utterances, 90% were designated for training purposes, with 604 utterances classified as very-low severity-level, 563 as low severity-level, and 616 as high severity-level. The remaining 10% of utterances were reserved for testing (Table 1).

Table 1. Class-wise Patient Details. After [10]

Dysarthric Severity-Level	TORGO
Very Low	F04, M03
Low	F01, M05
Medium	M01, M04

3.2   Details of the Feature Sets Used

In this study, the performance of the whisper encoder-based features is compared with the state-of-the-art MFCC.

3.3   Generating Noisy Data

In this study, we investigate to assess the noise robustness of the Whisper-encoder features proposed in this study, via the introduction of two types of noise: stationary Additive White Gaussian noise (AWGN), and non-stationary babble noise. We also evaluate the performance of these features relative to MFCCs. A thorough evaluation is ensured through the inclusion of both station-ary and non-stationary noise sources. Furthermore, the impact of noise power on the proposed approach is analyzed by considering different SNR levels of -5 dB, 0 dB, 5 dB, and 10 dB for both types of noise.

Convolutional Neural Network (CNN). To take advantage of its ability to emulate the way the human brain perceives images or visual features, we utilized a CNN as our classifier. Our model comprised of four convolutional layers and one fully-connected (FC) layer, with corresponding kernel sizes of 3×3, 3×3, 5×5, and 5×5, respectively. Our CNN model implemented Rectified Linear activation Units (ReLU) and included max-pool layers following each convolutional layer. To avoid overfitting, we integrated 2D spatial dropout layers with a probability of 0.225 after each convolution layer. We trained our CNN model using stochastic gradient descent optimizer, over 100 epochs. During training, we esimated the loss using a categorical cross-entropy function with a learning rate of 0.01 for the first 20 epochs, which was subsequently reduced to 0.003.

3.4   Performance Evaluation

To evaluate the performance of our model, we utilized several widely accepted metrics, including the F1-Score, Jaccard's Index, which measures the similarity and dissimilarity of two classes, Mathew's Correlation Coefficient (MCC), which indicates the degree of association between the expected and the actual class, and Hamming Loss, which is estimated based on the number of samples that are inaccurately predicted.

4   Experimental Results

This Section presents the analysis of experimental results obtained in the study.

4.1   Effect of Whisper Model Size

In this study, we have evaluated the performance of two different Whisper model features, namely, the *tiny* and *base* models. The pre-trained Whisper model has multiple models with increasing layers and parameters, namely, tiny, base, small, medium, and large. The tiny model has the smallest number of layers and parameters, while the base model is relatively larger and more complex.

We have compared the performance of Whisper features extracted from tiny and base models. It can be observed from Fig. 2 that Base Whisper model gives relatively better results than its Tiny counterpart.

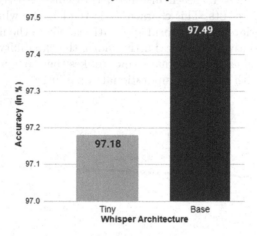

Fig. 2. Effect of Whisper Model Size.

4.2   Effect of Noisy Conditions

In this study, the effect of noise on the proposed Whisper encoder features has been investigated. The experiments were performed on multiple levels of noise using the proposed pipeline. The results obtained indicate that as the power of augmented noise increases, the performance gap between the MFCC and the proposed Whisper encoder features widens, suggesting that the proposed features are more noise-robust than the MFCC feature sets. This finding demonstrate the potential of the proposed approach to provide accurate classification of dysarthric speech under noisy conditions, which is crucial for practical applications. The results are presented and discussed in detail in Fig. 3.

4.3   Analysis of Latency Period

As observed from the results presented in Fig. 4, the performance of the Whisper-Encoder features surpasses that of the state-of-the-art MFCC feature set.

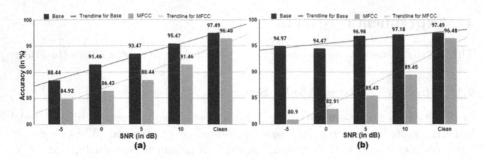

Fig. 3. Performance of CNN classifier on TORGO dataset with different SNR levels of noises, (a) Babble Noise, and (b) AWGN

Notably, even for shorter speech instances, the whisper-based system demonstrates comparable results. This characteristic renders the whisper-encoder features more appropriate for real-world applications, where the input speech duration tends to be relatively shorter. Furthermore, the capability to yield superior results even for smaller speech signal frames makes them particularly well-suited for the machines with limited computational capabilities.

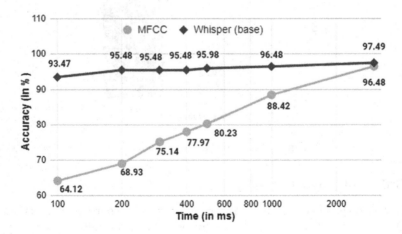

Fig. 4. Analysis of Latency Period.

5   Summary and Conclusions

Overall, this study highlights the potential of utilizing pre-trained models for developing novel feature sets for speech-related problems. The results obtained through this study demonstrate the effectiveness of the proposed Whisper-Encoder features for dysarthric severity-level classification, which has an important clinical applications. Additionally, the analysis of the effect of noise on the proposed feature set showcases its robustness and its practicality for real-world applications under signal degradation conditions. The large and diverse dataset used to train the Whisper model allows it to capture a wide range of speech characteristics and variations, making it more adaptable to different environments and microphone setups. This, in turn, leads to better performance of the Whisper encoder features in noise-robust speech applications, such as dysarthric severity-level classification. Furthermore, the proposed features perform better even for a shorter duration of speech segments, as indicated in the latency period analysis, making them more suitable for practical purposes. Due to limited computational resources, we have not been able to test the performance of larger whisper models. Our future work would be directed toward testing and analysing the performance obtained using larger whisper models.

References

1. Al-Qatab, B.A., Mustafa, M.B.: Classification of dysarthric speech according to the severity of impairment: an analysis of acoustic features. IEEE Access **9**, 18183–18194 (2021)
2. Bhat, C., Strik, H.: Automatic assessment of sentence-level dysarthria intelligibility using BLSTM. IEEE J. Sel. Top. Signal Process. **14**(2), 322–330 (2020)
3. Gupta, S., et al.: Residual neural network precisely quantifies dysarthria severity-level based on short-duration speech segments. Neural Netw. **139**, 105–117 (2021)
4. Iwamoto, Y., Shinozaki, T.: Unsupervised spoken term discovery using wav2vec 2.0. In: 2021 Asia-Pacific Signal and Information Processing Association Annual Summit and Conference (APSIPA ASC), Tokyo, Japan, pp. 1082–1086 (2021)
5. Joshy, A.A., Rajan, R.: Automated dysarthria severity classification using deep learning frameworks. In: 28th European Signal Processing Conference (EUSIPCO), Amsterdam, Netherlands, pp. 116–120 (2021)
6. Kim, M.J., Yoo, J., Kim, H.: Dysarthric speech recognition using dysarthria-severity-dependent and speaker-adaptive models. In: Interspeech, Lyon, France, pp. 3622–3626 (2013)
7. Lieberman, P.: Primate vocalizations and human linguistic ability. J. Acoust. Soc. Am. (JASA) **44**(6), 1574–1584 (1968)
8. Sekhar, S.M., Kashyap, G., Bhansali, A., Singh, K.: Dysarthric-speech detection using transfer learning with convolutional neural networks. ICT Express **8**(1), 61–64 (2022)
9. Radford, A., Kim, J.W., Xu, T., Brockman, G., McLeavey, C., Sutskever, I.: Robust speech recognition via large-scale weak supervision. arXiv preprint arXiv:2212.04356 (2022). Accessed 6 Mar 2023
10. Rudzicz, F., Namasivayam, A.K., Wolff, T.: The TORGO database of acoustic and articulatory speech from speakers with dysarthria. Lang. Resour. Eval. **46**, 523–541 (2012)
11. Vaswani, A., et al.: Attention is all you need. In: Advances in Neural Information Processing Systems (NIPS), Long Beach, USA, vol. 30 (2017)

Multilingual Speech Identification Framework (MSIF) A Novel Approach in Language Identification

Swapnil Sawalkar[1]([✉]) and Pinki Roy[2]

[1] Sipna College of Engineering and Technology Amravati, Amravati, M.S., India
swapnil21_rs@cse.nits.ac.in
[2] National Institute of Technology Silchar, Silchar, Assam, India

Abstract. Multilingual language detection is the process of automatically identifying the language(s) present in a given speech corpus that may contain multiple languages. Several approaches have been proposed for multilingual speech corpus detection, including statistical methods, machine learning algorithms, and deep learning models. These models have difficulty determining specific language, especially when dealing with biased towards certain accents, dialects, or languages, and reduce the accuracy of the model. Hence a novel framework named **"Multilingual Speech Identification Framework (MSIF)"** is developed to solve this problem by data augmentation and increase the accuracy of language identification. There is a limited amount of datasets available for languages except English makes it difficult to train the Indian regional language. So the proposed framework uses a novel Superintendence Neuvised Network, which combines GAN and CNN for data augmentation and transfer learning for feature extraction. The existing multilingual models have been implemented to identify the languages but these models were not able to detect dialect variations because these model does not utilize the attention mechanism. For this reason, the proposed model uses a novel Duel Atenuative memory network, which integrates a Generalized self-attention mechanism with bi-LSTM to understand dialect variations thereby providing better language detection in the Indian regional language.

Keywords: Speech corpus · back translation · transfer learning · attention mechanism · deep learning · multilingual language detection

1 Introduction

The components of the source text are often distinguished by having various degrees of relevance to the job at hand in problems involving the processing of natural language. In aspect-based sentiment analysis, for instance, cue words like "good" or "poor" may be applicable to some aspects but not to others. Certain words in the source text may not apply to the next word while it is being translated by a machine. The goal of the field of "natural language processing" (NLP), a subfield of artificial intelligence (AI), is to create computer systems that can recognize, interpret, and produce human language. NLP is the

P. Maji et al. (Eds.): PReMI 2023, LNCS 14301, pp. 716–723, 2023.
https://doi.org/10.1007/978-3-031-45170-6_75

application of computational tools and algorithms to analyze as well as to process natural language data such as written text, spoken speech, and other kinds of communication. Since the development of machine learning techniques like supervised and unsupervised learning, natural language processing (NLP) has advanced significantly. In order to provide predictions and judgements, machine learning algorithms exploit the patterns they discover in language data. Neural networks are a sort of machine learning algorithm that discovers complicated correlations between data elements by learning from enormous volumes of data. Natural language processing (NLP) has made use of neural networks to enhance speech recognition, machine translation, and language modelling the creation of NLP applications like chatbots and virtual assistants has also benefited from AI. Chatbots employ natural language processing techniques to replicate human communication, allowing them to do activities such as answering inquiries and providing recommendations.

Each of the 7,100 languages spoken around the world has its own set of linguistic principles, and other languages just function differently. The similarities between Italian, French, and Spanish, for instance, are evident, but these three languages are completely distinct from a particular group of Asian languages, namely Chinese, Japanese, and Korean, which share some comparable symbols and ideographs The study and creation of computing models and algorithms that process and comprehend human language in several languages are known as multilingual natural language processing (NLP).

Multilingual NLP models are designed to handle many languages at the same time, Training machine learning algorithms on huge, diverse datasets in different languages using language-specific characteristics, structures to increase accuracy and performance are standard components of these models. The multilingual transformer, which is built on the transformer architecture and trained on substantial volumes of multilingual data, is one common type of multilingual NLP model. Using language-specific models trained on sizable monolingual datasets and then transferring the obtained knowledge to additional languages is another typical strategy for multilingual NLP using deep learning. To train efficiently, deep learning models for multilingual NLP need a lot of data in several languages. The major contributions of this study are determined below:

- Development of a Multilingual Speech Identification Framework (MSIF) for the identification of four Indian languages. viz. Marathi, Gujrati, Konkani and Hindi.
- To obtain highly sensitive feature-level representation for language identification the proposed framework uses the Superintendence Neuvised Network.
- Utilization generalized self-attention mechanism to identify and recognize dialect variations of the language the proposed framework uses Duel Attenuative memory network.

Hence, the advanced technique proposed in this research paper provides an enhancement in multilingual language identification [1–8].

2 Literature Survey

A contemporary method to extract the triplet of fact from the web-document collection was put out by Khairova et al. The essential mathematical building blocks of the logical-linguistic model are logical-algebraic equations with finite predicates algebra.

Deep learning was used by Al-Smadi et al. to introduce transfer learning for Arabic-named entity recognition. The findings show that the Deep Learning method outperforms the previous model for Standard Arabic Named Entity Recognition. The main objective of a new model is to provide better fine-grained outcomes for applications in Natural Language Processing disciplines.

3 Multilingual Speech Identification Framework (MSIF)

Multilingualism is common place in the globalized world of today when content is accessible on many different platforms in a variety of languages. A multilingual framework would be able to identify multiple languages, providing wider coverage for language identification tasks. The existing multilingual model has difficulty in determining the language, like dialects or languages and reduces the accuracy of the model. Hence a novelty named **"Multilingual Speech Identification Framework (MSIF)"** is developed to solve the data augmentation problem which increases the accuracy in the identification of the language. A limited amount of data dataset is available for languages except English such as Gujarati, Marathi, Konkani, and Hindi. To produce high-quality audio waveforms for voice synthesis and other audio production, the suggested model leverages the Superintendence Neuvised Network, which employs Generative Adversarial Networks (GAN). This helps in processing languages with low datasets such as Gujarati, Marathi, Konkani, and Hindi. The Convolutional Neural Network is used for the feature extraction process from the generated data and original data using a process called transfer learning, which takes the weight of the model to adjust the output to solve the problem. In the context of feature extraction for text and speech, transfer learning is used to leverage pre-trained models. Hence the proposed model uses Duel attenuative memory network, which uses a generalized self-attention mechanism, which is integrated with bi-LSTM to detect dialect variations for better language identification. The generalized self-attention mechanism is a powerful technique in natural language processing that is used to detect dialect variations in speech. The input sequence is converted into a collection of vectors in this mechanism and then transmitted via a number of self-attention levels. The proposed framework is able to provide better language detection in the Indian regional language Python is used to implement the suggested innovative framework, greatly enhancing its usability. The suggested framework's architectural diagram is shown in Fig. 1.

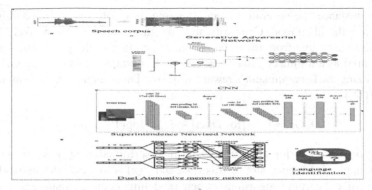

Fig. 1. Multilingual Speech Identification Framework (MSIF)

Figure 1 shows the architectural diagram of the Multilingual Speech Identification Framework (MSIF) for language identification.

3.1 Superintendence Neuvised Network

The speech corpus dataset available for Gujarati, Marathi, Konkani, and Hindi is not efficient to train the model without under fitting the model. The proposed system therefore makes use of generative adversarial networks (GAN). to generate audio data using data augmentation. For creating high-quality audio waveforms, generative adversarial networks (GANs) have demonstrated considerable promise. A discriminator and a generator are the two neural networks that make up a GAN. The discriminator makes the distinction between real and artificial audio waveforms, whereas the generator creates phony audio waveforms (Fig. 2).

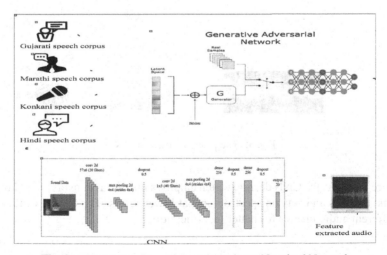

Fig. 2. The process flow of Superintendence Neuvised Network

720 S. Sawalkar and P. Roy

In this instance, the generative model represents the data distribution and is trained to maximize the likelihood. Contrarily, a model that determines how likely it is that the sample it got came from the training data as opposed to the generator. The GANs are structured as a minimax game in which the Generator wants to maximize its loss by minimizing the Discriminator's reward while the Discriminator tries to minimize its reward V(D, G).

$$V(D, G) = E_{p(x)}\left[\log D(x)\right] + E_{p(z)}\left[\log(1 - D(G(Z)))\right] \tag{1}$$

Equation (1): G is for generator, D is for discriminator, p(x) is for actual data distribution, p(z) is for generator distribution, and G(z) is for generator network.

In machine Learning algorithms when modeling complex data sets, especially unstructured data the existing approach run into a computational bottleneck and over-fitting problems. A typical CNN architecture consists of alternating Convolutional and Max Pooling layers, before flattening or global-average pooling into a one-dimensional feature layer and passing into a fully-connected layer to extract features. Transfer learning is the process of picking up new information from an existing or trained model.

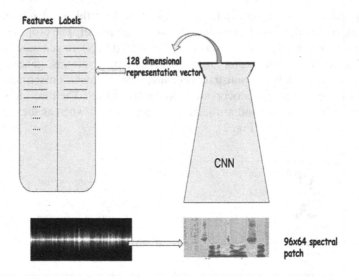

Fig. 3. The process flow of CNN

Figure 3 depicts the CNN design, which employs numerous convolutional layers and fully linked layers and acts on spectrograms at lower levels. The CNN extract features from different audio classes for better identification.

The pre-trained CNN is then used as a feature extractor for the speech corpus by passing each speech signal through the network to obtain a set of feature vectors that represent the speech signal. CNN. Once extracted features for all the data it is sent to the bi-LSTM model for language identification is explained in detail in Sect. 3.2.

3.2 Duel Attenuative Memory Network

The proposed framework makes use of bidirectional long short-term memory from speech corpus to distinguish between the many regional languages spoken in India. The proposed framework combines a convolutional neural network (CNN) and bi-LSTM layers to extract features from the input speech signal and then applies language identification. The bi-directional Long Short-Term Memory (bi-LSTM) is a type of recurrent neural network (RNN) that is used in speech recognition. A bi-LSTM differs from a standard LSTM in that our input travels in two ways when it is bidirectional. Make input flow in only one way, either backwards or forwards, using the standard LSTM. However, in bi-directional, make the input flow in both directions to preserve future and past information. As a result, the voice stream has context-specific characteristics. Modelling sequence context correlations offers considerable benefits for Bi-LSTM.

4   Performance Metrics of the Proposed Multilingual Speech Identification Framework

The performance of the proposed Multilingual Speech Identification Framework for language identification achieved outcomes in terms of accuracy, recall and precision on finite epochs was explained in detail in this section (Fig. 4 and Table 1).

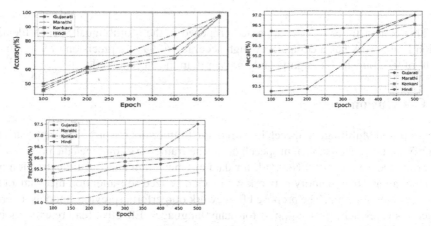

Fig. 4. Performance of Proposed Framework

Table 1. Performance of Proposed Framework

Language/Parameters	Accuracy (At 500 epochs)	Recall (At 500 epochs)	Precision (At 500 epochs)
Gujrati	97%	97%	96%
Marathi	97.2	96%	95.50%
Konkani	96%	96.50%	95.50%
Hindi	96.50%	97%	97.50%
Average	96.75%	96.62%	96.10%

5 Comparison Between Previous Models and Proposed Model

This section highlights the proposed Multilingual Speech Identification Framework for language identification by comparing it to the outcomes of existing approaches such as Visual Geometry Group (VGG-16), and Residual neural networks 50-layer (ResNet50) [9] (Table 2).

Table 2. Comparison between previous model and proposed model

Model/Parameters	Accuracy	Recall	Precision
VGG	96.20%	96.40%	94.30%
ResNet-50	98.20%	96.50%	97%
Proposed Model	99%	97.50%	98%

This demonstrates that the approach proposed in the Multilingual Speech Identification Framework has a comparably high accuracy of 99%, a precision of 97%, and a recall of 97.5%, which is significantly greater than the current model.

6 Conclusion

The proposed Multilingual Speech Identification Framework is a promising approach for identifying languages spoken in speech data. The framework combines the power of the Superintendence Neuvised Network for data augmentation and feature extraction and the Duel attenuative memory network with a Generalized self-attention mechanism for language identification. The proposed framework outperforms previous models in terms of accuracy, resilience, and support for many languages. Effective feature extraction is made possible by the Superintendence Neuvised Network, and the model's capacity to recognize the language of speech is increased by the Duel Atenuative memory network with a generalized self-attention mechanism. The proposed framework Multilingual Speech Identification Framework for language identification attained high accuracy of 99%, a precision of 97%, and a recall of 97.5%.

References

1. Galassi, A., Lippi, M., Torroni, P.: Attention in natural language processing. IEEE Trans. Neural Netw. Learn. Syst. **32**(10), 4291–4308 (2020)
2. Kumar Attar, R., Komal: The emergence of natural language processing (NLP) techniques in healthcare AI. In: Parah, S.A., Rashid, M., Varadarajan, V. (eds.) Artificial Intelligence for Innovative Healthcare Informatics, pp. 285–307. Springer, Cham (2022). https://doi.org/10.1007/978-3-030-96569-3_14
3. Dreisbach, C., Koleck, T.A., Bourne, P.E., Bakken, S.: A systematic review of natural language processing and text mining of symptoms from electronic patient-authored text data. Int. J. Med. Inform. **125**, 37–46 (2019)
4. Tyagi, N., Bhushan, B.: Demystifying the role of natural language processing (NLP) in smart city applications: background, motivation, recent advances, and future research directions. Wirel. Pers. Commun. **130**(2), 857–908 (2023). https://doi.org/10.1007/s11277-023-10312-8
5. Dave, E., Suhartono, D., Arymurthy, A.M.: Enhancing argumentation component classification using contextual language model. J. Big Data **8**, 1–17 (2021)
6. Malte, A., Ratadiya, P.: Multilingual cyber abuse detection using advanced transformer architecture. In: 2019 IEEE Region 10 Conference (TENCON), TENCON 2019, pp. 784–789. IEEE (2019)
7. Al-Smadi, M., Al-Zboon, S., Jararweh, Y., Juola, P.: Transfer learning for Arabic named entity recognition with deep neural networks. IEEE Access **8**, 37736–37745 (2020)
8. Cabot, C., Darmoni, S., Soualmia, L.F.: Cimind: a phonetic-based tool for multilingual named entity recognition in biomedical texts. J. Biomed. Inform. **94**, 103176 (2019)
9. Das, H.S., Roy, P.: A CNN-BiLSTM based hybrid model for Indian language identification. Appl. Acoust. **182**, 108274 (2021)

Spoken Language Identification Using Linear Frequency Residual Cepstral Coefficients

Krishna Parmar[1]([✉])[iD], Baveet Singh Hora[1][iD], Shrey Machhar[1][iD],
Hemant Arjun Patil[1][iD], Kiran Praveen[2][iD], and Balaji Radhakrishnan[2][iD]

[1] Speech Research Lab, Dhirubhai Ambani Institute of Information
and Communication Technology, Gandhinagar, Gujarat, India
{201901155,201901256,201901151,hemant_patil}@daiict.ac.in
[2] Samsung Research Institute, Bengaluru, Karnataka, India
{kiran.praveen.t,balaji.r}@samsung.com

Abstract. This paper aims to identify the spoken language of the person given the utterances using Linear Frequency Residual Cepstral Coefficients (LFRCC). Experiments were performed on statistically meaningful and computationally challenging VoxLingua107 database. For the fair comparison of the efficiency and use-fullness, LFRCC, Mel Frequency Cepstral Coefficients (MFCC) and Linear Frequency Cepstral Coefficients (LFCC) were extracted and considered as features. We have used one classifier, namely, Residual Network (ResNet). With this classifier, we achieved EER of 10.19%, 9.46%, and 9.37% for ResNet on MFCC, LFCC, and LFRCC, respectively. Additionally, we improved overall performance using score-level and feature-level fusion of the said feature sets on the said classifier. This helped us achieve EER of 7.4875% on the score-level fusion of MFCC and LFRCC and 7.01% on the feature-level fusion of LFRCC and MFCC. In this paper, we discuss how linear prediction (LP) residual captures pitch source harmonic information, melodic, and prosody information, which is found to be helpful in Spoken Language Identification (SLID).

Keywords: LP Residual · Residual Network · Pitch Strength · Spoken Language Identification · Score-Level Fusion · Feature-Level Fusion

1 Introduction

Automatic Speech Recognition (ASR) tasks have been getting globally popular and challenging in the past years of development in the industry. Spoken Language Identification (SLID) refers to identifying one's spoken language given the utterances. It is a crucial and fundamental block for developing multiple multilingual speech communication applications, such as Spoken Language Translation, Speech-To-Text Transcription, and Forensic and Security. Identifying the language is getting more challenging and demanding because humans are generating speech data at an enormous rate, and discoveries of several dialects of a language is making current systems fail. As much as dialects affect the identification systems, the accent also contributes a harmful component drastically affecting performance. In the context of India, 22 different languages are currently spoken according to the language included in the eight schedules of the constitution of India [11]. In [9], the researchers have shown increased interest in identifying the Indic languages in the last decade. In recent studies, many researchers have proposed methods for the task using Deep Neural Networks (DNN), Convolutional Neural Networks (CNN) [13], and traditional models, namely, Gaussian Mixture Models (GMM) and Hidden Markov Models (HMM) [12]. These methods use low-level acoustic features, namely, Mel Frequency Cepstral Coefficients, Shifted Delta Cepstrals, Linear Frequency Cepstral Coefficients, or Linear Prediction Cepstral Coefficients (LPCC) [10]. These acoustic features are appended with delta and double-delta cepstrum to model the temporal contexts in the speech signal. These structures enable the models to learn the linguistic structure of the language. These acoustic features have their limitations. As the development of the SLID systems mainly focuses on using Spectral information as they provide the vocaltract information, they are easily affected by noisy environments.

The use of models which provide longer temporal context has increased as vanilla CNN and DNN, as well as HMM and GMM, do not capture global context but are limited to the supplied context in the features. Both GMM and HMM are statistical models in which GMM assumes the probability density of each speech class as a mixture of Gaussians, and HMM assumes that the hidden state is stationary over time. DNN and CNN can learn local information but must be more complex to capture the global context. Our present study uses the Residual Network. ResNets are now adapted to speech processing tasks, although they were introduced for image processing tasks [1]. The works [4,6] are among the many that utilize the ResNet.

The key objective of our paper is to investigate the capability of the Linear Frequency Residual Cepstral Coefficients (LFRCC) for the purposes of SLID. These features were first introduced in [2] and are good at detecting spoofs in audio due to the ability of the feature to capture speaker-specific information [3]. We study how the prosodic information provided by Linear Prediction (LP) residual in LFRCC contributes to the SLID. Further, we also explore how different order of LP affects prosodic features, such as pitch.

The rest of the paper is structured as follows: Sect. 2 presents details of the proposed LFRCC feature set and the effects of different LP orders on the performance of the LFRCC in terms of SLID. Section 3 provides the technical details of the experimental setup and model architectures used. Section 4 represents the results, and finally, Sect. 5 concludes the study and gives directions about future work.

2   Linear Prediction (LP) Residual Analysis

LP is a powerful and widely used technique for analyzing and forecasting the behavior of dynamic systems. In LP, the number of past samples used for predicting the future sample is referred to as the prediction order. Model order and linear prediction filter order are other names for the prediction order. In other words, the linear prediction filter predicts the subsequent sample using p past samples if the prediction order is set to p.

The signal s_n can be predicted from a linearly weighted summation of past samples. Where a_k is Linear Prediction Coefficient [5].

$$\tilde{s}_n = -\sum_{k=1}^{p} a_k s_{n-k}. \tag{1}$$

Then, the error between the actual value s_n and the predicted value $\tilde{s}_n$ is given by [5],

$$e_n = s_n - \tilde{s}_n = s_n + \sum_{k=1}^{p} a_k s_{n-k}, \tag{2}$$

where e_n is known as the LP residual. The LFRCC features described in Sect. 3.2, are designed to capture the spectral envelope of the glottal excitation source, which is well known to be a reliable clue for tasks such as speaker and language recognition [5].

In order to make accurate predictions, the best prediction order must be selected. Poor predictions could result from the model not capturing all the crucial signal features if the prediction order is too low. On the other hand, if the prediction order is set too high, the model might overfit the data, leading to significant generalization loss and high prediction errors.

2.1   LP Order Analysis for SLID

As basic intuition, in terms of SLID, suprasegmental features are used to present the speech, showing the linguistic structure that can uniquely represent the speech. There are numerous acoustic similarities regarding suprasegmental aspects of sentences in different languages [8]. Prosodic information is one of such suprasegmental features, which can help distinguish language-specific and speaker-specific information. Prosody contains pitch, intonations, rhythm (or melody), and duration. The physical representation of the pitch is the fundamental frequency (F_0) originating from the vocal fold vibrations during the speech production mechanism. The main components of intonation are accent, attitude, and grammar. These features are not limited to a particular phone or sound but are extended over syllables, phrases, and words and convey crucial language-specific information. Due to the different speaking styles, these features can also extract speaker-specific information.

We can group languages into three main classes: syllable-time, stress-timed, and mora-timed [8,9]. Stress-timed languages, such as English, maintain a rhythm, and syllables have different lengths. For syllable-timed languages, such as Hindi, Tamil, and Bengali, syllables are said to be near-equal length. The language structure mainly depends on the prosodic information derived from the excitation source. Additionally, these features are not affected by channel variations and noise. The LP residual helps us gain prosodic information. Hence, we have used the LP residual followed by parameterization by the linearly spaced filterbank.

To find the optimal LP order in our task, we extracted Linear Frequency Residual Cepstral Coefficients (LFRCC) described in Sect. 3.2 for different LP orders. These different LP order LFRCC features were trained over the ResNet model described in Sect. 3.3 over classes described in Sect. 3.1. As can be observed from Fig. 1, the highest accuracy has been achieved at LP order 16. Hence, all the experiments described in Sect. 3 are reported for LP order (= 16) during LFRCC feature extraction.

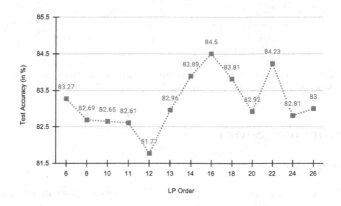

Fig. 1. Test accuracy of different LP orders

2.2 Spectographic Analysis of LP Residual

To further understand the contribution of LP Residual in providing language-specific information, we examine the pitch dynamics for the least accuracy LP order 12 and highest accuracy LP order 16. We calculate the pitch strength using the autocorrelation method to show better how these different LP order residuals w.r.t duration capture changes in the speech signal. We perform this for syllable-timed languages, such as Hindi and stress-timed English to better derive a statement.

From the Fig. 2, it can be observed that the changes in pitch strength of normal speech, LP order 12 residual speech and LP order 16 residual speech for syllable-timed and stress-timed language. We can observe how LP order 16 better preserves the speech structure instead of LP order 12. This preservation of speech structure contributes to the language-specific information as prosodic information is mainly dependent on language [8].

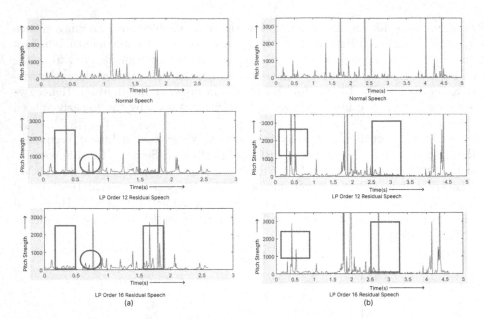

Fig. 2. (a) Pitch Strength for Syllable-timed Language, such as Hindi, (b) Pitch Strength for Stress-timed Language, such as English

3   Experimental Setup

3.1   Corpus Used

The speech corpus we desire should provide speech utterances from real-life instances and having different recording environments, etc. We can find such data in VoxLingua107 [7]. The corpus is designed explicitly for spoken language recognition tasks. The author Valk J *et al.* [7] scraped the audio from random YouTube videos by a similar search prompt for each language and validated the gained data using crowd-sourcing. The resulting database contains 6628 h of speech samples.

We take five classes, namely, English, Hindi, Panjabi, Bengali, and Tamil. First, we divided the speech samples per language class in terms of duration (i.e., speech samples less than 5 s duration, speech samples between 5 s to 10 s duration, speech samples between 10 s to 15 s duration, and speech samples more than 15 s duration). The same number of samples (= 1300) were taken from each duration class. Due to the computational limitations, we limit the number of samples per language to 5200. In the case of the English language, one of the duration classes had less than 1300 samples, resulting in a total sample size of 5132. Our motivation to do this was to have a balanced dataset to avoid any bias. We have used 80% of the samples from the described data for the models' training, 10% for test, and 10% for the validation set.

3.2   Feature Extraction

From the corpus, we extracted the MFCC, LFCC and LFRCC. For all the feature sets, we kept the window size to 30 ms with overlap length to 15ms. We extracted 13 coefficients for each feature set. Each of those was appended with 13 Δ and 13 $\Delta\Delta$ features to give the temporal context. Resulting feature sets (13 Coefficients, 13 Δ, 13 $\Delta\Delta$) were given input to our model described in Sect. 3.3.

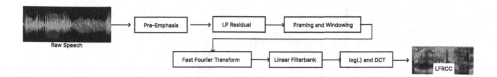

Fig. 3. Functional Block Diagram of Extraction of LFRCC

LFRCC are extracted using LP residual. To emphasize the high-frequency components, the speech signal is passed through a pre-emphasis filter. The pre-emphasized speech signal is processed by the LP analysis block, yielding the LP residual (r(n)) waveform. Furthermore, frame blocking and windowing are applied to the LP residual waveform for a short duration of 30 ms with a frameshift of 15 ms. Following that, the power spectrum for each LP residual frame is computed. This power spectrum is passed through 40 linearly-spaced triangular filterbanks to obtain the filterbank energies. The Discrete Cosine Transform (DCT) is used to compute low-dimensional feature representation in order to decorrelate the feature set. Figure 3 shows the functional block diagram of the proposed method.

3.3   Model Architectures

Residual Network. The main motivation behind using the ResNet architecture in our task is its ability to capture the complex information such as, vocal track information, and language-specific information. With the help of its skip connection, it can mitigate the vanishing gradient problem, and converge the training more rapidly than other deep neural network architectures which allows us to go more deeper. Due to its attribute of skip connections, it can capture both temporal acoustic features and global language information, enabling model to learn discriminatory information among languages. We can also see the adoption of the ResNet in speech processing tasks [4,6].

We utilize 6 residual blocks with an increasing number of channels followed by a fully connected layer and adaptive average pooling. The structure of a single residual block contains two convolutional layers. The structure of the adopted ResNet is similar to ResNet50. The weights are updated using the Adam optimizer during training

4   Experimental Results

It can be observed from Fig. 3, the individual accuracy and EER scores of the feature sets described in Sect. 3.2. Further, LFRCC gives better results than the traditional MFCC features for ResNet. This shows that, information provided by LP residual in LFRCC features, helps in identifying one's spoken language.

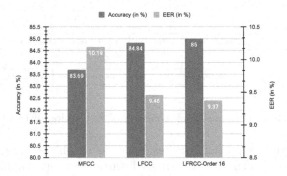

Fig. 4. Individual Feature Accuracy (in %) and EER (in %)Scores

4.1   Results for Score-Level Fusion

We fused the scores of different feature sets, described in Sect. 3.2 while keeping the same model, i.e., ResNet (described in Sect. 3.3). We have used the data fusion Eq. 3, where α is the weight factor. $L_{feature1}$ represents the score of either MFCC, LFCC or LFRCC feature and $L_{feature2}$ represents the score of feature apart from the feature used in $L_{feature1}$.

$$L_{fusion} = \alpha L_{feature1} + (1 - \alpha)L_{feature2}. \tag{3}$$

From score-level fusion, we can get insights about the importance of individual feature and how better they perform when combined with other feature sets. For the score-level fusion, the results can be found in Fig. 4. The scores for different α values for such can be found in Table 1. As it can be observed that for α=0.5, we get the best results for all the combinations. It shows that proposed LFRCC features are compatible in fusion with other feature sets, as well as, increases the overall performance of the system.

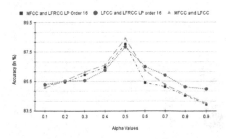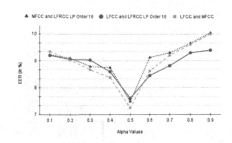

Fig. 5. Results of Score-Level Fusion on ResNet (a) Accuracy (in %), and (b) EER (in %)

Table 1. Score-Level Fusion Scores

For ResNet

α Values	MFCC and LFRCC LP order 16		LFCC and LFRCC LP order 16		MFCC and LFCC	
	Accuracy (in %)	EER (in %)	Accuracy (in %)	EER (in %)	Accuracy (in %)	EER (in %)
0.1	85.25	9.2208	85.29	9.1986	85.06	9.3420
0.2	85.45	9.1003	85.52	9.0524	85.56	9.0287
0.3	85.95	8.7873	85.56	9.0286	86.14	8.6680
0.4	86.45	8.7471	85.25	8.5949	86.60	8.3791
0.5	**88.02**	**7.4875**	**87.83**	**7.6067**	**88.41**	**7.2486**
0.6	85.40	9.1269	86.48	8.4504	86.21	8.6220
0.7	85.13	9.2961	85.91	8.8123	85.28	9.2001
0.8	84.55	9.6569	85.13	9.2944	84.63	9.6090
0.9	83.94	10.0425	84.98	9.3904	84.01	9.9944

4.2 Results for Feature-Level Fusion

As described in Sect. 3.2, we extracted (39, T) features, where 39 is the number of coefficients, and T is the number of timeframes. We now stacked the features in the timeframe domain, and performed classification. Hence, after fusing two-different feature sets, the resulting feature vector will have a size of (78, T), and after fusing three of them together, the resulting vector will have a size of (117, T). Unlike Score-level fusion, in feature-level fusion, we can get insights about how information preserved in these feature sets complement each other and their fusion help in increasing system performance. The results can be found in Fig. 5 for the feature-level fusion. As it can be observed, MFCC and LFRCC LP order 16 outperformed MFCC and LFCC. We can infer from our discussions in Sect. 2, LP residual contains language-specific information (Fig. 6).

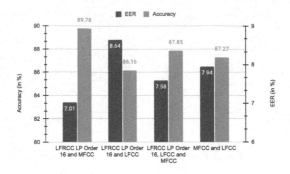

Fig. 6. Feature-Level Fusion using ResNet

5   Summary and Conclusions

Our study scrutinizes the significance, relevancy, and efficiency of the LFRCC feature set for the SLID. The feature set is evaluated on five language classes (described in Sect. 3.2) from VoxLingua107 [7]. The evaluation uses model architecture (described in Sect. 3.3) followed by score-level, and feature-level fusion. From the results presented, we can conclude that LFRCC plays an important role in the task of SLID. As presented, language structure mainly depends on the prosodic information, enabling LFRCC to be useful in SLID as LP residual in the said feature set plays an important part in extracting the prosody information from the utterances. Further, we can also observe how crucial the linear filterbank is instead of the Mel filterbank. One of the limitations of the study is results presented are only on five language classes. Our future research will be directed towards including more language classes.

Acknowledgements. Authors would like to thank the authorities of DA-IICT, Gandhinagar for their resources, support, and cooperation in carrying out this research work. Additionally, the authors would like to extend a vote of thanks to Abhishek Pandey from Samsung Research Institute, Bangalore.

References

1. He, K., Zhang, X., Ren, S., Sun, J.: Deep residual learning for image recognition. In: Proceedings of the IEEE Conference on Computer Vision and Pattern Recognition, pp. 770–778 (2016)
2. Tak, H., Patil, H.A.: Novel linear frequency residual cepstral features for replay attack detection. In: INTERSPEECH 2018, Hyderabad, India, pp. 726–730 (2018)
3. Gupta, P., Patil, H.A.: Linear frequency residual cepstral features for replay spoof detection on ASVSpoof 2019. In: 30th European Signal Processing Conference (EUSIPCO), pp. 349–353 (2022)
4. Tripathi, S., Kumar, A., Ramesh, A., Singh, C., Yenigalla, P.: Focal loss based residual convolutional neural network for speech emotion recognition (2019)
5. Makhoul, J.: Linear prediction: a tutorial review. Proc. IEEE **63**, 561–580 (1975)

6. Vuddagiri, R.K., Vydana, H.K., Vuppala, A.K.: Improved language identification using stacked SDC features and residual neural network. In: SLTU, pp. 210–214 (2018)

7. Valk, J., Alumäe, T.: VoxLingua107: a dataset for spoken language recognition. In: 2021 IEEE Spoken Language Technology Workshop (SLT), pp. 652–658 (2021)

8. Mary, L., Yegnanarayana, B.: Extraction and representation of prosodic features for language and speaker recognition. Speech Commun. **50**(10), 782–796 (2008)

9. Aarti, B., Kopparapu, S.K.: Spoken Indian language identification: a review of features and databases. Sādhanā **43** (2018). Article number: 53. https://doi.org/10.1007/s12046-018-0841-y

10. Deshwal, D., Sangwan, P., Kumar, D.: Feature extraction methods in language identification: a survey. Wireless Pers. Commun. **107**, 2071–2103 (2020). https://doi.org/10.1007/s11277-019-06373-3

11. Indian Constitution: The Constitution of India, Government of India (2021)

12. Jothilakshmi, S., Ramalingam, V., Palanivel, S.: A hierarchical language identification system for Indian languages. Digit. Sig. Process. **22**(3), 544–553 (2012)

13. Arla, L.R., Bonthu, S., Dayal, A.: Multiclass spoken language identification for Indian languages using deep learning. In: 2020 IEEE Bombay Section Signature Conference (IBSSC), Mumbai, India, pp. 42–45 (2020)

Computational Neurology

Multi-modal Multi-class Parkinson Disease Classification Using CNN and Decision Level Fusion

Sushanta Kumar Sahu[✉][iD] and Ananda S. Chowdhury[iD]

Jadavpur University, Kolkata, West Bengal, India
{sksahu.etce.rs,as.chowdhury}@jadavpuruniversity.in

Abstract. Parkinson's disease (PD) is the second most common neurodegenerative disorder, as reported by the World Health Organization (WHO). In this paper, we propose a direct three-Class PD classification using two different modalities, namely, MRI and DTI. The three classes used for classification are PD, Scans Without Evidence of Dopamine Deficit (SWEDD) and Healthy Control (HC). We use white matter (WM) and gray matter (GM) from the MRI and fractional anisotropy (FA) and mean diffusivity (MD) from the DTI to achieve our goal. We train four separate CNNs on the above four types of data. At the decision level, the outputs of the four CNN models are fused with an optimal weighted average fusion technique. We achieve an accuracy of 95.53% for the direct three-class classification of PD, HC and SWEDD on the publicly available PPMI database. Extensive comparisons including a series of ablation studies clearly demonstrate the effectiveness of our proposed solution.

Keywords: Parkinson's disease (PD) · Direct three-Class classification · Multi-modal Data · Decision level fusion

1 Introduction

Parkinson's disease is the second most common neurological disorder that affects movement and can cause tremors, stiffness, and difficulty with coordination [1]. Early diagnosis of PD is important for effective treatment, as there is currently no cure for the disease. However, diagnosis can be challenging due to the variability of symptoms and lack of definitive biomarkers. According to the World Health Organization (WHO), PD affects approximately 1% of people aged 60 years and older worldwide. However there are approximately 10% of clinically diagnosed patients with early stage PD who exhibit normal dopaminergic functional scans. This class, which signifies a medical condition distinct from PD, is known as Scans Without Evidence of Dopamine Deficit (SWEDD) [2,3]. As a result of the evolution of this new class, difficulty of diagnosing PD has increased manifold, leading to a three-class classification problem of PD vs. SWEDD vs. HC with class overlaps [3].

MRI, SPECT and PET are commonly used imaging techniques for PD diagnosis. However, PET and SPECT are not preferred by doctors due to invasiveness and cost [4]. DTI is a newer technique that measures water molecule movement to analyze white

© The Author(s), under exclusive license to Springer Nature Switzerland AG 2023
P. Maji et al. (Eds.): PReMI 2023, LNCS 14301, pp. 737–745, 2023.
https://doi.org/10.1007/978-3-031-45170-6_77

matter microstructure which gets affected in PD. In the literature, quite a few works were reported on PD classification based on machine learning (ML) and deep learning (DL) models applied to neuroimaging data. Salat et al. [5] found correlations between gray or white matter changes and age using Voxel-based Morphometry (VBM). Adeli et al. [1] used a recursive feature elimination approach for two-class classification with 81.9% accuracy. Cigdem et al. [6] proposed a total intracranial volume method with 93.7% accuracy. Singh et al. [2] presented a ML framework for three two-class classifications. Chakraborty et al. [7] presented an DL model with 95.29% accuracy. A DL-based ensemble learning technique was reported by [8] with 97.8% accuracy.

Recent research indicates that combining features from multiple imaging modalities can improve the classification accuracy. For example, Li et al. [9] show that combining DTI and MRI features improves classification accuracy in Alzheimer's disease. In light of the above findings, we anticipate that MRI and DTI can be effectively combined to better analyze PD. To improve decision accuracy, various decision-level fusion techniques are considered. Majority voting technique is the most common techniques used in late fusion [10]. This strategy, however, may not be appropriate for multi-class classification applications. Instead of using a majority voting strategy, a modified scheme called modulated rank averaging is employed in [11]. We feel the accuracy may be enhanced even further by fine-tuning the weights computed in the modulated rank averaging approach.

As a summary, we can say that there is a clear dearth of direct three-class PD classification strategies and that too with multi-modal data. In this paper, we present a direct three-class PD classification using CNNs and decision level fusion. We investigate full potential of multimodal data *i.e.,* FA & MD from DTI and WM & GM from MRI. We use four CNNs to analyze these four types of data. Outputs from all these four models are finally fused using an Optimal Weighted Average Fusion (OWAF) technique at the decision level. Since neuroimaging datasets are small, data augmentation is adopted to ensure proper training with the CNNs [11]. We now summarize our contributions as below:

1. We address a direct three-class classification task (PD, HC and SWEDD) for Parkinson's disease, which is certainly more challenging than the current trend of a single binary classification (for 2-class problem) or multiple binary classifications (for 3-class problem).
2. We make effective use of the underlying potential of multi-modal neuroimaging, namely T1-weighted MRI and DTI. In particular, we train four different CNNs on WM, GM data from MRI and FA, MD data from DTI. Such in-depth analysis of multi-modal neuroimaging data is largely missing in the analysis of PD.
3. Finally, at the decision level, the outputs of each CNN model are fused using an Optimal Weighted Average Fusion (OWAF) strategy to achieve state-of-the-art classification accuracy.

2 Proposed Method

Our solution pipeline for an end-to-end direct three-class classification of PD from DTI and MRI consists of four CNN networks. Each CNN network yields a 3×1 probability vector, which represents the probability that the data falls into one of three classes, *i.e.*, PD, HC or SWEDD. The probability vectors are then combined using the OWAF technique. In Sect. 2.1, we discuss how WM and GM are obtained from MRI data and MD and FA are used from DTI data. Section 2.2 presents the proposed CNN architecture. In Sect. 2.3, we discuss the decision level fusion. Figure 1 illustrates the overall pipeline of our solution.

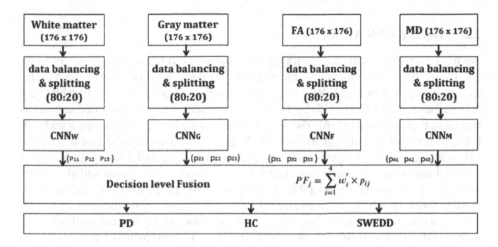

Fig. 1. Direct three-class Parkinson's disease classification framework

2.1 Data Pre-processing and Balancing

In this work, voxel-based morphometry (VBM) is used to prepare MRI data. The data is preprocessed using SPM-12 tools and images are normalized using the diffeomorphic anatomical registration with exponentiated lie algebra (DARTEL) method [12]. This SPM-12 tool segments the whole MRI data into GM, WM and cerebrospinal fluid, as well as the anatomical normalization of all images to the same stereotactic space employing linear affine translation, non-linear warping, smoothing and statistical analysis. After registration, GM and WM volumetric images were obtained and the unmodulated image is defined as the density map of grey matter (GMD) and white matter (WMD). The PPMI database contains all information regarding DTI indices, including FA and MD. Brain scans from PD groups as well as HC have distinct voxel MD values. MD and FA can be expressed mathematically expressed as [13]:

$$MD = \frac{\lambda_1 + \lambda_2 + \lambda_3}{3} = \frac{D_{xx} + D_{yy} + D_{zz}}{3} \tag{1}$$

$$FA = \sqrt{\frac{1}{2}} \sqrt{\frac{(\lambda_1 - \lambda_2)^2 + (\lambda_2 - \lambda_3)^2 + (\lambda_3 - \lambda_1)^2}{\lambda_1^2 + \lambda_2^2 + \lambda_3^2}} \tag{2}$$

In Eq. 1 the diagonal terms of the diffusion tensor are D_{xx}, D_{yy} and D_{zz} and the sum of these diagonal terms constitutes its trace. After prepossessing, four types of data are made available, namely, grey matter (GM), white matter (WM), fractional anisotropy (FA) and mean diffusivity (MD). We find each of GM, WM, FA, MD to be highly imbalanced across the three classes. Further, the number of training samples required to feed a DL model is insufficient. So, ADASYN, an oversampling method is used to increase the number of samples for each minority class [14]. The primary idea behind the use of an ADASYN technique is to compute the weighted distribution of minority samples based on a wide range of out-of-elegance neighbors.

2.2   Proposed CNN Architecture

We use four CNN models, each with ten convolutional layers and four dense (FC) layers, for the direct three-class classification task of PD. The proposed network's architecture is depicted in Fig. 2. We chose fewer parameters in the proposed architecture than in the original VGG16 [15] by decreasing network depth. Our proposed network is similar to that proposed in [16]. The number of layers are limited to maintain a trade-off between accuracy and computational cost. To generate feature representations of brain MR scans, convolution layers are used. The final FC layer and a soft max operation are used for the classification task. The volumetric input data is processed slice-wise, with each slice having a size of 176×176 pixels. We have used max-pooling in the pooling layers to reduce the image size. The flattened layers convert the reduced feature maps to a one-dimensional feature map. The fully connected layers classify this feature map into three classes: HC, PD and SWEDD. The cross-entropy loss function (CELF) is the most common loss function used for classification problems since it has better convergence speeds for training deep CNNs than MSE and hinge loss. As a result, we consider CELF for this work, which is mathematically expressed as:

$$L_{CELF} = - \sum_{k=1}^{K} p\left(y_k|\mathbf{x}\right) \log \widehat{p}\left(y_k|\mathbf{x}\right) \qquad (3)$$

where $p(y_k|\mathbf{x})$ is the original class label distribution and $\widehat{p}(y_k|\mathbf{x})$ is the predicted label distribution from the CNN network. Here K represent number of classes, and for our problem $K = 3$.

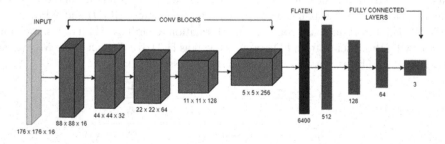

Fig. 2. Architecture of the proposed CNN

2.3 Decision Level Fusion of CNN Networks

We use four CNN models, one each for GM, WM, FA and MD. We fuse these predicted probabilities with the help of suitable weights. The weights are generated in two stages. In the first stage, the weights are generated using the modulated rank averaging (MRA) method [11]. The weights in the MRA method are given by:

$$w_i = \frac{f_i}{\sum_{i=1}^{N-1} f_i + R_{max}} \tag{4}$$

In Eq. 4, f_i and R_{max} indicate the normalizing factor and the rank of the model having highest accuracy respectively. The normalizing factor is calculated based on the rank of the current model and the difference between the accuracy of the current and next model. In the second stage, these weights are optimised using the grid search method [17]. Let the final optimized weights be denoted by w_i'. Note that this weight vector is fixed for all 3 classes. We combine this optimal weight vector with the respective probability vectors to obtain the overall probability of occurrence of respective classes. Let us denote by PF_j; $j = 1, 2, 3$, the overall probability of occurrence of the jth class as a result of fusion.

$$PF_j = \sum_{i=1}^{4} w_i' \times p_{ij} \tag{5}$$

The final class will be the one for which PF_j is maximum.

3 Experimental Results

In this section, we present the experimental results for three-class PD classification. The section is divided into three subsections. The first subsection provides an overview of the PPMI database. In addition, it also describes data preparation, System configuration, parameter settings, and evaluation metrics. The second subsection demonstrates ablation studies on the impacts of MRI and DTI data and the proposed fusion strategy. Finally, we include comparisons with ten state-of-the-art methods to showcase the effectiveness of our proposed solution.

Table 1. Demographics of the subjects

	Healthy Control	Parkinson's Disease	SWEDD
Number of subjects	67	177	37
Sex (Female/Male)	24/43	65/122	14/23
Age*	60.12 ± 10.71	61.24 ± 9.47	59.97 ± 10.71

*mean ± standard deviation

3.1 Data Preparation and Implementation Details

For our study, we included 281 subjects with baseline visits having both DTI and MRI data from the PPMI database. This consisted of 67 HC, 177 PD, and 37 SWEDD subjects. Table 1 shows the demographics of the individuals used in this investigation. The system used for experiments had 16.0 GB DDR4 RAM, an Intel® Core™ i7-10750H CPU @ 2.60 GHz, and an NVIDIA GeForce RTX 3060 GPU @ 6 GB. The data is divided randomly into an 80% training set and a 20% test set. Four CNN models were trained for 100 epochs on GM, WM, FA, and MD data. ADAM optimizer and ReLU activation functions are employed. The learning rate is initialized at 1×10^{-4} with a batch size of 32. The same training parameters were used for each model to facilitate fusion at the decision level. We evaluate the classification performance using four different metrics. These are accuracy, precision, recall and F1 score. All the measures are calculated using the Scikit Learn packages [18].

Table 2. Impact of DTI and MRI data on direct 3-class classification

Data	Accuracy in (%)	Precision in (%)	Recall in (%)	F1 Score in (%)
MRI (WM)	88.6	86.57	82.50	88.94
MRI (GM)	84.2	81.76	82.50	84.80
DTI (MD)	88.2	88.85	89.50	88.11
DTI(FA)	80.94	80.35	81.00	81.59
WM and GM (MRI)	90.02	90.17	90.02	90.09
FA and MD (DTI)	91.14	91.23	91.14	91.18
WM, GM, FA, MD (MRI + DTI) using OWAF	**95.53**	**93.64**	**91.99**	**92.74**

Table 3. Impact of fusion strategies on direct 3-class classification

Fusion Technique	Accuracy in (%)	Precision in (%)	Recall in (%)	F1 Score in (%)
Majority Voting	92.19	92.5	**94.87**	92.34
Model Average Fusion	88.6	82.5	86.57	85.44
Modulated Rank Average	94.6	91.5	93.92	**93.02**
OWAF (proposed)	**95.53**	**93.64**	91.99	92.74

3.2 Ablation Studies

We conduct two ablation studies. The first study demonstrates the utility of using both MRI and DTI data, while the second study conveys the benefits of the proposed fusion strategy, OWAF. The results of the direct three-class classification are presented in Table 2. The results clearly show that combining both DTI and MRI data leads to superior results compared to using them in isolation. Notably, incorporating multi-modal data significantly improves the performance, particularly for the challenging three-class classification problem.

The four CNNs are combined using different fusion strategies at the decision level: majority voting, model average fusion, modulated rank averaging [11], and our proposed optimal weighted average fusion (OWAF) based on a grid search approach. Majority voting selects the class with the majority of votes, while the model average fusion method multiplies the output probabilities of each model by the weight assigned based on its accuracy. The modulated rank averaging method updates the output probabilities using a weight calculated from the rank and the difference in probabilities between the models. In this work, we initially obtain weights using the modulated rank averaging method and further optimize them through a grid search. These optimized weights are employed in our OWAF technique. Table 3 presents the effects of the various fusion strategies, considering both MRI and DTI data in all cases for a fair comparison. The experimental results clearly demonstrate that our proposed OWAF outperforms other fusion strategies in terms of classification accuracy. Table 3 presents the effects of the various fusion strategies. For fare comparison, we consider both MRI and DTI data in all cases. The experimental results in Table 3 clearly demonstrate that our proposed OWAF outperforms other fusion strategies.

Table 4. Comparisons of the proposed method with State-of-the-art Approaches

Approach	ML/DL	MODALITY	PD vs HC			PD vs. SWEDD	HC vs. SWEDD	PD vs. HC vs SWEDD
			Ac	Pr	Re	Ac	Ac	Ac
Adeli 2016 [1]	ML	MRI	81.9	-	-	-	-	-
Cigdem 2018 [6]	ML	MRI	93.7	-	95	-	-	-
Prashanth 2018 [19]	ML	SPECT	95	-	96.7	-	-	-
Singh 2018 [2]	ML	MRI	95.37	-	-	96.04	93.03	-
Gabriel 2021 [20]	ML	MRI	99.01(M) 87.10(F) 93.05 (A)	100(M) 97.2(F) -	99.3(M) 100(F) -	-	-	-
Li 2019 [21]	DL (AE)	MRI + DTI	85.24	95.8	68.1	-	89.67	-
Tremblay 2020 [22]	DL	MRI	88.3	88.2	88.4	-	-	-
Chakraborty 2020 [7]	DL	MRI	95.3	92.7	91.4	-	-	-
Sivaranjini 2020 [23]	DL	MRI	88.9	-	89.3	-	-	-
Rajanbabu 2022 [8]	DL (EL)	MRI	97.5	97.9	97.1	-	-	-
Proposed method	DL	MRI + DTI	97.8	97.2	97.6	94.5	95.7	95.53 Pr: 93.64 Re: 91.99

Ac, Pr, Re, M, F, A, AE, EL, - Indicates Accuracy, Precision, Recall, Male, Female, Average, Auto Encoder, Ensemble Learning & *data* not available respectively. All the values are in %.

3.3   Comparisons with State-of-the-Art Approaches

We compare our method with ten state-of-the-art approaches. There are no results available for a direct 3-class PD classification. So, we compare our results with those papers that have addressed the PD classification on the PPMI database using single or multiple modalities and with three or fewer two-class classifications. The results of comparisons are shown in Table 4. Out of the ten methods we have considered, five are based on machine learning (ML) and the rest five are based on deep learning (DL). Further, in four out of five DL based approaches, only a single modality, namely, MRI is used for classification. Also note that eight of these ten techniques have only addressed a single two-class classification problem between PD and HC and did not consider the challenging SWEDD class at all. The remaining two approaches did consider SWEDD as a third class but have divided the three-class classification problem into multiple binary classes [2,21]. However, Li at al. [21] did not report the classification results for PD vs. SWEDD in their paper. In order to have fair comparisons, we have also included three binary classifications as obtained from our method in this table. Our direct three-class classification accuracy turns out to be superior than two-class classification accuracy of at least eight out of 10 methods. It is also higher than two out of three binary classification accuracy of [2]. Note that in [2], the authors used a somewhat different experimental protocol by considering two publicly available databases of ADNI and PPMI. In our work, we explicitly consider data with both MRI and DTI for the same individual as available solely in the PPMI database. Though the authors in [20] reported superior classification accuracy for male, the accuracy is much less for female and also for the average case (both male and female taken into account). Only, [8] has reported a higher classification accuracy than ours. But, they have considered only a single binary class classification of PD vs HC and ignored the more challenging SWEDD class. If we consider the binary classification results of our method, then we straightway outperform nine of the ten state-of-the-art competitors and even beat the remaining method [2] in two out of three classifications.

4   Conclusion

In this paper, we present an automated solution for the direct three-class classification of Parkinson's disease (PD) using both MRI and DTI data. Initially, we utilize four different CNNs to obtain direct three-class classification from WM, GM, MD, and FA data. Subsequently, an optimal weighted average decision fusion method is applied to integrate the individual classification outcomes. The achieved overall three-class classification accuracy is 95.53%. Extensive comparisons, including a number of ablation studies on the publicly available PPMI database, clearly establish the efficacy of our proposed formulation.

In the future, our plan is to deploy our model in clinical practice using data from other modalities such as gait, handwriting, and speech. Additionally, we intend to investigate the role of the attention mechanism on the classification performance.

References

1. Adeli, E., et al.: Joint feature-sample selection and robust diagnosis of Parkinson's disease from MRI data. Neuroimage **141**, 206–219 (2016)
2. Singh, G., Samavedham, L., Lim, E.C.-H.: Determination of imaging biomarkers to decipher disease trajectories and differential diagnosis of neurodegenerative diseases (disease trend). J. Neurosci. Methods **305**, 105–116 (2018)
3. Kim, M., Park, H.: Using tractography to distinguish SWEDD from Parkinson's disease patients based on connectivity. Parkinson's Disease **2016**, Article no. 8704910 (2016)

4. Long, D., et al.: Automatic classification of early Parkinson's disease with multi-modal MR imaging. PLoS ONE **7**, e47714 (2012)
5. Salat, D.H., Lee, S.Y., Van der Kouwe, A., Greve, D.N., Fischl, B., Rosas, H.D.: Age-associated alterations in cortical gray and white matter signal intensity and gray to white matter contrast. Neuroimage **48**(1), 21–28 (2009)
6. Cigdem, O., Beheshti, I., Demirel, H.: Effects of different covariates and contrasts on classification of Parkinson's disease using structural MRI. Comput. Biol. Med. **99**, 173–181 (2018)
7. Chakraborty, S., Aich, S., Kim, H.-C.: Detection of Parkinson's disease from 3T T1 weighted MRI scans using 3D convolutional neural network. Diagnostics **10**(6), 402 (2020)
8. Rajanbabu, K., Veetil, I.K., Sowmya, V., Gopalakrishnan, E.A., Soman, K.P.: Ensemble of deep transfer learning models for Parkinson's disease classification. In: Reddy, V.S., Prasad, V.K., Wang, J., Reddy, K.T.V. (eds.) Soft Computing and Signal Processing. AISC, vol. 1340, pp. 135–143. Springer, Singapore (2022). https://doi.org/10.1007/978-981-16-1249-7_14
9. Li, M., Qin, Y., Gao, F., Zhu, W., He, X.: Discriminative analysis of multivariate features from structural MRI and diffusion tensor images. Magn. Reson. Imaging **32**(8), 1043–1051 (2014)
10. Daskalakis, A., Glotsos, D., Kostopoulos, S., Cavouras, D., Nikiforidis, G.: A comparative study of individual and ensemble majority vote CDNA microarray image segmentation schemes, originating from a spot-adjustable based restoration framework. Comput. Methods Programs Biomed. **95**(1), 72–88 (2009)
11. De, A., Chowdhury, A.S.: DTI based Alzheimer's disease classification with rank modulated fusion of CNNs and random forest. Expert Syst. Appl. **169**, 114338 (2021)
12. Ashburner, J.: A fast diffeomorphic image registration algorithm. Neuroimage **38**(1), 95–113 (2007)
13. Alexander, A.L., Lee, J.E., Lazar, M., Field, A.S.: Diffusion tensor imaging of the brain. Neurotherapeutics **4**(3), 316–329 (2007)
14. Pristyanto, Y., Nugraha, A.F., Dahlan, A., Wirasakti, L.A., Ahmad Zein, A., Pratama, I.: Multiclass imbalanced handling using ADASYN oversampling and stacking algorithm. In: 2022 16th International Conference on Ubiquitous Information Management and Communication (IMCOM), pp. 1–5 (2022)
15. Simonyan, K., Zisserman, A.: Very deep convolutional networks for large-scale image recognition. arXiv preprint arXiv:1409.1556
16. Wang, S.-H., Zhou, Q., Yang, M., Zhang, Y.-D.: ADVIAN: Alzheimer's disease VGG-inspired attention network based on convolutional block attention module and multiple way data augmentation. Front. Aging Neurosci. **13**, 687456 (2021)
17. Fayed, H.A., Atiya, A.F.: Speed up grid-search for parameter selection of support vector machines. Appl. Soft Comput. **80**, 202–210 (2019)
18. Pedregosa, F., et al.: Scikit-learn: machine learning in Python. J. Mach. Learn. Res. **12**, 2825–2830 (2011)
19. Prashanth, R., Roy, S.D.: Early detection of Parkinson's disease through patient questionnaire and predictive modelling. Int. J. Med. Inform. **119**, 75–87 (2018)
20. Solana-Lavalle, G., Rosas-Romero, R.: Classification of PPMI MRI scans with voxel-based morphometry and machine learning to assist in the diagnosis of Parkinson's disease. Comput. Methods Programs Biomed. **198**, 105793 (2021)
21. Li, S., Lei, H., Zhou, F., Gardezi, J., Lei, B.: Longitudinal and multi-modal data learning for Parkinson's disease diagnosis via stacked sparse auto-encoder. In: IEEE 16th International Symposium on Biomedical Imaging (ISBI 2019), pp. 384–387. IEEE (2019)
22. Tremblay, C., Mei, J., Frasnelli, J.: Olfactory bulb surroundings can help to distinguish Parkinson's disease from non-parkinsonian olfactory dysfunction. NeuroImage: Clin. **28**, 102457 (2020)
23. Sivaranjini, S., Sujatha, C.: Deep learning based diagnosis of Parkinson's disease using convolutional neural network. Multimed. Tools Appl. **79**(21), 15467–15479 (2020)

Mental Workload Classification with One-Dimensional CNN Using fNIRS Signal

Ashish Kumar, Subashis Karmakar$^{(\boxtimes)}$, Isha Agarwal, and Tandra Pal

Department of Computer Science and Engineering, National Institute of Technology Durgapur, Durgapur, West Bengal, India
ashishkumaras789@gmail.com, sk.21cs1108@phd.nitdgp.ac.in

Abstract. As one of the promising technology, Brain-Computer Interface assists people by exploring various aspects of brain functionality. Analyzing and decoding brain signals to classify mental workload can help in the diagnosis and treatment of various neurodegenerative diseases and neurological disorders like learning disability. In this pursuit, functional near-infrared spectroscopy has emerged as a promising non-invasive technique that uses blood flow patterns to analyze brain signals. In this study open-access functional near-infrared spectroscopy datasets are used for mental workload classification. We have considered it as a two class problem and proposed a one-dimensional convolutional neural network to distinguish between mental task and rest, and compared the performance with two other machine learning methods, support vector machine and deep neural network. The proposed one-dimensional convolutional neural network model eliminates the requirement for complex brain image processing providing a computationally efficient alternative and comparable accuracy.

Keywords: Brain-computer interface (BCI) · fNIRS · Cognitive Load · Mental Task · Convolutional Neural Network (CNN)

1 Introduction

Mental workload pertains to the cognitive demands of a specific task or activity, and it can significantly impact an individual's mental performance, cognitive function, and overall health. Precise mental workload evaluation enhances productivity, safety, comfort, decision-making, and learning outcomes by providing a better understanding and control over cognitive demands. [11]. Neural measures like functional magnetic resonance imaging (fMRI), electroencephalography (EEG) and functional near-infrared spectroscopy (fNIRS) can be used to measure brain activity to infer mental workload. fNIRS measures the concentration of oxygenated haemoglobin (HbO) and deoxygenated haemoglobin (HbR) in the brain by emitting near-infrared light through the scalp and measuring

This work is supported by Ministry of Electronics & Information Technology, Government of India (Sanctioned number: 4(16)/2019-ITEA).

the changes in light absorption. fNIRS offers several benefits compared to other physiological techniques. Firstly, it is a non-invasive method, which means it does not require any invasive procedures. Secondly, it provides better temporal resolution than fMRI and greater spatial resolution than EEG. Additionally, its portability, lightweight design, and simple data acquisition and processing make it a convenient option to measure brain activity during cognitive tasks and is effective in classifying mental workload [4].

Machine learning approaches and fNIRS have been employed in recent studies on mental computation to evaluate cognitive functioning to distinguish between different cognitive states of the brain. In-depth feature engineering and dimensionality reduction are two of the challenging aspects of conventional machine learning classification methods. Feature engineering techniques, such as feature selection, extraction, combinations, and dimensionality reduction, often lead to overfitting and bias in results. Machine learning approaches are computationally intensive and difficult to enhance overall outcomes because of the data preprocessing. The necessity for manual feature engineering has been eliminated by deep learning approaches, providing an alternative to overcome this issue.

Deep learning approaches have exhibited encouraging outcomes in the field of mental workload classification, providing a solution to the challenges posed by traditional machine learning algorithms. Previous studies have demonstrated the effectiveness of deep learning models in classifying mental workload levels based on fNIRS data. Zhang et al. [2] used a convolution neural network (CNN) to classify three levels of mental workload and achieved a classification accuracy of 91%. Mughal et al. [3] proposed a deep learning method by considering both long short-term memory (LSTM) and CNN for classifying multi-class mental workload and achieved a classification accuracy of 85.9%. These studies demonstrate the potential of deep learning approaches for accurately classifying the levels of mental workload using fNIRS data without the need for extensive feature engineering or dimensionality reduction.

In this study, we have proposed a one-dimensional (1D) CNN to classify mental workload using fNIRS data. 1D CNN is used to analyze the temporal dynamics of brain activity by learning features from the time series fNIRS data based on which it classifies the mental workload. To show the performance of the proposed model, it is compared with a support vector machine (SVM) that uses kernel as radial basis function (RBF) and deep neural network (DNN).

The remaining paper is structured as follows. The datasets description is provided in Sect. 2. The proposed methodology is illustrated in Sect. 3. The results and discussion on the performance of the proposed model are provided in Sect. 4. Thereafter, the work is concluded in Sect. 5.

2   Datasets

The two open-access datasets that are available in [9] and [10], are used in this work and, respectively, denoted them as Dataset A and Dataset B.

Dataset A [9]: This dataset consists of two tasks: mental arithmetic (MA) and baseline (BL). In this experiment, twenty nine subjects (15 females and 14 males)

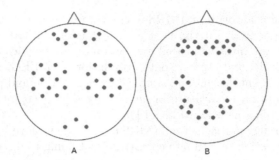

Fig. 1. The Placement of fNIRS channels. (A) Placement of fNIRS channels (red dots) for Dataset A. (B) Placement of fNIRS channels (red dots) for Dataset B. (Color figure online)

of an average age of 28.5 ± 3.7 (mean ± standard deviation) have participated. During the experiment, the data was collected by placing 36 fNIRS channels on the subjects' scalp. At 12.5 Hz of sampling rate, the fNIRS data was collected. In [9], three datasets are considered, but we have used only the MA vs BL dataset, relevant to our work. For MA, a subtraction problem was presented on the screen and the subjects were requested to remember the numbers. The subjects were requested to repeatedly perform the subtraction mentally during the task period while a black crosshair was presented on the screen during the rest period. When a black crosshair was shown on the screen, the subjects were asked to take rest to maintain a low cognitive load. Each session consisted of 1 min of pre-trial rest, 20 iterations of the task, and a post-trial rest period of 1 min. Task sessions began with a 2 s visual cue, succeeded by a 10 s task session and randomly assigned rest periods of 15–17 seconds. The BL task pertains to the resting period (Figs. 1 and 2).

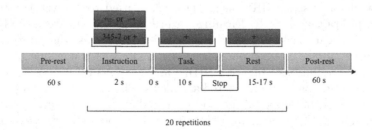

Fig. 2. The timing sequence diagram of the experimental setup for Dataset A.

Dataset B [10]: This dataset consists of two tasks: word generation (WG) and rest (BL). In this experiment, twenty-six subjects (17 females and 9 males) of an average age of 26.1 ± 3.5 (mean ± standard deviation) have participated. During the experiment, the data was collected by placing 36 fNIRS channels on

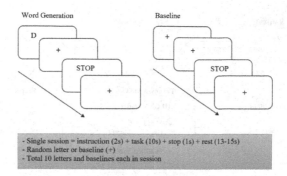

Fig. 3. The timing sequence diagram of the experimental setup for Dataset B.

the subjects' scalp. At 10.4 Hz of sampling rate, the fNIRS data was collected. In [10], three datasets are considered, but we have used only the dataset for WG vs rest as it is relevant to our study. The dataset includes three sessions per participant, with each session containing 10 trials of WG and BL. During the WG task, participants were asked to generate words starting with the letter presented on the screen, while avoiding repetition of any previously stated word. The trials were randomly arranged and spaced out over time. Each trial consists of a 2 s instruction period where a single letter was presented for the WG task or a cross treatment for the BL task, a task duration of 10 s and a rest of 13–15 second in which the crosshair was displayed. For BL, which pertains to the resting period, the subjects were instructed to relax to maintain a low cognitive load. In total, there were 60 trials (30 WG trials and 30 BL trials) (Fig. 3).

3 Proposed Methodology

This section consists of two subsections namely signal preprocessing which discusses the preprocessing steps applied to the fNIRS signal. The next subsection describes the proposed 1D CNN model. We have compared the proposed model with an SVM model ($C = 1.5$, where C is the regularization parameter) having RBF kernel and a DNN model. The DNN model, developed by us, has five fully connected (FC) layers respectively with 256, 128, 64, 32 and 16 neurons and a dropout layer (dropout rate $= 0.3$) between the second and third FC layers to prevent overfitting. Each FC layer utilizes the ReLU activation, while the output layer employs a sigmoid activation function with a single neuron for binary classification of mental workload, i.e., mental task or rest.

3.1 Signal Preprocessing

The measurement of cognitive load using the analysis of hemodynamic response can be carried out in a non-invasive manner through fNIRS. It operates based on the blood-oxygen-level dependent (BOLD) response. This neuroimaging method

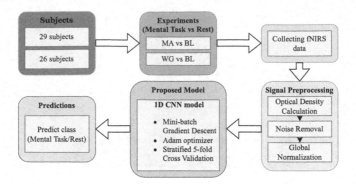

Fig. 4. The diagrammatic representation of the proposed methodology.

depends upon the principle that the brain tissues absorb light having wavelength lying in the near-infrared region of the spectrum and scatter the rest. To analyze the fNIRS data, concentrations of HbO and HbR are evaluated from optical intensity observed in the cerebral cortex of the brain.

The Modified Beer-Lambert law (MBLL) [1] as reported below in (1) is used to compute optical density from optical intensity data.

$$A = log_{10}\left(\frac{I_{inc}}{I_{det}}\right) = (\epsilon \times C \times DPF) + G \tag{1}$$

Here, A, I_{inc} and I_{det} respectively denote the optical density, incident light intensity and detected light intensity, ϵ is the coefficient of molar absorption, C denotes the concentration of the substance in media, DPF and G respectively represent differential path factor (i.e., lost intensity due to scattering). Further, Butterworth filter with sixth-order and zero-phase response and a passband of 0.01 to 0.1 Hz is used to eliminate the noise generated due to eye movement, cardiac (1–1.5 Hz) [6], respiration (0.2–0.5 Hz) and Mayer wave (0.1 Hz). Next, global normalization is performed for uniform scaling of the data (Fig. 4).

3.2 Proposed 1D CNN Model

The 1D CNN model is used to analyze 1D time series data to extract the representative features by performing 1D convolution using multiple kernels. In contrast to two-dimensional (2D) CNN that uses 2D arrays for kernels, 1D CNN utilizes 1D arrays [7] which results in low computational cost as the convolution operations are the linear weighted sum of two 1D arrays.

The proposed model comprises of six convolutional layers, two average pooling layers followed by FC layers. The notations used for different layers of the proposed model are mentioned in Fig. 5. The preprocessed signal data is fed into the first 1D convolutional layer (conv1D-L1) with input size 36×1 (number of channels × number of timesteps) and specifications are mentioned in Fig. 5. The layer uses 'same' type of padding, therefore the output size is the same as that of the input. The output of the conv1D-L1 layer is then passed into Rectified Linear Unit (ReLU), a nonlinear activation function. The 1D convolution operation followed by the ReLU activation is evaluated in (2) as follows.

$$y_k^l = \phi \left(\sum_{i=1}^{N^{l-1}} conv1D(w_{i,k}^l, x_i^{l-1} + b_k^l) \right) \qquad (2)$$

In (2), y_k^l represents the kth feature map in l^{th} layer, $w_{i,k}^l$ represents the trainable convolutional kernel, b_k^l is the bias of the kth feature map in the lth layer, N^{l-1} is the number of feature map in $(l-1)^{th}$ layer and ϕ denotes the ReLU activation function. The activation output of 16 kernels, each of size 36×1 is fed into the second 1D convolutional layer (conv1D-L2) having 32 kernels of size 11 with stride as 1. The resultant output of size 26×1 is then passed to the ReLU activation function to add nonlinearity to the feature maps. Next, the feature map is passed into a 1D average pooling layer (pool1D-L1) with a pool size of 3 and 'same' padding, where stride is 1. The 1D average pooling is shown in (3).

$$p_k^a = \frac{1}{s} \sum_{a'=a}^{a+s} p_k^{a'} \qquad (3)$$

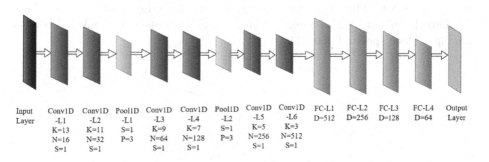

| Input Layer | Conv1D -L1 K=13 N=16 S=1 | Conv1D -L2 K=11 N=32 S=1 | Pool1D -L1 S=1 P=3 | Conv1D -L3 K=9 N=64 S=1 | Conv1D -L4 K=7 N=128 S=1 | Pool1D -L2 S=1 P=3 | Conv1D -L5 K=5 N=256 S=1 | Conv1D -L6 K=3 N=512 S=1 | FC-L1 D=512 | FC-L2 D=256 | FC-L3 D=128 | FC-L4 D=64 | Output Layer |

Fig. 5. The proposed 1D CNN model. Here, K, N, S, P and D denotes Kernel Size, Number of Kernels, Stride, Pool Size and Dimension, respectively.

Here, p_k^a is the output of the ath neuron after applying average pooling operation, $p_k^{a'}$ is the input to the ath neuron and s is the pooling window size. The generated 32 feature maps of size 26×1 are then fed into two 1D convolutional layers followed by another 1D average pooling layer. They are conv1D-L3, conv1D-L4 and pool1D-L2 as described in Fig. 5. The pool1D-L2 uses 'same' padding, and the ReLU activation function is applied to each convolutional layer to further help in feature extraction. The result contains 128 feature maps of dimension 12×1 which are then fed into other two convolutional layers, namely conv1D-L5 and conv1D-L6 with ReLU activation layers as mentioned in Fig. 5. In order to avoid overfitting in the proposed model, L2 regularization with a coefficient $\lambda = 0.03$ is applied to the conv1D-L6 layer. The resultant 512 feature maps of dimension 6×1 are then flattened and fed into 4 FC layers for the purpose of learning. These FC layers are FC-L1, FC-L2, FC-L3 and FC-L4 with 512, 256, 128 and 64 neurons respectively. The ReLU activation is applied after each of the FC layers. There is also a dropout layer between FC-L2 and FC-L3 with a dropout rate of 0.15 to avoid overfitting. Finally, the output of 64 neurons from FC-L4 is fed into another FC layer with a sigmoid activation layer to generate output for binary classification task, i.e., mental task or rest. The proposed model uses mini-batch gradient descent which means that the model's parameters are updated after processing each mini-batch (subset of training data) where mini-batch size is 256. The proposed model is validated using stratified 5-fold cross-validation where each fold retains the same proportion of samples for every class.

To enhance the performance of the proposed model, we have used certain optimization techniques such as 'early stop' and 'reduced learning rate'. The proposed model monitors the training loss and applies 'early stop' when the loss stop decreasing. Learning rate is reduced on the plateau using a scheduling technique when the training loss runs into stagnation.

4   Results and Discussion

The proposed 1D CNN model's performance on two datasets, Dataset A and Dataset B, is described in this section. To evaluate the performance of the proposed model, we have performed a comparative analysis with two other models, SVM and DNN. The experiment is conducted in Python3 with TensorFlow2 framework on 16 GB of System RAM and AMD Radeon Graphics Processor having a clock speed of 400 MHz.

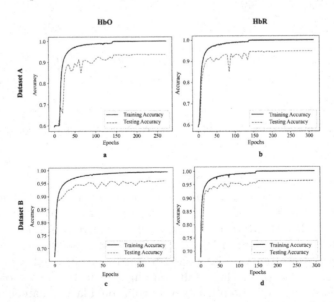

Fig. 6. Classification accuracies of training and testing of Dataset A and Dataset B for the proposed model. (a) and (b) shows the training and testing accuracies, respectively, for HbO and HbR data of Dataset A. (c) and (d) shows the training and testing accuracies, respectively, for HbO and HbR data of Dataset B.

The training and testing accuracies of the proposed model for both HbO and HbR data of both the datasets, Dataset A and Dataset B, are given in Fig. 6. For Dataset A, Fig. 6(a) and (b) depicts that the training accuracy of the proposed model reaches 97% and 98% in 50 epochs, respectively, for the HbO and HbR data, whereas the testing accuracy for HbO and HbR are, respectively, 89% and 92%. For Dataset A, the training accuracy gets saturated at 99% for both HbO and HbR data while the testing accuracy gets saturated at 94% and 95%, respectively for HbO and HbR data. For Dataset B, it is also observed from the Fig. 6(c) and (d) that the training and testing accuracies of the proposed model reach 98% and 95% in 50 epochs, respectively, for both the HbO and HbR data. The training accuracy gets saturated at 99% for both HbO and HbR data while the testing accuracy gets saturated at 96% and 97%, respectively, for HbO and HbR data for Dataset B. The training and the testing accuracy of the proposed model are increasing faster with respect to each epoch for Dataset B because of the larger sample and consequently increased number of mini-batches.

For comparison purposes, the proposed model is compared with SVM [13] and DNN [12] models. Table 1 shows the performance comparison of the proposed model. The proposed model is able to perform superior with an accuracy difference of 12.86% and 8.41%, respectively, for HbO and HbR data. Also, for Dataset B, the proposed model performs better than SVM with an accuracy difference of 6.84% on HbO data and 7.83% on HbR data. Further, the proposed model and the DNN have comparable performance with the proposed model performing superior with an accuracy difference of 0.01% on HbO data while in the case of HbR data, DNN has better performance with the difference of 0.94% in the accuracies on HbR data of Dataset A. For Dataset B, the given model performs better than DNN with the accuracy difference of 1.67% and 2.15%,

Table 1. The performance comparison of the proposed model with SVM and DNN for Dataset A and Dataset B

Dataset	Methods	Activity	Accuracy	Precision	Recall	F1-Score
Dataset A	SVM	HbO	80.71	86.45	61.30	80.71
		HbR	86.37	89.07	75.08	86.37
	DNN	HbO	93.56	**94.13**	89.47	91.73
		HbR	**95.72**	**95.53**	**93.68**	**94.59**
	Proposed Model	HbO	**93.57**	92.50	**91.30**	**91.89**
		HbR	94.78	93.50	93.35	93.46
Dataset B	SVM	HbO	88.58	90.52	73.42	88.58
		HbR	88.38	89.34	73.97	88.38
	DNN	HbO	93.75	91.76	89.28	90.49
		HbR	94.06	92.98	88.91	90.89
	Proposed Model	HbO	**95.42**	**93.98**	**92.28**	**93.06**
		HbR	**96.21**	**94.57**	**94.02**	**94.29**

respectively, for HbO and HbR data. We have also evaluated precision, recall and f1-score as performance metrics as defined respectively in (4), (5) and (6) to compare the proposed model with SVM and DNN.

$$Precision = \frac{TP}{TP + FP} \tag{4}$$

$$Recall = \frac{TP}{TP + FN} \tag{5}$$

$$F1 - Score = 2 \times \frac{Precision \times Recall}{Precision + Recall} \tag{6}$$

Here, the values of TP (True Positive), FN (False Negative) and FP (False Positive), respectively, represent the number of mental tasks being correctly, the number of mental tasks being wrongly and the number of rest tasks being wrongly classified. It can be observed from Table 1 that the precision of DNN are highest for both the data (i.e., HbO and HbR for Dataset A) while the proposed model has the highest precision for Dataset B, i.e., 93.98% and 94.57%. In case of recall, for HbR data of Dataset A, DNN has the highest recall while for HbO data, the proposed model has the highest recall of 91.30%. For Dataset B, the proposed model also achieved the highest recall with 92.28% and 94.02%, respectively on HbO and HbR data. For Dataset A, the proposed model also has the highest f1-score of 91.89% for HbO data while DNN holds the higher f1-score of 94.59% for HbR data. The proposed model also has the highest f1-score of 93.06% and 94.29% for HbO and HbR data, respectively, for Dataset B. Hence, it is apparent from the metrics that the proposed model has comparable performance to DNN for Dataset A, while it has superior performance for Dataset B.

5 Conclusion

In the present study, we have proposed a 1D CNN to classify mental workload as mental task or rest using fNIRS data. To observe the performance of the proposed model we have used two open-access datasets. The proposed model attains an average testing accuracy of 94.18% and 95.82%, respectively, for Dataset A and Dataset B. The proposed model has performed significantly better than SVM. Also, the proposed model is able to give comparable testing accuracies as that of DNN in case of Dataset A while it is able to perform superior to DNN in case of Dataset B. The proposed model has the advantage over the standard 2D CNN models as it works on time-series data which requires less computational time than 2D CNN models which work on image data [8].

Although the proposed model is able to classify mental workload as either mental task or rest with promising accuracy, still there are a few limitations that require attention. Firstly, there is a need to further reduce the computational time without compromising the attained accuracies, which can be accomplished by better tuning of the hyperparameters. Secondly, due to the requirement of manual labelling, the model needs a significant amount of labelled training data, which is a time-consuming process [5]. In future, these limitations can be addressed.

References

1. Baker, W.B., Parthasarathy, A.B., Busch, D.R., Mesquita, R.C., Greenberg, J.H., Yodh, A.: Modified beer-lambert law for blood flow. Biomed. Opt. Express **5**(11), 4053–4075 (2014)
2. Jiao, Z., Gao, X., Wang, Y., Li, J., Xu, H.: Deep convolutional neural networks for mental load classification based on EEG data. Pattern Recogn. **76**, 582–595 (2018)
3. Mughal, N.E., Khalil, K., Khan, M.J.: fNIRS based multi-class mental workload classification using recurrence plots and CNN-LSTM. In: 2021 International Conference on Artificial Intelligence and Mechatronics Systems (AIMS), pp. 1–6. IEEE (2021)
4. Naseer, N., Hong, K.S.: fNIRS-based brain-computer interfaces: a review. Front. Hum. Neurosci. **9**, 3 (2015)
5. Pham, T.T., Nguyen, T.D., Van Vo, T.: Sparse fNIRS feature estimation via unsupervised learning for mental workload classification. In: Bassis, S., Esposito, A., Morabito, F.C., Pasero, E. (eds.) Advances in Neural Networks. SIST, vol. 54, pp. 283–292. Springer, Cham (2016). https://doi.org/10.1007/978-3-319-33747-0_28
6. Pinti, P., Scholkmann, F., Hamilton, A., Burgess, P., Tachtsidis, I.: Current status and issues regarding pre-processing of fNIRS neuroimaging data: an investigation of diverse signal filtering methods within a general linear model framework. Front. Hum. Neurosci. **12**, 505 (2019)
7. Rai, A.A., Ahirwal, M.K.: Cognitive load classification during arithmetic task using single convolution layer-based 2D-CNN model. In: Doriya, R., Soni, B., Shukla, A., Gao, X.Z. (eds.) Machine Learning, Image Processing, Network Security and Data Sciences. LNEE, vol. 946, pp. 209–216. Springer, Singapore (2023). https://doi.org/10.1007/978-981-19-5868-7_16
8. Saadati, M., Nelson, J., Ayaz, H.: Mental workload classification from spatial representation of fNIRS recordings using convolutional neural networks. In: 2019 IEEE 29th International Workshop on Machine Learning for Signal Processing (MLSP), pp. 1–6. IEEE (2019)
9. Shin, J., et al.: Open access dataset for EEG+NIRS single-trial classification. IEEE Trans. Neural Syst. Rehabil. Eng. **25**(10), 1735–1745 (2017). https://doi.org/10.1109/TNSRE.2016.2628057
10. Shin, J., Von Lühmann, A., Kim, D.W., Mehnert, J., Hwang, H.J., Müller, K.R.: Simultaneous acquisition of EEG and NIRS during cognitive tasks for an open access dataset. Sci. Data **5**(1), 1–16 (2018)
11. da Silva, F.P.: Mental workload, task demand and driving performance: what relation? Procedia Soc. Behav. Sci. **162**, 310–319 (2014)
12. Zeng, D., Liu, K., Lai, S., Zhou, G., Zhao, J.: Relation classification via convolutional deep neural network. In: Proceedings of COLING 2014, The 25th International Conference on Computational Linguistics: Technical Papers, pp. 2335–2344 (2014)
13. Zhang, Y.: Support vector machine classification algorithm and its application. In: Liu, C., Wang, L., Yang, A. (eds.) ICICA 2012. CCIS, vol. 308, pp. 179–186. Springer, Heidelberg (2012). https://doi.org/10.1007/978-3-642-34041-3_27

An Effective Centrality-Based Community Detection Approach Using scRNA-Seq Data for Critical Neuro-Degenerative Diseases

Tonmoya Sarmah$^{(\boxtimes)}$ ⓘ and Dhruba K. Bhattacharyya ⓘ

Tezpur University, Tezpur, Assam, India
tonmoya.22@gmail.com

Abstract. The process of community detection in a network uncovers groups of closely connected nodes, known as communities. In the context of gene correlation networks and neuro-degenerative diseases, this study introduces a systematic pipeline for centrality-based community detection using scRNA-Seq data. Comparisons with existing methods demonstrate its superior performance in terms of modularity. Furthermore, the resulting communities undergo biological validation and hub-gene analysis, which reveal disease-specific pathways and gene ontology associated with the genes within these communities.

Keywords: Community detection · Graph centrality · Modularity · Gene correlation network · scRNA Seq data

1 Introduction

The advent of single-cell RNA sequencing (scRNA-seq) technology has transformed our ability to study gene expression at the cellular level, enabling the exploration of expression diversity within complex tissues and the identification of previously unrecognized cell types and states. Co-expression analysis of scRNA-seq data is a powerful approach for uncovering functionally related genes and pathways within specific cell populations. By examining gene expression patterns across individual cells, we can identify cells with similar gene expression profiles, offering fresh insights into cellular function and disease mechanisms. However, the analysis of scRNA-seq data is challenging due to technical noise, data sparsity, and the vast number of genes and cells involved. To overcome these challenges, researchers have developed algorithms and methodologies that focus on detecting co-expressed gene modules and interpreting their implications. Clustering-based and network-based methods are among the prominent strategies employed for these analyses. Clustering-based methods group genes with similar expression patterns across cells into co-expression modules using similarity calculations and clustering algorithms like hierarchical clustering and

© The Author(s), under exclusive license to Springer Nature Switzerland AG 2023
P. Maji et al. (Eds.): PReMI 2023, LNCS 14301, pp. 756–763, 2023.
https://doi.org/10.1007/978-3-031-45170-6_79

k-means. Network-based methods detect co-expressed gene modules by representing gene interactions as a network, where genes are nodes and the strength of their co-expression is represented by edges. Densely connected subgraphs are identified as co-expression modules. An example is the Louvain method [13], which identifies cell clusters and gene modules in scRNA-seq data.

Gene coexpression networks (GCNs) have been valuable in uncovering relationships and annotating functions of uncharacterized genes. Existing GCN methods, like WGCNA [16], DiffCorr [17], DiffCoEx [18], CEMiTool [19], etc. were designed for microarray and bulk RNA-seq data and are unsuitable for scRNA-seq due to data sparsity [14,15]. Therefore, this study aims to introduce a systematic framework for analyzing scRNA-seq data, including preprocessing, differential gene expression, GCN construction, and identification of key gene modules associated with critical functions in diverse cell types.

2   Materials and Methods

2.1   Dataset

We have used a scRNA Seq dataset for Schizophrenia as case study for the implementation of our method. The data is downloaded from NCBI Gene Expression Omnibus [1] with accession ID GSE184878. This dataset consists of 4 control and 3 diseased samples, and each of these samples comprises of 33538 features (genes) and 27793 cell samples.

2.2   Method

This paper presents a systematic pipeline for centrality-based community detection in gene correlation networks using scRNA-Seq data. The pipeline involves three steps: preprocessing, cell clustering and marker gene identification using the Seurat pipeline [20], construction of a gene correlation network using marker genes, and community detection to identify functionally related gene communities. The workflow is illustrated in Fig. 1, and the implementation can be found on GitHub (https://github.com/Tonmoya/Community-detection-in-scRNA-Seq-data).

Step 1: The scRNA-Seq data undergoes preprocessing using the Seurat pipeline [20]. This includes quality control, normalization, identification of highly variable features, batch effect removal, and dimensionality reduction using PCA (Principal Component Analysis) and UMAP (Uniform Manifold Approximation and Projection). Cell clustering is performed using the Louvain community detection method, and marker genes are identified using three methods, viz, Wilcoxon RankSum Text, MAST and t-test. The top 20 marker genes from each cluster are integrated to create a list of common marker genes for subsequent gene network analysis and community detection.

Step 2: The centrality-based community detection method in this paper utilizes marker genes to construct a gene correlation network. To address dropout events in scRNA sequencing data, the SAVER method is employed to impute zero values before calculating gene correlations [2]. Dropout events occurs when gene expression values fail to get detected and this leads to biases in many calculations. Pearson correlation is then computed to construct the gene correlation network.

Step 3: To determine the importance of nodes in the gene correlation network, various centrality measures such as Average Distance, Barycenter Centrality, Closeness Centrality (Freeman), Decay Centrality, Eigenvector centrality, Lin Centrality, and Radiality Centrality were applied using the *CINNA* package in R [3]. PCA and t-SNE analysis are used on the computed centrality values to identify the most informative measure [3], which was found to be Lin centrality in this case. Nodes with top Lin centrality values were selected as community centers for subsequent analysis, and the following steps for community detection were then implemented.

1. Detection of sub-communities - Each node's correlation with the center nodes is examined. The node is assigned to the center with the highest correlation, and this process is repeated until all nodes are visited, resulting in a set of sub-communities.
2. Calculation of a merging factor - A merging factor as described in Eq. 1 is calculated to find the pairs of sub-communities that can be merged.

Definition 1. *Merging Factor (MEF) of pair of sub-communities: The MEF of a pair of sub-communities SC_i and SC_j, denoted by $MEF(SC_i, SC_j)$, is the average of edge weights of edge-cut of the pair of sub-communities SC_i and SC_j, divided by the sum of average edge weights of the two communities SC_i and SC_j.*

$$MEF(SC_i, SC_j) = \frac{\frac{\sum EC_{ij}}{n_{ei}+n_{ej}}}{\frac{\sum W_i}{n_{ei}} + \frac{\sum W_j}{n_{ej}}} \qquad (1)$$

$\sum EC_{ij}$ is the sum of edge weights of the edge cut of the pair of sub-communities SC_i and SC_j. Edge cut in a graph refers to a subset of edges which, when removed separates the graph into two or more disconnected components. $\sum W_i$ and $\sum W_j$ are the sum of edge weights of sub-community SC_i and SC_j respectively, and n_{ei} and n_{ej} are number of edges in sub-communities SC_i and SC_j respectively.

3. Merge sub-communities - Pairs of sub-communities are merged, and the modularity of the resulting network is evaluated. If the change in modularity surpasses the previous change, the merge is accepted; otherwise, the merge is rejected. This process continues until all potential pairs of sub-communities have been considered.

After completion of this process, we get a gene network that comprises of the detected communities.

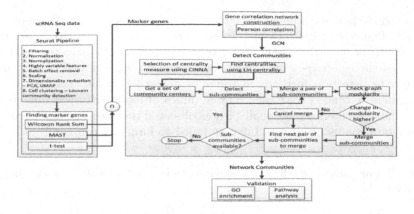

Fig. 1. Workflow followed for the community detection of gene correlation network.

3 Results

Quality control, visualization and cell clustering is carried out on the scRNA-Seq data using the Seurat pipeline. The data is filtered to exclude cells that have unique feature counts less than 500 and gene expression less than 800 and mitochondrial percentage of over 5%. This resulted in 33538 remaining features and 25275 remaining cell samples, out of which 2000 highly variable features are used for further downstream analysis.

The remaining data is log normalized to eliminate noise and biases. Scaling is applied to standardize gene expressions so that the variance across cells is 1 and mean expression across cells is 0, thus preventing highly variable genes from dominating downstream analysis. Next, dimensionality reduction is performed using PCA and UMAP to identify the most significant dimensions. Louvain community detection identifies 7 distinct cell clusters. Marker genes are identified in each cluster using three methods available in the Seurat pipeline, Wilcoxon Rank Sum Text, MAST and t-test, and the top 20 genes from each method are integrated, resulting in 135 common marker genes. These potential markers are then utilized for gene network construction and community detection as shown in Fig. 1. Using Pearson correlation, the gene-gene correlation is calculated, resulting in a correlation matrix. This matrix forms the gene correlation network with 135 nodes. To determine node centralities, Lin centrality is employed as it was identified as the most favorable measure among various centrality measures as described in Sect. 2.2. The top 10 nodes with the highest centrality values serve as community centers. These centers are then used to form 10 sub-communities. Merging factors are computed for each pair of sub-communities, and the pair with the highest factor is merged if the change in modularity surpasses the previous change; otherwise, it is rejected.

The algorithm is evaluated using various numbers of community centers to determine the optimal number. When the number of centers exceeded 10, the results became inconsistent with some communities being excessively large and others isolated. Thus, number of community centers more than 10 are not considered. The comparison of communities and network modularity is presented in Table 1, along with a comparison to other community detection methods. Based on the comparison in Table 1, our method outperformed other popular community detection methods in terms of achieving higher modularity when 10 community centers were used. Lower values of modularity was observed for fewer than 10 centers. Additionally, it was observed that Leading eigen produced inconsistent communities, and Infomap failed to form any communities.

Table 1. Comparison of different community detection methods with the proposed method

Method	Modularity	Communities	
		number	sizes
Proposed method (centers = 10)	0.6723389	6	34, 31, 19, 18, 19, 14
Proposed method (centers = 9)	0.4321331	5	37, 55, 8, 24, 11
Proposed method (centers = 8)	0.1875202	3	38, 77, 20
Proposed method (centers = 7)	0.1760786	4	44, 70, 3, 18
Louvain	0.2425762	5	34, 32, 21, 35, 13
Leading eigen	0.2168736	8	9, 24, 16, 36, 2, 31, 13, 4
Fast greedy	0.2053297	3	20, 54, 61
Infomap	$1.110223e-16$	1	135

3.1 Functional Analysis

Functional analysis of the communities generated by our centrality-based method uncovers functional relationships among the genes through GO enrichment and pathway analysis. The analysis is conducted using the functional annotation tools provided by the Database for Annotation, Visualization, and Integrated Discovery (DAVID) tool [4,5][1]. Table 2 provides details of the GO terms and pathways identified for each community using Count = 2, EASE = 0.1 and adjusted p-value < 0.05.

The functional analysis of the communities reveals that the functional relations of the genes within the communities are associated with schizophrenia. The GO terms *Detection of chemical stimulus involved in sensory perception of smell* and *Olfactory receptor activity* and *Olfactory transduction* pathway found for community 1 are associated with olfactory dysfunction in schizophrenia that helps in detecting early warning signs [6]. *G-protein coupled receptor activity* mediates slow synaptic transmission and most neurotransmitters involved in schizophrenia acts through G protein-coupled receptors (GPCRs) [7]. GO terms enriched in community 2 are also found to be associated with neuro-degenerative

---

[1] (https://david.ncifcrf.gov/).

Table 2. GO terms and pathways enriched for the resultant communities

Community	GO terms	Pathways
1	Detection of chemical stimulus involved in sensory perception of smell, Olfactory receptor activity, Signal transduction, G-protein coupled receptor activity	Olfactory transduction
2	Vascular endothelial growth factor-activated receptor activity, Semaphorin receptor activity	Olfactory transduction
3	Golgi transport complex, Retrograde transport, Vesicle recycling within Golgi	Cortisol synthesis and secretion, Aldosterone synthesis and secretion
4	G-protein coupled receptor signaling pathway, RNA polymerase II transcription factor activity, Sequence-specific DNA binding	Cortisol synthesis and secretion
5	Fatty acid beta-oxidation, Calcium ion binding	Fatty acid metabolism, PPAR signaling pathway
6	Golgi apparatus	Cortisol synthesis and secretion

disorders including schizophrenia [8,9]. *Golgi complex* found in community 3 is associated with various psychiatric disorders [10] and *Cortisol synthesis and secretion* pathway is related to cortisols which are biomarkers for mental disorder severity [11] and are also observed in women with schizophrenia [12]. Similarly, the other communities reveals pathways and GO terms associated with schizophrenia as described in Table 2.

Thus, it can be stated that the communities found using our method are functionally enriched and are consistent in size and has modularity higher than other widely used community detection methods.

3.2 Hub-Gene Analysis

The top 10 highly connected genes were selected from each individual community to reveal the corresponding hub genes as shown in Fig. 2.

On literature mining, it was found that hub genes RALGDS [21], RAP2A [22], RAPGEF2 [23] from community 1, SMAP2 [24], CROT [25], HOXA1 [26] from community 2, COG1 [27], COG8 [28], COG3 [29] from community 3, UBXN1 [22], PLAA [22] from community 4, DCP1A [22] from community 5 and TANGO2 [22] from community 6 were found to be associated with schizophrenia, whereas genes NRP2, DTX3 form community 2, RBM7 from community 5 and MDFI from community 6 were not yet found to be associated with schizophrenia. Thus, further studies will be required to find the relatedness of these genes with the target disease in consideration.

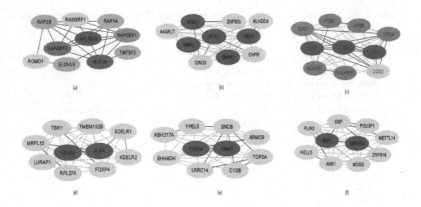

Fig. 2. Hub gene detection for communities

4   Conclusion

The clustering of genes in scRNA-seq data is a challenging task due to large sample sizes and high dimensionality. Marker genes identified in individual cell clusters can provide insights into gene functionality and relationships. Centrality-based community detection in gene correlation networks helps identify important genes and functionally relevant communities. As future work, community detection can be extended to other neuro-degenerative diseases to explore the biological significance of gene communities in scRNA-seq data.

References

1. Notaras, M., et al.: Schizophrenia is defined by cell-specific neuropathology and multiple neurodevelopmental mechanisms in patient-derived cerebral organoids. Mol. Psychiatry **27**(3), 1416–1434 (2022)
2. Huang, M., et al.: SAVER: gene expression recovery for single-cell RNA sequencing. Nat. Methods **15**(7), 539–542 (2018)
3. Ashtiani, M., Mirzaie, M., Jafari, M.: CINNA: an R/CRAN package to decipher Central Informative Nodes in Network Analysis. Bioinformatics **35**(8), 1436–1437 (2019)
4. Sherman, B.T., et al.: DAVID: a web server for functional enrichment analysis and functional annotation of gene lists (2021 update). Nucl. Acids Res. **50**(W1), W216–W221 (2022). https://doi.org/10.1093/nar/gkac194
5. Huang, D.W., Sherman, B.T., Lempicki, R.A.: Systematic and integrative analysis of large gene lists using DAVID bioinformatics resources. Nature Protoc. **4**(1), 44–57 (2009)
6. Turetsky, B.I., et al.: Olfactory receptor neuron dysfunction in schizophrenia. Neuropsychopharmacology **34**(3), 767–774 (2009)
7. Boczek, T., et al.: The role of G protein-coupled receptors (GPCRs) and calcium signaling in schizophrenia. Focus on GPCRs activated by neurotransmitters and chemokines. Cells **10**(5), 1228 (2021)

8. Daniela, C., De Winter, F., Verhaagen, J.: Semaphorins in adult nervous system plasticity and disease. Front. Synaptic Neurosci. **13**, 672891 (2021)
9. Saoud, H., et al.: Association of VEGF-A and KDR polymorphisms with the development of schizophrenia. Hum. Immunol. **83**(6), 528–537 (2022)
10. Caracci, M.O., Fuentealba, L.M., Marzolo, M.-P.: Golgi complex dynamics and its implication in prevalent neurological disorders. Front. Cell Dev. Biol. **7**, 75 (2019)
11. Dziurkowska, E., Wesolowski, M.: Cortisol as a biomarker of mental disorder severity. J. Clin. Med. **10**(21), 5204 (2021)
12. Mikulska, J., et al.: HPA axis in the pathomechanism of depression and schizophrenia: new therapeutic strategies based on its participation. Brain Sci. **11**(10), 1298 (2021)
13. Blondel, V.D., et al.: Fast unfolding of communities in large networks. J. Stat. Mech: Theory Exp. **2008**(10), P10008 (2008)
14. Sarmah, T., Bhattacharyya, D.K.: A study of tools for differential co-expression analysis for RNA-Seq data. Inform. Med. Unlocked **26**, 100740 (2021)
15. Cheng, C.W., Beech, D.J., Wheatcroft, S.B.: Advantages of CEMiTool for gene co-expression analysis of RNA-seq data. Comput. Biol. Med. **125**, 103975 (2020)
16. Langfelder, P., Horvath, S.: WGCNA: an R package for weighted correlation network analysis. BMC Bioinform. **9**(1), 1–13 (2008)
17. Fukushima, A.: DiffCorr: an R package to analyze and visualize differential correlations in biological networks. Gene **518**(1), 209–214 (2013)
18. Tesson, B.M., Breitling, R., Jansen, R.C.: DiffCoEx: a simple and sensitive method to find differentially coexpressed gene modules. BMC Bioinform. **11**(1), 1–9 (2010)
19. Russo, P.S.T., et al.: CEMiTool: a bioconductor package for performing comprehensive modular co-expression analyses. BMC Bioinform. **19**(1), 1–13 (2018)
20. Hao, Y., et al.: Integrated analysis of multimodal single-cell data. Cell **184**(13), 3573–3587 (2021)
21. Najmabadi, H., et al.: Deep sequencing reveals 50 novel genes for recessive cognitive disorders. Nature **478**(7367), 57–63 (2011)
22. Stelzer, G., et al.: The GeneCards suite: from gene data mining to disease genome sequence analyses. Curr. Protoc. Bioinform. **54**(1), 1–30 (2016)
23. Farag, M.I., et al.: Rapgef2, a guanine nucleotide exchange factor for Rap1 small GTPases, plays a crucial role in adherence junction (AJ) formation in radial glial cells through ERK-mediated upregulation of the AJ-constituent protein expression. Biochem. Biophys. Res. Commun. **493**(1), 139–145 (2017)
24. Xu, B., et al.: De novo gene mutations highlight patterns of genetic and neural complexity in schizophrenia. Nat. Genet. **44**(12), 1365–1369 (2012)
25. Richards, A.L., et al.: Exome arrays capture polygenic rare variant contributions to schizophrenia. Hum. Mol. Genet. **25**(5), 1001–1007 (2016)
26. Laroche, F., et al.: Polymorphisms of coding trinucleotide repeats of homeogenes in neurodevelopmental psychiatric disorders. Psychiatr. Genet. **18**(6), 295–301 (2008)
27. Huang, G., et al.: Overdispersed gene expression in schizophrenia. npj Schizophr. **6**(1), 9 (2020)
28. Reay, W.R., Cairns, M.J.: Pairwise common variant meta-analyses of schizophrenia with other psychiatric disorders reveals shared and distinct gene and gene-set associations. Transl. Psychiatry **10**(1), 134 (2020)
29. Tsivion-Visbord, H., et al.: Increased RNA editing in maternal immune activation model of neurodevelopmental disease. Nat. Commun. **11**(1), 5236 (2020)

Chronologically Arranged Convolutional Gated Recurrent Network for EEG-Based Schizophrenia Detection

Shipra Swati$^{(\boxtimes)}$ and Mukesh Kumar

Department of CSE, National Institute of Technology Patna, Patna, India
{shipras.phd18.cs,mukesh.kumar}@nitp.ac.in
https://www.nitp.ac.in/cse

Abstract. Schizophrenia is a severe brain disorder having disruptive effects on human behavior, which can progressively turn out to be worst if left undiagnosed and untreated in its early stages. Therefore, early detection of schizophrenia is crucial for effective treatment and limiting the extent of its effects. Electroencephalogram (EEG) is a widely used method for measuring brain activity in order to investigate the presence of any brain disorders such as schizophrenia. This paper aims to identify the cases of Schizophrenia by applying deep learning techniques to electrical signals recorded through the human brain. Here, chronologically arranged stacks of convolutional modules are used to learn features for further analyzing the temporal dynamics of EEG signals associated with schizophrenia. This hybrid deep learning architecture composed of multiple 1D convolution layers followed by deep gated recurrent units (GRU), achieves a classification score of 99.44% during experimental execution. The performance analysis demonstrates the potential of the proposed architecture for identifying schizophrenia using the EEG recordings of the affected subjects. Following similar footsteps, this study might also be of great help to clinicians in detecting other mental disorders as well.

Keywords: Schizophrenia · Electroencephalogram · CNN · GRU

1 Introduction

Schizophrenia is a mental disorder characterized by a range of symptoms, including delusions, hallucinations, disorganized speech and behavior, and social withdrawal. It is a chronic condition that can have a significant impact on a person's life and can also affect their relationships with family and friends. As per the report of World Health Organization (WHO), this complex mental disorder affects approximately 20 million people worldwide [1]. It also emphasizes the importance of early detection, diagnosis, and treatment of schizophrenia to improve outcomes and quality of life for affected individuals. The treatment typically involves a combination of medication, psychotherapy, and support services, such as vocational rehabilitation and social skills training.

P. Maji et al. (Eds.): PReMI 2023, LNCS 14301, pp. 764–771, 2023.
https://doi.org/10.1007/978-3-031-45170-6_80

EEG (electroencephalogram) data has been shown to provide valuable insights into the neurobiological conditions including schizophrenia [2]. EEG is a recording of electrical activity in the brain over time, that makes it a suitable candidate of signal processing and analysis. This time series data typically consists of a sequence of voltage measurements recorded through EEG channels at discrete time points, known as sampling rate. Treating EEG as a time series enables researchers to better understand the complex patterns of brain activity and to develop new insights into the functioning of the brain. Specific research studies have found that EEG data can differentiate between individuals with neurological disorders (NDs) and healthy controls based on differences in brain activity patterns. Various methods, such as time-frequency analysis and machine learning techniques, can be used to extract meaningful information from EEG time series, such as identifying specific brain states, detecting anomalies or abnormalities in brain activity, and predicting outcomes or responses to stimuli. Deep learning (DL), a subset of machine learning, has been applied to EEG data analysis to improve the accuracy of EEG-based diagnosis and classification [3]. Deep learning algorithms, such as convolutional neural networks (CNNs) and recurrent neural networks (RNNs), have shown promise in identifying and classifying abnormal EEG patterns associated with neurological disorders. CNNs are particularly well-suited for analyzing EEG signals because they can extract spatial and temporal features from the data, allowing for more accurate and reliable classification [4]. RNNs, on the other hand, can capture the temporal dynamics of EEG signals, which is important for identifying patterns of abnormal activity over time. An efficient deep learning architecture has been developed for analyzing and classifying EEG signals for a variety of applications, such as detecting seizures, sleep staging, and emotion recognition [5]. It uses convolutional layers to perform feature extraction by applying a set of filters to the input data, while the pooling layers downsample the output of the CNN layers to reduce the computational cost. The recurrent layers, such as LSTM or GRU, are used to capture the temporal dependencies and patterns in the EEG signals. The effective performance of this architecture promoted investigating the efficiency of similar framework for identifying the schizophrenic cases using EEG segments for varying length. These EEG recordings are fetched from an open source repository consisting of 14 effected subjects and 14 controlled subjects [6]. Following are the main contributions of the paper:

- The presented paper intends to effectively identify the traits of Schizophrenia at an early stage using end to end application of deep learning on EEG recordings.
- Here, a concatenated architecture of DL blocks is used to analyze and interpret the complex patterns of EEG, consisting of spatial and temporal features. It applies stacked layers of CNN with GRU blocks resulting in efficient Convolutional Gated Recurrent Network (C-GRN) for successful classification of healthy and diseased cases.

– The comparative analysis of experimental evaluation with existing works promote the feasibility of presented methodology to detect other neurological condition as well.

Rest of the paper is organized as follows: a brief overview of EEG based analysis for schizophrenia is given in Sect. 2. The architectural description of the proposed methodology is given in Sect. 3, whereas the results are listed in Sect. 4. Finally, the paper concludes in Sect. 5 along with the discussion of its future scope.

2   Literature Review

In recent times, remarkable progress has been made by utilizing machine learning (ML) and deep learning (DL) techniques, to diagnose and predict schizophrenia using EEG. Siuly et al. [7] utilized empirical mode decomposition (EMD) based scheme to extract features from EEG recordings of 49 individuals with SZ and 32 healthy controls. Further, performance of several classifiers, including Decision Tree (DT), k-Nearest Neighbor (k-NN), Support Vector Machine (SVM), and ensemble bagged tree (EBT) was observed. The EBT classifier outperformed the other reported classifiers, achieving a superior performance of 89.59%. In another approach proposed by Zülfikar and Mehmet [8], two dimensional features from raw EEG recordings are fetched using Short-time Fourier Transform (STFT) and scalogram. Then a state-of-the-art CNN architecture, VGG-16, is applied to achieve best possible classification accuracy of 97% and 99% for the same datasets considered in the presented analysis. Jie et al. [9] have applied a hybrid version of deep learning techniques for identifying the schizophrenic cases. They extracted the time-domain and frequency-domain features of preprocessed EEG time series for attaining the validation accuracy of 99.22%. Carla et al. [10] conducted their study on spatial impact caused by the quantity of electrodes on the classification task. Their results reveal the capability of proposed model to classify schizophrenia and healthy subjects with an average accuracy of 78% using only 5 midline channels of EEG recording. The effectiveness of unidimensional CNN is investigated by Hanife Göker [11], on three different feature sets extracted using popular techniques such as periodogram, welch, and multitaper. The presented neural network architecture delivered 0.991 sensitivity, 0.984 precision, and 0.983 specificity, along with an accuracy of 98.76%. Another study introduces the utility of deep residual network to fetch features from EEG effectively, which is passed to softmax classifier [12]. The proposed model performs quite better with a significant accuracy 99.23%.

From the study of existing methods, the idea of using deep neural architectures for analyzing EEG recordings to identify schizophrenic patients is positively supported. So, this work combines two state-of-the-art techniques of deep learning, namely Convolutional Neural Networks (CNN) and Gated Recurrent Units (GRU), to analyze their effectiveness for the considered classification task.

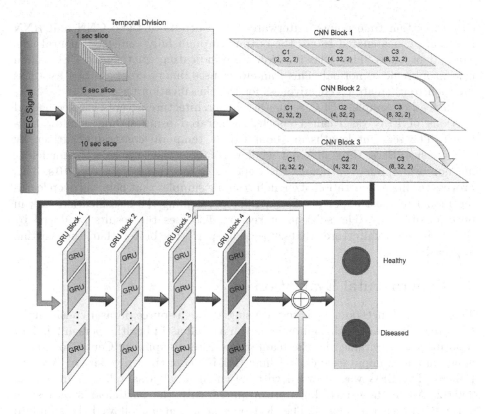

Fig. 1. Proposed framework.

3   Proposed Methodology

The presented deep learning architecture suggests chronological arrangements of CNN modules, stacked with GRU blocks, to carefully consider spatial and temporal aspects of the EEG data. As shown in Fig. 1, it starts with a convolutional neural network (CNN) to extract spatial features from the input time series data. This will help identify patterns in the data that are independent of time. Then it uses Gated Recurrent Units (GRU), a recurrent neural network (RNN) to capture temporal dependencies in the data. The stacks of GRU layers are arranged with multiple one-dimensional convolution layer having various filters of exponentially varying lengths. The availability of different filters in the Convolutional layers enable this architecture to extract and combine features from different time scales. For the task at hand, the optimum filter count of CNN layers are kept as 32 having lengths 2, 4, and 8. Additionally, the use of densely connected GRU layers enhances feature propagation and promotes feature reuse within the GRU layers along with handling the issue of training accuracy degradation due to vanishing or exploding gradients. The suggested architectural design will help to model the patterns of EEG signal that are specific to certain time points. Afterwards, the outputs of these CNN and RNN layers are concatenated to get the output through fully connected neural network. It provides binary classification score indicating whether the EEG signal is schizophrenic or normal. This framework uses binary cross entropy as a loss function to calculate its effectiveness for the classification task.

Instead of complete EEG sequence, this architecture accepts the segmented portions of EEG (also called epochs), generated using sliding window approach. The segment lengths are bounded by temporal constraints, driven by window size. Here, three different window configurations are selected for fetching non-overlapping continuous EEG epochs of lengths: 1 s, 5 s, and 10 s. This process results in generation of enough training samples that help the deep learning model to learn important features for performing the classification task in best possible way. The subsequent section discusses the results produced by the proposed architecture, that expectedly performs better than the existing approaches.

4 Experimental Evaluation

The suggested methodology is tested using an open-source dataset consisting of EEG recordings of 14 schizophrenic person as well as 14 healthy person [6]. This repository is maintained by the team of the Interdisciplinary Center for Mathematical and Computational Modelling (ICMCM) of the University of Warsaw, Poland. The EEG was recorded with 19 channels at a sampling frequency of 250 Hz. All of these recordings are acquired with the participants at resting state, with their eyes-closed. The electrodes arrangement followed the standard 10–20 system, with reference electrodes placed at FCz. The analysis phase re-reference the scalp EEG data by averaging the signals of all EEG channels. Then each of the acquired signal is divided into 1-s, 5-s, and 10-s epochs after applying primitive preprocessing steps, like downsampling to 125 Hz and filtering for a range of 1 Hz to 50 Hz. These three segmentation strategies generate 28863, 5771, and 2158 samples having respective spatial dimension as (125, 19), (625, 19), and (1250, 19). The proposed deep learning model uses learning rate of 0.0001 and batch size of 32 for the considered schizophrenia classification task. The learning behavior of this suggested approach during training and prediction is plotted in Fig. 2. It shows the quick convergence of the proposed model in case of 10 s epochs, which is closely followed by the model performance for 5 s epochs. The executional outcome of this trained model for new unseen data with these varying set of input sets is listed in Table 1 in terms of standard performance evaluation parameters. It clearly indicate the effectiveness of presented architecture for classifying the effected person. However, epochs with longer duration exhibit better performance, which is quite evident as they facilitate DL components with sufficient sample size to learn important features. Table 2 provides a comparative analytical overview for the classification accuracy achieved through state-of-the-art methods as well as proposed method. It confirms the potential of this chronological hybrid DL model as it delivers best classification score for the same set of EEG recordings.

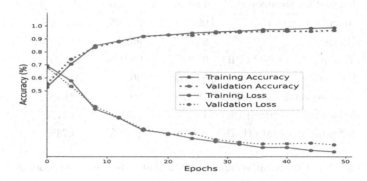

(a) EEG epochs of 1 second duration

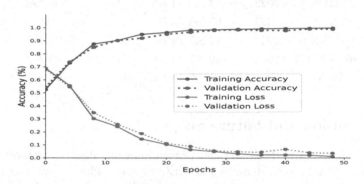

(b) EEG epochs of 5 second duration

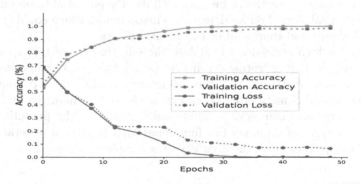

(c) EEG epochs of 10 second duration

Fig. 2. Accuracy and loss plots for training and validation sample set.

Table 1. Performance analysis of different EEG epoch configuration.

Evaluation parameters	1 s Epochs	5 s Epochs	10 s Epochs
Accuracy	96.41%	99.02%	99.44%
Precision	98.59%	99.23%	99.75%
True positive rate (TPR)	95.18%	98.97%	99.25%
F1-score	94.86%	96.85%	99.5%
True negative rate (TNR)	98.12%	99.08%	99.68%
False positive rate (FPR)	1.87%	0.91%	0.31%
False negative rate (FNR)	4.81%	1.02%	0.74%

Table 2. Comparative analysis with state-of-the-art approaches.

Approach	Year	#EEG samples	#Channels	Accuracy
VGG16 [8]	2022	14 SZ, 14 HC	19	99.35%
CNN [10]	2022	65 SZ, 63 HC	5	78%
1D-CNN [11]	2023	14 SZ, 14 HC	19	98.75%
ResNet [12]	2023	49 SZ, 32 HC	70	99.23%
C-GRN	Proposed	14 SZ, 14 HC	19	99.44%

5   Conclusion and Future Scope

The basic idea behind designing the Chronologically stacked architecture was to capture the temporal dynamics of EEG signals, which play a crucial role for identifying patterns associated with schizophrenia. The results of this presented work positively support using this deep learning architecture for EEG-based schizophrenia detection. This approach has the potential to provide a non-invasive and reliable method for detecting schizophrenia, which could greatly aid in early diagnosis and treatment of this mental illness.

Further research is needed to validate the effectiveness of this approach on a larger scale, including testing on diverse populations and comparing it with existing diagnostic methods. Also, the dependency of EEG-based diagnostic process on the spatial density of EEG sensors needs to be minimized by including devices with reduced complexity. Additionally, exploring the potential of integrating other types of data, such as functional MRI (fMRI) or genetic information, could help to improve the accuracy of schizophrenia detection.

References

1. Schizophrenia   (2022).   https://www.who.int/news-room/fact-sheets/detail/schizophrenia. Accessed 13 Mar 2023
2. Sharma, G., Joshi, A.M.: SzHNN: a novel and scalable deep convolution hybrid neural network framework for schizophrenia detection using multichannel EEG. IEEE Trans. Instrum. Meas. **71**, 1–9 (2022)

3. Roy, Y., Banville, H., Albuquerque, I., Gramfort, A., Falk, T.H., Faubert, J.: Deep learning-based electroencephalography analysis: a systematic review. J. Neural Eng. **16**(5), 051001 (2019)
4. Swati, S., Kumar, M.: Analysis of multichannel neurophysiological signal for detecting epilepsy using deep-nets. Int. J. Inf. Technol. **15**(3), 1–7 (2023). https://doi.org/10.1007/s41870-023-01186-x
5. Roy, S., Kiral-Kornek, I., Harrer, S.: ChronoNet: a deep recurrent neural network for abnormal EEG identification. In: Riaño, D., Wilk, S., ten Teije, A. (eds.) AIME 2019. LNCS (LNAI), vol. 11526, pp. 47–56. Springer, Cham (2019). https://doi.org/10.1007/978-3-030-21642-9_8
6. Olejarczyk, E., Jernajczyk, W.: EEG in schizophrenia (2017). https://doi.org/10.18150/repod.0107441. Accessed 13 Mar 2023
7. Siuly, S., Khare, S.K., Bajaj, V., Wang, H., Zhang, Y.: A computerized method for automatic detection of schizophrenia using EEG signals. IEEE Trans. Neural Syst. Rehabil. Eng. **28**(11), 2390–2400 (2020)
8. Aslan, Z., Akin, M.: A deep learning approach in automated detection of schizophrenia using scalogram images of EEG signals. Phys. Eng. Sci. Med. **45**(1), 83–96 (2022). https://doi.org/10.1007/s13246-021-01083-2
9. Sun, J., et al.: A hybrid deep neural network for classification of schizophrenia using EEG data. Sci. Rep. **11**(1), 1–16 (2021)
10. Barros, C., Roach, B., Ford, J.M., Pinheiro, A.P., Silva, C.A.: From sound perception to automatic detection of schizophrenia: an EEG-based deep learning approach. Front. Psych. **12**, 2659 (2022)
11. Göker, H.: 1D-convolutional neural network approach and feature extraction methods for automatic detection of schizophrenia. SIViP **17**(5), 2627–2636 (2023). https://doi.org/10.1007/s11760-022-02479-7
12. Siuly, S., Guo, Y., Alcin, O.F., Li, Y., Wen, P., Wang, H.: Exploring deep residual network based features for automatic schizophrenia detection from EEG. Phys. Eng. Sci. Med. **46**(2), 561–574 (2023). https://doi.org/10.1007/s13246-023-01225-8

A Novel Brain Connectivity-Powered Graph Signal Processing Approach for Automated Detection of Schizophrenia from Electroencephalogram Signals

Subrata Pain[1]($\boxtimes$), Naincy Vimal[2], Debasis Samanta[2], and Monalisa Sarma[3]

[1] Advanced Technology Development Center, Indian Institute of Technology, Kharagpur, Kharagpur 721302, India
subratabankata@gmail.com
[2] Department of Computer Science, Indian Institute of Technology, Kharagpur, Kharagpur 721302, India
[3] Subir Chowdhury School of Quality and Reliability, Indian Institute of Technology, Kharagpur, Kharagpur 721302, India

Abstract. Schizophrenia is a severe neural disorder that affects around 24 million individuals globally. In this context, Electroencephalogram (EEG) signal-based analysis and automated screening for Schizophrenia (SZ) have gained importance. EEG-based Schizophrenia (SZ-EEG) analysis is traditionally done by extracting features from individual EEG electrodes' signals and utilizing these features for Machine Learning (ML)-based classification models. However, these methods do not exploit the Schizophrenia-induced alteration of functional brain connectivity between neuronal masses. The present study proposes a novel graph-signal (GS) representation of multi-channel SZ-EEG data that fully encompasses local brain activation and global interactions between brain regions. The proposed GS representation comprises the underlying connectivity network and the signal values on the network's vertices. Here, the EEG signal's entropy at each electrode is used as GS values, and a phase lag index (PLI)-based functional connectivity measure is utilized as the underlying connectivity network. Further, these connectivity-informed GSs are transformed to the spectral domain by the Graph Fourier Transform (GFT), and relevant discriminatory features are extracted from them using the Graph Signal Processing (GSP) technique. Those features are fed to basic ML-based classification models. The efficacy of the proposed PLI-GSP framework is validated using a publicly available SZ-EEG dataset, and a 99.77% classification accuracy is achieved that outperforms most of the state-of-the-art models.

Keywords: Schizophrenia · Electroencephalogram Signals · Graphical Representations · Graph Signal Processing · Machine Learning

© The Author(s), under exclusive license to Springer Nature Switzerland AG 2023
P. Maji et al. (Eds.): PReMI 2023, LNCS 14301, pp. 772–779, 2023.
https://doi.org/10.1007/978-3-031-45170-6_81

1   Introduction

Schizophrenia is a complicated neuropsychological illness affecting 0.32% of the general population, per the World Health Organisation report [1] published in 2022. Hallucinations are one symptom of SZ, along with mental disturbances, delusions, negative emotions, and intellectual impairment. Early diagnosis of Schizophrenia can result in successful treatment, enhancing the quality of life for patients. However, the complexity and heterogeneity of Schizophrenia symptoms pose a challenge for an objective diagnosis. For that reason, several neuroimaging techniques, such as Electroencephalogram (EEG), come in handy to automatically detect neuro-disorders caused by Schizophrenia by recording brain signals.

EEG signal-based Schizophrenia analysis has been traditionally performed by extracting time-domain, frequency-domain, and time-frequency domain features from individual EEG channels' signals and utilizing ML classifiers. In [2] and [3], a set of entropy-based non-linear features were extracted from SZ-EEG time sequences, and classification was performed by Support Vector Machine (SVM) and Naive Bayes (NB) classifiers, respectively. Further, the frequency-domain features of SZ-EEG were investigated in [4] and [5], where the spectral powers of different EEG frequency bands are computed using Fast Fourier Transform (FFT) method. Moreover, due to the non-stationarity of EEG data, a time-frequency domain analysis was performed in [6] where the L1-norms of 6-level wavelet decomposition of EEG signal were considered features. On the other hand, with the recent advent of deep learning models in EEG classification, in [7], a Convolutional Neural Network (CNN)-based classification model was proposed. However, all the classification schemes mentioned above extract features from individual electrodes while neglecting the functional topological relationships between the electrodes. Specifically, the time-domain, FFT-based, or wavelet features represent the nature of brain activations at individual electrodes. However, the synchrony and information flow between the brain regions is still not captured. Recent brain connectivity analysis studies show significant brain connectivity alterations in Schizophrenia [8]. Therefore, exploring the nature of local EEG activations integrated with global connectivity patterns can provide more insights about SZ-EEG, but this approach is still to be investigated.

The recent advances in graph signal processing (GSP) provide an effective tool to describe local and global properties of many multi-component, mutually interacting systems, such as social networks, electric grids, etc. Attempts have been made to capture and characterize brain activities by representing the same as graph signals (GS). In the case of EEG, GSP has been utilized for classification, signal denoising [9], and spatial filtering purposes [10]. The underlying connectivity graphs for GSP are obtained from structural connectivity information or computed based on the physical distance between the brain regions. This poses an issue for implementing such techniques in EEG data, as the functional connectivity is not directly related to the physical distance.

To address the issue of integrating the local and global properties of SZ-EEG into a unified representation based on connectivity, this study proposes a novel graph signal (GS)-based representation of multivariable SZ-EEG. The proposed approach fuses the individual electrode features and the global functional interaction between brain regions into a unified GS representation. Further, different vertex-domain and spectral-domain GSP-based features are extracted from the GS representation. Lastly, we employ several ML models with low computational costs for the classification task. The significant contributions of the proposed model are as follows:

- An appropriate functional connectivity-based GS representation for multichannel SZ-EEG data.
- To extract discriminatory GSP-based features to facilitate high-performance automated detection of Schizophrenia.

2   Preliminary Concepts

Graph Signal Representation: A graph is defined as $G = \{V, E, W\}$, where V is the node set, E is the edge set, and $W \in \mathbb{R}^{N \times N}$ is the weighted adjacency matrix. A graph signal $X \in \mathbb{R}^N$, that resides on the nodes of the underlying graph G is defined as $X = \{x_1, x_2, .., x_N\}$. The degree normalized graph Laplacian is denoted as, $L = I - D_w^{-1/2} W D_w^{-1/2}$, where D_w is the diagonal degree matrix of W, and $I \in \mathbb{R}^{N \times N}$ the identity matrix. The normalized Laplacian provides the basis of GFT for the graph signals. Here, the graph signal X is represented as linear combinations of the eigenvectors of L. The eigendecomposition of normalized Laplacian is $L = U \Lambda U^H$, where Λ is a diagonal matrix consisting of the eigenvalues and U is the eigenvector matrix, and U_H is the Hermitian matrix of U. Then the GFT and the inverse-GFT (IGFT) [11] of the graph signal X is defined as $\tilde{X} = U^H X$, $X = U\tilde{X}$, thus forming a Fourier transform-pair.

3   Methodology

3.1   Overview

Figure 1 depicts the proposed PLI-GSP approach. Firstly, from the preprocessed EEG data of healthy and SZ patients, the Phase Lag Index-based connectivity matrix is computed for all the trials. The underlying network is obtained by averaging all the PLI matrices. Moreover, the permutation entropies for individual channels are calculated for a particular trial and used as node features. Afterward, the averaged connectivity matrix and the node features for individual trials are fused together to obtain the proposed GS representations. Then, a set of discriminatory GSP-based features is extracted from the GSs using GFT. Lastly, the classification is performed by feeding the GSP features of both classes to traditional ML models, and the classification performances are observed.

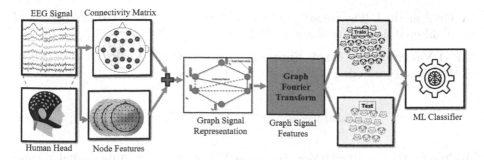

Fig. 1. Overview of the proposed classification framework.

3.2 Representing Multi-variable EEG Recordings as Graph Signals

Each preprocessed EEG epoch is represented in 2D form by $X_t \in \mathbb{R}^{N \times T}$, where N = number of EEG electrodes, and T = (Sampling frequency × epoch duration in seconds) is the number of time points of the epoch. Here, the brain network G consists of N nodes, each representing the individual electrode's location. The proposed GS representation of the EEG signal has two components, the underlying connectivity network ($W \in \mathbb{R}^{N \times N}$) and the signal values (Graph signal $X = \{x_1, x_2, .., x_N\}$) at each node.

Computing Connectivity Networks: From individual preprocessed EEG epochs (X_t), the functional connectivity networks are extracted by utilizing a phase-based estimator, namely, the Phase Lag Index, due to its robustness to the volume conduction effect that commonly hampers the efficiency of standard EEG connectivity measures. Given two signals, PLI is calculated using Eq. 1.

$$PLI = |n^{-1} \sum_{t=1}^{n} sgn(Im[e^{i(\Phi^j - \Phi^k)t}])|, \tag{1}$$

where n is the length of the original signals, *sgn* is the *signum* function, and ϕ_j and ϕ_k are the instantaneous phases of the signals, calculated using the Hilbert transform to the original time series. All the trials' PLI matrices are then averaged to get the underlying connectivity network of GS representation.

Computing the Graph Signal Values at Individual Nodes: For each trial $X_t \in \mathbb{R}^{N \times T}$, the Permutation Entropy [12] of each electrode's EEG signal is computed and considered as the GS values for that trial. The GS representation for each trial is obtained by combining the GS values with the connectivity network.

3.3 Graph Signal Processing-Based Feature Extraction

Utilizing GSP, several vertex-domain and spectral-domain features of the GSs of each trial are computed. The spectral-domain representation of GSs is obtained by GFT method. The smoothness and variation properties and the powers of graph-filtered signals are considered as features described below.

Total Variation of Graph Signal (gsp-norm-tv): $L2$ norm of the gradient of the signal over node i is a measure of local smoothness:

$$\text{Local variation} = \sqrt{\sum_{j=1}^{n^*} w_{ij}(x_i - x_j)^2}. \tag{2}$$

Adding all the local variations, the Total Variation of the graph signal is computed, which is defined as follows:

$$\text{gsp-norm-tv} = \sum_{i=0}^{N} \sqrt{\sum_{j=1}^{n^*} w_{ij}(x_i - x_j)^2}, \tag{3}$$

where N = total no of nodes, and $n*$ = no of nodes neighbor to ith node.

Tikhonov Norm of Graph Signal Variation (gsp-norm-tik): Tikhonov norm is defined as the $L1$ norm of the gradient of the signal-

$$\text{gsp-norm-tik} = \sum_{i=0}^{n} \sum_{j=1}^{n^*} \sqrt{w_{ij}}|x_i - x_j|, j = 1, 2, ...n^*. \tag{4}$$

Similar to classical signal processing, utilizing the notion of graph frequencies (how the graph signal's amplitude fluctuates throughout the network), graph signal filtering can be performed by converting the signal (X) into the spectral-domain using GFT and then by removing the desired graph frequency components from the spectral representation ($\tilde{X}$). We defined low-pass, band-pass, and high-pass filters for the SZ-EEG graph signals utilizing the graph frequencies described below. Overall, a total of 6 features, namely, gsp-norm-tv, gsp-norm-tik, and the four band-power features described below, are utilized in the ML models.

Full-band power: $Power_{FB} = \frac{1}{N} \sum \tilde{x}_i^2$
Low-band power: $Power_{LB} = \frac{1}{N} \sum (\tilde{x}_{lowpassfiltered})_i^2$
Mid-band power: $Power_{MB} = \frac{1}{N} \sum (\tilde{x}_{midband})_i^2$
High-band power: $Power_{HB} = \frac{1}{N} \sum (\tilde{x}_{highpassfiltered})_i^2$

4   Experimental Results and Discussion

The Dataset and Preprocessing: In the current study, a publicly available SZ-EEG dataset [8], obtained from an experiment performed at the Institute of Psychiatry and Neurology in Warsaw, Poland, has been utilized. The original study [8] included 14 paranoid schizophrenia patients and 14 healthy controls. A 19-channel EEG device recorded the eyes-closed, resting state data for 15 min at a sampling rate of 250 Hz. The preprocessing includes three steps: firstly, A Common Average Referencing (CAR) is done on the raw EEG data; secondly, a 0.1–50 Hz band-pass filter is applied to remove high-frequency noises; thirdly, the baseline correction is done. Further, each 15-min trial is fragmented into multiple 5-s segments to increase the number of training instances.

Obtaining Connectivity Matrices: As discussed previously, the PLI connectivity matrices are computed for the individual EEG segments. Obtained PLI matrices are then averaged to obtain a connectivity matrix further utilized as the underlying network for the GS representations. The averaged PLI matrices of healthy persons and SZ patients are shown in Fig. 2. Figure 2 shows that the number of connections for SZ patients is significantly lower with prominent disconnectivity observed in the C3, P3, Pz, and F3 channels.

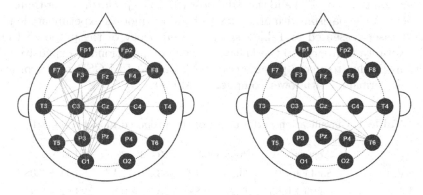

Fig. 2. Comparison of PLI-based averaged connectivity networks for healthy (on the left) and SZ (on the right) classes, with a threshold value of $T = 0.75$.

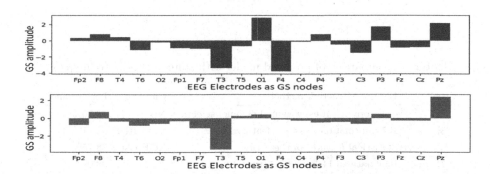

Fig. 3. Original GS (on top) and filtered GS (on bottom). The impact of low-pass filtering on the GS for the unhealthy subject '*h01*' is shown. The high-frequency variation of the GSs is reduced, and smoothness is increased.

Graph Signal Processing-Based Feature Extraction: Using a total of 19 graph frequencies, the low-frequency band is defined by considering the 6 lowest frequencies, the high-frequency band is defined as the 6 highest frequencies, and the other frequencies form the mid-band. A sample of GS filtering in Fig. 3 shows that the variation of the signal values in the nodes gets significantly reduced after applying the low-pass filter, and corresponding smoothness increases.

Classification Performance: Using the GSP features, a 10-fold cross-validated averaged classification is performed. The ML model names and the optimum hyperparameters as obtained by a grid search are SVM (C = 1, gamma = 1) with 'rbf' kernel, KNN (K = 5), D-Tree (max-features = 3), AdaBoost, XGB (n-estimators = 75, gamma = 0.02, and max-depth = 5), and LDA. From the classification results shown in Table 1, it is observed that the XGBoost model achieves the highest accuracy of 99.77% with a low standard deviation. Further, the Decision tree (96.27%) and the Adaboost (97.23%) perform better than other classifiers. A comparison with other state-of-the-art models experimented on the same dataset presented in Table 2 shows the efficiency of the proposed framework. Notably, compared to the 11-layer based computationally expensive CNN model in [7] due to many parameters, the proposed PLI-GSP model provides better performance with lower computational cost.

Table 1. Classification performance of the proposed model using ML

	Accuracy	Precision	Recall	F1 score
SVM	83.44 ± 1.08	83.58 ± 1.12	83.52 ± 1.17	83.41 ± 1.08
KNN	93.05 ± 0.85	93.24 ± 0.88	93.01 ± 0.80	93.02 ± 0.85
Decision Tree	96.27 ± 0.91	96.27 ± 0.91	96.28 ± 0.92	96.27 ± 0.91
XGBoost	**99.77 ± 0.52**	**99.33 ± 0.52**	**99.77 ± 0.51**	**99.77 ± 0.52**
Adaboost	97.23 ± 0.78	97.25 ± 0.75	97.24 ± 0.77	97.22 ± 0.78
LDA	86.83 ± 1.72	88.29 ± 1.46	87.02 ± 1.76	86.73 ± 1.75

Table 2. Comparison of proposed model with state-of-the-art techniques

Ref.	Feature extraction method	Classifier	Performance
[2]	6 entropy features, weighted channel selection	NB	93.75%
[3]	157 information-theoretic features	SVM-RBF	92.91%
[6]	Statistical features of theta-EEG	XGBoost	78.75%
[7]	Raw data to 11-layer CNN model		98.07%
[13]	Cyclic Group of Prime Order Patterns	KNN	**99.91%**
PLI-GSP	Graph Signal processing based features	XGBoost	99.77%

5   Conclusion

In this work, a novel GSP-based method for automated detection of Schizophrenia from EEG signals is proposed. The proposed PLI-GSP model integrates the local EEG activation and the global functional connectivity into a GS representation. Then, vertex-domain and spectral-domain discriminatory features are extracted from the graph signals using the GFT method. Using these features, a 99.77% average accuracy is obtained using the XGBoost model that outperforms most of the state-of-the-art models. One limitation of this study is that it only investigates the PLI as the connectivity measure for GS representation. In the future, connectivity measures other than PLI can be explored. Also, different graph learning algorithms may be attempted for a better connectivity network.

References

1. Schizophrenia (2022). https://www.who.int/news-room/fact-sheets/detail/schizophrenia. Accessed 12 July 2023
2. Goshvarpour, A., Goshvarpour, A.: Schizophrenia diagnosis by weighting the entropy measures of the selected EEG channel. J. Med. Biol. Eng. **42**, 898–908 (2022). https://doi.org/10.1007/s40846-022-00762-z
3. Jahmunah, V., et al.: Automated detection of schizophrenia using nonlinear signal processing methods. Artif. Intell. Med. **100**, 101698 (2019)
4. Kim, J.W., Lee, Y.S., Han, D.H., Min, K.J., Lee, J., Lee, K.: Diagnostic utility of quantitative EEG in un-medicated schizophrenia. Neurosci. Lett. **589**, 126–131 (2015)
5. Dvey-Aharon, Z., Fogelson, N., Peled, A., Intrator, N.: Schizophrenia detection and classification by advanced analysis of EEG recordings using a single electrode approach. PLoS ONE **10**(4), e0123033 (2015)
6. Sahu, P.K.: Artificial intelligence system for verification of schizophrenia via theta-EEG rhythm. Biomed. Sig. Process. Control **81**, 104485 (2023)
7. Oh, S.L., Vicnesh, J., Ciaccio, E.J., Yuvaraj, R., Acharya, U.R.: Deep convolutional neural network model for automated diagnosis of schizophrenia using EEG signals. Appl. Sci. **9**(14), 2870 (2019)
8. Olejarczyk, E., Jernajczyk, W.: Graph-based analysis of brain connectivity in schizophrenia. PLoS ONE **12**(11), e0188629 (2017)
9. Pentari, A., Tzagkarakis, G., Marias, K., Tsakalides, P.: Graph denoising of impulsive EEG signals and the effect of their graph representation. Biomed. Sig. Process. Control **78**, 103886 (2022)
10. Humbert, P., Oudre, L., Dubost, C.: Learning spatial filters from EEG signals with graph signal processing methods. In: 2021 43rd Annual International Conference of the IEEE Engineering in Medicine & Biology Society (EMBC), pp. 657–660. IEEE (2021)
11. Sandryhaila, A., Moura, J.M.F.: Discrete signal processing on graphs: graph Fourier transform. In: 2013 IEEE International Conference on Acoustics, Speech and Signal Processing, pp. 6167–6170. IEEE (2013)
12. Bandt, C., Pompe, B.: Permutation entropy: a natural complexity measure for time series. Phys. Rev. Lett. **88**(17), 174102 (2002)
13. E. Aydemir, et al.: CGP17Pat: automated schizophrenia detection based on a cyclic group of prime order patterns using EEG signals. In: Healthcare, vol. 10, p. 643. MDPI (2022)

Biometrics

FVINet: Translating Thermograms to Facial Vasculature Imprints

Anushree Basu[1], Anirban Dasgupta[2(✉)] [iD], Aurobinda Routray[1],
and Pabitra Mitra[1]

[1] Indian Institute of Technology Kharagpur, Kharagpur 721302, West Bengal, India
[2] Indian Institute of Technology Guwahati, Guwahati 781039, Assam, India
anirban1828@gmail.com

Abstract. Facial vasculature is the arrangement of blood vessels and adjacent tissues inside the facial surface. This arrangement is useful in biometrics, healthcare, and psychological analysis. The blood flow in these vessels monitors the spatiotemporal temperature distribution, which makes vasculature estimation possible using facial thermal images. The existing methods are inaccurate due to the noisy capture of thermal images and variations of the facial vasculature imprints (FVI) across subjects. In this paper, we solve this issue using a data-driven approach. We propose a neural network architecture named FVINet to convert facial thermograms to their corresponding FVI. We manually mark the FVIs in the thermograms and then train the FVINet to output the FVI, given the corresponding facial thermograms. The testing results show significant improvements compared to existing methods.

Keywords: Thermogram · Vasculature · Generative Adversarial Network

1 Introduction

The arrangement of the superficial arteries and veins in the face is called the facial vasculature [1], as shown in Fig. 1. The flow of blood in these vessels alters the superficial skin temperature. This creates a facial vasculature imprint (FVI), which can be captured using a thermal camera. The manual observation of the FVI in the facial thermogram is useful in several applications, such as biometric identification, stress, and emotion analysis, vital sign monitoring, etc. However, automation of this process is challenging as it is not accurate. This is because we cannot find a perfect function $f(.)$ which maps an input facial thermogram $\mathbb{I}(x,y)$ to the FVI image $\mathbb{V}(x,y)$, as $\mathbb{V}(x,y) = f(\mathbb{I}(x,y))$. This is due to thermal noise and variability across individuals. The existing attempts to solve this problem are by Buddharaju et $al.$ [2], and Guzmman et $al.$ [3]. These methods use morphological operations on the facial thermograms to highlight the vasculature. However, noise and subject variability pose serious challenges to these

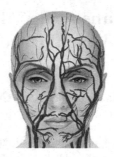

Fig. 1. Blood vascular network consisting of Veins and arteries overlaying the human face, Courtesy [1]

methods. The advent of deep learning has helped to solve such problems, specifically, denoising autoencoders [4]. However, autoencoders sometimes produce blurry outputs during reconstruction.

This work proposes a data-driven approach to solve the problem. The objectives of the work are as follows:

- Ground-truth data preparation through manually marking the vasculature regions
- Training a suitable network that can translate the thermogram to FVI.

The main contribution of this work is the trained deep neural network, named the FVINet, that maps the input facial thermal image to its corresponding FVI.

2   Facial Vasculature Imprint Network (FVINet)

The objective of the neural network is to translate the facial thermogram to its corresponding FVI. The available architectures [5] for image-to-image translation tasks include denoising autoencoders and conditional Generative Adversarial Networks (cGAN). Owing to the limitations of lossy outputs in denoising autoencoders, we select cGAN for the end-to-end learning of FVI from its corresponding thermal face image, inspired by the work of Isola *et al.* [5].

2.1   Conditional Generative Adversarial Neural Network

Here, we train a conditional generative model G to learn a mapping from thermal face image $\mathbb{I}$, a random noise image $\mathbb{Z}$ to vasculature image $\mathbb{V}$, $G : (\mathbb{I}, \mathbb{Z}) \longrightarrow \mathbb{V}$. We provide the noise image $\mathbb{Z}$ in the form of dropout, applied on several layers of our generator at training and testing times. The generator G produces synthetic vasculature images that cannot be distinguished from real vasculature images by the adversarially trained discriminator, D. The discriminator, D is trained to detect the synthesized vasculature images output by the generator G.

The objective function $\mathcal{L}_c(G, D)$ of the FVINet can be expressed as:

$$\mathcal{L}_c(G, D) = \mathbb{E}(\log D(\mathbb{I}, \mathbb{V})) + \mathbb{E}(\log(1 - D(\mathbb{I}, G(\mathbb{I}, \mathbb{Z})))) \qquad (1)$$

Here, $\mathbb{E}(.)$ denotes the expectation operator. The generator G tries to minimize this objective against an adversarial discriminator D that tries to maximize it, *i.e.*,

$$G^* = \arg \min_G \max_D \mathcal{L}_c(G, D) \tag{2}$$

The conditioning of the discriminator D by comparing it to an unconditional variant in which D does not observe $\mathbb{I}$ is given by the loss function $\mathcal{L}(G, D)$ as:

$$\mathcal{L}(G, D) = \mathbb{E}(\log D(\mathbb{V})) + \mathbb{E}(\log(1 - D(\mathbb{I}, \mathbb{Z}))) \tag{3}$$

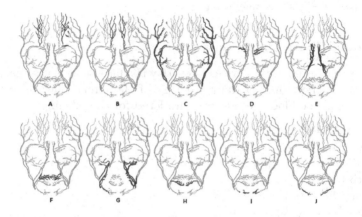

Fig. 2. Highlighted Arteries and Veins in Different Facial Parts A: Supraorbital (SO), B: Supratrochlear (STr), C: Superficial Temporal (ST), D: Infraorbital (IO), E: Angular (A), F: Superior Labial (SL), G: Facial(F), H: Inferior Labial (IL), I: Mental (M), J: Submental (SM)

Fig. 3. The overall blood vessel anatomy showing the distribution of different venous and arterial networks

The task of the generator G is to deceive the discriminator and generate an output as close as possible to the ground truth vasculature imprint. This generator output with respect to the ground truth vasculature imprint is computed using the L1 norm as:

$$\mathcal{L}_{L1}(G) = \mathbb{E}(|\mathbb{V} - G(\mathbb{I}, \mathbb{Z})|) \tag{4}$$

The final optimization can be formulated as

$$G^* = \arg \min_{G} \max_{D} [\mathcal{L}_c(G, D) + \lambda \mathcal{L}_{L1}(G)] \tag{5}$$

We have used $\lambda = 100$, as suggested in [5].

2.2 Ground Truth Data Preparation

For ground truth preparation, we must overlay the face image's vasculature. This requires an understanding of the physiology of the human face. The following location sites of the blood vessels are considered for the labeling.

- Supraorbital (SO)
- Supratrochlear (STr)
- Superficial Temporal (ST)
- Infraorbital (IO)
- Angular (A)
- Superior Labial (SL)
- Facial (F)
- Inferior Labial (IL)
- Mental (M)
- Submental (SM)

Figure 2 shows highlighted important blood vessels manually marked properly for ground truth data preparation. This approach of labeling the vasculature is carried out by manually marking the vasculature region in the facial thermograms, with the help of subject matter experts, as followed in segmentation tasks [6]. We have involved two physiologists and a Computer Vision expert. Each facial thermogram is analyzed pixel-wise and labeled with a graphics tablet and COCO annotator tool [7].

We have collected 2000 facial thermograms randomly selected from the Heteroface [8] database. Each such image pair is further resized to 178×228. The data pair order is reshuffled to remove any training bias, maintaining the thermogram-FVI pair correspondence intact.

2.3 Network Architecture

The generator and the discriminator blocks of the FVINet are shown in Fig. 4. The generator architecture constitutes the encoder and decoder blocks with skip connections between the encoding and corresponding decoding layers, forming a

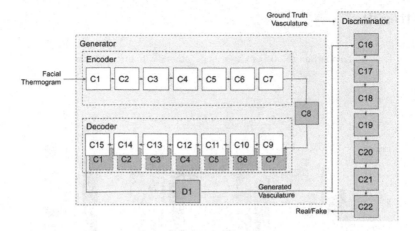

Fig. 4. Architecture of FVINet

U-Net. The encoder block has seven conv2D layers of size 4×4, strides of 2×2, same padding followed by a Leaky ReLU activation layer up to the penultimate convolution layer. The numbers of Conv2D filters for the seven layers are 64, 128, 256, 512, 512, 512, and 512, respectively. The decoder model is the exact replica of the encoder model but in reverse order. The final layer activation is a tanh function to scale the output from -1 to $+1$. The discriminator is based on a patch-GAN model where each output prediction of the model maps to 70×70 patch of the input thermogram. Each value provides a probability that a 70×70 patch in the input image is real. The input thermogram is passed through six conv2D layers with 4×4 filters with a stride of 2×2, the same padding, each followed by a Leaky ReLU activation layer, up to the penultimate convolution layer. The Conv2D filters for the seven layers are 64, 128, 256, 512, 512, and 1, respectively. The final activation layer is sigmoid. For training, the real and fake images are assigned 1 and 0, respectively.

2.4 Training

The $\mathcal{G}$ model is trained using back-propagation with the loss given in (5). The $\mathcal{D}$ model is compiled with a loss function of binary cross-entropy h, with p being the output and b being the ground truth value, as

$$h = -b \log(p) - (1 - b) \log(1 - p) \tag{6}$$

We have used an Adam optimizer with a learning rate of 0.0002. The FVINet was trained for 100 epochs with a single paired image sample constituting a batch as suggested in [5].

3 Results

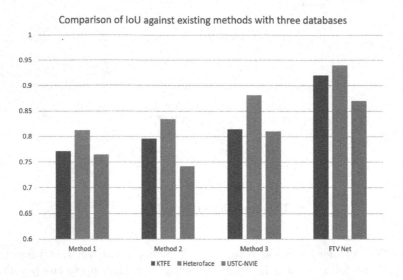

Fig. 5. Comparison of IoU against existing methods, Method 1 (Buddaraju *et al.* [9]), Method 2 (Guzman *et al.* [3]), Method 3 (Autoencoder [4]) with FVINet

Table 1. Comparison of different methods for the extraction of each vein: Method 1 (Buddaraju *et al.* [9]), Method 2 (Guzman *et al.* [3]), Method 3 (Autoencoder [4]) with FVINet

Vessel	Method 1	Method 2	Method 3	FVINet
SO	0.79	0.86	0.84	0.93
STr	0.78	0.84	0.83	0.88
ST	0.54	0.64	0.75	0.83
IO	0.24	0.44	0.59	0.67
A	0.49	0.45	0.51	0.85
SL	0.43	0.38	0.47	0.61
F	0.30	0.69	0.55	0.91
IL	0.62	0.63	0.78	0.87
M	0.72	0.77	0.67	0.78
SM	0.34	0.37	0.52	0.59

We use a total of 900 images for testing. We use the vasculature of Fig. 3 as our reference to compute the detectability of a specific blood vessel from the vasculature imprint obtained by the FVINet and its competing methods. We have used the blood vessels *viz.* SO, STr, ST, IO, A, SL, F, IL, M, SM for the comparison. For a correct extraction of a particular blood vessel, we give a score

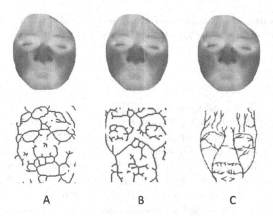

A   B   C

Fig. 6. Comparison between test results using A. Method 1 (Buddaraju *et al.* [9]), B. Method 2 (Guzman *et al.* [3]), C. FVINet

of 1, otherwise a 0. Finally, we execute the algorithms across all the N frames and find ^iN_v true detections of a specific vein $i \in$ SO, STr, ST, IO, A, SL, F, IL, M, SM. We define the detectability factor $^i\delta$ for a blood vessel i as

$$^i\delta = \frac{^iN_v}{N} \tag{7}$$

Table 1 shows the detectability of a blood vessel using different techniques. The methods compared with the FVINet are with those of Buddaraju *et al.* [9], Guzman *et al.* [3], as well as with a seven-layered convolutional Autoencoder [4]. To evaluate the correctness of the FVI estimation, the best performance metric is the intersection over union (IoU) (Fig. 6).

The observations obtained in Table 1 reveal that the detectability is better in the proposed method for SO, STr, ST, A, SL, F, IL, and M as compared to the competing methods. However, the detectability is found to be low in the case of SM and IO. The IoU performance comparisons are provided in Fig. 5 across the three databases.

4 Conclusion

In this paper, we have proposed a deep-learning method to extract of facial vasculature imprint (FVI) from thermograms. The trained network is based on a conditional generative adversarial neural network, which we named the FVINet. We use a manual marking scheme under the guidance of experts for the ground truth data of FVI. The superior performance over the existing methods is mainly due to the guided training of the network by the experts to achieve the desired results. The technique will be used to compare the FVI under different physiological conditions across subjects.

Acknowledgements. The authors are extremely grateful to the experts and participants for manually marking the ground truths for the vasculature.

References

1. UFO Themes. 7: The head by regions (2015)
2. Buddharaju, P., Pavlidis, I.T., Tsiamyrtzis, P.: Pose-invariant physiological face recognition in the thermal infrared spectrum. In: 2006 Conference on Computer Vision and Pattern Recognition Workshop (CVPRW 2006), p. 53. IEEE (2006)
3. Guzman, A.M., Goryawala, M., Adjouadi, M.: Generating thermal facial signatures using thermal infrared images. In: 2012 IEEE International Conference on Emerging Signal Processing Applications, pp. 21–24. IEEE (2012)
4. García-González, J., Ortiz-de Lazcano-Lobato, J.M., Luque-Baena, R.M., Molina-Cabello, M.A., López-Rubio, E.: Foreground detection by probabilistic modeling of the features discovered by stacked denoising autoencoders in noisy video sequences. Pattern Recogn. Lett. **125**, 481–487 (2019)
5. Isola, P., Zhu, J.-Y., Zhou, T., Efros, A.A.: Image-to-image translation with conditional adversarial networks. In: Proceedings of the IEEE Conference on Computer Vision and Pattern Recognition, pp. 1125–1134 (2017)
6. Qureshi, T.A., Habib, M., Hunter, A., Al-Diri, B.: A manually-labeled, artery/vein classified benchmark for the DRIVE dataset. In: Proceedings of the 26th IEEE International Symposium on Computer-Based Medical Systems, pp. 485–488. IEEE (2013)
7. Carbonari, M., Vallasciani, G., Migliorelli, L., Frontoni, E., Moccia, S.: End-to-end semantic joint detection and limb-pose estimation from depth images of preterm infants in NICUs. In: 2021 IEEE Symposium on Computers and Communications (ISCC), pp. 1–6. IEEE (2021)
8. Basu, A., Dasgupta, A., Thyagharajan, A., Routray, A., Guha, R., Mitra, P.: A portable personality recognizer based on affective state classification using spectral fusion of features. IEEE Trans. Affect. Comput. **9**(3), 330–342 (2018)
9. Buddharaju, P., Pavlidis, I.T., Tsiamyrtzis, P., Bazakos, M.: Physiology-based face recognition in the thermal infrared spectrum. IEEE Trans. Pattern Anal. Mach. Intell. **29**(4), 613–626 (2007)

Enforcement of DNN with LDA-PCA-ELM for PIE Invariant Few-Shot Face Recognition

Anvaya Rai[1,2]([✉]), Brejesh Lall[2], Astha Zalani[1], Raghwender Prakash[1], and Shikha Srivastava[1]

[1] Centre for Development of Telematics, New Delhi, India
anvayarai@gmail.com
[2] Indian Institute of Technology Delhi, New Delhi, India

Abstract. Face Recognition has been an active area of research but limited work has been done in the domains where the captured face images are of very low resolution, blurred and occluded. The other challenges in the domains like face recognition at a distance or unconstrained face recognition, include pose and expression variations. Additionally, for use cases like person re-identification and surveillance, the availability of limited amount of annotated data for various classes, makes it a highly probable candidate for Few-shot face recognition. In this work, we present a deep learning architecture that uses Deep Neural Networks (DNN) along with Extreme Learning Machines (ELM) to address the problem of generating compact and discriminating face representations, while accounting for the few-shot constraints of the novel dataset. We have used three types of ELMs namely, PCA-ELM, LDA-ELM and LDA-PCA-ELM, to augment the DNN and achieve better accuracy with lower computational cost at the time of inference.

Keywords: Low-shot Recognition · Dimensionality Reduction · Hyperspherical Manifold · Extreme Learning Machines (ELM) · Principal Component Analysis Extreme Learning Machine (PCA-ELM) · Linear Discriminant Analysis Extreme Learning Machine (LDA-ELM)

1 Introduction

Facial recognition system is a technology capable of recognition or verifying a human face from a digital image and in few-shot face recognition, a person is recognized by seeing only once or a few number of times. The holistic machine learning approaches of face recognition used to derive a low-dimensional representation of classes through certain assumptions about the distribution of the available face image samples. These representations included linear sub-space [2], manifold [3], and sparse representation [4]. As most methods addressed each aspect of unconstrained face recognition separately, such as disguise, illumination, pose or expression, there was a lack of a technique to address these challenges integrally. Thus, these approaches were unable to address the facial changes that deviated from the prior assumptions.

These challenges are better addressed by deep learning. The use of multiple layers of cascaded filters enable deep neural networks (DNN) learn reliable features that are distinct and compact, while the output space remains well generalised. The drawback with these techniques is the requirement of huge dataset. This problem is addressed by Low-shot learning techniques. They aim to achieve good generalisation performance using the limited number of training samples. Most Low-shot learning methods use a meta-learning strategy [5], where a meta-learner is trained to classify well on new, unseen samples. Low-shot learning methods use episodic meta-learning and include architectures like prototypical networks [6], relation networks [7], model agnostic meta-learning frameworks [8] and LSTM-based meta-learning [9]. In addition to episodic meta-learning methods, Low-shot learning also uses transfer learning, where large datasets are used to first train the models and then this knowledge is transferred to smaller datasets that contain the novel target classes; examples include SimCLR [12], MoCo [14], SimSiam [13] etc.

In this work, we use the concept of transfer learning and augment it with the traditional approach of feature space transformation and manifold extraction. To ensure faster training of the classifier and to investigate the quantum of performance improvement (if we are provided with limited amount of domain specific data), we make the use of Extreme Learning Machine (ELM) [10] algorithms to implement this feature space transformation and manifold extraction.

2   Methodology

In the face recognition task, it is important to generate features that are agnostic to constraints like pose, illumination, expression, occlusion etc. The few-shot constraint, makes it further more challenging to learn the optimal representation of the samples in the novel dataset. Thus, we need to learn representations that focus only on the physiognomic features that make it possible to tell one person from another by their face's form, their nose, lips, eyes, and other skeletal characteristics.

To meet this requirement for learning an optimal representation of the samples in the novel dataset, we propose a new topology comprising of a domain specific Pre-Trained DNN, followed by a Single-hidden Layer Feedforward Network (SLFN), called *Feature Space Transformer Network* - motivated by ELM. It performs the task of extracting a relevant dense subspace from the original generalised latent feature space and helps in classification based on only those sets of features which contain information about the samples in the novel dataset. The suggested pipeline is depicted in Fig. 1(b).

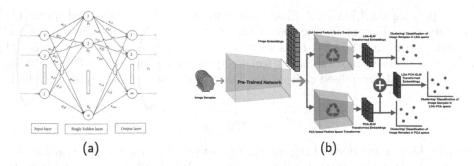

(a)   (b)

Fig. 1. (a) ELM Architecture using Single-hidden Layer Feedforward Network. (b) Proposed pipelines using the PCA-ELM, LDA-ELM and LDA-PCA-ELM initialised Feature Space Transformer Network following a Pre-trained Deep Neural Network.

2.1 Determining Feature Transformed Latent Space

The ELM framework is implemented using a Single-hidden Layer Feedforward Network (SLFN), as shown in Fig. 1(a). A SLFN consists of three layers, namely Input Layer, Hidden Layer and Output Layer. The D-dimensional input layer, in our case, comprises of the 128-dimensional or 2048-dimensional embedding generated by the last fully connected layer of FaceNet or ResNet-50, respectively. This is then followed by a n-dimensional hidden layer. Let $\boldsymbol{a}_s = (a_{1s}, a_{2s}, a_{3s}, ..., a_{Ds})^{\mathrm{T}}$ denote the weight vector connecting the input layer to the sth hidden layer node, $s \in (1, n)$ and $\boldsymbol{v}_j = (v_{1j}, v_{2j}, v_{3j}, ..., v_{nj})^{\mathrm{T}}$ represents the vector containing the weights of the edges connecting the hidden layer to the jth output layer node, $j \in (1, m)$, where m is the number of novel dataset classes. Each node in the output layer corresponds to a novel dataset class. As a process for identifying an optimally dense and uncorrelated feature space, henceforth called as *Feature Transformed Latent Space*, we need to determine the optimal value of n and the corresponding weights of $\boldsymbol{a}_s$ that connect the last fully connected layer of the DNN to the hidden layer of the SLFN.

In case of PCA-ELM [11], $n \in [1, D]$ and the $\boldsymbol{a}_s$ correspond to the sth basis vector of the eigen space, and in case of LDA-ELM [11], $n \in [1, m-1]$ and the $\boldsymbol{a}_s$ correspond to the sth basis vector of the LDA space of the embedding generated by pre-trained DNN. We also concatenate PCA and LDA feature space and generate an extended *Feature Transformed Latent Space*. While PCA captures the overall variance of the training sample space, LDA enhances the discriminability between the classes in the training sample space. Through our experiments, we will show that the hybrid LDA-PCA-ELM framework [11] results in better generalization performance compared to the two individual frameworks (PCA-ELM or LDA-ELM). Thus, corresponding to k^{th} input pattern $(\boldsymbol{x}_k)$, the input to the sth hidden layer node $(b_k{}^{\mathrm{s}})$, is represented as:

$$b_k{}^{\mathrm{s}} = \boldsymbol{a}_s{}^{\mathrm{T}} \boldsymbol{x}_k \qquad (1)$$

Applying the LDA-PCA-ELM algorithm, we extract a dense subspace (U) of the original latent feature space. The columns of U are initailised using the eigen vectors and the LDA basis vectors, estimated by projecting the images of the novel dataset into the latent feature space and performing PCA/ LDA on the generated normalised embedding. The transformed latent variable model is as follows:

$$x = Uz + \tau \tag{2}$$

where, U is a transformed representation of the latent feature space and represents a matrix with D rows and n columns (with $n <= D + m - 1$, m being the number of classes in the novel dataset), x is a D-dimensional embedding of input image from novel dataset, z is a n-dimensional latent variable, τ is a constant (mean) vector in the transformed latent space. The maximum dimensionality of the subspace spanned by U is motivated by the fact that PCA over the original D-dimensional latent space will result in at most D-dimensional orthogonal space (when 100% variance is captured) and LDA will result in at most $m - 1$ feature projections, where m is the number of target classes in the novel dataset. As U represents a combination of both the spaces, thus the dimension of U is at most $D + m - 1$.

Unlike the PCA-ELM or LDA-PCA-ELM [11] proposed by Castaño et al., in our case, the choice of n is not restricted to the number of principal components that capture 90% of the variance in the training set. Instead, we propose to choose multiple number of PCA and LDA components, thereby capturing different levels of variance for the training data. Thus, to create this Feature Space Transformer Network, we need to freeze the weights of the pre-trained network and estimate the optimum weights of ELM framework. The freezing of the pre-trained network should ensure that the embedding generated for the samples of novel set, should be deterministic. This requirement also leads to removal of Drop-out layers from the pre-trained network during this stage.

After initialising the Feature Space Transformer Network with the weights estimated using PCA and LDA, we further proceed to choose an activation function (Φ) to generate the hidden layer output matrix $\mathbf{H}$, as defined by (3). For our experiments, we have used sigmoidal activation function.

$$\mathbf{H} = \begin{bmatrix} \Phi(a_1{}^T x_1) & \Phi(a_2{}^T x_1) & .. & \Phi(a_n{}^T x_1) \\ \Phi(a_1{}^T x_2) & \Phi(a_2{}^T x_2) & .. & \Phi(a_n{}^T x_2) \\ & . & & \\ & . & & \\ \Phi(a_1{}^T x_N) & \Phi(a_2{}^T x_N) & .. & \Phi(a_n{}^T x_N) \end{bmatrix}_{N \times n} \tag{3}$$

where, a_i is the ith basis vector of Feature Transformed Latent Space, x_j is the embedding of the jth training sample (generated by pre-trained DNN), N is the number of Training examples and n is the dimension of Feature Transformed Latent Space i.e. the number of hidden units.

Finally, as proposed by Huang [10], the output layer weights are estimated by solving the linear system $\mathbf{H}V = \mathbf{Y}$ using the Moore-Penrose generalized inverse. Thus, the values of the V parameters are estimated as:

$$V = \mathbf{H}^{\dagger}\mathbf{Y} \tag{4}$$

where $\mathbf{H}^{\dagger}$ is the Moore-Penrose generalized inverse of the hidden layer output matrix ($\mathbf{H}$) and $\mathbf{Y}$ is a training data target label matrix. This solution minimizes the training error, as it is the least-square solutions of the general linear system $\mathbf{H}V = \mathbf{Y}$. Also it has good generalization performance as it is unique, and has the smallest norm for the weights.

3 Experimental Framework

Ultra - Lowshot Dataset. The dataset we used here is LFW [1] and considered only those classes which had images greater than or equal to 5. We used 4 images per class to train our model and used the rest of the image samples for testing the model. By this criteria we have chose 423 classes having 1692 images for training our model. For testing purpose, we had additional 4293 face images.

Lowshot Dataset. The dataset we used here is LFW [1] and considered only those classes which had images greater than or equal to 16. We used 15 images per class to train our model and used the rest of the image samples for testing the model. By this criteria we have chose 96 classes having 1440 images for training our model. For testing purpose, we had additional 2155 face images.

The testing set, in both the above cases, had normalised low resolution blurred samples from varied poses, orientations and lighting conditions. The blur was applied synthetically using a 5×5 Gaussian kernel over the test images.

Recognition Pipeline. Our model pipeline contains a pre-trained DNN (FaceNet/ ResNet-50 model) followed by a Feature Space Transformer Network. We have done our implementation by varying the amount of variance captured across the face embedding generated from pre-trained DNN. The results for different experiments, have been tabulated and discussed in the following sections. The proposed approaches are evaluated over *Classification Accuracy* and *Dimension of Feature Space*. We use the following convention to represent the various topology of the experiments conducted over the above dataset:

1. Original Latent Feature Space - FaceNet (OLFS-F): 128-dimensional output latent feature space generated by the pre-trained FaceNet network.
2. Original Latent Feature Space - ResNet-50 (OLFS-R): 2048-dimensional output latent feature space generated by the pre-trained ResNet-50 network.
3. Feature Transformed Latent Space - PCA (FTLS-P ($\alpha\%$)): q-dimensional feature space generated using PCA-ELM. The weights being initialised by first q number of eigen vectors accounting for $\alpha\%$ of captured variance.

4. Feature Transformed Latent Space - LDA (FTLS-L): q-dimensional feature space generated using LDA-ELM. The weights being initialised by first q number of basis vectors accounting for maximum variance.
5. Feature Transformed Latent Space - LDA-PCA (FTLS-LP (l,p)): q-dimensional feature space generated using LDA-PCA-ELM. The weights being initialised by l basis vectors generated from LDA transformation and p eigen vectors generated from PCA transformation.

4   Results and Discussion

We list the comparative analysis of the experimental results in the following section. The values in terms of classification accuracy rate, that are observed for Top 5, Top 3 and Top 1 matches in the Original Latent Feature Space (FaceNet/ResNet-50), serve as the benchmarks for defining the weights and output dimensions of the Feature Space Transformer Network and Feature Transformed Latent Space respectively. The same is highlighted in the tabulated results and color coded in Fig. 2, 3, 4 and 5. The inlay in the figures is showing the zoomed in view of the curves for the selected range of feature vectors.

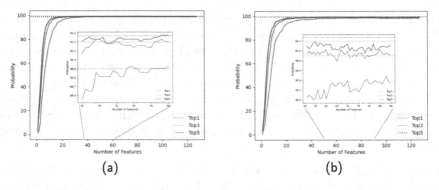

Fig. 2. Benchmark comparison over Ultra-Lowshot Dataset after appending (a) PCA and (b) LDA based Feature Space Transformer Network with Facenet.

Table 1 shows that if we use only FaceNet as a pre-trained network over Ultra-lowshot Dataset, then Top 5 Top 3 and Top 1 accuracy that serve as benchmark, are 99.27%, 99.20% and 98.90% respectively in the 128-dimensional latent feature space. However, Fig. 2(a) shows that with the same pre-trained network (FaceNet) followed by a PCA initialised Feature Space Transformer Network, with 99% energy captured, the benchmarks are matched, with the Transformed Latent Space being 59 dimensional only. The reduced feature vector can improve the response time and memory footprint of the applications that use database queries or feature matching techniques.

Table 1. Results on various Pre-Trained Networks & Dataset

Dataset	Pipeline	Top 1	Top 3	Top 5	Dimension (q)
Ultra-lowshot Dataset with FaceNet	OLFS-F	**98.90**	**99.20**	**99.27**	128
	FTLS-P (93%)	**98.92**	99.16	99.23	49
	FTLS-P (99%)	**98.90**	**99.20**	**99.27**	59
	FTLS-L	98.04	98.92	99.18	55
	FTLS-L	98.48	98.95	99.06	88
	FTLS-LP (55, 59)	98.27	99.02	99.16	114
	FTLS-LP (88, 49)	98.46	98.46	99.06	137
Ultra-lowshot Dataset with Resnet-50	OLFS-R	**99.18**	**99.27**	**99.30**	2048
	FTLS-P (45%)	98.92	99.18	**99.32**	45
	FTLS-P (64%)	**99.23**	99.27	99.27	95
	FTLS-P (70%)	**99.20**	**99.30**	99.30	**121**
	FTLS-L	99.09	99.25	**99.34**	312
	FTLS-L	99.06	**99.30**	99.30	320
	FTLS-L	**99.20**	99.27	**99.32**	**348**
	FTLS-LP (348, 45)	99.16	**99.30**	**99.32**	393
	FTLS-LP (348, 121)	**99.20**	**99.30**	**99.34**	469
Lowshot Dataset with FaceNet	OLFS-F	**99.35**	**99.53**	**99.67**	128
	FTLS-P (82%)	**99.44**	**99.58**	99.58	32
	FTLS-P (84%)	**99.39**	**99.62**	99.62	34
	FTLS-P (96%)	99.35	**99.58**	**99.72**	49
	FTLS-L	99.30	**99.62**	99.67	**56**
	FTLS-L	**99.48**	99.53	99.58	85
	FTLS-LP (56, 34)	99.35	**99.62**	99.67	90
	FTLS-LP (85, 32)	**99.48**	99.53	99.58	117
	FTLS-LP (85, 34)	**99.48**	**99.58**	99.67	119
Lowshot Dataset with Resnet-50	OLFS-R	**99.67**	**99.72**	**99.72**	2048
	FTLS-P (90%)	99.62	99.72	99.72	224
	FTLS-P (93%)	99.67	99.72	99.72	296
	FTLS-L	**99.72**	99.72	**99.76**	86
	FTLS-L	99.67	**99.76**	**99.76**	95
	FTLS-LP (95, 224)	**99.72**	**99.76**	**99.76**	319

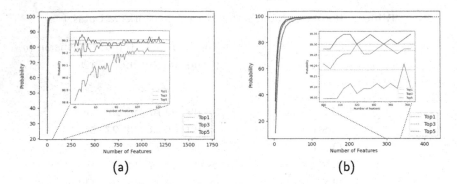

(a)   (b)

Fig. 3. Benchmark comparison over Ultra-Lowshot Dataset after appending (a) PCA and (b) LDA based Feature Space Transformer Network with ResNet-50.

Claim 1: When we use LDA in place of PCA to initialize the Feature Space Transformer Network, then results are not very encouraging. In Fig. 2(b), we can see that in this case the results comes out to be closer to benchmark but are not able to beat it. This attributes to the following 2 limitations:

1. Only 4 samples per class are not sufficient for LDA to learn the discriminating features.
2. In case of Ultra-lowshot dataset, LDA needs large number of basis vectors to generate discriminating features, but the maximum number of possible basis vectors (l) is constrained by the dimensionality of the original latent feature space (D) because if $D \gg m$ then $l = max(D, m - 1)$, where D is the dimensionality of the original latent feature space (128 in case of Facenet) and m is the number of classes in the novel dataset (423 in our Ultra-lowshot dataset). Since, $D \ll m$ hence $l = D$, resulting in sub-optimal output space.

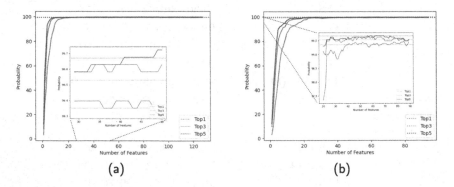

(a)   (b)

Fig. 4. Benchmark comparison over Lowshot Dataset after appending (a) PCA and (b) LDA based Feature Space Transformer Network with Facenet.

Similarly, if we use ResNet-50 as a pre-trained network over Ultra-lowshot Dataset, the Top 5, Top 3 and Top 1 accuracy are 99.30%, 99.27% and 99.18% respectively in 2048-dimensional latent feature space. However, Fig. 3(a) shows that with the same pre-trained network (ResNet-50) followed by a PCA initialised Feature Space Transformer Network, with 64% energy captured, the Top 1 accuracy is 99.23% (*higher than benchmarks for both pre-trained FaceNet and pre-trained ResNet-50*) and the output Feature Transformed Latent Space being 95 dimensional (*lower than dimensions for both pre-trained FaceNet and pre-trained ResNet-50*). While the same network having been initialised at 70% energy, the Top 5 accuracy is 99.30%, the Top 3 accuracy is 99.30% and Top 1 accuracy is 99.20% with only 121 dimensional output Feature Transformed Latent Space. Thus, this network topology performs much better than original FaceNet, both in terms of accuracy and latent space dimension, considering the size of the generated embedding. Here, we can see that if we use LDA over Ultra-lowshot Dataset along with ResNet-50, the results are able to beat the corresponding benchmarks but with a choice of higher number of basis vectors (348). This observation is also consistent with the **claim** 1 made above. The performance of LDA with Resnet-50 (as shown in the inlay of Fig. 3(b)) is better than that of LDA with FaceNet (as shown in the inlay of Fig. 2(b)). It is important to observe that when the same pre-trained network is followed by the Feature Space Transformer Network initialised with PCA and LDA both, the attained performance is even better, both in terms of accuracy and latent space dimensionality reduction. It can be seen in Table 1 that if we append the 348 dimensional embedding of the LDA transformed feature space, with 121 dimensional embedding of the PCA transformed feature space, then the 469 dimensional resultant feature space has the Top 5, Top 3 and Top 1 accuracy of 99.34%, 99.30% and 99.20% respectively. These accuracy are much higher than the benchmark values, while the dimensionality of the transformed latent space is close to only 25% of the original latent feature space.

Similar observations were made with Lowshot dataset. We can see that when we used more number of training samples while combining the LDA and PCA latent feature space, the dimensionality of the Feature Transformed Latent Space got highly reduced, while the accuracy remained significantly better than the benchmark values. It is also important to note that deeper pre-trained network like ResNet-50 followed by the Feature Space Transformer Network initialised with LDA alone, results in better accuracy than the pre-trained FaceNet, while projecting the test data into a space with dimensions (86) much lesser than that of the pre-trained FaceNet network (128). Thus the suggested approach enables us to use deeper network like ResNet-50 along with Feature Space Transformer Network, instead of shallow networks like FaceNet.

The datasets contained low resolution samples with high intra-class variance. The high intra-class variance is accounted to varied expression, lighting, pose, occlusion, disguise like makeup etc. We can see that the use of deeper networks, helps us extract better invariant features and the application of the Feature Space Transformer Network to these networks, helps us extract a very con-

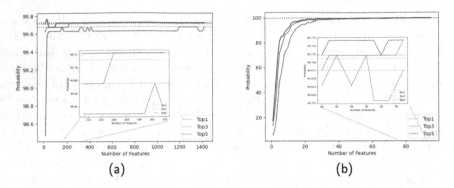

Fig. 5. Benchmark comparison over Lowshot Dataset after appending (a) PCA and (b) LDA based Feature Space Transformer Network with Resnet-50.

fined subspace of the original latent feature space and transform it to maximise the inter-class variance while minimising the intra-class variance. This subspace serves as an optimal latent feature space for any classifier to learn its decision boundaries and the lower uncorrelated dimensions of this Feature Transformed Latent Space help in faster comparison of the embedding, there by improving the inference time and reducing the memory footprint of the models.

5   Conclusion

In case of lowshot face recognition, when most of the features are not captured well by the limited number of training sample embedding, the classifiers find it further difficult to create a decision boundary along those features. A test sample that contains information along such under-represented features makes it worse for the classifier to classify correctly. LDA/PCA of FaceNet/ResNet-50 latent space results in generation of a transformed latent space where the features are discriminatory and uncorrelated. The feature initialisation algorithm, being deterministic instead of stochastic, does not impact model complexity and performance. Also, the PCA based suggested approach can be applied to both regression and classification problems as it determines the number of hidden nodes by accounting for the cumulative variance expressed through PCA, but the LDA based suggested approach can be applied to only to classification or verification problems as it determines the number of hidden nodes by accounting for the inter-class and intra-class variance.

References

1. Huang, G.B., Ramesh, M., Berg, T., Learned-Miller, E.: Labeled faces in the wild: a database for studying face recognition in unconstrained environments. University of Massachusetts, Amherst, Technical report (2007)
2. Deng, W., Hu, J., Lu, J., Guo, J.: Transform-invariant PCA: a unified approach to fully automatic face alignment, representation, and recognition. IEEE Trans. Pattern Anal. Mach. Intell. **36**(6), 1275–1284 (2014)
3. He, X., Yan, S., Hu, Y., Niyogi, P., Zhang, H.-J.: Face recognition using Laplacian faces. IEEE Trans. Pattern Anal. Mach. Intell. **27**(3), 328–340 (2005)
4. Deng, W., Hu, J., Guo, J.: Face recognition via collaborative representation: its discriminant nature and superposed representation. IEEE Trans. Pattern Anal. Mach. Intell. **40**, 2513–2521 (2018)
5. Vinyals, O., Blundell, C., Lillicrap, T., Wierstra, D.: Matching networks for one shot learning. In: Proceedings of the Advances in Neural Information Processing Systems, Barcelona, Spain, 5–10 December 2016, pp. 3630–3638 (2016)
6. Snell, J., Swersky, K., Zemel, R.: Prototypical networks for few-shot learning. In: Proceedings of the Advances in Neural Information Processing Systems, Long Beach, CA, USA, 4–9 December 2017, pp. 4077–4087 (2017)
7. Sung, F., Yang, Y., Zhang, L., Xiang, T., Torr, P.H.S., Hospedales, T.M.: Learning to compare: relation network for few-shot learning. In: Proceedings of the 2018 IEEE/CVF Conference on Computer Vision and Pattern Recognition, Salt Lake City, UT, USA, 18–23 June 2018, pp. 1199–1208 (2018)
8. Finn, C., Abbeel, P., Levine, S.: Model-agnostic meta-learning for fast adaptation of deep networks. In: Proceedings of the International Conference on Machine Learning, Sydney, Australia, 6–11 August 2017, pp. 1126–1135 (2017)
9. Ravi, S., Larochelle, H.: Optimization as a model for few-shot learning. In: Proceedings of the International Conference on Learning Representations, Toulon, France, 24–26 April 2017 (2017)
10. Huang, G.B., Zhou, H., Ding, X., Zhang, R.: Extreme learning machine for regression and multiclass classification. IEEE Trans. Syst. Man Cybern. Part B **42**(2), 513–529 (2012)
11. Castaño, A., Fernández-Navarro, F., Riccardi, A., et al.: Enforcement of the principal component analysis-extreme learning machine algorithm by linear discriminant analysis. Neural Comput. Appl. **27**, 1749–1760 (2016)
12. Chen, T., Kornblith, S., Norouzi, M., Hinton, G.: A simple framework for contrastive learning of visual representations. In: International Conference on Machine Learning, pp. 1597–1607. PMLR (2020)
13. Chen, X., He, K.: Exploring simple Siamese representation learning. In: Proceedings of the IEEE/CVF Conference on Computer Vision and Pattern Recognition, pp. 15750–15758 (2021)
14. He, K., Fan, H., Wu, Y., Xie, S., Girshick, R.: Momentum contrast for unsupervised visual representation learning. In: Proceedings of the IEEE/CVF Conference on Computer Vision and Pattern Recognition, pp. 9729–9738 (2020)

Identifying a Person in Mask: Fusion of Masked Face and Iris

Shadab Ahmad[1], Rajarshi Pal[2(✉)], and Avatharam Ganivada[3]

[1] Department of Data Science and Artificial Intelligence, Faculty of Science and Technology, (IcfaiTech), ICFAI Foundation for Higher Education, Hyderabad, India
shadab.ahmad@ifheindia.org
[2] Institute for Development and Research in Banking Technology (IDRBT), Hyderabad, India
iamrajarshi@yahoo.co.in
[3] University of Hyderabad, Hyderabad, India
avatharg@uohyd.ac.in

Abstract. In a face recognition system, effect of occlusion due to a face mask can be mitigated by fusing other available biometric information (such as the periocular region or iris) with the face. Therefore, a novel approach involving fusion of masked face and iris is presented in this paper to identify a person. The proposed approach suggests a generative adversarial network (GAN) based approach for mask removal and reconstruction of the face image (unmasking the face). Fusion of this unmasked face and iris biometrics is performed at score level. Here, an optimization based approach is presented for the said score level fusion. A new search space-reduced and quality-weighted particle swarm optimization based method is introduced for this score level fusion.

1 Introduction

Face recognition systems are generally trained on unmasked face images. Several recent studies [8,22,26] show that the pre-covid19 existing face recognition systems perform significantly poor in the presence of face mask. Recently, a masked face recognition challenge has been organized as part of international joint conference on biometrics (IJCB 2021) [6]. The problem being posed to traditional face recognition system due to wearing mask has been highlighted in this challenge.

In order to deal with this challenge, face unmasking methods are presented using convolutional neural network (CNN) [5] and generative adversarial network (GAN) [11]. In contrast, occluded region removal based masked face recognition system is proposed in [16]. In [10], a deep-learning based dynamic ensemble model is presented. If a face mask is detected, then it dynamically changes to the ocular region for recognition.

Alternatively, iris based biometric recognition systems are unaffected by the presence of masks as the iris region is clearly visible in a masked face image. Though the iris based recognition systems have shown improved performance,

P. Maji et al. (Eds.): PReMI 2023, LNCS 14301, pp. 802–812, 2023.
https://doi.org/10.1007/978-3-031-45170-6_84

this biometric modality faces several challenges [13,23]. Therefore, it is important to use a combination of biometric modalities to improve recognition accuracy. Fusion of face and iris is extensively studied in literature [7] and the results are astonishing. Various establishments [12,14] frequently use multimodal biometric systems for authentication.

The current paper presents a novel approach involving fusion of masked face and iris for improving performance of biometric system in presence of mask. Here, a GAN based approach [11] is used for mask removal and reconstruction of face image (unmasking the face). This unmasked face image is passed to an ArcFace based face recognition system [9] to compute the matching scores for face modality. Similarly, the iris image is passed to the iris recognition system [27] to generate the matching scores for iris modality. For each one of these two modalities, the matching scores of a probe with every enrolled subject (gallery) are used to construct the score list. Fusion of these two score lists for unmasked face and iris is performed at score level. Here, an optimization framework is used for this fusion at score level. This optimization problem formulation is inspired form the work in [2]. Here, objective is to generate an aggregated list of scores. This aggregated score list is having minimum weighted summation of distances from every input score list. In [2], the stated optimization problem is solved using genetic algorithm (GA). Similarly, genetic algorithm is also used in [3], but in case of rank level fusion. On the contrary, in this paper, particle swarm optimization (PSO) based fusion is used. In this work, PSO is preferred over GA to achieve faster convergence. Significant reduction of the search space to achieve fast convergence and quality-derived weight are two major aspects of the proposed approach. Incorporation of quality-derived weight for each modality aids in assigning significance to each modality. It helps in achieving enhanced performance. Therefore, the term 'search space-Reduced and Quality-weighted Particle Swarm Optimization' (RQ-PSO) is introduced in this paper to describe the proposed PSO based score level fusion approach. The suitability of the proposed masked face and iris based multimodal biometric recognition for person identification in the presence of mask is justified experimentally. The experiment also demonstrates superiority of the proposed RQ-PSO based score level fusion over state-of-the-art score level fusion approaches.

Remainder of this paper is organized as following: Overview of the proposed approach for identifying a person wearing a mask is presented in Sect. 2. In Sect. 3, the problem formulation of score level fusion is shown as optimization problem. Search space-reduced and quality-weighted particle swarm optimization (RQ-PSO) based approach is also presented for score level fusion in this section. Experimental results are discussed in Sect. 4. Concluding remarks are drawn in Sect. 5.

2   Overview of the Proposed Approach

State-of-the-art face recognition systems fail to correctly identify a person due to the occlusion by face mask [8,22,26]. In this work, multimodal biometric fusion for person identification in masked faces is proposed. Figure 1 presents an overview of the proposed approach. This approach contains following three stages: (i) matching score generation for masked face modality, (ii) matching score generation for iris modality and (iii) score level fusion of these two modalities. In the face biometrics stage, a masked face image of probe user is unmasked using a generative adversarial network (GAN) based approach [11]. This generated unmasked face image is passed to the ArcFace based face recognition system [9] for matching score generation. The generated matching scores are used for constructing the matching score list for face modality. In the iris biometrics stage, an iris image of probe user is passed as an input to the iris recognition system [27] and matching scores are generated. These matching scores are used to construct the matching score list for iris modality. Finally, in the fusion stage, the matching score lists of both the modalities are fused using the proposed search space-reduced and quality-weighted PSO (RQ-PSO) based fusion approach to identify the person (probe user).

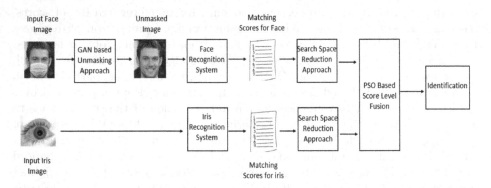

Fig. 1. Stages of the proposed masked face and iris fusion approach

3   Score Level Fusion

The work in [2] conceptualized the fusion of multimodal biometrics at the score level as optimization problem. The current work is inspired from the work in [2] and adopts the same optimization problem formulation.

Let S_f and S_i be the generated score lists for face and iris modalities, respectively. Normalization of these matching scores using min-max normalization [1] brings them into same range. Let S'_f and S'_i be the normalized score lists for face and iris modalities, respectively. Aggregation of the two normalized score lists produces the aggregated score list δ^*. Here, generation of the aggregated score list δ^* is treated as optimization problem. Minimization of a weighted summation of distances of the fused score list from the input score lists S'_f and S'_i is attempted here. Objective function for generating the aggregated score list is stated below:

$$minimize \quad \Phi(\delta) = w_f \times d(\delta, S_f') + w_i \times d(\delta, S_i') \qquad (1)$$

A candidate fused score list is represented by δ. Here, weights w_f and w_i are associated with face and iris biometric modalities, respectively. The weight represents the significance of the corresponding biometric modality. The function $d()$ in Eq. 1 denotes the distance between an aggregated and the normalized input score lists. In the current work, weighted Spearman footrule [2] metric is used as distance measure. For solving this optimization problem, a search space-reduced and quality-weighted score level fusion using PSO (RQ-PSO) is introduced in this paper.

3.1   The Proposed Search Space-Reduction Approach

In a meta-heuristic optimization algorithm (e.g., particle swarm optimization), a search space constitutes all possible (candidate) solutions for a given problem. The search space in these algorithms depends on the dimension of a candidate solution. In context of multimodal biometrics fusion at score level, this dimension is equal to the total number of enrolled users in score list. If there are n enrolled users, then each candidate solution is of n-dimension. Therefore, the amount of time for convergence is proportional to n. The current work proposes the search space-reduction approach to achieve faster convergence. Hence, the dimension of a score list is being reduced through the proposed approach.

Let the proposed search space-reduction approach be explained using an example. Let there be seven enrolled subjects A to G. The normalized score lists S_f' and S_i' for face and iris modalities, respectively, contain the normalized scores for these seven subjects as shown in Fig. 2a. Thus, the initial dimension of the normalized score lists is 7. Firstly, a sorted list of subject identities is created for each modality by considering the normalized similarity scores in descending order. Let L_f and L_i be the sorted list of subject identities for face and iris biometrics, respectively (Fig. 2a). Subjects appearing at first position in each of the lists L_f and L_i are identified. Subjects A and D appear at first position in L_f and L_i, respectively (Fig. 2a).

Now the position of subject A (appearing at top position in L_f list) is identified in the list L_i (Fig. 2a). The subject A appears at 2nd position in the sorted list of iris modality (Fig. 2a). Similarly, the subject D (appearing at top position in L_i list) is identified at 4th position in the sorted list of face modality L_f (Fig. 2a). Now the maximum position values for face and iris modalities are identified as 4 and 2, respectively, as shown in Fig. 2a. For each modality, the maximum position value indicates the number of first few subjects to be considered in the reduced list. The justification for this approach can be understood with the help of the same example as above (Fig. 2a). As both subjects A and D appear in the first position in L_f and L_i lists, respectively, these subjects are potential matches with the probe. For face modality, subject D appears in the fourth position (Fig. 2a). In this approach, the assumption is that all the preceding subjects to D in the sorted list L_f are also potential matches with the probe.

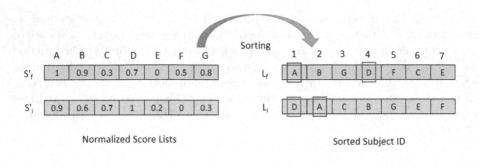

(a)

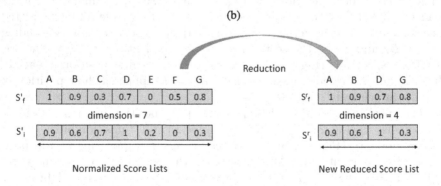

(b)

(c)

Fig. 2. Illustration of proposed search space-reduction approach: (a) Generating sorted subject identity lists, (b) Finding important subject IDs and (c) Generating reduced score lists

Similar discussion is applicable on the sorted list of iris modality L_i. Therefore, all the potential matches must be considered in the reduced score list. Union of potential matches from both the lists generates an exhaustive list of potential matches (Fig. 2b). In this example, the set of potential matches includes subjects A, B, D and G as shown in Fig. 2b. Finally, the normalized scores of the selected subjects are only used to construct the reduced score list in each modality. The initial normalized score lists S'_f and S'_i had dimension n as 7. The reduced dimension n^r of the new reduced score lists S^r_f and S^r_i is 4 (Fig. 2c).

3.2   Quality Estimated Weight

Weights w_f and w_i are associated with face and iris biometric modalities, respectively (Eq. 1). A weight represents the significance of the corresponding biometric modality. In this work, similarity scores between probe and gallery are considered for estimating the quality-derived weight for each modality of the probe user. The weight w_j for a biometric modality j (face or iris) is derived by considering the difference between the first maximum normalized similarity score $max_1(S^r_j)$ and the second maximum normalized similarity score $max_2(S^r_j)$. This difference is then divided by the difference between the first maximum normalized similarity score $max_1(S^r_j)$ and the average of all other normalized similarity scores (excluding the first maximum normalized similarity score $max_1(S^r_j)$). The proposed weight estimation is defined in Eq. 2.

$$w_j = \frac{max_1(S^r_j) - max_2(S^r_j)}{max_1(S^r_j) - \frac{1}{n^r-1}\left(\sum_{l=1}^{n^r} S^r_j - max_1(S^r_j)\right)} \qquad (2)$$

The underlying philosophy of the above estimation is mentioned here. Distinction between the first best match and the second best match is clear for a good quality probe image. However, in case of a bad quality problem image, this does not hold true. In the second case, any single subject does not stand out as different than others.

3.3   Particle Swarm Optimization Based Score Level Fusion

Finally, a particle swarm optimization (PSO) based score level fusion approach is proposed in this paper for solving the stated optimization problem (Eq. 1). The proposed approach is termed as search space-reduced and quality-weighted particle swarm optimization (RQ-PSO) based fusion approach at score level. A particle position in the proposed RQ-PSO based fusion approach at score level represents a reduced candidate score list δ (Sect. 3.1). It indicates the similarity scores of the probe with the subjects in reduced score lists. Moreover, the objective function (in Eq. 1) of the proposed RQ-PSO based approach uses the quality derived weight to indicate significance of face and iris modality for particular probe (Sect. 3.2). In RQ-PSO, the particle's velocity and position in the solution space are updated iteratively until a stopping criteria is met. When the personal best positions of all the particles do not change over a certain period of iterations, the proposed search space-reduced and quality-weighted particle swarm optimization based fusion approach at score level is considered to have converged.

4   Performance Evaluation and Discussion

A virtually created multimodal biometric dataset is used for this purpose. The virtual dataset contains CelebFaces Attributes face dataset (CelebA) [20] and IIT Delhi iris dataset [19]. The CelebA face dataset contains 200K celebrity images with varying face attributes for 10177 unique subjects. The IIT Delhi iris dataset contains left and right iris images from 224 unique subjects. For the reported experiments in this paper, left and right iris images are considered to be part of different subjects. Therefore, there are 2175 iris images corresponding to 435 subjects, as right iris images are missing for the remaining 13 subjects. As the iris dataset has only 435 subjects, unique 435 subjects are randomly selected from the CelebA face datasets [20] to create a virtual multimodal biometric datasets.

4.1   Experimental Setup

Generating Masked Face Dataset: Several researches [5,16,21] have used synthetically applied mask face dataset for training the model. To carry out the experiments in this work, a similar approach is used. The mask is applied on all the selected images of CelebA face dataset [20] using synthetic mask generation approach [4]. The synthetic mask generation approach is widely used by researchers [6,21] to generate synthetic masked face dataset.

Division of Dataset: The selected images from CelebA face dataset [20] containing 435 classes are divided into training (gallery) and test (probe) set. The training set contains 9565 masked face images and corresponding ground truth face images (without mask). The test set contains 435 masked face images corresponding to 435 classes. The training dataset is used to train the GAN based model [11]. The evaluation of trained model is performed on the test (probe) dataset.

4.2   Experimental Results

At first, the effect of mask on the face recognition system is studied. For the person identification task, the masked face (probe) is compared with the gallery face images (without mask). The similarity scores for few such probe images with their ground truth are illustrated in Fig. 3a. It can be observed form the presented similarity scores in Fig. 3a that the ArcFace based face recognition system [9] is not able to correctly identify the genuine subject from the gallery. Therefore, the proposed method involves an unmasking stage using a GAN based approach [11]. Figure 3b illustrates the similarity scores of unmasked face

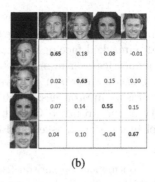

	0.02	-0.01	-0.03	0.09
	0.07	-0.01	0.02	0.07
	0.01	0.01	-0.03	-0.06
	0.04	0.01	0.05	0.03

(a)

	0.65	0.18	0.08	-0.01
	0.02	0.63	0.15	0.10
	0.07	0.14	0.55	0.15
	0.04	0.10	-0.04	0.67

(b)

Fig. 3. a. Similarity scores between masked face images (probe) and corresponding gallery images, b. Similarity scores between unmasked faces images and corresponding gallery images

images as probe against the gallery images (without mask). It is to be noted that these unmasked face images in Fig. 3b correspond to the masked face images of Fig. 3a. It is observed from the Fig. 3b that the unmasked face images are close to the actual images (gallery). Therefore, persons are correctly identified based on the similarity scores in Fig. 3b. Thus, the results establish the effectiveness of GAN based approach [11] to generate the unmasked face images from the masked images.

Furthermore, the fusion of unmasked face and iris modalities is performed using the proposed search space-reduced and quality-weighted RQ-PSO based fusion approach at score level. The subject having the highest score in the fused list is identified as a match for the probe. Performance of the proposed approach is compared against the performances of state-of-the-art score level fusion approaches [1,15,17,18,24,25]. The effect of combining unmasked face and iris modalities using the proposed as well as existing score level fusion approach is presented in Table 1. The performance of each approach is represented as its ability to recognize a probe correctly. Additionally, experiments are performed without removing the mask. The recognition accuracies for masked face and iris fusion are also presented in Table 1 for the RQ-PSO and state-of-the-art score level fusion approaches.

There are a few interesting observations in Table 1. (i) The recognition accuracy of only masked face modality is very less (0.92%). It establishes the known fact that a masked face can not be used for person identification. (ii) Recognition accuracy using iris modality is 89.66%. The proposed RQ-PSO based fusion approach at score level as well as existing score level fusion approaches perform worse than the individual iris modality. This is because the masked face modality brings down the performances of the fusion based approaches. Though the fusion based approaches perform much better than only masked face modality, iris modality is the best method for person identification in the presence of face mask. (iii) The recognition accuracy of the face modality after unmasking the face image has significantly increased from 0.92% to 88.05% (Table 1). It justifies the usefulness of the GAN based unmasking of the masked faces. (iv) Fusion based approaches of unmasked face and iris modalities perform even better than individual unmasked face or iris modalities. This justifies the usefulness of multimodal biometrics over unimodal biometrics. (v) The proposed RQ-PSO based score level fusion approach achieves better performance than state-of-the-art score level fusion approaches. At the end, the experimental results establish the superiority of the proposed GAN based unmasking of face and RQ-PSO based score level fusion of unmasked and iris biometrics.

Table 1. Performance comparison (recognition accuracies in %) between of the proposed RQ-PSO based score level fusion approach and state-of-the-art score level fusion approaches in the context of masked face and unmasked face.

Method		Masked Face and Iris	Unmasked Face and Iris
Unimodal	Face	0.92	88.05
	Iris	89.66	89.66
Score Level Fusion (Multimodal)	Sum-OEBA [17]	7.36	89.89
	Sum-MOEBA [17]	54.02	92.41
	Sum-OEVBA [18]	78.62	92.18
	Hamacher t-norm [15]	7.57	92.18
	Frank t-norm [15]	8.28	92.41
	WQAM cos [1]	63.22	96.32
	WQAM coŝr [1]	57.24	97.01
	WQAM tan [1]	63.22	97.24
	WQAM sin [1]	36.55	94.02
	WQAM r̂(1/s) [1]	69.89	97.01
	Proposed RQ-PSO	78.62	**97.93**

5   Conclusion

The major contributions of the paper are summarized in this section. In this work, a novel approach involving fusion of masked face and iris is presented to improve recognition performance of the biometric system. A GAN based approach [11] is suggested to generate the unmasked face images. The fusion at score level is conceptualized as an optimization problem. Furthermore, a search space-reduced and quality-weighted particle swarm optimization (RQ-PSO) based fusion approach at score level is proposed to solve the stated optimization problem. The search space-reduction and quality-derived weight estimation approaches are the major highlights of the proposed score level fusion. The reported experimental results highlight that the fusion of masked face (through GAN based unmasking) and iris achieves better recognition accuracy in post-covid19 era. The proposed RQ-PSO based score level fusion approach also exhibits superior performance than the existing score level fusion approaches.

This justifies the introduction of a novel RQ-PSO based score level fusion approach in this paper. Therefore, the proposed fusion of masked face (through GAN based unmasking) and iris using RQ-PSO based score level fusion can be utilized to identify a person wearing mask.

References

1. Abderrahmane, H., Noubeil, G., Lahcene, Z., Akhtar, Z., Dasgupta, D.: Weighted quasi-arithmetic mean based score level fusion for multi-biometric systems. IET Biometrics **9**(3), 91–99 (2020)
2. Ahmad, S., Pal, R., Ganivada, A.: Score level fusion of multimodal biometrics using genetic algorithm. In: IEEE Congress on Evolutionary Computation, pp. 2242–2250 (2021)
3. Ahmad, S., Pal, R., Ganivada, A.: Rank level fusion of multimodal biometrics using genetic algorithm. Multimedia Tools Appl. **81**(28), 40931–40958 (2022). https://doi.org/10.1007/s11042-022-12688-4
4. Anwar, A., Raychowdhury, A.: Masked face recognition for secure authentication. arXiv preprint arXiv:2008.11104 (2020)
5. Boutros, F., Damer, N., Kirchbuchner, F., Kuijper, A.: Self-restrained triplet loss for accurate masked face recognition. Pattern Recogn. **124**, 108473 (2022)
6. Boutros, F., et al.: MFR 2021: masked face recognition competition. In: Proceedings of IEEE International Joint Conference on Biometrics, pp. 1–10 (2021)
7. Brown, D.: Deep face-iris recognition using robust image segmentation and hyperparameter tuning. In: Smys, S., Bestak, R., Palanisamy, R., Kotuliak, I. (eds.) Computer Networks and Inventive Communication Technologies. LNDECT, vol. 75, pp. 259–275. Springer, Singapore (2022). https://doi.org/10.1007/978-981-16-3728-5_19
8. Damer, N., Grebe, J.H., Chen, C., Boutros, F., Kirchbuchner, F., Kuijper, A.: The effect of wearing a mask on face recognition performance: an exploratory study. In: Proceedings of International Conference of the Biometrics Special Interest Group, pp. 1–6. IEEE (2020)
9. Deng, J., Guo, J., Xue, N., Zafeiriou, S.: ArcFace: additive angular margin loss for deep face recognition. In: Proceedings of the IEEE/CVF Conference on Computer Vision and Pattern Recognition, pp. 4690–4699 (2019)
10. Dharanesh, S., Rattani, A.: Post-COVID-19 mask-aware face recognition system. In: Proceedings of IEEE International Symposium on Technologies for Homeland Security, pp. 1–7 (2021)
11. Din, N.U., Javed, K., Bae, S., Yi, J.: A novel GAN-based network for unmasking of masked face. IEEE Access **8**, 44276–44287 (2020)
12. Emirates Media-Centre: Emirates launches integrated biometric path at the airport for added convenience. https://www.emirates.com/media-centre/emirates-biometric-path-at-the-airport-for-added-convenience/. Accessed 23 Oct 2020
13. Fathee, H., Sahmoud, S.: Iris segmentation in uncooperative and unconstrained environments: state-of-the-art, datasets and future research directions. Digit. Sig. Process. **118**, 103244 (2021)
14. Government of Philippine: Philippine identification system act (philsys). https://psa.gov.ph/system/files/kmcd/IRR%20of%20the%20RA%2011055%20or%20PhilSys%20Law.pdf. Accessed 14 Apr 2022

15. Hanmandlu, M., Grover, J., Gureja, A., Gupta, H.M.: Score level fusion of multimodal biometrics using triangular norms. Pattern Recognition Letters, Elsevier **32**(14), 1843–1850 (2011)
16. Hariri, W.: Efficient masked face recognition method during the COVID-19 pandemic. Sig. Image Video Process. **16**(3), 605–612 (2022). https://doi.org/10.1007/s11760-021-02050-w
17. Kabir, W., Ahmad, M.O., Swamy, M.N.S.: Normalization and weighting techniques based on genuine-impostor score fusion in multi-biometric systems. IEEE Trans. Inf. Forensics Secur. **13**(8), 1989–2000 (2018)
18. Kabir, W., Ahmad, M.O., Swamy, M.N.S.: A multi-biometric system based on feature and score level fusions. IEEE Access **7**, 59437–59450 (2019)
19. Kumar, A., Passi, A.: Comparison and combination of iris matchers for reliable personal authentication. Pattern Recogn. **43**(3), 1016–1026 (2010)
20. Liu, Z., Luo, P., Wang, X., Tang, X.: Deep learning face attributes in the wild. In: Proceedings of International Conference on Computer Vision, pp. 3730–3738. IEEE (2015)
21. Montero, D., Nieto, M., Leskovsky, P., Aginako, N.: Boosting masked face recognition with multi-task arcface. arXiv preprint arXiv:2104.09874 (2021)
22. Ngan, M.L., Grother, P.J., Hanaoka, K.K., et al.: Ongoing face recognition vendor test (FRVT) part 6B: face recognition accuracy with face masks using post-COVID-19 algorithms. NIST Interagency/Internal Report. Accessed 5 July 2022
23. Nguyen, K., Fookes, C., Jillela, R., Sridharan, S., Ross, A.: Long range iris recognition: a survey. Pattern Recogn. **72**, 123–143 (2017)
24. Ross, A.A., Nandakumar, K., Jain, A.K.: Handbook of Multibiometrics, vol. 6. Springer, New York (2006). https://doi.org/10.1007/0-387-33123-9
25. Soltanpour, S., Wu, Q.J.: Multimodal 2D–3D face recognition using local descriptors: pyramidal shape map and structural context. IET Biometrics **6**(1), 27–35 (2016)
26. Vemury, A., Hasselgren, A., Howard, J., Sirotin, Y.: 2020 biometric rally results - face masks face recognition performance (2022). https://mdtf.org/Rally2020/Results2020
27. Zhao, Z., Kumar, A.: Towards more accurate iris recognition using deeply learned spatially corresponding features. In: Proceedings of the IEEE International Conference on Computer Vision, pp. 3809–3818 (2017)

A PCA-Based Keypoint Tracking Approach to Automated Facial Expressions Encoding

Shivansh Chandra Tripathi(✉) ⓘ and Rahul Garg ⓘ

Indian Institute of Technology Delhi, New Delhi, India
{shivansh,rahulgarg}@cse.iitd.ac.in

Abstract. The Facial Action Coding System (FACS) for studying facial expressions is manual and requires significant effort and expertise. This paper explores using automated techniques to generate Action Units (AUs) for studying facial expressions. We propose an unsupervised approach based on Principal Component Analysis (PCA) and facial keypoint tracking to generate data-driven AUs called PCA AUs using the publicly available DISFA dataset. The PCA AUs comply with the direction of facial muscle movements and can explain over 92.83% of the variance in other public test datasets (BP4D-Spontaneous and CK+), indicating their capability to generalize facial expressions. The PCA AUs are also comparable to a keypoint-based equivalence of FACS AUs in terms of variance explained on the test datasets. Besides, PCA AUs can code at 30 fps on AMD EPYC 7402 24-Core Processor. In conclusion, our research demonstrates the potential of an automated coding system as an alternative to manual FACS, which could lead to efficient real-time analysis of facial expressions in psychology and related fields. To promote further research, we have made the code publicly available.

Keywords: Facial expressions · Action Units (AUs) · FACS · PCA

1 Introduction

Facial expressions are essential for non-verbal communication in humans.[1] They are reliable indicators of vital emotions such as happiness, fear, disgust, anger, surprise, and sadness. Owing to their importance in emotion analysis, facial expressions have a wide range of applications in marketing, healthcare, cinematics, security, etc., and are extensively investigated in affective computing [1]. The most comprehensive and descriptive tool to manually study facial expressions is the Facial Action Coding System (FACS) [2], which has been adapted for non-human primates as well [3]. Facial expressions arise due to the anatomical pull of the facial muscles in different directions. FACS groups the most granular

---

[1] The code can be found here: https://github.com/Shivansh-ct/PCA-AUs.

P. Maji et al. (Eds.): PReMI 2023, LNCS 14301, pp. 813–823, 2023.
https://doi.org/10.1007/978-3-031-45170-6_85

movement on the face produced by a facial muscle or a few of their combinations as Action Units (AUs). Any facial expression can be encoded in terms of AUs, demonstrating the universality of FACS. Experts trained to annotate facial expressions with AUs are called FACS coders.

However, FACS coding is extremely time-intensive [4], limiting its applications in real-time systems such as online marketing and healthcare. A FACS coder requires approximately 100 h of training before certifying to code AUs and takes more than one hour to code 100 static images [2,5]. Also, different coders can interpret facial expressions slightly differently, leading to inconsistent coding. Therefore, to eliminate the manual dependency on facial expressions coding, various automated systems for AU analysis are developed using machine learning [1,6–9]. Most of these techniques are supervised [1,6,7] and rely heavily on large annotated datasets of AUs, which again imposes a dependency on manual FACS coding. Unsupervised techniques [1,8,9] have been utilized in facial expression research and can eliminate the need for manual coding. However, these unsupervised techniques primarily focus on feature generation to improve AU recognition rather than developing a facial coding system that uses AUs which comply with facial muscle movements. Also, the ability of the generated features to code multiple datasets to establish their universality, like FACS AUs, stands unexamined.

We propose an unsupervised learning method based on Principal Component Analysis (PCA) for facial expression coding. Results show that the PCA components termed PCA AUs can explain significant variances in different datasets. The PCA AUs in which the facial keypoint movements are as per the direction of facial muscle movement are defined as interpretable. We show that 50% of the PCA AUs are interpretable. These AUs also explain variances in the test datasets comparable to a keypoint-based equivalence of FACS AUs and are efficient for real-time analysis.

The subsequent section describes the preprocessing of facial keypoints and constructing the PCA model. Section 3 discusses the experimentation and results, and Sect. 4 concludes with our work's limitations and future scope.

2   Facial Keypoint-Based Automated Coding System

In order to track facial expressions in a video sequence, specific keypoints in various points of the face (such as eyes, eyebrows, nose, lips, and jawline) are labeled and tracked. Labeling these keypoints can be done manually or using automated algorithms [10]. We use the facial keypoints provided in the following three publicly available datasets- DISFA [6,11] (66 keypoints), BP4D-Spontaneous [12,13] (49 keypoints), and CK+ [14,15] (68 keypoints). These keypoints were tracked using Active Appearance Model (AAM) [16] for DISFA and CK+ and the Constrained Local Model (CLM) [17] for BP4D-Spontaneous. To maintain consistent representation, all the datasets are vectorized to 68 keypoint templates (Fig. 1[2]),

---

[2] Modification of image https://github.com/Fang-Haoshu/Halpe-FullBody/blob/master/docs/face.jpg.

filling the keypoint indices with zero values that are absent in the corresponding data. We preprocess these keypoints to eliminate geometric variabilities across multiple subjects, such as head movement, the difference in face sizes, or the relative position of face parts. Finally, these keypoints are converted into features that are representative of facial expressions. Further, we present our PCA model and prepare a keypoint-based equivalence of the FACS AUs. We first discuss the geometric corrections in detail:

CK+   DISFA   BP4D

Fig. 1. Keypoint locations for the 68-keypoint template in the three datasets. Yellow keypoints indicate the standard affine co-ordinates (Color figure online)

2.1 Geometric Corrections

There are three steps in eliminating the geometric variabilities, frontalization, affine registration, and similarity registration, as described below:

To isolate pure facial muscle movements, we eliminate any head movement from our analysis and bring the keypoints to a front-facing image using the algorithm proposed by Vonikakis et al. [18].

Next, an affine registration [19] registers the keypoints to a standard space to remove face size and position-related variabilities. A set of six fixated facial keypoints are chosen for estimating the geometric parameters in a face image, and the remaining keypoints in that image are registered using those parameters. For DISFA and CK+, the six keypoints are: 0,16,39,42,27,33 (Fig. 1). BP4D Spontaneous has the jawline keypoints (0,16) missing; therefore, we use the following keypoints: 39,42,36,45,27,33 (Fig. 1).

Lastly, using similarity registration [19], we eliminate variabilities such as the distance between the eye corners, the length of the nose and eyebrows, and so forth. The following fixated keypoints are used for registration: (42,45) keypoints for the left eyebrow and left eye, (36,39) for the right eyebrow and right eye, (27) for the nose, and (0,16) for the jawline. Lips have no fixated keypoints, so they are not similarity registered.

2.2   Feature Generation

A feature is defined as a vector representing changes in facial keypoint positions from a neutral face. To generate features, we subtract the x and y values of the neutral frame keypoints from their corresponding values in all other frames of the same subject. The data from all subjects are compactly represented in a matrix $X \in \mathbb{R}^{136 \times m}$, where m represents the total number of frames in the corresponding dataset.

2.3   Principal Component Analysis (PCA)

In facial expression research, PCA is widely employed for feature extraction and analyzing various facial representations [1,8,9]. PCA is a typical example of a dimensionality reduction problem and aims to find a lower dimensional representation of data while retaining maximum information. Mathematically, given $X \in \mathbb{R}^{p \times m}$(p=136) where each sample x_i is represented in a p-dimensional space, PCA finds a set of k basis vectors $u_i \in \mathbb{R}^p (i = 1, 2, ..., k)$, which can represent the samples in a much lower dimensional space such that $k << p$. In matrix notation, the PCA decomposition is written as $X \approx UDV$ where $U \in \mathbb{R}^{p \times k}$, $D \in \mathbb{R}^{k \times k}$ and $V \in \mathbb{R}^{k \times m}$ and, D is a diagonal matrix, U and V are orthonormal matrices. D can be absorbed in matrix V as $DV \to V$, and the decomposition can be stated as $X \approx UV$. Any x_i is thus a linear combination of the k u_i's as $x_i \approx \sum_{j=1}^{k} u_j v_{ij}$, linear weights given by matrix V. The columns of U are called principal components, and V is called the encoding matrix. The k basis vectors represent facial keypoint movements from a neutral face. Since only k basis vectors can represent the entire dataset, X, they are similar to FACS AUs that can encode any facial expression, excluding head movements using only 26 AUs. We call the basis vectors in the matrix U as PCA AUs.

Computing Encoding Matrix for Test Data: This step shows how a test data $Y \in \mathbb{R}^{p \times n}$ is represented in terms of the PCA AUs such that $Y \approx \hat{Y} = UV'$ or equivalently $\hat{y}_i = \sum_{j=1}^{k} u_j v'_{ij}$. Since U is an orthonormal matrix, V' is computed by projecting Y onto the columns of matrix U as $U^T Y$. So, $\hat{Y} = UU^T Y$.

Addressing Keypoint Disparity: We define the keypoints that are initially present in any dataset as non-redundant and redundant otherwise. A 136-dimensional PCA component contains 66,49,68 non-redundant keypoints for the three training datasets- DISFA, BP4D-Spontaneous, and CK+, respectively. A PCA model can only reconstruct non-redundant keypoints from its training dataset during testing. For instance, if BP4D-Spontaneous is trained and DISFA is tested, the jawline keypoints in DISFA would not be reconstructed. Similarly, if CK+ is trained and BP4D-Spontaneous is tested, the reconstructed jawline keypoints in BP4D-Spontaneous lack ground truth labeling for comparison. To avoid these discrepancies, only the common non-redundant keypoints between train and test data are kept in the PCA components U (derived from the train) and test data Y when computing the encoding matrix for $\hat{Y}$. Also, only these keypoints are kept in test data Y and $\hat{Y}$ when we compute the evaluation metrics for performance.

2.4 Feature Generation for FACS AUs

To compare the PCA AUs with FACS AUs, we convert the FACS AUs to equivalent facial keypoint movements. First, we select a single subject and extract its image for the APEX frame of each AU and AU combination that excludes head movement from the images used in the FACS manual. A neutral image of the same subject is also selected. Using a keypoint tracking algorithm [10], we generate 68 facial keypoints on each image. Next, these keypoints undergo the same preprocessing steps mentioned in Sects. 2.1 and 2.2 to give a 136-dimensional feature vector representing the keypoint motion from neutral to APEX frame. We compile the preprocessed data for 26 pure AUs in a matrix $U_{AU} \in \mathbb{R}^{136 \times 26}$. Data for pure AUs and their combinations (total 113 in numbers) given in the FACS manual are compiled in a matrix $U_{AUC} \in \mathbb{R}^{136 \times 113}$ called comb AUs.

Computing Encoding Matrix for PCA vs. FACS Comparison: This step shows how a test data $Y \in \mathbb{R}^{p \times n}$ is represented in terms of the PCA AUs and FACS AUs such as $Y \approx UV'$, $Y \approx U_{AU}V'$, or $Y \approx U_{AUC}V'$. PCA gives an ordered list of components in decreasing order of importance. However, there is no such ordering for FACS AUs. For a fair comparison between PCA AUs and FACS AUs, we use lasso for feature selection and regression for computing the encoding matrix for these AUs. We employ the lasso modification to LARS, the LARS-EN algorithm [20] for this purpose and solve the lasso regression objective with a least angle regression to learn V'. The lasso regression objective is $\min \|y_i - Uv_i'\|_2^2 + \alpha\|v_i'\|_1$ where y_i and v_i are columns of Y,V, $\|\|_2$ is L2-norm, and $\|\|_1$ is L1-norm. To limit the number of components used by y_i, the number of non-zero weights in v_i' can be constrained using an early stop on the number of LARS-EN algorithmic steps [20]. The keypoint disparity between any of the AU types (PCA AUs, pure AUs, or comb AUs) and the test data while computing the encoding matrix and the evaluation metrics is handled in the same manner as in Sect. 2.3.

3 Experiments

We first outline the datasets and the evaluation metrics used. We then investigate the PCA AUs generated by these datasets for their coding power and interpretability. We finally compare the PCA AUs with the keypoint-based equivalence of the FACS AUs and show their real-time efficiency.

3.1 Datasets

We used the datasets CK+ [14,15], DISFA [6,11], and BP4D-Spontaneous [12, 13] to evaluate our PCA model. Below we describe the details:

CK+: This dataset contains posed facial expressions of 123 subjects and consists of nearly 10,100 video frames. The keypoint movement features extracted from this data on 10,100 frames is called CK+.

DISFA: This dataset contains spontaneous facial expressions recording of 27 subjects and nearly 1,14,000 video frames. The keypoint movement features extracted on all the frames are called DISFA_full. To compare with a model trained on CK+, we randomly extract features on the same number of frames as CK+, i.e., on 10,100 frames from DISFA_full to use for training and call it DISFA_train.

BP4D-Spontaneous: This dataset contains spontaneous facial expressions recording of 41 subjects and comprises nearly 1,36,000 video frames. The keypoint movement features extracted on all the frames are called BP4D_full. Again, for a fair comparison, we randomly extract features on 10,100 frames from BP4D_full for training and call it BP4D_train.

3.2   Evaluation Metrics

We used the following three evaluation metrics:

1. **Train Variance Explained (Train VE)** -   Normalized sum-of-squares error ($NSSE$) is used to evaluate algorithms for image reconstruction [21]. We use $NSSE$ to compute the variance explained for the dataset reconstructed by our proposed AUs. Let $X, X \in \mathbb{R}^{p \times m}$ be the training data of a model and $\hat{X}, \hat{X} \in \mathbb{R}^{p \times m}$ is reconstructed using the model parameters such that $\hat{X} = UV$, then $NSSE(X)$ is defined as $\frac{\|X - \hat{X}\|_F^2}{\|X\|_F^2}$. We define Train VE as $100(1 - NSSE(X))$.

2. **Test Variance Explained (Test VE)** -   In the case of test data Y and its approximation $\hat{Y} = UV'$, we define Test VE as $100(1 - NSSE(Y))$ for test time performance.

3. **Mean Components (MC)** -   MC is the average number of components a sample uses in a dataset. Formally, if $X \in \mathbb{R}^{p \times m}$ is the dataset approximated as $\hat{X} = UV$, then $MC(\hat{X})$ is equal to $\frac{\sum_{i=1}^{i=m} \|v_i\|_0}{m}$, where $\|v_i\|_0$ is the L0-norm of v_i. For test data $Y \approx \hat{Y} = UV'$, $MC(\hat{Y})$ can be computed similarly.

3.3   PCA AUs

To train a PCA algorithm on dataset X, we tune the hyperparameter k representing the number of components from $k = 1$ to $k = 136$. For a given train dataset, at each k, we compute the Train VE and the average of the Test VE on the remaining two datasets and plot it (Fig. 2). The average Test VE of the DISFA_train and BP4D_train are comparable, while both have consistently better average Test VE than CK+. However, despite their similar performance, DISFA_train can better visualize facial keypoint movements than the

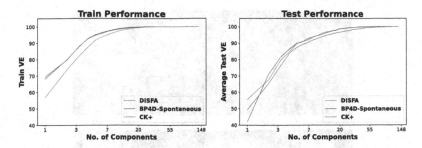

Fig. 2. Train VE and the average of the Test VE on the remaining two datasets when PCA is trained on either DISFA, BP4D-Spontaneous, or CK+ with $k = 1$ to $k = 136$ (x-axis on the log scale)

BP4D_train, which lacks the entire jawline. Further, Table 1 shows that for a PCA trained with 95% Train VE on the three datasets, the DISFA_train outperforms the other two datasets. Therefore, we select the PCA components from the DISFA_train as the final PCA AUs.

Table 1. Variance Explained (VE) results for PCA. (Paired t-test using Test VE values on 30 test folds shows that DISFA_train performs significantly better than BP4D_train ($p < 0.001$) on CK+ and significantly better than CK+ ($p < 0.001$) on BP4D_full. CK+ performs significantly better than BP4D_train on DISFA_full($p < 0.001$))

Train Data	Test Data	Train VE	Test VE
DISFA_train	BP4D_full	95.51	90.76
DISFA_train	CK+	95.51	94.90
Average		**95.51**	**92.83**
BP4D_train	DISFA_full	96.10	88.72
BP4D_train	CK+	96.10	92.97
Average		**96.10**	**90.85**
CK+	DISFA_full	95.74	90.06
CK+	BP4D_full	95.74	88.08
Average		**95.74**	**89.07**

To further investigate the interpretability of keypoint movements in PCA AUs, we select the first eight components that account for 95% of the Train VE. Figure 3 shows the visualization of these components in PCA AUs when projected on a neutral face. Figure 4 shows major facial muscles responsible for AUs according to FACS that do not include head movements. In PCA component 3, the lower lip move along the line of the lower lip towards the center, as shown by blue dots in Fig. 3, and in PCA component 6, the lower and upper parts of the lip compress against each other. LF1 and LF2 show that the lower lip is pushed

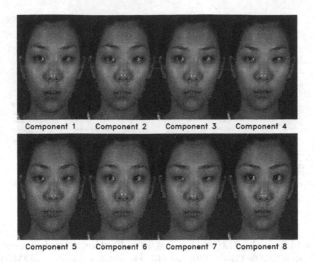

Fig. 3. PCA AUs- red represents the keypoint position on a neutral face, green on an expression face, and blue is a non-interpretable movement. The arrow indicates the direction of keypoint movement. (Face image source: BP4D-Spontaneous [12,13] (Color figure online))

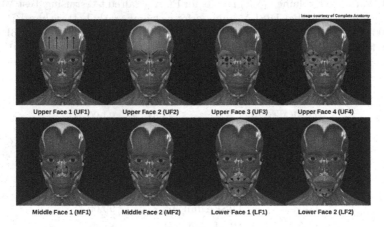

Fig. 4. Muscle movements generating AUs that exclude head movements as per FACS

radially towards the center or pulled sideways or downwards, but not unlike in component 3 and component 6. Also, UF1, UF2, UF3, and UF4 show that eyebrows are either pulled upward, diagonally towards the nose, or towards the eye socket, but not diagonally down towards the ears as occurring in component 7,8 (Fig. 3). We conclude that components 3,6,7, and 8 contain movements that are non-interpretable. Therefore, among the top eight components of PCA AUs, 50% are interpretable and can account for 92.83% variance explained in the test datasets on average.

3.4   Comparison of PCA AUs with FACS AUs

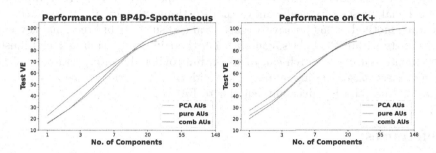

Fig. 5. Comparison of PCA AUs, pure AUs, and comb AUs (x-axis on the log scale)

As mentioned in Sect. 2.4, we use a LARS-EN algorithm to compute the encoding matrix for comparing PCA and FACS AUs. On a given test data Y and AU type (PCA AUs, pure AUs, or comb AUs), we early stop the LARS-EN algorithm when the average number of components used by $\hat{Y}$ reaches a given value N_c such that $MC(\hat{Y}) = N_c$. We vary N_c from 1 to the maximum number of AUs present in the given AU type and plot the Test VE for the two datasets-BP4D-Spontaneous and CK+ (Fig. 5). In both BP4D-Spontaneous and CK+ datasets, PCA AUs outperform FACS AUs when the number of components is small. However, asymptotically the PCA AUs and FACS AUs performance becomes comparable.

Keypoint-based FACS AUs are 100% interpretable as they are directly extracted from the facial expressions in human images. Overall, we conclude, that the PCA AUs outperform FACS AUs when $N_c < 11$ and have a comparable performance for large N_c. However, they are less interpretable than the keypoint-based FACS AUs.

3.5   Real-Time Efficiency

We assess the computational efficiency of PCA AUs coding using the tracking algorithm [10]. From tracking to PCA AUs code generation on a frame, the process achieves a speed of around 30 fps or 108k frames per hour on AMD EPYC 7402 24-Core Processor. This surpasses manual FACS coding (100 frames per hour) and is suitable for real-time applications.

4   Conclusion

We propose an unsupervised technique for facial expression coding to eliminate the need for manual FACS, reducing tremendous effort. Our proposed PCA AUs can encode various facial expression samples across different datasets, and demonstrate a coding ability comparable to FACS AUs in terms of variance explained. PCA AUs can also code in real-time at approximately 30 fps. However, PCA AUs exhibit less interpretability compared to FACS AUs. Moreover, while facial muscles typically move unidirectionally from a neutral face, our encoding method (using positive/negative values) suggests bidirectional keypoint movements within PCA AUs, complicating their interpretation as facial muscle movements. Future research can focus on improving the interpretability of the unsupervised based coding system and validating its performance across many datasets to establish universality similar to FACS AUs.

References

1. Zhi, R., Liu, M., Zhang, D.: A comprehensive survey on automatic facial action unit analysis. Vis. Comput. **36**, 1067–1093 (2020)
2. Ekman, P., Friesen, W., Hager, J.: Facial action coding system. A Human Face, Salt Lake City, UT (2002)
3. Waller, B., Julle-Daniere, E., Micheletta, J.: Measuring the evolution of facial 'expression' using multi-species FACS. Neurosci. Biobehav. Rev. **113**, 1–11 (2020)
4. Bartlett, M., Hager, J., Ekman, P., Sejnowski, T.: Measuring facial expressions by computer image analysis. Psychophysiology **36**, 253–263 (1999)
5. Bartlett, M., Littlewort, G., Frank, M., Lainscsek, C., Fasel, I., Movellan, J., et al.: Automatic recognition of facial actions in spontaneous expressions. J. Multimed. **1**, 22–35 (2006)
6. Mavadati, S., Mahoor, M., Bartlett, K., Trinh, P.: Automatic detection of non-posed facial action units. In: 2012 19th IEEE International Conference On Image Processing, pp. 1817–1820 (2012)
7. Shao, Z., Liu, Z., Cai, J., Ma, L.: Deep adaptive attention for joint facial action unit detection and face alignment. In: ECCV 2018. LNCS, vol. 11217, pp. 725–740. Springer, Cham (2018). https://doi.org/10.1007/978-3-030-01261-8_43
8. Torre, F., Cohn, J.: Facial expression analysis. Visual Analysis Of Humans: Looking At People, pp. 377–409 (2011)
9. Sariyanidi, E., Gunes, H., Cavallaro, A.: Automatic analysis of facial affect: a survey of registration, representation, and recognition. IEEE Trans. Pattern Anal. Mach. Intell. **37**, 1113–1133 (2014)
10. Dong, X., Yang, Y., Wei, S., Weng, X., Sheikh, Y., Yu, S.: Supervision by registration and triangulation for landmark detection. IEEE Trans. Pattern Anal. Mach. Intell. **43**, 3681–3694 (2020)
11. Mavadati, S., Mahoor, M., Bartlett, K., Trinh, P., Cohn, J.: DISFA: a spontaneous facial action intensity database. IEEE Trans. Affect. Comput. **4**, 151–160 (2013)
12. Zhang, X., et al.: A high-resolution spontaneous 3D dynamic facial expression database. In: 2013 10th IEEE International Conference And Workshops On Automatic Face And Gesture Recognition (FG), pp. 1–6 (2013)
13. Zhang, X., et al.: Bp4d-spontaneous: a high-resolution spontaneous 3d dynamic facial expression database. Image Vis. Comput. **32**, 692–706 (2014)
14. Kanade, T., Cohn, J., Tian, Y.: Comprehensive database for facial expression analysis. In: Proceedings Fourth IEEE International Conference On Automatic Face And Gesture Recognition (cat. No. PR00580), pp. 46–53 (2000)

15. Lucey, P., Cohn, J., Kanade, T., Saragih, J., Ambadar, Z., Matthews, I.: The extended cohn-kanade dataset (CK+): a complete dataset for action unit and emotion-specified expression. In: 2010 IEEE Computer Society Conference On Computer Vision And Pattern Recognition-Workshops, pp. 94–101 (2010)
16. Cootes, T., Edwards, G., Taylor, C.: Active appearance models. IEEE Trans. Pattern Anal. Mach. Intell. **23**, 681–685 (2001)
17. Saragih, J., Lucey, S., Cohn, J.: Deformable model fitting by regularized landmark mean-shift. Int. J. Comput. Vis. **91**, 200–215 (2011)
18. Vonikakis, V., Winkler, S.: Identity-invariant facial landmark frontalization for facial expression analysis. In: 2020 IEEE International Conference On Image Processing (ICIP), pp. 2281–2285 (2020)
19. Hartley, R., Zisserman, A.: Multiple View Geometry in Computer Vision. Cambridge University Press, Cambridge (2003)
20. Zou, H., Hastie, T.: Regularization and variable selection via the elastic net. J. R. Stat. Soc. Ser. B (Stat. Methodol.) **67**, 301–320 (2005)
21. Fienup, J.: Invariant error metrics for image reconstruction. Appl. Opt. **36**, 8352–8357 (1997)

A Clustering-Based Approach for the Extraction of ROI from Fingerprint Images

Santhoshkumar Peddi$^{(\boxtimes)}$, Nishkal Prakash, Rakesh Krishna Konduru, Alka Ranjan, and Debasis Samanta

Indian Institute of Technology, Kharagpur, West Bengal, India
santhoshpps11@gmail.com

Abstract. Fingerprint-based verification systems require a certain amount of pre-processing on the fingerprint images before they can be applied. The complete fingerprint image is usually never used during authentication. A specific region of interest (ROI) is extracted for the feature extraction, which is then used for matching. In this paper, the ROI is extracted using a clustering-based approach. The entire fingerprint is first segmented into blocks; then, several features are extracted from each block using a Sobel filter. These features are clustered based on similarity, after which an agglomerative clustering algorithm combines similar clusters and separates dissimilar clusters leading to an accurate ROI. When used in a fingerprint recognition pipeline, the ROI extracted improves the matching accuracy significantly. The extracted ROI will always contain a core point if it exists in the initial fingerprint. A generalized algorithm is proposed to find the ROI consistently on fingerprints while invariant to translation and rotation.

Keywords: Fingerprint Biometric · Region of Interest · Fingerprint recognition · Agglomerative Clustering

1 Introduction

Fingerprint biometrics are extensively employed to identify individuals based on their distinct physical characteristics. This recognition method ensures permanence and distinctiveness, establishing a foundation for non-repudiation. While current recognition techniques are satisfactory, there is room for improvement by extracting a Region of Interest (ROI) that remains consistent across multiple impressions and exhibits unique distinguishing features. By employing this ROI, computational resources are optimized, resulting in more efficient and faster fingerprint recognition systems. Moreover, this extraction process helps mitigate challenges associated with noise, image quality, and partial acquisition. The extracted ROI also contributes to reducing false acceptance or rejection rates and enhances compatibility and interoperability among different fingerprint recognition systems and databases. Nevertheless, extracting the ROI from a fingerprint image remains a challenging task due to factors such as noise, quality, partial capture, etc.

P. Maji et al. (Eds.): PReMI 2023, LNCS 14301, pp. 824–832, 2023.
https://doi.org/10.1007/978-3-031-45170-6_86

In contrast to existing literature, which typically involves cropping a region around a reference point after some enhancement, the proposed method systematically analyzes the fingerprint to extract the ROI.

Five statistical features from each segmented region are computed, after which clustering is done based on the extracted parameters, leading to the ROI extraction.

To evaluate the performance of the proposed approach, experiments were conducted on publicly available fingerprint databases. The experimental results demonstrate that the proposed approach achieves higher accuracy and is more efficient than existing methods. Furthermore, the approach is robust to noise and variations in fingerprint patterns, making it suitable for real-world applications. Overall, the proposed clustering-based approach provides an effective solution for the extraction of ROI from fingerprint images, which can be applied in various biometric applications like authentication, verification, indexing and data protection, to name a few.

2 Related Work

Fingerprint recognition has been widely studied, and various approaches have been proposed for ROI extraction. Processing the entire fingerprint image is a computationally expensive task. Extracting the ROI from the fingerprint image before processing it further is necessary. A brief overview of some of the related works is presented in this section. Various approaches have been proposed in the past for extracting ROI (Region of Interest) from fingerprint images. These approaches can be broadly classified into the following categories:

- **Segmentation-Based Approach:** This approach involves using techniques such as watershed segmentation [10], or active contour models [2] to segment the fingerprint image and extract the ROI. However, this approach may suffer from over-segmentation or under-segmentation, which can affect the accuracy of ROI extraction.
- **Filtering-Based Approach:** This approach involves using filters such as Sobel, Prewitt, or Canny [9], to detect the edges in the fingerprint image, followed by thresholding [7] to extract the ROI. However, this approach may be affected by noise and variations in fingerprint patterns, which can limit its accuracy.
- **Clustering-Based Approach:** This approach involves using clustering techniques such as K-means clustering [8] to group similar pixels in the fingerprint image and extract the ROI. However, the accuracy of clustering may be affected by the choice of initial centroids and the number of clusters.
- **Hybrid Approaches:** These approaches combine the advantages of different methods, such as filtering and segmentation [3], to improve the accuracy and efficiency of ROI extraction. The proposed approach combines segmentation with filtering using statistical measures and agglomerative clustering to extract the ROI from fingerprint images.
- **Deep Learning-Based Approaches:** In recent years, deep learning-based approaches [5,11], such as convolutional neural networks (CNNs) [6], have been used for ROI extraction from fingerprint images. These approaches can achieve high accuracy but require large training data and computing resources.

The proposed clustering-based hybrid approach aims to overcome the limitations of existing methods and provide a more accurate and efficient solution for ROI extraction. The approach is computationally inexpensive and can be used for real-time applications while being able to handle noise and variations in fingerprint patterns. This allows for generalizing the approach to a wide range of fingerprint images obtained from different sensors with different noise levels and variations in fingerprint patterns.

3   Proposed Method

The proposed method (shown in Fig. 1) involves dividing the fingerprint image into blocks of equal size. These blocks are used as the basis for feature extraction, which is the process of identifying and isolating essential characteristics of the image. Once the features have been extracted, they are grouped into three clusters. These clusters represent different parts of the fingerprint image that share similar characteristics, and one of them is mapped to the fingerprint image to form the ROI.

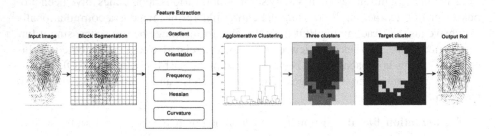

Fig. 1. The overview of the proposed method

The method involves five key steps: block segmentation of the fingerprint image, feature extraction from each block, feature clustering based on the distance matrix, identification of a target cluster and mapping the target cluster to a region in the fingerprint image, which is considered as the ROI.

3.1   Block Segmentation

The block segmentation involves dividing an input fingerprint image I of size $m \times n$ into non-overlapping blocks of size $p \times p$, where p is the size of the blocks.

$$B_{i,j} = I_{(i-1)\times p+1:i\times p,(j-1)\times p+1:j\times p} \tag{1}$$

As shown in the Eq. 1, the i, jth block is denoted by $B_{i,j}$, and is obtained by extracting the pixels in rows $(i-1)\times p+1$ to $i\times p$ and columns $(j-1)\times p+1$ to $j\times p$ from the original image I. The resulting block matrix B is of size $(m/p)\times(n/p)$.

3.2 Feature Extraction

For each block $B_{i,j}$ of size $p \times p$, the five features $F^1_{i,j}$, $F^2_{i,j}$, $F^3_{i,j}$, $F^4_{i,j}$, and $F^5_{i,j}$ are calculated, which represent the gradient, ridge orientation, curvature, Hessian and ridge frequency features, respectively.

Then, the mean of these five features is taken to form a 5-dimensional feature vector for the block $B_{i,j}$, which is denoted as $V(B_{i,j})$ and is defined as:

$$V(B_{i,j}) = [\text{mean}(F^1_{i,j}), \text{mean}(F^2_{i,j}), \text{mean}(F^3_{i,j}), \text{mean}(F^4_{i,j}), \text{mean}(F^5_{i,j})]$$

In other words, the 5-dimensional feature vector $V(B_{i,j})$ is formed by taking the mean of the five features calculated for the block $B_{i,j}$. The feature vector is generated for each block in the fingerprint image to obtain a set of feature vectors representing the entire fingerprint.

The gradient features $F^1_{i,j}$ of the blocks are obtained using the Sobel operator, as shown below:

$$F^1_{i,j} = \sqrt{G^2_x + G^2_y} \quad , \text{where} \quad G_x = B_{i,j} * K_x, \quad G_y = B_{i,j} * K_y \tag{2}$$

Here, K_x and K_y are Sobel operator kernels for the X and Y direction.

The ridge orientation feature $F^2_{i,j}$ captures the direction of the fingerprint ridges at each pixel in the block $B_{i,j}$. A gradient-based approach is used to extract the direction of the ridges in the blocks using the equations,

$$F^2_{i,j} = \frac{\pi}{2} + \frac{\arctan(2G_{xy}/(G_{xx} - G_{yy}))}{2} \tag{3}$$
$$\text{where,} \quad G_{xx} = \Sigma_B G^2_x, G_{yy} = \Sigma_B G^2_y \text{ and } G_{xy} = \Sigma_B G_x G_y$$

The local curvature $F^3_{i,j}$ of the ridges and the ridge frequency $F^5_{i,j}$ are calculated using the Hessian matrix $F^4_{i,j}$ and second-order gradients, as shown in the equation below. The Hessian matrix is also considered a separate feature.

$$F^3_{i,j} = \frac{F^4_{i,j}}{(1 + G^2_x + G^2_y)^2} \qquad F^5_{i,j} = \frac{1}{2\pi}\sqrt{\frac{\lambda_1 \lambda_2}{\lambda_1 + \lambda_2}} \tag{4}$$

where, λ_1 and λ_2 are the eigenvalues of the Hessian matrix and $F^4_{i,j} = (G_{xx} \cdot G_{yy}) - (G_{xy} \cdot G_{yx})$.

3.3 Agglomerative Clustering

After extracting the feature vectors for each block, a distance matrix is calculated based on the Euclidean distance. The Euclidean distance between two feature vectors V_i and V_j is defined as d_{ij} and the distance matrix as D.

By using this distance matrix D, agglomerative clustering is used to form the clusters. Agglomerative clustering is a hierarchical clustering technique that starts with each vector V as a separate cluster and iteratively merges the most similar cluster until the desired number of clusters is obtained, which, in this case, is three. These three clusters are assumed to be the background, ROI, and other parts of the fingerprint image. Here, the distance between clusters is defined as the minimum distance between any two feature vectors belonging to different clusters. Then, the two closest clusters are merged, and the distance matrix is updated accordingly. This process is repeated until the desired number of clusters is obtained.

3.4   Identification of Target Cluster

Once the agglomerative clustering algorithm generates three clusters, a specific cluster is selected to represent the ROI in the fingerprint image. This selection is based on calculating the cosine similarity (CS) between the feature vectors within each cluster, with the cluster displaying the highest average cosine similarity (ACS(Ci)) being chosen. To account for background similarity, additional metrics like curvature and orientation are employed. Among the remaining two clusters, the one with more dissimilarities in the edge regions, where ridges may terminate or exhibit varying orientations, is disregarded. Instead, priority is given to the cluster that shows greater consistency and similarity in terms of ridge orientation and curvature. This meticulous approach ensures accurate identification of the desired ROI. The cosine similarity between two feature vectors V_i and V_j can be computed as follows:

$$ACS(C_i) = \frac{\Sigma_{i,j} CS(V_i, V_j)}{N(N-1)/2} \qquad CS(V_i, V_j) = \frac{V_i \cdot V_j}{\|V_i\| \cdot \|V_j\|} \tag{5}$$

Here, $V_i \cdot V_j$ denotes the dot product of the feature vectors, and $\|V_i\|$, $\|V_j\|$ represent their Euclidean norms, C_i represents the i-th cluster, N represents the number of feature vectors in the cluster, and the sum is taken over all unique pairs of feature vectors within the cluster. Finally, the cluster with the highest average cosine similarity is selected as the target cluster.

3.5   Identification of ROI

After selecting the target cluster with the highest average cosine similarity, it can be mapped back to the original fingerprint image to identify the ROI by finding the corresponding block indices of features in the cluster. To calculate the block indices i,j the following formulae have been used.

$$i = \left\lfloor \frac{(k-1)}{p} \right\rfloor + 1 \qquad j = (k-1) \bmod p + 1$$

where k is the index of the feature vector in an array of feature vectors.

Then each block is mapped to the original image by calculating the top left (r, c) and bottom right (r', c') indices of that block in the original image.

$$r = (i-1) \times p + 1, \qquad c = (j-1) \times p + 1, \qquad r' = i \times p, \qquad c' = j \times p$$

After mapping the block indices to the original fingerprint, the next step is to determine the coordinates of the bounding box that encloses the target cluster. This is done by comparing the indices of all the blocks that are selected for the cluster and finding the minimum and maximum values for the row and column indices. The top left corner of the bounding box is given by the minimum row and column indices, while the bottom right corner is given by the maximum row and column indices. Once these four indices are determined, a bounding box is drawn using them to indicate the ROI.

4 Experimental Results

For this experiment, two datasets, FVC2002 DB2 and SPD2010, have been used to check the region consistency and prove the core point's existence in the ROI, respectively. For the block size, statistical metrics, and clustering methods both datasets are used combinedly.

Region Consistency: To prove that the region obtained is consistent across all impressions of the same fingerprint, a fingerprint is considered from the FVC dataset. The ROI computed for these fingerprints is shown in Fig. 2, and it can be seen that the ROI is consistent.

Fig. 2. ROI obtained for different impressions of a fingerprint.

ROI with Corepoint: As the SPD dataset contains the core point labels, it has been used to show that the ROI always contains a core point. Six fingerprints are selected at random, and their core points and ROI are shown in Fig. 3.

Fig. 3. A set of images from the SPD dataset with their ROI and core point.

Block Size: Based on the observation of the ROI generated by the method, the corresponding block size is given a score of '1' if the ROI contains the core point, and a '0' otherwise. Thus, the scores for different block sizes are compared, and the block sizes within the range of 16 to 35 have a score of '1'. A block size of 23 is chosen for the method as it is close to the mid-point of the range of the optimal block sizes.

Statistical Metrics: Different statistical metrics like mean, variance, median and mode are used to reshape features in Sect. 3.2. The features obtained from these statistical metrics are checked for their miss rate, and it can be seen from Fig. 4a that the mean of features has the least amount of miss. For this study, it is considered to be a miss whenever the ROI doesn't contain the core point.

Clustering Methods: The features are clustered based on the k-means and agglomerative algorithms. The silhouette scores for the k-means and agglomerative clustering algorithms are computed, and as can be seen in Fig. 4b, agglomerative clustering has the best score for the three clusters.

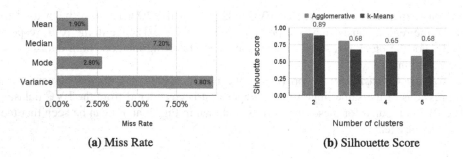

(a) Miss Rate   (b) Silhouette Score

Fig. 4. Analysis of the Miss Rate and Silhouette Score.

Fingerprint Recognition: The evaluation of fingerprint recognition accuracy involves using half of the data from each dataset as genuine data and the other half as imposter data. A random fingerprint is selected from either half of the data and compared with all fingerprints from the genuine half. Based on the harris corner matching score [1], the selected fingerprint is declared to either have a match or no match. The performance of the method for a set of fingerprints with and without ROI is shown in Fig. 6 (Fig. 5).

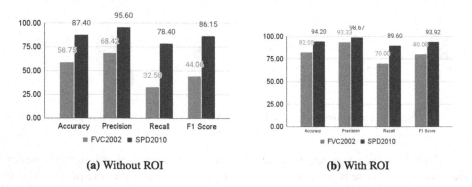

(a) Without ROI   (b) With ROI

Fig. 5. Performance of the fingerprint recognition method

Additionally, the performance of the fingerprint recognition method in terms of FAR, FRR, GAR and GRR is tabulated in Table 1. It can be seen that the performance of the method is better when the fingerprint is used along with an ROI.

Comaprison of Time and Accuracy: The average identification time is compared between the full fingerprint and the ROI in the dataset, as shown in Fig. 6a. Additionally, Fig. 6b provides a comparison of the proposed method's accuracy with existing Cluster-based [8] and Filter-based [4] methods.

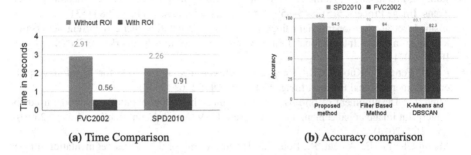

(a) Time Comparison   (b) Accuracy comparison

Fig. 6. Time comparison and Accuracy comparison

Table 1. Fingerprint Recognition Performance

Type	Dataset	Accuracy	FAR	FRR	GAR	GRR
Without ROI	SPD2010	87.4%	3.60%	21.6%	78.4%	96.4%
	FVC2002 DB2	58.7%	15%	67.5%	32.5%	85%
With ROI	SPD2010	**94.2%**	**1.2%**	**10.45%**	**89.6%**	**98.8%**
	FVC2002 DB2	**82.5%**	**5%**	**30%**	**70%**	**95%**

5 Conclusion and Future Work

The proposed method extracts the ROI from a fingerprint image using agglomerative clustering, surpassing existing methods that use threshold values or morphological operations for region cropping. It consistently and efficiently extracts the ROI, regardless of scanner/sensor variations, while maintaining translation and rotation invariance. The experiment successfully extracted the ROI for each fingerprint in the two datasets and achieved notable improvements in fingerprint recognition accuracy: 6.8% for SPD2010 and 24.4% for FVC2002. Moreover, the proposed method significantly reduced processing time by 80.75% for SPD2010 and 59.29% for FVC2002. To further enhance the method, alternative filters or machine learning approaches can be explored, and different clustering approaches could be investigated.

References

1. Derpanis, K.G.: The harris corner detector. York Univ. **2**, 1–2 (2004)
2. Hilles, S.M., et al.: Adaptive latent fingerprint image segmentation and matching using Chan-Vese technique based on EDTV model. In: 2021 2nd International Conference on Smart Computing and Electronic Enterprise (ICSCEE), pp. 2–7. IEEE (2021)
3. Hilles, S.M., et al.: Latent fingerprint enhancement and segmentation technique based on hybrid edge adaptive DTV model. In: 2021 2nd International Conference on Smart Computing and Electronic Enterprise (ICSCEE), pp. 8–13. IEEE (2021)
4. Jain, A., Prabhakar, S., Hong, L., Pankanti, S.: Filterbank-based fingerprint matching. IEEE Trans. Image Process. **9**(5), 846–859 (2000). https://doi.org/10.1109/83.841531
5. Joshi, I., et al.: Sensor-invariant fingerprint ROI segmentation using recurrent adversarial learning. In: 2021 International Joint Conference on Neural Networks (IJCNN), pp. 1–8. IEEE (2021)
6. Li, J., Feng, J., Kuo, C.C.J.: Deep convolutional neural network for latent fingerprint enhancement. Signal Process. Image Commun. **60**, 52–63 (2018)
7. Lupu, C.: Development of optimal filters obtained through convolution methods, used for fingerprint image enhancement and restoration. USV Annal. Econ. Public Adm. **14**(2 (20)), 156–167 (2014)
8. Mehdi Cherrat, E., Alaoui, R., Bouzahir, H.: Improving of fingerprint segmentation images based on k-means and DBSCAN clustering. Int. J. Electr. Comput. Eng. (IJECE) **9**(4), 2425–2432 (2019)
9. Sujatha, P., Sudha, K.: Performance analysis of different edge detection techniques for image segmentation. Indian J. Sci. Technol. **8**(14), 1 (2015)
10. Sumijan, S., Arlis, S., Widya Purnama, P.A.: Fingerprint identification using the hybrid thresholding and edge detection for the room security. TEM J. **9**(4), 1396–1400 (2020)
11. Wan, G.C., Li, M.M., Xu, H., Kang, W.H., Rui, J.W., Tong, M.S.: Xfinger-net: pixel-wise segmentation method for partially defective fingerprint based on attention gates and u-net. Sensors **20**(16), 4473 (2020)

Bioinformatics

Encoded Deep Vectors for Eukaryotic Exon Prediction

Praveen Kumar Vesapogu[1]([⊠])[iD] and Bapi Raju Surampudi[2][iD]

[1] School of Computer and Information Sciences, University of Hyderabad,
Hyderabad, India
praveencs@uohyd.ac.in
[2] Cognitive Science Lab, IIIT Hyderabad, Hyderabad, India
raju.bapi@iiit.ac.in

Abstract. In bioinformatics, identifying protein-coding regions in genomic sequences is a vital problem. The majority of methods used to locate protein-coding regions(exons) in genomic sequences rely on the 3-base periodicity signal. Additionally based on encoding also, many machine learning approaches have been devised for exon prediction. They transform a sequence of DNA into numerical values and use those values to predict protein-coding regions using a machine learning model. Encoding strategies, however, have a direct impact on the classifier's capacity to extract coding information, and it is yet unclear how to select the best encoding scheme. In this article, we proposed a hybrid encoding scheme, where the DNA nucleotide sequences are encoded into multiple vectors that were fed as multi-dimensional input channels to the Convolutional neural network. The effectiveness of the proposed hybrid encoding scheme using a Convolutional neural network is compared with the existing methods from the literature. The presented approach performed better than the existing approaches on benchmark datasets of the eukaryotic organisms, H.sapiens, D.melanogaster, C.elegans, A.thaliana, Cow, and Rat.

Keywords: CNN · Exon · Intron

1 Introduction

Exons are distinct portions within genes that hold the genetic instructions for manufacturing a certain protein. These instructions are passed down from parent to offspring via generations. Introns are the sections of a gene that do not include any coding at all. In most cases, non-coding sections (introns) divide exons, which code for proteins, from other regions of the gene. Locating protein-coding regions in genomic sequences is one of the hardest bioinformatics challenges to solve. The majority of methods for locating protein-coding regions in

---

Supported by organization x.

genomic sequences rely on spectrum analysis techniques and the Fourier representation of the nucleotide sequence. Typically, these approaches take into account, the presence of a 3-base periodicity signal. Numerous machine learning techniques for exon prediction have also been proposed, and many of them are based on encoding. Several computational techniques have been developed to detect protein-coding areas, however, small exons are still challenging to locate. In this article, we have proposed a hybrid encoding scheme using a convolutional neural network for classifying protein-coding and non-coding genetic sequences. Each DNA nucleotide sequence is encoded into multiple numeric vectors. The multiple numeric vectors are given as two-dimensional input channels to the convolutional neural network.

2 Related Work

Several techniques for differentiating between protein-coding regions (exons) and non-coding regions (introns) have been devised over the past few decades such as Exon prediction by nucleotide distribution [21], Spectral envelope [15], Neural networks [3,14], Hidden Markov models [8,20], and Fast Fourier spectrum analysis [16]. The 3-base periodicity of coding areas of protein was denoised by Yin et al. [22] employing a complex Tracking-Differentiator. Relying on the nucleotide distributions at three codon locations, Yin and Yau [21] presented the EPND algorithm. Lapedes et al. [3] employed neural networks to locate the regions of DNA sequences that code for proteins. For the purpose of locating protein-coding areas, Krogh et al. built Hidden Markov models [8]. To enhance the accuracy of identifying protein-coding areas in sequences of DNA, Saberkari et al. [9] applied a discrete Fourier transform (DFT) and a notch filter. Gao et al. [4] employed fractal characteristics of DNA sequences in conjunction with 3-base periodicity to identify genes in genetic sequences. In order to predict genes from DNA sequences, Kotlar et al. [7] retrieved and implemented spectral rotation techniques. For detecting protein-coding areas in sequences of DNA, Stoffer et al. suggested employing the principal components method based on frequency called a spectral envelope [15]. Tiwari et al. [16] employed the Fourier Transform on binary digit sequences derived from nucleotide sequences of DNA to determine the 1/3 periodicity. The fundamental idea behind using Fourier analysis is to derive the special attribute of protein-coding regions, which is their 1/3 periodicity.

An artificial neural network model was implemented by Hatzigeorgiou et al. [6] for the purpose of predicting the initiation of translation in human DNA. They have utilized two different modules, one of which looks for the coding and non-coding patterns that are nearby the start codon. In order to anticipate protein-coding areas, Shuo et al. [12] developed and published an SVM, based machine-learning model. For the purpose of predicting protein-coding areas, Wei et al. [19] proposed using a bidirectional neural network. Singh et al. [13] developed the method using LSTM with the objective of predicting exon regions through the identification of splice sites.

3   Materials and Methods

3.1   Data Sets

Saxonav et al. [10] published experimentally derived datasets EID to assist the research, available at http://mcb.harvard.edu/gilbert/EID. The Advances in EID datasets were published by Shepelev et al. [11]. In this paper, we have used datasets of six different organisms. The datasets of the organisms D. melanogaster, C.elegans, and A.thaliana were taken from the EID database [10]. The datasets of the organisms H.sapiens, Cow, and Rat were taken from Advances in EID database [11]. For all six organisms in this experiment, 10000 sequences of positive exons and 10000 sequences of negative introns were taken each of length 150. Both positive exon and negative introns sequences are taken randomly.

3.2   Proposed Method

An encoding scheme is what decides the procedures for pattern identification and signal processing in genome analysis. Also, it determines the extent to which genetic attributes can be exploited to discover the features of certain regions. As a result, a great many encoding strategies have been devised to accommodate various purposes. For instance, the Voss [17] representation is the encoding scheme that is utilized the most frequently. This is due to the fact that it only consists of 0 s and 1 s in sequences, making it simple to implement in Discrete Fourier Transform (DFT)-related applications. These applications are used to locate three base periodicity signals in protein-coding areas. Akthar et al. [1] used frequency of occurrence encoding for finding the period-3 signal in the protein-coding regions. Even though many encoding methods were proposed in the literature, still there is a need to improve the results. In this article, we have implemented a new hybrid encoding method using a Convolutional neural network for exon prediction.

For color image classification the pixel values of each color red, blue, and green is given as three separate input channels to the CNN. Each channel contains a two-dimensional array of pixel values of the height and width of the image, corresponding to the particular RGB colors. For classifying exons and introns we have proposed a hybrid encoding with the Convolutional neural network. In our hybrid encoding, we have combined three popular encoding methods, they are One-Hot encoding, Complimentary encoding, and Frequency encoding. In the proposed encoding each DNA sequence is converted into six one-dimensional vectors, corresponding to the three below-mentioned three encodings, and these six one-dimensional vectors are fed as six input channels to the Convolutional neural network. Each DNA nucleotide sequence containing A, C, G, and T nucleotides, of length N is encoded into one to four sequences of one-dimensional vectors of length N, depending on the encoding. For one-hot encoding, each sequence of

DNA is converted into four one-dimensional vectors one for each nucleotide A, C, G, and T. For complimentary and frequency encoding each DNA sequence is converted into one one-dimensional vector.

All these six one-dimensional vectors are given as six channels to the convolutional neural network for the classification of exons and introns.

One-Hot Encoding. The famous Voss [17] representation uses one-hot encoding for finding the period-3 signal in the coding regions of protein using a discrete Fourier transform. In our proposed hybrid encoding we have chosen one-hot encoding as one of the three encodings for predicting exons. One-hot encoding can capture the global features of the DNA sequence. In one-hot encoding, each genetic sequence S of length N is transformed into four one-hot vectors of length N, S_k where $k \epsilon \{A, C, G, T\}$. For example, genetic sequence S = "acgttcgtacgt" is converted into $S_a = 1\ 0\ 0\ 0\ 0\ 0\ 0\ 0\ 1\ 0\ 0\ 0$, $S_c = 0\ 1\ 0\ 0\ 0\ 1\ 0\ 0\ 0\ 1\ 0\ 0$, $S_g = 0\ 0\ 1\ 0\ 0\ 0\ 1\ 0\ 0\ 0\ 1\ 0$, and $S_t = 0\ 0\ 0\ 1\ 1\ 0\ 0\ 1\ 0\ 0\ 0\ 1$. All these four one-dimensional vectors of length N are given as four different input channels to the CNN.

Complimentary Encoding. The complementary encoding approach is highly popular among those who study neural networks [23]. This is due to the fact that its differences are symmetric and its mean is zero. Base pairing occurs in the DNA double helix structure, where each base is paired with its complementary base (C with G, A with T) [2]. The inherent symmetry of DNA sequences can be captured through complementary encoding, which also preserves biological information. Both the learning of features and the training of data can benefit from features that are symmetric and complementary to one another. In complementary encoding, each genetic segment S of length N is transformed into a one-dimensional vector of length N, and each nucleotide is encoded as $C = +1$, $G = +1$, $A = -1$, and $T = -1$. For the example, the nucleotide sequence S = "acgttcgtacgt", is encoded as $S_e = -1\ 1\ 1\ -1\ -1\ 1\ 1\ -1\ -1\ 1\ 1\ -1$.

Frequency Encoding. There is a possibility that the occurrences of DNA nucleotides will differ among the specific segments of the genome, such as the intron and the exon. It is possible to statistically analyze the fractional occurrence by using the percentages of occurrence of individual nucleotides as the basis, and it can then be utilized as a critical parameter in the process of detecting these regions. They exhibit varied frequencies between species, suggesting that the DNA genomes of individual species, each having distinctively distinct statistical profiles. As a result, this particular method of encoding could have a variety of appearances in the various DNA genomes. In our proposed hybrid encoding we have chosen the frequency of single nucleotides as one of the three encoding methods. Every nucleotide in the sequence of DNA is represented by the frequency with which that nucleotide occurs in the sequence in this frequency encoding. The DNA nucleotide sequence S is converted as

$$\hat{s} = \left(\frac{f_x}{\frac{n}{m}} \right) \quad \forall x, \quad x \in \{A, C, G, T\} \tag{1}$$

Algorithm 1 Proposed algorithm for exon prediction with hybrid encoding using Convolutional neural network

---

Input: Advances in EID dataset E.

Output: Sn, Sp, P, Acc, AUC.

$\aleph = 20000$: No. of DNA sequences, $n = 50$: Len. of the DNA sequence, ξ : Encoding, $K = 10$: No. of folds, $p = 1$: No. of input rows, $q = 6$: No. of input channels.

procedure PREPROCESS(E, $\aleph$)
    $exons, introns \leftarrow$ EXTRACT(E, $\aleph$)
    $X, Y \leftarrow$ BUILDDATASET($exons, introns$)
return X, Y

procedure ENCODE($X, \aleph, n, \xi$)
    $j \leftarrow 0$
    for each sequence s in X **do**
        $j \leftarrow j + 1$ ▷ Encode s with encoding ξ_j
        for each nucleotide η in $\{A, T, G, C\}$ **do**
            if $s_i = \eta$ **then**
                $X_{ej} \leftarrow freq(\eta)$
        $j \leftarrow j + 1$ ▷ Encode s with encoding ξ_j
        for each nucleotide η in s **do**
            if $s_i = A \parallel s_i = T$ **then**
                $X_{ej} \leftarrow -1$
            if $s_i = G \parallel s_i = C$ **then**
                $X_{ej} \leftarrow 1$
        $j \leftarrow j + 1$ ▷ Encode s with encoding ξ_j
        if $s_i = A$ **then**
            $X_{ej} \leftarrow 1$
        else
            $X_{ej} \leftarrow 0$
        $j \leftarrow j + 1$ ▷ Encode s with encoding ξ_j
        if $s_i = C$ **then**
            $X_{ej} \leftarrow 1$
        else
            $X_{ej} \leftarrow 0$
        $j \leftarrow j + 1$ ▷ Encode s with encoding ξ_j
        if $s_i = G$ **then**
            $X_{ej} \leftarrow 1$
        else
            $X_{ej} \leftarrow 0$
        $j \leftarrow j + 1$ ▷ Encode s with encoding ξ_j
        if $s_i = T$ **then**
            $X_{ej} \leftarrow 1$
        else
            $X_{ej} \leftarrow 0$
return CONCATENATE($X_{e1}, ...X_{eq}$), Y

procedure TRAINTEST(X_{eq}, Y, K)
    for each fold in K **do**
        $M \leftarrow$ BUILDMODEL( )
        $M \leftarrow$ TRAINMODEL(M, X_{train}, Y_{train})
        $Sn, Sp, P, Acc, AUC \leftarrow$ TESTMODEL(M, X_{test}, Y_{test})
    return $Avg.Sn, Sp, P, Acc, AUC$

where f_x is the frequency with which the nucleotide x occurs, n is the length of the DNA nucleotide sequence, and m is the count of letters in the DNA nucleotide alphabet i.e., 4. For all the organisms studied in this experimentation we took genetic sequences of length, $n = 150$.

4   Results and Discussion

We evaluated the effectiveness of the presented method with the current approaches to exon prediction in this section. Hatzigeorgiou et.al. [5] used 2-bit binary encoding for representing DNA sequences. For predicting functional sites, they have implemented a feed-forward neural network. Shuo et al. [12] employed four-bit one-hot encoding for finding protein-coding regions using a support vector machine. The findings of a convolutional neural network with 2-bit binary encoding for identifying exon regions in sequences of DNA were published by Wei et al. [18]. We have reimplemented all these three methods for exon prediction on datasets of six different organisms. With all three of these approaches from the literature, we have contrasted the effectiveness of our proposed approach.

Table 1 presents the details of the performances of the current methods and the proposed approach in terms of sensitivity, specificity, precision, the area under receiver operating curve, and accuracy. Every single experiment that was carried out was validated by employing 10-fold cross-validation. The proposed approach performed superior to the approaches that are published in classifying exons and introns on all the datasets in terms of accuracy. In conclusion, all the methods studied in this paper performed well with accuracy around 90% for only the plant species A.thaliana and C.elegans for exon prediction. For remaining species like D.melanogaster i.e., fruit flies and other mammals H.sapiens, Cows, and, Rats, all the studied methods failed to give accuracy above 90%. For the first two species, there can be better dissimilarities between non-coding areas and the coding regions of the protein. The remaining last four species might have better similarities between non-coding portions and the protein-coding portions. Further different encoding methods and their combinations need to be studied in specific for individual species, and the proposed hybrid encoding method showed significant improvement in predicting exons compared to the existing methods in all the six organisms studied.

Table 1. Performance evaluation and comparison of proposed hybrid encoding and existing methods in terms of Sensitivity(S), Specificity(Sp), Precision(P), Accuracy(Acc), and Area under receiver operating curve(AUC).

Organism	Method	S	Sp	P	Acc	AUC
A.thaliana	2-bit Binary + CNN [18]	0.86	0.91	0.91	0.89	0.96
	4-bit One-Hot +MLP [5]	0.87	0.91	0.91	0.95	0.89
	4-bit One-Hot +SVM [12]	0.87	0.93	0.93	0.90	0.95
	Proposed + CNN	0.88	0.94	0.94	0.92	0.97
C.elegans	2-bit Binary + CNN [18]	0.91	0.89	0.90	0.90	0.97
	4-bit One-Hot +MLP [5]	0.85	0.79	0.80	0.82	0.90
	4-bit One-Hot +SVM [12]	0.87	0.79	0.81	0.83	0.91
	Proposed + CNN	0.92	0.92	0.91	0.92	0.97
D.melanogaster	2-bit Binary + CNN [18]	0.70	0.83	0.81	0.77	0.85
	4-bit One-Hot +MLP [5]	0.72	0.75	0.74	0.80	0.89
	4-bit One-Hot +SVM [12]	0.72	0.79	0.77	0.75	0.82
	Proposed + CNN	0.74	0.87	0.85	0.81	0.87
H.sapiens	2-bit Binary + CNN [18]	0.68	0.80	0.78	0.74	0.83
	4-bit One-Hot +MLP [5]	0.69	0.72	0.72	0.79	0.89
	4-bit One-Hot +SVM [12]	0.73	0.70	0.71	0.72	0.80
	Proposed + CNN	0.73	0.82	0.83	0.78	0.87
Cow	2-bit Binary + CNN [18]	0.60	0.84	0.80	0.72	0.81
	4-bit One-Hot +MLP [5]	0.64	0.69	0.67	0.66	0.73
	4-bit One-Hot +SVM [12]	0.64	0.71	0.69	0.68	0.75
	Proposed + CNN	0.69	0.83	0.82	0.76	0.85
Rat	2-bit Binary + CNN [18]	0.67	0.83	0.81	0.75	0.84
	4-bit One-Hot +MLP [5]	0.71	0.75	0.74	0.73	0.81
	4-bit One-Hot +SVM [12]	0.70	0.79	0.77	0.75	0.82
	Proposed + CNN	0.71	0.86	0.87	0.78	0.87

5 Conclusion

In this research, we employed a convolutional neural network for classifying exon and intron genetic sequences using the proposed hybrid encoding method. The experiments were conducted on genome sequences of various eukaryotic organisms. The efficacy of the proposed approach proves to be superior to all the studied methods on all the species investigated when the results of the tests are juxtaposed with the existing approaches from the literature in terms of sensitivity, accuracy, and ROC. From the results, it can be concluded that the proposed hybrid encoding scheme is effective in representing the DNA sequences, discriminating the features of coding regions of protein and non-coding regions, for identifying the exon regions in the genome sequences.

References

1. Akhtar, M., Epps, J., Ambikairajah, E.: On DNA numerical representations for period-3 based exon prediction. In: 2007 IEEE International Workshop on Genomic Signal Processing and Statistics, pp. 1–4. IEEE (2007)
2. Elliott, D., Ladomery, M.: Molecular Biology of RNA. Oxford University Press, Oxford (2017)
3. Farber, R., Lapedes, A., Sirotkin, K.: Determination of eukaryotic protein coding regions using neural networks and information theory. J. Mol. Biol. **226**(2), 471–479 (1992)
4. Gao, J., Qi, Y., Cao, Y., Tung, W.E.: Protein coding sequence identification by simultaneously characterizing the periodic and random features of DNA sequences. J. Biomed. Biotechnol. **2005**(2), 139 (2005)
5. Hatzigeorgiou, A., Mache, N., Reczko, M.: Functional site prediction on the dna sequence by artificial neural networks. In: Proceedings IEEE International Joint Symposia on Intelligence and Systems, pp. 12–17. IEEE (1996)
6. Hatzigeorgiou, A.G.: Translation initiation start prediction in human CDNAs with high accuracy. Bioinformatics **18**(2), 343–350 (2002)
7. Kotlar, D., Lavner, Y.: Gene prediction by spectral rotation measure: a new method for identifying protein-coding regions. Genome Res. **13**(8), 1930–1937 (2003)
8. Krogh, A., Mian, I.S., Haussler, D.: A hidden Markov model that finds genes in E. coli DNA. Nucleic Acids Res. **22**(22), 4768–4778 (1994)
9. Saberkari, H., Shamsi, M., Sedaaghi, M., Golabi, F.: Prediction of protein coding regions in DNA sequences using signal processing methods. In: 2012 IEEE Symposium on Industrial Electronics and Applications, pp. 355–360. IEEE (2012)
10. Saxonov, S., Daizadeh, I., Fedorov, A., Gilbert, W.: EID: the exon-intron database an exhaustive database of protein-coding intron-containing genes. Nucleic Acids Res. **28**(1), 185–190 (2000)
11. Shepelev, V., Fedorov, A.: Advances in the exon-intron database (EID). Brief. Bioinform. **7**(2), 178–185 (2006)
12. Shuo, G., Yi-sheng, Z.: Prediction of protein coding regions by support vector machine. In: 2009 International Symposium on Intelligent Ubiquitous Computing and Education, pp. 185–188. IEEE (2009)
13. Singh, N., Nath, R., Singh, D.B.: Splice-site identification for exon prediction using bidirectional LSTM-RNN approach. Biochem. Biophys. Rep. **30**, 101285 (2022)
14. Snyder, E.E., Stormo, G.D.: Identification of coding regions in genomic DNA sequences: an application of dynamic programming and neural networks. Nucleic Acids Res. **21**(3), 607–613 (1993)
15. Stoffer, D.S., Tyler, D.E., Wendt, D.A.: The spectral envelope and its applications. Stat. Sci. **15**, 224–253 (2000)
16. Tiwari, S., Ramachandran, S., Bhattacharya, A., Bhattacharya, S., Ramaswamy, R.: Prediction of probable genes by Fourier analysis of genomic sequences. Bioinformatics **13**(3), 263–270 (1997)
17. Voss, R.F.: Evolution of long-range fractal correlations and 1/f noise in DNA base sequences. Phys. Rev. Lett. **68**(25), 3805 (1992)
18. Wei, C., Zhang, J., Yuan, X., He, Z., Liu, G.: A deep learning framework with hybrid encoding for protein coding regions prediction in biological sequences. bioRxiv (2020)
19. Wei, C., Zhang, J., Yuan, X., He, Z., Liu, G., Wu, J.: NeuroTIS: enhancing the prediction of translation initiation sites in mRNA sequences via a hybrid dependency network and deep learning framework. Knowl.-Based Syst. **212**, 106459 (2021)

20. Yada, T., Hirosawa, M.: Detection of short protein coding regions within the cyanobacterium genome: application of the hidden Markov model. DNA Res. **3**(6), 355–361 (1996)
21. Yin, C., Yau, S.S.T.: Prediction of protein coding regions by the 3-base periodicity analysis of a DNA sequence. J. Theor. Biol. **247**(4), 687–694 (2007)
22. Yin, C., Yoo, D., Yau, S.S.T.: Tracking the 3-base periodicity of protein-coding regions by the nonlinear tracking-differentiator. In: Proceedings of the 45th IEEE Conference on Decision and Control, pp. 2094–2097. IEEE (2006)
23. Yu, N., Yu, Z., Gu, F., Pan, Y.: Evaluating the impact of encoding schemes on deep auto-encoders for DNA annotation. In: Cai, Z., Daescu, O., Li, M. (eds.) ISBRA 2017. LNCS, vol. 10330, pp. 390–395. Springer, Cham (2017). https://doi.org/10.1007/978-3-319-59575-7_40

Quantifying Intratumor Heterogeneity by Key Genes Selected Using Concrete Autoencoder

Raihanul Bari Tanvir[✉], Ricardo Ruiz, Samuel Ebert, Masrur Sobhan,
Abdullah Al Mamun, and Ananda Mohan Mondal

Knight Foundation School of Computing and Information Sciences, Florida International
University, Miami, FL 33199, USA
{rtanv003,rruiz101,seber007,msobh002,mmamu009,amondal}@fiu.edu

Abstract. The tumor cell population in cancer tissue has distinct molecular characteristics and exhibits different phenotypes, thus, resulting in different subpopulations. This phenomenon is known as Intratumor Heterogeneity (ITH), a major contributor to drug resistance, poor prognosis, etc. Therefore, quantifying the levels of ITH in cancer patients is essential, and many algorithms do so in different ways, using different types of omics data. DEPTH2 algorithm utilizes transcriptomic data to assess ITH scores and exhibits promising performance. However, it quantifies ITH using all genes, limiting the identification of ITH-related prognostic genes. We hypothesize that a subset of key genes is sufficient to quantify the ITH level, and this subset of key genes could be ITH-related prognostic genes. To prove our hypothesis, we propose an unsupervised deep learning-based framework using Concrete Autoencoder (CAE) to select a subset of cancer-specific key genes for ITH evaluation. For the experiment, we used gene expression profile data of breast, kidney, and lung cancer tumor cohorts from the TCGA repository. Multi-run CAE identified three sets of key genes for each cancer cohort. Comparing ITH scores derived from all genes and CAE-selected key genes showed similar prognostic outcomes. Subtypes of lung cancer displayed consistent ITH distributions for both gene sets. Based on these observations, it can be concluded that a subset of key genes, instead of all, is sufficient for ITH quantification. Our results also showed that many key genes are prognostically significant and can be used as therapeutic targets.

Keywords: Concrete Autoencoder · Deep Learning · Gene Expression ·
Intratumor Heterogeneity · ITH

1 Introduction

Intratumor Heterogeneity (ITH) refers to different types of tumor cell subpopulations within a tumor [1]. Even though these cell subpopulations have the same origin (tumor tissue, patient), they exhibit different phenotypes and molecular characteristics. ITH is one of the main challenges for targeted cancer therapy, as the difference in tumor cells and their microenvironments makes it harder for targeted cancer therapy to eradicate cancer cells [2, 3]. Therefore, an accurate assessment of ITH is essential to understand

P. Maji et al. (Eds.): PReMI 2023, LNCS 14301, pp. 844–852, 2023.
https://doi.org/10.1007/978-3-031-45170-6_88

the tumor dynamics and the development of effective and durable therapeutic strategies. ITH causes can vary depending on different levels, such as the genome, epigenome, transcriptome, etc. [4]. For example, reduced DNA damage mechanisms, microenvironmental factors (hypoxia, acidosis, etc.) [5], subclonal evolution [2], etc., contribute to ITH at the genomic level. The methylation of tumor suppressor genes is an example of ITH at the epigenomic level [6]. Different gene expression patterns contribute to ITH at the transcriptome level, which is observed to mirror ITH at the genomic or epigenomic level or both [5, 7]. This makes transcriptomic data suitable for quantifying ITH.

Different algorithms for quantifying ITH exist, such as ABSOLUTE [8], MATH [9], EXPANDS [10], and PhyloWGS [11]. These algorithms use genomic data, such as – copy number alterations (CNA), somatic mutation profiles, etc. Some algorithms take advantage of transcriptome profile that mirrors ITH at the genomic and epigenomic level, such as – tITH [12], sITH [13], DEPTH [14], and DEPTH2 [15]. In contrast to other ITH evaluation techniques, such as DEPTH and others, the DEPTH2 method assesses ITH independently of normal controls. This implies that it can be utilized for all tumor gene expression profiles regardless of the availability of corresponding normal samples' gene expression data. tITH requires protein-protein interaction (PPI) network along with gene expression data. Unlike tITH, DEPTH2 calculates the ITH score using only gene expression data.

Though the DEPTH2 method is statistically sound, the drawbacks are- (i) it uses expression values of all genes (~20,000) in calculating the ITH score and (ii) it cannot guide finding the prognostically significant genes. We argue that not all genes are related to ITH, and a subset of key genes is sufficient to calculate the ITH score at the transcriptome level.

This study presents a deep learning-based computational framework that utilizes an unsupervised concrete autoencoder (CAE) to identify key genes for quantifying Intratumor Heterogeneity (ITH). The framework selects a subset of key genes from Breast Invasive Carcinoma (BRCA), Kidney Renal Carcinoma (KIRC), and Lung Adenocarcinoma (LUAD) using expression profile data from the TCGA repository. The ITH scores are then calculated using all genes and the selected key genes. The results demonstrate that using the subset of 100 key genes outperforms all ~20,000 genes in terms of survival and prognostic outcomes for the three cancer types. The key genes exhibit consistent levels of ITH across cancer subtypes and show potential as prognostic markers and therapeutic targets. This study highlights the effectiveness of a reduced set of key genes in quantifying ITH at the transcriptome level. The overall framework is depicted in Supplementary Fig. S1.

2 Materials and Methods

2.1 Dataset Collection

We collected gene expression datasets of BRCA,LUAD, and KIRC cancers from the UCSC Xena Browser database [16]. Each dataset contains expression profiles of 20,530 mRNAs. The number of tumor samples for each cancer type was as follows: BRCA (1097 samples), LUAD (533 samples), and KIRC (517 samples).

2.2 Concrete Autoencoder to Select Cancer-Specific Key Genes

Concrete Autoencoder (CAE) [17], an unsupervised deep learning approach is used to identify cancer-specific key genes. CAE identifies features most informative for a given dataset [18–23]. CAE differs from the standard Autoencoder in the encoder part, where CAE employs a concrete selector layer (See Fig. S2). This selector layer is based on Concrete distribution [24], a relaxed variant of discrete distribution. Unlike the encoder part of the CAE, the decoder part resembles closely with the standard Autoencoder. The selector layer is used to incorporate discrete distribution into deep learning algorithms. For example, CAE uses it to learn a subset of the most informative features and produce minimum reconstruction error. In the learning phase, the selector layer learns a subset of features, which depends on a hyperparameter called Temperature (T), which is gradually lowered during the training phase to a low value using a simple annealing scheduling. This gradual decrease in temperature helps the concrete distribution to learn and select a definite subset of features [17]. In the selector layer, each unit selects a unique feature with the highest probability from the original feature space. Thus, CAE selects the most informative subset of features, and the reconstruction of the original feature space using the selected subset of features produces minimum reconstruction error. In the original Autoencoder, the features learned at the encoder part are latent features, whereas those learned at CAE are actual features. CAE was trained on each gene expression data of BRCA, KIRC, and LUAD, and 100 features were selected in each run. While training CAE, the dataset was divided randomly into 80/20 split for training and testing. Details of hyperparameter tuning are in Table S1.

2.3 Training CAE

Figure S3 shows the characteristics curve for CAE or an instance of the training behaviors of CAE for the LUAD dataset. The hyperparameter, Temperature (T), was reduced using a simple annealing schedule from 10 to 0.1 from the start epoch to the last. The reconstruction errors (loss) for the training and validation sets are plotted using blue and red curves, respectively. It shows that both errors were relatively high during the early training phase, as expected, and both reached a minimum plateau at the end. Also, the mean-max probability finally approaches 1.0 (yellow curve). The CAE was implemented using Keras (https://keras.io/). Experiments were conducted on the high-performance cluster with NVIDIA Quatro K620 GPU with 384 cores and 2 GB memory devices.

2.4 ITH Level Estimation Method

To calculate the Intratumor Heterogeneity (ITH) score, we used a scoring method named - Deviating Gene Expression Profiling Tumor Heterogeneity, or DEPTH2 in short [15], defined as –

$$\sqrt{\frac{\sum_{i=1}^{m}\left(z(ex(G_i, T)) - \frac{1}{m}\sum_{j=1}^{m}z(ex(G_j, T))\right)^2}{m - 1}} \tag{1}$$

where,

$$z(ex(G_i, T) = \frac{\left| (ex(G_i, T) - \frac{1}{t}\sum_{j=1}^{t} ex(G_i, TS_j) \right|}{SD_i} \tag{2}$$

and,

$$SD_i = \sqrt{\frac{\sum_{j}^{t} \left((ex(G_i, T) - \frac{1}{t}\sum_{j=1}^{t} ex(G_i, TS_j) \right)^2}{t-1}} \tag{3}$$

where T is the tumor sample for which the score is being calculated. G_i is the i-th gene, and m is the number of genes. $ex(G_i, T)$ expression of gene G_i in sample T. It assigns a score to each patient. It is based on standard deviations of the z-score of the gene expression value variations. If a tumor displays similar z-scored expression values across most genes, it will have a low DEPTH2 score and a lower ITH level. In contrast, if there is variation in gene expression alterations, the tumor will receive a higher DEPTH2 score. This score indicates how much the gene expressions deviate from the norm for all tumors and genes within the matrix. We calculated the ITH score for each cancer patient of BRCA, KIRC, and LUAD employing DEPTH2 using two sets of genes. One score uses all the genes, and the other uses only the key genes selected by multi-run CAE.

2.5 Survival Analysis

Survival Analysis was performed to check whether two groups of patients based on high and low ITH scores are significantly distinguishable in prognosis. In our analysis, the event of interest is the death of cancer patients.

Survival Analysis Based on ITH Scores: Samples were sorted in descending order of the ITH score, and then the top and bottom of the total samples were taken as two groups. This analysis compared the prognostic importance of ITH scores derived using all genes and key genes (our study).

Survival Analysis Based on Each Key Gene: The cohort was divided into two groups based on the median gene expression values. This survival analysis helped identify prognostically significant genes.

After forming two groups, the Kaplan-Meier curves were plotted, and the Log-rank test was performed to check the statistical significance of the difference in survival function.

3 Results and Discussion

3.1 Multi-run CAE to Select Key Genes

Due to the stochastic nature of CAE, the model was trained ten times, and in each run, 100 features were selected for each cancer cohort - BRCA, KIRC, and LUAD. Figure 1(a) shows the stochastic nature of CAE since only 16 genes are common between three single-run CAE. In the case of 10-run CAE, the top 100 features were selected from the combined list sorted in descending order based on the frequency of appearance of a feature in 10 runs. It is clear from Fig. 1(b) that there are 53 genes common between three batches of 10 runs, which is more than the common genes (16 genes) in three single runs. Thus, a multi-run approach was adopted to select the robust set of features.

The top 100 frequent features were chosen to select the key features based on the assumption that the more frequent a feature in different runs, the more informative the feature is. The combined lists of features derived from 10-run CAE consist of 469, 527, and 435 genes for BRCA, KIRC, and LUAD, respectively. The frequency range of the top 100 features is 3 to 10 for each cancer cohort, which means that the most frequent features appeared in all ten runs, and the least frequent one appeared in 3 runs.

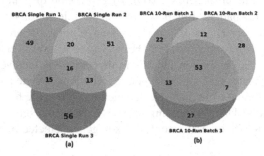

Fig. 1. Selecting the robust set of features. (a) Venn diagram of three sets of 100 genes from three single-run CAE; CAE produces only 16 features common between single runs. (b) three sets of most frequent 100 features from 10-run CAE. 10-run CAE produces more features (53 genes) common between three batches of runs. Thus, multi-run CAE produces a robust set of features.

3.2   Multi-run CAE Selects Cancer-specific Genes

We investigated whether there were any common genes between two sets or among the three sets of key genes derived from three cancers, shown by the Venn diagram in Fig. S4. It shows that there is no common gene between the three gene sets. However, a few genes are common between each pair of gene sets: 5 between BRCA and LUAD, 3 between KIRC and BRCA, and 3 between KIRC and LUAD. Since the size of each set is 100 and there are only a few genes common between two sets and none between the three sets, thus, the key gene sets are cancer-specific.

3.3   All Genes vs. Key Genes in ITH Scoring: Whole Cancer Cohorts

We compared the ITH scores calculated for BRCA, KIRC, and LUAD cohorts using two different sets of genes: (i) DEPTH2 score calculated using all genes and (ii) DEPTH2 score calculated using only the key genes selected by the multi-run CAE system (our work). Survival analysis is used to compare the two ITH scores. Figure 2 presents the results of survival analyses, Kaplan Meier plots, for cancer cohort - BRCA based on ITH scores derived from all genes (Fig. 2a) and key genes (Fig. 2b).

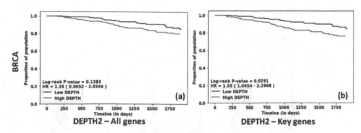

Fig. 2. Survival analysis of BRCA cohort. Kaplan Meier plots based on DEPTH2 score calculated using all genes (a) and key genes (b).

It is evident from Kaplan Meier plots that high DEPTH2 scores are related to poor prognosis, and low DEPTH2 scores have a higher chance of survival.

Survival analysis of BRCA showed a P-value of 0.1383 (not significant) and Hazard Ratio (HR) of 1.36 using all genes (Fig. 2a), while key genes produced a significant result with a P-value of 0.0291 and HR of 1.55 (Fig. 2b). The latter case is prognostically significant (P-value $\leq$ 0.05) compared to the former, thus validating our claim.

Similarly, better results were found using key genes than all genes both in LUAD (P-value: 0.0019 vs. 0.109; HR: 1.79 vs. 1.34) and KIRC (P-value: 5.18e−07 vs. 0.0018, HR: 2.67 vs. 1.78), as shown in Fig. S5a–b and S5c–d.

Our investigation showed that 100 key genes produced better results than all genes (~20,000) in three types of cancers. Thus, we do not need all genes to evaluate the ITH scores.

3.4 All Genes vs. Key Genes in ITH Scoring: LUAD Subtypes

In this section, we show the comparison of ITH scores (DEPTH2) for LUAD subtypes calculated using all genes versus key genes. Of 435 LUAD patients, 55, 34, and 54 are labeled as Terminal Respiratory Unit (TRU), Proximal Proliferation (PP), and Proximal Inflammation (PI), respectively. The remaining patients did not have any subtype-based labels. This molecular subtyping was done in [25]. It is evident from survival analysis that the TRU subtype is prognostically favorable and has a higher chance of survival than the PI and PP subtypes combined (Fig. S6).

Figure 3 shows the ITH score distribution for three subtypes, using all genes and key genes. Min-max normalization on DEPTH2 scores was performed to bring the distribution to the same scale. It is seen that the subtype TRU has comparatively lower values in ITH score than other subtypes, which supports the higher chance of survival for the TRU subtype than PI and PP combined (Fig. S6). It is also clear that the distribution of ITH scores for three subtypes remained the same for all genes and key genes.

We performed correlation analysis to compare the distribution of the DEPTH2 scores using all genes and key genes, and the results are shown in Table S2. It is observed that there is a relatively high correlation between DEPTH2 scores of each subtype of LUAD cancer using all and key genes. It is clear from the P-values (ns: not significant) in Fig. 3 that the two scores for each subtype derived using all genes and key genes are not significantly different. Both all genes and key genes produced the same level of

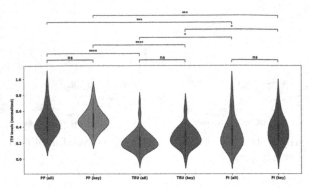

Fig. 3. Comparison of ITH scores of three molecular subtypes of LUAD using all genes (labeled as 'all') and key genes (labeled as 'key'). Distribution of Min-max normalized ITH score (DEPTH2) in three molecular subtypes of LUAD in violin plots. The Mann-Whitney-Wilcoxon test between two distributions was performed, and stars marked the p-value significance. P-value annotation legend: ns (not significant): $0.05 < p \le 1$, *: $0.01 < p \le 0.05$, **: $0.001 < p \le 0.01$, ***: $0.0001 < p \le 0.001$, ****: $p \le 0.0001$

difference in ITH between two subtypes. For example, PP and TRU (****), TRU and PI (*), and PP and PI (***).

Based on these observations, we do not need ~20,000 genes to calculate the ITH score; only 100 key genes will suffice.

3.5 Survival Analysis of Key Genes

Survival analysis was performed on each key gene from their respective cancer cohort to identify whether they possess prognostic capabilities. Figure S5 shows the forest plot of the prognostically significant genes and the summary of survival analyses in terms of Logrank P-value and Hazard Ratio with a 95% confidence interval. The thresholds for prognostically significant genes are Logrank P-value ≤ 0.05 and Hazard Ratio, HR $\neq 1$. Of 100 key genes for BRCA, 15 were prognostically significant, as shown in the forest plot in Fig. S7. Similarly, for KIRC and LUAD, 30 and 61 genes were prognostically significant. The list of genes with prognostically significant genes marked as bold is given in Table S3.

4   Conclusion and Future Direction

This study proposes that a subset of key genes instead of all genes (~20,000) is adequate for evaluating the ITH scores of individual tumors. To test this hypothesis, a computational framework was developed using a multi-run concrete autoencoder to select the key genes from gene expression profile data. Results showed that using only the selected 100 key genes instead of all ~20,000 genes produced better survival and prognostic outcomes for three cancers (BRCA, KIRC, and LUAD). Our investigation showed that key genes produce the same levels of ITH at the cancer subtype levels. We also showed that many of these key genes are prognostically significant, which can be investigated further as possible therapeutic targets. This study concludes that a subset of key genes is sufficient to quantify the ITH at the transcriptome level.

However, this study has its limitations. The intratumor heterogeneity (ITH) is determined by genetic and epigenetic variation within an individual's tumor. The transcriptome reflects both types of heterogeneity, meaning that a unique set of genes may dictate ITH for each patient. However, our study used the same key genes to assess ITH across all patients for a specific type of tumor, which presents a limitation. The selection of 10 runs in multi-run CAE was arbitrary and may not be optimal for identifying a stable set of features for BRCA, KIRC, and LUAD cohorts. Despite these limitations, the study demonstrated that a short list of key genes is effective in assessing ITH levels. In future research, we will extend this study to determine the ideal number of runs needed to select a reliable feature set across different cohorts using multi-run CAE. Additionally, we aim to create an approach that identifies patient-specific key genes for evaluating ITH.

Acknowledgment. This work has been partially supported by the NSF CAREER Award #1901628.

Supplementary Materials. The supplementary materials are available at GitHub. https://github.com/mldag/ITH-Key-Genes-mrCAE/blob/main/supplementary.pdf.

References

1. Jamal-Hanjani, M., Quezada, S.A., Larkin, J., Swanton, C.: Translational implications of tumor heterogeneity. Clin. Cancer Res. **21**, 1258–1266 (2015)
2. Qazi, M.A., et al.: Intratumoral heterogeneity: pathways to treatment resistance and relapse in human glioblastoma. Ann. Oncol. **28**(7), 1448–1456 (2017). https://doi.org/10.1093/annonc/mdx169
3. Reinartz, R., et al.: Functional Subclone profiling for prediction of treatment-induced intratumor population shifts and discovery of rational drug combinations in human glioblastoma. Clin. Cancer Res. **23**(2), 562–574 (2017). https://doi.org/10.1158/1078-0432.CCR-15-2089
4. Grzywa, T.M., Paskal, W., Włodarski, P.K.: Intratumor and intertumor heterogeneity in melanoma. Transl. Oncol. **10**(6), 956–975 (2017). https://doi.org/10.1016/j.tranon.2017.09.007
5. Gillies, R.J., Verduzco, D., Gatenby, R.A.: Evolutionary dynamics of carcinogenesis and why targeted therapy does not work. Nat. Rev. Cancer **12**(7), 487–493 (2012). https://doi.org/10.1038/nrc3298
6. Takamizawa, J., et al.: Reduced expression of the let-7 MicroRNAs in human lung cancers in association with shortened postoperative survival. Cancer Res. **64**(11), 3753–3756 (2004)
7. Sigalotti, L., et al.: Intratumor heterogeneity of cancer/testis antigens expression in human cutaneous melanoma is methylation-regulated and functionally reverted by 5-Aza-2'-deoxycytidine. Cancer Res. **64**(24), 9167–9171 (2004). https://doi.org/10.1158/0008-5472.CAN-04-1442
8. Carter, S.L., et al.: Absolute quantification of somatic DNA alterations in human cancer. Nat. Biotechnol. **30**(5), 413–421 (2012). https://doi.org/10.1038/nbt.2203
9. Mroz, E.A., Rocco, J.W.: MATH, a novel measure of intratumor genetic heterogeneity, is high in poor-outcome classes of head and neck squamous cell carcinoma. Oral Oncol. **49**(3), 211–215 (2013). https://doi.org/10.1016/j.oraloncology.2012.09.007

10. Andor, N., Harness, J.V., Müller, S., Mewes, H.W., Petritsch, C.: Expands: expanding ploidy and allele frequency on nested subpopulations. Bioinformatics **30**(1), 50–60 (2014). https://doi.org/10.1093/bioinformatics/btt622

11. Deshwar, A.G., Vembu, S., Yung, C.K., Jang, G.H., Stein, L., Morris, Q.: PhyloWGS: reconstructing subclonal composition and evolution from whole-genome sequencing of tumors. Genome Biol. **16**, 1–20 (2015)

12. Park, Y., Lim, S., Nam, J.-W., Kim, S.: Measuring intratumor heterogeneity by network entropy using RNA-seq data. Sci. Rep. **6**(1), 37767 (2016). https://doi.org/10.1038/srep37767

13. Kim, M., Lee, S., Lim, S., Kim, S.: SpliceHetero: an information theoretic approach for measuring spliceomic intratumor heterogeneity from bulk tumor RNA-seq. PLoS ONE **14**(10), e0223520 (2019). https://doi.org/10.1371/journal.pone.0223520

14. Li, M., Zhang, Z., Li, L., Wang, X.: An algorithm to quantify intratumor heterogeneity based on alterations of gene expression profiles. Commun. Biol. **3**(1), 505 (2020). https://doi.org/10.1038/s42003-020-01230-7

15. Song, D., Wang, X.: DEPTH2: an mRNA-based algorithm to evaluate intratumor heterogeneity without reference to normal controls. J. Transl. Med. **20**(1), 150 (2022)

16. Goldman, M., et al.: The UCSC Xena platform for public and private cancer genomics data visualization and interpretation. bioRxiv (2018)

17. Abid, A., Balin, M.F., Zou, J.: Concrete autoencoders: differentiable feature selection and reconstruction. In: 36th International Conference on Machine Learning, ICML 2019 (2019)

18. Tanvir, R.B., Sobhan, M., Mondal, A.M.: An autoencoder based bioinformatics framework for predicting prognosis of breast cancer patients. In: 2022 IEEE International Conference on Bioinformatics and Biomedicine (BIBM), pp. 3160–3166 (2022)

19. Sobhan, M., Al Mamun, A., Tanvir, R.B., Alfonso, M.J., Valle, P., Mondal, A.M.: Deep learning to discover genomic signatures for racial disparity in lung cancer. In: 2020 IEEE International Conference on Bioinformatics and Biomedicine (BIBM), pp. 2990–2992 (2020)

20. Sobhan, M., Kalie, K., Al Mamun, A., Godavarty, A., Mondal, A.M.: Skin tone benchmark dataset for diabetic foot ulcers and machine learning to discover the salient features. In: International Conference on Image Processing, Computer Vision, & Pattern Recognition (2022)

21. Al Mamun, A., et al.: Multi-run concrete autoencoder to identify prognostic lncRNAs for 12 cancers. Int. J. Mol. Sci. **22**, 11919 (2021)

22. Al Mamun, A., Sobhan, M., Tanvir, R.B., Dimitroff, C.J., Mondal, A.M.: Deep learning to discover cancer glycome genes signifying the origins of cancer. In: Proceedings of the 2020 IEEE International Conference on Bioinformatics and Biomedicine, BIBM 2020 (2020)

23. Al Mamun, A., Duan, W., Mondal, A.M.: Pan-cancer feature selection and classification reveals important long non-coding RNAs. In: Proceedings of the 2020 IEEE International Conference on Bioinformatics and Biomedicine, BIBM 2020, pp. 2417–2424 (2020)

24. Maddison, C.J., Mnih, A., Teh, Y.W.: The concrete distribution: a continuous relaxation of discrete random variables. In: 5th International Conference on Learning Representations, ICLR 2017 - Conference Track Proceedings (2017)

25. Comprehensive molecular profiling of lung adenocarcinoma. Nature (2014)

Identification of Potential Prognostic Biomarkers for ESCC Using Single-Cell RNA Sequencing Data Analysis

Pallabi Patowary[1]([✉])(iD), Dhruba K. Bhattacharyya[1](iD), and Pankaj Barah[2]

[1] Department of Computer Science and Engineering, Tezpur University, Assam, India
{ppallabi,dkb}@tezu.ernet.in
[2] Department of Molecular Biology and Biotechnology,
Tezpur University, Assam, India
barah@tezu.ernet.in
http://www.springer.com/gp/computer-science/lncs

Abstract. This paper analyses the difference between parental cells and cells that acquired radioresistance using scRNA-seq data and investigates the dynamic changes of the transcriptome of cells in response to fractionated irradiation (FIR) towards the identification of potential biomarkers for Esophageal Squamous Cell Carcinoma (ESCC). The divergence of gene expressions is analyzed in response to FIR and the dynamic changes in differentially expressed genes (DEGs) of KYSE-180 cells with two different cumulative doses of FIR (12-Gy and 30-Gy). We construct several biological networks and observe relative to control (0-Gy), 30-Gy induced higher variability of genes. We identified four hub genes TXN, IER2, PCNA, and CENPF involved in ESCC progression.

Keywords: ESCC · Biomarkers · Esophageal squamous cell carcinoma · sc-RNAseq · Hub gene · Differential expression analysis

1 Introduction

ESCC is one of the main histological subtypes of Esophageal cancer. Several risk factors are associated with ESCC, although there is no specific ESCC biomarker available, which ultimately results in inadequate treatment modalities for patients suffering from ESCC. Due to the advancement of Next Generation Sequencing (NGS), it is now possible to identify genomic alterations and gene expression changes that are associated with cancer development and pathogenesis. scRNA-seq enables researchers to identify rare subpopulations of cancer cells that are involved with cancer progression, which helps in developing targeted therapeutics for cancer. Biomarkers are molecules that can be used to identify a particular cell type or state. These molecules are helpful in the investigation of cancer cells, for example, to determine how healthy a cell is. Biomarkers can be identified by studying the proteins or genes that are expressed by a cell.

Single-cell RNA sequencing data can be used to identify biomarkers that are specific to a particular cell type or state. This helps improve the accuracy of biomarker identification. This study reveals that scRNA-seq data analysis is helpful in analyzing gene expression patterns and uncovering biological insights. By leveraging the scRNA-seq data, one can gain a better understanding of gene expression patterns in different cell types and use this knowledge to develop more effective treatments for diseases. We analyse the ESCC scRNA-seq dataset using (i) a consensus function of differential expression analysis (DEA) methods and (ii) a novel measure called SNMRS and its application in clustering. We identify four potential genes that have been found to have a close association with ESCC development.

2   Related Work

Biomarker identification in scRNA-seq data begins with the selection of a set of DEGs that are significantly associated with a given phenotype. Once the differential expressions of the genes have been identified, the next step is to perform functional enrichment analysis to identify markers that are associated with specific biological pathways. The analysis of scRNA-seq data is challenging because of replication noise, sparsity in transcripts, and outlier cell populations [2]. Seth et al. [11] discuss the application of dimensionality reduction and hierarchical clustering for cluster-specific potential biomarker discovery in scRNA-seq data. We observe that the authors have not used an imputed matrix and multiple DEA tools to eliminate biased DEGs. Wang et al. [13] identify novel biomarkers for diabetic kidney disease by combining scRNA-seq and bulk RNA-seq data. The authors use the Seurat package and identify key biomarkers by the method of MCODE. Cui et al. [4] establish a framework for analyzing scRNA-seq data, including DEA, differential correlation analysis, network analysis (WGCNA), and differential network analysis. Algabri et al. [2] present a framework based on co-expression network analysis for scRNA-seq data. They used Seurat's MAST method to perform a DEA and WGCNA package for GCN analysis. From the above discussion, it is evident that the Seurat framework with some variations has been successfully used in scRNA-seq gene data analysis, towards the identification of crucial genes for a given disease.

3   Materials and Methods

A scRNA-seq ESCC dataset of size 18938 Genes x 314 cells with accession number: GSE81812 downloaded from cancerSEA[1] has been used. scRNA-seq data obtained from KYSE-180 cells before exposure to fractionated irradiation serves as a control and post-fractionated irradiation data are obtained after cumulative doses of 12-Gy and 30-Gy.

---

[1] http://biocc.hrbmu.edu.cn/CancerSEA/home.jsp.

This framework shown in Fig. 1 is proposed to (i) compare the behaviour of genes in different sample types and (ii) identify crucial genes associated with the disease ESCC. First, the dataset is pre-processed. Highly variable genes are identified and performed scaling and dimensionality reduction. Next, the nearest neighbour graph and SNNs are computed to find all markers. We identify the clusters using the Louvain algorithm that match the cell types of data. After clustering, differentially expressed genes are identified for each sample type i.e. 0 Gy (Control), 12 Gy (ESCC) and 30 Gy (ESCC) individually using three different DEA methods i.e., Wilcox [15], MAST [5], and t-test [14]. A consensus of DEA is performed independently to avoid biases for each sample type. A set of DEGs considered as common DEGs for 0-Gy sample type w.r.t. a user-defined threshold α = logfc.threshold = 0.25 (default) which are identified using mentioned three different methods. Similarly, common DEGs are obtained for 12-Gy and 30-Gy.

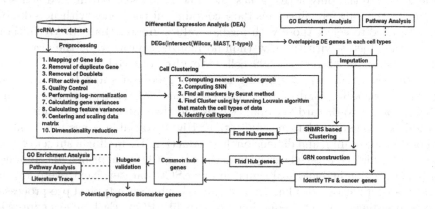

Fig. 1. Framework of the proposed method.

With these DEGs, Gene Regulatory Networks (GRN) are constructed individually for each sample type and identify already established transcription factors and ESCC cancer genes. GO enrichment analysis and KEGG pathways are analyzed for all these selected DEGs and if found significantly enriched in GO and pathways then we consider them for downstream analysis. In order to reduce the effect of noise and dropout events, an imputation method SAVER [6] has been used in the datasets with DEGs for each sample type individually to impute the missing gene expression values. Co-expression networks are generated from imputed datasets of DEGs for each sample type by computing a measure of co-expression between pairs of genes. Here, SNMRS measure [10] is applied to compute co-expression between genes and extracted modules using the hierarchical clustering method for each sample type. Also, a list of hub genes is extracted from these modules based on degree information and considering those genes having degree values≥mean(degree). From GRNs, a list of the top five hub genes or central genes is identified for each sub-network in the different sample types and accordingly, a list of hub genes has been identified. Next, the common hub genes from GCN modules and GRN are matched with the transcription factors and if found valid, consider them as the most crucial hub genes for ESCC. After biological validation and literature trace, the identified crucial hub genes are considered the most crucial genes associated with ESCC progression.

4   Results

In this section preprocessing and results obtained during our analysis are presented. At first, ensemble Ids from the raw dataset are mapped into gene symbols and removed 39 duplicate genes and 1 "NA" gene. Next, doublet cells are removed and cell size is reduced to 309. Genes that have a median of zFPKM value > -3 are the only active genes and now 10684 selected filtered genes are present in the dataset. Since this data contains all the genes with non-doublet cells, we need to select those with median values greater than -3. We initialize the Seurat objects with the raw (non-normalized) data. Now, the size of our data becomes 10684 genes x 309 cells. We filter out cells having (1) greater than 200 genes and (ii) cells having less than 2500 genes and keep only those cells that have mitochondrial percentage less than 5%. Next, performed quality control analysis to discard low-quality cells and the global-scaling normalization method is applied for data normalization. Highly variable genes are identified and performed scaling and dimensionality reduction. By finding a subset of genes that exhibit high cell-to-cell variation in the dataset helps in principal component analysis to highlight biological signal in our ESCC dataset. Next, we perform a linear transformation, also known as "scaling," which is a typical pre-processing step before dimensionality reduction methods like PCA. Each gene's expression is changed via the ScaleData function, resulting in a mean expression across cells of 0 scales each gene's expression so that the variation between cells is 1. In order to prevent highly expressed genes from dominating, this step assigns equal weight to downstream analyses.

In the next step, the nearest neighbour graph and SNNs are computed to find all potential markers. The clusters are identified by running Louvain algorithm that matches the cell types of data. We extracted the information of Celltypes from the meta dataset and combined with the dataset. After clustering, differentially expressed genes are identified for each sample type i.e. 0 Gy (Control), 12 Gy (ESCC) and 30 Gy (ESCC). A consensus of DEA method is performed to avoid biases. For this, three DEA methods i.e., Wilcox, MAST, and t-type are used. A total of 138 DEGs from 0-Gy, 289 DEGs from 12-Gy, and 763 DEGs from 30-Gy were obtained. SAVER is used to impute the missing gene expression values in the sub-matrix of DEGs. With these DEGs, GRNs are constructed individually for each sample type and identified already established transcription factors and ESCC cancer genes. It has been found that in the 30-Gy type, the number of identified transcription factors and ESCC cancer genes are comparatively more than the 0-Gy type. All the 1363 DEGs were significantly enriched in DNA replication, cell cycle, RNA transport, and oocyte meiosis pathways.

A hub gene can be defined as the central gene to a network which has comparatively more connectivity in the case of an undirected graph and in the case of a directed graph a node which has more outgoing edges. We know that a hub gene always has a significant role in disease progression and investigating these genes might provide a clue related to disease or dug discovery to researchers. Here, we aim to find hub genes from different angles such as from co-expression networks, GRNs, and transcription factor lists.

(a) Constructing gene co-expression networks (GCN): GCNs are generated from gene expression data by computing a measure of co-expression between pairs of genes. Here, we apply SNMRS measure [10] to compute co-expression between genes and found modules using the hierarchical clustering method for each sample type. Also, a list of hub genes is extracted using degree and taking genes above mean(degree) reported in Table 1. It has been observed that the number of modules extracted is comparatively more in the case of the 30-Gy sample type.

Table 1. Details of GCN Analysis

Sample Type	Module Name	Hub Gene from GCN Modules
0-Gy	brown	TXN, LAMTOR5, B2M, PDIA3, SRSF7, ACP1, SUMO1, KDELR2, PGK1, ITM2B, CAPZA1
	turquoise	IER2, TPI1, EIF3I, SKP1, UBE2N, MRPL17, CD55, POLD4, FTH1, EBP, CTSB, OAZ2, PLD3, RHOC, LGALS3BP, DUSP1, SH3BGRL3, TMED10, CNBP, CFL1, GPX3, LGALS3, CD164, CNIH1, CST3, S100A14, TMBIM6, AKR1B1 PRDX2, TIMP1, ELOF1, FTL, GAPDH, CSNK2B
	blue	MCM4, MCM2, PCNA, CDC6, THAP7, RFC4, GINS2, PPIF, WDR76, DTL, FAM111B, LIPH, GMNN, RFC2, SNX8, TM2D2
12-Gy	turquoise	KRT8, FBLN1, MDH2, TAGLN2, SPINT2
	blue	CCNB1, CKS2, DEPDC1, FAM83D, TOP2A, PLK1, AURKB, NEK2, CCNA2, CENPF, TPX2, CDC20, SPAG5, HMMR, CDKN3, CDCA8, DLGAP5, KPNA2
	brown	UBB, EPS8, ATP5F1B, MT1X
30-Gy	blue	RPL22, RPS25, RPL37A
	red	TOP2A, H2AX, MKI67, PRC1
	turquoise	CHCHD10, LDLRAD2, BASP1, STUB1, FAM83H
	yellow	DDX56, PRPF38B

(b) Finding Transcription Factors (TFs) and cancer genes: TFs are the key players in GRN interactions. Based on human transcriptional regulatory factors extracted from the HumanTFDB database[2] and TFCheckpoint, a

---

[2] bioinfo.life.hust.edu.cn/HumanTFDB/.

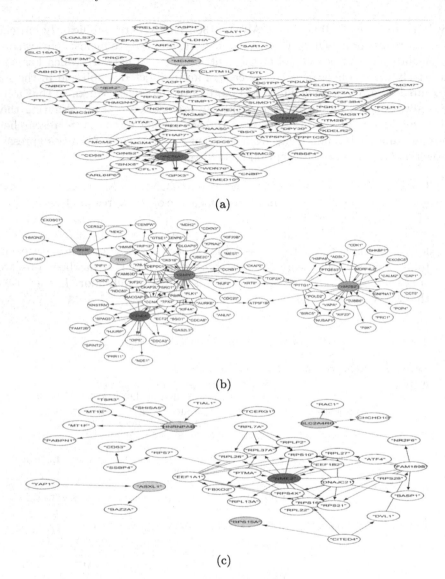

Fig. 2. GRN and hub genes of their subnetworks obtained by cytoHubba for (a) 0-Gy (b) 12-Gy (c) 30-Gy

total of 22, 33, and 179 TFs were detected in DEGs of 0-Gy, 12-Gy, and 30-Gy samples, respectively. Further, a list of ESCC cancer driver genes is downloaded from cBioportal https://www.cbioportal.org/ and intOGen https://www.intogen.org/ and found a total of 11, and 36 cancer genes in DEGs of 12-Gy, and 30-Gy samples, respectively.

(c) Constructing gene regulatory network (GRN): GRN is used to obtain information regarding the regulatory interactions between transcriptional regulators and their target genes. We used the significant DEGs as input to construct the GRN so as to observe the regulatory behaviour of the corresponding genes. We apply the GENIE3 R tool for the prediction of GRN from gene expression data and it uses the random forest approach. The resulting GRNs are in the form of an adjacency list with weighted directed edges from regulatory genes to other target genes. In Cytoscape, tool GRNs are plotted (shown in Fig. 2) and by applying cytoHubba tool [3] a list of the top five hub genes or central genes which act as regulators are found for each sub-network in the different sample types. It is seen that PCNA, FOS, TXN, IER2, and MCM6 are the hub gene regulators extracted from sub-networks of 0-Gy GRN. CENPA, CENPF, BRD8, HMGB2, and TTK are the hub gene regulators extracted from sub-networks of 12-Gy GRN. NME2, HNRNPAB, SLC2A4RG, RPS15A, and ASXL1 are the hub gene regulators extracted from sub-networks of 30-Gy GRN.

(d) Selection of hub genes: From a different perspective, we found a good number of hub genes. Therefore, the common hub genes from GCN modules and GRN are matched with the transcription factors and if found then considered as the most crucial genes in ESCC. After biological validation and literature trace TXN, IER2, PCNA, and CENPF genes are considered as the prognostic biomarkers for ESCC.

(e) Biological analysis of hub genes: Biological analysis (Biological Process, Cellular Component and Molecular Function) are performed for each crucial gene in DAVID https://david.ncifcrf.gov. The GO enrichment term nucleoplasm, Acetylation, and nucleus are associated with genes CENPF, PCNA, TXN, and IER2 genes. Protein C-terminus binding, chromatin binding, and centrosome GO terms are associated with CENPF and PCNA genes.

(f) Literature Trace: From the literature of established wet lab results, some observations have been made. The protein TXN helps catalyze dithiol-disulfide exchange reactions and participates in various redox reactions [1]. IER2 is also known to play a role in promoting tumour motility and metastasis and is a potential prognostic and therapeutic target [8]. Talukder et al. [12] performed Pearson correlation network link analysis for ESCC and found one of the most linked genes in the tumour network was IER2. PCNA is a nuclear protein that is known to be present in proliferating cells, including normal proliferating cells and cancer cells [7]. The expression level of PCNA has been found to be appreciably correlated with the TNM stage of ESCC patients. CENPF is found upregulated in ESCC [9]. The expression of CENPE is associated with DNA methylation status in esophageal adenocarcinoma and is an independent predictor of unfavourable overall survival [16].

5   Conclusion

In this piece of work, an effective framework is introduced to find highly similar patterns containing genes with high biological relevance. In this work, a consensus model is used to identify DEGs with high biological relevance in ESCC development. This study shows significant changes in gene expression after receiving a 12-Gy or 30-Gy cumulative radiation dose. This study suggests that TXN, IER2, PCNA, and CENPF are potential prognostic biomarkers for ESCC diagnosis and can be considered as potential therapeutic targets for ESCC.

References

1. Abdo, J., et al.: Discovery of novel and clinically relevant markers in formalin-fixed paraffin-embedded esophageal cancer specimen. Front. Oncol. **8**, 157 (2018)
2. Algabri, Y.A., Li, L., Liu, Z.P.: scGENA: a single-cell gene coexpression network analysis framework for clustering cell types and revealing biological mechanisms. Bioengineering **9**(8), 353 (2022)
3. Chin, C.H., Chen, S.H., Wu, H.H., Ho, C.W., Ko, M.T., Lin, C.Y.: cytoHubba: identifying hub objects and sub-networks from complex interactome. BMC Syst. Biol. **8**(4), 1–7 (2014)
4. Cui, L., Wang, B., Ren, C., Wang, A., An, H., Liang, W.: A novel method to identify the differences between two single cell groups at single gene, gene pair, and gene module levels. Front. Genet. **12**, 648898 (2021)
5. Finak, G., et al.: MAST: a flexible statistical framework for assessing transcriptional changes and characterizing heterogeneity in single-cell RNA sequencing data. Genome Biol. **16**(1), 1–13 (2015)
6. Huang, M., et al.: SAVER: gene expression recovery for single-cell RNA sequencing. Nat. Methods **15**(7), 539–542 (2018)
7. Kim, S., et al.: ATAD5 restricts R-loop formation through PCNA unloading and RNA helicase maintenance at the replication fork. Nucleic Acids Res. **48**(13), 7218–7238 (2020)
8. Neeb, A., et al.: The immediate early gene Ier2 promotes tumor cell motility and metastasis, and predicts poor survival of colorectal cancer patients. Oncogene **31**(33), 3796–3806 (2012)
9. Osako, Y., et al.: Regulation of MMP13 by antitumor microRNA-375 markedly inhibits cancer cell migration and invasion in esophageal squamous cell carcinoma. Int. J. Oncol. **49**(6), 2255–2264 (2016)
10. Patowary, P., Bhattacharyya, D.K., Barah, P.: SNMRS: an advanced measure for co-expression network analysis. Comput. Biol. Med. 105222 (2022)
11. Seth, S., Mallik, S., Bhadra, T., Zhao, Z.: Dimensionality reduction and louvain agglomerative hierarchical clustering for cluster-specified frequent biomarker discovery in single-cell sequencing data. Front. Genet. **13**, 32 (2022)
12. Talukder, A.K., Agarwal, M., Buetow, K.H., Denèfle, P.P.: Tracking cancer genetic evolution using oncotrack. Sci. Rep. **6**(1), 1–15 (2016)
13. Wang, Y., Zhao, M., Zhang, Y.: Integrated analysis of single-cell RNA-seq and bulk RNA-seq in the identification of a novel ceRNA network and key biomarkers in diabetic kidney disease. Int. J. Gener. Med. 1985–2001 (2022)
14. Welch, B.L.: The generalization of 'STUDENT'S' problem when several different population varlances are involved. Biometrika **34**(1–2), 28–35 (1947)

15. Wilcoxon, F.: Individual comparisons by ranking methods. Biom. Bull. **1**, 80–83 (1945)
16. Zhu, X., et al.: CENPE expression is associated with its DNA methylation status in esophageal adenocarcinoma and independently predicts unfavorable overall survival. PLoS ONE **14**(2), e0207341 (2019)

Litchi Fruit Instance Segmentation from UAV Sensed Images Using Spatial Attention-Based Deep Learning Model

Debarun Chakraborty and Bhabesh Deka[(✉)]

Department of ECE, Tezpur University, Tezpur 784028, Assam, India
{dkdeb20,bdeka}@tezu.ernet.in

Abstract. This paper highlights the importance of deep learning-based litchi segmentation in precision agriculture using machine vision. The proposed method involves preparing a mixed UAV litchi and MinneApple database, consisting of 2000 images of the same size 256×256. This paper introduces a modified Mask-RCNN-based instance segmentation model; incorporating a spatial attention block in the backbone network ResNet101, to mitigate one of the significant challenges in litchi counting, i.e., occlusion. The results demonstrate that the proposed model achieves a mean Average Precision (mAP), recall, and F1-score of 90.81%, 89.00%, and 90.35%, respectively, for separated and unoccluded litchis, and an mAP, recall, and F1-score of 81.41%, 82.42%, and 81.91%, respectively, for occluded litchis. The proposed model provides better detection accuracy while minimizing computational burden, showing its potential for efficient and accurate litchi detection and counting in precision agriculture.

Keywords: Unmanned Aerial Vehicle (UAV) · Deep Learning · Instance Segmentation · Litchi · Precision Agriculture · Spatial Attention Module (SAM)

1 Introduction

The field of precision agriculture and autonomous industries is rapidly growing, driven by advancements in technologies, like unmanned aerial vehicle (UAV) and state-of-the-art deep learning (DL) models to optimize crop production and health monitoring using minimum resources [3]. One critical aspect of horticulture production is the accurate detection and counting of crops, which allows farmers and industry professionals to make data-driven decisions prior to their operation. In recent years, litchi fruit detection and counting has emerged as a particularly important area of focus in the field of precision agriculture, because of its high value in international market. Traditionally, litchi fruit counting has been a time-consuming and labor-intensive process, requiring manual counting and data collection. However, with the advent of modern UAV sensing technology and deep learning-based approaches for image analysis, this process has been

P. Maji et al. (Eds.): PReMI 2023, LNCS 14301, pp. 862–870, 2023.
https://doi.org/10.1007/978-3-031-45170-6_90

revolutionized [7]. Now, high-resolution images of the litchi crop can be captured in no time [2], which can then be processed using advanced algorithms to accurately count litchi and assess overall crop health. One of the main drawbacks for crop detection during UAV-based data acquisition is due to the occlusion with leaves and branches, which makes it difficult for the DL model to detect and localize the fruit and results in the reduction of detection and counting accuracy. In recent years, many studies have been reported on the detection of fruits in complex growth environment using UAV sensing images; Xu *et al.* [10] proposed a deep learning-based study using UAV images for the detection and counting of maize leaves. Findings show that Mask-RCNN perform better with SmoothLR than L1 Loss. Authors could obtain bounding box and mask average precision of 96.9% and 95.2%, respectively. Shiu *et al.* [5] proposed a DL-based method to detect pineapple using high resolution UAV images with ground sampling distance (GSD) of 3 cm. The model used Faster-RCNN for the localization and detection of pineapples and further Mask-RCNN was used to get an instance segmentation mask of the target object. The outcomes showed a kappa coefficient of 0.908 and an overall classification accuracy of 97.46%. Zhu *et al.* [11] proposed an improved You Only Look Once v4 (YOLOv4) for fruit tree canopy recognition and counting in complex natural environment. The model used UAV-based fruit tree canopy custom dataset and trained with Mobilenetv3 network. To enhance multi-scale feature extraction capability, author incorporated convolutional block attention module (CBAM) and adaptive spatial feature fusion (ASFF) with the existing model. The model reached mAP, and F1-Score of 98.21% and 93.60%, respectively. Apolo-Apolo *et al.* [1] proposed deep learning techniques to identify, count, and estimate the size of citrus fruits on individual trees using UAV images. Model was trained with Faster-RCNN network and obtained average standard error (SE) of 6.59% between visual counting and the model's fruit detection. Further more, the model was trained with Long Short-term Memory (LSTM) for total yield prediction.

In this paper, we study the possibility of deep learning-based instance segmentation on UAV images for litchi fruit detection as an application of precision agriculture and robotic applications. In order to address one of the key challenges of fruit occlusion, the paper presents a cutting-edge data collecting strategy based on UAV and dependable DL approach where Mask-RCNN is modified with SAM. Following are the major contributions of the paper:

1. Prepared a robust and diverse mix UAV dataset for litchi detection and instance segmentation.
2. Proposed a spatial attention module (SAM)-based Mask-RCNN model for litchi instance segmentation.
3. Compared the proposed model with few others instance segmentation models and provide a possible solution for occlusion in context to precision agriculture with minimum computational burden.

2   Materials and Methods

This section describes the approach and resources used in the study. The data acquisition protocol using UAV sensing and mix dataset preparation procedures are detailed. Based on our target application of occluded litchi detection a modified Mask-RCNN architecture is proposed for litchi instance segmentation-based on spatial attention.

2.1   Data Acquisition and Dataset Preparation

The data collection site is a litchi garden in the city of Tezpur, Assam, India. The garden is spread over an area of 1.5 acres situated at a distance of 5 km away from Tezpur University with geographical co-ordinates having latitude $26°45'30''$N and longitude $92°48'43''$E. UAV images were collected during the month of May-June 2022, using "DJI Phantom 4 pro". The UAV is equipped with three-axis stabilized camera having a spatial resolution of 1-in. (25 mm), 20 MP RGB sensor. The flight campaign is executed in two different locations of the garden in different lighting conditions to provide more generic approach to the dataset. The two sample areas are randomly selected based on the tree size and count uniformity, the individual sample area consists of 15 trees with 5 trees in each row. Therefore, the entire dataset consists of images of 30 litchi trees approximately.

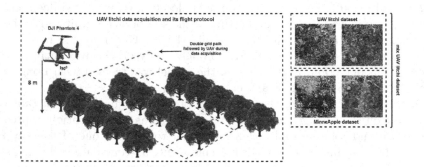

Fig. 1. 3D representation of UAV data acquisition flight protocol and few sample images from UAV litchi and MinneApple datasets

For the proposed work we took 600 high resolution images of size 5472 × 3648 with an overlap of 90% at a height of 8 m from the ground. The high resolution UAV images were transformed into 1000 image pathes, each of size 256 × 256. The images pathes were annotated with the LabelImg python toolkit. Further, we introduce a unique data augmentation technique, where we integrate data from two different sources of similar category to provide detailed, thorough, and cohesive knowledge about an situation. The approach increase the efficiency of the models, as it can also mitigate the problem of crop data scarcity for training.

By this method, we intend to expose to the model to adapt to the real environments and situations by incorporating new data sources. Therefore, to increase the model efficacy and better training, we prepared a fusion dataset by mixing the UAV-based litchi images with benchmark MinneApple [4] dataset. MinneApple dataset consists of 1000 images of size 256×256 captured by standard Samsung Galaxy S4 cell phone at the University of Minnesota's Horticultural Research Center (HRC). The combined dataset consists of total 2000 images, where 75% of the data is used for training and rest 15% and 10% are used for validation and testing, respectively. Figure 1 shows UAV data acquisition flight protocol and few sample images of mix dataset.

2.2 Significance of Spatial Attention in Convolutional Block Attention Module(CBAM)

Convolutional block attention module (CBAM) [9] is a popular attention module most widely used in computer vision tasks, like image classification and object detection. It helps to enhance the representation of CNNs by selectively emphasizing informative features and suppressing irrelevant ones. CBAM consists of to two sequential modules: channel attention module (CAM) followed by spatial attention module (SAM) as shown in Fig. 2. CAM determines the relative relevance of various feature channels by constructing a channel-wise attention map using global average pooling and two fully linked layers. SAM, on the other hand, captures the spatial context of feature maps by computing a spatial attention map using max-pooling and two fully connected layers. Given, an intermediate feature map say, $F \in \mathbb{R}^{C \times H \times W}$, CBAM infers the channel attention map as $M_c \in \mathbb{R}^{C \times 1 \times 1}$ and spatial attention map as $M_s \in \mathbb{R}^{1 \times H \times W}$. The overall attention process can be mathematically expressed as:

$$F' = M_c(F) \bigotimes F \tag{1}$$

$$F'' = M_s(F') \bigotimes F' \tag{2}$$

where $\bigotimes$ denotes element wise operation, M_c and M_s are the ID and 2D, channel and spatial attention maps respectively. F' be the intermediate refined attention feature maps, and F'' be the final refined feature map. Both the attention module in CBAM can be utilized separately-based on the challenges in object detection. However, Integrating the entire CBAM module in the backbone network may increase the computational burden of the architecture. Moreover, to mitigate the issue of occlusion of litchis with leaves and branches spatial features are more significant, therefore, we intend to integrate only the SAM in the backbone network making the network highly rich in spatial features.

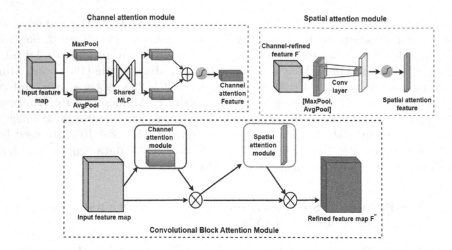

Fig. 2. Architecture of the Convolutional Block Attention Module (CBAM).

2.3 Proposed Methodology

Instance segmentation being one of the most widely used segmentation techniques where it allows the machine to learn and detect object with pixel level information [6]. Precision agriculture applications, like fruit detection and localization, diseases detection, yield estimation etc., demand instance or panoptic segmentation approach. It is not only capable of distinctly detect and localize the object, but also provide more insightful information for precise segmentation. Mask-RCNN being one of the most popular detection method for instance segmentation, involves identifying and delineating of objects within an image. Implementation of Mask-RCNN in precision agriculture is being relatively new and state-of-the-art development, and there is enough room for modifying the current model to further increase its accuracy and effectiveness in complex agricultural environments and crop management.

The performance of the model can be affected by variations in lighting conditions, occlusions, and complex background scenes. To address these challenges, we are exploring new approaches of mix-data augmentation technique and integrating the SAM into the proposed DL-model for better detection of litchis in complex environment. The proposed architecture is based on the baseline Mask-RCNN model, which is modified by incorporating SAM module in the backbone network i.e.; ResNet101. SAM can address the issue by selectively emphasizing pertinent elements using attention mechanism, allowing ResNet101 architecture to concentrate more effectively on the spatial features. To enhance the spatial features we targeted the initial bottleneck blocks of ResNet101 and pass it through the SAM which contain rich spatial information about the image as shown in the Fig. 3. Among the five feature scales (CA1, CA2, CA3, CA4, CA5) as produced by ResNet101, we intend to incorporate the SAM to some of the selective feature scales say (CA1, CA2, CA3), where the network learns most of the spatial fea-

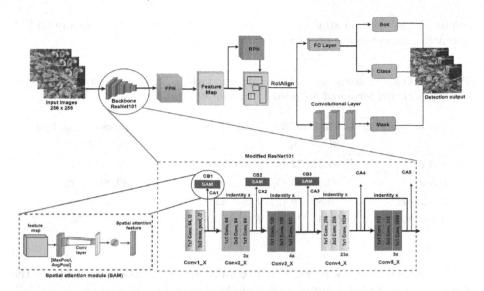

Fig. 3. Complete architecture of the proposed method.

ture of the objects. By adding SAM to the high resolution but low level feature maps of the backbone we intend to improve the spatial features such as edges, corner etc. It effectively helps the model to overcome the challenges of detecting litchis in occluded conditions and provide better detection accuracy with negligible rise in inference time as compared to baseline Mask-RCNN model. The above theoretical proposition are verified by experimental results in the next section.

2.4 Experimental Setup

The experiments were conducted on a 32 GB Tesla V-100 GPU, 128 GB RAM, and 1TB hard drive using Python 3.7.12 environment equipped with general purpose graphics processing unit (GPGPU). For training 75% data was used, while 15% and 10% were used for validation and testing. The model was trained for 200 epochs, with a batch size of 8, initial learning rate of 0.001, and weight delay of 0.0001. The optimizer used was Stochastic Gradient Descent (SGD) method. All the results are averaged over several runs using the mix dataset detailed in Subsect. 2.1.

3 Results and Discussion

Three sets of experiments are conducted for the ablation study on the mix dataset as shown in Table 1. From the experiments results as shown in Fig. 4, it can be observed that CBAM performs better than Mask-RCNN in terms of detection accuracy but faces false detection and higher inference time. The results of the ablation study suggest that the proposed method does provide a significant improvement over the baseline Mask-RCNN model.

Table 1. Ablation study on UAV mix dataset, where SU and OL stands for separated/unoccluded litchi and occluded litchi, respectively.

Evaluation metrics	Mask-RCNN		Mask-RCNN + CBAM		proposed method	
	SU	OL	SU	OL	SU	OL
mAP	86.32	72.94	89.69	77.83	90.81	81.41
Recall	92.10	86.45	93.54	85.45	89.00	82.42
F1-Score	90.80	79.12	91.57	81.42	90.35	81.91
Time (sec)	7.34	7.52	7.41	7.55	7.37	7.56

A comparison study is conducted to validate the proposed model with the state-of-the-art instance segmentation model reported in [8], as shown in Table 2. The study revealed that the proposed method enhances the accuracy of detection by 5% for SU and 6% for OL compared to the transformer attention model. Additionally, the proposed method achieves this improvement while reducing the computation burden by 0.55 s. The findings mentioned above are further supported by the visual representation in Fig. 4, which clearly demonstrates that the inclusion of SAM eliminates any instances of missed detection in the proposed model, thereby mitigating the challenge of litchi occlusion with leaves and branches. Finally, the proposed approach shows great potential as a solution for object detection and instance segmentation, particularly when dealing with small and occluded objects.

Table 2. Comparison of model accuracy and test time (sec) with state-of-the-art methods on mix dataset.

Evaluation metrics	Mask-RCNN		Mask-RCNN + transformer attention		proposed method	
	SU	OL	SU	OL	SU	OL
mAP	86.32	72.94	85.79	74.92	90.81	81.41
Recall	92.10	86.45	93.33	83.22	89.00	82.42
F1-Score	90.80	79.12	90.21	80.32	90.35	81.91
Time (sec)	7.34	7.52	7.55	7.93	7.37	7.56

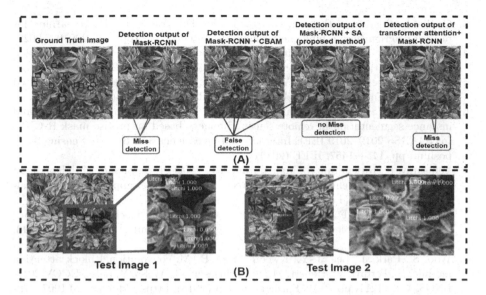

Fig. 4. (A) Detection outputs of various models and the proposed model (B) Zoom in portion of the detected outputs using the proposed model.

4   Conclusion

This paper presents a novel approach to detect and count litchi in precision agriculture by combining UAV litchi and MinneApple datasets. A modified Mask-RCNN instance segmentation model is proposed, integrating a spatial attention model. The model achieves promising performance with mAP, recall, and F1-scores of 90.81%, 89.00%, and 90.35% for separated and unoccluded litchis, and a mAP, recall, and F1-score of 81.41%, 82.42%, and 81.91% for occluded litchis, respectively. The model offers better detection accuracy with minimizing computational burden.

Acknowledgements. Authors are grateful to the proprietors of Ram Narayan Singh Lychee Garden, Parmaighuli, Tezpur, Assam 784501 for generously giving their consent for UAV data collection for the current research.

References

1. Apolo-Apolo, O., Martínez-Guanter, J., Egea, G., Raja, P., Pérez-Ruiz, M.: Deep learning techniques for estimation of the yield and size of citrus fruits using a UAV. Eur. J. Agron. **115**, 126030 (2020)
2. Chakraborty, D., Deka, B.: UAV sensing-based semantic image segmentation of litchi tree crown using deep learning. In: 2023 IEEE Applied Sensing Conference (APSCON), pp. 1–3 (2023). https://doi.org/10.1109/APSCON56343.2023.10101133

3. Couliably, S., Kamsu-Foguem, B., Kamissoko, D., Traore, D.: Deep learning for precision agriculture: a bibliometric analysis. Intell. Syst. Appl. **16**, 200102 (2022)
4. Häni, N., Roy, P., Isler, V.: Minneapple: a benchmark dataset for apple detection and segmentation. IEEE Robot. Autom. Lett. **5**(2), 852–858 (2020)
5. Shiu, Y.S., Lee, R.Y., Chang, Y.C.: Pineapples detection and segmentation based on faster and mask R-CNN in UAV imagery. Remote Sens. **15**(3), 814 (2023)
6. Su, H., Wei, S., Yan, M., Wang, C., Shi, J., Zhang, X.: Object detection and instance segmentation in remote sensing imagery based on precise mask R-CNN. In: IGARSS 2019–2019 IEEE International Geoscience and Remote Sensing Symposium, pp. 1454–1457. IEEE (2019)
7. Velusamy, P., Rajendran, S., Mahendran, R.K., Naseer, S., Shafiq, M., Choi, J.G.: Unmanned aerial vehicles (UAV) in precision agriculture: applications and challenges. Energies **15**(1), 217 (2021)
8. Wang, D., He, D.: Fusion of mask RCNN and attention mechanism for instance segmentation of apples under complex background. Comput. Electron. Agric. **196**, 106864 (2022)
9. Woo, S., Park, J., Lee, J.-Y., Kweon, I.S.: CBAM: convolutional block attention module. In: Ferrari, V., Hebert, M., Sminchisescu, C., Weiss, Y. (eds.) ECCV 2018. LNCS, vol. 11211, pp. 3–19. Springer, Cham (2018). https://doi.org/10.1007/978-3-030-01234-2_1
10. Xu, X., et al.: Detection and counting of maize leaves based on two-stage deep learning with UAV-based RGB image. Remote Sens. **14**(21), 5388 (2022)
11. Zhu, Y., Zhou, J., Yang, Y., Liu, L., Liu, F., Kong, W.: Rapid target detection of fruit trees using UAV imaging and improved light YOLOv4 algorithm. Remote Sens. **14**(17), 4324 (2022)

ccLoopER: Deep Prediction of *C*TCF and *c*ohesin Mediated Chromatin *loop*ing Using DNA Transform*er* Model

Anup Kumar Halder[1,2] (iD), Abhishek Agarwal[2] (iD), Sevastianos Korsak[1,2] (iD), Karolina Jodkowska[2] (iD), and Dariusz Plewczynski[1,2(✉)] (iD)

[1] Laboratory of Bioinformatics and Computational Genomics, Faculty of Mathematics and Information Science, Warsaw University of Technology, Warsaw, Poland
{anup.halder,Dariusz.Plewczynski}@pw.edu.pl, s.korsak@datascience.edu.pl
[2] Laboratory of Functional and Structural Genomics, Centre of New Technologies, University of Warsaw, Warsaw, Poland
{a.halder,a.agarwal,s.korsak,k.jodkowska,d.plewczynski}@cent.uw.edu.pl

Abstract. Chromosome conformation capture technologies have advanced the understanding of chromatin organization and interaction in three dimensions, giving insight into gene regulation, disease development, and cell differentiation. However, due to experimental and technical limitations, it is only possible to identify a limited number of potential genome-wide chromatin loops in all tissues or cell types of interest. Therefore we developed the "ccLoopER" method to predict genome-wide chromatin loops mediated by architectural proteins (CTCF and Cohesin) using the DNA language model and DNA-based transformer model. The ccLoopER shows significant performance improvement compared to the state-of-the-art approaches. In addition, a polymer model-specific validation shows the high similarity between real and insilico interactions (Pearson correlation: 0.955).

Keywords: Chromatin loop · CTCF · Cohesin · HiChIP · ChIA-PIPE · ChIA-PET · DNA sequence · Deep Transformer model · polymer modeling

1 Introduction

The spatial arrangement of chromatin inside the nucleus is known as the three-dimensional (3D) organization of the genome, and it plays a crucial role in regulating gene expression and other cellular processes [2]. The genome is packaged into chromosomes and arranged inside the nucleus, where it interacts with a variety of nuclear bodies that have a significant impact on its higher-order organization and function. Although there have been significant advances in genome-wide mapping techniques and chromosome conformation capture technologies over the decade, the mechanisms governing the interactions between

P. Maji et al. (Eds.): PReMI 2023, LNCS 14301, pp. 871–878, 2023.
https://doi.org/10.1007/978-3-031-45170-6_91

large-scale chromatin structures and functional nuclear bodies are not yet fully understood. The identification of multiscale structures of the nuclear genome, such as A/B compartments [10], subcompartments [12], topologically associating domains (TADs) [3], and chromatin loops [13], has been made possible through these techniques.

Protein-mediated loops can be mapped using chromatin conformation capture (3C)-based approaches, with Hi-C [10,12] offering the most comprehensive coverage for spotting looping events, albeit at the cost of requiring billions of reads to attain kilobase resolution. Alternatively, Chromatin Interaction Analysis using Paired-End Tags (ChIA-PET) [5,9,13] can increase resolution by focusing on chromatin interactions associated with a specific protein of interest, although it may be less sensitive and cost-effective than newer protocols such as Hi-ChIP [11] and PLAC-seq [4]. Even with recent technology advancements, only a few different cell types have been thoroughly studied thus far, making experimental profiling of CTCF and Cohesin (SMC1, RAD21) mediated interactions difficult and expensive. In order to effectively direct the exploration of the significant interaction in certain cell types of interest, it can be helpful to leverage computational machine-learning prediction frameworks that make use of easily available sequence data.

Deep learning models have emerged as a promising area of research for predicting chromatin interactions/loops. These models use advanced neural network architectures and are trained on large amounts of genomic data to accurately predict the spatial proximity between distant genomic elements. One major advantage of these models is their ability to capture complex, non-linear relationships between genomic features, which can be challenging to achieve using traditional statistical methods. Recently, deep transformer models such as Bidirectional Encoder Representations from Transformers (BERT) [8] have shown promising performances on genomic sequence data. One significant advantage of using BERT for chromatin interaction prediction is its ability to learn from large datasets and extract complex patterns and features from DNA sequences. This enables the development of more accurate models capable of predicting chromatin interactions with greater precision than traditional methods. Additionally, BERT models can be fine-tuned for specific tasks, such as identifying regulatory elements or predicting specific types of chromatin interactions, making them highly adaptable to various research needs.

In NLP, pre-training with large-scale unlabelled data has resolved the insufficient data problem. In contrast, convolutional models are able to extract the local features but are not suitable for long DNA sequences. In addition, CNN architectures rely on large amounts of labelled data whereas the BERT architecture is pre-trained on a large corpus of DNA sequences from the human reference genome [7]. By leveraging this pre-trained language model, DNABERT showed significant performance improvement in different sequence-based prediction tasks. However, downstream predictive task-specific models required task-specific labelled datasets. In recent work by Chiliński et al. [1] has proposed a deep hybrid learning (DHL) strategy by incorporating the pre-trained language

model from DNABERT along with traditional machine learning-based classification. In DHL, authors trained the model for loop prediction from a pair
of genomic regions (anchor). Due to the memory issue of positional encoding
of maximum length 512, they consider the mid-position-based flanking regions
limited to 256 bp for each anchor representation. However, it causes important information loss for the learning estimation as all the binding factors are
not located within the considered flanking region. To overcome this problem we
incorporated motif finding script to localise the protein factors within the anchor
region before the predictive learning module. As a fine-tuning task, we proposed
the transformer-based predictive model *ccLoopER* for 3D genome-wide chromatin interaction prediction from DNA sequence. The proposed approach finds
the motif regions among the interacting anchor regions. The model is trained and
tested on individual datasets for different cells with two architectural proteins
(CTCF and Cohesin) from different experimental setups.

2   Materials and Method

2.1   Data Processing

We conducted experiments on the B-Lymphocyte cell types, specifically
GM12878 and HG00731 cells. Experimental data included CTCF ChIA-PET,
Rad21 ChIA-PET, SMC1 HiChIP, and CTCF HiChIP interactions. The ChIA-
PIPE pipeline was employed to process and map the data to the human hg38
reference genome. Following a series of data processing and filtering steps, we
retained only clustered and merged intra-chromosomal PETs that met certain
criteria. The number of significant interactions for each sample is detailed in
Fig. 1A, with CTCF interactions collected from the 4DN data portal and Cohesin
interactions from ENCODE.

The genomic interactions are represented as two anchors, connecting distal parts of the genome where these distal regions represent the anchors. We
extracted the highest-scoring CTCF motifs and their orientations within anchor
regions for each chromatin interaction. Interactions without motif regions in
both anchors are excluded from the learning mechanism. Finally, we have 75743
and 38122 CTCF interactions and 53565 and 94386 cohesin interactions from
GM12878 and HG00731 cells, respectively, for the deep predictive module across
all 23 chromosomes (see Fig. 1A).

We represent each genomic subsequence of length 250 bp retrieved from
respective anchors regions considering motif location at the middle of the subsequences (± 125 bp from the motif). Finally, the chromatin loop is represented
as the pair of such subsequences delimited by [SEP] token resulting in 500 bp
input data. We prepared a negative set of interactions by randomly selecting
two genomic regions with motifs at the middle of each region and excluding positive interactions. In training the deep predictive module, the interactions from
chromosome 9 are considered the validation data, while the rest of the interactions from the remaining 22 chromosomes are for training in each cell. To ensure
balanced learning, the positive and negative ratio is kept at 1:1.

2.2   Model Architecture

In this experiment, we presented a deep transformer-based model ccLoopER that will predict genome-wide chromatin loops mediated by CTCF and Cohesin proteins. The proposed module ccLoopER for interacting loop prediction is developed based on the DNABERT pre-trained language model, where all the sequences are processed using k-mer methods for tokenization. The task-specific fine-tuning module is initiated with the embedding layer by processing the input nucleotide sequence pair as k-mer representation (k = 6) to capture contextual information compared to a single base as words. The embedding layer consists of token and positional encoding. The basic transformer block consist of 12 layers of transformer encoders where each encoder block is composed of a multi-head self-attention (MHA) layer, feed-forward layer followed by normalization layer as detailed in Fig. 1B. Incorporating Multi-Head Attention (MHA) expands the model's ability to consider diverse positions and more effectively comprehend contextual information.

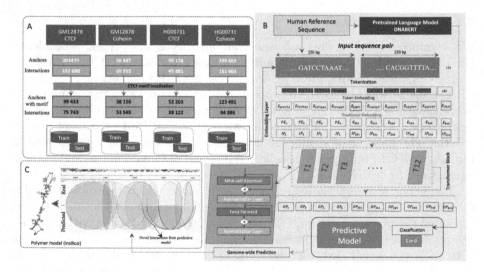

Fig. 1. Workflow of ccLoopER for chromatin loop prediction from single tissue specificity. A) Represents the data set preparation details. B) ccLoopER basic architecture representation, C) The in silico interactions from the model for a given region and the corresponding polymer model representation.

Subsequently, the output embedding is gathered and fed into a classifier layer, which includes a dropout layer, a fully connected neural network, and a softmax function. The learning rate is set as $2e - 4$ with a warmup of 10%. The hidden dropout rate is set to 0.01 to prevent overfitting. The model employs binary cross-entropy as its loss function,

$$loss = -\frac{1}{N}\sum_{n=1}^{N}[y_n * log(x_n) + (1 - y_n) * log(1 - x_n)] \qquad (1)$$

3   Results and Discussion

The model is trained and tested on each individual data set as described in above data preparation section. Our model ccLoopER was evaluated and compared with state-of-the-art approaches, DNABERT [7] and DHL enhanced DNABERT [1], using accuracy, precision, recall, F-1, and MCC metrics. The ccLoopER model demonstrated promising performance across all metrics for both HG00731 and GM12878 cell lines. The performance evaluations are depicted in Table 1. The ccLoopER show significant improvement prediction performance compared to DNABERT and almost equal accuracy compared to DNABERT advanced DHL on GM12878 CTCF dataset. In addition, ccLoopER surpass DHL in F1 and MCC scores (see Table 1). DNABERT [7] and DHL [1] show performance only on the GM12878_CTCF dataset. Therefore, the comparison with the proposed ccLoopER is depicted on the same dataset.

Table 1. Classification Performances evaluation of ccLoopER comparison with state of the art approaches on different datasets

Model	Cell line	Accuracy	Precision	Recall	F-1	MCC
ccLoopER	HG00731_Cohesin	0.827	0.848	0.827	0.825	0.676
	GM12878_Cohesin	0.887	0.888	0.887	0.886	0.775
	HG00731_CTCF	0.857	0.86	0.857	0.857	0.718
	GM12878_CTCF	0.84	0.851	0.84	0.839	0.692
DNABERT [7]	GM12878_CTCF	0.78	0.782	0.780	0.780	0.562
DHL [1]	GM12878_CTCF	0.840	0.856	0.819	0.837	0.682

3.1   Performance Evaluation on Self and Cross Protein Binding Factors

We have evaluated the performance of ccLoopER at self and cross cell types with two architectural protein factors (CTCF and Cohesin). A heatmap plot is shown in Fig. 2A to depicts different performance metrics. All the evaluation in self and cross cell type and protein factors in Fig. 2A are based on the prediction performance on validation data from chromosome 9. Row wise represent the training model and column wise plots represent the testing performance. We have evaluated the model on human B-Lymphocyte cell type, specifically GM12878 and

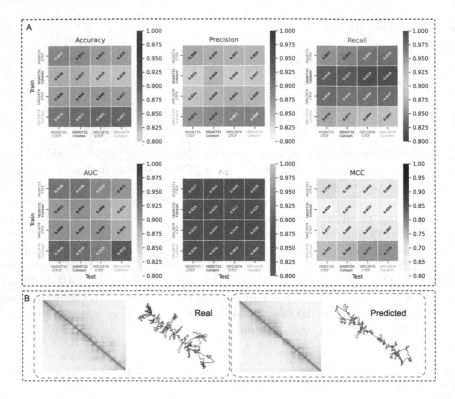

Fig. 2. Performance Assessment. A) Prediction performances on chromatin loops with cross cell type and with self and cross protein factors. B) Polymer model and heatmap representation of real and predicted interactions for the example region chr9: 135567737-138146487 from GM12878 CTCF.

HG00731 cells with two protein factors CTCF and Cohesin, which results four different variation of interaction datasets (see Fig. 1A). The individual model is evaluated and tested for each dataset on self and other validation data from remaining dataset variations. It has been observed that the GM12878-Cohesin-based model achieves the highest accuracy of 0.887 for self-prediction, and the best score is 0.884 while tested on GM12878-CTCF. However, in HG00731 cell type, CTCF based model performs better than the HG00731-Cohesin-based model. This performance trend is consistent over all other matrices (see Fig. 2A for details).

3.2 Polymer Model Specific Evaluation

We employed a specialized evaluation strategy to assess the effectiveness of the ccLoopER model. This involved constructing polymer models for both real and predicted interactions, based on the biophysical principles of loop extrusion and cohesin movement [6]. To create these models, we utilized a stochastic simulation method in which cohesins acted as loop extruders, while CTCF where interpreted as boundary elements which block the motion of cohesin and were linked to energy minima. The simulation allows for three types of cohesin moves: sliding left, sliding right, and relocating. The thermodynamic system follows the Boltzmann probability distribution with energy,

$$E = f \sum_{i=1}^{N_{coh}} \log\left(n_i - m_i\right) + \kappa \sum_{i,j} K(m_i, n_i; m_j, n_j) + b \sum_{i=1}^{N_{coh}} \left(L(m_i)\right) + R(n_i)) \quad (2)$$

where m_i and n_i are the left and right polymer cites that the cohesin i connect. The first term is negative and represents the folding or entropic gain, which gives lower energy to conformations with bigger loops, consequently it makes the loops extrude. The second term is positive and it is a Langragian multiplier that forbids knotted conformations. Therefore, $K(m_i, n_i \, m_j, n_j)$ is equal to 1 if $m_i \leq m_j \leq n_i \leq n_j$, and 0 otherwise, while κ takes high values. The last term is negative and represents the binding energy, which is minimum when cohesin meets CTCF occupied beads. The binding energy is constructed by taking into account CTCF interaction data, and the probabilities that a CTCF is tandem-left or tandem-right. By following a simulated annealing approach, we end up with an ensemble of positions $(m_i(t_j), n_i(t_j))$ for each cohesin i, which is used to create realistic 3D polymer structures by translating them into time-dependent covalent harmonic bonds. The averaged all-versus-all inverse distance heatmaps over the 3D structure ensembles calculated for both real and predicted data show high similarities (pearson correlation 0.955). A polymer model and its corresponding heatmap for the example region of chr9 (chr9:135567737-138146487) for both real and in silico interactions from GM12878 CTCF dataset are shown in Fig. 2B.

4   Conclusion

Our study introduces a deep learning model named *ccLoopER*, based on the Transformer architecture, for predicting chromatin loops throughout the genome mediated by architectural proteins, CTCF and Cohesin. The model primarily identifies the position of motifs across given genomic regions and predicts interactions between them. We evaluated the model's performance on B-Lymphocyte cells (GM12878 and HG00731) by considering two protein factors. The stability and robustness of the model were assessed through its prediction performance in different cell-specific and protein factor combinations. Finally, we evaluated the model by comparing the polymer model between actual and predicted interactions..

Acknowledgement. Research was co-funded by Warsaw University of Technology within the Excellence Initiative: Research University (IDUB) programme. The work was co-supported by EU-funded the Marie Sklodowska-Curie action (MSCA) Innovative Training Network named Enhpathy (www.enhpathy.eu) 'Molecular Basis of Human enhanceropathies' and Polish National Science Centre (2019/35/O/ST6/02484 and

2020/37/B/NZ2/03757). Computations were performed at the Laboratory of Bioinformatics and Computational Genomics, Faculty of Mathematics and Information Science, Warsaw University of Technology using Artificial Intelligence HPC platform financed by Polish Ministry of Science and Higher Education (decision no. 7054/IA/SP/2020 of 2020-08-28).

References

1. Chiliński, M., Halder, A.K., Plewczynski, D.: Prediction of chromatin looping using deep hybrid learning (DHL). Quant. Biol. **11**(2), 155–162 (2023)
2. Dekker, J., Mirny, L.: The 3D genome as moderator of chromosomal communication. Cell **164**(6), 1110–1121 (2016)
3. Dixon, J.R., et al.: Topological domains in mammalian genomes identified by analysis of chromatin interactions. Nature **485**(7398), 376–380 (2012)
4. Fang, R., et al.: Comprehensive analysis of single cell ATAC-seq data with SnapATAC. Nat. Commun. **12**(1), 1337 (2021)
5. Fang, R., et al.: Mapping of long-range chromatin interactions by proximity ligation-assisted ChIP-seq. Cell Res. **26**(12), 1345–1348 (2016)
6. Ganji, M., et al.: Real-time imaging of DNA loop extrusion by condensin. Science **360**(6384), 102–105 (2018)
7. Ji, Y., Zhou, Z., Liu, H., Davuluri, R.V.: DNABERT: pre-trained bidirectional encoder representations from transformers model for DNA-language in genome. Bioinformatics **37**(15), 2112–2120 (2021)
8. Kenton, J.D.M.W.C., Toutanova, L.K.: BERT: pre-training of deep bidirectional transformers for language understanding. In: Proceedings of naacL-HLT, vol. 1, p. 2 (2019)
9. Li, G., et al.: Extensive promoter-centered chromatin interactions provide a topological basis for transcription regulation. Cell **148**(1–2), 84–98 (2012)
10. Lieberman-Aiden, E., et al.: Comprehensive mapping of long-range interactions reveals folding principles of the human genome. Science **326**(5950), 289–293 (2009)
11. Mumbach, M.R., et al.: Hichip: efficient and sensitive analysis of protein-directed genome architecture. Nat. Methods **13**(11), 919–922 (2016)
12. Rao, S.S., et al.: A 3D map of the human genome at kilobase resolution reveals principles of chromatin looping. Cell **159**(7), 1665–1680 (2014)
13. Tang, Z., et al.: CTCF-mediated human 3D genome architecture reveals chromatin topology for transcription. Cell **163**(7), 1611–1627 (2015)

Author Index

P. Maji et al. (Eds.): PReMI 2023, LNCS 14301, pp. 879–882, 2023.
https://doi.org/10.1007/978-3-031-45170-6